FEDERAL RULES OF CIVIL PROCEDURE

As Amended Through April 1, 2010

Together with:

in conjunction with an online Statutory Companion site
at http://www.ClermontStatutorySupplements.com

FOUNDATION PRESS
2010

THOMSON REUTERS

© 1986 through 2004 FOUNDATION PRESS
© 2005 through 2009 THOMSON REUTERS/FOUNDATION PRESS
© 2010 By THOMSON REUTERS/FOUNDATION PRESS

      195 Broadway, 9th Floor
      New York, NY 10007
      Phone Toll Free 1–877–888–1330
      Fax (212) 367–6799
      foundation–press.com

ISBN 978-1-59941-843-8   **ISSN** 1082-9024
Cover Photos: SUPREME COURT HISTORICAL SOCIETY and USDA Photos

Mat # 40999972

PREFACE

Welcome to the world of the Federal Rules of Civil Procedure. Here is a roadmap to the interior:

1. Federal Rules of Civil Procedure

This booklet begins with the Civil Rules themselves or, more exactly, with (i) the Table of Rules, which allows you to see the structure of the Federal Rules of Civil Procedure, (ii) the main corpus of Civil Rules 1–86, (iii) the Appendix of Forms, and (iv) the Supplemental Rules for Admiralty or Maritime Claims and Asset Forfeiture Actions.

The most important pointer on use of this portion of the booklet regards the history of amendments. After each amended Rule or Form appears a line listing by year the effective date of all amendments. Details of these amendments appear immediately after Federal Rule of Civil Procedure 86—there the booklet tells which particular subdivisions underwent amendment in each year, and it gives both an official citation to the amendatory order or statute and a reference to a readily available source containing any Advisory Committee's Notes. For example, you might want to know how Fed.R.Civ.P. 11 read when some 1980 case came down: Rule 11 in this booklet closes with an indication of amendment in 1983, 1987, 1993, and 2007. Referring to the sources cited after after Rule 86 would tell you that Rule 11 underwent a significant amendment in 1983, a minor change in 1987 to neutralize gender-specific language, a major amendment in 1993, and mainly a "restyling" in 2007; for 1983 in particular, the Supreme Court's amendatory order appears at 461 U.S. 1095, while the Advisory Committee's Notes appear at 97 F.R.D. 165. The latter source will tell you exactly how Rule 11 looked in 1980, because the Advisory Committee Notes show the Rules before and after amendment.

It is worth specially noting that all the Rules and Forms underwent massive, albeit mainly stylistic, amendments on December 1, 2007. This "restyling" was intended to make the Rules and Forms clearer and simpler, but not to alter their meaning. It included some redesignation of the Rules' subdivisions and a re-numbering of all Forms.

2. Civil Advisory Committee's Notes

This booklet in fact reprints the most significant of the Advisory Committee's Notes on the Federal Rules of Civil Procedure. These come right after the booklet's Civil Rules portion, with the primary organization of the Notes being by Rule number. Thus, the

1

important Notes on Rule 11 for 1983 and 1993 appear in the subpart devoted to Rule 11.

The most important pointer on using this portion of the booklet regards the style of Advisory Committee's Notes. For each amendment, the Rule appears with its changes (new matter is in italics; omitted matter appears with a line through it) and then the following Note allows the Advisory Committee to explain the changes. All this enables you to reconstruct the former Rule. Using the same example, and referring to the 1983 amendment, you can see that in 1980 Rule 11 was much shorter. Indeed, you have reconstructed Rule 11 as it existed from the beginning in 1938, and you can find the Advisory Committee's Note on that original Rule 11 at the beginning of the set of Advisory Committee's Notes dealing with Rule 11.

Incidentally, you can find a complete repository of Committee reports, as well as many other useful features, in the online Statutory Companion site for this booklet, at http://www.Clermont StatutorySupplements.com. There you can see even the minor changes to Rule 11 by the Advisory Committee in 1987 and 2007.

3. Federal Rules of Appellate Procedure

This booklet's next portion contains most of the Appellate Rules and Forms. The organization is similar to the booklet's treatment of the Civil Rules.

Also, you can trace the history of amendments in the same way, using the detailed information that appears after Federal Rule of Appellate Procedure 48.

4. Constitution and Procedural Statutes

This booklet next reprints selected provisions of the United States Constitution, title 28 of the United States Code, and other procedural statutes—all preceded by this portion's own table of contents. The editing effort centered on including those provisions most effectively considered in connection with the study of civil procedure. For example, the selection of "other procedural statutes" includes a few key federal statutes that lie outside title 28 (antitrust procedural provisions and civil rights statutes) and also illustrative state statutes in a few key procedural subjects (California's long-arm statute and New York's statute of limitations and jurisdiction, service, and venue provisions).

Title 28 is of course the centerpiece, and accordingly the booklet contains many of its sections. This systematization of statutes on the federal judiciary and judicial procedure comes from the Act of June 25, 1948, ch. 646, § 1, 62 Stat. 869 ("Act to revise, codify, and enact into law title 28 of the United States Code").

PREFACE

After each reprinted statutory section, the booklet lists all amending statutes since the 1948 Act.

5. Federal Rules of Evidence

This booklet sets out the complete Rules of Evidence for United States Courts and Magistrates. Although the Evidence Rules constitute a statute, the booklet presents them in a format similar to that of the Civil and Appellate Rules.

Again, you can trace the history of amendments in the same way, using the detailed information that appears after Federal Rule of Evidence 1103.

6. Sample Local Rules

This booklet finally presents, for illustrative purposes, the local rules of the United States District Court for the Northern District of New York.

7. General Comments

The foregoing descriptions evince an editing effort to select thoughtfully a collection of procedural provisions. Also, this preface and the closing consolidated index represent a similarly serious attempt to facilitate the collection's use. We nevertheless want to continue improving this booklet. That does not establish an easy goal, however, because users' widely varying desires are not always obvious. Accordingly, I sincerely request the users to send suggestions for improvement to me.

The booklet also reflects a dedication to keeping it up to date. The Court and Congress are surprisingly active in the procedural arena. We update the Civil Rules through the date shown on the booklet's title page. We update the various other provisions at least through the end of the preceding congressional session, which roughly corresponds to the beginning of the year that appears on the booklet's cover.

KEVIN M. CLERMONT
Ziff Professor of Law
Myron Taylor Hall
Cornell Law School
Ithaca, NY 14853

P.S. Notwithstanding all the above, this booklet still gives you only the raw materials. To get into the immense body of legal doctrine adhering to these materials, you should consult the secondary literature. I especially recommend Charles Alan Wright and Mary Kay Kane's single-volume hornbook on Federal Courts and the multi-volume Federal Practice and Procedure by Professors Wright and Miller and others. To give you a sample, while also providing you with valuable background information on the Federal

Rules that are the subject of the booklet, I close this preface with an excerpt from the former reference work, reprinted here with kind permission:

CHARLES ALAN WRIGHT & MARY KAY
KANE, LAW OF FEDERAL COURTS

429–35, 764 (6th ed. 2002).

§ 62. The Federal Rules of Civil Procedure [1]

... An erratic conformity to state procedure, an anachronistic survival of the separation between law and equity, and a failure to take advantage of the possibilities of judicial rulemaking were hallmarks of the system [of federal procedure prior to 1938]. The last of these points, that procedure is better regulated by the courts than by legislative bodies, was seen to be the key to the problem. It is doubtful whether, as some have contended, the legislature lacks constitutional power to regulate procedure,[2] but it is certainly clear that this power can be delegated by the legislature to the courts.[3] It cannot be doubted that legislative regulation is less satisfactory than regulation by court-made rules.[4]

---

1. 4 Wright & Miller, Civil 2d §§ 1003–1008; Burbank, The Transformation of American Civil Procedure: The Example of Rule 11, 1989, 137 U.Pa.L.Rev. 1925; Chandler, Some Major Advances in the Federal Judicial System, 1922–1947, 1963, 31 F.R.D. 307, 477–516; Clark, Two Decades of the Federal Civil Rules, 1958, 58 Col.L.Rev. 435; Clark, The Role of the Supreme Court in Federal Rule–Making, 1963, 46 J.Am.Jud.Soc. 250; Goodman, On the Fiftieth Anniversary of the Federal Rules of Civil Procedure: What Did the Drafters Intend?, 1987, 21 Suffolk U.L.Rev. 351; Holtzoff, Origin and Sources of the Federal Rules of Civil Procedure, 1955, 30 N.Y.U.L.Rev. 1057; Subrin, How Equity Conquered Common Law: The Federal Rules of Civil Procedure in Historical Perspective, 1987, 135 U.Pa.L.Rev. 909; Sunderland, The Grant of Rule–Making Power to the Supreme Court of the United States, 1934, 32 Mich.L.Rev. 1116; Tolman, Historical Beginnings of Procedural Reform, 1936, 22 A.B.A.J. 783; Toran, 'Tis A Gift To Be Simple: Aesthetics and Procedural Reform, 1990, 89 Mich.L.Rev. 352; Weinstein, The Ghost of Process Past: The Fiftieth Anniversary of the Federal Rules of Civil Procedure and Erie, 1988, 54 Brooklyn L.Rev. 1.

2. Compare Wigmore, Legislative Rules for Judicial Procedure are Void Constitutionally, 1928, 23 Ill.L.Rev. 276, with Kaplan & Greene, The Legislature's Relation to Judicial Rule–Making: An Appraisal of Winberry v. Salisbury, 1951, 65 Harv. L.Rev. 234.

Indeed Professor Whitten argues that separation-of-powers principles restrict the authority of the Court to make even "purely procedural" rules under a general delegation of rulemaking power if Congress has occupied the procedural field in question. Whitten, Separation of Powers Restrictions on Judicial Rulemaking: A Case Study of Federal Rule 4, 1988, 40 Me.L.Rev. 41.

3. See Mistretta v. U.S., 1989, 109 S.Ct. 647, 662–664, 488 U.S. 361, 386–390, 102 L.Ed.2d 714, and cases there cited. The principle was recognized as early as Wayman v. Southard, 1825, 10 Wheat. 1, 43, 6 L.Ed. 253.

4. 4 Wright & Miller, Civil 2d § 1001; Clark & Wright, The Judicial Council and the Rule–Making Power: A Dissent and a Protest, 1950, 1 Syracuse L.Rev. 346; Joiner & Miller, Rules of Practice and Procedure: A Study of Judicial Rule–Making, 1957, 55 Mich.L.Rev. 623; Levin & Amsterdam, Legislative Control over Judicial Rule–Making: A Problem in Constitutional Revision, 1958, 107 U.Pa.L.Rev. 1.

PREFACE

The fight for court-made rules of civil procedure for the federal courts began in 1911 when the American Bar Association, at the instigation of Thomas Shelton, adopted a resolution favoring such a system. For almost 20 years a bill to give the Supreme Court power to make such rules was introduced in every Congress, but never was passed, despite the gallant efforts of Mr. Shelton. In later years, in response to a suggestion by Chief Justice Taft,[5] the bill included a provision authorizing the Court to unify law and equity. Opposition to the bill was led by Senator Walsh of Montana, and was based in large measure on the fear that grant of the rulemaking power would result in the rather simplified code practice of the western states being superseded by the involved practice that had developed in New York.[6] In 1930 Mr. Shelton died, and the American Bar Association lost interest, even to the point of abolishing its committee that had been pressing for this reform.

Senator Walsh was to have been appointed Attorney General in 1933, which would surely have ended, for the time at least, any hope of obtaining rulemaking power for the Supreme Court. He died, however, on the eve of his appointment, and the new Attorney General, Homer Cummings, assumed sponsorship of the bill authorizing the court to make procedural rules and to unite law and equity. So effective was his leadership that the bill was adopted unanimously by Congress in 1934 with very little discussion.[7]

It is a long step from a grant of rulemaking power to the adoption of effective rules. Indeed one familiar argument against rulemaking power is that it will not be exercised. For almost a year after the Enabling Act was passed the Supreme Court took no action with regard to it. The Department of Justice and the Conference of Senior Circuit Judges apparently contemplated that no more would be required than the drafting of uniform rules for actions at law to supplement the existing Equity Rules of 1912.[8]

That the reform was not so limited, that law and equity were merged under a single set of simple and effective rules, was due primarily to the efforts of William D. Mitchell, a former Attorney General of the United States, and Charles E. Clark, then Dean of

---

5. Taft, Three Needed Steps of Progress, 1922, 8 A.B.A.J. 34, 35; Taft, Possible and Needed Reforms in the Administration of Justice in Federal Courts, 1922, 8 A.B.A.J. 601, 604, 607.

6. Walsh, Rule–Making Power on Law Side of Federal Practice, 1927, 13 A.B.A.J. 84. See Clark, Code Pleading, 2d ed. 1947, p. 35.

7. Act of June 19, 1934, c. 651, 48 Stat. 1064; 4 Wright & Miller, Civil 2d § 1003; Burbank, The Rules Enabling Act of 1934, 1982, 130 U.Pa.L.Rev. 1015. See Cummings, Immediate Problems of the Bar, 1934, 20 A.B.A.J. 212. The Enabling Act, as subsequently revised, is now 28 U.S.C.A. §§ 2072–2074.

8. Subrin, Charles E. Clark and His Procedural Outlook: The Disciplined Champion of Undisciplined Rules, in Judge Charles E. Clark, Petruck ed. 1991, p. 115.

the Yale Law School and later Chief Judge of the Court of Appeals for the Second Circuit. In January 1935, Dean Clark, in collaboration with James Wm. Moore, published a major article summarizing the history of federal procedure and predicting that reform would be a failure unless it included a merger of law and equity.[9] Aroused by this article, General Mitchell wrote Chief Justice Hughes, on February 9, 1935, setting forth powerfully and persuasively the need for the full reform.[10] Three months later the Chief Justice, addressing the American Law Institute, made the dramatic announcement that the rules would not be limited to common-law cases, but would unify the procedure for cases in equity and actions at law "so as to secure one form of civil action and procedure for both."[11] A few weeks later the Court appointed an Advisory Committee of the most distinguished lawyers and law professors in the country to prepare and submit a draft of unified rules. General Mitchell was named by the Court as chairman, a post he filled with distinction until his death in 1955, and Dean Clark was designated as Reporter for the Committee.[12]

The Committee circulated three printed drafts for comment and criticism by the profession. The third draft, which was the Final Report of the Committee, was submitted to the Supreme Court in November 1937, and on December 20, 1937, the Court adopted the rules proposed by the Committee with some changes of its own.[13] The rules were submitted to Congress, as the Enabling Act required, and when Congress adjourned without any adverse legislation,[14] the rules became effective September 16, 1938.

Even the best system of court rules cannot remain static. Experience under the rules, and continued scholarly thinking about problems of procedure, will disclose places in which improvement is possible. Amendment will be necessary in other instances to

9. Clark & Moore, A New Federal Civil Procedure: I. The Background, 1935, 44 Yale L.J. 387.

10. Subrin, note 8 above, at pp. 128–131. The letter appears in full in Mitchell, The Federal Rules of Civil Procedure, in David Dudley Field Centenary Essays, 1949, pp. 73, 76–78.

11. Address of Chief Justice Hughes, 1935, 55 S.Ct. xxxv, xxxvii, 21 A.B.A.J. 340, 12 A.L.I.Proc. 54.

12. Order of June 3, 1935, 295 U.S. 774. For a full list of members of the committee, see 4 Wright & Miller, Civil 2d § 1003, pp. 21–24.

The contributions of Dean—later Judge—Clark are described in Smith, Judge Charles E. Clark and The Federal Rules of Civil Procedure, 1976, 85 Yale L.J. 914. See also Subrin, note 8 above.

13. Order of Dec. 20, 1937, 302 U.S. 783. Justice Brandeis dissented from adoption of the rules.

14. There was opposition to the rules in the Senate, but that body took no action, since the House of Representatives favored the rules, and concurrent action of both houses would have been required to delay or defeat adoption of the rules. See Chandler, Some Major Advances in the Federal Judicial System, 1922–1947, 1963, 31 F.R.D. 307, 505–512.

remove unsound judicial glosses on the rules, or to codify desirable lines of decision. It is essential, therefore, that there be a continuing body charged with the responsibility of examining the rules in action and recommending change to the Court when this seems desirable.[15] The Advisory Committee that drafted the federal rules was reconstituted in 1942 to serve this function, and did so until its discharge in 1956. Various amendments were made by the Court, on the recommendation of that Committee, but the most significant was the set of amendments adopted in 1946, effective March 19, 1948, which reflected the results of a general study of the rules in operation.

The old Advisory Committee was discharged in 1956. In 1958 Congress amended the act creating the Judicial Conference to include among the duties of that body advising the Supreme Court with regard to necessary changes in the various rules the Court has power to make or amend.[16] An elaborate structure was created to assist the Judicial Conference, and ultimately the Court, in this task. There have been, as needed, advisory committees of practitioners, judges, and scholars for civil procedure, criminal procedure, appellate procedure, admiralty, bankruptcy, and evidence. These report to a standing Committee on Rules of Practice and Procedure and it in turn reports to the Judicial Conference.[17] The Judicial Conference transmits those recommendations it approves to the Supreme Court, for under this new plan, as under that in effect from 1934 to 1956, the Court retains ultimate responsibility for the adoption of amendments to the rules.

This new machinery led to significant amendments to the Civil Rules in 1961, 1963, 1966, 1970, 1980, and 1983. More recently there have been amendments almost every other year.

The success of the Federal Rules of Civil Procedure has been quite phenomenal. They provide for the federal courts a uniform procedure in civil actions. This in itself would be a fine accomplishment, but the rules go beyond this to create a uniform procedure that is flexible, simple, clear, and efficient. It may smack of hyperbole to say, as one commentator has, that the rules are "one

15. Clark, "Clarifying" Amendments to the Federal Rules, 1953, 14 Ohio St.L.J. 241; Wright, Rule 56(e): A Case Study on the Need for Amending the Federal Rules, 1956, 69 Harv.L.Rev. 839; Wright, Amendments to the Federal Rules: The Function of a Continuing Rules Committee, 1954, 7 Vand.L.Rev. 521.

16. 28 U.S.C.A. § 331, as amended by Act of July 11, 1958, 72 Stat. 356. For discussion of this amendment prior to its adoption, see Symposium, 1957, 21 F.R.D. 117.

17. The work of the new committees is described by the chairman of the Judicial Conference's Standing Committee on Rules of Practice and Procedure in Maris, Federal Procedural Rule–Making: The Program of the Judicial Conference, 1961, 37 A.B.A.J. 772. Their members are listed in 4 Wright & Miller, Civil 2d § 1007.

of the greatest contributions to the free and unhampered administration of law and justice ever struck off by any group of men since the dawn of civilized law."[18] It is nevertheless true that the chorus of approval of the rules by judges, lawyers, and commentators had been, until very recently, unanimous, unstinted, and spontaneous.[19] In the last few years, however, there has been questioning and reexamination of the assumptions about the proper goals of procedure that are at the heart of the Civil Rules.[20] This questioning has been sparked particularly by what some think is abuse of the discovery procedures made available by the rules.

The impact of the rules has not been limited to the federal courts. The excellence of the rules is such that in more than half the states the rules have been adapted for state use virtually unchanged, and there is not a jurisdiction that has not revised its procedure in some way that reflects the influence of the federal rules.[22]

The Enabling Act declares that the rules are to regulate only "practice and procedure" and are not to "abridge, enlarge or modify any substantive rights."[23] Particular rules have been attacked as affecting matters of substance, but the Supreme Court, in a notable series of decisions, has upheld all such rules challenged before it.[24]

18. Carey, In Favor of Uniformity, 1943, 3 F.R.D. 507, 18 Temp.L.Q. 145.

19. See 4 Wright & Miller, Civil 2d § 1008, and particularly n. 6.

20. Subrin, The New Era in American Civil Procedure, 1981, 67 A.B.A.J. 1648.

22. A commentator has pointed out, however, that certain provisions in the Civil Rules respond to special problems of a federal system and of courts of constitutionally limited jurisdiction, and that those provisions ought not be blindly adopted by the states. Rowe, A Comment on the Federalism of the Federal Rules, 1979 Duke L.J. 843.

23. 28 U.S.C.A. § 2072(b). See Carrington, "Substance" and "Procedure" in the Rules Enabling Act, 1989 Duke L.J. 281.

24. Hanna v. Plumer, 1965, 85 S.Ct. 1136, 380 U.S. 460, 14 L.Ed.2d 8 (Rule 4(d)(1)); Cold Metal Process Co. v. United Engineering & Foundry Co., 1956, 76 S.Ct. 904, 351 U.S. 445, 100 L.Ed. 1311 (amended Rule 54(b)); Mississippi Pub. Co. v. Murphree, 1946, 66 S.Ct. 242, 326 U.S. 438, 90 L.Ed. 185 (Rule 4(f)); Sibbach v. Wilson & Co., 1941, 61 S.Ct. 422, 312 U.S. 1, 85 L.Ed. 479 (Rule 35(a)).

It has been argued, however, that the Court has been too permissive in upholding rules that do affect substantive rights, contrary to the Enabling Act. Ely, The Irrepressible Myth of Erie, 1974, 87 Harv.L.Rev. 693. Professor Ely's view is rejected, in the course of a thoughtful decision holding that Rule 25(a) is valid, in Boggs v. Blue Diamond Coal Co., D.C.Ky.1980, 497 F.Supp. 1105, 1118–1121, noted 1981, 11 Mem.St.U.L.Rev. 413.

It has also been argued that the Supreme Court has become increasingly fond of using the plain-meaning doctrine to interpret the Federal Rules. Moore, The Supreme Court's Role in Interpreting the Federal Rules of Civil Procedure, 1993, 44 Hastings L.J. 1039. The author argues that because of the Court's dual roles as rulemaker and rule interpreter, the determination of the proper interpretation and application of a rule should be informed by many considerations beyond the simple literal language of the rule.

The success of the Civil Rules caused many to think that formulation of Federal Rules of Evidence would be desirable. An Advisory Committee on Rules of Evidence was created in 1965 and followed the methods of the committee that had drafted the Civil Rules in its work. Ultimately Federal Rules of Evidence became effective July 1, 1975, but their gestation period was as troubled as it was lengthy. ... [A] draft of Evidence Rules was promulgated by the Supreme Court in 1972, but they caused so much controversy that Congress passed a statute providing that they could not take effect until they were expressly approved by Act of Congress. Congress then made very substantial revisions in the rules as they had been promulgated by the Supreme Court before [enacting] them [as a statute,] to become effective in 1975.

The controversy over the Evidence Rules, and a similar furor over amendments to the Criminal Rules that the Supreme Court had approved in 1974, has led to some reappraisal of the rulemaking process.[27] The critics have not been directing themselves particularly to the Civil Rules, but insofar as the criticism goes to the methods that the rulemaking committees have used over the years, they must inevitably have an impact on future amendments of the Civil Rules. Legislation in 1988 amended the Enabling Act to respond to some of the arguments of the critics,[28] but the more important changes go to rules made by district courts and courts of appeals. Rulemaking by the Supreme Court for the federal courts generally is now subjected to closer public and congressional scrutiny, but is not changed in substance.[29]

Another threat to the integrity of the Civil Rules has come from the proliferation of local rules for particular districts. Although Rule 83 authorizes local rules, it had been expected that these would be few in number and confined to purely housekeeping matters. Instead the use of local rules has been extensive and they cover a great variety of important matters.[30] This in itself is a

27. Weinstein, Reform of Court Rule–Making Procedures, 1977 (shorter versions of this book appeared in 1977, 63 A.B.A.J. 47, and 1976, 76 Col.L.Rev. 905). See also Clinton, Rule 9 of the Federal Habeas Corpus Rules: A Case Study on the Need for Reform of the Rules Enabling Acts, 1977, 63 Iowa L.Rev. 15; Friedenthal, The Rulemaking Power of the Supreme Court: A Contemporary Crisis, 1975, 27 Stan.L.Rev. 673; Lesnick, The Federal Rule–Making Process: Time for Re-examination, 1975, 61 A.B.A.J. 579; Wright, Book Review, 1978, 9 St. Mary's L.J. 652.

28. Act of Nov. 19, 1988, Pub.L. 100–702, Title IV, 102 Stat. 4648.

29. Carrington, The New Order in Judicial Rulemaking, 1991, 75 Judicature 161; Mullenix, Hope Over Experience: Mandatory Informal Discovery and the Politics of Rulemaking, 1991, 69 N.C.L.Rev. 795.

It has been argued that recent controversies suggest that rulemaking should be reformed and follow what is done in modern administrative law. Walker, A Comprehensive Reform for Federal Civil Rulemaking, 1993, 61 Geo.Wash.L.Rev. 455.

30. 12 Wright, Miller & Marcus, Civil 2d § 3154. See also Coquilette, Squiers & Subrin, The Role of Local Rules, A.B.A.J., Jan. 1989, p. 62; Subrin, Federal Rules,

threat to uniformity of procedure throughout the country, the local rules often provide "a series of traps" [31] for lawyers from other districts, and the casual manner in which until recently the judges in a district have decided to adopt a rule or set of rules is in striking contrast to the care with which the Civil Rules themselves are made and amended. Almost every study of experience with local rules has demonstrated how unsatisfactory it has been.[32]

The Supreme Court sought to provide a check when it ruled in 1960 that the power to make local rules is not to be used to introduce "basic procedural innovations," [33] but it seemed to retreat from this when it later held that local rules reducing the size of civil juries from 12 to six did not fall afoul of that restriction.[34] Many local rules have been held invalid for this reason, or because they are inconsistent with the Civil Rules, an Act of Congress, or the Constitution,[35] but patently there are many other invalid local rules on the books that have escaped scrutiny in a contested case.[36]

Rule 83 was amended in 1985 to provide that local rules can be made only after appropriate public notice and an opportunity to comment, and to give the judicial council of the circuit power to abrogate any local rule of a district. These provisions were made

Local Rules, and State Rules: Uniformity, Divergence, and Emerging Procedural Patterns, 1989, 137 U.Pa.L.Rev. 1999.

31. Woodham v. American Cystoscope Co. of Pelham, C.A.5th, 1964, 335 F.2d 551, 552.

The difficulty in finding out what local rules are in effect is illustrated by Doran v. U.S., C.A.1st, 1973, 475 F.2d 742, where the United States attorney had no knowledge of a local rule in effect for 20 years. See also U.S. v. Ferretti, C.A.3d, 1980, 635 F.2d 1089, in which the judges in the district were uncertain about the continued existence of a local rule.

32. 12 Wright, Miller & Marcus, Civil 2d § 3152; Weinstein, note 27 above, at pp. 117–137; Roberts, The Myth of Uniformity in Federal Civil Procedure: Federal Civil Rule 83 and District Court Local Rulemaking Powers, 1985, 8 U.Puget Sound L.Rev. 537; Tobias, Civil Justice Reform and the Balkanization of Federal Civil Procedure, 1992, 24 Ariz.St.L.J. 1393, 1397–1401; Note, Rule 83 and the Local Federal Rules, 1967, 67 Col.L.Rev. 1251; Note, The Local Rules of Civil Procedure in the Federal District Courts—A Survey, 1966 Duke L.J. 1011.

But see Flanders, Local Rules in Federal District Courts: Usurpation, Legislation, or Information?, 1981, 14 Loy.L.A.L.Rev. 213; Flanders, In Praise of Local Rules, 1978, 62 Judicature 28.

33. Miner v. Atlass, 1960, 80 S.Ct. 1300, 1306, 363 U.S. 641, 650, 4 L.Ed.2d 1462.

34. Colgrove v. Battin, 1973, 93 S.Ct. 2448, 2456 n. 23, 413 U.S. 149, 163 n. 23, 37 L.Ed.2d 522.

35. See Frazier v. Heebe, 1987, 107 S.Ct. 2607, 482 U.S. 641, 96 L.Ed.2d 557; Carver v. Bunch, C.A.6th, 1991, 946 F.2d 451; Bailey v. Systems Innovation, Inc., C.A.3d, 1988, 852 F.2d 93; Carter v. Clark, C.A.5th, 1980, 616 F.2d 228; and cases cited in 12 Wright, Miller & Marcus, Civil 2d § 3153 nn. 77–79.

36. "[A]nother failure of rule 83 flows from the fact that occasions for judicially testing local rules have been and will continue to be infrequent. Given practical realities and economic constraints, few litigants will venture into battle over issues that seem so arcane." Roberts, note 32 above, at 546–547.

statutory in 1988. The statutes also require each district court and court of appeals to appoint an advisory committee to study and make recommendations about the rules of the court [37] and they give the Judicial Conference of the United States power to modify or abrogate a rule adopted by any court other than a district court or the Supreme Court.[38] These changes, if they stood alone, could improve the local rulemaking process. But the Civil Justice Reform Act of 1990 [39] has led to the adoption in many districts of procedures that vary among themselves and that are often inconsistent with the Federal Rules of Civil Procedure....

One of the most striking achievements in the federal rules from the first has been the simplified procedures they introduced for taking appeals. These matters were dealt with until 1968 by Civil Rules 73 to 76 and Criminal Rules 37 to 39. In that year the Federal Rules of Appellate Procedure were adopted, applicable to all cases, and the former civil and criminal provisions were repealed. The Appellate Rules incorporate in general the portions of the Civil Rules and Criminal Rules that they replaced but they also make uniform provision for a number of other matters of appellate practice that prior to 1968 were dealt with in varying ways by the rules of the eleven courts of appeals.

37. 28 U.S.C.A. §§ 2071, 2077(b). See also 28 U.S.C.A. § 332(d)(4).

38. 28 U.S.C.A. § 2071(c)(2).

39. 28 U.S.C.A. §§ 471–482, added by Act of Dec. 1, 1990, Pub.L. No. 101–650, 104 Stat. 5089.

*

RULES OF CIVIL PROCEDURE FOR THE UNITED STATES DISTRICT COURTS

TABLE OF RULES

RULES OF CIVIL PROCEDURE

RULES OF CIVIL PROCEDURE

RULES OF CIVIL PROCEDURE

Rule

APPENDIX OF FORMS

SUPPLEMENTAL RULES FOR ADMIRALTY OR MARITIME CLAIMS AND ASSET FORFEITURE ACTIONS

Rule

RULES OF CIVIL PROCEDURE

RULES OF CIVIL PROCEDURE FOR THE UNITED STATES DISTRICT COURTS

I. SCOPE OF RULES; FORM OF ACTION

Rule 1.

SCOPE AND PURPOSE

These rules govern the procedure in all civil actions and proceedings in the United States district courts, except as stated in Rule 81. They should be construed and administered to secure the just, speedy, and inexpensive determination of every action and proceeding.

As amended 1949, 1966, 1993, 2007.

Rule 2.

ONE FORM OF ACTION

There is one form of action—the civil action.

As amended 2007.

II. COMMENCING AN ACTION; SERVICE OF PROCESS, PLEADINGS, MOTIONS, AND ORDERS

Rule 3.

COMMENCING AN ACTION

A civil action is commenced by filing a complaint with the court.

As amended 2007.

Rule 4.

SUMMONS

(a) Contents; Amendments.

(1) *Contents.* A summons must:

   (A) name the court and the parties;

   (B) be directed to the defendant;

   (C) state the name and address of the plaintiff's attorney or—if unrepresented—of the plaintiff;

   (D) state the time within which the defendant must appear and defend;

   (E) notify the defendant that a failure to appear and defend will result in a default judgment against the defendant for the relief demanded in the complaint;

   (F) be signed by the clerk; and

   (G) bear the court's seal.

(2) *Amendments.* The court may permit a summons to be amended.

(b) Issuance. On or after filing the complaint, the plaintiff may present a summons to the clerk for signature and seal. If the summons is properly completed, the clerk must sign, seal, and issue it to the plaintiff for service on the defendant. A summons—or a copy of a summons that is addressed to multiple defendants—must be issued for each defendant to be served.

(c) Service.

(1) *In General.* A summons must be served with a copy of the complaint. The plaintiff is responsible for having the summons and complaint served within the time allowed by Rule 4(m) and must furnish the necessary copies to the person who makes service.

(2) *By Whom.* Any person who is at least 18 years old and not a party may serve a summons and complaint.

(3) *By a Marshal or Someone Specially Appointed.* At the plaintiff's request, the court may order that service be made by a United States marshal or deputy marshal or by a person specially appointed by the court. The court must so order if the plaintiff is authorized to proceed in forma pauperis under 28 U.S.C. § 1915 or as a seaman under 28 U.S.C. § 1916.

(d) Waiving Service.

(1) *Requesting a Waiver.* An individual, corporation, or association that is subject to service under Rule 4(e), (f), or (h) has a duty

to avoid unnecessary expenses of serving the summons. The plaintiff may notify such a defendant that an action has been commenced and request that the defendant waive service of a summons. The notice and request must:

(A) be in writing and be addressed:

(i) to the individual defendant; or

(ii) for a defendant subject to service under Rule 4(h), to an officer, a managing or general agent, or any other agent authorized by appointment or by law to receive service of process;

(B) name the court where the complaint was filed;

(C) be accompanied by a copy of the complaint, two copies of a waiver form, and a prepaid means for returning the form;

(D) inform the defendant, using text prescribed in Form 5, of the consequences of waiving and not waiving service;

(E) state the date when the request is sent;

(F) give the defendant a reasonable time of at least 30 days after the request was sent—or at least 60 days if sent to the defendant outside any judicial district of the United States—to return the waiver; and

(G) be sent by first-class mail or other reliable means.

(2) *Failure to Waive.* If a defendant located within the United States fails, without good cause, to sign and return a waiver requested by a plaintiff located within the United States, the court must impose on the defendant:

(A) the expenses later incurred in making service; and

(B) the reasonable expenses, including attorney's fees, of any motion required to collect those service expenses.

(3) *Time to Answer After a Waiver.* A defendant who, before being served with process, timely returns a waiver need not serve an answer to the complaint until 60 days after the request was sent—or until 90 days after it was sent to the defendant outside any judicial district of the United States.

(4) *Results of Filing a Waiver.* When the plaintiff files a waiver, proof of service is not required and these rules apply as if a summons and complaint had been served at the time of filing the waiver.

(5) *Jurisdiction and Venue Not Waived.* Waiving service of a summons does not waive any objection to personal jurisdiction or to venue.

(e) Serving an Individual Within a Judicial District of the United States. Unless federal law provides otherwise, an individual—other than a minor, an incompetent person, or a person whose waiver has been filed—may be served in a judicial district of the United States by:

(1) following state law for serving a summons in an action brought in courts of general jurisdiction in the state where the district court is located or where service is made; or

(2) doing any of the following:

(A) delivering a copy of the summons and of the complaint to the individual personally;

(B) leaving a copy of each at the individual's dwelling or usual place of abode with someone of suitable age and discretion who resides there; or

(C) delivering a copy of each to an agent authorized by appointment or by law to receive service of process.

(f) Serving an Individual in a Foreign Country. Unless federal law provides otherwise, an individual—other than a minor, an incompetent person, or a person whose waiver has been filed—may be served at a place not within any judicial district of the United States:

(1) by any internationally agreed means of service that is reasonably calculated to give notice, such as those authorized by the Hague Convention on the Service Abroad of Judicial and Extrajudicial Documents;

(2) if there is no internationally agreed means, or if an international agreement allows but does not specify other means, by a method that is reasonably calculated to give notice:

(A) as prescribed by the foreign country's law for service in that country in an action in its courts of general jurisdiction;

(B) as the foreign authority directs in response to a letter rogatory or letter of request; or

(C) unless prohibited by the foreign country's law, by:

(i) delivering a copy of the summons and of the complaint to the individual personally; or

(ii) using any form of mail that the clerk addresses and sends to the individual and that requires a signed receipt; or

(3) by other means not prohibited by international agreement, as the court orders.

(g) Serving a Minor or an Incompetent Person. A minor or an incompetent person in a judicial district of the United States must be served by following state law for serving a summons or like process on such a defendant in an action brought in the courts of general jurisdiction of the state where service is made. A minor or an incompetent person who is not within any judicial district of the United States must be served in the manner prescribed by Rule 4(f)(2)(A), (f)(2)(B), or (f)(3).

(h) Serving a Corporation, Partnership, or Association. Unless federal law provides otherwise or the defendant's waiver has been filed, a domestic or foreign corporation, or a partnership or other unincorporated association that is subject to suit under a common name, must be served:

(1) in a judicial district of the United States:

(A) in the manner prescribed by Rule 4(e)(1) for serving an individual; or

(B) by delivering a copy of the summons and of the complaint to an officer, a managing or general agent, or any other agent authorized by appointment or by law to receive service of process and—if the agent is one authorized by statute and the statute so requires—by also mailing a copy of each to the defendant; or

(2) at a place not within any judicial district of the United States, in any manner prescribed by Rule 4(f) for serving an individual, except personal delivery under (f)(2)(C)(i).

(i) Serving the United States and Its Agencies, Corporations, Officers, or Employees.

(1) *United States.* To serve the United States, a party must:

(A)(i) deliver a copy of the summons and of the complaint to the United States attorney for the district where the action is brought—or to an assistant United States attorney or clerical employee whom the United States attorney designates in a writing filed with the court clerk—or

(ii) send a copy of each by registered or certified mail to the civil-process clerk at the United States attorney's office;

(B) send a copy of each by registered or certified mail to the Attorney General of the United States at Washington, D.C.; and

(C) if the action challenges an order of a nonparty agency or officer of the United States, send a copy of each by registered or certified mail to the agency or officer.

(2) *Agency; Corporation; Officer or Employee Sued in an Official Capacity.* To serve a United States agency or corporation, or a

United States officer or employee sued only in an official capacity, a party must serve the United States and also send a copy of the summons and of the complaint by registered or certified mail to the agency, corporation, officer, or employee.

(3) *Officer or Employee Sued Individually.* To serve a United States officer or employee sued in an individual capacity for an act or omission occurring in connection with duties performed on the United States' behalf (whether or not the officer or employee is also sued in an official capacity), a party must serve the United States and also serve the officer or employee under Rule 4(e), (f), or (g).

(4) *Extending Time.* The court must allow a party a reasonable time to cure its failure to:

(A) serve a person required to be served under Rule 4(i)(2), if the party has served either the United States attorney or the Attorney General of the United States; or

(B) serve the United States under Rule 4(i)(3), if the party has served the United States officer or employee.

(j) Serving a Foreign, State, or Local Government.

(1) *Foreign State.* A foreign state or its political subdivision, agency, or instrumentality must be served in accordance with 28 U.S.C. § 1608.

(2) *State or Local Government.* A state, a municipal corporation, or any other state-created governmental organization that is subject to suit must be served by:

(A) delivering a copy of the summons and of the complaint to its chief executive officer; or

(B) serving a copy of each in the manner prescribed by that state's law for serving a summons or like process on such a defendant.

(k) Territorial Limits of Effective Service.

(1) *In General.* Serving a summons or filing a waiver of service establishes personal jurisdiction over a defendant:

(A) who is subject to the jurisdiction of a court of general jurisdiction in the state where the district court is located;

(B) who is a party joined under Rule 14 or 19 and is served within a judicial district of the United States and not more than 100 miles from where the summons was issued; or

(C) when authorized by a federal statute.

(2) *Federal Claim Outside State–Court Jurisdiction.* For a claim that arises under federal law, serving a summons or filing a waiver of service establishes personal jurisdiction over a defendant if:

(A) the defendant is not subject to jurisdiction in any state's courts of general jurisdiction; and

(B) exercising jurisdiction is consistent with the United States Constitution and laws.

(*l*) Proving Service.

(1) *Affidavit Required.* Unless service is waived, proof of service must be made to the court. Except for service by a United States marshal or deputy marshal, proof must be by the server's affidavit.

(2) *Service Outside the United States.* Service not within any judicial district of the United States must be proved as follows:

(A) if made under Rule 4(f)(1), as provided in the applicable treaty or convention; or

(B) if made under Rule 4(f)(2) or (f)(3), by a receipt signed by the addressee, or by other evidence satisfying the court that the summons and complaint were delivered to the addressee.

(3) *Validity of Service; Amending Proof.* Failure to prove service does not affect the validity of service. The court may permit proof of service to be amended.

(m) Time Limit for Service. If a defendant is not served within 120 days after the complaint is filed, the court—on motion or on its own after notice to the plaintiff—must dismiss the action without prejudice against that defendant or order that service be made within a specified time. But if the plaintiff shows good cause for the failure, the court must extend the time for service for an appropriate period. This subdivision (m) does not apply to service in a foreign country under Rule 4(f) or 4(j)(1).

(n) Asserting Jurisdiction over Property or Assets.

(1) *Federal Law.* The court may assert jurisdiction over property if authorized by a federal statute. Notice to claimants of the property must be given as provided in the statute or by serving a summons under this rule.

(2) *State Law.* On a showing that personal jurisdiction over a defendant cannot be obtained in the district where the action is brought by reasonable efforts to serve a summons under this rule, the court may assert jurisdiction over the defendant's assets found in the district. Jurisdiction is acquired by seizing the assets under the circumstances and in the manner provided by state law in that district.

As amended 1963, 1966, 1980, 1983, 1987, 1993, 2000, 2007.

Rule 4.1.

SERVING OTHER PROCESS

(a) In General. Process—other than a summons under Rule 4 or a subpoena under Rule 45—must be served by a United States marshal or deputy marshal or by a person specially appointed for that purpose. It may be served anywhere within the territorial limits of the state where the district court is located and, if authorized by a federal statute, beyond those limits. Proof of service must be made under Rule 4(*l*).

(b) Enforcing Orders: Committing for Civil Contempt. An order committing a person for civil contempt of a decree or injunction issued to enforce federal law may be served and enforced in any district. Any other order in a civil-contempt proceeding may be served only in the state where the issuing court is located or elsewhere in the United States within 100 miles from where the order was issued.

Added 1993; as amended 2007.

Rule 5.

SERVING AND FILING PLEADINGS AND OTHER PAPERS

(a) Service: When Required.

(1) *In General.* Unless these rules provide otherwise, each of the following papers must be served on every party:

(A) an order stating that service is required;

(B) a pleading filed after the original complaint, unless the court orders otherwise under Rule 5(c) because there are numerous defendants;

(C) a discovery paper required to be served on a party, unless the court orders otherwise;

(D) a written motion, except one that may be heard ex parte; and

(E) a written notice, appearance, demand, or offer of judgment, or any similar paper.

(2) *If a Party Fails to Appear.* No service is required on a party who is in default for failing to appear. But a pleading that asserts a new claim for relief against such a party must be served on that party under Rule 4.

(3) *Seizing Property.* If an action is begun by seizing property and no person is or need be named as a defendant, any service

required before the filing of an appearance, answer, or claim must be made on the person who had custody or possession of the property when it was seized.

(b) Service: How Made.

(1) *Serving an Attorney.* If a party is represented by an attorney, service under this rule must be made on the attorney unless the court orders service on the party.

(2) *Service in General.* A paper is served under this rule by:

(A) handing it to the person;

(B) leaving it:

(i) at the person's office with a clerk or other person in charge or, if no one is in charge, in a conspicuous place in the office; or

(ii) if the person has no office or the office is closed, at the person's dwelling or usual place of abode with someone of suitable age and discretion who resides there;

(C) mailing it to the person's last known address—in which event service is complete upon mailing;

(D) leaving it with the court clerk if the person has no known address;

(E) sending it by electronic means if the person consented in writing—in which event service is complete upon transmission, but is not effective if the serving party learns that it did not reach the person to be served; or

(F) delivering it by any other means that the person consented to in writing—in which event service is complete when the person making service delivers it to the agency designated to make delivery.

(3) *Using Court Facilities.* If a local rule so authorizes, a party may use the court's transmission facilities to make service under Rule 5(b)(2)(E).

(c) Serving Numerous Defendants.

(1) *In General.* If an action involves an unusually large number of defendants, the court may, on motion or on its own, order that:

(A) defendants' pleadings and replies to them need not be served on other defendants;

(B) any crossclaim, counterclaim, avoidance, or affirmative defense in those pleadings and replies to them will be treated as denied or avoided by all other parties; and

(C) filing any such pleading and serving it on the plaintiff constitutes notice of the pleading to all parties.

(2) *Notifying Parties.* A copy of every such order must be served on the parties as the court directs.

(d) Filing.

(1) *Required Filings; Certificate of Service.* Any paper after the complaint that is required to be served—together with a certificate of service—must be filed within a reasonable time after service. But disclosures under Rule 26(a)(1) or (2) and the following discovery requests and responses must not be filed until they are used in the proceeding or the court orders filing: depositions, interrogatories, requests for documents or tangible things or to permit entry onto land, and requests for admission.

(2) *How Filing Is Made—In General.* A paper is filed by delivering it:

(A) to the clerk; or

(B) to a judge who agrees to accept it for filing, and who must then note the filing date on the paper and promptly send it to the clerk.

(3) *Electronic Filing, Signing, or Verification.* A court may, by local rule, allow papers to be filed, signed, or verified by electronic means that are consistent with any technical standards established by the Judicial Conference of the United States. A local rule may require electronic filing only if reasonable exceptions are allowed. A paper filed electronically in compliance with a local rule is a written paper for purposes of these rules.

(4) *Acceptance by the Clerk.* The clerk must not refuse to file a paper solely because it is not in the form prescribed by these rules or by a local rule or practice.

As amended 1963, 1970, 1980, 1987, 1991, 1993, 1996, 2000, 2001, 2006, 2007.

Rule 5.1.

CONSTITUTIONAL CHALLENGE TO A STATUTE— NOTICE, CERTIFICATION, AND INTERVENTION

(a) Notice by a Party. A party that files a pleading, written motion, or other paper drawing into question the constitutionality of a federal or state statute must promptly:

(1) file a notice of constitutional question stating the question and identifying the paper that raises it, if:

(A) a federal statute is questioned and the parties do not include the United States, one of its agencies, or one of its officers or employees in an official capacity; or

(B) a state statute is questioned and the parties do not include the state, one of its agencies, or one of its officers or employees in an official capacity; and

(2) serve the notice and paper on the Attorney General of the United States if a federal statute is questioned—or on the state attorney general if a state statute is questioned—either by certified or registered mail or by sending it to an electronic address designated by the attorney general for this purpose.

(b) Certification by the Court. The court must, under 28 U.S.C. § 2403, certify to the appropriate attorney general that a statute has been questioned.

(c) Intervention; Final Decision on the Merits. Unless the court sets a later time, the attorney general may intervene within 60 days after the notice is filed or after the court certifies the challenge, whichever is earlier. Before the time to intervene expires, the court may reject the constitutional challenge, but may not enter a final judgment holding the statute unconstitutional.

(d) No Forfeiture. A party's failure to file and serve the notice, or the court's failure to certify, does not forfeit a constitutional claim or defense that is otherwise timely asserted.

Added 2006; as amended 2007.

Rule 5.2.

PRIVACY PROTECTION FOR FILINGS MADE WITH THE COURT

(a) Redacted Filings. Unless the court orders otherwise, in an electronic or paper filing with the court that contains an individual's social-security number, taxpayer-identification number, or birth date, the name of an individual known to be a minor, or a financial-account number, a party or nonparty making the filing may include only:

(1) the last four digits of the social-security number and taxpayer-identification number;

(2) the year of the individual's birth;

(3) the minor's initials; and

(4) the last four digits of the financial-account number.

(b) Exemptions from the Redaction Requirement. The redaction requirement does not apply to the following:

(1) a financial-account number that identifies the property allegedly subject to forfeiture in a forfeiture proceeding;

(2) the record of an administrative or agency proceeding;

(3) the official record of a state-court proceeding;

(4) the record of a court or tribunal, if that record was not subject to the redaction requirement when originally filed;

(5) a filing covered by Rule 5.2(c) or (d); and

(6) a pro se filing in an action brought under 28 U.S.C. §§ 2241, 2254, or 2255.

(c) Limitations on Remote Access to Electronic Files; Social–Security Appeals and Immigration Cases. Unless the court orders otherwise, in an action for benefits under the Social Security Act, and in an action or proceeding relating to an order of removal, to relief from removal, or to immigration benefits or detention, access to an electronic file is authorized as follows:

(1) the parties and their attorneys may have remote electronic access to any part of the case file, including the administrative record;

(2) any other person may have electronic access to the full record at the courthouse, but may have remote electronic access only to:

(A) the docket maintained by the court; and

(B) an opinion, order, judgment, or other disposition of the court, but not any other part of the case file or the administrative record.

(d) Filings Made Under Seal. The court may order that a filing be made under seal without redaction. The court may later unseal the filing or order the person who made the filing to file a redacted version for the public record.

(e) Protective Orders. For good cause, the court may by order in a case:

(1) require redaction of additional information; or

(2) limit or prohibit a nonparty's remote electronic access to a document filed with the court.

(f) Option for Additional Unredacted Filing Under Seal. A person making a redacted filing may also file an unredacted copy under seal. The court must retain the unredacted copy as part of the record.

(g) Option for Filing a Reference List. A filing that contains redacted information may be filed together with a reference list that identifies each item of redacted information and specifies an appropriate identifier that uniquely corresponds to each item listed. The list must be filed under seal and may be amended as of right. Any reference in the case to a listed identifier will be construed to refer to the corresponding item of information.

(h) Waiver of Protection of Identifiers. A person waives the protection of Rule 5.2(a) as to the person's own information by filing it without redaction and not under seal.

Added 2007.

Rule 6.

COMPUTING AND EXTENDING TIME; TIME FOR MOTION PAPERS

(a) Computing Time. The following rules apply in computing any time period specified in these rules, in any local rule or court order, or in any statute that does not specify a method of computing time.

(1) *Period Stated in Days or a Longer Unit.* When the period is stated in days or a longer unit of time:

(A) exclude the day of the event that triggers the period;

(B) count every day, including intermediate Saturdays, Sundays, and legal holidays; and

(C) include the last day of the period, but if the last day is a Saturday, Sunday, or legal holiday, the period continues to run until the end of the next day that is not a Saturday, Sunday, or legal holiday.

(2) *Period Stated in Hours.* When the period is stated in hours:

(A) begin counting immediately on the occurrence of the event that triggers the period;

(B) count every hour, including hours during intermediate Saturdays, Sundays, and legal holidays; and

(C) if the period would end on a Saturday, Sunday, or legal holiday, the period continues to run until the same time on the next day that is not a Saturday, Sunday, or legal holiday.

(3) *Inaccessibility of the Clerk's Office.* Unless the court orders otherwise, if the clerk's office is inaccessible:

(A) on the last day for filing under Rule 6(a)(1), then the time for filing is extended to the first accessible day that is not a Saturday, Sunday, or legal holiday; or

(B) during the last hour for filing under Rule 6(a)(2), then the time for filing is extended to the same time on the first accessible day that is not a Saturday, Sunday, or legal holiday.

(4) *"Last Day" Defined.* Unless a different time is set by a statute, local rule, or court order, the last day ends:

(A) for electronic filing, at midnight in the court's time zone; and

(B) for filing by other means, when the clerk's office is scheduled to close.

(5) *"Next Day" Defined.* The "next day" is determined by continuing to count forward when the period is measured after an event and backward when measured before an event.

(6) *"Legal Holiday" Defined.* "Legal holiday" means:

(A) the day set aside by statute for observing New Year's Day, Martin Luther King Jr.'s Birthday, Washington's Birthday, Memorial Day, Independence Day, Labor Day, Columbus Day, Veterans' Day, Thanksgiving Day, or Christmas Day;

(B) any day declared a holiday by the President or Congress; and

(C) for periods that are measured after an event, any other day declared a holiday by the state where the district court is located.

(b) Extending Time.

(1) *In General.* When an act may or must be done within a specified time, the court may, for good cause, extend the time:

(A) with or without motion or notice if the court acts, or if a request is made, before the original time or its extension expires; or

(B) on motion made after the time has expired if the party failed to act because of excusable neglect.

(2) *Exceptions.* A court must not extend the time to act under Rules 50(b) and (d), 52(b), 59(b), (d), and (e), and 60(b).

(c) Motions, Notices of Hearing, and Affidavits.

(1) *In General.* A written motion and notice of the hearing must be served at least 14 days before the time specified for the hearing, with the following exceptions:

(A) when the motion may be heard ex parte;

(B) when these rules set a different time; or

(C) when a court order—which a party may, for good cause, apply for ex parte—sets a different time.

(2) *Supporting Affidavit.* Any affidavit supporting a motion must be served with the motion. Except as Rule 59(c) provides otherwise, any opposing affidavit must be served at least 7 days before the hearing, unless the court permits service at another time.

(d) Additional Time After Certain Kinds of Service. When a party may or must act within a specified time after service and service is made under Rule 5(b)(2)(C), (D), (E), or (F), 3 days are added after the period would otherwise expire under Rule 6(a).

As amended 1948, 1963, 1966, 1968, 1971, 1983, 1985, 1987, 1999, 2001, 2005, 2007, 2009.

III. PLEADINGS AND MOTIONS

Rule 7.

PLEADINGS ALLOWED; FORM OF MOTIONS AND OTHER PAPERS

(a) Pleadings. Only these pleadings are allowed:

(1) a complaint;

(2) an answer to a complaint;

(3) an answer to a counterclaim designated as a counterclaim;

(4) an answer to a crossclaim;

(5) a third-party complaint;

(6) an answer to a third-party complaint; and

(7) if the court orders one, a reply to an answer.

(b) Motions and Other Papers.

(1) *In General.* A request for a court order must be made by motion. The motion must:

(A) be in writing unless made during a hearing or trial;

(B) state with particularity the grounds for seeking the order; and

(C) state the relief sought.

(2) *Form.* The rules governing captions and other matters of form in pleadings apply to motions and other papers.

As amended 1948, 1963, 1983, 2007.

Rule 7.1.

DISCLOSURE STATEMENT

(a) Who Must File; Contents. A nongovernmental corporate party must file two copies of a disclosure statement that:

(1) identifies any parent corporation and any publicly held corporation owning 10% or more of its stock; or

(2) states that there is no such corporation.

(b) Time to File; Supplemental Filing. A party must:

(1) file the disclosure statement with its first appearance, pleading, petition, motion, response, or other request addressed to the court; and

(2) promptly file a supplemental statement if any required information changes.

Added 2002; as amended 2007.

Rule 8.

GENERAL RULES OF PLEADING

(a) Claim for Relief. A pleading that states a claim for relief must contain:

(1) a short and plain statement of the grounds for the court's jurisdiction, unless the court already has jurisdiction and the claim needs no new jurisdictional support;

(2) a short and plain statement of the claim showing that the pleader is entitled to relief; and

(3) a demand for the relief sought, which may include relief in the alternative or different types of relief.

(b) Defenses; Admissions and Denials.

(1) *In General.* In responding to a pleading, a party must:

(A) state in short and plain terms its defenses to each claim asserted against it; and

(B) admit or deny the allegations asserted against it by an opposing party.

(2) *Denials—Responding to the Substance.* A denial must fairly respond to the substance of the allegation.

(3) *General and Specific Denials.* A party that intends in good faith to deny all the allegations of a pleading—including the jurisdictional grounds—may do so by a general denial. A party that does not intend to deny all the allegations must either specifically deny designated allegations or generally deny all except those specifically admitted.

(4) *Denying Part of an Allegation.* A party that intends in good faith to deny only part of an allegation must admit the part that is true and deny the rest.

(5) *Lacking Knowledge or Information.* A party that lacks knowledge or information sufficient to form a belief about the truth

of an allegation must so state, and the statement has the effect of a denial.

(6) *Effect of Failing to Deny.* An allegation—other than one relating to the amount of damages—is admitted if a responsive pleading is required and the allegation is not denied. If a responsive pleading is not required, an allegation is considered denied or avoided.

(c) Affirmative Defenses.

(1) *In General.* In responding to a pleading, a party must affirmatively state any avoidance or affirmative defense, including:

- accord and satisfaction;
- arbitration and award;
- assumption of risk;
- contributory negligence;
- discharge in bankruptcy;
- duress;
- estoppel;
- failure of consideration;
- fraud;
- illegality;
- injury by fellow servant;
- laches;
- license;
- payment;
- release;
- res judicata;
- statute of frauds;
- statute of limitations; and
- waiver.

(2) *Mistaken Designation.* If a party mistakenly designates a defense as a counterclaim, or a counterclaim as a defense, the court must, if justice requires, treat the pleading as though it were correctly designated, and may impose terms for doing so.

(d) Pleading to Be Concise and Direct; Alternative Statements; Inconsistency.

(1) *In General.* Each allegation must be simple, concise, and direct. No technical form is required.

(2) *Alternative Statements of a Claim or Defense.* A party may set out two or more statements of a claim or defense alternatively or hypothetically, either in a single count or defense or in separate ones. If a party makes alternative statements, the pleading is sufficient if any one of them is sufficient.

(3) *Inconsistent Claims or Defenses.* A party may state as many separate claims or defenses as it has, regardless of consistency.

(e) Construing Pleadings. Pleadings must be construed so as to do justice.

As amended 1966, 1987, 2007.

Rule 9.

PLEADING SPECIAL MATTERS

(a) Capacity or Authority to Sue; Legal Existence.

(1) *In General.* Except when required to show that the court has jurisdiction, a pleading need not allege:

(A) a party's capacity to sue or be sued;

(B) a party's authority to sue or be sued in a representative capacity; or

(C) the legal existence of an organized association of persons that is made a party.

(2) *Raising Those Issues.* To raise any of those issues, a party must do so by a specific denial, which must state any supporting facts that are peculiarly within the party's knowledge.

(b) Fraud or Mistake; Conditions of Mind. In alleging fraud or mistake, a party must state with particularity the circumstances constituting fraud or mistake. Malice, intent, knowledge, and other conditions of a person's mind may be alleged generally.

(c) Conditions Precedent. In pleading conditions precedent, it suffices to allege generally that all conditions precedent have occurred or been performed. But when denying that a condition precedent has occurred or been performed, a party must do so with particularity.

(d) Official Document or Act. In pleading an official document or official act, it suffices to allege that the document was legally issued or the act legally done.

(e) Judgment. In pleading a judgment or decision of a domestic or foreign court, a judicial or quasi-judicial tribunal, or a board or officer, it suffices to plead the judgment or decision without showing jurisdiction to render it.

(f) Time and Place. An allegation of time or place is material when testing the sufficiency of a pleading.

(g) Special Damages. If an item of special damage is claimed, it must be specifically stated.

(h) Admiralty or Maritime Claim.

(1) *How Designated.* If a claim for relief is within the admiralty or maritime jurisdiction and also within the court's subject-matter jurisdiction on some other ground, the pleading may designate the claim as an admiralty or maritime claim for purposes of Rules 14(c), 38(e), and 82 and the Supplemental Rules for Admiralty or Maritime Claims and Asset Forfeiture Actions. A claim cognizable only in the admiralty or maritime jurisdiction is an admiralty or maritime claim for those purposes, whether or not so designated.

(2) *Designation for Appeal.* A case that includes an admiralty or maritime claim within this subdivision (h) is an admiralty case within 28 U.S.C. § 1292(a)(3).

As amended 1966, 1968, 1970, 1987, 1997, 2006, 2007.

Rule 10.

FORM OF PLEADINGS

(a) Caption; Names of Parties. Every pleading must have a caption with the court's name, a title, a file number, and a Rule 7(a) designation. The title of the complaint must name all the parties; the title of other pleadings, after naming the first party on each side, may refer generally to other parties.

(b) Paragraphs; Separate Statements. A party must state its claims or defenses in numbered paragraphs, each limited as far as practicable to a single set of circumstances. A later pleading may refer by number to a paragraph in an earlier pleading. If doing so would promote clarity, each claim founded on a separate transaction or occurrence—and each defense other than a denial—must be stated in a separate count or defense.

(c) Adoption by Reference; Exhibits. A statement in a pleading may be adopted by reference elsewhere in the same pleading or in any other pleading or motion. A copy of a written instrument that is an exhibit to a pleading is a part of the pleading for all purposes.

As amended 2007.

Rule 11.

SIGNING PLEADINGS, MOTIONS, AND OTHER PAPERS; REPRESENTATIONS TO THE COURT; SANCTIONS

(a) Signature. Every pleading, written motion, and other paper must be signed by at least one attorney of record in the attorney's name—or by a party personally if the party is unrepresented. The paper must state the signer's address, e-mail address, and telephone number. Unless a rule or statute specifically states otherwise, a pleading need not be verified or accompanied by an affidavit. The court must strike an unsigned paper unless the omission is promptly corrected after being called to the attorney's or party's attention.

(b) Representations to the Court. By presenting to the court a pleading, written motion, or other paper—whether by signing, filing, submitting, or later advocating it—an attorney or unrepresented party certifies that to the best of the person's knowledge, information, and belief, formed after an inquiry reasonable under the circumstances:

(1) it is not being presented for any improper purpose, such as to harass, cause unnecessary delay, or needlessly increase the cost of litigation;

(2) the claims, defenses, and other legal contentions are warranted by existing law or by a nonfrivolous argument for extending, modifying, or reversing existing law or for establishing new law;

(3) the factual contentions have evidentiary support or, if specifically so identified, will likely have evidentiary support after a reasonable opportunity for further investigation or discovery; and

(4) the denials of factual contentions are warranted on the evidence or, if specifically so identified, are reasonably based on belief or a lack of information.

(c) Sanctions.

(1) *In General.* If, after notice and a reasonable opportunity to respond, the court determines that Rule 11(b) has been violated, the court may impose an appropriate sanction on any attorney, law firm, or party that violated the rule or is responsible for the violation. Absent exceptional circumstances, a law firm must be held jointly responsible for a violation committed by its partner, associate, or employee.

(2) *Motion for Sanctions.* A motion for sanctions must be made separately from any other motion and must describe the specific conduct that allegedly violates Rule 11(b). The motion must be served under Rule 5, but it must not be filed or be presented to the court if the challenged paper, claim, defense, contention, or denial is withdrawn or appropriately corrected within 21 days after service or within another time the court sets. If warranted, the court may award to the prevailing party the reasonable expenses, including attorney's fees, incurred for the motion.

(3) *On the Court's Initiative.* On its own, the court may order an attorney, law firm, or party to show cause why conduct specifically described in the order has not violated Rule 11(b).

(4) *Nature of a Sanction.* A sanction imposed under this rule must be limited to what suffices to deter repetition of the conduct or comparable conduct by others similarly situated. The sanction may include nonmonetary directives; an order to pay a penalty into court; or, if imposed on motion and warranted for effective deterrence, an order directing payment to the movant of part or all of the reasonable attorney's fees and other expenses directly resulting from the violation.

(5) *Limitations on Monetary Sanctions.* The court must not impose a monetary sanction:

    (A) against a represented party for violating Rule 11(b)(2); or

    (B) on its own, unless it issued the show-cause order under Rule 11(c)(3) before voluntary dismissal or settlement of the claims made by or against the party that is, or whose attorneys are, to be sanctioned.

(6) *Requirements for an Order.* An order imposing a sanction must describe the sanctioned conduct and explain the basis for the sanction.

(d) Inapplicability to Discovery. This rule does not apply to disclosures and discovery requests, responses, objections, and motions under Rules 26 through 37.

As amended 1983, 1987, 1993, 2007.

Rule 12.

DEFENSES AND OBJECTIONS: WHEN AND HOW PRESENTED; MOTION FOR JUDGMENT ON THE PLEADINGS; CONSOLIDATING MOTIONS; WAIVING DEFENSES; PRETRIAL HEARING

(a) Time to Serve a Responsive Pleading.

(1) *In General.* Unless another time is specified by this rule or a federal statute, the time for serving a responsive pleading is as follows:

(A) A defendant must serve an answer:

(i) within 21 days after being served with the summons and complaint; or

(ii) if it has timely waived service under Rule 4(d), within 60 days after the request for a waiver was sent, or within 90 days after it was sent to the defendant outside any judicial district of the United States.

(B) A party must serve an answer to a counterclaim or crossclaim within 21 days after being served with the pleading that states the counterclaim or crossclaim.

(C) A party must serve a reply to an answer within 21 days after being served with an order to reply, unless the order specifies a different time.

(2) *United States and Its Agencies, Officers, or Employees Sued in an Official Capacity.* The United States, a United States agency, or a United States officer or employee sued only in an official capacity must serve an answer to a complaint, counterclaim, or crossclaim within 60 days after service on the United States attorney.

(3) *United States Officers or Employees Sued in an Individual Capacity.* A United States officer or employee sued in an individual capacity for an act or omission occurring in connection with duties performed on the United States' behalf must serve an answer to a complaint, counterclaim, or crossclaim within 60 days after service on the officer or employee or service on the United States attorney, whichever is later.

(4) *Effect of a Motion.* Unless the court sets a different time, serving a motion under this rule alters these periods as follows:

(A) if the court denies the motion or postpones its disposition until trial, the responsive pleading must be served within 14 days after notice of the court's action; or

(B) if the court grants a motion for a more definite statement, the responsive pleading must be served within 14 days after the more definite statement is served.

(b) How to Present Defenses. Every defense to a claim for relief in any pleading must be asserted in the responsive pleading if one is required. But a party may assert the following defenses by motion:

(1) lack of subject-matter jurisdiction;

(2) lack of personal jurisdiction;

(3) improper venue;

(4) insufficient process;

(5) insufficient service of process;

(6) failure to state a claim upon which relief can be granted; and

(7) failure to join a party under Rule 19.

A motion asserting any of these defenses must be made before pleading if a responsive pleading is allowed. If a pleading sets out a claim for relief that does not require a responsive pleading, an opposing party may assert at trial any defense to that claim. No defense or objection is waived by joining it with one or more other defenses or objections in a responsive pleading or in a motion.

(c) Motion for Judgment on the Pleadings. After the pleadings are closed—but early enough not to delay trial—a party may move for judgment on the pleadings.

(d) Result of Presenting Matters Outside the Pleadings. If, on a motion under Rule 12(b)(6) or 12(c), matters outside the pleadings are presented to and not excluded by the court, the motion must be treated as one for summary judgment under Rule 56. All parties must be given a reasonable opportunity to present all the material that is pertinent to the motion.

(e) Motion for a More Definite Statement. A party may move for a more definite statement of a pleading to which a responsive pleading is allowed but which is so vague or ambiguous that the party cannot reasonably prepare a response. The motion must be made before filing a responsive pleading and must point out the defects complained of and the details desired. If the court orders a more definite statement and the order is not obeyed within 14 days after notice of the order or within the time the court sets, the court may strike the pleading or issue any other appropriate order.

(f) Motion to Strike. The court may strike from a pleading an insufficient defense or any redundant, immaterial, impertinent, or scandalous matter. The court may act:

(1) on its own; or

(2) on motion made by a party either before responding to the pleading or, if a response is not allowed, within 21 days after being served with the pleading.

(g) Joining Motions.

(1) *Right to Join.* A motion under this rule may be joined with any other motion allowed by this rule.

(2) *Limitation on Further Motions.* Except as provided in Rule 12(h)(2) or (3), a party that makes a motion under this rule must not make another motion under this rule raising a defense or objection that was available to the party but omitted from its earlier motion.

(h) Waiving and Preserving Certain Defenses.

(1) *When Some Are Waived.* A party waives any defense listed in Rule 12(b)(2)–(5) by:

(A) omitting it from a motion in the circumstances described in Rule 12(g)(2); or

(B) failing to either:

(i) make it by motion under this rule; or

(ii) include it in a responsive pleading or in an amendment allowed by Rule 15(a)(1) as a matter of course.

(2) *When to Raise Others.* Failure to state a claim upon which relief can be granted, to join a person required by Rule 19(b), or to state a legal defense to a claim may be raised:

(A) in any pleading allowed or ordered under Rule 7(a);

(B) by a motion under Rule 12(c); or

(C) at trial.

(3) *Lack of Subject–Matter Jurisdiction.* If the court determines at any time that it lacks subject-matter jurisdiction, the court must dismiss the action.

(i) Hearing Before Trial. If a party so moves, any defense listed in Rule 12(b)(1)–(7)—whether made in a pleading or by motion—and a motion under Rule 12(c) must be heard and decided before trial unless the court orders a deferral until trial.

As amended 1948, 1963, 1966, 1987, 1993, 2000, 2007, 2009.

Rule 13.

COUNTERCLAIM AND CROSSCLAIM

(a) Compulsory Counterclaim.

(1) *In General.* A pleading must state as a counterclaim any claim that—at the time of its service—the pleader has against an opposing party if the claim:

(A) arises out of the transaction or occurrence that is the subject matter of the opposing party's claim; and

(B) does not require adding another party over whom the court cannot acquire jurisdiction.

(2) *Exceptions.* The pleader need not state the claim if:

(A) when the action was commenced, the claim was the subject of another pending action; or

(B) the opposing party sued on its claim by attachment or other process that did not establish personal jurisdiction over the pleader on that claim, and the pleader does not assert any counterclaim under this rule.

(b) Permissive Counterclaim. A pleading may state as a counterclaim against an opposing party any claim that is not compulsory.

(c) Relief Sought in a Counterclaim. A counterclaim need not diminish or defeat the recovery sought by the opposing party. It may request relief that exceeds in amount or differs in kind from the relief sought by the opposing party.

(d) Counterclaim Against the United States. These rules do not expand the right to assert a counterclaim—or to claim a credit—against the United States or a United States officer or agency.

(e) Counterclaim Maturing or Acquired After Pleading. The court may permit a party to file a supplemental pleading asserting a counterclaim that matured or was acquired by the party after serving an earlier pleading.

(f) [Abrogated.]

(g) Crossclaim Against a Coparty. A pleading may state as a crossclaim any claim by one party against a coparty if the claim arises out of the transaction or occurrence that is the subject matter of the original action or of a counterclaim, or if the claim relates to any property that is the subject matter of the original action. The crossclaim may include a claim that the coparty is or

43

may be liable to the crossclaimant for all or part of a claim asserted in the action against the crossclaimant.

(h) **Joining Additional Parties.** Rules 19 and 20 govern the addition of a person as a party to a counterclaim or crossclaim.

(i) **Separate Trials; Separate Judgments.** If the court orders separate trials under Rule 42(b), it may enter judgment on a counterclaim or crossclaim under Rule 54(b) when it has jurisdiction to do so, even if the opposing party's claims have been dismissed or otherwise resolved.

As amended 1948, 1963, 1966, 1987, 2007, 2009.

Rule 14.

THIRD–PARTY PRACTICE

(a) **When a Defending Party May Bring in a Third Party.**

(1) *Timing of the Summons and Complaint.* A defending party may, as third-party plaintiff, serve a summons and complaint on a nonparty who is or may be liable to it for all or part of the claim against it. But the third-party plaintiff must, by motion, obtain the court's leave if it files the third-party complaint more than 14 days after serving its original answer.

(2) *Third-Party Defendant's Claims and Defenses.* The person served with the summons and third-party complaint—the "third-party defendant":

    (A) must assert any defense against the third-party plaintiff's claim under Rule 12;

    (B) must assert any counterclaim against the third-party plaintiff under Rule 13(a), and may assert any counterclaim against the third-party plaintiff under Rule 13(b) or any crossclaim against another third-party defendant under Rule 13(g);

    (C) may assert against the plaintiff any defense that the third-party plaintiff has to the plaintiff's claim; and

    (D) may also assert against the plaintiff any claim arising out of the transaction or occurrence that is the subject matter of the plaintiff's claim against the third-party plaintiff.

(3) *Plaintiff's Claims Against a Third–Party Defendant.* The plaintiff may assert against the third-party defendant any claim arising out of the transaction or occurrence that is the subject matter of the plaintiff's claim against the third-party plaintiff. The third-party defendant must then assert any defense under Rule 12 and any counterclaim under Rule 13(a), and may assert any counterclaim under Rule 13(b) or any crossclaim under Rule 13(g).

(4) *Motion to Strike, Sever, or Try Separately.* Any party may move to strike the third-party claim, to sever it, or to try it separately.

(5) *Third-Party Defendant's Claim Against a Nonparty.* A third-party defendant may proceed under this rule against a non-party who is or may be liable to the third-party defendant for all or part of any claim against it.

(6) *Third-Party Complaint In Rem.* If it is within the admiralty or maritime jurisdiction, a third-party complaint may be in rem. In that event, a reference in this rule to the "summons" includes the warrant of arrest, and a reference to the defendant or third-party plaintiff includes, when appropriate, a person who asserts a right under Supplemental Rule C(6)(a)(i) in the property arrested.

(b) When a Plaintiff May Bring in a Third Party. When a claim is asserted against a plaintiff, the plaintiff may bring in a third party if this rule would allow a defendant to do so.

(c) Admiralty or Maritime Claim.

(1) *Scope of Impleader.* If a plaintiff asserts an admiralty or maritime claim under Rule 9(h), the defendant or a person who asserts a right under Supplemental Rule C(6)(a)(i) may, as a third-party plaintiff, bring in a third-party defendant who may be wholly or partly liable—either to the plaintiff or to the third-party plaintiff—for remedy over, contribution, or otherwise on account of the same transaction, occurrence, or series of transactions or occurrences.

(2) *Defending Against a Demand for Judgment for the Plaintiff.* The third-party plaintiff may demand judgment in the plaintiff's favor against the third-party defendant. In that event, the third-party defendant must defend under Rule 12 against the plaintiff's claim as well as the third-party plaintiff's claim; and the action proceeds as if the plaintiff had sued both the third-party defendant and the third-party plaintiff.

As amended 1948, 1963, 1966, 1987, 2000, 2006, 2007, 2009.

Rule 15.

AMENDED AND SUPPLEMENTAL PLEADINGS

(a) Amendments Before Trial.

(1) *Amending as a Matter of Course.* A party may amend its pleading once as a matter of course within:

(A) 21 days after serving it, or

(B) if the pleading is one to which a responsive pleading is required, 21 days after service of a responsive pleading or 21 days after service of a motion under Rule 12(b), (e), or (f), whichever is earlier.

(2) *Other Amendments.* In all other cases, a party may amend its pleading only with the opposing party's written consent or the court's leave. The court should freely give leave when justice so requires.

(3) *Time to Respond.* Unless the court orders otherwise, any required response to an amended pleading must be made within the time remaining to respond to the original pleading or within 14 days after service of the amended pleading, whichever is later.

(b) Amendments During and After Trial.

(1) *Based on an Objection at Trial.* If, at trial, a party objects that evidence is not within the issues raised in the pleadings, the court may permit the pleadings to be amended. The court should freely permit an amendment when doing so will aid in presenting the merits and the objecting party fails to satisfy the court that the evidence would prejudice that party's action or defense on the merits. The court may grant a continuance to enable the objecting party to meet the evidence.

(2) *For Issues Tried by Consent.* When an issue not raised by the pleadings is tried by the parties' express or implied consent, it must be treated in all respects as if raised in the pleadings. A party may move—at any time, even after judgment—to amend the pleadings to conform them to the evidence and to raise an unpleaded issue. But failure to amend does not affect the result of the trial of that issue.

(c) Relation Back of Amendments.

(1) *When an Amendment Relates Back.* An amendment to a pleading relates back to the date of the original pleading when:

   (A) the law that provides the applicable statute of limitations allows relation back;

   (B) the amendment asserts a claim or defense that arose out of the conduct, transaction, or occurrence set out—or attempted to be set out—in the original pleading; or

   (C) the amendment changes the party or the naming of the party against whom a claim is asserted, if Rule 15(c)(1)(B) is satisfied and if, within the period provided by Rule 4(m) for serving the summons and complaint, the party to be brought in by amendment:

      (i) received such notice of the action that it will not be prejudiced in defending on the merits; and

(ii) knew or should have known that the action would have been brought against it, but for a mistake concerning the proper party's identity.

(2) *Notice to the United States.* When the United States or a United States officer or agency is added as a defendant by amendment, the notice requirements of Rule 15(c)(1)(C)(i) and (ii) are satisfied if, during the stated period, process was delivered or mailed to the United States attorney or the United States attorney's designee, to the Attorney General of the United States, or to the officer or agency.

(d) Supplemental Pleadings. On motion and reasonable notice, the court may, on just terms, permit a party to serve a supplemental pleading setting out any transaction, occurrence, or event that happened after the date of the pleading to be supplemented. The court may permit supplementation even though the original pleading is defective in stating a claim or defense. The court may order that the opposing party plead to the supplemental pleading within a specified time.

As amended 1963, 1966, 1987, 1991, 1993, 2007, 2009.

Rule 16.

PRETRIAL CONFERENCES; SCHEDULING; MANAGEMENT

(a) Purposes of a Pretrial Conference. In any action, the court may order the attorneys and any unrepresented parties to appear for one or more pretrial conferences for such purposes as:

(1) expediting disposition of the action;

(2) establishing early and continuing control so that the case will not be protracted because of lack of management;

(3) discouraging wasteful pretrial activities;

(4) improving the quality of the trial through more thorough preparation; and

(5) facilitating settlement.

(b) Scheduling.

(1) *Scheduling Order.* Except in categories of actions exempted by local rule, the district judge—or a magistrate judge when authorized by local rule—must issue a scheduling order:

(A) after receiving the parties' report under Rule 26(f); or

(B) after consulting with the parties' attorneys and any unrepresented parties at a scheduling conference or by telephone, mail, or other means.

(2) *Time to Issue.* The judge must issue the scheduling order as soon as practicable, but in any event within the earlier of 120 days after any defendant has been served with the complaint or 90 days after any defendant has appeared.

(3) *Contents of the Order.*

(A) *Required Contents.* The scheduling order must limit the time to join other parties, amend the pleadings, complete discovery, and file motions.

(B) *Permitted Contents.* The scheduling order may:

(i) modify the timing of disclosures under Rules 26(a) and 26(e)(1);

(ii) modify the extent of discovery;

(iii) provide for disclosure or discovery of electronically stored information;

(iv) include any agreements the parties reach for asserting claims of privilege or of protection as trial-preparation material after information is produced;

(v) set dates for pretrial conferences and for trial; and

(vi) include other appropriate matters.

(4) *Modifying a Schedule.* A schedule may be modified only for good cause and with the judge's consent.

(c) Attendance and Matters for Consideration at a Pretrial Conference.

(1) *Attendance.* A represented party must authorize at least one of its attorneys to make stipulations and admissions about all matters that can reasonably be anticipated for discussion at a pretrial conference. If appropriate, the court may require that a party or its representative be present or reasonably available by other means to consider possible settlement.

(2) *Matters for Consideration.* At any pretrial conference, the court may consider and take appropriate action on the following matters:

(A) formulating and simplifying the issues, and eliminating frivolous claims or defenses;

(B) amending the pleadings if necessary or desirable;

(C) obtaining admissions and stipulations about facts and documents to avoid unnecessary proof, and ruling in advance on the admissibility of evidence;

(D) avoiding unnecessary proof and cumulative evidence, and limiting the use of testimony under Federal Rule of Evidence 702;

(E) determining the appropriateness and timing of summary adjudication under Rule 56;

(F) controlling and scheduling discovery, including orders affecting disclosures and discovery under Rule 26 and Rules 29 through 37;

(G) identifying witnesses and documents, scheduling the filing and exchange of any pretrial briefs, and setting dates for further conferences and for trial;

(H) referring matters to a magistrate judge or a master;

(I) settling the case and using special procedures to assist in resolving the dispute when authorized by statute or local rule;

(J) determining the form and content of the pretrial order;

(K) disposing of pending motions;

(L) adopting special procedures for managing potentially difficult or protracted actions that may involve complex issues, multiple parties, difficult legal questions, or unusual proof problems;

(M) ordering a separate trial under Rule 42(b) of a claim, counterclaim, crossclaim, third-party claim, or particular issue;

(N) ordering the presentation of evidence early in the trial on a manageable issue that might, on the evidence, be the basis for a judgment as a matter of law under Rule 50(a) or a judgment on partial findings under Rule 52(c);

(O) establishing a reasonable limit on the time allowed to present evidence; and

(P) facilitating in other ways the just, speedy, and inexpensive disposition of the action.

(d) Pretrial Orders. After any conference under this rule, the court should issue an order reciting the action taken. This order controls the course of the action unless the court modifies it.

(e) Final Pretrial Conference and Orders. The court may hold a final pretrial conference to formulate a trial plan, including a plan to facilitate the admission of evidence. The conference must be held as close to the start of trial as is reasonable, and must be attended by at least one attorney who will conduct the trial for each party and by any unrepresented party. The court may modify the order issued after a final pretrial conference only to prevent manifest injustice.

(f) Sanctions.

(1) *In General.* On motion or on its own, the court may issue any just orders, including those authorized by Rule 37(b)(2)(A)(ii)–(vii), if a party or its attorney:

> (A) fails to appear at a scheduling or other pretrial conference;

> (B) is substantially unprepared to participate—or does not participate in good faith—in the conference; or

> (C) fails to obey a scheduling or other pretrial order.

(2) *Imposing Fees and Costs.* Instead of or in addition to any other sanction, the court must order the party, its attorney, or both to pay the reasonable expenses—including attorney's fees—incurred because of any noncompliance with this rule, unless the noncompliance was substantially justified or other circumstances make an award of expenses unjust.

As amended 1983, 1987, 1993, 2006, 2007.

IV. PARTIES

Rule 17.

PLAINTIFF AND DEFENDANT; CAPACITY; PUBLIC OFFICERS

(a) Real Party in Interest.

(1) *Designation in General.* An action must be prosecuted in the name of the real party in interest. The following may sue in their own names without joining the person for whose benefit the action is brought:

> (A) an executor;

> (B) an administrator;

> (C) a guardian;

> (D) a bailee;

> (E) a trustee of an express trust;

> (F) a party with whom or in whose name a contract has been made for another's benefit; and

> (G) a party authorized by statute.

(2) *Action in the Name of the United States for Another's Use or Benefit.* When a federal statute so provides, an action for another's use or benefit must be brought in the name of the United States.

(3) *Joinder of the Real Party in Interest.* The court may not dismiss an action for failure to prosecute in the name of the real party in interest until, after an objection, a reasonable time has been allowed for the real party in interest to ratify, join, or be substituted into the action. After ratification, joinder, or substitution, the action proceeds as if it had been originally commenced by the real party in interest.

(b) Capacity to Sue or Be Sued. Capacity to sue or be sued is determined as follows:

(1) for an individual who is not acting in a representative capacity, by the law of the individual's domicile;

(2) for a corporation, by the law under which it was organized; and

(3) for all other parties, by the law of the state where the court is located, except that:

(A) a partnership or other unincorporated association with no such capacity under that state's law may sue or be sued in its common name to enforce a substantive right existing under the United States Constitution or laws; and

(B) 28 U.S.C. §§ 754 and 959(a) govern the capacity of a receiver appointed by a United States court to sue or be sued in a United States court.

(c) Minor or Incompetent Person.

(1) *With a Representative.* The following representatives may sue or defend on behalf of a minor or an incompetent person:

(A) a general guardian;

(B) a committee;

(C) a conservator; or

(D) a like fiduciary.

(2) *Without a Representative.* A minor or an incompetent person who does not have a duly appointed representative may sue by a next friend or by a guardian ad litem. The court must appoint a guardian ad litem—or issue another appropriate order—to protect a minor or incompetent person who is unrepresented in an action.

(d) Public Officer's Title and Name. A public officer who sues or is sued in an official capacity may be designated by official title rather than by name, but the court may order that the officer's name be added.

As amended 1948, 1949, 1966, 1987, 1988, 2007.

Rule 18.

JOINDER OF CLAIMS

(a) In General. A party asserting a claim, counterclaim, crossclaim, or third-party claim may join, as independent or alternative claims, as many claims as it has against an opposing party.

(b) Joinder of Contingent Claims. A party may join two claims even though one of them is contingent on the disposition of the other; but the court may grant relief only in accordance with the parties' relative substantive rights. In particular, a plaintiff may state a claim for money and a claim to set aside a conveyance that is fraudulent as to that plaintiff, without first obtaining a judgment for the money.

As amended 1966, 1987, 2007.

Rule 19.

REQUIRED JOINDER OF PARTIES

(a) Persons Required to Be Joined if Feasible.

(1) *Required Party.* A person who is subject to service of process and whose joinder will not deprive the court of subject-matter jurisdiction must be joined as a party if:

(A) in that person's absence, the court cannot accord complete relief among existing parties; or

(B) that person claims an interest relating to the subject of the action and is so situated that disposing of the action in the person's absence may:

(i) as a practical matter impair or impede the person's ability to protect the interest; or

(ii) leave an existing party subject to a substantial risk of incurring double, multiple, or otherwise inconsistent obligations because of the interest.

(2) *Joinder by Court Order.* If a person has not been joined as required, the court must order that the person be made a party. A person who refuses to join as a plaintiff may be made either a defendant or, in a proper case, an involuntary plaintiff.

(3) *Venue.* If a joined party objects to venue and the joinder would make venue improper, the court must dismiss that party.

(b) When Joinder Is Not Feasible. If a person who is required to be joined if feasible cannot be joined, the court must determine whether, in equity and good conscience, the action should proceed among the existing parties or should be dismissed. The factors for the court to consider include:

(1) the extent to which a judgment rendered in the person's absence might prejudice that person or the existing parties;

(2) the extent to which any prejudice could be lessened or avoided by:

(A) protective provisions in the judgment;

(B) shaping the relief; or

(C) other measures;

(3) whether a judgment rendered in the person's absence would be adequate; and

(4) whether the plaintiff would have an adequate remedy if the action were dismissed for nonjoinder.

(c) Pleading the Reasons for Nonjoinder. When asserting a claim for relief, a party must state:

(1) the name, if known, of any person who is required to be joined if feasible but is not joined; and

(2) the reasons for not joining that person.

(d) Exception for Class Actions. This rule is subject to Rule 23.

As amended 1966, 1987, 2007.

Rule 20.

PERMISSIVE JOINDER OF PARTIES

(a) Persons Who May Join or Be Joined.

(1) *Plaintiffs.* Persons may join in one action as plaintiffs if:

(A) they assert any right to relief jointly, severally, or in the alternative with respect to or arising out of the same transaction, occurrence, or series of transactions or occurrences; and

(B) any question of law or fact common to all plaintiffs will arise in the action.

(2) *Defendants.* Persons—as well as a vessel, cargo, or other property subject to admiralty process in rem—may be joined in one action as defendants if:

(A) any right to relief is asserted against them jointly, severally, or in the alternative with respect to or arising out of the same transaction, occurrence, or series of transactions or occurrences; and

(B) any question of law or fact common to all defendants will arise in the action.

(3) *Extent of Relief.* Neither a plaintiff nor a defendant need be interested in obtaining or defending against all the relief demanded. The court may grant judgment to one or more plaintiffs according to their rights, and against one or more defendants according to their liabilities.

(b) Protective Measures. The court may issue orders—including an order for separate trials—to protect a party against embarrassment, delay, expense, or other prejudice that arises from including a person against whom the party asserts no claim and who asserts no claim against the party.

As amended 1966, 1987, 2007.

Rule 21.

MISJOINDER AND NONJOINDER OF PARTIES

Misjoinder of parties is not a ground for dismissing an action. On motion or on its own, the court may at any time, on just terms, add or drop a party. The court may also sever any claim against a party.

As amended 2007.

Rule 22.

INTERPLEADER

(a) Grounds.

(1) *By a Plaintiff.* Persons with claims that may expose a plaintiff to double or multiple liability may be joined as defendants and required to interplead. Joinder for interpleader is proper even though:

(A) the claims of the several claimants, or the titles on which their claims depend, lack a common origin or are adverse and independent rather than identical; or

(B) the plaintiff denies liability in whole or in part to any or all of the claimants.

(2) *By a Defendant.* A defendant exposed to similar liability may seek interpleader through a crossclaim or counterclaim.

(b) Relation to Other Rules and Statutes. This rule supplements—and does not limit—the joinder of parties allowed by

Rule 20. The remedy this rule provides is in addition to—and does not supersede or limit—the remedy provided by 28 U.S.C. §§ 1335, 1397, and 2361. An action under those statutes must be conducted under these rules.

As amended 1949, 1987, 2007.

Rule 23.

CLASS ACTIONS

(a) Prerequisites. One or more members of a class may sue or be sued as representative parties on behalf of all members only if:

(1) the class is so numerous that joinder of all members is impracticable;

(2) there are questions of law or fact common to the class;

(3) the claims or defenses of the representative parties are typical of the claims or defenses of the class; and

(4) the representative parties will fairly and adequately protect the interests of the class.

(b) Types of Class Actions. A class action may be maintained if Rule 23(a) is satisfied and if:

(1) prosecuting separate actions by or against individual class members would create a risk of:

(A) inconsistent or varying adjudications with respect to individual class members that would establish incompatible standards of conduct for the party opposing the class; or

(B) adjudications with respect to individual class members that, as a practical matter, would be dispositive of the interests of the other members not parties to the individual adjudications or would substantially impair or impede their ability to protect their interests;

(2) the party opposing the class has acted or refused to act on grounds that apply generally to the class, so that final injunctive relief or corresponding declaratory relief is appropriate respecting the class as a whole; or

(3) the court finds that the questions of law or fact common to class members predominate over any questions affecting only individual members, and that a class action is superior to other available methods for fairly and efficiently adjudicating the controversy. The matters pertinent to these findings include:

(A) the class members' interests in individually controlling the prosecution or defense of separate actions;

(B) the extent and nature of any litigation concerning the controversy already begun by or against class members;

(C) the desirability or undesirability of concentrating the litigation of the claims in the particular forum; and

(D) the likely difficulties in managing a class action.

(c) Certification Order; Notice to Class Members; Judgment; Issues Classes; Subclasses.

(1) *Certification Order.*

(A) *Time to Issue.* At an early practicable time after a person sues or is sued as a class representative, the court must determine by order whether to certify the action as a class action.

(B) *Defining the Class; Appointing Class Counsel.* An order that certifies a class action must define the class and the class claims, issues, or defenses, and must appoint class counsel under Rule 23(g).

(C) *Altering or Amending the Order.* An order that grants or denies class certification may be altered or amended before final judgment.

(2) *Notice.*

(A) *For (b)(1) or (b)(2) Classes.* For any class certified under Rule 23(b)(1) or (b)(2), the court may direct appropriate notice to the class.

(B) *For (b)(3) Classes.* For any class certified under Rule 23(b)(3), the court must direct to class members the best notice that is practicable under the circumstances, including individual notice to all members who can be identified through reasonable effort. The notice must clearly and concisely state in plain, easily understood language:

(i) the nature of the action;

(ii) the definition of the class certified;

(iii) the class claims, issues, or defenses;

(iv) that a class member may enter an appearance through an attorney if the member so desires;

(v) that the court will exclude from the class any member who requests exclusion;

(vi) the time and manner for requesting exclusion; and

(vii) the binding effect of a class judgment on members under Rule 23(c)(3).

(3) *Judgment.* Whether or not favorable to the class, the judgment in a class action must:

(A) for any class certified under Rule 23(b)(1) or (b)(2), include and describe those whom the court finds to be class members; and

(B) for any class certified under Rule 23(b)(3), include and specify or describe those to whom the Rule 23(c)(2) notice was directed, who have not requested exclusion, and whom the court finds to be class members.

(4) *Particular Issues.* When appropriate, an action may be brought or maintained as a class action with respect to particular issues.

(5) *Subclasses.* When appropriate, a class may be divided into subclasses that are each treated as a class under this rule.

(d) Conducting the Action.

(1) *In General.* In conducting an action under this rule, the court may issue orders that:

(A) determine the course of proceedings or prescribe measures to prevent undue repetition or complication in presenting evidence or argument;

(B) require—to protect class members and fairly conduct the action—giving appropriate notice to some or all class members of:

(i) any step in the action;

(ii) the proposed extent of the judgment; or

(iii) the members' opportunity to signify whether they consider the representation fair and adequate, to intervene and present claims or defenses, or to otherwise come into the action;

(C) impose conditions on the representative parties or on intervenors;

(D) require that the pleadings be amended to eliminate allegations about representation of absent persons and that the action proceed accordingly; or

(E) deal with similar procedural matters.

(2) *Combining and Amending Orders.* An order under Rule 23(d)(1) may be altered or amended from time to time and may be combined with an order under Rule 16.

(e) Settlement, Voluntary Dismissal, or Compromise. The claims, issues, or defenses of a certified class may be settled, voluntarily dismissed, or compromised only with the court's approval. The following procedures apply to a proposed settlement, voluntary dismissal, or compromise:

(1) The court must direct notice in a reasonable manner to all class members who would be bound by the proposal.

(2) If the proposal would bind class members, the court may approve it only after a hearing and on finding that it is fair, reasonable, and adequate.

(3) The parties seeking approval must file a statement identifying any agreement made in connection with the proposal.

(4) If the class action was previously certified under Rule 23(b)(3), the court may refuse to approve a settlement unless it affords a new opportunity to request exclusion to individual class members who had an earlier opportunity to request exclusion but did not do so.

(5) Any class member may object to the proposal if it requires court approval under this subdivision (e); the objection may be withdrawn only with the court's approval.

(f) Appeals. A court of appeals may permit an appeal from an order granting or denying class-action certification under this rule if a petition for permission to appeal is filed with the circuit clerk within 14 days after the order is entered. An appeal does not stay proceedings in the district court unless the district judge or the court of appeals so orders.

(g) Class Counsel.

(1) *Appointing Class Counsel.* Unless a statute provides otherwise, a court that certifies a class must appoint class counsel. In appointing class counsel, the court:

(A) must consider:

(i) the work counsel has done in identifying or investigating potential claims in the action;

(ii) counsel's experience in handling class actions, other complex litigation, and the types of claims asserted in the action;

(iii) counsel's knowledge of the applicable law; and

(iv) the resources that counsel will commit to representing the class;

(B) may consider any other matter pertinent to counsel's ability to fairly and adequately represent the interests of the class;

(C) may order potential class counsel to provide information on any subject pertinent to the appointment and to propose terms for attorney's fees and nontaxable costs;

(D) may include in the appointing order provisions about the award of attorney's fees or nontaxable costs under Rule 23(h); and

(E) may make further orders in connection with the appointment.

(2) *Standard for Appointing Class Counsel.* When one applicant seeks appointment as class counsel, the court may appoint that applicant only if the applicant is adequate under Rule 23(g)(1) and (4). If more than one adequate applicant seeks appointment, the court must appoint the applicant best able to represent the interests of the class.

(3) *Interim Counsel.* The court may designate interim counsel to act on behalf of a putative class before determining whether to certify the action as a class action.

(4) *Duty of Class Counsel.* Class counsel must fairly and adequately represent the interests of the class.

(h) Attorney's Fees and Nontaxable Costs. In a certified class action, the court may award reasonable attorney's fees and nontaxable costs that are authorized by law or by the parties' agreement. The following procedures apply:

(1) A claim for an award must be made by motion under Rule 54(d)(2), subject to the provisions of this subdivision (h), at a time the court sets. Notice of the motion must be served on all parties and, for motions by class counsel, directed to class members in a reasonable manner.

(2) A class member, or a party from whom payment is sought, may object to the motion.

(3) The court may hold a hearing and must find the facts and state its legal conclusions under Rule 52(a).

(4) The court may refer issues related to the amount of the award to a special master or a magistrate judge, as provided in Rule 54(d)(2)(D).

As amended 1966, 1987, 1998, 2003, 2007, 2009.

Rule 23.1.

DERIVATIVE ACTIONS

(a) Prerequisites. This rule applies when one or more shareholders or members of a corporation or an unincorporated association bring a derivative action to enforce a right that the corporation or association may properly assert but has failed to enforce. The derivative action may not be maintained if it appears that the plaintiff does not fairly and adequately represent the interests of shareholders or members who are similarly situated in enforcing the right of the corporation or association.

(b) Pleading Requirements. The complaint must be verified and must:

(1) allege that the plaintiff was a shareholder or member at the time of the transaction complained of, or that the plaintiff's share or membership later devolved on it by operation of law;

(2) allege that the action is not a collusive one to confer jurisdiction that the court would otherwise lack; and

(3) state with particularity:

(A) any effort by the plaintiff to obtain the desired action from the directors or comparable authority and, if necessary, from the shareholders or members; and

(B) the reasons for not obtaining the action or not making the effort.

(c) Settlement, Dismissal, and Compromise. A derivative action may be settled, voluntarily dismissed, or compromised only with the court's approval. Notice of a proposed settlement, voluntary dismissal, or compromise must be given to shareholders or members in the manner that the court orders.

Added 1966; as amended 1987, 2007.

Rule 23.2.

ACTIONS RELATING TO UNINCORPORATED ASSOCIATIONS

This rule applies to an action brought by or against the members of an unincorporated association as a class by naming certain members as representative parties. The action may be maintained only if it appears that those parties will fairly and adequately protect the interests of the association and its members. In conducting the action, the court may issue any appropriate orders corresponding with those in Rule 23(d), and the procedure for settlement, voluntary dismissal, or compromise must correspond with the procedure in Rule 23(e).

Added 1966; as amended 2007.

Rule 24.

INTERVENTION

(a) Intervention of Right. On timely motion, the court must permit anyone to intervene who:

(1) is given an unconditional right to intervene by a federal statute; or

(2) claims an interest relating to the property or transaction that is the subject of the action, and is so situated that disposing of the action may as a practical matter impair or impede the movant's ability to protect its interest, unless existing parties adequately represent that interest.

(b) Permissive Intervention.

(1) *In General.* On timely motion, the court may permit anyone to intervene who:

(A) is given a conditional right to intervene by a federal statute; or

(B) has a claim or defense that shares with the main action a common question of law or fact.

(2) *By a Government Officer or Agency.* On timely motion, the court may permit a federal or state governmental officer or agency to intervene if a party's claim or defense is based on:

(A) a statute or executive order administered by the officer or agency; or

(B) any regulation, order, requirement, or agreement issued or made under the statute or executive order.

(3) *Delay or Prejudice.* In exercising its discretion, the court must consider whether the intervention will unduly delay or prejudice the adjudication of the original parties' rights.

(c) Notice and Pleading Required. A motion to intervene must be served on the parties as provided in Rule 5. The motion must state the grounds for intervention and be accompanied by a pleading that sets out the claim or defense for which intervention is sought.

As amended 1948, 1949, 1963, 1966, 1987, 1991, 2006, 2007.

Rule 25.

SUBSTITUTION OF PARTIES

(a) Death.

(1) *Substitution if the Claim Is Not Extinguished.* If a party dies and the claim is not extinguished, the court may order substitution of the proper party. A motion for substitution may be made by any party or by the decedent's successor or representative. If the motion is not made within 90 days after service of a statement noting the death, the action by or against the decedent must be dismissed.

(2) *Continuation Among the Remaining Parties.* After a party's death, if the right sought to be enforced survives only to or against the remaining parties, the action does not abate, but proceeds in favor of or against the remaining parties. The death should be noted on the record.

(3) *Service.* A motion to substitute, together with a notice of hearing, must be served on the parties as provided in Rule 5 and on nonparties as provided in Rule 4. A statement noting death must be served in the same manner. Service may be made in any judicial district.

(b) Incompetency. If a party becomes incompetent, the court may, on motion, permit the action to be continued by or against the party's representative. The motion must be served as provided in Rule 25(a)(3).

(c) Transfer of Interest. If an interest is transferred, the action may be continued by or against the original party unless the court, on motion, orders the transferee to be substituted in the action or joined with the original party. The motion must be served as provided in Rule 25(a)(3).

(d) Public Officers; Death or Separation from Office. An action does not abate when a public officer who is a party in an official capacity dies, resigns, or otherwise ceases to hold office while the action is pending. The officer's successor is automatically substituted as a party. Later proceedings should be in the substituted party's name, but any misnomer not affecting the parties' substantial rights must be disregarded. The court may order substitution at any time, but the absence of such an order does not affect the substitution.

As amended 1949, 1961, 1963, 1987, 2007.

V. DISCLOSURES AND DISCOVERY

Rule 26.

DUTY TO DISCLOSE; GENERAL PROVISIONS GOVERNING DISCOVERY

(a) Required Disclosures.

(1) *Initial Disclosure.*

(A) *In General.* Except as exempted by Rule 26(a)(1)(B) or as otherwise stipulated or ordered by the court, a party must, without awaiting a discovery request, provide to the other parties:

(i) the name and, if known, the address and telephone number of each individual likely to have discoverable information—along with the subjects of that information—that the disclosing party may use to support its claims or defenses, unless the use would be solely for impeachment;

(ii) a copy—or a description by category and location—of all documents, electronically stored information, and tangible things that the disclosing party has in its possession, custody, or control and may use to support its claims or defenses, unless the use would be solely for impeachment;

(iii) a computation of each category of damages claimed by the disclosing party—who must also make available for inspection and copying as under Rule 34 the documents or other evidentiary material, unless privileged or protected from disclosure, on which each computation is based, including materials bearing on the nature and extent of injuries suffered; and

(iv) for inspection and copying as under Rule 34, any insurance agreement under which an insurance business may be liable to satisfy all or part of a possible judgment in the action or to indemnify or reimburse for payments made to satisfy the judgment.

(B) *Proceedings Exempt from Initial Disclosure.* The following proceedings are exempt from initial disclosure:

(i) an action for review on an administrative record;

(ii) a petition for habeas corpus or any other proceeding to challenge a criminal conviction or sentence;

(iii) an action brought without an attorney by a person in the custody of the United States, a state, or a state subdivision;

(iv) an action to enforce or quash an administrative summons or subpoena;

(v) an action by the United States to recover benefit payments;

(vi) an action by the United States to collect on a student loan guaranteed by the United States;

(vii) a proceeding ancillary to a proceeding in another court; and

(viii) an action to enforce an arbitration award.

(C) *Time for Initial Disclosures—In General.* A party must make the initial disclosures at or within 14 days after the parties' Rule 26(f) conference unless a different time is set by stipulation or court order, or unless a party objects during the conference that initial disclosures are not appropriate in this action and states the objection in the proposed discovery plan. In ruling on the objection, the court must determine what disclosures, if any, are to be made and must set the time for disclosure.

(D) *Time for Initial Disclosures—For Parties Served or Joined Later.* A party that is first served or otherwise joined after the Rule 26(f) conference must make the initial disclosures within 30 days after being served or joined, unless a different time is set by stipulation or court order.

(E) *Basis for Initial Disclosure; Unacceptable Excuses.* A party must make its initial disclosures based on the information then reasonably available to it. A party is not excused from making its disclosures because it has not fully investigated the case or because it challenges the sufficiency of another party's disclosures or because another party has not made its disclosures.

(2) *Disclosure of Expert Testimony.*

(A) *In General.* In addition to the disclosures required by Rule 26(a)(1), a party must disclose to the other parties the identity of any witness it may use at trial to present evidence under Federal Rule of Evidence 702, 703, or 705.

(B) *Written Report.* Unless otherwise stipulated or ordered by the court, this disclosure must be accompanied by a written report—prepared and signed by the witness—if the witness is one retained or specially employed to provide expert testimony in the case or one whose duties as the party's employee regularly involve giving expert testimony. The report must contain:

64

(i) a complete statement of all opinions the witness will express and the basis and reasons for them;

(ii) the data or other information considered by the witness in forming them;

(iii) any exhibits that will be used to summarize or support them;

(iv) the witness's qualifications, including a list of all publications authored in the previous ten years;

(v) a list of all other cases in which, during the previous four years, the witness testified as an expert at trial or by deposition; and

(vi) a statement of the compensation to be paid for the study and testimony in the case.

(C) *Time to Disclose Expert Testimony.* A party must make these disclosures at the times and in the sequence that the court orders. Absent a stipulation or a court order, the disclosures must be made:

(i) at least 90 days before the date set for trial or for the case to be ready for trial; or

(ii) if the evidence is intended solely to contradict or rebut evidence on the same subject matter identified by another party under Rule 26(a)(2)(B), within 30 days after the other party's disclosure.

(D) *Supplementing the Disclosure.* The parties must supplement these disclosures when required under Rule 26(e).

(3) *Pretrial Disclosures.*

(A) *In General.* In addition to the disclosures required by Rule 26(a)(1) and (2), a party must provide to the other parties and promptly file the following information about the evidence that it may present at trial other than solely for impeachment:

(i) the name and, if not previously provided, the address and telephone number of each witness—separately identifying those the party expects to present and those it may call if the need arises;

(ii) the designation of those witnesses whose testimony the party expects to present by deposition and, if not taken stenographically, a transcript of the pertinent parts of the deposition; and

(iii) an identification of each document or other exhibit, including summaries of other evidence—separately identifying those items the party expects to offer and those it may offer if the need arises.

(B) *Time for Pretrial Disclosures; Objections.* Unless the court orders otherwise, these disclosures must be made at least 30 days before trial. Within 14 days after they are made, unless the court sets a different time, a party may serve and promptly file a list of the following objections: any objections to the use under Rule 32(a) of a deposition designated by another party under Rule 26(a)(3)(A)(ii); and any objection, together with the grounds for it, that may be made to the admissibility of materials identified under Rule 26(a)(3)(A)(iii). An objection not so made—except for one under Federal Rule of Evidence 402 or 403—is waived unless excused by the court for good cause.

(4) *Form of Disclosures.* Unless the court orders otherwise, all disclosures under Rule 26(a) must be in writing, signed, and served.

(b) Discovery Scope and Limits.

(1) *Scope in General.* Unless otherwise limited by court order, the scope of discovery is as follows: Parties may obtain discovery regarding any nonprivileged matter that is relevant to any party's claim or defense—including the existence, description, nature, custody, condition, and location of any documents or other tangible things and the identity and location of persons who know of any discoverable matter. For good cause, the court may order discovery of any matter relevant to the subject matter involved in the action. Relevant information need not be admissible at the trial if the discovery appears reasonably calculated to lead to the discovery of admissible evidence. All discovery is subject to the limitations imposed by Rule 26(b)(2)(C).

(2) *Limitations on Frequency and Extent.*

(A) *When Permitted.* By order, the court may alter the limits in these rules on the number of depositions and interrogatories or on the length of depositions under Rule 30. By order or local rule, the court may also limit the number of requests under Rule 36.

(B) *Specific Limitations on Electronically Stored Information.* A party need not provide discovery of electronically stored information from sources that the party identifies as not reasonably accessible because of undue burden or cost. On motion to compel discovery or for a protective order, the party from whom discovery is sought must show that the information is not reasonably accessible because of undue burden or cost. If that showing is made, the court may nonetheless order discovery from such sources if the requesting party shows good cause, considering the limitations of Rule 26(b)(2)(C). The court may specify conditions for the discovery.

(C) *When Required.* On motion or on its own, the court must limit the frequency or extent of discovery otherwise allowed by these rules or by local rule if it determines that:

(i) the discovery sought is unreasonably cumulative or duplicative, or can be obtained from some other source that is more convenient, less burdensome, or less expensive;

(ii) the party seeking discovery has had ample opportunity to obtain the information by discovery in the action; or

(iii) the burden or expense of the proposed discovery outweighs its likely benefit, considering the needs of the case, the amount in controversy, the parties' resources, the importance of the issues at stake in the action, and the importance of the discovery in resolving the issues.

(3) *Trial Preparation: Materials.*

(A) *Documents and Tangible Things.* Ordinarily, a party may not discover documents and tangible things that are prepared in anticipation of litigation or for trial by or for another party or its representative (including the other party's attorney, consultant, surety, indemnitor, insurer, or agent). But, subject to Rule 26(b)(4), those materials may be discovered if:

(i) they are otherwise discoverable under Rule 26(b)(1); and

(ii) the party shows that it has substantial need for the materials to prepare its case and cannot, without undue hardship, obtain their substantial equivalent by other means.

(B) *Protection Against Disclosure.* If the court orders discovery of those materials, it must protect against disclosure of the mental impressions, conclusions, opinions, or legal theories of a party's attorney or other representative concerning the litigation.

(C) *Previous Statement.* Any party or other person may, on request and without the required showing, obtain the person's own previous statement about the action or its subject matter. If the request is refused, the person may move for a court order, and Rule 37(a)(5) applies to the award of expenses. A previous statement is either:

(i) a written statement that the person has signed or otherwise adopted or approved; or

      (ii) a contemporaneous stenographic, mechanical, electrical, or other recording—or a transcription of it—that recites substantially verbatim the person's oral statement.

(4) *Trial Preparation: Experts.*

      (A) *Expert Who May Testify.* A party may depose any person who has been identified as an expert whose opinions may be presented at trial. If Rule 26(a)(2)(B) requires a report from the expert, the deposition may be conducted only after the report is provided.

      (B) *Expert Employed Only for Trial Preparation.* Ordinarily, a party may not, by interrogatories or deposition, discover facts known or opinions held by an expert who has been retained or specially employed by another party in anticipation of litigation or to prepare for trial and who is not expected to be called as a witness at trial. But a party may do so only:

      (i) as provided in Rule 35(b); or

      (ii) on showing exceptional circumstances under which it is impracticable for the party to obtain facts or opinions on the same subject by other means.

      (C) *Payment.* Unless manifest injustice would result, the court must require that the party seeking discovery:

      (i) pay the expert a reasonable fee for time spent in responding to discovery under Rule 26(b)(4)(A) or (B); and

      (ii) for discovery under (B), also pay the other party a fair portion of the fees and expenses it reasonably incurred in obtaining the expert's facts and opinions.

(5) *Claiming Privilege or Protecting Trial–Preparation Materials.*

      (A) *Information Withheld.* When a party withholds information otherwise discoverable by claiming that the information is privileged or subject to protection as trial-preparation material, the party must:

      (i) expressly make the claim; and

      (ii) describe the nature of the documents, communications, or tangible things not produced or disclosed—and do so in a manner that, without revealing information itself privileged or protected, will enable other parties to assess the claim.

      (B) *Information Produced.* If information produced in discovery is subject to a claim of privilege or of protection as trial-preparation material, the party making the claim may notify any party that received the information of the claim and the basis for it. After being notified, a party must promptly return, sequester, or destroy the specified information and any copies it has; must not use or disclose the information until the claim is resolved; must take reasonable steps to retrieve the information if the party disclosed it before being notified; and may promptly present the information to the court under seal for a determination of the claim. The producing party must preserve the information until the claim is resolved.

(c) Protective Orders.

(1) *In General.* A party or any person from whom discovery is sought may move for a protective order in the court where the action is pending—or as an alternative on matters relating to a deposition, in the court for the district where the deposition will be taken. The motion must include a certification that the movant has in good faith conferred or attempted to confer with other affected parties in an effort to resolve the dispute without court action. The court may, for good cause, issue an order to protect a party or person from annoyance, embarrassment, oppression, or undue burden or expense, including one or more of the following:

(A) forbidding the disclosure or discovery;

(B) specifying terms, including time and place, for the disclosure or discovery;

(C) prescribing a discovery method other than the one selected by the party seeking discovery;

(D) forbidding inquiry into certain matters, or limiting the scope of disclosure or discovery to certain matters;

(E) designating the persons who may be present while the discovery is conducted;

(F) requiring that a deposition be sealed and opened only on court order;

(G) requiring that a trade secret or other confidential research, development, or commercial information not be revealed or be revealed only in a specified way; and

(H) requiring that the parties simultaneously file specified documents or information in sealed envelopes, to be opened as the court directs.

(2) *Ordering Discovery.* If a motion for a protective order is wholly or partly denied, the court may, on just terms, order that any party or person provide or permit discovery.

(3) *Awarding Expenses.* Rule 37(a)(5) applies to the award of expenses.

(d) Timing and Sequence of Discovery.

(1) *Timing.* A party may not seek discovery from any source before the parties have conferred as required by Rule 26(f), except in a proceeding exempted from initial disclosure under Rule 26(a)(1)(B), or when authorized by these rules, by stipulation, or by court order.

(2) *Sequence.* Unless, on motion, the court orders otherwise for the parties' and witnesses' convenience and in the interests of justice:

> (A) methods of discovery may be used in any sequence; and

> (B) discovery by one party does not require any other party to delay its discovery.

(e) Supplementing Disclosures and Responses.

(1) *In General.* A party who has made a disclosure under Rule 26(a)—or who has responded to an interrogatory, request for production, or request for admission—must supplement or correct its disclosure or response:

> (A) in a timely manner if the party learns that in some material respect the disclosure or response is incomplete or incorrect, and if the additional or corrective information has not otherwise been made known to the other parties during the discovery process or in writing; or

> (B) as ordered by the court.

(2) *Expert Witness.* For an expert whose report must be disclosed under Rule 26(a)(2)(B), the party's duty to supplement extends both to information included in the report and to information given during the expert's deposition. Any additions or changes to this information must be disclosed by the time the party's pretrial disclosures under Rule 26(a)(3) are due.

(f) Conference of the Parties; Planning for Discovery.

(1) *Conference Timing.* Except in a proceeding exempted from initial disclosure under Rule 26(a)(1)(B) or when the court orders otherwise, the parties must confer as soon as practicable—and in any event at least 21 days before a scheduling conference is to be held or a scheduling order is due under Rule 16(b).

(2) *Conference Content; Parties' Responsibilities.* In conferring, the parties must consider the nature and basis of their claims and defenses and the possibilities for promptly settling or resolving the case; make or arrange for the disclosures required by Rule 26(a)(1); discuss any issues about preserving discoverable information; and develop a proposed discovery plan. The attorneys of record and all unrepresented parties that have appeared in the case are jointly

responsible for arranging the conference, for attempting in good faith to agree on the proposed discovery plan, and for submitting to the court within 14 days after the conference a written report outlining the plan. The court may order the parties or attorneys to attend the conference in person.

(3) *Discovery Plan.* A discovery plan must state the parties' views and proposals on:

(A) what changes should be made in the timing, form, or requirement for disclosures under Rule 26(a), including a statement of when initial disclosures were made or will be made;

(B) the subjects on which discovery may be needed, when discovery should be completed, and whether discovery should be conducted in phases or be limited to or focused on particular issues;

(C) any issues about disclosure or discovery of electronically stored information, including the form or forms in which it should be produced;

(D) any issues about claims of privilege or of protection as trial-preparation materials, including—if the parties agree on a procedure to assert these claims after production—whether to ask the court to include their agreement in an order;

(E) what changes should be made in the limitations on discovery imposed under these rules or by local rule, and what other limitations should be imposed; and

(F) any other orders that the court should issue under Rule 26(c) or under Rule 16(b) and (c).

(4) *Expedited Schedule.* If necessary to comply with its expedited schedule for Rule 16(b) conferences, a court may by local rule:

(A) require the parties' conference to occur less than 21 days before the scheduling conference is held or a scheduling order is due under Rule 16(b); and

(B) require the written report outlining the discovery plan to be filed less than 14 days after the parties' conference, or excuse the parties from submitting a written report and permit them to report orally on their discovery plan at the Rule 16(b) conference.

(g) Signing Disclosures and Discovery Requests, Responses, and Objections.

(1) *Signature Required; Effect of Signature.* Every disclosure under Rule 26(a)(1) or (a)(3) and every discovery request, response, or objection must be signed by at least one attorney of record in the attorney's own name—or by the party personally, if unrepresented—and must state the signer's address, e-mail address, and tele-

phone number. By signing, an attorney or party certifies that to the best of the person's knowledge, information, and belief formed after a reasonable inquiry:

(A) with respect to a disclosure, it is complete and correct as of the time it is made; and

(B) with respect to a discovery request, response, or objection, it is:

(i) consistent with these rules and warranted by existing law or by a nonfrivolous argument for extending, modifying, or reversing existing law, or for establishing new law;

(ii) not interposed for any improper purpose, such as to harass, cause unnecessary delay, or needlessly increase the cost of litigation; and

(iii) neither unreasonable nor unduly burdensome or expensive, considering the needs of the case, prior discovery in the case, the amount in controversy, and the importance of the issues at stake in the action.

(2) *Failure to Sign.* Other parties have no duty to act on an unsigned disclosure, request, response, or objection until it is signed, and the court must strike it unless a signature is promptly supplied after the omission is called to the attorney's or party's attention.

(3) *Sanction for Improper Certification.* If a certification violates this rule without substantial justification, the court, on motion or on its own, must impose an appropriate sanction on the signer, the party on whose behalf the signer was acting, or both. The sanction may include an order to pay the reasonable expenses, including attorney's fees, caused by the violation.

As amended 1948, 1963, 1966, 1970, 1980, 1983, 1987, 1993, 2000, 2006, 2007.

Rule 27.

DEPOSITIONS TO PERPETUATE TESTIMONY

(a) Before an Action Is Filed.

(1) *Petition.* A person who wants to perpetuate testimony about any matter cognizable in a United States court may file a verified petition in the district court for the district where any expected adverse party resides. The petition must ask for an order authorizing the petitioner to depose the named persons in order to perpetuate their testimony. The petition must be titled in the petitioner's name and must show:

(A) that the petitioner expects to be a party to an action cognizable in a United States court but cannot presently bring it or cause it to be brought;

(B) the subject matter of the expected action and the petitioner's interest;

(C) the facts that the petitioner wants to establish by the proposed testimony and the reasons to perpetuate it;

(D) the names or a description of the persons whom the petitioner expects to be adverse parties and their addresses, so far as known; and

(E) the name, address, and expected substance of the testimony of each deponent.

(2) *Notice and Service.* At least 21 days before the hearing date, the petitioner must serve each expected adverse party with a copy of the petition and a notice stating the time and place of the hearing. The notice may be served either inside or outside the district or state in the manner provided in Rule 4. If that service cannot be made with reasonable diligence on an expected adverse party, the court may order service by publication or otherwise. The court must appoint an attorney to represent persons not served in the manner provided in Rule 4 and to cross-examine the deponent if an unserved person is not otherwise represented. If any expected adverse party is a minor or is incompetent, Rule 17(c) applies.

(3) *Order and Examination.* If satisfied that perpetuating the testimony may prevent a failure or delay of justice, the court must issue an order that designates or describes the persons whose depositions may be taken, specifies the subject matter of the examinations, and states whether the depositions will be taken orally or by written interrogatories. The depositions may then be taken under these rules, and the court may issue orders like those authorized by Rules 34 and 35. A reference in these rules to the court where an action is pending means, for purposes of this rule, the court where the petition for the deposition was filed.

(4) *Using the Deposition.* A deposition to perpetuate testimony may be used under Rule 32(a) in any later-filed district-court action involving the same subject matter if the deposition either was taken under these rules or, although not so taken, would be admissible in evidence in the courts of the state where it was taken.

(b) Pending Appeal.

(1) *In General.* The court where a judgment has been rendered may, if an appeal has been taken or may still be taken, permit a party to depose witnesses to perpetuate their testimony for use in the event of further proceedings in that court.

(2) *Motion.* The party who wants to perpetuate testimony may move for leave to take the depositions, on the same notice and service as if the action were pending in the district court. The motion must show:

>(A) the name, address, and expected substance of the testimony of each deponent; and

>(B) the reasons for perpetuating the testimony.

(3) *Court Order.* If the court finds that perpetuating the testimony may prevent a failure or delay of justice, the court may permit the depositions to be taken and may issue orders like those authorized by Rules 34 and 35. The depositions may be taken and used as any other deposition taken in a pending district-court action.

(c) Perpetuation by an Action. This rule does not limit a court's power to entertain an action to perpetuate testimony.

As amended 1948, 1949, 1971, 1987, 2005, 2007, 2009.

Rule 28.

PERSONS BEFORE WHOM DEPOSITIONS MAY BE TAKEN

(a) Within the United States.

(1) *In General.* Within the United States or a territory or insular possession subject to United States jurisdiction, a deposition must be taken before:

>(A) an officer authorized to administer oaths either by federal law or by the law in the place of examination; or

>(B) a person appointed by the court where the action is pending to administer oaths and take testimony.

(2) *Definition of "Officer."* The term "officer" in Rules 30, 31, and 32 includes a person appointed by the court under this rule or designated by the parties under Rule 29(a).

(b) In a Foreign Country.

(1) *In General.* A deposition may be taken in a foreign country:

>(A) under an applicable treaty or convention;

>(B) under a letter of request, whether or not captioned a "letter rogatory";

>(C) on notice, before a person authorized to administer oaths either by federal law or by the law in the place of examination; or

(D) before a person commissioned by the court to administer any necessary oath and take testimony.

(2) *Issuing a Letter of Request or a Commission.* A letter of request, a commission, or both may be issued:

(A) on appropriate terms after an application and notice of it; and

(B) without a showing that taking the deposition in another manner is impracticable or inconvenient.

(3) *Form of a Request, Notice, or Commission.* When a letter of request or any other device is used according to a treaty or convention, it must be captioned in the form prescribed by that treaty or convention. A letter of request may be addressed "To the Appropriate Authority in [name of country]." A deposition notice or a commission must designate by name or descriptive title the person before whom the deposition is to be taken.

(4) *Letter of Request—Admitting Evidence.* Evidence obtained in response to a letter of request need not be excluded merely because it is not a verbatim transcript, because the testimony was not taken under oath, or because of any similar departure from the requirements for depositions taken within the United States.

(c) Disqualification. A deposition must not be taken before a person who is any party's relative, employee, or attorney; who is related to or employed by any party's attorney; or who is financially interested in the action.

As amended 1948, 1963, 1980, 1987, 1993, 2007.

Rule 29.

STIPULATIONS ABOUT DISCOVERY PROCEDURE

Unless the court orders otherwise, the parties may stipulate that:

(a) a deposition may be taken before any person, at any time or place, on any notice, and in the manner specified—in which event it may be used in the same way as any other deposition; and

(b) other procedures governing or limiting discovery be modified—but a stipulation extending the time for any form of discovery must have court approval if it would interfere with the time set for completing discovery, for hearing a motion, or for trial.

As amended 1970, 1993, 2007.

Rule 30.

DEPOSITIONS BY ORAL EXAMINATION

(a) When a Deposition May Be Taken.

(1) *Without Leave.* A party may, by oral questions, depose any person, including a party, without leave of court except as provided in Rule 30(a)(2). The deponent's attendance may be compelled by subpoena under Rule 45.

(2) *With Leave.* A party must obtain leave of court, and the court must grant leave to the extent consistent with Rule 26(b)(2):

(A) if the parties have not stipulated to the deposition and:

(i) the deposition would result in more than 10 depositions being taken under this rule or Rule 31 by the plaintiffs, or by the defendants, or by the third-party defendants;

(ii) the deponent has already been deposed in the case; or

(iii) the party seeks to take the deposition before the time specified in Rule 26(d), unless the party certifies in the notice, with supporting facts, that the deponent is expected to leave the United States and be unavailable for examination in this country after that time; or

(B) if the deponent is confined in prison.

(b) Notice of the Deposition; Other Formal Requirements.

(1) *Notice in General.* A party who wants to depose a person by oral questions must give reasonable written notice to every other party. The notice must state the time and place of the deposition and, if known, the deponent's name and address. If the name is unknown, the notice must provide a general description sufficient to identify the person or the particular class or group to which the person belongs.

(2) *Producing Documents.* If a subpoena duces tecum is to be served on the deponent, the materials designated for production, as set out in the subpoena, must be listed in the notice or in an attachment. The notice to a party deponent may be accompanied by a request under Rule 34 to produce documents and tangible things at the deposition.

(3) *Method of Recording.*

(A) *Method Stated in the Notice.* The party who notices the deposition must state in the notice the method for recording the testimony. Unless the court orders otherwise, testimony may be recorded by audio, audiovisual, or stenographic means. The noticing party bears the recording costs. Any party may arrange to transcribe a deposition.

(B) *Additional Method.* With prior notice to the deponent and other parties, any party may designate another method for recording the testimony in addition to that specified in the original notice. That party bears the expense of the additional record or transcript unless the court orders otherwise.

(4) *By Remote Means.* The parties may stipulate—or the court may on motion order—that a deposition be taken by telephone or other remote means. For the purpose of this rule and Rules 28(a), 37(a)(2), and 37(b)(1), the deposition takes place where the deponent answers the questions.

(5) *Officer's Duties.*

(A) *Before the Deposition.* Unless the parties stipulate otherwise, a deposition must be conducted before an officer appointed or designated under Rule 28. The officer must begin the deposition with an on-the-record statement that includes:

(i) the officer's name and business address;

(ii) the date, time, and place of the deposition;

(iii) the deponent's name;

(iv) the officer's administration of the oath or affirmation to the deponent; and

(v) the identity of all persons present.

(B) *Conducting the Deposition; Avoiding Distortion.* If the deposition is recorded nonstenographically, the officer must repeat the items in Rule 30(b)(5)(A)(i)–(iii) at the beginning of each unit of the recording medium. The deponent's and attorneys' appearance or demeanor must not be distorted through recording techniques.

(C) *After the Deposition.* At the end of a deposition, the officer must state on the record that the deposition is complete and must set out any stipulations made by the attorneys about custody of the transcript or recording and of the exhibits, or about any other pertinent matters.

(6) *Notice or Subpoena Directed to an Organization.* In its notice or subpoena, a party may name as the deponent a public or private corporation, a partnership, an association, a governmental agency, or other entity and must describe with reasonable particularity the matters for examination. The named organization must then designate one or more officers, directors, or managing agents, or designate other persons who consent to testify on its behalf; and

it may set out the matters on which each person designated will testify. A subpoena must advise a nonparty organization of its duty to make this designation. The persons designated must testify about information known or reasonably available to the organization. This paragraph (6) does not preclude a deposition by any other procedure allowed by these rules.

(c) Examination and Cross–Examination; Record of the Examination; Objections; Written Questions.

(1) *Examination and Cross–Examination*. The examination and cross-examination of a deponent proceed as they would at trial under the Federal Rules of Evidence, except Rules 103 and 615. After putting the deponent under oath or affirmation, the officer must record the testimony by the method designated under Rule 30(b)(3)(A). The testimony must be recorded by the officer personally or by a person acting in the presence and under the direction of the officer.

(2) *Objections*. An objection at the time of the examination—whether to evidence, to a party's conduct, to the officer's qualifications, to the manner of taking the deposition, or to any other aspect of the deposition—must be noted on the record, but the examination still proceeds; the testimony is taken subject to any objection. An objection must be stated concisely in a nonargumentative and nonsuggestive manner. A person may instruct a deponent not to answer only when necessary to preserve a privilege, to enforce a limitation ordered by the court, or to present a motion under Rule 30(d)(3).

(3) *Participating Through Written Questions*. Instead of participating in the oral examination, a party may serve written questions in a sealed envelope on the party noticing the deposition, who must deliver them to the officer. The officer must ask the deponent those questions and record the answers verbatim.

(d) Duration; Sanction; Motion to Terminate or Limit.

(1) *Duration*. Unless otherwise stipulated or ordered by the court, a deposition is limited to 1 day of 7 hours. The court must allow additional time consistent with Rule 26(b)(2) if needed to fairly examine the deponent or if the deponent, another person, or any other circumstance impedes or delays the examination.

(2) *Sanction*. The court may impose an appropriate sanction—including the reasonable expenses and attorney's fees incurred by any party—on a person who impedes, delays, or frustrates the fair examination of the deponent.

(3) *Motion to Terminate or Limit*.

(A) *Grounds*. At any time during a deposition, the deponent or a party may move to terminate or limit it on the ground that it is being conducted in bad faith or in a manner that unreasonably annoys, embarrasses, or oppresses the deponent or party. The motion may be filed in the court where the action is pending or the deposition is being taken. If the objecting deponent or party so demands, the deposition must be suspended for the time necessary to obtain an order.

(B) *Order.* The court may order that the deposition be terminated or may limit its scope and manner as provided in Rule 26(c). If terminated, the deposition may be resumed only by order of the court where the action is pending.

(C) *Award of Expenses.* Rule 37(a)(5) applies to the award of expenses.

(e) Review by the Witness; Changes.

(1) *Review; Statement of Changes.* On request by the deponent or a party before the deposition is completed, the deponent must be allowed 30 days after being notified by the officer that the transcript or recording is available in which:

(A) to review the transcript or recording; and

(B) if there are changes in form or substance, to sign a statement listing the changes and the reasons for making them.

(2) *Changes Indicated in the Officer's Certificate.* The officer must note in the certificate prescribed by Rule 30(f)(1) whether a review was requested and, if so, must attach any changes the deponent makes during the 30–day period.

(f) Certification and Delivery; Exhibits; Copies of the Transcript or Recording; Filing.

(1) *Certification and Delivery.* The officer must certify in writing that the witness was duly sworn and that the deposition accurately records the witness's testimony. The certificate must accompany the record of the deposition. Unless the court orders otherwise, the officer must seal the deposition in an envelope or package bearing the title of the action and marked "Deposition of [witness's name]" and must promptly send it to the attorney who arranged for the transcript or recording. The attorney must store it under conditions that will protect it against loss, destruction, tampering, or deterioration.

(2) *Documents and Tangible Things.*

(A) *Originals and Copies.* Documents and tangible things produced for inspection during a deposition must, on a party's request, be marked for identification and attached to the deposition. Any party may inspect and copy them. But if the person who produced them wants to keep the originals, the person may:

> (i) offer copies to be marked, attached to the deposition, and then used as originals—after giving all parties a fair opportunity to verify the copies by comparing them with the originals; or

> (ii) give all parties a fair opportunity to inspect and copy the originals after they are marked—in which event the originals may be used as if attached to the deposition.

(B) *Order Regarding the Originals.* Any party may move for an order that the originals be attached to the deposition pending final disposition of the case.

(3) *Copies of the Transcript or Recording.* Unless otherwise stipulated or ordered by the court, the officer must retain the stenographic notes of a deposition taken stenographically or a copy of the recording of a deposition taken by another method. When paid reasonable charges, the officer must furnish a copy of the transcript or recording to any party or the deponent.

(4) *Notice of Filing.* A party who files the deposition must promptly notify all other parties of the filing.

(g) Failure to Attend a Deposition or Serve a Subpoena; Expenses. A party who, expecting a deposition to be taken, attends in person or by an attorney may recover reasonable expenses for attending, including attorney's fees, if the noticing party failed to:

(1) attend and proceed with the deposition; or

(2) serve a subpoena on a nonparty deponent, who consequently did not attend.

As amended 1963, 1970, 1971, 1975, 1980, 1987, 1993, 2000, 2007.

Rule 31.

DEPOSITIONS BY WRITTEN QUESTIONS

(a) When a Deposition May Be Taken.

(1) *Without Leave.* A party may, by written questions, depose any person, including a party, without leave of court except as provided in Rule 31(a)(2). The deponent's attendance may be compelled by subpoena under Rule 45.

(2) *With Leave.* A party must obtain leave of court, and the court must grant leave to the extent consistent with Rule 26(b)(2):

> (A) if the parties have not stipulated to the deposition and:

> > (i) the deposition would result in more than 10 depositions being taken under this rule or Rule 30 by the

plaintiffs, or by the defendants, or by the third-party defendants;

(ii) the deponent has already been deposed in the case; or

(iii) the party seeks to take a deposition before the time specified in Rule 26(d); or

(B) if the deponent is confined in prison.

(3) *Service; Required Notice.* A party who wants to depose a person by written questions must serve them on every other party, with a notice stating, if known, the deponent's name and address. If the name is unknown, the notice must provide a general description sufficient to identify the person or the particular class or group to which the person belongs. The notice must also state the name or descriptive title and the address of the officer before whom the deposition will be taken.

(4) *Questions Directed to an Organization.* A public or private corporation, a partnership, an association, or a governmental agency may be deposed by written questions in accordance with Rule 30(b)(6).

(5) *Questions from Other Parties.* Any questions to the deponent from other parties must be served on all parties as follows: cross-questions, within 14 days after being served with the notice and direct questions; redirect questions, within 7 days after being served with cross-questions; and recross-questions, within 7 days after being served with redirect questions. The court may, for good cause, extend or shorten these times.

(b) Delivery to the Officer; Officer's Duties. The party who noticed the deposition must deliver to the officer a copy of all the questions served and of the notice. The officer must promptly proceed in the manner provided in Rule 30(c), (e), and (f) to:

(1) take the deponent's testimony in response to the questions;

(2) prepare and certify the deposition; and

(3) send it to the party, attaching a copy of the questions and of the notice.

(c) Notice of Completion or Filing.

(1) *Completion.* The party who noticed the deposition must notify all other parties when it is completed.

(2) *Filing.* A party who files the deposition must promptly notify all other parties of the filing.

As amended 1970, 1987, 1993, 2007.

Rule 32.

USING DEPOSITIONS IN COURT PROCEEDINGS

(a) Using Depositions.

(1) *In General.* At a hearing or trial, all or part of a deposition may be used against a party on these conditions:

(A) the party was present or represented at the taking of the deposition or had reasonable notice of it;

(B) it is used to the extent it would be admissible under the Federal Rules of Evidence if the deponent were present and testifying; and

(C) the use is allowed by Rule 32(a)(2) through (8).

(2) *Impeachment and Other Uses.* Any party may use a deposition to contradict or impeach the testimony given by the deponent as a witness, or for any other purpose allowed by the Federal Rules of Evidence.

(3) *Deposition of Party, Agent, or Designee.* An adverse party may use for any purpose the deposition of a party or anyone who, when deposed, was the party's officer, director, managing agent, or designee under Rule 30(b)(6) or 31(a)(4).

(4) *Unavailable Witness.* A party may use for any purpose the deposition of a witness, whether or not a party, if the court finds:

(A) that the witness is dead;

(B) that the witness is more than 100 miles from the place of hearing or trial or is outside the United States, unless it appears that the witness's absence was procured by the party offering the deposition;

(C) that the witness cannot attend or testify because of age, illness, infirmity, or imprisonment;

(D) that the party offering the deposition could not procure the witness's attendance by subpoena; or

(E) on motion and notice, that exceptional circumstances make it desirable—in the interest of justice and with due regard to the importance of live testimony in open court—to permit the deposition to be used.

(5) *Limitations on Use.*

(A) *Deposition Taken on Short Notice.* A deposition must not be used against a party who, having received less than 14 days' notice of the deposition, promptly moved for a protective order under Rule 26(c)(1)(B) requesting that it not be taken or be taken at a different time or place—and this motion was still pending when the deposition was taken.

(B) *Unavailable Deponent; Party Could Not Obtain an Attorney.* A deposition taken without leave of court under the unavailability provision of Rule 30(a)(2)(A)(iii) must not be used against a party who shows that, when served with the notice, it could not, despite diligent efforts, obtain an attorney to represent it at the deposition.

(6) *Using Part of a Deposition.* If a party offers in evidence only part of a deposition, an adverse party may require the offeror to introduce other parts that in fairness should be considered with the part introduced, and any party may itself introduce any other parts.

(7) *Substituting a Party.* Substituting a party under Rule 25 does not affect the right to use a deposition previously taken.

(8) *Deposition Taken in an Earlier Action.* A deposition lawfully taken and, if required, filed in any federal- or state-court action may be used in a later action involving the same subject matter between the same parties, or their representatives or successors in interest, to the same extent as if taken in the later action. A deposition previously taken may also be used as allowed by the Federal Rules of Evidence.

(b) Objections to Admissibility. Subject to Rules 28(b) and 32(d)(3), an objection may be made at a hearing or trial to the admission of any deposition testimony that would be inadmissible if the witness were present and testifying.

(c) Form of Presentation. Unless the court orders otherwise, a party must provide a transcript of any deposition testimony the party offers, but may provide the court with the testimony in nontranscript form as well. On any party's request, deposition testimony offered in a jury trial for any purpose other than impeachment must be presented in nontranscript form, if available, unless the court for good cause orders otherwise.

(d) Waiver of Objections.

(1) *To the Notice.* An objection to an error or irregularity in a deposition notice is waived unless promptly served in writing on the party giving the notice.

(2) *To the Officer's Qualification.* An objection based on disqualification of the officer before whom a deposition is to be taken is waived if not made:

(A) before the deposition begins; or

(B) promptly after the basis for disqualification becomes known or, with reasonable diligence, could have been known.

(3) *To the Taking of the Deposition.*

(A) *Objection to Competence, Relevance, or Materiality.* An objection to a deponent's competence—or to the competence, relevance, or materiality of testimony—is not waived by a failure to make the objection before or during the deposition, unless the ground for it might have been corrected at that time.

(B) *Objection to an Error or Irregularity.* An objection to an error or irregularity at an oral examination is waived if:

(i) it relates to the manner of taking the deposition, the form of a question or answer, the oath or affirmation, a party's conduct, or other matters that might have been corrected at that time; and

(ii) it is not timely made during the deposition.

(C) *Objection to a Written Question.* An objection to the form of a written question under Rule 31 is waived if not served in writing on the party submitting the question within the time for serving responsive questions or, if the question is a recross-question, within 7 days after being served with it.

(4) *To Completing and Returning the Deposition.* An objection to how the officer transcribed the testimony—or prepared, signed, certified, sealed, endorsed, sent, or otherwise dealt with the deposition—is waived unless a motion to suppress is made promptly after the error or irregularity becomes known or, with reasonable diligence, could have been known.

As amended 1970, 1975, 1980, 1987, 1993, 2007, 2009.

Rule 33.

INTERROGATORIES TO PARTIES

(a) In General.

(1) *Number.* Unless otherwise stipulated or ordered by the court, a party may serve on any other party no more than 25 written interrogatories, including all discrete subparts. Leave to serve additional interrogatories may be granted to the extent consistent with Rule 26(b)(2).

(2) *Scope.* An interrogatory may relate to any matter that may be inquired into under Rule 26(b). An interrogatory is not objectionable merely because it asks for an opinion or contention that relates to fact or the application of law to fact, but the court may order that the interrogatory need not be answered until designated discovery is complete, or until a pretrial conference or some other time.

(b) Answers and Objections.

(1) *Responding Party.* The interrogatories must be answered:

(A) by the party to whom they are directed; or

(B) if that party is a public or private corporation, a partnership, an association, or a governmental agency, by any officer or agent, who must furnish the information available to the party.

(2) *Time to Respond.* The responding party must serve its answers and any objections within 30 days after being served with the interrogatories. A shorter or longer time may be stipulated to under Rule 29 or be ordered by the court.

(3) *Answering Each Interrogatory.* Each interrogatory must, to the extent it is not objected to, be answered separately and fully in writing under oath.

(4) *Objections.* The grounds for objecting to an interrogatory must be stated with specificity. Any ground not stated in a timely objection is waived unless the court, for good cause, excuses the failure.

(5) *Signature.* The person who makes the answers must sign them, and the attorney who objects must sign any objections.

(c) Use. An answer to an interrogatory may be used to the extent allowed by the Federal Rules of Evidence.

(d) Option to Produce Business Records. If the answer to an interrogatory may be determined by examining, auditing, compiling, abstracting, or summarizing a party's business records (including electronically stored information), and if the burden of deriving or ascertaining the answer will be substantially the same for either party, the responding party may answer by:

(1) specifying the records that must be reviewed, in sufficient detail to enable the interrogating party to locate and identify them as readily as the responding party could; and

(2) giving the interrogating party a reasonable opportunity to examine and audit the records and to make copies, compilations, abstracts, or summaries.

As amended 1948, 1970, 1980, 1993, 2006, 2007.

Rule 34.

PRODUCING DOCUMENTS, ELECTRONICALLY STORED INFORMATION, AND TANGIBLE THINGS, OR ENTERING ONTO LAND, FOR INSPECTION AND OTHER PURPOSES

(a) In General. A party may serve on any other party a request within the scope of Rule 26(b):

(1) to produce and permit the requesting party or its representative to inspect, copy, test, or sample the following items in the responding party's possession, custody, or control:

(A) any designated documents or electronically stored information—including writings, drawings, graphs, charts, photographs, sound recordings, images, and other data or data compilations—stored in any medium from which information can be obtained either directly or, if necessary, after translation by the responding party into a reasonably usable form; or

(B) any designated tangible things; or

(2) to permit entry onto designated land or other property possessed or controlled by the responding party, so that the requesting party may inspect, measure, survey, photograph, test, or sample the property or any designated object or operation on it.

(b) Procedure.

(1) *Contents of the Request.* The request:

(A) must describe with reasonable particularity each item or category of items to be inspected;

(B) must specify a reasonable time, place, and manner for the inspection and for performing the related acts; and

(C) may specify the form or forms in which electronically stored information is to be produced.

(2) *Responses and Objections.*

(A) *Time to Respond.* The party to whom the request is directed must respond in writing within 30 days after being served. A shorter or longer time may be stipulated to under Rule 29 or be ordered by the court.

(B) *Responding to Each Item.* For each item or category, the response must either state that inspection and related activities will be permitted as requested or state an objection to the request, including the reasons.

(C) *Objections.* An objection to part of a request must specify the part and permit inspection of the rest.

(D) *Responding to a Request for Production of Electronically Stored Information.* The response may state an objection to a requested form for producing electronically stored information. If the responding party objects to a requested form—or if no form was specified in the request—the party must state the form or forms it intends to use.

(E) *Producing the Documents or Electronically Stored Information.* Unless otherwise stipulated or ordered by the court, these procedures apply to producing documents or electronically stored information:

(i) A party must produce documents as they are kept in the usual course of business or must organize and label them to correspond to the categories in the request;

(ii) If a request does not specify a form for producing electronically stored information, a party must produce it in a form or forms in which it is ordinarily maintained or in a reasonably usable form or forms; and

(iii) A party need not produce the same electronically stored information in more than one form.

(c) Nonparties. As provided in Rule 45, a nonparty may be compelled to produce documents and tangible things or to permit an inspection.

As amended 1948, 1970, 1980, 1987, 1991, 1993, 2006, 2007.

Rule 35.

PHYSICAL AND MENTAL EXAMINATIONS

(a) Order for an Examination.

(1) *In General.* The court where the action is pending may order a party whose mental or physical condition—including blood group—is in controversy to submit to a physical or mental examination by a suitably licensed or certified examiner. The court has the same authority to order a party to produce for examination a person who is in its custody or under its legal control.

(2) *Motion and Notice; Contents of the Order.* The order:

(A) may be made only on motion for good cause and on notice to all parties and the person to be examined; and

(B) must specify the time, place, manner, conditions, and scope of the examination, as well as the person or persons who will perform it.

(b) Examiner's Report.

(1) *Request by the Party or Person Examined.* The party who moved for the examination must, on request, deliver to the requester a copy of the examiner's report, together with like reports of all earlier examinations of the same condition. The request may be made by the party against whom the examination order was issued or by the person examined.

(2) *Contents.* The examiner's report must be in writing and must set out in detail the examiner's findings, including diagnoses, conclusions, and the results of any tests.

(3) *Request by the Moving Party.* After delivering the reports, the party who moved for the examination may request—and is entitled to receive—from the party against whom the examination order was issued like reports of all earlier or later examinations of the same condition. But those reports need not be delivered by the party with custody or control of the person examined if the party shows that it could not obtain them.

(4) *Waiver of Privilege.* By requesting and obtaining the examiner's report, or by deposing the examiner, the party examined waives any privilege it may have—in that action or any other action involving the same controversy—concerning testimony about all examinations of the same condition.

(5) *Failure to Deliver a Report.* The court on motion may order—on just terms—that a party deliver the report of an examination. If the report is not provided, the court may exclude the examiner's testimony at trial.

(6) *Scope.* This subdivision (b) applies also to an examination made by the parties' agreement, unless the agreement states otherwise. This subdivision does not preclude obtaining an examiner's report or deposing an examiner under other rules.

As amended 1970, 1987, 1988, 1991, 2007.

Rule 36.

REQUESTS FOR ADMISSION

(a) Scope and Procedure.

(1) *Scope.* A party may serve on any other party a written request to admit, for purposes of the pending action only, the truth of any matters within the scope of Rule 26(b)(1) relating to:

    (A) facts, the application of law to fact, or opinions about either; and

    (B) the genuineness of any described documents.

(2) *Form; Copy of a Document.* Each matter must be separately stated. A request to admit the genuineness of a document must be accompanied by a copy of the document unless it is, or has been, otherwise furnished or made available for inspection and copying.

(3) *Time to Respond; Effect of Not Responding.* A matter is admitted unless, within 30 days after being served, the party to whom the request is directed serves on the requesting party a written answer or objection addressed to the matter and signed by the party or its attorney. A shorter or longer time for responding may be stipulated to under Rule 29 or be ordered by the court.

(4) *Answer.* If a matter is not admitted, the answer must specifically deny it or state in detail why the answering party cannot truthfully admit or deny it. A denial must fairly respond to the substance of the matter; and when good faith requires that a party qualify an answer or deny only a part of a matter, the answer must specify the part admitted and qualify or deny the rest. The answering party may assert lack of knowledge or information as a reason for failing to admit or deny only if the party states that it has made reasonable inquiry and that the information it knows or can readily obtain is insufficient to enable it to admit or deny.

(5) *Objections.* The grounds for objecting to a request must be stated. A party must not object solely on the ground that the request presents a genuine issue for trial.

(6) *Motion Regarding the Sufficiency of an Answer or Objection.* The requesting party may move to determine the sufficiency of an answer or objection. Unless the court finds an objection justified, it must order that an answer be served. On finding that an answer does not comply with this rule, the court may order either that the matter is admitted or that an amended answer be served. The court may defer its final decision until a pretrial conference or a specified time before trial. Rule 37(a)(5) applies to an award of expenses.

(b) Effect of an Admission; Withdrawing or Amending It. A matter admitted under this rule is conclusively established unless the court, on motion, permits the admission to be withdrawn or amended. Subject to Rule 16(e), the court may permit withdrawal or amendment if it would promote the presentation of the merits of the action and if the court is not persuaded that it would prejudice the requesting party in maintaining or defending the action on the merits. An admission under this rule is not an admission for any other purpose and cannot be used against the party in any other proceeding.

As amended 1948, 1970, 1987, 1993, 2007.

Rule 37.

FAILURE TO MAKE DISCLOSURES OR TO COOPERATE IN DISCOVERY; SANCTIONS

(a) Motion for an Order Compelling Disclosure or Discovery.

(1) *In General.* On notice to other parties and all affected persons, a party may move for an order compelling disclosure or discovery. The motion must include a certification that the movant has in good faith conferred or attempted to confer with the person or party failing to make disclosure or discovery in an effort to obtain it without court action.

(2) *Appropriate Court.* A motion for an order to a party must be made in the court where the action is pending. A motion for an order to a nonparty must be made in the court where the discovery is or will be taken.

(3) *Specific Motions.*

(A) *To Compel Disclosure.* If a party fails to make a disclosure required by Rule 26(a), any other party may move to compel disclosure and for appropriate sanctions.

(B) *To Compel a Discovery Response.* A party seeking discovery may move for an order compelling an answer, designation, production, or inspection. This motion may be made if:

(i) a deponent fails to answer a question asked under Rule 30 or 31;

(ii) a corporation or other entity fails to make a designation under Rule 30(b)(6) or 31(a)(4);

(iii) a party fails to answer an interrogatory submitted under Rule 33; or

(iv) a party fails to respond that inspection will be permitted—or fails to permit inspection—as requested under Rule 34.

(C) *Related to a Deposition.* When taking an oral deposition, the party asking a question may complete or adjourn the examination before moving for an order.

(4) *Evasive or Incomplete Disclosure, Answer, or Response.* For purposes of this subdivision (a), an evasive or incomplete disclosure, answer, or response must be treated as a failure to disclose, answer, or respond.

(5) *Payment of Expenses; Protective Orders.*

(A) *If the Motion Is Granted (or Disclosure or Discovery Is Provided After Filing).* If the motion is granted—or if the disclosure or requested discovery is provided after the motion was filed—the court must, after giving an opportunity to be heard, require the party or deponent whose conduct necessitated the motion, the party or attorney advising that conduct, or both to pay the movant's reasonable expenses incurred in making the motion, including attorney's fees. But the court must not order this payment if:

(i) the movant filed the motion before attempting in good faith to obtain the disclosure or discovery without court action;

(ii) the opposing party's nondisclosure, response, or objection was substantially justified; or

(iii) other circumstances make an award of expenses unjust.

(B) *If the Motion Is Denied.* If the motion is denied, the court may issue any protective order authorized under Rule 26(c) and must, after giving an opportunity to be heard, require the movant, the attorney filing the motion, or both to pay the party or deponent who opposed the motion its reasonable expenses incurred in opposing the motion, including attorney's fees. But the court must not order this payment if the motion was substantially justified or other circumstances make an award of expenses unjust.

(C) *If the Motion Is Granted in Part and Denied in Part.* If the motion is granted in part and denied in part, the court may issue any protective order authorized under Rule 26(c) and may, after giving an opportunity to be heard, apportion the reasonable expenses for the motion.

(b) Failure to Comply with a Court Order.

(1) *Sanctions in the District Where the Deposition Is Taken.* If the court where the discovery is taken orders a deponent to be sworn or to answer a question and the deponent fails to obey, the failure may be treated as contempt of court.

(2) *Sanctions in the District Where the Action Is Pending.*

(A) *For Not Obeying a Discovery Order.* If a party or a party's officer, director, or managing agent—or a witness designated under Rule 30(b)(6) or 31(a)(4)—fails to obey an order to provide or permit discovery, including an order under Rule 26(f), 35, or 37(a), the court where the action is pending may issue further just orders. They may include the following:

(i) directing that the matters embraced in the order or other designated facts be taken as established for purposes of the action, as the prevailing party claims;

(ii) prohibiting the disobedient party from supporting or opposing designated claims or defenses, or from introducing designated matters in evidence;

(iii) striking pleadings in whole or in part;

(iv) staying further proceedings until the order is obeyed;

(v) dismissing the action or proceeding in whole or in part;

(vi) rendering a default judgment against the disobedient party; or

(vii) treating as contempt of court the failure to obey any order except an order to submit to a physical or mental examination.

(B) *For Not Producing a Person for Examination.* If a party fails to comply with an order under Rule 35(a) requiring it to produce another person for examination, the court may issue any of the orders listed in Rule 37(b)(2)(A)(i)–(vi), unless the disobedient party shows that it cannot produce the other person.

(C) *Payment of Expenses.* Instead of or in addition to the orders above, the court must order the disobedient party, the attorney advising that party, or both to pay the reasonable expenses, including attorney's fees, caused by the failure, unless the failure was substantially justified or other circumstances make an award of expenses unjust.

(c) Failure to Disclose, to Supplement an Earlier Response, or to Admit.

(1) *Failure to Disclose or Supplement.* If a party fails to provide information or identify a witness as required by Rule 26(a) or (e), the party is not allowed to use that information or witness to supply evidence on a motion, at a hearing, or at a trial, unless the failure was substantially justified or is harmless. In addition to or instead of this sanction, the court, on motion and after giving an opportunity to be heard:

(A) may order payment of the reasonable expenses, including attorney's fees, caused by the failure;

(B) may inform the jury of the party's failure; and

(C) may impose other appropriate sanctions, including any of the orders listed in Rule 37(b)(2)(A)(i)–(vi).

(2) *Failure to Admit.* If a party fails to admit what is requested under Rule 36 and if the requesting party later proves a document to be genuine or the matter true, the requesting party may move

that the party who failed to admit pay the reasonable expenses, including attorney's fees, incurred in making that proof. The court must so order unless:

(A) the request was held objectionable under Rule 36(a);

(B) the admission sought was of no substantial importance;

(C) the party failing to admit had a reasonable ground to believe that it might prevail on the matter; or

(D) there was other good reason for the failure to admit.

(d) Party's Failure to Attend Its Own Deposition, Serve Answers to Interrogatories, or Respond to a Request for Inspection.

(1) *In General.*

(A) *Motion; Grounds for Sanctions.* The court where the action is pending may, on motion, order sanctions if:

(i) a party or a party's officer, director, or managing agent—or a person designated under Rule 30(b)(6) or 31(a)(4)—fails, after being served with proper notice, to appear for that person's deposition; or

(ii) a party, after being properly served with interrogatories under Rule 33 or a request for inspection under Rule 34, fails to serve its answers, objections, or written response.

(B) *Certification.* A motion for sanctions for failing to answer or respond must include a certification that the movant has in good faith conferred or attempted to confer with the party failing to act in an effort to obtain the answer or response without court action.

(2) *Unacceptable Excuse for Failing to Act.* A failure described in Rule 37(d)(1)(A) is not excused on the ground that the discovery sought was objectionable, unless the party failing to act has a pending motion for a protective order under Rule 26(c).

(3) *Types of Sanctions.* Sanctions may include any of the orders listed in Rule 37(b)(2)(A)(i)–(vi). Instead of or in addition to these sanctions, the court must require the party failing to act, the attorney advising that party, or both to pay the reasonable expenses, including attorney's fees, caused by the failure, unless the failure was substantially justified or other circumstances make an award of expenses unjust.

(e) Failure to Provide Electronically Stored Information. Absent exceptional circumstances, a court may not impose sanctions under these rules on a party for failing to provide electronically stored information lost as a result of the routine, good-faith operation of an electronic information system.

(f) Failure to Participate in Framing a Discovery Plan. If a party or its attorney fails to participate in good faith in developing and submitting a proposed discovery plan as required by Rule 26(f), the court may, after giving an opportunity to be heard, require that party or attorney to pay to any other party the reasonable expenses, including attorney's fees, caused by the failure.

As amended 1949, 1970, 1980, 1981, 1987, 1993, 2000, 2006, 2007.

VI. TRIALS

Rule 38.

RIGHT TO A JURY TRIAL; DEMAND

(a) Right Preserved. The right of trial by jury as declared by the Seventh Amendment to the Constitution—or as provided by a federal statute—is preserved to the parties inviolate.

(b) Demand. On any issue triable of right by a jury, a party may demand a jury trial by:

(1) serving the other parties with a written demand—which may be included in a pleading—no later than 14 days after the last pleading directed to the issue is served; and

(2) filing the demand in accordance with Rule 5(d).

(c) Specifying Issues. In its demand, a party may specify the issues that it wishes to have tried by a jury; otherwise, it is considered to have demanded a jury trial on all the issues so triable. If the party has demanded a jury trial on only some issues, any other party may—within 14 days after being served with the demand or within a shorter time ordered by the court—serve a demand for a jury trial on any other or all factual issues triable by jury.

(d) Waiver; Withdrawal. A party waives a jury trial unless its demand is properly served and filed. A proper demand may be withdrawn only if the parties consent.

(e) Admiralty and Maritime Claims. These rules do not create a right to a jury trial on issues in a claim that is an admiralty or maritime claim under Rule 9(h).

As amended 1966, 1987, 1993, 2007, 2009.

Rule 39.

TRIAL BY JURY OR BY THE COURT

(a) When a Demand Is Made. When a jury trial has been demanded under Rule 38, the action must be designated on the docket as a jury action. The trial on all issues so demanded must be by jury unless:

(1) the parties or their attorneys file a stipulation to a nonjury trial or so stipulate on the record; or

(2) the court, on motion or on its own, finds that on some or all of those issues there is no federal right to a jury trial.

(b) When No Demand Is Made. Issues on which a jury trial is not properly demanded are to be tried by the court. But the court may, on motion, order a jury trial on any issue for which a jury might have been demanded.

(c) Advisory Jury; Jury Trial by Consent. In an action not triable of right by a jury, the court, on motion or on its own:

(1) may try any issue with an advisory jury; or

(2) may, with the parties' consent, try any issue by a jury whose verdict has the same effect as if a jury trial had been a matter of right, unless the action is against the United States and a federal statute provides for a nonjury trial.

As amended 2007.

Rule 40.

SCHEDULING CASES FOR TRIAL

Each court must provide by rule for scheduling trials. The court must give priority to actions entitled to priority by a federal statute.

As amended 2007.

Rule 41.

DISMISSAL OF ACTIONS

(a) Voluntary Dismissal.

(1) *By the Plaintiff.*

(A) *Without a Court Order.* Subject to Rules 23(e), 23.1(c), 23.2, and 66 and any applicable federal statute, the plaintiff may dismiss an action without a court order by filing:

(i) a notice of dismissal before the opposing party serves either an answer or a motion for summary judgment; or

(ii) a stipulation of dismissal signed by all parties who have appeared.

(B) *Effect.* Unless the notice or stipulation states otherwise, the dismissal is without prejudice. But if the plaintiff previously dismissed any federal- or state-court action based on or including the same claim, a notice of dismissal operates as an adjudication on the merits.

(2) *By Court Order; Effect.* Except as provided in Rule 41(a)(1), an action may be dismissed at the plaintiff's request only by court order, on terms that the court considers proper. If a defendant has pleaded a counterclaim before being served with the plaintiff's motion to dismiss, the action may be dismissed over the defendant's objection only if the counterclaim can remain pending for independent adjudication. Unless the order states otherwise, a dismissal under this paragraph (2) is without prejudice.

(b) Involuntary Dismissal; Effect. If the plaintiff fails to prosecute or to comply with these rules or a court order, a defendant may move to dismiss the action or any claim against it. Unless the dismissal order states otherwise, a dismissal under this subdivision (b) and any dismissal not under this rule—except one for lack of jurisdiction, improper venue, or failure to join a party under Rule 19—operates as an adjudication on the merits.

(c) Dismissing a Counterclaim, Crossclaim, or Third–Party Claim. This rule applies to a dismissal of any counterclaim, crossclaim, or third-party claim. A claimant's voluntary dismissal under Rule 41(a)(1)(A)(i) must be made:

(1) before a responsive pleading is served; or

(2) if there is no responsive pleading, before evidence is introduced at a hearing or trial.

(d) Costs of a Previously Dismissed Action. If a plaintiff who previously dismissed an action in any court files an action based on or including the same claim against the same defendant, the court:

(1) may order the plaintiff to pay all or part of the costs of that previous action; and

(2) may stay the proceedings until the plaintiff has complied.

As amended 1948, 1963, 1966, 1968, 1987, 1991, 2007.

Rule 42.

CONSOLIDATION; SEPARATE TRIALS

(a) Consolidation. If actions before the court involve a common question of law or fact, the court may:

(1) join for hearing or trial any or all matters at issue in the actions;

(2) consolidate the actions; or

(3) issue any other orders to avoid unnecessary cost or delay.

(b) Separate Trials. For convenience, to avoid prejudice, or to expedite and economize, the court may order a separate trial of one or more separate issues, claims, crossclaims, counterclaims, or third-party claims. When ordering a separate trial, the court must preserve any federal right to a jury trial.

As amended 1966, 2007.

Rule 43.

TAKING TESTIMONY

(a) In Open Court. At trial, the witnesses' testimony must be taken in open court unless a federal statute, the Federal Rules of Evidence, these rules, or other rules adopted by the Supreme Court provide otherwise. For good cause in compelling circumstances and with appropriate safeguards, the court may permit testimony in open court by contemporaneous transmission from a different location.

(b) Affirmation Instead of an Oath. When these rules require an oath, a solemn affirmation suffices.

(c) Evidence on a Motion. When a motion relies on facts outside the record, the court may hear the matter on affidavits or may hear it wholly or partly on oral testimony or on depositions.

(d) Interpreter. The court may appoint an interpreter of its choosing; fix reasonable compensation to be paid from funds provided by law or by one or more parties; and tax the compensation as costs.

As amended 1966, 1975, 1987, 1996, 2007.

Rule 44.

PROVING AN OFFICIAL RECORD

(a) Means of Proving.

(1) *Domestic Record.* Each of the following evidences an official record—or an entry in it—that is otherwise admissible and is kept within the United States, any state, district, or commonwealth, or any territory subject to the administrative or judicial jurisdiction of the United States:

(A) an official publication of the record; or

(B) a copy attested by the officer with legal custody of the record—or by the officer's deputy—and accompanied by a certificate that the officer has custody. The certificate must be made under seal:

(i) by a judge of a court of record in the district or political subdivision where the record is kept; or

(ii) by any public officer with a seal of office and with official duties in the district or political subdivision where the record is kept.

(2) *Foreign Record.*

(A) *In General.* Each of the following evidences a foreign official record—or an entry in it—that is otherwise admissible:

(i) an official publication of the record; or

(ii) the record—or a copy—that is attested by an authorized person and is accompanied either by a final certification of genuineness or by a certification under a treaty or convention to which the United States and the country where the record is located are parties.

(B) *Final Certification of Genuineness.* A final certification must certify the genuineness of the signature and official position of the attester or of any foreign official whose certificate of genuineness relates to the attestation or is in a chain of certificates of genuineness relating to the attestation. A final certification may be made by a secretary of a United States embassy or legation; by a consul general, vice consul, or consular agent of the United States; or by a diplomatic or consular official of the foreign country assigned or accredited to the United States.

(C) *Other Means of Proof.* If all parties have had a reasonable opportunity to investigate a foreign record's authenticity and accuracy, the court may, for good cause, either:

(i) admit an attested copy without final certification; or

(ii) permit the record to be evidenced by an attested summary with or without a final certification.

(b) Lack of a Record. A written statement that a diligent search of designated records revealed no record or entry of a specified tenor is admissible as evidence that the records contain no such record or entry. For domestic records, the statement must be authenticated under Rule 44(a)(1). For foreign records, the statement must comply with (a)(2)(C)(ii).

(c) Other Proof. A party may prove an official record—or an entry or lack of an entry in it—by any other method authorized by law.

As amended 1966, 1987, 1991, 2007.

Rule 44.1.

DETERMINING FOREIGN LAW

A party who intends to raise an issue about a foreign country's law must give notice by a pleading or other writing. In determining foreign law, the court may consider any relevant material or source, including testimony, whether or not submitted by a party or admissible under the Federal Rules of Evidence. The court's determination must be treated as a ruling on a question of law.

Added 1966; as amended 1975, 1987, 2007.

Rule 45.

SUBPOENA

(a) In General.

(1) *Form and Contents.*

(A) *Requirements—In General.* Every subpoena must:

(i) state the court from which it issued;

(ii) state the title of the action, the court in which it is pending, and its civil-action number;

(iii) command each person to whom it is directed to do the following at a specified time and place: attend and testify; produce designated documents, electronically stored information, or tangible things in that person's possession, custody, or control; or permit the inspection of premises; and

(iv) set out the text of Rule 45(c) and (d).

(B) *Command to Attend a Deposition—Notice of the Recording Method.* A subpoena commanding attendance at a deposition must state the method for recording the testimony.

(C) *Combining or Separating a Command to Produce or to Permit Inspection; Specifying the Form for Electronically Stored Information.* A command to produce documents, electronically stored information, or tangible things or to permit the inspection of premises may be included in a subpoena commanding attendance at a deposition, hearing, or trial, or may be set out in a separate subpoena. A subpoena may specify the form or forms in which electronically stored information is to be produced.

(D) *Command to Produce; Included Obligations.* A command in a subpoena to produce documents, electronically stored information, or tangible things requires the responding party to permit inspection, copying, testing, or sampling of the materials.

(2) *Issued from Which Court.* A subpoena must issue as follows:

(A) for attendance at a hearing or trial, from the court for the district where the hearing or trial is to be held;

(B) for attendance at a deposition, from the court for the district where the deposition is to be taken; and

(C) for production or inspection, if separate from a subpoena commanding a person's attendance, from the court for the district where the production or inspection is to be made.

(3) *Issued by Whom.* The clerk must issue a subpoena, signed but otherwise in blank, to a party who requests it. That party must complete it before service. An attorney also may issue and sign a subpoena as an officer of:

(A) a court in which the attorney is authorized to practice; or

(B) a court for a district where a deposition is to be taken or production is to be made, if the attorney is authorized to practice in the court where the action is pending.

(b) Service.

(1) *By Whom; Tendering Fees; Serving a Copy of Certain Subpoenas.* Any person who is at least 18 years old and not a party may serve a subpoena. Serving a subpoena requires delivering a copy to the named person and, if the subpoena requires that person's attendance, tendering the fees for 1 day's attendance and the mileage allowed by law. Fees and mileage need not be tendered when the subpoena issues on behalf of the United States or any of

its officers or agencies. If the subpoena commands the production of documents, electronically stored information, or tangible things or the inspection of premises before trial, then before it is served, a notice must be served on each party.

(2) *Service in the United States.* Subject to Rule 45(c)(3)(A)(ii), a subpoena may be served at any place:

(A) within the district of the issuing court;

(B) outside that district but within 100 miles of the place specified for the deposition, hearing, trial, production, or inspection;

(C) within the state of the issuing court if a state statute or court rule allows service at that place of a subpoena issued by a state court of general jurisdiction sitting in the place specified for the deposition, hearing, trial, production, or inspection; or

(D) that the court authorizes on motion and for good cause, if a federal statute so provides.

(3) *Service in a Foreign Country.* 28 U.S.C. § 1783 governs issuing and serving a subpoena directed to a United States national or resident who is in a foreign country.

(4) *Proof of Service.* Proving service, when necessary, requires filing with the issuing court a statement showing the date and manner of service and the names of the persons served. The statement must be certified by the server.

(c) Protecting a Person Subject to a Subpoena.

(1) *Avoiding Undue Burden or Expense; Sanctions.* A party or attorney responsible for issuing and serving a subpoena must take reasonable steps to avoid imposing undue burden or expense on a person subject to the subpoena. The issuing court must enforce this duty and impose an appropriate sanction—which may include lost earnings and reasonable attorney's fees—on a party or attorney who fails to comply.

(2) *Command to Produce Materials or Permit Inspection.*

(A) *Appearance Not Required.* A person commanded to produce documents, electronically stored information, or tangible things, or to permit the inspection of premises, need not appear in person at the place of production or inspection unless also commanded to appear for a deposition, hearing, or trial.

(B) *Objections.* A person commanded to produce documents or tangible things or to permit inspection may serve on the party or attorney designated in the subpoena a written objection to inspecting, copying, testing or sampling any or all of the materials or to inspecting the premises—or to producing

electronically stored information in the form or forms requested. The objection must be served before the earlier of the time
specified for compliance or 14 days after the subpoena is
served. If an objection is made, the following rules apply:

(i) At any time, on notice to the commanded person,
the serving party may move the issuing court for an order
compelling production or inspection.

(ii) These acts may be required only as directed in the
order, and the order must protect a person who is neither
a party nor a party's officer from significant expense
resulting from compliance.

(3) *Quashing or Modifying a Subpoena.*

(A) *When Required.* On timely motion, the issuing court
must quash or modify a subpoena that:

(i) fails to allow a reasonable time to comply;

(ii) requires a person who is neither a party nor a
party's officer to travel more than 100 miles from where
that person resides, is employed, or regularly transacts
business in person—except that, subject to Rule
45(c)(3)(B)(iii), the person may be commanded to attend a
trial by traveling from any such place within the state
where the trial is held;

(iii) requires disclosure of privileged or other protected matter, if no exception or waiver applies; or

(iv) subjects a person to undue burden.

(B) *When Permitted.* To protect a person subject to or
affected by a subpoena, the issuing court may, on motion,
quash or modify the subpoena if it requires:

(i) disclosing a trade secret or other confidential research, development, or commercial information;

(ii) disclosing an unretained expert's opinion or information that does not describe specific occurrences in dispute and results from the expert's study that was not
requested by a party; or

(iii) a person who is neither a party nor a party's
officer to incur substantial expense to travel more than
100 miles to attend trial.

(C) *Specifying Conditions as an Alternative.* In the circumstances described in Rule 45(c)(3)(B), the court may, instead of
quashing or modifying a subpoena, order appearance or production under specified conditions if the serving party:

(i) shows a substantial need for the testimony or material that cannot be otherwise met without undue hardship; and

(ii) ensures that the subpoenaed person will be reasonably compensated.

(d) Duties in Responding to a Subpoena.

(1) *Producing Documents or Electronically Stored Information.* These procedures apply to producing documents or electronically stored information:

(A) *Documents.* A person responding to a subpoena to produce documents must produce them as they are kept in the ordinary course of business or must organize and label them to correspond to the categories in the demand.

(B) *Form for Producing Electronically Stored Information Not Specified.* If a subpoena does not specify a form for producing electronically stored information, the person responding must produce it in a form or forms in which it is ordinarily maintained or in a reasonably usable form or forms.

(C) *Electronically Stored Information Produced in Only One Form.* The person responding need not produce the same electronically stored information in more than one form.

(D) *Inaccessible Electronically Stored Information.* The person responding need not provide discovery of electronically stored information from sources that the person identifies as not reasonably accessible because of undue burden or cost. On motion to compel discovery or for a protective order, the person responding must show that the information is not reasonably accessible because of undue burden or cost. If that showing is made, the court may nonetheless order discovery from such sources if the requesting party shows good cause, considering the limitations of Rule 26(b)(2)(C). The court may specify conditions for the discovery.

(2) *Claiming Privilege or Protection.*

(A) *Information Withheld.* A person withholding subpoenaed information under a claim that it is privileged or subject to protection as trial-preparation material must:

(i) expressly make the claim; and

(ii) describe the nature of the withheld documents, communications, or tangible things in a manner that, without revealing information itself privileged or protected, will enable the parties to assess the claim.

(B) *Information Produced.* If information produced in response to a subpoena is subject to a claim of privilege or of protection as trial-preparation material, the person making the claim may notify any party that received the information of the claim and the basis for it. After being notified, a party must promptly return, sequester, or destroy the specified information and any copies it has; must not use or disclose the information until the claim is resolved; must take reasonable steps to retrieve the information if the party disclosed it before being notified; and may promptly present the information to the court under seal for a determination of the claim. The person who produced the information must preserve the information until the claim is resolved.

(e) Contempt. The issuing court may hold in contempt a person who, having been served, fails without adequate excuse to obey the subpoena. A nonparty's failure to obey must be excused if the subpoena purports to require the nonparty to attend or produce at a place outside the limits of Rule 45(c)(3)(A)(ii).

As amended 1948, 1949, 1970, 1980, 1985, 1987, 1991, 2005, 2006, 2007.

Rule 46.

OBJECTING TO A RULING OR ORDER

A formal exception to a ruling or order is unnecessary. When the ruling or order is requested or made, a party need only state the action that it wants the court to take or objects to, along with the grounds for the request or objection. Failing to object does not prejudice a party who had no opportunity to do so when the ruling or order was made.

As amended 1987, 2007.

Rule 47.

SELECTING JURORS

(a) Examining Jurors. The court may permit the parties or their attorneys to examine prospective jurors or may itself do so. If the court examines the jurors, it must permit the parties or their attorneys to make any further inquiry it considers proper, or must itself ask any of their additional questions it considers proper.

(b) Peremptory Challenges. The court must allow the number of peremptory challenges provided by 28 U.S.C. § 1870.

(c) Excusing a Juror. During trial or deliberation, the court may excuse a juror for good cause.

As amended 1966, 1991, 2007.

Rule 48.

NUMBER OF JURORS; VERDICT; POLLING

(a) Number of Jurors. A jury must begin with at least 6 and no more than 12 members, and each juror must participate in the verdict unless excused under Rule 47(c).

(b) Verdict. Unless the parties stipulate otherwise, the verdict must be unanimous and must be returned by a jury of at least 6 members.

(c) Polling. After a verdict is returned but before the jury is discharged, the court must on a party's request, or may on its own, poll the jurors individually. If the poll reveals a lack of unanimity or lack of assent by the number of jurors that the parties stipulated to, the court may direct the jury to deliberate further or may order a new trial.

As amended 1991, 2007, 2009.

Rule 49.

SPECIAL VERDICT; GENERAL VERDICT AND QUESTIONS

(a) Special Verdict.

(1) *In General.* The court may require a jury to return only a special verdict in the form of a special written finding on each issue of fact. The court may do so by:

(A) submitting written questions susceptible of a categorical or other brief answer;

(B) submitting written forms of the special findings that might properly be made under the pleadings and evidence; or

(C) using any other method that the court considers appropriate.

(2) *Instructions.* The court must give the instructions and explanations necessary to enable the jury to make its findings on each submitted issue.

(3) *Issues Not Submitted.* A party waives the right to a jury trial on any issue of fact raised by the pleadings or evidence but not submitted to the jury unless, before the jury retires, the party demands its submission to the jury. If the party does not demand submission, the court may make a finding on the issue. If the court makes no finding, it is considered to have made a finding consistent with its judgment on the special verdict.

(b) General Verdict with Answers to Written Questions.

(1) *In General.* The court may submit to the jury forms for a general verdict, together with written questions on one or more issues of fact that the jury must decide. The court must give the instructions and explanations necessary to enable the jury to render a general verdict and answer the questions in writing, and must direct the jury to do both.

(2) *Verdict and Answers Consistent.* When the general verdict and the answers are consistent, the court must approve, for entry under Rule 58, an appropriate judgment on the verdict and answers.

(3) *Answers Inconsistent with the Verdict.* When the answers are consistent with each other but one or more is inconsistent with the general verdict, the court may:

    (A) approve, for entry under Rule 58, an appropriate judgment according to the answers, notwithstanding the general verdict;

    (B) direct the jury to further consider its answers and verdict; or

    (C) order a new trial.

(4) *Answers Inconsistent with Each Other and the Verdict.* When the answers are inconsistent with each other and one or more is also inconsistent with the general verdict, judgment must not be entered; instead, the court must direct the jury to further consider its answers and verdict, or must order a new trial.

As amended 1963, 1987, 2007.

Rule 50.

JUDGMENT AS A MATTER OF LAW IN A JURY TRIAL; RELATED MOTION FOR A NEW TRIAL; CONDITIONAL RULING

(a) Judgment as a Matter of Law.

(1) *In General.* If a party has been fully heard on an issue during a jury trial and the court finds that a reasonable jury would not have a legally sufficient evidentiary basis to find for the party on that issue, the court may:

    (A) resolve the issue against the party; and

    (B) grant a motion for judgment as a matter of law against the party on a claim or defense that, under the controlling law, can be maintained or defeated only with a favorable finding on that issue.

(2) *Motion.* A motion for judgment as a matter of law may be made at any time before the case is submitted to the jury. The motion must specify the judgment sought and the law and facts that entitle the movant to the judgment.

(b) Renewing the Motion After Trial; Alternative Motion for a New Trial. If the court does not grant a motion for judgment as a matter of law made under Rule 50(a), the court is considered to have submitted the action to the jury subject to the court's later deciding the legal questions raised by the motion. No later than 28 days after the entry of judgment—or if the motion addresses a jury issue not decided by a verdict, no later than 28 days after the jury was discharged—the movant may file a renewed motion for judgment as a matter of law and may include an alternative or joint request for a new trial under Rule 59. In ruling on the renewed motion, the court may:

(1) allow judgment on the verdict, if the jury returned a verdict;

(2) order a new trial; or

(3) direct the entry of judgment as a matter of law.

(c) Granting the Renewed Motion; Conditional Ruling on a Motion for a New Trial.

(1) *In General.* If the court grants a renewed motion for judgment as a matter of law, it must also conditionally rule on any motion for a new trial by determining whether a new trial should be granted if the judgment is later vacated or reversed. The court must state the grounds for conditionally granting or denying the motion for a new trial.

(2) *Effect of a Conditional Ruling.* Conditionally granting the motion for a new trial does not affect the judgment's finality; if the judgment is reversed, the new trial must proceed unless the appellate court orders otherwise. If the motion for a new trial is conditionally denied, the appellee may assert error in that denial; if the judgment is reversed, the case must proceed as the appellate court orders.

(d) Time for a Losing Party's New-Trial Motion. Any motion for a new trial under Rule 59 by a party against whom judgment as a matter of law is rendered must be filed no later than 28 days after the entry of the judgment.

(e) Denying the Motion for Judgment as a Matter of Law; Reversal on Appeal. If the court denies the motion for judgment as a matter of law, the prevailing party may, as appellee, assert grounds entitling it to a new trial should the appellate court conclude that the trial court erred in denying the motion. If the appellate court reverses the judgment, it may order a new trial,

107

direct the trial court to determine whether a new trial should be granted, or direct the entry of judgment.

As amended 1963, 1987, 1991, 1993, 1995, 2006, 2007, 2009.

Rule 51.

INSTRUCTIONS TO THE JURY; OBJECTIONS; PRESERVING A CLAIM OF ERROR

(a) Requests.

(1) *Before or at the Close of the Evidence.* At the close of the evidence or at any earlier reasonable time that the court orders, a party may file and furnish to every other party written requests for the jury instructions it wants the court to give.

(2) *After the Close of the Evidence.* After the close of the evidence, a party may:

(A) file requests for instructions on issues that could not reasonably have been anticipated by an earlier time that the court set for requests; and

(B) with the court's permission, file untimely requests for instructions on any issue.

(b) Instructions. The court:

(1) must inform the parties of its proposed instructions and proposed action on the requests before instructing the jury and before final jury arguments;

(2) must give the parties an opportunity to object on the record and out of the jury's hearing before the instructions and arguments are delivered; and

(3) may instruct the jury at any time before the jury is discharged.

(c) Objections.

(1) *How to Make.* A party who objects to an instruction or the failure to give an instruction must do so on the record, stating distinctly the matter objected to and the grounds for the objection.

(2) *When to Make.* An objection is timely if:

(A) a party objects at the opportunity provided under Rule 51(b)(2); or

(B) a party was not informed of an instruction or action on a request before that opportunity to object, and the party objects promptly after learning that the instruction or request will be, or has been, given or refused.

(d) Assigning Error; Plain Error.

(1) *Assigning Error.* A party may assign as error:

(A) an error in an instruction actually given, if that party properly objected; or

(B) a failure to give an instruction, if that party properly requested it and—unless the court rejected the request in a definitive ruling on the record—also properly objected.

(2) *Plain Error.* A court may consider a plain error in the instructions that has not been preserved as required by Rule 51(d)(1) if the error affects substantial rights.

As amended 1987, 2003, 2007.

Rule 52.

FINDINGS AND CONCLUSIONS BY THE COURT; JUDGMENT ON PARTIAL FINDINGS

(a) Findings and Conclusions.

(1) *In General.* In an action tried on the facts without a jury or with an advisory jury, the court must find the facts specially and state its conclusions of law separately. The findings and conclusions may be stated on the record after the close of the evidence or may appear in an opinion or a memorandum of decision filed by the court. Judgment must be entered under Rule 58.

(2) *For an Interlocutory Injunction.* In granting or refusing an interlocutory injunction, the court must similarly state the findings and conclusions that support its action.

(3) *For a Motion.* The court is not required to state findings or conclusions when ruling on a motion under Rule 12 or 56 or, unless these rules provide otherwise, on any other motion.

(4) *Effect of a Master's Findings.* A master's findings, to the extent adopted by the court, must be considered the court's findings.

(5) *Questioning the Evidentiary Support.* A party may later question the sufficiency of the evidence supporting the findings, whether or not the party requested findings, objected to them, moved to amend them, or moved for partial findings.

(6) *Setting Aside the Findings.* Findings of fact, whether based on oral or other evidence, must not be set aside unless clearly erroneous, and the reviewing court must give due regard to the trial court's opportunity to judge the witnesses' credibility.

(b) Amended or Additional Findings. On a party's motion filed no later than 28 days after the entry of judgment, the court

may amend its findings—or make additional findings—and may amend the judgment accordingly. The motion may accompany a motion for a new trial under Rule 59.

(c) Judgment on Partial Findings. If a party has been fully heard on an issue during a nonjury trial and the court finds against the party on that issue, the court may enter judgment against the party on a claim or defense that, under the controlling law, can be maintained or defeated only with a favorable finding on that issue. The court may, however, decline to render any judgment until the close of the evidence. A judgment on partial findings must be supported by findings of fact and conclusions of law as required by Rule 52(a).

As amended 1948, 1963, 1983, 1985, 1991, 1993, 1995, 2007, 2009.

Rule 53.

MASTERS

(a) Appointment.

(1) *Scope.* Unless a statute provides otherwise, a court may appoint a master only to:

(A) perform duties consented to by the parties;

(B) hold trial proceedings and make or recommend findings of fact on issues to be decided without a jury if appointment is warranted by:

(i) some exceptional condition; or

(ii) the need to perform an accounting or resolve a difficult computation of damages; or

(C) address pretrial and posttrial matters that cannot be effectively and timely addressed by an available district judge or magistrate judge of the district.

(2) *Disqualification.* A master must not have a relationship to the parties, attorneys, action, or court that would require disqualification of a judge under 28 U.S.C. § 455, unless the parties, with the court's approval, consent to the appointment after the master discloses any potential grounds for disqualification.

(3) *Possible Expense or Delay.* In appointing a master, the court must consider the fairness of imposing the likely expenses on the parties and must protect against unreasonable expense or delay.

(b) Order Appointing a Master.

(1) *Notice.* Before appointing a master, the court must give the parties notice and an opportunity to be heard. Any party may suggest candidates for appointment.

(2) *Contents.* The appointing order must direct the master to proceed with all reasonable diligence and must state:

(A) the master's duties, including any investigation or enforcement duties, and any limits on the master's authority under Rule 53(c);

(B) the circumstances, if any, in which the master may communicate ex parte with the court or a party;

(C) the nature of the materials to be preserved and filed as the record of the master's activities;

(D) the time limits, method of filing the record, other procedures, and standards for reviewing the master's orders, findings, and recommendations; and

(E) the basis, terms, and procedure for fixing the master's compensation under Rule 53(g).

(3) *Issuing.* The court may issue the order only after:

(A) the master files an affidavit disclosing whether there is any ground for disqualification under 28 U.S.C. § 455; and

(B) if a ground is disclosed, the parties, with the court's approval, waive the disqualification.

(4) *Amending.* The order may be amended at any time after notice to the parties and an opportunity to be heard.

(c) Master's Authority.

(1) *In General.* Unless the appointing order directs otherwise, a master may:

(A) regulate all proceedings;

(B) take all appropriate measures to perform the assigned duties fairly and efficiently; and

(C) if conducting an evidentiary hearing, exercise the appointing court's power to compel, take, and record evidence.

(2) *Sanctions.* The master may by order impose on a party any noncontempt sanction provided by Rule 37 or 45, and may recommend a contempt sanction against a party and sanctions against a nonparty.

(d) Master's Orders. A master who issues an order must file it and promptly serve a copy on each party. The clerk must enter the order on the docket.

(e) Master's Reports. A master must report to the court as required by the appointing order. The master must file the report and promptly serve a copy on each party, unless the court orders otherwise.

(f) Action on the Master's Order, Report, or Recommendations.

(1) *Opportunity for a Hearing; Action in General.* In acting on a master's order, report, or recommendations, the court must give the parties notice and an opportunity to be heard; may receive evidence; and may adopt or affirm, modify, wholly or partly reject or reverse, or resubmit to the master with instructions.

(2) *Time to Object or Move to Adopt or Modify.* A party may file objections to—or a motion to adopt or modify—the master's order, report, or recommendations no later than 21 days after a copy is served, unless the court sets a different time.

(3) *Reviewing Factual Findings.* The court must decide de novo all objections to findings of fact made or recommended by a master, unless the parties, with the court's approval, stipulate that:

    (A) the findings will be reviewed for clear error; or

    (B) the findings of a master appointed under Rule 53(a)(1)(A) or (C) will be final.

(4) *Reviewing Legal Conclusions.* The court must decide de novo all objections to conclusions of law made or recommended by a master.

(5) *Reviewing Procedural Matters.* Unless the appointing order establishes a different standard of review, the court may set aside a master's ruling on a procedural matter only for an abuse of discretion.

(g) Compensation.

(1) *Fixing Compensation.* Before or after judgment, the court must fix the master's compensation on the basis and terms stated in the appointing order, but the court may set a new basis and terms after giving notice and an opportunity to be heard.

(2) *Payment.* The compensation must be paid either:

    (A) by a party or parties; or

    (B) from a fund or subject matter of the action within the court's control.

(3) *Allocating Payment.* The court must allocate payment among the parties after considering the nature and amount of the controversy, the parties' means, and the extent to which any party is more responsible than other parties for the reference to a master. An interim allocation may be amended to reflect a decision on the merits.

(h) Appointing a Magistrate Judge. A magistrate judge is subject to this rule only when the order referring a matter to the magistrate judge states that the reference is made under this rule.

As amended 1966, 1983, 1987, 1991, 1993, 2003, 2007, 2009.

VII. JUDGMENT

Rule 54.

JUDGMENT; COSTS

(a) Definition; Form. "Judgment" as used in these rules includes a decree and any order from which an appeal lies. A judgment should not include recitals of pleadings, a master's report, or a record of prior proceedings.

(b) Judgment on Multiple Claims or Involving Multiple Parties. When an action presents more than one claim for relief—whether as a claim, counterclaim, crossclaim, or third-party claim—or when multiple parties are involved, the court may direct entry of a final judgment as to one or more, but fewer than all, claims or parties only if the court expressly determines that there is no just reason for delay. Otherwise, any order or other decision, however designated, that adjudicates fewer than all the claims or the rights and liabilities of fewer than all the parties does not end the action as to any of the claims or parties and may be revised at any time before the entry of a judgment adjudicating all the claims and all the parties' rights and liabilities.

(c) Demand for Judgment; Relief to Be Granted. A default judgment must not differ in kind from, or exceed in amount, what is demanded in the pleadings. Every other final judgment should grant the relief to which each party is entitled, even if the party has not demanded that relief in its pleadings.

(d) Costs; Attorney's Fees.

(1) *Costs Other Than Attorney's Fees.* Unless a federal statute, these rules, or a court order provides otherwise, costs—other than attorney's fees—should be allowed to the prevailing party. But costs against the United States, its officers, and its agencies may be imposed only to the extent allowed by law. The clerk may tax costs on 14 days' notice. On motion served within the next 7 days, the court may review the clerk's action.

(2) *Attorney's Fees.*

(A) *Claim to Be by Motion.* A claim for attorney's fees and related nontaxable expenses must be made by motion unless the substantive law requires those fees to be proved at trial as an element of damages.

(B) *Timing and Contents of the Motion.* Unless a statute or a court order provides otherwise, the motion must:

(i) be filed no later than 14 days after the entry of judgment;

(ii) specify the judgment and the statute, rule, or other grounds entitling the movant to the award;

(iii) state the amount sought or provide a fair estimate of it; and

(iv) disclose, if the court so orders, the terms of any agreement about fees for the services for which the claim is made.

(C) *Proceedings.* Subject to Rule 23(h), the court must, on a party's request, give an opportunity for adversary submissions on the motion in accordance with Rule 43(c) or 78. The court may decide issues of liability for fees before receiving submissions on the value of services. The court must find the facts and state its conclusions of law as provided in Rule 52(a).

(D) *Special Procedures by Local Rule; Reference to a Master or a Magistrate Judge.* By local rule, the court may establish special procedures to resolve fee-related issues without extensive evidentiary hearings. Also, the court may refer issues concerning the value of services to a special master under Rule 53 without regard to the limitations of Rule 53(a)(1), and may refer a motion for attorney's fees to a magistrate judge under Rule 72(b) as if it were a dispositive pretrial matter.

(E) *Exceptions.* Subparagraphs (A)–(D) do not apply to claims for fees and expenses as sanctions for violating these rules or as sanctions under 28 U.S.C. § 1927.

As amended 1948, 1961, 1987, 1993, 2002, 2003, 2007, 2009.

Rule 55.

DEFAULT; DEFAULT JUDGMENT

(a) Entering a Default. When a party against whom a judgment for affirmative relief is sought has failed to plead or otherwise defend, and that failure is shown by affidavit or otherwise, the clerk must enter the party's default.

(b) Entering a Default Judgment.

(1) *By the Clerk.* If the plaintiff's claim is for a sum certain or a sum that can be made certain by computation, the clerk—on the plaintiff's request, with an affidavit showing the amount due—must enter judgment for that amount and costs against a defendant

who has been defaulted for not appearing and who is neither a minor nor an incompetent person.

(2) *By the Court.* In all other cases, the party must apply to the court for a default judgment. A default judgment may be entered against a minor or incompetent person only if represented by a general guardian, conservator, or other like fiduciary who has appeared. If the party against whom a default judgment is sought has appeared personally or by a representative, that party or its representative must be served with written notice of the application at least 7 days before the hearing. The court may conduct hearings or make referrals—preserving any federal statutory right to a jury trial—when, to enter or effectuate judgment, it needs to:

(A) conduct an accounting;

(B) determine the amount of damages;

(C) establish the truth of any allegation by evidence; or

(D) investigate any other matter.

(c) Setting Aside a Default or a Default Judgment. The court may set aside an entry of default for good cause, and it may set aside a default judgment under Rule 60(b).

(d) Judgment Against the United States. A default judgment may be entered against the United States, its officers, or its agencies only if the claimant establishes a claim or right to relief by evidence that satisfies the court.

As amended 1987, 2007, 2009.

Rule 56.

SUMMARY JUDGMENT

(a) By a Claiming Party. A party claiming relief may move, with or without supporting affidavits, for summary judgment on all or part of the claim.

(b) By a Defending Party. A party against whom relief is sought may move, with or without supporting affidavits, for summary judgment on all or part of the claim.

(c) Time for a Motion, Response, and Reply; Proceedings.

(1) These times apply unless a different time is set by local rule or the court orders otherwise:

(A) a party may move for summary judgment at any time until 30 days after the close of all discovery;

(B) a party opposing the motion must file a response within 21 days after the motion is served or a responsive pleading is due, whichever is later; and

(C) the movant may file a reply within 14 days after the response is served.

(2) The judgment sought should be rendered if the pleadings, the discovery and disclosure materials on file, and any affidavits show that there is no genuine issue as to any material fact and that the movant is entitled to judgment as a matter of law.

(d) Case Not Fully Adjudicated on the Motion.

(1) *Establishing Facts.* If summary judgment is not rendered on the whole action, the court should, to the extent practicable, determine what material facts are not genuinely at issue. The court should so determine by examining the pleadings and evidence before it and by interrogating the attorneys. It should then issue an order specifying what facts—including items of damages or other relief—are not genuinely at issue. The facts so specified must be treated as established in the action.

(2) *Establishing Liability.* An interlocutory summary judgment may be rendered on liability alone, even if there is a genuine issue on the amount of damages.

(e) Affidavits; Further Testimony.

(1) *In General.* A supporting or opposing affidavit must be made on personal knowledge, set out facts that would be admissible in evidence, and show that the affiant is competent to testify on the matters stated. If a paper or part of a paper is referred to in an affidavit, a sworn or certified copy must be attached to or served with the affidavit. The court may permit an affidavit to be supplemented or opposed by depositions, answers to interrogatories, or additional affidavits.

(2) *Opposing Party's Obligation to Respond.* When a motion for summary judgment is properly made and supported, an opposing party may not rely merely on allegations or denials in its own pleading; rather, its response must—by affidavits or as otherwise provided in this rule—set out specific facts showing a genuine issue for trial. If the opposing party does not so respond, summary judgment should, if appropriate, be entered against that party.

(f) When Affidavits Are Unavailable. If a party opposing the motion shows by affidavit that, for specified reasons, it cannot present facts essential to justify its opposition, the court may:

(1) deny the motion;

(2) order a continuance to enable affidavits to be obtained, depositions to be taken, or other discovery to be undertaken; or

(3) issue any other just order.

(g) Affidavit Submitted in Bad Faith. If satisfied that an affidavit under this rule is submitted in bad faith or solely for delay, the court must order the submitting party to pay the other party the reasonable expenses, including attorney's fees, it incurred as a result. An offending party or attorney may also be held in contempt.

As amended 1948, 1963, 1987, 2007, 2009.

Rule 57.

DECLARATORY JUDGMENT

These rules govern the procedure for obtaining a declaratory judgment under 28 U.S.C. § 2201. Rules 38 and 39 govern a demand for a jury trial. The existence of another adequate remedy does not preclude a declaratory judgment that is otherwise appropriate. The court may order a speedy hearing of a declaratory-judgment action.

As amended 1949, 2007.

Rule 58.

ENTERING JUDGMENT

(a) Separate Document. Every judgment and amended judgment must be set out in a separate document, but a separate document is not required for an order disposing of a motion:

(1) for judgment under Rule 50(b);

(2) to amend or make additional findings under Rule 52(b);

(3) for attorney's fees under Rule 54;

(4) for a new trial, or to alter or amend the judgment, under Rule 59; or

(5) for relief under Rule 60.

(b) Entering Judgment.

(1) *Without the Court's Direction.* Subject to Rule 54(b) and unless the court orders otherwise, the clerk must, without awaiting the court's direction, promptly prepare, sign, and enter the judgment when:

(A) the jury returns a general verdict;

(B) the court awards only costs or a sum certain; or

(C) the court denies all relief.

(2) *Court's Approval Required.* Subject to Rule 54(b), the court must promptly approve the form of the judgment, which the clerk must promptly enter, when:

(A) the jury returns a special verdict or a general verdict with answers to written questions; or

(B) the court grants other relief not described in this subdivision (b).

(c) Time of Entry. For purposes of these rules, judgment is entered at the following times:

(1) if a separate document is not required, when the judgment is entered in the civil docket under Rule 79(a); or

(2) if a separate document is required, when the judgment is entered in the civil docket under Rule 79(a) and the earlier of these events occurs:

(A) it is set out in a separate document; or

(B) 150 days have run from the entry in the civil docket.

(d) Request for Entry. A party may request that judgment be set out in a separate document as required by Rule 58(a).

(e) Cost or Fee Awards. Ordinarily, the entry of judgment may not be delayed, nor the time for appeal extended, in order to tax costs or award fees. But if a timely motion for attorney's fees is made under Rule 54(d)(2), the court may act before a notice of appeal has been filed and become effective to order that the motion have the same effect under Federal Rule of Appellate Procedure 4(a)(4) as a timely motion under Rule 59.

As amended 1948, 1963, 1993, 2002, 2007.

Rule 59.

NEW TRIAL; ALTERING OR AMENDING A JUDGMENT

(a) In General.

(1) *Grounds for New Trial.* The court may, on motion, grant a new trial on all or some of the issues—and to any party—as follows:

(A) after a jury trial, for any reason for which a new trial has heretofore been granted in an action at law in federal court; or

(B) after a nonjury trial, for any reason for which a rehearing has heretofore been granted in a suit in equity in federal court.

(2) *Further Action After a Nonjury Trial.* After a nonjury trial, the court may, on motion for a new trial, open the judgment if one has been entered, take additional testimony, amend findings of fact and conclusions of law or make new ones, and direct the entry of a new judgment.

(b) Time to File a Motion for a New Trial. A motion for a new trial must be filed no later than 28 days after the entry of judgment.

(c) Time to Serve Affidavits. When a motion for a new trial is based on affidavits, they must be filed with the motion. The opposing party has 14 days after being served to file opposing affidavits. The court may permit reply affidavits.

(d) New Trial on the Court's Initiative or for Reasons Not in the Motion. No later than 28 days after the entry of judgment, the court, on its own, may order a new trial for any reason that would justify granting one on a party's motion. After giving the parties notice and an opportunity to be heard, the court may grant a timely motion for a new trial for a reason not stated in the motion. In either event, the court must specify the reasons in its order.

(e) Motion to Alter or Amend a Judgment. A motion to alter or amend a judgment must be filed no later than 28 days after the entry of the judgment.

As amended 1948, 1966, 1995, 2007, 2009.

Rule 60.

RELIEF FROM A JUDGMENT OR ORDER

(a) Corrections Based on Clerical Mistakes; Oversights and Omissions. The court may correct a clerical mistake or a mistake arising from oversight or omission whenever one is found in a judgment, order, or other part of the record. The court may do so on motion or on its own, with or without notice. But after an appeal has been docketed in the appellate court and while it is pending, such a mistake may be corrected only with the appellate court's leave.

(b) Grounds for Relief from a Final Judgment, Order, or Proceeding. On motion and just terms, the court may relieve a party or its legal representative from a final judgment, order, or proceeding for the following reasons:

(1) mistake, inadvertence, surprise, or excusable neglect;

(2) newly discovered evidence that, with reasonable diligence, could not have been discovered in time to move for a new trial under Rule 59(b);

(3) fraud (whether previously called intrinsic or extrinsic), misrepresentation, or misconduct by an opposing party;

(4) the judgment is void;

(5) the judgment has been satisfied, released or discharged; it is based on an earlier judgment that has been reversed or vacated; or applying it prospectively is no longer equitable; or

(6) any other reason that justifies relief.

(c) Timing and Effect of the Motion.

(1) *Timing.* A motion under Rule 60(b) must be made within a reasonable time—and for reasons (1), (2), and (3) no more than a year after the entry of the judgment or order or the date of the proceeding.

(2) *Effect on Finality.* The motion does not affect the judgment's finality or suspend its operation.

(d) Other Powers to Grant Relief. This rule does not limit a court's power to:

(1) entertain an independent action to relieve a party from a judgment, order, or proceeding;

(2) grant relief under 28 U.S.C. § 1655 to a defendant who was not personally notified of the action; or

(3) set aside a judgment for fraud on the court.

(e) Bills and Writs Abolished. The following are abolished: bills of review, bills in the nature of bills of review, and writs of coram nobis, coram vobis, and audita querela.

As amended 1948, 1949, 1987, 2007.

Rule 61.

HARMLESS ERROR

Unless justice requires otherwise, no error in admitting or excluding evidence—or any other error by the court or a party—is ground for granting a new trial, for setting aside a verdict, or for vacating, modifying, or otherwise disturbing a judgment or order. At every stage of the proceeding, the court must disregard all errors and defects that do not affect any party's substantial rights.

As amended 2007.

Rule 62.

STAY OF PROCEEDINGS TO ENFORCE A JUDGMENT

(a) Automatic Stay; Exceptions for Injunctions, Receiverships, and Patent Accountings. Except as stated in this rule, no execution may issue on a judgment, nor may proceedings be taken to enforce it, until 14 days have passed after its entry. But unless the court orders otherwise, the following are not stayed after being entered, even if an appeal is taken:

(1) an interlocutory or final judgment in an action for an injunction or a receivership; or

(2) a judgment or order that directs an accounting in an action for patent infringement.

(b) Stay Pending the Disposition of a Motion. On appropriate terms for the opposing party's security, the court may stay the execution of a judgment—or any proceedings to enforce it—pending disposition of any of the following motions:

(1) under Rule 50, for judgment as a matter of law;

(2) under Rule 52(b), to amend the findings or for additional findings;

(3) under Rule 59, for a new trial or to alter or amend a judgment; or

(4) under Rule 60, for relief from a judgment or order.

(c) Injunction Pending an Appeal. While an appeal is pending from an interlocutory order or final judgment that grants, dissolves, or denies an injunction, the court may suspend, modify, restore, or grant an injunction on terms for bond or other terms that secure the opposing party's rights. If the judgment appealed from is rendered by a statutory three-judge district court, the order must be made either:

(1) by that court sitting in open session; or

(2) by the assent of all its judges, as evidenced by their signatures.

(d) Stay with Bond on Appeal. If an appeal is taken, the appellant may obtain a stay by supersedeas bond, except in an action described in Rule 62(a)(1) or (2). The bond may be given upon or after filing the notice of appeal or after obtaining the order allowing the appeal. The stay takes effect when the court approves the bond.

(e) Stay Without Bond on an Appeal by the United States, Its Officers, or Its Agencies. The court must not require a bond, obligation, or other security from the appellant when granting a stay on an appeal by the United States, its officers, or its agencies or on an appeal directed by a department of the federal government.

(f) Stay in Favor of a Judgment Debtor Under State Law. If a judgment is a lien on the judgment debtor's property under the law of the state where the court is located, the judgment debtor is entitled to the same stay of execution the state court would give.

(g) Appellate Court's Power Not Limited. This rule does not limit the power of the appellate court or one of its judges or justices:

(1) to stay proceedings—or suspend, modify, restore, or grant an injunction—while an appeal is pending; or

(2) to issue an order to preserve the status quo or the effectiveness of the judgment to be entered.

(h) Stay with Multiple Claims or Parties. A court may stay the enforcement of a final judgment entered under Rule 54(b) until it enters a later judgment or judgments, and may prescribe terms necessary to secure the benefit of the stayed judgment for the party in whose favor it was entered.

As amended 1948, 1949, 1961, 1987, 2007, 2009.

Rule 62.1.

INDICATIVE RULING ON A MOTION FOR RELIEF THAT IS BARRED BY A PENDING APPEAL

(a) Relief Pending Appeal. If a timely motion is made for relief that the court lacks authority to grant because of an appeal that has been docketed and is pending, the court may:

(1) defer considering the motion;

(2) deny the motion; or

(3) state either that it would grant the motion if the court of appeals remands for that purpose or that the motion raises a substantial issue.

(b) Notice to the Court of Appeals. The movant must promptly notify the circuit clerk under Federal Rule of Appellate Procedure 12.1 if the district court states that it would grant the motion or that the motion raises a substantial issue.

(c) Remand. The district court may decide the motion if the court of appeals remands for that purpose.

Added 2009.

Rule 63.

JUDGE'S INABILITY TO PROCEED

If a judge conducting a hearing or trial is unable to proceed, any other judge may proceed upon certifying familiarity with the record and determining that the case may be completed without prejudice to the parties. In a hearing or a nonjury trial, the successor judge must, at a party's request, recall any witness whose testimony is material and disputed and who is available to testify again without undue burden. The successor judge may also recall any other witness.

As amended 1987, 1991, 2007.

VIII.   PROVISIONAL AND FINAL REMEDIES

Rule 64.

SEIZING A PERSON OR PROPERTY

(a) Remedies Under State Law—In General. At the commencement of and throughout an action, every remedy is available that, under the law of the state where the court is located, provides for seizing a person or property to secure satisfaction of the potential judgment. But a federal statute governs to the extent it applies.

(b) Specific Kinds of Remedies. The remedies available under this rule include the following—however designated and regardless of whether state procedure requires an independent action:

- arrest;
- attachment;
- garnishment;
- replevin;
- sequestration; and
- other corresponding or equivalent remedies.

As amended 2007.

Rule 65.

INJUNCTIONS AND RESTRAINING ORDERS

(a) Preliminary Injunction.

(1) *Notice*. The court may issue a preliminary injunction only on notice to the adverse party.

(2) *Consolidating the Hearing with the Trial on the Merits*. Before or after beginning the hearing on a motion for a preliminary injunction, the court may advance the trial on the merits and consolidate it with the hearing. Even when consolidation is not ordered, evidence that is received on the motion and that would be admissible at trial becomes part of the trial record and need not be

repeated at trial. But the court must preserve any party's right to a jury trial.

(b) Temporary Restraining Order.

(1) *Issuing Without Notice.* The court may issue a temporary restraining order without written or oral notice to the adverse party or its attorney only if:

> (A) specific facts in an affidavit or a verified complaint clearly show that immediate and irreparable injury, loss, or damage will result to the movant before the adverse party can be heard in opposition; and

> (B) the movant's attorney certifies in writing any efforts made to give notice and the reasons why it should not be required.

(2) *Contents; Expiration.* Every temporary restraining order issued without notice must state the date and hour it was issued; describe the injury and state why it is irreparable; state why the order was issued without notice; and be promptly filed in the clerk's office and entered in the record. The order expires at the time after entry—not to exceed 14 days—that the court sets, unless before that time the court, for good cause, extends it for a like period or the adverse party consents to a longer extension. The reasons for an extension must be entered in the record.

(3) *Expediting the Preliminary–Injunction Hearing.* If the order is issued without notice, the motion for a preliminary injunction must be set for hearing at the earliest possible time, taking precedence over all other matters except hearings on older matters of the same character. At the hearing, the party who obtained the order must proceed with the motion; if the party does not, the court must dissolve the order.

(4) *Motion to Dissolve.* On 2 days' notice to the party who obtained the order without notice—or on shorter notice set by the court—the adverse party may appear and move to dissolve or modify the order. The court must then hear and decide the motion as promptly as justice requires.

(c) Security. The court may issue a preliminary injunction or a temporary restraining order only if the movant gives security in an amount that the court considers proper to pay the costs and damages sustained by any party found to have been wrongfully enjoined or restrained. The United States, its officers, and its agencies are not required to give security.

(d) Contents and Scope of Every Injunction and Restraining Order.

(1) *Contents.* Every order granting an injunction and every restraining order must:

    (A) state the reasons why it issued;

    (B) state its terms specifically; and

    (C) describe in reasonable detail—and not by referring to the complaint or other document—the act or acts restrained or required.

(2) *Persons Bound.* The order binds only the following who receive actual notice of it by personal service or otherwise:

    (A) the parties;

    (B) the parties' officers, agents, servants, employees, and attorneys; and

    (C) other persons who are in active concert or participation with anyone described in Rule 65(d)(2)(A) or (B).

(e) Other Laws Not Modified. These rules do not modify the following:

    (1) any federal statute relating to temporary restraining orders or preliminary injunctions in actions affecting employer and employee;

    (2) 28 U.S.C. § 2361, which relates to preliminary injunctions in actions of interpleader or in the nature of interpleader; or

    (3) 28 U.S.C. § 2284, which relates to actions that must be heard and decided by a three-judge district court.

(f) Copyright Impoundment. This rule applies to copyright-impoundment proceedings.

As amended 1948, 1949, 1966, 1987, 2001, 2007, 2009.

Rule 65.1.

PROCEEDINGS AGAINST A SURETY

Whenever these rules (including the Supplemental Rules for Admiralty or Maritime Claims and Asset Forfeiture Actions) require or allow a party to give security, and security is given through a bond or other undertaking with one or more sureties, each surety submits to the court's jurisdiction and irrevocably appoints the court clerk as its agent for receiving service of any papers that affect its liability on the bond or undertaking. The surety's liability may be enforced on motion without an independent action. The motion and any notice that the court orders may be served on the court clerk, who must promptly mail a copy of each to every surety whose address is known.

Added 1966; as amended 1987, 2006, 2007.

Rule 66.

RECEIVERS

These rules govern an action in which the appointment of a receiver is sought or a receiver sues or is sued. But the practice in administering an estate by a receiver or a similar court-appointed officer must accord with the historical practice in federal courts or with a local rule. An action in which a receiver has been appointed may be dismissed only by court order.

As amended 1948, 1949, 2007.

Rule 67.

DEPOSIT INTO COURT

(a) **Depositing Property.** If any part of the relief sought is a money judgment or the disposition of a sum of money or some other deliverable thing, a party—on notice to every other party and by leave of court—may deposit with the court all or part of the money or thing, whether or not that party claims any of it. The depositing party must deliver to the clerk a copy of the order permitting deposit.

(b) **Investing and Withdrawing Funds.** Money paid into court under this rule must be deposited and withdrawn in accordance with 28 U.S.C. §§ 2041 and 2042 and any like statute. The money must be deposited in an interest-bearing account or invested in a court-approved, interest-bearing instrument.

As amended 1949, 1983, 2007.

Rule 68.

OFFER OF JUDGMENT

(a) **Making an Offer; Judgment on an Accepted Offer.** At least 14 days before the date set for trial, a party defending against a claim may serve on an opposing party an offer to allow judgment on specified terms, with the costs then accrued. If, within 14 days after being served, the opposing party serves written notice accepting the offer, either party may then file the offer and notice of acceptance, plus proof of service. The clerk must then enter judgment.

(b) **Unaccepted Offer.** An unaccepted offer is considered withdrawn, but it does not preclude a later offer. Evidence of an unaccepted offer is not admissible except in a proceeding to determine costs.

(c) Offer After Liability Is Determined. When one party's liability to another has been determined but the extent of liability remains to be determined by further proceedings, the party held liable may make an offer of judgment. It must be served within a reasonable time—but at least 14 days—before the date set for a hearing to determine the extent of liability.

(d) Paying Costs After an Unaccepted Offer. If the judgment that the offeree finally obtains is not more favorable than the unaccepted offer, the offeree must pay the costs incurred after the offer was made.

As amended 1948, 1966, 1987, 2007, 2009.

Rule 69.

EXECUTION

(a) In General.

(1) *Money Judgment; Applicable Procedure.* A money judgment is enforced by a writ of execution, unless the court directs otherwise. The procedure on execution—and in proceedings supplementary to and in aid of judgment or execution—must accord with the procedure of the state where the court is located, but a federal statute governs to the extent it applies.

(2) *Obtaining Discovery.* In aid of the judgment or execution, the judgment creditor or a successor in interest whose interest appears of record may obtain discovery from any person—including the judgment debtor—as provided in these rules or by the procedure of the state where the court is located.

(b) Against Certain Public Officers. When a judgment has been entered against a revenue officer in the circumstances stated in 28 U.S.C. § 2006, or against an officer of Congress in the circumstances stated in 2 U.S.C. § 118, the judgment must be satisfied as those statutes provide.

As amended 1949, 1970, 1987, 2007.

Rule 70.

ENFORCING A JUDGMENT FOR A SPECIFIC ACT

(a) Party's Failure to Act; Ordering Another to Act. If a judgment requires a party to convey land, to deliver a deed or other document, or to perform any other specific act and the party fails to comply within the time specified, the court may order the act to be done—at the disobedient party's expense—by another person appointed by the court. When done, the act has the same effect as if done by the party.

(b) Vesting Title. If the real or personal property is within the district, the court—instead of ordering a conveyance—may enter a judgment divesting any party's title and vesting it in others. That judgment has the effect of a legally executed conveyance.

(c) Obtaining a Writ of Attachment or Sequestration. On application by a party entitled to performance of an act, the clerk must issue a writ of attachment or sequestration against the disobedient party's property to compel obedience.

(d) Obtaining a Writ of Execution or Assistance. On application by a party who obtains a judgment or order for possession, the clerk must issue a writ of execution or assistance.

(e) Holding in Contempt. The court may also hold the disobedient party in contempt.

As amended 2007.

Rule 71.

ENFORCING RELIEF FOR OR AGAINST A NONPARTY

When an order grants relief for a nonparty or may be enforced against a nonparty, the procedure for enforcing the order is the same as for a party.

As amended 1987, 2007.

IX.   SPECIAL PROCEEDINGS

Rule 71.1.

CONDEMNING REAL OR PERSONAL PROPERTY

(a) Applicability of Other Rules. These rules govern proceedings to condemn real and personal property by eminent domain, except as this rule provides otherwise.

(b) Joinder of Properties. The plaintiff may join separate pieces of property in a single action, no matter whether they are owned by the same persons or sought for the same use.

(c) Complaint.

(1) *Caption.* The complaint must contain a caption as provided in Rule 10(a). The plaintiff must, however, name as defendants both the property—designated generally by kind, quantity, and location—and at least one owner of some part of or interest in the property.

(2) *Contents.* The complaint must contain a short and plain statement of the following:

(A) the authority for the taking;

(B) the uses for which the property is to be taken;

(C) a description sufficient to identify the property;

(D) the interests to be acquired; and

(E) for each piece of property, a designation of each defendant who has been joined as an owner or owner of an interest in it.

(3) *Parties.* When the action commences, the plaintiff need join as defendants only those persons who have or claim an interest in the property and whose names are then known. But before any hearing on compensation, the plaintiff must add as defendants all those persons who have or claim an interest and whose names have become known or can be found by a reasonably diligent search of the records, considering both the property's character and value and the interests to be acquired. All others may be made defendants under the designation "Unknown Owners."

(4) *Procedure.* Notice must be served on all defendants as provided in Rule 71.1(d), whether they were named as defendants when the action commenced or were added later. A defendant may answer as provided in Rule 71.1(e). The court, meanwhile, may order any distribution of a deposit that the facts warrant.

(5) *Filing; Additional Copies.* In addition to filing the complaint, the plaintiff must give the clerk at least one copy for the defendants' use and additional copies at the request of the clerk or a defendant.

(d) Process.

(1) *Delivering Notice to the Clerk.* On filing a complaint, the plaintiff must promptly deliver to the clerk joint or several notices directed to the named defendants. When adding defendants, the plaintiff must deliver to the clerk additional notices directed to the new defendants.

(2) *Contents of the Notice.*

(A) *Main Contents.* Each notice must name the court, the title of the action, and the defendant to whom it is directed. It must describe the property sufficiently to identify it, but need not describe any property other than that to be taken from the named defendant. The notice must also state:

(i) that the action is to condemn property;

(ii) the interest to be taken;

(iii) the authority for the taking;

(iv) the uses for which the property is to be taken;

(v) that the defendant may serve an answer on the plaintiff's attorney within 21 days after being served with the notice;

(vi) that the failure to so serve an answer constitutes consent to the taking and to the court's authority to proceed with the action and fix the compensation; and

(vii) that a defendant who does not serve an answer may file a notice of appearance.

(B) *Conclusion.* The notice must conclude with the name, telephone number, and e-mail address of the plaintiff's attorney and an address within the district in which the action is brought where the attorney may be served.

(3) *Serving the Notice.*

(A) *Personal Service.* When a defendant whose address is known resides within the United States or a territory subject to the administrative or judicial jurisdiction of the United States, personal service of the notice (without a copy of the complaint) must be made in accordance with Rule 4.

(B) *Service by Publication.*

(i) A defendant may be served by publication only when the plaintiff's attorney files a certificate stating that the attorney believes the defendant cannot be personally served, because after diligent inquiry within the state where the complaint is filed, the defendant's place of residence is still unknown or, if known, that it is beyond the territorial limits of personal service. Service is then made by publishing the notice—once a week for at least three successive weeks—in a newspaper published in the county where the property is located or, if there is no such newspaper, in a newspaper with general circulation where the property is located. Before the last publication, a copy of the notice must also be mailed to every defendant who cannot be personally served but whose place of residence is then known. Unknown owners may be served by publication in the same manner by a notice addressed to "Unknown Owners."

(ii) Service by publication is complete on the date of the last publication. The plaintiff's attorney must prove publication and mailing by a certificate, attach a printed copy of the published notice, and mark on the copy the newspaper's name and the dates of publication.

(4) *Effect of Delivery and Service.* Delivering the notice to the clerk and serving it have the same effect as serving a summons under Rule 4.

(5) *Proof of Service; Amending the Proof or Notice.* Rule 4(*l*) governs proof of service. The court may permit the proof or the notice to be amended.

(e) Appearance or Answer.

(1) *Notice of Appearance.* A defendant that has no objection or defense to the taking of its property may serve a notice of appearance designating the property in which it claims an interest. The defendant must then be given notice of all later proceedings affecting the defendant.

(2) *Answer.* A defendant that has an objection or defense to the taking must serve an answer within 21 days after being served with the notice. The answer must:

> (A) identify the property in which the defendant claims an interest;

> (B) state the nature and extent of the interest; and

> (C) state all the defendant's objections and defenses to the taking.

(3) *Waiver of Other Objections and Defenses; Evidence on Compensation.* A defendant waives all objections and defenses not stated in its answer. No other pleading or motion asserting an additional objection or defense is allowed. But at the trial on compensation, a defendant—whether or not it has previously appeared or answered—may present evidence on the amount of compensation to be paid and may share in the award.

(f) Amending Pleadings. Without leave of court, the plaintiff may—as often as it wants—amend the complaint at any time before the trial on compensation. But no amendment may be made if it would result in a dismissal inconsistent with Rule 71.1(i)(1) or (2). The plaintiff need not serve a copy of an amendment, but must serve notice of the filing, as provided in Rule 5(b), on every affected party who has appeared and, as provided in Rule 71.1(d), on every affected party who has not appeared. In addition, the plaintiff must give the clerk at least one copy of each amendment for the defendants' use, and additional copies at the request of the clerk or a defendant. A defendant may appear or answer in the time and manner and with the same effect as provided in Rule 71.1(e).

(g) Substituting Parties. If a defendant dies, becomes incompetent, or transfers an interest after being joined, the court may, on motion and notice of hearing, order that the proper party be substituted. Service of the motion and notice on a nonparty must be made as provided in Rule 71.1(d)(3).

(h) Trial of the Issues.

(1) *Issues Other Than Compensation; Compensation.* In an action involving eminent domain under federal law, the court tries all issues, including compensation, except when compensation must be determined:

(A) by any tribunal specially constituted by a federal statute to determine compensation; or

(B) if there is no such tribunal, by a jury when a party demands one within the time to answer or within any additional time the court sets, unless the court appoints a commission.

(2) *Appointing a Commission; Commission's Powers and Report.*

(A) *Reasons for Appointing.* If a party has demanded a jury, the court may instead appoint a three-person commission to determine compensation because of the character, location, or quantity of the property to be condemned or for other just reasons.

(B) *Alternate Commissioners.* The court may appoint up to two additional persons to serve as alternate commissioners to hear the case and replace commissioners who, before a decision is filed, the court finds unable or disqualified to perform their duties. Once the commission renders its final decision, the court must discharge any alternate who has not replaced a commissioner.

(C) *Examining the Prospective Commissioners.* Before making its appointments, the court must advise the parties of the identity and qualifications of each prospective commissioner and alternate, and may permit the parties to examine them. The parties may not suggest appointees, but for good cause may object to a prospective commissioner or alternate.

(D) *Commission's Powers and Report.* A commission has the powers of a master under Rule 53(c). Its action and report are determined by a majority. Rule 53(d), (e), and (f) apply to its action and report.

(i) Dismissal of the Action or a Defendant.

(1) *Dismissing the Action.*

(A) *By the Plaintiff.* If no compensation hearing on a piece of property has begun, and if the plaintiff has not acquired title or a lesser interest or taken possession, the plaintiff may, without a court order, dismiss the action as to that property by filing a notice of dismissal briefly describing the property.

(B) *By Stipulation.* Before a judgment is entered vesting the plaintiff with title or a lesser interest in or possession of property, the plaintiff and affected defendants may, without a court order, dismiss the action in whole or in part by filing a stipulation of dismissal. And if the parties so stipulate, the court may vacate a judgment already entered.

(C) *By Court Order.* At any time before compensation has been determined and paid, the court may, after a motion and hearing, dismiss the action as to a piece of property. But if the plaintiff has already taken title, a lesser interest, or possession as to any part of it, the court must award compensation for the title, lesser interest, or possession taken.

(2) *Dismissing a Defendant.* The court may at any time dismiss a defendant who was unnecessarily or improperly joined.

(3) *Effect.* A dismissal is without prejudice unless otherwise stated in the notice, stipulation, or court order.

(j) Deposit and Its Distribution.

(1) *Deposit.* The plaintiff must deposit with the court any money required by law as a condition to the exercise of eminent domain and may make a deposit when allowed by statute.

(2) *Distribution; Adjusting Distribution.* After a deposit, the court and attorneys must expedite the proceedings so as to distribute the deposit and to determine and pay compensation. If the compensation finally awarded to a defendant exceeds the amount distributed to that defendant, the court must enter judgment against the plaintiff for the deficiency. If the compensation awarded to a defendant is less than the amount distributed to that defendant, the court must enter judgment against that defendant for the overpayment.

(k) Condemnation Under a State's Power of Eminent Domain.
This rule governs an action involving eminent domain under state law. But if state law provides for trying an issue by jury—or for trying the issue of compensation by jury or commission or both—that law governs.

(l) Costs.
Costs are not subject to Rule 54(d).

Added 1951; as amended 1963, 1985, 1987, 1988, 1993, 2003, 2007, 2009.

Rule 72.

MAGISTRATE JUDGES: PRETRIAL ORDER

(a) **Nondispositive Matters.** When a pretrial matter not dispositive of a party's claim or defense is referred to a magistrate judge to hear and decide, the magistrate judge must promptly conduct the required proceedings and, when appropriate, issue a written order stating the decision. A party may serve and file objections to the order within 14 days after being served with a copy. A party may not assign as error a defect in the order not timely objected to. The district judge in the case must consider timely objections and modify or set aside any part of the order that is clearly erroneous or is contrary to law.

(b) Dispositive Motions and Prisoner Petitions.

(1) *Findings and Recommendations.* A magistrate judge must promptly conduct the required proceedings when assigned, without the parties' consent, to hear a pretrial matter dispositive of a claim or defense or a prisoner petition challenging the conditions of confinement. A record must be made of all evidentiary proceedings and may, at the magistrate judge's discretion, be made of any other proceedings. The magistrate judge must enter a recommended disposition, including, if appropriate, proposed findings of fact. The clerk must promptly mail a copy to each party.

(2) *Objections.* Within 14 days after being served with a copy of the recommended disposition, a party may serve and file specific written objections to the proposed findings and recommendations. A party may respond to another party's objections within 14 days after being served with a copy. Unless the district judge orders otherwise, the objecting party must promptly arrange for transcribing the record, or whatever portions of it the parties agree to or the magistrate judge considers sufficient.

(3) *Resolving Objections.* The district judge must determine de novo any part of the magistrate judge's disposition that has been properly objected to. The district judge may accept, reject, or modify the recommended disposition; receive further evidence; or return the matter to the magistrate judge with instructions.

Added 1983; as amended 1991, 1993, 2007, 2009.

Rule 73.

MAGISTRATE JUDGES: TRIAL BY CONSENT; APPEAL

(a) Trial by Consent. When authorized under 28 U.S.C. § 636(c), a magistrate judge may, if all parties consent, conduct a civil action or proceeding, including a jury or nonjury trial. A record must be made in accordance with 28 U.S.C. § 636(c)(5).

(b) Consent Procedure.

(1) *In General.* When a magistrate judge has been designated to conduct civil actions or proceedings, the clerk must give the parties written notice of their opportunity to consent under 28 U.S.C. § 636(c). To signify their consent, the parties must jointly or

separately file a statement consenting to the referral. A district judge or magistrate judge may be informed of a party's response to the clerk's notice only if all parties have consented to the referral.

(2) *Reminding the Parties About Consenting.* A district judge, magistrate judge, or other court official may remind the parties of the magistrate judge's availability, but must also advise them that they are free to withhold consent without adverse substantive consequences.

(3) *Vacating a Referral.* On its own for good cause—or when a party shows extraordinary circumstances—the district judge may vacate a referral to a magistrate judge under this rule.

(c) Appealing a Judgment. In accordance with 28 U.S.C. § 636(c)(3), an appeal from a judgment entered at a magistrate judge's direction may be taken to the court of appeals as would any other appeal from a district-court judgment.

Added 1983; as amended 1987, 1993, 1997, 2007.

Rule 74.

METHOD OF APPEAL FROM MAGISTRATE JUDGE TO DISTRICT JUDGE UNDER TITLE 28, U.S.C. § 636(c)(4) AND RULE 73(d)

Abrogated 1997

Rule 75.

PROCEEDINGS ON APPEAL FROM MAGISTRATE JUDGE TO DISTRICT JUDGE UNDER RULE 73(d)

Abrogated 1997

Rule 76.

JUDGMENT OF THE DISTRICT JUDGE ON THE APPEAL UNDER RULE 73(d) AND COSTS

Abrogated 1997

X. DISTRICT COURTS AND CLERKS: CONDUCTING BUSINESS; ISSUING ORDERS

Rule 77.

CONDUCTING BUSINESS; CLERK'S AUTHORITY; NOTICE OF AN ORDER OR JUDGMENT

(a) When Court Is Open. Every district court is considered always open for filing any paper, issuing and returning process, making a motion, or entering an order.

(b) Place for Trial and Other Proceedings. Every trial on the merits must be conducted in open court and, so far as convenient, in a regular courtroom. Any other act or proceeding may be done or conducted by a judge in chambers, without the attendance of the clerk or other court official, and anywhere inside or outside the district. But no hearing—other than one ex parte—may be conducted outside the district unless all the affected parties consent.

(c) Clerk's Office Hours; Clerk's Orders.

(1) *Hours.* The clerk's office—with a clerk or deputy on duty—must be open during business hours every day except Saturdays, Sundays, and legal holidays. But a court may, by local rule or order, require that the office be open for specified hours on Saturday or a particular legal holiday other than one listed in Rule 6(a)(4)(A).

(2) *Orders.* Subject to the court's power to suspend, alter, or rescind the clerk's action for good cause, the clerk may:

(A) issue process;

(B) enter a default;

(C) enter a default judgment under Rule 55(b)(1); and

(D) act on any other matter that does not require the court's action.

(d) Serving Notice of an Order or Judgment.

(1) *Service.* Immediately after entering an order or judgment, the clerk must serve notice of the entry, as provided in Rule 5(b), on each party who is not in default for failing to appear. The clerk must record the service on the docket. A party also may serve notice of the entry as provided in Rule 5(b).

(2) *Time to Appeal Not Affected by Lack of Notice.* Lack of notice of the entry does not affect the time for appeal or relieve—or authorize the court to relieve—a party for failing to appeal within

the time allowed, except as allowed by Federal Rule of Appellate Procedure (4)(a).

As amended 1948, 1963, 1968, 1971, 1987, 1991, 2001, 2007.

Rule 78.

HEARING MOTIONS; SUBMISSION ON BRIEFS

(a) Providing a Regular Schedule for Oral Hearings. A court may establish regular times and places for oral hearings on motions.

(b) Providing for Submission on Briefs. By rule or order, the court may provide for submitting and determining motions on briefs, without oral hearings.

As amended 1987, 2007.

Rule 79.

RECORDS KEPT BY THE CLERK

(a) Civil Docket.

(1) *In General.* The clerk must keep a record known as the "civil docket" in the form and manner prescribed by the Director of the Administrative Office of the United States Courts with the approval of the Judicial Conference of the United States. The clerk must enter each civil action in the docket. Actions must be assigned consecutive file numbers, which must be noted in the docket where the first entry of the action is made.

(2) *Items to be Entered.* The following items must be marked with the file number and entered chronologically in the docket:

(A) papers filed with the clerk;

(B) process issued, and proofs of service or other returns showing execution; and

(C) appearances, orders, verdicts, and judgments.

(3) *Contents of Entries; Jury Trial Demanded.* Each entry must briefly show the nature of the paper filed or writ issued, the substance of each proof of service or other return, and the substance and date of entry of each order and judgment. When a jury trial has been properly demanded or ordered, the clerk must enter the word "jury" in the docket.

(b) Civil Judgments and Orders. The clerk must keep a copy of every final judgment and appealable order; of every order affecting title to or a lien on real or personal property; and of any other order that the court directs to be kept. The clerk must keep these in the form and manner prescribed by the Director of the Administrative Office of the United States Courts with the approval of the Judicial Conference of the United States.

(c) Indexes; Calendars. Under the court's direction, the clerk must:

(1) keep indexes of the docket and of the judgments and orders described in Rule 79(b); and

(2) prepare calendars of all actions ready for trial, distinguishing jury trials from nonjury trials.

(d) Other Records. The clerk must keep any other records required by the Director of the Administrative Office of the United States Courts with the approval of the Judicial Conference of the United States.

As amended 1948, 1949, 1963, 2007.

Rule 80.

STENOGRAPHIC TRANSCRIPT AS EVIDENCE

If stenographically reported testimony at a hearing or trial is admissible in evidence at a later trial, the testimony may be proved by a transcript certified by the person who reported it.

As amended 1948, 2007.

XI.   GENERAL PROVISIONS

Rule 81.

APPLICABILITY OF THE RULES IN GENERAL; REMOVED ACTIONS

(a) Applicability to Particular Proceedings.

(1) *Prize Proceedings.* These rules do not apply to prize proceedings in admiralty governed by 10 U.S.C. §§ 7651–7681.

(2) *Bankruptcy.* These rules apply to bankruptcy proceedings to the extent provided by the Federal Rules of Bankruptcy Procedure.

(3) *Citizenship.* These rules apply to proceedings for admission to citizenship to the extent that the practice in those proceedings is not specified in federal statutes and has previously conformed to the practice in civil actions. The provisions of 8 U.S.C. § 1451 for service by publication and for answer apply in proceedings to cancel citizenship certificates.

(4) *Special Writs.* These rules apply to proceedings for habeas corpus and for quo warranto to the extent that the practice in those proceedings:

(A) is not specified in a federal statute, the Rules Governing Section 2254 Cases, or the Rules Governing Section 2255 Cases; and

(B) has previously conformed to the practice in civil actions.

(5) *Proceedings Involving a Subpoena.* These rules apply to proceedings to compel testimony or the production of documents through a subpoena issued by a United States officer or agency under a federal statute, except as otherwise provided by statute, by local rule, or by court order in the proceedings.

(6) *Other Proceedings.* These rules, to the extent applicable, govern proceedings under the following laws, except as these laws provide other procedures:

(A) 7 U.S.C. §§ 292, 499g(c), for reviewing an order of the Secretary of Agriculture;

(B) 9 U.S.C., relating to arbitration;

(C) 15 U.S.C. § 522, for reviewing an order of the Secretary of the Interior;

(D) 15 U.S.C. § 715d(c), for reviewing an order denying a certificate of clearance;

(E) 29 U.S.C. §§ 159, 160, for enforcing an order of the National Labor Relations Board;

(F) 33 U.S.C. §§ 918, 921, for enforcing or reviewing a compensation order under the Longshore and Harbor Workers' Compensation Act; and

(G) 45 U.S.C. § 159, for reviewing an arbitration award in a railway-labor dispute.

(b) Scire Facias and Mandamus. The writs of scire facias and mandamus are abolished. Relief previously available through them may be obtained by appropriate action or motion under these rules.

(c) Removed Actions.

(1) *Applicability.* These rules apply to a civil action after it is removed from a state court.

(2) *Further Pleading.* After removal, repleading is unnecessary unless the court orders it. A defendant who did not answer before removal must answer or present other defenses or objections under these rules within the longest of these periods:

(A) 21 days after receiving—through service or otherwise—a copy of the initial pleading stating the claim for relief;

(B) 21 days after being served with the summons for an initial pleading on file at the time of service; or

(C) 7 days after the notice of removal is filed.

(3) *Demand for a Jury Trial.*

(A) *As Affected by State Law.* A party who, before removal, expressly demanded a jury trial in accordance with state law need not renew the demand after removal. If the state law did not require an express demand for a jury trial, a party need not make one after removal unless the court orders the parties to do so within a specified time. The court must so order at a party's request and may so order on its own. A party who fails to make a demand when so ordered waives a jury trial.

(B) *Under Rule 38.* If all necessary pleadings have been served at the time of removal, a party entitled to a jury trial under Rule 38 must be given one if the party serves a demand within 14 days after:

(i) it files a notice of removal; or

(ii) it is served with a notice of removal filed by another party.

(d) Law Applicable.

(1) *"State Law" Defined.* When these rules refer to state law, the term "law" includes the state's statutes and the state's judicial decisions.

(2) *"State" Defined.* The term "state" includes, where appropriate, the District of Columbia and any United States commonwealth or territory.

(3) *"Federal Statute" Defined in the District of Columbia.* In the United States District Court for the District of Columbia, the term "federal statute" includes any Act of Congress that applies locally to the District.

As amended 1941, 1948, 1949, 1951, 1963, 1966, 1968, 1971, 1987, 2001, 2002, 2007, 2009.

Rule 82.

JURISDICTION AND VENUE UNAFFECTED

These rules do not extend or limit the jurisdiction of the district courts or the venue of actions in those courts. An admiralty or maritime claim under Rule 9(h) is not a civil action for purposes of 28 U.S.C. §§ 1391–1392.

As amended 1949, 1966, 2001, 2007.

Rule 83.

RULES BY DISTRICT COURTS; JUDGE'S DIRECTIVES

(a) Local Rules.

(1) *In General.* After giving public notice and an opportunity for comment, a district court, acting by a majority of its district judges, may adopt and amend rules governing its practice. A local rule must be consistent with—but not duplicate—federal statutes and rules adopted under 28 U.S.C. §§ 2072 and 2075, and must conform to any uniform numbering system prescribed by the Judicial Conference of the United States. A local rule takes effect on the date specified by the district court and remains in effect unless amended by the court or abrogated by the judicial council of the circuit. Copies of rules and amendments must, on their adoption, be furnished to the judicial council and the Administrative Office of the United States Courts and be made available to the public.

(2) *Requirement of Form.* A local rule imposing a requirement of form must not be enforced in a way that causes a party to lose any right because of a nonwillful failure to comply.

(b) Procedure When There Is No Controlling Law. A judge may regulate practice in any manner consistent with federal law, rules adopted under 28 U.S.C. §§ 2072 and 2075, and the district's local rules. No sanction or other disadvantage may be imposed for noncompliance with any requirement not in federal law, federal rules, or the local rules unless the alleged violator has been furnished in the particular case with actual notice of the requirement.

As amended 1985, 1995, 2007.

Rule 84.

FORMS

The forms in the Appendix suffice under these rules and illustrate the simplicity and brevity that these rules contemplate.

As amended 1948, 2007.

Rule 85.

TITLE

These rules may be cited as the Federal Rules of Civil Procedure.

As amended 2007.

Rule 86.

EFFECTIVE DATES

(a) In General. These rules and any amendments take effect at the time specified by the Supreme Court, subject to 28 U.S.C. § 2074. They govern:

(1) proceedings in an action commenced after their effective date; and

(2) proceedings after that date in an action then pending unless:

(A) the Supreme Court specifies otherwise; or

(B) the court determines that applying them in a particular action would be infeasible or work an injustice.

(b) December 1, 2007 Amendments. If any provision in Rules 1–5.1, 6–73, or 77–86 conflicts with another law, priority in time for the purpose of 28 U.S.C. § 2072(b) is not affected by the amendments taking effect on December 1, 2007.

As amended 1948, 1949, 1961, 1963, 2007.

[The order of the Supreme Court of December 20, 1937, adopted the rules, to be known as the Federal Rules of Civil Procedure. The Rules became effective on September 16, 1938. 302 U.S. 783, 308 U.S. 645; see 12A Wright, Miller, Kane & Marcus, Federal Practice and Procedure app. C.]

[Rule 81(a) was amended by the order of the Supreme Court of December 28, 1939, to be effective February 3, 1941. 308 U.S. 642; see 1 F.R.D. 79.]

[Rules 6(b) and (c), 7(a), 12(a), (b), (c), (d), (e), (f), (g), and (h), 13(a), (g), and (i), 14(a), 17(b), 24(a) and (b), 26, 27(a) and (b), 28(a), 33, 34, 36(a), 41(a) and (b), 45(b) and (d), 52(a), 54(b), 56(a) and (c), 58, 59(b) and (e), 60 (a) and (b), 62(b) and (h), 65(c), 66, 68, 73, 75, 77(d), 79(a), (b), (c), and (d), 80(a) and (b), 81(a), (c), and (f), 84, and 86 and Forms 17, 20, 22, and 25 were amended by the order of the Supreme Court of December 27, 1946, to be effective March 19, 1948. 329 U.S. 839; cf. 5 F.R.D. 433; 6 F.R.D. 229.]

———

[Rules 1, 17(b), 22(2), 24(c), 25(d), 27(a), 37(e), 45(e), 57, 60(b), 62(g), 65(e), 66, 67, 69(b), 72, 73, 74, 75, 76, 79(a), (b), and (d), 81(a), (c), (d), and (e), 82, and 86(c) and Forms 1, 19, 22, 23, and 27 were amended by the order of the Supreme Court of December 29, 1948, to be effective October 20, 1949. 335 U.S. 919; see 8 F.R.D. 591.]

———

[Rule 81(a) was amended, and Rule 71A and Forms 28 and 29 added, by the order of the Supreme Court of April 30, 1951, to be effective August 1, 1951. 341 U.S. 959; see 11 F.R.D. 213.]

———

[Rules 25(d), 54(b), 62(h), and 86(d) and Forms 2 and 19 were amended by the order of the Supreme Court of April 17, 1961, to be effective July 19, 1961. 368 U.S. 1009; see 27 F.R.D. xxxvii; 12A Wright, Miller, Kane & Marcus, Federal Practice and Procedure app. C.]

———

[Rules 4(b), (d), (e), (f), and (i), 5(a), 6(a) and (b), 7(a), 12(a), 13(a), 14(a), 15(d), 24(c), 25(a), 26, 28(b), 30(f), 41(b), 49(b), 50(a), (b), (c), and (d), 52(a), 56(c) and (e), 58, 71A(d), 77(c) and (d), 79(a), 81(a), (c), and (f), and 86(e) and Forms 3, 4, 5, 6, 7, 8, 9, 10, 11, 12, 13, 16, 18, and 21 were amended, Form 22 eliminated, and Forms 22–A, 22–B, 30, 31, and 32 added, by the orders of the Supreme Court of January 21, 1963, and March 18, 1963, to be effective July 1, 1963. 374 U.S. 861; see 31 F.R.D. 587.]

———

[Rules 1, 4(f), 6(c), 8(e), 9(h), 12(b), (g), and (h), 13(h), 14(a) and (c), 15(c), 17(a), 18(a), 19, 20(a), 23, 24(a), 26, 38(e), 41(b), 42(b), 43(f), 44(a), (b), and (c), 47(b), 53(a) and (b), 59(d), 65(a), (b), and (c), 68, 73, 74, 75, 81(a), and 82 and Forms 2 and 15 were amended, and Rules 23.1, 23.2, 44.1, and 65.1 and Supplemental Rules A–F added, by the order of the Supreme Court of February

143

28, 1966, to be effective July 1, 1966. 383 U.S. 1029; see 39 F.R.D. 69.]

———

[Rules 6(b), 9(h), 41(a), 77(d), and 81(a) were amended, and former Rules 72–76 and Form 27 abrogated, by the order of the Supreme Court of December 4, 1967, to be effective July 1, 1968. 389 U.S. 1121; see 43 F.R.D. 163.]

———

[Rules 5(a), 9(h), 26, 29, 30, 31, 32, 33, 34, 35, 36, 37, 45(d), and 69(a) and Form 24 were amended by the order of the Supreme Court of March 30, 1970, to be effective July 1, 1970. 398 U.S. 977; see 48 F.R.D. 485.] The Advisory Committee provided this table showing the rearrangement of Rules:

Former Rule No.	*New Rule No.*
26(a)	30(a), 31(a)
26(c)	30(c)
26(d)	32(a)
26(e)	32(b)
26(f)	32(c)
30(a)	30(b)
30(b)	26(c)
32	32(d)]

———

[Rules 6(a), 27(a), 30(b), 77(c), and 81(a) were amended by the order of the Supreme Court of March 1, 1971, to be effective July 1, 1971. 401 U.S. 1017; see 52 F.R.D. 79.]

———

[Rules 30(c), 32(c), 43(a), (b), and (c), and 44.1 were amended by the orders of the Supreme Court of November 20, 1972, and December 18, 1972. 419 U.S. 1133; see 56 F.R.D. 355. Those amendments were expressly approved by Congress January 2, 1975, Pub.L. 93–595, § 3, 88 Stat. 1949, to be effective July 1, 1975.]

———

[Rules 4(a) and (c), 5(d), 26(f), 28(a), 30(b) and (f), 32(a), 33(c), 34(b), 37(b), (e), and (g), and 45(d) and (e) were amended by the order of the Supreme Court of April 29, 1980, to be effective August 1, 1980. 446 U.S. 995; see 85 F.R.D. 521.]

———

[Rule 37(f) was repealed October 21, 1980, Pub.L. 96–481, Title II, § 205(a), 94 Stat. 2330, to be effective October 1, 1981.]

———

[Rule 4(a), (c), (d), (e), (g), and (j) was amended by the order of the Supreme Court of April 28, 1982, to be effective August 1, 1982. 456 U.S. 1013; see 93 F.R.D. 255. That amendment was suspended by Congress August 2, 1982, Pub.L. 97–227, 96 Stat. 246, effective August 1, 1982. See 94 F.R.D. 221. Rule 4(a), (c), (d), (e), (g), and (j) was then amended, and Form 18–A added, January 12, 1983, Pub.L. 97–462, 96 Stat. 2527, to be effective February 26, 1983. See 96 F.R.D. 75.]

———

[Rules 6(b), 7(b), 11, 16, 26(a), (b), and (g), 52(a), 53(a), (b), (c), and (f), and 67 were amended, and Rules 72–76 and Forms 33 and 34 added, by the order of the Supreme Court of April 28, 1983, to be effective August 1, 1983. 461 U.S. 1095; see 97 F.R.D. 165.]

———

[Rules 6(a), 45(d), 52(a), 71A(h), and 83, Form 18–A, and Supplemental Rules B(1), C(3), and E(4) were amended by the order of the Supreme Court of April 29, 1985, to be effective August 1, 1985. 471 U.S. 1153; see 105 F.R.D. 202.]

———

[Rules 51 and 77(c) were amended, and gender-specific language was neutralized in numerous Rules and Supplemental Rules, by the order of the Supreme Court of March 2, 1987, to be effective August 1, 1987. 480 U.S. 953; see 113 F.R.D. 189.]

———

[Technical corrections to Rules 17(a) and 71A(e) were made by the order of the Supreme Court of April 25, 1988, to be effective August 1, 1988. 485 U.S. 1043; see 119 F.R.D. 261.]

———

[Rule 35 was amended November 18, 1988, Pub.L. 100–690, Title VII, § 7047, 102 Stat. 4401. See 122 F.R.D. 276.]

––––––

[Rules 5(d) and (e), 15(c), 24(c), 34(c), 35, 41(b), 44(a), 45, 47(b) and (c), 48, 50, 52(a) and (c), 53(e), 63, 72(a), and 77(d) and Supplemental Rules C(3) and (5) and E(4), (5), and (9) were amended by the order of the Supreme Court of April 30, 1991, to be effective December 1, 1991. 500 U.S. 963; see 134 F.R.D. 525. A technical correction to Rule 15(c) was made December 9, 1991, Pub.L. 102–198, § 11(a), 105 Stat. 1626.]

––––––

[Rules 1, 4, 5(e), 11, 12(a), 15(c), 16(b) and (c), 26, 28(b), 29, 30(a), (b), (c), (d), (e), and (f), 31(a), 32(a) and (c), 33, 34(b), 36(a), 37(a), (c), (d), and (g), 38(b) and (d), 50(a), 52(c), 53(a), (b), and (f), 54(d), 58, 71A(d), 72, 73, 74(a) and (c), 75(b), and 76(a) and (c) and Forms 2, 33, and 34 were amended, Form 18–A abrogated, and Rule 4.1 and Forms 1A, 1B, 34A, and 35 added, by the order of the Supreme Court of April 22, 1993, to be effective December 1, 1993. 507 U.S. 1089; see 146 F.R.D. 401.]

––––––

[Rules 50(b) and (c), 52(b), 59(b), (c), (d), and (e), and 83 were amended by the order of the Supreme Court of April 27, 1995, to be effective December 1, 1995. 514 U.S. 1151; see 161 F.R.D. 149.]

––––––

[Rules 5(e) and 43(a) were amended by the order of the Supreme Court of April 23, 1996, to be effective December 1, 1996. 517 U.S. 1279; see 167 F.R.D. 209.]

––––––

[Rules 9(h) and 73(a), (c), and (d) and Forms 33 and 34 were amended, and Rules 74–76 abrogated, by the order of the Supreme Court of April 11, 1997, to be effective December 1, 1997. 520 U.S. 1305; see 171 F.R.D. 679.]

––––––

[Rule 23(f) was added by the order of the Supreme Court of April 24, 1998, to be effective December 1, 1998. 523 U.S. 1221; see 177 F.R.D. 530; 12A Wright, Miller, Kane & Marcus, Federal Practice and Procedure app. C.]

———

[Rule 6(b) and Form 2 were amended by the order of the Supreme Court of April 26, 1999, to be effective December 1, 1999. 526 U.S. 1183; see 185 F.R.D. 27.]

———

[Rules 4(i), 5(d), 12(a), 14(a) and (c), 26(a), (b), (d), and (f), 30(d) and (f), and 37(c) and Supplemental Rules B(1) and (2), C(2), (3), (4), and (6), and E(3), (7), (8), (9), and (10) were amended by the order of the Supreme Court of April 17, 2000, to be effective December 1, 2000. 529 U.S. 1155; see 192 F.R.D. 340.]

———

[Rules 5(b), 6(e), 65(f), 77(d), 81(a), and 82 were amended by the order of the Supreme Court of April 23, 2001, to be effective December 1, 2001. 532 U.S. 1085; see 200 F.R.D. 52.]

———

[Rules 54(d), 58, and 81(a) and Supplemental Rule C(3) and (6) were amended, and Rule 7.1 added, by the order of the Supreme Court of April 29, 2002, to be effective December 1, 2002. 535 U.S. 1147; see 207 F.R.D. 50.]

———

[Rules 23(c), (e), (g), and (h), 51, and 53 were amended, with technical changes to Rules 54(d) and 71A(h) and Forms 19, 31, and 32, by the order of the Supreme Court of March 27, 2003, to be effective December 1, 2003. 538 U.S. 1083; see 215 F.R.D. 158.]

———

[Rules 6(e), 27(a), and 45(a) and Supplemental Rules B(1) and C(6) were amended by the order of the Supreme Court of April 25,

2005, to be effective December 1, 2005. 544 U.S. 1173; see http://www.uscourts.gov/rules/archive.htm.]

––––––––––

[Rules 5(e), 9(h), 14(a) and (c), 16(b), 24(c), 26(a), (b), and (f), 33(d), 34(a) and (b), 37(f), 45, 50(a) and (b), and 65.1, Form 35, and Supplemental Rules A, C(2), (3), and (6), and E(3), (5), and (9) were amended, and Rule 5.1 and Supplemental Rule G added, by the order of the Supreme Court of April 12, 2006, to be effective December 1, 2006. 547 U.S. 1233; see 234 F.R.D. 219.]

––––––––––

[Rules 4(k), 9(h), 11(a), 14(b), 16(c), 26(g), 30(b), 31(c), 40, 71.1(d), and 78 were amended, and Rule 5.2 added and all Rules and Forms restyled, by the order of the Supreme Court of April 30, 2007, to be effective December 1, 2007. 550 U.S. 1003; see ____ F.R.D. ____. The Advisory Committee provided these tables showing the rearrangement of Rules and Forms:

Former Rule No.	*Restyled Rule No.*
5(e)	5(d)(2)–(4)
6(d)	6(c)
6(e)	6(d)
7(c)	Deleted
8(d)	8(b)(6)
8(e)	8(d)
8(f)	8(e)
12(b)(final sentence) and 12(c)(final sentence)	12(d)
12(d)	12(i)
16(d)	16(e)
16(e)	16(d)
22(1)	22(a)
22(1)(final sentence) and 22(2)	22(b)
23.1	23.1(a)–(c)
25(d)(2)	17(d)
26(a)(5)	Deleted
30(d)(1)	30(c)(2)(second and third sentence)
33(a)(part of first sentence)	33(b)(1)
33(c)(part of first sentence, second paragraph)	33(a)(2)
37(f)	37(e)
37(g)	37(f)
43(d)	43(b)
43(e)	43(c)
43(f)	43(d)

Former Rule No.	*Restyled Rule No.*
50(c)(2)	50(d)
50(d)	50(e)
52(b)(final sentence)	52(a)(5)
53(d)	53(c)(1)(C)
53(e)	53(d)
53(f)	53(e)
53(g)	53(f)
53(h)	53(g)
53(i)	53(h)
55(d)	Deleted
55(e)	55(d)
56(c)(final sentence)	56(d)(2)
58(a)(2)	58(b)
58(b)	58(c)
58(c)	58(e)
60(b)(second sentence)	60(c)
60(b)(third sentence)	60(d)
60(b)(fourth sentence)	60(e)
80(c)	80
81(e)	81(d)
81(f)	Deleted

Restyled Form No.	*Former Form No.*
1	1
2	1
3	1
4	22–A
5	1A
6	1B
7	2
8	26
9	30
10	3, 4, 5, 6, 7, and 8
11	9
12	10
13	14
14	15
15	11
16	22–A
17	12
18	16
19	17
20	18
21	13
30	20
31	21
40	19
41	22–B
42	23
50	24
51	25

Restyled Form No.	*Former Form No.*
52	35
60	28
61	29
70	31
71	32
80	33
81	34
82	34A]

———

[Supplemental Rule C(6) was amended by the order of the Supreme Court of April 23, 2008, to be effective December 1, 2008. ___ U.S. ___; see ___ F.R.D. ___.]

———

[Rules 6(a), (b), and (c), 12(a), (e), and (f), 13(f), 14(a), 15(a), 23(f), 27(a), 32(a) and (d), 38(b) and (c), 48, 50(b) and (d), 52(b), 53(f), 54(d), 55(b), 56(a), (b), and (c), 59(b), (c), (d), and (e), 62(a), 65(b), 68(a) and (c), 71.1(d) and (e), 72, and 81(c) and (d), Forms 3, 4, and 60, and Supplemental Rules B(3), C(4) and (6), and G(4), (5), and (6) were amended, and Rule 62.1 added, by the order of the Supreme Court of March 26, 2009, to be effective December 1, 2009. ___ U.S. ___; see ___ F.R.D. ___.]

APPENDIX OF FORMS

(See Rule 84)

Form 1.

CAPTION

(Use on every summons, complaint, answer, motion, or other document.)

United States District Court
for the
_____ District of _____

A B, Plaintiff	)	
	)	
v.	)	
	)	Civil Action No. _____
C D, Defendant	)	
	)	
v.	)	
	)	
E F, Third–Party Defendant	)	
(Use if needed.)	)	

(Name of Document)

As amended 1949, 2007.

Form 2.

DATE, SIGNATURE, ADDRESS, E–MAIL ADDRESS, AND TELEPHONE NUMBER

(Use at the conclusion of pleadings and other papers that require a signature.)

Date _____

_____
(Signature of the attorney
or unrepresented party)

_____
(Printed name)

_____
(Address)

_____
(E-mail address)

_____

(Telephone number)

As amended 1949, 2007.

Form 3.

SUMMONS

(Caption—See Form 1.)

To *name the defendant*:

A lawsuit has been filed against you.

Within 21 days after service of this summons on you (not counting the day you received it), you must serve on the plaintiff an answer to the attached complaint or a motion under Rule 12 of the Federal Rules of Civil Procedure. The answer or motion must be served on the plaintiff's attorney, _____, whose address is _____. If you fail to do so, judgment by default will be entered against you for the relief demanded in the complaint. You also must file your answer or motion with the court.

Date _____

_____

Clerk of Court

(Court Seal)

(Use 60 days if the defendant is the United States or a United States agency, or is an officer or employee of the United States allowed 60 days by Rule 12(a)(3).)

As amended 1949, 2007, 2009.

Form 4.

SUMMONS ON A THIRD–PARTY COMPLAINT

(Caption—See Form 1.)

To *name the third-party defendant*:

A lawsuit has been filed against defendant _____, who as third-party plaintiff is making this claim against you to pay part or all of what [he] may owe to the plaintiff _____.

Within 21 days after service of this summons on you (not counting the day you received it), you must serve on the plaintiff and on the defendant an answer to the attached third-party complaint or a motion under Rule 12 of the Federal Rules of Civil Procedure. The answer or motion must be served on the defendant's attorney, _____, whose address is _____, and also on the plaintiff's attorney, _____, whose address is _____. If you fail to do so, judgment by default will be entered against you for the relief demanded in the third-party complaint. You also must file the answer or motion with the court and serve it on any other parties.

A copy of the plaintiff's complaint is also attached. You may—but are not required to—respond to it.

Date _____   _____

                                       Clerk of Court

(Court Seal)

Added 1963; as amended 2007, 2009.

Form 5.

NOTICE OF A LAWSUIT AND REQUEST TO WAIVE SERVICE OF A SUMMONS

(Caption—See Form 1.)

To (*name the defendant—or if the defendant is a corporation, partnership, or association name an officer or agent authorized to receive service*):

Why are you getting this?

A lawsuit has been filed against you, or the entity you represent, in this court under the number shown above. A copy of the complaint is attached.

This is not a summons, or an official notice from the court. It is a request that, to avoid expenses, you waive formal service of a summons by signing and returning the enclosed waiver. To avoid these expenses, you must return the signed waiver within (*give at least 30 days or at least 60 days if the defendant is outside any judicial district of the United States*) from the date shown below, which is the date this notice was sent. Two copies of the waiver form are enclosed, along with a stamped, self-addressed envelope or other prepaid means for returning one copy. You may keep the other copy.

What happens next?

If you return the signed waiver, I will file it with the court. The action will then proceed as if you had been served on the date the waiver is filed, but no summons will be served on you and you will have 60 days from the date this notice is sent (see the date below) to answer the complaint (or 90 days if this notice is sent to you outside any judicial district of the United States).

153

If you do not return the signed waiver within the time indicated, I will arrange to have the summons and complaint served on you. And I will ask the court to require you, or the entity you represent, to pay the expenses of making service.

Please read the enclosed statement about the duty to avoid unnecessary expenses.

I certify that this request is being sent to you on the date below.

(Date and sign—See Form 2.)

Added 1993; as amended 2007.

Form 6.

WAIVER OF THE SERVICE OF SUMMONS

(Caption—See Form 1.)

To *name the plaintiff's attorney or the unrepresented plaintiff*:

I have received your request to waive service of a summons in this action along with a copy of the complaint, two copies of this waiver form, and a prepaid means of returning one signed copy of the form to you.

I, or the entity I represent, agree to save the expense of serving a summons and complaint in this case.

I understand that I, or the entity I represent, will keep all defenses or objections to the lawsuit, the court's jurisdiction, and the venue of the action, but that I waive any objections to the absence of a summons or of service.

I also understand that I, or the entity I represent, must file and serve an answer or a motion under Rule 12 within 60 days from _____, the date when this request was sent (or 90 days if it was sent outside the United States). If I fail to do so, a default judgment will be entered against me or the entity I represent.

(Date and sign—See Form 2.)

(Attach the following to Form 6.)

Duty to Avoid Unnecessary Expenses of Serving a Summons

Rule 4 of the Federal Rules of Civil Procedure requires certain defendants to cooperate in saving unnecessary expenses of serving a summons and complaint. A defendant who is located in the United States and who fails to return a signed waiver of service requested by a plaintiff located in the United States will be required to pay the expenses of service, unless the defendant shows good cause for the failure.

"Good cause" does *not* include a belief that the lawsuit is groundless, or that it has been brought in an improper venue, or that the court has no jurisdiction over this matter or over the defendant or the defendant's property.

If the waiver is signed and returned, you can still make these and all other defenses and objections, but you cannot object to the absence of a summons or of service.

If you waive service, then you must, within the time specified on the waiver form, serve an answer or a motion under Rule 12 on the plaintiff and file a copy with the court. By signing and returning the waiver form, you are allowed more time to respond than if a summons had been served.

Added 1993; as amended 2007.

Form 7.

STATEMENT OF JURISDICTION

a. (*For diversity-of-citizenship jurisdiction.*) The plaintiff is [a citizen of *Michigan*] [a corporation incorporated under the laws of *Michigan* with its principal place of business in *Michigan*]. The defendant is [a citizen of *New York*] [a corporation incorporated under the laws of *New York* with its principal place of business in *New York*]. The amount in controversy, without interest and costs, exceeds the sum or value specified by 28 U.S.C. § 1332.

b. (*For federal-question jurisdiction.*) This action arises under [the United States Constitution, *specify the article or amendment and the section*] [a United States treaty *specify*] [a federal statute, ___ U.S.C. § ___].

c. (*For a claim in the admiralty or maritime jurisdiction.*) This is a case of admiralty or maritime jurisdiction. (*To invoke admiralty status under Rule 9(h) use the following:* This is an admiralty or maritime claim within the meaning of Rule 9(h).)

As amended 1961, 1966, 1993, 1999, 2007.

Form 8.

STATEMENT OF REASONS FOR OMITTING A PARTY

(*If a person who ought to be made a party under Rule 19(a) is not named, include this statement in accordance with Rule 19(c).*)

This complaint does not join as a party *name* who [is not subject to this court's personal jurisdiction] [cannot be made a party without depriving this court of subject-matter jurisdiction] because *state the reason*.

As amended 2007.

Form 9.

STATEMENT NOTING A PARTY'S DEATH

(Caption—See Form 1.)

In accordance with Rule 25(a) *name the person*, who is [a party to this action] [a representative of or successor to the deceased party], notes the death during the pendency of this action of *name*, [*describe as party* in this action].

(Date and sign—See Form 2.)

Added 1963; as amended 2007.

Form 10.

COMPLAINT TO RECOVER A SUM CERTAIN

(Caption—See Form 1.)

1.   (Statement of Jurisdiction—See Form 7.)

(Use one or more of the following as appropriate and include a demand for judgment.)

(a) On a Promissory Note

2.   On *date*, the defendant executed and delivered a note promising to pay the plaintiff on *date* the sum of $_____ with interest at the rate of __ percent. A copy of the note [is attached as Exhibit A] [is summarized as follows: _____].

3.   The defendant has not paid the amount owed.

(b) On an Account

2.   The defendant owes the plaintiff $_____ according to the account set out in Exhibit A.

(c) For Goods Sold and Delivered

2.   The defendant owes the plaintiff $_____ for goods sold and delivered by the plaintiff to the defendant from *date* to *date*.

(d) For Money Lent

2.   The defendant owes the plaintiff $_____ for money lent by the plaintiff to the defendant on *date*.

(e) For Money Paid by Mistake

2.   The defendant owes the plaintiff $_____ for money paid by mistake to the defendant on *date* under these circumstances: *describe with particularity in accordance with Rule 9(b)*.

(f) For Money Had and Received

2.   The defendant owes the plaintiff $_____ for money that was received from *name* on *date* to be paid by the defendant to the plaintiff.

Demand for Judgment

Therefore, the plaintiff demands judgment against the defendant for $_____, plus interest and costs.

(Date and sign—See Form 2.)

As amended 1963, 2007.

Form 11.

COMPLAINT FOR NEGLIGENCE

(Caption—See Form 1.)

1.   (Statement of Jurisdiction—See Form 7.)

2.   On *date*, at *place*, the defendant negligently drove a motor vehicle against the plaintiff.

3.   As a result, the plaintiff was physically injured, lost wages or income, suffered physical and mental pain, and incurred medical expenses of $_____.

Therefore, the plaintiff demands judgment against the defendant for $_____, plus costs.

(Date and sign—See Form 2.)

As amended 1963, 2007.

Form 12.

COMPLAINT FOR NEGLIGENCE WHEN THE PLAINTIFF DOES NOT KNOW WHO IS RESPONSIBLE

(Caption—See Form 1.)

1.   (Statement of Jurisdiction—See Form 7.)

2.   On *date*, at *place*, defendant *name* or defendant *name* or both of them willfully or recklessly or negligently drove, or caused to be driven, a motor vehicle against the plaintiff.

3.   As a result, the plaintiff was physically injured, lost wages or income, suffered mental and physical pain, and incurred medical expenses of $_____.

Therefore, the plaintiff demands judgment against one or both defendants for $_____, plus costs.

(Date and sign—See Form 2.)

As amended 1963, 2007.

Form 13.

COMPLAINT FOR NEGLIGENCE UNDER THE FEDERAL EMPLOYERS' LIABILITY ACT

(Caption—See Form 1.)

1. (Statement of Jurisdiction—See Form 7.)

2. At the times below, the defendant owned and operated in interstate commerce a railroad line that passed through a tunnel located at _____.

3. On *date*, the plaintiff was working to repair and enlarge the tunnel to make it convenient and safe for use in interstate commerce.

4. During this work, the defendant, as the employer, negligently put the plaintiff to work in a section of the tunnel that the defendant had left unprotected and unsupported.

5. The defendant's negligence caused the plaintiff to be injured by a rock that fell from an unsupported portion of the tunnel.

6. As a result, the plaintiff was physically injured, lost wages or income, suffered mental and physical pain, and incurred medical expenses of $_____.

Therefore, the plaintiff demands judgment against the defendant for $_____, and costs.

(Date and sign—See Form 2.)

As amended 2007.

Form 14.

COMPLAINT FOR DAMAGES UNDER THE MERCHANT MARINE ACT

(Caption—See Form 1.)

1. (Statement of Jurisdiction—See Form 7.)

2. At the times below, the defendant owned and operated the vessel *name* and used it to transport cargo for hire by water in interstate and foreign commerce.

3. On *date*, at *place*, the defendant hired the plaintiff under seamen's articles of customary form for a voyage from _____ to

_____ and return at a wage of $_____ a month and found, which is equal to a shore worker's wage of $_____ a month.

4. On _date_, the vessel was at sea on the return voyage. (_Describe the weather and the condition of the vessel._)

5. (_Describe as in Form 11 the defendant's negligent conduct._)

6. As a result of the defendant's negligent conduct and the unseaworthiness of the vessel, the plaintiff was physically injured, has been incapable of any gainful activity, suffered mental and physical pain, and has incurred medical expenses of $_____.

Therefore, the plaintiff demands judgment against the defendant for $_____, plus costs.

(Date and sign—See Form 2.)

As amended 1966, 2007.

Form 15.

COMPLAINT FOR THE CONVERSION OF PROPERTY

(Caption—See Form 1.)

1. (Statement of Jurisdiction—See Form 7.)

2. On _date_, at _place_, the defendant converted to the defendant's own use property owned by the plaintiff. The property converted consists of _describe_.

3. The property is worth $_____.

Therefore, the plaintiff demands judgment against the defendant for $_____, plus costs.

(Date and sign—See Form 2.)

As amended 1963, 2007.

Form 16.

THIRD–PARTY COMPLAINT

(Caption—See Form 1.)

1. Plaintiff _name_ has filed against defendant _name_ a complaint, a copy of which is attached.

2. (_State grounds entitling defendant's name to recover from third-party defendant's name for (all or an identified share) of any judgment for plaintiff's name against defendant's name._)

Therefore, the defendant demands judgment against _third-party defendant's name_ for _all or an identified share_ of sums that may be adjudged against the defendant in the plaintiff's favor.

159

(Date and sign—See Form 2.)

Added 1963; as amended 2007.

Form 17.

COMPLAINT FOR SPECIFIC PERFORMANCE OF A CONTRACT TO CONVEY LAND

(Caption—See Form 1.)

1.   (Statement of Jurisdiction—See Form 7.)

2.   On *date*, the parties agreed to the contract [attached as Exhibit A] [summarize the contract].

3.   As agreed, the plaintiff tendered the purchase price and requested a conveyance of the land, but the defendant refused to accept the money or make a conveyance.

4.   The plaintiff now offers to pay the purchase price.

Therefore, the plaintiff demands that:

(a) the defendant be required to specifically perform the agreement and pay damages of $_____, plus interest and costs, or

(b) if specific performance is not ordered, the defendant be required to pay damages of $_____, plus interest and costs.

(Date and sign—See Form 2.)

As amended 1963, 2007.

Form 18.

COMPLAINT FOR PATENT INFRINGEMENT

(Caption—See Form 1.)

1.   (Statement of Jurisdiction—See Form 7.)

2.   On *date*, United States Letters Patent No. _____ were issued to the plaintiff for an invention in an *electric motor*. The plaintiff owned the patent throughout the period of the defendant's infringing acts and still owns the patent.

3.   The defendant has infringed and is still infringing the Letters Patent by making, selling, and using *electric motors* that embody the patented invention, and the defendant will continue to do so unless enjoined by this court.

4.   The plaintiff has complied with the statutory requirement of placing a notice of the Letters Patent on all *electric motors* it manufactures and sells and has given the defendant written notice of the infringement.

Therefore, the plaintiff demands:

(a) a preliminary and final injunction against the continuing infringement;

(b) an accounting for damages; and

(c) interest and costs.

(Date and sign—See Form 2.)

As amended 1963, 2007.

Form 19.

COMPLAINT FOR COPYRIGHT INFRINGEMENT AND UNFAIR COMPETITION

(Caption—See Form 1.)

1. (Statement of Jurisdiction—See Form 7.)

2. Before *date*, the plaintiff, a United States citizen, wrote a book entitled _____.

3. The book is an original work that may be copyrighted under United States law. A copy of the book is attached as Exhibit A.

4. Between *date* and *date*, the plaintiff applied to the copyright office and received a certificate of registration dated _____ and identified as *date, class, number*.

5. Since *date*, the plaintiff has either published or licensed for publication all copies of the book in compliance with the copyright laws and has remained the sole owner of the copyright.

6. After the copyright was issued, the defendant infringed the copyright by publishing and selling a book entitled _____, which was copied largely from the plaintiff's book. A copy of the defendant's book is attached as Exhibit B.

7. The plaintiff has notified the defendant in writing of the infringement.

8. The defendant continues to infringe the copyright by continuing to publish and sell the infringing book in violation of the copyright, and further has engaged in unfair trade practices and unfair competition in connection with its publication and sale of the infringing book, thus causing irreparable damage.

Therefore, the plaintiff demands that:

(a) until this case is decided the defendant and the defendant's agents be enjoined from disposing of any copies of the defendant's book by sale or otherwise;

(b) the defendant account for and pay as damages to the plaintiff all profits and advantages gained from unfair trade practices and unfair competition in selling the defendant's book, and all profits and advantages gained from infringing the plaintiff's copyright (but no less than the statutory minimum);

(c) the defendant deliver for impoundment all copies of the book in the defendant's possession or control and deliver for destruction all infringing copies and all plates, molds, and other materials for making infringing copies;

(d) the defendant pay the plaintiff interest, costs, and reasonable attorney's fees; and

(e) the plaintiff be awarded any other just relief.

(Date and sign—See Form 2.)

As amended 1948, 2007.

Form 20.

COMPLAINT FOR INTERPLEADER AND DECLARATORY RELIEF

(Caption—See Form 1.)

1.   (Statement of Jurisdiction—See Form 7.)

2.   On *date*, the plaintiff issued a life insurance policy on the life of *name* with *name* as the named beneficiary.

3.   As a condition for keeping the policy in force, the policy required payment of a premium during the first year and then annually.

4.   The premium due on *date* was never paid, and the policy lapsed after that date.

5.   On *date*, after the policy had lapsed, both the insured and the named beneficiary died in an automobile collision.

6.   Defendant *name* claims to be the beneficiary in place of *name* and has filed a claim to be paid the policy's full amount.

7.   The other two defendants are representatives of the deceased persons' estates. Each defendant has filed a claim on behalf of each estate to receive payment of the policy's full amount.

8.   If the policy was in force at the time of death, the plaintiff is in doubt about who should be paid.

Therefore, the plaintiff demands that:

(a) each defendant be restrained from commencing any action against the plaintiff on the policy;

(b) a judgment be entered that no defendant is entitled to the proceeds of the policy or any part of it, but if the court determines that the policy was in effect at the time of the insured's death, that the defendants be required to interplead and settle among themselves their rights to the proceeds, and that the plaintiff be discharged from all liability except to the defendant determined to be entitled to the proceeds; and

(c) the plaintiff recover its costs.

(Date and sign—See Form 2.)

As amended 1963, 2007.

Form 21.

COMPLAINT ON A CLAIM FOR A DEBT AND TO SET ASIDE A FRAUDULENT CONVEYANCE UNDER RULE 18(b)

(Caption—See Form 1.)

1. (Statement of Jurisdiction—See Form 7.)

2. On *date*, defendant *name* signed a note promising to pay to the plaintiff on *date* the sum of $_____ with interest at the rate of ___ percent. [The pleader may, but need not, attach a copy or plead the note verbatim.]

3. Defendant *name* owes the plaintiff the amount of the note and interest.

4. On *date*, defendant *name* conveyed all defendant's real and personal property *if less than all, describe it fully* to defendant *name* for the purpose of defrauding the plaintiff and hindering or delaying the collection of the debt.

Therefore, the plaintiff demands that:

(a) judgment for $_____, plus costs, be entered against defendant(s) *name(s)*; and

(b) the conveyance to defendant *name* be declared void and any judgment granted be made a lien on the property.

(Date and sign—See Form 2.)

As amended 1963, 2007.

Form 30.

ANSWER PRESENTING DEFENSES UNDER RULE 12(b)

(Caption—See Form 1.)

Responding to Allegations in the Complaint

1. Defendant admits the allegations in paragraphs _____.

2. Defendant lacks knowledge or information sufficient to form a belief about the truth of the allegations in paragraphs _____.

3.   Defendant admits *identify part of the allegation* in paragraph _____ and denies or lacks knowledge or information sufficient to form a belief about the truth of the rest of the paragraph.

Failure to State a Claim

4.   The complaint fails to state a claim upon which relief can be granted.

Failure to Join a Required Party

5.   If there is a debt, it is owed jointly by the defendant and *name* who is a citizen of _____. This person can be made a party without depriving this court of jurisdiction over the existing parties.

Affirmative Defense—Statute of Limitations

6.   The plaintiff's claim is barred by the statute of limitations because it arose more than _____ years before this action was commenced.

Counterclaim

7.   (*Set forth any counterclaim in the same way a claim is pleaded in a complaint. Include a further statement of jurisdiction if needed.*)

Crossclaim

8.   (*Set forth a crossclaim against a coparty in the same way a claim is pleaded in a complaint. Include a further statement of jurisdiction if needed.*)

(Date and sign—See Form 2.)

As amended 1948, 2007.

Form 31.

ANSWER TO A COMPLAINT FOR MONEY HAD AND RECEIVED WITH A COUNTERCLAIM FOR INTERPLEADER

(Caption—See Form 1.)

Response to the Allegations in the Complaint
(See Form 30.)

Counterclaim for Interpleader

1.   The defendant received from *name* a deposit of $_____.

2.   The plaintiff demands payment of the deposit because of a purported assignment from *name*, who has notified the defendant

that the assignment is not valid and who continues to hold the defendant responsible for the deposit.

Therefore, the defendant demands that:

(a) *name* be made a party to this action;

(b) the plaintiff and *name* be required to interplead their respective claims;

(c) the court decide whether the plaintiff or *name* or either of them is entitled to the deposit and discharge the defendant of any liability except to the person entitled to the deposit; and

(d) the defendant recover costs and attorney's fees.

(Date and sign—See Form 2.)

As amended 1963, 2007.

Form 40.

MOTION TO DISMISS UNDER RULE 12(b) FOR LACK OF JURISDICTION, IMPROPER VENUE, INSUFFICIENT SERVICE OF PROCESS, OR FAILURE TO STATE A CLAIM

(Caption—See Form 1.)

The defendant moves to dismiss the action because:

1. the amount in controversy is less than the sum or value specified by 28 U.S.C. § 1332;

2. the defendant is not subject to the personal jurisdiction of this court;

3. venue is improper (this defendant does not reside in this district and no part of the events or omissions giving rise to the claim occurred in the district);

4. the defendant has not been properly served, as shown by the attached affidavits of _____; or

5. the complaint fails to state a claim upon which relief can be granted.

(Date and sign—See Form 2.)

As amended 1949, 1961, 2003, 2007.

Form 41.

MOTION TO BRING IN A THIRD–PARTY DEFENDANT

(Caption—See Form 1.)

The defendant, as third-party plaintiff, moves for leave to serve on *name* a summons and third-party complaint, copies of which are attached.

(Date and sign—See Form 2.)

Added 1963; as amended 2007.

Form 42.

MOTION TO INTERVENE AS A DEFENDANT UNDER RULE 24

(Caption—See Form 1.)

1.   *name* moves for leave to intervene as a defendant in this action and to file the attached answer.

(State grounds under Rule 24(a) or (b).)

2.   The plaintiff alleges patent infringement. We manufacture and sell to the defendant the articles involved, and we have a defense to the plaintiff's claim.

3.   Our defense presents questions of law and fact that are common to this action.

(Date and sign—See Form 2.)

[An Intervener's Answer must be attached. See Form 30.]

As amended 1949, 2007.

Form 50.

REQUEST TO PRODUCE DOCUMENTS AND TANGIBLE THINGS, OR TO ENTER ONTO LAND UNDER RULE 34

(Caption—See Form 1.)

The plaintiff *name* requests that the defendant *name* respond within _____ days to the following requests:

1.   To produce and permit the plaintiff to inspect and copy and to test or sample the following documents, including electronically stored information:

(Describe each document and the electronically stored information, either individually or by category.)

(State the time, place, and manner of the inspection and any related acts.)

2.   To produce and permit the plaintiff to inspect and copy— and to test or sample—the following tangible things:

(Describe each thing, either individually or by category.)

*(State the time, place, and manner of the
inspection and any related acts.)*

3.   To permit the plaintiff to enter onto the following land to inspect, photograph, test, or sample the property or an object or operation on the property.

(Describe the property and each object or operation.)

*(State the time and manner of the inspection
and any related acts.)*

(Date and sign—See Form 2.)

As amended 1970, 2007.

Form 51.

REQUEST FOR ADMISSIONS UNDER RULE 36

(Caption—See Form 1.)

The plaintiff *name* asks the defendant *name* to respond within 30 days to these requests by admitting, for purposes of this action only and subject to objections to admissibility at trial:

1.   The genuineness of the following documents, copies of which [are attached] [are or have been furnished or made available for inspection and copying].

(List each document.)

2.   The truth of each of the following statements:

(List each statement.)

(Date and sign—See Form 2.)

As amended 1948, 2007.

Form 52.

REPORT OF THE PARTIES' PLANNING MEETING

(Caption—See Form 1.)

1.   The following persons participated in a Rule 26(f) conference on *date* by *state the method of conferring*:

(e.g., name representing the plaintiff.)

2.   Initial Disclosures. The parties [have completed] [will complete by *date*] the initial disclosures required by Rule 26(a)(1).

3.   Discovery Plan. The parties propose this discovery plan:

*(Use separate paragraphs or subparagraphs
if the parties disagree.)*

(a) Discovery will be needed on these subjects: (*describe.*)

(b) (Dates for commencing and completing discovery, including discovery to be commenced or completed before other discovery.)

(c) (Maximum number of interrogatories by each party to another party, along with the dates the answers are due.)

(d) (Maximum number of requests for admission, along with the dates responses are due.)

(e) (Maximum number of depositions by each party.)

(f) (Limits on the length of depositions, in hours.)

(g) (Dates for exchanging reports of expert witnesses.)

(h) (Dates for supplementations under Rule 26(e).)

4.   Other Items:

(a) (A date if the parties ask to meet with the court before a scheduling order.)

(b) (Requested dates for pretrial conferences.)

(c) (Final dates for the plaintiff to amend pleadings or to join parties.)

(d) (Final dates for the defendant to amend pleadings or to join parties.)

(e) (Final dates to file dispositive motions.)

(f) (State the prospects for settlement.)

(g) (Identify any alternative dispute resolution procedure that may enhance settlement prospects.)

(h) (Final dates for submitting Rule 26(a)(3) witness lists, designations of witnesses whose testimony will be presented by deposition, and exhibit lists.)

(i) (Final dates to file objections under Rule 26(a)(3).)

(j) (Suggested trial date and estimate of trial length.)

(k) (Other matters.)

(Date and sign—See Form 2.)

Added 1993; as amended 2006, 2007.

Form 60.

NOTICE OF CONDEMNATION

(Caption—See Form 1.)

To *name the defendant*.

1.   A complaint in condemnation has been filed in the United States District Court for the _____ District of _____, to take property to use for *purpose*. The interest to be taken is *describe*. The court is located in the United States courthouse at this address: _____.

2.   The property to be taken is described below. You have or claim an interest in it.

(Describe the property.)

3.   The authority for taking this property is *cite*.

4.   If you want to object or present any defense to the taking you must serve an answer on the plaintiff's attorney within 21 days [after being served with this notice] [from *(insert the date of the last publication of notice)*]. Send your answer to this address: _____.

5.   Your answer must identify the property in which you claim an interest, state the nature and extent of that interest, and state all your objections and defenses to the taking. Objections and defenses not presented are waived.

6.   If you fail to answer you consent to the taking and the court will enter a judgment that takes your described property interest.

7.   Instead of answering, you may serve on the plaintiff's attorney a notice of appearance that designates the property in which you claim an interest. After you do that, you will receive a notice of any proceedings that affect you. Whether or not you have previously appeared or answered, you may present evidence at a trial to determine compensation for the property and share in the overall award.

(Date and sign—See Form 2.)

Added 1951; as amended 2007, 2009.

Form 61.

COMPLAINT FOR CONDEMNATION

(Caption—See Form 1; name as defendants
the property and at least one owner.)

1.   (Statement of Jurisdiction—See Form 7.)

2. This is an action to take property under the power of eminent domain and to determine just compensation to be paid to the owners and parties in interest.

3. The authority for the taking is _____.

4. The property is to be used for _____.

5. The property to be taken is (*describe in enough detail for identification—or attach the description and state "is described in Exhibit A, attached"*).

6. The interest to be acquired is _____.

7. The persons known to the plaintiff to have or claim an interest in the property are: _____. (*For each person include the interest claimed.*)

8. There may be other persons who have or claim an interest in the property and whose names could not be found after a reasonably diligent search. They are made parties under the designation "Unknown Owners."

Therefore, the plaintiff demands judgment:

(a) condemning the property;

(b) determining and awarding just compensation; and

(c) granting any other lawful and proper relief.

(Date and sign—See Form 2.)

Added 1951; as amended 2007.

Form 70.

JUDGMENT ON A JURY VERDICT

(Caption—See Form 1.)

This action was tried by a jury with Judge _____ presiding, and the jury has rendered a verdict.

It is ordered that:

[the plaintiff *name* recover from the defendant *name* the amount of $_____ with interest at the rate of __%, along with costs.]

[the plaintiff recover nothing, the action be dismissed on the merits, and the defendant *name* recover costs from the plaintiff *name*.]

Date _____

_____
Clerk of Court

Added 1963; as amended 2003, 2007.

Form 71.

JUDGMENT BY THE COURT WITHOUT A JURY

(Caption—See Form 1.)

This action was tried by Judge _____ without a jury and the following decision was reached:

It is ordered that [the plaintiff *name* recover from the defendant *name* the amount of $_____, with prejudgment interest at the rate of _%, postjudgment interest at the rate of _%, along with costs.] [the plaintiff recover nothing, the action be dismissed on the merits, and the defendant *name* recover costs from the plaintiff *name*.]

Date _____   _____
                                Clerk of Court

Added 1963; as amended 2003, 2007.

Form 80.

NOTICE OF A MAGISTRATE JUDGE'S AVAILABILITY

1. A magistrate judge is available under title 28 U.S.C. § 636(c) to conduct the proceedings in this case, including a jury or nonjury trial and the entry of final judgment. But a magistrate judge can be assigned only if all parties voluntarily consent.

2. You may withhold your consent without adverse substantive consequences. The identity of any party consenting or withholding consent will not be disclosed to the judge to whom the case is assigned or to any magistrate judge.

3. If a magistrate judge does hear your case, you may appeal directly to a United States court of appeals as you would if a district judge heard it.

A form called *Consent to an Assignment to a United States Magistrate Judge* is available from the court clerk's office.

Added 1983; as amended 1993, 1997, 2007.

Form 81.

CONSENT TO AN ASSIGNMENT
TO A MAGISTRATE JUDGE

(Caption—See Form 1.)

I voluntarily consent to have a United States magistrate judge conduct all further proceedings in this case, including a trial, and order the entry of final judgment. (Return this form to the court clerk—not to a judge or magistrate judge.)

Date _____   _____
                                          Signature of the Party

Added 1983; as amended 1993, 1997, 2007.

Form 82.

ORDER OF ASSIGNMENT TO A MAGISTRATE JUDGE

(Caption—See Form 1.)

With the parties' consent it is ordered that this case be assigned to United States Magistrate Judge _____ of this district to conduct all proceedings and enter final judgment in accordance with 28 U.S.C. § 636(c).

Date _____   _____
                                          United States District Judge

Added 1993; as amended 2007.

SUPPLEMENTAL RULES FOR ADMIRALTY OR MARITIME CLAIMS AND ASSET FORFEITURE ACTIONS

Adopted February 28, 1966, effective July 1, 1966

Rule A.

SCOPE OF RULES

(1) These Supplemental Rules apply to:

(A) the procedure in admiralty and maritime claims within the meaning of Rule 9(h) with respect to the following remedies:

(i) maritime attachment and garnishment,

(ii) actions in rem,

(iii) possessory, petitory, and partition actions, and

(iv) actions for exoneration from or limitation of liability;

(B) forfeiture actions in rem arising from a federal statute; and

(C) the procedure in statutory condemnation proceedings analogous to maritime actions in rem, whether within the admiralty and maritime jurisdiction or not. Except as otherwise provided, references in these Supplemental Rules to actions in rem include such analogous statutory condemnation proceedings.

(2) The Federal Rules of Civil Procedure also apply to the foregoing proceedings except to the extent that they are inconsistent with these Supplemental Rules.

As amended 2006.

Rule B.

IN PERSONAM ACTIONS: ATTACHMENT AND GARNISHMENT

(1) When Available; Complaint, Affidavit, Judicial Authorization, and Process. In an in personam action:

(a) If a defendant is not found within the district when a verified complaint praying for attachment and the affidavit required by Rule B(1)(b) are filed, a verified complaint may contain a prayer for process to attach the defendant's tangible or intangible personal property—up to the amount sued for—in the hands of garnishees named in the process.

(b) The plaintiff or the plaintiff's attorney must sign and file with the complaint an affidavit stating that, to the affiant's knowledge, or on information and belief, the defendant cannot be found within the district. The court must review the complaint and affidavit and, if the conditions of this Rule B appear to exist, enter an order so stating and authorizing process of attachment and garnishment. The clerk may issue supplemental process enforcing the court's order upon application without further court order.

(c) If the plaintiff or the plaintiff's attorney certifies that exigent circumstances make court review impracticable, the clerk must issue the summons and process of attachment and garnishment. The plaintiff has the burden in any post-attachment hearing under Rule E(4)(f) to show that exigent circumstances existed.

(d)(i) If the property is a vessel or tangible property on board a vessel, the summons, process, and any supplemental process must be delivered to the marshal for service.

(ii) If the property is other tangible or intangible property, the summons, process, and any supplemental process must be delivered to a person or organization authorized to serve it, who may be (A) a marshal; (B) someone under contract with the United States; (C) someone specially appointed by the court for that purpose; or, (D) in an action brought by the United States, any officer or employee of the United States.

(e) The plaintiff may invoke state-law remedies under Rule 64 for seizure of person or property for the purpose of securing satisfaction of the judgment.

(2) Notice to Defendant. No default judgment may be entered except upon proof—which may be by affidavit—that:

(a) the complaint, summons, and process of attachment or garnishment have been served on the defendant in a manner authorized by Rule 4;

(b) the plaintiff or the garnishee has mailed to the defendant the complaint, summons, and process of attachment or garnishment, using any form of mail requiring a return receipt; or

(c) the plaintiff or the garnishee has tried diligently to give notice of the action to the defendant but could not do so.

(3) Answer.

(a) By Garnishee. The garnishee shall serve an answer, together with answers to any interrogatories served with the complaint, within 21 days after service of process upon the garnishee. Interrogatories to the garnishee may be served with the complaint without leave of court. If the garnishee refuses or neglects to answer on oath as to the debts, credits, or effects of the defendant in the garnishee's hands, or any interrogatories concerning such debts, credits, and effects that may be propounded by the plaintiff, the court may award compulsory process against the garnishee. If the garnishee admits any debts, credits, or effects, they shall be held in the garnishee's hands or paid into the registry of the court, and shall be held in either case subject to the further order of the court.

(b) By Defendant. The defendant shall serve an answer within 30 days after process has been executed, whether by attachment of property or service on the garnishee.

As amended 1985, 1987, 2000, 2005, 2009.

Rule C.

IN REM ACTIONS: SPECIAL PROVISIONS

(1) When Available. An action in rem may be brought:

(a) To enforce any maritime lien;

(b) Whenever a statute of the United States provides for a maritime action in rem or a proceeding analogous thereto.

Except as otherwise provided by law a party who may proceed in rem may also, or in the alternative, proceed in personam against any person who may be liable.

Statutory provisions exempting vessels or other property owned or possessed by or operated by or for the United States from arrest or seizure are not affected by this rule. When a statute so provides, an action against the United States or an instrumentality thereof may proceed on in rem principles.

(2) Complaint. In an action in rem the complaint must:

(a) be verified;

(b) describe with reasonable particularity the property that is the subject of the action; and

(c) state that the property is within the district or will be within the district while the action is pending.

(3) Judicial Authorization and Process.

(a) Arrest Warrant.

(i) The court must review the complaint and any supporting papers. If the conditions for an in rem action appear to exist, the court must issue an order directing the clerk to issue a warrant for the arrest of the vessel or other property that is the subject of the action.

(ii) If the plaintiff or the plaintiff's attorney certifies that exigent circumstances make court review impracticable, the clerk must promptly issue a summons and a warrant for the arrest of the vessel or other property that is the subject of the action. The plaintiff has the burden in any post-arrest hearing under Rule E(4)(f) to show that exigent circumstances existed.

(b) Service.

(i) If the property that is the subject of the action is a vessel or tangible property on board a vessel, the warrant and any supplemental process must be delivered to the marshal for service.

(ii) If the property that is the subject of the action is other property, tangible or intangible, the warrant and any supplemental process must be delivered to a person or organization authorized to enforce it, who may be: (A) a marshal; (B) someone under contract with the United States; (C) someone specially appointed by the court for that purpose; or, (D) in an action brought by the United States, any officer or employee of the United States.

(c) Deposit in Court. If the property that is the subject of the action consists in whole or in part of freight, the proceeds of property sold, or other intangible property, the clerk must issue—in addition to the warrant—a summons directing any person controlling the property to show cause why it should not be deposited in court to abide the judgment.

(d) Supplemental Process. The clerk may upon application issue supplemental process to enforce the court's order without further court order.

(4) Notice. No notice other than execution of process is required when the property that is the subject of the action has been released under Rule E(5). If the property is not released within 14 days after execution, the plaintiff must promptly—or within the time that the court allows—give public notice of the action and arrest in a newspaper designated by court order and having general circulation in the district, but publication may be terminated if the property is released before publication is completed. The notice must specify the time under Rule C(6) to file a statement of interest in or right against the seized property and to answer. This rule does not affect the notice requirements in an action to foreclose a preferred ship mortgage under 46 U.S.C. § 31301 et seq., as amended.

(5) Ancillary Process. In any action in rem in which process has been served as provided by this rule, if any part of the property that is the subject of the action has not been brought within the control of the court because it has been removed or sold, or because it is intangible property in the hands of a person who has not been served with process, the court may, on motion, order any person having possession or control of such property or its proceeds to show cause why it should not be delivered into the custody of the marshal or other person or organization having a warrant for the arrest of the property, or paid into court to abide the judgment; and, after hearing, the court may enter such judgment as law and justice may require.

(6) Responsive Pleading; Interrogatories.

(a) Statement of Interest; Answer. In an action in rem:

(i) a person who asserts a right of possession or any ownership interest in the property that is the subject of the action must file a verified statement of right or interest:

(A) within 14 days after the execution of process, or

(B) within the time that the court allows;

(ii) the statement of right or interest must describe the interest in the property that supports the person's demand for its restitution or right to defend the action;

(iii) an agent, bailee, or attorney must state the authority to file a statement of right or interest on behalf of another; and

(iv) a person who asserts a right of possession or any ownership interest must serve an answer within 21 days after filing the statement of interest or right.

(b) Interrogatories. Interrogatories may be served with the complaint in an in rem action without leave of court. Answers to the interrogatories must be served with the answer to the complaint.

As amended 1985, 1987, 1991, 2000, 2002, 2005, 2006, 2008, 2009.

Rule D.

POSSESSORY, PETITORY, AND PARTITION ACTIONS

In all actions for possession, partition, and to try title maintainable according to the course of the admiralty practice with respect to a vessel, in all actions so maintainable with respect to the possession of cargo or other maritime property, and in all actions by one or more part owners against the others to obtain security for the return of the vessel from any voyage undertaken without their consent, or by one or more part owners against the others to obtain possession of the vessel for any voyage on giving security for its safe return, the process shall be by a warrant of arrest of the vessel, cargo, or other property, and by notice in the manner provided by Rule B(2) to the adverse party or parties.

Rule E.

ACTIONS IN REM AND QUASI IN REM: GENERAL PROVISIONS

(1) Applicability. Except as otherwise provided, this rule applies to actions in personam with process of maritime attachment and garnishment, actions in rem, and petitory, possessory, and partition actions, supplementing Rules B, C, and D.

(2) Complaint; Security.

(a) Complaint. In actions to which this rule is applicable the complaint shall state the circumstances from which the claim arises with such particularity that the defendant or claimant will be able, without moving for a more definite statement, to commence an investigation of the facts and to frame a responsive pleading.

(b) Security for Costs. Subject to the provisions of Rule 54(d) and of relevant statutes, the court may, on the filing of the complaint or on the appearance of any defendant, claimant, or any other party, or at any later time, require the plaintiff, defendant, claimant, or other party to give security, or additional security, in such sum as the court shall direct to pay all costs and expenses that shall be awarded against the party by any interlocutory order or by the final judgment, or on appeal by any appellate court.

(3) Process.

(a) In admiralty and maritime proceedings process in rem or of maritime attachment and garnishment may be served only within the district.

(b) Issuance and Delivery. Issuance and delivery of process in rem, or of maritime attachment and garnishment, shall be held in abeyance if the plaintiff so requests.

(4) Execution of Process; Marshal's Return; Custody of Property; Procedures for Release.

(a) In General. Upon issuance and delivery of the process, or, in the case of summons with process of attachment and garnishment, when it appears that the defendant cannot be found within the district, the marshal or other person or organization having a

warrant shall forthwith execute the process in accordance with this subdivision (4), making due and prompt return.

(b) Tangible Property. If tangible property is to be attached or arrested, the marshal or other person or organization having the warrant shall take it into the marshal's possession for safe custody. If the character or situation of the property is such that the taking of actual possession is impracticable, the marshal or other person executing the process shall affix a copy thereof to the property in a conspicuous place and leave a copy of the complaint and process with the person having possession or the person's agent. In furtherance of the marshal's custody of any vessel the marshal is authorized to make a written request to the collector of customs not to grant clearance to such vessel until notified by the marshal or a deputy marshal or by the clerk that the vessel has been released in accordance with these rules.

(c) Intangible Property. If intangible property is to be attached or arrested the marshal or other person or organization having the warrant shall execute the process by leaving with the garnishee or other obligor a copy of the complaint and process requiring the garnishee or other obligor to answer as provided in Rules B(3)(a) and C(6); or the marshal may accept for payment into the registry of the court the amount owed to the extent of the amount claimed by the plaintiff with interest and costs, in which event the garnishee or other obligor shall not be required to answer unless alias process shall be served.

(d) Directions with Respect to Property in Custody. The marshal or other person or organization having the warrant may at any time apply to the court for directions with respect to property that has been attached or arrested, and shall give notice of such application to any or all of the parties as the court may direct.

(e) Expenses of Seizing and Keeping Property; Deposit. These rules do not alter the provisions of Title 28, U.S.C., § 1921, as amended, relative to the expenses of seizing and keeping property attached or arrested and to the requirement of deposits to cover such expenses.

(f) Procedure for Release from Arrest or Attachment. Whenever property is arrested or attached, any person claiming an interest in it shall be entitled to a prompt hearing at which the plaintiff shall be required to show why the arrest or attachment should not be vacated or other relief granted consistent with these rules. This subdivision shall have no application to suits for seamen's wages when process is issued upon a certification of sufficient cause filed pursuant to Title 46, U.S.C. §§ 603 and 604 or to actions by the United States for forfeitures for violation of any statute of the United States.

(5) Release of Property.

(a) Special Bond. Whenever process of maritime attachment and garnishment or process in rem is issued the execution of such process shall be stayed, or the property released, on the giving of security, to be approved by the court or clerk, or by stipulation of the parties, conditioned to answer the judgment of the court or of any appellate court. The parties may stipulate the amount and nature of such security. In the event of the inability or refusal of the parties so to stipulate the court shall fix the principal sum of the bond or stipulation at an amount sufficient to cover the amount of the plaintiff's claim fairly stated with accrued interest and costs; but the principal sum shall in no event exceed (i) twice the amount of the plaintiff's claim or (ii) the value of the property on due appraisement, whichever is smaller. The bond or stipulation shall be conditioned for the payment of the principal sum and interest thereon at 6 per cent per annum.

(b) General Bond. The owner of any vessel may file a general bond or stipulation, with sufficient surety, to be approved by the court, conditioned to answer the judgment of such court in all or any actions that may be brought thereafter in such court in which the vessel is attached or arrested. Thereupon the execution of all such process against such vessel shall be stayed so long as the amount secured by such bond or stipulation is at least double the aggregate amount claimed by plaintiffs in all actions begun and pending in which such vessel has been attached or arrested. Judgments and remedies may be had on such bond or stipulation as if a special bond or stipulation had been filed in each of such actions. The district court may make necessary orders to carry this rule into effect, particularly as to the giving of proper notice of any action against or attachment of a vessel for which a general bond has been filed. Such bond or stipulation shall be indorsed by the clerk with a minute of the actions wherein process is so stayed. Further security may be required by the court at any time.

If a special bond or stipulation is given in a particular case, the liability on the general bond or stipulation shall cease as to that case.

(c) Release by Consent or Stipulation; Order of Court or Clerk; Costs. Any vessel, cargo, or other property in the custody of the marshal or other person or organization having the warrant may be released forthwith upon the marshal's acceptance and approval of a stipulation, bond, or other security, signed by the party on whose behalf the property is detained or the party's attorney and expressly authorizing such release, if all costs and charges of the court and its officers shall have first been paid. Otherwise no property in the custody of the marshal, other person or organization having the

warrant, or other officer of the court shall be released without an order of the court; but such order may be entered as of course by the clerk, upon the giving of approved security as provided by law and these rules, or upon the dismissal or discontinuance of the action; but the marshal or other person or organization having the warrant shall not deliver any property so released until the costs and charges of the officers of the court shall first have been paid.

(d) Possessory, Petitory, and Partition Actions. The foregoing provisions of this subdivision (5) do not apply to petitory, possessory, and partition actions. In such cases the property arrested shall be released only by order of the court, on such terms and conditions and on the giving of such security as the court may require.

(6) Reduction or Impairment of Security. Whenever security is taken the court may, on motion and hearing, for good cause shown, reduce the amount of security given; and if the surety shall be or become insufficient, new or additional sureties may be required on motion and hearing.

(7) Security on Counterclaim.

(a) When a person who has given security for damages in the original action asserts a counterclaim that arises from the transaction or occurrence that is the subject of the original action, a plaintiff for whose benefit the security has been given must give security for damages demanded in the counterclaim unless the court, for cause shown, directs otherwise. Proceedings on the original claim must be stayed until this security is given, unless the court directs otherwise.

(b) The plaintiff is required to give security under Rule E(7)(a) when the United States or its corporate instrumentality counterclaims and would have been required to give security to respond in damages if a private party but is relieved by law from giving security.

(8) Restricted Appearance. An appearance to defend against an admiralty and maritime claim with respect to which there has issued process in rem, or process of attachment and garnishment, may be expressly restricted to the defense of such claim, and in that event is not an appearance for the purposes of any other claim with respect to which such process is not available or has not been served.

(9) Disposition of Property; Sales.

(a) Interlocutory Sales; Delivery.

(i) On application of a party, the marshal, or other person having custody of the property, the court may order all or part of the property sold—with the sales proceeds, or as much of them as will satisfy the judgment, paid into court to await further orders of the court—if:

(A) the attached or arrested property is perishable, or liable to deterioration, decay, or injury by being detained in custody pending the action;

(B) the expense of keeping the property is excessive or disproportionate; or

(C) there is an unreasonable delay in securing release of the property.

(ii) In the circumstances described in Rule E(9)(a)(i), the court, on motion by a defendant or a person filing a statement of interest or right under Rule C(6), may order that the property, rather than being sold, be delivered to the movant upon giving security under these rules.

(b) Sales, Proceeds. All sales of property shall be made by the marshal or a deputy marshal, or by other person or organization having the warrant, or by any other person assigned by the court where the marshal or other person or organization having the warrant is a party in interest; and the proceeds of sale shall be forthwith paid into the registry of the court to be disposed of according to law.

(10) Preservation of Property. When the owner or another person remains in possession of property attached or arrested under the provisions of Rule E(4)(b) that permit execution of process without taking actual possession, the court, on a party's motion or on its own, may enter any order necessary to preserve the property and to prevent its removal.

As amended 1985, 1987, 1991, 2000, 2006.

Rule F.

LIMITATION OF LIABILITY

(1) Time for Filing Complaint; Security. Not later than six months after receipt of a claim in writing, any vessel owner may file a complaint in the appropriate district court, as provided in subdivision (9) of this rule, for limitation of liability pursuant to statute. The owner (a) shall deposit with the court, for the benefit of claimants, a sum equal to the amount or value of the owner's interest in the vessel and pending freight, or approved security therefor, and in addition such sums, or approved security therefor, as the court may from time to time fix as necessary to carry out the provisions of the statutes as amended; or (b) at the owner's option shall transfer to a trustee to be appointed by the court, for the benefit of claimants, the owner's interest in the vessel and pending freight, together with such sums, or approved security therefor, as the court may from time to time fix as necessary to carry out the provisions of the statutes as amended. The plaintiff shall also give security for costs and, if the plaintiff elects to give security, for interest at the rate of 6 percent per annum from the date of the security.

(2) Complaint. The complaint shall set forth the facts on the basis of which the right to limit liability is asserted, and all facts necessary to enable the court to determine the amount to which the owner's liability shall be limited. The complaint may demand exoneration from as well as limitation of liability. It shall state the voyage, if any, on which the demands sought to be limited arose, with the date and place of its termination; the amount of all demands including all unsatisfied liens or claims of lien, in contract or in tort or otherwise, arising on that voyage, so far as known to the plaintiff, and what actions and proceedings, if any, are pending thereon; whether the vessel was damaged, lost, or abandoned, and, if so, when and where; the value of the vessel at the close of the voyage or, in case of wreck, the value of her wreckage, strippings, or proceeds, if any, and where and in whose possession they are; and the amount of any pending freight recovered or recoverable. If the plaintiff elects to transfer the plaintiff's interest in the vessel to a trustee, the complaint must further show any prior paramount liens thereon, and what voyages or trips, if any, she has made since the voyage or trip on which the claims sought to be limited arose, and any existing liens arising upon any such subsequent voyage or trip, with the amounts and causes thereof, and the names and addresses of the lienors, so far as known; and whether the vessel sustained any injury upon or by reason of such subsequent voyage or trip.

(3) Claims Against Owner; Injunction. Upon compliance by the owner with the requirements of subdivision (1) of this rule all claims and proceedings against the owner or the owner's property with respect to the matter in question shall cease. On application of the plaintiff the court shall enjoin the further prosecution of any action or proceeding against the plaintiff or the plaintiff's property with respect to any claim subject to limitation in the action.

(4) Notice to Claimants. Upon the owner's compliance with subdivision (1) of this rule the court shall issue a notice to all persons asserting claims with respect to which the complaint seeks limitation, admonishing them to file their respective claims with the clerk of the court and to serve on the attorneys for the plaintiff a copy thereof on or before a date to be named in the notice. The date so fixed shall not be less than 30 days after issuance of the notice. For cause shown, the court may enlarge the time within which claims may be filed. The notice shall be published in such newspaper or newspapers as the court may direct once a week for four successive weeks prior to the date fixed for the filing of claims. The plaintiff not later than the day of second publication shall also mail a copy of the notice to every person known to have made any claim against the vessel or the plaintiff arising out the voyage or trip on which the claims sought to be limited arose. In cases involving death a copy of such notice shall be mailed to the decedent at the decedent's last known address, and also to any person who shall be known to have made any claim on account of such death.

(5) Claims and Answer. Claims shall be filed and served on or before the date specified in the notice provided for in subdivision (4) of this rule. Each claim shall specify the facts upon which the claimant relies in support of the claim, the items thereof, and the dates on which the same accrued. If a claimant desires to contest either the right to exoneration from or the right to limitation of liability the claimant shall file and serve an answer to the complaint unless the claim has included an answer.

(6) Information to Be Given Claimants. Within 30 days after the date specified in the notice for filing claims, or within such time as the court thereafter may allow, the plaintiff shall mail to the attorney for each claimant (or if the claimant has no attorney to the claimant) a list setting forth (a) the name of each claimant, (b) the name and address of the claimant's attorney (if the claimant is known to have one), (c) the nature of the claim, i.e., whether property loss, property damage, death, personal injury, etc., and (d) the amount thereof.

(7) Insufficiency of Fund or Security. Any claimant may by motion demand that the funds deposited in court or the security given by the plaintiff be increased on the ground that they are less than the value of the plaintiff's interest in the vessel and pending freight. Thereupon the court shall cause due appraisement to be made of the value of the plaintiff's interest in the vessel and pending freight; and if the court finds that the deposit or security is either insufficient or excessive it shall order its increase or reduction. In like manner any claimant may demand that the deposit or security be increased on the ground that it is insufficient to carry out the provisions of the statutes relating to claims in respect of loss of life or bodily injury; and, after notice and hearing, the court may similarly order that the deposit or security be increased or reduced.

(8) Objections to Claims: Distribution of Fund. Any interested party may question or controvert any claim without filing an objection thereto. Upon determination of liability the fund deposited or secured, or the proceeds of the vessel and pending freight, shall be divided pro rata, subject to all relevant provisions of law, among the several claimants in proportion to the amounts of their respective claims, duly proved, saving, however, to all parties any priority to which they may be legally entitled.

(9) Venue; Transfer. The complaint shall be filed in any district in which the vessel has been attached or arrested to answer for any claim with respect to which the plaintiff seeks to limit liability; or, if the vessel has not been attached or arrested, then in any district in which the owner has been sued with respect to any such claim. When the vessel has not been attached or arrested to answer the matters aforesaid, and suit has not been commenced against the owner, the proceedings may be had in the district in which the vessel may be, but if the vessel is not within any district and no suit has been commenced in any district, then the complaint may be filed in any district. For the convenience of parties and witnesses, in the interest of justice, the court may transfer the action to any district; if venue is wrongly laid the court shall dismiss or, if it be in the interest of justice, transfer the action to any district in which it could have been brought. If the vessel shall have been sold, the proceeds shall represent the vessel for the purposes of these rules.

As amended 1987.

Rule G.

FORFEITURE ACTIONS IN REM

(1) Scope. This rule governs a forfeiture action in rem arising from a federal statute. To the extent that this rule does not address an issue, Supplemental Rules C and E and the Federal Rules of Civil Procedure also apply.

(2) Complaint. The complaint must:

(a) be verified;

(b) state the grounds for subject-matter jurisdiction, in rem jurisdiction over the defendant property, and venue;

(c) describe the property with reasonable particularity;

(d) if the property is tangible, state its location when any seizure occurred and—if different—its location when the action is filed;

(e) identify the statute under which the forfeiture action is brought; and

(f) state sufficiently detailed facts to support a reasonable belief that the government will be able to meet its burden of proof at trial.

(3) Judicial Authorization and Process.

(a) *Real Property.* If the defendant is real property, the government must proceed under 18 U.S.C. § 985.

(b) *Other Property; Arrest Warrant.* If the defendant is not real property:

(i) the clerk must issue a warrant to arrest the property if it is in the government's possession, custody, or control;

(ii) the court—on finding probable cause—must issue a warrant to arrest the property if it is not in the government's possession, custody, or control and is not subject to a judicial restraining order; and

(iii) a warrant is not necessary if the property is subject to a judicial restraining order.

(c) *Execution of Process.*

(i) The warrant and any supplemental process must be delivered to a person or organization authorized to execute it, who may be: (A) a marshal or any other United States officer or employee; (B) someone under contract with the United States; or (C) someone specially appointed by the court for that purpose.

(ii) The authorized person or organization must execute the warrant and any supplemental process on property in the United States as soon as practicable unless:

(A) the property is in the government's possession, custody, or control; or

(B) the court orders a different time when the complaint is under seal, the action is stayed before the warrant and supplemental process are executed, or the court finds other good cause.

(iii) The warrant and any supplemental process may be executed within the district or, when authorized by statute, outside the district.

(iv) If executing a warrant on property outside the United States is required, the warrant may be transmitted to an appropriate authority for serving process where the property is located.

(4) Notice.

(a) *Notice by Publication.*

(i) *When Publication Is Required.* A judgment of forfeiture may be entered only if the government has published notice of the action within a reasonable time after filing the complaint or at a time the court orders. But notice need not be published if:

(A) the defendant property is worth less than $1,000 and direct notice is sent under Rule G(4)(b) to every person the government can reasonably identify as a potential claimant; or

(B) the court finds that the cost of publication exceeds the property's value and that other means of notice would satisfy due process.

(ii) *Content of the Notice.* Unless the court orders otherwise, the notice must:

(A) describe the property with reasonable particularity;

(B) state the times under Rule G(5) to file a claim and to answer; and

(C) name the government attorney to be served with the claim and answer.

(iii) *Frequency of Publication.* Published notice must appear:

(A) once a week for three consecutive weeks; or

(B) only once if, before the action was filed, notice of nonjudicial forfeiture of the same property was published on an official internet government forfeiture site for at least 30 consecutive days, or in a newspaper of general circulation for three consecutive weeks in a district where publication is authorized under Rule G(4)(a)(iv).

(iv) *Means of Publication.* The government should select from the following options a means of publication reasonably calculated to notify potential claimants of the action:

(A) if the property is in the United States, publication in a newspaper generally circulated in the district where the action is filed, where the property was seized, or where property that was not seized is located;

(B) if the property is outside the United States, publication in a newspaper generally circulated in a district where the action is filed, in a newspaper generally circulated in the country where the property is located, or in legal notices published and generally circulated in the country where the property is located; or

(C) instead of (A) or (B), posting a notice on an official internet government forfeiture site for at least 30 consecutive days.

(b) Notice to Known Potential Claimants.

(i) *Direct Notice Required.* The government must send notice of the action and a copy of the complaint to any person who reasonably appears to be a potential claimant on the facts known to the government before the end of the time for filing a claim under Rule G(5)(a)(ii)(B).

(ii) *Content of the Notice.* The notice must state:

(A) the date when the notice is sent;

(B) a deadline for filing a claim, at least 35 days after the notice is sent;

(C) that an answer or a motion under Rule 12 must be filed no later than 21 days after filing the claim; and

(D) the name of the government attorney to be served with the claim and answer.

(iii) *Sending Notice.*

(A) The notice must be sent by means reasonably calculated to reach the potential claimant.

(B) Notice may be sent to the potential claimant or to the attorney representing the potential claimant with respect to the seizure of the property or in a related investigation, administrative forfeiture proceeding, or criminal case.

(C) Notice sent to a potential claimant who is incarcerated must be sent to the place of incarceration.

(D) Notice to a person arrested in connection with an offense giving rise to the forfeiture who is not incarcerated when notice is sent may be sent to the address that person last gave to the agency that arrested or released the person.

(E) Notice to a person from whom the property was seized who is not incarcerated when notice is sent may be sent to the last address that person gave to the agency that seized the property.

(iv) *When Notice Is Sent.* Notice by the following means is sent on the date when it is placed in the mail, delivered to a commercial carrier, or sent by electronic mail.

(v) *Actual Notice.* A potential claimant who had actual notice of a forfeiture action may not oppose or seek relief from forfeiture because of the government's failure to send the required notice.

(5) Responsive Pleadings.

(a) *Filing a Claim.*

(i) A person who asserts an interest in the defendant property may contest the forfeiture by filing a claim in the court where the action is pending. The claim must:

(A) identify the specific property claimed;

188

(B) identify the claimant and state the claimant's interest in the property;

(C) be signed by the claimant under penalty of perjury; and

(D) be served on the government attorney designated under Rule G(4)(a)(ii)(C) or (b)(ii)(D).

(ii) Unless the court for good cause sets a different time, the claim must be filed:

(A) by the time stated in a direct notice sent under Rule G(4)(b);

(B) if notice was published but direct notice was not sent to the claimant or the claimant's attorney, no later than 30 days after final publication of newspaper notice or legal notice under Rule G(4)(a) or no later than 60 days after the first day of publication on an official internet government forfeiture site; or

(C) if notice was not published and direct notice was not sent to the claimant or the claimant's attorney:

(1) if the property was in the government's possession, custody, or control when the complaint was filed, no later than 60 days after the filing, not counting any time when the complaint was under seal or when the action was stayed before execution of a warrant issued under Rule G(3)(b); or

(2) if the property was not in the government's possession, custody, or control when the complaint was filed, no later than 60 days after the government complied with 18 U.S.C. § 985(c) as to real property, or 60 days after process was executed on the property under Rule G(3).

(iii) A claim filed by a person asserting an interest as a bailee must identify the bailor, and if filed on the bailor's behalf must state the authority to do so.

(b) *Answer.* A claimant must serve and file an answer to the complaint or a motion under Rule 12 within 21 days after filing the claim. A claimant waives an objection to in rem jurisdiction or to venue if the objection is not made by motion or stated in the answer.

(6) Special Interrogatories.

(a) *Time and Scope.* The government may serve special interrogatories limited to the claimant's identity and relationship to the defendant property without the court's leave at any time after the claim is filed and before discovery is closed. But if the claimant serves a motion to dismiss the action, the government must serve the interrogatories within 21 days after the motion is served.

(b) Answers or Objections. Answers or objections to these interrogatories must be served within 21 days after the interrogatories are served.

(c) Government's Response Deferred. The government need not respond to a claimant's motion to dismiss the action under Rule G(8)(b) until 21 days after the claimant has answered these interrogatories.

(7) Preserving, Preventing Criminal Use, and Disposing of Property; Sales.

(a) Preserving and Preventing Criminal Use of Property. When the government does not have actual possession of the defendant property the court, on motion or on its own, may enter any order necessary to preserve the property, to prevent its removal or encumbrance, or to prevent its use in a criminal offense.

(b) Interlocutory Sale or Delivery.

(i) *Order to Sell.* On motion by a party or a person having custody of the property, the court may order all or part of the property sold if:

(A) the property is perishable or at risk of deterioration, decay, or injury by being detained in custody pending the action;

(B) the expense of keeping the property is excessive or is disproportionate to its fair market value;

(C) the property is subject to a mortgage or to taxes on which the owner is in default; or

(D) the court finds other good cause.

(ii) *Who Makes the Sale.* A sale must be made by a United States agency that has authority to sell the property, by the agency's contractor, or by any person the court designates.

(iii) *Sale Procedures.* The sale is governed by 28 U.S.C. §§ 2001, 2002, and 2004, unless all parties, with the court's approval, agree to the sale, aspects of the sale, or different procedures.

(iv) *Sale Proceeds.* Sale proceeds are a substitute res subject to forfeiture in place of the property that was sold. The proceeds must be held in an interest-bearing account maintained by the United States pending the conclusion of the forfeiture action.

(v) *Delivery on a Claimant's Motion.* The court may order that the property be delivered to the claimant pending the conclusion of the action if the claimant shows circumstances that would permit sale under Rule G(7)(b)(i) and gives security under these rules.

(c) Disposing of Forfeited Property. Upon entry of a forfeiture judgment, the property or proceeds from selling the property must be disposed of as provided by law.

(8) Motions.

(a) Motion to Suppress Use of the Property as Evidence. If the defendant property was seized, a party with standing to contest the lawfulness of the seizure may move to suppress use of the property as evidence. Suppression does not affect forfeiture of the property based on independently derived evidence.

(b) Motion to Dismiss the Action.

(i) A claimant who establishes standing to contest forfeiture may move to dismiss the action under Rule 12(b).

(ii) In an action governed by 18 U.S.C. § 983(a)(3)(D) the complaint may not be dismissed on the ground that the government did not have adequate evidence at the time the complaint was filed to establish the forfeitability of the property. The sufficiency of the complaint is governed by Rule G(2).

(c) Motion to Strike a Claim or Answer.

(i) At any time before trial, the government may move to strike a claim or answer:

(A) for failing to comply with Rule G(5) or (6), or

(B) because the claimant lacks standing.

(ii) The motion:

(A) must be decided before any motion by the claimant to dismiss the action; and

(B) may be presented as a motion for judgment on the pleadings or as a motion to determine after a hearing or by summary judgment whether the claimant can carry the burden of establishing standing by a preponderance of the evidence.

(d) Petition to Release Property.

(i) If a United States agency or an agency's contractor holds property for judicial or nonjudicial forfeiture under a statute governed by 18 U.S.C. § 983(f), a person who has filed a claim to the property may petition for its release under § 983(f).

(ii) If a petition for release is filed before a judicial forfeiture action is filed against the property, the petition may be filed either in the district where the property was seized or in the district where a warrant to seize the property issued. If a judicial forfeiture action against the property is later filed in another district—or if the government shows that the action will be filed in another district—the petition may be transferred to that district under 28 U.S.C. § 1404.

(e) Excessive Fines. A claimant may seek to mitigate a forfeiture under the Excessive Fines Clause of the Eighth Amendment by motion for summary judgment or by motion made after entry of a forfeiture judgment if:

> (i) the claimant has pleaded the defense under Rule 8; and

> (ii) the parties have had the opportunity to conduct civil discovery on the defense.

(9) Trial. Trial is to the court unless any party demands trial by jury under Rule 38.

Added 2006; as amended 2009.

CERTAIN OF THE CIVIL ADVISORY COMMITTEE'S NOTES

[The following selected Notes, arranged by Rule number, come from certain years: 1938, 1948, 1961, 1963, 1966, 1970, 1980, 1983, 1985, 1991, 1993, 2000, 2003, and 2006. All the other original Notes and amendatory Notes, arranged by year, appear in this booklet's online Statutory Companion site, which is discussed in the Preface to this booklet.]

Rule 4. Process

Advisory Committee's Note to Original Rule

Note to Subdivision (a). With the provision permitting additional summons upon request of the plaintiff, compare Equity Rule 14 (Alias Subpoena) and the last sentence of Equity Rule 12 (Issue of Subpoena—Time for Answer).

Note to Subdivision (b). This rule prescribes a form of summons which follows substantially the requirements stated in Equity Rules 12 (Issue of Subpoena—Time for Answer) and 7 (Process, Mesne and Final).

U.S.C., Title 28, § 721 [now § 1691] (Sealing and testing of writs) is substantially continued in so far as it applies to a summons, but its requirements as to teste of process are superseded. U.S.C., Title 28, § 722 [1946 ed.] (Teste of process, day of) is superseded.

See Rule 12(a) for a statement of the time within which the defendant is required to appear and defend.

Note to Subdivision (c). This Rule does not affect U.S.C., Title 28, § 503, as amended June 15, 1935 [1946 ed.] (Marshals; duties) and such statutes as the following in so far as they provide for service of process by a marshal, but modifies them in so far as they may imply service by a marshal only:

U.S.C., Title 15:

§ 5   (Bringing in additional parties) (Sherman Act)

§ 10   (Bringing in additional parties)

§ 25   (Restraining violations; procedure)

U.S.C., Title 28:

§ 45   [1946 ed.] (Practice and procedure in certain cases under the interstate commerce laws)

Compare Equity Rule 15 (Process, by Whom Served).

Note to Subdivision (d). Under this rule the complaint must always be served with the summons.

Paragraph (1). For an example of a statute providing for service upon an agent of an individual see U.S.C., Title 28, § 109 [now §§ 1400, 1694] (Patent cases).

Paragraph (3). This enumerates the officers and agents of a corporation or of a partnership or other unincorporated association upon whom service of process may be made, and permits service of process only upon the officers, managing or general

---

New matter is shown in italics; matter to be omitted is lined through

agents, or agents authorized by appointment or by law, of the corporation, partnership or unincorporated association against which the action is brought. See *Christian v. International Ass'n of Machinists,* 7 F.(2d) 481 (D.C.Ky.,1925) and *Singleton v. Order of Railway Conductors of America,* 9 F.Supp. 417 (D.C.Ill.,1935). Compare *Operative Plasterers' and Cement Finishers' International Ass'n of the United States and Canada v. Case,* 93 F.(2d) 56 (App.D.C.,1937).

For a statute authorizing service upon a specified agent and requiring mailing to the defendant, see U.S.C., Title 6, § 7 (Surety companies as sureties; appointment of agents; service of process).

Paragraphs (4) and (5) provide a uniform and comprehensive method of service for all actions against the United States or an officer or agency thereof. For statutes providing for such service, see U.S.C., Title 7, §§ 217 (Proceedings for suspension of orders), 499k (Injunctions; application of injunction laws governing orders of Interstate Commerce Commission), 608c(15)(B) (Court review of ruling of Secretary of Agriculture), and 855 (making § 608c(15)(B) applicable to orders of the Secretary of Agriculture as to handlers of anti-hog-cholera serum and hog-cholera virus); U.S.C., Title 26, § 1569 (Bill in chancery to clear title to realty on which the United States has a lien for taxes); U.S.C., Title 28, §§ 45 [1946 ed.] (District Courts; practice and procedure in certain cases under the interstate commerce laws), 763 [1946 ed.] (Petition in suit against the United States; service; appearance by district attorney), 766 [now § 2409] (Partition suits where United States is tenant in common or joint tenant), 902 [now § 2410] (Foreclosure of mortgages or other liens on property in which the United States has an interest). These and similar statutes are modified in so far as they prescribe a different method of service or dispense with the service of a summons.

For the Equity Rule on service, see Equity Rule 13 (Manner of Serving Subpoena).

Note to Subdivision (e). The provisions for the service of a summons or of notice or of an order in lieu of summons contained in U.S.C., Title 8, § 405 (Cancellation of certificates of citizenship fraudulently or illegally procured) (service by publication in accordance with state law); U.S.C., Title 28, § 118 [now § 1655] (Absent defendants in suits to enforce liens); U.S.C., Title 35, § 72a (Jurisdiction of District Court of United States for the District of Columbia in certain equity suits where adverse parties reside elsewhere) (service by publication against parties residing in foreign countries); U.S.C., Title 38, § 445 (Action against the United States on a veteran's contract of insurance) (parties not inhabitants of or not found within the district may be served with an order of the court, personally or by publication) and similar statutes are continued by this rule. Title 24, § 378 of the Code of the District of Columbia (Publication against non-resident; those absent for six months; unknown heirs or devisees; for divorce or in rem; actual service beyond District) is continued by this rule.

Note to Subdivision (f). This rule enlarges to some extent the present rule as to where service may be made. It does not, however, enlarge the jurisdiction of the district courts.

U.S.C., Title 28, §§ 113 [now § 1392] (Suits in States containing more than one district) (where there are two or more defendants residing in different districts), 115 [1946 ed.] (Suits of a local nature), 116 [now § 1392] (Property in different districts in same state), 838 [1946 ed.] (Executions run in all districts of state); U.S.C., Title 47, § 13 (Action for damages against a railroad or telegraph company whose officer or agent in control of a telegraph line refuses or fails to operate such line in a certain manner—"upon any agent of the company found in such state"); U.S.C., Title 49, § 321(c) (Requiring designation of a process agent by interstate motor carriers and

---

New matter is shown in italics; matter to be omitted is lined through

in case of failure so to do, service may be made upon any agent in the state) and similar statutes, allowing the running of process throughout a state, are substantially continued.

U.S.C., Title 15, §§ 5 (Bringing in additional parties) (Sherman Act), 25 (Restraining violations; procedure); U.S.C., Title 28, §§ 44 [now § 2321] (Procedure in certain cases under interstate commerce laws; service of processes of court), 117 [now §§ 754, 1692] (Property in different states in same circuit; jurisdiction of receiver), 839 [now § 2413] (Executions; run in every State and Territory) and similar statutes, providing for the running of process beyond the territorial limits of a state, are expressly continued.

Note to Subdivision (g). With the second sentence compare Equity Rule 15 (Process, by Whom Served).

Note to Subdivision (h). This rule substantially continues U.S.C., Title 28, § 767 [1946 ed.] (Amendment of process).

Advisory Committee's Note to 1963 Amendment

(b) Same: Form. The summons shall be signed by the clerk, be under the seal of the court, contain the name of the court and the names of the parties, be directed to the defendant, state the name and address of the plaintiff's attorney, if any, otherwise the plaintiff's address, and the time within which these rules require the defendant to appear and defend, and shall notify him that in case of his failure to do so judgment by default will be rendered against him for the relief demanded in the complaint. *When, under Rule 4(e), service is made pursuant to a statute or rule of court of a state, the summons, or notice, or order in lieu of summons shall correspond as nearly as may be to that required by the statute or rule.*

(d) Summons: Personal Service.

(4) Upon the United States, by delivering a copy of the summons and of the complaint to the United States attorney for the district in which the action is brought or to an assistant United States attorney or clerical employee designated by the United States attorney in a writing filed with the clerk of the court and by sending a copy of the summons and of the complaint by registered *or certified* mail to the Attorney General of the United States at Washington, District of Columbia, and in any action attacking the validity of an order of an officer or agency of the United States not made a party, by also sending a copy of the summons and of the complaint by registered *or certified* mail to such officer or agency.

(7) Upon a defendant of any class referred to in paragraph (1) or (3) of this subdivision of this rule, it is also sufficient if the summons and complaint are served in the manner prescribed by

---

New matter is shown in italics; matter to be omitted is lined through

any statute of the United States or in the manner prescribed by the law of the state in which the ~~service is made~~ *district court is held* for the service of summons or other like process upon any such defendant in an action brought in the courts of general jurisdiction of that state.

(e) Same: ~~Other Service~~ *Service Upon Party Not Inhabitant of or Found Within State.* Whenever a statute of the United States or an order of court *thereunder* provides for service of a summons, or of a notice, or of an order in lieu of summons upon a party not an inhabitant of or found within the state *in which the district court is held,* service ~~shall~~ *may* be made under the circumstances and in the manner prescribed by the statute~~, rule,~~ or order~~.~~*, or, if there is no provision therein prescribing the manner of service, in a manner stated in this rule. Whenever a statute or rule of court of the state in which the district court is held provides (1) for service of a summons, or of a notice, or of an order in lieu of summons upon a party not an inhabitant of or found within the state, or (2) for service upon or notice to him to appear and respond or defend in an action by reason of the attachment or garnishment or similar seizure of his property located within the state, service may in either case be made under the circumstances and in the manner prescribed in the statute or rule.*

(f) Territorial Limits of Effective Service. All process other than a subpoena may be served anywhere within the territorial limits of the state in which the district court is held, and, when *authorized by* a statute of the United States *or by these rules,* ~~so provides,~~ beyond the territorial limits of that state. *In addition, persons who are brought in as parties pursuant to Rule 13(h) or Rule 14, or as additional parties to a pending action pursuant to Rule 19, may be served in the manner stated in paragraphs (1)–(6) of subdivision (d) of this rule at all places outside the state but within the United States that are not more than 100 miles from the place in which the action is commenced, or to which it is assigned or transferred for trial; and persons required to respond to an order of commitment for civil contempt may be served at the same places. A* subpoena may be served within the territorial limits provided in Rule 45.

(i) *Alternative Provisions for Service in a Foreign Country.*

(1) Manner. When the federal or state law referred to in subdivision (e) of this rule authorizes service upon a party not an inhabitant of or found within the state in which the district court is held, and service is to be effected upon the party in a foreign country, it is also sufficient if service of the summons and complaint is made:

New matter is shown in italics; matter to be omitted is lined through

(A) in the manner prescribed by the law of the foreign country for service in that country in an action in any of its courts of general jurisdiction, or (B) as directed by the foreign authority in response to a letter rogatory, when service in either case is reasonably calculated to give actual notice; or (C) upon an individual, by delivery to him personally, and upon a corporation or partnership or association, by delivery to an officer, a managing or general agent; or (D) by any form of mail, requiring a signed receipt, to be addressed and dispatched by the clerk of the court to the party to be served; or (E) as directed by order of the court. Service under (C) or (E) above may be made by any person who is not a party and is not less than 18 years of age or who is designated by order of the district court or by the foreign court. On request, the clerk shall deliver the summons to the plaintiff for transmission to the person or the foreign court or officer who will make the service.

(2) Return. Proof of service may be made as prescribed by subdivision (g) of this rule, or by the law of the foreign country, or by order of the court. When service is made pursuant to subparagraph (1)(D) of this subdivision, proof of service shall include a receipt signed by the addressee or other evidence of delivery to the addressee satisfactory to the court.

————

Subdivision (b). Under amended subdivision (e) of this rule, an action may be commenced against a nonresident of the State in which the district court is held by complying with State procedures. Frequently the form of the summons or notice required in these cases by State law differs from the Federal form of summons described in present subdivision (b) and exemplified in Form 1. To avoid confusion, the amendment of subdivision (b) states that a form of summons or notice, corresponding "as nearly as may be" to the State form, shall be employed. See also a corresponding amendment of Rule 12(a) with regard to the time to answer.

Subdivision (d)(4). This paragraph, governing service upon the United States, is amended to allow the use of certified mail as an alternative to registered mail for sending copies of the papers to the Attorney General or to a United States officer or agency. *Cf.* N.J. Rule 4:5–2. See also the amendment of Rule 30(f)(1).

Subdivision (d)(7). Formerly a question was raised whether this paragraph, in the context of the rule as a whole, authorized service in original Federal actions pursuant to State statutes permitting service on a State official as a means of bringing a nonresident motorist defendant into court. It was argued in *McCoy v. Siler,* 205 F.2d 498, 501–2 (3d Cir.) (concurring opinion), *cert. denied,* 346 U.S. 872, 74 S.Ct. 120, 98 L.Ed. 380 (1953), that the effective service in those cases occurred not when the State official was served but when notice was given to the defendant outside the State, and that subdivision (f) (Territorial limits of effective service), as then worded, did not authorize out-of-State service. This contention found little support. A considerable number of cases held the service to be good, either by fixing upon the service on the official within the State as the effective service, thus satisfying the wording of subdivision (f) as it then stood, see *Holbrook v. Cafiero,* 18 F.R.D. 218 (D.Md.1955); *Pasternack v. Dalo,* 17 F.R.D. 420 (W.D.Pa.1955); *cf. Super*

New matter is shown in italics;   matter to be omitted is lined through

Prods. Corp. v. Parkin, 20 F.R.D. 377 (S.D.N.Y.1957), or by reading paragraph (7) as not limited by subdivision (f). See *Giffin v. Ensign,* 234 F.2d 307 (3d Cir.1956); 2 *Moore's Federal Practice,* ¶ 4.19 (2d ed. 1948); 1 Barron & Holtzoff, *Federal Practice & Procedure* § 182.1 (Wright ed. 1960); Comment, 27 U. of Chi.L.Rev. 751 (1960). See also *Olberding v. Illinois Central R. R.,* 201 F.2d 582 (6th Cir.), *rev'd on other grounds,* 346 U.S. 338, 74 S.Ct. 83, 98 L.Ed. 39 (1953); *Feinsinger v. Bard,* 195 F.2d 45 (7th Cir. 1952).

An important and growing class of State statutes base personal jurisdiction over nonresidents on the doing of acts or on other contacts within the State, and permit notice to be given the defendant outside the State without any requirement of service on a local State official. See, *e.g.,* Ill.Ann.Stat., c. 110, §§ 16, 17 (Smith–Hurd 1956); Wis.Stat. § 262.06 (1959). This service, employed in original Federal actions pursuant to paragraph (7), has also been held proper. See *Farr & Co. v. Cia. Intercontinental de Nav. de Cuba,* 243 F.2d 342 (2d Cir. 1957); *Kappus v. Western Hills Oil, Inc.,* 24 F.R.D. 123 (E.D.Wis.1959); *Star v. Rogalny,* 162 F.Supp. 181 (E.D.Ill.1957). It has also been held that the clause of paragraph (7) which permits service "in the manner prescribed by the law of the state," etc., is not limited by subdivision (c) requiring that service of all process be made by certain designated persons. See *Farr & Co. v. Cia. Intercontinental de Nav. de Cuba, supra. But cf. Sappia v. Lauro Lines,* 130 F.Supp. 810 (S.D.N.Y.1955).

The salutary results of these cases are intended to be preserved. See paragraph (7), with a clarified reference to State law, and amended subdivisions (e) and (f).

Subdivision (e). For the general relation between subdivisions (d) and (e), see 2 Moore, *supra,* ¶ 4.32.

The amendment of the first sentence inserting the word "thereunder" supports the original intention that the "order of court" must be authorized by a specific United States statute. See 1 Barron & Holtzoff, *supra,* at 731. The clause added at the end of the first sentence expressly adopts the view taken by commentators that, if no manner of service is prescribed in the statute or order, the service may be made in a manner stated in Rule 4. See 2 Moore, *supra,* ¶ 4.32, at 1004; Smit, *International Aspects of Federal Civil Procedure,* 61 Colum.L.Rev. 1031, 1036–39 (1961). *But see* Commentary, 5 Fed. Rules Serv. 791 (1942).

Examples of the statutes to which the first sentence relates are 28 U.S.C. § 2361 (Interpleader; process and procedure); 28 U.S.C. § 1655 (Lien enforcement; absent defendants).

The second sentence, added by amendment, expressly allows resort in original Federal actions to the procedures provided by State law for effecting service on nonresident parties (as well as on domiciliaries not found within the State). See, as illustrative, the discussion under amended subdivision (d)(7) of service pursuant to State nonresident motorist statutes and other comparable State statutes. Of particular interest is the change brought about by the reference in this sentence to State procedures for commencing actions against nonresidents by attachment and the like, accompanied by notice. Although an action commenced in a State court by attachment may be removed to the Federal court if ordinary conditions for removal are satisfied, see 28 U.S.C. § 1450; *Rorick v. Devon Syndicate, Ltd.,* 307 U.S. 299, 59 S.Ct. 877, 83 L.Ed. 1303 (1939); Clark v. Wells, 203 U.S. 164, 27 S.Ct. 43, 51 L.Ed. 138 (1906), there has heretofore been no provision recognized by the courts for commencing an original Federal civil action by attachment. See Currie, *Attachment and Garnishment in the Federal Courts,* 59 Mich.L.Rev. 337 (1961), arguing that this result came about through historical anomaly. Rule 64, which refers to attachment, garnishment, and similar procedures under State law, furnishes only provisional remedies in actions otherwise validly commenced. See *Big Vein Coal Co. v. Read,* 229

New matter is shown in italics; matter to be omitted is lined through

U.S. 31, 33 S.Ct. 694, 57 L.Ed. 1053 (1913); *Davis v. Ensign–Bickford Co.,* 139 F.2d 624 (8th Cir. 1944); 7 *Moore's Federal Practice* ¶ 64.05 (2d ed. 1954); 3 Barron & Holtzoff, *Federal Practice & Procedure* § 1423 (Wright ed. 1958); *but cf.* Note, 13 So.Calif.L.Rev. 361 (1940). The amendment will now permit the institution of original Federal actions against nonresidents through the use of familiar State procedures by which property of these defendants is brought within the custody of the court and some appropriate service is made upon them.

The necessity of satisfying subject-matter jurisdictional requirements and requirements of venue will limit the practical utilization of these methods of effecting service. Within those limits, however, there appears to be no reason for denying plaintiffs means of commencing actions in Federal courts which are generally available in the State courts. See 1 Barron & Holtzoff, *supra,* at 374–80; Nordbye, *Comments on Proposed Amendments to Rules of Civil Procedure for the United States District Courts,* 18 F.R.D. 105, 106 (1956); Note, 34 Corn.L.Q. 103 (1948); Note, 13 So.Calif.L.Rev. 361 (1940).

If the circumstances of a particular case satisfy the applicable Federal law (first sentence of Rule 4(e), as amended) and the applicable State law (second sentence), the party seeking to make the service may proceed under the Federal or the State law, at his option.

See also amended Rule 13(a), and the Advisory Committee's Note thereto.

Subdivision (f). The first sentence is amended to assure the effectiveness of service outside the territorial limits of the State in all the cases in which any of the rules authorize service beyond those boundaries. Besides the preceding provisions of Rule 4, see Rule 71A(d)(3). In addition, the new second sentence of the subdivision permits effective service within a limited area outside the State in certain special situations, namely, to bring in additional parties to a counterclaim or cross-claim (Rule 13(h)), impleaded parties (Rule 14), and indispensable or conditionally necessary parties to a pending action (Rule 19); and to secure compliance with an order of commitment for civil contempt. In those situations effective service can be made at points not more than 100 miles distant from the courthouse in which the action is commenced, or to which it is assigned or transferred for trial.

The bringing in of parties under the 100–mile provision in the limited situations enumerated is designed to promote the objective of enabling the court to determine entire controversies. In the light of present-day facilities for communication and travel, the territorial range of the service allowed, analogous to that which applies to the service of a subpoena under Rule 45(e)(1), can hardly work hardship on the parties summoned. The provision will be especially useful in metropolitan areas spanning more than one State. Any requirements of subject-matter jurisdiction and venue will still have to be satisfied as to the parties brought in, although these requirements will be eased in some instances when the parties can be regarded as "ancillary." See *Pennsylvania R.R. v. Erie Avenue Warehouse Co.,* 5 F.R. Serv. 2d 14a.62, Case 2 (3d Cir. 1962); *Dery v. Wyer,* 265 F.2d 804 (2d Cir. 1959); *United Artists Corp. v. Masterpiece Productions, Inc.,* 221 F.2d 213 (2d Cir. 1955); *Lesnik v. Public Industrials Corp.,* 144 F.2d 968 (2d Cir. 1944); *Vaughn v. Terminal Transp. Co.,* 162 F.Supp. 647 (E.D.Tenn.1957); and compare the fifth paragraph of the Advisory Committee's Note to Rule 4(e), as amended. The amendment is but a moderate extension of the territorial reach of Federal process and has ample practical justification. See 2 Moore, *supra,* § 4.01[13] (Supp.1960); 1 Barron & Holtzoff, *supra,* § 184; Note, 51 Nw.U.L.Rev. 354 (1956). *But cf.* Nordbye, *Comments on Proposed Amendments to Rules of Civil Procedure for the United States District Courts,* 18 F.R.D. 105, 106 (1956).

New matter is shown in italics; matter to be omitted is lined through

As to the need for enlarging the territorial area in which orders of commitment for civil contempt may be served, see *Graber v. Graber,* 93 F.Supp. 281 (D.D.C.1950); *Teele Soap Mfg. Co. v. Pine Tree Products Co., Inc.,* 8 F.Supp. 546 (D.N.H.1934); *Mitchell v. Dexter,* 244 Fed. 926 (1st Cir.1917); *In re Graves,* 29 Fed. 60 (N.D.Iowa 1886).

As to the Court's power to amend subdivisions (e) and (f) as here set forth, see *Mississippi Pub. Corp. v. Murphree,* 326 U.S. 438, 66 S.Ct. 242, 90 L.Ed. 185 (1946).

Subdivision (i). The continual increase of civil litigation having international elements makes it advisable to consolidate, amplify, and clarify the provisions governing service upon parties in foreign countries. See generally Jones, *International Judicial Assistance: Procedural Chaos and a Program for Reform,* 62 Yale L.J. 515 (1953); Longley, *Serving Process, Subpoenas and Other Documents in Foreign Territory,* Proc.A.B.A., Sec.Int'l & Comp.L. 34 (1959); Smit, *International Aspects of Federal Civil Procedure,* 61 Colum.L.Rev. 1031 (1961).

As indicated in the opening lines of new subdivision (i), referring to the provisions of subdivision (e), the authority for effecting foreign service must be found in a statute of the United States or a statute or rule of court of the State in which the district court is held providing in terms or upon proper interpretation for service abroad upon persons not inhabitants of or found within the State. See the Advisory Committee's Note to amended Rule 4(d)(7) and Rule 4(e). For examples of Federal and State statutes expressly authorizing such service, see 8 U.S.C. § 1451(b); 35 U.S.C. §§ 146, 293; Me.Rev.Stat., ch. 22, § 70 (Supp.1961); Minn.Stat. Ann. § 303.13 (1947); N.Y.Veh. & Tfc. Law § 253. Several decisions have construed statutes to permit service in foreign countries, although the matter is not expressly mentioned in the statutes. See, *e.g., Chapman v. Superior Court,* 162 Cal.App.2d 421, 328 P.2d 23 (Dist.Ct.App.1958); *Sperry v. Fliegers,* 194 Misc. 438, 86 N.Y.S.2d 830 (Sup.Ct.1949); *Ewing v. Thompson,* 233 N.C. 564, 65 S.E.2d 17 (1951); *Rushing v. Bush,* 260 S.W.2d 900 (Tex.Ct.Civ.App.1953). Federal and State statutes authorizing service on nonresidents in such terms as to warrant the interpretation that service abroad is permissible include 15 U.S.C. §§ 77v(a), 78aa, 79y; 28 U.S.C. § 1655; 38 U.S.C. § 784(a); Ill.Ann.Stat., c. 110, §§ 16, 17 (Smith–Hurd 1956); Wis.Stat. § 262.06 (1959).

Under subdivisions (e) and (i), when authority to make foreign service is found in a Federal statute or statute or rule of court of a State, it is always sufficient to carry out the service in the manner indicated therein. Subdivision (i) introduces considerable further flexibility by permitting the foreign service and the return thereof to be carried out in any of a number of other alternative ways that are also declared to be sufficient. Other aspects of foreign service continue to be governed by the other provisions of Rule 4. Thus, for example, subdivision (i) effects no change in the form of the summons, or the issuance of separate or additional summons, or the amendment of service.

Service of process beyond the territorial limits of the United States may involve difficulties not encountered in the case of domestic service. Service abroad may be considered by a foreign country to require the performance of judicial, and therefore "sovereign," acts within its territory, which that country may conceive to be offensive to its policy or contrary to its law. See Jones, *supra,* at 537. For example, a person not qualified to serve process according to the law of the foreign country may find himself subject to sanctions if he attempts service therein. See Inter–American Juridical Committee, *Report on Uniformity of Legislation on International Cooperation in Judicial Procedures* 20 (1952). The enforcement of a judgment in the foreign country in which the service was made may be embarrassed or prevented if the service did not comport with the law of that country. See *ibid.*

New matter is shown in italics; matter to be omitted is lined through

One of the purposes of subdivision (i) is to allow accommodation to the policies and procedures of the foreign country. It is emphasized, however, that the attitudes of foreign countries vary considerably and that the question of recognition of United States judgments abroad is complex. Accordingly, if enforcement is to be sought in the country of service, the foreign law should be examined before a choice is made among the methods of service allowed by subdivision (i).

Subdivision (i)(1). Subparagraph (a) of paragraph (1), permitting service by the method prescribed by the law of the foreign country for service on a person in that country in a civil action in any of its courts of general jurisdiction, provides an alternative that is likely to create least objection in the place of service and also is likely to enhance the possibilities of securing ultimate enforcement of the judgment abroad. See *Report on Uniformity of Legislation on International Cooperation in Judicial Procedures, supra.*

In certain foreign countries service in aid of litigation pending in other countries can lawfully be accomplished only upon request to the foreign court, which in turn directs the service to be made. In many countries this has long been a customary way of accomplishing the service. See *In re Letters Rogatory out of First Civil Court of City of Mexico,* 261 Fed. 652 (S.D.N.Y.1919); Jones, *supra,* at 543; Comment, 44 Colum.L.Rev. 72 (1944); Note, 58 Yale L.J. 1193 (1949). Subparagraph (B) of paragraph (1), referring to a letter rogatory, validates this method. A proviso, applicable to this subparagraph and the preceding one, requires, as a safeguard, that the service made shall be reasonably calculated to give actual notice of the proceedings to the party. See *Milliken v. Meyer,* 311 U.S. 457, 61 S.Ct. 339, 85 L.Ed. 278 (1940).

Subparagraph (C) of paragraph (1), permitting foreign service by personal delivery on individuals and corporations, partnerships, and associations, provides for a manner of service that is not only traditionally preferred, but also is most likely to lead to actual notice. Explicit provision for this manner of service was thought desirable because a number of Federal and State statutes permitting foreign service do not specifically provide for service by personal delivery abroad, see *e.g.,* 35 U.S.C. §§ 146, 293; 46 U.S.C. § 1292; Calif.Ins.Code § 1612; N.Y.Veh. & Tfc. Law § 253, and it also may be unavailable under the law of the country in which the service is made.

Subparagraph (D) of paragraph (1), permitting service by certain types of mail, affords a manner of service that is inexpensive and expeditious, and requires a minimum of activity within the foreign country. Several statutes specifically provide for service in a foreign country by mail, *e.g.,* Hawaii Rev. Laws §§ 230–31, 230–32 (1955); Minn.Stat.Ann. § 303.13 (1947); N.Y.Civ.Prac.Act, § 229–b; N.Y.Veh. & Tfc. Law § 253, and it has been sanctioned by the courts even in the absence of statutory provision specifying that form of service. *Zurini v. United States,* 189 F.2d 722 (8th Cir. 1951); *United States v. Cardillo,* 135 F.Supp. 798 (W.D.Pa.1955); *Autogiro Co. v. Kay Gyroplanes, Ltd.,* 55 F.Supp. 919 (D.D.C.1944). Since the reliability of postal service may vary from country to country, service by mail is proper only when it is addressed to the party to be served and a form of mail requiring a signed receipt is used. An additional safeguard is provided by the requirement that the mailing be attended to by the clerk of the court. See also the provisions of paragraph (2) of this subdivision (i) regarding proof of service by mail.

Under the applicable law it may be necessary, when the defendant is an infant or incompetent person, to deliver the summons and complaint to a guardian, committee, or similar fiduciary. In such a case it would be advisable to make service under subparagraph (A), (B), or (E).

New matter is shown in italics; matter to be omitted is lined through

Subparagraph (E) of paragraph (1) adds flexibility by permitting the court by order to tailor the manner of service to fit the necessities of a particular case or the peculiar requirements of the law of the country in which the service is to be made. A similar provision appears in a number of statutes, *e.g.*, 35 U.S.C. §§ 146, 293; 38 U.S.C. § 784(a); 46 U.S.C. § 1292.

The next-to-last sentence of paragraph (1) permits service under (C) and (E) to be made by any person who is not a party and is not less than 18 years of age or who is designated by court order or by the foreign court. *Cf.* Rule 45(c); N.Y.Civ.Prac.Act §§ 233, 235. This alternative increases the possibility that the plaintiff will be able to find a process server who can proceed unimpeded in the foreign country; it also may improve the chances of enforcing the judgment in the country of service. Especially is this alternative valuable when authority for the foreign service is found in a statute or rule of court that limits the group of eligible process servers to designated officials or special appointees who, because directly connected with another "sovereign," may be particularly offensive to the foreign country. See generally Smit, *supra*, at ___-___. When recourse is had to subparagraph (A) or (B) the identity of the process server always will be determined by the law of the foreign country in which the service is made.

The last sentence of paragraph (1) sets forth an alternative manner for the issuance and transmission of the summons for service. After obtaining the summons from the clerk, the plaintiff must ascertain the best manner of delivering the summons and complaint to the person, court, or officer who will make the service. Thus the clerk is not burdened with the task of determining who is permitted to serve process under the law of a particular country or the appropriate governmental or nongovernmental channel for forwarding a letter rogatory. Under (D), however, the papers must always be posted by the clerk.

Subdivision (i)(2). When service is made in a foreign country, paragraph (2) permits methods for proof of service in addition to those prescribed by subdivision (g). Proof of service in accordance with the law of the foreign country is permitted because foreign process servers, unaccustomed to the form or the requirement of return of service prevalent in the United States, have on occasion been unwilling to execute the affidavit required by Rule 4(g). See Jones, *supra*, at 537; Longley, *supra*, at 35. As a corollary of the alternate manner of service in subdivision (i)(1)(E), proof of service as directed by order of the court is permitted. The special provision for proof of service by mail is intended as an additional safeguard when that method is used. On the type of evidence of delivery that may be satisfactory to a court in lieu of a signed receipt, see *Aero Associates, Inc. v. La Metropolitana*, 183 F.Supp. 357 (S.D.N.Y.1960).

Advisory Committee's Note to 1993 Amendment

Rule 4. ~~Process~~ *Summons*

(a) **Summons: Issuance.** ~~Upon the filing of the complaint the clerk shall forthwith issue a summons and deliver the summons to the plaintiff or the plaintiff's attorney, who shall be responsible for prompt service of the summons and a copy of the complaint. Upon request of the plaintiff separate or additional summons shall issue against any defendants.~~

New matter is shown in italics; matter to be omitted is lined through

(b) ~~Same:~~ Form. The summons shall be signed by the clerk, ~~be under~~ *bear* the seal of the court, ~~contain the name of~~ *identify* the court and ~~the names of~~ the parties, be directed to the defendant, *and* state the name and address of the plaintiff's attorney, ~~if any, otherwise the plaintiff's address~~ *or, if unrepresented, of the plaintiff, and. It shall also state* the time within which ~~these rules require~~ the defendant ~~to~~ *must* appear and defend, and ~~shall~~ notify the defendant that ~~in case of the defendant's~~ failure to do so *will result in a* judgment by default ~~will be rendered~~ against the defendant for the relief demanded in the complaint. ~~When, under Rule 4(e), service is made pursuant to a statute or rule of court of a state, the summons, or notice, or order in lieu of summons shall correspond as nearly as may be to that required by the statute or rule.~~ *The court may allow a summons to be amended.*

*(b) **Issuance.** Upon or after filing the complaint, the plaintiff may present a summons to the clerk for signature and seal. If the summons is in proper form, the clerk shall sign, seal, and issue it to the plaintiff for service on the defendant. A summons, or a copy of the summons if addressed to multiple defendants, shall be issued for each defendant to be served.*

(c) Service *with Complaint; by Whom Made.*

(1) ~~Process, other than a subpoena or a summons and complaint, shall be served by a United States marshal or deputy United States marshal, or by a person specially appointed for that purpose.~~ *A summons shall be served together with a copy of the complaint. The plaintiff is responsible for service of a summons and complaint within the time allowed under subdivision (m) and shall furnish the person effecting service with the necessary copies of the summons and complaint.*

(2) ~~(A) A summons and complaint shall, except as provided in subparagraphs (B) and (C) of this paragraph, be served~~ *Service may be effected* by any person who is not a party and *who* is ~~not less than~~ *at least* 18 years of age. *At the request of the plaintiff, however, the court may direct that service be effected by a United States marshal, deputy United States marshal, or other person or officer specially appointed by the court for that purpose. Such an appointment must be made when the plaintiff is*

~~(B) A summons and complaint shall, at the request of the party seeking service or such party's attorney, be served by a United States marshal or deputy United States marshal, or by a person specially appointed by the court for that purpose, only~~

~~(i) on behalf of a party~~ authorized to proceed in forma pauperis pursuant to ~~Title 28,~~ U.S.C. § 1915, or ~~of a seaman~~ *is*

New matter is shown in italics; matter to be omitted is lined through

authorized to proceed *as a seaman* under ~~Title~~ 28~~,~~ U.S.C. § 1916~~,~~.

~~(ii) on behalf of the United States or an officer or agency of the United States, or~~

~~(iii) pursuant to an order issued by the court stating that a United States marshal or deputy United States marshal, or a person specially appointed for that purpose, is required to serve the summons and complaint in order that service be properly effected in that particular action.~~

~~(C) A summons and complaint may be served upon a defendant of any class referred to in paragraph (1) or (3) of subdivision (d) of this rule~~

~~(i) pursuant to the law of the State in which the district court is held for the service of summons or other like process upon such defendant in an action brought in the courts of general jurisdiction of that State, or~~

~~(ii) by mailing a copy of the summons and of the complaint (by first class mail, postage prepaid) to the person to be served, together with two copies of a notice and acknowledgment conforming substantially to form 18-A and a return envelope, postage prepaid, addressed to the sender. If no acknowledgment of service under this subdivision of this rule is received by the sender within 20 days after the date of mailing, service of such summons and complaint shall be made under subparagraph (A) or (B) of this paragraph in the manner prescribed by subdivision (d)(1) or (d)(3).~~

~~(D) Unless good cause is shown for not doing so the court shall order the payment of the costs of personal service by the person served if such person does not complete and return within 20 days after mailing, the notice and acknowledgment of receipt of summons.~~

~~(E) The notice and acknowledgment of receipt of summons and complaint shall be executed under oath or affirmation.~~

~~(3) The court shall freely make special appointments to serve summonses and complaints under paragraph (2)(B) of this subdivision of this rule and all other process under paragraph (1) of this subdivision of this rule.~~

(d) Summons and Complaint: Person to be Served. *Waiver of Service; Duty to Save Costs of Service; Request to Waive.* ~~The summons and complaint shall be served together. The plaintiff shall furnish the person making service with such copies as are necessary. Service shall be made as follows:~~

New matter is shown in italics; matter to be omitted is lined through

(1) A defendant who waives service of a summons does not thereby waive any objection to the venue or to the jurisdiction of the court over the person of the defendant.

(2) An individual, corporation, or association that is subject to service under subdivision (e), (f), or (h) and that receives notice of an action in the manner provided in this paragraph has a duty to avoid unnecessary costs of serving the summons. To avoid costs, the plaintiff may notify such a defendant of the commencement of the action and request that the defendant waive service of a summons. The notice and request

> *(A) shall be in writing and shall be addressed directly to the defendant, if an individual, or else to an officer or managing or general agent (or other agent authorized by appointment or law to receive service of process) of a defendant subject to service under subdivision (h);*

> *(B) shall be dispatched through first-class mail or other reliable means;*

> *(C) shall be accompanied by a copy of the complaint and shall identify the court in which it has been filed;*

> *(D) shall inform the defendant, by means of a text prescribed in an official form promulgated pursuant to Rule 84, of the consequences of compliance and of a failure to comply with the request;*

> *(E) shall set forth the date on which the request is sent;*

> *(F) shall allow the defendant a reasonable time to return the waiver, which shall be at least 30 days from the date on which the request is sent, or 60 days from that date if the defendant is addressed outside any judicial district of the United States; and*

> *(G) shall provide the defendant with an extra copy of the notice and request, as well as a prepaid means of compliance in writing.*

If a defendant located within the United States fails to comply with a request for waiver made by a plaintiff located within the United States, the court shall impose the costs subsequently incurred in effecting service on the defendant unless good cause for the failure be shown.

(3) A defendant that, before being served with process, timely returns a waiver so requested is not required to serve an answer to the complaint until 60 days after the date on which the request for waiver of service was sent, or 90 days after that date if the defendant was addressed outside any judicial district of the United States.

New matter is shown in italics; matter to be omitted is lined through

(4) When the plaintiff files a waiver of service with the court, the action shall proceed, except as provided in paragraph (3), as if a summons and complaint had been served at the time of filing the waiver, and no proof of service shall be required.

(5) The costs to be imposed on a defendant under paragraph (2) for failure to comply with a request to waive service of a summons shall include the costs subsequently incurred in effecting service under subdivision (e), (f), or (h), together with the costs, including a reasonable attorney's fee, of any motion required to collect the costs of service.

(e~1~) *Service Upon Individuals Within a Judicial District of the United States. Unless otherwise provided by federal law,* service ~U~u~pon~ an individual *from whom a waiver has not been obtained and filed,* other than an infant or an incompetent person, *may be effected in any judicial district of the United States:*

(1) pursuant to the law of the state in which the district court is located, or in which service is effected, for the service of a summons upon the defendant in an action brought in the courts of general jurisdiction of the State; or

(2) by delivering a copy of the summons and of the complaint to the individual personally or by leaving copies thereof at the individual's dwelling house or usual place of abode with some person of suitable age and discretion then residing therein or by delivering a copy of the summons and of the complaint to an agent authorized by appointment or by law to receive service of process.

(f) Service Upon Individuals in a Foreign Country. Unless otherwise provided by federal law, service upon an individual from whom a waiver has not been obtained and filed, other than an infant or an incompetent person, may be effected in a place not within any judicial district of the United States:

(1) by any internationally agreed means reasonably calculated to give notice, such as those means authorized by the Hague Convention on the Service Abroad of Judicial and Extrajudicial Documents; or

(2) if there is no internationally agreed means of service or the applicable international agreement allows other means of service, provided that service is reasonably calculated to give notice:

(A) in the manner prescribed by the law of the foreign country for service in that country in an action in any of its courts of general jurisdiction; or

---

New matter is shown in italics; matter to be omitted is lined through

(B) as directed by the foreign authority in response to a letter rogatory or letter of request; or

(C) unless prohibited by the law of the foreign country, by

(i) delivery to the individual personally of a copy of the summons and the complaint; or

(ii) any form of mail requiring a signed receipt, to be addressed and dispatched by the clerk of the court to the party to be served; or

(3) by other means not prohibited by international agreement as may be directed by the court.

(g2) Service Upon Infants and Incompetent Persons. Service uUpon an infant or an incompetent person, by serving the summons and complaint in a judicial district of the United States shall be effected in the manner prescribed by the law of the state in which the service is made for the service of summons or other like process upon any such defendant in an action brought in the courts of general jurisdiction of that state. Service upon an infant or an incompetent person in a place not within any judicial district of the United States shall be effected in the manner prescribed by paragraph (2)(A) or (2)(B) of subdivision (f) or by such means as the court may direct.

(h3) Service Upon Corporations and Associations. Unless otherwise provided by federal law, service uUpon a domestic or foreign corporation or upon a partnership or other unincorporated association which that is subject to suit under a common name, and from which a waiver of service has not been obtained and filed, shall be effected:

(1) in a judicial district of the United States in the manner prescribed for individuals by subdivision (e)(1), or by delivering a copy of the summons and of the complaint to an officer, a managing or general agent, or to any other agent authorized by appointment or by law to receive service of process and, if the agent is one authorized by statute to receive service and the statute so requires, by also mailing a copy to the defendant. , or

(2) in a place not within any judicial district of the United States in any manner prescribed for individuals by subdivision (f) except personal delivery as provided in paragraph (2)(C)(i) thereof.

(i4) Service Upon the United States, and Its Agencies, Corporations, or Officers.

(1) Service uUpon the United States, shall be effected

New matter is shown in italics; matter to be omitted is lined through

(A) by delivering a copy of the summons and of the complaint to the United States attorney for the district in which the action is brought or to an assistant United States attorney or clerical employee designated by the United States attorney in a writing filed with the clerk of the court *or by sending a copy of the summons and of the complaint by registered or certified mail addressed to the civil process clerk at the office of the United States attorney* and

(B) by *also* sending a copy of the summons and of the complaint by registered or certified mail to the Attorney General of the United States at Washington, District of Columbia, and

(C) in any action attacking the validity of an order of an officer or agency of the United States not made a party, by also sending a copy of the summons and of the complaint by registered or certified mail to ~~such~~ *the* officer or agency.

(5̶2) *Service* ~~U~~*u*pon an officer, ~~or~~ agency, *or corporation* of the United States~~,~~ *shall be effected* by serving the United States *in the manner prescribed by paragraph (1) of this subdivision* and by *also* sending a copy of the summons and of the complaint by registered or certified mail to ~~such~~ *the* officer, ~~or~~ agency, *or corporation.* ~~If the agency is a corporation the copy shall be delivered as provided in paragraph (3) of this subdivision of this rule.~~

(3) The court shall allow a reasonable time for service of process under this subdivision for the purpose of curing the failure to serve multiple officers, agencies, or corporations of the United States if the plaintiff has effected service on either the United States attorney or the Attorney General of the United States.

(j̶6̶) *Service Upon Foreign, State, or Local Governments.*

(1) Service upon a foreign state or a political subdivision, agency, or instrumentality thereof shall be effected pursuant to 28 U.S.C. § 1608.

(2) *Service* ~~u~~*U*pon a state, ~~or~~ municipal corporation, or other governmental organization ~~thereof~~ subject to suit~~,~~ *shall be effected* by delivering a copy of the summons and of the complaint to ~~the~~ *its* chief executive officer ~~thereof~~ or by serving the summons and complaint in the manner prescribed by the law of that state for the service of summons or other like process upon any such defendant.

~~**(e) Summons: Service Upon Party Not Inhabitant of or Found Within State.** Whenever a statute of the United States or an order of court thereunder provides for service of a summons, or of a notice, or of an order in lieu of summons upon a party not an inhabitant of or found within the state in which the district court is~~

New matter is shown in italics; matter to be omitted is lined through

~~held, service may be made under the circumstances and in the manner prescribed by the statute or order, or, if there is no provision therein prescribing the manner of service, in a manner stated in this rule. Whenever a statute or rule of court of the state in which the district court is held provides (1) for service of a summons, or of a notice, or of an order in lieu of summons upon a party not an inhabitant of or found within the state, or (2) for service upon or notice to such a party to appear and respond or defend in an action by reason of the attachment or garnishment or similar seizure of the party's property located within the state, service may in either case be made under the circumstances and in the manner prescribed in the statute or rule.~~

(*fk*) Territorial Limits of Effective Service. ~~All process other than a subpoena may be served anywhere within the territorial limits of the state in which the district court is held, and, when authorized by a statute of the United States or by these rules, beyond the territorial limits of that state. In addition, persons who are brought in as parties pursuant to Rule 14, or as additional parties to a pending action or a counterclaim or cross claim therein pursuant to Rule 19, may be served in the manner stated in paragraphs (1)–(6) of subdivision (d) of this rule at all places outside the state but within the United States that are not more than 100 miles from the place in which the action is commenced, or to which it is assigned or transferred for trial; and persons required to respond to an order of commitment for civil contempt may be served at the same places. A subpoena may be served within the territorial limits provided in Rule 45.~~

(1) Service of a summons or filing a waiver of service is effective to establish jurisdiction over the person of a defendant

(A) who could be subjected to the jurisdiction of a court of general jurisdiction in the state in which the district court is located, or

(B) who is a party joined under Rule 14 or Rule 19 and is served at a place within a judicial district of the United States and not more than 100 miles from the place from which the summons issues, or

(C) who is subject to the federal interpleader jurisdiction under 28 U.S.C. § 1335, or

(D) when authorized by a statute of the United States.

(2) If the exercise of jurisdiction is consistent with the Constitution and laws of the United States, serving a summons or filing a waiver of service is also effective, with respect to claims arising under federal law, to establish personal jurisdiction over the person

---

New matter is shown in italics; matter to be omitted is lined through

of any defendant who is not subject to the jurisdiction of the courts of general jurisdiction of any state.

(g~l~) Return. *Proof of Service.* *If service is not waived, t*~T~he person ~serving the process~ *effecting* service shall make proof ~of service~ thereof to the court ~promptly and in any event within the time during which the person served must respond to the process.~ If service is made by a person other than a United States marshal or deputy United States marshal, ~such~ *the* person shall make affidavit thereof. *Proof of service in a place not within any judicial district of the United States shall, if effected under paragraph (1) of subdivision (f), be made pursuant to the applicable treaty or convention, and shall, if effected under paragraph (2) or (3) thereof, include a receipt signed by the addressee or other evidence of delivery to the addressee satisfactory to the court.* ~If service is made under subdivision (c)(2)(C)(ii) of this rule, return shall be made by the sender's filing with the court the acknowledgment received pursuant to such subdivision.~ Failure to make proof of service does not affect the validity of the service. *The court may allow proof of service to be amended.*

(h) Amendment. ~At any time in its discretion and upon such terms as it deems just, the court may allow any process or proof of service thereof to be amended, unless it clearly appears that material prejudice would result to the substantial rights of the party against whom the process issued.~

(i) ~Alternative Provisions for Service in a Foreign Country.~

~(1) Manner. When the federal or state law referred to in subdivision (e) of this rule authorizes service upon a party not an inhabitant of or found within the state in which the district court is held, and service is to be effected upon the party in a foreign country, it is also sufficient if service of the summons and complaint is made: (A) in the manner prescribed by the law of the foreign country for service in that country in an action in any of its courts of general jurisdiction; or (B) as directed by the foreign authority in response to a letter rogatory, when service in either case is reasonably calculated to give actual notice; or (C) upon an individual, by delivery to the individual personally, and upon a corporation or partnership or association, by delivery to an officer, a managing or general agent; or (D) by any form of mail, requiring a signed receipt, to be addressed and dispatched by the clerk of the court to the party to be served; or (E) as directed by order of the court. Service under (C) or (E) above may be made by any person who is not a party and is not less than 18 years of age or who is designated by order of the district court or by the foreign court. On~

New matter is shown in italics; matter to be omitted is lined through

210

request, the clerk shall deliver the summons to the plaintiff for transmission to the person or the foreign court or officer who will make the service.

(2) Return. Proof of service may be made as prescribed by subdivision (g) of this rule, or by the law of the foreign country, or by order of the court. When service is made pursuant to subparagraph (1)(D) of this subdivision, proof of service shall include a receipt signed by the addressee or other evidence of delivery to the addressee satisfactory to the court.

(~~jm~~) ~~Summons:~~ Time Limit for Service. If ~~a~~ service of the summons and complaint is not made upon a defendant within 120 days after the filing of the complaint ~~and the party on whose behalf such service was required cannot show good cause why such service was not made within that period~~, the *court* ~~action shall be dismissed as to that defendant without prejudice~~, upon ~~the court's~~ *motion or on its* own initiative ~~with~~ *after* notice to ~~such party or upon motion~~ *the plaintiff, shall dismiss the action without prejudice as to that defendant or direct that service be effected within a specified time; provided that if the plaintiff shows good cause for the failure, the court shall extend the time for service for an appropriate period.* This subdivision ~~shall~~ *does* not apply to service in a foreign country pursuant to subdivision (~~i~~*f*) *or (j)(1)* ~~of this rule~~.

(n) Seizure of Property; Service of Summons Not Feasible.

(1) If a statute of the United States so provides, the court may assert jurisdiction over property. Notice to claimants of the property shall then be sent in the manner provided by the statute or by service of a summons under this rule.

(2) Upon a showing that personal jurisdiction over a defendant cannot, in the district where the action is brought, be obtained with reasonable efforts by service of summons in any manner authorized by this rule, the court may assert jurisdiction over any of the defendant's assets found within the district by seizing the assets under the circumstances and in the manner provided by the law of the state in which the district court is located.

SPECIAL NOTE: Mindful of the constraints of the Rules Enabling Act, the Committee calls the attention of the Supreme Court and Congress to new subdivision (k)(2). Should this limited extension of service be disapproved, the Committee nevertheless recommends adoption of the balance of the rule, with subdivision (k)(1) becoming simply subdivision (k). The Committee Notes would be revised to eliminate references to subdivision (k)(2).

New matter is shown in italics; matter to be omitted is lined through

Purposes of Revision. The general purpose of this revision is to facilitate the service of the summons and complaint. The revised rule explicitly authorizes a means for service of the summons and complaint on any defendant. While the methods of service so authorized always provide appropriate notice to persons against whom claims are made, effective service under this rule does not assure that personal jurisdiction has been established over the defendant served.

First, the revised rule authorizes the use of any means of service provided by the law not only of the forum state, but also of the state in which a defendant is served, unless the defendant is a minor or incompetent.

Second, the revised rule clarifies and enhances the cost-saving practice of securing the assent of the defendant to dispense with actual service of the summons and complaint. This practice was introduced to the rule in 1983 by an act of Congress authorizing "service-by-mail," a procedure that effects economic service with cooperation of the defendant. Defendants that magnify costs of service by requiring expensive service not necessary to achieve full notice of an action brought against them are required to bear the wasteful costs. This provision is made available in actions against defendants who cannot be served in the districts in which the actions are brought.

Third, the revision reduces the hazard of commencing an action against the United States or its officers, agencies, and corporations. A party failing to effect service on all the offices of the United States as required by the rule is assured adequate time to cure defects in service.

Fourth, the revision calls attention to the important effect of the Hague Convention and other treaties bearing on service of documents in foreign countries and favors the use of internationally agreed means of service. In some respects, these treaties have facilitated service in foreign countries but are not fully known to the bar.

Finally, the revised rule extends the reach of federal courts to impose jurisdiction over the person of all defendants against whom federal law claims are made and who can be constitutionally subjected to the jurisdiction of the courts of the United States. The present territorial limits on the effectiveness of service to subject a defendant to the jurisdiction of the court over the defendant's person are retained for all actions in which there is a state in which personal jurisdiction can be asserted consistently with state law and the Fourteenth Amendment. A new provision enables district courts to exercise jurisdiction, if permissible under the Constitution and not precluded by statute, when a federal claim is made against a defendant not subject to the jurisdiction of any single state.

The revised rule is reorganized to make its provisions more accessible to those not familiar with all of them. Additional subdivisions in this rule allow for more captions; several overlaps among subdivisions are eliminated; and several disconnected provisions are removed, to be relocated in a new Rule 4.1.

The Caption of the Rule. Prior to this revision, Rule 4 was entitled "Process" and applied to the service of not only the summons but also other process as well, although these are not covered by the revised rule. Service of process in eminent domain proceedings is governed by Rule 71A. Service of a subpoena is governed by Rule 45, and service of papers such as orders, motions, notices, pleadings, and other documents is governed by Rule 5.

The revised rule is entitled "Summons" and applies only to that form of legal process. Unless service of the summons is waived, a summons must be served whenever a person is joined as a party against whom a claim is made. Those few

---

New matter is shown in italics; matter to be omitted is lined through

provisions of the former rule which relate specifically to service of process other than a summons are relocated in Rule 4.1 in order to simplify the text of this rule.

Subdivision (a). Revised subdivision (a) contains most of the language of the former subdivision (b). The second sentence of the former subdivision (b) has been stricken, so that the federal court summons will be the same in all cases. Few states now employ distinctive requirements of form for a summons and the applicability of such a requirement in federal court can only serve as a trap for an unwary party or attorney. A sentence is added to this subdivision authorizing an amendment of a summons. This sentence replaces the rarely used former subdivision 4(h). *See* 4A Wright & Miller, *Federal Practice and Procedure* § 1131 (2d ed. 1987).

Subdivision (b). Revised subdivision (b) replaces the former subdivision (a). The revised text makes clear that the responsibility for filling in the summons falls on the plaintiff, not the clerk of the court. If there are multiple defendants, the plaintiff may secure issuance of a summons for each defendant, or may serve copies of a single original bearing the names of multiple defendants if the addressee of the summons is effectively identified.

Subdivision (c). Paragraph (1) of revised subdivision (c) retains language from the former subdivision (d)(1). Paragraph (2) retains language from the former subdivision (a), and adds an appropriate caution regarding the time limit for service set forth in subdivision (m).

The 1983 revision of Rule 4 relieved the marshals' offices of much of the burden of serving the summons. Subdivision (c) eliminates the requirement for service by the marshal's office in actions in which the party seeking service is the United States. The United States, like other civil litigants, is now permitted to designate any person who is 18 years of age and not a party to serve its summons.

The court remains obligated to appoint a marshal, a deputy, or some other person to effect service of a summons in two classes of cases specified by statute: actions brought *in forma pauperis* or by a seaman. 28 U.S.C. §§ 1915, 1916. The court also retains discretion to appoint a process server on motion of a party. If a law enforcement presence appears to be necessary or advisable to keep the peace, the court should appoint a marshal or deputy or other official person to make the service. The Department of Justice may also call upon the Marshals Service to perform services in actions brought by the United States. 28 U.S.C. § 651.

Subdivision (d). This text is new, but is substantially derived from the former subdivisions (c)(2)(C) and (D), added to the rule by Congress in 1983. The aims of the provision are to eliminate the costs of service of a summons on many parties and to foster cooperation among adversaries and counsel. The rule operates to impose upon the defendant those costs that could have been avoided if the defendant had cooperated reasonably in the manner prescribed. This device is useful in dealing with defendants who are furtive, who reside in places not easily reached by process servers, or who are outside the United States and can be served only at substantial and unnecessary expense. Illustratively, there is no useful purpose achieved by requiring a plaintiff to comply with all the formalities of service in a foreign country, including costs of translation, when suing a defendant manufacturer, fluent in English, whose products are widely distributed in the United States. *See Bankston v. Toyota Motor Corp.,* 889 F.2d 172 (8th Cir.1989).

The former text described this process as service-by-mail. This language misled some plaintiffs into thinking that service could be effected by mail without the affirmative cooperation of the defendant. *E.g., Gulley v. Mayo Foundation,* 886 F.2d 161 (8th Cir.1989). It is more accurate to describe the communication sent to the defendant as a request for a waiver of formal service.

New matter is shown in italics; matter to be omitted is lined through

The request for waiver of service may be sent only to defendants subject to service under subdivision (e), (f), or (h). The United States is not expected to waive service for the reason that its mail receiving facilities are inadequate to assure that the notice is actually received by the correct person in the Department of Justice. The same principle is applied to agencies, corporations, and officers of the United States and to other governments and entities subject to service under subdivision (j). Moreover, there are policy reasons why governmental entities should not be confronted with the potential for bearing costs of service in cases in which they ultimately prevail. Infants or incompetent persons likewise are not called upon to waive service because, due to their presumed inability to understand the request and its consequences, they must generally be served through fiduciaries.

It was unclear whether the former rule authorized mailing of a request for "acknowledgement of service" to defendants outside the forum state. *See* 1 R. Casad, *Jurisdiction in Civil Actions* (2d Ed.) 5–29, 30 (1991) and cases cited. But, as Professor Casad observed, there was no reason not to employ this device in an effort to obtain service outside the state, and there are many instances in which it was in fact so used, with respect both to defendants within the United States and to defendants in other countries.

The opportunity for waiver has distinct advantages to a foreign defendant. By waiving service, the defendant can reduce the costs that may ultimately be taxed against it if unsuccessful in the lawsuit, including the sometimes substantial expense of translation that may be wholly unnecessary for defendants fluent in English. Moreover, a foreign defendant that waives service is afforded substantially more time to defend against the action than if it had been formally served: under Rule 12, a defendant ordinarily has only 20 days after service in which to file its answer or raise objections by motion, but by signing a waiver it is allowed 90 days after the date the request for waiver was mailed in which to submit its defenses. Because of the additional time needed for mailing and the unreliability of some foreign mail services, a period of 60 days (rather than the 30 days required for domestic transmissions) is provided for a return of a waiver sent to a foreign country.

It is hoped that, since transmission of the notice and waiver forms is a private nonjudicial act, does not purport to effect service, and is not accompanied by any summons or directive from a court, use of the procedure will not offend foreign sovereignties, even those that have withheld their assent to formal service by mail or have objected to the "service-by-mail" provisions of the former rule. Unless the addressee consents, receipt of the request under the revised rule does not give rise to any obligation to answer the lawsuit, does not provide a basis for default judgment, and does not suspend the statute of limitations in those states where the period continues to run until service. Nor are there any adverse consequences to a foreign defendant, since the provisions for shifting the expense of service to a defendant that declines to waive service apply only if the plaintiff and defendant are both located in the United States.

With respect to a defendant located in a foreign country like the United Kingdom, which accepts documents in English, whose Central Authority acts promptly in effecting service, and whose policies discourage its residents from waiving formal service, there will be little reason for a plaintiff to send the notice and request under subdivision (d) rather than use convention methods. On the other hand, the procedure offers significant potential benefits to a plaintiff when suing a defendant that, though fluent in English, is located in a country where, as a condition to formal service under a convention, documents must be translated into another language or where formal service will be otherwise costly or time-consuming.

New matter is shown in italics; matter to be omitted is lined through

Paragraph (1) is explicit that a timely waiver of service of a summons does not prejudice the right of a defendant to object by means of a motion authorized by Rule 12(b)(2) to the absence of jurisdiction over the defendant's person, or to assert other defenses that may be available. The only issues eliminated are those involving the sufficiency of the summons or the sufficiency of the method by which it is served.

Paragraph (2) states what the present rule implies: the defendant has a duty to avoid costs associated with the service of a summons not needed to inform the defendant regarding the commencement of an action. The text of the rule also sets forth the requirements for a Notice and Request for Waiver sufficient to put the cost-shifting provision in place. These requirements are illustrated in Forms 1A and 1B, which replace the former Form 18–A.

Paragraph (2)(A) is explicit that a request for waiver of service by a corporate defendant must be addressed to a person qualified to receive service. The general mail rooms of large organizations cannot be required to identify the appropriate individual recipient for an institutional summons.

Paragraph (2)(B) permits the use of alternatives to the United States mails in sending the Notice and Request. While private messenger services or electronic communications may be more expensive than the mail, they may be equally reliable and on occasion more convenient to the parties. Especially with respect to transmissions to foreign countries, alternative means may be desirable, for in some countries facsimile transmission is the most efficient and economical means of communication. If electronic means such as facsimile transmission are employed, the sender should maintain a record of the transmission to assure proof of transmission if receipt is denied, but a party receiving such a transmission has a duty to cooperate and cannot avoid liability for the resulting cost of formal service if the transmission is prevented at the point of receipt.

A defendant failing to comply with a request for waiver shall be given an opportunity to show good cause for the failure, but sufficient cause should be rare. It is not a good cause for failure to waive service that the claim is unjust or that the court lacks jurisdiction. Sufficient cause not to shift the cost of service would exist, however, if the defendant did not receive the request or was insufficiently literate in English to understand it. It should be noted that the provisions for shifting the cost of service apply only if the plaintiff and the defendant are both located in the United States, and accordingly a foreign defendant need not show "good cause" for its failure to waive service.

Paragraph (3) extends the time for answer if, before being served with process, the defendant waives formal service. The extension is intended to serve as an inducement to waive service and to assure that a defendant will not gain any delay by declining to waive service and thereby causing the additional time needed to effect service. By waiving service, a defendant is not called upon to respond to the complaint until 60 days from the date the notice was sent to it—90 days if the notice was sent to a foreign country—rather than within the 20 day period from date of service specified in Rule 12.

Paragraph (4) clarifies the effective date of service when service is waived; the provision is needed to resolve an issue arising when applicable law requires service of process to toll the statute of limitations. *E.g., Morse v. Elmira Country Club,* 752 F.2d 35 (2d Cir.1984). *Cf. Walker v. Armco Steel Corp.,* 446 U.S. 740 (1980).

The provisions in former subdivision (c)(2)(C)(ii) of this rule may have been misleading to some parties. Some plaintiffs, not reading the rule carefully, supposed that receipt by the defendant of the mailed complaint had the effect both of establishing the jurisdiction of the court over the defendant's person and of tolling the statute of limitations in actions in which service of the summons is required to

New matter is shown in italics; matter to be omitted is lined through

toll the limitations period. The revised rule is clear that, if the waiver is not returned and filed, the limitations period under such a law is not tolled and the action will not otherwise proceed until formal service of process is effected.

Some state limitations laws may toll an otherwise applicable statute at the time when the defendant receives notice of the action. Nevertheless, the device of requested waiver of service is not suitable if a limitations period which is about to expire is not tolled by filing the action. Unless there is ample time, the plaintiff should proceed directly to the formal methods for service identified in subdivisions (e), (f), or (h).

The procedure of requesting waiver of service should also not be used if the time for service under subdivision (m) will expire before the date on which the waiver must be returned. While a plaintiff has been allowed additional time for service in that situation, *e.g., Prather v. Raymond Constr. Co.,* 570 F.Supp. 278 (N.D.Ga.1983), the court could refuse a request for additional time unless the defendant appears to have evaded service pursuant to subdivision (e) or (h). It may be noted that the presumptive time limit for service under subdivision (m) does not apply to service in a foreign country.

Paragraph (5) is a cost-shifting provision retained from the former rule. The costs that may be imposed on the defendant could include, for example, the cost of the time of a process server required to make contact with a defendant residing in a guarded apartment house or residential development. The paragraph is explicit that the costs of enforcing the cost-shifting provision are themselves recoverable from a defendant who fails to return the waiver. In the absence of such a provision, the purpose of the rule would be frustrated by the cost of its enforcement, which is likely to be high in relation to the small benefit secured by the plaintiff.

Some plaintiffs may send a notice and request for waiver and, without waiting for return of the waiver, also proceed with efforts to effect formal service on the defendant. To discourage this practice, the cost-shifting provisions in paragraphs (2) and (5) are limited to costs of effecting service incurred after the time expires for the defendant to return the waiver. Moreover, by returning the waiver within the time allowed and before being served with process, a defendant receives the benefit of the longer period for responding to the complaint afforded for waivers under paragraph (3).

Subdivision (e). This subdivision replaces former subdivisions (c)(2)(C)(i) and (d)(1). It provides a means for service of summons on individuals within a judicial district of the United States. Together with subdivision (f), it provides for service on persons anywhere, subject to constitutional and statutory constraints.

Service of the summons under this subdivision does not conclusively establish the jurisdiction of the court over the person of the defendant. A defendant may assert the territorial limits of the court's reach set forth in subdivision (k), including the constitutional limitations that may be imposed by the Due Process Clause of the Fifth Amendment.

Paragraph (1) authorizes service in any judicial district in conformity with state law. This paragraph sets forth the language of former subdivision (c)(2)(C)(i), which authorized the use of the law of the state in which the district court sits, but adds as an alternative the use of the law of the state in which the service is effected.

Paragraph (2) retains the text of the former subdivision (d)(1) and authorizes the use of the familiar methods of personal or abode service or service on an authorized agent in any judicial district.

To conform to these provisions, the former subdivision (e) bearing on proceedings against parties not found within the state is stricken. Likewise stricken is the

New matter is shown in italics; matter to be omitted is lined through

first sentence of the former subdivision (f), which had restricted the authority of the federal process server to the state in which the district court sits.

Subdivision (f). This subdivision provides for service on individuals who are in a foreign country, replacing the former subdivision (i) that was added to Rule 4 in 1963. Reflecting the pattern of Rule 4 in incorporating state law limitations on the exercise of jurisdiction over persons, the former subdivision (i) limited service outside the United States to cases in which extraterritorial service was authorized by state or federal law. The new rule eliminates the requirement of explicit authorization. On occasion, service in a foreign country was held to be improper for lack of statutory authority. *E.g., Martens v. Winder,* 341 F.2d 197 (9th Cir.), *cert. denied,* 382 U.S. 937 (1965). This authority, however, was found to exist by implication. *E.g., SEC v. VTR, Inc.,* 39 F.R.D. 19 (S.D.N.Y.1966). Given the substantial increase in the number of international transactions and events that are the subject of litigation in federal courts, it is appropriate to infer a general legislative authority to effect service on defendants in a foreign country.

A secondary effect of this provision for foreign service of a federal summons is to facilitate the use of federal long-arm law in actions brought to enforce the federal law against defendants who cannot be served under any state law but who can be constitutionally subjected to the jurisdiction of the federal court. Such a provision is set forth in paragraph (2) of subdivision (k) of this rule, applicable only to persons not subject to the territorial jurisdiction of any particular state.

Paragraph (1) gives effect to the Hague Convention on the Service Abroad of Judicial and Extrajudicial Documents, which entered into force for the United States on February 10, 1969. See 28 U.S.C.A., Fed.R.Civ.P. 4 (Supp.1986). This Convention is an important means of dealing with problems of service in a foreign country. *See generally* 1 B. Ristau, *International Judicial Assistance* §§ 4–1–1 to 4–5–2 (1990). Use of the Convention procedures, when available, is mandatory if documents must be transmitted abroad to effect service. *See Volkswagenwerk Aktiengesellschaft v. Schlunk,* 486 U.S. 694 (1988) (noting that voluntary use of these procedures may be desirable even when service could constitutionally be effected in another manner); J. Weis, *The Federal Rules and the Hague Conventions: Concerns of Conformity and Comity,* 50 *U.Pitt.L.Rev.* 903 (1989). Therefore, this paragraph provides that, when service is to be effected outside a judicial district of the United States, the methods of service appropriate under an applicable treaty shall be employed if available and if the treaty so requires.

The Hague Convention furnishes safeguards against the abridgment of rights of parties through inadequate notice. Article 15 provides for verification of actual notice or a demonstration that process was served by a method prescribed by the internal laws of the foreign state before a default judgment may be entered. Article 16 of the Convention also enables the judge to extend the time for appeal after judgment if the defendant shows a lack of adequate notice either to defend or to appeal the judgment, or has disclosed a prima facie case on the merits.

The Hague Convention does not specify a time within which a foreign country's Central Authority must effect service, but Article 15 does provide that alternate methods may be used if a Central Authority does not respond within six months. Generally, a Central Authority can be expected to respond much more quickly than that limit might permit, but there have been occasions when the signatory state was dilatory or refused to cooperate for substantive reasons. In such cases, resort may be had to the provision set forth in subdivision (f)(3).

Two minor changes in the text reflect the Hague Convention. First, the term "letter of request" has been added. Although these words are synonymous with "letter rogatory," "letter of request" is preferred in modern usage. The provision

---

New matter is shown in italics; matter to be omitted is lined through

should not be interpreted to authorize use of a letter of request when there is in fact no treaty obligation on the receiving country to honor such a request from this country or when the United States does not extend diplomatic recognition to the foreign nation. Second, the passage formerly found in subdivision (i)(1)(B), "when service in either case is reasonably calculated to give actual notice," has been relocated.

Paragraph (2) provides alternative methods for use when internationally agreed methods are not intended to be exclusive, or where there is no international agreement applicable. It contains most of the language formerly set forth in subdivision (i) of the rule. Service by methods that would violate foreign law is not generally authorized. Subparagraphs (A) and (B) prescribe the more appropriate methods for conforming to local practice or using a local authority. Subparagraph (C) prescribes other methods authorized by the former rule.

Paragraph (3) authorizes the court to approve other methods of service not prohibited by international agreements. The Hague Convention, for example, authorizes special forms of service in cases of urgency if convention methods will not permit service within the time required by the circumstances. Other circumstances that might justify the use of additional methods include the failure of the foreign country's Central Authority to effect service within the six-month period provided by the Convention, or the refusal of the Central Authority to serve a complaint seeking punitive damages or to enforce the antitrust laws of the United States. In such cases, the court may direct a special method of service not explicitly authorized by international agreement if not prohibited by the agreement. Inasmuch as our Constitution requires that reasonable notice be given, an earnest effort should be made to devise a method of communication that is consistent with due process and minimizes offense to foreign law. A court may in some instances specially authorize use of ordinary mail. *Cf. Levin v. Ruby Trading Corp.,* 248 F.Supp. 537 (S.D.N.Y. 1965).

Subdivision (g). This subdivision retains the text of former subdivision (d)(2). Provision is made for service upon an infant or incompetent person in a foreign country.

Subdivision (h). This subdivision retains the text of former subdivision (d)(3), with changes reflecting those made in subdivision (e). It also contains the provisions for service on a corporation or association in a foreign country, as formerly found in subdivision (i).

Frequent use should be made of the Notice and Request procedure set forth in subdivision (d) in actions against corporations. Care must be taken, however, to address the request to an individual officer or authorized agent of the corporation. It is not effective use of the Notice and Request procedure if the mail is sent undirected to the mail room of the organization.

Subdivision (i). This subdivision retains much of the text of former subdivisions (d)(4) and (d)(5). Paragraph (1) provides for service of a summons on the United States; it amends former subdivision (d)(4) to permit the United States attorney to be served by registered or certified mail. The rule does not authorize the use of the Notice and Request procedure of revised subdivision (d) when the United States is the defendant. To assure proper handling of mail in the United States attorney's office, the authorized mail service must be specifically addressed to the civil process clerk of the office of the United States attorney.

Paragraph (2) replaces former subdivision (d)(5). Paragraph (3) saves the plaintiff from the hazard of losing a substantive right because of failure to comply with the complex requirements of multiple service under this subdivision. That risk has proved to be more than nominal. *E.g., Whale v. United States,* 792 F.2d 951 (9th

---

New matter is shown in italics; matter to be omitted is lined through

Cir.1986). This provision should be read in connection with the provisions of subdivision (c) of Rule 15 to preclude the loss of substantive rights against the United States or its agencies, corporations, or officers resulting from a plaintiff's failure to correctly identify and serve all the persons who should be named or served.

Subdivision (j). This subdivision retains the text of former subdivision (d)(6) without material change. The waiver-of-service provision is also inapplicable to actions against governments subject to service pursuant to this subdivision.

The revision adds a new paragraph (1) referring to the statute governing service of a summons on a foreign state and its political subdivisions, agencies, and instrumentalities, the Foreign Sovereign Immunities Act of 1976, 28 U.S.C. § 1608. The caption of the subdivision reflects that change.

Subdivision (k). This subdivision replaces the former subdivision (f), with no change in the title. Paragraph (1) retains the substance of the former rule in explicitly authorizing the exercise of personal jurisdiction over persons who can be reached under state long-arm law, the "100–mile bulge" provision added in 1963, or the federal interpleader act. Paragraph (1)(D) is new, but merely calls attention to federal legislation that may provide for nationwide or even world-wide service of process in cases arising under particular federal laws. Congress has provided for nationwide service of process and full exercise of territorial jurisdiction by all district courts with respect to specified federal actions. *See* 1 R. Casad, *Jurisdiction in Civil Actions* (2d Ed.) chap. 5 (1991).

Paragraph (2) is new. It authorizes the exercise of territorial jurisdiction over the person of any defendant against whom is made a claim arising under any federal law if that person is subject to personal jurisdiction in no state. This addition is a companion to the amendments made in revised subdivisions (e) and (f).

This paragraph corrects a gap in the enforcement of federal law. Under the former rule, a problem was presented when the defendant was a non-resident of the United States having contacts with the United States sufficient to justify the application of United States law and to satisfy federal standards of forum selection, but having insufficient contact with any single state to support jurisdiction under state long-arm legislation or meet the requirements of the Fourteenth Amendment limitation on state court territorial jurisdiction. In such cases, the defendant was shielded from the enforcement of federal law by the fortuity of a favorable limitation on the power of state courts, which was incorporated into the federal practice by the former rule. In this respect, the revision responds to the suggestion of the Supreme Court made in *Omni Capital Int'l v. Rudolf Wolff & Co., Ltd.,* 484 U.S. 97, 111 (1987).

There remain constitutional limitations on the exercise of territorial jurisdiction by federal courts over persons outside the United States. These restrictions arise from the Fifth Amendment rather than from the Fourteenth Amendment, which limits state-court reach and which was incorporated into federal practice by the reference to state law in the text of the former subdivision (e) that is deleted by this revision. The Fifth Amendment requires that any defendant have affiliating contacts with the United States sufficient to justify the exercise of personal jurisdiction over that party. *Cf. Wells Fargo & Co. v. Wells Fargo Express Co.,* 556 F.2d 406, 418 (9th Cir.1977). There also may be a further Fifth Amendment constraint in that a plaintiff's forum selection might be so inconvenient to a defendant that it would be a denial of "fair play and substantial justice" required by the due process clause, even though the defendant had significant affiliating contacts with the United States. *See DeJames v. Magnificent Carriers,* 654 F.2d 280, 286 n.3 (3rd Cir.), *cert. denied,* 454 U.S. 1085 (1981). *Compare World–Wide Volkswagen Corp. v. Woodson,* 444 U.S. 286, 293–294 (1980); *Insurance Corp. of Ireland v. Compagnie des Bauxites de Guinee,*

New matter is shown in italics; matter to be omitted is lined through

456 U.S. 694, 702–03 (1982); *Burger King Corp. v. Rudzewicz,* 471 U.S. 462, 476–78 (1985); *Asahi Metal Indus. v. Superior Court of Cal., Solano County,* 480 U.S. 102, 108–13 (1987). *See generally* R. Lusardi, *Nationwide Service of Process: Due Process Limitations on the Power of the Sovereign,* 33 *Vill.L.Rev.* 1 (1988).

This provision does not affect the operation of federal venue legislation. *See generally* 28 U.S.C. § 1391. Nor does it affect the operation of federal law providing for the change of venue. 28 U.S.C. §§ 1404, 1406. The availability of transfer for fairness and convenience under § 1404 should preclude most conflicts between the full exercise of territorial jurisdiction permitted by this rule and the Fifth Amendment requirement of "fair play and substantial justice."

The district court should be especially scrupulous to protect aliens who reside in a foreign country from forum selections so onerous that injustice could result. "[G]reat care and reserve should be exercised when extending our notions of personal jurisdiction into the international field." *Asahi Metal Indus. v. Superior Court of Cal., Solano County,* 480 U.S. 102, 115 (1987), quoting *United States v. First Nat'l City Bank,* 379 U.S. 378, 404 (1965) (Harlan, J., dissenting).

This narrow extension of the federal reach applies only if a claim is made against the defendant under federal law. It does not establish personal jurisdiction if the only claims are those arising under state law or the law of another country, even though there might be diversity or alienage subject matter jurisdiction as to such claims. If, however, personal jurisdiction is established under this paragraph with respect to a federal claim, then 28 U.S.C. § 1367(a) provides supplemental jurisdiction over related claims against that defendant, subject to the court's discretion to decline exercise of that jurisdiction under 28 U.S.C. § 1367(c).

Subdivision (l). This subdivision assembles in one place all the provisions of the present rule bearing on proof of service. No material change in the rule is effected. The provision that proof of service can be amended by leave of court is retained from the former subdivision (h). *See generally* 4A Wright & Miller, *Federal Practice and Procedure* § 1132 (2d ed. 1987).

Subdivision (m). This subdivision retains much of the language of the present subdivision (j).

The new subdivision explicitly provides that the court shall allow additional time if there is good cause for the plaintiff's failure to effect service in the prescribed 120 days, and authorizes the court to relieve a plaintiff of the consequences of an application of this subdivision even if there is no good cause shown. Such relief formerly was afforded in some cases, partly in reliance on Rule 6(b). Relief may be justified, for example, if the applicable statute of limitations would bar the refiled action, or if the defendant is evading service or conceals a defect in attempted service. *E.g., Ditkof v. Owens–Illinois, Inc.,* 114 F.R.D. 104 (E.D.Mich.1987). A specific instance of good cause is set forth in paragraph (3) of this rule, which provides for extensions if necessary to correct oversights in compliance with the requirements of multiple service in actions against the United States or its officers, agencies, and corporations. The district court should also take care to protect *pro se* plaintiffs from consequences of confusion or delay attending the resolution of an *in forma pauperis* petition. *Robinson v. America's Best Contacts & Eyeglasses,* 876 F.2d 596 (7th Cir.1989).

The 1983 revision of this subdivision referred to the "party on whose behalf such service was required," rather than to the "plaintiff," a term used generically elsewhere in this rule to refer to any party initiating a claim against a person who is not a party to the action. To simplify the text, the revision returns to the usual practice in the rule of referring simply to the plaintiff even though its principles

---

New matter is shown in italics; matter to be omitted is lined through

apply with equal force to defendants who may assert claims against non-parties under Rules 13(h), 14, 19, 20, or 21.

Subdivision (n). This subdivision provides for in rem and quasi-in-rem jurisdiction. Paragraph (1) incorporates any requirements of 28 U.S.C. § 1655 or similar provisions bearing on seizures or liens.

Paragraph (2) provides for other uses of quasi-in-rem jurisdiction but limits its use to exigent circumstances. Provisional remedies may be employed as a means to secure jurisdiction over the property of a defendant whose person is not within reach of the court, but occasions for the use of this provision should be rare, as where the defendant is a fugitive or assets are in imminent danger of disappearing. Until 1963, it was not possible under Rule 4 to assert jurisdiction in a federal court over the property of a defendant not personally served. The 1963 amendment to subdivision (e) authorized the use of state law procedures authorizing seizures of assets as a basis for jurisdiction. Given the liberal availability of long-arm jurisdiction, the exercise of power quasi-in-rem has become almost an anachronism. Circumstances too spare to affiliate the defendant to the forum state sufficiently to support long-arm jurisdiction over the defendant's person are also inadequate to support seizure of the defendant's assets fortuitously found within the state. *Shaffer v. Heitner,* 433 U.S. 186 (1977).

Rule 4.1.   Service of Other Process

Advisory Committee's Note to Rule Added in 1993

This is a new rule. Its purpose is to separate those few provisions of the former Rule 4 bearing on matters other than service of a summons to allow greater textual clarity in Rule 4. Subdivision (a) contains no new language.

Subdivision (b) replaces the final clause of the penultimate sentence of the former subdivision 4(f), a clause added to the rule in 1963. The new rule provides for nationwide service of orders of civil commitment enforcing decrees of injunctions issued to compel compliance with federal law. The rule makes no change in the practice with respect to the enforcement of injunctions or decrees not involving the enforcement of federally-created rights.

Service of process is not required to notify a party of a decree or injunction, or of an order that the party show cause why that party should not be held in contempt of such an order. With respect to a party who has once been served with a summons, the service of the decree or injunction itself or of an order to show cause can be made pursuant to Rule 5. Thus, for example, an injunction may be served on a party through that person's attorney. *Chagas v. United States,* 369 F.2d 643 (5th Cir. 1966). The same is true for service of an order to show cause. *Waffenschmidt v. Mackay,* 763 F.2d 711 (5th Cir.1985).

The new rule does not affect the reach of the court to impose criminal contempt sanctions. Nationwide enforcement of federal decrees and injunctions is already available with respect to criminal contempt: a federal court may effect the arrest of a criminal contemnor anywhere in the United States, 28 U.S.C. § 3041, and a contemnor when arrested may be subject to removal to the district in which punishment may be imposed. Fed.R.Crim.P. 40. Thus, the present law permits criminal contempt enforcement against a contemnor wherever that person may be found.

The effect of the revision is to provide a choice of civil or criminal contempt sanctions in those situations to which it applies. Contempt proceedings, whether civil or criminal, must be brought in the court that was allegedly defied by a contuma-

---

New matter is shown in italics;   matter to be omitted is lined through

cious act. *Ex parte Bradley,* 74 U.S. 366 (1869). This is so even if the offensive conduct or inaction occurred outside the district of the court in which the enforcement proceeding must be conducted. *E.g., McCourtney v. United States,* 291 Fed. 497 (8th Cir.), *cert. denied,* 263 U.S. 714 (1923). For this purpose, the rule as before does not distinguish between parties and other persons subject to contempt sanctions by reason of their relation or connection to parties.

Rule 11. Signing of Pleadings

Advisory Committee's Note to Original Rule

This is substantially the content of Equity Rules 24 (Signature of Counsel) and 21 (Scandal and Impertinence) consolidated and unified. Compare Equity Rule 36 (Officers Before Whom Pleadings Verified). Compare to similar purposes, English Rules Under the Judicature Act (The Annual Practice, 1937) O. 19, r. 4, and *Great Australian Gold Mining Co. v. Martin,* L. R. 5 Ch.Div. 1, 10 (1877). Subscription of pleadings is required in many codes. 2 Minn.Stat. (Mason, 1927) § 9265; N.Y.R.C.P. (1937) Rule 91; 2 N.D.Comp.Laws Ann. (1913) § 7455.

This rule expressly continues any statute which requires a pleading to be verified or accompanied by an affidavit, such as:

U.S.C., Title 28:

§ 381   (Preliminary injunctions and temporary restraining orders)

§ 762   (Suit against the United States)

U.S.C., Title 28, § 829 (Costs; attorney liable for, when) is unaffected by this rule.

For complaints which must be verified under these rules, see Rule 23(b) (Secondary Action by Shareholders) and 65 (Injunctions).

For abolition of the rule in equity that the averments of an answer under oath must be overcome by the testimony of two witnesses or of one witness sustained by corroborating circumstances, see Pa.Stat.Ann. (Purdon, 1931) tit. 12, § 1222; for the rule in equity itself, see *Greenfield v. Blumenthal,* 69 F.(2d) 294 (C.C.A.3d, 1934).

Advisory Committee's Note to 1983 Amendment

Rule 11. Signing of Pleadings, *Motions, and Other Papers; Sanctions*

Every pleading, *motion, and other paper* of a party represented by an attorney shall be signed by at least one attorney of record in his individual name, whose address shall be stated. A party who is not represented by an attorney shall sign his pleading, *motion, or other paper* and state his address. Except when otherwise specifically provided by rule or statute, pleadings need not be verified or accompanied by affidavit. The rule in equity that the averments of an answer under oath must be overcome by the testimony of two witnesses or of one witness sustained by corroborating circumstances is abolished. The signature of an attorney *or party* consti-

---

New matter is shown in italics; matter to be omitted is lined through

tutes a certificate by him that he has read the pleading, *motion, or other paper*; that to the best of his knowledge, information, and belief ~~there is good ground to support it; and that it is not interposed for delay~~ *formed after reasonable inquiry it is well grounded in fact and is warranted by existing law or a good faith argument for the extension, modification, or reversal of existing law, and that it is not interposed for any improper purpose, such as to harass or to cause unnecessary delay or needless increase in the cost of litigation. If a pleading, motion, or other paper* is not signed, *it shall be stricken unless it is signed promptly after the omission is called to the attention of the pleader or movant.* ~~or is signed with intent to defeat the purpose of this rule; it may be stricken as sham and false and the action may proceed as though the pleading had not been served. For a wilful violation of this rule an attorney may be subjected to appropriate disciplinary action. Similar action may be taken if scandalous or indecent matter is inserted.~~ *If a pleading, motion, or other paper is signed in violation of this rule, the court, upon motion or upon its own initiative, shall impose upon the person who signed it, a represented party, or both, an appropriate sanction, which may include an order to pay to the other party or parties the amount of the reasonable expenses incurred because of the filing of the pleading, motion, or other paper, including a reasonable attorney's fee.*

Since its original promulgation, Rule 11 has provided for the striking of pleadings and the imposition of disciplinary sanctions to check abuses in the signing of pleadings. Its provisions have always applied to motions and other papers by virtue of incorporation by reference in Rule 7(b)(2). The amendment and the addition of Rule 7(b)(3) expressly confirms this applicability.

Experience shows that in practice Rule 11 has not been effective in deterring abuses. See 6 Wright & Miller, *Federal Practice and Procedure: Civil* § 1334 (1971). There has been considerable confusion as to (1) the circumstances that should trigger striking a pleading or motion or taking disciplinary action, (2) the standard of conduct expected of attorneys who sign pleadings and motions, and (3) the range of available and appropriate sanctions. See Rodes, Ripple & Mooney, *Sanctions Imposable for Violations of the Federal Rules of Civil Procedure* 64–65, Federal Judicial Center (1981). The new language is intended to reduce the reluctance of courts to impose sanctions, see Moore, *Federal Practice* ¶ 7.05, at 1547, by emphasizing the responsibilities of the attorney and reenforcing those obligations by the imposition of sanctions.

The amended rule attempts to deal with the problem by building upon and expanding the equitable doctrine permitting the court to award expenses, including attorney's fees, to a litigant whose opponent acts in bad faith in instituting or conducting litigation. See, *e.g., Roadway Express, Inc. v. Piper*, 447 U.S. 752 (1980); *Hall v. Cole*, 412 U.S. 1, 5 (1973). Greater attention by the district courts to pleading and motion abuses and the imposition of sanctions when appropriate, should

---

New matter is shown in italics; matter to be omitted is lined through

discourage dilatory or abusive tactics and help to streamline the litigation process by lessening frivolous claims or defenses.

The expanded nature of the lawyer's certification in the fifth sentence of amended Rule 11 recognizes that the litigation process may be abused for purposes other than delay. See, *e.g., Browning Debenture Holders' Committee v. DASA Corp.,* 560 F.2d 1078 (2d Cir.1977).

The words "good ground to support" the pleading in the original rule were interpreted to have both factual and legal elements. See, *e.g., Heart Disease Research Foundation v. General Motors Corp.,* 15 Fed.R.Serv.2d 1517, 1519 (S.D.N.Y.1972). They have been replaced by a standard of conduct that is more focused.

The new language stresses the need for some prefiling inquiry into both the facts and the law to satisfy the affirmative duty imposed by the rule. The standard is one of reasonableness under the circumstances. See *Kinee v. Abraham Lincoln Fed. Sav. & Loan Ass'n,* 365 F.Supp. 975 (E.D.Pa.1973). This standard is more stringent than the original good-faith formula and thus it is expected that a greater range of circumstances will trigger its violation. See *Nemeroff v. Abelson,* 620 F.2d 339 (2d Cir.1980).

The rule is not intended to chill an attorney's enthusiasm or creativity in pursuing factual or legal theories. The court is expected to avoid using the wisdom of hindsight and should test the signer's conduct by inquiring what was reasonable to believe at the time the pleading, motion, or other paper was submitted. Thus, what constitutes a reasonable inquiry may depend on such factors as how much time for investigation was available to the signer; whether he had to rely on a client for information as to the facts underlying the pleading, motion, or other paper; whether the pleading, motion, or other paper was based on a plausible view of the law; or whether he depended on forwarding counsel or another member of the bar.

The rule does not require a party or an attorney to disclose privileged communications or work product in order to show that the signing of the pleading, motion, or other paper is substantially justified. The provisions of Rule 26(c), including appropriate orders after *in camera* inspection by the court, remain available to protect a party claiming privilege or work product protection.

Amended Rule 11 continues to apply to anyone who signs a pleading, motion, or other paper. Although the standard is the same for unrepresented parties, who are obliged themselves to sign the pleadings, the court has sufficient discretion to take account of the special circumstances that often arise in *pro se* situations. See *Haines v. Kerner,* 404 U.S. 519 (1972).

The provision in the original rule for striking pleadings and motions as sham and false has been deleted. The passage has rarely been utilized, and decisions thereunder have tended to confuse the issue of attorney honesty with the merits of the action. See generally Risinger, *Honesty in Pleading and its Enforcement: Some "Striking" Problems with Fed.R.Civ.P. 11,* 61 Minn.L.Rev. 1 (1976). Motions under this provision generally present issues better dealt with under Rules 8, 12, or 56. See *Murchison v. Kirby,* 27 F.R.D. 14 (S.D.N.Y.1961); 5 Wright & Miller, *Federal Practice and Procedure: Civil* § 1334 (1969).

The former reference to the inclusion of scandalous or indecent matter, which is itself strong indication that an improper purpose underlies the pleading, motion, or other paper, also has been deleted as unnecessary. Such matter may be stricken under Rule 12(f) as well as dealt with under the more general language of amended Rule 11.

The text of the amended rule seeks to dispel apprehensions that efforts to obtain enforcement will be fruitless by insuring that the rule will be applied when properly

---

New matter is shown in italics; matter to be omitted is lined through

invoked. The word "sanctions" in the caption, for example, stresses a deterrent orientation in dealing with improper pleadings, motions or other papers. This corresponds to the approach in imposing sanctions for discovery abuses. See *National Hockey League v. Metropolitan Hockey Club,* 427 U.S. 639 (1976) (per curiam). And the words "shall impose" in the last sentence focus the court's attention on the need to impose sanctions for pleading and motion abuses. The court, however, retains the necessary flexibility to deal appropriately with violations of the rule. It has discretion to tailor sanctions to the particular facts of the case, with which it should be well acquainted.

The reference in the former text to wilfulness as a prerequisite to disciplinary action has been deleted. However, in considering the nature and severity of the sanctions to be imposed, the court should take account of the state of the attorney's or party's actual or presumed knowledge when the pleading or other paper was signed. Thus, for example, when a party is not represented by counsel, the absence of legal advice is an appropriate factor to be considered.

Courts currently appear to believe they may impose sanctions on their own motion. See *North American Trading Corp. v. Zale Corp.,* 73 F.R.D. 293 (S.D.N.Y. 1979). Authority to do so has been made explicit in order to overcome the traditional reluctance of courts to intervene unless requested by one of the parties. The detection and punishment of a violation of the signing requirement, encouraged by the amended rule, is part of the court's responsibility for securing the system's effective operation.

If the duty imposed by the rule is violated, the court should have the discretion to impose sanctions on either the attorney, the party the signing attorney represents, or both, or on an unrepresented party who signed the pleading, and the new rule so provides. Although Rule 11 has been silent on the point, courts have claimed the power to impose sanctions on an attorney personally, either by imposing costs or employing the contempt technique. See 5 Wright & Miller, *Federal Practice and Procedure: Civil* § 1334 (1969); 2A Moore, *Federal Practice* ¶ 11.02, at 2104 n. 8. This power has been used infrequently. The amended rule should eliminate any doubt as to the propriety of assessing sanctions against the attorney.

Even though it is the attorney whose signature violates the rule, it may be appropriate under the circumstances of the case to impose a sanction on the client. See *Browning Debenture Holders' Committee v. DASA Corp., supra.* This modification brings Rule 11 in line with practice under Rule 37, which allows sanctions for abuses during discovery to be imposed upon the party, the attorney, or both.

A party seeking sanctions should give notice to the court and the offending party promptly upon discovering a basis for doing so. The time when sanctions are to be imposed rests in the discretion of the trial judge. However, it is anticipated that in the case of pleadings the sanctions issue under Rule 11 normally will be determined at the end of the litigation, and in the case of motions at the time when the motion is decided or shortly thereafter. The procedure obviously must comport with due process requirements. The particular format to be followed should depend on the circumstances of the situation and the severity of the sanction under consideration. In many situations the judge's participation in the proceedings provides him with full knowledge of the relevant facts and little further inquiry will be necessary.

To assure that the efficiencies achieved through more effective operation of the pleading regimen will not be offset by the cost of satellite litigation over the imposition of sanctions, the court must to the extent possible limit the scope of sanction proceedings to the record. Thus, discovery should be conducted only by leave of the court, and then only in extraordinary circumstances.

New matter is shown in italics; matter to be omitted is lined through

Although the encompassing reference to "other papers" in new Rule 11 literally includes discovery papers, the certification requirement in that context is governed by proposed new Rule 26(g). Discovery motions, however, fall within the ambit of Rule 11.

Advisory Committee's Note to 1993 Amendment

Rule 11. Signing of Pleadings, Motions, and Other Papers; *Representations to Court;* Sanctions

(a) Signature. Every pleading, *written* motion, and other paper ~~of a party represented by an attorney~~ shall be signed by at least one attorney of record in the attorney's individual name, *or, if the party is not represented by an attorney, shall be signed by the party.* ~~whose address shall be stated. A party who is not represented by an attorney shall sign the party's pleading, motion, or other paper and state the party's address.~~ *Each paper shall state the signer's address and telephone number, if any.* Except when otherwise specifically provided by rule or statute, pleadings need not be verified or accompanied by affidavit. ~~The rule in equity that the averments of an answer under oath must be overcome by the testimony of two witnesses or of one witness sustained by corroborating circumstances is abolished. The signature of an attorney or party constitutes a certificate by the signer that the signer has read the pleading, motion, or other paper; that to the best of the signer's knowledge, information, and belief formed after reasonable inquiry it is well grounded in fact and is warranted by existing law or a good faith argument for the extension, modification, or reversal of existing law, and that it is not interposed for any improper purpose, such as to harass or to cause unnecessary delay or needless increase in the cost of litigation. If a pleading, motion, or other~~ *An unsigned* paper ~~is not signed, it~~ shall be stricken unless ~~it is signed promptly after the~~ omission *of the signature is corrected promptly after being* called to the attention of the ~~pleader or movant~~ *attorney or party.*

(b) Representations to Court. ~~If a pleading, motion, or other paper is signed in violation of this rule, the court, upon motion or upon its own initiative, shall impose upon the person who signed it, a represented party, or both, an appropriate sanction, which may include an order to pay to the other party or parties the amount of the reasonable expenses incurred because of the filing of the pleading, motion, or other paper, including a reasonable attorney's fee.~~ *By presenting to the court (whether by signing, filing, submitting, or later advocating) a pleading, written motion, or other paper, an attorney or unrepresented party is certifying that to the best of the*

New matter is shown in italics; matter to be omitted is lined through

person's knowledge, information, and belief, formed after an inquiry reasonable under the circumstances,—

(1) it is not being presented for any improper purpose, such as to harass or to cause unnecessary delay or needless increase in the cost of litigation;

(2) the claims, defenses, and other legal contentions therein are warranted by existing law or by a nonfrivolous argument for the extension, modification, or reversal of existing law or the establishment of new law;

(3) the allegations and other factual contentions have evidentiary support or, if specifically so identified, are likely to have evidentiary support after a reasonable opportunity for further investigation or discovery; and

(4) the denials of factual contentions are warranted on the evidence or, if specifically so identified, are reasonably based on a lack of information or belief.

(c) Sanctions. If, after notice and a reasonable opportunity to respond, the court determines that subdivision (b) has been violated, the court may, subject to the conditions stated below, impose an appropriate sanction upon the attorneys, law firms, or parties that have violated subdivision (b) or are responsible for the violation.

(1) How Initiated.

(A) By Motion. A motion for sanctions under this rule shall be made separately from other motions or requests and shall describe the specific conduct alleged to violate subdivision (b). It shall be served as provided in Rule 5, but shall not be filed with or presented to the court unless, within 21 days after service of the motion (or such other period as the court may prescribe), the challenged paper, claim, defense, contention, allegation, or denial is not withdrawn or appropriately corrected. If warranted, the court may award to the party prevailing on the motion the reasonable expenses and attorney's fees incurred in presenting or opposing the motion. Absent exceptional circumstances, a law firm shall be held jointly responsible for violations committed by its partners, associates, and employees.

(B) On Court's Initiative. On its own initiative, the court may enter an order describing the specific conduct that appears to violate subdivision (b) and directing an attorney, law firm, or party to show cause why it has not violated subdivision (b) with respect thereto.

New matter is shown in italics; matter to be omitted is lined through

(2) Nature of Sanction; Limitations. A sanction imposed for violation of this rule shall be limited to what is sufficient to deter repetition of such conduct or comparable conduct by others similarly situated. Subject to the limitations in subparagraphs (A) and (B), the sanction may consist of, or include, directives of a nonmonetary nature, an order to pay a penalty into court, or, if imposed on motion and warranted for effective deterrence, an order directing payment to the movant of some or all of the reasonable attorneys' fees and other expenses incurred as a direct result of the violation.

(A) Monetary sanctions may not be awarded against a represented party for a violation of subdivision (b)(2).

(B) Monetary sanctions may not be awarded on the court's initiative unless the court issues its order to show cause before a voluntary dismissal or settlement of the claims made by or against the party which is, or whose attorneys are, to be sanctioned.

(3) Order. When imposing sanctions, the court shall describe the conduct determined to constitute a violation of this rule and explain the basis for the sanction imposed.

(d) Inapplicability to Discovery. *Subdivisions (a) through (c) of this rule do not apply to disclosures and discovery requests, responses, objections, and motions that are subject to the provisions of Rules 26 through 37.*

Purpose of revision. This revision is intended to remedy problems that have arisen in the interpretation and application of the 1983 revision of the rule. For empirical examination of experience under the 1983 rule, see, *e.g.*, New York State Bar Committee on Federal Courts, *Sanctions and Attorneys' Fees* (1987); T. Willging, *The Rule 11 Sanctioning Process* (1989); American Judicature Society, *Report of the Third Circuit Task Force on Federal Rule of Civil Procedure 11* (S. Burbank ed., 1989); E. Wiggins, T. Willging, and D. Stienstra, *Report on Rule 11* (Federal Judicial Center 1991). For book-length analyses of the case law, see G. Joseph, *Sanctions: The Federal Law of Litigation Abuse* (1989); J. Solovy, *The Federal Law of Sanctions* (1991); G. Vairo, *Rule 11 Sanctions: Case Law Perspectives and Preventive Measures* (1991).

The rule retains the principle that attorneys and pro se litigants have an obligation to the court to refrain from conduct that frustrates the aims of Rule 1. The revision broadens the scope of this obligation, but places greater constraints on the imposition of sanctions and should reduce the number of motions for sanctions presented to the court. New subdivision (d) removes from the ambit of this rule all discovery requests, responses, objections, and motions subject to the provisions of Rule 26 through 37.

Subdivision (a). Retained in this subdivision are the provisions requiring signatures on pleadings, written motions, and other papers. Unsigned papers are to be

New matter is shown in italics; matter to be omitted is lined through

received by the Clerk, but then are to be stricken if the omission of the signature is not corrected promptly after being called to the attention of the attorney or pro se litigant. Correction can be made by signing the paper on file or by submitting a duplicate that contains the signature. A court may require by local rule that papers contain additional identifying information regarding the parties or attorneys, such as telephone numbers to facilitate facsimile transmissions, though, as for omission of a signature, the paper should not be rejected for failure to provide such information.

The sentence in the former rule relating to the effect of answers under oath is no longer needed and has been eliminated. The provision in the former rule that signing a paper constitutes a certificate that it has been read by the signer also has been eliminated as unnecessary. The obligations imposed under subdivision (b) obviously require that a pleading, written motion, or other paper be read before it is filed or submitted to the court.

Subdivisions (b) and (c). These subdivisions restate the provisions requiring attorneys and pro se litigants to conduct a reasonable inquiry into the law and facts before signing pleadings, written motions, and other documents, and prescribing sanctions for violation of these obligations. The revision in part expands the responsibilities of litigants to the court, while providing greater constraints and flexibility in dealing with infractions of the rule. The rule continues to require litigants to "stop-and-think" before initially making legal or factual contentions. It also, however, emphasizes the duty of candor by subjecting litigants to potential sanctions for insisting upon a position after it is no longer tenable and by generally providing protection against sanctions if they withdraw or correct contentions after a potential violation is called to their attention.

The rule applies only to assertions contained in papers filed with or submitted to the court. It does not cover matters arising for the first time during oral presentations to the court, when counsel may make statements that would not have been made if there had been more time for study and reflection. However, a litigant's obligations with respect to the contents of these papers are not measured solely as of the time they are filed with or submitted to the court, but include reaffirming to the court and advocating positions contained in those pleadings and motions after learning that they cease to have any merit. For example, an attorney who during a pretrial conference insists on a claim or defense should be viewed as "presenting to the court" that contention and would be subject to the obligations of subdivision (b) measured as of that time. Similarly, if after a notice of removal is filed, a party urges in federal court the allegations of a pleading filed in state court (whether as claims, defenses, or in disputes regarding removal or remand), it would be viewed as "presenting"—and hence certifying to the district court under Rule 11—those allegations.

The certification with respect to allegations and other factual contentions is revised in recognition that sometimes a litigant may have good reason to believe that a fact is true or false but may need discovery, formal or informal, from opposing parties or third persons to gather and confirm the evidentiary basis for the allegation. Tolerance of factual contentions in initial pleadings by plaintiffs or defendants when specifically identified as made on information and belief does not relieve litigants from the obligation to conduct an appropriate investigation into the facts that is reasonable under the circumstances; it is not a license to join parties, make claims, or present defenses without any factual basis or justification. Moreover, if evidentiary support is not obtained after a reasonable opportunity for further investigation or discovery, the party has a duty under the rule not to persist with that contention. Subdivision (b) does not require a formal amendment to pleadings for which evidentiary support is not obtained, but rather calls upon a litigant not thereafter to advocate such claims or defenses.

New matter is shown in italics; matter to be omitted is lined through

The certification is that there is (or likely will be) "evidentiary support" for the allegation, not that the party will prevail with respect to its contention regarding the fact. That summary judgment is rendered against a party does not necessarily mean, for purposes of this certification, that it had no evidentiary support for its position. On the other hand, if a party has evidence with respect to a contention that would suffice to defeat a motion for summary judgment based thereon, it would have sufficient "evidentiary support" for purposes of Rule 11.

Denials of factual contentions involve somewhat different considerations. Often, of course, a denial is premised upon the existence of evidence contradicting the alleged fact. At other times a denial is permissible because, after an appropriate investigation, a party has no information concerning the matter or, indeed, has a reasonable basis for doubting the credibility of the only evidence relevant to the matter. A party should not deny an allegation it knows to be true; but it is not required, simply because it lacks contradictory evidence, to admit an allegation that it believes is not true.

The changes in subdivisions (b)(3) and (b)(4) will serve to equalize the burden of the rule upon plaintiffs and defendants, who under Rule 8(b) are in effect allowed to deny allegations by stating that from their initial investigation they lack sufficient information to form a belief as to the truth of the allegation. If, after further investigation or discovery, a denial is no longer warranted, the defendant should not continue to insist on that denial. While sometimes helpful, formal amendment of the pleadings to withdraw an allegation or denial is not required by subdivision (b).

Arguments for extensions, modifications, or reversals of existing law or for creation of new law do not violate subdivision (b)(2) provided they are "nonfrivolous." This establishes an objective standard, intended to eliminate any "empty-head pure-heart" justification for patently frivolous arguments. However, the extent to which a litigant has researched the issues and found some support for its theories even in minority opinions, in law review articles, or through consultation with other attorneys should certainly be taken into account in determining whether paragraph (2) has been violated. Although arguments for a change of law are not required to be specifically so identified, a contention that is so identified should be viewed with greater tolerance under the rule.

The court has available a variety of possible sanctions to impose for violations, such as striking the offending paper; issuing an admonition, reprimand, or censure; requiring participation in seminars or other educational programs; ordering a fine payable to the court; referring the matter to disciplinary authorities (or, in the case of government attorneys, to the Attorney General, Inspector General, or agency head), etc. *See Manual for Complex Litigation, Second,* § 42.3. The rule does not attempt to enumerate the factors a court should consider in deciding whether to impose a sanction or what sanctions would be appropriate in the circumstances; but, for emphasis, it does specifically note that a sanction may be nonmonetary as well as monetary. Whether the improper conduct was willful, or negligent; whether it was part of a pattern of activity, or an isolated event; whether it infected the entire pleading, or only one particular count or defense; whether the person has engaged in similar conduct in other litigation; whether it was intended to injure; what effect it had on the litigation process in time or expense; whether the responsible person is trained in the law; what amount, given the financial resources of the responsible person, is needed to deter that person from repetition in the same case; what amount is needed to deter similar activity by other litigants: all of these may in a particular case be proper considerations. The court has significant discretion in determining what sanctions, if any, should be imposed for a violation, subject to the principle that the sanctions should not be more severe than reasonably necessary to

---

New matter is shown in italics; matter to be omitted is lined through

deter repetition of the conduct by the offending person or comparable conduct by similarly situated persons.

Since the purpose of Rule 11 sanctions is to deter rather than to compensate, the rule provides that, if a monetary sanction is imposed, it should ordinarily be paid into court as a penalty. However, under unusual circumstances, particularly for (b)(1) violations, deterrence may be ineffective unless the sanction not only requires the person violating the rule to make a monetary payment, but also directs that some or all of this payment be made to those injured by the violation. Accordingly, the rule authorizes the court, if requested in a motion and if so warranted, to award attorney's fees to another party. Any such award to another party, however, should not exceed the expenses and attorneys' fees for the services directly and unavoidably caused by the violation of the certification requirement. If, for example, a wholly unsupportable count were included in a multi-count complaint or counterclaim for the purpose of needlessly increasing the cost of litigation to an impecunious adversary, any award of expenses should be limited to those directly caused by inclusion of the improper count, and not those resulting from the filing of the complaint or answer itself. The award should not provide compensation for services that could have been avoided by an earlier disclosure of evidence or an earlier challenge to the groundless claims or defenses. Moreover, partial reimbursement of fees may constitute a sufficient deterrent with respect to violations by persons having modest financial resources. In cases brought under statutes providing for fees to be awarded to prevailing parties, the court should not employ cost-shifting under this rule in a manner that would be inconsistent with the standards that govern the statutory award of fees, such as stated in *Christiansburg Garment Co. v. EEOC,* 434 U.S. 412 (1978).

The sanction should be imposed on the persons—whether attorneys, law firms, or parties—who have violated the rule or who may be determined to be responsible for the violation. The person signing, filing, submitting, or advocating a document has a nondelegable responsibility to the court, and in most situations is the person to be sanctioned for a violation. Absent exceptional circumstances, a law firm is to be held also responsible when, as a result of a motion under subdivision (c)(1)(A), one of its partners, associates, or employees is determined to have violated the rule. Since such a motion may be filed only if the offending paper is not withdrawn or corrected within 21 days after service of the motion, it is appropriate that the law firm ordinarily be viewed as jointly responsible under established principles of agency. This provision is designed to remove the restrictions of the former rule. *Cf. Pavelic & LeFlore v. Marvel Entertainment Group,* 493 U.S. 120 (1989) (1983 version of Rule 11 does not permit sanctions against law firm of attorney signing groundless complaint).

The revision permits the court to consider whether other attorneys in the firm, co-counsel, other law firms, or the party itself should be held accountable for their part in causing a violation. When appropriate, the court can make an additional inquiry in order to determine whether the sanction should be imposed on such persons, firms, or parties either in addition to or, in unusual circumstances, instead of the person actually making the presentation to the court. For example, such an inquiry may be appropriate in cases involving governmental agencies or other institutional parties that frequently impose substantial restrictions on the discretion of individual attorneys employed by it.

Sanctions that involve monetary awards (such as a fine or an award of attorney's fees) may not be imposed on a represented party for causing a violation of subdivision (b)(2), involving frivolous contentions of law. Monetary responsibility for such violations is more properly placed solely on the party's attorneys. With this limitation, the rule should not be subject to attack under the Rules Enabling Act.

New matter is shown in italics; matter to be omitted is lined through

See Willy v. Coastal Corp., 503 U.S. 131 (1992); *Business Guides, Inc. v. Chromatic Communications Enter. Inc.,* 498 U.S. 533 (1991). This restriction does not limit the court's power to impose sanctions or remedial orders that may have collateral financial consequences upon a party, such as dismissal of a claim, preclusion of a defense, or preparation of amended pleadings.

Explicit provision is made for litigants to be provided notice of the alleged violation and an opportunity to respond before sanctions are imposed. Whether the matter should be decided solely on the basis of written submissions or should be scheduled for oral argument (or, indeed, for evidentiary presentation) will depend on the circumstances. If the court imposes a sanction, it must, unless waived, indicate its reasons in a written order or on the record; the court should not ordinarily have to explain its denial of a motion for sanctions. Whether a violation has occurred and what sanctions, if any, to impose for a violation are matters committed to the discretion of the trial court; accordingly, as under current law, the standard for appellate review of these decisions will be for abuse of discretion. *See Cooter & Gell v. Hartmarx Corp.,* 496 U.S. 384 (1990) (noting, however, that an abuse would be established if the court based its ruling on an erroneous view of the law or on a clearly erroneous assessment of the evidence).

The revision leaves for resolution on a case-by-case basis, considering the particular circumstances involved, the question as to when a motion for violation of Rule 11 should be served and when, if filed, it should be decided. Ordinarily the motion should be served promptly after the inappropriate paper is filed, and, if delayed too long, may be viewed as untimely. In other circumstances, it should not be served until the other party has had a reasonable opportunity for discovery. Given the "safe harbor" provisions discussed below, a party cannot delay serving its Rule 11 motion until conclusion of the case (or judicial rejection of the offending contention).

Rule 11 motions should not be made or threatened for minor, inconsequential violations of the standards prescribed by subdivision (b). They should not be employed as a discovery device or to test the legal sufficiency or efficacy of allegations in the pleadings; other motions are available for those purposes. Nor should Rule 11 motions be prepared to emphasize the merits of a party's position, to exact an unjust settlement, to intimidate an adversary into withdrawing contentions that are fairly debatable, to increase the costs of litigation, to create a conflict of interest between attorney and client, or to seek disclosure of matters otherwise protected by the attorney-client privilege or the work-product doctrine. As under the prior rule, the court may defer its ruling (or its decision as to the identity of the persons to be sanctioned) until final resolution of the case in order to avoid immediate conflicts of interest and to reduce the disruption created if a disclosure of attorney-client communications is needed to determine whether a violation occurred or to identify the person responsible for the violation.

The rule provides that requests for sanctions must be made as a separate motion, *i.e.,* not simply included as an additional prayer for relief contained in another motion. The motion for sanctions is not, however, to be filed until at least 21 days (or such other period as the court may set) after being served. If, during this period, the alleged violation is corrected, as by withdrawing (whether formally or informally) some allegation or contention, the motion should not be filed with the court. These provisions are intended to provide a type of "safe harbor" against motions under Rule 11 in that a party will not be subject to sanctions on the basis of another party's motion unless, after receiving the motion, it refuses to withdraw that position or to acknowledge candidly that it does not currently have evidence to support a specified allegation. Under the former rule, parties were sometimes reluctant to abandon a questionable contention lest that be viewed as evidence of a

---

New matter is shown in italics; matter to be omitted is lined through

violation of Rule 11; under the revision, the timely withdrawal of a contention will protect a party against a motion for sanctions.

To stress the seriousness of a motion for sanctions and to define precisely the conduct claimed to violate the rule, the revision provides that the "safe harbor" period begins to run only upon service of the motion. In most cases, however, counsel should be expected to give informal notice to the other party, whether in person or by a telephone call or letter, of a potential violation before proceeding to prepare and serve a Rule 11 motion.

As under former Rule 11, the filing of a motion for sanctions is itself subject to the requirements of the rule and can lead to sanctions. However, service of a cross motion under Rule 11 should rarely be needed since under the revision the court may award to the person who prevails on a motion under Rule 11—whether the movant or the target of the motion—reasonable expenses, including attorney's fees, incurred in presenting or opposing the motion.

The power of the court to act on its own initiative is retained, but with the condition that this be done through a show cause order. This procedure provides the person with notice and an opportunity to respond. The revision provides that a monetary sanction imposed after a court-initiated show cause order be limited to a penalty payable to the court and that it be imposed only if the show cause order is issued before any voluntary dismissal or an agreement of the parties to settle the claims made by or against the litigant. Parties settling a case should not be subsequently faced with an unexpected order from the court leading to monetary sanctions that might have affected their willingness to settle or voluntarily dismiss a case. Since show cause orders will ordinarily be issued only in situations that are akin to a contempt of court, the rule does not provide a "safe harbor" to a litigant for withdrawing a claim, defense, etc., after a show cause order has been issued on the court's own initiative. Such corrective action, however, should be taken into account in deciding what—if any—sanction to impose if, after consideration of the litigant's response, the court concludes that a violation has occurred.

Subdivision (d). Rules 26(g) and 37 establish certification standards and sanctions that apply to discovery disclosures, requests, responses, objections, and motions. It is appropriate that Rules 26 through 37, which are specially designed for the discovery process, govern such documents and conduct rather than the more general provisions of Rule 11. Subdivision (d) has been added to accomplish this result.

Rule 11 is not the exclusive source for control of improper presentations of claims, defenses, or contentions. It does not supplant statutes permitting awards of attorney's fees to prevailing parties or alter the principles governing such awards. It does not inhibit the court in punishing for contempt, in exercising its inherent powers, or in imposing sanctions, awarding expenses, or directing remedial action authorized under other rules or under 28 U.S.C. § 1927. *See Chambers v. NASCO,* 501 U.S. 32 (1991). *Chambers* cautions, however, against reliance upon inherent powers if appropriate sanctions can be imposed under provisions such as Rule 11, and the procedures specified in Rule 11—notice, opportunity to respond, and findings—should ordinarily be employed when imposing a sanction under the court's inherent powers. Finally, it should be noted that Rule 11 does not preclude a party from initiating an independent action for malicious prosecution or abuse of process.

New matter is shown in italics; matter to be omitted is lined through

Rule 12.   Defenses and Objections—When and How Presented—By Pleading or Motion— Motion for Judgment on Pleadings

Advisory Committee's Note to Original Rule

Note to Subdivision (a). 1. Compare Equity Rules 12 (Issue of Subpoena—Time for Answer) and 31 (Reply—When Required—When Cause at Issue); 4 Mont.Rev. Codes Ann. (1935) §§ 9107, 9158; N.Y.C.P.A. (1937) § 263; N.Y.R.C.P. (1937) Rules 109–111.

2. U.S.C., Title 28, § 763 [1946 ed.] (Petition in action against United States; service; appearance by district attorney) provides that the United States as a defendant shall have 60 days within which to answer or otherwise defend. This and other statutes which provide 60 days for the United States or an officer or agency thereof to answer or otherwise defend are continued by this rule. In so far as any statutes not excepted in Rule 81 provide a different time for a defendant to defend, such statutes are modified. See U.S.C., Title 28, § 45 [1946 ed.] (District courts; practice and procedure in certain cases under the interstate commerce laws) (30 days).

3. Compare the last sentence of Equity Rule 29 (Defenses—How Presented) and N.Y.C.P.A. (1937) § 283. See Rule 15(a) for time within which to plead to an amended pleading.

Note to Subdivisions (b) and (d). 1. See generally Equity Rules 29 (Defenses— How Presented), 33 (Testing Sufficiency of Defense), 43 (Defect of Parties—Resisting Objection), and 44 (Defect of Parties—Tardy Objection); N.Y.C.P.A. (1937) §§ 277–280; N.Y.R.C.P. (1937) Rules 106–112; English Rules Under the Judicature Act (The Annual Practice, 1937) O. 25, r. r. 1–4; Clark, Code Pleading (1928) pp. 371–381.

2. For provisions authorizing defenses to be made in the answer or reply see English Rules Under the Judicature Act (The Annual Practice, 1937) O. 25, r. r. 1–4; 1 Miss.Code Ann. (1930) §§ 378, 379. Compare Equity Rule 29 (Defenses—How Presented); U.S.C., Title 28, § 45 [1946 ed.] (District Courts; practice and procedure in certain cases under the interstate commerce laws). U.S.C., Title 28, § 45, [1946 ed.] substantially continued by this rule, provides: "No replication need be filed to the answer, and objections to the sufficiency of the petition or answer as not setting forth a cause of action or defense must be taken at the final hearing or by motion to dismiss the petition based on said grounds, which motion may be made at any time before answer is filed." Compare Calif.Code Civ.Proc. (Deering, 1937) § 433; 4 Nev.Comp.Laws (Hillyer, 1929) § 8600. For provisions that the defendant may demur and answer at the same time, see Calif.Code Civ.Proc. (Deering, 1937) § 431; 4 Nev.Comp.Laws (Hillyer, 1929) § 8598.

3. Equity Rule 29 (Defenses—How Presented) abolished demurrers and provided that defenses in point of law arising on the face of the bill should be made by motion to dismiss or in the answer, with further provision that every such point of law going to the whole or material part of the cause or causes stated might be called up and disposed of before final hearing "at the discretion of the court." Likewise many state practices have abolished the demurrer, or retain it only to attack substantial and not formal defects. See 6 Tenn.Code Ann. (Williams, 1934) § 8784; Ala.Code Ann. (Michie, 1928) § 9479; 2 Mass.Gen.Laws (Ter.Ed., 1932) ch. 231, §§ 15–18; Kansas Gen.Stat.Ann. (1935) §§ 60–705, 60–706.

Note to Subdivision (c). Compare Equity Rule 33 (Testing Sufficiency of Defense); N.Y.R.C.P. (1937) Rules 111 and 112.

New matter is shown in italics;   matter to be omitted is lined through

Note to Subdivisions (e) and (f). Compare Equity Rules 20 (Further and Particular Statement in Pleading May Be Required) and 21 (Scandal and Impertinence); English Rules Under the Judicature Act (The Annual Practice, 1937) O. 19, r. r. 7, 7a, 7b, 8; 4 Mont.Rev.Codes Ann. (1935) §§ 9166, 9167; N.Y.C.P.A. (1937) § 247; N.Y.R.C.P. (1937) Rules 103, 115, 116, 117; Wyo.Rev.Stat.Ann. (Courtright, 1931) §§ 89–1033, 89–1034.

Note to Subdivision (g). Compare Rules of the District Court of the United States for the District of Columbia (1937), Equity Rule 11; N.M. Rules of Pleading, Practice and Procedure, 38 N.M.Rep. vii [105–408] (1934); Wash.Gen.Rules of the Superior Courts, 1 Wash.Rev.Stat.Ann. (Remington, 1932) p. 160, Rule VI(e) and (f).

Note to Subdivision (h). Compare Calif.Code Civ.Proc. (Deering, 1937) § 434; 2 Minn.Stat. (Mason, 1927) § 9252; N.Y.C.P.A. (1937) §§ 278 and 279; Wash.Gen. Rules of the Superior Courts, 1 Wash.Rev.Stat.Ann. (Remington, 1932) p. 160, Rule VI(e). This rule continues U.S.C., Title 28, § 80 [now §§ 1359, 1447, 1919] (Dismissal or remand) (of action over which district court lacks jurisdiction), while U.S.C., Title 28, § 399 [now § 1653] (Amendments to show diverse citizenship) is continued by Rule 15.

Advisory Committee's Note to 1948 Amendment

(a) When Presented. A defendant shall serve his answer within 20 days after the service of the summons and complaint upon him, unless the court directs otherwise when service of process is made pursuant to Rule 4(e). A party served with a pleading stating a cross-claim against him shall serve an answer thereto within 20 days after the service upon him. The plaintiff shall serve his reply to a counterclaim in the answer within 20 days after service of the answer or, if a reply is ordered by the court, within 20 days after service of the order, unless the order otherwise directs. The United States or an officer or agency thereof shall serve an answer to the complaint or to a cross-claim, or a reply to a counterclaim, within 60 days after the service upon the United States attorney of the pleading in which the claim is asserted. The service of ~~any~~ *a* motion ~~provided for in~~ *permitted under* this rule alters ~~the time fixed by these rules for serving any required responsive pleading~~ *these periods of time* as follows, unless a different time is fixed by order of the court: (1) if the court denies the motion or postpones its disposition until the trial on the merits, the responsive pleading ~~may~~ *shall* be served within 10 days after notice of the court's action; (2) if the court grants a motion for a more definite statement ~~or for a bill of particulars,~~ the responsive pleading ~~may~~ *shall* be served within ~~ten~~ *10* days after the service of the more definite statement ~~or bill of particulars. In either case the time for service of the responsive pleading shall be not less than~~ *remains of the time* which would have been allowed under these rules if the motion had not been made.

New matter is shown in italics; matter to be omitted is lined through

(b) How Presented. Every defense, in law or fact, to a claim for relief in any pleading, whether a claim, counterclaim, cross-claim, or third-party claim, shall be asserted in the responsive pleading thereto if one is required, except that the following defenses may at the option of the pleader be made by motion: (1) lack of jurisdiction over the subject matter, (2) lack of jurisdiction over the person, (3) improper venue, (4) insufficiency of process, (5) insufficiency of service of process, (6) failure to state a claim upon which relief can be granted, *(7) failure to join an indispensable party.* A motion making any of these defenses shall be made before pleading if a further pleading is permitted. No defense or objection is waived by being joined with one or more other defenses or objections in a responsive pleading or motion. If a pleading sets forth a claim for relief to which the adverse party is not required to serve a responsive pleading, he may assert at the trial any defense in law or fact to that claim for relief. *If, on a motion asserting the defense numbered (6) to dismiss for failure of the pleading to state a claim upon which relief can be granted, matters outside the pleading are presented to and not excluded by the court, the motion shall be treated as one for summary judgment and disposed of as provided in Rule 56, and all parties shall be given reasonable opportunity to present all material made pertinent to such a motion by Rule 56.*

(c) Motion for Judgment on the Pleadings. After the pleadings are closed but within such time as not to delay the trial, any party may move for judgment on the pleadings. *If, on a motion for judgment on the pleadings, matters outside the pleadings are presented to and not excluded by the court, the motion shall be treated as one for summary judgment and disposed of as provided in Rule 56, and all parties shall be given reasonable opportunity to present all material made pertinent to such a motion by Rule 56.*

(d) Preliminary Hearings. The defenses specifically enumerated (1)-~~(6)~~ *(7)* in subdivision (b) of this rule, whether made in a pleading or by motion, and the motion for judgment mentioned in subdivision (c) of this rule shall be heard and determined before trial on application of any party, unless the court orders that the hearing and determination thereof be deferred until the trial.

(e) Motion for More Definite Statement ~~or for Bill of Particulars.~~ ~~Before responding to a pleading or, if no responsive pleading is permitted by these rules, within 20 days after the service of the pleading upon him, a party may move for a more definite statement or for a bill of particulars of any matter which is not averred with sufficient definiteness or particularity to enable him properly to prepare his responsive pleading or to prepare for trial.~~ *If a pleading to which a responsive pleading is permitted is so*

New matter is shown in italics; matter to be omitted is lined through

vague or ambiguous that a party cannot reasonably be required to frame a responsive pleading, he may move for a more definite statement before interposing his responsive pleading. The motion shall point out the defects complained of and the details desired. If the motion is granted and the order of the court is not obeyed within 10 days after notice of the order or within such other time as the court may fix, the court may strike the pleading to which the motion was directed or make such order as it deems just. ~~A bill of particulars becomes part of the pleading which it supplements.~~

(f) Motion to Strike. Upon motion made by a party before responding to a pleading or, if no responsive pleading is permitted by these rules, upon motion made by a party within 20 days after the service of the pleading upon him or upon the court's own initiative at any time, the court may order *stricken from any pleading any insufficient defense or* any redundant, immaterial, impertinent, or scandalous matter ~~stricken from any pleading~~.

(g) Consolidation of ~~Motions~~ *Defenses*. A party who makes a motion under this rule may join with it the other motions herein provided for and then available to him. If a party makes a motion under this rule and does not include therein all defenses and objections then available to him which this rule permits to be raised by motion, he shall not thereafter make a motion based on any of the defenses or objections so omitted, except ~~that prior to making any other motions under this rule he may make a motion in which are joined all the defenses numbered (1) to (5) in subdivision (b) of this rule which he cares to assert~~ *as provided in subdivision (h) of this rule.*

(h) Waiver of Defenses. A party waives all defenses and objections which he does not present either by motion as hereinbefore provided or, if he has made no motion, in his answer or reply, except (1) that the defense of failure to state a claim upon which relief can be granted, *the defense of failure to join an indispensable party,* and the objection of failure to state a legal defense to a claim may also be made by a later pleading, if one is permitted, or by motion for judgment on the pleadings or at the trial on the merits, and except (2) that, whenever it appears by suggestion of the parties or otherwise that the court lacks jurisdiction of the subject matter, the court shall dismiss the action. The objection or defense, if made at the trial, shall be disposed of as provided in Rule 15(b) in the light of any evidence that may have been received.

———

New matter is shown in italics; matter to be omitted is lined through

Subdivision (a). Various minor alterations in language have been made to improve the statement of the rule. All references to bills of particulars have been stricken in accordance with changes made in subdivision (e).

Subdivision (b). The addition of defense (7), "failure to join an indispensable party", cures an omission in the rules, which are silent as to the mode of raising such failure. See Commentary, *Manner of Raising Objection of Non–Joinder of Indispensable Party,* 1940, 2 Fed.Rules Serv. 658 and, 1942, 5 Fed.Rules Serv. 820. In one case, *United States v. Metropolitan Life Ins. Co.,* E.D.Pa.1941, 36 F.Supp. 399, the failure to join an indispensable party was raised under Rule 12(c).

Rule 12(b)(6), permitting a motion to dismiss for failure of the complaint to state a claim on which relief can be granted, is substantially the same as the old demurrer for failure of a pleading to state a cause of action. Some courts have held that as the rule by its terms refers to statements in the complaint, extraneous matter on affidavits, depositions or otherwise, may not be introduced in support of the motion, or to resist it. On the other hand, in many cases the district courts have permitted the introduction of such material. When these cases have reached circuit courts of appeals in situations where the extraneous material so received shows that there is no genuine issue as to any material question of fact and that on the undisputed facts as disclosed by the affidavits or depositions, one party or the other is entitled to judgment as a matter of law, the circuit courts, properly enough, have been reluctant to dispose of the case merely on the face of the pleading, and in the interest of prompt disposition of the action have made a final disposition of it. In dealing with such situations the Second Circuit has made the sound suggestion that whatever its label or original basis, the motion may be treated as a motion for summary judgment and disposed of as such. *Samara v. United States,* C.C.A.2d, 1942, 129 F.2d 594, cert. den., 1942, 317 U.S. 686, 63 S.Ct. 258; *Boro Hall Corp. v. General Motors Corp.,* C.C.A.2d, 1942, 124 F.2d 822, cert. den., 1943, 317 U.S. 695, 63 S.Ct. 436. See also *Kithcart v. Metropolitan Life Ins. Co.,* C.C.A.8th, 1945, 150 F.2d 997, aff'g 62 F.Supp. 93.

It has also been suggested that this practice could be justified on the ground that the federal rules permit "speaking" motions. The Committee entertains the view that on motion under Rule 12(b)(6) to dismiss for failure of the complaint to state a good claim, the trial court should have authority to permit the introduction of extraneous matter, such as may be offered on a motion for summary judgment, and if it does not exclude such matter the motion should then be treated as a motion for summary judgment and disposed of in the manner and on the conditions stated in Rule 56 relating to summary judgments, and, of course, in such a situation, when the case reaches the circuit court of appeals, that court should treat the motion in the same way. The Committee believes that such practice, however, should be tied to the summary judgment rule. The term "speaking motion" is not mentioned in the rules, and if there is such a thing its limitations are undefined. Where extraneous matter is received, by tying further proceedings to the summary judgment rule the courts have a definite basis in the rules for disposing of the motion.

The Committee emphasizes particularly the fact that the summary judgment rule does not permit a case to be disposed of by judgment on the merits on affidavits, which disclose a conflict on a material issue of fact, and unless this practice is tied to the summary judgment rule, the extent to which a court, on the introduction of such extraneous matter, may resolve questions of fact on conflicting proof would be left uncertain.

The decisions dealing with this general situation may be generally grouped as follows: (1) cases dealing with the use of affidavits and other extraneous material on

---

New matter is shown in italics; matter to be omitted is lined through

motions; (2) cases reversing judgments to prevent final determination on mere pleading allegations alone.

Under group (1) are: *Boro Hall Corp. v. General Motors Corp.*, C.C.A.2d, 1942, 124 F.2d 822, cert. den., 1943, 317 U.S. 695, 63 S.Ct. 436; *Gallup v. Caldwell*, C.C.A.3d, 1941, 120 F.2d 90; *Central Mexico Light & Power Co. v. Munch*, C.C.A.2d, 1940, 116 F.2d 85; *National Labor Relations Board v. Montgomery Ward & Co.*, App.D.C.1944, 79 U.S.App.D.C. 200, 144 F.2d 528, cert. den., 1944, 65 S.Ct. 134; *Urquhart v. American–La France Foamite Corp.*, App.D.C.1944, 79 U.S.App.D.C. 219, 144 F.2d 542; *Samara v. United States*, C.C.A.2d, 1942, 129 F.2d 594; *Cohen v. American Window Glass Co.*, C.C.A.2d, 1942, 126 F.2d 111; *Sperry Products Inc. v. Association of American Railroads*, C.C.A.2d, 1942, 132 F.2d 408; *Joint Council Dining Car Employees Local 370 v. Delaware, Lackawanna and Western R. Co.*, C.C.A.2d, 1946, 157 F.2d 417; *Weeks v. Bareco Oil Co.*, C.C.A.7th, 1941, 125 F.2d 84; *Carroll v. Morrison Hotel Corp.*, C.C.A.7th, 1945, 149 F.2d 404; *Victory v. Manning*, C.C.A.3rd, 1942, 128 F.2d 415; *Locals No. 1470, No. 1469, and No. 1512 of International Longshoremen's Association v. Southern Pacific Co.*, C.C.A.5th, 1942, 131 F.2d 605; *Lucking v. Delano*, C.C.A.6th, 1942, 129 F.2d 283; *San Francisco Lodge No. 68 of International Association of Machinists v. Forrestal*, N.D.Cal.1944, 58 F.Supp. 466; *Benson v. Export Equipment Corp.*, N.Mex.1945, 164 P.2d 380, construing New Mexico rule identical with Rule 12(b)(6); *F.E. Myers & Bros. Co. v. Gould Pumps, Inc.*, W.D.N.Y.1946, 9 Fed.Rules Serv. 12b.33, Case 2, 5 F.R.D. 132. Cf. *Kohler v. Jacobs*, C.C.A.5th, 1943, 138 F.2d 440; *Cohen v. United States*, C.C.A.8th, 1942, 129 F.2d 733.

Under group (2) are: *Sparks v. England*, C.C.A.8th, 1940, 113 F.2d 579; *Continental Collieries, Inc. v. Shober*, C.C.A.3d, 1942, 130 F.2d 631; *Downey v. Palmer*, C.C.A.2d, 1940, 114 F.2d 116; *DeLoach v. Crowley's Inc.*, C.C.A.5th, 1942, 128 F.2d 378; *Leimer v. State Mutual Life Assurance Co. of Worcester, Mass.*, C.C.A.8th, 1940, 108 F.2d 302; *Rossiter v. Vogel*, C.C.A.2d, 1943, 134 F.2d 908, compare s.c., C.C.A.2d, 1945, 148 F.2d 292; *Karl Kiefer Machine Co. v. United States Bottlers Machinery Co.*, C.C.A.7th, 1940, 113 F.2d 356; *Chicago Metallic Mfg. Co. v. Edward Katzinger Co.*, C.C.A.7th, 1941, 123 F.2d 518; *Louisiana Farmers' Protective Union, Inc. v. Great Atlantic & Pacific Tea Co. of America, Inc.*, C.C.A.8th, 1942, 131 F.2d 419; *Publicity Bldg. Realty Corp. v. Hannegan*, C.C.A.8th, 1943, 139 F.2d 583; *Dioguardi v. Durning*, C.C.A.2d, 1944, 139 F.2d 774; *Package Closure Corp. v. Sealright Co., Inc.*, C.C.A.2d, 1944, 141 F.2d 972; *Tahir Erk v. Glenn L. Martin Co.*, C.C.A.4th, 1941, 116 F.2d 865; *Bell v. Preferred Life Assurance Society of Montgomery, Ala.*, 1943, 320 U.S. 238, 64 S.Ct. 5.

The addition at the end of subdivision (b) makes it clear that on a motion under Rule 12(b)(6) extraneous material may not be considered if the court excludes it, but that if the court does not exclude such material the motion shall be treated as a motion for summary judgment and disposed of as provided in Rule 56. It will also be observed that if a motion under Rule 12(b)(6) is thus converted into a summary judgment motion, the amendment insures that both parties shall be given a reasonable opportunity to submit affidavits and extraneous proofs to avoid taking a party by surprise through the conversion of the motion into a motion for summary judgment. In this manner and to this extent the amendment regularizes the practice above described. As the courts are already dealing with cases in this way, the effect of this amendment is really only to define the practice carefully and apply the requirements of the summary judgment rule in the disposition of the motion.

Subdivision (c). The sentence appended to subdivision (c) performs the same function and is grounded on the same reasons as the corresponding sentence added in subdivision (b).

New matter is shown in italics; matter to be omitted is lined through

Subdivision (d). The change here was made necessary because of the addition of defense (7) in subdivision (b).

Subdivision (e). References in this subdivision to a bill of particulars have been deleted, and the motion provided for is confined to one for a more definite statement, to be obtained only in cases where the movant cannot reasonably be required to frame an answer or other responsive pleading to the pleading in question. With respect to preparations for trial, the party is properly relegated to the various methods of examination and discovery provided in the rules for that purpose. *Slusher v. Jones,* E.D.Ky.1943, 7 Fed.Rules Serv. 12e.231, Case 5, 3 F.R.D. 168; *Best Foods, Inc. v. General Mills, Inc.,* D.Del.1943, 7 Fed.Rules Serv. 12e.231, Case 7, 3 F.R.D. 275; *Braden v. Callaway,* E.D.Tenn.1943, 8 Fed.Rules Serv. 12e.231, Case 1 (" ... most courts ... conclude that the definiteness required is only such as will be sufficient for the party to prepare responsive pleadings"). Accordingly, the reference to the 20 day time limit has also been eliminated, since the purpose of this present provision is to state a time period where the motion for a bill is made for the purpose or preparing for trial.

Rule 12(e) as originally drawn has been the subject of more judicial rulings than any other part of the rules, and has been much criticized by commentators, judges and members of the bar. See general discussion and cases cited in 1 *Moore's Federal Practice,* 1938, Cum.Supplement § 12.07, under "Page 657"; also, Holtzoff, *New Federal Procedure and the Courts,* 1940, 35–41. And compare vote of Second Circuit Conference of Circuit and District Judges, June 1940, recommending the abolition of the bill of particulars; *Sun Valley Mfg. Co. v. Mylish,* E.D.Pa.1944, 8 Fed.Rules Serv. 12e.231, Case 6 ("Our experience ... has demonstrated not only that 'the office of the bill of particulars is fast becoming obsolete' ... but that in view of the adequate discovery procedure available under the Rules, motions for bills of particulars should be abolished altogether."); *Walling v. American Steamship Co.,* W.D.N.Y.1945, 4 F.R.D. 355, 8 Fed.Rules Serv. 12e.244, Case 8 (" ... the adoption of the rule was ill advised. It has led to confusion, duplication and delay.") The tendency of some courts freely to grant extended bills of particulars has served to neutralize any helpful benefits derived from Rule 8, and has overlooked the intended use of the rules on depositions and discovery. The words "or to prepare for trial"—eliminated by the proposed amendment—have sometimes been seized upon as grounds for compulsory statement in the opposing pleading of all the details which the movant would have to meet at the trial. On the other hand, many courts have in effect read these words out of the rule. See *Walling v. Alabama Pipe Co.,* W.D.Mo.1942, 3 F.R.D. 159, 6 Fed.Rules Serv. 12e.244, Case 7; *Fleming v. Mason & Dixon Lines, Inc.,* E.D.Tenn.1941, 42 F.Supp. 230; *Kellogg Co. v. National Biscuit Co.,* D.N.J.1941, 38 F.Supp. 643; *Brown v. H.L. Green Co.,* S.D.N.Y.1943, 7 Fed.Rules Serv. 12e.231, Case 6; *Pedersen v. Standard Accident Ins. Co.,* W.D.Mo.1945, 8 Fed.Rules Serv. 12e.231, Case 8; *Bowles v. Ohse,* D.Neb.1945, 4 F.R.D. 403, 9 Fed.Rules Serv. 12e.231, Case 1; *Klages v. Cohen,* E.D.N.Y.1945, 9 Fed.Rules Serv. 8a.25, Case 4; *Bowles v. Lawrence,* D.Mass.1945, 8 Fed.Rules Serv. 12e.231, Case 19; *McKinney Tool & Mfg. Co. v. Hoyt,* N.D.Ohio 1945, 9 Fed.Rules Serv. 12e.235, Case 1; *Bowles v. Jack,* D.Minn.1945, 5 F.R.D. 1, 9 Fed.Rules Serv. 12e.244, Case 9. And it has been urged from the bench that the phrase be stricken. *Poole v. White,* N.D.W.Va.1941, 5 Fed.Rules Serv. 12e.231, Case 4, 2 F.R.D. 40. See also *Bowles v. Gabel,* W.D.Mo.1946, 9 Fed.Rules Serv. 12e.244, Case 10 ("The courts have never favored that portion of the rules which undertook to justify a motion of this kind for the purpose of aiding counsel in preparing his case for trial.").

Subdivision (f). This amendment affords a specific method of raising the insufficiency of a defense, a matter which has troubled some courts, although attack has been permitted in one way or another. See *Dysart v. Remington–Rand, Inc.,*

New matter is shown in italics; matter to be omitted is lined through

D.Conn.1939, 31 F.Supp. 296; *Eastman Kodak Co. v. McAuley,* S.D.N.Y.1941, 4 Fed.Rules Serv. 12f.21, Case 8, 2 F.R.D. 21; *Schenley Distillers Corp. v. Renken,* E.D.S.C.1940, 34 F.Supp. 678; *Yale Transport Corp. v. Yellow Truck & Coach Mfg. Co.,* S.D.N.Y.1944, 3 F.R.D. 440; *United States v. Turner Milk Co.,* N.D.Ill.1941, 4 Fed.Rules Serv. 12b.51, Case 3, 1 F.R.D. 643; *Teiger v. Stephan Oderwald, Inc.,* S.D.N.Y.1940, 31 F.Supp. 626; *Teplitsky v. Pennsylvania R. Co.,* N.D.Ill.1941, 38 F.Supp. 535; *Gallagher v. Carroll,* E.D.N.Y.1939, 27 F.Supp. 568; *United States v. Palmer,* S.D.N.Y.1939, 28 F.Supp. 936. And see *Indemnity Ins. Co. of North America v. Pan American Airways, Inc.,* S.D.N.Y.1944, 58 F.Supp. 338; Commentary, *Modes of Attacking Insufficient Defenses in the Answer,* 1939, 1 Fed.Rules Serv. 669, 1940, 2 Fed.Rules Serv. 640.

Subdivision (g). The change in title conforms with the companion provision in subdivision (h).

The alteration of the "except" clause requires that other than provided in subdivision (h) a party who resorts to a motion to raise defenses specified in the rule, must include in one motion all that are then available to him. Under the original rule defenses which could be raised by motion were divided into two groups which could be the subjects of two successive motions.

Subdivision (h). The addition of the phrase relating to indispensable parties is one of necessity.

Advisory Committee's Note to 1966 Amendment

Defenses and Objections—When and How Presented— By Pleading or Motion—Motion for Judgment on *the* Pleadings

(b) How Presented. Every defense, in law or fact, to a claim for relief in any pleading, whether a claim, counterclaim, cross-claim, or third-party claim, shall be asserted in the responsive pleading thereto if one is required, except that the following defenses may at the option of the pleader be made by motion: (1) lack of jurisdiction over the subject matter, (2) lack of jurisdiction over the person, (3) improper venue, (4) insufficiency of process, (5) insufficiency of service of process, (6) failure to state a claim upon which relief can be granted, (7) failure to join ~~an indispensable~~ *a* party *under Rule 19.* A motion making any of these defenses shall be made before pleading if a further pleading is permitted. No defense or objection is waived by being joined with one or more other defenses or objections in a responsive pleading or motion. If a pleading sets forth a claim for relief to which the adverse party is not required to serve a responsive pleading, he may assert at the trial any defense in law or fact to that claim for relief. If, on a motion asserting the defense numbered (6) to dismiss for failure of the pleading to state a claim upon which relief can be granted,

---

New matter is shown in italics; matter to be omitted is lined through

matters outside the pleading are presented to and not excluded by the court, the motion shall be treated as one for summary judgment and disposed of as provided in Rule 56, and all parties shall be given reasonable opportunity to present all material made pertinent to such a motion by Rule 56.

(g) Consolidation of Defenses *in Motion.* A party who makes a motion under this rule may join with it any other motions herein provided for and then available to him. If a party makes a motion under this rule but ~~does not include therein all defenses and objections~~ *omits therefrom any defense or objection* then available to him which this rule permits to be raised by motion, he shall not thereafter make a motion based on ~~any of the defenses or objections~~ *the defense or objection* so omitted, except *a* motion as provided in subdivision (h)*(2)* ~~of this rule~~ *hereof on any of the grounds there stated.*

(h) Waiver or Preservation of Certain Defenses. ~~A party waives all defenses and objections which he does not present either by motion as hereinbefore provided or, if he has made no motion, in his answer or reply, except (1) that the defense of failure to state a claim upon which relief can be granted, the defense of failure to join an indispensable party, and the objection of failure to state a legal defense to a claim may also be made by a later pleading, if one is permitted, or by motion for judgment on the pleadings or at the trial on the merits, and except (2) that, whenever it appears by suggestion of the parties or otherwise that the court lacks jurisdiction of the subject matter, the court shall dismiss the action. The objection or defense, if made at the trial, shall be disposed of as provided in Rule 15(b) in the light of any evidence that may have been received.~~

(1) A defense of lack of jurisdiction over the person, improper venue, insufficiency of process, or insufficiency of service of process is waived (A) if omitted from a motion in the circumstances described in subdivision (g), or (B) if it is neither made by motion under this rule nor included in a responsive pleading or an amendment thereof permitted by Rule 15(a) to be made as a matter of course.

(2) A defense of failure to state a claim upon which relief can be granted, a defense of failure to join a party indispensable under Rule 19, and an objection of failure to state a legal defense to a claim may be made in any pleading permitted or ordered under Rule 7(a), or by motion for judgment on the pleadings, or at the trial on the merits.

New matter is shown in italics; matter to be omitted is lined through

(3) Whenever it appears by suggestion of the parties or otherwise that the court lacks jurisdiction of the subject matter, the court shall dismiss the action.

―――――

Subdivision (b)(7). The terminology of this subdivision is changed to accord with the amendment of Rule 19. See the Advisory Committee's Note to Rule 19, as amended, especially the third paragraph therein before the caption "Subdivision (c)."

Subdivision (g). Subdivision (g) has forbidden a defendant who makes a preanswer motion under this rule from making a further motion presenting any defense or objection which was available to him at the time he made the first motion and which he could have included, but did not in fact include therein. Thus if the defendant moves before answer to dismiss the complaint for failure to state a claim, he is barred from making a further motion presenting the defense of improper venue, if that defense was available to him when he made his original motion. Amended subdivision (g) is to the same effect. This required consolidation of defenses and objections in a Rule 12 motion is salutary in that it works against piecemeal consideration of a case. For exceptions to the requirement of consolidation, see the last clause of subdivision (g), referring to new subdivision (h)(2).

Subdivision (h). The question has arisen whether an omitted defense which cannot be made the basis of a second motion may nevertheless be pleaded in the answer. Subdivision (h) called for waiver of " * * * defenses and objections which he [defendant] does not present * * * by motion * * * or, if he has made no motion, in his answer * * *." If the clause "if he has made no motion," was read literally, it seemed that the omitted defense was waived and could not be pleaded in the answer. On the other hand, the clause might be read as adding nothing of substance to the preceding words; in that event it appeared that a defense was not waived by reason of being omitted from the motion and might be set up in the answer. The decisions were divided. Favoring waiver, see *Keefe v. Derounian,* 6 F.R.D. 11 (N.D.Ill.1946); *Elbinger v. Precision Metal Workers Corp.,* 18 F.R.D. 467 (E.D.Wis.1956); see also *Rensing v. Turner Aviation Corp.,* 166 F.Supp. 790 (N.D.Ill.1958); *P. Beiersdorf & Co. v. Duke Laboratories, Inc.,* 10 F.R.D. 282 (S.D.N.Y.1950); *Neset v. Christensen,* 92 F.Supp. 78 (E.D.N.Y.1950). Opposing waiver, see *Phillips v. Baker,* 121 F.2d 752 (9th Cir.1941); *Crum v. Graham,* 32 F.R.D. 173 (D.Mont.1963) (regretfully following the Phillips case); see also *Birnbaum v. Birrell,* 9 F.R.D. 72 (S.D.N.Y.1948); *Johnson v. Joseph Schlitz Brewing Co.,* 33 F.Supp. 176 (E.D.Tenn.1940); *cf. Carter v. American Bus Lines, Inc.,* 22 F.R.D. 323 (D.Neb.1958).

Amended subdivision (h)(1)(A) eliminates the ambiguity and states that certain specified defenses which were available to a party when he made a preanswer motion, but which he omitted from the motion, are waived. The specified defenses are lack of jurisdiction over the person, improper venue, insufficiency of process, and insufficiency of service of process (see Rule 12(b)(2)–(5)). A party who by motion invites the court to pass upon a threshold defense should bring forward all the specified defenses he then has and thus allow the court to do a reasonably complete job. The waiver reinforces the policy of subdivision (g) forbidding successive motions.

By amended subdivision (h)(1)(B), the specified defenses, even if not waived by the operation of (A), are waived by the failure to raise them by a motion under Rule 12 or in the responsive pleading or any amendment thereof to which the party is entitled as a matter of course. The specified defenses are of such a character that

New matter is shown in italics; matter to be omitted is lined through

they should not be delayed and brought up for the first time by means of an application to the court to amend the responsive pleading.

Since the language of the subdivisions is made clear, the party is put on fair notice of the effect of his actions and omissions and can guard himself against unintended waiver. It is to be noted that while the defenses specified in subdivision (h)(1) are subject to waiver as there provided, the more substantial defenses of failure to state a claim upon which relief can be granted, failure to join a party indispensable under Rule 19, and failure to state a legal defense to a claim (see Rule 12(b)(6), (7), (f)), as well as the defense of lack of jurisdiction over the subject matter (see Rule 12(b)(1)), are expressly preserved against waiver by amended subdivision (h)(2) and (3).

Rule 13. Counterclaim and Cross–Claim

Advisory Committee's Note to Original Rule

1. This is substantially Equity Rule 30 (Answer—Contents—Counterclaim), broadened to include legal as well as equitable counterclaims.

2. Compare the English practice, English Rules Under the Judicature Act (The Annual Practice, 1937) O. 19, r. r. 2 and 3, and O. 21, r. r. 10–17; *Beddall v. Maitland,* L. R. 17 Ch.Div. 174, 181, 182 (1881).

3. Certain states have also adopted almost unrestricted provisions concerning both the subject matter of and the parties to a counterclaim. This seems to be the modern tendency. Ark.Civ.Code (Crawford, 1934) §§ 117 (as amended) and 118; N.J.Comp.Stat., (2 Cum.Supp. 1911–1924) tit. 163, § 288; N.Y.C.P.A. (1937) §§ 262, 266, 267 (all as amended, Laws of 1936, ch. 324), 268, 269, and 271; Wis.Stat. (1935) § 263.14(1)(c).

4. Most codes do not expressly provide for a counterclaim in the reply. Clark, *Code Pleading* (1928), p. 486. Ky.Codes (Carroll, 1932) Civ.Pract. § 98 does provide, however, for such counterclaim.

5. The provisions of this rule respecting counterclaims are subject to Rule 82 (Jurisdiction and Venue Unaffected). For a discussion of federal jurisdiction and venue in regard to counterclaims and cross-claims, see Shulman and Jaegerman, *Some Jurisdictional Limitations in Federal Procedure* (1936), 45 Yale L.J. 393, 410 *et seq.*

6. This rule does not affect such statutes of the United States as U.S.C., Title 28, § 41(1) [now §§ 1331, 1332, 1341, 1342, 1345, 1354, 1359] (United States as plaintiff; civil suits at common law and in equity), relating to assigned claims in actions based on diversity of citizenship.

7. If the action proceeds to judgment without the interposition of a counterclaim as required by subdivision (a) of this rule, the counterclaim is barred. See *American Mills Co. v. American Surety Co.,* 260 U.S. 360, 43 S.Ct. 149, 67 L.Ed. 306 (1922); *Marconi Wireless Telegraph Co. v. National Electric Signalling Co.,* 206 Fed. 295 (E.D.N.Y., 1913); Hopkins, *Federal Equity Rules* (8th ed., 1933), p. 213; Simkins, *Federal Practice* (1934), p. 663.

8. For allowance of credits against the United States see U.S.C., Title 26, §§ 1672–1673 (Suits for refunds of internal revenue taxes—limitations); U.S.C., Title 28, §§ 774 [now § 2406] (Suits by United States against individuals; credits),

---

New matter is shown in italics; matter to be omitted is lined through

775 [1946 ed.] (Suits under postal laws; credits); U.S.C., Title 31, § 227 (Offsets against judgments and claims against United States).

Advisory Committee's Note to 1948 Amendment

(a) Compulsory Counterclaims. A pleading shall state as a counterclaim any claim, ~~not the subject of a pending action,~~ which at the time of ~~filing~~ *serving* the pleading the pleader has against any opposing party, if it arises out of the transaction or occurrence that is the subject matter of the opposing party's claim and does not require for its adjudication the presence of third parties of whom the court cannot acquire jurisdiction, *except that such a claim need not be so stated if at the time the action was commenced the claim was the subject of another pending action.*

(g) Cross–Claim Against Co–Party. A pleading may state as a cross-claim any claim by one party against a co-party arising out of the transaction or occurrence that is the subject matter either of the original action or of a counterclaim therein *or relating to any property that is the subject matter of the original action.* Such cross-claim may include a claim that the party against whom it is asserted is or may be liable to the cross-claimant for all or part of a claim asserted in the action against the cross-claimant.

(i) Separate Trials; Separate Judgments. If the court orders separate trials as provided in Rule 42(b), judgment on a counterclaim or cross-claim may be rendered *in accordance with the terms of Rule 54(b)* when the court has jurisdiction so to do, even if the claims of the opposing party have been dismissed or otherwise disposed of.

Subdivision (a). The use of the word "filing" was inadvertent. The word "serving" conforms with subdivision (e) and with usage generally throughout the rules.

The removal of the phrase "not the subject of a pending action" and the addition of the new clause at the end of the subdivision is designed to eliminate the ambiguity noted in *Prudential Insurance Co. of America v. Saxe*, App.D.C.1943, 77 U.S.App.D.C. 144, 134 F.2d 16, 33–34, cert. den., 1943, 319 U.S. 745, 63 S.Ct. 1033. The rewording of the subdivision in this respect insures against an undesirable possibility presented under the original rule whereby a party having a claim which would be the subject of a compulsory counterclaim could avoid stating it as such by bringing an independent action in another court after the commencement of the federal action but before serving his pleading in the federal action.

Subdivision (g). The amendment is to care for a situation such as where a second mortgagee is made defendant in a foreclosure proceeding and wishes to file a

---

New matter is shown in italics; matter to be omitted is lined through

cross-complaint against the mortgagor in order to secure a personal judgment for the indebtedness and foreclose his lien. A claim of this sort by the second mortgagee may not necessarily arise out of the transaction or occurrence that is the subject matter of the original action under the terms of Rule 13(g).

Subdivision (i). The change clarifies the interdependence of Rules 13(i) and 54(b).

Advisory Committee's Note to 1963 Amendment

(a) Compulsory Counterclaims. A pleading shall state as a counterclaim any claim which at the time of serving the pleading the pleader has against any opposing party, if it arises out of the transaction or occurrence that is the subject matter of the opposing party's claim and does not require for its adjudication the presence of third parties of whom the court cannot acquire jurisdiction~,~. ~except that such a claim need not be so stated~ *But the pleader need not state the claim* if *(1)* at the time the action was commenced the claim was the subject of another pending action~,~*, or (2) the opposing party brought suit upon his claim by attachment or other process by which the court did not acquire jurisdiction to render a personal judgment on that claim, and the pleader is not stating any counterclaim under this Rule 13.*

When a defendant, if he desires to defend his interest in property, is obliged to come in and litigate in a court to whose jurisdiction he could not ordinarily be subjected, fairness suggests that he should not be required to assert counterclaims, but should rather be permitted to do so at his election. If, however, he does elect to assert a counterclaim, it seems fair to require him to assert any other which is compulsory within the meaning of Rule 13(a). Clause (2), added by amendment to Rule 13(a), carries out this idea. It will apply to various cases described in Rule 4(e), as amended, where service is effected through attachment or other process by which the court does not acquire jurisdiction to render a personal judgment against the defendant. Clause (2) will also apply to actions commenced in State courts jurisdictionally grounded on attachment or the like, and removed to the Federal courts.

Rule 15. Amended and Supplemental Pleadings

Advisory Committee's Note to Original Rule

See generally for the present federal practice, Equity Rules 19 (Amendments Generally), 28 (Amendment of Bill as of Course), 32 (Answer to Amended Bill), 34 (Supplemental Pleading), and 35 (Bills of Revivor and Supplemental Bills—Form); U.S.C., Title 28, §§ 399 [now § 1653] (Amendments to show diverse citizenship) and 777 [1946 ed.] (Defects of form; amendments). See English Rules Under the Judicature Act (The Annual Practice, 1937) O. 28, r. r. 1–13; O. 20, r. 4; O. 24, r. r. 1–3.

New matter is shown in italics; matter to be omitted is lined through

Note to Subdivision (a). The right to serve an amended pleading once as of course is common. 4 Mont.Rev.Codes Ann. (1935) § 9186; 1 Ore.Code Ann. (1930) § 1–904; 1 S.C.Code (Michie, 1932) § 493; English Rules Under the Judicature Act (The Annual Practice, 1937) O. 28, r. 2. Provision for amendment of pleading before trial, by leave of court, is in almost every code. If there is no statute the power of the court to grant leave is said to be inherent. Clark, *Code Pleading* (1928), pp. 498, 509.

Note to Subdivision (b). Compare Equity Rule 19 (Amendments Generally) and code provisions which allow an amendment "at any time in furtherance of justice," (e.g., Ark.Civ.Code (Crawford, 1934) § 155) and which allow an amendment of pleadings to conform to the evidence, where the adverse party has not been misled and prejudiced (e.g., N.M.Stat.Ann. (Courtright, 1929) §§ 105–601, 105–602).

Note to Subdivision (c). "Relation back" is a well recognized doctrine of recent and now more frequent application. Compare Ala.Code Ann. (Michie, 1928) § 9513; Ill.Rev.Stat. (1937) ch. 110, § 170(2); 2 Wash.Rev.Stat.Ann. (Remington, 1932) § 308–3(4). See U.S.C., Title 28, § 399 [now § 1653] (Amendments to show diverse citizenship) for a provision for "relation back".

Note to Subdivision (d). This is an adaptation of Equity Rule 34 (Supplemental Pleading).

Advisory Committee's Note to 1966 Amendment

(c) Relation Back of Amendments. Whenever the claim or defense asserted in the amended pleading arose out of the conduct, transaction, or occurrence set forth or attempted to be set forth in the original pleading, the amendment relates back to the date of the original pleading. *An amendment changing the party against whom a claim is asserted relates back if the foregoing provision is satisfied and, within the period provided by law for commencing the action against him, the party to be brought in by amendment (1) has received such notice of the institution of the action that he will not be prejudiced in maintaining his defense on the merits, and (2) knew or should have known that, but for a mistake concerning the identity of the proper party, the action would have been brought against him.*

The delivery or mailing of process to the United States Attorney, or his designee, or the Attorney General of the United States, or an agency or officer who would have been a proper defendant if named, satisfies the requirement of clauses (1) and (2) hereof with respect to the United States or any agency or officer thereof to be brought into the action as a defendant.

Rule 15(c) is amplified to state more clearly when an amendment of a pleading changing the party against whom a claim is asserted (including an amendment to correct a misnomer or misdescription of a defendant) shall "relate back" to the date of the original pleading.

New matter is shown in italics; matter to be omitted is lined through

The problem has arisen most acutely in certain actions by private parties against officers or agencies of the United States. Thus an individual denied social security benefits by the Secretary of Health, Education, and Welfare may secure review of the decision by bringing a civil action against that officer within sixty days. 42 U.S.C. § 405(g) (Supp. III, 1962). In several recent cases the claimants instituted timely action but mistakenly named as defendant the United States, the Department of HEW, the "Federal Security Administration" (a nonexistent agency), and a Secretary who had retired from the office nineteen days before. Discovering their mistakes, the claimants moved to amend their complaints to name the proper defendant; by this time the statutory sixty-day period had expired. The motions were denied on the ground that the amendment "would amount to the commencement of a new proceeding and would not relate back in time so as to avoid the statutory provision * * * that suit be brought within sixty days. * * * *" *Cohn v. Federal Security Adm.,* 199 F.Supp. 884, 885 (W.D.N.Y.1961); see also *Cunningham v. United States,* 199 F.Supp. 541 (W.D.Mo.1958); *Hall v. Department of HEW,* 199 F.Supp. 833 (S.D.Tex.1960); *Sandridge v. Folsom, Secretary of HEW,* 200 F.Supp. 25 (M.D.Tenn.1959). [The Secretary of Health, Education, and Welfare has approved certain ameliorative regulations under 42 U.S.C. § 405(g). See 29 Fed.Reg. 8209 (June 30, 1964); Jacoby, *The Effect of Recent Changes in the Law of "Nonstatutory" Judicial Review,* 53 Geo.L.J. 19, 42–43 (1964); see also *Simmons v. United States Dept. HEW,* 328 F.2d 86 (3d Cir.1964).]

Analysis in terms of "new proceeding" is traceable to *Davis v. L. L. Cohen & Co.,* 268 U.S. 638 (1925), and *Mellon v. Arkansas Land & Lumber Co.,* 275 U.S. 460 (1928), but those cases antedate the adoption of the rules which import different criteria for determining when an amendment is to "relate back". As lower courts have continued to rely on the *Davis* and *Mellon* cases despite the contrary intent of the rules, clarification of Rule 15(c) is considered advisable.

Relation back is intimately connected with the policy of the statute of limitations. The policy of the statute limiting the time for suit against the Secretary of HEW would not have been offended by allowing relation back in the situations described above. For the government was put on notice of the claim within the stated period—in the particular instances, by means of the initial delivery of process to a responsible government official (see Rule 4(d)(4) and (5)). In these circumstances, characterization of the amendment as a new proceeding is not responsive to the reality, but is merely question-begging; and to deny relation back is to defeat unjustly the claimant's opportunity to prove his case. See the full discussion by Byse, *Suing the "Wrong" Defendant in Judicial Review of Federal Administrative Action: Proposals for Reform,* 77 Harv.L.Rev. 40 (1963); see also Ill.Civ.P.Act § 46(4).

Much the same question arises in other types of actions against the government (see Byse, *supra,* at 45 n. 15). In actions between private parties, the problem of relation back of amendments changing defendants has generally been better handled by the courts, but incorrect criteria have sometimes been applied, leading sporadically to doubtful results. See 1A Barron & Holtzoff, *Federal Practice & Procedure* § 451 (Wright ed. 1960); 1 *id.* § 186 (1960); 2 *id.* § 543 (1961); 3 *Moore's Federal Practice* ¶ 15.15 (Cum.Supp.1962); Annot., *Change in Party After Statute of Limitations Has Run,* 8 A.L.R.2d 6 (1949). Rule 15(c) has been amplified to provide a general solution. An amendment changing the party against whom a claim is asserted relates back if the amendment satisfies the usual condition of Rule 15(c) of "arising out of the conduct * * * set forth * * * in the original pleading," and if, within the applicable limitations period, the party brought in by amendment, *first,* received such notice of the institution of the action—the notice need not be formal—that he would not be prejudiced in defending the action, and, *second,* knew or should have known that the action would have been brought against him initially had there not

---

New matter is shown in italics; matter to be omitted is lined through

been a mistake concerning the identity of the proper party. Revised Rule 15(c) goes on to provide specifically in the government cases that the *first* and *second* requirements are satisfied when the government has been notified in the manner there described (see Rule 4(d)(4) and (5)). As applied to the government cases, revised Rule 15(c) further advances the objectives of the 1961 amendment of Rule 25(d) (substitution of public officers).

The relation back of amendments changing plaintiffs is not expressly treated in revised Rule 15(c) since the problem is generally easier. Again the chief consideration of policy is that of the statute of limitations, and the attitude taken in revised Rule 15(c) toward change of defendants extends by analogy to amendments changing plaintiffs. Also relevant is the amendment of Rule 17(a) (real party in interest). To avoid forfeitures of just claims, revised Rule 17(a) would provide that no action shall be dismissed on the ground that it is not prosecuted in the name of the real party in interest until a reasonable time has been allowed for correction of the defect in the manner there stated.

Advisory Committee's Note to 1991 Amendment

(c) Relation Back of Amendments. *An amendment of a pleading relates back to the date of the original pleading when*

(1) relation back is permitted by the law that provides the statute of limitations applicable to the action, or

(2) ~~Whenever~~ the claim or defense asserted in the amended pleading arose out of the conduct, transaction, or occurrence set forth or attempted to be set forth in the original pleading, ~~the amendment relates back to the date of the original pleading.~~ *or*

(3) ~~An~~ *the* amendment ~~changing~~ *changes* the party *or the naming of the party* against whom a claim is asserted ~~relates back~~ if the foregoing provision *(2)* is satisfied and, within the period provided by ~~law~~ *Rule 4(m)* for ~~commencing the action against~~ *service of the summons and complaint,* the party to be brought in by amendment~~, that party~~ (*1A*) has received such notice of the institution of the action that the party will not be prejudiced in maintaining a defense on the merits, and (*2B*) knew or should have known that, but for a mistake concerning the identity of the proper party, the action would have been brought against the party.

The delivery or mailing of process to the United States Attorney, or United States Attorney's designee, or the Attorney General of the United States, or an agency or officer who would have been a proper defendant if named, satisfies the requirement of ~~clauses~~ *subparagraphs* (*1A*) and (*2B*) ~~hereof~~ *this paragraph (3)* with respect to the United States or any

---

New matter is shown in italics; matter to be omitted is lined through

agency or officer thereof to be brought into the action as a defendant.

———

The rule has been revised to prevent parties against whom claims are made from taking unjust advantage of otherwise inconsequential pleading errors to sustain a limitations defense.

Paragraph (c)(1). This provision is new. It is intended to make it clear that the rule does not apply to preclude any relation back that may be permitted under the applicable limitations law. Generally, the applicable limitations law will be state law. If federal jurisdiction is based on the citizenship of the parties, the primary reference is the law of the state in which the district court sits. *Walker v. Armco Steel Corp.,* 446 U.S. 740 (1980). If federal jurisdiction is based on a federal question, the reference may be to the law of the state governing relations between the parties. *E.g., Board of Regents v. Tomanio,* 446 U.S. 478 (1980). In some circumstances, the controlling limitations law may be federal law. *E.g., West v. Conrail, Inc.,* 107 S.Ct. 1538 (1987). Cf. *Burlington Northern R. Co. v. Woods,* 480 U.S. 1 (1987); *Stewart Organization v. Ricoh,* 108 S.Ct. 2239 (1988). Whatever may be the controlling body of limitations law, if that law affords a more forgiving principle of relation back than the one provided in this rule, it should be available to save the claim. Accord, *Marshall v. Mulrenin,* 508 F.2d 39 (1st Cir.1974). If *Schiavone v. Fortune,* 106 S.Ct. 2379 (1986) implies the contrary, this paragraph is intended to make a material change in the rule.

Paragraph (c)(3). This paragraph has been revised to change the result in *Schiavone v. Fortune, supra,* with respect to the problem of a misnamed defendant. An intended defendant who is notified of an action within the period allowed by Rule 4(m) for service of a summons and complaint may not under the revised rule defeat the action on account of a defect in the pleading with respect to the defendant's name, provided that the requirements of clauses (A) and (B) have been met. If the notice requirement is met within the Rule 4(m) period, a complaint may be amended at any time to correct a formal defect such as a misnomer or misidentification. On the basis of the text of the former rule, the Court reached a result in *Schiavone v. Fortune* that was inconsistent with the liberal pleading practices secured by Rule 8. See Bauer, Schiavone: *An Un–Fortune–ate Illustration of the Supreme Court's Role as Interpreter of the Federal Rules of Civil Procedure,* 63 Notre Dame L.Rev. 720 (1988); Brussack, *Outrageous Fortune: The Case for Amending Rule 15(c) Again,* 61 S.Cal.L.Rev. 671 (1988); Lewis, *The Excessive History of Federal Rule 15(c) and Its Lessons for Civil Rules Revision,* 86 Mich.L.Rev. 1507 (1987).

In allowing a name-correcting amendment within the time allowed by Rule 4(m), this rule allows not only the 120 days specified in that rule, but also any additional time resulting from any extension ordered by the court pursuant to that rule, as may be granted, for example, if the defendant is a fugitive from service of the summons.

This revision, together with the revision of Rule 4(i) with respect to the failure of a plaintiff in an action against the United States to effect timely service on all the appropriate officials, is intended to produce results contrary to those reached in *Gardner v. Gartman,* 880 F.2d 797 (4th Cir.1989), *Rys v. U.S. Postal Service,* 886 F.2d 443 (1st Cir.1989), *Martin's Food & Liquor, Inc. v. U.S. Dept. of Agriculture,* 702 F.Supp. 215 (N.D.Ill.1988). But cf. *Montgomery v. United States Postal Service,* 867 F.2d 900 (5th Cir.1989), *Warren v. Department of the Army,* 867 F.2d 1156 (8th Cir.1989); *Miles v. Department of the Army,* 881 F.2d 777 (9th Cir.1989), *Barsten v.*

New matter is shown in italics; matter to be omitted is lined through

Department of the Interior, 896 F.2d 422 (9th Cir.1990); *Brown v. Georgia Dept. of Revenue,* 881 F.2d 1018 (11th Cir.1989).

Advisory Committee's Note to 2009 Amendment

(a) Amendments Before Trial.

(1) Amending as a Matter of Course. A party may amend its pleading once as a matter of course *within*:

(A) ~~before being served with a responsive pleading;~~ *21 days after serving it,* or

(B) ~~within 20 days after serving the pleading if a responsive pleading is not allowed and the action is not yet on the trial calendar~~ *if the pleading is one to which a responsive pleading is required, 21 days after service of a responsive pleading or 21 days after service of a motion under Rule 12(b), (e), or (f), whichever is earlier.*

(2) Other Amendments. In all other cases, a party may amend its pleading only with the opposing party's written consent or the court's leave. The court should freely give leave when justice so requires.

(3) Time to Respond. Unless the court orders otherwise, any required response to an amended pleading must be made within the time remaining to respond to the original pleading or within ~~10~~ *14* days after service of the amended pleading, whichever is later.

Rule 15(a)(1) is amended to make three changes in the time allowed to make one amendment as a matter of course.

Former Rule 15(a) addressed amendment of a pleading to which a responsive pleading is required by distinguishing between the means used to challenge the pleading. Serving a responsive pleading terminated the right to amend. Serving a motion attacking the pleading did not terminate the right to amend, because a motion is not a "pleading" as defined in Rule 7. The right to amend survived beyond decision of the motion unless the decision expressly cut off the right to amend.

The distinction drawn in former Rule 15(a) is changed in two ways. First, the right to amend once as a matter of course terminates 21 days after service of a motion under Rule 12(b), (e), or (f). This provision will force the pleader to consider carefully and promptly the wisdom of amending to meet the arguments in the motion. A responsive amendment may avoid the need to decide the motion or reduce the number of issues to be decided, and will expedite determination of issues that otherwise might be raised seriatim. It also should advance other pretrial proceedings.

Second, the right to amend once as a matter of course is no longer terminated by service of a responsive pleading. The responsive pleading may point out issues

---

New matter is shown in italics;   matter to be omitted is lined through

that the original pleader had not considered and persuade the pleader that amendment is wise. Just as amendment was permitted by former Rule 15(a) in response to a motion, so the amended rule permits one amendment as a matter of course in response to a responsive pleading. The right is subject to the same 21–day limit as the right to amend in response to a motion.

The 21–day periods to amend once as a matter of course after service of a responsive pleading or after service of a designated motion are not cumulative. If a responsive pleading is served after one of the designated motions is served, for example, there is no new 21–day period.

Finally, amended Rule 15(a)(1) extends from 20 to 21 days the period to amend a pleading to which no responsive pleading is allowed and omits the provision that cuts off the right if the action is on the trial calendar. Rule 40 no longer refers to a trial calendar, and many courts have abandoned formal trial calendars. It is more effective to rely on scheduling orders or other pretrial directions to establish time limits for amendment in the few situations that otherwise might allow one amendment as a matter of course at a time that would disrupt trial preparations. Leave to amend still can be sought under Rule 15(a)(2), or at and after trial under Rule 15(b).

Abrogation of Rule 13(f) establishes Rule 15 as the sole rule governing amendment of a pleading to add a counterclaim.

Amended Rule 15(a)(3) extends from 10 to 14 days the period to respond to an amended pleading.

Rule 16. Pre–Trial Procedure; Formulating Issues

Advisory Committee's Note to Original Rule

1. Similar rules of pre-trial procedure are now in force in Boston, Cleveland, Detroit, and Los Angeles, and a rule substantially like this one has been proposed for the urban centers of New York state. For a discussion of the successful operation of pre-trial procedure in relieving the congested condition of trial calendars of the courts in such cities and for the proposed New York plan, see *A Proposal for Minimizing Calendar Delay in Jury Cases* (Dec. 1936—published by The New York Law Society); *Pre–Trial Procedure and Administration,* Third Annual Report of the Judicial Council of the State of New York (1937), pages 207–243; *Report of the Commission on the Administration of Justice in New York State* (1934), pp. (288)–(290). See also *Pre–trial Procedure in the Wayne Circuit Court, Detroit, Michigan,* Sixth Annual Report of the Judicial Council of Michigan (1936), pp. 63–75; and Sunderland, *The Theory and Practice of Pre–Trial Procedure* (Dec. 1937) 36 Mich.L.Rev. 215–226, 21 J.Am.Jud.Soc. 125. Compare the English procedure known as the "summons for directions", English Rules Under the Judicature Act (The Annual Practice, 1937) O. 38a; and a similar procedure in New Jersey, N.J.Comp.Stat. (2 Cum.Supp. 1911–1924) tit. 163, § 293, (Supp. 1925–1930) tit. 163, § 347a, N.J.Supreme Court Rules, 2 N.J.Misc.Rep. (1924) 1230, Rules 94, 92, 93, 95 (the last three as amended 1933, 11 N.J.Misc.Rep. (1933) 955).

2. Compare the similar procedure under rule 56(d) (Summary Judgment—Case Not Fully Adjudicated on Motion). Rule 12(g) (Consolidation of Motions), by requiring to some extent the consolidation of motions dealing with matters preliminary to trial, is a step in the same direction. In connection with clause (5) of this rule, see Rules 53(b) (Masters; Reference) and 53(e)(3) (Master's Report: In Jury Actions).

New matter is shown in italics; matter to be omitted is lined through

Rule 16. *Pretrial Conferences; Scheduling; Management*
~~Pre-Trial Procedure; Formulating Issues~~

(a) Pretrial Conferences; Objectives. In any action, the court may in its discretion direct the attorneys for the parties *and any unrepresented parties* to appear before it for a conference *or conferences before trial* ~~to consider~~ *for such purposes as*

(1) *expediting the disposition of the action;*

(2) *establishing early and continuing control so that the case will not be protracted because of lack of management;*

(3) *discouraging wasteful pretrial activities;*

(4) *improving the quality of the trial through more thorough preparation, and;*

(5) *facilitating the settlement of the case.*

(b) Scheduling and Planning. Except in categories of actions exempted by district court rule as inappropriate, the judge, or a magistrate when authorized by district court rule, shall, after consulting with the attorneys for the parties and any unrepresented parties, by a scheduling conference, telephone, mail, or other suitable means, enter a scheduling order that limits the time

(1) *to join other parties and to amend the pleadings;*

(2) *to file and hear motions; and*

(3) *to complete discovery.*

The scheduling order also may include

(4) *the date or dates for conferences before trial, a final pretrial conference, and trial; and*

(5) *any other matters appropriate in the circumstances of the case.*

The order shall issue as soon as practicable but in no event more than 120 days after filing of the complaint. A schedule shall not be modified except by leave of the judge or a magistrate when authorized by district court rule upon a showing of good cause.

(c) Subjects to Be Discussed at Pretrial Conferences. The participants at any conference under this rule may consider and take action with respect to

(1) the *formulation and* simplification of the issues, *including the elimination of frivolous claims or defenses;*

New matter is shown in italics; matter to be omitted is lined through

(2) the necessity or desirability of amendments to the pleadings;

(3) the possibility of obtaining admissions of fact and of documents which will avoid unnecessary proof, *stipulations regarding the authenticity of documents, and advance rulings from the court on the admissibility of evidence*;

(4) the avoidance of unnecessary proof and of cumulative evidence;

(5)~~(4)~~ the ~~limitation of the number of expert~~ *identification of* witnesses *and documents, the need and schedule for filing and exchanging pretrial briefs, and the date or dates for further conferences and for trial*;

(6)~~(5)~~ the advisability of ~~a preliminary reference of~~ *refer*ring ~~issues~~ *matters* to a *magistrate or* master ~~for findings to be used as evidence when the trial is to be by jury~~;

(7) the possibility of settlement or the use of extrajudicial procedures to resolve the dispute;

(8) the form and substance of the pretrial order;

(9) the disposition of pending motions;

(10) the need for adopting special procedures for managing potentially difficult or protracted actions that may involve complex issues, multiple parties, difficult legal questions, or unusual proof problems; and

(11)~~(6)~~ such other matters as may aid in the disposition of the action.

At least one of the attorneys for each party participating in any conference before trial shall have authority to enter into stipulations and to make admissions regarding all matters that the participants may reasonably anticipate may be discussed.

(d) Final Pretrial Conference. Any final pretrial conference shall be held as close to the time of trial as reasonable under the circumstances. The participants at any such conference shall formulate a plan for trial, including a program for facilitating the admission of evidence. The conference shall be attended by at least one of the attorneys who will conduct the trial for each of the parties and by any unrepresented parties.

(e) Pretrial Orders. After any conference held pursuant to this rule, an order shall be entered reciting the action taken. This order shall control the subsequent course of the action unless modified by a subsequent order. The order following a final pretrial conference shall be modified only to prevent manifest injustice.

New matter is shown in italics; matter to be omitted is lined through

(f) Sanctions. If a party or party's attorney fails to obey a scheduling or pretrial order, or if no appearance is made on behalf of a party at a scheduling or pretrial conference, or if a party or party's attorney is substantially unprepared to participate in the conference, or if a party or party's attorney fails to participate in good faith, the judge, upon motion or his own initiative, may make such orders with regard thereto as are just, and among others any of the orders provided in Rule 37(b)(2)(B), (C), (D). In lieu of or in addition to any other sanction, the judge shall require the party or the attorney representing him or both to pay the reasonable expenses incurred because of any noncompliance with this rule, including attorney's fees, unless the judge finds that the noncompliance was substantially justified or that other circumstances make an award of expenses unjust.

~~The court shall make an order which recites the action taken at the conference, the amendments allowed to the pleadings, and the agreements made by the parties as to any of the matters considered, and which limits the issues for trial to those not disposed of by admissions or agreements of counsel; and such order when entered controls the subsequent course of the action, unless modified at the trial to prevent manifest injustice. The court in its discretion may establish by rule a pretrial calendar on which actions may be placed for consideration as above provided and may either confine the calendar to jury actions or to non-jury actions or extend it to all actions.~~

Introduction

Rule 16 has not been amended since the Federal Rules were promulgated in 1938. In many respects, the rule has been a success. For example, there is evidence that pretrial conferences may improve the quality of justice rendered in the federal courts by sharpening the preparation and presentation of cases, tending to eliminate trial surprise, and improving, as well as facilitating, the settlement process. See 6 Wright & Miller, *Federal Practice and Procedure: Civil* § 1522 (1971). However, in other respects particularly with regard to case management, the rule has not always been as helpful as it might have been. Thus there has been a widespread feeling that amendment is necessary to encourage pretrial management that meets the needs of modern litigation. See *Report of the National Commission for the Review of Antitrust Laws and Procedures* (1979).

Major criticism of Rule 16 has centered on the fact that its application can result in over-regulation of some cases and under-regulation of others. In simple, run-of-the-mill cases, attorneys have found pretrial requirements burdensome. It is claimed that over-administration leads to a series of mini-trials that result in a waste of an attorney's time and needless expense to a client. Pollack, *Pretrial Procedures More Effectively Handled,* 65 F.R.D. 475 (1974). This is especially likely to be true when pretrial proceedings occur long before trial. At the other end of the spectrum, the discretionary character of Rule 16 and its orientation toward a single conference late

---

New matter is shown in italics; matter to be omitted is lined through

in the pretrial process has led to under-administration of complex or protracted cases. Without judicial guidance beginning shortly after institution, these cases often become mired in discovery.

Four sources of criticism of pretrial have been identified. First, conferences often are seen as a mere exchange of legalistic contentions without any real analysis of the particular case. Second, the result frequently is nothing but a formal agreement on minutiae. Third, the conferences are seen as unnecessary and time-consuming in cases that will be settled before trial. Fourth, the meetings can be ceremonial and ritualistic, having little effect on the trial and being of minimal value, particularly when the attorneys attending the sessions are not the ones who will try the case or lack authority to enter into binding stipulations. See generally *McCargo v. Hedrick*, 545 F.2d 393 (4th Cir. 1976); Pollack, *Pretrial Procedures More Effectively Handled*, 65 F.R.D. 475 (1974); Rosenberg, *The Pretrial Conference and Effective Justice* 45 (1964).

There also have been difficulties with the pretrial orders that issue following Rule 16 conferences. When an order is entered far in advance of trial, some issues may not be properly formulated. Counsel naturally are cautious and often try to preserve as many options as possible. If the judge who tries the case did not conduct the conference, he could find it difficult to determine exactly what was agreed to at the conference. But any insistence on a detailed order may be too burdensome, depending on the nature or posture of the case.

Given the significant changes in federal civil litigation since 1938 that are not reflected in Rule 16, it has been extensively rewritten and expanded to meet the challenges of modern litigation. Empirical studies reveal that when a trial judge intervenes personally at an early stage to assume judicial control over a case and to schedule dates for completion by the parties of the principal pretrial steps, the case is disposed of by settlement or trial more efficiently and with less cost and delay than when the parties are left to their own devices. Flanders, *Case Management and Court Management in United States District Courts* 17, Federal Judicial Center (1977). Thus, the rule mandates a pretrial scheduling order. However, although scheduling and pretrial conferences are encouraged in appropriate cases, they are not mandated.

Discussion

Subdivision (a); Pretrial Conferences; Objectives. The amended rule makes scheduling and case management an express goal of pretrial procedure. This is done in Rule 16(a) by shifting the emphasis away from a conference focused solely on the trial and toward a process of judicial management that embraces the entire pretrial phase, especially motions and discovery. In addition, the amendment explicitly recognizes some of the objectives of pretrial conferences and the powers that many courts already have assumed. Rule 16 thus will be a more accurate reflection of actual practice.

Subdivision (b); Scheduling and Planning. The most significant change in Rule 16 is the mandatory scheduling order described in Rule 16(b), which is based in part on Wisconsin Civil Procedure Rule 802.10. The idea of scheduling orders is not new. It has been used by many federal courts. See, *e.g.*, Southern District of Indiana, Local Rule 19.

Although a mandatory scheduling order encourages the court to become involved in case management early in the litigation, it represents a degree of judicial involvement that is not warranted in many cases. Thus, subdivision (b) permits each district court to promulgate a local rule under Rule 83 exempting certain categories of cases in which the burdens of scheduling orders exceed the administrative

---

New matter is shown in italics; matter to be omitted is lined through

efficiencies that would be gained. See Eastern District of Virginia, Local Rule 12(1). Logical candidates for this treatment include social security disability matters, habeas corpus petitions, forfeitures, and reviews of certain administrative actions.

A scheduling conference may be requested either by the judge, a magistrate when authorized by district court rule, or a party within 120 days after the summons and complaint are filed. If a scheduling conference is not arranged within that time and the case is not exempted by local rule, a scheduling order must be issued under Rule 16(b), after some communication with the parties, which may be by telephone or mail rather than in person. The use of the term "judge" in subdivision (b) reflects the Advisory Committee's judgment that it is preferable that this task should be handled by a district judge rather than a magistrate, except when the magistrate is acting under 28 U.S.C. § 636(c). While personal supervision by the trial judge is preferred, the rule, in recognition of the impracticality or difficulty of complying with such a requirement in some districts, authorizes a district by local rule to delegate the duties to a magistrate. In order to formulate a practicable scheduling order, the judge, or a magistrate when authorized by district court rule, and attorneys are required to develop a timetable for the matters listed in Rule 16(b)(1)–(3). As indicated in Rule 16(b)(4)–(5), the order may also deal with a wide range of other matters. The rule is phrased permissively as to clauses (4) and (5), however, because scheduling these items at an early point may not be feasible or appropriate. Even though subdivision (b) relates only to scheduling, there is no reason why some of the procedural matters listed in Rule 16(c) cannot be addressed at the same time, at least when a scheduling conference is held.

Item (1) assures that at some point both the parties and the pleadings will be fixed, by setting a time within which joinder of parties shall be completed and the pleadings amended.

Item (2) requires setting time limits for interposing various motions that otherwise might be used as stalling techniques.

Item (3) deals with the problem of procrastination and delay by attorneys in a context in which scheduling is especially important—discovery. Scheduling the completion of discovery can serve some of the same functions as the conference described in Rule 26(f).

Item (4) refers to setting dates for conferences and for trial. Scheduling multiple pretrial conferences may well be desirable if the case is complex and the court believes that a more elaborate pretrial structure, such as that described in the *Manual for Complex Litigation,* should be employed. On the other hand, only one pretrial conference may be necessary in an uncomplicated case.

As long as the case is not exempted by local rule, the court must issue a written scheduling order even if no scheduling conference is called. The order, like pretrial orders under the former rule and those under new Rule 16(c), normally will "control the subsequent course of the action." See Rule 16(e). After consultation with the attorneys for the parties and any unrepresented parties—a formal motion is not necessary—the court may modify the schedule on a showing of good cause if it cannot reasonably be met despite the diligence of the party seeking the extension. Since the scheduling order is entered early in the litigation, this standard seems more appropriate than a "manifest injustice" or "substantial hardship" test. Otherwise, a fear that extensions will not be granted may encourage counsel to request the longest possible periods for completing pleading, joinder, and discovery. Moreover, changes in the court's calendar sometimes will oblige the judge or magistrate when authorized by district court rule to modify the scheduling order.

The district courts undoubtedly will develop several prototype scheduling orders for different types of cases. In addition, when no formal conference is held, the court

---

New matter is shown in italics; matter to be omitted is lined through

may obtain scheduling information by telephone, mail, or otherwise. In many instances this will result in a scheduling order better suited to the individual case than a standard order, without taking the time that would be required by a formal conference.

Rule 16(b) assures that the judge will take some early control over the litigation, even when its character does not warrant holding a scheduling conference. Despite the fact that the process of preparing a scheduling order does not always bring the attorneys and judge together, the fixing of time limits serves

> to stimulate litigants to narrow the areas of inquiry and advocacy to those they believe are truly relevant and material. Time limits not only compress the amount of time for litigation, they should also reduce the amount of resources invested in litigation. Litigants are forced to establish discovery priorities and thus to do the most important work first.

Report of the National Commission for the Review of Antitrust Laws and Procedures 28 (1979).

Thus, except in exempted cases, the judge or a magistrate when authorized by district court rule will have taken some action in every case within 120 days after the complaint is filed that notifies the attorneys that the case *will* be moving toward trial. Subdivision (b) is reenforced by subdivision (f), which makes it clear that the sanctions for violating a scheduling order are the same as those for violating a pretrial order.

Subdivision (c); Subjects to be Discussed at Pretrial Conferences. This subdivision expands upon the list of things that may be discussed at a pretrial conference that appeared in original Rule 16. The intention is to encourage better planning and management of litigation. Increased judicial control during the pretrial process accelerates the processing and termination of cases. Flanders, *Case Management and Court Management in United States District Courts,* Federal Judicial Center (1977). See also *Report of the National Commission for the Review of Antitrust Laws and Procedures* (1979).

The reference in Rule 16(c)(1) to "formulation" is intended to clarify and confirm the court's power to identify the litigable issues. It has been added in the hope of promoting efficiency and conserving judicial resources by identifying the real issues prior to trial, thereby saving time and expense for everyone. See generally *Meadow Gold Prods. Co. v. Wright,* 278 F.2d 867 (D.C. Cir. 1960). The notion is emphasized by expressly authorizing the elimination of frivolous claims or defenses at a pretrial conference. There is no reason to require that this await a formal motion for summary judgment. Nor is there any reason for the court to wait for the parties to initiate the process called for in Rule 16(c)(1).

The timing of any attempt at issue formulation is a matter of judicial discretion. In relatively simple cases it may not be necessary or may take the form of a stipulation between counsel or a request by the court that counsel work together to draft a proposed order.

Counsel bear a substantial responsibility for assisting the court in identifying the factual issues worthy of trial. If counsel fail to identify an issue for the court, the right to have the issue tried is waived. Although an order specifying the issues is intended to be binding, it may be amended at trial to avoid manifest injustice. See Rule 16(e). However, the rule's effectiveness depends on the court employing its discretion sparingly.

Clause (6) acknowledges the widespread availability and use of magistrates. The corresponding provision in the original rule referred only to masters and limited the function of the reference to the making of "findings to be used as evidence" in a case

---

New matter is shown in italics; matter to be omitted is lined through

to be tried to a jury. The new text is not limited and broadens the potential use of a magistrate to that permitted by the Magistrate's Act.

Clause (7) explicitly recognizes that it has become commonplace to discuss settlement at pretrial conferences. Since it obviously eases crowded court dockets and results in savings to the litigants and the judicial system, settlement should be facilitated at as early a stage of the litigation as possible. Although it is not the purpose of Rule 16(b)(7) [*sic*] to impose settlement negotiations on unwilling litigants, it is believed that providing a neutral forum for discussing the subject might foster it. See Moore's *Federal Practice* ¶ 16.17; 6 Wright & Miller, *Federal Practice and Procedure: Civil* § 1522 (1971). For instance, a judge to whom a case has been assigned may arrange, on his own motion or at a party's request, to have settlement conferences handled by another member of the court or by a magistrate. The rule does not make settlement conferences mandatory because they would be a waste of time in many cases. See Flanders, *Case Management and Court Management in the United States District Courts,* 39, Federal Judicial Center (1977). Requests for a conference from a party indicating a willingness to talk settlement normally should be honored, unless thought to be frivolous or dilatory.

A settlement conference is appropriate at any time. It may be held in conjunction with a pretrial or discovery conference, although various objectives of pretrial management, such as moving the case toward trial, may not always be compatible with settlement negotiations, and thus a separate settlement conference may be desirable. See 6 Wright & Miller, *Federal Practice and Procedure: Civil* § 1522, at p. 571 (1971).

In addition to settlement, Rule 16(c)(7) refers to exploring the use of procedures other than litigation to resolve the dispute. This includes urging the litigants to employ adjudicatory techniques outside the courthouse. See, for example, the experiment described in Green, Marks & Olson, *Settling Large Case Litigation: An Alternative Approach,* 11 Loyola of L.A.L.Rev. 493 (1978).

Rule 16(c)(10) authorizes the use of special pretrial procedures to expedite the adjudication of potentially difficult or protracted cases. Some district courts obviously have done so for many years. See Rubin, *The Managed Calendar: Some Pragmatic Suggestions About Achieving the Just, Speedy and Inexpensive Determination of Civil Cases in Federal Courts,* 4 Just.Sys.J. 135 (1976). Clause 10 provides an explicit authorization for such procedures and encourages their use. No particular techniques have been described; the Committee felt that flexibility and experience are the keys to efficient management of complex cases. Extensive guidance is offered in such documents as the *Manual for Complex Litigation.*

The rule simply identifies characteristics that make a case a strong candidate for special treatment. The four mentioned are illustrative, not exhaustive, and overlap to some degree. But experience has shown that one or more of them will be present in every protracted or difficult case and it seems desirable to set them out. See Kendig, *Procedures for Management of Non–Routine Cases,* 3 Hofstra L.Rev. 701 (1975).

The last sentence of subdivision (c) is new. See Wisconsin Civil Procedure Rule 802.11(2). It has been added to meet one of the criticisms of the present practice described earlier and insure proper preconference preparation so that the meeting is more than a ceremonial or ritualistic event. The reference to "authority" is not intended to insist upon the ability to settle the litigation. Nor should the rule be read to encourage the judge conducting the conference to compel attorneys to enter into stipulations or to make admissions that they consider to be unreasonable, that touch on matters that could not normally have been anticipated to arise at the

New matter is shown in italics; matter to be omitted is lined through

conference, or on subjects of a dimension that normally require prior consultation with and approval from the client.

Subdivision (d); Final Pretrial Conference. This provision has been added to make it clear that the time between any final pretrial conference (which in a simple case may be the *only* pretrial conference) and trial should be as short as possible to be certain that the litigants make substantial progress with the case and avoid the inefficiency of having that preparation repeated when there is a delay between the last pretrial conference and trial. An optimum time of 10 days to two weeks has been suggested by one federal judge. Rubin, *The Managed Calendar: Some Pragmatic Suggestions About Achieving the Just, Speedy and Inexpensive Determination of Civil Cases in Federal Courts,* 4 Just.Sys.J. 135, 141 (1976). The Committee, however, concluded that it would be inappropriate to fix a precise time in the rule, given the numerous variables that could bear on the matter. Thus the timing has been left to the court's discretion.

At least one of the attorneys who will conduct the trial for each party must be present at the final pretrial conference. At this late date there should be no doubt as to which attorney or attorneys this will be. Since the agreements and stipulations made at this final conference will control the trial, the presence of lawyers who will be involved in it is especially useful to assist the judge in structuring the case, and to lead to a more effective trial.

Subdivision (e); Pretrial Orders. Rule 16(e) does not substantially change the portion of the original rule dealing with pretrial orders. The purpose of an order is to guide the course of the litigation and the language of the original rule making that clear has been retained. No compelling reason has been found for major revision, especially since this portion of the rule has been interpreted and clarified by over forty years of judicial decisions with comparatively little difficulty. See 6 Wright & Miller, *Federal Practice and Procedure: Civil* §§ 1521–30 (1971). Changes in language therefore have been kept to a minimum to avoid confusion.

Since the amended rule encourages more extensive pretrial management than did the original, two or more conferences may be held in many cases. The language of Rule 16(e) recognizes this possibility and the corresponding need to issue more than one pretrial order in a single case.

Once formulated, pretrial orders should not be changed lightly; but total inflexibility is undesirable. See, *e.g., Clark v. Pennsylvania R.R. Co.,* 328 F.2d 591 (2d Cir. 1964). The exact words used to describe the standard for amending the pretrial order probably are less important than the meaning given them in practice. By not imposing any limitation on the ability to modify a pretrial order, the rule reflects the reality that in any process of continuous management what is done at one conference may have to be altered at the next. In the case of the final pretrial order, however, a more stringent standard is called for and the words "to prevent manifest injustice," which appeared in the original rule, have been retained. They have the virtue of familiarity and adequately describe the restraint the trial judge should exercise.

Many local rules make the plaintiff's attorney responsible for drafting a proposed pretrial order, either before or after the conference. Others allow the court to appoint any of the attorneys to perform the task, and others leave it to the court. See Note, *Pretrial Conference: A Critical Examination of Local Rules Adopted by Federal District Courts,* 64 Va.L.Rev. 467 (1978). Rule 16 has never addressed this matter. Since there is no consensus about which method of drafting the order works best and there is no reason to believe that nationwide uniformity is needed, the rule has been left silent on the point. See *Handbook for Effective Pretrial Procedure,* 37 F.R.D. 225 (1964).

New matter is shown in italics; matter to be omitted is lined through

Subdivision (f); Sanctions. Original Rule 16 did not mention the sanctions that might be imposed for failing to comply with the rule. However, courts have not hesitated to enforce it by appropriate measures. See, *e.g., Link v. Wabash R. Co.,* 370 U.S. 628 (1962) (district court's dismissal under Rule 41(b) after plaintiff's attorney failed to appear at a pretrial conference upheld); *Admiral Theatre Corp. v. Douglas Theatre,* 585 F.2d 877 (8th Cir. 1978) (district court has discretion to exclude exhibits or refuse to permit the testimony of a witness not listed prior to trial in contravention of its pretrial order).

To reflect that existing practice, and to obviate dependence upon Rule 41(b) or the court's inherent power to regulate litigation, *cf. Societe Internationale Pour Participations Industrielles et Commerciales, S.A. v. Rogers,* 357 U.S. 197 (1958), Rule 16(f) expressly provides for imposing sanctions on disobedient or recalcitrant parties, their attorneys, or both in four types of situations. Rodes, Ripple & Mooney, *Sanctions Imposable for Violations of the Federal Rules of Civil Procedure* 65–67, 80–84, Federal Judicial Center (1981). Furthermore, explicit reference to sanctions reenforces the rule's intention to encourage forceful judicial management.

Rule 16(f) incorporates portions of Rule 37(b)(2), which prescribes sanctions for failing to make discovery. This should facilitate application of Rule 16(f), since courts and lawyers already are familiar with the Rule 37 standards. Among the sanctions authorized by the new subdivision are: preclusion order, striking a pleading, staying the proceeding, default judgment, contempt, and charging a party, his attorney, or both with the expenses, including attorney's fees, caused by noncompliance. The contempt sanction, however, is only available for a violation of a court order. The references in Rule 16(f) are not exhaustive.

As is true under Rule 37(b)(2), the imposition of sanctions may be sought by either the court or a party. In addition, the court has discretion to impose whichever sanction it feels is appropriate under the circumstances. Its action is reviewable under the abuse-of-discretion standard. See *National Hockey League v. Metropolitan Hockey Club, Inc.,* 427 U.S. 639 (1976).

————

Advisory Committee's Note to 1993 Amendment

(b) Scheduling and Planning. Except in categories of actions exempted by district court rule as inappropriate, the *district* judge, or a magistrate *judge* when authorized by district court rule, shall, *after receiving the report from the parties under Rule 26(f) or* after consulting with the attorneys for the parties and any unrepresented parties, by a scheduling conference, telephone, mail, or other suitable means, enter a scheduling order that limits the time

    (1) to join other parties and to amend the pleadings;

    (2) to file and hear motions; and

    (3) to complete discovery.

The scheduling order may also include

    (4) modifications of the times for disclosures under Rules 26(a) and 26(e)(1) and of the extent of discovery to be permitted;

New matter is shown in italics; matter to be omitted is lined through

(45) the date or dates for conferences before trial, a final pretrial conference, and trial; and

(56) any other matters appropriate in the circumstances of the case.

The order shall issue as soon as practicable but in ~~no~~ *any* event ~~more than 120~~ *within 90* days after ~~filing of the complaint~~ *the appearance of a defendant and within 120 days after the complaint has been served on a defendant*. A schedule shall not be modified except *upon a showing of good cause and* by leave of the *district* judge or, *when authorized by local rule,* by a magistrate *judge* ~~when authorized by district court rule upon a showing of good cause~~.

(c) Subjects ~~to be Discussed~~ *for Consideration* at Pretrial Conferences. ~~The participants a~~*At* any conference under this rule ~~may consider and take action~~ *consideration may be given, and the court may take appropriate action,* with respect to

(1) the formulation and simplification of the issues, including the elimination of frivolous claims or defenses;

(2) the necessity or desirability of amendments to the pleadings;

(3) the possibility of obtaining admissions of fact and of documents which will avoid unnecessary proof, stipulations regarding the authenticity of documents, and advance rulings from the court on the admissibility of evidence;

(4) the avoidance of unnecessary proof and of cumulative evidence, *and limitations or restrictions on the use of testimony under Rule 702 of the Federal Rules of Evidence*;

(5) the appropriateness and timing of summary adjudication under Rule 56;

(6) the control and scheduling of discovery, including orders affecting disclosures and discovery pursuant to Rule 26 and Rules 29 through 37;

(57) the identification of witnesses and documents, the need and schedule for filing and exchanging pretrial briefs, and the date or dates for further conferences and for trial;

(68) the advisability of referring matters to a magistrate *judge* or master;

(79) ~~the possibility of~~ settlement ~~or~~ *and* the use of ~~extrajudicial~~ *special* procedures to ~~resolve~~ *assist in resolving* the dispute *when authorized by statute or local rule*;

(810) the form and substance of the pretrial order;

(911) the disposition of pending motions;

New matter is shown in italics; matter to be omitted is lined through

(1~~0~~2) the need for adopting special procedures for managing potentially difficult or protracted actions that may involve complex issues, multiple parties, difficult legal questions, or unusual proof problems;

(13) an order for a separate trial pursuant to Rule 42(b) with respect to a claim, counterclaim, cross-claim, or third-party claim, or with respect to any particular issue in the case;

(14) an order directing a party or parties to present evidence early in the trial with respect to a manageable issue that could, on the evidence, be the basis for a judgment as a matter of law under Rule 50(a) or a judgment on partial findings under Rule 52(c);

(15) an order establishing a reasonable limit on the time allowed for presenting evidence; and

(1~~1~~6) such other matters as may ~~aid in~~ *facilitate* the *just, speedy, and inexpensive* disposition of the action.

At least one of the attorneys for each party participating in any conference before trial shall have authority to enter into stipulations and to make admissions regarding all matters that the participants may reasonably anticipate may be discussed. *If appropriate, the court may require that a party or its representative be present or reasonably available by telephone in order to consider possible settlement of the dispute.*

Subdivision (b). One purpose of this amendment is to provide a more appropriate deadline for the initial scheduling order required by the rule. The former rule directed that the order be entered within 120 days from the filing of the complaint. This requirement has created problems because Rule 4(m) allows 120 days for service and ordinarily at least one defendant should be available to participate in the process of formulating the scheduling order. The revision provides that the order is to be entered within 90 days after the date a defendant first appears (whether by answer or by a motion under Rule 12) or, if earlier (as may occur in some actions against the United States or if service is waived under Rule 4), within 120 days after service of the complaint on a defendant. The longer time provided by the revision is not intended to encourage unnecessary delays in entering the scheduling order. Indeed, in most cases the order can and should be entered at a much earlier date. Rather, the additional time is intended to alleviate problems in multi-defendant cases and should ordinarily be adequate to enable participation by all defendants initially named in the action.

In many cases the scheduling order can and should be entered before this deadline. However, when setting a scheduling conference, the court should take into account the effect this setting will have in establishing deadlines for the parties to meet under revised Rule 26(f) and to exchange information under revised Rule 26(a)(1). While the parties are expected to stipulate to additional time for making their disclosures when warranted by the circumstances, a scheduling conference held

---

New matter is shown in italics; matter to be omitted is lined through

before defendants have had time to learn much about the case may result in diminishing the value of the Rule 26(f) meeting, the parties' proposed discovery plan, and indeed the conference itself.

New paragraph (4) has been added to highlight that it will frequently be desirable for the scheduling order to include provisions relating to the timing of disclosures under Rule 26(a). While the initial disclosures required by Rule 26(a)(1) will ordinarily have been made before entry of the scheduling order, the timing and sequence for disclosure of expert testimony and of the witnesses and exhibits to be used at trial should be tailored to the circumstances of the case and is a matter that should be considered at the initial scheduling conference. Similarly, the scheduling order might contain provisions modifying the extent of discovery (*e.g.*, number and length of depositions) otherwise permitted under these rules or by a local rule.

The report from the attorneys concerning their meeting and proposed discovery plan, as required by revised Rule 26(f), should be submitted to the court before the scheduling order is entered. Their proposals, particularly regarding matters on which they agree, should be of substantial value to the court in setting the timing and limitations on discovery and should reduce the time of the court needed to conduct a meaningful conference under Rule 16(b). As under the prior rule, while a scheduling order is mandated, a scheduling conference is not. However, in view of the benefits to be derived from the litigants and a judicial officer meeting in person, a Rule 16(b) conference should, to the extent practicable, be held in all cases that will involve discovery.

This subdivision, as well as subdivision (c)(8), also is revised to reflect the new title of United States Magistrate Judges pursuant to the Judicial Improvements Act of 1990.

Subdivision (c). The primary purposes of the changes in subdivision (c) are to call attention to the opportunities for structuring of trial under Rules 42, 50, and 52 and to eliminate questions that have occasionally been raised regarding the authority of the court to make appropriate orders designed either to facilitate settlement or to provide for an efficient and economical trial. The prefatory language of this subdivision is revised to clarify the court's power to enter appropriate orders at a conference notwithstanding the objection of a party. Of course settlement is dependent upon agreement by the parties and, indeed, a conference is most effective and productive when the parties participate in a spirit of cooperation and mindful of their responsibilities under Rule 1.

Paragraph (4) is revised to clarify that in advance of trial the court may address the need for, and possible limitations on, the use of expert testimony under Rule 702 of the Federal Rules of Evidence. Even when proposed expert testimony might be admissible under the standards of Rules 403 and 702 of the evidence rules, the court may preclude or limit such testimony if the cost to the litigants—which may include the cost to adversaries of securing testimony on the same subjects by other experts— would be unduly expensive given the needs of the case and the other evidence available at trial.

Paragraph (5) is added (and the remaining paragraphs renumbered) in recognition that use of Rule 56 to avoid or reduce the scope of trial is a topic that can, and often should, be considered at a pretrial conference. Renumbered paragraph (11) enables the court to rule on pending motions for summary adjudication that are ripe for decision at the time of the conference. Often, however, the potential use of Rule 56 is a matter that arises from discussions during a conference. The court may then call for motions to be filed.

Paragraph (6) is added to emphasize that a major objective of pretrial conferences should be to consider appropriate controls on the extent and timing of

---

New matter is shown in italics; matter to be omitted is lined through

discovery. In many cases the court should also specify the times and sequence for disclosure of written reports from experts under revised Rule 26(a)(2)(B) and perhaps direct changes in the types of experts from whom written reports are required. Consideration should also be given to possible changes in the timing or form of the disclosure of trial witnesses and documents under Rule 26(a)(3).

Paragraph (9) is revised to describe more accurately the various procedures that, in addition to traditional settlement conferences, may be helpful in settling litigation. Even if a case cannot immediately be settled, the judge and attorneys can explore possible use of alternative procedures such as mini-trials, summary jury trials, mediation, neutral evaluation, and nonbinding arbitration that can lead to consensual resolution of the dispute without a full trial on the merits. The rule acknowledges the presence of statutes and local rules or plans that may authorize use of some of these procedures even when not agreed to by the parties. See 28 U.S.C. §§ 473(a)(6), 473(b)(4), 651–58; Section 104(b)(2), Pub.L. 101–650. The rule does not attempt to resolve questions as to the extent a court would be authorized to require such proceedings as an exercise of its inherent powers.

The amendment of paragraph (9) should be read in conjunction with the sentence added to the end of subdivision (c), authorizing the court to direct that, in appropriate cases, a responsible representative of the parties be present or available by telephone during a conference in order to discuss possible settlement of the case. The sentence refers to participation by a party or its representative. Whether this would be the individual party, an officer of a corporate party, a representative from an insurance carrier, or someone else would depend on the circumstances. Particularly in litigation in which governmental agencies or large amounts of money are involved, there may be no one with on-the-spot settlement authority, and the most that should be expected is access to a person who would have a major role in submitting a recommendation to the body or board with ultimate decision-making responsibility. The selection of the appropriate representative should ordinarily be left to the party and its counsel. Finally, it should be noted that the unwillingness of a party to be available, even by telephone, for a settlement conference may be a clear signal that the time and expense involved in pursuing settlement is likely to be unproductive and that personal participation by the parties should not be required.

The explicit authorization in the rule to require personal participation in the manner stated is not intended to limit the reasonable exercise of the court's inherent powers, *e.g.,* G. Heileman Brewing Co. v. Joseph Oat Corp., 871 F.2d 648 (7th Cir.1989), or its power to require party participation under the Civil Justice Reform Act of 1990. See 28 U.S.C. § 473(b)(5) (civil justice expense and delay reduction plans adopted by district courts may include requirement that representatives "with authority to bind [parties] in settlement discussions" be available during settlement conferences).

New paragraphs (13) and (14) are added to call attention to the opportunities for structuring of trial under Rule 42 and under revised Rules 50 and 52.

Paragraph (15) is also new. It supplements the power of the court to limit the extent of evidence under Rules 403 and 611(a) of the Federal Rules of Evidence, which typically would be invoked as a result of developments during trial. Limits on the length of trial established at a conference in advance of trial can provide the parties with a better opportunity to determine priorities and exercise selectivity in presenting evidence than when limits are imposed during trial. Any such limits must be reasonable under the circumstances, and ordinarily the court should impose them only after receiving appropriate submissions from the parties outlining the nature of the testimony expected to be presented through various witnesses, and the expected duration of direct and cross-examination.

New matter is shown in italics; matter to be omitted is lined through

Rule 17. Parties Plaintiff and Defendant; Capacity

Advisory Committee's Note to 1966 Amendment

(a) **Real Party in Interest.** Every action shall be prosecuted in the name of the real party in interest;. ~~but~~ ~~a~~*A*n executor, administrator, guardian, *bailee,* trustee of an express trust, a party with whom or in whose name a contract has been made for the benefit of another, or a party authorized by statute may sue in his own name without joining with him the party for whose benefit the action is brought; and when a statute of the United States so provides, an action for the use or benefit of another shall be brought in the name of the United States. *No action shall be dismissed on the ground that it is not prosecuted in the name of the real party in interest until a reasonable time has been allowed after objection for ratification of commencement of the action by, or joinder or substitution of, the real party in interest; and such ratification, joinder, or substitution shall have the same effect as if the action had been commenced in the name of the real party in interest.*

The minor change in the text of the rule is designed to make it clear that the specific instances enumerated are not exceptions to, but illustrations of, the rule. These illustrations, of course, carry no negative implication to the effect that there are not other instances of recognition as the real party in interest of one whose standing as such may be in doubt. The enumeration is simply of cases in which there might be substantial doubt as to the issue but for the specific enumeration. There are other potentially arguable cases that are not excluded by the enumeration. For example, the enumeration states that the promisee in a contract for the benefit of a third party may sue as real party in interest; it does not say, because it is obvious, that the third-party beneficiary may sue (when the applicable law gives him that right.)

The rule adds to the illustrative list of real parties in interest a bailee— meaning, of course, a bailee suing on behalf of the bailor with respect to the property bailed. (When the possessor of property other than the owner sues for an invasion of the possessory interest he is the real party in interest.) The word "bailee" is added primarily to preserve the admiralty practice whereby the owner of a vessel as bailee of the cargo, or the master of the vessel as bailee of both vessel and cargo, sues for damage to either property interest or both. But there is no reason to limit such a provision to maritime situations. The owner of a warehouse in which household furniture is stored is equally entitled to sue on behalf of the numerous owners of the furniture stored. *Cf. Gulf Oil Corp. v. Gilbert,* 330 U.S. 501 (1947).

The provision that no action shall be dismissed on the ground that it is not prosecuted in the name of the real party in interest until a reasonable time has been allowed, after the objection has been raised, for ratification, substitution, etc., is added simply in the interests of justice. In its origin the rule concerning the real party in interest was permissive in purpose: it was designed to *allow* an assignee to sue in his own name. That having been accomplished, the modern function of the rule in its negative aspect is simply to protect the defendant against a subsequent

---

New matter is shown in italics; matter to be omitted is lined through

action by the party actually entitled to recover, and to insure generally that the judgment will have its proper effect as res judicata.

This provision keeps pace with the law as it is actually developing. Modern decisions are inclined to be lenient when an honest mistake has been made in choosing the party in whose name the action is to be filed—in both maritime and nonmaritime cases. See *Levinson v. Deupree,* 345 U.S. 648 (1953); *Link Aviation, Inc. v. Downs,* 325 F.2d 613 (D.C.Cir.1963). The provision should not be misunderstood or distorted. It is intended to prevent forfeiture when determination of the proper party to sue is difficult or when an understandable mistake has been made. It does not mean, for example, that, following an airplane crash in which all aboard were killed, an action may be filed in the name of John Doe (a fictitious person), as personal representative of Richard Roe (another fictitious person), in the hope that at a later time the attorney filing the action may substitute the real name of the real personal representative of a real victim, and have the benefit of suspension of the limitation period. It does not even mean, when an action is filed by the personal representative of John Smith, of Buffalo, in the good faith belief that he was aboard the flight, that upon discovery that Smith is alive and well, having missed the fatal flight, the representative of James Brown, of San Francisco, an actual victim, can be substituted to take advantage of the suspension of the limitation period. It is, in cases of this sort, intended to insure against forfeiture and injustice—in short, to codify in broad terms the salutary principle of *Levinson v. Deupree,* 345 U.S. 648 (1953), and *Link Aviation, Inc. v. Downs,* 325 F.2d 613 (D.C.Cir.1963).

Rule 19.   Necessary Joinder of Parties

Advisory Committee's Note to Original Rule

Note to Subdivision (a). The first sentence with verbal differences (e.g., "united" interest for "joint" interest) is to be found in Equity Rule 37 (Parties Generally—Intervention). Such compulsory joinder provisions are common. Compare Alaska Comp.Laws (1933) § 3392 (containing in same sentence a "class suit" provision); Wyo.Rev.Stat.Ann. (Courtright, 1931) § 89–515 (immediately followed by "class suit" provisions, § 89–516). See also Equity Rule 42 (Joint and Several Demands). For example of a proper case for involuntary plaintiff, see *Independent Wireless Telegraph Co. v. Radio Corp. of America,* 269 U.S. 459, 46 S.Ct. 166, 70 L.Ed. 357 (1926).

The joinder provisions of this rule are subject to Rule 82 (Jurisdiction and Venue Unaffected).

Note to Subdivision (b). For the substance of this rule see Equity Rule 39 (Absence of Persons who Would be Proper Parties) and U.S.C., Title 28, § 111 [now § 1391] (When part of several defendants cannot be served); *Camp v. Gress,* 250 U.S. 308, 39 S.Ct. 478, 63 L.Ed. 997 (1919). See also the second and third sentences of Equity Rule 37 (Parties Generally—Intervention).

Note to Subdivision (c). For the substance of this rule see the fourth subdivision of Equity Rule 25 (Bill of Complaint—Contents).

New matter is shown in italics; matter to be omitted is lined through

~~Rule 19.~~ ~~Necessary Joinder of Parties~~

~~**(a) Necessary Joinder.** Subject to the provisions of Rule 23 and of subdivision (b) of this rule, persons having a joint interest shall be made parties and be joined on the same side as plaintiffs or defendants. When a person who should join as a plaintiff refuses to do so, he may be made a defendant or, in proper cases, an involuntary plaintiff.~~

~~**(b) Effect of Failure to Join.** When persons who are not indispensable, but who ought to be parties if complete relief is to be accorded between those already parties, have not been made parties and are subject to the jurisdiction of the court as to both service of process and venue and can be made parties without depriving the court of jurisdiction of the parties before it, the court shall order them summoned to appear in the action. The court in its discretion may proceed in the action without making such persons parties, if its jurisdiction over them as to either service of process or venue can be acquired only by their consent or voluntary appearance or if, though they are subject to its jurisdiction, their joinder would deprive the court of jurisdiction of the parties before it, but the judgment rendered therein does not affect the rights or liabilities of absent persons.~~

~~**(c) Same: Names of Omitted Persons and Reasons for Non-Joinder to be Pleaded.** In any pleading in which relief is asked, the pleader shall set forth the names, if known to him, of persons who ought to be parties if complete relief is to be accorded between those already parties, but who are not joined, and shall state why they are omitted.~~

Rule 19. *Joinder of Persons Needed for Just Adjudication*

(a) Persons to be Joined if Feasible. A person who is subject to service of process and whose joinder will not deprive the court of jurisdiction over the subject matter of the action shall be joined as a party in the action if (1) in his absence complete relief cannot be accorded among those already parties, or (2) he claims an interest relating to the subject of the action and is so situated that the disposition of the action in his absence may (i) as a practical matter impair or impede his ability to protect that interest or (ii) leave any of the persons already parties subject to a substantial risk of incurring double, multiple, or otherwise inconsistent obligations by reason of his claimed interest. If he has not been so joined, the court shall order that he be made a party. If he should join as a

---

New matter is shown in italics; matter to be omitted is lined through

plaintiff but refuses to do so, he may be made a defendant, or, in a proper case, an involuntary plaintiff. If the joined party objects to venue and his joinder would render the venue of the action improper, he shall be dismissed from the action.

*(b) **Determination by Court Whenever Joinder Not Feasible.** If a person as described in subdivision (a)(1)–(2) hereof cannot be made a party, the court shall determine whether in equity and good conscience the action should proceed among the parties before it, or should be dismissed, the absent person being thus regarded as indispensable. The factors to be considered by the court include: first, to what extent a judgment rendered in the person's absence might be prejudicial to him, or those already parties; second, the extent to which, by protective provisions in the judgment, by the shaping of relief, or other measures, the prejudice can be lessened or avoided; third, whether a judgment rendered in the person's absence will be adequate; fourth, whether the plaintiff will have an adequate remedy if the action is dismissed for nonjoinder.*

*(c) **Pleading Reasons for Nonjoinder.** A pleading asserting a claim for relief shall state the names, if known to the pleader, of any persons as described in subdivision (a)(1)–(2) hereof who are not joined, and the reasons why they are not joined.*

*(d) **Exception of Class Actions.** This rule is subject to the provisions of Rule 23.*

General Considerations

Whenever feasible, the persons materially interested in the subject of an action—see the more detailed description of these persons in the discussion of new subdivision (a) below—should be joined as parties so that they may be heard and a complete disposition made. When this comprehensive joinder cannot be accomplished—a situation which may be encountered in Federal courts because of limitations on service of process, subject matter jurisdiction, and venue—the case should be examined pragmatically and a choice made between the alternatives of proceeding with the action in the absence of particular interested persons, and dismissing the action.

Even if the court is mistaken in its decision to proceed in the absence of an interested person, it does not by that token deprive itself of the power to adjudicate as between the parties already before it through proper service of process. But the court can make a legally binding adjudication only between the parties actually joined in the action. It is true that an adjudication between the parties before the court may on occasion adversely affect the absent person as a practical matter, or leave a party exposed to a later inconsistent recovery by the absent person. These are factors which should be considered in deciding whether the action should proceed, or should rather be dismissed; but they do not themselves negate the court's power to adjudicate as between the parties who have been joined.

New matter is shown in italics; matter to be omitted is lined through

Defects in the Original Rule

The foregoing propositions were well understood in the older equity practice, see Hazard, *Indispensable Party: The Historical Origin of a Procedural Phantom,* 61 Colum.L.Rev. 1254 (1961), and Rule 19 could be and often was applied in consonance with them. But experience showed that the rule was defective in its phrasing and did not point clearly to the proper basis of decision.

Textual defects. (1) The expression "persons * * * who ought to be parties if complete relief is to be accorded between those already parties," appearing in original subdivision (b), was apparently intended as a description of the persons whom it would be desirable to join in the action, all questions of feasibility of joinder being put to one side; but it was not adequately descriptive of those persons.

(2) The word "indispensable," appearing in original subdivision (b), was apparently intended as an inclusive reference to the interested persons in whose absence it would be advisable, all factors having been considered, to dismiss the action. Yet the sentence implied that there might be interested persons, not "indispensable," in whose absence the action ought also to be dismissed. Further, it seemed at least superficially plausible to equate the word "indispensable" with the expression "having a joint interest," appearing in subdivision (a). See *United States v. Washington Inst. of Tech., Inc.,* 138 F.2d 25, 26 (3d Cir.1943); *cf. Chidester v. City of Newark,* 162 F.2d 598 (3d Cir.1947). But persons holding an interest technically "joint" are not always so related to an action that it would be unwise to proceed without joining all of them, whereas persons holding an interest not technically "joint" may have this relation to an action. See Reed, *Compulsory Joinder of Parties in Civil Actions,* 55 Mich.L.Rev. 327, 356 ff., 483 (1957).

(3) The use of "indispensable" and "joint interest" in the context of original Rule 19 directed attention to the technical or abstract character of the rights or obligations of the persons whose joinder was in question, and correspondingly distracted attention from the pragmatic considerations which should be controlling.

(4) The original rule, in dealing with the feasibility of joining a person as a party to the action, besides referring to whether the person was "subject to the jurisdiction of the court as to both service of process and venue," spoke of whether the person could be made a party "without depriving the court of jurisdiction of the parties before it." The second quoted expression used "jurisdiction" in the sense of the competence of the court over the subject matter of the action, and in this sense the expression was apt. However, by a familiar confusion, the expression seems to have suggested to some that the absence from the lawsuit of a person who was "indispensable" or "who ought to be [a] part[y]" itself deprived the court of the power to adjudicate as between the parties already joined. See *Samuel Goldwyn, Inc. v. United Artists Corp.,* 113 F.2d 703, 707 (3d Cir. 1940); *McArthur v. Rosenbaum Co. of Pittsburgh,* 180 F.2d 617, 621 (3d Cir. 1949); *cf. Calcote v. Texas Pac. Coal & Oil Co.,* 157 F.2d 216 (5th Cir. 1946), *cert. denied,* 329 U.S. 782 (1946), noted in 56 Yale L.J. 1088 (1947); Reed, *supra,* 55 Mich.L.Rev. at 332–34.

Failure to point to correct basis of decision. The original rule did not state affirmatively what factors were relevant in deciding whether the action should proceed or be dismissed when joinder of interested persons was infeasible. In some instances courts did not undertake the relevant inquiry or were misled by the "jurisdiction" fallacy. In other instances there was undue preoccupation with abstract classifications of rights or obligations, as against consideration of the particular consequences of proceeding with the action and the ways by which these consequences might be ameliorated by the shaping of final relief or other precautions.

New matter is shown in italics; matter to be omitted is lined through

Although these difficulties cannot be said to have been general, analysis of the cases showed that there was good reason for attempting to strengthen the rule. The literature also indicated how the rule should be reformed. See Reed, *supra* (discussion of the important case of *Shields v. Barrow,* 17 How. (58 U.S.) 130 (1854), appears at 55 Mich.L.Rev., p. 340 ff.); Hazard, *supra;* N.Y. Temporary Comm. on Courts, *First Preliminary Report,* Legis.Doc. 1957, No. 6(b), pp. 28, 233; N.Y. Judicial Council, *Twelfth Ann. Rep.,* Legis.Doc. 1946, No. 17, p. 163; Joint Comm. on Michigan Procedural Revision, *Final Report,* Pt. III, p. 69 (1960); Note, *Indispensable Parties in the Federal Courts,* 65 Harv.L.Rev. 1050 (1952); *Developments in the Law—Multiparty Litigation in the Federal Courts,* 71 Harv.L.Rev. 874, 879 (1958); Mich.Gen.Court Rules, R. 205 (effective Jan. 1, 1963); N.Y.Civ.Prac. Law & Rules, § 1001 (effective Sept. 1, 1963).

The Amended Rule

New *subdivision (a)* defines the persons whose joinder in the action is desirable. Clause (1) stresses the desirability of joining those persons in whose absence the court would be obliged to grant partial or "hollow" rather than complete relief to the parties before the court. The interests that are being furthered here are not only those of the parties, but also that of the public in avoiding repeated lawsuits on the same essential subject matter. Clause (2)(i) recognizes the importance of protecting the person whose joinder is in question against the practical prejudice to him which may arise through a disposition of the action in his absence. Clause (2)(ii) recognizes the need for considering whether a party may be left, after the adjudication, in a position where a person not joined can subject him to a double or otherwise inconsistent liability. See Reed, *supra,* 55 Mich.L.Rev. at 330, 338; Note, *supra,* 65 Harv.L.Rev. at 1052–57; *Developments in the Law, supra,* 71 Harv.L.Rev. at 881–85.

The subdivision (a) definition of persons to be joined is not couched in terms of the abstract nature of their interests—"joint," "united," "separable," or the like. See N.Y. Temporary Comm. on Courts, *First Preliminary Report, supra; Developments in the Law, supra,* at ___. It should be noted particularly, however, that the description is not at variance with the settled authorities holding that a tortfeasor with the usual "joint-and-several" liability is merely a permissive party to an action against another with like liability. See 3 *Moore's Federal Practice,* § 2153 (2d ed. 1963); 2 Barron & Holtzoff, *Federal Practice & Procedure* § 513.8 (Wright ed. 1961). Joinder of these tortfeasors continues to be regulated by Rule 20; compare Rule 14 on third-party practice.

If a person as described in subdivision (a)(1)–(2) is amenable to service of process and his joinder would not deprive the court of jurisdiction in the sense of competence over the action, he should be joined as a party; and if he has not been joined, the court should order him to be brought into the action. If a party joined has a valid objection to the venue and chooses to assert it, he will be dismissed from the action.

Subdivision (b). When a person as described in subdivision (a)(1)–(2) cannot be made a party, the court is to determine whether in equity and good conscience the action should proceed among the parties already before it, or should be dismissed. That this decision is to be made in the light of pragmatic considerations has often been acknowledged by the courts. See *Roos v. Texas Co.,* 23 F.2d 171 (2d Cir. 1927), *cert. denied,* 277 U.S. 587 (1928); *Niles-Bement–Pond Co. v. Iron Moulders' Union,* 254 U.S. 77, 80 (1920). The subdivision sets out four relevant considerations drawn from the experience revealed in the decided cases. The factors are to a certain extent overlapping, and they are not intended to exclude other considerations which may be applicable in particular situations.

New matter is shown in italics; matter to be omitted is lined through

The *first factor* brings in a consideration of what a judgment in the action would mean to the absentee. Would the absentee by adversely affected in a practical sense, and if so, would the prejudice be immediate and serious, or remote and minor? The possible collateral consequences of the judgment upon the parties already joined are also to be appraised. Would any party be exposed to a fresh action by the absentee, and if so, how serious is the threat? See the elaborate discussion in Reed, *supra; cf. A. L. Smith Iron Co. v. Dickson,* 141 F.2d 3 (2d Cir. 1944); *Caldwell Mfg. Co. v. Unique Balance Co.,* 18 F.R.D. 258 (S.D.N.Y.1955).

The *second factor* calls attention to the measures by which prejudice may be averted or lessened. The "shaping of relief" is a familiar expedient to this end. See, *e.g.,* the award of money damages in lieu of specific relief where the latter might affect an absentee adversely. *Ward v. Deavers,* 203 F.2d 72 (D.C.Cir. 1953); *Miller & Lux, Inc. v. Nickel,* 141 F.Supp. 41 (N.D.Calif.1956). On the use of "protective provisions," see *Roos v. Texas Co., supra; Atwood v. Rhode Island Hosp. Trust Co.,* 275 Fed. 513, 519 (1st Cir. 1921), *cert. denied,* 257 U.S. 661 (1922); *cf. Stumpf v. Fidelity Gas Co.,* 294 F.2d 886 (9th Cir. 1961); and the general statement in *National Licorice Co. v. Labor Board,* 309 U.S. 350, 363 (1940).

Sometimes the party is himself able to take measures to avoid prejudice. Thus a defendant faced with a prospect of a second suit by an absentee may be in a position to bring the latter into the action by defensive interpleader. See *Hudson v. Newell,* 172 F.2d 848, 852, *mod.,* 176 F.2d 546 (5th Cir. 1949); *Gauss v. Kirk,* 198 F.2d 83, 86 (D.C.Cir. 1952); *Abel v. Brayton Flying Service, Inc.,* 248 F.2d 713, 716 (5th Cir. 1957) (suggestion of possibility of counterclaim under Rule 13(h)); *cf. Parker Rust–Proof Co. v. Western Union Tel. Co.,* 105 F.2d 976 (2d Cir. 1939), *cert. denied,* 308 U.S. 597 (1939). So also the absentee may sometimes be able to avert prejudice to himself by voluntarily appearing in the action or intervening on an ancillary basis. See *Developments in the Law, supra,* 71 Harv.L.Rev. at 882; Annot., *Intervention or Subsequent Joinder of Parties as Affecting Jurisdiction of Federal Court Based on Diversity of Citizenship,* 134 A.L.R. 335 (1941); *Johnson v. Middleton,* 175 F.2d 535 (7th Cir. 1949); *Kentucky Nat. Gas Corp. v. Duggins,* 165 F.2d 1011 (6th Cir. 1948); *McComb v. McCormack,* 159 F.2d 219 (5th Cir. 1947). The court should consider whether this, in turn, would impose undue hardship on the absentee. (For the possibility of the court's informing an absentee of the pendency of the action, see comment under subdivision (c) below.)

The *third factor*—whether an "adequate" judgment can be rendered in the absence of a given person—calls attention to the extent of the relief that can be accorded among the parties joined. It meshes with the other factors, especially the "shaping of relief" mentioned under the second factor. *Cf. Kroese v. General Steel Castings Corp.,* 179 F.2d 760 (3d Cir. 1949), *cert. denied,* 339 U.S. 983 (1950).

The *fourth factor,* looking to the practical effects of a dismissal, indicates that the court should consider whether there is any assurance that the plaintiff, if dismissed, could sue effectively in another forum where better joinder would be possible. See *Fitzgerald v. Haynes,* 241 F.2d 417, 420 (3d Cir. 1957); *Fouke v. Schenewerk,* 197 F.2d 234, 236 (5th Cir. 1952); *cf. Warfield v. Marks,* 190 F.2d 178 (5th Cir. 1951).

The subdivision uses the word "indispensable" only in a conclusory sense, that is, a person is "regarded as indispensable" when he cannot be made a party and, upon consideration of the factors above-mentioned, it is determined that in his absence it would be preferable to dismiss the action, rather than to retain it.

A person may be added as a party at any stage of the action on motion or on the court's initiative (see Rule 21); and a motion to dismiss, on the ground that a person has not been joined and justice requires that the action should not proceed in his

New matter is shown in italics; matter to be omitted is lined through

absence, may be made as late as the trial on the merits (see Rule 12(h)(2), as amended; *cf.* Rule 12(b)(7), as amended). However, when the moving party is seeking dismissal in order to protect himself against a later suit by the absent person (subdivision (a)(2)(ii)), and is not seeking vicariously to protect the absent person against a prejudicial judgment (subdivision (a)(2)(i)), his undue delay in making the motion can properly be counted against him as a reason for denying the motion. A joinder question should be decided with reasonable promptness, but decision may properly be deferred if adequate information is not available at the time. Thus the relationship of an absent person to the action, and the practical effects of an adjudication upon him and others, may not be sufficiently revealed at the pleading state; in such a case it would be appropriate to defer decision until the action was further advanced. *Cf.* Rule 12(d).

The amended rule makes no special provision for the problem arising in suits against subordinate Federal officials where it has often been set up as a defense that some superior officer must be joined. Frequently this defense has been accompanied by or intermingled with defenses of sovereign immunity or lack of consent of the United States to suit. So far as the issue of joinder can be isolated from the rest, the new subdivision seems better adapted to handle it than the predecessor provision. See the discussion in *Johnson v. Kirkland,* 290 F.2d 440, 446–47 (5th Cir. 1961) (stressing the practical orientation of the decisions); *Shaughnessy v. Pedreiro,* 349 U.S. 48, 54 (1955). Recent legislation, P.L. 87–748, 76 Stat. 744, approved October 5, 1962, adding §§ 1361, 1391(e) to Title 28, U.S.C., vests original jurisdiction in the district courts over actions in the nature of mandamus to compel officials of the United States to perform their legal duties, and extends the range of service of process and liberalizes venue in these actions. If, then, it is found that a particular official should be joined in the action, the legislation will make it easy to bring him in.

Subdivision (c) parallels the predecessor subdivision (c) of Rule 19. In some situations it may be desirable to advise a person who has not been joined of the fact that the action is pending, and in particular cases the court in its discretion may itself convey this information by directing a letter or other informal notice to the absentee.

Subdivision (d) repeats the exception contained in the first clause of the predecessor subdivision (a).

Rule 23.   Class Actions

Advisory Committee's Note to Original Rule

Note to Subdivision (a). This is a substantial restatement of Equity Rule 38 (Representatives of Class) as that rule has been construed. It applies to all actions, whether formerly denominated legal or equitable. For a general analysis of class actions, effect of judgment, and requisites of jurisdiction see Moore, *Federal Rules of Civil Procedure: Some Problems Raised by the Preliminary Draft,* 25 Georgetown L.J. 551, 570 *et seq.* (1937); Moore and Cohn, *Federal Class Actions,* 32 Ill.L.Rev. 307 (1937); Moore and Cohn, *Federal Class Actions—Jurisdiction and Effect of Judgment,* 32 Ill.L.Rev. 555–567 (1938); Lesar, *Class Suits and the Federal Rules,* 22 Minn.L.Rev. 34 (1937); *cf.* Arnold and James, *Cases on Trials, Judgments and Appeals* (1936) 175; and see Blume, *Jurisdictional Amount in Representative Suits,* 15 Minn.L.Rev. 501 (1931).

The general test of Equity Rule 38 (Representatives of Class) that the question should be "one of common or general interest to many persons constituting a class so numerous as to make it impracticable to bring them all before the court," is a

---

New matter is shown in italics; matter to be omitted is lined through

common test. For states which require the two elements of a common or general interest *and* numerous persons, as provided for in Equity Rule 38, see Del.Ch.Rule 113; Fla.Comp.Gen.Laws Ann. (Supp., 1936) § 4918(7); Georgia Code (1933) § 37–1002, and see English Rules Under the Judicature Act (The Annual Practice, 1937) O. 16, r. 9. For statutory provisions providing for class actions when the question is one of common or general interest *or* when the parties are numerous, see Ala.Code Ann. (Michie, 1928) § 5701; 2 Ind.Stat.Ann. (Burns, 1933) § 2–220; N.Y.C.P.A. (1937) § 195; Wis.Stat. (1935) § 260.12. These statutes have, however, been uniformly construed as though phrased in the conjunctive. See *Garfein v. Stiglitz,* 260 Ky. 430, 86 S.W.(2d) 155 (1935). The rule adopts the test of Equity Rule 38, but defines what constitutes a "common or general interest". Compare with code provisions which make the action dependent upon the propriety of joinder of the parties. See Blume, *The "Common Questions" Principle in the Code Provision for Representative Suits,* 30 Mich.L.Rev. 878 (1932). For discussion of what constitutes "numerous persons" see Wheaton, *Representative Suits Involving Numerous Litigants,* 19 Corn.L.Q. 399 (1934); Note, 36 Harv.L.Rev. 89 (1922).

Clause (1). Joint, Common, or Secondary Right. This clause is illustrated in actions brought by or against representatives of an unincorporated association. See *Oster v. Brotherhood of Locomotive Firemen and Enginemen,* 271 Pa. 419, 114 Atl. 377 (1921); *Pickett v. Walsh,* 192 Mass 572, 78 N.E. 753, 6 L.R.A.(N.S.) 1067 (1906); *Colt v. Hicks,* 97 Ind.App. 177, 179 N.E. 335 (1932). Compare Rule 17(b) as to when an unincorporated association has capacity to sue or be sued in its common name; *United Mine Workers of America v. Coronado Coal Co.,* 259 U.S. 344, 42 S.Ct. 570, 66 L.Ed. 975, 27 A.L.R. 762 (1922) (an unincorporated association was sued as an entity for the purpose of enforcing against it a federal substantive right); Moore, *Federal Rules of Civil Procedure: Some Problems Raised by the Preliminary Draft,* 25 Georgetown L.J. 551, 566 (for discussion of jurisdictional requisites when an unincorporated association sues or is sued in its common name and jurisdiction is founded upon diversity of citizenship). For an action brought by representatives of one group against representatives of another group for distribution of a fund held by an unincorporated association, see *Smith v. Swormstedt,* 16 How. 288, 14 L.Ed. 942 (U.S., 1853). Compare *Christopher, et al. v. Brusselback,* 302 U.S. 500, 58 S.Ct. 350, 82 L.Ed. 388 (1938).

For an action to enforce rights held in common by policyholders against the corporate issuer of the policies, see *Supreme Tribe of Ben Hur v. Cauble,* 255 U.S. 356, 41 S.Ct. 338, 65 L.Ed. 673 (1921). See also *Terry v. Little,* 101 U.S. 216, 25 L.Ed. 864 (1880); *John A. Roebling's Sons Co. v. Kinnicutt,* 248 Fed. 596 (D.C.N.Y., 1917) dealing with the right held in common by creditors to enforce the statutory liability of stockholders.

Typical of a secondary action is a suit by stockholders to enforce a corporate right. For discussion of the general nature of these actions see *Ashwander v. Tennessee Valley Authority,* 297 U.S. 288, 56 S.Ct. 466, 80 L.Ed. 688 (1936); Glenn, *The Stockholder's Suit—Corporate and Individual Grievances,* 33 Yale L.J. 580 (1924); McLaughlin, *Capacity of Plaintiff-Stockholder to Terminate a Stockholder's Suit,* 46 Yale L.J. 421 (1937). See also Subdivision (b) of this rule which deals with Shareholder's Action; note, 15 Minn.L.Rev. 453 (1931).

Clause (2). A creditor's action for liquidation or reorganization of a corporation is illustrative of this clause. An action by a stockholder against certain named defendants as representatives of numerous claimants presents a situation converse to the creditor's action.

Clause (3). See *Everglades Drainage League v. Napoleon Broward Drainage Dist.,* 253 Fed. 246 (D.C.Fla., 1918); *Gramling v. Maxwell,* 52 F.2d 256 (D.C.N.C.,

1931), approved in 30 Mich.L.Rev. 624 (1932); *Skinner v. Mitchell,* 108 Kan. 861, 197 Pac. 569 (1921); *Duke of Bedford v. Ellis* (1901) A.C. 1, for class actions when there were numerous persons and there was only a question of law or fact common to them; and see Blume, *The "Common Questions" Principle in the Code Provision for Representative Suits,* 30 Mich.L.Rev. 878 (1932).

Note to Subdivision (b). This is Equity Rule 27 (Stockholder's Bill) with verbal changes. See also *Hawes v. Oakland,* 104 U.S. 450, 26 L.Ed. 827 (1882) and former Equity Rule 94, promulgated January 23, 1882, 104 U.S. IX.

Note to Subdivision (c). See McLaughlin, *Capacity of Plaintiff–Stockholder to Terminate a Stockholder's Suit,* 46 Yale L.J. 421 (1937).

Advisory Committee's Note to 1966 Amendment

(a) Representation. If persons constituting a class are so numerous as to make it impracticable to bring them all before the court, such of them, one or more, as will fairly insure the adequate representation of all may, on behalf of all, sue or be sued, when the character of the right sought to be enforced for or against the class is

(1) joint or common, or secondary in the sense that the owner of a primary right refuses to enforce that right and a member of the class thereby becomes entitled to enforce it;

(2) several, and the object of the action is the adjudication of claims which do or may affect specific property involved in the action; or

(3) several, and there is a common question of law or fact affecting the several rights and a common relief is sought.

(b) Secondary Action by Shareholders. In an action brought to enforce a secondary right on the part of one or more shareholders in an association, incorporated or unincorporated, because the association refuses to enforce rights which may properly be asserted by it, the complaint shall be verified by oath and shall aver (1) that the plaintiff was a shareholder at the time of the transaction of which he complains or that his share thereafter devolved on him by operation of law and (2) that the action is not a collusive one to confer on a court of the United States jurisdiction of any action of which it would not otherwise have jurisdiction. The complaint shall also set forth with particularity the efforts of the plaintiff to secure from the managing directors or trustees and, if necessary, from the shareholders such action as he desires, and the reasons for his failure to obtain such action or the reasons for not making such effort.

New matter is shown in italics; matter to be omitted is lined through

(c) Dismissal or Compromise. A class action shall not be dismissed or compromised without the approval of the court. If the right sought to be enforced is one defined in paragraph (1) of subdivision (a) of this rule notice of the proposed dismissal or compromise shall be given to all members of the class in such manner as the court directs. If the right is one defined in paragraphs (2) or (3) of subdivision (a) notice shall be given only if the court requires it.

(a) Prerequisites to a Class Action. One or more members of a class may sue or be sued as representative parties on behalf of all only if (1) the class is so numerous that joinder of all members is impracticable, (2) there are questions of law or fact common to the class, (3) the claims or defenses of the representative parties are typical of the claims or defenses of the class, and (4) the representative parties will fairly and adequately protect the interests of the class.

(b) Class Actions Maintainable. An action may be maintained as a class action if the prerequisites of subdivision (a) are satisfied, and in addition:

(1) the prosecution of separate actions by or against individual members of the class would create a risk of

(A) inconsistent or varying adjudications with respect to individual members of the class which would establish incompatible standards of conduct for the party opposing the class, or

(B) adjudications with respect to individual members of the class which would as a practical matter be dispositive of the interests of the other members not parties to the adjudications or substantially impair or impede their ability to protect their interests; or

(2) the party opposing the class has acted or refused to act on grounds generally applicable to the class, thereby making appropriate final injunctive relief or corresponding declaratory relief with respect to the class as a whole; or

(3) the court finds that the questions of law or fact common to the members of the class predominate over any questions affecting only individual members, and that a class action is superior to other available methods for the fair and efficient adjudication of the controversy. The matters pertinent to the findings include: (A) the interest of members of the class in individually controlling the prosecution or defense of separate actions; (B) the extent and nature of any litigation concerning the controversy already commenced by or against members of

New matter is shown in italics; matter to be omitted is lined through

the class; (C) the desirability or undesirability of concentrating the litigation of the claims in the particular forum; (D) the difficulties likely to be encountered in the management of a class action.

(c) Determination by Order Whether Class Action to be Maintained; Notice; Judgment; Actions Conducted Partially as Class Actions.

(1) As soon as practicable after the commencement of an action brought as a class action, the court shall determine by order whether it is to be so maintained. An order under this subdivision may be conditional, and may be altered or amended before the decision on the merits.

(2) In any class action maintained under subdivision (b)(3), the court shall direct to the members of the class the best notice practicable under the circumstances, including individual notice to all members who can be identified through reasonable effort. The notice shall advise each member that (A) the court will exclude him from the class if he so requests by a specified date; (B) the judgment, whether favorable or not, will include all members who do not request exclusion; and (C) any member who does not request exclusion may, if he desires, enter an appearance through his counsel.

(3) The judgment in an action maintained as a class action under subdivision (b)(1) or (b)(2), whether or not favorable to the class, shall include and describe those whom the court finds to be members of the class. The judgment in an action maintained as a class action under subdivision (b)(3), whether or not favorable to the class, shall include and specify or describe those to whom the notice provided in subdivision (c)(2) was directed, and who have not requested exclusion, and whom the court finds to be members of the class.

(4) When appropriate (A) an action may be brought or maintained as a class action with respect to particular issues, or (B) a class may be divided into subclasses and each subclass treated as a class, and the provisions of this rule shall then be construed and applied accordingly.

(d) Orders in Conduct of Actions. *In the conduct of actions to which this rule applies, the court may make appropriate orders: (1) determining the course of proceedings or prescribing measures to prevent undue repetition or complication in the presentation of evidence or argument; (2) requiring, for the protection of the members of the class or otherwise for the fair conduct of the action, that notice be given in such manner as the court may direct to some or all of the members of any step in the action, or of the proposed extent of*

New matter is shown in italics; matter to be omitted is lined through

the judgment, or of the opportunity of members to signify whether they consider the representation fair and adequate, to intervene and present claims or defenses, or otherwise to come into the action; (3) imposing conditions on the representative parties or on intervenors; (4) requiring that the pleadings be amended to eliminate therefrom allegations as to representation of absent persons, and that the action proceed accordingly; (5) dealing with similar procedural matters. The orders may be combined with an order under Rule 16, and may be altered or amended as may be desirable form time to time.

*(e) **Dismissal or Compromise.** A class action shall not be dismissed or compromised without the approval of the court, and notice of the proposed dismissal or compromise shall be given to all members of the class in such manner as the court directs.*

Difficulties with the original rule. The categories of class actions in the original rule were defined in terms of the abstract nature of the rights involved: the so-called "true" category was defined as involving "joint, common, or secondary rights"; the "hybrid" category, as involving "several" rights related to "specific property"; the "spurious" category, as involving "several" rights affected by a common question and related to common relief. It was thought that the definitions accurately described the situations amenable to the class-suit device, and also would indicate the proper extent of the judgment in each category, which would in turn help to determine the *res judicata* effect of the judgment if questioned in a later action. Thus the judgments in "true" and "hybrid" class actions would extend to the class (although in somewhat different ways); the judgment in a "spurious" class action would extend only to the parties including intervenors. See Moore, *Federal Rules of Civil Procedure: Some Problems Raised by the Preliminary Draft,* 25 Geo.L.J. 551, 570–76 (1937).

In practice the terms "joint," "common," etc., which were used as the basis of the Rule 23 classification proved obscure and uncertain. See Chafee, *Some Problems of Equity* 245–46, 256–57 (1950); Kalven & Rosenfield, *The Contemporary Function of the Class Suit,* 8 U. of Chi.L.Rev. 684, 707 & n. 73 (1941); Keeffe, Levy & Donovan, *Lee Defeats Ben Hur,* 33 Corn.L.Q. 327, 329–36 (1948); *Developments in the Law: Multiparty Litigation in the Federal Courts,* 71 Harv.L.Rev. 874, 931 (1958); Advisory Committee's Note to Rule 19, as amended. The courts had considerable difficulty with these terms. See, *e.g., Gullo v. Veterans' Coop. H. Assn.,* 13 F.R.D. 11 (D.D.C.1952); *Shipley v. Pittsburgh & L. E. R. Co.,* 70 F.Supp. 870 (W.D.Pa.1947); *Deckert v. Independence Shares Corp.,* 27 F.Supp. 763 (E.D.Pa.1939), *rev'd,* 108 F.2d 51 (3d Cir. 1939), *rev'd,* 311 U.S. 282 (1940), *on remand,* 39 F.Supp. 592 (E.D.Pa.1941), *rev'd sub nom. Pennsylvania Co. for Ins. on Lives v. Deckert,* 123 F.2d 979 (3d Cir. 1941) (see Chafee, *supra,* at 264–65).

Nor did the rule provide an adequate guide to the proper extent of the judgments in class actions. First, we find instances of the courts classifying actions as "true" or intimating that the judgments would be decisive for the class where these results seemed appropriate but were reached by dint of depriving the word "several" of coherent meaning. See, *e.g., System Federation No. 91 v. Reed,* 180 F.2d 991 (6th Cir. 1950); *Wilson v. City of Paducah,* 100 F.Supp. 116 (W.D.Ky.1951);

New matter is shown in italics; matter to be omitted is lined through

Citizens Banking Co. v. Monticello State Bank, 143 F.2d 261 (8th Cir. 1944); *Redmond v. Commerce Trust Co.,* 144 F.2d 140 (8th Cir. 1944), *cert. denied,* 323 U.S. 776 (1944); *United States v. American Optical Co.,* 97 F.Supp. 66 (N.D.Ill.1951); *National Hairdressers' & C. Assn. v. Philad Co.,* 34 F.Supp. 264 (D.Del.1940); 41 F.Supp. 701 (D.Del.1940), *aff'd mem.,* 129 F.2d 1020 (3d Cir. 1942). Second, we find cases classified by the courts as "spurious" in which, on a realistic view, it would seem fitting for the judgments to extend to the class. See, *e.g., Knapp v. Bankers Sec. Corp.,* 17 F.R.D. 245 (E.D.Pa.1954), *aff'd,* 230 F.2d 717 (3d Cir. 1956); *Giesecke v. Denver Tramway Corp.,* 81 F.Supp. 957 (D.Del.1949); *York v. Guaranty Trust Co.,* 143 F.2d 503 (2d Cir. 1944), *rev'd on grounds not here relevant,* 326 U.S. 99 (1945) (see Chafee, *supra,* at 208); *cf. Webster Eisenlohr, Inc. v. Kalodner,* 145 F.2d 316, 320 (3d Cir. 1944), *cert. denied,* 325 U.S. 867 (1945). But *cf.* the early decisions, *Duke of Bedford v. Ellis,* [1901] A.C. 1; *Sheffield Waterworks v. Yeomans,* L. R. 2 Ch.App. 8 (1866); *Brown v. Vermuden,* 1 Ch.Cas. 272, 22 Eng.Rep. 796 (1676).

The "spurious" action envisaged by original Rule 23 was in any event an anomaly because, although denominated a "class" action and pleaded as such, it was supposed not to adjudicate the rights or liabilities of any person not a party. It was believed to be an advantage of the "spurious" category that it would invite decisions that a member of the "class" could, like a member of the class in a "true" or "hybrid" action, intervene on an ancillary basis without being required to show an independent basis of Federal jurisdiction, and have the benefit of the date of the commencement of the action for purposes of the statute of limitations. See 3 *Moore's Federal Practice* ¶¶ 23.10[1], 23.12 (2d ed. 1963). These results were attained in some instances but not in others. On the statute of limitations, see *Union Carbide & Carbon Corp. v. Nisley,* 300 F.2d 561 (10th Cir. 1961), *pet. cert. dism.,* 371 U.S. 801 (1963); but *cf. P. W. Husserl, Inc. v. Newman,* 25 F.R.D. 264 (S.D.N.Y.1960); *Athas v. Day,* 161 F.Supp. 916 (D.Colo.1958). On ancillary intervention, see *Amen v. Black,* 234 F.2d 12 (10th Cir. 1956), *cert. granted,* 352 U.S. 888 (1956), *dism. on stip.,* 355 U.S. 600 (1958); but *cf. Wagner v. Kemper,* 13 F.R.D. 128 (W.D.Mo.1952). The results, however, can hardly depend upon the mere appearance of a "spurious" category in the rule; they should turn on more basic considerations. See discussion of subdivision (c)(1) below.

Finally, the original rule did not squarely address itself to the question of the measures that might be taken during the course of the action to assure procedural fairness, particularly giving notice to members of the class, which may in turn be related in some instances to the extension of the judgment to the class. See Chafee, *supra,* at 230–31; Keeffe, Levy & Donovan, *supra; Developments in the Law, supra,* 71 Harv.L.Rev. at 937–38; Note, *Binding Effect of Class Actions,* 67 Harv.L.Rev. 1059, 1062–65 (1954); Note, *Federal Class Actions: A Suggested Revision of Rule 23,* 46 Colum.L.Rev. 818, 833–36 (1946); Mich.Gen.Court R. 208.4 (effective Jan. 1, 1963); Idaho R.Civ.P. 23(d); Minn.R.Civ.P. 23.04; N.Dak.R.Civ.P. 23(d).

The amended rule describes in more practical terms the occasions for maintaining class action; provides that all class actions maintained to the end as such will result in judgments including those whom the court finds to be members of the class, whether or not the judgment is favorable to the class; and refers to the measures which can be taken to assure the fair conduct of these actions.

Subdivision (a) states the prerequisites for maintaining any class action in terms of the numerousness of the class making joinder of the members impracticable, the existence of questions common to the class, and the desired qualifications of the representative parties. See Weinstein, *Revision of Procedure: Some Problems in Class Actions,* 9 Buffalo L.Rev. 433, 458–59 (1960); 2 Barron & Holtzoff, *Federal Practice & Procedure* § 562, at 265, § 572, at 351–52 (Wright ed. 1961). These are necessary but not sufficient conditions for a class action. See *e.g., Giordano v. Radio*

New matter is shown in italics; matter to be omitted is lined through

Corp. of Am., 183 F.2d 558, 560 (3d Cir. 1950); *Zachman v. Erwin*, 186 F.Supp. 681 (S.D.Tex.1959); *Baim & Blank, Inc. v. Warren–Connelly Co., Inc.*, 19 F.R.D. 108 (S.D.N.Y.1956). Subdivision (b) describes the additional elements which in varying situations justify the use of a class action.

Subdivision (b)(1). The difficulties which would be likely to arise if resort were had to separate actions by or against the individual members of the class here furnish the reasons for, and the principal key to, the propriety and value of utilizing the class-action device. The considerations stated under clauses (A) and (B) are comparable to certain of the elements which define the persons whose joinder in an action is desirable as stated in Rule 19(a), as amended. See amended Rule 19(a)(2)(i) and (ii), and the Advisory Committee's Note thereto; Hazard, *Indispensable Party: The Historical Origin of a Procedural Phantom*, 61 Colum.L.Rev. 1254, 1259–60 (1961); *cf.* 3 Moore, *supra*, ¶ 23.08, at 3435.

Clause (A): One person may have rights against, or be under duties toward, numerous persons constituting a class, and be so positioned that conflicting or varying adjudications in lawsuits with individual members of the class might establish incompatible standards to govern his conduct. The class action device can be used effectively to obviate the actual or virtual dilemma which would thus confront the party opposing the class. The matter has been stated thus: "The felt necessity for a class action is greatest when the courts are called upon to order or sanction the alteration of the status quo in circumstances such that a large number of persons are in a position to call on a single person to alter the status quo, or to complain if it is altered, and the possibility exists that [the] actor might be called upon to act in inconsistent ways." Louisell & Hazard, *Pleading and Procedure: State and Federal* 719 (1962); see *Supreme Tribe of Ben–Hur v. Cauble*, 255 U.S. 356, 366–67 (1921). To illustrate: Separate actions by individuals against a municipality to declare a bond issue invalid or condition or limit it, to prevent or limit the making of a particular appropriation or to compel or invalidate an assessment, might create a risk of inconsistent or varying determinations. In the same way, individual litigations of the rights and duties of riparian owners, or of landowners' rights and duties respecting a claimed nuisance, could create a possibility of incompatible adjudications. Actions by or against a class provide a ready and fair means of achieving unitary adjudication. See *Maricopa County Mun. Water Con. Dist. v. Looney*, 219 F.2d 529 (9th Cir. 1955); *Rank v. Krug*, 142 F.Supp. 1, 154–59 (S.D.Calif.1956), *on app., State of California v. Rank*, 293 F.2d 340, 348 (9th Cir. 1961); *Gart v. Cole*, 263 F.2d 244 (2d Cir. 1959), *cert. denied*, 359 U.S. 978 (1959); *cf. Martinez v. Maverick Cty. Water Con. & Imp. Dist.*, 219 F.2d 666 (5th Cir. 1955); 3 Moore, *supra*, ¶ 23.11[2], at 3458–59.

Clause (B): This clause takes in situations where the judgment in a nonclass action by or against an individual member of the class, while not technically concluding the other members, might do so as a practical matter. The vice of an individual action would lie in the fact that the other members of the class, thus practically concluded, would have had no representation in the lawsuit. In an action by policy holders against a fraternal benefit association attacking a financial reorganization of the society, it would hardly have been practical, if indeed it would have been possible, to confine the effects of a validation of the reorganization to the individual plaintiffs. Consequently a class action was called for with adequate representation of all members of the class. See *Supreme Tribe of Ben–Hur v. Cauble*, 255 U.S. 356 (1921); *Waybright v. Columbian Mut. Life Ins. Co.*, 30 F.Supp. 885 (W.D.Tenn.1939); *cf. Smith v. Swormstedt*, 16 How. (57 U.S.) 288 (1853). For much the same reason actions by shareholders to compel the declaration of a dividend, the proper recognition and handling of redemption or pre-emption rights, or the like (or actions by the corporation for corresponding declaration of rights), should ordinarily

---

New matter is shown in italics; matter to be omitted is lined through

be conducted as class actions, although the matter has been much obscured by the insistence that each shareholder has an individual claim. See *Knapp v. Bankers Securities Corp.* 17 F.R.D. 245 (E.D.Pa.1954), *aff'd*, 230 F.2d 717 (3d Cir. 1956); *Giesecke v. Denver Tramway Corp.*, 81 F.Supp. 957 (D.Del.1949); *Zahn v. Transamerica Corp.*, 162 F.2d 36 (3d Cir. 1947); *Speed v. Transamerica Corp.*, 100 F.Supp. 461 (D.Del.1951); *Sobel v. Whittier Corp.*, 95 F.Supp. 643 (E.D.Mich.1951), *app. dism.*, 195 F.2d 361 (6th Cir. 1952); *Goldberg v. Whittier Corp.*, 111 F.Supp. 382 (E.D.Mich.1953); *Dann v. Studebaker–Packard Corp.*, 288 F.2d 201 (6th Cir. 1961); *Edgerton v. Armour & Co.*, 94 F.Supp. 549 (S.D.Calif.1950); *Ames v. Mengel Co.*, 190 F.2d 344 (2d Cir. 1951). (These shareholders' actions are to be distinguished from derivative actions by shareholders dealt with in new Rule 23.1). The same reasoning applies to an action which charges a breach of trust by an indenture trustee or other fiduciary similarly affecting the members of a large class of security holders or other beneficiaries, and which requires an accounting or like measures to restore the subject of the trust. See *Boesenberg v. Chicago T. & T. Co.*, 128 F.2d 245 (7th Cir. 1942); *Citizens Banking Co. v. Monticello State Bank*, 143 F.2d 261 (8th Cir. 1944); *Redmond v. Commerce Trust Co.* 144 F.2d 140 (8th Cir. 1944), *cert. denied*, 323 U.S. 776 (1944); *cf. York v. Guaranty Trust Co.*, 143 F.2d 503 (2d Cir. 1944), *rev'd on grounds not here relevant*, 326 U.S. 99 (1945).

In various situations an adjudication as to one or more members of the class will necessarily or probably have an adverse practical effect on the interests of other members who should therefore be represented in the lawsuit. This is plainly the case when claims are made by numerous persons against a fund insufficient to satisfy all claims. A class action by or against representative members to settle the validity of the claims as a whole, or in groups, followed by separate proof of the amount of each valid claim and proportionate distribution of the fund, meets the problem. *Cf. Dickinson v. Burnham*, 197 F.2d 973 (2d Cir. 1952), *cert. denied*, 344 U.S. 875 (1952); 3 Moore, *supra*, at ¶ 23.09. The same reasoning applies to an action by a creditor to set aside a fraudulent conveyance by the debtor and to appropriate the property to his claim, when the debtor's assets are insufficient to pay all creditors' claims. See *Heffernan v. Bennett & Armour*, 110 Cal.App.2d 564, 243 P.2d 846 (1952); *cf. City & County of San Francisco v. Market Street Ry.*, 95 Cal.App.2d 648, 213 P.2d 780 (1950). Similar problems, however, can arise in the absence of a fund either present or potential. A negative or mandatory injunction secured by one of a numerous class may disable the opposing party from performing claimed duties toward the other members of the class or materially affect his ability to do so. An adjudication as to movie "clearances and runs" nominally affecting only one exhibitor would often have practical effects on all the exhibitors in the same territorial area. *Cf. United States v. Paramount Pictures, Inc.*, 66 F.Supp. 323, 341–46 (S.D.N.Y. 1946); 334 U.S. 131, 144–48 (1948). Assuming a sufficiently numerous class of exhibitors, a class action would be advisable. (Here representation of subclasses of exhibitors could become necessary; see subdivision (c)(3)(B).)

Subdivision (b)(2). This subdivision is intended to reach situations where a party has taken action or refused to take action with respect to a class, and final relief of an injunctive nature or of a corresponding declaratory nature, settling the legality of the behavior with respect to the class as a whole, is appropriate. Declaratory relief "corresponds" to injunctive relief when as a practical matter it affords injunctive relief or serves as a basis for later injunctive relief. The subdivision does not extend to cases in which the appropriate final relief relates exclusively or predominantly to money damages. Action or inaction is directed to a class within the meaning of this subdivision even if it has taken effect or is threatened only as to one or a few members of the class, provided it is based on grounds which have general application to the class.

New matter is shown in italics; matter to be omitted is lined through

Illustrative are various actions in the civil-rights field where a party is charged with discriminating unlawfully against a class, usually one whose members are incapable of specific enumeration. See *Potts v. Flax*, 313 F.2d 284 (5th Cir. 1963); *Bailey v. Patterson*, 323 F.2d 201 (5th Cir. 1963), *cert. denied*, 377 U.S. 972 (1964); *Brunson v. Board of Trustees of School District No. 1, Clarendon Cty., S. C.*, 311 F.2d 107 (4th Cir. 1962), *cert. denied*, 373 U.S. 933 (1963); *Green v. School Bd. of Roanoke, Va.*, 304 F.2d 118 (4th Cir. 1962); *Orleans Parish School Bd. v. Bush*, 242 F.2d 156 (5th Cir. 1957), *cert. denied*, 354 U.S. 921 (1957); *Mannings v. Board of Public Inst. of Hillsborough County, Fla.*, 277 F.2d 370 (5th Cir. 1960); *Northcross v. Board of Ed. of City of Memphis*, 302 F.2d 818 (6th Cir. 1962), *cert. denied*, 370 U.S. 944 (1962); *Frasier v. Board of Trustees of Univ. of N. C.*, 134 F.Supp. 589 (M.D.N.C.1955, 3–judge court), *aff'd*, 350 U.S. 979 (1956). Subdivision (b)(2) is not limited to civil-rights cases. Thus an action looking to specific or declaratory relief could be brought by a numerous class of purchasers, say retailers of a given description, against a seller alleged to have undertaken to sell to that class at prices higher than those set for other purchasers, say retailers of another description, when the applicable law forbids such a pricing differential. So also a patentee of a machine, charged with selling or licensing the machine on condition that purchasers or licensees also purchase or obtain licenses to use an ancillary unpatented machine, could be sued on a class basis by a numerous group of purchasers or licensees, or by a numerous group of competing sellers or licensors of the unpatented machine, to test the legality of the "tying" condition.

Subdivision (b)(3). In the situations to which this subdivision relates, class-action treatment is not as clearly called for as in those described above, but it may nevertheless be convenient and desirable depending upon the particular facts. Subdivision (b)(3) encompasses those cases in which a class action would achieve economies of time, effort, and expense, and promote uniformity of decision as to persons similarly situated, without sacrificing procedural fairness or bringing about other undesirable results. *Cf.* Chafee, *supra*, at 201.

The court is required to find, as a condition of holding that a class action may be maintained under this subdivision, that the questions common to the class predominate over the questions affecting individual members. It is only where this predominance exists that economies can be achieved by means of the class-action device. In this view, a fraud perpetrated on numerous persons by the use of similar misrepresentations may be an appealing situation for a class action, and it may remain so despite the need, if liability is found, for separate determination of the damages suffered by individuals within the class. On the other hand, although having some common core, a fraud case may be unsuited for treatment as a class action if there was material variation in the representations made or in the kinds or degrees of reliance by the persons to whom they were addressed. See *Oppenheimer v. F. J. Young & Co., Inc.*, 144 F.2d 387 (2d Cir. 1944); *Miller v. National City Bank of N. Y.*, 166 F.2d 723 (2d Cir. 1948); and for like problems in other contexts, see *Hughes v. Encyclopaedia Britannica*, 199 F.2d 295 (7th Cir. 1952); *Sturgeon v. Great Lakes Steel Corp.*, 143 F.2d 819 (6th Cir. 1944). A "mass accident" resulting in injuries to numerous persons is ordinarily not appropriate for a class action because of the likelihood that significant questions, not only of damages but of liability and defenses to liability, would be present, affecting the individuals in different ways. In these circumstances an action conducted nominally as a class action would degenerate in practice into multiple lawsuits separately tried. See *Pennsylvania R. R. v. United States*, 111 F.Supp. 80 (D.N.J.1953); *cf.* Weinstein, *supra*, 9 Buffalo L.Rev. at 469. Private damage claims by numerous individuals arising out of concerted antitrust violations may or may not involve predominating common questions. See *Union Carbide & Carbon Corp. v. Nisley*, 300 F.2d 561 (10th Cir. 1961), *pet. cert. dism.*, 371 U.S. 801 (1963); *cf. Weeks v. Bareco Oil Co.*, 125 F.2d 84 (7th Cir. 1941);

New matter is shown in italics; matter to be omitted is lined through

Kainz v. Anheuser–Busch, Inc., 194 F.2d 737 (7th Cir. 1952); *Hess v. Anderson, Clayton & Co.,* 20 F.R.D. 466 (S.D.Calif.1957).

That common questions predominate is not itself sufficient to justify a class action under subdivision (b)(3), for another method of handling the litigious situation may be available which has greater practical advantages. Thus one or more actions agreed to by the parties as test or model actions may be preferable to a class action; or it may prove feasible and preferable to consolidate actions. *Cf.* Weinstein, *supra,* 9 Buffalo L.Rev. at 438–54. Even when a number of separate actions are proceeding simultaneously, experience shows that the burdens on the parties and the courts can sometimes be reduced by arrangements for avoiding repetitious discovery or the like. Currently the Coordinating Committee on Multiple Litigation in the United States District Courts (a subcommittee of the Committee on Trial Practice and Technique of the Judicial Conference of the United States) is charged with developing methods for expediting such massive litigation. To reinforce the point that the court with the aid of the parties ought to assess the relative advantages of alternative procedures for handling the total controversy, subdivision (b)(3) requires, as a further condition of maintaining the class action, that the court shall find that that procedure is "superior" to the others in the particular circumstances.

Factors (A)–(D) are listed, non-exhaustively, as pertinent to the findings. The court is to consider the interests of individual members of the class in controlling their own litigations and carrying them on as they see fit. See *Weeks v. Bareco Oil Co.,* 125 F.2d 84, 88–90, 93–94 (7th Cir.1941) (anti-trust action); see also *Pentland v. Dravo Corp.,* 152 F.2d 851 (3d Cir.1945), and Chafee, *supra,* at 273–75, regarding policy of Fair Labor Standards Act of 1938, § 16(b), 29 U.S.C. § 216(b), prior to amendment by Portal-to-Portal Act of 1947, § 5(a). [The present provisions of 29 U.S.C. § 216(b) are not intended to be affected by Rule 23, as amended.] In this connection the court should inform itself of any litigation actually pending by or against the individuals. The interests of individuals in conducting separate lawsuits may be so strong as to call for denial of a class action. On the other hand, these interests may be theoretic rather than practical: the class may have a high degree of cohesion and prosecution of the action through representatives would be quite unobjectionable, or the amounts at stake for individuals may be so small that separate suits would be impracticable. The burden that separate suits would impose on the party opposing the class, or upon the court calendars, may also fairly be considered. (See the discussion, under subdivision (c)(2) below, of the right of members to be excluded from the class upon their request.)

Also pertinent is the question of the desirability of concentrating the trial of the claims in the particular forum by means of a class action, in contrast to allowing the claims to be litigated separately in forums to which they would ordinarily be brought. Finally, the court should consider the problems of management which are likely to arise in the conduct of a class action.

Subdivision (c)(1). In order to give clear definition to the action, this provision requires the court to determine, as early in the proceedings as may be practicable, whether an action brought as a class action is to be so maintained. The determination depends in each case on satisfaction of the terms of subdivision (a) and the relevant provisions of subdivision (b).

An order embodying a determination can be conditional; the court may rule, for example, that a class action may be maintained only if the representation is improved through intervention of additional parties of a stated type. A determination once made can be altered or amended before the decision on the merits if, upon full development of the facts, the original determination appears unsound. A

New matter is shown in italics; matter to be omitted is lined through

negative determination means that the action should be stripped of its character as a class action. See subdivision (d)(4). Although an action thus becomes a nonclass action, the court may still be receptive to interventions before the decision on the merits so that the litigation may cover as many interests as can be conveniently handled; the questions whether the intervenors in the nonclass action shall be permitted to claim "ancillary" jurisdiction or the benefit of the date of the commencement of the action for purposes of the statute of limitations are to be decided by reference to the laws governing jurisdiction and limitations as they apply in particular contexts.

Whether the court should require notice to be given to members of the class of its intention to make a determination, or of the order embodying it, is left to the court's discretion under subdivision (d)(2).

Subdivision (c)(2) makes special provision for class actions maintained under subdivision (b)(3). As noted in the discussion of the latter subdivision, the interests of the individuals in pursuing their own litigations may be so strong here as to warrant denial of a class action altogether. Even when a class action is maintained under subdivision (b)(3), this individual interest is respected. Thus the court is required to direct notice to the members of the class of the right of each member to be excluded from the class upon his request. A member who does not request exclusion may, if he wishes, enter an appearance in the action through his counsel; whether or not he does so, the judgment in the action will embrace him.

The notice, setting forth the alternatives open to the members of the class, is to be the best practicable under the circumstances, and shall include individual notice to the members who can be identified through reasonable effort. (For further discussion of this notice, see the statement under subdivision (d)(2) below.)

Subdivision (c)(3). The judgment in a class action maintained as such to the end will embrace the class, that is, in a class action under subdivision (b)(1) or (b)(2), those found by the court to be class members; in a class action under subdivision (b)(3), those to whom the notice prescribed by subdivision (c)(2) was directed, excepting those who requested exclusion or who are ultimately found by the court not to be members of the class. The judgment has this scope whether it is favorable or unfavorable to the class. In a (b)(1) or (b)(2) action the judgment "describes" the members of the class, but need not specify the individual members; in a (b)(3) action the judgment "specifies" the individual members who have been identified and describes the others.

Compare subdivision (c)(4) as to actions conducted as class actions only with respect to particular issues. Where the class-action character of the lawsuit is based solely on the existence of a "limited fund," the judgment, while extending to all claims of class members against the fund, has ordinarily left unaffected the personal claims of nonappearing members against the debtor. See 3 Moore, *supra,* ¶ 23.11[4].

Hitherto, in a few actions conducted as "spurious" class actions and thus nominally designed to extend only to parties and others intervening *before* the determination of liability, courts have held or intimated that class members might be permitted to intervene *after* a decision on the merits favorable to their interests, in order to secure the benefits of the decision for themselves, although they would presumably be unaffected by an unfavorable decision. See, as to the propriety of this so-called "one-way" intervention in "spurious" actions, the conflicting views expressed in *Union Carbide & Carbon Corp. v. Nisley,* 300 F.2d 561 (10th Cir.1961), *pet. cert. dism.,* 371 U.S. 801 (1963); *York v. Guaranty Trust Co.,* 143 F.2d 503, 529 (2d Cir.1944), *rev'd on grounds not here relevant,* 326 U.S. 99 (1945); *Pentland v. Dravo Corp.,* 152 F.2d 851, 856 (3d Cir.1945); *Speed v. Transamerica Corp.,* 100 F.Supp. 461, 463 (D.Del.1951); *State Wholesale Grocers v. Great Atl. & Pac. Tea Co.,*

New matter is shown in italics; matter to be omitted is lined through

24 F.R.D. 510 (N.D.Ill.1959); *Alabama Ind. Serv. Stat. Assn. v. Shell Pet. Corp.*, 28 F.Supp. 386, 390 (N.D.Ala.1939); *Tolliver v. Cudahy Packing Co.*, 39 F.Supp. 337, 339 (E.D.Tenn.1941); Kalven & Rosenfield, *supra*, 8 U. of Chi.L.Rev. 684 (1941); Comment, 53 Nw.U.L.Rev. 627, 632–33 (1958); *Developments in the Law, supra*, 71 Harv.L.Rev. at 935; 2 Barron & Holtzoff, *supra*, § 568; but *cf. Lockwood v. Hercules Powder Co.*, 7 F.R.D. 24, 28–29 (W.D.Mo.1947); *Abram v. San Joaquin Cotton Oil Co.*, 46 F.Supp. 969, 976–77 (S.D.Calif.1942); Chafee, *supra*, at 280, 285; 3 Moore, *supra*, ¶ 23.12, at 3476. Under proposed subdivision (c)(3), one-way intervention is excluded; the action will have been early determined to be a class or nonclass action, and in the former case the judgment, whether or not favorable, will include the class, as above stated.

Although thus declaring that the judgment in a class action includes the class, as defined, subdivision (c)(3) does not disturb the recognized principle that the court conducting the action cannot predetermine the *res judicata* effect of the judgment; this can be tested only in a subsequent action. See Restatement, *Judgments* § 86, comment (h), § 116 (1942). The court, however, in framing the judgment in any suit brought as a class action, must decide what its extent or coverage shall be, and if the matter is carefully considered, questions of *res judicata* are less likely to be raised at a later time and if raised will be more satisfactorily answered. See Chafee, *supra*, at 294; Weinstein, *supra*, 9 Buffalo L.Rev. at 460.

Subdivision (c)(4). This provision recognizes that an action may be maintained as a class action as to particular issues only. For example, in a fraud or similar case the action may retain its "class" character only through the adjudication of liability to the class; the members of the class may thereafter be required to come in individually and prove the amounts of their respective claims.

Two or more classes may be represented in a single action. Where a class is found to include subclasses divergent in interest, the class may be divided correspondingly, and each subclass treated as a class.

Subdivision (d) is concerned with the fair and efficient conduct of the action and lists some types of orders which may be appropriate.

The court should consider how the proceedings are to be arranged in sequence, and what measures should be taken to simplify the proof and argument. See subdivision (d)(1). The orders resulting from this consideration, like the others referred to in subdivision (d), may be combined with a pretrial order under Rule 16, and are subject to modification as the case proceeds.

Subdivision (d)(2) sets out a non-exhaustive list of possible occasions for orders requiring notice to the class. Such notice is not a novel conception. For example, in "limited fund" cases, members of the class have been notified to present individual claims after the basic class decision. Notice has gone to members of a class so that they might express any opposition to the representation, see *United States v. American Optical Co.*, 97 F.Supp. 66 (N.D.Ill.1951), and 1950–51 CCH Trade Cases 64573–74 (¶ 62869); *cf. Weeks v. Bareco Oil Co.*, 125 F.2d 84, 94 (7th Cir.1941), and notice may encourage interventions to improve the representation of the class. *Cf. Oppenheimer v. F.J. Young & Co.*, 144 F.2d 387 (2d Cir.1944). Notice has been used to poll members on a proposed modification of a consent decree. See record in *Sam Fox Publishing Co. v. United States*, 366 U.S. 683 (1961).

Subdivision (d)(2) does not require notice at any stage, but rather calls attention to its availability and invokes the court's discretion. In the degree that there is cohesiveness or unity in the class and the representation is effective, the need for notice to the class will tend toward a minimum. These indicators suggest that notice under subdivision (d)(2) may be particularly useful and advisable in certain class actions maintained under subdivision (b)(3), for example, to permit members of the

New matter is shown in italics; matter to be omitted is lined through

class to object to the representation. Indeed, under subdivision (c)(2), notice must be ordered, and is not merely discretionary, to give the members in a subdivision (b)(3) class action an opportunity to secure exclusion from the class. This mandatory notice pursuant to subdivision (c)(2), together with any discretionary notice which the court may find it advisable to give under subdivision (d)(2), is designed to fulfill requirements of due process to which the class action procedure is of course subject. See *Hansberry v. Lee,* 311 U.S. 32 (1940); *Mullane v. Central Hanover Bank & Trust Co.,* 339 U.S. 306 (1950); *cf. Dickinson v. Burnham,* 197 F.2d 973, 979 (2d Cir.1952), and studies cited at 979 n. 4; see also *All American Airways, Inc. v. Eldered,* 209 F.2d 247, 249 (2d Cir.1954); *Gart v. Cole,* 263 F.2d 244, 248–49 (2d Cir.1959), *cert. denied,* 359 U.S. 978 (1959).

Notice to members of the class, whenever employed under amended Rule 23, should be accommodated to the particular purpose but need not comply with the formalities for service of process. See Chafee, *supra,* at 230–31; *Brendle v. Smith,* 7 F.R.D. 119 (S.D.N.Y.1946). The fact that notice is given at one stage of the action does not mean that it must be given at subsequent stages. Notice is available fundamentally "for the protection of the members of the class or otherwise for the fair conduct of the action" and should not be used merely as a device for the undesirable solicitation of claims. See the discussion in *Cherner v. Transitron Electronic Corp.,* 201 F.Supp. 934 (D.Mass.1962); *Hormel v. United States,* 17 F.R.D. 303 (S.D.N.Y.1955).

In appropriate cases the court should notify interested government agencies of the pendency of the action or of particular steps therein.

Subdivision (d)(3) reflects the possibility of conditioning the maintenance of a class action, *e.g.,* on the strengthening of the representation, see subdivision (c)(1) above; and recognizes that the imposition of conditions on intervenors may be required for the proper and efficient conduct of the action.

As to orders under subdivision (d)(4), see subdivision (c)(1) above.

Subdivision (e) requires approval of the court, after notice, for the dismissal or compromise of any class action.

————

Advisory Committee's Note to 2003 Amendment

(c) Determin*ing*ation by Order Whether *to Certify a* Class Action ~~to Be Maintained~~; *Appointing Class Counsel;* Notice *and Membership in Class*; Judgment; ~~Actions Conducted Partially as Class Actions~~ *Multiple Classes and Subclasses.*

(1)(A) ~~As soon as practicable after the commencement of an action brought as a class action, the court shall determine by order whether it is to be so maintained.~~ *When a person sues or is sued as a representative of a class, the court must—at an early practicable time—determine by order whether to certify the action as a class action.*

New matter is shown in italics; matter to be omitted is lined through

(B) An order certifying a class action must define the class and the class claims, issues, or defenses, and must appoint class counsel under Rule 23(g).

(C) An order under ~~this subdivision~~ *Rule 23(c)(1)* ~~may be conditional, and~~ may be altered or amended before ~~the decision on the merits~~ *final judgment.*

(2)(A) For any class certified under Rule 23(b)(1) or (2), the court may direct appropriate notice to the class.

(B) For ~~In~~ any class ~~action maintained~~ *certified* under ~~subdivision~~ *Rule 23*(b)(3), the court ~~shall~~ *must* direct to *class* ~~the~~ members ~~of the class~~ the best notice practicable under the circumstances, including individual notice to all members who can be identified through reasonable effort. *The notice must concisely and clearly state in plain, easily understood language:*

- *the nature of the action,*

- *the definition of the class certified,*

- *the class claims, issues, or defenses,*

- *that a class member may enter an appearance through counsel if the member so desires,*

- *that the court will exclude from the class any member who requests exclusion, stating when and how members may elect to be excluded, and*

- *the binding effect of a class judgment on class members under Rule 23(c)(3).*

~~The notice shall advise each member that (A) the court will exclude the member from the class if the member so requests by a specified date; (B) the judgment, whether favorable or not, will include all members who do not request exclusion; and (C) any member who does not request exclusion may, if the member desires, enter an appearance through counsel.~~

(3) The judgment in an action maintained as a class action under subdivision (b)(1) or (b)(2), whether or not favorable to the class, shall include and describe those whom the court finds to be members of the class. The judgment in an action maintained as a class action under subdivision (b)(3), whether or not favorable to the class, shall include and specify or describe those to whom the notice provided in subdivision (c)(2) was directed, and who have not requested exclusion, and whom the court finds to be members of the class.

(4) When appropriate (A) an action may be brought or maintained as a class action with respect to particular issues, or (B) a

---

New matter is shown in italics; matter to be omitted is lined through

class may be divided into subclasses and each subclass treated as a class, and the provisions of this rule shall then be construed and applied accordingly.

(e) *Settlement, Voluntary* **Dismissal, or Compromise.** ~~A class action shall not be dismissed or compromised without the approval of the court, and notice of the proposed dismissal or compromise shall be given to all members of the class in such manner as the court directs.~~

(1)(A) The court must approve any settlement, voluntary dismissal, or compromise of the claims, issues, or defenses of a certified class.

(B) The court must direct notice in a reasonable manner to all class members who would be bound by a proposed settlement, voluntary dismissal, or compromise.

(C) The court may approve a settlement, voluntary dismissal, or compromise that would bind class members only after a hearing and on finding that the settlement, voluntary dismissal, or compromise is fair, reasonable, and adequate.

(2) The parties seeking approval of a settlement, voluntary dismissal, or compromise under Rule 23(e)(1) must file a statement identifying any agreement made in connection with the proposed settlement, voluntary dismissal, or compromise.

(3) In an action previously certified as a class action under Rule 23(b)(3), the court may refuse to approve a settlement unless it affords a new opportunity to request exclusion to individual class members who had an earlier opportunity to request exclusion but did not do so.

(4)(A) Any class member may object to a proposed settlement, voluntary dismissal, or compromise that requires court approval under Rule 23(e)(1)(A).

(B) An objection made under Rule 23(e)(4)(A) may be withdrawn only with the court's approval.

(g) Class Counsel.

(1) Appointing Class Counsel.

(A) Unless a statute provides otherwise, a court that certifies a class must appoint class counsel.

(B) An attorney appointed to serve as class counsel must fairly and adequately represent the interests of the class.

(C) In appointing class counsel, the court

(i) must consider:

New matter is shown in italics; matter to be omitted is lined through

- *the work counsel has done in identifying or investigating potential claims in the action,*

- *counsel's experience in handling class actions, other complex litigation, and claims of the type asserted in the action,*

- *counsel's knowledge of the applicable law, and*

- *the resources counsel will commit to representing the class;*

(ii) may consider any other matter pertinent to counsel's ability to fairly and adequately represent the interests of the class;

(iii) may direct potential class counsel to provide information on any subject pertinent to the appointment and to propose terms for attorney fees and nontaxable costs; and

(iv) may make further orders in connection with the appointment.

(2) Appointment Procedure.

(A) The court may designate interim counsel to act on behalf of the putative class before determining whether to certify the action as a class action.

(B) When there is one applicant for appointment as class counsel, the court may appoint that applicant only if the applicant is adequate under Rule 23(g)(1)(B) and (C). If more than one adequate applicant seeks appointment as class counsel, the court must appoint the applicant best able to represent the interests of the class.

(C) The order appointing class counsel may include provisions about the award of attorney fees or nontaxable costs under Rule 23(h).

(h) Attorney Fees Award. In an action certified as a class action, the court may award reasonable attorney fees and nontaxable costs authorized by law or by agreement of the parties as follows:

(1) Motion for Award of Attorney Fees. A claim for an award of attorney fees and nontaxable costs must be made by motion under Rule 54(d)(2), subject to the provisions of this subdivision, at a time set by the court. Notice of the motion must be served on all parties and, for motions by class counsel, directed to class members in a reasonable manner.

(2) Objections to Motion. A class member, or a party from whom payment is sought, may object to the motion.

New matter is shown in italics; matter to be omitted is lined through

(3) Hearing and Findings. The court may hold a hearing and must find the facts and state its conclusions of law on the motion under Rule 52(a).

(4) Reference to Special Master or Magistrate Judge. The court may refer issues related to the amount of the award to a special master or to a magistrate judge as provided in Rule 54(d)(2)(D).

Subdivision (c). Subdivision (c) is amended in several respects. The requirement that the court determine whether to certify a class "as soon as practicable after commencement of an action" is replaced by requiring determination "at an early practicable time." The notice provisions are substantially revised.

Paragraph (1). Subdivision (c)(1)(A) is changed to require that the determination whether to certify a class be made "at an early practicable time." The "as soon as practicable" exaction neither reflects prevailing practice nor captures the many valid reasons that may justify deferring the initial certification decision. See Willging, Hooper & Niemic, *Empirical Study of Class Actions in Four Federal District Courts: Final Report to the Advisory Committee on Civil Rules 26–36* (Federal Judicial Center 1996).

Time may be needed to gather information necessary to make the certification decision. Although an evaluation of the probable outcome on the merits is not properly part of the certification decision, discovery in aid of the certification decision often includes information required to identify the nature of the issues that actually will be presented at trial. In this sense it is appropriate to conduct controlled discovery into the "merits," limited to those aspects relevant to making the certification decision on an informed basis. Active judicial supervision may be required to achieve the most effective balance that expedites an informed certification determination without forcing an artificial and ultimately wasteful division between "certification discovery" and "merits discovery." A critical need is to determine how the case will be tried. An increasing number of courts require a party requesting class certification to present a "trial plan" that describes the issues likely to be presented at trial and tests whether they are susceptible of class-wide proof. See Manual For Complex Litigation Third, § 21.213, p. 44; § 30.11, p. 214; § 30.12, p. 215.

Other considerations may affect the timing of the certification decision. The party opposing the class may prefer to win dismissal or summary judgment as to the individual plaintiffs without certification and without binding the class that might have been certified. Time may be needed to explore designation of class counsel under Rule 23(g), recognizing that in many cases the need to progress toward the certification determination may require designation of interim counsel under Rule 23(g)(2)(A).

Although many circumstances may justify deferring the certification decision, active management may be necessary to ensure that the certification decision is not unjustifiably delayed.

Subdivision (c)(1)(C) reflects two amendments. The provision that a class certification "may be conditional" is deleted. A court that is not satisfied that the requirements of Rule 23 have been met should refuse certification until they have been met. The provision that permits alteration or amendment of an order granting or denying class certification is amended to set the cut-off point at final judgment

---

New matter is shown in italics; matter to be omitted is lined through

rather than "the decision on the merits." This change avoids the possible ambiguity in referring to "the decision on the merits." Following a determination of liability, for example, proceedings to define the remedy may demonstrate the need to amend the class definition or subdivide the class. In this setting the final judgment concept is pragmatic. It is not the same as the concept used for appeal purposes, but it should be flexible, particularly in protracted litigation.

The authority to amend an order under Rule 23(c)(1) before final judgment does not restore the practice of "one-way intervention" that was rejected by the 1966 revision of Rule 23. A determination of liability after certification, however, may show a need to amend the class definition. Decertification may be warranted after further proceedings.

If the definition of a class certified under Rule 23(b)(3) is altered to include members who have not been afforded notice and an opportunity to request exclusion, notice—including an opportunity to request exclusion—must be directed to the new class members under Rule 23(c)(2)(B).

Paragraph (2). The first change made in Rule 23(c)(2) is to call attention to the court's authority—already established in part by Rule 23(d)(2)—to direct notice of certification to a Rule 23(b)(1) or (b)(2) class. The present rule expressly requires notice only in actions certified under Rule 23(b)(3). Members of classes certified under Rules 23(b)(1) or (b)(2) have interests that may deserve protection by notice.

The authority to direct notice to class members in a (b)(1) or (b)(2) class action should be exercised with care. For several reasons, there may be less need for notice than in a (b)(3) class action. There is no right to request exclusion from a (b)(1) or (b)(2) class. The characteristics of the class may reduce the need for formal notice. The cost of providing notice, moreover, could easily cripple actions that do not seek damages. The court may decide not to direct notice after balancing the risk that notice costs may deter the pursuit of class relief against the benefits of notice.

When the court does direct certification notice in a (b)(1) or (b)(2) class action, the discretion and flexibility established by subdivision (c)(2)(A) extend to the method of giving notice. Notice facilitates the opportunity to participate. Notice calculated to reach a significant number of class members often will protect the interests of all. Informal methods may prove effective. A simple posting in a place visited by many class members, directing attention to a source of more detailed information, may suffice. The court should consider the costs of notice in relation to the probable reach of inexpensive methods.

If a Rule 23(b)(3) class is certified in conjunction with a (b)(2) class, the (c)(2)(B) notice requirements must be satisfied as to the (b)(3) class.

The direction that class-certification notice be couched in plain, easily understood language is a reminder of the need to work unremittingly at the difficult task of communicating with class members. It is difficult to provide information about most class actions that is both accurate and easily understood by class members who are not themselves lawyers. Factual uncertainty, legal complexity, and the complication of class-action procedure raise the barriers high. The Federal Judicial Center has created illustrative clear-notice forms that provide a helpful starting point for actions similar to those described in the forms.

Subdivision (e). Subdivision (e) is amended to strengthen the process of reviewing proposed class-action settlements. Settlement may be a desirable means of resolving a class action. But court review and approval are essential to assure adequate representation of class members who have not participated in shaping the settlement.

New matter is shown in italics; matter to be omitted is lined through

Paragraph (1). Subdivision (e)(1)(A) expressly recognizes the power of a class representative to settle class claims, issues, or defenses.

Rule 23(e)(1)(A) resolves the ambiguity in former Rule 23(e)'s reference to dismissal or compromise of "a class action." That language could be—and at times was—read to require court approval of settlements with putative class representatives that resolved only individual claims. See Manual for Complex Litigation Third, § 30.41. The new rule requires approval only if the claims, issues, or defenses of a certified class are resolved by a settlement, voluntary dismissal, or compromise.

Subdivision (e)(1)(B) carries forward the notice requirement of present Rule 23(e) when the settlement binds the class through claim or issue preclusion; notice is not required when the settlement binds only the individual class representatives. Notice of a settlement binding on the class is required either when the settlement follows class certification or when the decisions on certification and settlement proceed simultaneously.

Reasonable settlement notice may require individual notice in the manner required by Rule 23(c)(2)(B) for certification notice to a Rule 23(b)(3) class. Individual notice is appropriate, for example, if class members are required to take action—such as filing claims—to participate in the judgment, or if the court orders a settlement opt-out opportunity under Rule 23(e)(3).

Subdivision (e)(1)(C) confirms and mandates the already common practice of holding hearings as part of the process of approving settlement, voluntary dismissal, or compromise that would bind members of a class.

Subdivision (e)(1)(C) states the standard for approving a proposed settlement that would bind class members. The settlement must be fair, reasonable, and adequate. A helpful review of many factors that may deserve consideration is provided by *In re: Prudential Ins. Co. America Sales Practice Litigation Agent Actions*, 148 F.3d 283, 316–324 (3d Cir. 1998). Further guidance can be found in the Manual for Complex Litigation.

The court must make findings that support the conclusion that the settlement is fair, reasonable, and adequate. The findings must be set out in sufficient detail to explain to class members and the appellate court the factors that bear on applying the standard.

Settlement review also may provide an occasion to review the cogency of the initial class definition. The terms of the settlement themselves, or objections, may reveal divergent interests of class members and demonstrate the need to redefine the class or to designate subclasses. Redefinition of a class certified under Rule 23(b)(3) may require notice to new class members under Rule 23(c)(2)(B). See Rule 23(c)(1)(C).

Paragraph (2). Subdivision (e)(2) requires parties seeking approval of a settlement, voluntary dismissal, or compromise under Rule 23(e)(1) to file a statement identifying any agreement made in connection with the settlement. This provision does not change the basic requirement that the parties disclose all terms of the settlement or compromise that the court must approve under Rule 23(e)(1). It aims instead at related undertakings that, although seemingly separate, may have influenced the terms of the settlement by trading away possible advantages for the class in return for advantages for others. Doubts should be resolved in favor of identification.

Further inquiry into the agreements identified by the parties should not become the occasion for discovery by the parties or objectors. The court may direct the parties to provide to the court or other parties a summary or copy of the full terms of any agreement identified by the parties. The court also may direct the parties to

New matter is shown in italics; matter to be omitted is lined through

provide a summary or copy of any agreement not identified by the parties that the court considers relevant to its review of a proposed settlement. In exercising discretion under this rule, the court may act in steps, calling first for a summary of any agreement that may have affected the settlement and then for a complete version if the summary does not provide an adequate basis for review. A direction to disclose a summary or copy of an agreement may raise concerns of confidentiality. Some agreements may include information that merits protection against general disclosure. And the court must provide an opportunity to claim work-product or other protections.

Paragraph (3). Subdivision (e)(3) authorizes the court to refuse to approve a settlement unless the settlement affords class members a new opportunity to request exclusion from a class certified under Rule 23(b)(3) after settlement terms are known. An agreement by the parties themselves to permit class members to elect exclusion at this point by the settlement agreement may be one factor supporting approval of the settlement. Often there is an opportunity to opt out at this point because the class is certified and settlement is reached in circumstances that lead to simultaneous notice of certification and notice of settlement. In these cases, the basic opportunity to elect exclusion applies without further complication. In some cases, particularly if settlement appears imminent at the time of certification, it may be possible to achieve equivalent protection by deferring notice and the opportunity to elect exclusion until actual settlement terms are known. This approach avoids the cost and potential confusion of providing two notices and makes the single notice more meaningful. But notice should not be delayed unduly after certification in the hope of settlement.

Rule 23(e)(3) authorizes the court to refuse to approve a settlement unless the settlement affords a new opportunity to elect exclusion in a case that settles after a certification decision if the earlier opportunity to elect exclusion provided with the certification notice has expired by the time of the settlement notice. A decision to remain in the class is likely to be more carefully considered and is better informed when settlement terms are known.

The opportunity to request exclusion from a proposed settlement is limited to members of a (b)(3) class. Exclusion may be requested only by individual class members; no class member may purport to opt out other class members by way of another class action.

The decision whether to approve a settlement that does not allow a new opportunity to elect exclusion is confided to the court's discretion. The court may make this decision before directing notice to the class under Rule 23(e)(1)(B) or after the Rule 23(e)(1)(C) hearing. Many factors may influence the court's decision. Among these are changes in the information available to class members since expiration of the first opportunity to request exclusion, and the nature of the individual class members' claims.

The terms set for permitting a new opportunity to elect exclusion from the proposed settlement of a Rule 23(b)(3) class action may address concerns of potential misuse. The court might direct, for example, that class members who elect exclusion are bound by rulings on the merits made before the settlement was proposed for approval. Still other terms or conditions may be appropriate.

Paragraph (4). Subdivision (e)(4) confirms the right of class members to object to a proposed settlement, voluntary dismissal, or compromise. The right is defined in relation to a disposition that, because it would bind the class, requires court approval under subdivision (e)(1)(C).

Subdivision (e)(4)(B) requires court approval for withdrawal of objections made under subdivision (e)(4)(A). Review follows automatically if the objections are withdrawn on terms that lead to modification of the settlement with the class. Review also is required if the objector formally withdraws the objections. If the objector simply abandons pursuit of the objection, the court may inquire into the circumstances.

Approval under paragraph (4)(B) may be given or denied with little need for further inquiry if the objection and the disposition go only to a protest that the individual treatment afforded the objector under the proposed settlement is unfair because of factors that distinguish the objector from other class members. Different considerations may apply if the objector has protested that the proposed settlement is not fair, reasonable, or adequate on grounds that apply generally to a class or subclass. Such objections, which purport to represent class-wide interests, may augment the opportunity for obstruction or delay. If such objections are surrendered on terms that do not affect the class settlement or the objector's participation in the class settlement, the court often can approve withdrawal of the objections without elaborate inquiry.

Once an objector appeals, control of the proceeding lies in the court of appeals. The court of appeals may undertake review and approval of a settlement with the objector, perhaps as part of appeal settlement procedures, or may remand to the district court to take advantage of the district court's familiarity with the action and settlement.

Subdivision (g). Subdivision (g) is new. It responds to the reality that the selection and activity of class counsel are often critically important to the successful handling of a class action. Until now, courts have scrutinized proposed class counsel as well as the class representative under Rule 23(a)(4). This experience has recognized the importance of judicial evaluation of the proposed lawyer for the class, and this new subdivision builds on that experience rather than introducing an entirely new element into the class certification process. Rule 23(a)(4) will continue to call for scrutiny of the proposed class representative, while this subdivision will guide the court in assessing proposed class counsel as part of the certification decision. This subdivision recognizes the importance of class counsel, states the obligation to represent the interests of the class, and provides a framework for selection of class counsel. The procedure and standards for appointment vary depending on whether there are multiple applicants to be class counsel. The new subdivision also provides a method by which the court may make directions from the outset about the potential fee award to class counsel in the event the action is successful.

Paragraph (1) sets out the basic requirement that class counsel be appointed if a class is certified and articulates the obligation of class counsel to represent the interests of the class, as opposed to the potentially conflicting interests of individual class members. It also sets out the factors the court should consider in assessing proposed class counsel.

Paragraph (1)(A) requires that the court appoint class counsel to represent the class. Class counsel must be appointed for all classes, including each subclass that the court certifies to represent divergent interests.

Paragraph (1)(A) does not apply if "a statute provides otherwise." This recognizes that provisions of the Private Securities Litigation Reform Act of 1995, Pub. L. No. 104–67, 109 Stat. 737 (1995) (codified in various sections of 15 U.S.C.), contain directives that bear on selection of a lead plaintiff and the retention of counsel. This subdivision does not purport to supersede or to affect the interpretation of those provisions, or any similar provisions of other legislation.

Paragraph (1)(B) recognizes that the primary responsibility of class counsel, resulting from appointment as class counsel, is to represent the best interests of the class. The rule thus establishes the obligation of class counsel, an obligation that

---

New matter is shown in italics; matter to be omitted is lined through

may be different from the customary obligations of counsel to individual clients. Appointment as class counsel means that the primary obligation of counsel is to the class rather than to any individual members of it. The class representatives do not have an unfettered right to "fire" class counsel. In the same vein, the class representatives cannot command class counsel to accept or reject a settlement proposal. To the contrary, class counsel must determine whether seeking the court's approval of a settlement would be in the best interests of the class as a whole.

Paragraph (1)(C) articulates the basic responsibility of the court to appoint class counsel who will provide the adequate representation called for by paragraph (1)(B). It identifies criteria that must be considered and invites the court to consider any other pertinent matters. Although couched in terms of the court's duty, the listing also informs counsel seeking appointment about the topics that should be addressed in an application for appointment or in the motion for class certification.

The court may direct potential class counsel to provide additional information about the topics mentioned in paragraph (1)(C) or about any other relevant topic. For example, the court may direct applicants to inform the court concerning any agreements about a prospective award of attorney fees or nontaxable costs, as such agreements may sometimes be significant in the selection of class counsel. The court might also direct that potential class counsel indicate how parallel litigation might be coordinated or consolidated with the action before the court.

The court may also direct counsel to propose terms for a potential award of attorney fees and nontaxable costs. Attorney fee awards are an important feature of class action practice, and attention to this subject from the outset may often be a productive technique. Paragraph (2)(C) therefore authorizes the court to provide directions about attorney fees and costs when appointing class counsel. Because there will be numerous class actions in which this information is not likely to be useful, the court need not consider it in all class actions.

Some information relevant to class counsel appointment may involve matters that include adversary preparation in a way that should be shielded from disclosure to other parties. An appropriate protective order may be necessary to preserve confidentiality.

In evaluating prospective class counsel, the court should weigh all pertinent factors. No single factor should necessarily be determinative in a given case. For example, the resources counsel will commit to the case must be appropriate to its needs, but the court should be careful not to limit consideration to lawyers with the greatest resources.

If, after review of all applicants, the court concludes that none would be satisfactory class counsel, it may deny class certification, reject all applications, recommend that an application be modified, invite new applications, or make any other appropriate order regarding selection and appointment of class counsel.

Paragraph (2). This paragraph sets out the procedure that should be followed in appointing class counsel. Although it affords substantial flexibility, it provides the framework for appointment of class counsel in all class actions. For counsel who filed the action, the materials submitted in support of the motion for class certification may suffice to justify appointment so long as the information described in paragraph (g)(1)(C) is included. If there are other applicants, they ordinarily would file a formal application detailing their suitability for the position.

In a plaintiff class action the court usually would appoint as class counsel only an attorney or attorneys who have sought appointment. Different considerations may apply in defendant class actions.

New matter is shown in italics; matter to be omitted is lined through

The rule states that the court should appoint "class counsel." In many instances, the applicant will be an individual attorney. In other cases, however, an entire firm, or perhaps numerous attorneys who are not otherwise affiliated but are collaborating on the action will apply. No rule of thumb exists to determine when such arrangements are appropriate; the court should be alert to the need for adequate staffing of the case, but also to the risk of overstaffing or an ungainly counsel structure.

Paragraph (2)(A) authorizes the court to designate interim counsel during the pre-certification period if necessary to protect the interests of the putative class. Rule 23(c)(1)(B) directs that the order certifying the class include appointment of class counsel. Before class certification, however, it will usually be important for an attorney to take action to prepare for the certification decision. The amendment to Rule 23(c)(1) recognizes that some discovery is often necessary for that determination. It also may be important to make or respond to motions before certification. Settlement may be discussed before certification. Ordinarily, such work is handled by the lawyer who filed the action. In some cases, however, there may be rivalry or uncertainty that makes formal designation of interim counsel appropriate. Rule 23(g)(2)(A) authorizes the court to designate interim counsel to act on behalf of the putative class before the certification decision is made. Failure to make the formal designation does not prevent the attorney who filed the action from proceeding in it. Whether or not formally designated interim counsel, an attorney who acts on behalf of the class before certification must act in the best interests of the class as a whole. For example, an attorney who negotiates a pre-certification settlement must seek a settlement that is fair, reasonable, and adequate for the class.

Rule 23(c)(1) provides that the court should decide whether to certify the class "at an early practicable time," and directs that class counsel should be appointed in the order certifying the class. In some cases, it may be appropriate for the court to allow a reasonable period after commencement of the action for filing applications to serve as class counsel. The primary ground for deferring appointment would be that there is reason to anticipate competing applications to serve as class counsel. Examples might include instances in which more than one class action has been filed, or in which other attorneys have filed individual actions on behalf of putative class members. The purpose of facilitating competing applications in such a case is to afford the best possible representation for the class. Another possible reason for deferring appointment would be that the initial applicant was found inadequate, but it seems appropriate to permit additional applications rather than deny class certification.

Paragraph (2)(B) states the basic standard the court should use in deciding whether to certify the class and appoint class counsel in the single applicant situation—that the applicant be able to provide the representation called for by paragraph (1)(B) in light of the factors identified in paragraph (1)(C).

If there are multiple adequate applicants, paragraph (2)(B) directs the court to select the class counsel best able to represent the interests of the class. This decision should also be made using the factors outlined in paragraph (1)(C), but in the multiple applicant situation the court is to go beyond scrutinizing the adequacy of counsel and make a comparison of the strengths of the various applicants. As with the decision whether to appoint the sole applicant for the position, no single factor should be dispositive in selecting class counsel in cases in which there are multiple applicants. The fact that a given attorney filed the instance action, for example, might not weigh heavily in the decision if that lawyer had not done significant work identifying or investigating claims. Depending on the nature of the case, one important consideration might be the applicant's existing attorney-client relationship with the proposed class representative.

New matter is shown in italics; matter to be omitted is lined through

Paragraph (2)(C) builds on the appointment process by authorizing the court to include provisions regarding attorney fees in the order appointing class counsel. Courts may find it desirable to adopt guidelines for fees or nontaxable costs, or to direct class counsel to report to the court at regular intervals on the efforts undertaken in the action, to facilitate the court's later determination of a reasonable attorney fee.

Subdivision (h). Subdivision (h) is new. Fee awards are a powerful influence on the way attorneys initiate, develop, and conclude class actions. Class action attorney fee awards have heretofore been handled, along with all other attorney fee awards, under Rule 54(d)(2), but that rule is not addressed to the particular concerns of class actions. This subdivision is designed to work in tandem with new subdivision (g) on appointment of class counsel, which may afford an opportunity for the court to provide an early framework for an eventual fee award, or for monitoring the work of class counsel during the pendency of the action.

Subdivision (h) applies to "an action certified as a class action." This includes cases in which there is a simultaneous proposal for class certification and settlement even though technically the class may not be certified unless the court approves the settlement pursuant to review under Rule 23(e). When a settlement is proposed for Rule 23(e) approval, either after certification or with a request for certification, notice to class members about class counsel's fee motion would ordinarily accompany the notice to the class about the settlement proposal itself.

This subdivision does not undertake to create new grounds for an award of attorney fees or nontaxable costs. Instead, it applies when such awards are authorized by law or by agreement of the parties. Against that background, it provides a format for all awards of attorney fees and nontaxable costs in connection with a class action, not only the award to class counsel. In some situations, there may be a basis for making an award to other counsel whose work produced a beneficial result for the class, such as attorneys who acted for the class before certification but were not appointed class counsel, or attorneys who represented objectors to a proposed settlement under Rule 23(e) or to the fee motion of class counsel. Other situations in which fee awards are authorized by law or by agreement of the parties may exist.

This subdivision authorizes an award of "reasonable" attorney fees and nontaxable costs. This is the customary term for measurement of fee awards in cases in which counsel may obtain an award of fees under the "common fund" theory that applies in many class actions, and is used in many fee-shifting statutes. Depending on the circumstances, courts have approached the determination of what is reasonable in different ways. In particular, there is some variation among courts about whether in "common fund" cases the court should use the lodestar or a percentage method of determining what fee is reasonable. The rule does not attempt to resolve the question whether the lodestar or percentage approach should be viewed as preferable.

Active judicial involvement in measuring fee awards is singularly important to the proper operation of the class-action process. Continued reliance on caselaw development of fee-award measures does not diminish the court's responsibility. In a class action, the district court must ensure that the amount and mode of payment of attorney fees are fair and proper whether the fees come from a common fund or are otherwise paid. Even in the absence of objections, the court bears this responsibility.

Courts discharging this responsibility have looked to a variety of factors. One fundamental focus is the result actually achieved for class members, a basic consideration in any case in which fees are sought on the basis of a benefit achieved for class members. The Private Securities Litigation Reform Act of 1995 explicitly makes this factor a cap for a fee award in actions to which it applies. See 15 U.S.C.

New matter is shown in italics; matter to be omitted is lined through

§§ 77z–1(a)(6); 78u–4(a)(6) (fee award should not exceed a "reasonable percentage of the amount of any damages and prejudgment interest actually paid to the class"). For a percentage approach to fee measurement, results achieved is the basic starting point.

In many instances, the court may need to proceed with care in assessing the value conferred on class members. Settlement regimes that provide for future payments, for example, may not result in significant actual payments to class members. In this connection, the court may need to scrutinize the manner and operation of any applicable claims procedure. In some cases, it may be appropriate to defer some portion of the fee award until actual payouts to class members are known. Settlement involving nonmonetary provisions for class members also deserve careful scrutiny to ensure that these provisions have actual value to the class. On occasion the court's Rule 23(e) review will provide a solid basis for this sort of evaluation, but in any event it is also important to assessing the fee award for the class.

At the same time, it is important to recognize that in some class actions the monetary relief obtained is not the sole determinant of an appropriate attorney fees award. Cf. *Blanchard v. Bergeron*, 489 U.S. 87, 95 (1989) (cautioning in an individual case against an "undesirable emphasis" on "the importance of the recovery of damages in civil rights litigation" that might "shortchange efforts to seek effective injunctive or declaratory relief").

Any directions or orders made by the court in connection with appointing class counsel under Rule 23(g) should weigh heavily in making a fee award under this subdivision.

Courts have also given weight to agreements among the parties regarding the fee motion, and to agreements between class counsel and others about the fees claimed by the motion. Rule 54(d)(2)(B) provides: "If directed by the court, the motion shall also disclose the terms of any agreement with respect to fees to be paid for the services for which claim is made." The agreement by a settling party not to oppose a fee application up to a certain amount, for example, is worthy of consideration, but the court remains responsible to determine a reasonable fee. "Side agreements" regarding fees provide at least perspective pertinent to an appropriate fee award.

In addition, courts may take account of the fees charged by class counsel or other attorneys for representing individual claimants or objectors in the case. In determining a fee for class counsel, the court's objective is to ensure an overall fee that is fair for counsel and equitable within the class. In some circumstances individual fee agreements between class counsel and class members might have provisions inconsistent with those goals, and the court might determine that adjustments in the class fee award were necessary as a result.

Finally, it is important to scrutinize separately the application for an award covering nontaxable costs. If costs were addressed in the order appointing class counsel, those directives should be a presumptive starting point in determining what is an appropriate award.

Paragraph (1). Any claim for an award of attorney fees must be sought by motion under Rule 54(d)(2), which invokes the provisions for timing of appeal in Rule 58 and Appellate Rule 4. Owing to the distinctive features of class action fee motions, however, the provisions of this subdivision control disposition of fee motions in class actions, while Rule 54(d)(2) applies to matters not addressed in this subdivision.

New matter is shown in italics; matter to be omitted is lined through

The court should direct when the fee motion must be filed. For motions by class counsel in cases subject to court review of a proposed settlement under Rule 23(e), it would be important to require the filing of at least the initial motion in time for inclusion of information about the motion in the notice to the class about the proposed settlement that is required by Rule 23(e). In cases litigated to judgment, the court might also order class counsel's motion to be filed promptly so that notice to the class under this subdivision (h) can be given.

Besides service of the motion on all parties, notice of class counsel's motion for attorney fees must be "directed to the class in a reasonable manner." Because members of the class have an interest in the arrangements for payment of class counsel whether that payment comes from the class fund or is made directly by another party, notice is required in all instances. In cases in which settlement approval is contemplated under Rule 23(e), notice of class counsel's fee motion should be combined with notice of the proposed settlement, and the provision regarding notice to the class is parallel to the requirements for notice under Rule 23(e). In adjudicated class actions, the court may calibrate the notice to avoid undue expense.

Paragraph (2). A class member and any party from whom payment is sought may object to the fee motion. Other parties—for example, nonsettling defendants—may not object because they lack a sufficient interest in the amount the court awards. The rule does not specify a time limit for making an objection. In setting the date objections are due, the court should provide sufficient time after the full fee motion is on file to enable potential objectors to examine the motion.

The court may allow an objector discovery relevant to the objections. In determining whether to allow discovery, the court should weigh the need for the information against the cost and delay that would attend discovery. See Rule 26(b)(2). One factor in determining whether to authorize discovery is the completeness of the material submitted in support of the fee motion, which depends in part on the fee measurement standard applicable to the case. If the motion provides thorough information, the burden should be on the objector to justify discovery to obtain further information.

Paragraph (3). Whether or not there are formal objections, the court must determine whether a fee award is justified and, if so, set a reasonable fee. The rule does not require a formal hearing in all cases. The form and extent of a hearing depend on the circumstances of the case. The rule does require findings and conclusions under Rule 52(a).

Paragraph (4). By incorporating Rule 54(d)(2), this provision gives the court broad authority to obtain assistance in determining the appropriate amount to award. In deciding whether to direct submission of such questions to a special master or magistrate judge, the court should give appropriate consideration to the cost and delay that such a process might entail.

Rule 23.1. Derivative Actions by Shareholders

Advisory Committee's Note to Rule Added in 1966

A derivative action by a shareholder of a corporation or by a member of an unincorporated association has distinctive aspects which require the special provisions set forth in the new rule. The next-to-the-last sentence recognizes that the question of adequacy of representation may arise when the plaintiff is one of a group of shareholders or members. *Cf.* 3 *Moore's Federal Practice* ¶ 23.08 (2d ed.1963).

The court has inherent power to provide for the conduct of the proceedings in a derivative action, including the power to determine the course of the proceedings and require that any appropriate notice be given to shareholders or members.

New matter is shown in italics; matter to be omitted is lined through

Rule 23.2. Actions Relating to Unincorporated Associations

Advisory Committee's Note to Rule Added in 1966

Although an action by or against representatives of the membership of an unincorporated association has often been viewed as a class action, the real or main purpose of this characterization has been to give "entity treatment" to the association when for formal reasons it cannot sue or be sued as a jural person under Rule 17(b). See Louisell & Hazard, *Pleading and Procedure: State and Federal* 718 (1962); 3 *Moore's Federal Practice* ¶ 23.08 (2d ed.1963); Story, J. in *West v. Randall*, 29 Fed.Cas. 718, 722–23, No. 17,424 (C.C.D.R.I.1820); and, for examples, *Gibbs v. Buck*, 307 U.S. 66 (1939); *Tunstall v. Brotherhood of Locomotive F. & E.*, 148 F.2d 403 (4th Cir.1945); *Oskoian v. Canuel*, 269 F.2d 311 (1st Cir.1959). Rule 23.2 deals separately with these actions, referring where appropriate to Rule 23.

Rule 24. Intervention

Advisory Committee's Note to 1966 Amendment

(a) Intervention of Right. Upon timely application anyone shall be permitted to intervene in an action: (1) when a statute of the United States confers an unconditional right to intervene; or (2) when the ~~representation of the applicant's interest by existing parties is or may be inadequate and the applicant is or may be bound by a judgment in the action; or (3) when the applicant is so situated as to be adversely affected by a distribution or other disposition of property which is in the custody or subject to the control or disposition of the court or an officer thereof.~~ *applicant claims an interest relating to the property or transaction which is the subject of the action and he is so situated that the disposition of the action may as a practical matter impair or impede his ability to protect that interest, unless the applicant's interest is adequately represented by existing parties.*

In attempting to overcome certain difficulties which have arisen in the application of present Rule 24(a)(2) and (3), this amendment draws upon the revision of the related Rules 19 (joinder of persons needed for just adjudication) and 23 (class actions), and the reasoning underlying that revision.

Rule 24(a)(3) as amended in 1948 provided for intervention of right where the applicant established that he would be adversely affected by the distribution or disposition of property involved in an action to which he had not been made a party. Significantly, some decided cases virtually disregarded the language of this provision. Thus Professor Moore states: "The concept of a fund has been applied so loosely that it is possible for a court to find a fund in almost any in personam action." 4 *Moore's Federal Practice*, ¶ 24.09[3], at 55 (2d ed. 1962), and see, *e.g.*, *Formulabs, Inc. v. Hartley Pen Co.*, 275 F.2d 52 (9th Cir.1960). This development was quite natural, for Rule 24(a)(3) was unduly restricted. If an absentee would be substantially affected in a practical sense by the determination made in an action, he should, as a general rule, be entitled to intervene, and his right to do so should not depend on whether

New matter is shown in italics; matter to be omitted is lined through

there is a fund to be distributed or otherwise disposed of. Intervention of right is here seen to be a kind of counterpart to Rule 19(a)(2)(i) on joinder of persons needed for a just adjudication: where, upon motion of a party in an action, an absentee should be joined so that he may protect his interest which as a practical matter may be substantially impaired by the disposition of the action, he ought to have a right to intervene in the action on his own motion. See Louisell & Hazard, *Pleading and Procedure: State and Federal* 749–50 (1962).

The general purpose of original Rule 24(a)(2) was to entitle an absentee, purportedly represented by a party, to intervene in the action if he could establish with fair probability that the representation was inadequate. Thus, where an action is being prosecuted or defended by a trustee, a beneficiary of the trust should have a right to intervene if he can show that the trustee's representation of his interest probably is inadequate; similarly a member of a class should have the right to intervene in a class action if he can show the inadequacy of the representation of his interest by the representative parties before the court.

Original Rule 24(a)(2), however, made it a condition of intervention that "the applicant is or may be bound by a judgment in the action," and this created difficulties with intervention in class actions. If the "bound" language was read literally in the sense of res judicata, it could defeat intervention in some meritorious cases. A member of a class to whom a judgment in a class action extended by its terms (see Rule 23(c)(3), as amended) might be entitled to show in a later action, when the judgment in the class action was claimed to operate as res judicata against him, that the "representative" in the class action had not in fact adequately represented him. If he could make this showing, the class-action judgment might be held not to bind him. See *Hansberry v. Lee*, 311 U.S. 32 (1940). If a class member sought to intervene in the class action proper, while it was still pending, on grounds of inadequacy of representation, he could be met with the argument: if the representation was in fact inadequate, he would not be "bound" by the judgment when it was subsequently asserted against him as res judicata, hence he was not entitled to intervene; if the representation was in fact adequate, there was no occasion or ground for intervention. See *Sam Fox Publishing Co. v. United States*, 366 U.S. 683 (1961); *cf. Sulphen Estates, Inc. v. United States*, 342 U.S. 19 (1951). This reasoning might be linguistically justified by original Rule 24(a)(2); but it could lead to poor results. Compare the discussion in *International M. & I. Corp. v. Von Clemm*, 301 F.2d 857 (2d Cir.1962); *Atlantic Refining Co. v. Standard Oil Co.*, 304 F.2d 387 (D.C.Cir.1962). A class member who claims that his "representative" does not adequately represent him, and is able to establish that proposition with sufficient probability should not be put to the risk of having a judgment entered in the action which by its terms extends to him, and be obliged to test the validity of the judgment as applied to his interest by a later collateral attack. Rather he should, as a general rule, be entitled to intervene in the action.

The amendment provides that an applicant is entitled to intervene in an action when his position is comparable to that of a person under Rule 19(a)(2)(i), as amended, unless his interest is already adequately represented in the action by existing parties. The Rule 19(a)(2)(i) criterion imports practical considerations, and the deletion of the "bound" language similarly frees the rule from undue preoccupation with strict considerations of res judicata.

The representation whose adequacy comes into question under the amended rule is not confined to formal representation like that provided by a trustee for his beneficiary or a representative party in a class action for a member of the class. A party to a action may provide practical representation to the absentee seeking intervention although no such formal relationship exists between them, and the adequacy of this practical representation will then have to be weighed. See *Interna-*

New matter is shown in italics; matter to be omitted is lined through

tional M. & I. Corp. v. Von Clemm, and *Atlantic Refining Co. v. Standard Oil Co.*, both supra; *Wolpe v. Poretsky*, 144 F.2d 505 (D.C.Cir.1944), cert. denied, 323 U.S. 777 (1944); *cf. Ford Motor Co. v. Bisanz Bros.*, 249 F.2d 22 (8th Cir.1957); and generally Annot., 84 A.L.R.2d 1412 (1962).

An intervention of right under the amended rule may be subject to appropriate conditions or restrictions responsive among other things to the requirements of efficient conduct of the proceedings.

Rule 26.   Depositions Pending Action

Advisory Committee's Note to 1970 Amendment

Rule 26.   ~~Depositions Pending Action~~ *General Provisions Governing Discovery*

(a) ~~When Depositions May Be Taken.~~ ~~Any party may take the testimony of any person, including a party, by deposition upon oral examination or written interrogatories for the purpose of discovery or for use as evidence in the action or for both purposes. After commencement of the action the deposition may be taken without leave of court, except that leave, granted with or without notice, must be obtained if notice of the taking is served by the plaintiff within 20 days after commencement of the action. The attendance of witnesses may be compelled by the use of subpoena as provided in Rule 45. Depositions shall be taken only in accordance with these rules, except that in admiralty and maritime claims within the meaning of Rule 9(h) depositions may also be taken under and used in accordance with sections 863, 864, and 865 of the Revised Statutes (see note preceding 28 U.S.C. § 1781). The deposition of a person confined in prison may be taken only by leave of court on such terms as the court prescribes.~~

(a) Discovery Methods. Parties may obtain discovery by one or more of the following methods: depositions upon oral examination or written questions; written interrogatories; production of documents or things or permission to enter upon land or other property, for inspection and other purposes; physical and mental examinations; and requests for admission. Unless the court orders otherwise under subdivision (c) of this rule, the frequency of use of these methods is not limited.

(b) Scope of ~~Examination~~ *Discovery.* Unless otherwise ~~ordered by~~ *limited by order of* the court ~~as provided by Rule 30(b) or (d), the deponent may be examined~~ *in accordance with these rules, the scope of discovery is as follows:*

(1) In General. Parties may obtain discovery regarding any matter, not privileged, which is relevant to the subject matter

involved in the pending action, whether it relates to the claim or defense of the ~~examining~~ party *seeking discovery* or to the claim or defense of any other party, including the existence, description, nature, custody, condition and location of any books, documents, or other tangible things and the identity and location of persons having knowledge of *any discoverable matter* ~~relevant facts.~~ It is not ground for objection that the ~~testimony~~ *information sought* will be inadmissible at the trial if the ~~testimony~~ *information* sought appears reasonably calculated to lead to the discovery of admissible evidence.

(2) Insurance Agreements. A party may obtain discovery of the existence and contents of any insurance agreement under which any person carrying on an insurance business may be liable to satisfy part or all of a judgment which may be entered in the action or to indemnify or reimburse for payments made to satisfy the judgment. Information concerning the insurance agreement is not by reason of disclosure admissible in evidence at trial. For purposes of this paragraph, an application for insurance shall not be treated as part of an insurance agreement.

(3) Trial Preparation: Materials. Subject to the provisions of subdivision (b)(4) of this rule, a party may obtain discovery of documents and tangible things otherwise discoverable under subdivision (b)(1) of this rule and prepared in anticipation of litigation or for trial by or for another party or by or for that other party's representative (including his attorney, consultant, surety, indemnitor, insurer, or agent) only upon a showing that the party seeking discovery has substantial need of the materials in the preparation of his case and that he is unable without undue hardship to obtain the substantial equivalent of the materials by other means. In ordering discovery of such materials when the required showing has been made, the court shall protect against disclosure of the mental impressions, conclusions, opinions, or legal theories of an attorney or other representative of a party concerning the litigation.

A party may obtain without the required showing a statement concerning the action or its subject matter previously made by that party. Upon request, a person not a party may obtain without the required showing a statement concerning the action or its subject matter previously made by that person. If the request is refused, the person may move for a court order. The provisions of Rule 37(a)(4) apply to the award of expenses incurred in relation to the motion. For purposes of this paragraph, a statement previously made is (A) a written statement

---

New matter is shown in italics; matter to be omitted is lined through

signed or otherwise adopted or approved by the person making it, or (B) a stenographic, mechanical, electrical, or other recording, or a transcription thereof, which is a substantially verbatim recital of an oral statement by the person making it and contemporaneously recorded.

(4) Trial Preparation: Experts. Discovery of facts known and opinions held by experts, otherwise discoverable under the provisions of subdivision (b)(1) of this rule and acquired or developed in anticipation of litigation or for trial, may be obtained only as follows:

(A)(i) A party may through interrogatories require any other party to identify each person whom the other party expects to call as an expert witness at trial, to state the subject matter on which the expert is expected to testify, and to state the substance of the facts and opinions to which the expert is expected to testify and a summary of the grounds for each opinion. (ii) Upon motion the court may order further discovery by other means, subject to such restrictions as to scope and such provisions, pursuant to subdivision (b)(4)(C) of this rule, concerning fees and expenses as the court may deem appropriate.

(B) A party may discover facts known or opinions held by an expert who has been retained or specially employed by another party in anticipation of litigation or preparation for trial and who is not expected to be called as a witness at trial, only as provided in Rule 35(b) or upon a showing of exceptional circumstances under which it is impracticable for the party seeking discovery to obtain facts or opinions on the same subject by other means.

(C) Unless manifest injustice would result, (i) the court shall require that the party seeking discovery pay the expert a reasonable fee for time spent in responding to discovery under subdivisions (b)(4)(A)(ii) and (b)(4)(B) of this rule; and (ii) with respect to discovery obtained under subdivision (b)(4)(A)(ii) of this rule the court may require, and with respect to discovery obtained under subdivision (b)(4)(B) of this rule the court shall require, the party seeking discovery to pay the other party a fair portion of the fees and expenses reasonably incurred by the latter party in obtaining facts and opinions from the expert.

(c) Examination and Cross Examination. Examination and cross-examination of deponents may proceed as permitted at the trial under the provisions of Rule 43(b).

New matter is shown in italics; matter to be omitted is lined through

(d) Use of Depositions. ~~At the trial or upon the hearing of a motion or an interlocutory proceeding, any part or all of a deposition, so far as admissible under the rules of evidence, may be used against any party who was present or represented at the taking of the deposition or who had due notice thereof, in accordance with any one of the following provisions:~~

~~(1) Any deposition may be used by any party for the purpose of contradicting or impeaching the testimony of deponent as a witness.~~

~~(2) The deposition of a party or of any one who at the time of taking the deposition was an officer, director, or managing agent of a public or private corporation, partnership, or association which is a party may be used by an adverse party for any purpose.~~

~~(3) The deposition of a witness, whether or not a party, may be used by any party for any purpose if the court finds: 1, that the witness is dead; or 2, that the witness is at a greater distance than 100 miles from the place of trial or hearing, or is out of the United States, unless it appears that the absence of the witness was procured by the party offering the deposition; or 3, that the witness is unable to attend or testify because of age, sickness, infirmity, or imprisonment; or 4, that the party offering the deposition has been unable to procure the attendance of the witness by subpoena; or 5, upon application and notice, that such exceptional circumstances exist as to make it desirable, in the interest of justice and with due regard to the importance of presenting the testimony of witnesses orally in open court, to allow the deposition to be used.~~

~~(4) If only part of a deposition is offered in evidence by a party, an adverse party may require him to introduce all of it which is relevant to the part introduced, and any party may introduce any other parts.~~

~~Substitution of parties does not affect the right to use depositions previously taken; and, when an action in any court of the United States or of any state has been dismissed and another action involving the same subject matter is afterward brought between the same parties or their representatives or successors in interest, all depositions lawfully taken and duly filed in the former action may be used in the latter as if originally taken therefor.~~

(e) Objections to Admissibility. ~~Subject to the provisions of Rules 28(b) and 32(c) objection may be made at the trial or hearing to receiving in evidence any deposition or part thereof for any~~

New matter is shown in italics; matter to be omitted is lined through

~~reason which would require the exclusion of the evidence if the witness were then present and testifying.~~

~~**(f) Effect of Taking or Using Depositions.** A party shall not be deemed to make a person his own witness for any purpose by taking his deposition. The introduction in evidence of the deposition or any part thereof for any purpose other than that of contradicting or impeaching the deponent makes the deponent the witness of the party introducing the deposition, but this shall not apply to the use by an adverse party of a deposition as described in paragraph (2) of subdivision (d) of this rule. At the trial or hearing any party may rebut any relevant evidence contained in a deposition whether introduced by him or by any other party.~~

(c) Protective Orders. Upon motion by a party or by the person from whom discovery is sought, and for good cause shown, the court in which the action is pending or alternatively, on matters relating to a deposition, the court in the district where the deposition is to be taken may make any order which justice requires to protect a party or person from annoyance, embarrassment, oppression, or undue burden or expense, including one or more of the following: (1) that the discovery not be had; (2) that the discovery may be had only on specified terms and conditions, including a designation of the time or place; (3) that the discovery may be had only by a method of discovery other than that selected by the party seeking discovery; (4) that certain matters not be inquired into, or that the scope of the discovery be limited to certain matters; (5) that discovery be conducted with no one present except persons designated by the court; (6) that a deposition after being sealed be opened only by order of the court; (7) that a trade secret or other confidential research, development, or commercial information not be disclosed or be disclosed only in a designated way; (8) that the parties simultaneously file specified documents or information enclosed in sealed envelopes to be opened as directed by the court.

If the motion for a protective order is denied in whole or in part, the court may, on such terms and conditions as are just, order that any party or person provide or permit discovery. The provisions of Rule 37(a)(4) apply to the award of expenses incurred in relation to the motion.

(d) Sequence and Timing of Discovery. Unless the court upon motion, for the convenience of parties and witnesses and in the interests of justice, orders otherwise, methods of discovery may be used in any sequence and the fact that a party is conducting discovery, whether by deposition or otherwise, shall not operate to delay any other party's discovery.

New matter is shown in italics; matter to be omitted is lined through

(e) Supplementation of Responses. A party who has responded to a request for discovery with a response that was complete when made is under no duty to supplement his response to include information thereafter acquired, except as follows:

(1) A party is under a duty seasonably to supplement his response with respect to any question directly addressed to (A) the identity and location of persons having knowledge of discoverable matters, and (B) the identity of each person expected to be called as an expert witness at trial, the subject matter on which he is expected to testify, and the substance of his testimony.

(2) A party is under a duty seasonably to amend a prior response if he obtains information upon the basis of which (A) he knows that the response was incorrect when made, or (B) he knows that the response though correct when made is no longer true and the circumstances are such that a failure to amend the response is in substance a knowing concealment.

(3) A duty to supplement responses may be imposed by order of the court, agreement of the parties, or at any time prior to trial through new requests for supplementation of prior responses.

A limited rearrangement of the discovery rules is made, whereby certain rule provisions are transferred, as follows: Existing Rule 26(a) is transferred to Rules 30(a) and 31(a). Existing Rule 26(c) is transferred to Rule 30(c). Existing Rules 26(d), (e), and (f) are transferred to Rule 32. Revisions of the transferred provisions, if any, are discussed in the notes appended to Rules 30, 31, and 32. In addition, Rule 30(b) is transferred to Rule 26(c). The purpose of this rearrangement is to establish Rule 26 as a rule governing discovery in general. (The reasons are set out in the Advisory Committee's explanatory statement.)

Subdivision (a)—Discovery Devices. This is a new subdivision listing all of the discovery devices provided in the discovery rules and establishing the relationship between the general provisions of Rule 26 and the specific rules for particular discovery devices. The provision that the frequency of use of these methods is not limited confirms existing law. It incorporates in general form a provision now found in Rule 33.

Subdivision (b)—Scope of Discovery. This subdivision is recast to cover the scope of discovery generally. It regulates the discovery obtainable through any of the discovery devices listed in Rule 26(a).

All provisions as to scope of discovery are subject to the initial qualification that the court may limit discovery in accordance with these rules. Rule 26(c) (transferred from 30(b)) confers broad powers on the courts to regulate or prevent discovery even though the materials sought are within the scope of 26(b), and these powers have always been freely exercised. For example, a party's income tax return is generally held not privileged, 2A Barron & Holtzoff, *Federal Practice and Procedure,* § 651.2 (Wright ed. 1961), and yet courts have recognized that interests in privacy may call for a measure of extra protection. *E.g., Wiesenberger v. W. E. Hutton & Co.,* 35 F.R.D. 556 (S.D.N.Y.1964). Similarly, the courts have in appropriate circumstances

----

New matter is shown in italics; matter to be omitted is lined through

protected materials that are primarily of an impeaching character. These two types of materials merely illustrate the many situations, not capable of governance by precise rule, in which courts must exercise judgment. The new subsections in Rule 26(b) do not change existing law with respect to such situations.

Subdivision (b)(1)—In General. The language is changed to provide for the scope of discovery in general terms. The existing subdivision, although in terms applicable only to depositions, is incorporated by reference in existing Rules 33 and 34. Since decisions as to relevance to the subject matter of the action are made for discovery purposes well in advance of trial, a flexible treatment of relevance is required and the making of discovery, whether voluntary or under court order, is not a concession or determination of relevance for purposes of trial. *Cf. 4 Moore's Federal Practice* ¶ 26–16[1] (2d ed. 1966).

Subdivision (b)(2)—Insurance Policies. Both the cases and commentators are sharply in conflict on the question whether defendant's liability insurance coverage is subject to discovery in the usual situation when the insurance coverage is not itself admissible and does not bear on another issue in the case. Examples of Federal cases requiring disclosure and supporting comments: *Cook v. Welty,* 253 F.Supp. 875 (D.D.C.1966) (cases cited); *Johanek v. Aberle,* 27 F.R.D. 272 (D.Mont.1961); Williams, *Discovery of Dollar Limits in Liability Policies in Automobile Tort Cases,* 10 Ala.L.Rev. 355 (1958); Thode, *Some Reflections on the 1957 Amendments to the Texas Rules,* 37 Tex.L.Rev. 33, 40–42 (1958). Examples of Federal cases refusing disclosure and supporting comments: *Bisserier v. Manning,* 207 F.Supp. 476 (D.N.J. 1962); *Cooper v. Stender,* 30 F.R.D. 389 (E.D.Tenn.1962); Frank, *Discovery and Insurance, Coverage* 1959 Ins.L.J. 281; Fournier, *Pre-Trial Discovery of Insurance Coverage and Limits,* 28 Ford.L.Rev. 215 (1959).

The division in reported cases is close. State decisions based on provisions similar to the federal rules are similarly divided. See cases collected in 2A Barron & Holtzoff, *Federal Practice and Procedure* § 647.1, nn. 45.5, 45.6 (Wright ed. 1961). It appears to be difficult if not impossible to obtain appellate review of the issue. Resolution by rule amendment is indicated. The question is essentially procedural in that it bears upon preparation for trial and settlement before trial, and courts confronting the question, however they have decided it, have generally treated it as procedural and governed by the rules.

The amendment resolves this issue in favor of disclosure. Most of the decisions denying discovery, some explicitly, reason from the text of Rule 26(b) that it permits discovery only of matters which will be admissible in evidence or appear reasonably calculated to lead to such evidence; they avoid considerations of policy, regarding them as foreclosed. See *Bisserier v. Manning, supra.* Some note also that facts about a defendant's financial status are not discoverable as such, prior to judgment with execution unsatisfied, and fear that, if courts hold insurance coverage discoverable, they must extend the principle to other aspects of the defendant's financial status. The cases favoring disclosure rely heavily on the practical significance of insurance in the decisions lawyers make about settlement and trial preparation. In *Clauss v. Danker,* 264 F.Supp. 246 (S.D.N.Y.1967), the court held that the rules forbid disclosure but called for an amendment to permit it.

Disclosure of insurance coverage will enable counsel for both sides to make the same realistic appraisal of the case, so that settlement and litigation strategy are based on knowledge and not speculation. It will conduce to settlement and avoid protracted litigation in some cases, though in others it may have an opposite effect. The amendment is limited to insurance coverage, which should be distinguished from any other facts concerning defendant's financial status (1) because insurance is an asset created specifically to satisfy the claim; (2) because the insurance company

---

New matter is shown in italics; matter to be omitted is lined through

ordinarily controls the litigation; (3) because information about coverage is available only from defendant or his insurer; and (4) because disclosure does not involve a significant invasion of privacy.

Disclosure is required when the insurer "may be liable" on part or all of the judgment. Thus, an insurance company must disclose even when it contests liability under the policy, and such disclosure does not constitute a waiver of its claim. It is immaterial whether the liability is to satisfy the judgment directly or merely to indemnify or reimburse another after he pays the judgment.

The provision applies only to persons "carrying on an insurance business" and thus covers insurance companies and not the ordinary business concern that enters into a contract of indemnification. *Cf.* N.Y.Ins.Law § 41. Thus, the provision makes no change in existing law on discovery of indemnity agreements other than insurance agreements by persons carrying on an insurance business. Similarly, the provision does not cover the business concern that creates a reserve fund for purposes of self-insurance.

For some purposes other than discovery, an application for insurance is treated as a part of the insurance agreement. The provision makes clear that, for discovery purposes, the application is not to be so treated. The insurance application may contain personal and financial information concerning the insured, discovery of which is beyond the purpose of this provision.

In no instance does disclosure make the facts concerning insurance coverage admissible in evidence.

Subdivision (b)(3)—Trial Preparation: Materials. Some of the most controversial and vexing problems to emerge from the discovery rules have arisen out of requests for the production of documents or things prepared in anticipation of litigation or for trial. The existing rules make no explicit provision for such materials. Yet, two verbally distinct doctrines have developed, each conferring a qualified immunity on these materials—the "good cause" requirement in Rule 34 (now generally held applicable to discovery of documents via deposition under Rule 45 and interrogatories under Rule 33) and the work-product doctrine of *Hickman v. Taylor,* 329 U.S. 495 (1947). Both demand a showing of justification before production can be had, the one of "good cause" and the other variously described in the *Hickman* case: "necessity or justification," "denial * * * would unduly prejudice the preparation of petitioner's case," or "cause hardship or injustice" 329 U.S. at 509–510.

In deciding the *Hickman* case, the Supreme Court appears to have expressed a preference in 1947 for an approach to the problem of trial preparation materials by judicial decision rather than by rule. Sufficient experience has accumulated, however, with lower court applications of the *Hickman* decision to warrant a reappraisal.

The major difficulties visible in the existing case law are (1) confusion and disagreement as to whether "good cause" is made out by a showing of relevance and lack of privilege, or requires an additional showing of necessity, (2) confusion and disagreement as to the scope of the *Hickman* work-product doctrine, particularly whether it extends beyond work actually performed by lawyers, and (3) the resulting difficulty of relating the "good cause" required by Rule 34 and the "necessity or justification" of the work-product doctrine, so that their respective roles and the distinctions between them are understood.

Basic Standard.—Since Rule 34 in terms requires a showing of "good cause" for the production of all documents and things, whether or not trial preparation is involved, courts have felt that a single formula is called for and have differed over whether a showing of relevance and lack of privilege is enough or whether more must be shown. When the facts of the cases are studied, however, a distinction

New matter is shown in italics; matter to be omitted is lined through

emerges based upon the type of materials. With respect to documents not obtained or prepared with an eye to litigation, the decisions, while not uniform, reflect a strong and increasing tendency to relate "good cause" to a showing that the documents are relevant to the subject matter of the action. *E.g., Connecticut Mutual Life Ins. Co. v. Shields*, 17 F.R.D. 273 (S.D.N.Y.1959), with cases cited; *Houdry Process Corp. v. Commonwealth Oil Refining Co.*, 24 F.R.D. 58 (S.D.N.Y.1955); see *Bell v. Commercial Ins. Co.*, 280 F.2d 514, 517 (3d Cir.1960). When the party whose documents are sought shows that the request for production is unduly burdensome or oppressive, courts have denied discovery for lack of "good cause", although they might just as easily have based their decision on the protective provisions of existing Rule 30(b) (new Rule 26(c)). *E.g., Lauer v. Tankrederi*, 39 F.R.D. 334 (E.D.Pa.1966).

As to trial-preparation materials, however, the courts are increasingly interpreting "good cause" as requiring more than relevance. When lawyers have prepared or obtained the materials for trial, all courts require more than relevance; so much is clearly commanded by *Hickman*. But even as to the preparatory work of nonlawyers, while some courts ignore work-product and equate "good cause" with relevance, *e.g., Brown v. New York, N.H. & H.R.R.*, 17 F.R.D. 324 (S.D.N.Y.1955), the more recent trend is to read "good cause" as requiring inquiry into the importance of and need for the materials, as well as into alternative sources for securing the same information. In *Guilford Nat'l Bank v. Southern Ry.*, 297 F.2d 921 (4th Cir.1962), statements of witnesses obtained by claim agents were held not discoverable because both parties had had equal access to the witnesses at about the same time, shortly after the collision in question. The decision was based solely on Rule 34 and "good cause"; the court declined to rule on whether the statements were work-product. The court's treatment of "good cause" is quoted at length and with approval in *Schlagenhauf v. Holder*, 379 U.S. 104, 117–118 (1964). See also *Mitchell v. Bass*, 252 F.2d 513 (8th Cir.1958); *Hauger v. Chicago, R.I. & Pac. R.R.*, 216 F.2d 501 (7th Cir.1954); *Burke v. United States*, 32 F.R.D. 213 (E.D.N.Y.1963). While the opinions dealing with "good cause" do not often draw an explicit distinction between trial preparation materials and other materials, in fact an overwhelming proportion of the cases in which a special showing is required are cases involving trial preparation materials.

The rules are amended by eliminating the general requirement of "good cause" from Rule 34 but retaining a requirement of a special showing for trial preparation materials in this subdivision. The required showing is expressed, not in terms of "good cause" whose generality has tended to encourage confusion and controversy, but in terms of the elements of the special showing to be made: substantial need of the materials in the preparation of the case and inability without undue hardship to obtain the substantial equivalent of the materials by other means.

These changes conform to the holdings of the cases, when viewed in light of their facts. Apart from trial preparation, the fact that the materials sought are documentary does not in and of itself require a special showing beyond relevance and absence of privilege. The protective provisions are of course available, and if the party from whom production is sought raises a special issue of privacy (as with respect to income tax returns or grand jury minutes) or points to evidence primarily impeaching, or can show serious burden or expense, the court will exercise its traditional power to decide whether to issue a protective order. On the other hand, the requirement of a special showing for discovery of trial preparation materials reflects the view that each side's informal evaluation of its case should be protected, that each side should be encouraged to prepare independently, and that one side should not automatically have the benefit of the detailed preparatory work of the other side. See Field and McKusick, *Maine Civil Practice* 264 (1959).

Elimination of a "good cause" requirement from Rule 34 and the establishment of a requirement of a special showing in this subdivision will eliminate the confusion

---

New matter is shown in italics; matter to be omitted is lined through

caused by having two verbally distinct requirements of justification that the courts have been unable to distinguish clearly. Moreover, the language of the subdivision suggests the factors which the courts should consider in determining whether the requisite showing has been made. The importance of the materials sought to the party seeking them in preparation of his case and the difficulty he will have obtaining them by other means are factors noted in the *Hickman* case. The courts should also consider the likelihood that the party, even if he obtains the information by independent means, will not have the substantial equivalent of the documents the production of which he seeks.

Consideration of these factors may well lead the court to distinguish between witness statements taken by an investigator, on the one hand, and other parts of the investigative file, on the other. The court in *Southern Ry. v. Lanham,* 403 F.2d 119 (5th Cir.1968), while it naturally addressed itself to the "good cause" requirements of Rule 34, set forth as controlling considerations the factors contained in the language of this subdivision. The analysis of the court suggests circumstances under which witness statements will be discoverable. The witness may have given a fresh and contemporaneous account in a written statement while he is available to the party seeking discovery only a substantial time thereafter. *Lanham, supra* at 127–128; *Guilford, supra* at 926. Or he may be reluctant or hostile, *Lanham, supra* at 128–129; *Brookshire v. Pennsylvania R.R.,* 14 F.R.D. 154 (N.D.Ohio 1953); *Diamond v. Mohawk Rubber Co.,* 33 F.R.D. 264 (D.Colo.1963). Or he may have a lapse of memory. *Tannenbaum v. Walker,* 16 F.R.D. 570 (E.D.Pa.1954). Or he may probably be deviating from his prior statement. *Cf. Hauger v. Chicago, R.I. & Pac. R.R.,* 216 F.2d 501 (7th Cir.1954). On the other hand, a much stronger showing is needed to obtain evaluative materials in an investigator's reports. *Lanham, supra* at 131–133; *Pickett v. L. R. Ryan, Inc.,* 237 F.Supp. 198 (E.D.S.C.1965).

Materials assembled in the ordinary course of business, or pursuant to public requirements unrelated to litigation, or for other nonlitigation purposes are not under the qualified immunity provided by this subdivision. *Goosman v. A. Duie Pyle, Inc.,* 320 F.2d 45 (4th Cir.1963); *cf. United States v. New York Foreign Trade Zone Operators, Inc.,* 304 F.2d 792 (2d Cir.1962). No change is made in the existing doctrine, noted in the *Hickman* case, that one party may discover relevant facts known or available to the other party, even though such facts are contained in a document which is not itself discoverable.

Treatment of Lawyers; Special Protection of Mental Impressions, Conclusions, Opinions, and Legal Theories Concerning the Litigation.—The courts are divided as to whether the work-product doctrine extends to the preparatory work only of lawyers. The *Hickman* case left this issue open since the statements in that case were taken by a lawyer. As to courts of appeals, *compare Alltmont v. United States,* 177 F.2d 971, 976 (3d Cir.1949), *cert. denied,* 339 U.S. 967 (1950) (*Hickman* applied to statements obtained by FBI agents on theory it should apply to "all statements of prospective witnesses which a party has obtained for his trial counsel's use"), with *Southern Ry. v. Campbell,* 309 F.2d 569 (5th Cir.1962) (statements taken by claim agents not work-product), and *Guilford Nat'l Bank v. Southern Ry.,* 297 F.2d 921 (4th Cir.1962) (avoiding issue of work-product as to claim agents, deciding case instead under Rule 34 "good cause"). Similarly, the district courts are divided on statements obtained by claim agents, *compare, e.g., Brown v. New York, N.H. & H. R.R.,* 17 F.R.D. 324 (S.D.N.Y.1955) with *Hanke v. Milwaukee Electric Ry. & Transp. Co.,* 7 F.R.D. 540 (E.D.Wis.1947); investigators, *compare Burke v. United States,* 32 F.R.D. 213 (E.D.N.Y.1963) with *Snyder v. United States,* 20 F.R.D. 7 (E.D.N.Y.1956); and insurers, *compare Gottlieb v. Bresler,* 24 F.R.D. 371 (D.D.C.1959) with *Burns v. Mulder,* 20 F.R.D. 605 (E.D.Pa.1957). See 4 *Moore's Federal Practice* ¶ 26.23[8.1] (2d

---

New matter is shown in italics; matter to be omitted is lined through

311

ed. 1966); 2A Barron & Holtzoff, *Federal Practice and Procedure* § 652.2 (Wright ed. 1961).

A complication is introduced by the use made by courts of the "good cause" requirement of Rule 34, as described above. A court may conclude that trial preparation materials are not work-product because not the result of lawyer's work and yet hold that they are not producible because "good cause" has not been shown. *Cf. Guilford Nat'l Bank v. Southern Ry.*, 297 F.2d 921 (4th Cir.1962), cited and described above. When the decisions on "good cause" are taken into account, the weight of authority affords protection of the preparatory work of both lawyers and nonlawyers (though not necessarily to the same extent) by requiring more than a showing of relevance to secure production.

Subdivision (b)(3) reflects the trend of the cases by requiring a special showing, not merely as to materials prepared by an attorney, but also as to materials prepared in anticipation of litigation or preparation for trial by or for a party or any representative acting on his behalf. The subdivision then goes on to protect against disclosure the mental impressions, conclusions, opinions, or legal theories concerning the litigation of an attorney or other representative of a party. The *Hickman* opinion drew special attention to the need for protecting an attorney against discovery of memoranda prepared from recollect of oral interviews. The courts have steadfastly safeguarded against disclosure of lawyers' mental impressions and legal theories, as well as mental impressions and subjective evaluations of investigators and claim-agents. In enforcing this provision of the subdivision, the courts will sometimes find it necessary to order disclosure of a document but with portions deleted.

Rules 33 and 36 have been revised in order to permit discovery calling for opinions, contentions, and admissions relating not only to fact but also to the application of law to fact. Under those rules, a party and his attorney or other representative may be required to disclose, to some extent, mental impressions, opinions, or conclusions. But documents or parts of documents containing these matters are protected against discovery by this subdivision. Even though a party may ultimately have to disclose in response to interrogatories or requests to admit, he is entitled to keep confidential documents containing such matters prepared for internal use.

Party's Right to Own Statement.—An exception to the requirement of this subdivision enables a party to secure production of his own statement without any special showing. The cases are divided. *Compare, e.g., Safeway Stores, Inc. v. Reynolds*, 176 F.2d 476 (D.C.Cir.1949); *Shupe v. Pennsylvania R. R.*, 19 F.R.D. 144 (W.D.Pa.1956); with *e.g., New York Central R. R. v. Carr*, 251 F.2d 433 (4th Cir.1957); *Belback v. Wilson Freight Forwarding Co.*, 40 F.R.D. 16 (W.D.Pa.1966).

Courts which treat a party's statement as though it were that of any witness overlook the fact that the party's statement is, without more, admissible in evidence. Ordinarily, a party gives a statement without insisting on a copy because he does not yet have a lawyer and does not understand the legal consequences of his actions. Thus, the statement is given at a time when he functions at a disadvantage. Discrepancies between his trial testimony and earlier statement may result from lapse of memory or ordinary inaccuracy; a written statement produced for the first time at trial may give such discrepancies a prominence which they do not deserve. In appropriate cases the court may order a party to be deposed before his statement is produced. *E.g., Smith v. Central Linen Service Co.*, 39 F.R.D. 15 (D.Md.1966); *McCoy v. General Motors Corp.*, 33 F.R.D. 354 (W.D.Pa.1963).

Commentators strongly support the view that a party be able to secure his statement without a showing. 4 *Moore's Federal Practice* ¶ 26.23[8.4] (2d ed. 1966); 2A Barron & Holtzoff, *Federal Practice and Procedure* § 652.3 (Wright ed. 1961); see

---

New matter is shown in italics; matter to be omitted is lined through

also Note, *Developments in the Law—Discovery*, 74 Harv.L.Rev. 940, 1039 (1961). The following states have by statute or rule taken the same position: *Statutes:* Fla.Stat.Ann. § 92.33; Ga.Code Ann. § 38–2109(b); La.Stat.Ann.R.S. 13:3732; Mass. Gen.Laws Ann. c. 271, § 44; Minn.Stat.Ann. § 602.01; N.Y.C.P.L.R. § 3101(e). *Rules:* Mo.R.C.P. 56.01(a); N.Dak.R.C.P. 34(b); Wyo.R.C.P. 34(b); *cf.* Mich.G.C.R. 306.2.

In order to clarify and tighten the provision on statements by a party, the term "statement" is defined. The definition is adapted from 18 U.S.C. § 3500(e) (Jencks Act). The statement of a party may of course be that of plaintiff or defendant, and it may be that of an individual or of a corporation or other organization.

Witness' Right to Own Statement.—A second exception to the requirement of this subdivision permits a non-party witness to obtain a copy of his own statement without any special showing. Many, though not all, of the considerations supporting a party's right to obtain his statement apply also to the non-party witness. Insurance companies are increasingly recognizing that a witness is entitled to a copy of his statement and are modifying their regular practice accordingly.

Subdivision (b)(4)—Trial Preparation: Experts. This is a new provision dealing with discovery of information (including facts and opinions) obtained by a party from an expert retained by that party in relation to litigation or obtained by the expert and not yet transmitted to the party. The subdivision deals separately with those experts whom the party expects to call as trial witnesses and with those experts who have been retained or specially employed by the party but who are not expected to be witnesses. It should be noted that the subdivision does not address itself to the expert whose information was not acquired in preparation for trial but rather because he was an actor or viewer with respect to transactions or occurrences that are part of the subject matter of the lawsuit. Such an expert should be treated as an ordinary witness.

Subsection (b)(4)(A) deals with discovery of information obtained by or through experts who will be called as witnesses at trial. The provision is responsive to problems suggested by a relatively recent line of authorities. Many of these cases present intricate and difficult issues as to which expert testimony is likely to be determinative. Prominent among them are food and drug, patent, and condemnation cases. See, *e.g., United States v. Nysco Laboratories, Inc.*, 26 F.R.D. 159, 162 (E.D.N.Y.1960) (food and drug); *E. I. du Pont de Nemours & Co. v. Phillips Petroleum Co.*, 24 F.R.D. 416, 421 (D.Del.1959) (patent); *Cold Metal Process Co. v. Aluminum Co. of America*, 7 F.R.D. 425 (N.D.Ohio 1947), aff'd, *Sachs v. Aluminum Co. of America*, 167 F.2d 570 (6th Cir.1948) (same); *United States v. 50.34 Acres of Land*, 13 F.R.D. 19 (E.D.N.Y.1952) (condemnation).

In cases of this character, a prohibition against discovery of information held by expert witnesses produces in acute form the very evils that discovery has been created to prevent. Effective cross-examination of an expert witness requires advance preparation. The lawyer even with the help of his own experts frequently cannot anticipate the particular approach his adversary's expert will take or the data on which he will base his judgment on the stand. McGlothlin, *Some Practical Problems in Proof of Economic, Scientific, and Technical Facts*, 23 F.R.D. 467, 478 (1958). A California study of discovery and pretrial in condemnation cases notes that the only substitute for discovery of experts' valuation materials is "lengthy—and often fruitless—cross-examination during trial," and recommends pretrial exchange of such material. Calif.Law Rev.Comm'n, *Discovery in Eminent Domain Proceedings* 707–710 (Jan.1963). Similarly, effective rebuttal requires advance knowledge of the line of testimony of the other side. If the latter is foreclosed by a rule against

---

New matter is shown in italics; matter to be omitted is lined through

discovery, then the narrowing of issues and elimination of surprise which discovery normally produces are frustrated.

These considerations appear to account for the broadening of discovery against experts in the cases cited where expert testimony was central to the case. In some instances, the opinions are explicit in relating expanded discovery to improved cross-examination and rebuttal at trial. *Franks v. National Dairy Products Corp.*, 41 F.R.D. 234 (W.D.Tex.1966); *United States v. 23.76 Acres*, 32 F.R.D. 593 (D.Md.1963); see also an unpublished opinion of Judge Hincks, quoted in *United States v. 48 Jars, etc.*, 23 F.R.D. 192, 198 (D.D.C.1958). On the other hand, the need for new provision is shown by the many cases in which discovery of expert trial witnesses is needed for effective cross-examination and rebuttal, and yet courts apply the traditional doctrine and refuse disclosure. *E.g., United States v. Certain Parcels of Land*, 25 F.R.D. 192 (N.D.Cal.1959); *United States v. Certain Acres*, 18 F.R.D. 98 (M.D.Ga.1955).

Although the trial problems flowing from lack of discovery of expert witnesses are most acute and noteworthy when the case turns largely on experts, the same problems are encountered when a single expert testifies. Thus, subdivision (b)(4)(A) draws no line between complex and simple cases, or between cases with many experts and those with but one. It establishes by rule substantially the procedure adopted by decision of the court in *Knighton v. Villian & Fassio*, 39 F.R.D. 11 (D.Md.1965). For a full analysis of the problem and strong recommendations to the same effect, see Friedenthal, *Discovery and Use of an Adverse Party's Expert Information*, 14 Stan.L.Rev. 455, 485–488 (1962); Long, *Discovery and Experts under the Federal Rules of Civil Procedure*, 38 F.R.D. 111 (1965).

Past judicial restrictions on discovery of an adversary's expert, particularly as to his opinions, reflect the fear that one side will benefit unduly from the other's better preparation. The procedure established in subsection (b)(4)(A) holds the risk to a minimum. Discovery is limited to trial witnesses, and may be obtained only at a time when the parties know who their expert witnesses will be. A party must as a practical matter prepare his own case in advance of that time, for he can hardly hope to build his case out of his opponent's experts.

Subdivision (b)(4)(A) provides for discovery of an expert who is to testify at the trial. A party can require one who intends to use the expert to state the substance of the testimony that the expert is expected to give. The court may order further discovery, and it has ample power to regulate its timing and scope and to prevent abuse. Ordinarily, the order for further discovery shall compensate the expert for his time, and may compensate the party who intends to use the expert for past expenses reasonably incurred in obtaining facts or opinions from the expert. Those provisions are likely to discourage abusive practices.

Subdivision (b)(4)(B) deals with an expert who has been retained or specially employed by the party in anticipation of litigation or preparation for trial (thus excluding an expert who is simply a general employee of the party not specially employed on the case), but who is not expected to be called as a witness. Under its provisions, a party may discover facts known or opinions held by such an expert only on a showing of exceptional circumstances under which it is impracticable for the party seeking discovery to obtain facts or opinions on the same subject by other means.

Subdivision (b)(4)(B) is concerned only with experts retained or specially consulted in relation to trial preparation. Thus the subdivision precludes discovery against experts who were informally consulted in preparation for trial, but not retained or specially employed. As an ancillary procedure, a party may on a proper showing require the other party to name experts retained or specially employed, but not those informally consulted.

New matter is shown in italics; matter to be omitted is lined through

These new provisions of subdivision (b)(4) repudiate the few decisions that have held an expert's information privileged simply because of his status as an expert, *e.g., American Oil Co. v. Pennsylvania Petroleum Products Co.*, 23 F.R.D. 680, 685–686 (D.R.I.1959). See Louisell, *Modern California Discovery* 315–316 (1963). They also reject as ill-considered the decisions which have sought to bring expert information within the work-product doctrine. See *United States v. McKay*, 372 F.2d 174, 176–177 (5th Cir.1967). The provisions adopt a form of the more recently developed doctrine of "unfairness". See *e.g., United States v. 23.76 Acres of Land*, 32 F.R.D. 593, 597 (D.Md.1963); Louisell, *supra*, at 317–318; 4 *Moore's Federal Practice* ¶ 26.24 (2d ed. 1966).

Under subdivision (b)(4)(C), the court is directed or authorized to issue protective orders, including an order that the expert be paid a reasonable fee for time spent in responding to discovery, and that the party whose expert is made subject to discovery be paid a fair portion of the fees and expenses that the party incurred in obtaining information from the expert. The court may issue the latter order as a condition of discovery, or it may delay the order until after discovery is completed. These provisions for fees and expenses meet the objection that it is unfair to permit one side to obtain without cost the benefit of an expert's work for which the other side has paid, often a substantial sum. *E.g., Lewis v. United Air Lines Transp. Corp.*, 32 F.Supp. 21 (W.D.Pa.1940); *Walsh v. Reynolds Metal Co.*, 15 F.R.D. 376 (D.N.J. 1954). On the other hand, a party may not obtain discovery simply by offering to pay fees and expenses. *Cf. Boynton v. R. J. Reynolds Tobacco Co.*, 36 F.Supp. 593 (D.Mass.1941).

In instances of discovery under subdivision (b)(4)(B), the court is directed to award fees and expenses to the other party, since the information is of direct value to the discovering party's preparation of his case. In ordering discovery under (b)(4)(A)(ii), the court has discretion whether to award fees and expenses to the other party; its decision should depend upon whether the discovering party is simply learning about the other party's case or is going beyond this to develop his own case. Even in cases where the court is directed to issue a protective order, it may decline to do so if it finds that manifest injustice would result. Thus, the court can protect, when necessary and appropriate, the interests of an indigent party.

Subdivision (c)—Protective Orders. The provisions of existing Rule 30(b) are transferred to this subdivision (c), as part of the rearrangement of Rule 26. The language has been changed to give it application to discovery generally. The subdivision recognizes the power of the court in the district where a deposition is being taken to make protective orders. Such power is needed when the deposition is being taken far from the court where the action is pending. The court in the district where the deposition is being taken may, and frequently will, remit the deponent or party to the court where the action is pending.

In addition, drafting changes are made to carry out and clarify the sense of the rule. Insertions are made to avoid any possible implication that a protective order does not extend to "time" as well as to "place" or may not safeguard against "undue burden or expense."

The new reference to trade secrets and other confidential commercial information reflects existing law. The courts have not given trade secrets automatic and complete immunity against disclosure, but have in each case weighed their claim to privacy against the need for disclosure. Frequently, they have been afforded a limited protection. See, *e.g., Covey Oil Co. v. Continental Oil Co.*, 340 F.2d 993 (10th Cir.1965); *Julius M. Ames Co. v. Bostitch, Inc.*, 235 F.Supp. 856 (S.D.N.Y.1964).

The subdivision contains new matter relating to sanctions. When a motion for a protective order is made and the court is disposed to deny it, the court may go a step

---

New matter is shown in italics; matter to be omitted is lined through

further and issue an order to provide or permit discovery. This will bring the sanctions of Rule 37(b) directly into play. Since the court has heard the contentions of all interested persons, an affirmative order is justified. See Rosenberg, *Sanctions to Effectuate Pretrial Discovery*, 58 Col.L.Rev. 480, 492–493 (1958). In addition, the court may require the payment of expenses incurred in relation to the motion.

Subdivision (d)—Sequence and Priority. This new provision is concerned with the sequence in which parties may proceed with discovery and with related problems of timing. The principal effects of the new provision are first, to eliminate any fixed priority in the sequence of discovery, and second, to make clear and explicit the court's power to establish priority by an order issued in a particular case.

A priority rule developed by some courts, which confers priority on the party who first serves notice of taking a deposition, is unsatisfactory in several important respects:

First, this priority rule permits a party to establish a priority running to all depositions as to which he has given earlier notice. Since he can on a given day serve notice of taking many depositions he is in a position to delay his adversary's taking of depositions for an inordinate time. Some courts have ruled that deposition priority also permits a party to delay his answers to interrogatories and production of documents. *E.g., E. I. du Pont de Nemours & Co. v. Phillips Petroleum Co.*, 23 F.R.D. 237 (D.Del.1959); *but cf. Sturdevant v. Sears, Roebuck & Co.*, 32 F.R.D. 426 (W.D.Mo.1963).

Second, since notice is the key to priority, if both parties wish to take depositions first a race results. See *Caldwell–Clements, Inc. v. McGraw–Hill Pub. Co.*, 11 F.R.D. 156 (S.D.N.Y.1951) (description of tactics used by parties). But the existing rules on notice of deposition create a race with runners starting from different positions. The plaintiff may not give notice without leave of court until 20 days after commencement of the action, whereas the defendant may serve notice at any time after commencement. Thus, a careful and prompt defendant can almost always secure priority. This advantage of defendants is fortuitous, because the purpose of requiring plaintiff to wait 20 days is to afford defendant an opportunity to obtain counsel, not to confer priority.

Third, although courts have ordered a change in the normal sequence of discovery on a number of occasions, *e.g., Kaeppler v. James H. Matthews & Co.*, 200 F.Supp. 229 (E.D.Pa.1961); *Park & Tilford Distillers Corp. v. Distillers Co.*, 19 F.R.D. 169 (S.D.N.Y.1956), and have at all times avowed discretion to vary the usual priority, most commentators are agreed that courts in fact grant relief only for "the most obviously compelling reasons." 2A Barron & Holtzoff, *Federal Practice and Procedure* 44–47 (Wright ed. 1961); see also Younger, *Priority of Pretrial Examination in the Federal Courts—A Comment*, 34 N.Y.U.L.Rev. 1271 (1959); Freund, *The Pleading and Pretrial of an Antitrust Claim*, 46 Corn.L.Q. 555, 564 (1964). Discontent with the fairness of actual practice has been evinced by other observers. Comment, 59 Yale L.J. 117, 134–136 (1949); Yudkin, *Some Refinements in Federal discovery Procedure*, 11 Fed.B.J. 289, 296–297 (1951); *Developments in the Law—Discovery*, 74 Harv.L.Rev. 940, 954–958 (1961).

Despite these difficulties, some courts have adhered to the priority rule, presumably because it provides a test which is easily understood and applied by the parties without much court intervention. It thus permits deposition discovery to function extrajudicially, which the rules provide for and the courts desire. For these same reasons, courts are reluctant to make numerous exceptions to the rule.

The Columbia Survey makes clear that the problem of priority does not affect litigants generally. It found that most litigants do not move quickly to obtain discovery. In over half of the cases, both parties waited at least 50 days. During the

---

New matter is shown in italics; matter to be omitted is lined through

first 20 days after commencement of the action—the period when defendant might assure his priority by noticing depositions—16 percent of the defendants acted to obtain discovery. A race could not have occurred in more than 16 percent of the cases and it undoubtedly occurred in fewer. On the other hand, five times as many defendants as plaintiffs served notice of deposition during the first 19 days. To the same effect, see Comment, *Tactical Use and Abuse of Depositions Under the Federal Rules*, 59 Yale L.J. 117, 134 (1949).

These findings do not mean, however, that the priority rule is satisfactory or that a problem of priority does not exist. The court decisions show that parties do battle on this issue and carry their disputes to court. The statistics show that these court cases are not typical. By the same token, they reveal that more extensive exercise of judicial discretion to vary the priority will not bring a flood of litigation, and that a change in the priority rule will in fact affect only a small fraction of the cases.

It is contended by some that there is no need to alter the existing priority practice. In support, it is urged that there is no evidence that injustices in fact result from present practice and that, in any event, the courts can and do promulgate local rules, as in New York, to deal with local situations and issue orders to avoid possible injustice in particular cases.

Subdivision (d) is based on the contrary view that the rule of priority based on notice is unsatisfactory and unfair in its operation. Subdivision (d) follows an approach adapted from Civil Rule 4 of the District Court for the Southern District of New York. That rule provides that starting 40 days after commencement of the action, unless otherwise ordered by the court, the fact that one party is taking a deposition shall not prevent another party from doing so "concurrently." In practice, the depositions are not usually taken simultaneously; rather, the parties work out arrangements for alternation in the taking of depositions. One party may take a complete deposition and then the other, or, if the depositions are extensive, one party deposes for a set time, and then the other. See *Caldwell-Clements, Inc. v. McGraw-Hill Pub. Co.*, 11 F.R.D. 156 (S.D.N.Y.1951).

In principle, one party's initiation of discovery should not wait upon the other's completion, unless delay is dictated by special considerations. Clearly the principle is feasible with respect to all methods of discovery other than depositions. And the experience of the Southern District of New York shows that the principle can be applied to depositions as well. The courts have not had an increase in motion business on this matter. Once it is clear to lawyers that they bargain on an equal footing, they are usually able to arrange for an orderly succession of depositions without judicial intervention. Professor Moore has called attention to Civil Rule 4 and suggested that it may usefully be extended to other areas. 4 *Moore's Federal Practice* 1154 (2d ed. 1966).

The court may upon motion and by order grant priority in a particular case. But a local court rule purporting to confer priority in certain classes of cases would be inconsistent with this subdivision and thus void.

Subdivision (e)—Supplementation of Responses. The rules do not now state whether interrogatories (and questions at deposition as well as requests for inspection and admissions) impose a "continuing burden" on the responding party to supplement his answers if he obtains new information. The issue is acute when new information renders substantially incomplete or inaccurate an answer which was complete and accurate when made. It is essential that the rules provide an answer to this question. The parties can adjust to a rule either way, once they know what it is. See 4 *Moore's Federal Practice* ¶ 33.25[4] (2d ed. 1966).

New matter is shown in italics; matter to be omitted is lined through

Arguments can be made both ways. Imposition of a continuing burden reduces the proliferation of additional sets of interrogatories. Some courts have adopted local rules establishing such a burden. *E.g.*, E.D.Pa.R. 20(f), quoted in *Taggart v. Vermont Transp. Co.*, 32 F.R.D. 587 (E.D.Pa.1963); D.Me.R.15(c). Others have imposed the burden by decision. *E.g.*, *Chenault v. Nebraska Farm Products, Inc.*, 9 F.R.D. 529, 533 (D.Nebr.1949). On the other hand, there are serious objections to the burden, especially in protracted cases. Although the party signs the answers, it is his lawyer who understands their significance and bears the responsibility to bring answers up to date. In a complex case all sorts of information reaches the party, who little understands its bearing on answers previously given to interrogatories. In practice, therefore, the lawyer under a continuing burden must periodically recheck all interrogatories and canvass all new information. But a full set of new answers may no longer be needed by the interrogating party. Some issues will have been dropped from the case, some questions are now seen as unimportant, and other questions must in any event by reformulated. See *Novick v. Pennsylvania R. R.*, 18 F.R.D. 296, 298 (W.D.Pa.1955).

Subdivision (e) provides that a party is not under a continuing burden except as expressly provided. *Cf.* Note, 68 Harv.L.Rev. 673, 677 (1955). An exception is made as to the identity of persons having knowledge of discoverable matters, because of the obvious importance to each side of knowing all witnesses and because information about witnesses routinely comes to each lawyer's attention. Many of the decisions on the issue of a continuing burden have in fact concerned the identity of witnesses. An exception is also made as to expert trial witnesses in order to carry out the provisions of Rule 26(b)(4). See *Diversified Products Corp. v. Sports Center Co.*, 42 F.R.D. 3 (D.Md.1967).

Another exception is made for the situation in which a party, or more frequently his lawyer, obtains actual knowledge that a prior response is incorrect. This exception does not impose a duty to check the accuracy of prior responses, but it prevents knowing concealment by a party or attorney. Finally, a duty to supplement may be imposed by order of the court in a particular case (including an order resulting from a pretrial conference) or by agreement of the parties. A party may of course make a new discovery request which requires supplementation of prior responses.

The duty will normally be enforced, in those limited instances where it is imposed, through sanctions imposed by the trial court, including exclusion of evidence, continuance, or other action, as the court may deem appropriate.

————————

Advisory Committee's Note to 1980 Amendment

(f) Discovery Conference. At any time after commencement of an action the court may direct the attorneys for the parties to appear before it for a conference on the subject of discovery. The court shall do so upon motion by the attorney for any party if the motion includes:

    (1) A statement of the issues as they then appear;

    (2) A proposed plan and schedule of discovery;

    (3) Any limitations proposed to be placed on discovery;

New matter is shown in italics; matter to be omitted is lined through

(4) Any other proposed orders with respect to discovery; and

(5) A statement showing that the attorney making the motion has made a reasonable effort to reach agreement with opposing attorneys on the matters set forth in the motion. Each party and his attorney are under a duty to participate in good faith in the framing of a discovery plan if a plan is proposed by the attorney for any party. Notice of the motion shall be served on all parties. Objections or additions to matters set forth in the motion shall be served not later than 10 days after service of the motion.

Following the discovery conference, the court shall enter an order tentatively identifying the issues for discovery purposes, establishing a plan and schedule for discovery, setting limitations on discovery, if any; and determining such other matters, including the allocation of expenses, as are necessary for the proper management of discovery in the action. An order may be altered or amended whenever justice so requires.

Subject to the right of a party who properly moves for a discovery conference to prompt convening of the conference, the court may combine the discovery conference with a pretrial conference authorized by Rule 16.

Subdivision (f). This subdivision is new. There has been widespread criticism of abuse of discovery. The Committee has considered a number of proposals to eliminate abuse, including a change in Rule 26(b)(1) with respect to the scope of discovery and a change in Rule 33(a) to limit the number of questions that can be asked by interrogatories to parties.

The Committee believes that abuse of discovery, while very serious in certain cases, is not so general as to require such basic changes in the rules that govern discovery in all cases. A very recent study of discovery in selected metropolitan districts tends to support its belief. P. Connolly, E. Holleman, & M. Kuhlman, *Judicial Controls and the Civil Litigative Process: Discovery* (Federal Judicial Center, 1978). In the judgment of the Committee abuse can best be prevented by intervention by the court as soon as abuse is threatened.

To this end this subdivision provides that counsel who has attempted without success to effect with opposing counsel a reasonable program or plan for discovery is entitled to the assistance of the court.

It is not contemplated that requests for discovery conferences will be made routinely. A relatively narrow discovery dispute should be resolved by resort to Rules 26(c) or 37(a), and if it appears that a request for a conference is in fact grounded in such a dispute, the court may refer counsel to those rules. If the court is persuaded that a request is frivolous or vexatious, it can strike it. See Rules 11 and 7(b)(2).

A number of courts routinely consider discovery matters in preliminary pretrial conferences held shortly after the pleadings are closed. This subdivision does not

---

New matter is shown in italics; matter to be omitted is lined through

interfere with such a practice. It authorizes the court to combine a discovery conference with a pretrial conference under Rule 16 if a pretrial conference is held sufficiently early to prevent or curb abuse.

Advisory Committee's Note to 1983 Amendment

(a) Discovery Methods. Parties may obtain discovery by one or more of the following methods: depositions upon oral examination or written questions; written interrogatories; production of documents or things or permission to enter upon land or other property, for inspection and other purposes; physical and mental examinations; and requests for admission. ~~Unless the court orders otherwise under subdivision (e) of this rule, the frequency of use of these methods is not limited.~~

(b) ~~Scope of Discovery~~ *Discovery Scope and Limits.* Unless other wise limited by order of the court in accordance with these rules, the scope of discovery is as follows:

(1) In General. Parties may obtain discovery regarding any matter, not privileged, which is relevant to the subject matter involved in the pending action, whether it relates to the claim or defense of the party seeking discovery or to the claim or defense of any other party, including the existence, description, nature, custody, condition and location of any books, documents, or other tangible things and the identity and location of persons having knowledge of any discoverable matter. It is not ground for objection that the information sought will be inadmissible at the trial if the information sought appears reasonably calculated to lead the discovery of admissible evidence.

The frequency or extent of use of the discovery methods set forth in subdivision (a) shall be limited by the court if it determines that: (i) the discovery sought is unreasonably cumulative or duplicative, or is obtainable from some other source that is more convenient, less burdensome, or less expensive; (ii) the party seeking discovery has had ample opportunity by discovery in the action to obtain the information sought; or (iii) the discovery is unduly burdensome or expensive, taking into account the needs of the case, the amount in controversy, limitations on the parties' resources, and the importance of the issues at stake in the litigation. The court may act upon its own initiative after reasonable notice or pursuant to a motion under subdivision (c).

(g) *Signing of Discovery Requests, Responses, and Objections.* *Every request for discovery or response or objection thereto*

New matter is shown in italics; matter to be omitted is lined through

made by a party represented by an attorney shall be signed by at least one attorney of record in his individual name, whose address shall be stated. A party who is not represented by an attorney shall sign the request, response, or objection and state his address. The signature of the attorney or party constitutes a certification that he has read the request, response, or objection, and that to the best of his knowledge, information, and belief formed after a reasonable inquiry it is: (1) consistent with these rules and warranted by existing law or a good faith argument for the extension, modification, or reversal of existing law; (2) not interposed for any improper purpose, such as to harass or to cause unnecessary delay or needless increase in the cost of litigation; and (3) not unreasonable or unduly burdensome or expensive, given the needs of the case, the discovery already had in the case, the amount in controversy, and the importance of the issues at stake in the litigation. If a request, response, or objection is not signed, it shall be stricken unless it is signed promptly after the omission is called to the attention of the party making the request, response or objection and a party shall not be obligated to take any action with respect to it until it is signed.

If a certification is made in violation of the rule, the court, upon motion or upon its own initiative, shall impose upon the person who made the certification, the party on whose behalf the request, response, or objection is made, or both, an appropriate sanction, which may include an order to pay the amount of the reasonable expenses incurred because of the violation, including a reasonable attorney's fee.

Excessive discovery and evasion or resistance to reasonable discovery requests pose significant problems. Recent studies have made some attempt to determine the sources and extent of the difficulties. See Brazil, *Civil Discovery: Lawyers' Views of its Effectiveness, Principal Problems and Abuses,* American Bar Foundation (1980); Connolly, Holleman & Kuhlman, *Judicial Controls and the Civil Litigative Process: Discovery,* Federal Judicial Center (1978); Ellington, *A Study of Sanctions for Discovery Abuse,* Department of Justice (1979); Schroeder & Frank, *The Proposed Changes in the Discovery Rules,* 1978 Ariz.St.L.J. 475.

The purpose of discovery is to provide a mechanism for making relevant information available to the litigants. "Mutual knowledge of all the relevant facts gathered by both parties is essential to proper litigation." *Hickman v. Taylor,* 329 U.S. 495, 507 (1947). Thus the spirit of the rules is violated when advocates attempt to use discovery tools as tactical weapons rather than to expose the facts and illuminate the issues by overuse of discovery or unnecessary use of defensive weapons or evasive responses. All of this results in excessively costly and time-consuming activities that are disproportionate to the nature of the case, the amount involved, or the issues or values at stake.

Given our adversary tradition and the current discovery rules, is it not surprising that there are many opportunities, if not incentives, for attorneys to engage in

New matter is shown in italics; matter to be omitted is lined through

discovery that, although authorized by the broad, permissive terms of the rules, nevertheless results in delay. See Brazil, *The Adversary Character of Civil Discovery: A Critique and Proposals for Change*, 31 Vand.L.Rev. 1259 (1978). As a result, it has been said that the rules have "not infrequently [been] exploited to the disadvantage of justice." *Herbert v. Lando*, 441 U.S. 153, 179 (1979) (Powell, J., concurring). These practices impose costs on an already overburdened system and impede the fundamental goal of the "just, speedy, and inexpensive determination of every action." Fed.R.Civ.P. 1.

Subdivision (a); Discovery Methods. The deletion of the last sentence of Rule 26(a)(1), which provided that unless the court ordered otherwise under Rule 26(c) "the frequency of use" of the various discovery methods was not to be limited, is an attempt to address the problem of duplicative, redundant, and excessive discovery and to reduce it. The amendment, in conjunction with the changes in Rule 26(b)(1), is designed to encourage district judges to identify instances of needless discovery and to limit the use of the various discovery devices accordingly. The question may be raised by one of the parties, typically on a motion for a protective order, or by the court on its own initiative. It is entirely appropriate to consider a limitation on the frequency of use of discovery at a discovery conference under Rule 26(f) or at any other pretrial conference authorized by these rules. In considering the discovery needs of a particular case, the court should consider the factors described in Rule 26(b)(1).

Subdivision (b); Discovery Scope and Limits. Rule 26(b)(1) has been amended to add a sentence to deal with the problem of over-discovery. The objective is to guard against redundant or disproportionate discovery by giving the court authority to reduce the amount of discovery that may be directed to matters that are otherwise proper subjects of inquiry. The new sentence is intended to encourage judges to be more aggressive in identifying and discouraging discovery overuse. The grounds mentioned in the amended rule for limiting discovery reflect the existing practice of many courts in issuing protective orders under Rule 26(c). See, *e.g., Carlson Cos. v. Sperry & Hutchinson Co.*, 374 F.Supp. 1080 (D.Minn.1974); *Dolgow v. Anderson*, 53 F.R.D. 661 (E.D.N.Y.1971); *Mitchell v. American Tobacco Co.*, 33 F.R.D. 262 (M.D.Pa.1963); *Welty v. Clute*, 1 F.R.D. 446 (W.D.N.Y.1941). On the whole, however, district judges have been reluctant to limit the use of the discovery devices. See, *e.g., Apco Oil Co. v. Certified Transp., Inc.*, 46 F.R.D. 428 (W.D.Mo.1969). See generally 8 Wright & Miller, *Federal Practice and Procedure: Civil* §§ 2036, 2037, 2039, 2040 (1970).

The first element of the standard, Rule 26(b)(1)(i), is designed to minimize redundancy in discovery and encourage attorneys to be sensitive to the comparative costs of different methods of securing information. Subdivision (b)(1)(ii) also seeks to reduce repetitiveness and to oblige lawyers to think through their discovery activities in advance so that full utilization is made of each deposition, document request, or set of interrogatories. The elements of Rule 26(b)(1)(iii) address the problem of discovery that is disproportionate to the individual lawsuit as measured by such matters as its nature and complexity, the importance of the issues at stake in a case seeking damages, the limitations on a financially weak litigant to withstand extensive opposition to a discovery program or to respond to discovery requests, and the significance of the substantive issues, as measured in philosophic, social, or institutional terms. Thus the rule recognizes that many cases in public policy spheres, such as employment practices, free speech, and other matters, may have importance far beyond the monetary amount involved. The court must apply the standards in an even-handed manner that will prevent use of discovery to wage a war of attrition or as a device to coerce a party, whether financially weak or affluent.

New matter is shown in italics; matter to be omitted is lined through

The rule contemplates greater judicial involvement in the discovery process and thus acknowledges the reality that it cannot always operate on a self-regulating basis. See Connolly, Holleman & Kuhlman, *Judicial Controls and the Civil Litigative Process: Discovery* 77, Federal Judicial Center (1978). In an appropriate case the court could restrict the number of depositions, interrogatories, or the scope of a production request. But the court must be careful not to deprive a party of discovery that is reasonably necessary to afford a fair opportunity to develop and prepare the case.

The court may act on motion, or its own initiative. It is entirely appropriate to resort to the amended rule in conjunction with a discovery conference under Rule 26(f) or one of the other pretrial conferences authorized by the rules.

Subdivision (g); Signing of Discovery Requests, Responses, and Objections. Rule 26(g) imposes an affirmative duty to engage in pretrial discovery in a responsible manner that is consistent with the spirit and purposes of Rules 26 through 37. In addition, Rule 26(g) is designed to curb discovery abuse by explicitly encouraging the imposition of sanctions. The subdivision provides a deterrent to both excessive discovery and evasion by imposing a certification requirement that obliges each attorney to stop and think about the legitimacy of a discovery request, a response thereto, or an objection. The term "response" includes answers to interrogatories and to requests to admit as well as responses to production requests.

If primary responsibility for conducting discovery is to continue to rest with the litigants, they must be obliged to act responsibly and avoid abuse. With this in mind, Rule 26(g), which parallels the amendments to Rule 11, requires an attorney or unrepresented party to sign each discovery request, response, or objection. Motions relating to discovery are governed by Rule 11. However, since a discovery request, response, or objection usually deals with more specific subject matter than motions or papers, the elements that must be certified in connection with the former are spelled out more completely. The signature is a certification of the elements set forth in Rule 26(g).

Although the certification duty requires the lawyer to pause and consider the reasonableness of his request, response, or objection, it is not meant to discourage or restrict necessary and legitimate discovery. The rule simply requires that the attorney make a reasonable inquiry into the factual basis of his response, request, or objection.

The duty to make a "reasonable inquiry" is satisfied if the investigation undertaken by the attorney and the conclusions drawn therefrom are reasonable under the circumstances. It is an objective standard similar to the one imposed by Rule 11. See the Advisory Committee Note to Rule 11. See also *Kinee v. Abraham Lincoln Fed. Sav. & Loan Ass'n,* 365 F.Supp. 975 (E.D.Pa.1973). In making the inquiry, the attorney may rely on assertions by the client and on communications with other counsel in the case as long as that reliance is appropriate under the circumstances. Ultimately, what is reasonable is a matter for the court to decide on the totality of the circumstances.

Rule 26(g) does not require the signing attorney to certify the truthfulness of the client's factual responses to a discovery request. Rather, the signature certifies that the lawyer has made a reasonable effort to assure that the client has provided all the information and documents available to him that are responsive to the discovery demand. Thus, the lawyer's certification under Rule 26(g) should be distinguished from other signature requirements in the rules, such as those in Rules 30(e) and 33.

Nor does the rule require a party or an attorney to disclose privileged communications or work product in order to show that a discovery request, response, or

---

New matter is shown in italics; matter to be omitted is lined through

323

objection is substantially justified. The provisions of Rule 26(c), including appropriate orders after *in camera* inspection by the court, remain available to protect a party claiming privilege or work product protection.

The signing requirement means that every discovery request, response, or objection should be grounded on a theory that is reasonable under the precedents or a good faith belief as to what should be the law. This standard is heavily dependent on the circumstances of each case. The certification speaks as of the time it is made. The duty to supplement discovery responses continues to be governed by Rule 26(e).

Concern about discovery abuse has led to widespread recognition that there is a need for more aggressive judicial control and supervision. *ACF Industries, Inc. v. EEOC*, 439 U.S. 1081 (1979) (certiorari denied) (Powell, J., dissenting). Sanctions to deter discovery abuse would be more effective if they were diligently applied "not merely to penalize those whose conduct may be deemed to warrant such a sanction, but to deter those who might be tempted to such conduct in the absence of such a deterrent." *National Hockey League v. Metropolitan Hockey Club*, 427 U.S. 639, 643 (1976). See also Note, *The Emerging Deterrence Orientation in the Imposition of Discovery Sanctions*, 91 Harv.L.Rev. 1033 (1978). Thus the premise of Rule 26(g) is that imposing sanctions on attorneys who fail to meet the rule's standards will significantly reduce abuse by imposing disadvantages therefor.

Because of the asserted reluctance to impose sanctions on attorneys who abuse the discovery rules, see Brazil, *Civil Discovery: Lawyers' Views of its Effectiveness, Principal Problems and Abuses*, American Bar Foundation (1980); Ellington, *A Study of Sanctions for Discovery Abuse*, Department of Justice (1979), Rule 26(g) makes explicit the authority judges now have to impose appropriate sanctions and requires them to use it. This authority derives from Rule 37, 28 U.S.C. § 1927, and the court's inherent power. See *Roadway Express, Inc. v. Piper*, 447 U.S. 752 (1980); *Martin v. Bell Helicopter Co.*, 85 F.R.D. 654, 661–62 (D.Col.1980); Note, *Sanctions Imposed by Courts on Attorneys Who Abuse the Judicial Process*, 44 U.Chi.L.Rev. 619 (1977). The new rule mandates that sanctions be imposed on attorneys who fail to meet the standards established in the first portion of Rule 26(g). The nature of the sanction is a matter of judicial discretion to be exercised in light of the particular circumstances. The court may take into account any failure by the party seeking sanctions to invoke protection under Rule 26(c) at an early stage in the litigation.

The sanctioning process must comport with due process requirements. The kind of notice and hearing required will depend on the facts of the case and the severity of the sanction being considered. To prevent the proliferation of the sanction procedure and to avoid multiple hearings, discovery in any sanction proceeding normally should be permitted only when it is clearly required by the interests of justice. In most cases the court will be aware of the circumstances and only a brief hearing should be necessary.

Advisory Committee's Note to 1993 Amendment

Rule 26. General Provisions Governing Discovery; *Duty of Disclosure*

(a) *Required Disclosures;* ~~Discovery~~ Methods *to Discover Additional Matter.*

(1) Initial Disclosures. Except to the extent otherwise stipulated or directed by order or local rule, a party shall, without awaiting a discovery request, provide to other parties:

New matter is shown in italics; matter to be omitted is lined through

(A) the name and, if known, the address and telephone number of each individual likely to have discoverable information relevant to disputed facts alleged with particularity in the pleadings, identifying the subjects of the information;

(B) a copy of, or a description by category and location of, all documents, data compilations, and tangible things in the possession, custody, or control of the party that are relevant to disputed facts alleged with particularity in the pleadings;

(C) a computation of any category of damages claimed by the disclosing party, making available for inspection and copying as under Rule 34 the documents or other evidentiary material, not privileged or protected from disclosure, on which such computation is based, including materials bearing on the nature and extent of injuries suffered; and

(D) for inspection and copying as under Rule 34 any insurance agreement under which any person carrying on an insurance business may be liable to satisfy part or all of a judgment which may be entered in the action or to indemnify or reimburse for payments made to satisfy the judgment.

Unless otherwise stipulated or directed by the court, these disclosures shall be made at or within 10 days after the meeting of the parties under subdivision (f). A party shall make its initial disclosures based on the information then reasonably available to it and is not excused from making its disclosures because it has not fully completed its investigation of the case or because it challenges the sufficiency of another party's disclosures or because another party has not made its disclosures.

(2) Disclosure of Expert Testimony.

(A) In addition to the disclosures required by paragraph (1), a party shall disclose to other parties the identity of any person who may be used at trial to present evidence under Rules 702, 703, or 705 of the Federal Rules of Evidence.

(B) Except as otherwise stipulated or directed by the court, this disclosure shall, with respect to a witness who is retained or specially employed to provide expert testimony in the case or whose duties as an employee of the party regularly involve giving expert testimony, be accompanied by a written report prepared and signed by the witness. The report shall contain a complete statement of all opinions to be expressed and the basis and reasons therefor; the data or other information considered by the witness in forming the opinions; any exhibits to be used as a summary of or support for the opinions; the qualifications of the witness, including a list of all publications authored by

---

New matter is shown in italics; matter to be omitted is lined through

the witness within the preceding ten years; the compensation to be paid for the study and testimony; and a listing of any other cases in which the witness has testified as an expert at trial or by deposition within the preceding four years.

(C) These disclosures shall be made at the times and in the sequence directed by the court. In the absence of other directions from the court or stipulation by the parties, the disclosures shall be made at least 90 days before the trial date or the date the case is to be ready for trial or, if the evidence is intended solely to contradict or rebut evidence on the same subject matter identified by another party under paragraph (2)(B), within 30 days after the disclosure made by the other party. The parties shall supplement these disclosures when required under subdivision (e)(1).

(3) Pretrial Disclosures. In addition to the disclosures required in the preceding paragraphs, a party shall provide to other parties the following information regarding the evidence that it may present at trial other than solely for impeachment purposes:

(A) the name and, if not previously provided, the address and telephone number of each witness, separately identifying those whom the party expects to present and those whom the party may call if the need arises;

(B) the designation of those witnesses whose testimony is expected to be presented by means of a deposition and, if not taken stenographically, a transcript of the pertinent portions of the deposition testimony; and

(C) an appropriate identification of each document or other exhibit, including summaries of other evidence, separately identifying those which the party expects to offer and those which the party may offer if the need arises.

Unless otherwise directed by the court, these disclosures shall be made at least 30 days before trial. Within 14 days thereafter, unless a different time is specified by the court, a party may serve and file a list disclosing (i) any objections to the use under Rule 32(a) of a deposition designated by another party under subparagraph (B) and (ii) any objection, together with the grounds therefor, that may be made to the admissibility of materials identified under subparagraph (C). Objections not so disclosed, other than objections under Rules 402 and 403 of the Federal Rules of Evidence, shall be deemed waived unless excused by the court for good cause shown.

(4) Form of Disclosures; Filing. Unless otherwise directed by order or local rule, all disclosures under paragraphs (1) through (3)

New matter is shown in italics;   matter to be omitted is lined through

shall be made in writing, signed, served, and promptly filed with the court.

(5) Methods to Discover Additional Matter. Parties may obtain discovery by one or more of the following methods: depositions upon oral examination or written questions; written interrogatories; production of documents or things or permission to enter upon land or other property *under Rule 34 or 45(a)(1)(C)*, for inspection and other purposes; physical and mental examinations; and requests for admission.

(b) Discovery Scope and Limits. Unless otherwise limited by order of the court in accordance with these rules, the scope of discovery is as follows:

(1) In General. Parties may obtain discovery regarding any matter, not privileged, which is relevant to the subject matter involved in the pending action, whether it relates to the claim or defense of the party seeking discovery or to the claim or defense of any other party, including the existence, description, nature, custody, condition, and location of any books, documents, or other tangible things and the identity and location of persons having knowledge of any discoverable matter. ~~It is not a ground for objection that t~~*T*he information sought *need not be* ~~will be in~~admissible at the trial if the information sought appears reasonably calculated to lead to the discovery of admissible evidence.

(2) Limitations. By order or by local rule, the court may alter the limits in these rules on the number of depositions and interrogatories and may also limit the length of depositions under Rule 30 and the number of requests under Rule 36. The frequency or extent of use of the discovery methods ~~set forth in subdivision (a)~~ *otherwise permitted under these rules and by any local rule* shall be limited by the court if it determines that: (i) the discovery sought is unreasonably cumulative or duplicative, or is obtainable from some other source that is more convenient, less burdensome, or less expensive; (ii) the party seeking discovery has had ample opportunity by discovery in the action to obtain the information sought; or (iii) ~~the discovery is unduly burdensome or expensive~~ *the burden or expense of the proposed discovery outweighs its likely benefit,* taking into account the needs of the case, the amount in controversy, ~~limitations on~~ the parties' resources, ~~and~~ the importance of the issues at stake in the litigation, *and the importance of the proposed discovery in resolving the issues.* The court may act upon its own initiative after reasonable notice or pursuant to a motion under subdivision (c).

New matter is shown in italics; matter to be omitted is lined through

(2) ~~Insurance Agreements. A party may obtain discovery of the existence and contents of any insurance agreement under which any person carrying on an insurance business may be liable to satisfy part or all of a judgment which may be entered in the action or to indemnify or reimburse for payments made to satisfy the judgment. Information concerning the insurance agreement is not by reason of disclosure admissible in evidence at trial. For purposes of this paragraph, an application for insurance shall not be treated as part of an insurance agreement.~~

(4) Trial Preparation: Experts. ~~Discovery of facts known and opinions held by experts, otherwise discoverable under the provisions of subdivision (b)(1) of this rule and acquired or developed in anticipation of litigation or for trial, may be obtained only as follows.~~

(A)~~(i)~~ A party may ~~through interrogatories require any other party to identify each person whom the other party expects to call as an expert witness at trial, to state the subject matter on which the expert is expected to testify, and to state the substance of the facts and opinions to which the expert is expected to testify and a summary of the grounds for each opinion. (ii) Upon motion, the court may order further discovery by other means, subject to such restrictions as to scope and such provisions, pursuant to subdivision (b)(4)(C) of this rule, concerning fees and expenses as the court may deem appropriate.~~ *depose any person who has been identified as an expert whose opinions may be presented at trial. If a report from the expert is required under subdivision (a)(2)(B), the deposition shall not be conducted until after the report is provided.*

(B) A party may, *through interrogatories or by deposition,* discover facts known or opinions held by an expert who has been retained or specially employed by another party in anticipation of litigation or preparation for trial and who is not expected to be called as a witness at trial~~,~~ only as provided in Rule 35(b) or upon a showing of exceptional circumstances under which it is impracticable for the party seeking discovery to obtain facts or opinions on the same subject by other means.

(C) Unless manifest injustice would result, (i) the court shall require that the party seeking discovery pay the expert a reasonable fee for time spent in responding to discovery under *this* subdivision~~s (b)(4)(A)(ii) and (b)(4)(B) of this rule~~; and (ii) with respect to discovery obtained

---

New matter is shown in italics; matter to be omitted is lined through

under ~~subdivision (b)(4)(A)(ii) of this rule the court may require, and with respect to discovery obtained under~~ subdivision (b)(4)(B) of this rule the court shall require~~,~~ the party seeking discovery to pay the other party a fair portion of the fees and expenses reasonably incurred by the latter party in obtaining facts and opinions from the expert.

(5) Claims of Privilege or Protection of Trial Preparation Materials. When a party withholds information otherwise discoverable under these rules by claiming that it is privileged or subject to protection as trial preparation material, the party shall make the claim expressly and shall describe the nature of the documents, communications, or things not produced or disclosed in a manner that, without revealing information itself privileged or protected, will enable other parties to assess the applicability of the privilege or protection.

(c) Protective Orders. Upon motion by a party or by the person from whom discovery is sought, *accompanied by a certification that the movant has in good faith conferred or attempted to confer with other affected parties in an effort to resolve the dispute without court action,* and for good cause shown, the court in which the action is pending or alternatively, on matters relating to a deposition, the court in the district where the deposition is to be taken may make any order which justice requires to protect a party or person from annoyance, embarrassment, oppression, or undue burden or expense, including one or more of the following:

(1) that the *disclosure or* discovery not be had;

(2) that the *disclosure or* discovery may be had only on specified terms and conditions, including a designation of the time or place;

(3) that the discovery may be had only by a method of discovery other than that selected by the party seeking discovery;

(4) that certain matters not be inquired into, or that the scope of the *disclosure or* discovery be limited to certain matters;

(5) that discovery be conducted with no one present except persons designated by the court;

(6) that a deposition, after being sealed, be opened only by order of the court;

New matter is shown in italics; matter to be omitted is lined through

(7) that a trade secret or other confidential research, development, or commercial information not be ~~disclosed~~ *revealed* or be ~~disclosed~~ *revealed* only in a designated way; *and*

(8) that the parties simultaneously file specified documents or information enclosed in sealed envelopes to be opened as directed by the court.

If the motion for a protective order is denied in whole or in part, the court may, on such terms and conditions as are just, order that any party or *other* person provide or permit discovery. The provisions of Rule 37(a)(4) apply to the award of expenses incurred in relation to the motion.

(d) ~~Sequence and~~ Timing *and Sequence* of Discovery. *Except when authorized under these rules or by local rule, order, or agreement of the parties, a party may not seek discovery from any source before the parties have met and conferred as required by subdivision (f).* Unless the court upon motion, for the convenience of parties and witnesses and in the interests of justice, orders otherwise, methods of discovery may be used in any sequence, and the fact that a party is conducting discovery, whether by deposition or otherwise, shall not operate to delay any other party's discovery.

(e) Supplementation of *Disclosures and* Responses. A party who has *made a disclosure under subdivision (a) or* responded to a request for discovery with a *disclosure or* response ~~that was complete when made~~ is under ~~no~~ *a* duty to supplement *or correct* the *disclosure or* response to include information thereafter acquired~~, except as follows~~ *if ordered by the court or in the following circumstances*:

(1) A party is under a duty ~~seasonably~~ to supplement ~~the response with respect to any question directly addressed to (A) the identity and location of persons having knowledge of discoverable matters, and (B) the identity of each person expected to be called as an expert witness at trial, the subject matter on which the person is expected to testify, and the substance of the person's testimony.~~ *at appropriate intervals its disclosures under subdivision (a) if the party learns that in some material respect the information disclosed is incomplete or incorrect and if the additional or corrective information has not otherwise been made known to the other parties during the discovery process or in writing. With respect to testimony of an expert from whom a report is required under subdivision (a)(2)(B) the duty extends both to information contained in the report and to information provided through a deposition of the expert, and any additions or other changes to this information shall be*

New matter is shown in italics; matter to be omitted is lined through

disclosed by the time the party's disclosures under Rule 26(a)(3) are due.

(2) A party is under a duty seasonally to amend a prior response *to an interrogatory, request for production, or request for admission* if the party *learns* ~~obtains information upon the basis of which (A) the party knows~~ that the response ~~was incorrect when made, or (B) the party knows that the response though correct when made is no longer true and the circumstances are such that a failure to amend the response is in substance a knowing concealment~~ *is in some material respect incomplete or incorrect and if the additional or corrective information has not otherwise been made known to the other parties during the discovery process or in writing.*

~~(3) A duty to supplement responses may be imposed by order of the court, agreement of the parties, or at any time prior to trial through new requests for supplementation of prior responses.~~

(f) *Meeting of Parties; Planning for Discovery* **Confer-ence.** ~~At any time after commencement of an action the court may direct the attorneys for the parties to appear before it for a conference on the subject of discovery. The court shall do so upon motion by the attorney for any party if the motion includes~~ *Except in actions exempted by local rule or when otherwise ordered, the parties shall, as soon as practicable and in any event at least 14 days before a scheduling conference is held or a scheduling order is due under Rule 16(b), meet to discuss the nature and basis of their claims and defenses and the possibilities for a prompt settlement or resolution of the case, to make or arrange for the disclosures required by subdivision (a)(1), and to develop a proposed discovery plan. The plan shall indicate the parties' views and proposals concerning:*

(1) ~~A statement of the issues as they then appear;~~ *what changes should be made in the timing, form, or requirement for disclosures under subdivision (a) or local rule, including a statement as to when disclosures under subdivision (a)(1) were made or will be made;*

(2) ~~A proposed plan and schedule of discovery;~~ *the subjects on which discovery may be needed, when discovery should be completed, and whether discovery should be conducted in phases or be limited to or focused upon particular issues;*

(3) ~~Any limitations proposed to be placed on discovery;~~ *what changes should be made in the limitations on discovery*

New matter is shown in italics; matter to be omitted is lined through

imposed under these rules or by local rule, and what other limitations should be imposed; and

(4) ~~A~~*any other* ~~proposed~~ *orders* ~~with respect to discovery~~ *that should be entered by the court under subdivision (c) or under Rule 16(b) and (c).*~~; and~~

~~(5) A statement showing that the attorney making the motion has made a reasonable effort to reach agreement with opposing attorneys on the matters set forth in the motion. Each party and each party's attorney are under a duty to participate in good faith in the framing of a discovery plan if a plan is proposed by the attorney for any party. Notice of the motion shall be served on all parties. Objections or additions to matters set forth in the motion shall be served not later than 10 days after service of the motion.~~

The attorneys of record and all unrepresented parties that have appeared in the case are jointly responsible for arranging and being present or represented at the meeting, for attempting in good faith to agree on the proposed discovery plan, and for submitting to the court within 10 days after the meeting a written report outlining the plan. ~~Following the discovery conference, the court shall enter an order tentatively identifying the issues for discovery purposes, establishing a plan and schedule for discovery, setting limitations on discovery, if any; and determining such other matters, including the allocation of expenses, as are necessary for the proper management of discovery in the action. An order may be altered or amended whenever justice so requires.~~

~~Subject to the right of a party who properly moves for a discovery conference to prompt convening of the conference, the court may combine the discovery conference with a pretrial conference authorized by Rule 16.~~

(g) Signing of *Disclosures*, Discovery Requests, Responses, and Objections.

(1) Every disclosure made pursuant to subdivision (a)(1) or subdivision (a)(3) shall be signed by at least one attorney of record in the attorney's individual name, whose address shall be stated. An unrepresented party shall sign the disclosure and state the party's address. The signature of the attorney or party constitutes a certification that to the best of the signer's knowledge, information, and belief, formed after a reasonable inquiry, the disclosure is complete and correct as of the time it is made.

(2) Every *discovery* request, ~~for discovery or~~ response, or objection ~~thereto~~ made by a party represented by an attorney shall be signed by at least one attorney of record in the attorney's individual

---

New matter is shown in italics;   matter to be omitted is lined through

name, whose address shall be stated. A*n unrepresented* party who is not represented by an attorney shall sign the request, response, or objection and state the party's address. The signature of the attorney or party constitutes a certification that the signer has read the request, response, or objection, and that to the best of the signer's knowledge, information, and belief, formed after a reasonable inquiry, it *the request, response, or objection* is:

(~~1~~*A*) consistent with these rules and warranted by existing law or a good faith argument for the extension, modification, or reversal of existing law;

(~~2~~*B*) not interposed for any improper purpose, such as to harass or to cause unnecessary delay or needless increase in the cost of litigation; and

(~~3~~*C*) not unreasonable or unduly burdensome or expensive, given the needs of the case, the discovery already had in the case, the amount in controversy, and the importance of the issues at stake in the litigation.

If a request, response, or objection is not signed, it shall be stricken unless it is signed promptly after the omission is called to the attention of the party making the request, response, or objection, and a party shall not be obligated to take any action with respect to it until it is signed.

(3) If *without substantial justification* a certification is made in violation of the rule, the court, upon motion or upon its own initiative, shall impose upon the person who made the certification, the party on whose behalf the *disclosure,* request, response, or objection is made, or both, an appropriate sanction, which may include an order to pay the amount of the reasonable expenses incurred because of the violation, including a reasonable attorney's fee.

Subdivision (a). Through the addition of paragraphs (1)–(4), this subdivision imposes on parties a duty to disclose, without awaiting formal discovery requests, certain basic information that is needed in most cases to prepare for trial or make an informed decision about settlement. The rule requires all parties (1) early in the case to exchange information regarding potential witnesses, documentary evidence, damages, and insurance, (2) at an appropriate time during the discovery period to identify expert witnesses and provide a detailed written statement of the testimony that may be offered at trial through specially retained experts, and (3) as the trial date approaches to identify the particular evidence that may be offered at trial. The enumeration in Rule 26(a) of items to be disclosed does not prevent a court from requiring by order or local rule that the parties disclose additional information without a discovery request. Nor are parties precluded from using traditional discovery methods to obtain further information regarding these matters, as for

---

New matter is shown in italics; matter to be omitted is lined through

example asking an expert during a deposition about testimony given in other litigation beyond the four-year period specified in Rule 26(a)(2)(B).

A major purpose of the revision is to accelerate the exchange of basic information about the case and to eliminate the paper work involved in requesting such information, and the rule should be applied in a manner to achieve those objectives. The concepts of imposing a duty of disclosure were set forth in Brazil, *The Adversary Character of Civil Discovery: A Critique and Proposals for Change,* 31 *Vand.L.Rev.* 1348 (1978), and Schwarzer, *The Federal Rules, the Adversary Process, and Discovery Reform,* 50 *U.Pitt.L.Rev.* 703, 721–23 (1989).

The rule is based upon the experience of district courts that have required disclosure of some of this information through local rules, court-approved standard interrogatories, and standing orders. Most have required pretrial disclosure of the kind of information described in Rule 26(a)(3). Many have required written reports from experts containing information like that specified in Rule 26(a)(2)(B). While far more limited, the experience of the few state and federal courts that have required pre-discovery exchange of core information such as is contemplated in Rule 26(a)(1) indicates that savings in time and expense can be achieved, particularly if the litigants meet and discuss the issues in the case as a predicate for this exchange and if a judge supports the process, as by using the results to guide further proceedings in the case. Courts in Canada and the United Kingdom have for many years required disclosure of certain information without awaiting a request from an adversary.

Paragraph (1). As the functional equivalent of court-ordered interrogatories, this paragraph requires early disclosure, without need for any request, of four types of information that have been customarily secured early in litigation through formal discovery. The introductory clause permits the court, by local rule, to exempt all or particular types of cases from these disclosure requirement[s] or to modify the nature of the information to be disclosed. It is expected that courts would, for example, exempt cases like Social Security reviews and government collection cases in which discovery would not be appropriate or would be unlikely. By order the court may eliminate or modify the disclosure requirements in a particular case, and similarly the parties, unless precluded by order or local rule, can stipulate to elimination or modification of the requirements for that case. The disclosure obligations specified in paragraph (1) will not be appropriate for all cases, and it is expected that changes in these obligations will be made by the court or parties when the circumstances warrant.

Authorization of these local variations is, in large measure, included in order to accommodate the Civil Justice Reform Act of 1990, which implicitly directs districts to experiment during the study period with differing procedures to reduce the time and expense of civil litigation. The civil justice delay and expense reduction plans adopted by the courts under the Act differ as to the type, form, and timing of disclosures required. Section 105(c)(1) of the Act calls for a report by the Judicial Conference to Congress by December 31, 1995, comparing experience in twenty of these courts; and section 105(c)(2)(B) contemplates that some changes in the Rules may then be needed. While these studies may indicate the desirability of further changes in Rule 26(a)(1), these changes probably could not become effective before December 1998 at the earliest. In the meantime, the present revision puts in place a series of disclosure obligations that, unless a court acts affirmatively to impose other requirements or indeed to reject all such requirements for the present, are designed to eliminate certain discovery, help focus the discovery that is needed, and facilitate preparation for trial or settlement.

Subparagraph (A) requires identification of all persons who, based on the investigation conducted thus far, are likely to have discoverable information relevant

---

New matter is shown in italics; matter to be omitted is lined through

to the factual disputes between the parties. All persons with such information should be disclosed, whether or not their testimony will be supportive of the position of the disclosing party. As officers of the court, counsel are expected to disclose the identity of those persons who may be used by them as witnesses or who, if their potential testimony were known, might reasonably be expected to be deposed or called as a witness by any of the other parties. Indicating briefly the general topics on which such persons have information should not be burdensome, and will assist other parties in deciding which depositions will actually be needed.

Subparagraph (B) is included as a substitute for the inquiries routinely made about the existence and location of documents and other tangible things in the possession, custody, or control of the disclosing party. Although, unlike subdivision (a)(3)(C), an itemized listing of each exhibit is not required, the disclosure should describe and categorize, to the extent identified during the initial investigation, the nature and location of potentially relevant documents and records, including computerized data and other electronically-recorded information, sufficiently to enable opposing parties (1) to make an informed decision concerning which documents might need to be examined, at least initially, and (2) to frame their document requests in a manner likely to avoid squabbles resulting from the wording of the requests. As with potential witnesses, the requirement for disclosure of documents applies to all potentially relevant items then known to the party, whether or not supportive of its contentions in the case.

Unlike subparagraphs (C) and (D), subparagraph (B) does not require production of any documents. Of course, in cases involving few documents a disclosing party may prefer to provide copies of the documents rather than describe them, and the rule is written to afford this option to the disclosing party. If, as will be more typical, only the description is provided, the other parties are expected to obtain the documents desired by proceeding under Rule 34 or through informal requests. The disclosing party does not, by describing documents under subparagraph (B), waive its right to object to production on the basis of privilege or work product protection, or to assert that the documents are not sufficiently relevant to justify the burden or expense of production.

The initial disclosure requirements of subparagraphs (A) and (B) are limited to identification of potential evidence "relevant to disputed facts alleged with particularity in the pleadings." There is no need for a party to identify potential evidence with respect to allegations that are admitted. Broad, vague, and conclusory allegations sometimes tolerated in notice pleading—for example, the assertion that a product with many component parts is defective in some unspecified manner—should not impose upon responding parties the obligation at that point to search for and identify all persons possibly involved in, or all documents affecting, the design, manufacture, and assembly of the product. The greater the specificity and clarity of the allegations in the pleadings, the more complete should be the listing of potential witnesses and types of documentary evidence. Although paragraphs (1)(A) and (1)(B) by their terms refer to the factual disputes defined in the pleadings, the rule contemplates that these issues would be informally refined and clarified during the meeting of the parties under subdivision (f) and that the disclosure obligations would be adjusted in the light of these discussions. The disclosure requirements should, in short, be applied with common sense in light of the principles of Rule 1, keeping in mind the salutary purposes that the rule is intended to accomplish. The litigants should not indulge in gamesmanship with respect to the disclosure obligations.

Subparagraph (C) imposes a burden of disclosure that includes the functional equivalent of a standing Request for Production under Rule 34. A party claiming damages or other monetary relief must, in addition to disclosing the calculation of such damages, make available the supporting documents for inspection and copying

---

New matter is shown in italics; matter to be omitted is lined through

as if a request for such materials had been made under Rule 34. This obligation applies only with respect to documents then reasonably available to it and not privileged or protected as work product. Likewise, a party would not be expected to provide a calculation of damages which, as in many patent infringement actions, depends on information in the possession of another party or person.

Subparagraph (D) replaces subdivision (b)(2) of Rule 26, and provides that liability insurance policies be made available for inspection and copying. The last two sentences of that subdivision have been omitted as unnecessary, not to signify any change of law. The disclosure of insurance information does not thereby render such information admissible in evidence. See Rule 411, Federal Rules of Evidence. Nor does subparagraph (D) require disclosure of applications for insurance, though in particular cases such information may be discoverable in accordance with revised subdivision (a)(5).

Unless the court directs a different time, the disclosures required by subdivision (a)(1) are to be made at or within 10 days after the meeting of the parties under subdivision (f). One of the purposes of this meeting is to refine the factual disputes with respect to which disclosures should be made under paragraphs (1)(A) and (1)(B), particularly if an answer has not been filed by a defendant, or, indeed, to afford the parties an opportunity to modify by stipulation the timing or scope of these obligations. The time of this meeting is generally left to the parties provided it is held at least 14 days before a scheduling conference is held or before a scheduling order is due under Rule 16(b). In cases in which no scheduling conference is held, this will mean that the meeting must ordinarily be held within 75 days after a defendant has first appeared in the case and hence that the initial disclosures would be due no later than 85 days after the first appearance of a defendant.

Before making its disclosures, a party has the obligation under subdivision (g)(1) to make a reasonable inquiry into the facts of the case. The rule does not demand an exhaustive investigation at this stage of the case, but one that is reasonable under the circumstances, focusing on the facts that are alleged with particularity in the pleadings. The type of investigation that can be expected at this point will vary based upon such factors as the number and complexity of the issues; the location, nature, number, and availability of potentially relevant witnesses and documents; the extent of past working relationships between the attorney and the client, particularly in handling related or similar litigation; and of course how long the party has to conduct an investigation, either before or after filing of the case. As provided in the last sentence of subdivision (a)(1), a party is not excused from the duty of disclosure merely because its investigation is incomplete. The party should make its initial disclosures based on the pleadings and the information then reasonably available to it. As its investigation continues and as the issues in the pleadings are clarified, it should supplement its disclosures as required by subdivision (e)(1). A party is not relieved from its obligation of disclosure merely because another party has not made its disclosures or has made an inadequate disclosure.

It will often be desirable, particularly if the claims made in the complaint are broadly stated, for the parties to have their Rule 26(f) meeting early in the case, perhaps before a defendant has answered the complaint or had time to conduct other than a cursory investigation. In such circumstances, in order to facilitate more meaningful and useful initial disclosures, they can and should stipulate to a period of more than 10 days after the meeting in which to make these disclosures, at least for defendants who had no advance notice of the potential litigation. A stipulation at an early meeting affording such a defendant at least 60 days after receiving the complaint in which to make its disclosures under subdivision (a)(1)—a period that is two weeks longer than the time formerly specified for responding to interrogatories served with a complaint—should be adequate and appropriate in most cases.

New matter is shown in italics; matter to be omitted is lined through

Paragraph (2). This paragraph imposes an additional duty to disclose information regarding expert testimony sufficiently in advance of trial that opposing parties have a reasonable opportunity to prepare for effective cross examination and perhaps arrange for expert testimony from other witnesses. Normally the court should prescribe a time for these disclosures in a scheduling order under Rule 16(b), and in most cases the party with the burden of proof on an issue should disclose its expert testimony on that issue before other parties are required to make their disclosures with respect to that issue. In the absence of such a direction, the disclosures are to be made by all parties at least 90 days before the trial date or the date by which the case is to be ready for trial, except that an additional 30 days is allowed (unless the court specifies another time) for disclosure of expert testimony to be used solely to contradict or rebut the testimony that may be presented by another party's expert. For a discussion of procedures that have been used to enhance the reliability of expert testimony, see M. Graham, *Expert Witness Testimony and the Federal Rules of Evidence: Insuring Adequate Assurance of Trustworthiness,* 1986 *U.Ill.L.Rev.* 90.

Paragraph (2)(B) requires that persons retained or specially employed to provide expert testimony, or whose duties as an employee of the party regularly involve the giving of expert testimony, must prepare a detailed and complete written report, stating the testimony the witness is expected to present during direct examination, together with the reasons therefor. The information disclosed under the former rule in answering interrogatories about the "substance" of expert testimony was frequently so sketchy and vague that it rarely dispensed with the need to depose the expert and often was even of little help in preparing for a deposition of the witness. Revised Rule 37(c)(1) provides an incentive for full disclosure; namely, that a party will not ordinarily be permitted to use on direct examination any expert testimony not so disclosed. Rule 26(a)(2)(B) does not preclude counsel from providing assistance to experts in preparing the reports, and indeed, with experts such as automobile mechanics, this assistance may be needed. Nevertheless, the report, which is intended to set forth the substance of the direct examination, should be written in a manner that reflects the testimony to be given by the witness and it must be signed by the witness.

The report is to disclose the data and other information considered by the expert and any exhibits or charts that summarize or support the expert's opinions. Given this obligation of disclosure, litigants should no longer be able to argue that materials furnished to their experts to be used in forming their opinions—whether or not ultimately relied upon by the expert—are privileged or otherwise protected from disclosure when such persons are testifying or being deposed.

Revised subdivision (b)(4)(A) authorizes the deposition of expert witnesses. Since depositions of experts required to prepare a written report may be taken only after the report has been has been served, the length of the deposition of such experts should be reduced, and in many cases the report may eliminate the need for a deposition. Revised subdivision (e)(1) requires disclosure of any material changes made in the opinions of an expert from whom a report is required, whether the changes are in the written report or in testimony given at a deposition.

For convenience, this rule and revised Rule 30 continue to use the term "expert" to refer to those persons who will testify under Rule 702 of the Federal Rules of Evidence with respect to scientific, technical, and other specialized matters. The requirement of a written report in paragraph (2)(B), however, applies only to those experts who are retained or specially employed to provide such testimony in the case or whose duties as an employee of a party regularly involve the giving of such testimony. A treating physician, for example, can be deposed or called to testify at trial without any requirement for a written report. By local rule, order, or written

---

New matter is shown in italics; matter to be omitted is lined through

stipulation, the requirement of a written report may be waived for particular experts or imposed upon additional persons who will provide opinions under Rule 702.

Paragraph (3). This paragraph imposes an additional duty to disclose, without any request, information customarily needed in final preparation for trial. These disclosures are to be made in accordance with schedules adopted by the court under Rule 16(b) or by special order. If no such schedule is directed by the court, the disclosures are to be made at least 30 days before commencement of the trial. By its terms, rule 26(a)(3) does not require disclosure of evidence to be used solely for impeachment purposes; however, disclosure of such evidence—as well as other items relating to conduct of trial—may be required by local rule or a pretrial order.

Subparagraph (A) requires the parties to designate the persons whose testimony they may present as substantive evidence at trial, whether in person or by deposition. Those who will probably be called as witnesses should be listed separately from those who are not likely to be called but who are being listed in order to preserve the right to do so if needed because of developments during trial. Revised Rule 37(c)(1) provides that only persons so listed may be used at trial to present substantive evidence. This restriction does not apply unless the omission was "without substantial justification" and hence would not bar an unlisted witness if the need for such testimony is based upon developments during trial that could not reasonably have been anticipated—*e.g.*, a change of testimony.

Listing a witness does not obligate the party to secure the attendance of the person at trial, but should preclude the party from objecting if the person is called to testify by another party who did not list the person as a witness.

Subparagraph (B) requires the party to indicate which of these potential witnesses will be presented by deposition at trial. A party expecting to use at trial a deposition not recorded by stenographic means is required by revised Rule 32 to provide the court with a transcript of the pertinent portions of such depositions. This rule requires that copies of the transcript of a nonstenographic deposition be provided to other parties in advance of trial for verification, an obvious concern since counsel often utilize their own personnel to prepare transcripts from audio or video tapes. By order or local rule, the court may require that parties designate the particular portions of stenographic depositions to be used at trial.

Subparagraph (C) requires disclosure of exhibits, including summaries (whether to be offered in lieu of other documentary evidence or to be used as an aid in understanding such evidence), that may be offered as substantive evidence. The rule requires a separate listing of each such exhibit, though it should permit voluminous items of a similar or standardized character to be described by meaningful categories. For example, unless the court has otherwise directed, a series of vouchers might be shown collectively as a single exhibit with their starting and ending dates. As with witnesses, the exhibits that will probably be offered are to be listed separately from those which are unlikely to be offered but which are listed in order to preserve the right to do so if needed because of developments during trial. Under revised Rule 37(c)(1) the court can permit use of unlisted documents the need for which could not reasonably have been anticipated in advance of trial.

Upon receipt of these final pretrial disclosures, other parties have 14 days (unless a different time is specified by the court) to disclose any objections they wish to preserve to the usability of the deposition testimony or to the admissibility of the documentary evidence (other than under Rules 402 and 403 of the Federal Rules of Evidence). Similar provisions have become commonplace either in pretrial orders or by local rules, and significantly expedite the presentation of evidence at trial, as well as eliminate the need to have available witnesses to provide "foundation" testimony for most items of documentary evidence. The listing of a potential objection does not

---

New matter is shown in italics; matter to be omitted is lined through

constitute the making of that objection or require the court to rule on the objection; rather, it preserves the right of the party to make the objection when and as appropriate during trial. The court may, however, elect to treat the listing as a motion "in limine" and rule upon the objections in advance of trial to the extent appropriate.

The time specified in the rule for the final pretrial disclosures is relatively close to the trial date. The objective is to eliminate the time and expense in making these disclosures of evidence and objections in those cases that settle shortly before trial, while affording a reasonable time for final preparation for trial in those cases that do not settle. In many cases, it will be desirable for the court in a scheduling or pretrial order to set an earlier time for disclosures of evidence and provide more time for disclosing potential objections.

Paragraph (4). This paragraph prescribes the form of disclosures. A signed written statement is required, reminding the parties and counsel of the solemnity of the obligations imposed; and the signature on the initial or pretrial disclosure is a certification under subdivision (g)(1) that it is complete and correct as of the time when made. Consistent with Rule 5(d), these disclosures are to be filed with the court unless otherwise directed. It is anticipated that many courts will direct that expert reports required under paragraph (2)(B) not be filed until needed in connection with a motion or for trial.

Paragraph (5). This paragraph is revised to take note of the availability of revised Rule 45 for inspection from non-parties of documents and premises without the need for a deposition.

Subdivision (b). This subdivision is revised in several respects. First, former paragraph (1) is subdivided into two paragraphs for ease of reference and to avoid renumbering of paragraphs (3) and (4). Textual changes are then made in new paragraph (2) to enable the court to keep tighter rein on the extent of discovery. The information explosion of recent decades has greatly increased both the potential cost of wide-ranging discovery and the potential for discovery to be used as an instrument for delay or oppression. Amendments to Rules 30, 31, and 33 place presumptive limits on the number of depositions and interrogatories, subject to leave of court to pursue additional discovery. The revisions in Rule 26(b)(2) are intended to provide the court with broader discretion to impose additional restrictions on the scope and extent of discovery and to authorize courts that develop case tracking systems based on the complexity of cases to increase or decrease by local rule the presumptive number of depositions and interrogatories allowed in particular types or classifications of cases. The revision also dispels any doubt as to the power of the court to impose limitations on the length of depositions under Rule 30 or on the number of requests for admission under Rule 36.

Second, former paragraph (2), relating to insurance, has been relocated as part of the required initial disclosures under subdivision (a)(1)(D), and revised to provide for disclosure of the policy itself.

Third, paragraph (4)(A) is revised to provide that experts who are expected to be witnesses will be subject to deposition prior to trial, conforming the norm stated in the rule to the actual practice followed in most courts, in which depositions of experts have become standard. Concerns regarding the expense of such depositions should be mitigated by the fact that the expert's fees for the deposition will ordinarily be borne by the party taking the deposition. The requirement under subdivision (a)(2)(B) of a complete and detailed report of the expected testimony of certain forensic experts may, moreover, eliminate the need for some such depositions or at least reduce the length of the depositions. Accordingly, the deposition of an

---

New matter is shown in italics; matter to be omitted is lined through

expert required by subdivision (a)(2)(B) to provide a written report may be taken only after the report has been served.

Paragraph (4)(C), bearing on compensation of experts, is revised to take account of the changes in paragraph (4)(A).

Paragraph (5) is a new provision. A party must notify other parties if it is withholding materials otherwise subject to disclosure under the rule or pursuant to a discovery request because it is asserting a claim of privilege or work product protection. To withhold materials without such notice is contrary to the rule, subjects the party to sanctions under Rule 37(b)(2), and may be viewed as a waiver of the privilege or protection.

The party must also provide sufficient information to enable other parties to evaluate the applicability of the claimed privilege or protection. Although the person from whom the discovery is sought decides whether to claim a privilege or protection, the court ultimately decides whether, if this claim is challenged, the privilege or protection applies. Providing information pertinent to the applicability of the privilege or protection should reduce the need for in camera examination of the documents.

The rule does not attempt to define for each case what information must be provided when a party asserts a claim of privilege or work product protection. Details concerning time, persons, general subject matter, etc., may be appropriate if only a few items are withheld, but may be unduly burdensome when voluminous documents are claimed to be privileged or protected, particularly if the items can be described by categories. A party can seek relief through a protective order under subdivision (c) if compliance with the requirement for providing this information would be an unreasonable burden. In rare circumstances some of the pertinent information affecting applicability of the claim, such as the identity of the client, may itself be privileged; the rule provides that such information need not be disclosed.

The obligation to provide pertinent information concerning withheld privileged materials applies only to items "otherwise discoverable." If a broad discovery request is made—for example, for all documents of a particular type during a twenty year period—and the responding party believes in good faith that production of documents for more than the past three years would be unduly burdensome, it should make its objection to the breadth of the request and, with respect to the documents generated in that three year period, produce the unprivileged documents and describe those withheld under the claim of privilege. If the court later rules that documents for a seven year period are properly discoverable, the documents for the additional four years should then be either produced (if not privileged) or described (if claimed to be privileged).

Subdivision (c). The revision requires that before filing a motion for a protective order the movant must confer—either in person or by telephone—with the other affected parties in a good faith effort to resolve the discovery dispute without the need for court intervention. If the movant is unable to get opposing parties even to discuss the matter, the efforts in attempting to arrange such a conference should be indicated in the certificate.

Subdivision (d). This subdivision is revised to provide that formal discovery—as distinguished from interviews of potential witnesses and other informal discovery—not commence until the parties have met and conferred as required by subdivision (f). Discovery can begin earlier if authorized under Rule 30(a)(2)(C) (deposition of person about to leave the country) or by local rule, order, or stipulation. This will be appropriate in some cases, such as those involving requests for a preliminary injunction or motions challenging personal jurisdiction. If a local rule exempts any

---

New matter is shown in italics; matter to be omitted is lined through

types of cases in which discovery may be needed from the requirement of a meeting under Rule 26(f), it should specify when discovery may commence in those cases.

The meeting of counsel is to take place as soon as practicable and in any event at least 14 days before the date of the scheduling conference under Rule 16(b) or the date a scheduling order is due under Rule 16(b). The court can assure that discovery is not unduly delayed either by entering a special order or by setting the case for a scheduling conference.

Subdivision (e). This subdivision is revised to provide that the requirement for supplementation applies to all disclosures required by subdivisions (a)(1)–(3). Like the former rule, the duty, while imposed on a "party," applies whether the corrective information is learned by the client or by the attorney. Supplementations need not be made as each new item of information is learned but should be made at appropriate intervals during the discovery period, and with special promptness as the trial date approaches. It may be useful for the scheduling order to specify the time or times when supplementations should be made.

The revision also clarifies that the obligation to supplement responses to formal discovery requests applies to interrogatories, requests for production, and requests for admissions, but not ordinarily to deposition testimony. However, with respect to experts from whom a written report is required under subdivision (a)(2)(B), changes in the opinions expressed by the expert whether in the report or at a subsequent deposition are subject to a duty of supplemental disclosure under subdivision (e)(1).

The obligation to supplement disclosures and discovery responses applies whenever a party learns that its prior disclosures or responses are in some material respect incomplete or incorrect. There is, however, no obligation to provide supplemental or corrective information that has been otherwise made known to the parties in writing or during the discovery process, as when a witness not previously disclosed is identified during the taking of a deposition or when an expert during a deposition corrects information contained in an earlier report.

Subdivision (f). This subdivision was added in 1980 to provide a party threatened with abusive discovery with a special means for obtaining judicial intervention other than through discrete motions under Rules 26(c) and 37(a). The amendment envisioned a two-step process: first, the parties would attempt to frame a mutually agreeable plan; second, the court would hold a "discovery conference" and then enter an order establishing a schedule and limitations for the conduct of discovery. It was contemplated that the procedure, an elective one triggered on request of a party, would be used in special cases rather than as a routine matter. As expected, the device has been used only sparingly in most courts, and judicial controls over the discovery process have ordinarily been imposed through scheduling orders under Rule 16(b) or through rulings on discovery motions.

The provisions relating to a conference with the court are removed from subdivision (f). This change does not signal any lessening of the importance of judicial supervision. Indeed, there is a greater need for early judicial involvement to consider the scope and timing of the disclosure requirements of Rule 26(a) and the presumptive limits on discovery imposed under these rules or by local rules. Rather, the change is made because the provisions addressing the use of conferences with the court to control discovery are more properly included in Rule 16, which is being revised to highlight the court's powers regarding the discovery process.

The desirability of some judicial control of discovery can hardly be doubted. Rule 16, as revised, requires that the court set a time for completion of discovery and authorizes various other orders affecting the scope, timing, and extent of discovery and disclosures. Before entering such orders, the court should consider the views of the parties, preferably by means of a conference, but at the least through written

---

New matter is shown in italics; matter to be omitted is lined through

submissions. Moreover, it is desirable that the parties' proposals regarding discovery be developed through a process where they meet in person, informally explore the nature and basis of the issues, and discuss how discovery can be conducted most efficiently and economically.

As noted above, former subdivision (f) envisioned the development of proposed discovery plans as an optional procedure to be used in relatively few cases. The revised rule directs that in all cases not exempted by local rule or special order the litigants must meet in person and plan for discovery. Following this meeting, the parties submit to the court their proposals for a discovery plan and can begin formal discovery. Their report will assist the court in seeing that the timing and scope of disclosures under revised Rule 26(a) and the limitations on the extent of discovery under these rules and local rules are tailored to the circumstances of the particular case.

To assure that the court has the litigants' proposals before deciding on a scheduling order and that the commencement of discovery is not delayed unduly, the rule provides that the meeting of the parties take place as soon as practicable and in any event at least 14 days before a scheduling conference is held or before a scheduling order is due under Rule 16(b). (Rule 16(b) requires that a scheduling order be entered within 90 days after the first appearance of a defendant or, if earlier, within 120 days after the complaint has been served on any defendant.) The obligation to participate in the planning process is imposed on all parties that have appeared in the case, including defendants who, because of a pending Rule 12 motion, may not have yet filed an answer in the case. Each such party should attend the meeting, either through one of its attorneys or in person if unrepresented. If more parties are joined or appear after the initial meeting, an additional meeting may be desirable.

Subdivision (f) describes certain matters that should be accomplished at the meeting and included in the proposed discovery plan. This listing does not exclude consideration of other subjects, such as the time when any dispositive motions should be filed and when the case should be ready for trial.

The parties are directed under subdivision (a)(1) to make the disclosures required by that subdivision at or within 10 days after this meeting. In many cases the parties should use the meeting to exchange, discuss, and clarify their respective disclosures. In other cases, it may be more useful if the disclosures are delayed until after the parties have discussed at the meeting the claims and defenses in order to define the issues with respect to which the initial disclosures should be made. As discussed in the Notes to subdivision (a)(1), the parties may also need to consider whether a stipulation extending this 10–day period would be appropriate, as when a defendant would otherwise have less than 60 days after being served in which to make its initial disclosure. The parties should also discuss at the meeting what additional information, although not subject to the disclosure requirements, can be made available informally without the necessity for formal discovery requests.

The report is to be submitted to the court within 10 days after the meeting and should not be difficult to prepare. In most cases counsel should be able to agree that one of them will be responsible for its preparation and submission to the court. Form 35 has been added in the Appendix to the Rules, both to illustrate the type of report that is contemplated and to serve as a checklist for the meeting.

The litigants are expected to attempt in good faith to agree on the contents of the proposed discovery plan. If they cannot agree on all aspects of the plan, their report to the court should indicate the competing proposals of the parties on those items, as well as the matters on which they agree. Unfortunately, there may be cases in which, because of disagreements about time or place or for other reasons, the

---

New matter is shown in italics; matter to be omitted is lined through

meeting is not attended by all parties or, indeed, no meeting takes place. In such situations, the report—or reports—should describe the circumstances and the court may need to consider sanctions under Rule 37(g).

By local rule or special order, the court can exempt particular cases or types of cases from the meet-and-confer requirement of subdivision (f). In general this should include any types of cases which are exempted by local rule from the requirement for a scheduling order under Rule 16(b), such as cases in which there will be no discovery (*e.g.*, bankruptcy appeals and reviews of social security determinations). In addition, the court may want to exempt cases in which discovery is rarely needed (*e.g.*, government collection cases and proceedings to enforce administrative summonses) or in which a meeting of the parties might be impracticable (*e.g.*, actions by unrepresented prisoners). Note that if a court exempts from the requirements for a meeting any types of cases in which discovery may be needed, it should indicate when discovery may commence in those cases.

Subdivision (g). Paragraph (1) is added to require signatures on disclosures, a requirement that parallels the provisions of paragraph (2) with respect to discovery requests, responses, and objections. The provisions of paragraph (3) have been modified to be consistent with Rules 37(a)(4) and 37(c)(1); in combination, these rules establish sanctions for violation of the rules regarding disclosures and discovery matters. Amended Rule 11 no longer applies to such violations.

Advisory Committee's Note to 2000 Amendment

(a) Required Disclosures; Methods to Discover Additional Matter.

(1) Initial Disclosures. Except *in categories of proceedings specified in Rule 26(a)(1)(E), or* to the extent otherwise stipulated or directed by order ~~or local rule~~, a party ~~shall~~ *must*, without awaiting a discovery request, provide to other parties:

(A) the name and, if known, the address and telephone number of each individual likely to have discoverable information *that the disclosing party may use to support its claims or defenses, unless solely for impeachment* ~~relevant to disputed facts alleged with particularity in the pleadings~~, identifying the subjects of the information;

(B) a copy of, or a description by category and location of, all documents, data compilations, and tangible things *that are* in the possession, custody, or control of the party *and that the disclosing party may use to support its claims or defenses, unless solely for impeachment* ~~that are relevant to disputed facts alleged with particularity in the pleadings~~;

(C) a computation of any category of damages claimed by the disclosing party, making available for inspection and copying as under Rule 34 the documents or other evidentiary material, not privileged or protected from disclosure, on which

---

New matter is shown in italics; matter to be omitted is lined through

such computation is based, including materials bearing on the nature and extent of injuries suffered; and

(D) for inspection and copying as under Rule 34 any insurance agreement under which any person carrying on an insurance business may be liable to satisfy part or all of a judgment which may be entered in the action or to indemnify or reimburse for payments made to satisfy the judgment.

(E) The following categories of proceedings are exempt from initial disclosure under Rule 26(a)(1):

 (i) an action for review on an administrative record;

 (ii) a petition for habeas corpus or other proceeding to challenge a criminal conviction or sentence;

 (iii) an action brought without counsel by a person in custody of the United States, a state, or a state subdivision;

 (iv) an action to enforce or quash an administrative summons or subpoena;

 (v) an action by the United States to recover benefit payments;

 (vi) an action by the United States to collect on a student loan guaranteed by the United States;

 (vii) a proceeding ancillary to proceedings in other courts; and

 (viii) an action to enforce an arbitration award.

~~Unless otherwise stipulated or directed by the court,~~ *T*these disclosures *must* ~~shall~~ be made at or within *14* ~~10~~ days after the *Rule 26(f) conference* ~~meeting of the parties under subdivision (f).~~ *unless a different time is set by stipulation or court order, or unless a party objects during the conference that initial disclosures are not appropriate in the circumstances of the action and states the objection in the Rule 26(f) discovery plan. In ruling on the objection, the court must determine what disclosures—if any—are to be made, and set the time for disclosure. Any party first served or otherwise joined after the Rule 26(f) conference must make these disclosures within 30 days after being served or joined unless a different time is set by stipulation or court order.* A party *must* ~~shall~~ make its initial disclosures based on the information then reasonably available to it and is not excused from making its disclosures because it has not fully completed its investigation of the case or because it challenges the sufficiency of another party's disclosures or because another party has not made its disclosures.

New matter is shown in italics; matter to be omitted is lined through

(3) Pretrial Disclosures. In addition to the disclosures required *by Rule 26(a)(1) and (2)* in the preceding paragraphs, a party shall *must* provide to other parties *and promptly file with the court* the following information regarding the evidence that it may present at trial other than solely for impeachment purposes:

(A) the name and, if not previously provided, the address and telephone number of each witness, separately identifying those whom the party expects to present and those whom the party may call if the need arises;

(B) the designation of those witnesses whose testimony is expected to be presented by means of a deposition and, if not taken stenographically, a transcript of the pertinent portions of the deposition testimony; and

(C) an appropriate identification of each document or other exhibit, including summaries of other evidence, separately identifying those which the party expects to offer and those which the party may offer if the need arises.

Unless otherwise directed by the court, these disclosures shall *must* be made at least 30 days before trial. Within 14 days thereafter, unless a different time is specified by the court, a party may serve and *promptly* file a list disclosing (i) any objections to the use under Rule 32(a) of a deposition designated by another party under subparagraph (B) *Rule 26(a)(3)(B),* and (ii) any objection, together with the grounds therefor, that may be made to the admissibility of materials identified under subparagraph (C) *Rule 26(a)(3)(C).* Objections not so disclosed, other than objections under Rules 402 and 403 of the Federal Rules of Evidence, shall be deemed *are* waived unless excused by the court for good cause shown.

(4) Form of Disclosures; Filing. Unless *the court orders* otherwise directed by order or local rule, all disclosures under paragraphs *Rules 26(a)*(1) through (3) *must* shall be made in writing, signed, *and* served., and promptly filed with the court.

(b) Discovery Scope and Limits. Unless otherwise limited by order of the court in accordance with these rules. the scope of discovery is as follows:

(1) In General. Parties may obtain discovery regarding any matter, not privileged, *that* which is relevant to the subject matter involved in the pending action, whether it relates to the claim or defense of the party seeking discovery or to the claim or defense of any other party, including the existence, description, nature, custody, condition, and location of any books, documents, or other tangible things and the identity and location of persons having knowledge of any discoverable mat-

New matter is shown in italics; matter to be omitted is lined through

ter. *For good cause, the court may order discovery of any matter relevant to the subject matter involved in the action. Relevant* ~~The~~ information ~~sought~~ need not be admissible at the trial if the *discovery* ~~information sought~~ appears reasonably calculated to lead to the discovery of admissible evidence. *All discovery is subject to the limitations imposed by Rule 26(b)(2)(i), (ii), and (iii).*

(2) Limitations. By order ~~or by local rule~~, the court may alter the limits in these rules on the number of depositions and interrogatories, *or* ~~and may also limit~~ the length of depositions under Rule 30. ~~and~~ *By order or local rule, the court may also limit* the number of requests under Rule 36. The frequency or extent of use of the discovery methods otherwise permitted under these rules and by any local rule shall be limited by the court if it determines that: (i) the discovery sought is unreasonably cumulative or duplicative, or is obtainable from some other source that is more convenient, less burdensome, or less expensive; (ii) the party seeking discovery has had ample opportunity by discovery in the action to obtain the information sought; or (iii) the burden or expense of the proposed discovery outweighs its likely benefit, taking into account the needs of the case, the amount in controversy, the parties' resources, the importance of the issues at stake in the litigation, and the importance of the proposed discovery in resolving the issues. The court may act upon its own initiative after reasonable notice or pursuant to a motion under ~~subdivision~~ *Rule 26*(c).

(d) Timing and Sequence of Discovery. Except *in categories of proceedings exempted from initial disclosure under Rule 26(a)(1)(E), or* when authorized under these rules or by ~~local rule,~~ order~~,~~ or agreement of the parties, a party may not seek discovery from any source before the parties have ~~met and~~ conferred as required by ~~subdivision~~ *Rule 26*(f). Unless the court upon motion, for the convenience of parties and witnesses and in the interests of justice, orders otherwise, methods of discovery may be used in any sequence, and the fact that a party is conducting discovery, whether by deposition or otherwise, ~~shall~~ *does* not operate to delay any other party's discovery.

(f) Conference ~~Meeting~~ of Parties; Planning for Discovery. Except in *categories of proceedings* ~~actions~~ exempted *from initial disclosure under Rule 26(a)(1)(E)* ~~by local rule~~ or when otherwise ordered, the parties ~~shall~~ *must*, as soon as practicable and in any event at least *21* ~~14~~ days before a scheduling conference is held or a scheduling order is due under Rule 16(b), *confer* ~~meet~~ to *consider* ~~discuss~~ the nature and basis of their claims and defenses and the possibilities for a prompt settlement or resolution of the case, to make or arrange for the disclosures required by ~~subdivision~~ *Rule 26*(a)(1), and to develop a proposed discovery plan. ~~The plan shall~~ *that* indicates the parties' views and proposals concerning:

(1) what changes should be made in the timing, form, or requirement for disclosures under ~~subdivision~~ *Rule 26*(a) ~~or local rule~~, including a statement as to when disclosures under ~~subdivision~~ *Rule 26*(a)(1) were made or will be made;

(2) the subjects on which discovery may be needed, when discovery should be completed, and whether discovery should be conducted in phases or be limited to or focused upon particular issues;

(3) what changes should be made in the limitations on discovery imposed under these rules or by local rule, and what other limitations should be imposed; and

(4) any other orders that should be entered by the court under ~~subdivision~~ *Rule 26*(c) or under Rule 16(b) and (c).

The attorneys of record and all unrepresented parties that have appeared in the case are jointly responsible for arranging *the conference* ~~and being present or represented at the meeting~~, for attempting in good faith to agree on the proposed discovery plan, and for submitting to the court within *14*~~10~~ days after the *conference* ~~meeting~~ a written report outlining the plan. *A court may order that the parties or attorneys attend the conference in person. If necessary to comply with its expedited schedule for Rule 16(b) conferences, a court may by local rule (i) require that the conference between the parties occur fewer than 21 days before the scheduling conference is held or a scheduling order is due under Rule 16(b), and (ii) require that the written report outlining the discovery plan be filed fewer than 14 days after the conference between the parties, or excuse the parties from submitting a written report and permit them to report orally on their discovery plan at the Rule 16(b) conference.*

———

Purposes of amendments. The Rule 26(a)(1) initial disclosure provisions are amended to establish a nationally uniform practice. The scope of the disclosure obligation is narrowed to cover only information that the disclosing party may use to support its position. In addition, the rule exempts specified categories of proceedings from initial disclosure, and permits a party who contends that disclosure is not appropriate in the circumstances of the case to present its objections to the court, which must then determine whether disclosure should be made. Related changes are made in Rules 26(d) and (f).

New matter is shown in italics; matter to be omitted is lined through

The initial disclosure requirements added by the 1993 amendments permitted local rules directing that disclosure would not be required or altering its operation. The inclusion of the "opt out" provision reflected the strong opposition to initial disclosure felt in some districts, and permitted experimentation with differing disclosure rules in those districts that were favorable to disclosure. The local option also recognized that—partly in response to the first publication in 1991 of a proposed disclosure rule—many districts had adopted a variety of disclosure programs under the aegis of the Civil Justice Reform Act. It was hoped that developing experience under a variety of disclosure systems would support eventual refinement of a uniform national disclosure practice. In addition, there was hope that local experience could identify categories of actions in which disclosure is not useful.

A striking array of local regimes in fact emerged for disclosure and related features introduced in 1993. *See* D. Stienstra. *Implementation of Disclosure in United States District Courts, With Specific Attention to Courts' Responses to Selected Amendments to Federal Rule of Civil Procedure 26* (Federal Judicial Center, March 30, 1998) (describing and categorizing local regimes). In its final report to Congress on the CJRA experience, the Judicial Conference recommended reexamination of the need for national uniformity, particularly in regard to initial disclosure. Judicial Conference, *Alternative Proposals for Reduction of Cost and Delay: Assessment of Principles, Guidelines and Techniques,* 175 F.R.D. 62, 98 (1997).

At the Committee's request, the Federal Judicial Center undertook a survey in 1997 to develop information on current disclosure and discovery practices. *See* T. Willging, J. Shapard, D. Stienstra & D. Miletich, *Discovery and Disclosure Practice, Problems, and Proposals for Change* (Federal Judicial Center, 1997). In addition, the Committee convened two conferences on discovery involving lawyers from around the country and received reports and recommendations on possible discovery amendments from a number of bar groups. Papers and other proceedings from the second conference are published in 39 Boston Col. L. Rev. 517–840 (1998).

The Committee has discerned widespread support for national uniformity. Many lawyers have experienced difficulty in coping with divergent disclosure and other practices as they move from one district to another. Lawyers surveyed by the Federal Judicial Center ranked adoption of a uniform national disclosure rule second among proposed rule changes (behind increased availability of judges to resolve discovery disputes) as a means to reduce litigation expenses without interfering with fair outcomes. *Discovery and Disclosure Practice, supra,* at 44–45. National uniformity is also a central purpose of the Rules Enabling Act of 1934, as amended, 28 U.S.C. §§ 2072–2077.

These amendments restore national uniformity to disclosure practice. Uniformity is also restored to other aspects of discovery by deleting most of the provisions authorizing local rules that vary the number of permitted discovery events or the length of depositions. Local rule options are also deleted from Rules 26(d) and (f).

Subdivision(a)(1). The amendments remove the authority to alter or opt out of the national disclosure requirements by local rule, invalidating not only formal local rules but also informal "standing" orders of an individual judge or court that purport to create exemptions from—or limit or expand—the disclosure provided under the national rule. *See* Rule 83. Case-specific orders remain proper, however, and are expressly required if a party objects that initial disclosure is not appropriate in the circumstances of the action. Specified categories of proceedings are excluded from initial disclosure under subdivision (a)(1)(E). In addition, the parties can stipulate to forgo disclosure, as was true before. But even in a case excluded by subdivision (a)(1)(E) or in which the parties stipulate to bypass disclosure, the court can order exchange of similar information in managing the action under Rule 16.

New matter is shown in italics; matter to be omitted is lined through

The initial disclosure obligation of subdivisions (a)(1)(A) and (B) has been narrowed to identification of witnesses and documents that the disclosing party may use to support its claims or defenses. "Use" includes any use at a pretrial conference, to support a motion, or at trial. The disclosure obligation is also triggered by intended use in discovery, apart from use to respond to a discovery request; use of a document to question a witness during a deposition is a common example. The disclosure obligation attaches both to witnesses and documents a party intends to use and also to witnesses and to documents the party intends to use if—in the language of Rule 26(a)(3)—"the need arises."

A party is no longer obligated to disclose witnesses or documents, whether favorable or unfavorable, that it does not intend to use. The obligation to disclose information the party may use connects directly to the exclusion sanction of Rule 37(c)(1). Because the disclosure obligation is limited to material that the party may use, it is no longer tied to particularized allegations in the pleadings. Subdivision (e)(1), which is unchanged, requires supplementation if information later acquired would have been subject to the disclosure requirement. As case preparation continues, a party must supplement its disclosures when it determines that it may use a witness or document that it did not previously intend to use.

The disclosure obligation applies to "claims and defenses," and therefore requires a party to disclose information it may use to support its denial or rebuttal of the allegations, claim, or defense of another party. It thereby bolsters the requirements of Rule 11(b)(4), which authorizes denials "warranted on the evidence," and disclosure should include the identity of any witness or document that the disclosing party may use to support such denials.

Subdivision (a)(3) presently excuses pretrial disclosure of information solely for impeachment. Impeachment information is similarly excluded from the initial disclosure requirement.

Subdivisions (a)(1)(C) and (D) are not changed. Should a case be exempted from initial disclosure by Rule 26(a)(1)(E) or by agreement or order, the insurance information described by subparagraph (D) should be subject to discovery, as it would have been under the principles of former Rule 26(b)(2), which was added in 1970 and deleted in 1993 as redundant in light of the new initial disclosure obligation.

New subdivision (a)(1)(E) excludes eight specified categories of proceedings from initial disclosure. The objective of this listing is to identify cases in which there is likely to be little or no discovery, or in which initial disclosure appears unlikely to contribute to the effective development of the case. The list was developed after a review of the categories excluded by local rules in various districts from the operation of Rule 16(b) and the conference requirements of subdivision (f). Subdivision (a)(1)(E) refers to categories of "proceedings" rather than categories of "actions" because some might not properly be labeled "actions." Case designations made by the parties or the clerk's office at the time of filing do not control application of the exemptions. The descriptions in the rule are generic and are intended to be administered by the parties—and, when needed, the courts—with the flexibility needed to adapt to gradual evolution in the types of proceedings that fall within these general categories. The exclusion of an action for review on an administrative record, for example, is intended to reach a proceeding that is framed as an "appeal" based solely on an administrative record. The exclusion should not apply to a proceeding in a form that commonly permits admission of new evidence to supplement the record. Item (vii), excluding a proceeding ancillary to proceedings in other courts, does not refer to bankruptcy proceedings; application of the Civil Rules to bankruptcy proceedings is determined by the Bankruptcy Rules.

New matter is shown in italics; matter to be omitted is lined through

Subdivision (a)(1)(E) is likely to exempt a substantial proportion of the cases in most districts from the initial disclosure requirement. Based on 1996 and 1997 case filing statistics, Federal Judicial Center staff estimate that, nationwide, these categories total approximately one-third of all civil filings.

The categories of proceedings listed in subdivision (a)(1)(E) are also exempted from the subdivision (f) conference requirement and from the subdivision (d) moratorium on discovery. Although there is no restriction on commencement of discovery in these cases, it is not expected that this opportunity will often lead to abuse since there is likely to be little or no discovery in most such cases. Should a defendant need more time to respond to discovery requests filed at the beginning of an exempted action, it can seek relief by motion under Rule 26(c) if the plaintiff is unwilling to defer the due date by agreement.

Subdivision (a)(1)(E)'s enumeration of exempt categories is exclusive. Although a case-specific order can alter or excuse initial disclosure, local rules or "standing" orders that purport to create general exemptions are invalid. *See* Rule 83.

The time for initial disclosure is extended to 14 days after the subdivision (f) conference unless the court orders otherwise. This change is integrated with corresponding changes requiring that the subdivision (f) conference be held 21 days before the Rule 16(b) scheduling conference or scheduling order, and that the report on the subdivision (f) conference be submitted to the court 14 days after the meeting. These changes provide a more orderly opportunity for the parties to review the disclosures, and for the court to consider the report. In many instances, the subdivision (f) conference and the effective preparation of the case would benefit from disclosure before the conference, and earlier disclosure is encouraged.

The presumptive disclosure date does not apply if a party objects to initial disclosure during the subdivision (f) conference and states its objection in the subdivision (f) discovery plan. The right to object to initial disclosure is not intended to afford parties an opportunity to "opt out" of disclosure unilaterally. It does provide an opportunity for an objecting party to present to the court its position that disclosure would be "inappropriate in the circumstances of the action." Making the objection permits the objecting party to present the question to the judge before any party is required to make disclosure. The court must then rule on the objection and determine what disclosures—if any—should be made. Ordinarily, this determination would be included in the Rule 16(b) scheduling order, but the court could handle the matter in a different fashion. Even when circumstances warrant suspending some disclosure obligations, others—such as the damages and insurance information called for by subdivisions (a)(1)(C) and (D)—may continue to be appropriate.

The presumptive disclosure date is also inapplicable to a party who is "first served or otherwise joined" after the subdivision (f) conference. This phrase refers to the date of service of a claim on a party in a defensive posture (such as a defendant or third-party defendant), and the date of joinder of a party added as a claimant or an intervenor. Absent court order or stipulation, a new party has 30 days in which to make its initial disclosures. But it is expected that later-added parties will ordinarily be treated the same as the original parties when the original parties have stipulated to forgo initial disclosure, or the court has ordered disclosure in a modified form.

Subdivision (a)(3). The amendment to Rule 5(d) forbids filing disclosures under subdivisions (a)(1) and (a)(2) until they are used in the proceeding, and this change is reflected in an amendment to subdivision (a)(4). Disclosures under subdivision (a)(3), however, may be important to the court in connection with the final pretrial conference or otherwise in preparing for trial. The requirement that objections to certain matters be filed points up the court's need to be provided with these materials. Accordingly, the requirement that subdivision (a)(3) materials be filed has

---

New matter is shown in italics; matter to be omitted is lined through

been moved from subdivision (a)(4) to subdivision (a)(3), and it has also been made clear that they—and any objections—should be filed "promptly."

Subdivision (a)(4). The filing requirement has been removed from this subdivision. Rule 5(d) has been amended to provide that disclosures under subdivisions (a)(1) and (a)(2) must not be filed until used in the proceeding. Subdivision (a)(3) has been amended to require that the disclosures it directs, and objections to them, be filed promptly. Subdivision (a)(4) continues to require that all disclosures under subdivisions (a)(1), (a)(2), and (a)(3) be in writing, signed, and served.

"Shall" is replaced by "must" under the program to conform amended rules to current style conventions when there is no ambiguity.

Subdivision (b)(1). In 1978, the Committee published for comment a proposed amendment, suggested by the Section of Litigation of the American Bar Association, to refine the scope of discovery by deleting the "subject matter" language. This proposal was withdrawn, and the Committee has since then made other changes in the discovery rules to address concerns about overbroad discovery. Concerns about costs and delay of discovery have persisted nonetheless, and other bar groups have repeatedly renewed similar proposals for amendment to this subdivision to delete the "subject matter" language. Nearly one-third of the lawyers surveyed in 1997 by the Federal Judicial Center endorsed narrowing the scope of discovery as a means of reducing litigation expense without interfering with fair case resolutions. *Discovery and Disclosure Practice, supra,* at 44–45 (1997). The Committee has heard that in some instances, particularly cases involving large quantities of discovery, parties seek to justify discovery requests that sweep far beyond the claims and defenses of the parties on the ground that they nevertheless have a bearing on the "subject matter" involved in the action.

The amendments proposed for subdivision (b)(1) include one element of these earlier proposals but also differ from these proposals in significant ways. The similarity is that the amendments describe the scope of party-controlled discovery in terms of matter relevant to the claim or defense of any party. The court, however, retains authority to order discovery of any matter relevant to the subject matter involved in the action for good cause. The amendment is designed to involve the court more actively in regulating the breadth of sweeping or contentious discovery. The Committee has been informed repeatedly by lawyers that involvement of the court in managing discovery is an important method of controlling problems of inappropriately broad discovery. Increasing the availability of judicial officers to resolve discovery disputes and increasing court management of discovery were both strongly endorsed by the attorneys surveyed by the Federal Judicial Center. *See Discovery and Disclosure Practice, supra,* at 44. Under the amended provisions, if there is an objection that discovery goes beyond material relevant to the parties' claims or defenses, the court would become involved to determine whether the discovery is relevant to the claims or defenses and, if not, whether good cause exists for authorizing it so long as it is relevant to the subject matter of the action. The good-cause standard warranting broader discovery is meant to be flexible.

The Committee intends that the parties and the court focus on the actual claims and defenses involved in the action. The dividing line between information relevant to the claims and defenses and that relevant only to the subject matter of the action cannot be defined with precision. A variety of types of information not directly pertinent to the incident in suit could be relevant to the claims or defenses raised in a given action. For example, other incidents of the same type, or involving the same product, could be properly discoverable under the revised standard. Information about organizational arrangements or filing systems of a party could be discoverable if likely to yield or lead to the discovery of admissible information. Similarly,

New matter is shown in italics; matter to be omitted is lined through

information that could be used to impeach a likely witness, although not otherwise relevant to the claims or defenses, might be properly discoverable. In each instance, the determination whether such information is discoverable because it is relevant to the claims or defenses depends on the circumstances of the pending action.

The rule change signals to the court that it has the authority to confine discovery to the claims and defenses asserted in the pleadings, and signals to the parties that they have no entitlement to discovery to develop new claims or defenses that are not already identified in the pleadings. In general, it is hoped that reasonable lawyers can cooperate to manage discovery without the need for judicial intervention. When judicial intervention is invoked, the actual scope of discovery should be determined according to the reasonable needs of the action. The court may permit broader discovery in a particular case depending on the circumstances of the case, the nature of the claims and defenses, and the scope of the discovery requested.

The amendments also modify the provision regarding discovery of information not admissible in evidence. As added in 1946, this sentence was designed to make clear that otherwise relevant material could not be withheld because it was hearsay or otherwise inadmissible. The Committee was concerned that the "reasonably calculated to lead to the discovery of admissible evidence" standard set forth in this sentence might swallow any other limitation on the scope of discovery. Accordingly, this sentence has been amended to clarify that information must be relevant to be discoverable, even though inadmissible, and that discovery of such material is permitted if reasonably calculated to lead to the discovery of admissible evidence. As used here, "relevant" means within the scope of discovery as defined in this subdivision, and it would include information relevant to the subject matter involved in the action if the court has ordered discovery to that limit based on a showing of good cause.

Finally, a sentence has been added calling attention to the limitations of subdivision (b)(2)(i), (ii), and (iii). These limitations apply to discovery that is otherwise within the scope of subdivision (b)(1). The Committee has been told repeatedly that courts have not implemented these limitations with the vigor that was contemplated. *See 8 Federal Practice & Procedure* § 2008.1 at 121. This otherwise redundant cross-reference has been added to emphasize the need for active judicial use of subdivision (b)(2) to control excessive discovery. *Cf. Crawford–El v. Britton*, 118 S. Ct. 1584, 1597 (1998) (quoting Rule 26(b)(2)(iii) and stating that "Rule 26 vests the trial judge with broad discretion to tailor discovery narrowly").

Subdivision (b)(2). Rules 30, 31, and 33 establish presumptive national limits on the numbers of depositions and interrogatories. New Rule 30(d)(2) establishes a presumptive limit on the length of depositions. Subdivision (b)(2) is amended to remove the previous permission for local rules that establish different presumptive limits on these discovery activities. There is no reason to believe that unique circumstances justify varying these nationally-applicable presumptive limits in certain districts. The limits can be modified by court order or agreement in an individual action, but "standing" orders imposing different presumptive limits are not authorized. Because there is no national rule limiting the number of Rule 36 requests for admissions, the rule continues to authorize local rules that impose numerical limits on them. This change is not intended to interfere with differentiated case management in districts that use this technique by case-specific order as part of their Rule 16 process.

Subdivision (d). The amendments remove the prior authority to exempt cases by local rule from the moratorium on discovery before the subdivision (f) conference, but the categories of proceedings exempted from initial disclosure under subdivision (a)(1)(E) are excluded from subdivision (d). The parties may agree to disregard the

New matter is shown in italics; matter to be omitted is lined through

moratorium where it applies, and the court may so order in a case, out "standing" orders altering the moratorium are not authorized.

Subdivision (f). As in subdivision (d), the amendments remove the prior authority to exempt cases by local rule from the conference requirement. The Committee has been informed that the addition of the conference was one of the most successful changes made in the 1993 amendments, and it therefore has determined to apply the conference requirement nationwide. The categories of proceedings exempted from initial disclosure under subdivision (a)(1)(E) are exempted from the conference requirement for the reasons that warrant exclusion from initial disclosure. The court may order that the conference need not occur in a case where otherwise required, or that it occur in a case otherwise exempted by subdivision (a)(1)(E). "Standing" orders altering the conference requirement for categories of cases are not authorized.

The rule is amended to require only a "conference" of the parties, rather than a "meeting." There are important benefits to face-to-face discussion of the topics to be covered in the conference, and those benefits may be lost if other means of conferring were routinely used when face-to-face meetings would not impose burdens. Nevertheless, geographic conditions in some districts may exact costs far out of proportion to these benefits. The amendment allows the court by case-specific order to require a face-to-face meeting, but "standing" orders so requiring are not authorized.

As noted concerning the amendments to subdivision (a)(1), the time for the conference has been changed to at least 21 days before the Rule 16 scheduling conference, and the time for the report is changed to no more than 14 days after the Rule 26(f) conference. This should ensure that the court will have the report well in advance of the scheduling conference or the entry of the scheduling order.

Since Rule 16 was amended in 1983 to mandate some case management activities in all courts, it has included deadlines for Completing these tasks to ensure that all courts do so within a reasonable time. Rule 26(f) was fit into this scheme when it was adopted in 1993. It was never intended, however, that the national requirements that certain activities be completed by a certain time should delay case management in districts that move much faster than the national rules direct, and the rule is therefore amended to permit such a court to adopt a local rule that shortens the period specified for the completion of these tasks.

"Shall" is replaced by "must," "does," or an active verb under the program to conform amended rules to current style conventions when there is no ambiguity.

Advisory Committee's Note to 2006 Amendment

(a) Required Disclosures; Methods to Discover Additional Matter.

(1) Initial Disclosures. Except in categories of proceedings specified in Rule 26(a)(1)(E), or to the extent otherwise stipulated or directed by order, a party must, without awaiting a discovery request, provide to other parties:

(A) the name and, if known, the address and telephone number of each individual likely to have discoverable informa-

---

New matter is shown in italics; matter to be omitted is lined through

tion that the disclosing party may use to support its claims or defenses, unless solely for impeachment, identifying the subjects of the information;

(B) a copy of, or a description by category and location of, all documents, *electronically stored information,* ~~data compilations,~~ and tangible things that are in the possession, custody, or control of the party and that the disclosing party may use to support its claims or defenses, unless solely for impeachment;

(E) The following categories of proceedings are exempt from initial disclosure under Rule 26(a)(1):

(ii) *a forfeiture action in rem arising from a federal statute;*

(~~iii~~*ii*) a petition for habeas corpus or other proceeding to challenge a criminal conviction or sentence;

(~~iii~~*iv*) an action brought without counsel by a person in custody of the United States, a state, or a state subdivision;

(~~iv~~*v*) an action to enforce or quash an administrative summons or subpoena;

(~~v~~*vi*) an action by the United States to recover benefit payments;

(~~vi~~*vii*) an action by the United States to collect on a student loan guaranteed by the United States;

(~~vii~~*viii*) a proceeding ancillary to proceedings in other courts; and

(~~viii~~*ix*) an action to enforce an arbitration award.

(b) Discovery Scope and Limits. Unless otherwise limited by order of the court in accordance with these rules, the scope of discovery is as follows:

(2) Limitations.

(A) By order, the court may alter the limits in these rules on the number of depositions and interrogatories or the length of depositions under Rule 30. By order or local rule, the court may also limit the number of requests under Rule 36.

(B) A party need not provide discovery of electronically stored information from sources that the party identifies as not reasonably accessible because of undue burden or cost. On motion to compel discovery or for a protective order, the party from whom discovery is sought must show that the information is not reasonably accessible because of undue burden or cost. If that showing is made, the court may nonetheless order discovery

---

New matter is shown in italics; matter to be omitted is lined through

from such sources if the requesting party shows good cause, considering the limitations of Rule 26(b)(2)(C). The court may specify conditions for the discovery.

(C) The frequency or extent of use of the discovery methods otherwise permitted under these rules and by any local rule shall be limited by the court if it determines that: (i) the discovery sought is unreasonably cumulative or duplicative, or is obtainable from some other source that is more convenient, less burdensome, or less expensive; (ii) the party seeking discovery has had ample opportunity by discovery in the action to obtain the information sought; or (iii) the burden or expense of the proposed discovery outweighs its likely benefit, taking into account the needs of the case, the amount in controversy, the parties' resources, the importance of the issues at stake in the litigation, and the importance of the proposed discovery in resolving the issues. The court may act upon its own initiative after reasonable notice or pursuant to a motion under Rule 26(c).

(5) Claims of Privilege or Protection of Trial–Preparation Materials.

(A) Information Withheld. When a party withholds information otherwise discoverable under these rules by claiming that it is privileged or subject to protection as trial-preparation material, the party shall make the claim expressly and shall describe the nature of the documents, communications, or things not produced or disclosed in a manner that, without revealing information itself privileged or protected, will enable other parties to assess the applicability of the privilege or protection.

(B) Information Produced. If information is produced in discovery that is subject to a claim of privilege or of protection as trial-preparation material, the party making the claim may notify any party that received the information of the claim and the basis for it. After being notified, a party must promptly return, sequester, or destroy the specified information and any copies it has and may not use or disclose the information until the claim is resolved. A receiving party may promptly present the information to the court under seal for a determination of the claim. If the receiving party disclosed the information before being notified, it must take reasonable steps to retrieve it. The producing party must preserve the information until the claim is resolved.

(f) Conference of Parties; Planning for Discovery. Except in categories of proceedings exempted from initial disclosure under Rule 26(a)(1)(E) or when otherwise ordered, the parties must, as soon as practicable and in any event at least 21 days before a scheduling conference is held or a scheduling order is due under Rule 16(b), confer to consider the nature and basis of their claims and defenses and the possibilities for a prompt settlement or resolution of the case, to make or arrange for the disclosures required by Rule 26(a)(1), *to discuss any issues relating to preserving discoverable information,* and to develop a proposed discovery plan that indicates the parties' views and proposals concerning:

(1) what changes should be made in the timing, form, or requirement for disclosures under Rule 26(a), including a statement as to when disclosures under Rule 26(a)(1) were made or will be made;

(2) the subjects on which discovery may be needed, when discovery should be completed, and whether discovery should be conducted in phases or be limited to or focused upon particular issues;

(3) any issues relating to disclosure or discovery of electronically stored information, including the form or forms in which it should be produced;

(4) any issues relating to claims of privilege or of protection as trial-preparation material, including—if the parties agree on a procedure to assert such claims after production—whether to ask the court to include their agreement in an order;

(5~~3~~) what changes should be made in the limitations on discovery imposed under these rules or by local rule, and what other limitations should be imposed; and

(6~~4~~) any other orders that should be entered by the court under Rule 26(c) or under Rule 16(b) and (c).

Subdivision (a). Rule 26(a)(1)(B) is amended to parallel Rule 34(a) by recognizing that a party must disclose electronically stored information as well as documents that it may use to support its claims or defenses. The term "electronically stored information" has the same broad meaning in Rule 26(a)(1) as in Rule 34(a). This amendment is consistent with the 1993 addition of Rule 26(a)(1)(B). The term "data compilations" is deleted as unnecessary because it is a subset of both documents and electronically stored information.

Civil forfeiture actions are added to the list of exemptions from Rule 26(a)(1) disclosure requirements. These actions are governed by new Supplemental Rule G. Disclosure is not likely to be useful.

Subdivision (b)(2). The amendment to Rule 26(b)(2) is designed to address issues raised by difficulties in locating, retrieving, and providing discovery of some electronically stored information. Electronic storage systems often make it easier to locate and retrieve information. These advantages are properly taken into account in

----

New matter is shown in italics; matter to be omitted is lined through

determining the reasonable scope of discovery in a particular case. But some sources of electronically stored information can be accessed only with substantial burden and cost. In a particular case, these burdens and costs may make the information on such sources not reasonably accessible.

It is not possible to define in a rule the different types of technological features that may affect the burdens and costs of accessing electronically stored information. Information systems are designed to provide ready access to information used in regular ongoing activities. They also may be designed so as to provide ready access to information that is not regularly used. But a system may retain information on sources that are accessible only by incurring substantial burdens or costs. Subparagraph (B) is added to regulate discovery from such sources.

Under this rule, a responding party should produce electronically stored information that is relevant, not privileged, and reasonably accessible, subject to the (b)(2)(C) limitations that apply to all discovery. The responding party must also identify, by category or type, the sources containing potentially responsive information that it is neither searching nor producing. The identification should, to the extent possible, provide enough detail to enable the requesting party to evaluate the burdens and costs of providing the discovery and the likelihood of finding responsive information on the identified sources.

A party's identification of sources of electronically stored information as not reasonably accessible does not relieve the party of its common-law or statutory duties to preserve evidence. Whether a responding party is required to preserve unsearched sources of potentially responsive information that it believes are not reasonably accessible depends on the circumstances of each case. It is often useful for the parties to discuss this issue early in discovery.

The volume of—and the ability to search—much electronically stored information means that in many cases the responding party will be able to produce information from reasonably accessible sources that will fully satisfy the parties' discovery needs. In many circumstances the requesting party should obtain and evaluate the information from such sources before insisting that the responding party search and produce information contained on sources that are not reasonably accessible. If the requesting party continues to seek discovery of information from sources identified as not reasonably accessible, the parties should discuss the burdens and costs of accessing and retrieving the information, the needs that may establish good cause for requiring all or part of the requested discovery even if the information sought is not reasonably accessible, and conditions on obtaining and producing the information that may be appropriate.

If the parties cannot agree whether, or on what terms, sources identified as not reasonably accessible should be searched and discoverable information produced, the issue may be raised either by a motion to compel discovery or by a motion for a protective order. The parties must confer before bringing either motion. If the parties do not resolve the issue and the court must decide, the responding party must show that the identified sources of information are not reasonably accessible because of undue burden or cost. The requesting party may need discovery to test this assertion. Such discovery might take the form of requiring the responding party to conduct a sampling of information contained on the sources identified as not reasonably accessible; allowing some form of inspection of such sources; or taking depositions of witnesses knowledgeable about the responding party's information systems.

Once it is shown that a source of electronically stored information is not reasonably accessible, the requesting party may still obtain discovery by showing good cause, considering the limitations of Rule 26(b)(2)(C) that balance the costs and

---

New matter is shown in italics; matter to be omitted is lined through

potential benefits of discovery. The decision whether to require a responding party to search for and produce information that is not reasonably accessible depends not only on the burdens and costs of doing so, but also on whether those burdens and costs can be justified in the circumstances of the case. Appropriate considerations may include: (1) the specificity of the discovery request; (2) the quantity of information available from other and more easily accessed sources; (3) the failure to produce relevant information that seems likely to have existed but is no longer available on more easily accessed sources; (4) the likelihood of finding relevant, responsive information that cannot be obtained from other, more easily accessed sources; (5) predictions as to the importance and usefulness of the further information; (6) the importance of the issues at stake in the litigation; and (7) the parties' resources.

The responding party has the burden as to one aspect of the inquiry—whether the identified sources are not reasonably accessible in light of the burdens and costs required to search for, retrieve, and produce whatever responsive information may be found. The requesting party has the burden of showing that its need for the discovery outweighs the burdens and costs of locating, retrieving, and producing the information. In some cases, the court will be able to determine whether the identified sources are not reasonably accessible and whether the requesting party has shown good cause for some or all of the discovery, consistent with the limitations of Rule 26(b)(2)(C), through a single proceeding or presentation. The good-cause determination, however, may be complicated because the court and parties may know little about what information the sources identified as not reasonably accessible might contain, whether it is relevant, or how valuable it may be to the litigation. In such cases, the parties may need some focused discovery, which may include sampling of the sources, to learn more about what burdens and costs are involved in accessing the information, what the information consists of, and how valuable it is for the litigation in light of information that can be obtained by exhausting other opportunities for discovery.

The good-cause inquiry and consideration of the Rule 26(b)(2)(C) limitations are coupled with the authority to set conditions for discovery. The conditions may take the form of limits on the amount, type, or sources of information required to be accessed and produced. The conditions may also include payment by the requesting party of part or all of the reasonable costs of obtaining information from sources that are not reasonably accessible. A requesting party's willingness to share or bear the access costs may be weighed by the court in determining whether there is good cause. But the producing party's burdens in reviewing the information for relevance and privilege may weigh against permitting the requested discovery.

The limitations of Rule 26(b)(2)(C) continue to apply to all discovery of electronically stored information, including that stored on reasonably accessible electronic sources.

Subdivision (b)(5). The Committee has repeatedly been advised that the risk of privilege waiver, and the work necessary to avoid it, add to the costs and delay of discovery. When the review is of electronically stored information, the risk of waiver, and the time and effort required to avoid it, can increase substantially because of the volume of electronically stored information and the difficulty in ensuring that all information to be produced has in fact been reviewed. Rule 26(b)(5)(A) provides a procedure for a party that has withheld information on the basis of privilege or protection as trial-preparation material to make the claim so that the requesting party can decide whether to contest the claim and the court can resolve the dispute. Rule 26(b)(5)(B) is added to provide a procedure for a party to assert a claim of privilege or trial-preparation material protection after information is produced in discovery in the action and, if the claim is contested, permit any party that received the information to present the matter to the court for resolution.

New matter is shown in italics; matter to be omitted is lined through

Rule 26(b)(5)(B) does not address whether the privilege or protection that is asserted after production was waived by the production. The courts have developed principles to determine whether, and under what circumstances, waiver results from inadvertent production of privileged or protected information. Rule 26(b)(5)(B) provides a procedure for presenting and addressing these issues. Rule 26(b)(5)(B) works in tandem with Rule 26(f), which is amended to direct the parties to discuss privilege issues in preparing their discovery plan, and which, with amended Rule 16(b), allows the parties to ask the court to include in an order any agreements the parties reach regarding issues of privilege or trial-preparation material protection. Agreements reached under Rule 26(f)(4) and orders including such agreements entered under Rule 16(b)(6) may be considered when a court determines whether a waiver has occurred. Such agreements and orders ordinarily control if they adopt procedures different from those in Rule 26(b)(5)(B).

A party asserting a claim of privilege or protection after production must give notice to the receiving party. That notice should be in writing unless the circumstances preclude it. Such circumstances could include the assertion of the claim during a deposition. The notice should be as specific as possible in identifying the information and stating the basis for the claim. Because the receiving party must decide whether to challenge the claim and may sequester the information and submit it to the court for a ruling on whether the claimed privilege or protection applies and whether it has been waived, the notice should be sufficiently detailed so as to enable the receiving party and the court to understand the basis for the claim and to determine whether waiver has occurred. Courts will continue to examine whether a claim of privilege or protection was made at a reasonable time when delay is part of the waiver determination under the governing law.

After receiving notice, each party that received the information must promptly return, sequester, or destroy the information and any copies it has. The option of sequestering or destroying the information is included in part because the receiving party may have incorporated the information in protected trial-preparation materials. No receiving party may use or disclose the information pending resolution of the privilege claim. The receiving party may present to the court the questions whether the information is privileged or protected as trial preparation material, and whether the privilege or protection has been waived. If it does so, it must provide the court with the grounds for the privilege or protection specified in the producing party's notice, and serve all parties. In presenting the question, the party may use the content of the information only to the extent permitted by the applicable law of privilege, protection for trial-preparation material, and professional responsibility.

If a party disclosed the information to nonparties before receiving notice of a claim of privilege or protection as trial-preparation material, it must take reasonable steps to retrieve the information and to return it, sequester it until the claim is resolved, or destroy it.

Whether the information is returned or not, the producing party must preserve the information pending the court's ruling on whether the claim of privilege or of protection is properly asserted and whether it was waived. As with claims made under Rule 26(b)(5)(A), there may be no ruling if the other parties do not contest the claim.

Subdivision (f). Rule 26(f) is amended to direct the parties to discuss discovery of electronically stored information during their discovery-planning conference. The rule focuses on "issues relating to disclosure or discovery of electronically stored information"; the discussion is not required in cases not involving electronic discovery, and the amendment imposes no additional requirements in those cases. When

---

New matter is shown in italics; matter to be omitted is lined through

the parties do anticipate disclosure or discovery of electronically stored information, discussion at the outset may avoid later difficulties or ease their resolution.

When a case involves discovery of electronically stored information, the issues to be addressed during the Rule 26(f) conference depend on the nature and extent of the contemplated discovery and of the parties' information systems. It may be important for the parties to discuss those systems, and accordingly important for counsel to become familiar with those systems before the conference. With that information, the parties can develop a discovery plan that takes into account the capabilities of their computer systems. In appropriate cases identification of, and early discovery from, individuals with special knowledge of a party's computer systems may be helpful.

The particular issues regarding electronically stored information that deserve attention during the discovery planning stage depend on the specifics of the given case. *See Manual for Complex Litigation* (4th) § 40.25(2) (listing topics for discussion in a proposed order regarding meet-and-confer sessions). For example, the parties may specify the topics for such discovery and the time period for which discovery will be sought. They may identify the various sources of such information within a party's control that should be searched for electronically stored information. They may discuss whether the information is reasonably accessible to the party that has it, including the burden or cost of retrieving and reviewing the information. *See* Rule 26(b)(2)(B). Rule 26(f)(3) explicitly directs the parties to discuss the form or forms in which electronically stored information might be produced. The parties may be able to reach agreement on the forms of production, making discovery more efficient. Rule 34(b) is amended to permit a requesting party to specify the form or forms in which it wants electronically stored information produced. If the requesting party does not specify a form, Rule 34(b) directs the responding party to state the forms it intends to use in the production. Early discussion of the forms of production may facilitate the application of Rule 34(b) by allowing the parties to determine what forms of production will meet both parties' needs. Early identification of disputes over the forms of production may help avoid the expense and delay of searches or productions using inappropriate forms.

Rule 26(f) is also amended to direct the parties to discuss any issues regarding preservation of discoverable information during their conference as they develop a discovery plan. This provision applies to all sorts of discoverable information, but can be particularly important with regard to electronically stored information. The volume and dynamic nature of electronically stored information may complicate preservation obligations. The ordinary operation of computers involves both the automatic creation and the automatic deletion or overwriting of certain information. Failure to address preservation issues early in the litigation increases uncertainty and raises a risk of disputes.

The parties' discussion should pay particular attention to the balance between the competing needs to preserve relevant evidence and to continue routine operations critical to ongoing activities. Complete or broad cessation of a party's routine computer operations could paralyze the party's activities. *Cf. Manual for Complex Litigation* (4th) § 11.422 ("A blanket preservation order may be prohibitively expensive and unduly burdensome for parties dependent on computer systems for their day-to-day operations.") The parties should take account of these considerations in their discussions, with the goal of agreeing on reasonable preservation steps.

The requirement that the parties discuss preservation does not imply that courts should routinely enter preservation orders. A preservation order entered over

---

New matter is shown in italics; matter to be omitted is lined through

objections should be narrowly tailored. Ex parte preservation orders should issue only in exceptional circumstances.

Rule 26(f) is also amended to provide that the parties should discuss any issues relating to assertions of privilege or of protection as trial-preparation materials, including whether the parties can facilitate discovery by agreeing on procedures for asserting claims of privilege or protection after production and whether to ask the court to enter an order that includes any agreement the parties reach. The Committee has repeatedly been advised about the discovery difficulties that can result from efforts to guard against waiver of privilege and work-product protection. Frequently parties find it necessary to spend large amounts of time reviewing materials requested through discovery to avoid waiving privilege. These efforts are necessary because materials subject to a claim of privilege or protection are often difficult to identify. A failure to withhold even one such item may result in an argument that there has been a waiver of privilege as to all other privileged materials on that subject matter. Efforts to avoid the risk of waiver can impose substantial costs on the party producing the material and the time required for the privilege review can substantially delay access for the party seeking discovery.

These problems often become more acute when discovery of electronically stored information is sought. The volume of such data, and the informality that attends use of e-mail and some other types of electronically stored information, may make privilege determinations more difficult, and privilege review correspondingly more expensive and time consuming. Other aspects of electronically stored information pose particular difficulties for privilege review. For example, production may be sought of information automatically included in electronic files but not apparent to the creator or to readers. Computer programs may retain draft language, editorial comments, and other deleted matter (sometimes referred to as "embedded data" or "embedded edits") in an electronic file but not make them apparent to the reader. Information describing the history, tracking, or management of an electronic file (sometimes called "metadata") is usually not apparent to the reader viewing a hard copy or a screen image. Whether this information should be produced may be among the topics discussed in the Rule 26(f) conference. If it is, it may need to be reviewed to ensure that no privileged information is included, further complicating the task of privilege review.

Parties may attempt to minimize these costs and delays by agreeing to protocols that minimize the risk of waiver. They may agree that the responding party will provide certain requested materials for initial examination without waiving any privilege or protection—sometimes known as a "quick peek." The requesting party then designates the documents it wishes to have actually produced. This designation is the Rule 34 request. The responding party then responds in the usual course, screening only those documents actually requested for formal production and asserting privilege claims as provided in Rule 26(b)(5)(A). On other occasions, parties enter agreements—sometimes called "clawback agreements"—that production without intent to waive privilege or protection should not be a waiver so long as the responding party identifies the documents mistakenly produced, and that the documents should be returned under those circumstances. Other voluntary arrangements may be appropriate depending on the circumstances of each litigation. In most circumstances, a party who receives information under such an arrangement cannot assert that production of the information waived a claim of privilege or of protection as trial-preparation material.

Although these agreements may not be appropriate for all cases, in certain cases they can facilitate prompt and economical discovery by reducing delay before the discovering party obtains access to documents, and by reducing the cost and burden of review by the producing party. A case-management or other order including such

New matter is shown in italics; matter to be omitted is lined through

agreements may further facilitate the discovery process. Form 35 is amended to include a report to the court about any agreement regarding protections against inadvertent forfeiture or waiver of privilege or protection that the parties have reached, and Rule 16(b) is amended to recognize that the court may include such an agreement in a case management or other order. If the parties agree to entry of such an order, their proposal should be included in the report to the court.

Rule 26(b)(5)(B) is added to establish a parallel procedure to assert privilege or protection as trial-preparation material after production, leaving the question of waiver to later determination by the court.

Rule 30. Depositions Upon Oral Examination

Advisory Committee's Note to 1970 Amendment

(a) When Depositions May Be Taken. After commencement of the action, any party may take the testimony of any person, including a party, by deposition upon oral examination. Leave of court, granted with or without notice, must be obtained only if the plaintiff seeks to take a deposition prior to the expiration of 30 days after service of the summons and complaint upon any defendant or service made under Rule 4(e), except that leave is not required (1) if a defendant has served a notice of taking deposition or otherwise sought discovery, or (2) if special notice is given as provided in subdivision (b)(2) of this rule. The attendance of witnesses may be compelled by subpoena as provided in Rule 45. The deposition of a person confined in prison may be taken only by leave of court on such terms as the court prescribes.

(a)(b) Notice of Examination: Time and Place *General Requirements; Special Notice; Non–Stenographic Recording; Production of Documents and Things; Deposition of Organization.*

(1) A party desiring to take the deposition of any person upon oral examination shall give reasonable notice in writing to every other party to the action. The notice shall state the time and place for taking the deposition and the name and address of each person to be examined, if known, and, if the name is not known, a general description sufficient to identify him or the particular class or group to which he belongs. *If a subpoena duces tecum is to be served on the person to be examined, a designation of the materials to be produced as set forth in the subpoena shall be attached to or included in the notice.*

(2) Leave of court is not required for the taking of a deposition by plaintiff if the notice (A) states that the person to be examined is about to go out of the district where the action is pending and more than 100 miles from the place of trial, or is about to go out of the United States, or is bound on a voyage to sea, and will be unavail-

---

New matter is shown in italics; matter to be omitted is lined through

able for examination unless his deposition is taken before expiration of the 30–day period, and (B) sets forth facts to support the statement. The plaintiff's attorney shall sign the notice, and his signature constitutes a certification by him that to the best of his knowledge, information, and belief the statement and supporting facts are true. The sanctions provided by Rule 11 are applicable to the certification.

If a party shows that when he was served with notice under this subdivision (b)(2) he was unable through the exercise of diligence to obtain counsel to represent him at the taking of the deposition, the deposition may not be used against him.

(3) ~~On motion of any party upon whom the notice is served, the~~ *The* court may for cause shown enlarge or shorten the time~~.~~ *for taking the deposition.*

(4) The court may upon motion order that the testimony at a deposition be recorded by other than stenographic means, in which event the order shall designate the manner of recording, preserving, and filing the deposition, and may include other provisions to assure that the recorded testimony will be accurate and trustworthy. If the order is made, a party may nevertheless arrange to have a stenographic transcription made at his own expense.

(5) The notice to a party deponent may be accompanied by a request made in compliance with Rule 34 for the production of documents and tangible things at the taking of the deposition. The procedure of Rule 34 shall apply to the request.

(6) A party may in his notice name as the deponent a public or private corporation or a partnership or association or governmental agency and designate with reasonable particularity the matters on which examination is requested. The organization so named shall designate one or more officers, directors, or managing agents, or other persons who consent to testify on its behalf, and may set forth, for each person designated, the matters on which he will testify. The persons so designated shall testify as to matters known or reasonably available to the organization. This subdivision (b)(6) does not preclude taking a deposition by any other procedure authorized in these rules.

(b) ~~**Orders for the Protection of Parties and Deponents.** After notice is served for taking a deposition by oral examination, upon motion seasonably made by any party or by the person to be examined and upon notice and for good cause shown, the court in which the action is pending may make an order that the deposition shall not be taken, or that it may be taken only at some designated place other than that stated in the notice, or that it may be taken~~

New matter is shown in italics; matter to be omitted is lined through

~~only on written interrogatories, or that certain matters shall not be inquired into, or that the scope of the examination shall be limited to certain matters, or that the examination shall be held with no one present except the parties to the action and their officers or counsel, or that after being sealed the deposition shall be opened only by order of the court, or that secret processes, developments, or research need not be disclosed, or that the parties shall simultaneously file specified documents or information enclosed in sealed envelopes to be opened as directed by the court; or the court may make any other order which justice requires to protect the party or witness from annoyance, embarrassment, or oppression.~~

(c) *Examination and Cross–Examination;* **Record of Examination; Oath; Objections.** *Examination and cross-examination of witnesses may proceed as permitted at the trial under the provisions of Rule 43(b).* The officer before whom the deposition is to be taken shall put the witness on oath and shall personally, or by some one acting under his direction and in his presence, record the testimony of the witness. The testimony shall be taken stenographically *or recorded by any other means ordered in accordance with subdivision (b)(4) of this rule.* ~~and~~ *If requested by one of the parties, the testimony shall be* transcribed ~~unless the parties agree otherwise.~~

All objections made at the time of the examination to the qualifications of the officer taking the deposition, or to the manner of taking it, or to the evidence presented, or to the conduct of any party, and any other objection to the proceedings, shall be noted by the officer upon the deposition. Evidence objected to shall be taken subject to the objections. In lieu of participating in the oral examination, parties ~~served with notice of taking a deposition~~ may ~~transmit~~ *serve* written ~~interrogatories~~ *questions in a sealed envelope on the party taking the deposition and he shall transmit them* to the officer, who shall propound them to the witness and record the answers verbatim.

(d) **Motion To Terminate or Limit Examination.** At any time during the taking of the deposition, on motion of ~~any~~ *a* party or of the deponent and upon a showing that the examination is being conducted in bad faith or in such manner as unreasonably to annoy, embarrass, or oppress the deponent or party, the court in which the action is pending or the court in the district where the deposition is being taken may order the officer conducting the examination to cease forthwith from taking the deposition, or may limit the scope and manner of the taking of the deposition as provided in ~~subdivision (b)~~ *Rule 26(c).* If the order made terminates the examination, it shall be resumed thereafter only upon the order

---

New matter is shown in italics; matter to be omitted is lined through

of the court in which the action is pending. Upon demand of the objecting party or deponent, the taking of the deposition shall be suspended for the time necessary to make a motion for an order. ~~In granting or refusing such order the court may impose upon either party or upon the witness the requirement to pay such costs or expenses as the court may deem reasonable.~~ *The provisions of Rule 37(a)(4) apply to the award of expenses incurred in relation to the motion.*

(e) Submission to Witness; Changes; Signing. When the testimony is fully transcribed the deposition shall be submitted to the witness for examination and shall be read to or by him, unless such examination and reading are waived by the witness and by the parties. Any changes in form or substance which the witness desires to make shall be entered upon the deposition by the officer with a statement of the reasons given by the witness for making them. The deposition shall then be signed by the witness, unless the parties by stipulation waive the signing or the witness is ill or cannot be found or refuses to sign. If the deposition is not signed by the witness *within 30 days of its submission to him,* the officer shall sign it and state on the record the fact of the waiver or of the illness or absence of the witness or the fact of the refusal to sign together with the reason, if any, given therefor; and the deposition may then be used as fully as though signed, unless on a motion to suppress under Rule 32(d)*(4)* the court holds that the reasons given for the refusal to sign require rejection of the deposition in whole or in part.

(f) Certification and Filing by Officer; *Exhibits;* Copies; Notice of Filing.

(1) The officer shall certify on the deposition that the witness was duly sworn by him and that the deposition is a true record of the testimony given by the witness. He shall then securely seal the deposition in an envelope indorsed with the title of the action and marked "Deposition of [here insert name of witness]" and shall promptly file it with the court in which the action is pending or send it by registered or certified mail to the clerk thereof for filing.

Documents and things produced for inspection during the examination of the witness, shall, upon the request of a party, be marked for identification and annexed to and returned with the deposition, and may be inspected and copied by any party, except that (A) the person producing the materials may substitute copies to be marked for identification, if he affords to all parties fair opportunity to verify the copies by comparison with the originals, and (B) if the person producing the materials requests their return, the officer shall mark them, give each party an opportunity to inspect and copy

---

New matter is shown in italics; matter to be omitted is lined through

them, and return them to the person producing them, and the materials, may then be used in the same manner as if annexed to and returned with the deposition. Any party may move for an order that the original be annexed to and returned with the deposition to the court, pending final disposition of the case.

(2) Upon payment of reasonable charges therefor, the officer shall furnish a copy of the deposition to any party or to the deponent.

(3) The party taking the deposition shall give prompt notice of its filing to all other parties.

(g) Failure To Attend or To Serve Subpoena; Expenses.

(1) If the party giving the notice of the taking of a deposition fails to attend and proceed therewith and another party attends in person or by attorney pursuant to the notice, the court may order the party giving the notice to pay to such other party the ~~amount of the~~ reasonable expenses incurred by him and his attorney in ~~so~~ attending, including reasonable attorney's fees.

(2) If the party giving the notice of the taking of a deposition of a witness fails to serve a subpoena upon him and the witness because of such failure does not attend, and if another party attends in person or by attorney because he expects the deposition of that witness to be taken, the court may order the party giving the notice to pay to such other party the ~~amount of the~~ reasonable expenses incurred by him and his attorney in ~~so~~ attending, including reasonable attorney's fees.

Subdivision (a). This subdivision contains the provisions of the existing Rule 26(a), transferred here as part of the rearrangement relating to Rule 26. Existing Rule 30(a) is transferred to 30(b). Changes in language have been made to conform to the new arrangement.

This subdivision is further revised in regard to the requirement of leave of court for taking a deposition. The present procedure, requiring a plaintiff to obtain leave of court if he serves notice of taking a deposition within 20 days after commencement of the action, is changed in several respects. First, leave is required by reference to the time the deposition is to be taken rather than the date of serving notice of taking. Second, the 20–day period is extended to 30 days and runs from the service of summons and complaint on any defendant, rather than the commencement of the action. *Cf.* Ill.S.Ct.R. 19–1, S—H Ill.Ann.Stat. § 101.19–1. Third, leave is not required beyond the time that defendant initiates discovery, thus showing that he has retained counsel. As under the present practice, a party not afforded a reasonable opportunity to appear at a deposition, because he has not yet been served with process, is protected against use of the deposition at trial against him. See Rule 32(a), transferred from 26(d). Moreover, he can later redepose the witness if he so desires.

New matter is shown in italics; matter to be omitted is lined through

The purpose of requiring the plaintiff to obtain leave of court is, as stated by the Advisory Committee that proposed the present language of Rule 26(a), to protect "a defendant who has not had an opportunity to retain counsel and inform himself as to the nature of the suit." Note to 1948 amendment of Rule 26(a), quoted in 3A Barron & Holtzoff, *Federal Practice and Procedure* 455–456 (Wright ed. 1958). In order to assure defendant of this opportunity, the period is lengthened to 30 days. This protection, however, is relevant to the time of taking the deposition, not to the time that notice is served. Similarly, the protective period should run from the service of process rather than the filing of the complaint with the court. As stated in the note to Rule 26(d), the courts have used the service of notice as a convenient reference point for assigning priority in taking depositions, but with the elimination of priority in new Rule 26(d) the reference point is no longer needed. The new procedure is consistent in principle with the provisions of Rules 33, 34, and 36 as revised.

Plaintiff is excused from obtaining leave even during the initial 30–day period if he gives the special notice provided in subdivision (b)(2). The required notice must state that the person to be examined is about to go out of the district where the action is pending and more than 100 miles from the place of trial, or out of the United States, or on a voyage to sea, and will be unavailable for examination unless deposed within the 30–day period. These events occur most often in maritime litigation, when seamen are transferred from one port to another or are about to go to sea. Yet, there are analogous situations in nonmaritime litigation, and although the maritime problems are more common, a rule limited to claims in the admiralty and maritime jurisdiction is not justified.

In the recent unification of the civil and admiralty rules, this problem was temporarily met through addition in Rule 26(a) of a provision that depositions de bene esse may continue to be taken as to admiralty and maritime claims within the meaning of Rule 9(h). It was recognized at the time that "a uniform rule applicable alike to what are now civil actions and suits in admiralty" was clearly preferable, but the de bene esse procedure was adopted "for the time being at least." See Advisory Committee's note in *Report of the Judicial Conference: Proposed Amendments to Rules of Civil Procedure* 43–44 (1966).

The changes in Rule 30(a) and the new Rule 30(b)(2) provide a formula applicable to ordinary civil as well as maritime claims. They replace the provision for depositions de bene esse. They authorize an early deposition without leave of court where the witness is about to depart and, unless his deposition is promptly taken, (1) it will be impossible or very difficult to depose him before trial or (2) his deposition can later be taken but only with substantially increased effort and expense. *Cf.* S. S. Hai Chang, 1966 A.M.C. 2239 (S.D.N.Y.1966), in which the deposing party is required to prepay expenses and counsel fees of the other party's lawyer when the action is pending in New York and depositions are to be taken on the West Coast. Defendant is protected by a provision that the deposition cannot be used against him if he was unable through exercise of diligence to obtain counsel to represent him.

The distance of 100 miles from place of trial is derived from the de bene esse provision and also conforms to the reach of a subpoena of the trial court, as provided in Rule 45(e). See also S.D.N.Y.Civ.R. 5(a). Some parts of the de bene esse provision are omitted from Rule 30(b)(2). Modern deposition practice adequately covers the witness who lives more than 100 miles away from place of trial. If a witness is aged or infirm, leave of court can be obtained.

Subdivision (b). Existing Rule 30(b) on protective orders has been transferred to Rule 26(c), and existing Rule 30(a) relating to the notice of taking deposition has

---

New matter is shown in italics; matter to be omitted is lined through

been transferred to this subdivision. Because new material has been added, subsection numbers have been inserted.

Subdivision (b)(1). If a subpoena duces tecum is to be served, a copy thereof or a designation of the materials to be produced must accompany the notice. Each party is thereby enabled to prepare for the deposition more effectively.

Subdivision (b)(2). This subdivision is discussed in the note to subdivision (a), to which it relates.

Subdivision (b)(3). This provision is derived from existing Rule 30(a), with a minor change of language.

Subdivision (b)(4). In order to facilitate less expensive procedures, provision is made for the recording of testimony by other than stenographic means—*e.g.*, by mechanical, electronic, or photographic means. Because these methods give rise to problems of accuracy and trustworthiness, the party taking the deposition is required to apply for a court order. The order is to specify how the testimony is to be recorded, preserved, and filed, and it may contain whatever additional safeguards the court deems necessary.

Subdivision (b)(5). A provision is added to enable a party, through service of notice, to require another party to produce documents or things at the taking of his deposition. This may now be done as to a nonparty deponent through use of a subpoena duces tecum as authorized by Rule 45, but some courts have held that documents may be secured from a party only under Rule 34. See 2A Barron & Holtzoff, *Federal Practice and Procedure* § 644.1 n. 83.2, § 792 n. 16 (Wright ed. 1961). With the elimination of "good cause" from Rule 34, the reason for this restrictive doctrine has disappeared. *Cf.* N.Y.C.P.L.R. § 3111.

Whether production of documents or things should be obtained directly under rule 34 or at the deposition under this rule will depend on the nature and volume of the documents or things. Both methods are made available. When the documents are few and simple, and closely related to the oral examination, ability to proceed via this rule will facilitate discovery. If the discovering party insists on examining many and complex documents at the taking of the deposition, thereby causing undue burdens on others, the latter may, under Rules 26(c) or 30(d), apply for a court order that the examining party proceed via Rule 34 alone.

Subdivision (b)(6). A new provision is added, whereby a party may name a corporation, partnership, association, or governmental agency as the deponent and designate the matters on which he requests examination, and the organization shall then name one or more of its officers, directors, or managing agents, or other persons consenting to appear and testify on its behalf with respect to matters known or reasonably available to the organization. *Cf.* Alberta Sup.Ct. R. 255. The organization may designate persons other than officers, directors, and managing agents, but only with their consent. Thus, an employee or agent who has an independent or conflicting interest in the litigation—for example, in a personal injury case—can refuse to testify on behalf of the organization.

This procedure supplements the existing practice whereby the examining party designates the corporate official to be deposed. Thus, if the examining party believes that certain officials who have not testified pursuant to this subdivision have added information, he may depose them. On the other hand, a court's decision whether to issue a protective order may take account of the availability and use made of the procedures provided in this subdivision.

The new procedure should be viewed as an added facility for discovery, one which may be advantageous to both sides as well as an improvement in the deposition process. It will reduce the difficulties now encountered in determining,

---

New matter is shown in italics; matter to be omitted is lined through

prior to the taking of a deposition, whether a particular employee or agent is a "managing agent." See Note, *Discovery Against Corporations Under the Federal Rules,* 47 Iowa L.Rev. 1006–1016 (1962). It will curb the "bandying" by which officers or managing agents of a corporation are deposed in turn but each disclaims knowledge of facts that are clearly known to persons in the organization and thereby to it. *Cf. Haney v. Woodward & Lothrop, Inc.,* 330 F.2d 940, 944 (4th Cir.1964). The provision should also assist organizations which find that an unnecessarily large number of their officers and agents are being deposed by a party uncertain of who in the organization has knowledge. Some courts have held that under the existing rules a corporation should not be burdened with choosing which person is to appear for it. *E.g., United States v. Gahagan Dredging Corp.,* 24 F.R.D. 328, 329 (S.D.N.Y.1958). This burden is not essentially different from that of answering interrogatories under Rule 33, and is in any case lighter than that of an examining party ignorant of who in the corporation has knowledge.

Subdivision (c). A new sentence is inserted at the beginning, representing the transfer of existing Rule 26(c) to this subdivision. Another addition conforms to the new provision in subdivision (b)(4).

The present rule provides that transcription shall be carried out unless all parties waive it. In view of the many depositions taken from which nothing useful is discovered, the revised language provides that transcription is to be performed if any party requests it. The fact of the request is relevant to the exercise of the court's discretion in determining who shall pay for transcription.

Parties choosing to serve written questions rather than participate personally in an oral deposition are directed to serve their questions on the party taking the deposition, since the officer is often not identified in advance. Confidentiality is preserved, since the questions may be served in a sealed envelope.

Subdivision (d). The assessment of expenses incurred in relation to motions made under this subdivision (d) is made subject to the provisions of Rule 37(a). The standards for assessment of expenses are more fully set out in Rule 37(a), and these standards should apply to the essentially similar motions of this subdivision.

Subdivision (e). The provision relating to the refusal of a witness to sign his deposition is tightened through insertion of a 30–day time period.

Subdivision (f)(1). A provision is added which codifies in a flexible way the procedure for handling exhibits related to the deposition and at the same time assures each party that he may inspect and copy documents and things produced by a nonparty witness in response to a subpoena duces tecum. As a general rule and in the absence of agreement to the contrary or order of the court, exhibits produced without objection are to be annexed to and returned with the deposition, but a witness may substitute copies for purposes of marking and he may obtain return of the exhibits. The right of the parties to inspect exhibits for identification and to make copies is assured. *Cf.* N.Y.C.P.L.R. § 3116(c).

Advisory Committee's Note to 1993 Amendment

(a) When Depositions May Be Taken; *When Leave Required.*

(1) ~~After commencement of the action, any~~ party may take the testimony of any person, including a party, by deposition upon oral

New matter is shown in italics; matter to be omitted is lined through

examination *without leave of court except as provided in paragraph (2).* ~~Leave of court, granted with or without notice, must be obtained only if the plaintiff seeks to take a deposition prior to the expiration of 30 days after service of the summons and complaint upon any defendant or service made under Rule 4(e), except that leave is not required (1) if a defendant has served a notice of taking deposition or otherwise sought discovery, or (2) if special notice is given as provided in subdivision (b)(2) of this rule.~~ The attendance of witnesses may be compelled by subpoena as provided in Rule 45. ~~The deposition of a person confined in prison may be taken only by leave of court on such terms as the court prescribes.~~

(2) A party must obtain leave of court, which shall be granted to the extent consistent with the principles stated in Rule 26(b)(2), if the person to be examined is confined in prison or if, without the written stipulation of the parties,

(A) a proposed deposition would result in more than ten depositions being taken under this rule or Rule 31 by the plaintiffs, or by the defendants, or by third-party defendants;

(B) the person to be examined already has been deposed in the case; or

(C) a party seeks to take a deposition before the time specified in Rule 26(d) unless the notice contains a certification, with supporting facts, that the person to be examined is expected to leave the United States and be unavailable for examination in this country unless deposed before that time.

(b) Notice of Examination: General Requirements; ~~**Special Notice; Non–Stenographic**~~ *Method of* **Recording; Production of Documents and Things; Deposition of Organization; Deposition by Telephone.**

(1) A party desiring to take the deposition of any person upon oral examination shall give reasonable notice in writing to every other party to the action. The notice shall state the time and place for taking the deposition and the name and address of each person to be examined, if known, and, if the name is not known, a general description sufficient to identify the person or the particular class or group to which the person belongs. If a subpoena duces tecum is to be served on the person to be examined, the designation of the materials to be produced as set forth in the subpoena shall be attached to, or included in, the notice.

(2) ~~Leave of court is not required for the taking of a deposition by the plaintiff if the notice (A) states that the person to be examined is about to go out of the district where the action is pending and more than 100 miles from the place of trial, or is about~~

New matter is shown in italics; matter to be omitted is lined through

~~to go out of the United States, or is bound on a voyage to sea, and will be unavailable for examination unless the person's deposition is taken before expiration of the 30-day period, and (B) sets forth facts to support the statement. The plaintiff's attorney shall sign the notice, and the attorney's signature constitutes a certification by the attorney that to the best of the attorney's knowledge, information, and belief the statement and supporting facts are true. The sanctions provided by Rule 11 are applicable to the certification.~~

~~If a party shows that when the party was served with notice under this subdivision (b)(2) the party was unable through the exercise of diligence to obtain counsel to represent the party at the taking of the deposition, the deposition may not be used against the party.~~

The party taking the deposition shall state in the notice the method by which the testimony shall be recorded. Unless the court orders otherwise, it may be recorded by sound, sound-and-visual, or stenographic means, and the party taking the deposition shall bear the cost of the recording. Any party may arrange for a transcription to be made from the recording of a deposition taken by nonstenographic means.

(3) ~~The court may for cause shown enlarge or shorten the time for taking the deposition.~~ *With prior notice to the deponent and other parties, any party may designate another method to record the deponent's testimony in addition to the method specified by the person taking the deposition. The additional record or transcript shall be made at that party's expense unless the court otherwise orders.*

(4) ~~The parties may stipulate in writing or the court may upon motion order that the testimony at a deposition be recorded by other than stenographic means. The stipulation or order shall designate the person before whom the deposition shall be taken, the manner of recording, preserving and filing the deposition, and may include other provisions to assure that the recorded testimony will be accurate and trustworthy. A party may arrange to have a stenographic transcription made at the party's own expense. Any objections under subdivision (c), any changes made by the witness, the witness' signature identifying the deposition as the witness' own or the statement of the officer that is required if the witness does not sign, as provided in subdivision (c), and the certification of the officer required by subdivision (f) shall be set forth in a writing to accompany a deposition recorded by non-stenographic means.~~ *Unless otherwise agreed by the parties, a deposition shall be conducted before an officer appointed or designated under Rule 28 and*

New matter is shown in italics; matter to be omitted is lined through

shall begin with a statement on the record by the officer that includes (A) the officer's name and business address; (B) the date, time, and place of the deposition; (C) the name of the deponent; (D) the administration of the oath or affirmation to the deponent; and (E) an identification of all persons present. If the deposition is recorded other than stenographically, the officer shall repeat items (A) through (C) at the beginning of each unit of recorded tape or other recording medium. The appearance or demeanor of deponents or attorneys shall not be distorted through camera or sound-recording techniques. At the end of the deposition, the officer shall state on the record that the deposition is complete and shall set forth any stipulations made by counsel concerning the custody of the transcript or recording and the exhibits, or concerning other pertinent matters.

(7) The parties may stipulate in writing or the court may upon motion order that a deposition be taken by telephone *or other remote electronic means*. For the purposes of this rule and Rules 28(a), 37(a)(1), *and* 37(b)(1), and 45(d), a deposition taken by telephone *such means* is taken in the district and at the place where the deponent is to answer questions propounded to the deponent.

(c) Examination and Cross–Examination; Record of Examination; Oath; Objections. Examination and cross-examination of witnesses may proceed as permitted at the trial under the provisions of the Federal Rules of Evidence *except Rules 103 and 615*. The officer before whom the deposition is to be taken shall put the witness on oath *or affirmation* and shall personally, or by someone acting under the officer's direction and in the officer's presence, record the testimony of the witness. The testimony shall be taken stenographically or recorded by any other means ordered in accordance with *method authorized by* subdivision (b)(42) of this rule. If requested by one of the parties the testimony shall be transcribed. All objections made at the time of the examination to the qualifications of the officer taking the deposition, or to the manner of taking it, or to the evidence presented, or to the conduct of any party, and any other objection to *or to any other aspect of* the proceedings, shall be noted by the officer upon *the record of* the deposition. Evidence objected to shall be; *but the examination shall proceed, with the testimony being* taken subject to the objections. In lieu of participating in the oral examination, parties may serve written questions in a sealed envelope on the party taking the deposition and the party taking the deposition shall transmit them to the officer, who shall propound them to the witness and record the answers verbatim.

New matter is shown in italics; matter to be omitted is lined through

(d) *Schedule and Duration;* **Motion to Terminate or Limit Examination.**

(1) Any objection to evidence during a deposition shall be stated concisely and in a non-argumentative and non-suggestive manner. A party may instruct a deponent not to answer only when necessary to preserve a privilege, to enforce a limitation on evidence directed by the court, or to present a motion under paragraph (3).

(2) By order or local rule, the court may limit the time permitted for the conduct of a deposition, but shall allow additional time consistent with Rule 26(b)(2) if needed for a fair examination of the deponent or if the deponent or another party impedes or delays the examination. If the court finds such an impediment, delay, or other conduct that has frustrated the fair examination of the deponent, it may impose upon the persons responsible an appropriate sanction, including the reasonable costs and attorney's fees incurred by any parties as a result thereof.

(3) At any time during ~~the taking of the~~ *a* deposition, on motion of a party or of the deponent and upon a showing that the examination is being conducted in bad faith or in such manner as unreasonably to annoy, embarrass, or oppress the deponent or party, the court in which the action is pending or the court in the district where the deposition is being taken may order the officer conducting the examination to cease forthwith from taking the deposition, or may limit the scope and manner of the taking of the deposition as provided in Rule 26(c). If the order made terminates the examination, it shall be resumed thereafter only upon the order of the court in which the action is pending. Upon demand of the objecting party or deponent, the taking of the deposition shall be suspended for the time necessary to make a motion for an order. The provisions of Rule 37(a)(4) apply to the award of expenses incurred in relation to the motion.

(e) ~~Submission to~~ *Review by* **Witness; Changes; Signing.** ~~When the testimony is fully transcribed, the deposition shall be submitted to the witness for examination and shall be read to or by the witness, unless such examination and reading are waived by the witness and by the parties. Any changes in form or substance which the witness desires to make shall be entered upon the deposition by the officer with a statement of the reasons given by the witness for making them. The deposition shall then be signed by the witness, unless the parties by stipulation waive the signing or the witness is ill or cannot be found or refuses to sign. If the deposition is not signed by the witness within 30 days of its submission to the witness, the officer shall sign it and state on the record the fact of the waiver or of the illness or absence of the witness or the fact of~~

New matter is shown in italics; matter to be omitted is lined through

~~the refusal to sign, together with the reason, if any, given therefor; and the deposition may then be used as fully as though signed unless on a motion to suppress under Rule 32(d)(4) the court holds that the reasons given for the refusal to sign require rejection of the deposition in whole or in part.~~ *If requested by the deponent or a party before completion of the deposition, the deponent shall have 30 days after being notified by the officer that the transcript or recording is available in which to review the transcript or recording and, if there are changes in form or substance, to sign a statement reciting such changes and the reasons given by the deponent for making them. The officer shall indicate in the certificate prescribed by subdivision (f)(1) whether any review was requested and, if so, shall append any changes made by the deponent during the period allowed.*

(f) Certification and Filing by Officer; Exhibits; Copies; Notice of Filing.

(1) The officer shall certify ~~on the deposition~~ that the witness was duly sworn by the officer and that the deposition is a true record of the testimony given by the witness. *This certificate shall be in writing and accompany the record of the deposition.* Unless otherwise ordered by the court, the officer shall ~~then~~ securely seal the deposition in an envelope *or package* indorsed with the title of the action and marked "Deposition of [here insert name of witness]" and shall promptly file it with the court in which the action is pending ~~or send it by registered or certified mail to the clerk thereof for filing~~ *or send it to the attorney who arranged for the transcript or recording, who shall store it under conditions that will protect it against loss, destruction, tampering, or deterioration.* Documents and things produced for inspection during the examination of the witness, shall, upon the request of a party, be marked for identification and annexed to the deposition and may be inspected and copied by any party, except that if the person producing the materials desires to retain them the person may (A) offer copies to be marked for identification and annexed to the deposition and to serve thereafter as originals if the person affords to all parties fair opportunity to verify the copies by comparison with the originals, or (B) offer the originals to be marked for identification, after giving to each party an opportunity to inspect and copy them, in which event the materials may then be used in the same manner as if annexed to the deposition. Any party may move for an order that the original be annexed to and returned with the deposition to the court, pending final disposition of the case.

(2) *Unless otherwise ordered by the court or agreed by the parties, the officer shall retain stenographic notes of any deposition*

New matter is shown in italics; matter to be omitted is lined through

taken stenographically or a copy of the recording of any deposition taken by another method. Upon payment of reasonable charges therefor, the officer shall furnish a copy of the *transcript or other recording of the* deposition to any party or to the deponent.

Subdivision (a). Paragraph (1) retains the first and third sentences from the former subdivision (a) without significant modification. The second and fourth sentences are relocated.

Paragraph (2) collects all provisions bearing on requirements of leave of court to take a deposition.

Paragraph (2)(A) is new. It provides a limit on the number of depositions the parties may take, absent leave of court or stipulation with the other parties. One aim of this revision is to assure judicial review under the standards stated in Rule 26(b)(2) before any side will be allowed to take more than ten depositions in a case without agreement of the other parties. A second objective is to emphasize that counsel have a professional obligation to develop a mutual cost-effective plan for discovery in the case. Leave to take additional depositions should be granted when consistent with the principles of Rule 26(b)(2), and in some cases the ten-per-side limit should be reduced in accordance with those same principles. Consideration should ordinarily be given at the planning meeting of the parties under Rule 26(f) and at the time of a scheduling conference under Rule 16(b) as to enlargements or reductions in the number of depositions, eliminating the need for special motions.

A deposition under Rule 30(b)(6) should, for purposes of this limit, be treated as a single deposition even though more than one person may be designated to testify.

In multi-party cases, the parties on any side are expected to confer and agree as to which depositions are most needed, given the presumptive limit on the number of depositions they can take without leave of court. If these disputes cannot be amicably resolved, the court can be requested to resolve the dispute or permit additional depositions.

Paragraph (2)(B) is new. It requires leave of court if any witness is to be deposed in the action more than once. This requirement does not apply when a deposition is temporarily recessed for convenience of counsel or the deponent or to enable additional materials to be gathered before resuming the deposition. If significant travel costs would be incurred to resume the deposition, the parties should consider the feasibility of conducting the balance of the examination by telephonic means.

Paragraph (2)(C) revises the second sentence of the former subdivision (a) as to when depositions may be taken. Consistent with the changes made in Rule 26(d), providing that formal discovery ordinarily not commence until after the litigants have met and conferred as directed in revised Rule 26(f), the rule requires leave of court or agreement of the parties if a deposition is to be taken before that time (except when a witness is about to leave the country).

Subdivision (b). The primary change in subdivision (b) is that parties will be authorized to record deposition testimony by nonstenographic means without first having to obtain permission of the court or agreement from other counsel.

Former subdivision (b)(2) is partly relocated in subdivision (a)(2)(C) of this rule. The latter two sentences of the first paragraph are deleted, in part because they are redundant to Rule 26(g) and in part because Rule 11 no longer applies to discovery

New matter is shown in italics; matter to be omitted is lined through

requests. The second paragraph of the former subdivision (b)(2), relating to use of depositions at trial where a party was unable to obtain counsel in time for an accelerated deposition, is relocated in Rule 32.

New paragraph (2) confers on the party taking the deposition the choice of the method of recording, without the need to obtain prior court approval for one taken other than stenographically. A party choosing to record a deposition only by videotape or audiotape should understand that a transcript will be required by Rule 26(a)(3)(B) and Rule 32(c) if the deposition is later to be offered as evidence at trial or on a dispositive motion under Rule 56. Objections to the nonstenographic recording of a deposition, when warranted by the circumstances, can be presented to the court under Rule 26(c).

Paragraph (3) provides that other parties may arrange, at their own expense, for the recording of a deposition by a means (stenographic, visual, or sound) in addition to the method designated by the person noticing the deposition. The former provisions of this paragraph, relating to the court's power to change the date of a deposition, have been eliminated as redundant in view of Rule 26(c)(2).

Revised paragraph (4) requires that all depositions be recorded by an officer designated or appointed under Rule 28 and contains special provisions designed to provide basic safeguards to assure the utility and integrity of recordings taken other than stenographically.

Paragraph (7) is revised to authorize the taking of a deposition not only by telephone but also by other remote electronic means, such as satellite television, when agreed to by the parties or authorized by the court.

Subdivision (c). Minor changes are made in this subdivision to reflect those made in subdivision (b) and to complement the new provisions of subdivision (d)(1), aimed at reducing the number of interruptions during depositions.

In addition, the revision addresses a recurring problem as to whether other potential deponents can attend a deposition. Courts have disagreed, some holding that witnesses should be excluded through invocation of Rule 615 of the evidence rules, and others holding that witnesses may attend unless excluded by an order under Rule 26(c)(5). The revision provides that other witnesses are not automatically excluded from a deposition simply by the request of a party. Exclusion, however, can be ordered under Rule 26(c)(5) when appropriate; and, if exclusion is ordered, consideration should be given as to whether the excluded witnesses likewise should be precluded from reading, or being otherwise informed about, the testimony given in the earlier depositions. The revision addresses only the matter of attendance by potential deponents, and does not attempt to resolve issues concerning attendance by others, such as members of the public or press.

Subdivision (d). The first sentence of new paragraph (1) provides that any objections during a deposition must be made concisely and in a nonargumentative and non-suggestive manner. Depositions frequently have been unduly prolonged, if not unfairly frustrated, by lengthy objections and colloquy, often suggesting how the deponent should respond. While objections may, under the revised rule, be made during a deposition, they ordinarily should be limited to those that under Rule 32(d)(3) might be waived if not made at that time, *i.e.*, objections on grounds that might be immediately obviated, removed, or cured, such as to the form of a question or the responsiveness of an answer. Under Rule 32(b), other objections can, even without the so-called "usual stipulation" preserving objections, be raised for the first time at trial and therefore should be kept to a minimum during a deposition.

Directions to a deponent not to answer a question can be even more disruptive than objections. The second sentence of new paragraph (1) prohibits such directions

New matter is shown in italics; matter to be omitted is lined through

except in the three circumstances indicated: to claim a privilege or protection against disclosure (*e.g.*, as work product), to enforce a court directive limiting the scope or length of permissible discovery, or to suspend a deposition to enable presentation of a motion under paragraph (3).

Paragraph (2) is added to this subdivision to dispel any doubts regarding the power of the court by order or local rule to establish limits on the length of depositions. The rule also explicitly authorizes the court to impose the cost resulting from obstructive tactics that unreasonably prolong a deposition on the person engaged in such obstruction. This sanction may be imposed on a non-party witness as well as a party or attorney, but is otherwise congruent with Rule 26(g).

It is anticipated that limits on the length of depositions prescribed by local rules would be presumptive only, subject to modification by the court or by agreement of the parties. Such modifications typically should be discussed by the parties in their meeting under Rule 26(f) and included in the scheduling order required by Rule 16(b). Additional time, moreover, should be allowed under the revised rule when justified under the principles stated in Rule 26(b)(2). To reduce the number of special motions, local rules should ordinarily permit—and indeed encourage—the parties to agree to additional time, as when, during the taking of a deposition, it becomes clear that some additional examination is needed.

Paragraph (3) authorizes appropriate sanctions not only when a deposition is unreasonably prolonged, but also when an attorney engages in other practices that improperly frustrate the fair examination of the deponent, such as making improper objections or giving directions not to answer prohibited by paragraph (1). In general, counsel should not engage in any conduct during a deposition that would not be allowed in the presence of a judicial officer. The making of an excessive number of unnecessary objections may itself constitute sanctionable conduct, as may the refusal of an attorney to agree with other counsel on a fair apportionment of the time allowed for examination of a deponent or a refusal to agree to a reasonable request for some additional time to complete a deposition, when that is permitted by the local rule or order.

Subdivision (e). Various changes are made in this subdivision to reduce problems sometimes encountered when depositions are taken stenographically. Reporters frequently have difficulties obtaining signatures—and the return of depositions—from deponents. Under the revision pre-filing review by the deponent is required only if requested before the deposition is completed. If review is requested, the deponent will be allowed 30 days to review the transcript or recording and to indicate any changes in form or substance. Signature of the deponent will be required only if review is requested and changes are made.

Subdivision (f). Minor changes are made in this subdivision to reflect those made in subdivision (b). In courts which direct that depositions not be automatically filed, the reporter can transmit the transcript or recording to the attorney taking the deposition (or ordering the transcript or record), who then becomes custodian for the court of the original record of the deposition. Pursuant to subdivision (f)(2), as under the prior rule, any other party is entitled to secure a copy of the deposition from the officer designated to take the deposition; accordingly, unless ordered or agreed, the officer must retain a copy of the recording or the stenographic notes.

Advisory Committee's Note to 2000 Amendment

New matter is shown in italics; matter to be omitted is lined through

(d) Schedule and Duration; Motion to Terminate or Limit Examination.

(1) Any objection ~~to evidence~~ during a deposition ~~shall~~ *must* be stated concisely and in a non-argumentative and non-suggestive manner. A *person* ~~party~~ may instruct a deponent not to answer only when necessary to preserve a privilege, to enforce a limitation ~~on evidence~~ directed by the court, or to present a motion under ~~paragraph~~ *Rule 30(d)(4*3*)*.

(2) *Unless otherwise authorized by the court or stipulated by the parties, a deposition is limited to one day of seven hours.* ~~By order or local rule,t~~ *T*he court ~~may limit the time permitted for the conduct of a deposition, but shall~~ *must* allow additional time consistent with Rule 26(b)(2) if needed for a fair examination of the deponent or if the deponent or another *person* ~~party,~~ *or other circumstance,* impedes or delays the examination.

(3) If the court finds *that any* ~~such an~~ impediment, delay, or other conduct ~~that~~ has frustrated the fair examination of the deponent, it may impose upon the persons responsible an appropriate sanction, including the reasonable costs and attorney's fees incurred by any parties as a result thereof.

(*4*3) At any time during a deposition, on motion of a party or of the deponent and upon a showing that the examination is being conducted in bad faith or in such manner as unreasonably to annoy, embarrass, or oppress the deponent or party, the court in which the action is pending or the court in the district where the deposition is being taken may order the officer conducting the examination to cease forthwith from taking the deposition, or may limit the scope and manner of the taking of the deposition as provided in Rule 26(c). If the order made terminates the examination, it ~~shall~~ *may* be resumed thereafter only upon the order of the court in which the action is pending. Upon demand of the objecting party or deponent, the taking of the deposition ~~shall~~ *must* be suspended for the time necessary to make a motion for an order. The provisions of Rule 37(a)(4) apply to the award of expenses incurred in relation to the motion.

(f) Certification and *Delivery* ~~Filing~~ by Officer; Exhibits; Copies.~~; Notice of Filing.~~

(1) The officer ~~shall~~ *must* certify that the witness was duly sworn by the officer and that the deposition is a true record of the testimony given by the witness. This certificate ~~shall~~ *must* be in writing and accompany the record of the deposition. Unless otherwise ordered by the court, the officer ~~shall~~ *must* securely seal the deposition in an envelope or package indorsed with the title of the

---

New matter is shown in italics; matter to be omitted is lined through

action and marked "Deposition of [here insert name of witness]" and ~~shall~~ *must* promptly ~~file it with the court in which the action is pending or~~ send it to the attorney who arranged for the transcript or recording, who ~~shall~~ *must* store it under conditions that will protect it against loss, destruction, tampering, or deterioration. Documents and things produced for inspection during the examination of the witness, ~~shall~~ *must*, upon the request of a party, be marked for identification and annexed to the deposition and may be inspected and copied by any party, except that if the person producing the materials desires to retain them the person may (A) offer copies to be marked for identification and annexed to the deposition and to serve thereafter as originals if the person affords to all parties fair opportunity to verify the copies by comparison with the originals, or (B) offer the originals to be marked for identification, after giving to each party an opportunity to inspect and copy them, in which event the materials may then be used in the same manner as if annexed to the deposition. Any party may move for an order that the original be annexed to and returned with the deposition to the court, pending final disposition of the case.

———

Subdivision (d). Paragraph (1) has been amended to clarify the terms regarding behavior during depositions. The references to objections "to evidence" and limitations "on evidence" have been removed to avoid disputes about what is "evidence" and whether an objection is to, or a limitation is on, discovery instead. It is intended that the rule apply to any objection to a question or other issue arising during a deposition, and to any limitation imposed by the court in connection with a deposition, which might relate to duration or other matters.

The current rule places limitations on instructions that a witness not answer only when the instruction is made by a "party." Similar limitations should apply with regard to anyone who might purport to instruct a witness not to answer a question. Accordingly, the rule is amended to apply the limitation to instructions by any person. The amendment is not intended to confer new authority on nonparties to instruct witnesses to refuse to answer deposition questions. The amendment makes it clear that, whatever the legitimacy of giving such instructions, the nonparty is subject to the same limitations as parties.

Paragraph (2) imposes a presumptive durational limitation of one day of seven hours for any deposition. The Committee has been informed that overlong depositions can result in undue costs and delays in some circumstances. This limitation contemplates that there will be reasonable breaks during the day for lunch and other reasons, and that the only time to be counted is the time occupied by the actual deposition. For purposes of this durational limit, the deposition of each person designated under Rule 30(b)(6) should be considered a separate deposition. The presumptive duration may be extended, or otherwise altered, by agreement. Absent agreement, a court order is needed. The party seeking a court order to extend the examination, or otherwise alter the limitations, is expected to show good cause to justify such an order.

New matter is shown in italics; matter to be omitted is lined through

Parties considering extending the time for a deposition—and courts asked to order an extension—might consider a variety of factors. For example, if the witness needs an interpreter, that may prolong the examination. If the examination will cover events occurring over a long period of time, that may justify allowing additional time. In cases in which the witness will be questioned about numerous or lengthy documents, it is often desirable for the interrogating party to send copies of the documents to the witness sufficiently in advance of the deposition so that the witness can become familiar with them. Should the witness nevertheless not read the documents in advance, thereby prolonging the deposition, a court could consider that a reason for extending the time limit. If the examination reveals that documents have been requested but not produced, that may justify further examination once production has occurred. In multi-party cases, the need for each party to examine the witness may warrant additional time, although duplicative questioning should be avoided and parties with similar interests should strive to designate one lawyer to question about areas of common interest. Similarly, should the lawyer for the witness want to examine the witness, that may require additional time. Finally, with regard to expert witnesses, there may more often be a need for additional time—even after the submission of the report required by Rule 26(a)(2)—for full exploration of the theories upon which the witness relies.

It is expected that in most instances the parties and the witness will make reasonable accommodations to avoid the need for resort to the court. The limitation is phrased in terms of a single day on the assumption that ordinarily a single day would be preferable to a deposition extending over multiple days; if alternative arrangements would better suit the parties, they may agree to them. It is also assumed that there will be reasonable breaks during the day. Preoccupation with timing is to be avoided.

The rule directs the court to allow additional time where consistent with Rule 26(b)(2) if needed for a fair examination of the deponent. In addition, if the deponent or another person impedes or delays the examination, the court must authorize extra time. The amendment makes clear that additional time should also be allowed where the examination is impeded by an "other circumstance," which might include a power outage, a health emergency, or other event.

In keeping with the amendment to Rule 26(b)(2), the provision added in 1993 granting authority to adopt a local rule limiting the time permitted for depositions has been removed. The court may enter a case-specific order directing shorter depositions for all depositions in a case or with regard to a specific witness. The court may also order that a deposition be taken for limited periods on several days.

Paragraph (3) includes sanctions provisions formerly included in paragraph (2). It authorizes the court to impose an appropriate sanction on any person responsible for an impediment that frustrated the fair examination of the deponent. This could include the deponent, any party, or any other person involved in the deposition. If the impediment or delay results from an "other circumstance" under paragraph (2), ordinarily no sanction would be appropriate.

Former paragraph (3) has been renumbered (4) but is otherwise unchanged.

Subdivision (f)(1). This subdivision is amended because Rule 5(d) has been amended to direct that discovery materials, including depositions, ordinarily should not be filed. The rule already has provisions directing that the lawyer who arranged for the transcript or recording preserve the deposition. Rule 5(d) provides that, once the deposition is used in the proceeding, the attorney must file it with the court.

"Shall" is replaced by "must" or "may" under the program to conform amended rules to current style conventions when there is no ambiguity.

New matter is shown in italics; matter to be omitted is lined through

Rule 33.   Interrogatories to Parties

Advisory Committee's Note to 1970 Amendment

(a) Availability; Procedures for Use. Any party may serve upon any ~~adverse~~ *other* party written interrogatories to be answered by the party served or, if the party served is a public or private corporation or a partnership or association *or governmental agency,* by any officer or agent, who shall furnish such information as is available to the party. Interrogatories may, *without leave of court,* be served *upon the plaintiff* after commencement of the action *and upon any other party with or after service of the summons and complaint upon that party.* ~~and without leave of court, except that, if service is made by the plaintiff within 10 days after such commencement, leave of court granted with or without notice must first be obtained. The interrogatories~~

Each interrogatory shall be answered separately and fully in writing under oath~~,~~ *unless it is objected to, in which event the reasons for objection shall be stated in lieu of an answer.* The answers ~~shall~~ *are to* be signed by the person making them~~;~~ *and the objections signed by the attorney making them.* ~~t~~*T*he party upon whom the interrogatories have been served shall serve a copy of the answers, *and objections if any,* ~~on the party submitting the interrogatories within 15 days after the service of the interrogatories, unless the court, on motion and notice and for good cause shown, enlarges or shortens the time.~~ *within 30 days after the service of the interrogatories, except that a defendant may serve answers or objections within 45 days after service of the summons and complaint upon that defendant. The court may allow a shorter or longer time.* ~~Within 10 days after service of interrogatories a party may serve written objections thereto together with a notice of hearing the objections at the earliest practicable time. Answers to interrogatories to which objection is made shall be deferred until the objections are determined.~~ *The party submitting the interrogatories may move for an order under Rule 37(a) with respect to any objection to or other failure to answer an interrogatory.*

(b) Scope; Use at Trial. Interrogatories may relate to any matters which can be inquired into under Rule 26(b), and the answers may be used to the ~~same~~ extent *permitted by the rules of evidence.* ~~as provided in Rule 26(d) for the use of the deposition of a party. Interrogatories may be served after a deposition has been taken, and a deposition may be sought after interrogatories have been answered, but the court, on motion of the deponent or the party interrogated, may make such protective order as justice may require. The number of interrogatories or of sets of interrogatories to be served is not limited except as justice requires to protect the~~

New matter is shown in italics; matter to be omitted is lined through

~~party from annoyance, expense, embarrassment, or oppression. The~~
~~provisions of Rule 30(b) are applicable for the protection of the~~
~~party from whom answers to interrogatories are sought under this~~
~~rule.~~

An interrogatory otherwise proper is not necessarily objectionable merely because an answer to the interrogatory involves an opinion or contention that relates to fact or the application of law to fact, but the court may order that such an interrogatory need not be answered until after designated discovery has been completed or until a pre-trial conference or other later time.

(c) Option to Produce Business Records. Where the answer to an interrogatory may be derived or ascertained from the business records of the party upon whom the interrogatory has been served or from an examination, audit or inspection of such business records, or from a compilation, abstract or summary based thereon, and the burden of deriving or ascertaining the answer is substantially the same for the party serving the interrogatory as for the party served, it is a sufficient answer to such interrogatory to specify the records from which the answer may be derived or ascertained and to afford to the party serving the interrogatory reasonable opportunity to examine, audit or inspect such records and to make copies, compilations, abstracts or summaries.

Subdivision (a). The mechanics of the operation of Rule 33 are substantially revised by the proposed amendment, with a view to reducing court intervention. There is general agreement that interrogatories spawn a greater percentage of objections and motions than any other discovery device. The Columbia Survey shows that, although half of the litigants resorted to depositions and about one-third used interrogatories, about 65 percent of the objections were made with respect to interrogatories and 26 percent related to depositions. See also Speck, *The Use of Discovery in United States District Courts,* 60 Yale L.J. 1132, 1144, 1151 (1951); Note, 36 Minn.L.Rev. 364, 379 (1952).

The procedures now provided in Rule 33 seem calculated to encourage objections and court motions. The time periods now allowed for responding to interrogatories—15 days for answers and 10 days for objections—are too short. The Columbia Survey shows that tardy response to interrogatories is common, virtually expected. The same was reported in Speck, *supra,* 60 Yale L.J. 1132, 1144. The time pressures tend to encourage objections as a means of gaining time to answer.

The time for objections is even shorter than for answers, and the party runs the risk that if he fails to object in time he may have waived his objections. *E.g., Cleminshaw v. Beech Aircraft Corp.,* 21 F.R.D. 300 (D.Del.1957); see 4 *Moore's Federal Practice,* ¶ 33.27 (2d ed. 1966); 2A Barron & Holtzoff, *Federal Practice and Procedure* 372–373 (Wright ed. 1961). It often seems easier to object than to seek an extension of time. Unlike Rules 30(d) and 37(a), Rule 33 imposes no sanction of expenses on a party whose objections are clearly unjustified.

New matter is shown in italics;   matter to be omitted is lined through

Rule 33 assures that the objections will lead directly to court, through its requirement that they be served with a notice of hearing. Although this procedure does not preclude an out-of-court resolution of the dispute, the procedure tends to discourage informal negotiations. If answers are served and they are thought inadequate, the interrogating party may move under Rule 37(a) for an order compelling adequate answers. There is no assurance that the hearing on objections and that on inadequate answers will be heard together.

The amendment improves the procedure of Rule 33 in the following respects:

(1) The time allowed for response is increased to 30 days and this time period applies to both answers and objections, but a defendant need not respond in less than 45 days after service of the summons and complaint upon him. As is true under existing law, the responding party who believes that some parts or all of the interrogatories are objectionable may choose to seek a protective order under new Rule 26(c) or may serve objections under this rule. Unless he applies for a protective order, he is required to serve answers or objections in response to the interrogatories, subject to the sanctions provided in Rule 37(d). Answers and objections are served together, so that a response to each interrogatory is encouraged, and any failure to respond is easily noted.

(2) In view of the enlarged time permitted for response, it is no longer necessary to require leave of court for service of interrogatories. The purpose of this requirement—that defendant have time to obtain counsel before a response must be made—is adequately fulfilled by the requirement that interrogatories be served upon a party with or after service of the summons and complaint upon him.

Some would urge that the plaintiff nevertheless not be permitted to serve interrogatories with the complaint. They fear that a routine practice might be invited, whereby form interrogatories would accompany most complaints. More fundamentally, they feel that, since very general complaints are permitted in present-day pleading, it is fair that the defendant have a right to take the lead in serving interrogatories. (These views apply also to Rule 36.) The amendment of Rule 33 rejects these views, in favor of allowing both parties to go forward with discovery, each free to obtain the information he needs respecting the case.

(3) If objections are made, the burden is on the interrogating party to move under Rule 37(a) for a court order compelling answers, in the course of which the court will pass on the objections. The change in the burden of going forward does not alter the existing obligation of an objecting party to justify his objections. *E.g., Pressley v. Boehlke,* 33 F.R.D. 316 (W.D.N.C. 1963). If the discovering party asserts that an answer is incomplete or evasive, again he may look to Rule 37(a) for relief, and he should add this assertion to his motion to overrule objections. There is no requirement that the parties consult informally concerning their differences, but the new procedure should encourage consultation, and the court may by local rule require it.

The proposed changes are similar in approach to those adopted by California in 1961. See Calif.Code Civ.Proc. § 2030(a). The experience of the Los Angeles Superior Court is informally reported as showing that the California amendment resulted in a significant reduction in court motions concerning interrogatories. Rhode Island takes a similar approach. See R. 33, R.I.R. Civ.Proc. Official Draft, p. 74 (Boston Law Book Co.).

A change is made in subdivision (a) which is not related to the sequence of procedures. The restriction to "adverse" parties is eliminated. The courts have generally construed this restriction as precluding interrogatories unless an issue between the parties is disclosed by the pleadings—even though the parties may have conflicting interests. *E.g., Mozeika v. Kaufman Construction Co.,* 25 F.R.D. 233

New matter is shown in italics; matter to be omitted is lined through

(E.D.Pa.1960) (plaintiff and third-party defendant); *Biddle v. Hutchinson,* 24 F.R.D. 256 (M.D.Pa.1959) (codefendants). The resulting distinctions have often been highly technical. In *Schlagenhauf v. Holder,* 379 U.S. 104 (1964), the Supreme Court rejected a contention that examination under Rule 35 could be had only against an "opposing" party, as not in keeping "with the aims of a liberal, nontechnical application of the Federal Rules." 379 U.S. at 116. Eliminating the requirement of "adverse" parties from Rule 33 brings it into line with all other discovery rules.

A second change in subdivision (a) is the addition of the term "governmental agency" to the listing of organizations whose answers are to be made by any officer or agent of the organization. This does not involve any change in existing law. Compare the similar listing in Rule 30(b)(6).

The duty of a party to supplement his answers to interrogatories is governed by a new provision in Rule 26(e).

Subdivision (b). There are numerous and conflicting decisions on the question whether and to what extent interrogatories are limited to matters "of fact," or may elicit opinions, contentions, and legal conclusions. *Compare, e.g., Payer, Hewitt & Co. v. Bellanca Corp.,* 26 F.R.D. 219 (D.Del.1960) (opinions bad); *Zinsky v. New York Central R. R.,* 36 F.R.D. 680 (N.D.Ohio 1964) (factual opinion or contention good, but legal theory bad); *United States v. Carter Products, Inc.,* 28 F.R.D. 373 (S.D.N.Y. 1961) (factual contentions and legal theories bad) *with Taylor v. Sound Steamship Lines, Inc.,* 100 F.Supp. 388 (D.Conn.1951) (opinions good); *Bynum v. United States,* 36 F.R.D. 14 (E.D.La.1964) (contentions as to facts constituting negligence good). For lists of the many conflicting authorities, see 4 *Moore's Federal Practice* ¶ 33.17 (2d ed. 1966); 2A Barron & Holtzoff, *Federal Practice and Procedure* § 768 (Wright ed. 1961).

Rule 33 is amended to provide that an interrogatory is not objectionable merely because it calls for an opinion or contention that relates to fact or the application of law to fact. Efforts to draw sharp lines between facts and opinions have invariably been unsuccessful, and the clear trend of the cases is to permit "factual" opinions. As to requests for opinions or contentions that call for the application of law to fact, they can be most useful in narrowing and sharpening the issues, which is a major purpose of discovery. See *Diversified Products Corp. v. Sports Center Co.,* 42 F.R.D. 3 (D.Md.1967); Moore, *supra;* Field & McKusick, *Maine Civil Practice* § 26.18 (1959). On the other hand, under the new language interrogatories may not extend to issues of "pure law," *i.e.,* legal issues unrelated to the facts of the case. *Cf. United States v. Maryland & Va. Milk Producers Assn., Inc.,* 22 F.R.D. 300 (D.D.C.1958).

Since interrogatories involving mixed questions of law and fact may create disputes between the parties which are best resolved after much or all of the other discovery has been completed, the court is expressly authorized to defer an answer. Likewise, the court may delay determination until pretrial conference, if it believes that the dispute is best resolved in the presence of the judge.

The principal question raised with respect to the cases permitting such interrogatories is whether they reintroduce undesirable aspects of the prior pleading practice, whereby parties were chained to misconceived contentions or theories, and ultimate determination on the merits was frustrated. See James, *The Revival of Bills of Particulars under the Federal Rules,* 71 Harv.L.Rev. 1473 (1958). But there are few if any instances in the recorded cases demonstrating that such frustration has occurred. The general rule governing the use of answers to interrogatories is that under ordinary circumstances they do not limit proof. See, *e.g., McElroy v. United Air Lines, Inc.,* 21 F.R.D. 100 (W.D.Mo.1967); *Pressley v. Boehlke,* 33 F.R.D. 316, 317 (W.D.N.C.1963). Although in exceptional circumstances reliance on an answer may cause such prejudice that the court will hold the answering party bound to his

---

New matter is shown in italics; matter to be omitted is lined through

answer, *e.g., Zielinski v. Philadelphia Piers, Inc.,* 139 F.Supp. 408 (E.D.Pa.1956), the interrogating party will ordinarily not be entitled to rely on the unchanging character of the answers he receives and cannot base prejudice on such reliance. The rule does not affect the power of a court to permit withdrawal or amendment of answers to interrogatories.

The use of answers to interrogatories at trial is made subject to the rules of evidence. The provisions governing use of depositions, to which Rule 33 presently refers, are not entirely apposite to answers to interrogatories, since deposition practice contemplates that all parties will ordinarily participate through cross-examination. See 4 *Moore's Federal Practice* ¶ 33.29[1] (2d ed. 1966).

Certain provisions are deleted from subdivision (b) because they are fully covered by new Rule 26(c) providing for protective orders and Rules 26(a) and 26(d). The language of the subdivision is thus simplified without any change of substance.

Subdivision (c). This is a new subdivision, adapted from Calif.Code Civ.Proc. § 2030(c), relating especially to interrogatories which require a party to engage in burdensome or expensive research into his own business records in order to give an answer. The subdivision gives the party an option to make the records available and place the burden of research on the party who seeks the information. "This provision, without undermining the liberal scope of interrogatory discovery, places the burden of discovery upon its potential benefitee," Louisell, *Modern California Discovery,* 124–125 (1963), and alleviates a problem which in the past has troubled Federal courts. See Speck, *The Use of Discovery in United States District Courts,* 60 Yale L.J. 1132, 1142–1144 (1951). The interrogating party is protected against abusive use of this provision through the requirement that the burden of ascertaining the answer be substantially the same for both sides. A respondent may not impose on an interrogating party a mass of records as to which research is feasible only for one familiar with the records. At the same time, the respondent unable to invoke this subdivision does not on that account lose the protection available to him under new Rule 26(c) against oppressive or unduly burdensome or expensive interrogatories. And even when the respondent successfully invokes the subdivision, the court is not deprived of its usual power, in appropriate cases, to require that the interrogating party reimburse the respondent for the expense of assembling his records and making them intelligible.

Advisory Committee's Note to 1980 Amendment

(c) Option to Produce Business Records. Where the answer to an interrogatory may be derived or ascertained from the business records of the party upon whom the interrogatory has been served or from an examination, audit or inspection of such business records, ~~or from~~ *including* a compilation, abstract or summary ~~based thereon~~ *thereof*, and the burden of deriving or ascertaining the answer is substantially the same for the party serving the interrogatory as for the party served, it is a sufficient answer to such interrogatory to specify the records from which the answer may be derived or ascertained and to afford to the party serving the interrogatory reasonable opportunity to examine, audit or inspect such records and to make copies, compilations, abstracts

---

New matter is shown in italics; matter to be omitted is lined through

or summaries. *A specification shall be in sufficient detail to permit the interrogating party to locate and to identify, as readily as can the party served, the records from which the answer may be ascertained.*

Subdivision (c). The Committee is advised that parties upon whom interrogatories are served have occasionally responded by directing the interrogating party to a mass of business records or by offering to make all of their records available, justifying the response by the option provided by this subdivision. Such practices are an abuse of the option. A party who is permitted by the terms of this subdivision to offer records for inspection in lieu of answering an interrogatory should offer them in a manner that permits the same direct and economical access that is available to the party. If the information sought exists in the form of compilations, abstracts or summaries then available to the responding party, those should be made available to the interrogating party. The final sentence is added to make it clear that a responding party has the duty to specify, by category and location, the records from which answers to interrogatories can be derived.

Advisory Committee's Note to 1993 Amendment

(a) Availability; ~~Procedures for Use~~. *Without leave of court or written stipulation, a*~~A~~ny party may serve upon any other party written interrogatories, *not exceeding 25 in number including all discrete subparts,* to be answered by the party served or, if the party served is a public or private corporation or a partnership or association or governmental agency, by any officer or agent, who shall furnish such information as is available to the party. *Leave to serve additional interrogatories shall be granted to the extent consistent with the principles of Rule 26(b)(2). Without leave of court or written stipulation, i*~~I~~nterrogatories may~~, without leave of court,~~ *not* be served ~~upon the plaintiff after commencement of the action and upon any other party with or after service of the summons and complaint upon that party~~ *before the time specified in Rule 26(d).*

(b) Answers and Objections.

(1) Each interrogatory shall be answered separately and fully in writing under oath, unless it is objected to, in which event *the objecting party shall state* the reasons for objection ~~shall be stated in lieu of an answer~~ *and shall answer to the extent the interrogatory is not objectionable.*

(2) The answers are to be signed by the person making them, and the objections signed by the attorney making them.

(3) The party upon whom the interrogatories have been served shall serve a copy of the answers, and objections if any, within 30 days after the service of the interrogatories~~, except that a defendant~~

New matter is shown in italics; matter to be omitted is lined through

~~may serve answers or objections within 45 days after service of the~~ ~~summons and complaint upon that defendant. The court may allow~~ ~~a~~A shorter or longer time *may be directed by the court or, in the absence of such an order, agreed to in writing by the parties subject to Rule 29.*

(4) All grounds for an objection to an interrogatory shall be stated with specificity. Any ground not stated in a timely objection is waived unless the party's failure to object is excused by the court for good cause shown.

(5) The party submitting the interrogatories may move for an order under Rule 37(a) with respect to any objection to or other failure to answer an interrogatory.

(~~b~~c) Scope; Use at Trial. Interrogatories may relate to any matters which can be inquired into under Rule 26(b)*(1)*, and the answers may be used to the extent permitted by the rules of evidence.

An interrogatory otherwise proper is not necessarily objectionable merely because an answer to the interrogatory involves an opinion or contention that relates to fact or the application of law to fact, but the court may order that such an interrogatory need not be answered until after designated discovery has been completed or until a pre-trial conference or other later time.

(~~c~~d) Option to Produce Business Records.

Purpose of Revision. The purpose of this revision is to reduce the frequency and increase the efficiency of interrogatory practice. The revision is based on experience with local rules. For ease of reference, subdivision (a) is divided into two subdivisions and the remaining subdivisions renumbered.

Subdivision (a). Revision of this subdivision limits interrogatory practice. Because Rule 26(a)(1)–(3) requires disclosure of much of the information previously obtained by this form of discovery, there should be less occasion to use it. Experience in over half of the district courts has confirmed that limitations on the number of interrogatories are useful and manageable. Moreover, because the device can be costly and may be used as a means of harassment, it is desirable to subject its use to the control of the court consistent with the principles stated in Rule 26(b)(2), particularly in multi-party cases where it has not been unusual for the same interrogatory to be propounded to a party by more than one of its adversaries.

Each party is allowed to serve 25 interrogatories upon any other party, but must secure leave of court (or a stipulation from the opposing party) to serve a larger number. Parties cannot evade this presumptive limitation through the device of joining as "subparts" questions that seek information about discrete separate subjects. However, a question asking about communications of a particular type should be treated as a single interrogatory even though it requests that the time, place, persons present, and contents be stated separately for each such communication.

New matter is shown in italics; matter to be omitted is lined through

As with the number of depositions authorized by Rule 30, leave to serve additional interrogatories is to be allowed when consistent with Rule 26(b)(2). The aim is not to prevent needed discovery, but to provide judicial scrutiny before parties make potentially excessive use of this discovery device. In many cases it will be appropriate for the court to permit a larger number of interrogatories in the scheduling order entered under Rule 16(b).

Unless leave of court is obtained, interrogatories may not be served prior to the meeting of the parties under Rule 26(f).

When a case with outstanding interrogatories exceeding the number permitted by this rule is removed to federal court, the interrogating party must seek leave allowing the additional interrogatories, specify which twenty-five are to be answered, or resubmit interrogatories that comply with the rule. Moreover, under Rule 26(d), the time for response would be measured from the date of the parties' meeting under Rule 26(f). See Rule 81(c), providing that these rules govern procedures after removal.

Subdivision (b). A separate subdivision is made of the former second paragraph of subdivision (a). Language is added to paragraph (1) of this subdivision to emphasize the duty of the responding party to provide full answers to the extent not objectionable. If, for example, an interrogatory seeking information about numerous facilities or products is deemed objectionable, but an interrogatory seeking information about a lesser number of facilities or products would not have been objectionable, the interrogatory should be answered with respect to the latter even though an objection is raised as to the balance of the facilities or products. Similarly, the fact that additional time may be needed to respond to some questions (or to some aspects of questions) should not justify a delay in responding to those questions (or other aspects of questions) that can be answered within the prescribed time.

Paragraph (4) is added to make clear that objections must be specifically justified, and that unstated or untimely grounds for objection ordinarily are waived. Note also the provisions of revised Rule 26(b)(5), which require a responding party to indicate when it is withholding information under a claim of privilege or as trial preparation materials.

These provisions should be read in light of Rule 26(g), authorizing the court to impose sanctions on a party and attorney making an unfounded objection to an interrogatory.

Subdivisions (c) and (d). The provisions of former subdivisions (b) and (c) are renumbered.

Rule 34. Discovery and Production of Documents and Things for Inspection, Copying, or Photographing

Advisory Committee's Note to 1970 Amendment

~~Rule 34. Discovery and Production of Documents and Things for Inspection, Copying, or Photographing~~

~~Upon motion of any party showing good cause therefor and upon notice to all other parties, and subject to the provisions of Rule 30(b), the court in which an action is pending may (1) order any party to produce and permit the inspection and copying or photographing, by or on behalf of the moving party, of any desig-~~

New matter is shown in italics; matter to be omitted is lined through

~~nated documents, papers, books, accounts, letters, photographs, objects, or tangible things, not privileged, which constitute or contain evidence relating to any of the matters within the scope of the examination permitted by Rule 26(b) and which are in his possession, custody, or control; or (2) order any party to permit entry upon designated land or other property in his possession or control for the purpose of inspecting, measuring, surveying, or photographing the property or any designated object or operation thereon within the scope of the examination permitted by Rule 26(b). The order shall specify the time, place, and manner of making the inspection and taking the copies and photographs and may prescribe such terms and conditions as are just.~~

Rule 34. *Production of Documents and Things and Entry Upon Land for Inspection and Other Purposes*

*(a) **Scope.** Any party may serve on any other party a request (1) to produce and permit the party making the request, or someone acting on his behalf, to inspect and copy, any designated documents (including writings, drawings, graphs, charts, photographs, phonorecords, and other data compilations from which information can be obtained, translated, if necessary, by the respondent through detection devices into reasonable usable form), or to inspect and copy, test, or sample any tangible things which constitute or contain matters within the scope of Rule 26(b) and which are in the possession, custody or control of the party upon whom the request is served; or (2) to permit entry upon designated land or other property in the possession or control of the party upon whom the request is served for the purpose of inspection and measuring, surveying, photographing, testing, or sampling the property or any designated objection or operation thereon, within the scope of Rule 26(b).*

*(b) **Procedure.** The request may, without leave of court, be served upon the plaintiff after commencement of the action and upon any other party with or after service of the summons and complaint upon that party. The request shall set forth the items to be inspected either by individual item or by category, and describe each item and category with reasonable particularity. The request shall specify a reasonable time, place, and manner of making the inspection and performing the related acts.*

The party upon whom the request is served shall serve a written response within 30 days after the service of the request, except that a defendant may serve a response within 45 days after service of the summons and complaint upon that defendant. The court may allow a shorter or longer time. The response shall state, with respect to each item or category, that inspection and related activities will be

---

New matter is shown in italics; matter to be omitted is lined through

permitted as requested, unless the request is objected to, in which event the reasons for objection shall be stated. If objection is made to part of an item or category, the part shall be specified. The party submitting the request may move for an order under Rule 37(a) with respect to any objection to or other failure to respond to the request or any part thereof, or any failure to permit inspection as requested.

(c) Persons Not Parties. This rule does not preclude an independent action against a person not a party for production of documents and things and permission to enter upon land.

———

Rule 34 is revised to accomplish the following major changes in the existing rule: (1) to eliminate the requirement of good cause; (2) to have the rule operate extrajudicially; (3) to include testing and sampling as well as inspecting or photographing tangible things; and (4) to make clear that the rule does not preclude an independent action for analogous discovery against persons not parties.

Subdivision (a). Good cause is eliminated because it has furnished an uncertain and erratic protection to the parties from whom production is sought and is now rendered unnecessary by virtue of the more specific provisions added to Rule 26(b) relating to materials assembled in preparation for trial and to experts retained or consulted by parties.

The good cause requirement was originally inserted in Rule 34 as a general protective provision in the absence of experience with the specific problems that would arise thereunder. As the note to Rule 26(b)(3) on trial preparation materials makes clear, good cause has been applied differently to varying classes of documents, though not without confusion. It has often been said in court opinions that good cause requires a consideration of need for the materials and of alternative means of obtaining them, *i. e.*, something more than relevance and lack of privilege. But the overwhelming proportion of the cases in which the formula of good cause has been applied to require a special showing are those involving trial preparation. In practice, the courts have not treated documents as having a special immunity to discovery simply because of their being documents. Protection may be afforded to claims of privacy or secrecy or of undue burden or expense under what is now Rule 26(c) (previously Rule 30(b)). To be sure, an appraisal of "undue" burden inevitably entails consideration of the needs of the party seeking discovery. With special provisions added to govern trial preparation materials and experts, there is no longer any occasion to retain the requirement of good cause.

The revision of Rule 34 to have it operate extrajudicially, rather than by court order, is to a large extent a reflection of existing law office practice. The Columbia Survey shows that of the litigants seeking inspection of documents or things, only about 25 percent filed motions for court orders. This minor fraction nevertheless accounted for a significant number of motions. About half of these motions were uncontested and in almost all instances the party seeking production ultimately prevailed. Although an extrajudicial procedure will not drastically alter existing practice under Rule 34—it will conform to it in most cases—it has the potential of saving court time in a substantial though proportionately small number of cases tried annually.

The inclusion of testing and sampling of tangible things and objects or operations on land reflects a need frequently encountered by parties in preparation for trial. If the operation of a particular machine is the basis of a claim for negligent

New matter is shown in italics; matter to be omitted is lined through

injury, it will often be necessary to test its operating parts or to sample and test the products it is producing. *Cf.* Mich.Gen.Ct.R. 310.1(1) (1963) (testing authorized).

The inclusive description of "documents" is revised to accord with changing technology. It makes clear that Rule 34 applies to electronic data compilations from which information can be obtained only with the use of detection devices, and that when the data can as a practical matter be made usable by the discovering party only through respondent's devices, respondent may be required to use his devices to translate the data into usable form. In many instances, this means that respondent will have to supply a print-out of computer data. The burden thus placed on respondent will vary from case to case, and the courts have ample power under Rule 26(c) to protect respondent against undue burden or expense, either by restricting discovery or requiring that the discovering party pay costs. Similarly, if the discovering party needs to check the electronic source itself, the court may protect respondent with respect to preservation of his records, confidentiality of nondiscoverable matters, and costs.

Subdivision (b). The procedure provided in Rule 34 is essentially the same as that in Rule 33, as amended, and the discussion in the note appended to that rule is relevant to Rule 34 as well. Problems peculiar to Rule 34 relate to the specific arrangements that must be worked out for inspection and related acts of copying, photographing, testing, or sampling. The rule provides that a request for inspection shall set forth the items to be inspected either by item or category, describing each with reasonable particularity, and shall specify a reasonable time, place, and manner of making the inspection.

Subdivision (c). Rule 34 as revised continues to apply only to parties. Comments from the bar make clear that in the preparation of cases for trial it is occasionally necessary to enter land or inspect large tangible things in the possession of a person not a party, and that some courts have dismissed independent actions in the nature of bills in equity for such discovery on the ground that Rule 34 is preemptive. While an ideal solution to this problem is to provide for discovery against persons not parties in Rule 34, both the jurisdictional and procedural problems are very complex. For the present, this subdivision makes clear that Rule 34 does not preclude independent actions for discovery against persons not parties.

Advisory Committee's Note to 2006 Amendment

Rule 34. Production of Documents, *Electronically Stored Information,* and Things and Entry Upon Land for Inspection and Other Purposes

(a) Scope. Any party may serve on any other party a request (1) to produce and permit the party making the request, or someone acting on the requestor's behalf, to inspect, ~~and~~ copy, *test, or sample* any designated documents *or electronically stored information*—(including writings, drawings, graphs, charts, photographs, *sound recordings, images* ~~phonorecords~~, and other *data or* data compilations *stored in any medium* from which information can be obtained,—translated, if necessary, by the respondent ~~through detection devices~~ into reasonably usable form), or to inspect, ~~and~~

New matter is shown in italics; matter to be omitted is lined through

copy, test, or sample any *designated* tangible things which constitute or contain matters within the scope of Rule 26(b) and which are in the possession, custody or control of the party upon whom the request is served; or (2) to permit entry upon designated land or other property in the possession or control of the party upon whom the request is served for the purpose of inspection and measuring, surveying, photographing, testing, or sampling the property or any designated object or operation thereon, within the scope of Rule 26(b).

(b) Procedure. The request shall set forth, either by individual item or by category, the items to be inspected, and describe each with reasonable particularity. The request shall specify a reasonable time, place, and manner of making the inspection and performing the related acts. *The request may specify the form or forms in which electronically stored information is to be produced.* Without leave of court or written stipulation, a request may not be served before the time specified in Rule 26(d).

The party upon whom the request is served shall serve a written response within 30 days after the service of the request. A shorter or longer time may be directed by the court or, in the absence of such an order, agreed to in writing by the parties, subject to Rule 29. The response shall state, with respect to each item or category, that inspection and related activities will be permitted as requested, unless the request is objected to, *including an objection to the requested form or forms for producing electronically stored information,* in which event *stating* the reasons for the objection shall be stated. If objection is made to part of an item or category, the part shall be specified and inspection permitted of the remaining parts. *If objection is made to the requested form or forms for producing electronically stored information—or if no form was specified in the request—the responding party must state the form or forms it intends to use.* The party submitting the request may move for an order under Rule 37(a) with respect to any objection to or other failure to respond to the request or any part thereof, or any failure to permit inspection as requested.

Unless the parties otherwise agree, or the court otherwise orders:

    (i) Aa party who produces documents for inspection shall produce them as they are kept in the usual course of business or shall organize and label them to correspond with the categories in the request.*;*

    (ii) if a request does not specify the form or forms for producing electronically stored information, a responding party must produce the information in a form or forms in which it is

---

New matter is shown in italics; matter to be omitted is lined through

ordinarily maintained or in a form or forms that are reasonably usable; and

(iii) a party need not produce the same electronically stored information in more than one form.

Subdivision (a). As originally adopted, Rule 34 focused on discovery of "documents" and "things." In 1970, Rule 34(a) was amended to include discovery of data compilations, anticipating that the use of computerized information would increase. Since then, the growth in electronically stored information and in the variety of systems for creating and storing such information has been dramatic. Lawyers and judges interpreted the term "documents" to include electronically stored information because it was obviously improper to allow a party to evade discovery obligations on the basis that the label had not kept pace with changes in information technology. But it has become increasingly difficult to say that all forms of electronically stored information, many dynamic in nature, fit within the traditional concept of a "document." Electronically stored information may exist in dynamic databases and other forms far different from fixed expression on paper. Rule 34(a) is amended to confirm that discovery of electronically stored information stands on equal footing with discovery of paper documents. The change clarifies that Rule 34 applies to information that is fixed in a tangible form and to information that is stored in a medium from which it can be retrieved and examined. At the same time, a Rule 34 request for production of "documents" should be understood to encompass, and the response should include, electronically stored information unless discovery in the action has clearly distinguished between electronically stored information and "documents."

Discoverable information often exists in both paper and electronic form, and the same or similar information might exist in both. The items listed in Rule 34(a) show different ways in which information may be recorded or stored. Images, for example, might be hard-copy documents or electronically stored information. The wide variety of computer systems currently in use, and the rapidity of technological change, counsel against a limiting or precise definition of electronically stored information. Rule 34(a)(1) is expansive and includes any type of information that is stored electronically. A common example often sought in discovery is electronic communications, such as e-mail. The rule covers—either as documents or as electronically stored information—information "stored in any medium," to encompass future developments in computer technology. Rule 34(a)(1) is intended to be broad enough to cover all current types of computer-based information, and flexible enough to encompass future changes and developments.

References elsewhere in the rules to "electronically stored information" should be understood to invoke this expansive approach. A companion change is made to Rule 33(d), making it explicit that parties choosing to respond to an interrogatory by permitting access to responsive records may do so by providing access to electronically stored information. More generally, the term used in Rule 34(a)(1) appears in a number of other amendments, such as those to Rules 26(a)(1), 26(b)(2), 26(b)(5)(B), 26(f), 34(b), 37(f), and 45. In each of these rules, electronically stored information has the same broad meaning it has under Rule 34(a)(1). References to "documents" appear in discovery rules that are not amended, including Rules 30(f), 36(a), and 37(c)(2). These references should be interpreted to include electronically stored information as circumstances warrant.

New matter is shown in italics; matter to be omitted is lined through

The term "electronically stored information" is broad, but whether material that falls within this term should be produced, and in what form, are separate questions that must be addressed under Rules 26(b), 26(c), and 34(b).

The Rule 34(a) requirement that, if necessary, a party producing electronically stored information translate it into reasonably usable form does not address the issue of translating from one human language to another. *See In re Puerto Rico Elect. Power Auth.*, 687 F.2d 501, 504–510 (1st Cir.1989).

Rule 34(a)(1) is also amended to make clear that parties may request an opportunity to test or sample materials sought under the rule in addition to inspecting and copying them. That opportunity may be important for both electronically stored information and hard-copy materials. The current rule is not clear that such testing or sampling is authorized; the amendment expressly permits it. As with any other form of discovery, issues of burden and intrusiveness raised by requests to test or sample can be addressed under Rules 26(b)(2) and 26(c). Inspection or testing of certain types of electronically stored information or of a responding party's electronic information system may raise issues of confidentiality or privacy. The addition of testing and sampling to Rule 34(a) with regard to documents and electronically stored information is not meant to create a routine right of direct access to a party's electronic information system, although such access might be justified in some circumstances. Courts should guard against undue intrusiveness resulting from inspecting or testing such systems.

Rule 34(a)(1) is further amended to make clear that tangible things must—like documents and land sought to be examined—be designated in the request.

Subdivision (b). Rule 34(b) provides that a party must produce documents as they are kept in the usual course of business or must organize and label them to correspond with the categories in the discovery request. The production of electronically stored information should be subject to comparable requirements to protect against deliberate or inadvertent production in ways that raise unnecessary obstacles for the requesting party. Rule 34(b) is amended to ensure similar protection for electronically stored information.

The amendment to Rule 34(b) permits the requesting party to designate the form or forms in which it wants electronically stored information produced. The form of production is more important to the exchange of electronically stored information than of hard-copy materials, although a party might specify hard copy as the requested form. Specification of the desired form or forms may facilitate the orderly, efficient, and cost-effective discovery of electronically stored information. The rule recognizes that different forms of production may be appropriate for different types of electronically stored information. Using current technology, for example, a party might be called upon to produce word processing documents, e-mail messages, electronic spreadsheets, different image or sound files, and material from databases. Requiring that such diverse types of electronically stored information all be produced in the same form could prove impossible, and even if possible could increase the cost and burdens of producing and using the information. The rule therefore provides that the requesting party may ask for different forms of production for different types of electronically stored information.

The rule does not require that the requesting party choose a form or forms of production. The requesting party may not have a preference. In some cases, the requesting party may not know what form the producing party uses to maintain its electronically stored information, although Rule 26(f)(3) is amended to call for discussion of the form of production in the parties' prediscovery conference.

The responding party also is involved in determining the form of production. In the written response to the production request that Rule 34 requires, the responding

---

New matter is shown in italics; matter to be omitted is lined through

party must state the form it intends to use for producing electronically stored information if the requesting party does not specify a form or if the responding party objects to a form that the requesting party specifies. Stating the intended form before the production occurs may permit the parties to identify and seek to resolve disputes before the expense and work of the production occurs. A party that responds to a discovery request by simply producing electronically stored information in a form of its choice, without identifying that form in advance of the production in the response required by Rule 34(b), runs a risk that the requesting party can show that the produced form is not reasonably usable and that it is entitled to production of some or all of the information in an additional form. Additional time might be required to permit a responding party to assess the appropriate form or forms of production.

If the requesting party is not satisfied with the form stated by the responding party, or if the responding party has objected to the form specified by the requesting party, the parties must meet and confer under Rule 37(a)(2)(B) in an effort to resolve the matter before the requesting party can file a motion to compel. If they cannot agree and the court resolves the dispute, the court is not limited to the forms initially chosen by the requesting party, stated by the responding party, or specified in this rule for situations in which there is no court order or party agreement.

If the form of production is not specified by party agreement or court order, the responding party must produce electronically stored information either in a form or forms in which it is ordinarily maintained or in a form or forms that are reasonably usable. Rule 34(a) requires that, if necessary, a responding party "translate" information it produces into a "reasonably usable" form. Under some circumstances, the responding party may need to provide some reasonable amount of technical support, information on application software, or other reasonable assistance to enable the requesting party to use the information. The rule does not require a party to produce electronically stored information in the form it which it is ordinarily maintained, as long as it is produced in a reasonably usable form. But the option to produce in a reasonably usable form does not mean that a responding party is free to convert electronically stored information from the form in which it is ordinarily maintained to a different form that makes it more difficult or burdensome for the requesting party to use the information efficiently in the litigation. If the responding party ordinarily maintains the information it is producing in a way that makes it searchable by electronic means, the information should not be produced in a form that removes or significantly degrades this feature.

Some electronically stored information may be ordinarily maintained in a form that is not reasonably usable by any party. One example is "legacy" data that can be used only by superseded systems. The questions whether a producing party should be required to convert such information to a more usable form, or should be required to produce it at all, should be addressed under Rule 26(b)(2)(B).

Whether or not the requesting party specified the form of production, Rule 34(b) provides that the same electronically stored information ordinarily need be produced in only one form.

Rule 35. Physical and Mental Examination of Persons

Advisory Committee's Note to 1970 Amendment

(a) Order for Examination. In an action in which *When* the mental or physical condition *(including the blood group)* of a party, *or of a person in the custody or under the legal control of a party,* is

---

New matter is shown in italics; matter to be omitted is lined through

in controversy, the court in which the action is pending may order ~~him~~ *the party* to submit to a physical or mental examination by a physician *or to produce for examination the person in his custody or legal control*. The order may be made only on motion for good cause shown and upon notice to the ~~party~~ *person* to be examined and to all ~~other~~ parties and shall specify the time, place, manner, conditions, and scope of the examination and the person or persons by whom it is to be made.

(b) Report of *Examining Physician* ~~Findings.~~

(1) If requested by the *party against whom an order is made under Rule 35(a) or the* person examined, the party causing the examination to be made shall deliver to him a copy of a detailed written report of the examining physician setting out his findings, *including results of all tests made, diagnoses* and ~~conclusions.~~*, together with like reports of all earlier examinations of the same condition.* After ~~such request and~~ delivery the party causing the examination ~~to be made~~ shall be entitled upon request to receive from the party ~~examined~~ *against whom the order is made* a like report of any examination, previously or thereafter made, of the same ~~mental or physical~~ condition~~.~~*, unless, in the case of a report of examination of a person not a party, the party shows that he is unable to obtain it.* ~~If the party examined refuses to deliver such report t~~*T*he ͡court on motion ~~and notice~~ may make an order *against a party* requiring delivery of a *report* on such terms as are just, and if a physician fails or refuses to make ~~such~~ a report the court may exclude his testimony if offered at the trial.

(2) By requesting and obtaining a report of the examination so ordered or by taking the deposition of the examiner, the party examined waives any privilege he may have in that action or any other involving the same controversy, regarding the testimony of every other person who has examined or may thereafter examine him in respect of the same mental or physical condition.

(3) This subdivision applies to examinations made by agreement of the parties, unless the agreement expressly provides otherwise. This subdivision does not preclude discovery of a report of an examining physician or the taking of a deposition of the physician in accordance with the provisions of any other rule.

Subdivision (a). Rule 35(a) has hitherto provided only for an order requiring a party to submit to an examination. It is desirable to extend the rule to provide for an order against the party for examination of a person in his custody or under his legal control. As appears from the provisions of amended Rule 37(b)(2) and the comment

New matter is shown in italics; matter to be omitted is lined through

under that rule, an order to "produce" the third person imposes only an obligation to use good faith efforts to produce the person.

The amendment will settle beyond doubt that a parent or guardian suing to recover for injuries to a minor may be ordered to produce the minor for examination. Further, the amendment expressly includes blood examination within the kinds of examinations that can be ordered under the rule. See *Beach v. Beach,* 114 F.2d 479 (D.C.Cir.1940). Provisions similar to the amendment have been adopted in at least 10 States: Calif.Code Civ.Proc. § 2032; Ida.R.Civ.P. 35; Ill. S–H Ann. c. 110A, § 215; Md.R.P. 420; Mich.Gen.Ct.R. 311; Minn.R.Civ.P. 35; Mo.Vern.Ann.R.Civ.P. 60.01; N.Dak.R.Civ.P. 35; N.Y.C.P.L. § 3121; Wyo.R.Civ.R. 35.

The amendment makes no change in the requirements of Rule 35 that, before a court order may issue, the relevant physical or mental condition must be shown to be "in controversy" and "good cause" must be shown for the examination. Thus, the amendment has no effect on the recent decision of the Supreme Court in *Schlagenhauf v. Holder,* 379 U.S. 104 (1964), stressing the importance of these requirements and applying them to the facts of the case. The amendment makes no reference to employees of a party. Provisions relating to employees in the State statutes and rules cited above appear to have been virtually unused.

Subdivision (b)(1). This subdivision is amended to correct an imbalance in Rule 35(b)(1) as heretofore written. Under that text, a party causing a Rule 35(a) examination to be made is required to furnish to the party examined, on request, a copy of the examining physician's report. If he delivers this copy, he is in turn entitled to receive from the party examined reports of all examinations of the same condition previously or later made. But the rule has not in terms entitled the examined party to receive from the party causing the Rule 35(a) examination any reports of earlier examinations of the same condition to which the latter may have access. The amendment cures this defect. See La.Stat.Ann., Civ.Proc. art. 1495 (1960); Utah R.Civ.P. 35(c).

The amendment specifies that the written report of the examining physician includes results of all tests made, such as results of X-rays and cardiograms. It also embodies changes required by the broadening of Rule 35(a) to take in persons who are not parties.

Subdivision (b)(3). This new subdivision removes any possible doubt that reports of examination may be obtained although no order for examination has been made under Rule 35(a). Examinations are very frequently made by agreement, and sometimes before the party examined has an attorney. The courts have uniformly ordered that reports be supplied, see 4 *Moore's Federal Practice* ¶ 35.06, n. 1 (2d ed. 1966); 2A Barron & Holtzoff, *Federal Practice and Procedure* § 823, n. 22 (Wright ed. 1961), and it appears best to fill the technical gap in the present rule.

The subdivision also makes clear that reports of examining physicians are discoverable not only under Rule 35(b) but under other rules as well. To be sure, if the report is privileged, then discovery is not permissible under any rule other than Rule 35(b) and it is permissible under Rule 35(b) only if the party requests a copy of the report of examination made by the other party's doctor. *Sher v. De Haven,* 199 F.2d 777 (D.C.Cir.1952), *cert. denied* 345 U.S. 936 (1953). But if the report is unprivileged and is subject to discovery under the provisions of rules other than Rule 35(b)—such as Rules 34 or 26(b)(3) or (4)—discovery should not depend upon whether the person examined demands a copy of the report. Although a few cases have suggested the contrary, *e.g., Galloway v. National Dairy Products Corp.,* 24 F.R.D. 362 (E.D.Pa.1959), the better considered district court decisions hold that Rule 35(b) is not preemptive. *E.g., Leszynski v. Russ,* 29 F.R.D. 10, 12 (D.Md.1961)

New matter is shown in italics; matter to be omitted is lined through

and cases cited. The question was recently given full consideration in *Buffington v. Wood,* 351 F.2d 292 (3d Cir.1965), holding that Rule 35(b) is not preemptive.

Rule 36. Admission of Facts and of Genuineness of Documents

Advisory Committee's Note to 1970 Amendment

Rule 36. *Requests for* Admission ~~of Facts and of Genuineness of Documents~~

(a) Request for Admission. ~~After commencement of an action a party may serve upon any other party a written request for the admission by the latter of the genuineness of any relevant documents described in and exhibited with the request or of the truth of any relevant matters of fact set forth in the request. If a plaintiff desires to serve a request within 10 days after commencement of the action leave of court, granted with or without notice, must be obtained. Copies of the documents shall be served with the request unless copies have already been furnished.~~ *A party may serve upon any other party a written request for the admission, for purposes of the pending action only, of the truth of any matters within the scope of Rule 26(b) set forth in the request that relate to statements or opinions of fact or of the application of law to fact, including the genuineness of any documents described in the request. Copies of documents shall be served with the request unless they have been or are otherwise furnished or made available for inspection and copying. The request may, without leave of court, be served upon the plaintiff after commencement of the action and upon any other party with or after service of the summons and complaint upon that party.*

Each ~~of the matters~~ *matter* of which an admission is requested *shall be separately set forth.* ~~shall be deemed~~ *The matter is* admitted unless, within ~~a period designated in the request, not less than 10~~ *30* days after service ~~thereof~~ *of the request,* or within such shorter or longer time as the court may allow ~~on motion and notice~~, the party to whom the request is directed serves upon the party requesting the admission ~~either (1) a sworn statement denying~~ *a written answer or objection addressed to the matter, signed by the party or by his attorney, but, unless the court shortens the time, a defendant shall not be required to serve answers or objections before the expiration of 45 days after service of the summons and complaint upon him. If objection is made, the reasons therefor shall be stated. The answer shall* specifically *deny* the ~~matters of which an admission is requested~~ *matter* or ~~setting~~ *set* forth in detail the reasons why ~~he~~ *the answering party* cannot truthfully admit or deny ~~those~~

New matter is shown in italics; matter to be omitted is lined through

~~matters~~ *the matter.* ~~or (2) written objections on the ground that some or all of the requested admissions are privileged or irrelevant or that the request is otherwise improper in whole or in part, together with a notice of hearing the objections at the earliest practicable time. If written objections to a part of the request are made, the remainder of the request shall be answered within the period designated in the request.~~ A denial shall fairly meet the substance of the requested admission, and when good faith requires that a party *qualify his answer or* deny only a part ~~or a qualification~~ of ~~a~~ *the* matter of which an admission is requested, he shall specify so much of it as is true and *qualify or* deny ~~only~~ the remainder. *An answering party may not give lack of information or knowledge as a reason for failure to admit or deny unless he states that he has made reasonable inquiry and that the information known or readily obtainable by him is insufficient to enable him to admit or deny. A party who considers that a matter of which an admission has been requested presents a genuine issue for trial may not, on that ground alone, object to the request; he may, subject to the provisions of Rule 37(c), deny the matter or set forth reasons why he cannot admit or deny it.*

The party who has requested the admissions may move to determine the sufficiency of the answers or objections. Unless the court determines that an objection is justified, it shall order that an answer be served. If the court determines that an answer does not comply with the requirements of this rule, it may order either that the matter is admitted or that an amended answer be served. The court may, in lieu of these orders, determine that final disposition of the request be made at a pre-trial conference or at a designated time prior to trial. The provisions of Rule 37(a)(4) apply to the award of expenses incurred in relation to the motion.

(b) Effect of Admission. *Any matter admitted under this rule is conclusively established unless the court on motion permits withdrawal or amendment of the admission. Subject to the provisions of Rule 16 governing amendment of a pre-trial order, the court may permit withdrawal or amendment when the presentation of the merits of the action will be subserved thereby and the party who obtained the admission fails to satisfy the court that withdrawal or amendment will prejudice him in maintaining his action or defense on the merits.* Any admission made by a party ~~pursuant to such request~~ *under this rule* is for the purpose of the pending action only and ~~neither constitutes~~ *is not* an admission by him for any other purpose nor may *it* be used against him in any other proceeding.

New matter is shown in italics; matter to be omitted is lined through

Rule 36 serves two vital purposes, both of which are designed to reduce trial time. Admissions are sought, first to facilitate proof with respect to issues that cannot be eliminated from the case, and secondly, to narrow the issues by eliminating those that can be. The changes made in the rule are designed to serve these purposes more effectively. Certain disagreements in the courts about the proper scope of the rule are resolved. In addition, the procedural operation of the rule is brought into line with other discovery procedures, and the binding effect of an admission is clarified. See generally Finman, *The Request for Admissions in Federal Civil Procedure*, 71 Yale L.J. 371 (1962).

Subdivision (a). As revised, the subdivision provides that a request may be made to admit any matters within the scope of Rule 26(b) that relate to statements or opinions of fact or of the application of law to fact. It thereby eliminates the requirement that the matters be "of fact." This change resolves conflicts in the court decisions as to whether a request to admit matters of "opinion" and matters involving "mixed law and fact" is proper under the rule. As to "opinion," *compare, e.g., Jackson Bluff Corp. v. Marcelle*, 20 F.R.D. 139 (E.D.N.Y.1957); *California v. The S. S. Jules Fribourg*, 19 F.R.D. 432 (N.D.Calif.1955), *with e.g., Photon, Inc. v. Harris Intertype, Inc.*, 28 F.R.D. 327 (D.Mass.1961); *Hise v. Lockwood Grader Corp.*, 153 F.Supp. 276 (D.Nebr.1957). As to "mixed law and fact" the majority of courts sustain objections, *e.g., Minnesota Mining and Mfg. Co. v. Norton Co.*, 36 F.R.D. 1 (N.D.Ohio 1964), but *McSparran v. Hanigan*, 225 F.Supp. 628 (E.D.Pa.1963) is to the contrary.

Not only is it difficult as a practical matter to separate "fact" from "opinion," see 4 *Moore's Federal Practice* ¶ 36.04 (2d ed. 1966); *cf.* 2A Barron & Holtzoff, *Federal Practice and Procedure* 317 (Wright ed. 1961), but an admission on a matter of opinion may facilitate proof or narrow the issues or both. An admission of a matter involving the application of law to fact may, in a given case, even more clearly narrow the issues. For example, an admission that an employee acted in the scope of his employment may remove a major issue from the trial. In *McSparran v. Hanigan, supra,* plaintiff admitted that "the premises on which said accident occurred, were occupied or under the control" of one of the defendants, 225 F.Supp. at 636. This admission, involving law as well as fact, removed one of the issues from the lawsuit and thereby reduced the proof required at trial. The amended provision does not authorize requests for admissions of law unrelated to the facts of the case.

Requests for admission involving the application of law to fact may create disputes between the parties which are best resolved in the presence of the judge after much or all of the other discovery has been completed. Power is therefore expressly conferred upon the court to defer decision until a pretrial conference is held or until a designated time prior to trial. On the other hand, the court should not automatically defer decision; in many instances, the importance of the admission lies in enabling the requesting party to avoid the burdensome accumulation of proof prior to the pretrial conference.

Courts have also divided on whether an answering party may properly object to request for admission as to matters which that party regards as "in dispute." *Compare, e.g., Syracuse Broadcasting Corp. v. Newhouse*, 271 F.2d 910, 917 (2d Cir.1959); *Driver v. Gindy Mfg. Corp.*, 24 F.R.D. 473 (E.D.Pa.1959); *with, e.g., McGonigle v. Baxter*, 27 F.R.D. 504 (E.D.Pa.1961); *United States v. Ehbauer*, 13 F.R.D. 462 (W.D.Mo.1952). The proper response in such cases is an answer. The very purpose of the request is to ascertain whether the answering party is prepared to admit or regards the matter as presenting a genuine issue for trial. In his answer, the party may deny, or he may give as his reason for inability to admit or deny the existence of a genuine issue. The party runs no risk of sanctions if the matter is

---

New matter is shown in italics; matter to be omitted is lined through

genuinely in issue, since Rule 37(c) provides a sanction of costs only when there are no good reasons for a failure to admit.

On the other hand, requests to admit may be so voluminous and so framed that the answering party finds the task of identifying what is in dispute and what is not unduly burdensome. If so, the responding party may obtain a protective order under Rule 26(c). Some of the decisions sustaining objections on "disputability" grounds could have been justified by the burdensome character of the requests. See, *e.g., Syracuse Broadcasting Corp. v. Newhouse, supra.*

Another sharp split of authority exists on the question whether a party may base his answer on lack of information or knowledge without seeking out additional information. One line of cases has held that a party may answer on the basis of such knowledge as he has at the time he answers. *E.g., Jackson Buff Corp. v. Marcelle,* 20 F.R.D. 139 (E.D.N.Y.1957); *Sladek v. General Motors Corp.,* 16 F.R.D. 104 (S.D.Iowa 1954). A larger group of cases, supported by commentators, has taken the view that if the responding party lacks knowledge, he must inform himself in reasonable fashion. *E.g., Hise v. Lockwood Grader Corp.,* 153 F.Supp. 276 (D.Nebr.1957); *E. H. Tate Co. v. Jiffy Enterprises, Inc.,* 16 F.R.D. 571 (E.D.Pa.1954); Finman, *supra,* 71 Yale L.J. 371, 404–409; 4 *Moore's Federal Practice* ¶ 36.04 (2d ed. 1966); 2A Barron & Holtzoff, *Federal Practice and Procedure* 509 (Wright ed. 1961).

The rule as revised adopts the majority view, as in keeping with a basic principle of the discovery rules that a reasonable burden may be imposed on the parties when its discharge will facilitate preparation for trial and ease the trial process. It has been argued against this view that one side should not have the burden of "proving" the other side's case. The revised rule requires only that the answering party make reasonable inquiry and secure such knowledge and information as are readily obtainable by him. In most instances, the investigation will be necessary either to his own case or to preparation for rebuttal. Even when it is not, the information may be close enough at hand to be "readily obtainable." Rule 36 requires only that the party state that he has taken these steps. The sanction for failure of a party to inform himself before he answers lies in the award of costs after trial, as provided in Rule 37(c).

The requirement that the answer to a request for admission be sworn is deleted, in favor of a provision that the answer be signed by the party or by his attorney. The provisions of Rule 36 make it clear that admissions function very much as pleadings do. Thus, when a party admits in part and denies in part, his admission is for purposes of the pending action only and may not be used against him in any other proceeding. The broadening of the rule to encompass mixed questions of law and fact reinforces this feature. Rule 36 does not lack a sanction for false answers; Rule 37(c) furnishes an appropriate deterrent.

The existing language describing the available grounds for objection to a request for admission is eliminated as neither necessary nor helpful. The statement that objection may be made to any request which is "improper" adds nothing to the provisions that the party serve an answer or objection addressed to each matter and that he state his reasons for any objection. None of the other discovery rules sets forth grounds for objection, except so far as all are subject to the general provisions of Rule 26.

Changes are made in the sequence of procedures in Rule 36 so that they conform to the new procedures in Rules 33 and 34. The major changes are as follows:

(1) The normal time for response to a request for admissions is lengthened from 10 to 30 days, conforming more closely to prevailing practice. A defendant need not respond, however, in less than 45 days after service of the summons and complaint

---

New matter is shown in italics; matter to be omitted is lined through

upon him. The court may lengthen or shorten the time when special situations require it.

(2) The present requirement that the plaintiff wait 10 days to serve requests without leave of court is eliminated. The revised provision accords with those in Rules 33 and 34.

(3) The requirement that the objecting party move automatically for a hearing on his objection is eliminated, and the burden is on the requesting party to move for an order. The change in the burden of going forward does not modify present law on burden of persuasion. The award of expenses incurred in relation to the motion is made subject to the comprehensive provisions of Rule 37(a)(4).

(4) A problem peculiar to Rule 36 arises if the responding party serves answers that are not in conformity with the requirements of the rule—for example, a denial is not "specific," or the explanation of inability to admit or deny is not "in detail." Rule 36 now makes no provision for court scrutiny of such answers before trial, and it seems to contemplate that defective answers bring about admissions just as effectively as if no answer had been served. Some cases have so held. *E.g., Southern Ry. Co. v. Crosby*, 201 F.2d 878 (4th Cir.1953); *United States v. Laney*, 96 F.Supp. 482 (E.D.S.C.1951).

Giving a defective answer the automatic effect of an admission may cause unfair surprise. A responding party who purported to deny or to be unable to admit or deny will for the first time at trial confront the contention that he has made a binding admission. Since it is not always easy to know whether a denial is "specific" or an explanation is "in detail," neither party can know how the court will rule at trial and whether proof must be prepared. Some courts, therefore, have entertained motions to rule on defective answers. They have at times ordered that amended answers be served, when the defects were technical, and at other times have declared that the matter was admitted. *E.g., Woods v. Stewart*, 171 F.2d 544 (5th Cir.1948); *SEC v. Kaye, Real & Co.*, 122 F.Supp. 639 (S.D.N.Y.1954); *Sieb's Hatcheries, Inc. v. Lindley*, 13 F.R.D. 113 (W.D.Ark.1952). The rule as revised conforms to the latter practice.

Subdivision (b). The rule does not now indicate the extent to which a party is bound by his admission. Some courts view admissions as the equivalent of sworn testimony. *E.g., Ark–Tenn Distributing Corp. v. Breidt*, 209 F.2d 359 (3d Cir.1954); *United States v. Lemons*, 125 F.Supp. 686 (W.D.Ark.1954); 4 *Moore's Federal Practice* ¶ 36.08 (2d ed. 1966 Supp.). At least in some jurisdictions a party may rebut his own testimony, *e.g., Alamo v. Del Rosario*, 98 F.2d 328 (D.C.Cir.1938), and by analogy an admission made pursuant to Rule 36 may likewise be thought rebuttable. The courts in *Ark-Tenn* and *Lemons, supra*, reasoned in this way, although the results reached may be supported on different grounds. In *McSparran v. Hanigan*, 225 F.Supp. 628, 636–637 (E.D.Pa.1963), the court held that an admission is conclusively binding, though noting the confusion created by prior decisions.

The new provisions give an admission a conclusively binding effect, for purposes only of the pending action, unless the admission is withdrawn or amended. In form and substance a Rule 36 admission is comparable to an admission in pleadings or a stipulation drafted by counsel for use at trial, rather than to an evidentiary admission of a party. Louisell, *Modern California Discovery* § 8.07 (1963); 2A Barron & Holtzoff, *Federal Practice and Procedure* § 838 (Wright ed. 1961). Unless the party securing an admission can depend on its binding effect, he cannot safely avoid the expense of preparing to prove the very matters on which he has secured the admission, and the purpose of the rule is defeated. Field & McKusick, *Maine Civil Practice* § 36.4 (1959); Finman, *supra,* 71 Yale L.J. 371, 418–426; Comment, 56 Nw.U.L.Rev. 679, 682–683 (1961).

New matter is shown in italics; matter to be omitted is lined through

Provision is made for withdrawal or amendment of an admission. This provision emphasizes the importance of having the action resolved on the merits, while at the same time assuring each party that justified reliance on an admission in preparation for trial will not operate to his prejudice. *Cf. Moosman v. Joseph P. Blitz, Inc.,* 358 F.2d 686 (2d Cir.1966).

Rule 37. Refusal to Make Discovery: Consequences

Advisory Committee's Note to 1970 Amendment

Rule 37. ~~Refusal~~ *Failure* to Make Discovery: ~~Consequences~~ *Sanctions*

~~(a) Refusal to Answer.~~ ~~If a party or other deponent refuses to answer any question propounded upon oral examination, the examination shall be completed on other matters or adjourned, as the proponent of the question may prefer. Thereafter, on reasonable notice to all persons affected thereby, he may apply to the court in the district where the deposition is taken for an order compelling an answer. Upon the refusal of a deponent to answer any interrogatory submitted under Rule 31 or upon the refusal of a party to answer any interrogatory submitted under Rule 33, the proponent of the question may on like notice make like application for such an order. If the motion is granted and if the court finds that the refusal was without substantial justification the court shall require the refusing party or deponent and the party or attorney advising the refusal or either of them to pay to the examining party the amount of the reasonable expenses incurred in obtaining the order, including reasonable attorney's fees. If the motion is denied and if the court finds that the motion was made without substantial justification, the court shall require the examining party or the attorney advising the motion or both of them to pay to the refusing party or witness the amount of the reasonable expenses incurred in opposing the motion, including reasonable attorney's fees.~~

(a) Motion for Order Compelling Discovery. A party, upon reasonable notice to other parties and all persons affected thereby, may apply for an order compelling discovery as follows:

    (1) Appropriate Court. An application for an order to a party may be made to the court in which the action is pending, or, on matters relating to a deposition, to the court in the district where the deposition is being taken. An application for an order to a deponent who is not a party shall be made to the court in the district where the deposition is being taken.

    (2) Motion. If a deponent fails to answer a question propounded or submitted under Rule 30 or 31, or a corporation or

New matter is shown in italics; matter to be omitted is lined through

other entity fails to make a designation under Rule 30(b)(6) or 31(a), or a party fails to answer an interrogatory submitted under Rule 33, or if a party, in response to a request for inspection submitted under Rule 34, fails to respond that inspection will be permitted as requested or fails to permit inspection as requested, the discovering party may move for an order compelling an answer, or a designation, or an order compelling inspection in accordance with the request. When taking a deposition on oral examination, the proponent of the question may complete or adjourn the examination before he applies for an order.

If the court denies the motion in whole or in part, it may make such protective order as it would have been empowered to make on a motion made pursuant to Rule 26(c).

(3) Evasive or Incomplete Answer. For purposes of this subdivision an evasive or incomplete answer is to be treated as a failure to answer.

(4) Award of Expenses of Motion. If the motion is granted, the court shall, after opportunity for hearing, require the party or deponent whose conduct necessitated the motion or the party or attorney advising such conduct or both of them to pay to the moving party the reasonable expenses incurred in obtaining the order, including attorney's fees, unless the court finds that the opposition to the motion was substantially justified or that other circumstances make an award of expenses unjust.

If the motion is denied, the court shall, after opportunity for hearing, require the moving party or the attorney advising the motion or both of them to pay the party or deponent who opposed the motion the reasonable expenses incurred in opposing the motion, including attorney's fees, unless the court finds that the making of the motion was substantially justified or that other circumstances make an award of expenses unjust.

If the motion is granted in part and denied in part, the court may apportion the reasonable expenses incurred in relation to the motion among the parties and persons in a just manner.

(b) Failure to Comply With Order.

(1) ~~Contempt~~ *Sanctions by Court in District Where Deposition is Taken.* If a ~~party or other~~ *deponent* ~~witness refuses~~ *fails* to be sworn or ~~refuses~~ to answer ~~any~~ *a* question after being directed to do so by the court in the district in which the deposition is being taken, the ~~refusal~~ *failure* may be considered a contempt of that court.

New matter is shown in italics; matter to be omitted is lined through

(2) ~~Other Consequences~~ *Sanctions by Court in Which Action is Pending.* If ~~any~~ *a* party or an officer, *director,* or managing agent of a party *or a person designated under Rule 30(b)(6) or 31(a) to testify on behalf of a party* ~~refuses~~ *fails* to obey an order *to provide or permit discovery, including an order* made under subdivision (a) of this rule ~~requiring him to answer designated questions, or an order made under Rule 34 to produce any document or other thing for inspection, copying, or photographing or to permit it to be done, or to permit entry upon land or other property, or an order made under~~ *or* Rule 35 ~~requiring him to submit to a physical or mental examination~~, the court *in which the action is pending* may make such orders in regard to the ~~refusal~~ *failure* as are just, and among others the following:

~~(i)~~*(A)* An order that the matters regarding which the ~~questions were asked, or the character or description of the thing or land, or the contents of the paper, or the physical or mental condition of the party,~~ *order was made* or any other designated facts shall be taken to be established for the purposes of the action in accordance with the claim of the party obtaining the order;

~~(ii)~~*(B)* An order refusing to allow the disobedient party to support or oppose designated claims or defenses, or prohibiting him from introducing *designated matters* in evidence ~~designated documents or things or items of testimony, or from introducing evidence of physical or mental condition~~;

~~(iii)~~*(C)* An order striking out pleadings or parts thereof, or staying further proceedings until the order is obeyed, or dismissing the action or proceeding or any part thereof, or rendering a judgment by default against the disobedient party;

~~(iv)~~*(D)* In lieu of any of the foregoing orders or in addition thereto, an order ~~directing the arrest of any party or agent of a party for disobeying~~ *treating* as a contempt of court the failure to obey* any ~~of such~~ orders except an order to submit to a physical or mental examination~~.~~*;*

(E) Where a party has failed to comply with an order under Rule 35(a) requiring him to produce another for examination, such orders as are listed in paragraphs (A), (B), and (C) of this subdivision, unless the party failing to comply shows that he is unable to produce such person for examination.

In lieu of any of the foregoing orders or in addition thereto, the court shall require the party failing to obey the order or the attorney advising him or both to pay the reasonable expenses, including attorney's fees, caused by the failure, unless the court finds that the

---

New matter is shown in italics; matter to be omitted is lined through

failure was substantially justified or that other circumstances make an award of expenses unjust.

(c) Expenses on ~~Refusal~~ *Failure* To Admit. If a party ~~after being served with request under Rule 36,~~ *fails* to admit the genuineness of any documents or the truth of any matter~~s of fact~~ *as requested under Rule 36,* ~~serves a sworn denial thereof~~ and if the party requesting the admissions thereafter proves the genuineness of ~~any such~~ *the* document or the truth of ~~any such~~ *the* matter ~~of fact~~, he may apply to the court for an order requiring the other party to pay him the reasonable expenses incurred in making ~~such~~ *that* proof, including reasonable attorney's fees. ~~Unless the court finds that there were good reasons for the denial or that the admissions sought were of no substantial importance, the order shall be made.~~ *The court shall make the order unless it finds that (1) the request was held objectionable pursuant to Rule 36(a), or (2) the admission sought was of no substantial importance, or (3) the party failing to admit had reasonable ground to believe that he might prevail on the matter, or (4) there was other good reason for the failure to admit.*

(d) Failure of Party To Attend *at Own Deposition* or Serve Answers *to Interrogatories or Respond to Request for Inspection*. If a party or an officer, *director,* or managing agent of a party *or a person designated under Rule 30(b)(6) or 31(a) to testify on behalf of a party* ~~wilfully~~ fails *(1)* to appear before the officer who is to take his deposition, after being served with a proper notice, or ~~fails~~ *(2)* to serve answers *or objections* to interrogatories submitted under Rule 33, after proper service of ~~such~~ *the* interrogatories, *or (3) to serve a written response to a request for inspection submitted under Rule 34, after proper service of the request,* the court *in which the action is pending* on motion ~~and notice~~ may ~~strike out all or any part of any pleading of that party, or dismiss the action or proceeding or any part thereof, or enter a judgment by default against that party.~~ *make such orders in regard to the failure as are just, and among others it may take any action authorized under paragraph (A), (B), and (C) of subdivision (b)(2) of this rule. In lieu of any order or in addition thereto, the court shall require the party failing to act or the attorney advising him or both to pay the reasonable expenses, including attorney's fees, caused by the failure, unless the court finds that the failure was substantially justified or that other circumstances make an award of expenses unjust.*

The failure to act described in this subdivision may not be excused on the ground that the discovery sought is objectionable unless the party failing to act has applied for a protective order as provided by Rule 26(c).

New matter is shown in italics; matter to be omitted is lined through

(e) ~~Failure To Respond to Letters Rogatory.~~ *Subpoena of Person in Foreign Country.* A subpoena may be issued as provided in Title 28 U.S.C. § 1783, under the circumstances and conditions therein stated.

(f) **Expenses Against United States.** ~~Expenses and attorney's fees are not to be imposed upon~~ *Except to the extent permitted by statute, expenses and fees may not be awarded against* the United States under this rule.

Rule 37 provides generally for sanctions against parties or persons unjustifiably resisting discovery. Experience has brought to light a number of defects in the language of the rule as well as instances in which it is not serving the purposes for which it was designed. See Rosenberg, *Sanctions to Effectuate Pretrial Discovery,* 58 Col.L.Rev. 480 (1958). In addition, changes being made in other discovery rules require conforming amendments to Rule 37.

Rule 37 sometimes refers to a "failure" to afford discovery and at other times to a "refusal" to do so. Taking note of this dual terminology, courts have imported into "refusal" a requirement of "wilfullness." See *Roth v. Paramount Pictures Corp.,* 8 F.R.D. 31 (W.D.Pa.1948); *Campbell v. Johnson,* 101 F.Supp. 705, 707 (S.D.N.Y.1951). In *Societe Internationale v. Rogers,* 357 U.S. 197 (1958), the Supreme Court concluded that the rather random use of these two terms in Rule 37 showed no design to use them with consistently distinctive meanings, that "refused" in Rule 37(b)(2) meant simply a failure to comply, and that wilfullness was relevant only to the selection of sanctions, if any, to be imposed. Nevertheless, after the decision in *Societe,* the court in *Hinson v. Michigan Mutual Liability Co.,* 275 F.2d 537 (5th Cir.1960) once again ruled that "refusal" required wilfullness. Substitution of "failure" for "refusal" throughout Rule 37 should eliminate this confusion and bring the rule into harmony with the *Societe Internationale* decision. See Rosenberg, *supra,* 58 Col.L.Rev. 480, 489–490 (1958).

Subdivision (a). Rule 37(a) provides relief to a party seeking discovery against one who, with or without stated objections, fails to afford the discovery sought. It has always fully served this function in relation to depositions, but the amendments being made to Rules 33 and 34 give Rule 37(a) added scope and importance. Under existing Rule 33, a party objecting to interrogatories must make a motion for court hearing on his objections. The changes now made in Rules 33 and 37(a) make it clear that the interrogating party must move to compel answers, and the motion is provided for in Rule 37(a). Existing Rule 34, since it requires a court order prior to production of documents or things or permission to enter on land, has no relation to Rule 37(a). Amendments of Rules 34 and 37(a) create a procedure similar to that provided for Rule 33.

Subdivision (a)(1). This is a new provision making clear to which court a party may apply for an order compelling discovery. Existing Rule 37(a) refers only to the court in which the deposition is being taken; nevertheless, it has been held that the court where the action is pending has "inherent power" to compel a party deponent to answer. *Lincoln Laboratories, Inc. v. Savage Laboratories, Inc.,* 27 F.R.D. 476 (D.Del.1961). In relation to Rule 33 interrogatories and Rule 34 requests for inspection, the court where the action is pending is the appropriate enforcing tribunal. The new provision eliminates the need to resort to inherent power by spelling out the respective roles of the court where the action is pending and the

---

New matter is shown in italics; matter to be omitted is lined through

court where the deposition is taken. In some instances, two courts are available to a party seeking to compel answers from a party deponent. The party seeking discovery may choose the court to which he will apply, but the court has power to remit the party to the other court as a more appropriate forum.

Subdivision (a)(2). This subdivision contains the substance of existing provisions of Rule 37(a) authorizing motions to compel answers to questions put at depositions and to interrogatories. New provisions authorize motions for orders compelling designation under Rules 30(b)(6) and 31(a) and compelling inspection in accordance with a request made under Rule 34. If the court denies a motion, in whole or part, it may accompany the denial with issuance of a protective order. Compare the converse provision in Rule 26(c).

Subdivision (a)(3). This new provision makes clear that an evasive or incomplete answer is to be considered, for purposes of subdivision (a), a failure to answer. The courts have consistently held that they have the power to compel adequate answers. *E.g., Cone Mills Corp. v. Joseph Bancroft & Sons Co.,* 33 F.R.D. 318 (D.Del.1963). This power is recognized and incorporated into the rule.

Subdivision (a)(4). This subdivision amends the provisions for award of expenses, including reasonable attorney's fees, to the prevailing party or person when a motion is made for an order compelling discovery. At present, an award of expenses is made only if the losing party or person is found to have acted without substantial justification. The change requires that expenses be awarded unless the conduct of the losing party or person is found to have been substantially justified. The test of "substantial justification" remains, but the change in language is intended to encourage judges to be more alert to abuses occurring in the discovery process.

On many occasions, to be sure, the dispute over discovery between the parties is genuine, though ultimately resolved one way or the other by the court. In such cases, the losing party is substantially justified in carrying the matter to court. But the rules should deter the abuse implicit in carrying or forcing a discovery dispute to court when no genuine dispute exists. And the potential or actual imposition of expenses is virtually the sole formal sanction in the rules to deter a party from pressing to a court hearing frivolous requests for or objections to discovery.

The present provision of Rule 37(a) that the court shall require payment if it finds that the defeated party acted without "substantial justification" may appear adequate, but in fact it has been little used. Only a handful of reported cases include an award of expenses, and the Columbia Survey found that in only one instance out of about 50 motions decided under Rule 37(a) did the court award expenses. It appears that the courts do not utilize the most important available sanction to deter abusive resort to the judiciary.

The proposed change provides in effect that expenses should ordinarily be awarded unless a court finds that the losing party acted justifiably in carrying his point to court. At the same time, a necessary flexibility is maintained, since the court retains the power to find that other circumstances make an award of expenses unjust—as where, the prevailing party also acted unjustifiably. The amendment does not significantly narrow the discretion of the court, but rather presses the court to address itself to abusive practices. The present provision that expenses may be imposed upon either the party or his attorney or both is unchanged. But it is not contemplated that expenses will be imposed upon the attorney merely because the party is indigent.

Subdivision (b). This subdivision deals with sanctions for failure to comply with a court order. The present captions for subsections (1) and (2) entitled, "Contempt" and "Other Consequences," respectively, are confusing. One of the consequences

---

New matter is shown in italics; matter to be omitted is lined through

listed in (2) is the arrest of the party, representing the exercise of the contempt power. The contents of the subsections show that the first authorizes the sanction of contempt (and no other) by the court in which the deposition is taken, whereas the second subsection authorizes a variety of sanctions, including contempt, which may be imposed by the court in which the action is pending. The captions of the subsections are changed to reflect their contents.

The scope of Rule 37(b)(2) is broadened by extending it to include any order "to provide or permit discovery," including orders issued under Rules 37(a) and 35. Various rules authorize orders for discovery—*e.g.,* Rule 35(b)(1), Rule 26(c) as revised, Rule 37(d). See Rosenberg, *supra,* 58 Col.L.Rev. 480, 484–486. Rule 37(b)(2) should provide comprehensively for enforcement of all these orders. *Cf. Societe Internationale v. Rogers,* 357 U.S. 197, 207 (1958). On the other hand, the reference to Rule 34 is deleted to conform to the changed procedure in that rule.

A new subsection (E) provides that sanctions which have been available against a party for failure to comply with an order under Rule 35(a) to submit to examination will now be available against him for his failure to comply with a Rule 35(a) order to produce a third person for examination, unless he shows that he is unable to produce the person. In this context, "unable" means in effect "unable in good faith." See *Societe Internationale v. Rogers,* 357 U.S. 197 (1958).

Subdivision (b)(2) is amplified to provide for payment of reasonable expenses caused by the failure to obey the order. Although Rules 37(b)(2) and 37(d) have been silent as to award of expenses, courts have nevertheless ordered them on occasion. *E.g., United Sheeplined Clothing Co. v. Arctic Fur Cap Corp.,* 165 F.Supp. 193 (S.D.N.Y.1958); *Austin Theatre, Inc. v. Warner Bros. Pictures, Inc.,* 22 F.R.D. 302 (S.D.N.Y.1958). The provision places the burden on the disobedient party to avoid expenses by showing that his failure is justified or that special circumstances make an award of expenses unjust. Allocating the burden in this way conforms to the changed provisions as to expenses in Rule 37(a), and is particularly appropriate when a court order is disobeyed.

An added reference to directors of a party is similar to a change made in subdivision (d) and is explained in the note to that subdivision. The added reference to persons designated by a party under Rules 30(b)(6) or 31(a) to testify on behalf of the party carries out the new procedure in those rules for taking a deposition of a corporation or other organization.

Subdivision (c). Rule 37(c) provides a sanction for the enforcement of Rule 36 dealing with requests for admission. Rule 36 provides the mechanism whereby a party may obtain from another party in appropriate instances either (1) an admission, or (2) a sworn and specific denial, or (3) a sworn statement "setting forth in detail the reasons why he cannot truthfully admit or deny." If the party obtains the second or third of these responses, in proper form, Rule 36 does not provide for a pretrial hearing on whether the response is warranted by the evidence thus far accumulated. Instead, Rule 37(c) is intended to provide posttrial relief in the form of a requirement that the party improperly refusing the admission pay the expenses of the other side in making the necessary proof at trial.

Rule 37(c), as now written, addresses itself in terms only to the sworn denial and is silent with respect to the statement of reasons for an inability to admit or deny. There is no apparent basis for this distinction, since the sanction provided in Rule 37(c) should deter all unjustified failures to admit. This omission in the rule has caused confused and diverse treatment in the courts. One court has held that if a party gives inadequate reasons, he should be treated before trial as having denied the request, so that Rule 37(c) may apply. *Bertha Bldg. Corp. v. National Theatres Corp.,* 15 F.R.D. 339 (E.D.N.Y.1954). Another has held that the party should be

---

New matter is shown in italics; matter to be omitted is lined through

treated as having admitted the request. *Heng Hsin Co. v. Stern, Morgenthau & Co.,* 20 Fed.Rules Serv. 36a.52, Case 1 (S.D.N.Y. Dec. 10, 1954). Still another has ordered a new response, without indicating what the outcome should be if the new response were inadequate. *United States Plywood Corp. v. Hudson Lumber Co.,* 127 F.Supp. 489, 497–498 (S.D.N.Y.1954). See generally Finman, *The Request for Admissions in Federal Civil Procedure,* 71 Yale L.J. 371, 426–430 (1962). The amendment eliminates this defect in Rule 37(c) by bringing within its scope all failures to admit.

Additional provisions in Rule 37(c) protect a party from having to pay expenses if the request for admission was held objectionable under Rule 36(a) or if the party failing to admit had reasonable ground to believe that he might prevail on the matter. The latter provision emphasizes that the true test under Rule 37(c) is not whether a party prevailed at trial but whether he acted reasonably in believing that he might prevail.

Subdivision (d). The scope of subdivision (d) is broadened to include responses to requests for inspection under Rule 34, thereby conforming to the new procedures of Rule 34.

Two related changes are made in subdivision (d): the permissible sanctions are broadened to include such orders "as are just"; and the requirement that the failure to appear or respond be "wilful" is eliminated. Although Rule 37(d) in terms provides for only three sanctions, all rather severe, the courts have interpreted it as permitting softer sanctions than those which it sets forth. *E.g., Gill v. Stolow,* 240 F.2d 669 (2d Cir.1957); *Saltzman v. Birrell,* 156 F.Supp. 538 (S.D.N.Y.1957); 2A Barron & Holtzoff, *Federal Practice and Procedure* 554–557 (Wright ed. 1961). The rule is changed to provide the greater flexibility as to sanctions which the cases show is needed.

The resulting flexibility as to sanctions eliminates any need to retain the requirement that the failure to appear or respond be "wilful." The concept of "wilful failure" is at best subtle and difficult, and the cases do not supply a bright line. Many courts have imposed sanctions without referring to wilfullness. *E.g., Milewski v. Schneider Transportation Co.,* 238 F.2d 397 (6th Cir.1956); *Dictograph Products, Inc. v. Kentworth Corp.,* 7 F.R.D. 543 (W.D.Ky.1947). In addition, in view of the possibility of light sanctions, even a negligent failure should come within Rule 37(d). If default is caused by counsel's ignorance of Federal practice, *cf. Dunn v. Pa. R. R.,* 96 F.Supp. 597 (N.D.Ohio 1951), or by his preoccupation with another aspect of the case, *cf. Maurer–Neuer, Inc. v. United Packinghouse Workers,* 26 F.R.D. 139 (D.Kans.1960), dismissal of the action and default judgment are not justified, but the imposition of expenses and fees may well be. "Wilfullness" continues to play a role, along with various other factors, in the choice of sanctions. Thus, the scheme conforms to Rule 37(b) as construed by the Supreme Court in *Societe Internationale v. Rogers,* 357 U.S. 197, 208 (1958).

A provision is added to make clear that a party may not properly remain completely silent even when he regards a notice to take his deposition or a set of interrogatories or requests to inspect as improper and objectionable. If he desires not to appear or not to respond, he must apply for a protective order. The cases are divided on whether a protective order must be sought. Compare *Collins v. Wayland,* 139 F.2d 677 (9th Cir.1944), *cert. den.* 322 U.S. 744; *Bourgeois v. El Paso Natural Gas Co.,* 20 F.R.D. 358 (S.D.N.Y.1957); *Loosley v. Stone,* 15 F.R.D. 373 (S.D.Ill.1954), with *Scarlatos v. Kulukundis,* 21 F.R.D. 185 (S.D.N.Y.1957); *Ross v. True Temper Corp.,* 11 F.R.D. 307 (N.D.Ohio 1951). Compare also Rosenberg, *supra,* 58 Col.L.Rev. 480, 496 (1958) with 2A Barron & Holtzoff, *Federal Practice and Procedure* 530–531 (Wright ed. 1961). The party from whom discovery is sought is afforded, through Rule 26(c), a fair and effective procedure whereby he can challenge the request

---

New matter is shown in italics; matter to be omitted is lined through

made. At the same time, the total non-compliance with which Rule 37(d) is concerned may impose severe inconvenience or hardship on the discovering party and substantially delay the discovery process. *Cf.* 2B Barron & Holtzoff, *Federal Practice and Procedure* 306–307 (Wright ed. 1961) (response to a subpoena).

The failure of an officer or managing agent of a party to make discovery as required by present Rule 37(d) is treated as the failure of the party. The rule as revised provides similar treatment for a director of a party. There is slight warrant for the present distinction between officers and managing agents on the one hand and directors on the other. Although the legal power over a director to compel his making discovery may not be as great as over officers or managing agents, *Campbell v. General Motors Corp.*, 13 F.R.D. 331 (S.D.N.Y.1952), the practical differences are negligible. That a director's interests are normally aligned with those of his corporation is shown by the provisions of old Rule 26(d)(2), transferred to 32(a)(2) (deposition of director of party may be used at trial by an adverse party for any purpose) and of Rule 43(b) (director of party may be treated at trial as a hostile witness on direct examination by any adverse party). Moreover, in those rare instances when a corporation is unable through good faith efforts to compel a director to make discovery, it is unlikely that the court will impose sanctions. *Cf. Societe Internationale v. Rogers,* 357 U.S. 197 (1958).

Subdivision (e). The change in the caption conforms to the language of 28 U.S.C. § 1783, as amended in 1964.

Subdivision (f). Until recently, costs of a civil action could be awarded against the United States only when expressly provided by Act of Congress, and such provision was rarely made. See H.R.Rep.No.1535, 89th Cong., 2d Sess., 2–3 (1966). To avoid any conflict with this doctrine, Rule 37(f) has provided that expenses and attorney's fees may not be imposed upon the United States under Rule 37. See 2A Barron & Holtzoff, *Federal Practice and Procedure* 857 (Wright ed. 1961).

A major change in the law was made in 1966, 80 Stat. 308, 28 U.S.C. § 2412 (1966), whereby a judgment for costs may ordinarily be awarded to the prevailing party in any civil action brought by or against the United States. Costs are not to include the fees and expenses of attorneys. In light of this legislative development, Rule 37(f) is amended to permit the award of expenses and fees against the United States under Rule 37, but only to the extent permitted by statute. The amendment brings Rule 37(f) into line with present and future statutory provisions.

Advisory Committee's Note to 1980 Amendment

Rule 37. Failure to Make *or Cooperate in* Discovery: Sanctions

(b) Failure to Comply with Order.

(2) Sanctions by Court in Which Action is Pending. If a party or an officer, director, or managing agent of a party or a person designated under Rule 30(b)(6) or 31(a) to testify on behalf of a party fails to obey an order to provide or permit discovery, including an order made under subdivision (a) of this rule or Rule 35, *or if a party fails to obey an order entered under Rule 26(f),* the court in which the action is pending may make such orders in regard to the failure as are just, and among others the following:

New matter is shown in italics; matter to be omitted is lined through

(A) An order that the matters regarding which the order was made or any other designated facts shall be taken to be established for the purposes of the action in accordance with the claim of the party obtaining the order;

(B) An order refusing to allow the disobedient party to support or oppose designated claims or defenses, or prohibiting him from introducing designated matters in evidence;

(C) An order striking out pleadings or parts thereof, or staying further proceedings until the order is obeyed, or dismissing the action or proceeding or any part thereof, or rendering a judgment by default against the disobedient party;

(D) In lieu of any of the foregoing orders or in addition thereto, an order treating as a contempt of court the failure to obey any orders except an order to submit to a physical or mental examination;

(E) Where a party has failed to comply with an order under Rule 35(a) requiring him to produce another for examination, such orders as are listed in paragraphs (A), (B), and (C) of this subdivision, unless the party failing to comply shows that he is unable to produce such person for examination.

In lieu of any of the foregoing orders or in addition thereto, the court shall require the party failing to obey the order or the attorney advising him or both to pay the reasonable expenses, including attorney's fees, caused by the failure, unless the court finds that the failure was substantially justified or that other circumstances make an award of expenses unjust.

[(e) Subpoena of Person in Foreign Country.] A subpoena may be issued as provided in Title 28 U.S.C. § 1783, under the circumstances and conditions therein stated.

(g) Failure to Participate in the Framing of a Discovery Plan. If a party or his attorney fails to participate in good faith in the framing of a discovery plan by agreement as is required by Rule 26(f), the court may, after opportunity for hearing, require such party or his attorney to pay to any other party the reasonable expenses, including attorney's fees, caused by the failure.

Subdivision (b)(2). New Rule 26(f) provides that if a discovery conference is held, at its close the court shall enter an order respecting the subsequent conduct of discovery. The amendment provides that the sanctions available for violation of other court orders respecting discovery are available for violation of the discovery conference order.

New matter is shown in italics; matter to be omitted is lined through

Subdivision (e). Subdivision (e) is stricken. Title 28, U.S.C. § 1783 no longer refers to sanctions. The subdivision otherwise duplicates Rule 45(e)(2).

Subdivision (g). New Rule 26(f) imposes a duty on parties to participate in good faith in the framing of a discovery plan by agreement upon the request of any party. This subdivision authorizes the court to award to parties who participate in good faith in an attempt to frame a discovery plan the expenses incurred in the attempt if any party or his attorney fails to participate in good faith and thereby causes additional expense.

Failure of United States to Participate in Good Faith in Discovery. Rule 37 authorizes the court to direct that parties or attorneys who fail to participate in good faith in the discovery process pay the expenses, including attorneys' fees, incurred by other parties as a result of that failure. Since attorneys' fees cannot ordinarily be awarded against the United States (28 U.S.C. § 2412), there is often no practical remedy for the misconduct of its officers and attorneys. However, in the case of a government attorney who fails to participate in good faith in discovery, nothing prevents a court in an appropriate case from giving written notification of that fact to the Attorney General of the United States and other appropriate heads of offices or agencies thereof.

Advisory Committee's Note to 1993 Amendment

Rule 37. Failure to Make *Disclosure or* Cooperate in Discovery: Sanctions

(a) Motion for Order Compelling *Disclosure or* Discovery. A party, upon reasonable notice to other parties and all persons affected thereby, may apply for an order compelling *disclosure or* discovery as follows:

(1) Appropriate Court. An application for an order to a party ~~may~~ *shall* be made to the court in which the action is pending~~, or, on matters relating to a deposition, to the court in the district where the deposition is being taken~~. An application for an order to a ~~deponent~~ *person* who is not a party shall be made to the court in the district where the ~~deposition is being taken~~ *discovery is being, or is to be, taken.*

(2) Motion.

(A) If a party fails to make a disclosure required by Rule 26(a), any other party may move to compel disclosure and for appropriate sanctions. The motion must include a certification that the movant has in good faith conferred or attempted to confer with the party not making the disclosure in an effort to secure the disclosure without court action.

(B) If a deponent fails to answer a question propounded or submitted under Rules 30 or 31, or a corporation or

---

New matter is shown in italics; matter to be omitted is lined through

other entity fails to make a designation under Rule 30(b)(6) or 31(a), or a party fails to answer an interrogatory submitted under Rule 33, or if a party, in response to a request for inspection submitted under Rule 34, fails to respond that inspection will be permitted as requested or fails to permit inspection as requested, the discovering party may move for an order compelling an answer, or a designation, or an order compelling inspection in accordance with the request. *The motion must include a certification that the movant has in good faith conferred or attempted to confer with the person or party failing to make the discovery in an effort to secure the information or material without court action.* When taking a deposition on oral examination, the proponent of the question may complete or adjourn the examination before applying for an order.

~~If the court denies the motion in whole or in part, it may make such protective order as it would have been empowered to make on a motion made pursuant to Rule 26(c).~~

(3) Evasive or Incomplete *Disclosure,* Answer, *or Response.* For purposes of this subdivision an evasive or incomplete *disclosure,* answer, *or response* is to be treated as a failure to *disclose,* answer, *or respond.*

(4) ~~Award of~~ Expenses ~~of Motion~~ *and Sanctions.*

(A) If the motion is granted *or if the disclosure or requested discovery is provided after the motion was filed,* the court shall, after *affording an* opportunity ~~for hearing,~~ *to be heard,* require the party or deponent whose conduct necessitated the motion or the party or attorney advising such conduct or both of them to pay to the moving party the reasonable expenses incurred in ~~obtaining the order~~ *making the motion,* including attorney's fees, unless the court finds that the *motion was filed without the movant's first making a good faith effort to obtain the disclosure or discovery without court action, or that the* ~~opposition to the motion~~ *opposing party's nondisclosure, response, or objection* was substantially justified, or that other circumstances make an award of expenses unjust.

(B) If the motion is denied, the court *may enter any protective order authorized under Rule 26(c) and* shall, after *affording an* opportunity ~~for hearing,~~ *to be heard,* require the moving party or the attorney ~~advising~~ *filing* the motion or both of them to pay to the party or deponent

---

New matter is shown in italics; matter to be omitted is lined through

who opposed the motion the reasonable expenses incurred in opposing the motion, including attorney's fees, unless the court finds that the making of the motion was substantially justified or that other circumstances make an award of expenses unjust.

(C) If the motion is granted in part and denied in part, the court *may enter any protective order authorized under Rule 26(c) and* may, *after affording an opportunity to be heard,* apportion the reasonable expenses incurred in relation to the motion among the parties and persons in a just manner.

(c) ~~Expenses on~~ **Failure to *Disclose; False or Misleading Disclosure; Refusal to* Admit.**

(1) A party that without substantial justification fails to disclose information required by Rule 26(a) or 26(e)(1) shall not, unless such failure is harmless, be permitted to use as evidence at a trial, at a hearing, or on a motion any witness or information not so disclosed. In addition to or in lieu of this sanction, the court, on motion and after affording an opportunity to be heard, may impose other appropriate sanctions. In addition to requiring payment of reasonable expenses, including attorney's fees, caused by the failure, these sanctions may include any of the actions authorized under subparagraphs (A), (B), and (C) of subdivision (b)(2) of this rule and may include informing the jury of the failure to make the disclosure.

(2) If a party fails to admit the genuineness of any document or the truth of any matter as requested under Rule 36, and if the party requesting the admissions thereafter proves the genuineness of the document or the truth of the matter, the requesting party may apply to the court for an order requiring the other party to pay the reasonable expenses incurred in making that proof, including reasonable attorney's fees. The court shall make the order unless it finds that (~~1~~*A*) the request was held objectionable pursuant to Rule 36(a), or (~~2~~*B*) the admission sought was of no substantial importance, or (~~3~~*C*) the party failing to admit had reasonable ground to believe that the party might prevail on the matter, or (~~4~~*D*) there was other good reason for the failure to admit.

(d) Failure of Party to Attend at Own Deposition or Serve Answers to Interrogatories or Respond to Request for Inspection. If a party or an officer, director, or managing agent of a party or a person designated under Rule 30(b)(6) or 31(a) to testify on behalf of a party fails (1) to appear before the officer who is to take the deposition, after being served with a proper notice, or (2) to serve answers or objections to interrogatories submitted under Rule 33, after proper service of the interrogatories, or (3) to

---

New matter is shown in italics; matter to be omitted is lined through

serve a written response to a request for inspection submitted under Rule 34, after proper service of the request, the court in which the action is pending on motion may make such orders in regard to the failure as are just, and among others it may take any action authorized under *sub*paragraphs (A), (B), and (C) of subdivision (b)(2) of this rule. *Any motion specifying a failure under clause (2) or (3) of this subdivision shall include a certification that the movant has in good faith conferred or attempted to confer with the party failing to answer or respond in an effort to obtain such answer or response without court action.* In lieu of any order or in addition thereto, the court shall require the party failing to act or the attorney advising that party or both to pay the reasonable expenses, including attorney's fees, caused by the failure unless the court finds that the failure was substantially justified or that other circumstances make an award of expenses unjust.

The failure to act described in this subdivision may not be excused on the ground that the discovery sought is objectionable unless the party failing to act has ~~applied~~ *a pending motion* for a protective order as provided by Rule 26(c).

(g) Failure to Participate in the Framing of a Discovery Plan. If a party or a party's attorney fails to participate in good faith in the *development and submission* ~~framing~~ of a *proposed* discovery plan ~~by agreement~~ as ~~is~~ required by Rule 26(f), the court may, after opportunity for hearing, require such party or attorney to pay to any other party the reasonable expenses, including attorney's fees, caused by the failure.

Subdivision (a). This subdivision is revised to reflect the revision of Rule 26(a), requiring disclosure of matters without a discovery request.

Pursuant to new subdivision (a)(2)(A), a party dissatisfied with the disclosure made by an opposing party may under this rule move for an order to compel disclosure. In providing for such a motion, the revised rule parallels the provisions of the former rule dealing with failures to answer particular interrogatories. Such a motion may be needed when the information to be disclosed might be helpful to the party seeking the disclosure but not to the party required to make the disclosure. If the party required to make the disclosure would need the material to support its own contentions, the more effective enforcement of the disclosure requirement will be to exclude the evidence not disclosed, as provided in subdivision (c)(1) of this revised rule.

Language is included in the new paragraph and added to the subparagraph (B) that requires litigants to seek to resolve discovery disputes by informal means before filing a motion with the court. This requirement is based on successful experience with similar local rules of court promulgated pursuant to Rule 83.

The last sentence of paragraph (2) is moved into paragraph (4).

New matter is shown in italics; matter to be omitted is lined through

Under revised paragraph (3), evasive or incomplete disclosures and responses to interrogatories and production requests are treated as failures to disclose or respond. Interrogatories and requests for production should not be read or interpreted in an artificially restrictive or hypertechnical manner to avoid disclosure of information fairly covered by the discovery request, and to do so is subject to appropriate sanctions under subdivision (a).

Revised paragraph (4) is divided into three subparagraphs for ease of reference, and in each the phrase "after opportunity for hearing" is changed to "after affording an opportunity to be heard" to make clear that the court can consider such questions on written submissions as well as on oral hearings.

Subparagraph (A) is revised to cover the situation where information that should have been produced without a motion to compel is produced after the motion is filed but before it is brought on for hearing. The rule also is revised to provide that a party should not be awarded its expenses for filing a motion that could have been avoided by conferring with opposing counsel.

Subparagraph (C) is revised to include the provision that formerly was contained in subdivision (a)(2) and to include the same requirement of an opportunity to be heard that is specified in subparagraphs (A) and (B).

Subdivision (c). The revision provides a self-executing sanction for failure to make a disclosure required by Rule 26(a), without need for a motion under subdivision (a)(2)(A).

Paragraph (1) prevents a party from using as evidence any witnesses or information that, without substantial justification, has not been disclosed as required by Rules 26(a) and 26(e)(1). This automatic sanction provides a strong inducement for disclosure of material that the disclosing party would expect to use as evidence, whether at a trial, at a hearing, or on a motion, such as one under Rule 56. As disclosure of evidence offered solely for impeachment purposes is not required under those rules, this preclusion sanction likewise does not apply to that evidence.

Limiting the automatic sanction to violations "without substantial justification," coupled with the exception for violations that are "harmless," is needed to avoid unduly harsh penalties in a variety of situations: *e.g.,* the inadvertent omission from a Rule 26(a)(1)(A) disclosure of the name of a potential witness known to all parties; the failure to list as a trial witness a person so listed by another party; or the lack of knowledge of a pro se litigant of the requirement to make disclosures. In the latter situation, however, exclusion would be proper if the requirement for disclosure had been called to the litigant's attention by either the court or another party.

Preclusion of evidence is not an effective incentive to compel disclosure of information that, being supportive of the position of the opposing party, might advantageously be concealed by the disclosing party. However, the rule provides the court with a wide range of other sanctions—such as declaring specified facts to be established, preventing contradictory evidence, or, like spoliation of evidence, allowing the jury to be informed of the fact of nondisclosure—that, though not self-executing, can be imposed when found to be warranted after a hearing. The failure to identify a witness or document in a disclosure statement would be admissible under the Federal Rules of Evidence under the same principles that allow a party's interrogatory answers to be offered against it.

Subdivision (d). This subdivision is revised to require that, where a party fails to file any response to interrogatories or a Rule 34 request, the discovering party should informally seek to obtain such responses before filing a motion for sanctions.

New matter is shown in italics; matter to be omitted is lined through

The last sentence of this subdivision is revised to clarify that it is the pendency of a motion for protective order that may be urged as an excuse for a violation of subdivision (d). If a party's motion has been denied, the party cannot argue that its subsequent failure to comply would be justified. In this connection, it should be noted that the filing of a motion under Rule 26(c) is not self-executing—the relief authorized under that rule depends on obtaining the court's order to that effect.

Subdivision (g). This subdivision is modified to conform to the revision of Rule 26(f).

Advisory Committee's Note to 2006 Amendment

Rule 37.   Failure to Make Disclosures or Cooperate in Discovery: Sanctions

(f) Electronically Stored Information. Absent exceptional circumstances, a court may not impose sanctions under these rules on a party for failing to provide electronically stored information lost as a result of the routine, good-faith operation of an electronic information system.

Subdivision (f). Subdivision (f) is new. It focuses on a distinctive feature of computer operations, the routine alteration and deletion of information that attends ordinary use. Many steps essential to computer operation may alter or destroy information, for reasons that have nothing to do with how that information might relate to litigation. As a result, the ordinary operation of computer systems creates a risk that a party may lose potentially discoverable information without culpable conduct on its part. Under Rule 37(f), absent exceptional circumstances, sanctions cannot be imposed for loss of electronically stored information resulting from the routine, good-faith operation of an electronic information system.

Rule 37(f) applies only to information lost due to the "routine operation of an electronic information system"—the ways in which such systems are generally designed, programmed, and implemented to meet the party's technical and business needs. The "routine operation" of computer systems includes the alteration and overwriting of information, often without the operator's specific direction or awareness, a feature with no direct counterpart in hard-copy documents. Such features are essential to the operation of electronic information systems.

Rule 37(f) applies to information lost due to the routine operation of an information system only if the operation was in good faith. Good faith in the routine operation of an information system may involve a party's intervention to modify or suspend certain features of that routine operation to prevent the loss of information, if that information is subject to a preservation obligation. A preservation obligation may arise from many sources, including common law, statutes, regulations, or a court order in the case. The good faith requirement of Rule 37(f) means that a party is not permitted to exploit the routine operation of an information system to thwart discovery obligations by allowing that operation to continue in order to destroy specific stored information that it is required to preserve. When a party is under a duty to preserve information because of pending or reasonably anticipated litigation,

---

New matter is shown in italics; matter to be omitted is lined through

intervention in the routine operation of an information system is one aspect of what is often called a "litigation hold." Among the factors that bear on a party's good faith in the routine operation of an information system are the steps the party took to comply with a court order in the case or party agreement requiring preservation of specific electronically stored information.

Whether good faith would call for steps to prevent the loss of information on sources that the party believes are not reasonably accessible under Rule 26(b)(2) depends on the circumstances of each case. One factor is whether the party reasonably believes that the information on such sources is likely to be discoverable and not available from reasonably accessible sources.

The protection provided by Rule 37(f) applies only to sanctions "under these rules." It does not affect other sources of authority to impose sanctions or rules of professional responsibility.

This rule restricts the imposition of "sanctions." It does not prevent a court from making the kinds of adjustments frequently used in managing discovery if a party is unable to provide relevant responsive information. For example, a court could order the responding party to produce an additional witness for deposition, respond to additional interrogatories, or make similar attempts to provide substitutes or alternatives for some or all of the lost information.

Rule 41. Dismissal of Actions

Advisory Committee's Note to 1991 Amendment

(b) Involuntary Dismissal: Effect Thereof. For failure of the plaintiff to prosecute or to comply with these rules or any order of court, a defendant may move for dismissal of an action or of any claim against the defendant. ~~After the plaintiff, in an action tried by the court without a jury, has completed the presentation of evidence, the defendant, without waiving the right to offer evidence in the event the motion is not granted, may move for a dismissal on the ground that upon the facts and the law the plaintiff has shown no right to relief. The court as trier of the facts may then determine them and render judgment against the plaintiff or may decline to render any judgment until the close of all the evidence. If the court renders judgment on the merits against the plaintiff, the court shall make findings as provided in Rule 52(a).~~ Unless the court in its order for dismissal otherwise specifies, a dismissal under this subdivision and any dismissal not provided for in this rule, other than a dismissal for lack of jurisdiction, for improper venue, or for failure to join a party under Rule 19, operates as an adjudication upon the merits.

Language is deleted that authorized the use of this rule as a means of terminating a non-jury action on the merits when the plaintiff has failed to carry a burden of proof in presenting the plaintiff's case. The device is replaced by the new provisions of Rule 52(c), which authorize entry of judgment against the defendant as well as the plaintiff, and earlier than the close of the case of the party against whom

New matter is shown in italics; matter to be omitted is lined through

judgment is rendered. A motion to dismiss under Rule 41 on the ground that a plaintiff's evidence is legally insufficient should now be treated as a motion for judgment on partial findings as provided in Rule 52(c).

Rule 44.1. Determination of Foreign Law

Advisory Committee's Note to Rule Added in 1966

Rule 44.1 is added by amendment to furnish Federal courts with a uniform and effective procedure for raising and determining an issue concerning the law of a foreign country.

To avoid unfair surprise, the *first sentence* of the new rule requires that a party who intends to raise an issue of foreign law shall give notice thereof. The uncertainty under Rule 8(a) about whether foreign law must be pleaded—*compare Siegelman v. Cunard White Star, Ltd.*, 221 F.2d 189 (2d Cir.1955), and *Pedersen v. United States*, 191 F.Supp. 95 (D.Guam 1961) *with Harrison v. United Fruit Co.*, 143 F.Supp. 598 (S.D.N.Y.1956)—is eliminated by the provision that the notice shall be "written" and "reasonable." It may, but need not be, incorporated in the pleadings. In some situations the pertinence of foreign law is apparent from the outset; accordingly the necessary investigation of that law will have been accomplished by the party at the pleading stage, and the notice can be given conveniently in the pleadings. In other situations the pertinence of foreign law may remain doubtful until the case is further developed. A requirement that notice of foreign law be given only through the medium of the pleadings would tend in the latter instances to force the party to engage in a peculiarly burdensome type of investigation which might turn out to be unnecessary; and correspondingly the adversary would be forced into a possibly wasteful investigation. The liberal provisions for amendment of the pleadings afford help if the pleadings are used as the medium of giving notice of the foreign law; but it seems best to permit a written notice to be given outside of and later than the pleadings, provided the notice is reasonable.

The new rule does not attempt to set any definite limit on the party's time for giving the notice of an issue of foreign law; in some cases the issue may not become apparent until the trial, and notice then given may still be reasonable. The stage which the case has reached at the time of the notice, the reason proffered by the party for his failure to give earlier notice, and the importance to the case as a whole of the issue of foreign law sought to be raised, are among the factors which the court should consider in deciding a question of the reasonableness of a notice. If notice is given by one party it need not be repeated by any other and serves as a basis for presentation of material on the foreign law by all parties.

The *second sentence* of the new rule describes the materials to which the court may resort in determining an issue of foreign law. Heretofore the district courts, applying Rule 43(a), have looked in certain cases to State law to find the rules of evidence by which the content of foreign-country law is to be established. The State laws vary; some embody procedures which are inefficient, time consuming, and expensive. See, generally, Nussbaum, *Proving the Law of Foreign Countries*, 3 Am.J.Comp.L. 60 (1954). In all events the ordinary rules of evidence are often inapposite to the problem of determining foreign law and have in the past prevented examination of material which could have provided a proper basis for the determination. The new rule permits consideration by the court of any relevant material, including testimony, without regard to its admissibility under Rule 43. *Cf.* N.Y.Civ. Prac.Law & Rules, R. 4511 (effective Sept. 1, 1963); 2 Va.Code Ann. tit. 8, § 8–273; 2 W.Va.Code Ann. § 5711.

New matter is shown in italics; matter to be omitted is lined through

In further recognition of the peculiar nature of the issue of foreign law, the new rule provides that in determining this law the court is not limited by material presented by the parties; it may engage in its own research and consider any relevant material thus found. The court may have at its disposal better foreign law materials than counsel have presented, or may wish to reexamine and amplify material that has been presented by counsel in partisan fashion or in insufficient detail. On the other hand, the court is free to insist on a complete presentation by counsel.

There is no requirement that the court give formal notice to the parties of its intention to engage in its own research on an issue of foreign law which has been raised by them, or of its intention to raise and determine independently an issue not raised by them. Ordinarily the court should inform the parties of material it has found diverging substantially from the material which they have presented; and in general the court should give the parties an opportunity to analyze and counter new points upon which it proposes to rely. See Schlesinger, *Comparative Law* 142 (2d ed. 1959); Wyzanski, *A Trial Judge's Freedom and Responsibility*, 65 Harv.L.Rev. 1281, 1296 (1952); *cf. Siegelman v. Cunard White Star, Ltd., supra,* 221 F.2d at 197. To require, however, that the court give formal notice from time to time as it proceeds with its study of the foreign law would add an element of undesirable rigidity to the procedure for determining issues of foreign law.

The new rule refrains from imposing an obligation on the court to take "judicial notice" of foreign law because this would put an extreme burden on the court in many cases; and it avoids use of the concept of "judicial notice" in any form because of the uncertain meaning of that concept as applied to foreign law. See, *e.g.,* Stern, *Foreign Law in the Courts: Judicial Notice and Proof,* 45 Calif.L.Rev. 23, 43 (1957). Rather the rule provides flexible procedures for presenting and utilizing material on issues of foreign law by which a sound result can be achieved with fairness to the parties.

Under the *third sentence*, the court's determination of an issue of foreign law is to be treated as a ruling on a question of "law," not "fact," so that appellate review will not be narrowly confined by the "clearly erroneous" standard of Rule 52(a). *Cf.* Uniform Judicial Notice of Foreign Law Act § 3; Note, 72 Harv.L.Rev. 318 (1958).

The new rule parallels Article IV of the Uniform Interstate and International Procedure Act, approved by the Commissioners on Uniform State Laws in 1962, except that section 4.03 of Article IV states that "[t]he court, not the jury" shall determine foreign law. The new rule does not address itself to this problem, since the rules refrain from allocating functions as between the court and the jury. See Rule 38(a). It has long been thought, however, that the jury is not the appropriate body to determine issues of foreign law. See, *e.g.,* Story, *Conflict of Laws* § 638 (1st ed. 1834, 8th ed. 1883); 1 Greenleaf, *Evidence* § 486 (1st ed. 1842, 16th ed. 1899); 4 Wigmore, *Evidence* § 2558 (1st ed. 1905); 9 *id.* § 2558 (3d ed. 1940). The majority of the States have committed such issues to determination by the court. See Article 5 of the Uniform Judicial Notice of Foreign Law Act, adopted by twenty-six states, 9A U.L.A. 318 (1957) (Supp.1961, at 134); N.Y.Civ.Prac.Law & Rules, R. 4511 (effective Sept. 1, 1963); Wigmore, *loc. cit.* And Federal courts that have considered the problem in recent years have reached the same conclusion without reliance on statute. See *Jansson v. Swedish American Line,* 185 F.2d 212, 216 (1st Cir. 1950); *Bank of Nova Scotia v. San Miguel,* 196 F.2d 950, 957 n. 6 (1st Cir.1952); *Liechti v. Roche,* 198 F.2d 174 (5th Cir.1952); *Daniel Lumber Co. v. Empresas Hondurenas, S.A.,* 215 F.2d 465 (5th Cir.1954).

New matter is shown in italics; matter to be omitted is lined through

Rule 48. Juries of Less Than Twelve—Majority Verdict

Advisory Committee's Note to 1991 Amendment

Rule 48. ~~Juries of Less Than Twelve—Majority Verdict~~
Number of Jurors—Participation in Verdict

~~The parties may stipulate that the jury shall consist of any number less than twelve or that a verdict or a finding of a stated majority of the jurors shall be taken as the verdict or finding of the jury.~~

The court shall seat a jury of not fewer than six and not more than twelve members and all jurors shall participate in the verdict unless excused from service by the court pursuant to Rule 47(c). Unless the parties otherwise stipulate, (1) the verdict shall be unanimous and (2) no verdict shall be taken from a jury reduced in size to fewer than six members.

————

The former rule was rendered obsolete by the adoption in many districts of local rules establishing six as the standard size for a civil jury.

It appears that the minimum size of a jury consistent with the Seventh Amendment is six. *Cf. Ballew v. Georgia,* 435 U.S. 223 (1978) (holding that a conviction based on a jury of less than six is a denial of due process of law). If the parties agree to trial before a smaller jury, a verdict can be taken, but the parties should not other than in exceptional circumstances be encouraged to waive the right to a jury of six, not only because of the constitutional stature of the right, but also because smaller juries are more erratic and less effective in serving to distribute responsibility for the exercise of judicial power.

Because the institution of the alternate juror has been abolished by the proposed revision of Rule 47, it will ordinarily be prudent and necessary, in order to provide for sickness or disability among jurors, to seat more than six jurors. The use of jurors in excess of six increases the representativeness of the jury and harms no interest of a party. *Ray v. Parkside Surgery Center,* 13 F.R.Serv. 585 (6th Cir.1989).

If the court takes the precaution of seating a jury larger than six, an illness occurring during the deliberation period will not result in a mistrial, as it did formerly, because all seated jurors will participate in the verdict and a sufficient number will remain to render a unanimous verdict of six or more.

In exceptional circumstances, as where a jury suffers depletions during trial and deliberation that are greater than can reasonably be expected, the parties may agree to be bound by a verdict rendered by fewer than six jurors. The court should not, however, rely upon the availability of such an agreement, for the use of juries smaller than six is problematic for reasons fully explained in *Ballew v. Georgia,* supra.

New matter is shown in italics; matter to be omitted is lined through

Rule 50. Motion for a Directed Verdict

Advisory Committee's Note to Original Rule

Note to Subdivision (a). The present federal rule is changed to the extent that the formality of an express reservation of rights against waiver is no longer necessary. See *Sampliner v. Motion Picture Patents Co.,* 254 U.S. 233, 41 S.Ct. 79, 65 L.Ed. 240 (1920); *Union Indemnity Co. v. United States,* 74 F.(2d) 645 (C.C.A.6th, 1935). The requirement that specific grounds for the motion for a directed verdict must be stated settles a conflict in the federal cases. See Simkins, *Federal Practice* (1934) § 189.

Note to Subdivision (b). For comparable state practice upheld under the conformity act, see *Baltimore and Carolina Line v. Redman,* 295 U.S. 654, 55 S.Ct. 890, 79 L.Ed. 1636 (1935); compare *Slocum v. New York Life Ins. Co.,* 228 U.S. 364, 33 S.Ct. 523, 57 L.Ed. 879, Ann.Cas.1914D, 1029 (1913).

See *Northern Ry. Co. v. Page,* 274 U.S. 65, 47 S.Ct. 491, 71 L.Ed. 929 (1927), following the Massachusetts practice of alternative verdicts, explained in Thorndike, *Trial by Jury in United States Courts,* 26 Harv.L.Rev. 732 (1913). See also Thayer, *Judicial Administration,* 63 U. of Pa.L.Rev. 585, 600–601, and note 32 (1915); Scott, *Trial by Jury and the Reform of Civil Procedure,* 31 Harv.L.Rev. 669, 685 (1918); Comment, 34 Mich.L.Rev. 93, 98 (1935).

Advisory Committee's Note to 1963 Amendment

Rule 50. Motion for a Directed Verdict *and for Judgment Notwithstanding the Verdict*

(a) *Motion for Directed Verdict:* **When Made~~;~~ Effect.** A party who moves for a directed verdict at the close of the evidence offered by an opponent may offer evidence in the event that the motion is not granted, without having reserved the right so to do and to the same extent as if the motion had not been made. A motion for a directed verdict which is not granted is not a waiver of trial by jury even though all parties to the action have moved for directed verdicts. A motion for a directed verdict shall state the specific grounds therefor. *The order of the court granting a motion for a directed verdict is effective without any assent of the jury.*

(b) ~~Reservation of Decision on Motion.~~ *Motion for Judgment Notwithstanding the Verdict.* Whenever a motion for a directed verdict made at the close of all the evidence is denied or for any reason is not granted, the court is deemed to have submitted the action to the jury subject to a later determination of the legal questions raised by the motion. ~~Within 10 days after the reception of a verdict~~ *Not later than 10 days after entry of judgment,* a party who has moved for a directed verdict may move to have the verdict and any judgment entered thereon set aside and to have judgment entered in accordance with his motion for a directed verdict; or if a

---

New matter is shown in italics; matter to be omitted is lined through

verdict was not returned such party, within 10 days after the jury has been discharged, may move for judgment in accordance with his motion for a directed verdict. A motion for a new trial may be joined with this motion, or a new trial may be prayed for in the alternative. If a verdict was returned the court may allow the judgment to stand or may reopen the judgment and either order a new trial or direct the entry of judgment as if the requested verdict had been directed. If no verdict was returned the court may direct the entry of judgment as if the requested verdict had been directed or may order a new trial.

(c) Same: Conditional Rulings on Grant of Motion.

(1) If the motion for judgment notwithstanding the verdict, provided for in subdivision (b) of this rule, is granted, the court shall also rule on the motion for a new trial, if any, by determining whether it should be granted if the judgment is thereafter vacated or reversed, and shall specify the grounds for granting or denying the motion for the new trial. If the motion for a new trial is thus conditionally granted, the order thereon does not affect the finality of the judgment. In case the motion for a new trial has been conditionally granted and the judgment is reversed on appeal, the new trial shall proceed unless the appellate court has otherwise ordered. In case the motion for a new trial has been conditionally denied, the appellee on appeal may assert error in that denial; and if the judgment is reversed on appeal, subsequent proceedings shall be in accordance with the order of the appellate court.

(2) The party whose verdict has been set aside on motion for judgment notwithstanding the verdict may serve a motion for a new trial pursuant to Rule 59 not later than 10 days after entry of the judgment notwithstanding the verdict.

(d) Same: Denial of Motion. *If the motion for judgment notwithstanding the verdict is denied, the party who prevailed on that motion may, as appellee, assert grounds entitling him to a new trial in the event the appellate court concludes that the trial court erred in denying the motion for judgment notwithstanding the verdict. If the appellate court reverses the judgment, nothing in this rule precludes it from determining that the appellee is entitled to a new trial, or from directing the trial court to determine whether a new trial shall be granted.*

———

Subdivision (a). The practice, after the court has granted a motion for a directed verdict, of requiring the jury to express assent to a verdict they did not reach by their own deliberations serves no useful purpose and may give offense to the members of the jury. See 2B Barron & Holtzoff, *Federal Practice & Procedure*

New matter is shown in italics; matter to be omitted is lined through

§ 1072, at 367 (Wright ed. 1961); Blume, *Origin and Development of the Directed Verdict,* 48 Mich.L.Rev. 555, 582–85, 589–90 (1950). The final sentence of the subdivision, added by amendment, provides that the court's order granting a motion for a directed verdict is effective in itself, and that no action need be taken by the foreman or other members of the jury. See Ariz.R.Civ.P. 50(c); *cf.* Fed.R.Crim.P. 29(a). No change is intended in the standard to be applied in deciding the motion. To assure this interpretation, and in the interest of simplicity, the traditional term, "directed verdict," is retained.

Subdivision (b). A motion for judgment notwithstanding the verdict will not lie unless it was preceded by a motion for a directed verdict made at the close of all the evidence.

The amendment of the second sentence of this subdivision sets the time limit for making the motion for judgment n. o. v. at 10 days after the entry of judgment, rather than 10 days after the reception of the verdict. Thus the time provision is made consistent with that contained in Rule 59(b) (time for motion for new trial) and Rule 52(b) (time for motion to amend findings by the court).

Subdivision (c) deals with the situation where a party joins a motion for a new trial with his motion for judgment n. o. v., or prays for a new trial in the alternative, and the motion for judgment n. o. v. is granted. The procedure to be followed in making rulings on the motion for the new trial, and the consequences of the rulings thereon, were partly set out in *Montgomery Ward & Co. v. Duncan,* 311 U.S. 243, 253, 61 S.Ct. 189, 85 L.Ed. 147 (1940), and have been further elaborated in later cases. See *Cone v. West Virginia Pulp & Paper Co.,* 330 U.S. 212, 67 S.Ct. 752, 91 L.Ed. 849 (1947); *Globe Liquor Co., Inc. v. San Roman,* 332 U.S. 571, 68 S.Ct. 246, 92 L.Ed. 177 (1948); *Fountain v. Filson,* 336 U.S. 681, 69 S.Ct. 754, 93 L.Ed. 971 (1949); *Johnson v. New York, N. H. & H. R. R. Co.,* 344 U.S. 48, 73 S.Ct. 125, 97 L.Ed. 77 (1952). However, courts as well as counsel have often misunderstood the procedure, and it will be helpful to summarize the proper practice in the text of the rule. The amendments do not alter the effects of a jury verdict or the scope of appellate review.

In the situation mentioned, *subdivision (c)(1)* requires that the court make a "conditional" ruling on the new-trial motion, *i. e.,* a ruling which goes on the assumption that the motion for judgment n. o. v. was erroneously granted and will be reversed or vacated; and the court is required to state its grounds for the conditional ruling. Subdivision (c)(1) then spells out the consequences of a reversal of the judgment in the light of the conditional ruling on the new-trial motion.

If the motion for new trial has been conditionally granted, and the judgment is reversed, "the new trial shall proceed unless the appellate court has otherwise ordered." The party against whom the judgment n. o. v. was entered below may, as appellant, besides seeking to overthrow that judgment, also attack the conditional grant of the new trial. And the appellate court, if it reverses the judgment n. o. v., may in an appropriate case also reverse the conditional grant of the new trial and direct that judgment be entered on the verdict. See *Bailey v. Slentz,* 189 F.2d 406 (10th Cir. 1951); *Moist Cold Refrigerator Co. v. Lou Johnson Co.,* 249 F.2d 246 (9th Cir. 1957), *cert. denied,* 356 U.S. 968, 78 S.Ct. 1008, 2 L.Ed.2d 1074 (1958); *Peters v. Smith,* 221 F.2d 721 (3d Cir. 1955); *Dailey v. Timmer,* 292 F.2d 824 (3d Cir. 1961), explaining *Lind v. Schenley Industries, Inc.,* 278 F.2d 79 (3d Cir.), *cert. denied,* 364 U.S. 835, 81 S.Ct. 58, 5 L.Ed.2d 60 (1960); *Cox v. Pennsylvania R. R.,* 120 A.2d 214 (D.C.Mun.Ct.App.1956); 3 Barron & Holtzoff, *Federal Practice & Procedure* § 1302.1 at 346–47 (Wright ed. 1958); 6 *Moore's Federal Practice* ¶ 59.16 at 3915 n. 8a (2d ed. 1954).

New matter is shown in italics; matter to be omitted is lined through

If the motion for a new trial has been conditionally denied, and the judgment is reversed, "subsequent proceedings shall be in accordance with the order of the appellate court." The party in whose favor judgment n. o. v. was entered below may, as appellee, besides seeking to uphold that judgment, also urge on the appellate court that the trial court committed error in conditionally denying the new trial. The appellee may assert this error in his brief, without taking a cross-appeal. *Cf. Patterson v. Pennsylvania R. R.,* 238 F.2d 645, 650 (6th Cir. 1956); *Hughes v. St. Louis Nat. L. Baseball Club, Inc.,* 359 Mo. 993, 997, 224 S.W.2d 989, 992 (1949). If the appellate court concludes that the judgment cannot stand, but accepts the appellee's contention that there was error in the conditional denial of the new trial, it may order a new trial in lieu of directing the entry of judgment upon the verdict.

Subdivision (c)(2), which also deals with the situation where the trial court has granted the motion for judgment n. o. v., states that the verdict-winner may apply to the trial court for a new trial pursuant to Rule 59 after the judgment n. o. v. has been entered against him. In arguing to the trial court in opposition to the motion for judgment n. o. v., the verdict-winner may, and often will, contend that he is entitled, at the least, to a new trial, and the court has a range of discretion to grant a new trial or (where plaintiff won the verdict) to order a dismissal of the action without prejudice instead of granting judgment n. o. v. See *Cone v. West Virginia Pulp & Paper Co., supra,* 330 U.S. at 217, 218, 67 S.Ct. at 755, 756, 91 L.Ed. 849. Subdivision (c)(2) is a reminder that the verdict-winner is entitled, even after entry of judgment n. o. v. against him, to move for a new trial in the usual course. If in these circumstances the motion is granted, the judgment is superseded.

In some unusual circumstances, however, the grant of the new-trial motion may be only conditional, and the judgment will not be superseded. See the situation in *Tribble v. Bruin,* 279 F.2d 424 (4th Cir. 1960) (upon a verdict for plaintiff, defendant moves for and obtains judgment n. o. v.; plaintiff moves for a new trial on the ground of inadequate damages; trial court might properly have granted plaintiff's motion, conditional upon reversal of the judgment n. o. v.).

Even if the verdict-winner makes no motion for a new trial, he is entitled upon his appeal from the judgment n. o. v. not only to urge that that judgment should be reversed and judgment entered upon the verdict, but that errors were committed during the trial which at the least entitle him to a new trial.

Subdivision (d) deals with the situation where judgment has been entered on the jury verdict, the motion for judgment n. o. v. and any motion for a new trial having been denied by the trial court. The verdict-winner, as appellee, besides seeking to uphold the judgment, may urge upon the appellate court that in case the trial court is found to have erred in entering judgment on the verdict, there are grounds for granting him a new trial instead of directing the entry of judgment for his opponent. In appropriate cases the appellate court is not precluded from itself directing that a new trial be had. See *Weade v. Dichmann, Wright & Pugh, Inc.,* 337 U.S. 801, 69 S.Ct. 1326, 93 L.Ed. 1704 (1949). Nor is it precluded in proper cases from remanding the case for a determination by the trial court as to whether a new trial should be granted. The latter course is advisable where the grounds urged are suitable for the exercise of trial court discretion.

Subdivision (d) does not attempt a regulation of all aspects of the procedure where the motion for judgment n. o. v. and any accompanying motion for a new trial are denied, since the problems have not been fully canvassed in the decisions and the procedure is in some respects still in a formative stage. It is, however, designed to give guidance on certain important features of the practice.

New matter is shown in italics; matter to be omitted is lined through

Rule 50. ~~Motion for a Directed Verdict and for~~
Judgment ~~Notwithstanding the Verdict~~ *as a*
Matter of Law in Actions Tried by Jury;
Alternative Motion for New Trial;
Conditional Rulings

(a) ~~Motion for Directed Verdict: When Made; Effect.~~ ~~A party who moves for a directed verdict at the close of the evidence offered by an opponent may offer evidence in the event that the motion is not granted, without having reserved the right so to do and to the same extent as if the motion had not been made. A motion for a directed verdict which is not granted is not a waiver of trial by jury even though all parties to the action have moved for directed verdicts. A motion for a directed verdict shall state the specific grounds therefor. The order of the court granting a motion for a directed verdict is effective without any assent of the jury.~~ *Judgment as a Matter of Law.*

(1) If during a trial by jury a party has been fully heard with respect to an issue and there is no legally sufficient evidentiary basis for a reasonable jury to have found for that party with respect to that issue, the court may grant a motion for judgment as a matter of law against that party on any claim, counterclaim, cross-claim, or third party claim that cannot under the controlling law be maintained without a favorable finding on that issue.

(2) Motions for judgment as a matter of law may be made at any time before submission of the case to the jury. Such a motion shall specify the judgment sought and the law and the facts on which the moving party is entitled to the judgment.

(b) *Renewal of Motion for Judgment After Trial; Alternative* **Motion for** *New Trial* ~~Judgment Notwithstanding the Verdict.~~ Whenever a motion for a ~~directed verdict~~ *judgment as a matter of law* made at the close of all the evidence is denied or for any reason is not granted, the court is deemed to have submitted the action to the jury subject to a later determination of the legal questions raised by the motion. *Such a motion may be renewed by service and filing* N*n*ot later than 10 days after entry of judgment~~, a party who has moved for a directed verdict may move to have the verdict and any judgment entered thereon set aside and to have judgment entered in accordance with the party's motion for a directed verdict; or if a verdict was not returned such party, within 10 days after the jury has been discharged, may move for judgment in accordance with the party's motion for a directed verdict.~~ A motion for a new trial *under Rule 59* may be joined with *a renewal*

New matter is shown in italics; matter to be omitted is lined through

of the ~~this~~ motion *for judgment as a matter of law,* or a new trial may be ~~prayed for~~ *requested* in the alternative. If a verdict was returned, the court may, *in disposing of the renewed motion,* allow the judgment to stand or may reopen the judgment and either order a new trial or direct the entry of judgment as *a matter of law* ~~if the requested verdict had been directed~~. If no verdict was returned, the court may, *in disposing of the renewed motion,* direct the entry of judgment as *a matter of law* ~~if the requested verdict had been directed~~ or may order a new trial.

(c) Same: Conditional Rulings on Grant of Motion *for Judgment as a Matter of Law*.

(1) If the *renewed* motion for judgment ~~notwithstanding the verdict, provided for in subdivision (b) of this rule,~~ *as a matter of law* is granted, the court shall also rule on the motion for a new trial, if any, by determining whether it should be granted if the judgment is thereafter vacated or reversed, and shall specify the grounds for granting or denying the motion for the new trial. If the motion for a new trial is thus conditionally granted, the order thereon does not affect the finality of the judgment. In case the motion for a new trial has been conditionally granted and the judgment is reversed on appeal, the new trial shall proceed unless the appellate court has otherwise ordered. In case the motion for a new trial has been conditionally denied, the appellee on appeal may assert error in that denial; and if the judgment is reversed on appeal, subsequent proceedings shall be in accordance with the order of the appellate court.

(2) The party ~~whose verdict has been set aside on motion for judgment notwithstanding the verdict~~ *against whom judgment as a matter of law has been rendered* may serve a motion for a new trial pursuant to Rule 59 not later than 10 days after entry of the judgment ~~notwithstanding the verdict~~.

(d) Same: Denial of Motion *for Judgment as a Matter of Law*. If the motion for judgment ~~notwithstanding the verdict~~ *as a matter of law* is denied, the party who prevailed on that motion may, as appellee, assert grounds entitling the party to a new trial in the event the appellate court concludes that the trial court erred in denying the motion for judgment ~~notwithstanding the verdict~~. If the appellate court reverses the judgment, nothing in this rule precludes it from determining that the appellee is entitled to a new trial, or from directing the trial court to determine whether a new trial shall be granted.

New matter is shown in italics; matter to be omitted is lined through

Subdivision (a). The revision of this subdivision aims to facilitate the exercise by the court of its responsibility to assure the fidelity of its judgment to the controlling law, a responsibility imposed by the Due Process Clause of the Fifth Amendment. *Cf. Galloway v. United States,* 319 U.S. 372 (1943).

The revision abandons the familiar terminology of *direction of verdict* for several reasons. The term is misleading as a description of the relationship between judge and jury. It is also freighted with anachronisms some of which are the subject of the text of former subdivision (a) of this rule that is deleted in this revision. Thus, it should not be necessary to state in the text of this rule that a motion made pursuant to it is not a waiver of the right to jury trial, and only the antiquities of directed verdict practice suggest that it might have been. The term "judgment as a matter of law" is an almost equally familiar term and appears in the text of Rule 56; its use in Rule 50 calls attention to the relationship between the two rules. Finally, the change enables the rule to refer to preverdict and post-verdict motions with a terminology that does not conceal the common identity of two motions made at different times in the proceeding.

If a motion is denominated a motion for directed verdict or for judgment notwithstanding the verdict, the party's error is merely formal. Such a motion should be treated as a motion for judgment as a matter of law in accordance with this rule.

Paragraph (a)(1) articulates the standard for the granting of a motion for judgment as a matter of law. It effects no change in the existing standard. That existing standard was not expressed in the former rule, but was articulated in long-standing case law. *See generally* Cooper, *Directions for Directed Verdicts: A Compass for Federal Courts,* 55 Minn.L.Rev. 903 (1971). The expressed standard makes clear that action taken under the rule is a performance of the court's duty to assure enforcement of the controlling law and is not an intrusion on any responsibility for factual determinations conferred on the jury by the Seventh Amendment or any other provision of federal law. Because this standard is also used as a reference point for entry of summary judgment under 56(a), it serves to link the two related provisions.

The revision authorizes the court to perform its duty to enter judgment as a matter of law at any time during the trial, as soon as it is apparent that either party is unable to carry a burden of proof that is essential to that party's case. Thus, the second sentence of paragraph (a)(1) authorizes the court to consider a motion for judgment as a matter of law as soon as a party has completed a presentation on a fact essential to that party's case. Such early action is appropriate when economy and expedition will be served. In no event, however, should the court enter judgment against a party who has not been apprised of the materiality of the dispositive fact and been afforded an opportunity to present any available evidence bearing on that fact. In order further to facilitate the exercise of the authority provided by this rule, Rule 16 is also revised to encourage the court to schedule an order of trial that proceeds first with a presentation on an issue that is likely to be dispositive, if such an issue is identified in the course of pretrial. Such scheduling can be appropriate where the court is uncertain whether favorable action should be taken under Rule 56. Thus, the revision affords the court the alternative of denying a motion for summary judgment while scheduling a separate trial of the issue under Rule 42(b) or scheduling the trial to begin with a presentation on that essential fact which the opposing party seems unlikely to be able to maintain.

Paragraph (a)(2) retains the requirement that a motion for judgment be made prior to the close of the trial, subject to renewal after a jury verdict has been rendered. The purpose of this requirement is to assure the responding party an

New matter is shown in italics; matter to be omitted is lined through

opportunity to cure any deficiency in that party's proof that may have been overlooked until called to the party's attention by a late motion for judgment. Cf. *Farley Transp. Co. v. Santa Fe Trail Transp. Co.*, 786 F.2d 1342 (9th Cir.1986) ("If the moving party is then permitted to make a later attack on the evidence through a motion for judgment notwithstanding the verdict or an appeal, the opposing party may be prejudiced by having lost the opportunity to present additional evidence before the case was submitted to the jury"); *Benson v. Allphin*, 786 F.2d 268 (7th Cir.1986) ("the motion for directed verdict at the close of all the evidence provides the nonmovant an opportunity to do what he can to remedy the deficiencies in his case . . ."); *McLaughlin v. The Fellows Gear Shaper Co.*, 786 F.2d 592 (3d Cir.1986) (per Adams, J., dissenting: "This Rule serves important practical purposes in ensuring that neither party is precluded from presenting the most persuasive case possible and in preventing unfair surprise after a matter has been submitted to the jury"). At one time, this requirement was held to be of constitutional stature, being compelled by the Seventh Amendment. Cf. *Slocum v. New York Insurance Co.*, 228 U.S. 364 (1913). But cf. *Baltimore & Carolina Line v. Redman*, 295 U.S. 654 (1935).

The second sentence of paragraph (a)(2) does impose a requirement that the moving party articulate the basis on which a judgment as a matter of law might be rendered. The articulation is necessary to achieve the purpose of the requirement that the motion be made before the case is submitted to the jury, so that the responding party may seek to correct any overlooked deficiencies in the proof. The revision thus alters the result in cases in which courts have used various techniques to avoid the requirement that a motion for a directed verdict be made as a predicate to a motion for judgment notwithstanding the verdict. E.g., *Benson v. Allphin*, 786 F.2d 268 (7th Cir.1986) ("this circuit has allowed something less than a formal motion for directed verdict to preserve a party's right to move for judgment notwithstanding the verdict"). *See generally* 9 Wright & Miller, Federal Practice and Procedure § 2537 (1971 and Supp.). The information required with the motion may be supplied by explicit reference to materials and argument previously supplied to the court.

This subdivision deals only with the entry of judgment and not with the resolution of particular factual issues as a matter of law. The court may, as before, properly refuse to instruct a jury to decide an issue if a reasonable jury could on the evidence presented decide that issue in only one way.

Subdivision (b). This provision retains the concept of the former rule that the post-verdict motion is a renewal of an earlier motion made at the close of the evidence. One purpose of this concept was to avoid any question arising under the Seventh Amendment. *Montgomery Ward & Co. v. Duncan*, 311 U.S. 243 (1940). It remains useful as a means of defining the appropriate issue posed by the post-verdict motion. A post-trial motion for judgment can be granted only on grounds advanced in the pre-verdict motion. E.g., *Kutner Buick, Inc. v. American Motors Corp.*, 868 F.2d 614 (3d Cir.1989).

Often it appears to the court or to the moving party that a motion for judgment as a matter of law made at the close of the evidence should be reserved for a post-verdict decision. This is so because a jury verdict for the moving party moots the issue and because a preverdict ruling gambles that a reversal may result in a new trial that might have been avoided. For these reasons, the court may often wisely decline to rule on a motion for judgment as a matter of law made at the close of the evidence, and it is not inappropriate for the moving party to suggest such a postponement of the ruling until after the verdict has been rendered.

In ruling on such a motion, the court should disregard any jury determination for which there is no legally sufficient evidentiary basis enabling a reasonable jury to

---

New matter is shown in italics; matter to be omitted is lined through

make it. The court may then decide such issues as a matter of law and enter judgment if all other material issues have been decided by the jury on the basis of legally sufficient evidence, or by the court as a matter of law.

The revised rule is intended for use in this manner with Rule 49. Thus, the court may combine facts established as a matter of law either before trial under Rule 56 or at trial on the basis of the evidence presented with other facts determined by the jury under instructions provided under Rule 49 to support a proper judgment under this rule.

This provision also retains the former requirement that a post-trial motion under the rule must be made within 10 days after entry of a contrary judgment. The renewed motion must be served and filed as provided by Rule 5. A purpose of this requirement is to meet the requirements of F.R.App.P. 4(a)(4).

Subdivision (c). Revision of this subdivision conforms the language to the change in diction set forth in subdivision (a) of this revised rule.

Subdivision (d). Revision of this subdivision conforms the language to that of the previous subdivisions.

Advisory Committee's Note to 1993 Amendment

(a) Judgment as a Matter of Law.

(1) If during a trial by jury a party has been fully heard *on* ~~with respect to~~ an issue and there is no legally sufficient evidentiary basis for a reasonable jury to ~~have found~~ *find* for that party *on* ~~with respect to~~ that issue, the court may *determine the issue against that party and may* grant a motion for judgment as a matter of law against that party ~~on any~~ *with respect to a* claim~~,~~ ~~counterclaim, cross-claim, or third party claim~~ *or defense* that cannot under the controlling law be maintained *or defeated* without a favorable finding on that issue.

This technical amendment corrects an ambiguity in the text of the 1991 revision of the rule, which, as indicated in the Notes, was not intended to change the existing standards under which "directed verdicts" could be granted. This amendment makes clear that judgments as a matter of law in jury trials may be entered against both plaintiffs and defendants and with respect to issues or defenses that may not be wholly dispositive of a claim or defense.

Advisory Committee's Note to 2006 Amendment

(a) Judgment as a Matter of Law.

~~(1) If during a trial by jury a party has been fully heard on an issue and there is no legally sufficient evidentiary basis for a~~

New matter is shown in italics; matter to be omitted is lined through

~~reasonable jury to find for that party on that issue; the court may determine the issue against that party and may grant a motion for judgment as a matter of law against that party with respect to a claim or defense that cannot under the controlling law be maintained or defeated without a favorable finding on that issue.~~

~~(2) Motions for judgment as a matter of law may be made at any time before submission of the case to the jury. Such a motion shall specify the judgment sought and the law and the facts on which the moving party is entitled to the judgment.~~

(1) In General. If a party has been fully heard on an issue during a jury trial and the court finds that a reasonable jury would not have a legally sufficient evidentiary basis to find for the party on that issue, the court may:

> *(A) resolve the issue against the party; and*

> *(B) grant a motion for judgment as a matter of law against the party on a claim or defense that, under the controlling law, can be maintained or defeated only with a favorable finding on that issue.*

(2) Motion. A motion for judgment as a matter of law may be made at any time before the case is submitted to the jury. The motion must specify the judgment sought and the law and facts that entitle the movant to the judgment.

(b) Renewing *the* Motion ~~for Judgment~~ After Trial; Alternative Motion for *a* New Trial. If, ~~for any reason,~~ the court does not grant a motion for judgment as a matter of law made ~~at the close of all the evidence~~ *under subdivision (a)*, the court is considered to have submitted the action to the jury subject to the court's later deciding the legal questions raised by the motion. The movant may renew its request for judgment as a matter of law by filing a motion no later than 10 days after *the* entry of judgment *or—if the motion addresses a jury issue not decided by a verdict—no later than 10 days after the jury was discharged.*~~—and~~ *The* movant may alternatively request a new trial or join a motion for a new trial under Rule 59. In ruling on a renewed motion, the court may:

> (1) if a verdict was returned:

> > (A) allow the judgment to stand,

> > (B) order a new trial, or

> > (C) direct entry of judgment as a matter of law; or

> (2) if no verdict was returned:

> > (A) order a new trial, or

New matter is shown in italics; matter to be omitted is lined through

(B) direct entry of judgment as a matter of law.

The language of Rule 50(a) has been amended as part of the general restyling of the Civil Rules to make them more easily understood and to make style and terminology consistent throughout the rules. These changes are intended to be stylistic only.

Rule 50(b) is amended to permit renewal of any Rule 50(a) motion for judgment as a matter of law, deleting the requirement that a motion be made at the close of all the evidence. Because the Rule 50(b) motion is only a renewal of the preverdict motion, it can be granted only on grounds advanced in the preverdict motion. The earlier motion informs the opposing party of the challenge to the sufficiency of the evidence and affords a clear opportunity to provide additional evidence that may be available. The earlier motion also alerts the court to the opportunity to simplify the trial by resolving some issues, or even all issues, without submission to the jury. This fulfillment of the functional needs that underlie present Rule 50(b) also satisfies the Seventh Amendment. Automatic reservation of the legal questions raised by the motion conforms to the decision in *Baltimore & Carolina Line v. Redman*, 297 U.S. 654 (1935).

This change responds to many decisions that have begun to move away from requiring a motion for judgment as a matter of law at the literal close of all the evidence. Although the requirement has been clearly established for several decades, lawyers continue to overlook it. The courts are slowly working away from the formal requirement. The amendment establishes the functional approach that courts have been unable to reach under the present rule and makes practice more consistent and predictable.

Many judges expressly invite motions at the close of all the evidence. The amendment is not intended to discourage this useful practice.

Finally, an explicit time limit is added for making a posttrial motion when the trial ends without a verdict or with a verdict that does not dispose of all issues suitable for resolution by verdict. The motion must be made no later than 10 days after the jury was discharged.

Rule 51.   Instructions to Jury; Objections

Advisory Committee's Note to 2003 Amendment

Rule 51.   ~~Instructions to Jury; Objections~~

~~At the close of the evidence or at such earlier time during the trial as the court reasonably directs, any party may file written requests that the court instruct the jury on the law as set forth in the requests. The court shall inform counsel of its proposed action upon the requests prior to their arguments to the jury. The court, at its election, may instruct the jury before or after argument, or both. No party may assign as error the giving or the failure to give an instruction unless that party objects thereto before the jury retires to consider its verdict, stating distinctly the matter objected to and the grounds of the objection. Opportunity shall be given to make the objection out of the hearing of the jury.~~

New matter is shown in italics; matter to be omitted is lined through

Rule 51.   Instructions to Jury; Objections; Preserving a Claim of Error

(a) Requests.

(1) A party may, at the close of the evidence or at an earlier reasonable time that the court directs, file and furnish to every other party written requests that the court instruct the jury on the law as set forth in the requests.

(2) After the close of the evidence, a party may:

(A) file requests for instructions on issues that could not reasonably have been anticipated at an earlier time for requests set under Rule 51(a)(1), and

(B) with the court's permission file untimely requests for instructions on any issue.

(b) Instructions. *The court:*

(1) must inform the parties of its proposed instructions and proposed action on the requests before instructing the jury and before final jury arguments;

(2) must give the parties an opportunity to object on the record and out of the jury's hearing to the proposed instructions and actions on requests before the instructions and arguments are delivered; and

(3) may instruct the jury at any time after trial begins and before the jury is discharged.

(c) Objections.

(1) A party who objects to an instruction or the failure to give an instruction must do so on the record, stating distinctly the matter objected to and the grounds of the objection.

(2) An objection is timely if:

(A) a party that has been informed of an instruction or action on a request before the jury is instructed and before final jury arguments, as provided by Rule 51(b)(1), objects at the opportunity for objection required by Rule 51(b)(2); or

(B) a party that has not been informed of an instruction or action on a request before the time for objection provided under Rule 51(b)(2) objects promptly after learning that the instruction or request will be, or has been, given or refused.

(d) Assigning Error; Plain Error.

(1) A party may assign as error:

New matter is shown in italics; matter to be omitted is lined through

(A) an error in an instruction actually given if that party made a proper objection under Rule 51(c), or

(B) a failure to give an instruction if that party made a proper request under Rule 51(a), and—unless the court made a definitive ruling on the record rejecting the request—also made a proper objection under Rule 51(c).

(2) A court may consider a plain error in the instructions affecting substantial rights that has not been preserved as required by Rule 51(d)(1)(A) or (B).

Rule 51 is revised to capture many of the interpretations that have emerged in practice. The revisions in text will make uniform the conclusions reached by a majority of decisions on each point. Additions also are made to cover some practices that cannot now be anchored in the text of Rule 51.

Scope. Rule 51 governs instructions to the trial jury on the law that governs the verdict. A variety of other instructions cannot practicably be brought within Rule 51. Among these instructions are preliminary instructions to a venire, and cautionary or limiting instructions delivered in immediate response to events at trial.

Requests. Subdivision (a) governs requests. Apart from the plain error doctrine recognized in subdivision (d)(2), a court is not obliged to instruct the jury on issues raised by the evidence unless a party requests an instruction. The revised rule recognizes the court's authority to direct that requests be submitted before trial.

The close-of-the-evidence deadline may come before trial is completed on all potential issues. Trial may be formally bifurcated or may be sequenced in some less formal manner. The close of the evidence is measured by the occurrence of two events: completion of all intended evidence on an identified phase of the trial and impending submission to the jury with instructions.

The risk in directing a pretrial request deadline is that trial evidence may raise new issues or reshape issues the parties thought they had understood. Courts need not insist on pretrial requests in all cases. Even if the request time is set before trial or early in the trial, subdivision (a)(2)(A) permits requests after the close of the evidence to address issues that could not reasonably have been anticipated at the earlier time for requests set by the court.

Subdivision (a)(2)(B) expressly recognizes the court's discretion to act on an untimely request. The most important consideration in exercising the discretion confirmed by subdivision (a)(2)(B) is the importance of the issue to the case—the closer the issue lies to the "plain error" that would be recognized under subdivision (d)(2), the better the reason to give an instruction. The cogency of the reason for failing to make a timely request also should be considered. To be considered under subdivision (a)(2)(B) a request should be made before final instructions and before final jury arguments. What is a "final" instruction and argument depends on the sequence of submitting the case to the jury. If separate portions of the case are submitted to the jury in sequence, the final arguments and final instructions are those made on submitting to the jury the portion of the case addressed by the arguments and instructions.

Instructions. Subdivision (b)(1) requires the court to inform the parties, before instructing the jury and before final jury arguments related to the instruction, of the

---

New matter is shown in italics; matter to be omitted is lined through

proposed instructions as well as the proposed action on instruction requests. The time limit is addressed to final jury arguments to reflect the practice that allows interim arguments during trial in complex cases; it may not be feasible to develop final instructions before such interim arguments. It is enough that counsel know of the intended instructions before making final arguments addressed to the issue. If the trial is sequenced or bifurcated, the final arguments addressed to an issue may occur before the close of the entire trial.

Subdivision (b)(2) complements subdivision (b)(1) by carrying forward the opportunity to object established by present Rule 51. It makes explicit the opportunity to object on the record, ensuring a clear memorial of the objection.

Subdivision (b)(3) reflects common practice by authorizing instructions at any time after trial begins and before the jury is discharged.

Objections. Subdivision (c) states the right to object to an instruction or the failure to give an instruction. It carries forward the formula of present Rule 51 requiring that the objection state distinctly the matter objected to and the grounds of the objection, and makes explicit the requirement that the objection be made on the record. The provisions on the time to object make clear that it is timely to object promptly after learning of an instruction or action on a request when the court has not provided advance information as required by subdivision (b)(1). The need to repeat a request by way of objection is continued by new subdivision (d)(1)(B) except where the court made a definitive ruling on the record.

Preserving a claim of error and plain error. Many cases hold that a proper request for a jury instruction is not alone enough to preserve the right to appeal failure to give the instruction. The request must be renewed by objection. This doctrine is appropriate when the court may not have sufficiently focused on the request, or may believe that the request has been granted in substance although in different words. But this doctrine may also prove a trap for the unwary who fail to add an objection after the court has made it clear that the request has been considered and rejected on the merits. Subdivision (d)(1)(B) establishes authority to review the failure to grant a timely request, despite a failure to add an objection, when the court has made a definitive ruling on the record rejecting the request.

Many circuits have recognized that an error not preserved under Rule 51 may be reviewed in exceptional circumstances. The language adopted to capture these decisions in subdivision (d)(2) is borrowed from Criminal Rule 52. Although the language is the same, the context of civil litigation often differs from the context of criminal prosecution; actual application of the plain-error standard takes account of the differences. The Supreme Court has summarized application of Criminal Rule 52 as involving four elements: (1) there must be an error; (2) the error must be plain; (3) the error must affect substantial rights; and (4) the error must seriously affect the fairness, integrity, or public reputation of judicial proceedings. *Johnson v. U.S.*, 520 U.S. 461, 466–467, 469–470 (1997). (The Johnson case quoted the fourth element from its decision in a civil action, *U.S. v. Atkinson*, 297 U.S. 157, 160 (1936): "In exceptional circumstances, especially in criminal cases, appellate courts, in the public interest, may, of their own motion, notice errors to which no exception has been taken, if the errors are obvious, or if they otherwise substantially affect the fairness, integrity, or public reputation of judicial proceedings.")

The court's duty to give correct jury instructions in a civil action is shaped by at least four factors.

The factor most directly implied by a "plain" error rule is the obviousness of the mistake. The importance of the error is a second major factor. The costs of correcting an error reflect a third factor that is affected by a variety of circum-

---

New matter is shown in italics; matter to be omitted is lined through

stances. In a case that seems close to the fundamental error line, account also may be taken of the impact a verdict may have on nonparties.

Rule 52. Findings by the Court

Advisory Committee's Note to 1985 Amendment

(a) **Effect.** In all actions tried upon the facts without a jury or with an advisory jury, the court shall find the facts specially and state separately its conclusions of law thereon, and judgment shall be entered pursuant to Rule 58; and in granting or refusing interlocutory injunctions the court shall similarly set forth the findings of fact and conclusions of law which constitute the grounds of its action. Requests for findings are not necessary for purposes of review. Findings of fact, *whether based on oral or documentary evidence,* shall not be set aside unless clearly erroneous, and due regard shall be given to the opportunity of the trial court to judge of the credibility of the witnesses. The findings of a master, to the extent that the court adopts them, shall be considered as the findings of the court. It will be sufficient if the findings of fact and conclusions of law are stated orally and recorded in open court following the close of the evidence or appear in an opinion or memorandum of decision filed by the court. Findings of fact and conclusions of law are unnecessary on decisions of motions under Rules 12 or 56 or any other motion except as provided in Rule 41(b).

———

Rule 52(a) has been amended (1) to avoid continued confusion and conflicts among the circuits as to the standard of appellate review of findings of fact by the court, (2) to eliminate the disparity between the standard of review as literally stated in Rule 52(a) and the practice of some courts of appeals, and (3) to promote nationwide uniformity. See Note, *Rule 52(a): Appellate Review of Findings of Fact Based on Documentary or Undisputed Evidence,* 49 Va.L.Rev. 506, 536 (1963).

Some courts of appeal have stated that when a trial court's findings do not rest on demeanor evidence and evaluation of a witness' credibility, there is no reason to defer to the trial court's findings and the appellate court more readily can find them to be clearly erroneous. See, *e.g., Marcum v. United States,* 621 F.2d 142, 144–45 (5th Cir. 1980). Others go further, holding that appellate review may be had without application of the "clearly erroneous" test since the appellate court is in as good a position as the trial court to review a purely documentary record. See, *e.g., Atari, Inc. v. North American Philips Consumer Electronics Corp.,* 672 F.2d 607, 614 (7th Cir.), *cert. denied,* 459 U.S. 880 (1982); *Lydle v. United States,* 635 F.2d 763, 765 n. 1 (6th Cir. 1981); *Swanson v. Baker Indus., Inc.,* 615 F.2d 479, 483 (8th Cir. 1980); *Taylor v. Lombard,* 606 F.2d 371, 372 (2d Cir. 1979), *cert. denied,* 445 U.S. 946 (1980); *Jack Kahn Music Co. v. Baldwin Piano & Organ Co.,* 604 F.2d 755, 758 (2d Cir. 1979); *John R. Thompson Co. v. United States,* 477 F.2d 164, 167 (7th Cir. 1973).

New matter is shown in italics; matter to be omitted is lined through

A third group has adopted the view that the "clearly erroneous" rule applies in all nonjury cases even when findings are based solely on documentary evidence or on inferences from undisputed facts. See, *e.g.*, *Maxwell v. Sumner*, 673 F.2d 1031, 1036 (9th Cir.), *cert. denied*, 459 U.S. 976 (1982); *United States v. Texas Education Agency*, 647 F.2d 504, 506–07 (5th Cir. 1981), *cert. denied*, 454 U.S. 1143 (1982); *Constructora Maza, Inc. v. Banco de Ponce*, 616 F.2d 573, 576 (1st Cir. 1980); *In re Sierra Trading Corp.*, 482 F.2d 333, 337 (10th Cir. 1973); *Case v. Morrisette*, 475 F.2d 1300, 1306–07 (D.C. Cir. 1973).

The commentators also disagree as to the proper interpretation of the Rule. *Compare* Wright, *The Doubtful Omniscience of Appellate Courts*, 41 Minn. L. Rev. 751, 769–70 (1957) (language and intent of Rule support view that "clearly erroneous" test should apply to all forms of evidence), *and* 9 C. Wright & A. Miller, *Federal Practice and Procedure: Civil* § 2587, at 740 (1971) (language of the Rule is clear), *with* 5A J. Moore, *Federal Practice* ¶ 52.04, at 2687–88 (2d ed. 1982) (Rule as written supports broader review of findings based on non-demeanor testimony).

The Supreme Court has not clearly resolved the issue. See *Bose Corp. v. Consumers Union of United States, Inc.*, 104 S.Ct. 1949, 1958 (1984); *Pullman Standard v. Swint*, 456 U.S. 273, 293 (1982); *United States v. General Motors Corp.*, 384 U.S. 127, 141 n. 16 (1966); *United States v. United States Gypsum Co.*, 333 U.S. 364, 394–96 (1948).

The principal argument advanced in favor of a more searching appellate review of findings by the district court based solely on documentary evidence is that the rationale of Rule 52(a) does not apply when the findings do not rest on the trial court's assessment of credibility of the witnesses but on an evaluation of documentary proof and the drawing of inferences from it, thus eliminating the need for any special deference to the trial court's findings. These considerations are outweighed by the public interest in the stability and judicial economy that would be promoted by recognizing that the trial court, not the appellate tribunal, should be the finder of the facts. To permit courts of appeals to share more actively in the fact-finding function would tend to undermine the legitimacy of the district courts in the eyes of litigants, multiply appeals by encouraging appellate retrial of some factual issues, and needlessly reallocate judicial authority.

Advisory Committee's Note to 1991 Amendment

Rule 52. Findings by the Court; *Judgment on Partial Findings*

(a) Effect. In all actions tried upon the facts without a jury or with an advisory jury, the court shall find the facts specially and state separately its conclusions of law thereon, and judgment shall be entered pursuant to Rule 58; and in granting or refusing interlocutory injunctions the court shall similarly set forth the findings of fact and conclusions of law which constitute the grounds of its action. Requests for findings are not necessary for purposes of review. Findings of fact, whether based on oral or documentary evidence, shall not be set aside unless clearly erroneous, and due regard shall be given to the opportunity of the trial court to judge

New matter is shown in italics; matter to be omitted is lined through

of the credibility of the witnesses. The findings of a master, to the extent that the court adopts them, shall be considered as the findings of the court. It will be sufficient if the findings of fact and conclusions of law are stated orally and recorded in open court following the close of the evidence or appear in an opinion or memorandum of decision filed by the court. Findings of fact and conclusions of law are unnecessary on decisions of motions under Rule 12 or 56 or any other motion except as provided in ~~Rule 41(b)~~ *subdivision (c) of this rule.*

*(c) **Judgment on Partial Findings.** If during a trial without a jury a party has been fully heard with respect to an issue and the court finds against the party on that issue, the court may enter judgment as a matter of law against that party on any claim, counterclaim, cross-claim or third-party claim that cannot under the controlling law be maintained or defeated without a favorable finding on that issue, or the court may decline to render any judgment until the close of all the evidence. Such a judgment shall be supported by findings of fact and conclusions of law as required by subdivision (a) of this rule.*

Subdivision (c) is added. It parallels the revised Rule 50(a), but is applicable to non-jury trials. It authorizes the court to enter judgment at any time that it can appropriately make a dispositive finding of fact on the evidence.

The new subdivision replaces part of Rule 41(b), which formerly authorized a dismissal at the close of the plaintiff's case if the plaintiff had failed to carry an essential burden of proof. Accordingly, the reference to Rule 41 formerly made in subdivision (a) of this rule is deleted.

As under the former Rule 41(b), the court retains discretion to enter no judgment prior to the close of the evidence.

Judgment entered under this rule differs from a summary judgment under Rule 56 in the nature of the evaluation made by the court. A judgment on partial findings is made after the court has heard all the evidence bearing on the crucial issue of fact, and the finding is reversible only if the appellate court finds it to be "clearly erroneous." A summary judgment, in contrast, is made on the basis of facts established on account of the absence of contrary evidence or presumptions; such establishments of fact are rulings on questions of law as provided in Rule 56(a) and are not shielded by the "clear error" standard of review.

Rule 54.   Judgments; Costs

Advisory Committee's Note to Original Rule

Note to Subdivision (a). The second sentence is derived substantially from Equity Rule 71 (Form of Decree).

Note to Subdivision (b). This provides for the separate judgment of equity and code practice. See Wis.Stat. (1935) § 270.54; Compare N.Y.C.P.A. (1937) § 476.

New matter is shown in italics; matter to be omitted is lined through

Note to Subdivision (c). For the limitation on default contained in the first sentence, see 2 N.D.Comp.Laws Ann. (1913) § 7680; N.Y.C.P.A. (1937) § 479. Compare English Rules Under the Judicature Act (The Annual Practice, 1937) O. 13, r. r. 3–12. The remainder is a usual code provision. It makes clear that a judgment should give the relief to which a party is entitled, regardless of whether it is legal or equitable or both. This necessarily includes the deficiency judgment in foreclosure cases formerly provided for by Equity Rule 10 (Decree for Deficiency in Foreclosures, Etc.).

Note to Subdivision (d). For the present rule in common law actions, see *Ex parte Peterson,* 253 U.S. 300, 40 S.Ct. 543, 64 L.Ed. 919 (1920); Payne, *Costs in Common Law Actions in the Federal Courts* (1935), 21 Va.L.Rev. 397.

The provisions as to costs in actions in forma pauperis contained in U.S.C., Title 28, §§ 832–836 [now § 1915] are unaffected by this rule. Other sections of U.S.C., Title 28, which are unaffected by this rule are: §§ 815 [1946 ed.] (Costs; plaintiff not entitled to, when), 821 [now § 1928] (Costs; infringement of patent; disclaimer), 825 [1946 ed.] (Costs; several actions), 829 [now § 1927] (Costs; attorney liable for, when), and 830 [now § 1920] (Costs; bill of; taxation).

The provisions of the following and similar statutes as to costs against the United States and its officers and agencies are specifically continued:

U.S.C., Title 15, §§ 77v(a), 78aa, 79y (Securities and Exchange Commission)

U.S.C., Title 16, § 825p (Federal Power Commission)

U.S.C., Title 26, §§ 1569(d) and 1645(d) (Internal revenue actions)

U.S.C., Title 26, § 1670(b)(2) (Reimbursement of costs of recovery against revenue officers)

U.S.C., Title 28, § 817 [1946 ed.] (Internal revenue actions)

U.S.C., Title 28, § 836 [now § 1915] (United States—actions in forma pauperis)

U.S.C., Title 28, § 842 [now § 2006] (Actions against revenue officers)

U.S.C., Title 28, § 870 [now § 2408] (United States—in certain cases)

U.S.C., Title 28, § 906 [1946 ed.] (United States—foreclosure actions)

U.S.C., Title 47, § 401 (Communications Commission)

The provisions of the following and similar statutes as to costs are unaffected:

U.S.C., Title 7, § 210(f) (Actions for damages based on an order of the Secretary of Agriculture under Stockyards Act)

U.S.C., Title 7, § 499g(c) (Appeals from reparations orders of Secretary of Agriculture under Perishable Commodities Act)

U.S.C., Title 8, § 45 (Action against district attorneys in certain cases)

U.S.C., Title 15, § 15 (Actions for injuries due to violation of antitrust laws)

U.S.C., Title 15, § 72 (Actions for violation of law forbidding importation or sale of articles at less than market value or wholesale prices)

U.S.C., Title 15, § 77k (Actions by persons acquiring securities registered with untrue statements under Securities Act of 1933)

U.S.C., Title 15, § 78i(e) (Certain actions under the Securities Exchange Act of 1934)

U.S.C., Title 15, § 78r (Similar to 78i(e))

New matter is shown in italics; matter to be omitted is lined through

U.S.C., Title 15, § 96 (Infringement of trade-mark—damages)

U.S.C., Title 15, § 99 (Infringement of trade-mark—injunctions)

U.S.C., Title 15, § 124 (Infringement of trade-mark—damages)

U.S.C., Title 19, § 274 (Certain actions under customs law)

U.S.C., Title 30, § 32 (Action to determine right to possession of mineral lands in certain cases)

U.S.C., Title 31, §§ 232 and 234 (Action for making false claims upon United States)

U.S.C., Title 33, § 926 (Actions under Harbor Workers' Compensation Act)

U.S.C., Title 35, § 67 (Infringement of patent—damages)

U.S.C., Title 35, § 69 (Infringement of patent—pleading and proof)

U.S.C., Title 35, § 71 (Infringement of patent—when specification too broad)

U.S.C., Title 45, § 153p (Actions for non-compliance with an order of National R.R. Adjustment Board for payment of money)

U.S.C., Title 46, § 38 (Action for penalty for failure to register vessel)

U.S.C., Title 46, § 829 (Action based on non-compliance with an order of Maritime Commission for payment of money)

U.S.C., Title 46, § 941 (Certain actions under Ship Mortgage Act)

U.S.C., Title 46, § 1227 (Actions for damages for violation of certain provisions of the Merchant Marine Act, 1936)

U.S.C., Title 47, § 206 (Actions for certain violations of Communications Act of 1934)

U.S.C., Title 49, § 16(2) (Action based on non-compliance with an order of I.C.C. for payment of money)

Advisory Committee's Note to 1948 Amendment

(b) ~~**Judgment at Various Stages.** When more than one claim for relief is presented in an action, the court at any stage, upon a determination of the issues material to a particular claim and all counterclaims arising out of the transaction or occurrence which is the subject matter of the claim, may enter a judgment disposing of such claim. The judgment shall terminate the action with respect to the claim so disposed of and the action shall proceed as to the remaining claims. In case a separate judgment is so entered, the court by order may stay its enforcement until the entering of a subsequent judgment or judgments and may prescribe such conditions as are necessary to secure the benefit thereof to the party in whose favor the judgment is entered.~~ *Judgment Upon Multiple Claims. When more than one claim for relief is presented in an action, whether as a claim, counterclaim, cross-claim, or*

New matter is shown in italics; matter to be omitted is lined through

third-party claim, the court may direct the entry of a final judgment upon one or more but less than all of the claims only upon an express determination that there is no just reason for delay and upon an express direction for the entry of judgment. In the absence of such determination and direction, any order or other form of decision, however designated, which adjudicates less than all the claims shall not terminate the action as to any of the claims, and the order or other form of decision is subject to revision at any time before the entry of judgment adjudicating all the claims.

The historic rule in the federal courts has always prohibited piecemeal disposal of litigation and permitted appeals only from final judgments except in those special instances covered by statute. *Hohorst v. Hamburg–American Packet Co.*, 1893, 148 U.S. 262, 13 S.Ct. 590; *Rexford v. Brunswick–Balke–Collender Co.*, 1913, 228 U.S. 339, 33 S.Ct. 515; *Collins v. Miller*, 1920, 252 U.S. 364, 40 S.Ct. 347. Rule 54(b) was originally adopted in view of the wide scope and possible content of the newly created "civil action" in order to avoid the possible injustice of a delay in judgment of a distinctly separate claim to await adjudication of the entire case. It was not designed to overturn the settled federal rule stated above, which, indeed, has more recently been reiterated in *Catlin v. United States*, 1945, 324 U.S. 229, 65 S.Ct. 631. See also *United States v. Florian*, 1941, 312 U.S. 656, 61 S.Ct. 713, rev'g, and restoring the first opinion in, *Florian v. United States*, C.C.A.7th, 1940, 114 F.2d 990; *Reeves v. Beardall*, 1942, 316 U.S. 283, 62 S.Ct. 1085.

Unfortunately, this was not always understood, and some confusion ensued. Hence situations arose where district courts made a piecemeal disposition of an action and entered what the parties thought amounted to a judgment, although a trial remained to be had on other claims similar or identical with those disposed of. In the interim the parties did not know their ultimate rights, and accordingly took an appeal, thus putting the finality of the partial judgment in question. While most appellate courts have reached a result generally in accord with the intent of the rule, yet there have been divergent precedents and division of views which have served to render the issues more clouded to the parties appellant. It hardly seems a case where multiplicity of precedents will tend to remove the problem from debate. The problem is presented and discussed in the following cases: *Atwater v. North American Coal Corp.*, C.C.A.2d, 1940, 111 F.2d 125; *Rosenblum v. Dingfelder*, C.C.A.2d, 1940, 111 F.2d 406; *Audi-Vision, Inc. v. RCA Mfg. Co., Inc.*, C.C.A.2d, 1943, 136 F.2d 621; *Zalkind v. Scheinman*, C.C.A.2d, 1943, 139 F.2d 895; *Oppenheimer v. F.J. Young & Co., Inc.*, C.C.A.2d, 1944, 144 F.2d 387; *Libbey-Owens–Ford Glass Co. v. Sylvania Industrial Corp.*, C.C.A.2d, 1946, 154 F.2d 814, cert. den., 1946, 66 S.Ct. 1353; *Zarati Steamship Co. v. Park Bridge Corp.*, C.C.A.2d, 1946, 154 F.2d 377; *Baltimore and Ohio R. Co. v. United Fuel Gas Co.*, C.C.A.4th, 1946, 154 F.2d 545; *Jefferson Electric Co. v. Sola Electric Co.*, C.C.A.7th, 1941, 122 F.2d 124; *Leonard v. Socony–Vacuum Oil Co.*, C.C.A.7th, 1942, 130 F.2d 535; *Markham v. Kasper*, C.C.A.7th, 1945, 152 F.2d 270; *Hanney v. Franklin Fire Ins. Co. of Philadelphia*, C.C.A.9th, 1944, 142 F.2d 864; *Toomey v. Toomey*, App.D.C.1945, 80 U.S.App.D.C. 77, 149 F.2d 19.

In view of the difficulty thus disclosed, the Advisory Committee in its two preliminary drafts of proposed amendments attempted to redefine the original rule with particular stress upon the interlocutory nature of partial judgments which did not adjudicate all claims arising out of a single transaction or occurrence. This attempt appeared to meet with almost universal approval from those of the profes-

New matter is shown in italics; matter to be omitted is lined through

sion commenting upon it, although there were, of course, helpful suggestions for additional changes in language or clarification of detail. But *cf.* Circuit Judge Frank's dissenting opinion in *Libbey-Owens–Ford Glass Co. v. Sylvania Industrial Corp., supra,* n. 21 of the dissenting opinion. The Committee, however, became convinced on careful study of its own proposals that the seeds of ambiguity still remained, and that it had not completely solved the problem of piecemeal appeals. After extended consideration, it concluded that a retention of the older federal rule was desirable, and that this rule needed only the exercise of a discretionary power to afford a remedy in the infrequent harsh case to provide a simple, definite, workable rule. This is afforded by amended Rule 54(b). It re-establishes an ancient policy with clarity and precision. For the possibility of staying execution where not all claims are disposed of under Rule 54(b), see amended Rule 62(h).

Advisory Committee's Note to 1961 Amendment

(b) Judgment Upon Multiple Claims *or Involving Multiple Parties.* When more than one claim for relief is presented in an action, whether as a claim, counterclaim, cross-claim, or third-party claim, *or when multiple parties are involved,* the court may direct the entry of a final judgment ~~upon~~ *as to* one or more but ~~less~~ *fewer* than all of the claims *or parties* only upon an express determination that there is no just reason for delay and upon an express direction for the entry of judgment. In the absence of such determination and direction, any order or other form of decision, however designated, which adjudicates ~~less~~ *fewer* than all the claims *or the rights and liabilities of fewer than all the parties* shall not terminate the action as to any of the claims *or parties,* and the order or other form of decision is subject to revision at any time before the entry of judgment adjudicating all the claims *and the rights and liabilities of all the parties.*

This rule permitting appeal, upon the trial court's determination of "no just reason for delay," from a judgment upon one or more but fewer than all the claims in an action, has generally been given a sympathetic construction by the courts and its validity is settled. *Reeves v. Beardall,* 316 U.S. 283 (1942); *Sears, Roebuck & Co. v. Mackey,* 351 U.S. 427 (1956); *Cold Metal Process Co. v. United Engineering & Foundry Co.,* 351 U.S. 445 (1956).

A serious difficulty has, however, arisen because the rule speaks of claims but nowhere mentions parties. A line of cases has developed in the circuits consistently holding the rule to be inapplicable to the dismissal, even with the requisite trial court determination, of one or more but fewer than all defendants jointly charged in an action, *i.e.,* charged with various forms of concerted or related wrongdoing or related liability. See *Mull v. Ackerman,* 279 F.2d 25 (2d Cir.1960); *Richards v. Smith,* 276 F.2d 652 (5th Cir.1960); *Hardy v. Bankers Life & Cas. Co.,* 222 F.2d 827 (7th Cir.1955); *Steiner v. 20th Century–Fox Film Corp.,* 220 F.2d 105 (9th Cir.1955). For purposes of Rule 54(b) it was arguable that there were as many "claims" as

New matter is shown in italics; matter to be omitted is lined through

there were parties defendant and that the rule in its present text applied where fewer than all of the parties were dismissed, *cf. United Artists Corp. v. Masterpiece Productions, Inc.,* 221 F.2d 213, 215 (2d Cir.1955); *Bowling Machines, Inc. v. First Nat. Bank,* 283 F.2d 39 (1st Cir.1960); but the Courts of Appeals are now committed to an opposite view.

The danger of hardship through delay of appeal until the whole action is concluded may be at least as serious in the multiple-parties situations as in multiple-claims cases, see *Pabellon v. Grace Line, Inc.,* 191 F.2d 169, 179 (2d Cir.1951), *cert. denied,* 342 U.S. 893 (1951), and courts and commentators have urged that Rule 54(b) be changed to take in the former. See *Reagan v. Traders & General Ins. Co.,* 255 F.2d 845 (5th Cir.1958); *Meadows v. Greyhound Corp.,* 235 F.2d 233 (5th Cir.1956); *Steiner v. 20th Century–Fox Film Corp., supra;* 6 *Moore's Federal Practice* ¶ 54.34[2] (2d ed. 1953); 3 Barron & Holtzoff, *Federal Practice & Procedure* § 1193.2 (Wright ed. 1958); *Developments in the Law—Multiparty Litigation,* 71 Harv.L.Rev. 874, 981 (1958); Note, 62 Yale L.J. 263, 271 (1953); Ill.Ann.Stat. ch. 110, § 50(2) (Smith–Hurd 1956). The amendment accomplishes this purpose by referring explicitly to parties.

There has been some recent indication that interlocutory appeal under the provisions of 28 U.S.C. § 1292(b), added in 1958, may now be available for the multiple-parties cases here considered. See *Jaftex Corp. v. Randolph Mills, Inc.,* 282 F.2d 508 (2d Cir.1960). The Rule 54(b) procedure seems preferable for those cases, and § 1292(b) should be held inapplicable to them when the rule is enlarged as here proposed. See *Luckenbach Steamship Co., Inc., v. H. Muehlstein & Co., Inc.,* 280 F.2d 755, 757 (2d Cir.1960); 1 Barron & Holtzoff, *supra,* § 58.1, p. 321 (Wright ed. 1960).

Rule 56. Summary Judgment

Advisory Committee's Note to Original Rule

This rule is applicable to all actions, including those against the United States or an officer or agency thereof.

Summary judgment procedure is a method for promptly disposing of actions in which there is no genuine issue as to any material fact. It has been extensively used in England for more than 50 years and has been adopted in a number of American states. New York, for example, has made great use of it. During the first nine years after its adoption there, the records of New York county alone show 5,600 applications for summary judgments. *Report of the Commission on the Administration of Justice in New York State* (1934), p. 383. See also Third Annual Report of the Judicial Council of the State of New York (1937), p. 30.

In England it was first employed only in cases of liquidated claims, but there has been a steady enlargement of the scope of the remedy until it is now used in actions to recover land or chattels and in all other actions at law, for liquidated or unliquidated claims, except for a few designated torts and breach of promise of marriage. English Rules Under the Judicature Act (The Annual Practice, 1937) O. 3, r. 6; Orders 14, 14A, and 15; see also O. 32, r. 6, authorizing an application for judgment at any time upon admissions. In Michigan (3 Comp.Laws (1929) § 14260) and Illinois (Ill.Rev.Stat. (1937) ch. 110, §§ 181, 259.15, 259.16), it is not limited to liquidated demands. New York (N.Y.R.C.P. (1937) Rule 113; see also Rule 107) has brought so many classes of actions under the operation of the rule that the Commission on Administration of Justice in New York State (1934) recommend that all restrictions be removed and that the remedy be available "in any action" (p. 287). For the history and nature of the summary judgment procedure and citations of

New matter is shown in italics; matter to be omitted is lined through

state statutes, see Clark and Samenow, *The Summary Judgment* (1929), 38 Yale L.J. 423.

Note to Subdivision (d). See Rule 16 (Pre–Trial Procedure; Formulating Issues) and the Note thereto.

Note to Subdivisions (e) and (f). These are similar to rules in Michigan. Mich.Court Rules Ann. (Searl, 1933) Rule 30.

––––––

Advisory Committee's Note to 1948 Amendment

(a) For Claimant. A party seeking to recover upon a claim, counterclaim, or cross-claim or to obtain a declaratory judgment may, at any time after the ~~pleading in answer thereto has been served,~~ *expiration of 20 days from the commencement of the action or after service of a motion for summary judgment by the adverse party*, move with or without supporting affidavits for summary judgment in his favor upon all or any part thereof.

(c) Motion and Proceedings Thereon. The motion shall be served at least 10 days before the time ~~specified~~ *fixed* for the hearing. The adverse party prior to the day of hearing may serve opposing affidavits. The judgment sought shall be rendered forthwith if the pleadings, depositions, and admissions on file, together with the affidavits, if any, show that, ~~except as to the amount of damages,~~ there is no genuine issue as to any material fact and that the moving party is entitled to a judgment as a matter of law. *A summary judgment, interlocutory in character, may be rendered on the issue of liability alone although there is a genuine issue as to the amount of damages.*

––––––

Subdivision (a). The amendment allows a claimant to move for a summary judgment at any time after the expiration of 20 days from the commencement of the action or after service of a motion for summary judgment by the adverse party. This will normally operate to permit an earlier motion by the claimant than under the original rule, where the phrase "at any time after the pleading in answer thereto has been served" operates to prevent a claimant from moving for summary judgment, even in a case clearly proper for its exercise, until a former answer has been filed. Thus in *Peoples Bank v. Federal Reserve Bank of San Francisco,* N.D.Cal.1944, 58 F.Supp. 25, the plaintiff's counter-motion for a summary judgment was stricken as premature, because the defendant had not filed an answer. Since Rule 12(a) allows at least 20 days for an answer, that time plus the 10 days required in Rule 56(c) means that under original Rule 56(a) a minimum period of 30 days necessarily has to elapse in every case before the claimant can be heard on his right to a summary judgment. An extension of time by the court or the service of preliminary motions of any kind will prolong that period even further. In many cases this merely represents unnecessary delay. See *United States v. Adler's Creamery, Inc.,* C.C.A.2d, 1939, 107 F.2d 987. The changes are in the interest of more expeditious litigation. The 20–day

New matter is shown in italics; matter to be omitted is lined through

period, as provided, gives the defendant an opportunity to secure counsel and determine a course of action. But in a case where the defendant himself serves a motion for summary judgment within that time, there is no reason to restrict the plaintiff and the amended rule so provides.

Subdivision (c). The amendment of Rule 56(c), by the addition of the final sentence, resolves a doubt expressed in *Sartor v. Arkansas Natural Gas Corp.*, 1944, 321 U.S. 620, 64 S.Ct. 724. See also Commentary, *Summary Judgment as to Damages*, 1944, 7 Fed.Rules Serv. 974; *Madeirense Do Brasil S/A v. Stulman–Emrick Lumber Co.*, C.C.A.2d, 1945, 147 F.2d 399, cert. den., 1945, 325 U.S. 861, 65 S.Ct. 1201. It makes clear that although the question of recovery depends on the amount of damages, the summary judgment rule is applicable and summary judgment may be granted in a proper case. If the case is not fully adjudicated it may be dealt with as provided in subdivision (d) of Rule 56, and the right to summary recovery determined by a preliminary order, interlocutory in character, and the precise amount of recovery left for trial.

Subdivision (d). Rule 54(a) defines "judgment" as including a decree and "any order from which an appeal lies." Subdivision (d) of Rule 56 indicates clearly, however, that a partial summary "judgment" is not a final judgment, and, therefore, that it is not appealable, unless in the particular case some statute allows an appeal from the interlocutory order involved. The partial summary judgment is merely a pre-trial adjudication that certain issues shall be deemed established for the trial of the case. This adjudication is more nearly akin to the preliminary order under Rule 16, and likewise serves the purpose of speeding up litigation by eliminating before trial matters wherein there is no genuine issue of fact. See *Leonard v. Socony–Vacuum Oil Co.*, C.C.A.7th, 1942, 130 F.2d 535; *Biggins v. Oltmer Iron Works*, C.C.A.7th, 1946, 154 F.2d 214; 3 *Moore's Federal Practice*, 1938, 3190–3192. Since interlocutory appeals are not allowed, except where specifically provided by statute, see 3 *Moore, op. cit. supra*, 3155–3156, this interpretation is in line with that policy, *Leonard v. Socony–Vacuum Oil Co., supra*. See also *Audi Vision Inc. v. RCA Mfg. Co.*, C.C.A.2d, 1943, 136 F.2d 621; *Toomey v. Toomey*, App.D.C.1945, 80 U.S.App. D.C. 77, 149 F.2d 19; *Biggins v. Oltmer Iron Works, supra*; *Catlin v. United States*, 1945, 324 U.S. 229, 65 S.Ct. 631.

Advisory Committee's Note to 1963 Amendment

(c) Motion and Proceedings Thereon. The motion shall be served at least 10 days before the time fixed for the hearing. The adverse party prior to the day of hearing may serve opposing affidavits. The judgment sought shall be rendered forthwith if the pleadings, depositions, *answers to interrogatories,* and admissions on file, together with the affidavits, if any, show that there is no genuine issue as to any material fact and that the moving party is entitled to a judgment as a matter of law. A summary judgment, interlocutory in character, may be rendered on the issue of liability alone although there is a genuine issue as to the amount of damages.

(e) Form of Affidavits; Further Testimony; *Defense Required.* Supporting and opposing affidavits shall be made on per-

---

New matter is shown in italics; matter to be omitted is lined through

sonal knowledge, shall set forth such facts as would be admissible in evidence, and shall show affirmatively that the affiant is competent to testify to the matters stated therein. Sworn or certified copies of all papers or parts thereof referred to in an affidavit shall be attached thereto or served therewith. The court may permit affidavits to be supplemented or opposed by depositions, *answers to interrogatories,* or ~~by~~ further affidavits. *When a motion for summary judgment is made and supported as provided in this rule, an adverse party may not rest upon the mere allegations or denials of his pleading, but his response, by affidavits or as otherwise provided in this rule, must set forth specific facts showing that there is a genuine issue for trial. If he does not so respond, summary judgment, if appropriate, shall be entered against him.*

Subdivision (c). By the amendment "answers to interrogatories" are included among the materials which may be considered on motion for summary judgment. The phrase was inadvertently omitted from the rule, see 3 Barron & Holtzoff, *Federal Practice & Procedure* 159–60 (Wright ed. 1958), and the courts have generally reached by interpretation the result which will hereafter be required by the text of the amended rule. See Annot., 74 A.L.R.2d 984 (1960).

Subdivision (e). The words "answers to interrogatories" are added in the third sentence of this subdivision to conform to the amendment of subdivision (c).

The last two sentences are added to overcome a line of cases, chiefly in the Third Circuit, which has impaired the utility of the summary judgment device. A typical case is as follows: A party supports his motion for summary judgment by affidavits or other evidentiary matter sufficient to show that there is no genuine issue as to a material fact. The adverse party, in opposing the motion, does not produce any evidentiary matter, or produces some but not enough to establish that there is a genuine issue for trial. Instead, the adverse party rests on averments of his pleadings which on their face present an issue. In this situation Third Circuit cases have taken the view that summary judgment must be denied, at least if the averments are "well-pleaded," and not supposititious, conclusory, or ultimate. See *Frederick Hart & Co., Inc. v. Recordgraph Corp.,* 169 F.2d 580 (3d Cir. 1948); *United States ex rel. Kolton v. Halpern,* 260 F.2d 590 (3d Cir. 1958); *United States ex rel. Nobles v. Ivey Bros. Constr. Co., Inc.,* 191 F.Supp. 383 (D.Del.1961); *Jamison v. Pennsylvania Salt Mfg. Co.,* 22 F.R.D. 238 (W.D.Pa.1958); *Bunny Bear, Inc. v. Dennis Mitchell Industries,* 139 F.Supp. 542 (E.D.Pa.1956); *Levy v. Equitable Life Assur. Society,* 18 F.R.D. 164 (E.D.Pa.1955).

The very mission of the summary judgment procedure is to pierce the pleadings and to assess the proof in order to see whether there is a genuine need for trial. The Third Circuit doctrine, which permits the pleadings themselves to stand in the way of granting an otherwise justified summary judgment, is incompatible with the basic purpose of the rule. See 6 *Moore's Federal Practice* 2069 (2d ed. 1953); 3 Barron & Holtzoff, *supra,* § 1235.1.

It is hoped that the amendment will contribute to the more effective utilization of the salutary device of summary judgment.

The amendment is not intended to derogate from the solemnity of the pleadings. Rather it recognizes that, despite the best efforts of counsel to make his pleadings

---

New matter is shown in italics; matter to be omitted is lined through

accurate, they may be overwhelmingly contradicted by the proof available to his adversary.

Nor is the amendment designed to affect the ordinary standards applicable to the summary judgment motion. So, for example: Where an issue as to a material fact cannot be resolved without observation of the demeanor of witnesses in order to evaluate their credibility, summary judgment is not appropriate. Where the evidentiary matter in support of the motion does not establish the absence of a genuine issue, summary judgment must be denied even if no opposing evidentiary matter is presented. And summary judgment may be inappropriate where the party opposing it shows under subdivision (f) that he cannot at the time present facts essential to justify his opposition.

FEDERAL RULES OF APPELLATE PROCEDURE

(with some omissions)

TABLE OF RULES

RULES OF APPELLATE PROCEDURE

FEDERAL RULES OF APPELLATE PROCEDURE

(with some omissions)

TITLE I.   APPLICABILITY OF RULES

Rule 1.

SCOPE OF RULES;   TITLE

(a) Scope of Rules.

(1) These rules govern procedure in the United States courts of appeals.

(2) When these rules provide for filing a motion or other document in the district court, the procedure must comply with the practice of the district court.

(b) [Abrogated.]

(c) Title.   These rules are to be known as the Federal Rules of Appellate Procedure.

As amended 1979, 1989, 1994, 1998, 2002.

Rule 2.

SUSPENSION OF RULES

On its own or a party's motion, a court of appeals may—to expedite its decision or for other good cause—suspend any provision of these rules in a particular case and order proceedings as it directs, except as otherwise provided in Rule 26(b).

As amended 1998.

TITLE II.   APPEAL FROM A JUDGMENT OR ORDER OF A DISTRICT COURT

Rule 3.

APPEAL AS OF RIGHT—HOW TAKEN

(a) Filing the Notice of Appeal.

(1) An appeal permitted by law as of right from a district court to a court of appeals may be taken only by filing a notice of appeal

451

with the district clerk within the time allowed by Rule 4. At the time of filing, the appellant must furnish the clerk with enough copies of the notice to enable the clerk to comply with Rule 3(d).

(2) An appellant's failure to take any step other than the timely filing of a notice of appeal does not affect the validity of the appeal, but is ground only for the court of appeals to act as it considers appropriate, including dismissing the appeal.

(3) An appeal from a judgment by a magistrate judge in a civil case is taken in the same way as an appeal from any other district court judgment.

(4) An appeal by permission under 28 U.S.C. § 1292(b) or an appeal in a bankruptcy case may be taken only in the manner prescribed by Rules 5 and 6, respectively.

(b) Joint or Consolidated Appeals.

(1) When two or more parties are entitled to appeal from a district-court judgment or order, and their interests make joinder practicable, they may file a joint notice of appeal. They may then proceed on appeal as a single appellant.

(2) When the parties have filed separate timely notices of appeal, the appeals may be joined or consolidated by the court of appeals.

(c) Contents of the Notice of Appeal.

(1) The notice of appeal must:

(A) specify the party or parties taking the appeal by naming each one in the caption or body of the notice, but an attorney representing more than one party may describe those parties with such terms as "all plaintiffs," "the defendants," "the plaintiffs A, B, et al.," or "all defendants except X";

(B) designate the judgment, order, or part thereof being appealed; and

(C) name the court to which the appeal is taken.

(2) A pro se notice of appeal is considered filed on behalf of the signer and the signer's spouse and minor children (if they are parties), unless the notice clearly indicates otherwise.

(3) In a class action, whether or not the class has been certified, the notice of appeal is sufficient if it names one person qualified to bring the appeal as representative of the class.

(4) An appeal must not be dismissed for informality of form or title of the notice of appeal, or for failure to name a party whose intent to appeal is otherwise clear from the notice.

(5) Form 1 in the Appendix of Forms is a suggested form of a notice of appeal.

(d) Serving the Notice of Appeal.

(1) The district clerk must serve notice of the filing of a notice of appeal by mailing a copy to each party's counsel of record—excluding the appellant's—or, if a party is proceeding pro se, to the party's last known address. When a defendant in a criminal case appeals, the clerk must also serve a copy of the notice of appeal on the defendant, either by personal service or by mail addressed to the defendant. The clerk must promptly send a copy of the notice of appeal and of the docket entries—and any later docket entries—to the clerk of the court of appeals named in the notice. The district clerk must note, on each copy, the date when the notice of appeal was filed.

(2) If an inmate confined in an institution files a notice of appeal in the manner provided by Rule 4(c), the district clerk must also note the date when the clerk docketed the notice.

(3) The district clerk's failure to serve notice does not affect the validity of the appeal. The clerk must note on the docket the names of the parties to whom the clerk mails copies, with the date of mailing. Service is sufficient despite the death of a party or the party's counsel.

(e) Payment of Fees. Upon filing a notice of appeal, the appellant must pay the district clerk all required fees. The district clerk receives the appellate docket fee on behalf of the court of appeals.

As amended 1979, 1986, 1989, 1993, 1994, 1998.

Rule 3.1.

APPEAL FROM A JUDGMENT OF A MAGISTRATE JUDGE IN A CIVIL CASE

Abrogated 1998

Rule 4.

APPEAL AS OF RIGHT—WHEN TAKEN

(a) Appeal in a Civil Case.

(1) *Time for Filing a Notice of Appeal.*

(A) In a civil case, except as provided in Rules 4(a)(1)(B), 4(a)(4), and 4(c), the notice of appeal required by Rule 3 must be filed with the district clerk within 30 days after the judgment or order appealed from is entered.

(B) When the United States or its officer or agency is a party, the notice of appeal may be filed by any party within 60 days after the judgment or order appealed from is entered.

(C) An appeal from an order granting or denying an application for a writ of error coram nobis is an appeal in a civil case for purposes of Rule 4(a).

(2) *Filing Before Entry of Judgment.* A notice of appeal filed after the court announces a decision or order—but before the entry of the judgment or order—is treated as filed on the date of and after the entry.

(3) *Multiple Appeals.* If one party timely files a notice of appeal, any other party may file a notice of appeal within 14 days after the date when the first notice was filed, or within the time otherwise prescribed by this Rule 4(a), whichever period ends later.

(4) *Effect of a Motion on a Notice of Appeal.*

(A) If a party timely files in the district court any of the following motions under the Federal Rules of Civil Procedure, the time to file an appeal runs for all parties from the entry of the order disposing of the last such remaining motion:

(i) for judgment under Rule 50(b);

(ii) to amend or make additional factual findings under Rule 52(b), whether or not granting the motion would alter the judgment;

(iii) for attorney's fees under Rule 54 if the district court extends the time to appeal under Rule 58;

(iv) to alter or amend the judgment under Rule 59;

(v) for a new trial under Rule 59; or

(vi) for relief under Rule 60 if the motion is filed no later than 28 days after the judgment is entered.

(B)(i) If a party files a notice of appeal after the court announces or enters a judgment—but before it disposes of any motion listed in Rule 4(a)(4)(A)—the notice becomes effective to appeal a judgment or order, in whole or in part, when the order disposing of the last such remaining motion is entered.

(ii) A party intending to challenge an order disposing of any motion listed in Rule 4(a)(4)(A), or a judgment's alteration or amendment upon such a motion, must file a notice of appeal, or an amended notice of appeal—in compliance with Rule 3(c)—within the time prescribed by this Rule measured from the entry of the order disposing of the last such remaining motion.

(iii) No additional fee is required to file an amended notice.

(5) *Motion for Extension of Time.*

(A) The district court may extend the time to file a notice of appeal if:

(i) a party so moves no later than 30 days after the time prescribed by this Rule 4(a) expires; and

(ii) regardless of whether its motion is filed before or during the 30 days after the time prescribed by this Rule 4(a) expires, that party shows excusable neglect or good cause.

(B) A motion filed before the expiration of the time prescribed in Rule 4(a)(1) or (3) may be ex parte unless the court requires otherwise. If the motion is filed after the expiration of the prescribed time, notice must be given to the other parties in accordance with local rules.

(C) No extension under this Rule 4(a)(5) may exceed 30 days after the prescribed time or 14 days after the date when the order granting the motion is entered, whichever is later.

(6) *Reopening the Time to File an Appeal.* The district court may reopen the time to file an appeal for a period of 14 days after the date when its order to reopen is entered, but only if all the following conditions are satisfied:

(A) the court finds that the moving party did not receive notice under Federal Rule of Civil Procedure 77(d) of the entry of the judgment or order sought to be appealed within 21 days after entry;

(B) the motion is filed within 180 days after the judgment or order is entered or within 14 days after the moving party receives notice under Federal Rule of Civil Procedure 77(d) of the entry, whichever is earlier; and

(C) the court finds that no party would be prejudiced.

(7) *Entry Defined.*

(A) A judgment or order is entered for purposes of this Rule 4(a):

(i) if Federal Rule of Civil Procedure 58(a)(1) does not require a separate document, when the judgment or order is entered in the civil docket under Federal Rule of Civil Procedure 79(a); or

(ii) if Federal Rule of Civil Procedure 58(a)(1) requires a separate document, when the judgment or order is entered in the civil docket under Federal Rule of Civil Procedure 79(a) and when the earlier of these events occurs:

● the judgment or order is set forth on a separate document, or

- 150 days have run from entry of the judgment or order in the civil docket under Federal Rule of Civil Procedure 79(a).

(B) A failure to set forth a judgment or order on a separate document when required by Federal Rule of Civil Procedure 58(a)(1) does not affect the validity of an appeal from that judgment or order.

(b) Appeal in a Criminal Case.

(1) *Time for Filing a Notice of Appeal.*

(A) In a criminal case, a defendant's notice of appeal must be filed in the district court within 14 days after the later of:

(i) the entry of either the judgment or the order being appealed; or

(ii) the filing of the government's notice of appeal.

(B) When the government is entitled to appeal, its notice of appeal must be filed in the district court within 30 days after the later of:

(i) the entry of the judgment or order being appealed; or

(ii) the filing of a notice of appeal by any defendant.

(2) *Filing Before Entry of Judgment.* A notice of appeal filed after the court announces a decision, sentence, or order—but before the entry of the judgment or order—is treated as filed on the date of and after the entry.

(3) *Effect of a Motion on a Notice of Appeal.*

(A) If a defendant timely makes any of the following motions under the Federal Rules of Criminal Procedure, the notice of appeal from a judgment of conviction must be filed within 14 days after the entry of the order disposing of the last such remaining motion, or within 14 days after the entry of the judgment of conviction, whichever period ends later. This provision applies to a timely motion:

(i) for judgment of acquittal under Rule 29;

(ii) for a new trial under Rule 33, but if based on newly discovered evidence, only if the motion is made no later than 14 days after the entry of the judgment; or

(iii) for arrest of judgment under Rule 34.

(B) A notice of appeal filed after the court announces a decision, sentence, or order—but before it disposes of any of the motions referred to in Rule 4(b)(3)(A)—becomes effective upon the later of the following:

(i) the entry of the order disposing of the last such remaining motion; or

(ii) the entry of the judgment of conviction.

(C) A valid notice of appeal is effective—without amendment—to appeal from an order disposing of any of the motions referred to in Rule 4(b)(3)(A).

(4) *Motion for Extension of Time.* Upon a finding of excusable neglect or good cause, the district court may—before or after the time has expired, with or without motion and notice—extend the time to file a notice of appeal for a period not to exceed 30 days from the expiration of the time otherwise prescribed by this Rule 4(b).

(5) *Jurisdiction.* The filing of a notice of appeal under this Rule 4(b) does not divest a district court of jurisdiction to correct a sentence under Federal Rule of Criminal Procedure 35(a), nor does the filing of a motion under 35(a) affect the validity of a notice of appeal filed before entry of the order disposing of the motion. The filing of a motion under Federal Rule of Criminal Procedure 35(a) does not suspend the time for filing a notice of appeal from a judgment of conviction.

(6) *Entry Defined.* A judgment or order is entered for purposes of this Rule 4(b) when it is entered on the criminal docket.

(c) Appeal by an Inmate Confined in an Institution.

(1) If an inmate confined in an institution files a notice of appeal in either a civil or a criminal case, the notice is timely if it is deposited in the institution's internal mail system on or before the last day for filing. If an institution has a system designed for legal mail, the inmate must use that system to receive the benefit of this rule. Timely filing may be shown by a declaration in compliance with 28 U.S.C. § 1746 or by a notarized statement, either of which must set forth the date of deposit and state that first-class postage has been prepaid.

(2) If an inmate files the first notice of appeal in a civil case under this Rule 4(c), the 14–day period provided in Rule 4(a)(3) for another party to file a notice of appeal runs from the date when the district court dockets the first notice.

(3) When a defendant in a criminal case files a notice of appeal under this Rule 4(c), the 30–day period for the government to file its notice of appeal runs from the entry of the judgment or order appealed from or from the district court's docketing of the defendant's notice of appeal, whichever is later.

(d) Mistaken Filing in the Court of Appeals. If a notice of appeal in either a civil or a criminal case is mistakenly filed in the court of appeals, the clerk of that court must note on the notice the date when it was received and send it to the district clerk. The notice is then considered filed in the district court on the date so noted.

As amended 1979, 1988, 1991, 1993, 1995, 1998, 2002, 2005, 2009.

Rule 5.

APPEAL BY PERMISSION

(a) Petition for Permission to Appeal.

(1) To request permission to appeal when an appeal is within the court of appeals' discretion, a party must file a petition for permission to appeal. The petition must be filed with the circuit clerk with proof of service on all other parties to the district-court action.

(2) The petition must be filed within the time specified by the statute or rule authorizing the appeal or, if no such time is specified, within the time provided by Rule 4(a) for filing a notice of appeal.

(3) If a party cannot petition for appeal unless the district court first enters an order granting permission to do so or stating that the necessary conditions are met, the district court may amend its order, either on its own or in response to a party's motion, to include the required permission or statement. In that event, the time to petition runs from entry of the amended order.

(b) Contents of the Petition; Answer or Cross–Petition; Oral Argument.

(1) The petition must include the following:

(A) the facts necessary to understand the question presented;

(B) the question itself;

(C) the relief sought;

(D) the reasons why the appeal should be allowed and is authorized by a statute or rule; and

(E) an attached copy of:

(i) the order, decree, or judgment complained of and any related opinion or memorandum, and

(ii) any order stating the district court's permission to appeal or finding that the necessary conditions are met.

(2) A party may file an answer in opposition or a cross-petition within 10 days after the petition is served.

(3) The petition and answer will be submitted without oral argument unless the court of appeals orders otherwise.

(c) Form of Papers; Number of Copies. All papers must conform to Rule 32(c)(2). Except by the court's permission, a paper must not exceed 20 pages, exclusive of the disclosure statement, the proof of service, and the accompanying documents required by Rule 5(b)(1)(E). An original and 3 copies must be filed unless the court requires a different number by local rule or by order in a particular case.

(d) Grant of Permission; Fees; Cost Bond; Filing the Record.

(1) Within 14 days after the entry of the order granting permission to appeal, the appellant must:

(A) pay the district clerk all required fees; and

(B) file a cost bond if required under Rule 7.

(2) A notice of appeal need not be filed. The date when the order granting permission to appeal is entered serves as the date of the notice of appeal for calculating time under these rules.

(3) The district clerk must notify the circuit clerk once the petitioner has paid the fees. Upon receiving this notice, the circuit clerk must enter the appeal on the docket. The record must be forwarded and filed in accordance with Rules 11 and 12(c).

As amended 1979, 1994, 1998, 2002, 2009.

Rule 5.1.

APPEAL BY LEAVE UNDER 28 U.S.C. § 636(c)(5)

Abrogated 1998

Rule 6.

APPEAL IN A BANKRUPTCY CASE FROM A FINAL JUDGMENT, ORDER, OR DECREE OF A DISTRICT COURT OR BANKRUPTCY APPELLATE PANEL [OMITTED]

Rule 7.

BOND FOR COSTS ON APPEAL IN A CIVIL CASE

In a civil case, the district court may require an appellant to file a bond or provide other security in any form and amount necessary to ensure payment of costs on appeal. Rule 8(b) applies to a surety on a bond given under this rule.

As amended 1979, 1998.

Rule 8.

STAY OR INJUNCTION PENDING APPEAL

(a) Motion for Stay.

(1) *Initial Motion in the District Court.* A party must ordinarily move first in the district court for the following relief:

(A) a stay of the judgment or order of a district court pending appeal;

(B) approval of a supersedeas bond; or

(C) an order suspending, modifying, restoring, or granting an injunction while an appeal is pending.

(2) *Motion in the Court of Appeals; Conditions on Relief.* A motion for the relief mentioned in Rule 8(a)(1) may be made to the court of appeals or to one of its judges.

(A) The motion must:

(i) show that moving first in the district court would be impracticable; or

(ii) state that, a motion having been made, the district court denied the motion or failed to afford the relief requested and state any reasons given by the district court for its action.

(B) The motion must also include:

(i) the reasons for granting the relief requested and the facts relied on;

(ii) originals or copies of affidavits or other sworn statements supporting facts subject to dispute; and

(iii) relevant parts of the record.

(C) The moving party must give reasonable notice of the motion to all parties.

(D) A motion under this Rule 8(a)(2) must be filed with the circuit clerk and normally will be considered by a panel of the court. But in an exceptional case in which time requirements make that procedure impracticable, the motion may be made to and considered by a single judge.

(E) The court may condition relief on a party's filing a bond or other appropriate security in the district court.

(b) Proceeding Against a Surety. If a party gives security in the form of a bond or stipulation or other undertaking with one or more sureties, each surety submits to the jurisdiction of the district court and irrevocably appoints the district clerk as the

surety's agent on whom any papers affecting the surety's liability on the bond or undertaking may be served. On motion, a surety's liability may be enforced in the district court without the necessity of an independent action. The motion and any notice that the district court prescribes may be served on the district clerk, who must promptly mail a copy to each surety whose address is known.

(c) Stay in a Criminal Case. Rule 38 of the Federal Rules of Criminal Procedure governs a stay in a criminal case.

As amended 1986, 1995, 1998.

Rule 9.

RELEASE IN A CRIMINAL CASE

(a) Release Before Judgment of Conviction.

(1) The district court must state in writing, or orally on the record, the reasons for an order regarding the release or detention of a defendant in a criminal case. A party appealing from the order must file with the court of appeals a copy of the district court's order and the court's statement of reasons as soon as practicable after filing the notice of appeal. An appellant who questions the factual basis for the district court's order must file a transcript of the release proceedings or an explanation of why a transcript was not obtained.

(2) After reasonable notice to the appellee, the court of appeals must promptly determine the appeal on the basis of the papers, affidavits, and parts of the record that the parties present or the court requires. Unless the court so orders, briefs need not be filed.

(3) The court of appeals or one of its judges may order the defendant's release pending the disposition of the appeal.

(b) Release After Judgment of Conviction. A party entitled to do so may obtain review of a district-court order regarding release after a judgment of conviction by filing a notice of appeal from that order in the district court, or by filing a motion in the court of appeals if the party has already filed a notice of appeal from the judgment of conviction. Both the order and the review are subject to Rule 9(a). The papers filed by the party seeking review must include a copy of the judgment of conviction.

(c) Criteria for Release. The court must make its decision regarding release in accordance with the applicable provisions of 18 U.S.C. §§ 3142, 3143, and 3145(c).

As amended 1972, 1984, 1994, 1998.

Rule 10.

THE RECORD ON APPEAL

(a) Composition of the Record on Appeal. The following items constitute the record on appeal:

(1) the original papers and exhibits filed in the district court;

(2) the transcript of proceedings, if any; and

(3) a certified copy of the docket entries prepared by the district clerk.

(b) The Transcript of Proceedings.

(1) *Appellant's Duty to Order.* Within 14 days after filing the notice of appeal or entry of an order disposing of the last timely remaining motion of a type specified in Rule 4(a)(4)(A), whichever is later, the appellant must do either of the following:

(A) order from the reporter a transcript of such parts of the proceedings not already on file as the appellant considers necessary, subject to a local rule of the court of appeals and with the following qualifications:

(i) the order must be in writing;

(ii) if the cost of the transcript is to be paid by the United States under the Criminal Justice Act, the order must so state; and

(iii) the appellant must, within the same period, file a copy of the order with the district clerk; or

(B) file a certificate stating that no transcript will be ordered.

(2) *Unsupported Finding or Conclusion.* If the appellant intends to urge on appeal that a finding or conclusion is unsupported by the evidence or is contrary to the evidence, the appellant must include in the record a transcript of all evidence relevant to that finding or conclusion.

(3) *Partial Transcript.* Unless the entire transcript is ordered:

(A) the appellant must—within the 14 days provided in Rule 10(b)(1)—file a statement of the issues that the appellant intends to present on the appeal and must serve on the appellee a copy of both the order or certificate and the statement;

(B) if the appellee considers it necessary to have a transcript of other parts of the proceedings, the appellee must, within 14 days after the service of the order or certificate and

462

the statement of the issues, file and serve on the appellant a designation of additional parts to be ordered; and

(C) unless within 14 days after service of that designation the appellant has ordered all such parts, and has so notified the appellee, the appellee may within the following 14 days either order the parts or move in the district court for an order requiring the appellant to do so.

(4) *Payment.* At the time of ordering, a party must make satisfactory arrangements with the reporter for paying the cost of the transcript.

(c) Statement of the Evidence When the Proceedings Were Not Recorded or When a Transcript Is Unavailable. If the transcript of a hearing or trial is unavailable, the appellant may prepare a statement of the evidence or proceedings from the best available means, including the appellant's recollection. The statement must be served on the appellee, who may serve objections or proposed amendments within 14 days after being served. The statement and any objections or proposed amendments must then be submitted to the district court for settlement and approval. As settled and approved, the statement must be included by the district clerk in the record on appeal.

(d) Agreed Statement as the Record on Appeal. In place of the record on appeal as defined in Rule 10(a), the parties may prepare, sign, and submit to the district court a statement of the case showing how the issues presented by the appeal arose and were decided in the district court. The statement must set forth only those facts averred and proved or sought to be proved that are essential to the court's resolution of the issues. If the statement is truthful, it—together with any additions that the district court may consider necessary to a full presentation of the issues on appeal— must be approved by the district court and must then be certified to the court of appeals as the record on appeal. The district clerk must then send it to the circuit clerk within the time provided by Rule 11. A copy of the agreed statement may be filed in place of the appendix required by Rule 30.

(e) Correction or Modification of the Record.

(1) If any difference arises about whether the record truly discloses what occurred in the district court, the difference must be submitted to and settled by that court and the record conformed accordingly.

(2) If anything material to either party is omitted from or misstated in the record by error or accident, the omission or misstatement may be corrected and a supplemental record may be certified and forwarded:

(A) on stipulation of the parties;

(B) by the district court before or after the record has been forwarded; or

(C) by the court of appeals.

(3) All other questions as to the form and content of the record must be presented to the court of appeals.

As amended 1979, 1986, 1991, 1993, 1995, 1998, 2009.

Rule 11.

FORWARDING THE RECORD

(a) Appellant's Duty.   An appellant filing a notice of appeal must comply with Rule 10(b) and must do whatever else is necessary to enable the clerk to assemble and forward the record. If there are multiple appeals from a judgment or order, the clerk must forward a single record.

(b) Duties of Reporter and District Clerk.

(1) *Reporter's Duty to Prepare and File a Transcript.*   The reporter must prepare and file a transcript as follows:

(A) Upon receiving an order for a transcript, the reporter must enter at the foot of the order the date of its receipt and the expected completion date and send a copy, so endorsed, to the circuit clerk.

(B) If the transcript cannot be completed within 30 days of the reporter's receipt of the order, the reporter may request the circuit clerk to grant additional time to complete it. The clerk must note on the docket the action taken and notify the parties.

(C) When a transcript is complete, the reporter must file it with the district clerk and notify the circuit clerk of the filing.

(D) If the reporter fails to file the transcript on time, the circuit clerk must notify the district judge and do whatever else the court of appeals directs.

(2) *District Clerk's Duty to Forward.*   When the record is complete, the district clerk must number the documents constituting the record and send them promptly to the circuit clerk together with a list of the documents correspondingly numbered and reasonably identified. Unless directed to do so by a party or the circuit clerk, the district clerk will not send to the court of appeals documents of unusual bulk or weight, physical exhibits other than documents, or other parts of the record designated for omission by local rule of the court of appeals. If the exhibits are unusually

bulky or heavy, a party must arrange with the clerks in advance for their transportation and receipt.

(c) Retaining the Record Temporarily in the District Court for Use in Preparing the Appeal. The parties may stipulate, or the district court on motion may order, that the district clerk retain the record temporarily for the parties to use in preparing the papers on appeal. In that event the district clerk must certify to the circuit clerk that the record on appeal is complete. Upon receipt of the appellee's brief, or earlier if the court orders or the parties agree, the appellant must request the district clerk to forward the record.

(d) [Abrogated.]

(e) Retaining the Record by Court Order.

(1) The court of appeals may, by order or local rule, provide that a certified copy of the docket entries be forwarded instead of the entire record. But a party may at any time during the appeal request that designated parts of the record be forwarded.

(2) The district court may order the record or some part of it retained if the court needs it while the appeal is pending, subject, however, to call by the court of appeals.

(3) If part or all of the record is ordered retained, the district clerk must send to the court of appeals a copy of the order and the docket entries together with the parts of the original record allowed by the district court and copies of any parts of the record designated by the parties.

(f) Retaining Parts of the Record in the District Court by Stipulation of the Parties. The parties may agree by written stipulation filed in the district court that designated parts of the record be retained in the district court subject to call by the court of appeals or request by a party. The parts of the record so designated remain a part of the record on appeal.

(g) Record for a Preliminary Motion in the Court of Appeals. If, before the record is forwarded, a party makes any of the following motions in the court of appeals:

- for dismissal;

- for release;

- for a stay pending appeal;

- for additional security on the bond on appeal or on a supersedeas bond; or

- for any other intermediate order—

the district clerk must send the court of appeals any parts of the record designated by any party.

As amended 1979, 1986, 1998.

Rule 12.

DOCKETING THE APPEAL; FILING A REPRESENTATION STATEMENT; FILING THE RECORD

(a) Docketing the Appeal.   Upon receiving the copy of the notice of appeal and the docket entries from the district clerk under Rule 3(d), the circuit clerk must docket the appeal under the title of the district-court action and must identify the appellant, adding the appellant's name if necessary.

(b) Filing a Representation Statement.   Unless the court of appeals designates another time, the attorney who filed the notice of appeal must, within 14 days after filing the notice, file a statement with the circuit clerk naming the parties that the attorney represents on appeal.

(c) Filing the Record, Partial Record, or Certificate. Upon receiving the record, partial record, or district clerk's certificate as provided in Rule 11, the circuit clerk must file it and immediately notify all parties of the filing date.

As amended 1979, 1986, 1993, 1998, 2009.

Rule 12.1.

REMAND AFTER AN INDICATIVE RULING BY THE DISTRICT COURT ON A MOTION FOR RELIEF THAT IS BARRED BY A PENDING APPEAL

(a) Notice to the Court of Appeals. If a timely motion is made in the district court for relief that it lacks authority to grant because of an appeal that has been docketed and is pending, the movant must promptly notify the circuit clerk if the district court states either that it would grant the motion or that the motion raises a substantial issue.

(b) Remand After an Indicative Ruling. If the district court states that it would grant the motion or that the motion raises a substantial issue, the court of appeals may remand for further proceedings but retains jurisdiction unless it expressly dismisses the appeal. If the court of appeals remands but retains jurisdiction, the parties must promptly notify the circuit clerk when the district court has decided the motion on remand.

Added 2009.

TITLE III. REVIEW OF A DECISION OF THE UNITED STATES TAX COURT [OMITTED]

TITLE IV. REVIEW OR ENFORCEMENT OF AN ORDER OF AN ADMINISTRATIVE AGENCY, BOARD, COMMISSION, OR OFFICER [OMITTED]

TITLE V. EXTRAORDINARY WRITS

Rule 21.

WRITS OF MANDAMUS AND PROHIBITION, AND OTHER EXTRAORDINARY WRITS

(a) Mandamus or Prohibition to a Court: Petition, Filing, Service, and Docketing.

(1) A party petitioning for a writ of mandamus or prohibition directed to a court must file a petition with the circuit clerk with proof of service on all parties to the proceeding in the trial court. The party must also provide a copy to the trial-court judge. All parties to the proceeding in the trial court other than the petitioner are respondents for all purposes.

(2)(A) The petition must be titled "In re [name of petitioner]."

(B) The petition must state:

(i) the relief sought;

(ii) the issues presented;

(iii) the facts necessary to understand the issue presented by the petition; and

(iv) the reasons why the writ should issue.

(C) The petition must include a copy of any order or opinion or parts of the record that may be essential to understand the matters set forth in the petition.

(3) Upon receiving the prescribed docket fee, the clerk must docket the petition and submit it to the court.

(b) Denial; Order Directing Answer; Briefs; Precedence.

(1) The court may deny the petition without an answer. Otherwise, it must order the respondent, if any, to answer within a fixed time.

(2) The clerk must serve the order to respond on all persons directed to respond.

467

(3) Two or more respondents may answer jointly.

(4) The court of appeals may invite or order the trial-court judge to address the petition or may invite an amicus curiae to do so. The trial-court judge may request permission to address the petition but may not do so unless invited or ordered to do so by the court of appeals.

(5) If briefing or oral argument is required, the clerk must advise the parties, and when appropriate, the trial-court judge or amicus curiae.

(6) The proceeding must be given preference over ordinary civil cases.

(7) The circuit clerk must send a copy of the final disposition to the trial-court judge.

(c) Other Extraordinary Writs. An application for an extraordinary writ other than one provided for in Rule 21(a) must be made by filing a petition with the circuit clerk with proof of service on the respondents. Proceedings on the application must conform, so far as is practicable, to the procedures prescribed in Rule 21(a) and (b).

(d) Form of Papers; Number of Copies. All papers must conform to Rule 32(c)(2). Except by the court's permission, a paper must not exceed 30 pages, exclusive of the disclosure statement, the proof of service, and the accompanying documents required by Rule 21(a)(2)(C). An original and 3 copies must be filed unless the court requires the filing of a different number by local rule or by order in a particular case.

As amended 1994, 1996, 1998, 2002.

TITLE VI.   HABEAS CORPUS; PROCEEDINGS IN FORMA PAUPERIS

Rule 22.

HABEAS CORPUS AND SECTION 2255 PROCEEDINGS

(a) Application for the Original Writ. An application for a writ of habeas corpus must be made to the appropriate district court. If made to a circuit judge, the application must be transferred to the appropriate district court. If a district court denies an application made or transferred to it, renewal of the application before a circuit judge is not permitted. The applicant may, under 28 U.S.C. § 2253, appeal to the court of appeals from the district court's order denying the application.

(b) Certificate of Appealability.

(1) In a habeas corpus proceeding in which the detention complained of arises from process issued by a state court, or in a 28

U.S.C. § 2255 proceeding, the applicant cannot take an appeal unless a circuit justice or a circuit or district judge issues a certificate of appealability under 28 U.S.C. § 2253(c). If an applicant files a notice of appeal, the district clerk must send to the court of appeals the certificate (if any) and the statement described in Rule 11(a) of the Rules Governing Proceedings Under 28 U.S.C. § 2254 or § 2255 (if any), along with the notice of appeal and the file of the district-court proceedings. If the district judge has denied the certificate, the applicant may request a circuit judge to issue it.

(2) A request addressed to the court of appeals may be considered by a circuit judge or judges, as the court prescribes. If no express request for a certificate is filed, the notice of appeal constitutes a request addressed to the judges of the court of appeals.

(3) A certificate of appealability is not required when a state or its representative or the United States or its representative appeals.

As amended 1996, 1998, 2009.

Rule 23.

CUSTODY OR RELEASE OF A PRISONER IN A HABEAS CORPUS PROCEEDING

(a) Transfer of Custody Pending Review. Pending review of a decision in a habeas corpus proceeding commenced before a court, justice, or judge of the United States for the release of a prisoner, the person having custody of the prisoner must not transfer custody to another unless a transfer is directed in accordance with this rule. When, upon application, a custodian shows the need for a transfer, the court, justice, or judge rendering the decision under review may authorize the transfer and substitute the successor custodian as a party.

(b) Detention or Release Pending Review of Decision Not to Release. While a decision not to release a prisoner is under review, the court or judge rendering the decision, or the court of appeals, or the Supreme Court, or a judge or justice of either court, may order that the prisoner be:

(1) detained in the custody from which release is sought;

(2) detained in other appropriate custody; or

(3) released on personal recognizance, with or without surety.

(c) Release Pending Review of Decision Ordering Release. While a decision ordering the release of a prisoner is under review, the prisoner must—unless the court or judge rendering the decision, or the court of appeals, or the Supreme Court, or a judge or justice of either court orders otherwise—be released on personal recognizance, with or without surety.

(d) Modification of the Initial Order on Custody. An initial order governing the prisoner's custody or release, including any recognizance or surety, continues in effect pending review unless for special reasons shown to the court of appeals or the Supreme Court, or to a judge or justice of either court, the order is modified or an independent order regarding custody, release, or surety is issued.

As amended 1986, 1998.

Rule 24.

PROCEEDING IN FORMA PAUPERIS

(a) Leave to Proceed In Forma Pauperis.

(1) *Motion in the District Court.* Except as stated in Rule 24(a)(3), a party to a district-court action who desires to appeal in forma pauperis must file a motion in the district court. The party must attach an affidavit that:

    (A) shows in the detail prescribed by Form 4 of the Appendix of Forms, the party's inability to pay or to give security for fees and costs;

    (B) claims an entitlement to redress; and

    (C) states the issues that the party intends to present on appeal.

(2) *Action on the Motion.* If the district court grants the motion, the party may proceed on appeal without prepaying or giving security for fees and costs, unless a statute provides otherwise. If the district court denies the motion, it must state its reasons in writing.

(3) *Prior Approval.* A party who was permitted to proceed in forma pauperis in the district-court action, or who was determined to be financially unable to obtain an adequate defense in a criminal case, may proceed on appeal in forma pauperis without further authorization, unless:

    (A) the district court—before or after the notice of appeal is filed—certifies that the appeal is not taken in good faith or finds that the party is not otherwise entitled to proceed in forma pauperis and states in writing its reasons for the certification or finding; or

    (B) a statute provides otherwise.

(4) *Notice of District Court's Denial.* The district clerk must immediately notify the parties and the court of appeals when the district court does any of the following:

    (A) denies a motion to proceed on appeal in forma pauperis;

    (B) certifies that the appeal is not taken in good faith; or

    (C) finds that the party is not otherwise entitled to proceed in forma pauperis.

(5) *Motion in the Court of Appeals.* A party may file a motion to proceed on appeal in forma pauperis in the court of appeals within 30 days after service of the notice prescribed in Rule 24(a)(4). The motion must include a copy of the affidavit filed in the district court and the district court's statement of reasons for its action. If no affidavit was filed in the district court, the party must include the affidavit prescribed by Rule 24(a)(1).

(b) Leave to Proceed In Forma Pauperis on Appeal or Review of an Administrative Agency Proceeding. When an appeal or review of a proceeding before an administrative agency, board, commission, or officer (including for the purpose of this rule the United States Tax Court) proceeds directly in a court of appeals, a party may file in the court of appeals a motion for leave to proceed on appeal in forma pauperis with an affidavit prescribed by Rule 24(a)(1).

(c) Leave to Use Original Record. A party allowed to proceed on appeal in forma pauperis may request that the appeal be heard on the original record without reproducing any part.

As amended 1979, 1986, 1998, 2002.

TITLE VII. GENERAL PROVISIONS

Rule 25.

FILING AND SERVICE

(a) Filing.

(1) *Filing with the Clerk.* A paper required or permitted to be filed in a court of appeals must be filed with the clerk.

(2) *Filing: Method and Timeliness.*

    (A) In General. Filing may be accomplished by mail addressed to the clerk, but filing is not timely unless the clerk receives the papers within the time fixed for filing.

    (B) A Brief or Appendix. A brief or appendix is timely filed, however, if on or before the last day for filing, it is:

(i) mailed to the clerk by First–Class Mail, or other class of mail that is at least as expeditious, postage prepaid; or

(ii) dispatched to a third-party commercial carrier for delivery to the clerk within 3 days.

(C) Inmate Filing. A paper filed by an inmate confined in an institution is timely if deposited in the institution's internal mailing system on or before the last day for filing. If an institution has a system designed for legal mail, the inmate must use that system to receive the benefit of this rule. Timely filing may be shown by a declaration in compliance with 28 U.S.C. § 1746 or by a notarized statement, either of which must set forth the date of deposit and state that first-class postage has been prepaid.

(D) Electronic Filing. A court of appeals may by local rule permit or require papers to be filed, signed, or verified by electronic means that are consistent with technical standards, if any, that the Judicial Conference of the United States establishes. A local rule may require filing by electronic means only if reasonable exceptions are allowed. A paper filed by electronic means in compliance with a local rule constitutes a written paper for the purpose of applying these rules.

(3) *Filing a Motion with a Judge.* If a motion requests relief that may be granted by a single judge, the judge may permit the motion to be filed with the judge; the judge must note the filing date on the motion and give it to the clerk.

(4) *Clerk's Refusal of Documents.* The clerk must not refuse to accept for filing any paper presented for that purpose solely because it is not presented in proper form as required by these rules or by any local rule or practice.

(5) *Privacy Protection.* An appeal in a case whose privacy protection was governed by Federal Rule of Bankruptcy Procedure 9037, Federal Rule of Civil Procedure 5.2, or Federal Rule of Criminal Procedure 49.1 is governed by the same rule on appeal. In all other proceedings, privacy protection is governed by Federal Rule of Civil Procedure 5.2, except that Federal Rule of Criminal Procedure 49.1 governs when an extraordinary writ is sought in a criminal case.

(b) Service of All Papers Required. Unless a rule requires service by the clerk, a party must, at or before the time of filing a paper, serve a copy on the other parties to the appeal or review. Service on a party represented by counsel must be made on the party's counsel.

(c) Manner of Service.

(1) Service may be any of the following:

(A) personal, including delivery to a responsible person at the office of counsel;

(B) by mail;

(C) by third-party commercial carrier for delivery within 3 days; or

(D) by electronic means, if the party being served consents in writing.

(2) If authorized by local rule, a party may use the court's transmission equipment to make electronic service under Rule 25(c)(1)(D).

(3) When reasonable considering such factors as the immediacy of the relief sought, distance, and cost, service on a party must be by a manner at least as expeditious as the manner used to file the paper with the court.

(4) Service by mail or by commercial carrier is complete on mailing or delivery to the carrier. Service by electronic means is complete on transmission, unless the party making service is notified that the paper was not received by the party served.

(d) Proof of Service.

(1) A paper presented for filing must contain either of the following:

(A) an acknowledgment of service by the person served; or

(B) proof of service consisting of a statement by the person who made service certifying:

(i) the date and manner of service;

(ii) the names of the persons served; and

(iii) their mail or electronic addresses, facsimile numbers, or the addresses of the places of delivery, as appropriate for the manner of service.

(2) When a brief or appendix is filed by mailing or dispatch in accordance with Rule 25(a)(2)(B), the proof of service must also state the date and manner by which the document was mailed or dispatched to the clerk.

(3) Proof of service may appear on or be affixed to the papers filed.

(e) Number of Copies.   When these rules require the filing or furnishing of a number of copies, a court may require a different number by local rule or by order in a particular case.

As amended 1986, 1991, 1993, 1994, 1996, 1998, 2002, 2006, 2007, 2009.

Rule 26.

COMPUTING AND EXTENDING TIME

(a) Computing Time.   The following rules apply in computing any period of time specified in these rules or in any time period specified in these rules, in any local rule or court order, or in any statute that does not specify a method of computing time.

(1) *Period Stated in Days or a Longer Unit.* When the period is stated in days or a longer unit of time:

(A) exclude the day of the event that triggers the period;

(B) count every day, including intermediate Saturdays, Sundays, and legal holidays; and

(C) include the last day of the period, but if the last day is a Saturday, Sunday, or legal holiday, the period continues to run until the end of the next day that is not a Saturday, Sunday, or legal holiday.

(2) *Period Stated in Hours.* When the period is stated in hours:

(A) begin counting immediately on the occurrence of the event that triggers the period;

(B) count every hour, including hours during intermediate Saturdays, Sundays, and legal holidays; and

(C) if the period would end on a Saturday, Sunday, or legal holiday, the period continues to run until the same time on the next day that is not a Saturday, Sunday, or legal holiday.

(3) *Inaccessibility of the Clerk's Office.* Unless the court orders otherwise, if the clerk's office is inaccessible:

(A) on the last day for filing under Rule 26(a)(1), then the time for filing is extended to the first accessible day that is not a Saturday, Sunday, or legal holiday; or

(B) during the last hour for filing under Rule 26(a)(2), then the time for filing is extended to the same time on the first accessible day that is not a Saturday, Sunday, or legal holiday.

(4) *"Last Day" Defined.* Unless a different time is set by a statute, local rule, or court order, the last day ends:

(A) for electronic filing in the district court, at midnight in the court's time zone;

(B) for electronic filing in the court of appeals, at midnight in the time zone of the circuit clerk's principal office;

(C) for filing under Rules 4(c)(1), 25(a)(2)(B), and 25(a)(2)(C)—and filing by mail under Rule 13(b)—at the latest time for the method chosen for delivery to the post office, third-party commercial carrier, or prison mailing system; and

(D) for filing by other means, when the clerk's office is scheduled to close.

(5) *"Next Day" Defined.* The "next day" is determined by continuing to count forward when the period is measured after an event and backward when measured before an event.

(6) *"Legal Holiday" Defined.* "Legal holiday" means:

(A) the day set aside by statute for observing New Year's Day, Martin Luther King Jr.'s Birthday, Washington's Birthday, Memorial Day, Independence Day, Labor Day, Columbus Day, Veterans' Day, Thanksgiving Day, or Christmas Day;

(B) any day declared a holiday by the President or Congress; and

(C) for periods that are measured after an event, any other day declared a holiday by the state where either of the following is located: the district court that rendered the challenged judgment or order, or the circuit clerk's principal office.

(b) Extending Time. For good cause, the court may extend the time prescribed by these rules or by its order to perform any act, or may permit an act to be done after that time expires. But the court may not extend the time to file:

(1) a notice of appeal (except as authorized in Rule 4) or a petition for permission to appeal; or

(2) a notice of appeal from or a petition to enjoin, set aside, suspend, modify, enforce, or otherwise review an order of an administrative agency, board, commission, or officer of the United States, unless specifically authorized by law.

(c) Additional Time After Service. When a party may or must act within a specified time after service, 3 days are added after the period would otherwise expire Rule 26(a), unless the paper is delivered on the date of service stated in the proof of service. For purposes of this Rule 26(c), a paper that is served electronically is not treated as delivered on the date of service stated in the proof of service.

As amended 1971, 1986, 1989, 1991, 1996, 1998, 2002, 2005, 2009.

Rule 26.1.

CORPORATE DISCLOSURE STATEMENT

(a) Who Must File. Any nongovernmental corporate party to a proceeding in a court of appeals must file a statement that identifies any parent corporation and any publicly held corporation that owns 10% or more of its stock or states that there is no such corporation.

(b) Time for Filing; Supplemental Filing. A party must file the Rule 26.1(a) statement with the principal brief or upon filing a motion, response, petition, or answer in the court of appeals, whichever occurs first, unless a local rule requires earlier filing. Even if the statement has already been filed, the party's principal brief must include the statement before the table of contents. A party must supplement its statement whenever the information that must be disclosed under Rule 26.1(a) changes.

(c) Number of Copies. If the Rule 26.1(a) statement is filed before the principal brief, or if a supplemental statement is filed, the party must file an original and 3 copies unless the court requires a different number by local rule or by order in a particular case.

Added 1989; as amended 1991, 1994, 1998, 2002.

Rule 27.

MOTIONS

(a) In General.

(1) *Application for Relief.* An application for an order or other relief is made by motion unless these rules prescribe another form. A motion must be in writing unless the court permits otherwise.

(2) *Contents of a Motion.*

(A) Grounds and Relief Sought. A motion must state with particularity the grounds for the motion, the relief sought, and the legal argument necessary to support it.

(B) Accompanying Documents.

(i) Any affidavit or other paper necessary to support a motion must be served and filed with the motion.

(ii) An affidavit must contain only factual information, not legal argument.

(iii) A motion seeking substantive relief must include a copy of the trial court's opinion or agency's decision as a separate exhibit.

(C) Documents Barred or Not Required.

(i) A separate brief supporting or responding to a motion must not be filed.

(ii) A notice of motion is not required.

(iii) A proposed order is not required.

(3) *Response.*

(A) Time to File. Any party may file a response to a motion; Rule 27(a)(2) governs its contents. The response must be filed within 10 days after service of the motion unless the court shortens or extends the time. A motion authorized by Rules 8, 9, 18, or 41 may be granted before the 10–day period runs only if the court gives reasonable notice to the parties that it intends to act sooner.

(B) Request for Affirmative Relief. A response may include a motion for affirmative relief. The time to respond to the new motion, and to reply to that response, are governed by Rule 27(a)(3)(A) and (a)(4). The title of the response must alert the court to the request for relief.

(4) *Reply to Response.* Any reply to a response must be filed within 7 days after service of the response. A reply must not present matters that do not relate to the response.

(b) Disposition of a Motion for a Procedural Order. The court may act on a motion for a procedural order—including a motion under Rule 26(b)—at any time without awaiting a response, and may, by rule or by order in a particular case, authorize its clerk to act on specified types of procedural motions. A party adversely affected by the court's, or the clerk's, action may file a motion to reconsider, vacate, or modify that action. Timely opposition filed after the motion is granted in whole or in part does not constitute a request to reconsider, vacate, or modify the disposition; a motion requesting that relief must be filed.

(c) Power of a Single Judge to Entertain a Motion. A circuit judge may act alone on any motion, but may not dismiss or otherwise determine an appeal or other proceeding. A court of appeals may provide by rule or by order in a particular case that only the court may act on any motion or class of motions. The court may review the action of a single judge.

(d) Form of Papers; Page Limits; and Number of Copies.

(1) *Format.*

(A) Reproduction. A motion, response, or reply may be reproduced by any process that yields a clear black image on light paper.   The paper must be opaque and unglazed.   Only one side of the paper may be used.

(B) Cover.   A cover is not required but there must be a caption that includes the case number, the name of the court, the title of the case, and a brief descriptive title indicating the purpose of the motion and identifying the party or parties for whom it is filed. If a cover is used, it must be white.

(C) Binding.   The document must be bound in any manner that is secure, does not obscure the text, and permits the document to lie reasonably flat when open.

(D) Paper Size, Line Spacing, and Margins.   The document must be on 8½ by 11 inch paper.   The text must be double-spaced, but quotations more than two lines long may be indented and single-spaced.   Headings and footnotes may be single-spaced.   Margins must be at least one inch on all four sides.   Page numbers may be placed in the margins, but no text may appear there.

(E) Typeface and Type Styles. The document must comply with the typeface requirements of Rule 32(a)(5) and the type-style requirements of Rule 32(a)(6).

(2) *Page Limits.*   A motion or a response to a motion must not exceed 20 pages, exclusive of the corporate disclosure statement and accompanying documents authorized by Rule 27(a)(2)(B), unless the court permits or directs otherwise.   A reply to a response must not exceed 10 pages.

(3) *Number of Copies.*   An original and 3 copies must be filed unless the court requires a different number by local rule or by order in a particular case.

(e) Oral Argument.   A motion will be decided without oral argument unless the court orders otherwise.

As amended 1979, 1989, 1994, 1998, 2002, 2005, 2009.

Rule 28.

BRIEFS

(a) Appellant's Brief.   The appellant's brief must contain, under appropriate headings and in the order indicated:

(1) a corporate disclosure statement if required by Rule 26.1;

(2) a table of contents, with page references;

(3) a table of authorities—cases (alphabetically arranged), statutes, and other authorities—with references to the pages of the brief where they are cited;

(4) a jurisdictional statement, including:

(A) the basis for the district court's or agency's subject-matter jurisdiction, with citations to applicable statutory provisions and stating relevant facts establishing jurisdiction;

(B) the basis for the court of appeals' jurisdiction, with citations to applicable statutory provisions and stating relevant facts establishing jurisdiction;

(C) the filing dates establishing the timeliness of the appeal or petition for review; and

(D) an assertion that the appeal is from a final order or judgment that disposes of all parties' claims, or information establishing the court of appeals' jurisdiction on some other basis;

(5) a statement of the issues presented for review;

(6) a statement of the case briefly indicating the nature of the case, the course of proceedings, and the disposition below;

(7) a statement of facts relevant to the issues submitted for review with appropriate references to the record (see Rule 28(e));

(8) a summary of the argument, which must contain a succinct, clear, and accurate statement of the arguments made in the body of the brief, and which must not merely repeat the argument headings;

(9) the argument, which must contain:

(A) appellant's contentions and the reasons for them, with citations to the authorities and parts of the record on which the appellant relies; and

(B) for each issue, a concise statement of the applicable standard of review (which may appear in the discussion of the issue or under a separate heading placed before the discussion of the issues);

(10) a short conclusion stating the precise relief sought; and

(11) the certificate of compliance, if required by Rule 32(a)(7).

(b) Appellee's Brief. The appellee's brief must conform to the requirements of Rule 28(a)(1)–(9) and (11), except that none of the following need appear unless the appellee is dissatisfied with the appellant's statement:

(1) the jurisdictional statement;

(2) the statement of the issues;

(3) the statement of the case;

(4) the statement of the facts; and

(5) the statement of the standard of review.

(c) Reply Brief. The appellant may file a brief in reply to the appellee's brief. Unless the court permits, no further briefs may be filed. A reply brief must contain a table of contents, with page references, and a table of authorities—cases (alphabetically arranged), statutes, and other authorities—with references to the pages of the reply brief where they are cited.

(d) References to Parties. In briefs and at oral argument, counsel should minimize use of the terms "appellant" and "appellee." To make briefs clear, counsel should use the parties' actual names or the designations used in the lower court or agency proceeding, or such descriptive terms as "the employee," "the injured person," "the taxpayer," "the ship," "the stevedore."

(e) References to the Record. References to the parts of the record contained in the appendix filed with the appellant's brief must be to the pages of the appendix. If the appendix is prepared after the briefs are filed, a party referring to the record must follow one of the methods detailed in Rule 30(c). If the original record is used under Rule 30(f) and is not consecutively paginated, or if the brief refers to an unreproduced part of the record, any reference must be to the page of the original document. For example:

- Answer p. 7;
- Motion for Judgment p. 2;
- Transcript p. 231.

Only clear abbreviations may be used. A party referring to evidence whose admissibility is in controversy must cite the pages of the appendix or of the transcript at which the evidence was identified, offered, and received or rejected.

(f) Reproduction of Statutes, Rules, Regulations, etc. If the court's determination of the issues presented requires the study of statutes, rules, regulations, etc., the relevant parts must be set out in the brief or in an addendum at the end, or may be supplied to the court in pamphlet form.

(g) [Reserved.]

(h) [Reserved.]

(i) Briefs in a Case Involving Multiple Appellants or Appellees. In a case involving more than one appellant or appellee, including consolidated cases, any number of appellants or appellees may join in a brief, and any party may adopt by reference a part of another's brief. Parties may also join in reply briefs.

(j) Citation of Supplemental Authorities. If pertinent and significant authorities come to a party's attention after the party's brief has been filed—or after oral argument but before decision—a party may promptly advise the circuit clerk by letter, with a copy to all other parties, setting forth the citations. The letter must state the reasons for the supplemental citations, referring either to the page of the brief or to a point argued orally. The body of the letter must not exceed 350 words. Any response must be made promptly and must be similarly limited.

As amended 1979, 1986, 1989, 1991, 1993, 1994, 1998, 2002, 2005.

Rule 28.1

CROSS–APPEALS

(a) Applicability. This rule applies to a case in which a cross-appeal is filed. Rules 28(a)–(c), 31(a)(1), 32(a)(2), and 32(a)(7)(A)–(B) do not apply to such a case, except as otherwise provided in this rule.

(b) Designation of Appellant. The party who files a notice of appeal first is the appellant for the purposes of this rule and Rules 30 and 34. If notices are filed on the same day, the plaintiff in the proceeding below is the appellant. These designations may be modified by the parties' agreement or by court order.

(c) Briefs. In a case involving a cross-appeal:

(1) *Appellant's Principal Brief.* The appellant must file a principal brief in the appeal. That brief must comply with Rule 28(a).

(2) *Appellee's Principal and Response Brief.* The appellee must file a principal brief in the cross-appeal and must, in the same brief, respond to the principal brief in the appeal. That appellee's brief must comply with Rule 28(a), except that the brief need not include a statement of the case or a statement of the facts unless the appellee is dissatisfied with the appellant's statement.

(3) *Appellant's Response and Reply Brief.* The appellant must file a brief that responds to the principal brief in the cross-appeal and may, in the same brief, reply to the response in the appeal. That brief must comply with Rule 28(a)(2)–(9) and (11), except that none of the following need appear unless the appellant is dissatisfied with the appellee's statement in the cross-appeal:

(A) the jurisdictional statement;

(B) the statement of the issues;

(C) the statement of the case;

(D) the statement of the facts; and

(E) the statement of the standard of review.

(4) *Appellee's Reply Brief.* The appellee may file a brief in reply to the response in the cross-appeal. That brief must comply with

Rule 28(a)(2)–(3) and (11) and must be limited to the issues presented by the cross-appeal.

(5) *No Further Briefs.* Unless the court permits, no further briefs may be filed in a case involving a cross-appeal.

(d) Cover. Except for filings by unrepresented parties, the cover of the appellant's principal brief must be blue; the appellee's principal and response brief, red; the appellant's response and reply brief, yellow; the appellee's reply brief, gray; and intervenor's or amicus curiae's brief, green; and any supplemental brief, tan. The front cover of a brief must contain the information required by Rule 32(a)(2).

(e) Length.

(1) *Page Limitation.* Unless it complies with Rule 28.1(e)(2) and (3), the appellant's principal brief must not exceed 30 pages; the appellee's principal and response brief, 35 pages; the appellant's response and reply brief, 30 pages; and the appellee's reply brief, 15 pages.

(2) *Type-Volume Limitation.*

(A) The appellant's principal brief or the appellant's response and reply brief is acceptable if:

(i) it contains no more than 14,000 words; or

(ii) it uses a monospaced face and contains no more than 1,300 lines of text.

(B) The appellee's principal and response brief is acceptable if:

(i) it contains no more than 16,500 words; or

(ii) it uses a monospaced face and contains no more than 1,500 lines of text.

(C) The appellee's reply brief is acceptable if it contains no more than half of the type volume specified in Rule 28.1(e)(2)(A).

(3) *Certificate of Compliance.* A brief submitted under Rule 28.1(e)(2) must comply with Rule 32(a)(7)(C).

(f) Time to Serve and File a Brief. Briefs must be served and filed as follows:

(1) the appellant's principal brief, within 40 days after the record is filed;

(2) the appellee's principal and response brief, within 30 days after the appellant's principal brief is served;

(3) the appellant's response and reply brief, within 30 days after the appellee's principal and response brief is served; and

(4) the appellee's reply brief, within 14 days after the appellant's response and reply brief is served, but at least 7 days before argument unless the court, for good cause, allows a later filing.

Added 2005; as amended 2009.

Rule 29.

BRIEF OF AN AMICUS CURIAE

(a) When Permitted. The United States or its officer or agency, or a State, Territory, Commonwealth, or the District of Columbia may file an amicus-curiae brief without the consent of the parties or leave of court. Any other amicus curiae may file a brief only by leave of court or if the brief states that all parties have consented to its filing.

(b) Motion for Leave to File. The motion must be accompanied by the proposed brief and state:

(1) the movant's interest; and

(2) the reason why an amicus brief is desirable and why the matters asserted are relevant to the disposition of the case.

(c) Contents and Form. An amicus brief must comply with Rule 32. In addition to the requirements of Rule 32, the cover must identify the party or parties supported and indicate whether the brief supports affirmance or reversal. If an amicus curiae is a corporation, the brief must include a disclosure statement like that required of parties by Rule 26.1. An amicus brief need not comply with Rule 28, but must include the following:

(1) a table of contents, with page references;

(2) a table of authorities—cases (alphabetically arranged), statutes and other authorities—with references to the pages of the brief where they are cited;

(3) a concise statement of the identity of the amicus curiae, its interest in the case, and the source of its authority to file;

(4) an argument, which may be preceded by a summary and which need not include a statement of the applicable standard of review; and

(5) a certificate of compliance, if required by Rule 32(a)(7).

(d) Length. Except by the court's permission, an amicus brief may be no more than one-half the maximum length authorized by these rules for a party's principal brief. If the court grants a party permission to file a longer brief, that extension does not affect the length of an amicus brief.

(e) Time for Filing. An amicus curiae must file its brief, accompanied by a motion for filing when necessary, no later than 7 days after the principal brief of the party being supported is filed. An amicus curiae that does not support either party must file its brief no later than 7 days after the appellant's or petitioner's principal brief is filed. A court may grant leave for later filing, specifying the time within which an opposing party may answer.

(f) Reply Brief. Except by the court's permission, an amicus curiae may not file a reply brief.

(g) Oral Argument. An amicus curiae may participate in oral argument only with the court's permission.

As amended 1998.

Rule 30.

APPENDIX TO THE BRIEFS

(a) Appellant's Responsibility.

(1) *Contents of the Appendix.* The appellant must prepare and file an appendix to the briefs containing:

(A) the relevant docket entries in the proceeding below;

(B) the relevant portions of the pleadings, charge, findings, or opinion;

(C) the judgment, order, or decision in question; and

(D) other parts of the record to which the parties wish to direct the court's attention.

(2) *Excluded Material.* Memoranda of law in the district court should not be included in the appendix unless they have independent relevance. Parts of the record may be relied on by the court or the parties even though not included in the appendix.

(3) *Time to File; Number of Copies.* Unless filing is deferred under Rule 30(c), the appellant must file 10 copies of the appendix with the brief and must serve one copy on counsel for each party separately represented. An unrepresented party proceeding in forma pauperis must file 4 legible copies with the clerk, and one copy must be served on counsel for each separately represented party. The court may by local rule or by order in a particular case require the filing or service of a different number.

(b) All Parties' Responsibilities.

(1) *Determining the Contents of the Appendix.* The parties are encouraged to agree on the contents of the appendix. In the absence of an agreement, the appellant must, within 14 days after the record is filed, serve on the appellee a designation of the parts

of the record the appellant intends to include in the appendix and a statement of the issues the appellant intends to present for review. The appellee may, within 14 days after receiving the designation, serve on the appellant a designation of additional parts to which it wishes to direct the court's attention. The appellant must include the designated parts in the appendix. The parties must not engage in unnecessary designation of parts of the record, because the entire record is available to the court. This paragraph applies also to a cross-appellant and a cross-appellee.

(2) *Costs of Appendix.* Unless the parties agree otherwise, the appellant must pay the cost of the appendix. If the appellant considers parts of the record designated by the appellee to be unnecessary, the appellant may advise the appellee, who must then advance the cost of including those parts. The cost of the appendix is a taxable cost. But if any party causes unnecessary parts of the record to be included in the appendix, the court may impose the cost of those parts on that party. Each circuit must, by local rule, provide for sanctions against attorneys who unreasonably and vexatiously increase litigation costs by including unnecessary material in the appendix.

(c) Deferred Appendix.

(1) *Deferral Until After Briefs Are Filed.* The court may provide by rule for classes of cases or by order in a particular case that preparation of the appendix may be deferred until after the briefs have been filed and that the appendix may be filed 21 days after the appellee's brief is served. Even though the filing of the appendix may be deferred, Rule 30(b) applies; except that a party must designate the parts of the record it wants included in the appendix when it serves its brief, and need not include a statement of the issues presented.

(2) *References to the Record.*

(A) If the deferred appendix is used, the parties may cite in their briefs the pertinent pages of the record. When the appendix is prepared, the record pages cited in the briefs must be indicated by inserting record page numbers, in brackets, at places in the appendix where those pages of the record appear.

(B) A party who wants to refer directly to pages of the appendix may serve and file copies of the brief within the time required by Rule 31(a), containing appropriate references to pertinent pages of the record. In that event, within 14 days after the appendix is filed, the party must serve and file copies of the brief, containing references to the pages of the appendix in place of or in addition to the references to the pertinent pages of the record. Except for the correction of typographical errors, no other changes may be made to the brief.

(d) Format of the Appendix.   The appendix must begin with a table of contents identifying the page at which each part begins.   The relevant docket entries must follow the table of contents.   Other parts of the record must follow chronologically. When pages from the transcript of proceedings are placed in the appendix, the transcript page numbers must be shown in brackets immediately before the included pages.   Omissions in the text of papers or of the transcript must be indicated by asterisks.   Immaterial formal matters (captions, subscriptions, acknowledgments, etc.) should be omitted.

(e) Reproduction of Exhibits.   Exhibits designated for inclusion in the appendix may be reproduced in a separate volume, or volumes, suitably indexed.   Four copies must be filed with the appendix, and one copy must be served on counsel for each separately represented party.   If a transcript of a proceeding before an administrative agency, board, commission, or officer was used in a district-court action and has been designated for inclusion in the appendix, the transcript must be placed in the appendix as an exhibit.

(f) Appeal on the Original Record Without an Appendix. The court may, either by rule for all cases or classes of cases or by order in a particular case, dispense with the appendix and permit an appeal to proceed on the original record with any copies of the record, or relevant parts, that the court may order the parties to file.

As amended 1970, 1986, 1991, 1994, 1998, 2009.

Rule 31.

SERVING AND FILING BRIEFS

(a) Time to Serve and File a Brief.

(1) The appellant must serve and file a brief within 40 days after the record is filed.   The appellee must serve and file a brief within 30 days after the appellant's brief is served.   The appellant may serve and file a reply brief within 14 days after service of the appellee's brief but a reply brief must be filed at least 7 days before argument, unless the court, for good cause, allows a later filing.

(2) A court of appeals that routinely considers cases on the merits promptly after the briefs are filed may shorten the time to serve and file briefs, either by local rule or by order in a particular case.

(b) Number of Copies.   Twenty-five copies of each brief must be filed with the clerk and 2 copies must be served on each unrepresented party and on counsel for each separately represented party. An unrepresented party proceeding in forma pauperis must file 4 legible copies with the clerk, and one copy must be served on each unrepresented party and on counsel for each separately represented party. The court may by local rule or by order in a particular case require the filing or service of a different number.

(c) Consequence of Failure to File. If an appellant fails to file a brief within the time provided by this rule, or within an extended time, an appellee may move to dismiss the appeal. An appellee who fails to file a brief will not be heard at oral argument unless the court grants permission.

As amended 1970, 1986, 1994, 1998, 2002, 2009.

Rule 32.

FORM OF BRIEFS, APPENDICES, AND OTHER PAPERS

(a) Form of a Brief.

(1) *Reproduction.*

(A) A brief may be reproduced by any process that yields a clear black image on light paper. The paper must be opaque and unglazed. Only one side of the paper may be used.

(B) Text must be reproduced with a clarity that equals or exceeds the output of a laser printer.

(C) Photographs, illustrations, and tables may be reproduced by any method that results in a good copy of the original; a glossy finish is acceptable if the original is glossy.

(2) *Cover.* Except for filings by unrepresented parties, the cover of the appellant's brief must be blue; the appellee's, red; an intervenor's or amicus curiae's, green; any reply brief, gray; and any supplemental brief, tan. The front cover of a brief must contain:

(A) the number of the case centered at the top;

(B) the name of the court;

(C) the title of the case (see Rule 12(a));

(D) the nature of the proceeding (e.g., Appeal, Petition for Review) and the name of the court, agency, or board below;

(E) the title of the brief, identifying the party or parties for whom the brief is filed; and

(F) the name, office address, and telephone number of counsel representing the party for whom the brief is filed.

(3) *Binding.* The brief must be bound in any manner that is secure, does not obscure the text, and permits the brief to lie reasonably flat when open.

(4) *Paper Size, Line Spacing, and Margins.* The brief must be on 8½ by 11 inch paper. The text must be double-spaced, but quotations more than two lines long may be indented and single-spaced. Headings and footnotes may be single-spaced. Margins must be at least one inch on all four sides. Page numbers may be placed in the margins, but no text may appear there.

(5) *Typeface.* Either a proportionally spaced or a monospaced face may be used.

(A) A proportionally spaced face must include serifs, but sans-serif type may be used in headings and captions. A proportionally spaced face must be 14–point or larger.

(B) A monospaced face may not contain more than 10½ characters per inch.

(6) *Type Styles.* A brief must be set in a plain, roman style, although italics or boldface may be used for emphasis. Case names must be italicized or underlined.

(7) *Length.*

(A) Page limitation. A principal brief may not exceed 30 pages, or a reply brief 15 pages, unless it complies with Rule 32(a)(7)(B) and (C).

(B) Type-volume limitation.

(i) A principal brief is acceptable if:

• it contains no more than 14,000 words; or

• it uses a monospaced face and contains no more than 1,300 lines of text.

(ii) A reply brief is acceptable if it contains no more than half of the type volume specified in Rule 32(a)(7)(B)(i).

(iii) Headings, footnotes, and quotations count toward the word and line limitations. The corporate disclosure statement, table of contents, table of citations, statement with respect to oral argument, any addendum containing statutes, rules or regulations, and any certificates of counsel do not count toward the limitation.

(C) Certificate of compliance.

(i) A brief submitted under Rules 28.1(e)(2) or 32(a)(7)(B) must include a certificate by the attorney, or an unrepresented party, that the brief complies with the type-volume limitation. The person preparing the certificate may rely on the word or line count of the word-processing system used to prepare the brief. The certificate must state either:

- the number of words in the brief; or

- the number of lines of monospaced type in the brief.

(ii) Form 6 in the Appendix of Forms is a suggested form of a certificate of compliance. Use of Form 6 must be regarded as sufficient to meet the requirements of Rules 28.1(e)(3) and 32(a)(7)(C)(i).

(b) Form of an Appendix. An appendix must comply with Rule 32(a)(1), (2), (3), and (4), with the following exceptions:

(1) The cover of a separately bound appendix must be white.

(2) An appendix may include a legible photocopy of any document found in the record or of a printed judicial or agency decision.

(3) When necessary to facilitate inclusion of odd-sized documents such as technical drawings, an appendix may be a size other than 8½ by 11 inches, and need not lie reasonably flat when opened.

(c) Form of Other Papers.

(1) *Motion.* The form of a motion is governed by Rule 27(d).

(2) *Other Papers.* Any other paper, including a petition for panel rehearing and a petition for hearing or rehearing en banc, and any response to such a petition, must be reproduced in the manner prescribed by Rule 32(a), with the following exceptions:

(A) A cover is not necessary if the caption and signature page of the paper together contain the information required by Rule 32(a)(2). If a cover is used, it must be white.

(B) Rule 32(a)(7) does not apply.

(d) Signature. Every brief, motion, or other paper filed with the court must be signed by the party filing the paper or, if the party is represented, by one of the party's attorneys.

(e) Local Variation. Every court of appeals must accept documents that comply with the form requirements of this rule. By local rule or order in a particular case a court of appeals may accept documents that do not meet all of the form requirements of this rule.

As amended 1998, 2002, 2005.

Rule 32.1.

CITING JUDICIAL DISPOSITIONS

(a) Citation Permitted. A court may not prohibit or restrict the citation of federal judicial opinions, orders, judgments, or other written dispositions that have been:

(i) designated as "unpublished," "not for publication," "non-precedential," "not precedent," or the like; and

(ii) issued on or after January 1, 2007.

(b) Copies Required. If a party cites a federal judicial opinion, order, judgment, or other written disposition that is not available in a publicly accessible electronic database, the party must file and serve a copy of that opinion, order, judgment, or disposition with the brief or other paper in which it is cited.

Added 2006.

Rule 33.

APPEAL CONFERENCES

The court may direct the attorneys—and, when appropriate, the parties—to participate in one or more conferences to address any matter that may aid in disposing of the proceedings, including simplifying the issues and discussing settlement. A judge or other person designated by the court may preside over the conference, which may be conducted in person or by telephone. Before a settlement conference, the attorneys must consult with their clients and obtain as much authority as feasible to settle the case. The court may, as a result of the conference, enter an order controlling the course of the proceedings or implementing any settlement agreement.

As amended 1994, 1998.

Rule 34.

ORAL ARGUMENT

(a) In General.

(1) *Party's Statement.* Any party may file, or a court may require by local rule, a statement explaining why oral argument should, or need not, be permitted.

(2) *Standards.* Oral argument must be allowed in every case unless a panel of three judges who have examined the briefs and record unanimously agrees that oral argument is unnecessary for any of the following reasons:

(A) the appeal is frivolous;

(B) the dispositive issue or issues have been authoritatively decided; or

(C) the facts and legal arguments are adequately presented in the briefs and record, and the decisional process would not be significantly aided by oral argument.

(b) Notice of Argument; Postponement. The clerk must advise all parties whether oral argument will be scheduled, and, if so, the date, time, and place for it, and the time allowed for each side. A motion to postpone the argument or to allow longer argument must be filed reasonably in advance of the hearing date.

(c) Order and Contents of Argument. The appellant opens and concludes the argument. Counsel must not read at length from briefs, records, or authorities.

(d) Cross–Appeals and Separate Appeals. If there is a cross-appeal, Rule 28.1(b) determines which party is the appellant and which is the appellee for purposes of oral argument. Unless the court directs otherwise, a cross-appeal or separate appeal must be argued when the initial appeal is argued. Separate parties should avoid duplicative argument.

(e) Nonappearance of a Party. If the appellee fails to appear for argument, the court must hear appellant's argument. If the appellant fails to appear for argument, the court may hear the appellee's argument. If neither party appears, the case will be decided on the briefs, unless the court orders otherwise.

(f) Submission on Briefs. The parties may agree to submit a case for decision on the briefs, but the court may direct that the case be argued.

(g) Use of Physical Exhibits at Argument; Removal. Counsel intending to use physical exhibits other than documents at the argument must arrange to place them in the courtroom on the day of the argument before the court convenes. After the argument, counsel must remove the exhibits from the courtroom, unless the court directs otherwise. The clerk may destroy or dispose of the exhibits if counsel does not reclaim them within a reasonable time after the clerk gives notice to remove them.

As amended 1979, 1986, 1991, 1993, 1998, 2005.

Rule 35.

EN BANC DETERMINATION

(a) When Hearing or Rehearing En Banc May Be Ordered. A majority of the circuit judges who are in regular active service and who are not disqualified may order that an appeal or other proceeding be heard or reheard by the court of appeals en banc. An en banc hearing or rehearing is not favored and ordinarily will not be ordered unless:

(1) en banc consideration is necessary to secure or maintain uniformity of the court's decisions; or

(2) the proceeding involves a question of exceptional importance.

(b) Petition for Hearing or Rehearing En Banc. A party may petition for a hearing or rehearing en banc.

(1) The petition must begin with a statement that either:

(A) the panel decision conflicts with a decision of the United States Supreme Court or of the court to which the petition is addressed (with citation to the conflicting case or cases) and consideration by the full court is therefore necessary to secure and maintain uniformity of the court's decisions; or

(B) the proceeding involves one or more questions of exceptional importance, each of which must be concisely stated; for example, a petition may assert that a proceeding presents a question of exceptional importance if it involves an issue on which the panel decision conflicts with the authoritative decisions of other United States Courts of Appeals that have addressed the issue.

(2) Except by the court's permission, a petition for an en banc hearing or rehearing must not exceed 15 pages, excluding material not counted under Rule 32.

(3) For purposes of the page limit in Rule 35(b)(2), if a party files both a petition for panel rehearing and a petition for rehearing en banc, they are considered a single document even if they are filed separately, unless separate filing is required by local rule.

(c) Time for Petition for Hearing or Rehearing En Banc. A petition that an appeal be heard initially en banc must be filed by the date when the appellee's brief is due. A petition for a rehearing en banc must be filed within the time prescribed by Rule 40 for filing a petition for rehearing.

(d) Number of Copies. The number of copies to be filed must be prescribed by local rule and may be altered by order in a particular case.

(e) Response. No response may be filed to a petition for an en banc consideration unless the court orders a response.

(f) Call for a Vote. A vote need not be taken to determine whether the case will be heard or reheard en banc unless a judge calls for a vote.

As amended 1979, 1994, 1998, 2005.

Rule 36.

ENTRY OF JUDGMENT; NOTICE

(a) Entry. A judgment is entered when it is noted on the docket. The clerk must prepare, sign, and enter the judgment:

(1) after receiving the court's opinion—but if settlement of the judgment's form is required, after final settlement; or

(2) if a judgment is rendered without an opinion, as the court instructs.

(b) Notice. On the date when judgment is entered, the clerk must serve on all parties a copy of the opinion—or the judgment, if no opinion was written—and a notice of the date when the judgment was entered.

As amended 1998, 2002.

Rule 37.

INTEREST ON JUDGMENT

(a) When the Court Affirms. Unless the law provides otherwise, if a money judgment in a civil case is affirmed, whatever interest is allowed by law is payable from the date when the district court's judgment was entered.

(b) When the Court Reverses. If the court modifies or reverses a judgment with a direction that a money judgment be entered in the district court, the mandate must contain instructions about the allowance of interest.

As amended 1998.

Rule 38.

FRIVOLOUS APPEAL—DAMAGES AND COSTS

If a court of appeals determines that an appeal is frivolous, it may, after a separately filed motion or notice from the court and reasonable opportunity to respond, award just damages and single or double costs to the appellee.

As amended 1994, 1998.

Rule 39.

COSTS

(a) Against Whom Assessed. The following rules apply unless the law provides or the court orders otherwise:

(1) if an appeal is dismissed, costs are taxed against the appellant, unless the parties agree otherwise;

(2) if a judgment is affirmed, costs are taxed against the appellant;

(3) if a judgment is reversed, costs are taxed against the appellee;

(4) if a judgment is affirmed in part, reversed in part, modified, or vacated, costs are taxed only as the court orders.

(b) Costs For and Against the United States. Costs for or against the United States, its agency, or officer will be assessed under Rule 39(a) only if authorized by law.

(c) Costs of Copies. Each court of appeals must, by local rule, fix the maximum rate for taxing the cost of producing necessary copies of a brief or appendix, or copies of records authorized by Rule 30(f). The rate must not exceed that generally charged for such work in the area where the clerk's office is located and should encourage economical methods of copying.

(d) Bill of Costs: Objections; Insertion in Mandate.

(1) A party who wants costs taxed must—within 14 days after entry of judgment—file with the circuit clerk, with proof of service, an itemized and verified bill of costs.

(2) Objections must be filed within 14 days after service of the bill of costs, unless the court extends the time.

(3) The clerk must prepare and certify an itemized statement of costs for insertion in the mandate, but issuance of the mandate must not be delayed for taxing costs. If the mandate issues before costs are finally determined, the district clerk must—upon the circuit clerk's request—add the statement of costs, or any amendment of it, to the mandate.

(e) Costs on Appeal Taxable in the District Court. The following costs on appeal are taxable in the district court for the benefit of the party entitled to costs under this rule:

(1) the preparation and transmission of the record;

(2) the reporter's transcript, if needed to determine the appeal;

(3) premiums paid for a supersedeas bond or other bond to preserve rights pending appeal; and

(4) the fee for filing the notice of appeal.

As amended 1979, 1986, 1998, 2009.

Rule 40.

PETITION FOR PANEL REHEARING

(a) Time to File; Contents; Answer; Action by the Court if Granted.

(1) *Time.* Unless the time is shortened or extended by order or local rule, a petition for panel rehearing may be filed within 14 days after entry of judgment. But in a civil case, if the United States or its officer or agency is a party, the time within which any party may seek rehearing is 45 days after entry of judgment, unless an order shortens or extends the time.

(2) *Contents.* The petition must state with particularity each point of law or fact that the petitioner believes the court has overlooked or misapprehended and must argue in support of the petition. Oral argument is not permitted.

(3) *Answer.* Unless the court requests, no answer to a petition for panel rehearing is permitted. But ordinarily rehearing will not be granted in the absence of such a request.

(4) *Action by the Court.* If a petition for panel rehearing is granted, the court may do any of the following:

(A) make a final disposition of the case without reargument;

(B) restore the case to the calendar for reargument or resubmission; or

(C) issue any other appropriate order.

(b) Form of Petition; Length. The petition must comply in form with Rule 32. Copies must be served and filed as Rule 31 prescribes. Unless the court permits or a local rule provides otherwise, a petition for panel rehearing must not exceed 15 pages.

As amended 1979, 1994, 1998.

Rule 41.

MANDATE: CONTENTS; ISSUANCE AND EFFECTIVE DATE; STAY

(a) Contents. Unless the court directs that a formal mandate issue, the mandate consists of a certified copy of the judgment, a copy of the court's opinion, if any, and any direction about costs.

(b) When Issued. The court's mandate must issue 7 days after the time to file a petition for rehearing expires, or 7 days after entry of an order denying a timely petition for panel rehearing, petition for rehearing en banc, or motion for stay of mandate, whichever is later. The court may shorten or extend the time.

(c) Effective Date. The mandate is effective when issued.

(d) Staying the Mandate.

(1) *On Petition for Rehearing or Motion.* The timely filing of a petition for panel rehearing, petition for rehearing en banc, or motion for stay of mandate, stays the mandate until disposition of the petition or motion, unless the court orders otherwise.

(2) *Pending Petition for Certiorari.*

(A) A party may move to stay the mandate pending the filing of a petition for a writ of certiorari in the Supreme Court. The motion must be served on all parties and must show that the certiorari petition would present a substantial question and that there is good cause for a stay.

(B) The stay must not exceed 90 days, unless the period is extended for good cause or unless the party who obtained the stay files a petition for the writ and so notifies the circuit clerk in writing within the period of the stay. In that case, the stay continues until the Supreme Court's final disposition.

(C) The court may require a bond or other security as a condition to granting or continuing a stay of the mandate.

(D) The court of appeals must issue the mandate immediately when a copy of a Supreme Court order denying the petition for writ of certiorari is filed.

As amended 1994, 1998, 2002, 2009.

Rule 42.

VOLUNTARY DISMISSAL

(a) Dismissal in the District Court. Before an appeal has been docketed by the circuit clerk, the district court may dismiss the appeal on the filing of a stipulation signed by all parties or on the appellant's motion with notice to all parties.

(b) Dismissal in the Court of Appeals. The circuit clerk may dismiss a docketed appeal if the parties file a signed dismissal agreement specifying how costs are to be paid and pay any fees that are due. But no mandate or other process may issue without a court order. An appeal may be dismissed on the appellant's motion on terms agreed to by the parties or fixed by the court.

As amended 1998.

Rule 43.

SUBSTITUTION OF PARTIES

(a) Death of a Party.

(1) *After Notice of Appeal Is Filed.* If a party dies after a notice of appeal has been filed or while a proceeding is pending in the court of appeals, the decedent's personal representative may be substituted as a party on motion filed with the circuit clerk by the representative or by any party. A party's motion must be served on the representative in accordance with Rule 25. If the decedent has no representative, any party may suggest the death on the record, and the court of appeals may then direct appropriate proceedings.

(2) *Before Notice of Appeal Is Filed—Potential Appellant.* If a party entitled to appeal dies before filing a notice of appeal, the decedent's personal representative—or, if there is no personal representative, the decedent's attorney of record—may file a notice of appeal within the time prescribed by these rules. After the notice of appeal is filed, substitution must be in accordance with Rule 43(a)(1).

(3) *Before Notice of Appeal Is Filed—Potential Appellee.* If a party against whom an appeal may be taken dies after entry of a judgment or order in the district court, but before a notice of appeal is filed, an appellant may proceed as if the death had not occurred. After the notice of appeal is filed, substitution must be in accordance with Rule 43(a)(1).

(b) Substitution for a Reason Other Than Death. If a party needs to be substituted for any reason other than death, the procedure prescribed in Rule 43(a) applies.

(c) Public Officer: Identification; Substitution.

(1) *Identification of Party.* A public officer who is a party to an appeal or other proceeding in an official capacity may be described as a party by the public officer's official title rather than by name. But the court may require the public officer's name to be added.

(2) *Automatic Substitution of Officeholder.* When a public officer who is a party to an appeal or other proceeding in an official capacity dies, resigns, or otherwise ceases to hold office, the action does not abate. The public officer's successor is automatically substituted as a party. Proceedings following the substitution are to be in the name of the substituted party, but any misnomer that does not affect the substantial rights of the parties may be disre-

garded. An order of substitution may be entered at any time, but failure to enter an order does not affect the substitution.

As amended 1986, 1998.

Rule 44.

CASE INVOLVING A CONSTITUTIONAL QUESTION WHEN THE UNITED STATES OR THE RELEVANT STATE IS NOT A PARTY

(a) Constitutional Challenge to Federal Statute. If a party questions the constitutionality of an Act of Congress in a proceeding in which the United States or its agency, officer, or employee is not a party in an official capacity, the questioning party must give written notice to the circuit clerk immediately upon the filing of the record or as soon as the question is raised in the court of appeals. The clerk must then certify that fact to the Attorney General.

(b) Constitutional Challenge to State Statute. If a party questions the constitutionality of a statute of a State in a proceeding in which that State or its agency, officer, or employee is not a party in an official capacity, the questioning party must give written notice to the circuit clerk immediately upon the filing of the record or as soon as the question is raised in the court of appeals. The clerk must then certify that fact to the attorney general of the State.

As amended 1998, 2002.

Rule 45.

CLERK'S DUTIES

(a) General Provisions.

(1) *Qualifications.* The circuit clerk must take the oath and post any bond required by law. Neither the clerk nor any deputy clerk may practice as an attorney or counselor in any court while in office.

(2) *When Court Is Open.* The court of appeals is always open for filing any paper, issuing and returning process, making a motion, and entering an order. The clerk's office with the clerk or a deputy in attendance must be open during business hours on all days except Saturdays, Sundays, and legal holidays. A court may provide by local rule or by order that the clerk's office be open for specified hours on Saturdays or on legal holidays other than New Year's Day, Martin Luther King, Jr.'s Birthday, Washington's

Birthday, Memorial Day, Independence Day, Labor Day, Columbus Day, Veterans' Day, Thanksgiving Day, and Christmas Day.

(b) Records.

(1) *The Docket.* The circuit clerk must maintain a docket and an index of all docketed cases in the manner prescribed by the Director of the Administrative Office of the United States Courts. The clerk must record all papers filed with the clerk and all process, orders, and judgments.

(2) *Calendar.* Under the court's direction, the clerk must prepare a calendar of cases awaiting argument. In placing cases on the calendar for argument, the clerk must give preference to appeals in criminal cases and to other proceedings and appeals entitled to preference by law.

(3) *Other Records.* The clerk must keep other books and records required by the Director of the Administrative Office of the United States Courts, with the approval of the Judicial Conference of the United States, or by the court.

(c) Notice of an Order or Judgment. Upon the entry of an order or judgment, the circuit clerk must immediately serve a notice of entry on each party, with a copy of any opinion, and must note the date of service on the docket. Service on a party represented by counsel must be made on counsel.

(d) Custody of Records and Papers. The circuit clerk has custody of the court's records and papers. Unless the court orders or instructs otherwise, the clerk must not permit an original record or paper to be taken from the clerk's office. Upon disposition of the case, original papers constituting the record on appeal or review must be returned to the court or agency from which they were received. The clerk must preserve a copy of any brief, appendix, or other paper that has been filed.

As amended 1971, 1986, 1998, 2002, 2005.

Rule 46.

ATTORNEYS

(a) Admission to the Bar.

(1) *Eligibility.* An attorney is eligible for admission to the bar of a court of appeals if that attorney is of good moral and professional character and is admitted to practice before the Supreme Court of the United States, the highest court of a state, another United States court of appeals, or a United States district court (including the district courts for Guam, the Northern Mariana Islands, and the Virgin Islands).

(2) *Application.* An applicant must file an application for admission, on a form approved by the court that contains the applicant's personal statement showing eligibility for membership. The applicant must subscribe to the following oath or affirmation:

> "I, _____, do solemnly swear [or affirm] that I will conduct myself as an attorney and counselor of this court, uprightly and according to law; and that I will support the Constitution of the United States."

(3) *Admission Procedures.* On written or oral motion of a member of the court's bar, the court will act on the application. An applicant may be admitted by oral motion in open court. But, unless the court orders otherwise, an applicant need not appear before the court to be admitted. Upon admission, an applicant must pay the clerk the fee prescribed by local rule or court order.

(b) Suspension or Disbarment.

(1) *Standard.* A member of the court's bar is subject to suspension or disbarment by the court if the member:

(A) has been suspended or disbarred from practice in any other court; or

(B) is guilty of conduct unbecoming a member of the court's bar.

(2) *Procedure.* The member must be given an opportunity to show good cause, within the time prescribed by the court, why the member should not be suspended or disbarred.

(3) *Order.* The court must enter an appropriate order after the member responds and a hearing is held, if requested, or after the time prescribed for a response expires, if no response is made.

(c) Discipline. A court of appeals may discipline an attorney who practices before it for conduct unbecoming a member of the bar or for failure to comply with any court rule. First, however, the court must afford the attorney reasonable notice, an opportunity to show cause to the contrary, and, if requested, a hearing.

As amended 1986, 1998.

Rule 47.

LOCAL RULES BY COURTS OF APPEALS

(a) Local Rules.

(1) Each court of appeals acting by a majority of its judges in regular active service may, after giving appropriate public notice and opportunity for comment, make and amend rules governing its practice. A generally applicable direction to parties or lawyers

regarding practice before a court must be in a local rule rather than an internal operating procedure or standing order. A local rule must be consistent with—but not duplicative of—Acts of Congress and rules adopted under 28 U.S.C. § 2072 and must conform to any uniform numbering system prescribed by the Judicial Conference of the United States. Each circuit clerk must send the Administrative Office of the United States Courts a copy of each local rule and internal operating procedure when it is promulgated or amended.

(2) A local rule imposing a requirement of form must not be enforced in a manner that causes a party to lose rights because of a nonwillful failure to comply with the requirement.

(b) Procedure When There Is No Controlling Law. A court of appeals may regulate practice in a particular case in any manner consistent with federal law, these rules, and local rules of the circuit. No sanction or other disadvantage may be imposed for noncompliance with any requirement not in federal law, federal rules, or the local circuit rules unless the alleged violator has been furnished in the particular case with actual notice of the requirement.

As amended 1995, 1998.

Rule 48.

MASTERS

(a) Appointment; Powers. A court of appeals may appoint a special master to hold hearings, if necessary, and to recommend factual findings and disposition in matters ancillary to proceedings in the court. Unless the order referring a matter to a master specifies or limits the master's powers, those powers include, but are not limited to, the following:

(1) regulating all aspects of a hearing;

(2) taking all appropriate action for the efficient performance of the master's duties under the order;

(3) requiring the production of evidence on all matters embraced in the reference; and

(4) administering oaths and examining witnesses and parties.

(b) Compensation. If the master is not a judge or court employee, the court must determine the master's compensation and whether the cost is to be charged to any party.

As amended 1994, 1998.

———

[The order of the Supreme Court of December 4, 1967, stated that the rules therein set forth, to be known as the Federal Rules of Appellate Procedure, "be, and they hereby are, prescribed, pursuant to sections 3771 and 3772 of Title 18, United States Code, and sections 2072 and 2075 of Title 28, United States Code, to govern the procedure in appeals to United States courts of appeals from the United States district courts, in the review by United States courts of appeals of decisions of the Tax Court of the United States, in proceedings in the United States courts of appeals for the review or enforcement of orders of administrative agencies, boards, commissions and officers, and in applications for writs or other relief which a United States court of appeals or judge thereof is competent to give."]

[The order of December 4, 1967, further stated that the Rules "shall take effect on July 1, 1968, and shall govern all proceedings in appeals and petitions for review or enforcement of orders thereafter brought and in all such proceedings then pending, except to the extent that in the opinion of the court of appeals their application in a particular proceeding then pending would not be feasible or would work injustice, in which case the former procedure may be followed." 389 U.S. 1063, 1065; see 43 F.R.D. 61.]

———

[Rules 30(a) and (c) and 31(a) were amended by the order of the Supreme Court of March 30, 1970, to be effective July 1, 1970. 398 U.S. 971; see 48 F.R.D. 481.]

———

[Rules 26(a) and 45(a) were amended by the order of the Supreme Court of March 1, 1971, to be effective July 1, 1971. 401 U.S. 1029; see 52 F.R.D. 84.]

———

[Rule 9(c) was amended by the order of the Supreme Court of April 24, 1972, to be effective October 1, 1972. 406 U.S. 1005; see 56 F.R.D. 181.]

———

[Rules 1(a), 3(c), (d), and (e), 4(a), 5(d), 6(d), 7, 10(b), 11(a), (b), (c), and (d), 12(a), (b), and (c), 13(a), 24(b), 27(b), 28(g) and (j), 34(a) and (b), 35(b) and (c), 39(c) and (d), and 40(a) and (b) were amended by the order of the Supreme Court of April 30, 1979, to be effective August 1, 1979. 441 U.S. 969; see 16A Wright, Miller & Cooper, Federal Practice and Procedure app. B.]

———

[Rule 9(c) was amended October 12, 1984, Pub.L. 98–473, Title II, § 210, 98 Stat. 1987.]

––––––––

[Rules 19, 26(a), 28(c), 30(a) and (b), 39(c), and 45(a) and (b) were amended, and Rules 3.1, 5.1, and 15.1 added, by the order of the Supreme Court of March 10, 1986, to be effective July 1, 1986. That order also neutralized gender-specific language in numerous Rules. 475 U.S. 1153; see 109 F.R.D. 179.]

––––––––

[Rule 4(b) was amended November 18, 1988, Pub.L. 100–690, Title VII, § 7111, 102 Stat. 4419.]

––––––––

[Rules 1(a), 3(a), 6, 26(a), 27(a), and 28(g) were amended, and Rule 26.1 and Form 5 added, by the order of the Supreme Court of April 25, 1989, to be effective December 1, 1989. 490 U.S. 1125; see 124 F.R.D. 361.]

––––––––

[Rules 4(a), 6, 10(c), 25(a), 26(a), 26.1, 28(a), (b), and (h), 30(b), and 34(d) were amended by the order of the Supreme Court of April 30, 1991, to be effective December 1, 1991. 500 U.S. 1007; see 134 F.R.D. 725.]

––––––––

[Rules 3(c) and (d), 3.1, 4, 5.1(a), 6(b), 10(b), 12(b) and (c), 15(a) and (e), 25(a), 28(a) and (b), and 34(c) and Forms 1, 2, and 3 were amended by the order of the Supreme Court of April 22, 1993, to be effective December 1, 1993. 507 U.S. 1059; see 147 F.R.D. 287.]

––––––––

[Rules 1(c), 3(a), 5(c), 5.1(c), 9, 13(a), 21(d), 25(a), (d), and (e), 26.1, 27(d), 28(a), (b), and (g), 30(a), 31(b), 33, 35(d), 38, 40(a), 41, and 48 were amended by the order of the Supreme Court of April 29, 1994, to be effective December 1, 1994. 511 U.S. 1155; see 154 F.R.D. 329.]

––––––––

[Rules 4(a), 8(c), 10(a) and (b), and 47 were amended by the order of the Supreme Court of April 27, 1995, to be effective December 1, 1995. 514 U.S. 1137; see 161 F.R.D. 163.]

———

[Rule 22 was amended April 24, 1996, Pub.L. 104–132, Title I, § 103, 110 Stat. 1218.]

———

[Rules 21, 25(a), (c), and (d), and 26(c) were amended by the order of the Supreme Court of April 23, 1996, to be effective December 1, 1996. 517 U.S. 1255; see 167 F.R.D. 229.]

———

[Rules 3.1, 5, 5.1, 26.1, 27, 28, 29, 32, 35, and 41 and Form 4 were amended, and stylistic changes were made in all other Rules, by the order of the Supreme Court of April 24, 1998, to be effective December 1, 1998. 523 U.S. 1147; see 16A Wright, Miller & Cooper, Federal Practice and Procedure app. B.]

———

[Rules 1(b), 4(a) and (b), 5(c), 21(d), 24(a), 25(c) and (d), 26(a) and (c), 26.1, 27(a) and (d), 28(j), 31(b), 32(a), (c), (d), and (e), 36(b), 41(b), 44, and 45(c) were amended, and Form 6 added, by the order of the Supreme Court of April 29, 2002, to be effective December 1, 2002. 535 U.S. 1123; see 207 F.R.D. 655.]

———

[Forms 1, 2, 3, and 5 were amended by the order of the Supreme Court of March 27, 2003, to be effective December 1, 2003. 538 U.S. 1071; see 215 F.R.D. 377.]

———

[Rules 4(a), 26(a), 27(d), 28(c) and (h), 32(a), 34(d), 35(a), and 45(a) were amended, and Rule 28.1 added, by the order of the Supreme Court of April 25, 2005, to be effective December 1, 2005. 544 U.S. 1151; see 228 F.R.D. 267.]

———

[Rule 25(a) was amended, and Rule 32.1 added, by the order of the Supreme Court of April 12, 2006, to be effective December 1, 2006. 547 U.S. 1221; see 234 F.R.D. 543.]

———

[Rule 25(a) was amended by the order of the Supreme Court of April 30, 2007, to be effective December 1, 2007. 550 U.S. 983; see ___ F.R.D. ___.]

———

[Rules 4(a) and (b), 5(b) and (d), 6(b), 10(b) and (c), 12(b), 15(b), 19, 22(b), 25(a) and (c), 26(a) and (c), 27(a), 28.1(f), 30(b), 31(a), 39(d), and 41(b) were amended, and Rule 12.1 added, by the order of the Supreme Court of March 26, 2009, to be effective December 1, 2009. ___ U.S. ___; see ___ F.R.D. ___.]

APPENDIX OF FORMS

Form 1.

NOTICE OF APPEAL TO A COURT OF APPEALS FROM A JUDGMENT OR ORDER OF A DISTRICT COURT

United States District Court for the ....District of ....

File Number ....

A. B., Plaintiff	)	
v.	)	Notice of Appeal
C. D., Defendant	)	

Notice is hereby given that (here name all parties taking the appeal), (plaintiffs) (defendants) in the above named case,[1] hereby appeal to the United States Court of Appeals for the .... Circuit (from the final judgment) (from an order (describing it)) entered in this action on the ...... day of ...., 20....

(S) ....

Attorney for ....

....
(Address)

As amended 1993, 2003.

FORMS 2–6 [Omitted]

1. See Rule 3(c) for permissible ways of identifying appellants.

*

TABLE OF CONTENTS

SELECTED PROVISIONS OF THE CONSTITUTION OF THE UNITED STATES

SELECTED PROVISIONS OF TITLE 28, UNITED STATES CODE

507

TABLE OF CONTENTS

508

TABLE OF CONTENTS

509

TABLE OF CONTENTS

TABLE OF CONTENTS

SELECTED PROVISIONS OF OTHER PROCEDURAL STATUTES

SELECTED PROVISIONS OF THE CONSTITUTION OF THE UNITED STATES

* * *

ARTICLE. I.

* * *

Section 8. The Congress shall have Power To lay and collect Taxes, Duties, Imposts and Excises, to pay the Debts and provide for the common Defence and general Welfare of the United States; but all Duties, Imposts and Excises shall be uniform throughout the United States;

To borrow Money on the credit of the United States;

To regulate Commerce with foreign Nations, and among the several States, and with the Indian Tribes;

To establish an uniform Rule of Naturalization, and uniform Laws on the subject of Bankruptcies throughout the United States;

To coin Money, regulate the Value thereof, and of foreign Coin, and fix the Standard of Weights and Measures;

To provide for the Punishment of counterfeiting the Securities and current Coin of the United States;

To establish Post Offices and post Roads;

To promote the Progress of Science and useful Arts, by securing for limited Times to Authors and Inventors the exclusive Right to their respective Writings and Discoveries;

To constitute Tribunals inferior to the supreme Court;

To define and punish Piracies and Felonies committed on the high Seas, and Offences against the Law of Nations;

To declare War, grant Letters of Marque and Reprisal, and make Rules concerning Captures on Land and Water;

To raise and support Armies, but no Appropriation of Money to that Use shall be for a longer Term than two Years;

To provide and maintain a Navy;

To make Rules for the Government and Regulation of the land and naval Forces;

To provide for calling forth the Militia to execute the Laws of the Union, suppress Insurrections and repel Invasions;

To provide for organizing, arming, and disciplining, the Militia, and for governing such Part of them as may be employed in the Service of the United States, reserving to the States respectively, the Appointment of the

Officers, and the Authority of training the Militia according to the discipline prescribed by Congress;

To exercise exclusive Legislation in all Cases whatsoever, over such District (not exceeding ten Miles square) as may, by Cession of particular States, and the Acceptance of Congress, become the Seat of the Government of the United States, and to exercise like Authority over all Places purchased by the Consent of the Legislature of the State in which the same shall be, for the Erection of Forts, Magazines, Arsenals, dock-Yards, and other needful Buildings;—And

To make all Laws which shall be necessary and proper for carrying into Execution the foregoing Powers, and all other Powers vested by this Constitution in the Government of the United States, or in any Department or Officer thereof.

* * *

ARTICLE. III.

Section 1. The judicial Power of the United States, shall be vested in one supreme Court, and in such inferior Courts as the Congress may from time to time ordain and establish. The Judges, both of the supreme and inferior Courts, shall hold their Offices during good Behaviour, and shall, at stated Times, receive for their Services, a Compensation, which shall not be diminished during their Continuance in Office.

Section 2. The judicial Power shall extend to all Cases, in Law and Equity, arising under this Constitution, the Laws of the United States, and Treaties made, or which shall be made, under their Authority;—to all Cases affecting Ambassadors, other public Ministers and Consuls;—to all Cases of admiralty and maritime Jurisdiction;—to Controversies to which the United States shall be a Party;—to Controversies between two or more States;—between a State and Citizens of another State;—between Citizens of different States;—between Citizens of the same State claiming Lands under Grants of different States, and between a State, or the Citizens thereof, and foreign States, Citizens or Subjects.

In all Cases affecting Ambassadors, other public Ministers and Consuls, and those in which a State shall be Party, the supreme Court shall have original Jurisdiction. In all the other Cases before mentioned, the supreme Court shall have appellate Jurisdiction, both as to Law and Fact, with such Exceptions, and under such Regulations as the Congress shall make.

The Trial of all Crimes, except in Cases of Impeachment, shall be by Jury; and such Trial shall be held in the State where the said Crimes shall have been committed; but when not committed within any State, the Trial shall be at such Place or Places as the Congress may by Law have directed.

* * *

ARTICLE. IV.

Section 1. Full Faith and Credit shall be given in each State to the public Acts, Records, and judicial Proceedings of every other State. And the Congress may by general Laws prescribe the Manner in which such Acts, Records and Proceedings shall be proved, and the Effect thereof.

Section 2. The Citizens of each State shall be entitled to all Privileges and Immunities of Citizens in the several States.

* * *

ARTICLE. VI.

* * *

This Constitution, and the Laws of the United States which shall be made in Pursuance thereof; and all Treaties made, or which shall be made, under the Authority of the United States, shall be the supreme Law of the Land; and the Judges in every State shall be bound thereby, any Thing in the Constitution or Laws of any State to the Contrary notwithstanding.

* * *

AMENDMENT. I.

[1791]

Congress shall make no law respecting an establishment of religion, or prohibiting the free exercise thereof; or abridging the freedom of speech, or of the press; or the right of the people peaceably to assemble, and to petition the Government for a redress of grievances.

AMENDMENT. IV.

The right of the people to be secure in their persons, houses, papers, and effects, against unreasonable searches and seizures, shall not be violated, and no Warrants shall issue, but upon probable cause, supported by Oath or affirmation, and particularly describing the place to be searched, and the persons or things to be seized.

AMENDMENT. V.

No person shall be held to answer for a capital, or otherwise infamous crime, unless on a presentment or indictment of a Grand Jury, except in cases arising in the land or naval forces, or in the Militia, when in actual service in time of War or public danger; nor shall any person be subject for the same offence to be twice put in jeopardy of life or limb; nor shall be compelled in any criminal case to be a witness against himself, nor be deprived of life, liberty, or property, without due process of law; nor shall private property be taken for public use, without just compensation.

AMENDMENT. VI.

In all criminal prosecutions, the accused shall enjoy the right to a speedy and public trial, by an impartial jury of the State and district wherein the crime shall have been committed, which district shall have been previously ascertained by law, and to be informed of the nature and cause of the accusation; to be confronted with the Witnesses against him; to have compulsory process for obtaining witnesses in his favor, and to have the Assistance of Counsel for his defence.

AMENDMENT. VII.

In suits at common law, where the value in controversy shall exceed twenty dollars, the right of trial by jury shall be preserved, and no fact tried by a jury, shall be otherwise re-examined in any Court of the United States, than according to the rules of the common law.

AMENDMENT. IX.

The enumeration in the Constitution, of certain rights, shall not be construed to deny or disparage others retained by the people.

AMENDMENT. X.

The powers not delegated to the United States by the Constitution, nor prohibited by it to the States, are reserved to the States respectively, or to the people.

AMENDMENT. XI.

[1795*]

The Judicial power of the United States shall not be construed to extend to any suit in law or equity, commenced or prosecuted against one of the United States by Citizens of another State, or by Citizens or Subjects of any Foreign State.

AMENDMENT. XIV.

[1868]

Section 1. All persons born or naturalized in the United States, and subject to the jurisdiction thereof, are citizens of the United States and of the State wherein they reside. No State shall make or enforce any law which shall abridge the privileges or immunities of citizens of the United States; nor shall any State deprive any person of life, liberty, or property, without due process of law; nor deny to any person within its jurisdiction the equal protection of the laws.

Section 2. Representatives shall be apportioned among the several States according to their respective numbers, counting the whole number of persons in each State, excluding Indians not taxed. But when the right to vote at any election for the choice of electors for President and Vice President of the United States, Representatives in Congress, the Executive and Judicial officers of a State, or the members of the Legislature thereof, is denied to any of the male inhabitants of such State, being twenty-one years of age, and citizens of the United States, or in any way abridged, except for participation in rebellion, or other crime, the basis of representation therein shall be reduced in the proportion which the number of such male citizens shall bear to the whole number of male citizens twenty-one years of age in such State.

Section 3. No person shall be a Senator or Representative in Congress, or elector of President and Vice President, or hold any office, civil or military, under the United States, or under any State, who, having previ-

* Official announcement of ratification was not made until January 8, 1798, in a message from the President to Congress.

ously taken an oath, as a member of Congress, or as an officer of the United States, or as a member of any State legislature, or as an executive or judicial officer of any State, to support the Constitution of the United States, shall have engaged in insurrection or rebellion against the same, or given aid or comfort to the enemies thereof. But Congress may by a vote of two-thirds of each House, remove such disability.

Section 4. The validity of the public debt of the United States, authorized by law, including debts incurred for payment of pensions and bounties for services in suppressing insurrection or rebellion, shall not be questioned. But neither the United States nor any State shall assume or pay any debt or obligation incurred in aid of insurrection or rebellion against the United States, or any claim for the loss or emancipation of any slave; but all such debts, obligations and claims shall be held illegal and void.

Section 5. The Congress shall have power to enforce, by appropriate legislation, the provisions of this article.

*

SELECTED PROVISIONS OF TITLE 28, UNITED STATES CODE

§ 1. Number of justices; quorum

The Supreme Court of the United States shall consist of a Chief Justice of the United States and eight associate justices, any six of whom shall constitute a quorum.

§ 2. Terms of court

The Supreme Court shall hold at the seat of government a term of court commencing on the first Monday in October of each year and may hold such adjourned or special terms as may be necessary.

§ 3. Vacancy in office of Chief Justice; disability

Whenever the Chief Justice is unable to perform the duties of his office or the office is vacant, his powers and duties shall devolve upon the associate justice next in precedence who is able to act, until such disability is removed or another Chief Justice is appointed and duly qualified.

§ 4. Precedence of associate justices

Associate justices shall have precedence according to the seniority of their commissions. Justices whose commissions bear the same date shall have precedence according to seniority in age.

§ 41. Number and composition of circuits

The thirteen judicial circuits of the United States are constituted as follows:

Circuits	Composition
District of Columbia	District of Columbia.
First	Maine, Massachusetts, New Hampshire, Puerto Rico, Rhode Island.
Second	Connecticut, New York, Vermont.
Third	Delaware, New Jersey, Pennsylvania, Virgin Islands.
Fourth	Maryland, North Carolina, South Carolina, Virginia, West Virginia.
Fifth	District of the Canal Zone, Louisiana, Mississippi, Texas.
Sixth	Kentucky, Michigan, Ohio, Tennessee.
Seventh	Illinois, Indiana, Wisconsin.
Eighth	Arkansas, Iowa, Minnesota, Missouri, Nebraska, North Dakota, South Dakota.
Ninth	Alaska, Arizona, California, Idaho, Montana, Nevada, Oregon, Washington, Guam, Hawaii.

519

Circuits	Composition
Tenth	Colorado, Kansas, New Mexico, Oklahoma, Utah, Wyoming.
Eleventh	Alabama, Florida, Georgia.
Federal	All Federal judicial districts.

As amended Oct. 31, 1951, c. 655, § 34, 65 Stat. 723; Oct. 14, 1980, Pub.L. 96–452, § 2, 94 Stat. 1994; Apr. 2, 1982, Pub.L. 97–164, Title I, § 101, 96 Stat. 25.

§ 42. Allotment of Supreme Court justices to circuits

The Chief Justice of the United States and the associate justices of the Supreme Court shall from time to time be allotted as circuit justices among the circuits by order of the Supreme Court. The Chief Justice may make such allotments in vacation.

A justice may be assigned to more than one circuit, and two or more justices may be assigned to the same circuit.

§ 43. Creation and composition of courts

(a) There shall be in each circuit a court of appeals, which shall be a court of record, known as the United States Court of Appeals for the circuit.

(b) Each court of appeals shall consist of the circuit judges of the circuit in regular active service. The circuit justice and justices or judges designated or assigned shall also be competent to sit as judges of the court. As amended Nov. 13, 1963, Pub.L. 88–176, § 1(a), 77 Stat. 331.

§ 44. Appointment, tenure, residence and salary of circuit judges

(a) The President shall appoint, by and with the advice and consent of the Senate, circuit judges for the several circuits as follows:

Circuits	Number of Judges
District of Columbia	11
First	6
Second	13
Third	14
Fourth	15
Fifth	17
Sixth	16
Seventh	11
Eighth	11
Ninth	29
Tenth	12
Eleventh	12
Federal	12.

(b) Circuit judges shall hold office during good behavior.

(c) Except in the District of Columbia, each circuit judge shall be a resident of the circuit for which appointed at the time of his appointment and thereafter while in active service. While in active service, each circuit judge of the Federal judicial circuit appointed after the effective date of the Federal Courts Improvement Act of 1982, and the chief judge of the Federal judicial circuit, whenever appointed, shall reside within fifty miles of the District of Columbia. In each circuit (other than the Federal judicial) there shall be at least one circuit judge in regular active service appointed from the residents of each state in that circuit.

(d) Each circuit judge shall receive a salary at an annual rate determined under section 225 of the Federal Salary Act of 1967 (2 U.S.C. 351–361), as adjusted by section 461 of this title. Latest amendment Jan. 7, 2008, Pub.L. 110–177, Title V, § 509(a), 121 Stat. 2543.

§ 45. Chief judges; precedence of judges

(a)(1) The chief judge of the circuit shall be the circuit judge in regular active service who is senior in commission of those judges who—

(A) are sixty-four years of age or under;

(B) have served for one year or more as a circuit judge; and

(C) have not served previously as chief judge.

(2)(A) In any case in which no circuit judge meets the qualifications of paragraph (1), the youngest circuit judge in regular active service who is sixty-five years of age or over and who has served as circuit judge for one year or more shall act as the chief judge.

(B) In any case under subparagraph (A) in which there is no circuit judge in regular active service who has served as a circuit judge for one year or more, the circuit judge in regular active service who is senior in commission and who has not served previously as chief judge shall act as the chief judge.

(3)(A) Except as provided in subparagraph (C), the chief judge of the circuit appointed under paragraph (1) shall serve for a term of seven years and shall serve after expiration of such term until another judge is eligible under paragraph (1) to serve as chief judge of the circuit.

(B) Except as provided in subparagraph (C), a circuit judge acting as chief judge under subparagraph (A) or (B) of paragraph (2) shall serve until a judge has been appointed who meets the qualifications under paragraph (1).

(C) No circuit judge may serve or act as chief judge of the circuit after attaining the age of seventy years unless no other circuit judge is qualified to serve as chief judge of the circuit under paragraph (1) or is qualified to act as chief judge under paragraph (2).

(b) The chief judge shall have precedence and preside at any session of the court which he attends. Other circuit judges of the court in regular active service shall have precedence and preside according to the seniority of their commissions. Judges whose commissions bear the same date shall have precedence according to seniority in age. The circuit justice, however, shall have precedence over all the circuit judges and shall preside at any session which he attends.

(c) If the chief judge desires to be relieved of his duties as chief judge while retaining his active status as circuit judge, he may so certify to the Chief Justice of the United States, and thereafter the chief judge of the circuit shall be such other circuit judge who is qualified to serve or act as chief judge under subsection (a).

(d) If a chief judge is temporarily unable to perform his duties as such, they shall be performed by the circuit judge in active service, present in the circuit and able and qualified to act, who is next in precedence. As amended Oct. 31, 1951, c. 655, § 35, 65 Stat. 723; Aug. 6, 1958, Pub.L. 85–593, § 1, 72 Stat. 497; Apr. 2, 1982, Pub.L. 97–164, Title II, §§ 201, 204, 96 Stat. 51, 53.

§ 46. Assignment of judges; panels; hearings; quorum

(a) Circuit judges shall sit on the court and its panels in such order and at such times as the court directs.

(b) In each circuit the court may authorize the hearing and determination of cases and controversies by separate panels, each consisting of three judges, at lease a majority of whom shall be judges of that court, unless such judges cannot sit because recused or disqualified, or unless the chief judge of that court certifies that there is an emergency including, but not limited to, the unavailability of a judge of the court because of illness. Such panels shall sit at the times and places and hear the cases and controversies assigned as the court directs. The United States Court of Appeals for the Federal Circuit shall determine by rule a procedure for the rotation of judges from panel to panel to ensure that all of the judges sit on a representative cross section of the cases heard and, notwithstanding the first sentence of this subsection, may determine by rule the number of judges, not less than three, who constitute a panel.

(c) Cases and controversies shall be heard and determined by a court or panel of not more than three judges (except that the United States Court of Appeals for the Federal Circuit may sit in panels of more than three judges if its rules so provide), unless a hearing or rehearing before the court in banc is ordered by a majority of the circuit judges of the circuit who are in regular active service. A court in banc shall consist of all circuit judges in regular active service, or such number of judges as may be prescribed in accordance with section 6 of Public Law 95–486 (92 Stat. 1633), except that any senior circuit judge of the circuit shall be eligible (1) to participate, at his election and upon designation and assignment pursuant to section 294(c) of this title and the rules of the circuit, as a member of an in banc court reviewing a decision of a panel of which such judge was a member, or (2) to continue to participate in the decision of a case or controversy that was heard or reheard by the court in banc at a time when such judge was in regular active service.

(d) A majority of the number of judges authorized to constitute a court or panel thereof, as provided in paragraph (c), shall constitute a quorum. As amended Nov. 13, 1963, Pub.L. 88–176, § 1(b), 77 Stat. 331; Oct. 20, 1978, Pub.L. 95–486, § 5(a), (b), 92 Stat. 1633; Apr. 2, 1982, Pub.L. 97–164, Title I, § 103, Title II, § 205, 96 Stat. 25, 53; Aug. 6, 1996, Pub.L. 104–175, § 1, 110 Stat. 1556.

§ 47. Disqualification of trial judge to hear appeal

No judge shall hear or determine an appeal from the decision of a case or issue tried by him.

§ 48. Terms of court

(a) The courts of appeals shall hold regular sessions at the places listed below, and at such other places within the respective circuit as each court may designate by rule.

Circuits	*Places*
District of Columbia	Washington.
First	Boston.
Second	New York.
Third	Philadelphia.
Fourth	Richmond, Asheville.
Fifth	New Orleans, Fort Worth, Jackson.
Sixth	Cincinnati.
Seventh	Chicago.
Eighth	St. Louis, Kansas City, Omaha, St. Paul.
Ninth	San Francisco, Los Angeles, Portland, Seattle.
Tenth	Denver, Wichita, Oklahoma City.
Eleventh	Atlanta, Jacksonville, Montgomery.
Federal	District of Columbia, and in any other place listed above as the court by rule directs.

(b) Each court of appeals may hold special sessions at any place within its circuit as the nature of the business may require, and upon such notice as the court orders. The court may transact any business at a special session which it might transact at a regular session.

(c) Any court of appeals may pretermit any regular session of court at any place for insufficient business or other good cause.

(d) The times and places of the sessions of the Court of Appeals for the Federal Circuit shall be prescribed with a view to securing reasonable opportunity to citizens to appear before the court with as little inconvenience and expense to citizens as is practicable.

(e) Each court of appeals may hold special sessions at any place within the United States outside the circuit as the nature of the business may require and upon such notice as the court orders, upon a finding by either the chief judge of the court of appeals (or, if the chief judge is unavailable, the most senior available active judge of the court of appeals) or the judicial council of the circuit that, because of emergency conditions, no location within the circuit is reasonably available where such special sessions could be held. The court may transact any business at a special session outside the circuit which it might transact at a regular session.

(f) If a court of appeals issues an order exercising its authority under subsection (e), the court—

(1) through the Administrative Office of the United States Courts, shall—

    (A) send notice of such order, including the reasons for the issuance of such order, to the Committee on the Judiciary of the Senate and the Committee on the Judiciary of the House of Representatives; and

    (B) not later than 180 days after the expiration of such court order submit a brief report to the Committee on the Judiciary of the Senate and the Committee on the Judiciary of the House of Representatives describing the impact of such order, including—

        (i) the reasons for the issuance of such order;

        (ii) the duration of such order;

        (iii) the impact of such order on litigants; and

        (iv) the costs to the judiciary resulting from such order; and

(2) shall provide reasonable notice to the United States Marshals Service before the commencement of any special session held pursuant to such order. As amended Oct. 31, 1951, c. 655, § 36, 65 Stat. 723; Oct. 14, 1980, Pub.L. 96–452, § 4, 94 Stat. 1994; Apr. 2, 1982, Pub.L. 97–164, Title I, § 104, 96 Stat. 26; Oct. 29, 1992, Pub.L. 102–572, Title V, § 501, 106 Stat. 4512; Sept. 9, 2005, Pub.L 109–63, § 2(a), 119 Stat. 1993.

§ 132. Creation and composition of district courts

(a) There shall be in each judicial district a district court which shall be a court of record known as the United States District Court for the district.

(b) Each district court shall consist of the district judge or judges for the district in regular active service. Justices or judges designated or assigned shall be competent to sit as judges of the court.

(c) Except as otherwise provided by law, or rule or order of court, the judicial power of a district court with respect to any action, suit or proceeding may be exercised by a single judge, who may preside alone and hold a regular or special session of court at the same time other sessions are held by other judges. As amended Nov. 13, 1963, Pub.L. 88–176, § 2, 77 Stat. 331.

§ 133. Appointment and number of district judges

(a) The President shall appoint, by and with the advice and consent of the Senate, district judges for the several judicial districts, as follows:

Districts	Judges
Alabama:	
Northern	7
Middle	3
Southern	3
Alaska	3

Districts	Judges
Arizona	12
Arkansas:	
Eastern	5
Western	3
California:	
Northern	14
Eastern	6
Central	27
Southern	13
Colorado	7
Connecticut	8
Delaware	4
District of Columbia	15
Florida:	
Northern	4
Middle	15
Southern	17
Georgia:	
Northern	11
Middle	4
Southern	3
Hawaii	3
Idaho	2
Illinois:	
Northern	22
Central	4
Southern	4
Indiana:	
Northern	5
Southern	5
Iowa:	
Northern	2
Southern	3
Kansas	5
Kentucky:	
Eastern	5
Western	4
Eastern and Western *	1
Louisiana:	
Eastern	12
Middle	3
Western	7
Maine	3
Maryland	10
Massachusetts	13
Michigan:	
Eastern	15
Western	4
Minnesota	7

* A district judge may be appointed to serve in more than one district.—Ed.

Districts	Judges
Mississippi:	
Northern	3
Southern	6
Missouri:	
Eastern	6
Western	5
Eastern and Western	2
Montana	3
Nebraska	3
Nevada	7
New Hampshire	3
New Jersey	17
New Mexico	6
New York:	
Northern	5
Southern	28
Eastern	15
Western	4
North Carolina:	
Eastern	4
Middle	4
Western	4
North Dakota	2
Ohio:	
Northern	11
Southern	8
Oklahoma:	
Northern	3
Eastern	1
Western	6
Northern, Eastern, and Western	1
Oregon	6
Pennsylvania:	
Eastern	22
Middle	6
Western	10
Puerto Rico	7
Rhode Island	3
South Carolina	10
South Dakota	3
Tennessee:	
Eastern	5
Middle	4
Western	5
Texas:	
Northern	12
Southern	19
Eastern	7
Western	13
Utah	5
Vermont	2

Virginia:
    Eastern 11
    Western 4
Washington:
    Eastern 4
    Western 7
West Virginia:
    Northern 3
    Southern 5
Wisconsin:
    Eastern 5
    Western 2
Wyoming . . . . 3.

(b)(1) In any case in which a judge of the United States (other than a senior judge) assumes the duties of a full-time office of Federal judicial administration, the President shall appoint, by and with the advice and consent of the Senate, an additional judge for the court on which such judge serves. If the judge who assumes the duties of such full-time office leaves that office and resumes the duties as an active judge of the court, then the President shall not appoint a judge to fill the first vacancy which occurs thereafter in that court.

(2) For purposes of paragraph (1), the term "office of Federal judicial administration" means a position as Director of the Federal Judicial Center, Director of the Administrative Office of the United States Courts, or Counselor to the Chief Justice. Latest amendment Oct. 13, 2008, Pub.L. 110–402, § 1(b)(1), 122 Stat. 4254.

§ 134. Tenure and residence of district judges

(a) The district judges shall hold office during good behavior.

(b) Each district judge, except in the District of Columbia, the Southern District of New York, and the Eastern District of New York, shall reside in the district or one of the districts for which he is appointed. Each district judge of the Southern District of New York and the Eastern District of New York may reside within 20 miles of the district to which he or she is appointed.

(c) If the public interest and the nature of the business of a district court require that a district judge should maintain his adobe at or near a particular place for holding court in the district or within a particular part of the district the judicial council of the circuit may so declare and may make an appropriate order. If the district judges of such a district are unable to agree as to which of them shall maintain his adobe at or near the place or within the area specified in such an order the judicial council of the circuit may decide which of them shall do so. As amended Aug. 3, 1949, c. 387, § 2(b)(1), 63 Stat. 495; Feb. 10, 1954, c. 6, § 2(b)(13)(a), 68 Stat. 12; Mar. 18, 1959, Pub.L. 86–3, § 9(c), 73 Stat. 8; May 19, 1961, Pub.L. 87–36, § 2(e)(3), 75 Stat. 83; Sept. 12, 1966, Pub.L. 89–571, § 1, 80 Stat. 764; Dec. 18, 1971, Pub.L. 92–208, § 3(e), 85 Stat. 742; Oct. 19, 1996, Pub.L. 104–317, Title VI, § 607, 110 Stat. 3860.

§ 136. Chief judges; precedence of district judges

(a)(1) In any district having more than one district judge, the chief judge of the district shall be the district judge in regular active service who is senior in commission of those judges who—

    (A) are sixty-four years of age or under;

    (B) have served for one year or more as a district judge; and

    (C) have not served previously as chief judge.

(2)(A) In any case in which no district judge meets the qualifications of paragraph (1), the youngest district judge in regular active service who is sixty-five years of age or over and who has served as district judge for one year or more shall act as the chief judge.

(B) In any case under subparagraph (A) in which there is no district judge in regular active service who has served as a district judge for one year or more, the district judge in regular active service who is senior in commission and who has not served previously as chief judge shall act as the chief judge.

(3)(A) Except as provided in subparagraph (C), the chief judge of the district appointed under paragraph (1) shall serve for a term of seven years and shall serve after expiration of such term until another judge is eligible under paragraph (1) to serve as chief judge of the district.

(B) Except as provided in subparagraph (C), a district judge acting as chief judge under subparagraph (A) or (B) of paragraph (2) shall serve until a judge has been appointed who meets the qualifications under paragraph (1).

(C) No district judge may serve or act as chief judge of the district after attaining the age of seventy years unless no other district judge is qualified to serve as chief judge of the district under paragraph (1) or is qualified to act as chief judge under paragraph (2).

(b) The chief judge shall have precedence and preside at any session which he attends.

Other district judges shall have precedence and preside according to the seniority of their commissions. Judges whose commissions bear the same date shall have precedence according to seniority in age.

(c) A judge who commission extends over more than one district shall be junior to all district judges except in the district in which he resided at the time he entered upon the duties of his office.

(d) If the chief judge desires to be relieved of his duties as chief judge while retaining his active status as district judge, he may so certify to the Chief Justice of the United States, and thereafter, the chief judge of the district shall be such other district judge who is qualified to serve or act as chief judge under subsection (a).

(e) If a chief judge is temporarily unable to perform his duties as such, they shall be performed by the district judge in active service, present in the district and able and qualified to act, who is next in precedence. As amended Oct. 31, 1951, c. 655, § 37, 65 Stat. 723; Aug. 6, 1958, Pub.L.

85–593, § 2, 72 Stat. 497; Apr. 2, 1982, Pub.L. 97–164, Title II, § 202, 96 Stat. 52.

§ 137. Division of business among district judges

The business of a court having more than one judge shall be divided among the judges as provided by the rules and orders of the court.

The chief judge of the district court shall be responsible for the observance of such rules and orders, and shall divide the business and assign the cases so far as such rules and orders do not otherwise prescribe.

If the district judges in any district are unable to agree upon the adoption of rules or orders for that purpose the judicial council of the circuit shall make the necessary orders.

§ 144. Bias or prejudice of judge

Whenever a party to any proceeding in a district court makes and files a timely and sufficient affidavit that the judge before whom the matter is pending has a personal bias or prejudice either against him or in favor of any adverse party, such judge shall proceed no further therein, but another judge shall be assigned to hear such proceeding.

The affidavit shall state the facts and the reasons for the belief that bias or prejudice exists, and shall be filed not less than ten days before the beginning of the term at which the proceeding is to be heard, or good cause shall be shown for failure to file it within such time. A party may file only one such affidavit in any case. It shall be accompanied by a certificate of counsel of record stating that it is made in good faith. As amended May 24, 1949, c. 139, § 65, 63 Stat. 99.

§ 331. Judicial Conference of the United States

The Chief Justice of the United States shall summon annually the chief judge of each judicial circuit, the chief judge of the Court of International Trade, and a district judge from each judicial circuit to a conference at such time and place in the United States as he may designate. He shall preside at such conference which shall be known as the Judicial Conference of the United States. Special sessions of the Conference may be called by the Chief Justice at such times and places as he may designate.

* * *

The Conference shall make a comprehensive survey of the condition of business in the courts of the United States and prepare plans for assignment of judges to or from circuits or districts where necessary. It shall also submit suggestions and recommendations to the various courts to promote uniformity of management procedures and the expeditious conduct of court business. The Conference is authorized to exercise the authority provided in chapter 16 of this title as the Conference, or through a standing committee. If the Conference elects to establish a standing committee, it shall be appointed by the Chief Justice and all petitions for review shall be reviewed by that committee. The Conference or the standing committee may hold hearings, take sworn testimony, issue subpoenas and subpoenas duces tecum, and make necessary and appropriate orders in the exercise of its authority.   Subpoenas and subpoenas duces tecum shall be issued by the clerk of the Supreme Court or by the clerk of any court of appeals, at the direction of the Chief Justice or his designee and under the seal of the court, and shall be served in the manner provided in rule 45(c) of the Federal Rules of Civil Procedure for subpoenas and subpoenas duces tecum issued on behalf of the United States or an officer or any agency thereof.   The Conference may also prescribe and modify rules for the exercise of the authority provided in chapter 16 of this title. All judicial officers and employees of the United States shall promptly carry into effect all orders of the Judicial Conference or the standing committee established pursuant to this section.

The Conference shall also carry on a continuous study of the operation and effect of the general rules of practice and procedure now or hereafter in use as prescribed by the Supreme Court for the other courts of the United States pursuant to law.   Such changes in and additions to those rules as the Conference may deem desirable to promote simplicity in procedure, fairness in administration, the just determination of litigation, and the elimination of unjustifiable expense and delay shall be recommended by the Conference from time to time to the Supreme Court for its consideration and adoption, modification or rejection, in accordance with law.

The Judicial Conference shall review rules prescribed under section 2071 of this title by the courts, other than the Supreme Court and the district courts, for consistency with Federal law.   The Judicial Conference may modify or abrogate any such rule so reviewed found inconsistent in the course of such a review.

* * *

The Chief Justice shall submit to Congress an annual report of the proceedings of the Judicial Conference and its recommendations for legislation.

* * *

As amended July 9, 1956, c. 517, § 1(d), 70 Stat. 497; Aug. 28, 1957, Pub.L. 85–202, 71 Stat. 476; July 11, 1958, Pub.L. 85–513, 72 Stat. 356; Sept. 19, 1961, Pub.L. 87–253, §§ 1, 2, 75 Stat. 521; Oct. 15, 1980, Pub.L. 96–458, § 4, 94 Stat. 2040; Apr. 2, 1982, Pub.L. 97–164, Title I, § 111, 96 Stat. 29; Oct. 14, 1986, Pub.L. 99–466, § 1, 100 Stat. 1190; Nov. 19, 1988, Pub.L. 100–702, Title IV, § 402(b), 102 Stat. 4650; Oct. 19, 1996, Pub.L. 104–317, Title VI, § 601(a), 110 Stat. 3857; Nov. 2, 2002, Pub.L. 107–273, Div. C, Title I, § 11043(b), 116 Stat. 1855; Jan. 7, 2008, Pub.L. 110–177, Title I, § 101(b), 121 Stat. 2534.

§ 332.   Judicial councils of circuits

(a)(1) The chief judge of each judicial circuit shall call, at least twice in each year and at such places as he or she may designate, a meeting of the judicial council of the circuit, consisting of the chief judge of the circuit, who shall preside, and an equal number of circuit judges and district judges of the circuit, as such number is determined by majority vote of all such judges of the circuit in regular active service.

(2) Members of the council shall serve for terms established by a majority vote of all judges of the circuit in regular active service.

* * *

(d)(1) Each judicial council shall make all necessary and appropriate orders for the effective and expeditious administration of justice within its circuit. Any general order relating to practice and procedure shall be made or amended only after giving appropriate public notice and an opportunity for comment. Any such order so relating shall take effect upon the date specified by such judicial council. Copies of such orders so relating shall be furnished to the Judicial Conference and the Administrative Office of the United States Courts and be made available to the public. Each council is authorized to hold hearings, to take sworn testimony, and to issue subpoenas and subpoenas duces tecum. Subpoenas and subpoenas duces tecum shall be issued by the clerk of the court of appeals, at the direction of the chief judge of the circuit or his designee and under the seal of the court, and shall be served in the manner provided in rule 45(c) of the Federal Rules of Civil Procedure for subpoenas and subpoenas duces tecum issued on behalf of the United States or an officer or agency thereof.

(2) All judicial officers and employees of the circuit shall promptly carry into effect all orders of the judicial council. In the case of failure to comply with an order made under this subsection or a subpoena issued under chapter 16 of this title, a judicial council or a special committee appointed under section 353 of this title may institute a contempt proceeding in any district court in which the judicial officer or employee of the circuit who fails to comply with the order made under this subsection shall be ordered to show cause before the court why he or she should not be held in contempt of court.

(3) Unless an impediment to the administration of justice is involved, regular business of the courts need not be referred to the council.

(4) Each judicial council shall periodically review the rules which are prescribed under section 2071 of this title by district courts within its circuit for consistency with rules prescribed under section 2072 of this title. Each council may modify or abrogate any such rule found inconsistent in the course of such a review.

* * *

As amended Nov. 13, 1963, Pub.L. 88–176, § 3, 77 Stat. 331; Jan. 5, 1971, Pub.L. 91–647, 84 Stat. 1907; Oct. 15, 1980, Pub.L. 96–458, § 2(a)–(d)(1), 94 Stat. 2035; Oct. 1, 1988, Pub.L. 100–459, Title IV, § 407, 102 Stat. 2213; Nov. 19, 1988, Pub.L. 100–702, Title IV, § 403(a)(2), (b), Title X, §§ 1018, 1020(a)(1), 102 Stat. 4651, 4670, 4671; Dec. 1, 1990, Pub.L. 101–650, Title III, §§ 323, 325(b)(1), Title IV, § 403, 104 Stat. 5120, 5121, 5124; Dec. 9, 1991, Pub.L. 102–198, § 1, 105 Stat. 1623; Oct. 19, 1996, Pub.L. 104–317, Title II, § 208, 110 Stat. 3851; Nov. 13, 2000, Pub.L. 106–518, Title II, § 205, Title III, § 306, 114 Stat. 2414, 2418; Dec. 21, 2000, Pub.L. 106–553, § 1(a)(2)[306], 114 Stat. 2762A–202; Nov. 2, 2002, Pub.L. 107–273, Div. C, Title I, § 11043(c), 116 Stat. 1855.

§ 333. Judicial conferences of circuits

The chief judge of each circuit may summon biennially, and may summon annually, the circuit, district, magistrate, and bankruptcy judges of the circuit, in active service, to a conference at a time and place that he designates, for the purpose of considering the business of the courts and advising means of improving the administration of justice within such circuit. He may preside at such conference, which shall be known as the Judicial Conference of the circuit. The judges of the District Court of Guam, the District Court of the Virgin Islands, and the District Court of the Northern Mariana Islands may also be summoned biennially, and may be summoned annually, to the conferences of their respective circuits.

Every judge summoned may attend.

The court of appeals for each circuit shall provide by its rules for representation and active participation at such conference by members of the bar of such circuit. As amended Dec. 29, 1950, c. 1185, 64 Stat. 1128; Oct. 31, 1951, c. 655, § 38, 65 Stat. 723; July 7, 1958, Pub.L. 85–508, § 12(e), 72 Stat. 348; Nov. 6, 1978, Pub.L. 95–598, Title II, § 210, 92 Stat. 2661; Dec. 1, 1990, Pub.L. 101–650, Title III, § 320, 104 Stat. 5117; Apr. 26, 1996, Pub.L. 104–134, Title I, § 305, 110 Stat. 1321–36; Oct. 13, 2008, Pub.L. 110–406, § 9, 122 Stat. 4293.

§ 451. Definitions

As used in this title:

The term "court of the United States" includes the Supreme Court of the United States, courts of appeals, district courts constituted by chapter 5 of this title [§§ 81–144], including the Court of International Trade and any court created by Act of Congress the judges of which are entitled to hold office during good behavior.

The terms "district court" and "district court of the United States" mean the courts constituted by chapter 5 of this title.

The term "judge of the United States" includes judges of the courts of appeals, district courts, Court of International Trade and any court created by Act of Congress, the judges of which are entitled to hold office during good behavior.

The term "justice of the United States" includes the Chief Justice of the United States and the associate justices of the Supreme Court.

The term "district" and "judicial district" mean the districts enumerated in Chapter 5 of this title.

The term "department" means one of the executive departments enumerated in section 1 of Title 5, unless the context shows that such term was intended to describe the executive, legislative, or judicial branches of the government.

The term "agency" includes any department, independent establishment, commission, administration, authority, board or bureau of the United States or any corporation in which the United States has a proprietary interest, unless the context shows that such term was intended to be used in a more limited sense. As amended Mar. 18, 1959, Pub.L. 86–3, § 10, 73

Stat. 9; Sept. 12, 1966, Pub.L. 89–571, § 3, 80 Stat. 764; Nov. 6, 1978, Pub.L. 95–598, Title II, § 213, 92 Stat. 2661; Oct. 10, 1980, Pub.L. 96–417, Title V, § 501(10), 94 Stat. 1742; Apr. 2, 1982, Pub.L. 97–164, Title I, § 114, 96 Stat. 29.

§ 454. Practice of law by justices and judges

Any justice or judge appointed under the authority of the United States who engages in the practice of law is guilty of a high misdemeanor.

§ 455. Disqualification of justice, judge, or magistrate

(a) Any justice, judge, or magistrate of the United States shall disqualify himself in any proceeding in which his impartiality might reasonably be questioned.

(b) He shall also disqualify himself in the following circumstances:

(1) Where he has a personal bias or prejudice concerning a party, or personal knowledge of disputed evidentiary facts concerning the proceeding;

(2) Where in private practice he served as lawyer in the matter in controversy, or a lawyer with whom he previously practiced law served during such association as a lawyer concerning the matter, or the judge or such lawyer has been a material witness concerning it;

(3) Where he has served in governmental employment and in such capacity participated as counsel, adviser or material witness concerning the proceeding or expressed an opinion concerning the merits of the particular case in controversy;

(4) He knows that he, individually or as a fiduciary, or his spouse or minor child residing in his household, has a financial interest in the subject matter in controversy or in a party to the proceeding, or any other interest that could be substantially affected by the outcome of the proceeding;

(5) He or his spouse, or a person within the third degree of relationship to either of them, or the spouse of such a person:

(i) Is a party to the proceeding, or an officer, director, or trustee of a party;

(ii) Is acting as a lawyer in the proceeding;

(iii) Is known by the judge to have an interest that could be substantially affected by the outcome of the proceeding;

(iv) Is to the judge's knowledge likely to be a material witness in the proceeding.

(c) A judge should inform himself about his personal and fiduciary financial interests, and make a reasonable effort to inform himself about the personal financial interests of his spouse and minor children residing in his household.

(d) For the purposes of this section the following words or phrases shall have the meaning indicated:

(1) "proceeding" includes pretrial, trial, appellate review, or other stages of litigation;

(2) the degree of relationship is calculated according to the civil law system;

(3) "fiduciary" includes such relationships as executor, administrator, trustee, and guardian;

(4) "financial interest" means ownership of a legal or equitable interest, however small, or a relationship as director, adviser, or other active participant in the affairs of a party, except that:

    (i) Ownership in a mutual or common investment fund that holds securities is not a "financial interest" in such securities unless the judge participates in the management of the fund;

    (ii) An office in an educational, religious, charitable, fraternal, or civic organization is not a "financial interest" in securities held by the organization;

    (iii) The proprietary interest of a policyholder in a mutual insurance company, of a depositor in a mutual savings association, or a similar proprietary interest, is a "financial interest" in the organization only if the outcome of the proceeding could substantially affect the value of the interest;

    (iv) Ownership of government securities is a "financial interest" in the issuer only if the outcome of the proceeding could substantially affect the value of the securities.

(e) No justice, judge, or magistrate shall accept from the parties to the proceeding a waiver of any ground for disqualification enumerated in subsection (b). Where the ground for disqualification arises only under subsection (a), waiver may be accepted provided it is preceded by a full disclosure on the record of the basis for disqualification.

(f) Notwithstanding the preceding provisions of this section, if any justice, judge, magistrate, or bankruptcy judge to whom a matter has been assigned would be disqualified, after substantial judicial time has been devoted to the matter, because of the appearance or discovery, after the matter was assigned to him or her, that he or she individually or as a fiduciary, or his or her spouse or minor child residing in his or her household, has a financial interest in a party (other than an interest that could be substantially affected by the outcome), disqualification is not required if the justice, judge, magistrate, bankruptcy judge, spouse or minor child, as the case may be, divests himself or herself of the interest that provides the grounds for the disqualification. As amended Dec. 5, 1974, Pub.L. 93–512, § 1, 88 Stat. 1609; Nov. 6, 1978, Pub.L. 95–598, Title II, § 214(a), (b), 92 Stat. 2661; Nov. 19, 1988, Pub.L. 100–702, Title X, § 1007, 102 Stat. 4667.

§ 631. Appointment and tenure

(a) The judges of each United States district court and the district courts of the Virgin Islands, Guam, and the Northern Mariana Islands (including any judge in regular active service and any judge who has retired from regular active service under section 371(b) of this title, when designated and assigned to the court to which such judge was appointed) shall appoint United States magistrate judges in such numbers and to serve at such locations within the judicial districts as the Judicial Conference may determine under this chapter. In the case of a magistrate judge appointed by the district court of the Virgin Islands, Guam, or the Northern Mariana Islands, this chapter shall apply as though the court appointing such a magistrate judge were a United States district court. Where there is more than one judge of a district court, the appointment, whether an original appointment or a reappointment, shall be by the concurrence of a majority of all the judges of such district court, and when there is no such concurrence, then by the chief judge. Where the conference deems it desirable, a magistrate judge may be designated to serve in one or more districts adjoining the district for which he is appointed. Such a designation shall be made by the concurrence of a majority of the judges of each of the district courts involved and shall specify the duties to be performed by the magistrate judge in the adjoining district or districts.

(b) No individual may be appointed or reappointed to serve as a magistrate judge under this chapter unless:

(1) He has been for at least five years a member in good standing of the bar of the highest court of a State, the District of Columbia, the Commonwealth of Puerto Rico, the Territory of Guam, the Commonwealth of the Northern Mariana Islands, or the Virgin Islands of the United States, except that an individual who does not meet the bar membership requirements of this paragraph may be appointed and serve as a part-time magistrate judge if the appointing court or courts and the conference find that no qualified individual who is a member of the bar is available to serve at a specific location;

(2) He is determined by the appointing district court or courts to be competent to perform the duties of the office;

(3) In the case of an individual appointed to serve in a national park, he resides within the exterior boundaries of that park, or at some place reasonably adjacent thereto;

(4) He is not related by blood or marriage to a judge of the appointing court or courts at the time of his initial appointment; and

(5) He is selected pursuant to standards and procedures promulgated by the Judicial Conference of the United States. Such standards and procedures shall contain provision for public notice of all vacancies in magistrate judge positions and for the establishment by the district courts of merit selection panels, composed of residents of the individual judicial districts, to assist the courts in identifying and recommending persons who are best qualified to fill such positions.

(c) A magistrate judge may hold no other civil or military office or employment under the United States: *Provided, however,* That, with the approval of the conference, a part-time referee in bankruptcy or a clerk or deputy clerk of a court of the United States may be appointed and serve as a part-time United States magistrate judge, but the conference shall fix the aggregate amount of compensation to be received for performing the duties of part-time magistrate judge and part-time referee in bankruptcy, clerk or deputy clerk: *And provided further*, That retired officers and retired enlisted personnel of the Regular and Reserve components of the Army, Navy, Air Force, Marine Corps, and Coast Guard, members of the Reserve components of the Army, Navy, Air Force, Marine Corps, and Coast Guard, and members of the Army National Guard of the United States, the Air National Guard of the United States, and the Naval Militia and of the National Guard of a State, territory, or the District of Columbia, except the National Guard disbursing officers who are on a full-time salary basis, may be appointed and serve as United States magistrate judges.

(d) Except as otherwise provided in sections 375 and 636(h) of this title, no individual may serve under this chapter after having attained the age of seventy years: *Provided, however*, That upon a majority vote of all the judges of the appointing court or courts, which is taken upon the magistrate judge's attaining age seventy and upon each subsequent anniversary thereof, a magistrate judge who has attained the age of seventy years may continue to serve and may be reappointed under this chapter.

(e) The appointment of any individual as a full-time magistrate judge shall be for a term of eight years, and the appointment of any individuals as a part-time magistrate judge shall be for a term of four years, except that the term of a full-time or part-time magistrate judge appointed under subsection (k) shall expire upon—

(1) the expiration of the absent magistrate judge's term,

(2) the reinstatement of the absent magistrate judge in regular service in office as a magistrate judge,

(3) the failure of the absent magistrate judge to make timely application under subsection (j) of this section for reinstatement in regular service in office as a magistrate judge after discharge or release from military service,

(4) the death or resignation of the absent magistrate judge, or

(5) the removal from office of the absent magistrate judge pursuant to subsection (i) of this section, whichever may first occur.

(f) Upon the expiration of his term, a magistrate judge may, by a majority vote of the judges of the appointing district court or courts and with the approval of the judicial council of the circuit, continue to perform the duties of his office until his successor is appointed, or for 180 days after the date of the expiration of the magistrate judge's term, whichever is earlier.

(g) Each individual appointed as a magistrate judge under this section shall take the oath or affirmation prescribed by section 453 of this title before performing the duties of his office.

(h) Each appointment made by a judge or judges of a district court shall be entered of record in such court, and notice of such appointment shall be given at once by the clerk of that court to the Director.

(i) Removal of a magistrate judge during the term for which he is appointed shall be only for incompetency, misconduct, neglect of duty, or physical or mental disability, but a magistrate judge's office shall be terminated if the conference determines that the services performed by his office are no longer needed. Removal shall be by the judges of the district court for the judicial district in which the magistrate judge serves; where there is more than one judge of a district court, removal shall not occur unless a majority of all the judges of such court concur in the order of removal; and when there is a tie vote of the judges of the district court on the question of the removal or retention in office of a magistrate judge, then removal shall be only by a concurrence of a majority of all the judges of the council. In the case of a magistrate judge appointed under the third sentence of subsection (a) of this section, removal shall not occur unless a majority of all the judges of the appointing district courts concur in the order of removal; and where there is a tie vote on the question of the removal or retention in office of a magistrate judge, then removal shall be only by a concurrence of a majority of all the judges of the council or councils. Before any order or removal shall be entered, a full specification of the charges shall be furnished to the magistrate judge, and he shall be accorded by the judge or judges of the removing court, courts, council, or councils an opportunity to be heard on the charges.

(j) Upon the grant by the appropriate district court or courts of a leave of absence to a magistrate judge entitled to such relief under chapter 43 of title 38, such court or courts may proceed to appoint, in the manner specified in subsection (a) of this section, another magistrate judge, qualified for appointment and service under subsections (b), (c), and (d) of this section, who shall serve for the period specified in subsection (e) of this section.

(k) A United States magistrate judge appointed under this chapter shall be exempt from the provisions of subchapter I of chapter 63 of title 5. As amended May 24, 1949, c. 139, § 73, 63 Stat. 100; July 9, 1952, c. 609, § 1, 66 Stat. 509; July 25, 1956, c. 722, 70 Stat. 642; Oct. 17, 1968, Pub.L. 90–578, Title I, § 101, 82 Stat. 1108; Oct. 17, 1976, Pub.L. 94–520, § 2, 90 Stat. 2458; Nov. 6, 1978, Pub.L. 95–598, Title II, § 231, 92 Stat. 2665; Oct. 10, 1979, Pub.L. 96–82, § 3(a)-(d), 93 Stat. 644; Aug. 6, 1982, Pub.L. 97–230, 96 Stat. 255; Nov. 14, 1986, Pub.L. 99–651, Title II, § 201(a)(1), 100 Stat. 3646; Nov. 15, 1988, Pub.L. 100–659, § 5, 102 Stat. 3918; Nov. 19, 1988, Pub.L. 100–702, Title X, § 1003(a)(2), 102 Stat. 4665; June 30, 1989, Pub.L. 101–45, Title II, § 104, 103 Stat. 122; Dec. 1, 1990, Pub.L. 101–650, Title III, §§ 308(b), 321, 104 Stat. 5112, 5117; Oct. 13, 1994, Pub.L. 103–353, § 2(c), 108 Stat. 3169; Nov. 13, 2000, Pub.L. 106–518, Title II, § 201, 114 Stat. 2412; Jan. 7, 2008, Pub.L. 110–177, Title V, § 504, 121 Stat. 2542.

§ 632. Character of service

(a) Full-time United States magistrate judges may not engage in the practice of law, and may not engage in any other business, occupation, or employment inconsistent with the expeditious, proper, and impartial performance of their duties as judicial officers.

(b) Part-time United States magistrate judges shall render such service as judicial officers as is required by law. While so serving they may engage in the practice of law, but may not serve as counsel in any criminal action in any court of the United States, nor act in any capacity that is, under such regulations as the conference may establish, inconsistent with the proper discharge of their office. Within such restrictions, they may engage in any other business, occupation, or employment which is not inconsistent with the expeditious, proper, and impartial performance of their duties as judicial officers. As amended Oct. 17, 1968, Pub.L. 90–578, Title I, § 101, 82 Stat. 1110; Dec. 1, 1990, Pub.L. 101–650, Title III, § 321, 104 Stat. 5117.

§ 636. Jurisdiction, powers, and temporary assignment

(a) Each United States magistrate serving under this chapter shall have within the district in which sessions are held by the court that appointed the magistrate judge, at other places where that court may function, and elsewhere as authorized by law—

(1) all powers and duties conferred or imposed upon United States commissioners by law or by the Rules of Criminal Procedure for the United States District Courts;

(2) the power to administer oaths and affirmations, issue orders pursuant to section 3142 of title 18 concerning release or detention of persons pending trial, and take acknowledgments, affidavits, and depositions;

(3) the power to conduct trials under section 3401, title 18, United States Code, in conformity with and subject to the limitations of that section;

(4) the power to enter a sentence for a petty offense; and

(5) the power to enter a sentence for a class A misdemeanor in a case in which the parties have consented.

(b)(1) Notwithstanding any provision of law to the contrary—

(A) a judge may designate a magistrate to hear and determine any pretrial matter pending before the court, except a motion for injunctive relief, for judgment on the pleadings, for summary judgment, to dismiss or quash an indictment or information made by the defendant, to suppress evidence in a criminal case, to dismiss or to permit maintenance of a class action, to dismiss for failure to state a claim upon which relief can be granted, and to involuntarily dismiss an action. A judge of the court may reconsider any pretrial matter under this subparagraph (A) where it has been shown that the magistrate's order is clearly erroneous or contrary to law.

(B) a judge may also designate a magistrate to conduct hearings, including evidentiary hearings, and to submit to a judge of the court proposed findings of fact and recommendations for the disposition, by a judge of the court, of any motion excepted in subparagraph (A), of applications for posttrial relief made by individuals convicted of criminal offenses and of prisoner petitions challenging conditions of confinement.

(C) the magistrate shall file his proposed findings and recommendations under subparagraph (B) with the court and a copy shall forthwith be mailed to all parties.

Within fourteen days after being served with a copy, any party may serve and file written objections to such proposed findings and recommendations as provided by rules of court. A judge of the court shall make a de novo determination of those portions of the report or specified proposed findings or recommendations to which objection is made. A judge of the court may accept, reject, or modify, in whole or in part, the findings or recommendations made by the magistrate. The judge may also receive further evidence or recommit the matter to the magistrate with instructions.

(2) A judge may designate a magistrate to serve as a special master pursuant to the applicable provisions of this title and the Federal Rules of Civil Procedure for the United States district courts. A judge may designate a magistrate to serve as a special master in any civil case, upon consent of the parties, without regard to the provisions of rule 53(b) of the Federal Rules of Civil Procedure for the United States district courts.

(3) A magistrate may be assigned such additional duties as are not inconsistent with the Constitution and laws of the United States.

(4) Each district court shall establish rules pursuant to which the magistrates shall discharge their duties.

(c) Notwithstanding any provision of law to the contrary—

(1) Upon the consent of the parties, a full-time United States magistrate or a part-time United States magistrate who serves as a full-time judicial officer may conduct any or all proceedings in a jury or nonjury civil matter and order the entry of judgment in the case, when specially designated to exercise such jurisdiction by the district court or courts he serves. Upon the consent of the parties, pursuant to their specific written request, any other part-time magistrate may exercise such jurisdiction, if such magistrate meets the bar membership requirements set forth in section 631(b)(1) and the chief judge of the district court certifies that a full-time magistrate is not reasonably available in accordance with guidelines established by the judicial council of the circuit. When there is more than one judge of a district court, designation under this paragraph shall be by the concurrence of a majority of all the judges of such district court, and when there is no such concurrence, then by the chief judge.

(2) If a magistrate is designated to exercise civil jurisdiction under paragraph (1) of this subsection, the clerk of court shall, at the time the action is filed, notify the parties of the availability of a magistrate to exercise such jurisdiction. The decision of the parties shall be communicated to the clerk of court. Thereafter, either the district court judge or the magistrate may again advise the parties of the availability of the magistrate, but in so doing, shall also advise the parties that they are free to withhold consent without adverse substantive consequences. Rules of court for the reference of civil matters to magistrates shall include procedures to protect the voluntariness of the parties' consent.

(3) Upon entry of judgment in any case referred under paragraph (1) of this subsection, an aggrieved party may appeal directly to the appropriate United States court of appeals from the judgment of the

magistrate in the same manner as an appeal from any other judgment of a district court. The consent of the parties allows a magistrate designated to exercise civil jurisdiction under paragraph (1) of this subsection to direct the entry of a judgment of the district court in accordance with the Federal Rules of Civil Procedure. Nothing in this paragraph shall be construed as a limitation of any party's right to seek review by the Supreme Court of the United States.

(4) The court may, for good cause shown on its own motion, or under extraordinary circumstances shown by any party, vacate a reference of a civil matter to a magistrate under this subsection.

(5) The magistrate shall, subject to guidelines of the Judicial Conference, determine whether the record taken pursuant to this section shall be taken by electronic sound recording, by a court reporter, or by other means.

(d) The practice and procedure for the trial of cases before officers serving under this chapter shall conform to rules promulgated by the Supreme Court pursuant to section 2072 of this title.

(e) Contempt Authority.—

(1) In general.—A United States magistrate judge serving under this chapter shall have within the territorial jurisdiction prescribed by the appointment of such magistrate judge the power to exercise contempt authority as set forth in this subsection.

(2) Summary criminal contempt authority.—A magistrate judge shall have the power to punish summarily by fine or imprisonment, or both, such contempt of the authority of such magistrate judge constituting misbehavior of any person in the magistrate judge's presence so as to obstruct the administration of justice. The order of contempt shall be issued under the Federal Rules of Criminal Procedure.

(3) Additional criminal contempt authority in civil consent and misdemeanor cases.—In any case in which a United States magistrate judge presides with the consent of the parties under subsection (c) of this section, and in any misdemeanor case proceeding before a magistrate judge under section 3401 of title 18, the magistrate judge shall have the power to punish, by fine or imprisonment, or both, criminal contempt constituting disobedience or resistance to the magistrate judge's lawful writ, process, order, rule, decree, or command. Disposition of such contempt shall be conducted upon notice and hearing under the Federal Rules of Criminal Procedure.

(4) Civil contempt authority in civil consent and misdemeanor cases.—In any case in which a United States magistrate judge presides with the consent of the parties under subsection (c) of this section, and in any misdemeanor case proceeding before a magistrate judge under section 3401 of title 18, the magistrate judge may exercise the civil contempt authority of the district court. This paragraph shall not be construed to limit the authority of a magistrate judge to order sanctions under any other statute, the Federal Rules of Civil Procedure, or the Federal Rules of Criminal Procedure.

(5) Criminal contempt penalties.—The sentence imposed by a magistrate judge for any criminal contempt provided for in paragraphs (2) and (3) shall not exceed the penalties for a Class C misdemeanor as set forth in sections 3581(b)(8) and 3571(b)(6) of title 18.

(6) Certification of other contempts to the district court.—Upon the commission of any such act—

(A) in any case in which a United States magistrate judge presides with the consent of the parties under subsection (c) of this section, or in any misdemeanor case proceeding before a magistrate judge under section 3401 of title 18, that may, in the opinion of the magistrate judge, constitute a serious criminal contempt punishable by penalties exceeding those set forth in paragraph (5) of this subsection, or

(B) in any other case or proceeding under subsection (a) or (b) of this section, or any other statute, where—

(i) the act committed in the magistrate judge's presence may, in the opinion of the magistrate judge, constitute a serious criminal contempt punishable by penalties exceeding those set forth in paragraph (5) of this subsection,

(ii) the act that constitutes a criminal contempt occurs outside the presence of the magistrate judge, or

(iii) the act constitutes a civil contempt,

the magistrate judge shall forthwith certify the facts to a district judge and may serve or cause to be served, upon any person whose behavior is brought into question under this paragraph, an order requiring such person to appear before a district judge upon a day certain to show cause why that person should not be adjudged in contempt by reason of the facts so certified. The district judge shall thereupon hear the evidence as to the act or conduct complained of and, if it is such as to warrant punishment, punish such person in the same manner and to the same extent as for a contempt committed before a district judge.

(7) Appeals of magistrate judge contempt orders.—The appeal of an order of contempt under this subsection shall be made to the court of appeals in cases proceeding under subsection (c) of this section. The appeal of any other order of contempt issued under this section shall be made to the district court.

* * *

As amended Oct. 17, 1968, Pub.L. 90–578, Title I, § 101, 82 Stat. 1113; Mar. 1, 1972, Pub.L. 92–239, § 2, 86 Stat. 47; Oct. 21, 1976, Pub.L. 94–577, § 1, 90 Stat. 2729; Oct. 28, 1977, Pub.L. 95–144, § 2, 91 Stat. 1220; Oct. 10, 1979, Pub.L. 96–82, § 2, 93 Stat. 643; Oct. 12, 1984, Pub.L. 98–473, Title II, § 208, 98 Stat. 1986; Nov. 8, 1984, Pub.L. 98–620, Title IV, § 402(29)(B), 98 Stat. 3359; Nov. 14, 1986, Pub.L. 99–651, Title II, § 201(a)(2), 100 Stat. 3647; Nov. 15, 1988, Pub.L. 100–659, § 4(c), 102 Stat. 3918; Nov. 18, 1988, Pub.L. 100–690, Title VII, § 7322, 102 Stat. 4467; Nov. 19, 1988, Pub.L. 100–702, Title IV, § 404(b)(1), Title X, § 1014, 102 Stat. 4651, 4669; Dec. 1, 1990, Pub.L. 101–650, Title III, § 308(a), 104

Stat. 5112; Oct. 19, 1996, Pub.L. 104–317, Title II, §§ 201, 202(b), 207, 110 Stat. 3848, 3849, 3850; Nov. 13, 2000, Pub.L. 106–518, Title II, §§ 202, 203(b), 114 Stat. 2412, 2414; Nov. 2, 2002, Pub.L. 107–273, Div. B, Title III, § 3002(b), 116 Stat. 1805; Sept. 9, 2005, Pub.L. 109–63, § 2(d), 119 Stat. 1995; May 7, 2009, Pub.L. 111–16, § 6(1), 123 Stat. 1608, 1609.

§ 651. Authorization of alternative dispute resolution

(a) Definition.—For purposes of this chapter, an alternative dispute resolution process includes any process or procedure, other than an adjudication by a presiding judge, in which a neutral third party participates to assist in the resolution of issues in controversy, through processes such as early neutral evaluation, mediation, minitrial, and arbitration as provided in sections 654 through 658.

(b) Authority.—Each United States district court shall authorize, by local rule adopted under section 2071(a), the use of alternative dispute resolution processes in all civil actions, including adversary proceedings in bankruptcy, in accordance with this chapter, except that the use of arbitration may be authorized only as provided in section 654. Each United States district court shall devise and implement its own alternative dispute resolution program, by local rule adopted under section 2071(a), to encourage and promote the use of alternative dispute resolution in its district.

(c) Existing alternative dispute resolution programs.—In those courts where an alternative dispute resolution program is in place on the date of the enactment of the Alternative Dispute Resolution Act of 1998, the court shall examine the effectiveness of that program and adopt such improvements to the program as are consistent with the provisions and purposes of this chapter [§§ 651–658].

(d) Administration of alternative dispute resolution programs.—Each United States district court shall designate an employee, or a judicial officer, who is knowledgeable in alternative dispute resolution practices and processes to implement, administer, oversee, and evaluate the court's alternative dispute resolution program. Such person may also be responsible for recruiting, screening, and training attorneys to serve as neutrals and arbitrators in the court's alternative dispute resolution program.

(e) Title 9 not affected.—This chapter shall not affect title 9, United States Code.

(f) Program support.—The Federal Judicial Center and the Administrative Office of the United States Courts are authorized to assist the district courts in the establishment and improvement of alternative dispute resolution programs by identifying particular practices employed in successful programs and providing additional assistance as needed and appropriate. Added Nov. 19, 1988, Pub.L. 100–702, Title IX, § 901(a), 102 Stat. 4659; as amended Oct. 30, 1998, Pub.L. 105–315, § 3, 112 Stat. 2993.

§ 652. Jurisdiction

(a) Consideration of alternative dispute resolution in appropriate cases.—Notwithstanding any provision of law to the contrary and except as provided in subsections (b) and (c), each district court shall, by local rule adopted under section 2071(a), require that litigants in all civil cases consider the use of an alternative dispute resolution process at an appropriate stage in the litigation. Each district court shall provide litigants in all civil cases with at least one alternative dispute resolution process, including, but not limited to, mediation, early neutral evaluation, minitrial, and arbitration as authorized in sections 654 through 658. Any district court that elects to require the use of alternative dispute resolution in certain cases may do so only with respect to mediation, early neutral evaluation, and, if the parties consent, arbitration.

(b) Actions exempted from consideration of alternative dispute resolution.—Each district court may exempt from the requirements of this section specific cases or categories of cases in which use of alternative dispute resolution would not be appropriate. In defining these exemptions, each district court shall consult with members of the bar, including the United States Attorney for that district.

(c) Authority of the Attorney General.—Nothing in this section shall alter or conflict with the authority of the Attorney General to conduct litigation on behalf of the United States, with the authority of any Federal agency authorized to conduct litigation in the United States courts, or with any delegation of litigation authority by the Attorney General.

(d) Confidentiality provisions.—Until such time as rules are adopted under chapter 131 of this title [§§ 2071–2077] providing for the confidentiality of alternative dispute resolution processes under this chapter, each district court shall, by local rule adopted under section 2071(a), provide for the confidentiality of the alternative dispute resolution processes and to prohibit disclosure of confidential dispute resolution communications. Added Nov. 19, 1988, Pub.L. 100–702, Title IX, § 901(a), 102 Stat. 4659; as amended Oct. 30, 1998, Pub.L. 105–315, § 4, 112 Stat. 2994.

§ 653. Neutrals

(a) Panel of neutrals.—Each district court that authorizes the use of alternative dispute resolution processes shall adopt appropriate processes for making neutrals available for use by the parties for each category of process offered. Each district court shall promulgate its own procedures and criteria for the selection of neutrals on its panels.

(b) Qualifications and training.—Each person serving as a neutral in an alternative dispute resolution process should be qualified and trained to serve as a neutral in the appropriate alternative dispute resolution process. For this purpose, the district court may use, among others, magistrate judges who have been trained to serve as neutrals in alternative dispute resolution processes, professional neutrals from the private sector, and persons who have been trained to serve as neutrals in alternative dispute resolution processes. Until such time as rules are adopted under chapter 131 of this title relating to the disqualification of neutrals, each district court shall issue rules under section 2071(a) relating to the disqualification of neutrals (including, where appropriate, disqualification under section 455 of this title, other applicable law, and professional responsibility standards). Added Nov. 19, 1988, Pub.L. 100–702, Title IX, § 901(a), 102 Stat. 4660; as amended Oct. 30, 1998, Pub.L. 105–315, § 5, 112 Stat. 2995.

§ 654. Arbitration

(a) Referral of actions to arbitration.—Notwithstanding any provision of law to the contrary and except as provided in subsections (a), (b), and (c) of section 652 and subsection (d) of this section, a district court may allow the referral to arbitration of any civil action (including any adversary proceeding in bankruptcy) pending before it when the parties consent, except that referral to arbitration may not be made where—

(1) the action is based on an alleged violation of a right secured by the Constitution of the United States;

(2) jurisdiction is based in whole or in part on section 1343 of this title; or

(3) the relief sought consists of money damages in an amount greater than $150,000.

(b) Safeguards in consent cases.—Until such time as rules are adopted under chapter 131 of this title relating to procedures described in this subsection, the district court shall, by local rule adopted under section 2071(a), establish procedures to ensure that any civil action in which arbitration by consent is allowed under subsection (a)—

(1) consent to arbitration is freely and knowingly obtained; and

(2) no party or attorney is prejudiced for refusing to participate in arbitration.

(c) Presumptions.—For purposes of subsection (a)(3), a district court may presume damages are not in excess of $150,000 unless counsel certifies that damages exceed such amount.

(d) Existing programs.—Nothing in this chapter is deemed to affect any program in which arbitration is conducted pursuant to section title IX of the Judicial Improvements and Access to Justice Act (Public Law 100–702), as amended by section 1 of Public Law 105–53. Added Nov. 19, 1988, Pub.L. 100–702, Title IX, § 901(a), 102 Stat. 4660; as amended Oct. 30, 1998, Pub.L. 105–315, § 6, 112 Stat. 2995.

§ 655. Arbitrators

(a) Powers of arbitrators.—An arbitrator to whom an action is referred under section 654 shall have the power, within the judicial district of the district court which referred the action to arbitration—

(1) to conduct arbitration hearings;

(2) to administer oaths and affirmations; and

(3) to make awards.

(b) Standards for certification.—Each district court that authorizes arbitration shall establish standards for the certification of arbitrators and shall certify arbitrators to perform services in accordance with such standards and this chapter. The standards shall include provisions requiring that any arbitrator—

(1) shall take the oath or affirmation described in section 453; and

(2) shall be subject to the disqualification rules under section 455.

(c) Immunity.—All individuals serving as arbitrators in an alternative dispute resolution program under this chapter are performing quasi-judicial functions and are entitled to the immunities and protections that the law accords to persons serving in such capacity. Added Nov. 19, 1988, Pub.L. 100–702, Title IX, § 901(a), 102 Stat. 4661; as amended Oct. 30, 1998, Pub.L. 105–315, § 7, 112 Stat. 2996.

§ 656. Subpoenas

Rule 45 of the Federal Rules of Civil Procedure (relating to subpoenas) applies to subpoenas for the attendance of witnesses and the production of documentary evidence at an arbitration hearing under this chapter. Added Nov. 19, 1988, Pub.L. 100–702, Title IX, § 901(a), 102 Stat. 4662; as amended Oct. 30, 1998, Pub.L. 105–315, § 8, 112 Stat. 2996.

§ 657. Arbitration award and judgment

(a) Filing and effect of arbitration award.—An arbitration award made by an arbitrator under this chapter, along with proof of service of such award on the other party by the prevailing party or by the plaintiff, shall be filed promptly after the arbitration hearing is concluded with the clerk of the district court that referred the case to arbitration. Such award shall be entered as the judgment of the court after the time has expired for requesting a trial de novo. The judgment so entered shall be subject to the same provisions of law and shall have the same force and effect as a judgment of the court in a civil action, except that the judgment shall not be subject to review in any other court by appeal or otherwise.

(b) Sealing of arbitration award.—The district court shall provide, by local rule adopted under section 2071(a), that the contents of any arbitration award made under this chapter shall not be made known to any judge who might be assigned to the case until the district court has entered final judgment in the action or the action has otherwise terminated.

(c) Trial de novo of arbitration awards.—

(1) Time for filing demand.—Within 30 days after the filing of an arbitration award with a district court under subsection (a), any party may file a written demand for a trial de novo in the district court.

(2) Action restored to court docket.—Upon a demand for a trial de novo, the action shall be restored to the docket of the court and treated for all purposes as if it had not been referred to arbitration.

(3) Exclusion of evidence of arbitration.—The court shall not admit at the trial de novo any evidence that there has been an arbitration proceeding, the nature or amount of any award, or any other matter concerning the conduct of the arbitration proceeding, unless—

(A) the evidence would otherwise be admissible in the court under the Federal Rules of Evidence; or

(B) the parties have otherwise stipulated. Added Nov. 19, 1988, Pub.L. 100–702, Title IX, § 901(a), 102 Stat. 4662; as amended Oct. 30, 1998, Pub.L. 105–315, § 9, 112 Stat. 2997.

§ 658. Compensation of arbitrators and neutrals

(a) Compensation.—The district court shall, subject to regulations approved by the Judicial Conference of the United States, establish the amount of compensation, if any, that each arbitrator or neutral shall receive for services rendered in each case under this chapter.

(b) Transportation allowances.—Under regulations prescribed by the Director of the Administrative Office of the United States Courts, a district court may reimburse arbitrators and other neutrals for actual transportation expenses necessarily incurred in the performance of duties under this chapter. Added Nov. 19, 1988, Pub.L. 100–702, Title IX, § 901(a), 102 Stat. 4662; as amended Oct. 30, 1998, Pub.L. 105–315, § 10, 112 Stat. 2997.

§ 1251. Original jurisdiction

(a) The Supreme Court shall have original and exclusive jurisdiction of all controversies between two or more States.

(b) The Supreme Court shall have original but not exclusive jurisdiction of:

(1) All actions or proceedings to which ambassadors, other public ministers, consuls, or vice consuls of foreign states are parties;

(2) All controversies between the United States and a State;

(3) All actions or proceedings by a State against the citizens of another State or against aliens. As amended Sept. 30, 1978, Pub.L. 95–393, § 8(b), 92 Stat. 810.

§ 1253. Direct appeals from decisions of three-judge courts

Except as otherwise provided by law, any party may appeal to the Supreme Court from an order granting or denying, after notice and hearing, an interlocutory or permanent injunction in any civil action, suit or proceeding required by any Act of Congress to be heard and determined by a district court of three judges.

§ 1254. Courts of appeals; certiorari; certified questions

Cases in the courts of appeals may be reviewed by the Supreme Court by the following methods:

(1) By writ of certiorari granted upon the petition of any party to any civil or criminal case, before or after rendition of judgment or decree;

(2) By certification at any time by a court of appeals of any question of law in any civil or criminal case as to which instructions are desired, and upon such certification the Supreme Court may give binding instructions or require the entire record to be sent up for decision of the entire matter in controversy. As amended June 27, 1988, Pub.L. 100–352, § 2, 102 Stat. 662.

§ 1257. State courts; certiorari

(a) Final judgments or decrees rendered by the highest court of a State in which a decision could be had, may be reviewed by the Supreme Court by writ of certiorari where the validity of a treaty or statute of the United

States is drawn in question or where the validity of a statute of any State is drawn in question on the ground of its being repugnant to the Constitution, treaties, or laws of the United States, or where any title, right, privilege, or immunity is specially set up or claimed under the Constitution or the treaties or statutes of, or any commission held or authority exercised under, the United States.

(b) For the purposes of this section, the term "highest court of a State" includes the District of Columbia Court of Appeals. As amended July 29, 1970, Pub.L. 91–358, 84 Stat. 590; June 27, 1988, Pub.L. 100–352, § 3, 102 Stat. 662.

§ 1258. Supreme Court of Puerto Rico; certiorari

Final judgments or decrees rendered by the Supreme Court of the Commonwealth of Puerto Rico may be reviewed by the Supreme Court by writ of certiorari where the validity of a treaty or statute of the United States is drawn in question or where the validity of a statute of the Commonwealth of Puerto Rico is drawn in question on the ground of its being repugnant to the Constitution, treaties, or laws of the United States, or where any title, right, privilege, or immunity is specially set up or claimed under the Constitution or the treaties or statutes of, or any commission held or authority exercised under, the United States. Added Aug. 30, 1961, Pub.L. 87–189, § 1, 75 Stat. 417; as amended June 27, 1988, Pub.L. 100–352, § 4, 102 Stat. 662.

§ 1291. Final decisions of district courts

The courts of appeals (other than the United States Court of Appeals for the Federal Circuit) shall have jurisdiction of appeals from all final decisions of the district courts of the United States, the United States District Court for the District of the Canal Zone, the District Court of Guam, and the District Court of the Virgin Islands, except where a direct review may be had in the Supreme Court. The jurisdiction of the United States Court of Appeals for the Federal Circuit shall be limited to the jurisdiction described in sections 1292 (c) and (d) and 1295 of this title. As amended Oct. 31, 1951, c. 655, § 48, 65 Stat. 726; July 7, 1958, Pub.L. 85–508, § 12(e), 72 Stat. 348; Apr. 2, 1982, Pub.L. 97–164, Title I, § 124, 96 Stat. 36.

§ 1292. Interlocutory decisions

(a) Except as provided in subsections (c) and (d) of this section, the courts of appeals shall have jurisdiction of appeals from:

(1) Interlocutory orders of the district courts of the United States, the United States District Court for the District of the Canal Zone, the District Court of Guam, and the District Court of the Virgin Islands, or of the judges thereof, granting, continuing, modifying, refusing or dissolving injunctions, or refusing to dissolve or modify injunctions, except where a direct review may be had in the Supreme Court;

(2) Interlocutory orders appointing receivers, or refusing orders to wind up receiverships or to take steps to accomplish the purposes thereof, such as directing sales or other disposals of property;

(3) Interlocutory decrees of such district courts or the judges thereof determining the rights and liabilities of the parties to admiralty cases in which appeals from final decrees are allowed.

(b) When a district judge, in making in a civil action an order not otherwise appealable under this section, shall be of the opinion that such order involves a controlling question of law as to which there is substantial ground for difference of opinion and that an immediate appeal from the order may materially advance the ultimate termination of the litigation, he shall so state in writing in such order. The Court of Appeals which would have jurisdiction of an appeal of such action may thereupon, in its discretion, permit an appeal to be taken from such order, if application is made to it within ten days after the entry of the order: *Provided, however,* That application for an appeal hereunder shall not stay proceedings in the district court unless the district judge or the Court of Appeals or a judge thereof shall so order.

(c) The United States Court of Appeals for the Federal Circuit shall have exclusive jurisdiction—

(1) of an appeal from an interlocutory order or decree described in subsection (a) or (b) of this section in any case over which the court would have jurisdiction of an appeal under section 1295 of this title; and

(2) of an appeal from a judgment in a civil action for patent infringement which would otherwise be appealable to the United States Court of Appeals for the Federal Circuit and is final except for an accounting.

(d)(1) When the chief judge of the Court of International Trade issues an order under the provisions of section 256(b) of this title, or when any judge of the Court of International Trade, in issuing any other interlocutory order, includes in the order a statement that a controlling question of law is involved with respect to which there is a substantial ground for difference of opinion and that an immediate appeal from that order may materially advance the ultimate termination of the litigation, the United States Court of Appeals for the Federal Circuit may, in its discretion, permit an appeal to be taken from such order, if application is made to that Court within ten days after the entry of such order.

(2) When the chief judge of the United States Court of Federal Claims issues an order under section 798(b) of this title, or when any judge of the United States Court of Federal Claims, in issuing an interlocutory order, includes in the order a statement that a controlling question of law is involved with respect to which there is a substantial ground for difference of opinion and that an immediate appeal from that order may materially advance the ultimate termination of the litigation, the United States Court of Appeals for the Federal Circuit may, in its discretion, permit an appeal to be taken from such order, if application is made to that Court within ten days after the entry of such order.

(3) Neither the application for nor the granting of an appeal under this subsection shall stay proceedings in the Court of International Trade or in the Court of Federal Claims, as the case may be, unless a stay is

ordered by a judge of the Court of International Trade or of the Court of Federal Claims or by the United States Court of Appeals for the Federal Circuit or a judge of that court.

(4)(A) The United States Court of Appeals for the Federal Circuit shall have exclusive jurisdiction of an appeal from an interlocutory order of a district court of the United States, the District Court of Guam, the District Court of the Virgin Islands, or the District Court for the Northern Mariana Islands, granting or denying, in whole or in part, a motion to transfer an action to the United States Court of Federal Claims under section 1631 of this title.

(B) When a motion to transfer an action to the Court of Federal Claims is filed in a district court, no further proceedings shall be taken in the district court until 60 days after the court has ruled upon the motion. If an appeal is taken from the district court's grant or denial of the motion, proceedings shall be further stayed until the appeal has been decided by the Court of Appeals for the Federal Circuit. The stay of proceedings in the district court shall not bar the granting of preliminary or injunctive relief, where appropriate and where expedition is reasonably necessary. However, during the period in which proceedings are stayed as provided in this subparagraph, no transfer to the Court of Federal Claims pursuant to the motion shall be carried out.

(e) The Supreme Court may prescribe rules, in accordance with section 2072 of this title, to provide for an appeal of an interlocutory decision to the courts of appeals that is not otherwise provided for under subsection (a), (b), (c), or (d). As amended Oct. 31, 1951, c. 655, § 49, 65 Stat. 726; July 7, 1958, Pub.L. 85–508, § 12(e), 72 Stat. 348; Sept. 2, 1958, Pub.L. 85–919, 72 Stat. 1770; Apr. 2, 1982, Pub.L. 97–164, Title I, § 125, 96 Stat. 36; Nov. 8, 1984, Pub.L. 98–620, Title IV, § 412, 98 Stat. 3362; Nov. 19, 1988, Pub.L. 100–702, Title V, § 501, 102 Stat. 4652; Oct. 29, 1992, Pub.L. 102–572, Title I, § 101, Title IX, §§ 902(b), 906(c), 106 Stat. 4506, 4516, 4518.

§ 1294. Circuits in which decisions reviewable

Except as provided in sections 1292(c), 1292(d), and 1295 of this title, appeals from reviewable decisions of the district and territorial courts shall be taken to the courts of appeals as follows:

(1) From a district court of the United States to the court of appeals for the circuit embracing the district;

(2) From the United States District Court for the District of the Canal Zone, to the Court of Appeals for the Fifth Circuit;

(3) From the District Court of the Virgin Islands, to the Court of Appeals for the Third Circuit;

(4) From the District Court of Guam, to the Court of Appeals for the Ninth Circuit. As amended Oct. 31, 1951, c. 655, § 50(a), 65 Stat. 727; July 7, 1958, Pub.L. 85–508, § 12(g), 72 Stat. 348; Mar. 18, 1959, Pub.L. 86–3, § 14(c), 73 Stat. 10; Aug. 30, 1961, Pub.L. 87–189, § 5, 75 Stat. 417; Nov. 6, 1978, Pub.L. 95–598, Title II, § 237, 92 Stat. 2667; Apr. 2, 1982, Pub.L. 97–164, Title I, § 126, 96 Stat. 37.

§ 1295. Jurisdiction of the United States Court of Appeals for the Federal Circuit

(a) The United States Court of Appeals for the Federal Circuit shall have exclusive jurisdiction—

(1) of an appeal from a final decision of a district court of the United States, the United States District Court for the District of the Canal Zone, the District Court of Guam, the District Court of the Virgin Islands, or the District Court for the Northern Mariana Islands, if the jurisdiction of that court was based, in whole or in part, on section 1338 of this title, except that a case involving a claim arising under any Act of Congress relating to copyrights, exclusive rights in mask works, or trademarks and no other claims under section 1338(a) shall be governed by sections 1291, 1292, and 1294 of this title;

(2) of an appeal from a final decision of a district court of the United States, the United States District Court for the District of the Canal Zone, the District Court of Guam, the District Court of the Virgin Islands, or the District Court for the Northern Mariana Islands, if the jurisdiction of that court was based, in whole or in part, on section 1346 of this title, except that jurisdiction of an appeal in a case brought in a district court under section 1346(a)(1), 1346(b), 1346(e), or 1346(f) of this title or under section 1346(a)(2) when the claim is founded upon an Act of Congress or a regulation of an executive department providing for internal revenue shall be governed by sections 1291, 1292, and 1294 of this title;

(3) of an appeal from a final decision of the United States Court of Federal Claims;

(4) of an appeal from a decision of—

(A) the Board of Patent Appeals and Interferences of the United States Patent and Trademark Office with respect to patent applications and interferences, at the instance of an applicant for a patent or any party to a patent interference, and any such appeal shall waive the right of such applicant or party to proceed under section 145 or 146 of title 35;

(B) the Under Secretary of Commerce for Intellectual Property and Director of the United States Patent and Trademark Office or the Trademark Trial and Appeal Board with respect to applications for registration of marks and other proceedings as provided in section 21 of the Trademark Act of 1946 (15 U.S.C. 1071); or

(C) a district court to which a case was directed pursuant to section 145, 146, or 154(b) of title 35;

(5) of an appeal from a final decision of the United States Court of International Trade;

(6) to review the final determinations of the United States International Trade Commission relating to unfair practices in import trade, made under section 337 of the Tariff Act of 1930 (19 U.S.C. 1337);

(7) to review, by appeal on questions of law only, findings of the Secretary of Commerce under U.S. note 6 to subchapter X of chapter 98 of the Harmonized Tariff Schedule of the United States (relating to importation of instruments or apparatus);

(8) of an appeal under section 71 of the Plant Variety Protection Act (7 U.S.C. 2461);

(9) of an appeal from a final order or final decision of the Merit Systems Protection Board, pursuant to sections 7703(b)(1) and 7703(d) of title 5;

(10) of an appeal from a final decision of an agency board of contract appeals pursuant to section 8(g)(1) of the Contract Disputes Act of 1978 (41 U.S.C. 607(g)(1));

(11) of an appeal under section 211 of the Economic Stabilization Act of 1970;

(12) of an appeal under section 5 of the Emergency Petroleum Allocation Act of 1973;

(13) of an appeal under section 506(c) of the Natural Gas Policy Act of 1978; and

(14) of an appeal under section 523 of the Energy Policy and Conservation Act.

(b) The head of any executive department or agency may, with the approval of the Attorney General, refer to the Court of Appeals for the Federal Circuit for judicial review any final decision rendered by a board of contract appeals pursuant to the terms of any contract with the United States awarded by that department or agency which the head of such department or agency has concluded is not entitled to finality pursuant to the review standards specified in section 10(b) of the Contract Disputes Act of 1978 (41 U.S.C. 609(b)). The head of each executive department or agency shall make any referral under this section within one hundred and twenty days after the receipt of a copy of the final appeal decision.

(c) The Court of Appeals for the Federal Circuit shall review the matter referred in accordance with the standards specified in section 10(b) of the Contract Disputes Act of 1978. The court shall proceed with judicial review on the administrative record made before the board of contract appeals on matters so referred as in other cases pending in such court, shall determine the issue of finality of the appeal decision, and shall, if appropriate, render judgment thereon, or remand the matter to any administrative or executive body or official with such direction as it may deem proper and just. Added Apr. 2, 1982, Pub.L. 97–164, Title I, § 127(a), 96 Stat. 37; as amended Nov. 8, 1984, Pub.L. 98–622, Title II, § 205(a), 98 Stat. 3388; Aug. 23, 1988, Pub.L. 100–418, Title I, § 1214(a)(3), 102 Stat. 1156; Nov. 19, 1988, Pub.L. 100–702, Title X, § 1020(a)(3), 102 Stat. 4671; Oct. 29, 1992, Pub.L. 102–572, Title I, § 102(c), Title IX, § 902(b)(1), 106 Stat. 4507, 4516; Nov. 29, 1999, Pub.L. 106–113, Div. B, § 1000(a)(9)[4402(b)(2), 4732(b)(14)], 113 Stat. 1501A–560, –584.

§ 1330. Actions against foreign states

(a) The district courts shall have original jurisdiction without regard to amount in controversy of any nonjury civil action against a foreign state as defined in section 1603(a) of this title as to any claim for relief in personam with respect to which the foreign state is not entitled to immunity either under sections 1605–1607 of this title or under any applicable international agreement.

(b) Personal jurisdiction over a foreign state shall exist as to every claim for relief over which the district courts have jurisdiction under subsection (a) where service has been made under section 1608 of this title.

(c) For purposes of subsection (b), an appearance by a foreign state does not confer personal jurisdiction with respect to any claim for relief not arising out of any transaction or occurrence enumerated in sections 1605–1607 of this title. Added Oct. 21, 1976, Pub.L. 94–583, § 2(a), 90 Stat. 2891.

§ 1331. Federal question

The district courts shall have original jurisdiction of all civil actions arising under the Constitution, laws, or treaties of the United States. As amended July 25, 1958, Pub.L. 85–554, § 1, 72 Stat. 415; Oct. 21, 1976, Pub.L. 94–574, § 2, 90 Stat. 2721; Dec. 1, 1980, Pub.L. 96–486, § 2(a), 94 Stat. 2369.

§ 1332. Diversity of citizenship; amount in controversy; costs

(a) The district courts shall have original jurisdiction of all civil actions where the matter in controversy exceeds the sum or value of $75,000, exclusive of interest and costs, and is between—

(1) citizens of different States;

(2) citizens of a State and citizens or subjects of a foreign state;

(3) citizens of different States and in which citizens or subjects of a foreign state are additional parties; and

(4) a foreign state, defined in section 1603(a) of this title, as plaintiff and citizens of a State or of different States.

For the purposes of this section, section 1335, and section 1441, an alien admitted to the United States for permanent residence shall be deemed a citizen of the State in which such alien is domiciled.

(b) Except when express provision therefor is otherwise made in a statute of the United States, where the plaintiff who files the case originally in the Federal courts is finally adjudged to be entitled to recover less than the sum or value of $75,000, computed without regard to any setoff or counterclaim to which the defendant may be adjudged to be entitled, and exclusive of interest and costs, the district court may deny costs to the plaintiff and, in addition, may impose costs on the plaintiff.

(c) For the purposes of this section and section 1441 of this title—

(1) a corporation shall be deemed to be a citizen of any State by which it has been incorporated and of the State where it has its

principal place of business, except that in any direct action against the insurer of a policy or contract of liability insurance, whether incorporated or unincorporated, to which action the insured is not joined as a party-defendant, such insurer shall be deemed a citizen of the State of which the insured is a citizen, as well as of any State by which the insurer has been incorporated and of the State where it has its principal place of business; and

(2) the legal representative of the estate of a decedent shall be deemed to be a citizen only of the same State as the decedent, and the legal representative of an infant or incompetent shall be deemed to be a citizen only of the same State as the infant or incompetent.

(d)(1) In this subsection—

(A) the term "class" means all of the class members in a class action;

(B) the term "class action" means any civil action filed under rule 23 of the Federal Rules of Civil Procedure or similar State statute or rule of judicial procedure authorizing an action to be brought by 1 or more representative persons as a class action;

(C) the term "class certification order" means an order issued by a court approving the treatment of some or all aspects of a civil action as a class action; and

(D) the term "class members" means the persons (named or unnamed) who fall within the definition of the proposed or certified class in a class action.

(2) The district courts shall have original jurisdiction of any civil action in which the matter in controversy exceeds the sum or value of $5,000,000, exclusive of interest and costs, and is a class action in which—

(A) any member of a class of plaintiffs is a citizen of a State different from any defendant;

(B) any member of a class of plaintiffs is a foreign state or a citizen or subject of a foreign state and any defendant is a citizen of a State; or

(C) any member of a class of plaintiffs is a citizen of a State and any defendant is a foreign state or a citizen or subject of a foreign state.

(3) A district court may, in the interests of justice and looking at the totality of the circumstances, decline to exercise jurisdiction under paragraph (2) over a class action in which greater than one-third but less than two-thirds of the members of all proposed plaintiff classes in the aggregate and the primary defendants are citizens of the State in which the action was originally filed based on consideration of—

(A) whether the claims asserted involve matters of national or interstate interest;

(B) whether the claims asserted will be governed by laws of the State in which the action was originally filed or by the laws of other States;

(C) whether the class action has been pleaded in a manner that seeks to avoid Federal jurisdiction;

(D) whether the action was brought in a forum with a distinct nexus with the class members, the alleged harm, or the defendants;

(E) whether the number of citizens of the State in which the action was originally filed in all proposed plaintiff classes in the aggregate is substantially larger than the number of citizens from any other State, and the citizenship of the other members of the proposed class is dispersed among a substantial number of States; and

(F) whether, during the 3–year period preceding the filing of that class action, 1 or more other class actions asserting the same or similar claims on behalf of the same or other persons have been filed.

(4) A district court shall decline to exercise jurisdiction under paragraph (2)—

(A)(i) over a class action in which—

(I) greater than two-thirds of the members of all proposed plaintiff classes in the aggregate are citizens of the State in which the action was originally filed;

(II) at least 1 defendant is a defendant—

(aa) from whom significant relief is sought by members of the plaintiff class;

(bb) whose alleged conduct forms a significant basis for the claims asserted by the proposed plaintiff class; and

(cc) who is a citizen of the State in which the action was originally filed; and

(III) principal injuries resulting from the alleged conduct or any related conduct of each defendant were incurred in the State in which the action was originally filed; and

(ii) during the 3–year period preceding the filing of that class action, no other class action has been filed asserting the same or similar factual allegations against any of the defendants on behalf of the same or other persons; or

(B) two-thirds or more of the members of all proposed plaintiff classes in the aggregate, and the primary defendants, are citizens of the State in which the action was originally filed.

(5) Paragraphs (2) through (4) shall not apply to any class action in which—

(A) the primary defendants are States, State officials, or other governmental entities against whom the district court may be foreclosed from ordering relief; or

(B) the number of members of all proposed plaintiff classes in the aggregate is less than 100.

(6) In any class action, the claims of the individual class members shall be aggregated to determine whether the matter in controversy exceeds the sum or value of $5,000,000, exclusive of interest and costs.

(7) Citizenship of the members of the proposed plaintiff classes shall be determined for purposes of paragraphs (2) through (6) as of the date of filing of the complaint or amended complaint, or, if the case stated by the initial pleading is not subject to Federal jurisdiction, as of the date of service by plaintiffs of an amended pleading, motion, or other paper, indicating the existence of Federal jurisdiction.

(8) This subsection shall apply to any class action before or after the entry of a class certification order by the court with respect to that action.

(9) Paragraph (2) shall not apply to any class action that solely involves a claim—

(A) concerning a covered security as defined under 16(f)(3) of the Securities Act of 1933 (15 U.S.C. 78p(f)(3)) and section 28(f)(5)(E) of the Securities Exchange Act of 1934 (15 U.S.C. 78bb(f)(5)(E));

(B) that relates to the internal affairs or governance of a corporation or other form of business enterprise and that arises under or by virtue of the laws of the State in which such corporation or business enterprise is incorporated or organized; or

(C) that relates to the rights, duties (including fiduciary duties), and obligations relating to or created by or pursuant to any security (as defined under section 2(a)(1) of the Securities Act of 1933 (15 U.S.C. 77b(a)(1)) and the regulations issued thereunder).

(10) For purposes of this subsection and section 1453, an unincorporated association shall be deemed to be a citizen of the State where it has its principal place of business and the State under whose laws it is organized.

(11)(A) For purposes of this subsection and section 1453, a mass action shall be deemed to be a class action removable under paragraphs (2) through (10) if it otherwise meets the provisions of those paragraphs.

(B)(i) As used in subparagraph (A), the term "mass action" means any civil action (except a civil action within the scope of section 1711(2)) in which monetary relief claims of 100 or more persons are proposed to be tried jointly on the ground that the plaintiffs' claims involve common questions of law or fact, except that jurisdiction shall exist only over those plaintiffs whose claims in a mass action satisfy the jurisdictional amount requirements under subsection (a).

(ii) As used in subparagraph (A), the term "mass action" shall not include any civil action in which—

(I) all of the claims in the action arise from an event or occurrence in the State in which the action was filed, and that allegedly resulted in injuries in that State or in States contiguous to that State;

(II) the claims are joined upon motion of a defendant;

(III) all of the claims in the action are asserted on behalf of the general public (and not on behalf of individual claimants or members of a purported class) pursuant to a State statute specifically authorizing such action; or

(IV) the claims have been consolidated or coordinated solely for pretrial proceedings.

(C)(i) Any action(s) removed to Federal court pursuant to this subsection shall not thereafter be transferred to any other court pursuant to section 1407, or the rules promulgated thereunder, unless a majority of the plaintiffs in the action request transfer pursuant to section 1407.

(ii) This subparagraph will not apply—

(I) to cases certified pursuant to rule 23 of the Federal Rules of Civil Procedure; or

(II) if plaintiffs propose that the action proceed as a class action pursuant to rule 23 of the Federal Rules of Civil Procedure.

(D) The limitations periods on any claims asserted in a mass action that is removed to Federal court pursuant to this subsection shall be deemed tolled during the period that the action is pending in Federal court.

(e) The word "States", as used in this section, includes the Territories, the District of Columbia, and the Commonwealth of Puerto Rico.   As amended July 26, 1956, c. 740, 70 Stat. 658; July 25, 1958, Pub.L. 85–554, § 2, 72 Stat. 415; Aug. 14, 1964, Pub.L. 88–439, § 1, 78 Stat. 445; Oct. 21, 1976, Pub.L. 94–583, § 3, 90 Stat. 2891; Nov. 19, 1988, Pub.L. 100–702, Title II, §§ 201–203, 102 Stat. 4646; Oct. 19, 1996, Pub.L. 104–317, Title II, § 205, 110 Stat. 3850; Feb. 18, 2005, Pub.L. 109–2, § 4(a), 119 Stat. 9.

§ 1333.   Admiralty, maritime and prize cases

The district courts shall have original jurisdiction, exclusive of the courts of the States, of:

(1) Any civil case of admiralty or maritime jurisdiction, saving to suitors in all cases all other remedies to which they are otherwise entitled.

(2) Any prize brought into the United States and all proceedings for the condemnation of property taken as prize.   As amended May 24, 1949, c. 139, § 79, 63 Stat. 101.

§ 1334.   Bankruptcy cases and proceedings

(a) Except as provided in subsection (b) of this section, the district court shall have original and exclusive jurisdiction of all cases under title 11.

(b) Except as provided in subsection (e)(2), and notwithstanding any Act of Congress that confers exclusive jurisdiction on a court or courts other than the district courts, the district courts shall have original but not exclusive jurisdiction of all civil proceedings arising under title 11, or arising in or related to cases under title 11.

(c)(1) Except with respect to a case under chapter 15 of title 11, nothing in this section prevents a district court in the interest of justice, or in the interest of comity with State courts or respect for State law, from abstaining from hearing a particular proceeding arising under title 11 or arising in or related to a case under title 11.

(2) Upon timely motion of a party in a proceeding based upon a State law claim or State law cause of action, related to a case under title 11 but not arising under title 11 or arising in a case under title 11, with respect to which an action could not have been commenced in a court of the United States absent jurisdiction under this section, the district court shall abstain from hearing such proceeding if an action is commenced, and can be timely adjudicated, in a State forum of appropriate jurisdiction.

(d) Any decision to abstain or not to abstain made under subsection (c) (other than a decision not to abstain in a proceeding described in subsection (c)(2)) is not reviewable by appeal or otherwise by the court of appeals under section 158(d), 1291, or 1292 of this title or by the Supreme Court of the United States under section 1254 of this title. Subsection (c) and this subsection shall not be construed to limit the applicability of the stay provided for by section 362 of title 11, United States Code, as such section applies to an action affecting the property of the estate in bankruptcy.

(e) The district court in which a case under title 11 is commenced or is pending shall have exclusive jurisdiction—

(1) of all the property, wherever located, of the debtor as of the commencement of such case, and of property of the estate; and

(2) over all claims or causes of action that involve construction of section 327 of title 11, United States Code, or rules relating to disclosure requirements under section 327. As amended Nov. 6, 1978, Pub.L. 95–598, Title II, § 238(a), 92 Stat. 2667; July 10, 1984, Pub.L. 98–353, Title I, § 101(a), 98 Stat. 333; Oct. 27, 1986, Pub.L. 99–554, Title I, § 144(e), 100 Stat. 3096; Dec. 1, 1990, Pub.L. 101–650, Title III, § 309(b), 104 Stat. 5113; Oct. 22, 1994, Pub.L. 103–394, Title I, § 104(b), 108 Stat. 4109; Apr. 20, 2005, Pub.L. 109–8, Title III, § 324(a), Title VIII, § 802(c)(2), Title XII, § 1219, 119 Stat. 98, 145, 195.

§ 1335. Interpleader

(a) The district courts shall have original jurisdiction of any civil action of interpleader or in the nature of interpleader filed by any person, firm, or corporation, association, or society having in his or its custody or possession money or property of the value of $500 or more, or having issued a note, bond, certificate, policy of insurance, or other instrument of value or amount of $500 or more, or providing for the delivery or payment or the loan of money or property of such amount or value, or being under any obligation written or unwritten to the amount of $500 or more, if

(1) Two or more adverse claimants, of diverse citizenship as defined in subsection (a) or (d) of section 1332 of this title, are claiming or may claim to be entitled to such money or property, or to any one or more of the benefits arising by virtue of any note, bond, certificate, policy or other instrument, or arising by virtue of any such obligation; and if (2) the plaintiff has deposited such money or property or has paid the amount of or the loan or other value of such instrument or the amount due under such obligation into the registry of the court, there to abide the judgment of the court, or has given bond payable to the clerk of the court in such amount and with such surety as the court or judge may deem proper,

conditioned upon the compliance by the plaintiff with the future order or judgment of the court with respect to the subject matter of the controversy.

(b) Such an action may be entertained although the titles or claims of the conflicting claimants do not have a common origin, or are not identical, but are adverse to and independent of one another. As amended Feb. 18, 2005, Pub.L. 109–2, § 4(b)(1), 119 Stat. 12.

§ 1337. Commerce and antitrust regulations; amount in controversy, costs

(a) The district courts shall have original jurisdiction of any civil action or proceeding arising under any Act of Congress regulating commerce or protecting trade and commerce against restraints and monopolies: *Provided, however,* That the district courts shall have original jurisdiction of an action brought under section 11706 or 14706 of title 49, only if the matter in controversy for each receipt or bill of lading exceeds $10,000, exclusive of interest and costs.

(b) Except when express provision therefor is otherwise made in a statute of the United States, where a plaintiff who files the case under section 11706 or 14706 of title 49, originally in the Federal courts is finally adjudged to be entitled to recover less than the sum or value of $10,000, computed without regard to any setoff or counterclaim to which the defendant may be adjudged to be entitled, and exclusive of any interest and costs, the district court may deny costs to the plaintiff and, in addition, may impose costs on the plaintiff.

(c) The district courts shall not have jurisdiction under this section of any matter within the exclusive jurisdiction of the Court of International Trade under chapter 95 of this title. As amended Oct. 20, 1978, Pub.L. 95–486, § 9(a), 92 Stat. 1633; Oct. 10, 1980, Pub.L. 96–417, Title V, § 505, 94 Stat. 1743; Jan. 12, 1983, Pub.L. 97–449, § 5(f), 96 Stat. 2442; Dec. 29, 1995, Pub.L. 104–88, Title III, § 305(a)(3), 109 Stat. 944.

§ 1338. Patents, plant variety protection, copyrights, mask works, designs, trademarks, and unfair competition

(a) The district courts shall have original jurisdiction of any civil action arising under any Act of Congress relating to patents, plant variety protection, copyrights and trademarks. Such jurisdiction shall be exclusive of the courts of the states in patent, plant variety protection and copyright cases.

(b) The district courts shall have original jurisdiction of any civil action asserting a claim of unfair competition when joined with a substantial and related claim under the copyright, patent, plant variety protection or trademark laws.

(c) Subsections (a) and (b) apply to exclusive rights in mask works under chapter 9 of title 17, and to exclusive rights in designs under chapter 13 of title 17, to the same extent as such subsections apply to copyrights. As amended Dec. 24, 1970, Pub.L. 91–577, Title III, § 143(b), 84 Stat. 1559; Nov. 19, 1988, Pub.L. 100–702, Title X, § 1020(a)(4), 102 Stat. 4671; Oct. 28, 1998, Pub.L. 105–304, Title V, § 503(b), 112 Stat. 2917; Nov. 29, 1999, Pub.L. 106–113, Div. B, § 1000(a)(9)[3009(1)], 113 Stat. 1501A–551.

§ 1339. Postal matters

The district courts shall have original jurisdiction of any civil action arising under any Act of Congress relating to the postal service.

§ 1340. Internal revenue; customs duties

The district courts shall have original jurisdiction of any civil action arising under any Act of Congress providing for internal revenue, or revenue from imports or tonnage except matters within the jurisdiction of the Court of International Trade. As amended Oct. 10, 1980, Pub.L. 96–417, Title V, § 501(21), 94 Stat. 1742.

§ 1341. Taxes by States

The district courts shall not enjoin, suspend or restrain the assessment, levy or collection of any tax under State law where a plain, speedy and efficient remedy may be had in the courts of such State.

§ 1342. Rate orders of State agencies

The district courts shall not enjoin, suspend or restrain the operation of, or compliance with, any order affecting rates chargeable by a public utility and made by a State administrative agency or a rate-making body of a State political subdivision, where:

(1) Jurisdiction is based solely on diversity of citizenship or repugnance of the order to the Federal Constitution; and,

(2) The order does not interfere with interstate commerce; and,

(3) The order has been made after reasonable notice and hearing; and,

(4) A plain, speedy and efficient remedy may be had in the courts of such State.

§ 1343. Civil rights and elective franchise

(a) The district courts shall have original jurisdiction of any civil action authorized by law to be commenced by any person:

(1) To recover damages for injury to his person or property, or because of the deprivation of any right or privilege of a citizen of the United States, by any act done in furtherance of any conspiracy mentioned in section 1985 of Title 42;

(2) To recover damages from any person who fails to prevent or to aid in preventing any wrongs mentioned in section 1985 of Title 42 which he had knowledge were about to occur and power to prevent;

(3) To redress the deprivation, under color of any State law, statute, ordinance, regulation, custom or usage, of any right, privilege or immunity secured by the Constitution of the United States or by any Act of Congress providing for equal rights of citizens or of all persons within the jurisdiction of the United States;

(4) To recover damages or to secure equitable or other relief under any Act of Congress providing for the protection of civil rights, including the right to vote.

(b) For purposes of this section—

(1) the District of Columbia shall be considered to be a State; and

(2) any Act of Congress applicable exclusively to the District of Columbia shall be considered to be a statute of the District of Columbia. As amended Sept. 3, 1954, c. 1263, § 42, 68 Stat. 1241; Sept. 9, 1957, Pub.L. 85–315, Part III, § 121, 71 Stat. 637; Dec. 29, 1979, Pub.L. 96–170, § 2, 93 Stat. 1284.

§ 1344. Election disputes

The district courts shall have original jurisdiction of any civil action to recover possession of any office, except that of elector of President or Vice President, United States Senator, Representative in or delegate to Congress, or member of a state legislature, authorized by law to be commenced, wherein it appears that the sole question touching the title to office arises out of denial of the right to vote, to any citizen offering to vote, on account of race, color or previous condition of servitude.

The jurisdiction under this section shall extend only so far as to determine the rights of the parties to office by reason of the denial of the right, guaranteed by the Constitution of the United States and secured by any law, to enforce the right of citizens of the United States to vote in all the States.

§ 1345. United States as plaintiff

Except as otherwise provided by Act of Congress, the district courts shall have original jurisdiction of all civil actions, suits or proceedings commenced by the United States, or by any agency or officer thereof expressly authorized to sue by Act of Congress.

§ 1346. United States as defendant

(a) The district courts shall have original jurisdiction, concurrent with the United States Court of Federal Claims, of:

(1) Any civil action against the United States for the recovery of any internal-revenue tax alleged to have been erroneously or illegally assessed or collected, or any penalty claimed to have been collected without authority or any sum alleged to have been excessive or in any manner wrongfully collected under the internal-revenue laws;

(2) Any other civil action or claim against the United States, not exceeding $10,000 in amount, founded either upon the Constitution, or any Act of Congress, or any regulation of an executive department, or upon any express or implied contract with the United States, or for liquidated or unliquidated damages in cases not sounding in tort, except that the district courts shall not have jurisdiction of any civil action or claim against the United States founded upon any express or implied contract with the United States or for liquidated or unliquidated damages in cases not sounding in tort which are subject to sections 8(g)(1) and 10(a)(1) of the Contract Disputes Act of 1978. For the purpose of this paragraph, an express or implied contract with the Army and Air Force Exchange Service, Navy Exchanges, Marine Corps Exchanges, Coast Guard Exchanges, or

Exchange Councils of the National Aeronautics and Space Administration shall be considered an express or implied contract with the United States.

(b)(1) Subject to the provisions of chapter 171 of this title, the district courts, together with the United Stated District Court for the District of the Canal Zone and the District Court of the Virgin Islands, shall have exclusive jurisdiction of civil actions on claims against the United States, for money damages, accruing on and after January 1, 1945, for injury or loss of property, or personal injury or death caused by the negligent or wrongful act or omission of any employee of the government while acting within the scope of his office or employment, under circumstances where the United States, if a private person, would be liable to the claimant in accordance with the law of the place where the act or omission occurred.

(2) No person convicted of a felony who is incarcerated while awaiting sentencing or while serving a sentence may bring a civil action against the United States or an agency, officer, or employee of the Government, for mental or emotional injury suffered while in custody without a prior showing of physical injury.

(c) The jurisdiction conferred by this section includes jurisdiction of any set-off, counterclaim, or other claim or demand whatever on the part of the United States against any plaintiff commencing an action under this section.

(d) The district courts shall not have jurisdiction under this section of any civil action or claim for a pension.

(e) The district courts shall have original jurisdiction of any civil action against the United States provided in section 6226, 6228(a), 7426, or 7428 (in the case of the United States district court for the District of Columbia) or section 7429 of the Internal Revenue Code of 1954.

(f) The district courts shall have exclusive original jurisdiction of civil actions under section 2409a to quiet title to an estate or interest in real property in which an interest is claimed by the United States.

(g) Subject to the provisions of chapter 179, the district courts of the United States shall have exclusive jurisdiction over any civil action commenced under section 453(2) of title 3, by a covered employee under chapter 5 of such title. As amended Apr. 25, 1949, c. 92, § 2(a), 63 Stat. 62; May 24, 1949, c. 139, § 80(a, b), 63 Stat. 101; Oct. 31, 1951, c. 655, § 50(b), 65 Stat. 727; July 30, 1954, c. 648, § 1, 68 Stat. 589; July 7, 1958, Pub.L. 85–508, § 12(e), 72 Stat. 348; Aug. 30, 1964, Pub.L. 88–519, 78 Stat. 699; Nov. 2, 1966, Pub.L. 89–719, Title II, § 202(a), 80 Stat. 1148; July 23, 1970, Pub.L. 91–350, 84 Stat. 449; Oct. 25, 1972, Pub.L. 92–562, § 1, 86 Stat. 1176; Oct. 4, 1976, Pub.L. 94–455, Title XII, § 1204(c)(1), Title XIII, § 1306(b)(7), 90 Stat. 1697, 1719; Nov. 1, 1978, Pub.L. 95–563, § 14(a), 92 Stat. 2389; Apr. 2, 1982, Pub.L. 97–164, Title I, § 129, 96 Stat. 39; Sept. 3, 1982, Pub.L. 97–248, Title IV, § 402(c)(17), 96 Stat. 669; Oct. 29, 1992, Pub.L. 102–572, Title IX, § 902(b)(1), 106 Stat. 4516; Apr. 26, 1996, Pub.L. 104–134, Title I, § 806, 110 Stat. 1321–75; Oct. 26, 1996, Pub.L. 104–331, § 3(b)(1), 110 Stat. 4069.

§ 1350. Alien's action for tort

The district courts shall have original jurisdiction of any civil action by an alien for a tort only, committed in violation of the law of nations or a treaty of the United States.

§ 1351. Consuls, vice consuls, and members of a diplomatic mission as defendant

The district courts shall have original jurisdiction, exclusive of the courts of the States, of all civil actions and proceedings against—

(1) consuls or vice consuls of foreign states; or

(2) members of a mission or members of their families (as such terms are defined in section 2 of the Diplomatic Relations Act). As amended May 24, 1949, c. 139, § 80(c), 63 Stat. 101; Sept. 30, 1978, Pub.L. 95–393, § 8(a)(1), 92 Stat. 810.

§ 1355. Fine, penalty or forfeiture

(a) The district courts shall have original jurisdiction, exclusive of the courts of the States, of any action or proceeding for the recovery or enforcement of any fine, penalty, or forfeiture, pecuniary or otherwise, incurred under any Act of Congress, except matters within the jurisdiction of the Court of International Trade under section 1582 of this title.

(b)(1) A forfeiture action or proceeding may be brought in—

(A) the district court for the district in which any of the acts or omissions giving rise to the forfeiture occurred, or

(B) any other district where venue for the forfeiture action or proceeding is specifically provided for in section 1395 of this title or any other statute.

(2) Whenever property subject to forfeiture under the laws of the United States is located in a foreign country, or has been detained or seized pursuant to legal process or competent authority of a foreign government, an action or proceeding for forfeiture may be brought as provided in paragraph (1), or in the United States District court for the District of Columbia.

(c) In any case in which a final order disposing of property in a civil forfeiture action or proceeding is appealed, removal of the property by the prevailing party shall not deprive the court of jurisdiction. Upon motion of the appealing party, the district court or the court of appeals shall issue any order necessary to preserve the right of the appealing party to the full value of the property at issue, including a stay of the judgment of the district court pending appeal or requiring the prevailing party to post an appeal bond.

(d) Any court with jurisdiction over a forfeiture action pursuant to subsection (b) may issue and cause to be served in any other district such process as may be required to bring before the court the property that is the subject of the forfeiture action. As amended Oct. 10, 1980, Pub.L. 96–417, Title V, § 507, 94 Stat. 1743; Oct. 28, 1992, Pub.L. 102–550, Title XV, § 1521, 106 Stat. 4062.

§ 1359. Parties collusively joined or made

A district court shall not have jurisdiction of a civil action in which any party, by assignment or otherwise, has been improperly or collusively made or joined to invoke the jurisdiction of such court.

§ 1361. Action to compel an officer of the United States to perform his duty

The district courts shall have original jurisdiction of any action in the nature of mandamus to compel an officer or employee of the United States or any agency thereof to perform a duty owed to the plaintiff. Added Oct. 5, 1962, Pub.L. 87–748, § 1(a), 76 Stat. 744.

§ 1362. Indian tribes

The district courts shall have original jurisdiction of all civil actions, brought by any Indian tribe or band with a governing body duly recognized by the Secretary of the Interior, wherein the matter in controversy arises under the Constitution, laws, or treaties of the United States. Added Oct. 10, 1966, Pub.L. 89–635, § 1, 80 Stat. 880.

§ 1364. Direct actions against insurers of members of diplomatic missions and their families

(a) The district courts shall have original and exclusive jurisdiction, without regard to the amount in controversy, of any civil action commenced by any person against an insurer who by contract has insured an individual, who is, or was at the time of the tortious act or omission, a member of a mission (within the meaning of section 2(3) of the Diplomatic Relations Act (22 U.S.C. 254a(3))) or a member of the family of such a member of a mission, or an individual described in section 19 of the Convention on Privileges and Immunities of the United Nations of February 13, 1946, against liability for personal injury, death, or damage to property.

(b) Any direct action brought against an insurer under subsection (a) shall be tried without a jury, but shall not be subject to the defense that the insured is immune from suit, that the insured is an indispensable party, or in the absence of fraud or collusion, that the insured has violated a term of the contract, unless the contract was cancelled before the claim arose. Added Sept. 30, 1978, Pub.L. 95–393, § 7(a), 92 Stat. 809; as amended Aug. 24, 1982, Pub.L. 97–241, Title II, § 203(b)(4), 96 Stat. 291; Dec. 22, 1987, Pub.L. 100–204, Title I, § 138(a), 101 Stat. 1347.

§ 1366. Construction of references to laws of the United States or Acts of Congress

For the purposes of this chapter, references to laws of the United States or Acts of Congress do not include laws applicable exclusively to the District of Columbia. Added July 29, 1970, Pub.L. 91–358, Title I, § 172(c)(1), 84 Stat. 590; as amended Nov. 2, 1978, Pub.L. 95–572, § 6(b)(1), 92 Stat. 2456; June 19, 1986, Pub.L. 99–336, § 6(a)(1)(C), 100 Stat. 639.

§ 1367.   Supplemental jurisdiction

(a) Except as provided in subsections (b) and (c) or as expressly provided otherwise by Federal statute, in any civil action of which the district courts have original jurisdiction, the district courts shall have supplemental jurisdiction over all other claims that are so related to claims in the action within such original jurisdiction that they form part of the same case or controversy under Article III of the United States Constitution. Such supplemental jurisdiction shall include claims that involve the joinder or intervention of additional parties.

(b) In any civil action of which the district courts have original jurisdiction founded solely on section 1332 of this title, the district courts shall not have supplemental jurisdiction under subsection (a) over claims by plaintiffs against persons made parties under Rule 14, 19, 20, or 24 of the Federal Rules of Civil Procedure, or over claims by persons proposed to be joined as plaintiffs under Rule 19 of such rules, or seeking to intervene as plaintiffs under Rule 24 of such rules, when exercising supplemental jurisdiction over such claims would be inconsistent with the jurisdictional requirements of section 1332.

(c) The district courts may decline to exercise supplemental jurisdiction over a claim under subsection (a) if—

(1) the claim raises a novel or complex issue of State law,

(2) the claim substantially predominates over the claim or claims over which the district court has original jurisdiction,

(3) the district court has dismissed all claims over which it has original jurisdiction, or

(4) in exceptional circumstances, there are other compelling reasons for declining jurisdiction.

(d) The period of limitations for any claim asserted under subsection (a), and for any other claim in the same action that is voluntarily dismissed at the same time as or after the dismissal of the claim under subsection (a), shall be tolled while the claim is pending and for a period of 30 days after it is dismissed unless State law provides for a longer tolling period.

(e) As used in this section, the term "State" includes the District of Columbia, the Commonwealth of Puerto Rico, and any territory or possession of the United States. Added Dec. 1, 1990, Pub.L. 101–650, Title III, § 310(a), 104 Stat. 5113.

§ 1369.   Multiparty, multiforum jurisdiction

(a) In General.—The district courts shall have original jurisdiction of any civil action involving minimal diversity between adverse parties that arises from a single accident, where at least 75 natural persons have died in the accident at a discrete location, if—

(1) a defendant resides in a State and a substantial part of the accident took place in another State or other location, regardless of whether that defendant is also a resident of the State where a substantial part of the accident took place;

(2) any two defendants reside in different States, regardless of whether such defendants are also residents of the same State or States; or

(3) substantial parts of the accident took place in different States.

(b) Limitation of Jurisdiction of District Courts.—The district court shall abstain from hearing any civil action described in subsection (a) in which—

(1) the substantial majority of all plaintiffs are citizens of a single State of which the primary defendants are also citizens; and

(2) the claims asserted will be governed primarily by the laws of that State.

(c) Special Rules and Definitions.—For purposes of this section—

(1) minimal diversity exists between adverse parties if any party is a citizen of a State and any adverse party is a citizen of another State, a citizen or subject of a foreign state, or a foreign state as defined in section 1603(a) of this title;

(2) a corporation is deemed to be a citizen of any State, and a citizen or subject of any foreign state, in which it is incorporated or has its principal place of business, and is deemed to be a resident of any State in which it is incorporated or licensed to do business or is doing business;

(3) the term "injury" means—

(A) physical harm to a natural person; and

(B) physical damage to or destruction of tangible property, but only if physical harm described in subparagraph (A) exists;

(4) the term "accident" means a sudden accident, or a natural event culminating in an accident, that results in death incurred at a discrete location by at least 75 natural persons; and

(5) the term "State" includes the District of Columbia, the Commonwealth of Puerto Rico, and any territory or possession of the United States.

(d) Intervening Parties.—In any action in a district court which is or could have been brought, in whole or in part, under this section, any person with a claim arising from the accident described in subsection (a) shall be permitted to intervene as a party plaintiff in the action, even if that person could not have brought an action in a district court as an original matter.

(e) Notification of Judicial Panel on Multidistrict Litigation.—A district court in which an action under this section is pending shall promptly notify the judicial panel on multidistrict litigation of the pendency of the action. Added Nov. 2, 2002, Pub.L. 107–273, Div. C, Title I, § 11020(b)(1), 116 Stat. 1826.

§ 1391. Venue generally

(a) A civil action wherein jurisdiction is founded only on diversity of citizenship may, except as otherwise provided by law, be brought only in

(1) a judicial district where any defendant resides, if all defendants reside in the same State, (2) a judicial district in which a substantial part of the events or omissions giving rise to the claim occurred, or a substantial part of property that is the subject of the action is situated, or (3) a judicial district in which any defendant is subject to personal jurisdiction at the time the action is commenced, if there is no district in which the action may otherwise be brought.

(b) A civil action wherein jurisdiction is not founded solely on diversity of citizenship may, except as otherwise provided by law, be brought only in (1) a judicial district where any defendant resides, if all defendants reside in the same State, (2) a judicial district in which a substantial part of the events or omissions giving rise to the claim occurred, or a substantial part of property that is the subject of the action is situated, or (3) a judicial district in which any defendant may be found, if there is no district in which the action may otherwise be brought.

(c) For purposes of venue under this chapter, a defendant that is a corporation shall be deemed to reside in any judicial district in which it is subject to personal jurisdiction at the time the action is commenced. In a State which has more than one judicial district and in which a defendant that is a corporation is subject to personal jurisdiction at the time an action is commenced, such corporation shall be deemed to reside in any district in that State within which its contacts would be sufficient to subject it to personal jurisdiction if that district were a separate State, and, if there is no such district, the corporation shall be deemed to reside in the district within which it has the most significant contacts.

(d) An alien may be sued in any district.

(e) A civil action in which a defendant is an officer or employee of the United States or any agency thereof acting in his official capacity or under color of legal authority, or an agency of the United States, or the United States, may, except as otherwise provided by law, be brought in any judicial district in which (1) a defendant in the action resides, (2) a substantial part of the events or omissions giving rise to the claim occurred, or a substantial part of property that is the subject of the action is situated, or (3) the plaintiff resides if no real property is involved in the action. Additional persons may be joined as parties to any such action in accordance with the Federal Rules of Civil Procedure and with such other venue requirements as would be applicable if the United States or one of its officers, employees, or agencies were not a party.

The summons and complaint in such an action shall be served as provided by the Federal Rules of Civil Procedure except that the delivery of the summons and complaint to the officer or agency as required by the rules may be made by certified mail beyond the territorial limits of the district in which the action is brought.

(f) A civil action against a foreign state as defined in section 1603(a) of this title may be brought—

(1) in any judicial district in which a substantial part of the events or omissions giving rise to the claim occurred, or a substantial part of property that is the subject of the action is situated;

(2) in any judicial district in which the vessel or cargo of a foreign state is situated, if the claim is asserted under section 1605(b) of this title;

(3) in any judicial district in which the agency or instrumentality is licensed to do business or is doing business, if the action is brought against an agency or instrumentality of a foreign state as defined in section 1603(b) of this title; or

(4) in the United States District Court for the District of Columbia if the action is brought against a foreign state or political subdivision thereof.

(g) A civil action in which jurisdiction of the district court is based upon section 1369 of this title may be brought in any district in which any defendant resides or in which a substantial part of the accident giving rise to the action took place. As amended Oct. 5, 1962, Pub.L. 87–748, § 2, 76 Stat. 744; Dec. 23, 1963, Pub.L. 88–234, 77 Stat. 473; Nov. 2, 1966, Pub.L. 89–714, §§ 1, 2, 80 Stat. 1111; Oct. 21, 1976, Pub.L. 94–574, § 3, 90 Stat. 2721; Oct. 21, 1976, Pub.L. 94–583, § 5, 90 Stat. 2897; Nov. 19, 1988, Pub.L. 100–702, Title X, § 1013, 102 Stat. 4669; Dec. 1, 1990, Pub.L. 101–650, Title III, § 311, 104 Stat. 5114; Dec. 9, 1991, Pub.L. 102–198, § 3, 105 Stat. 1623; Oct. 29, 1992, Pub.L. 102–572, Title V, § 504, 106 Stat. 4513; Oct. 3, 1995, Pub.L. 104–34, § 1, 109 Stat. 293; Nov. 2, 2002, Pub.L. 107–273, Div. C, Title I, § 11020(b)(2), 116 Stat. 1827.

§ 1392. Defendants or property in different districts in same State

Any civil action, of a local nature, involving property located in different districts in the same State, may be brought in any of such districts. As amended Oct. 1, 1996, Pub.L. 104–220, § 1, 110 Stat. 3023.

§ 1395. Fine, penalty or forfeiture

(a) A civil proceeding for the recovery of a pecuniary fine, penalty or forfeiture may be prosecuted in the district where it accrues or the defendant is found.

(b) A civil proceeding for the forfeiture of property may be prosecuted in any district where such property is found.

(c) A civil proceeding for the forfeiture of property seized outside any judicial district may be prosecuted in any district into which the property is brought.

(d) A proceeding in admiralty for the enforcement of fines, penalties and forfeitures against a vessel may be brought in any district in which the vessel is arrested.

(e) Any proceeding for the forfeiture of a vessel or cargo entering a port of entry closed by the President in pursuance of law, or of goods and chattels coming from a State or section declared by proclamation of the President to be in insurrection, or of any vessel or vehicle conveying persons or property to or from such State or section or belonging in whole or in part to a resident thereof, may be prosecuted in any district into which the property is taken and in which the proceeding is instituted.

§ 1396. Internal revenue taxes

Any civil action for the collection of internal revenue taxes may be brought in the district where the liability for such tax accrues, in the district of the taxpayer's residence, or in the district where the return was filed.

§ 1397. Interpleader

Any civil action of interpleader or in the nature of interpleader under section 1335 of this title may be brought in the judicial district in which one or more of the claimants reside.

§ 1400. Patents and copyrights, mask works, and designs

(a) Civil actions, suits, or proceedings arising under any Act of Congress relating to copyrights or exclusive rights in mask works or designs may be instituted in the district in which the defendant or his agent resides or may be found.

(b) Any civil action for patent infringement may be brought in the judicial district where the defendant resides, or where the defendant has committed acts of infringement and has a regular and established place of business. As amended Nov. 19, 1988, Pub.L. 100–702, Title X, § 1020(a)(5), 102 Stat. 4671; Oct. 28, 1998, Pub.L. 105–304, Title V, § 503(c), 112 Stat. 2917; Aug. 5, 1999, Pub.L. 106–44, § 2(a), 113 Stat. 223.

§ 1401. Stockholder's derivative action

Any civil action by a stockholder on behalf of his corporation may be prosecuted in any judicial district where the corporation might have sued the same defendants.

§ 1402. United States as defendant

(a) Any civil action in a district court against the United States under subsection (a) of section 1346 of this title may be prosecuted only:

(1) Except as provided in paragraph (2), in the judicial district where the plaintiff resides;

(2) In the case of a civil action by a corporation under paragraph (1) of subsection (a) of section 1346, in the judicial district in which is located the principal place of business or principal office or agency of the corporation; or if it has no principal place of business or principal office or agency in any judicial district (A) in the judicial district in which is located the office to which was made the return of the tax in respect of which the claim is made, or (B) if no return was made, in the judicial district in which lies the District of Columbia. Notwithstanding the foregoing provisions of this paragraph a district court, for the convenience of the parties and witnesses, in the interest of justice, may transfer any such action to any other district or division.

(b) Any civil action on a tort claim against the United States under subsection (b) of section 1346 of this title may be prosecuted only in the judicial district where the plaintiff resides or wherein the act or omission complained of occurred.

(c) Any civil action against the United States under subsection (e) of section 1346 of this title may be prosecuted only in the judicial district where the property is situated at the time of levy, or if no levy is made, in the judicial district in which the event occurred which gave rise to the cause of action.

(d) Any civil action under section 2409a to quiet title to an estate or interest in real property in which an interest is claimed by the United States shall be brought in the district court of the district where the property is located or, if located in different districts, in any of such districts. As amended Sept. 2, 1958, Pub.L. 85–920, 72 Stat. 1770; Nov. 2, 1966, Pub.L. 89–719, Title II, § 202(b), 80 Stat. 1149; Oct. 25, 1972, Pub.L. 92–562, § 2, 86 Stat. 1176; Apr. 2, 1982, Pub.L. 97–164, Title I, § 131, 96 Stat. 39.

§ 1404. Change of venue

(a) For the convenience of parties and witnesses, in the interest of justice, a district court may transfer any civil action to any other district or division where it might have been brought.

(b) Upon motion, consent or stipulation of all parties, any action, suit or proceeding of a civil nature or any motion of hearing thereof, may be transferred, in the discretion of the court, from the division in which pending to any other division in the same district. Transfer of proceedings in rem brought by or on behalf of the United States may be transferred under this section without the consent of the United States where all other parties request transfer.

(c) A district court may order any civil action to be tried at any place within the division in which it is pending.

(d) As used in this section, the term "district court" includes the District Court of Guam, the District Court for the Northern Mariana Islands, and the District Court of the Virgin Islands, and the term "district" includes the territorial jurisdiction of each such court. As amended Oct. 18, 1962, Pub.L. 87–845, § 9, 76A Stat. 699; Oct. 19, 1996, Pub.L. 104–317, Title VI, § 610(a), 110 Stat. 3860.

§ 1406. Cure or waiver of defects

(a) The district court of a district in which is filed a case laying venue in the wrong division or district shall dismiss, or if it be in the interest of justice, transfer such case to any district or division in which it could have been brought.

(b) Nothing in this chapter shall impair the jurisdiction of a district court of any matter involving a party who does not interpose timely and sufficient objection to the venue.

(c) As used in this section, the term "district court" includes the District Court of Guam, the District Court for the Northern Mariana Islands, and the District Court of the Virgin Islands, and the term "district" includes the territorial jurisdiction of each such court. As amended May 24, 1949, c. 139, § 81, 63 Stat. 101; Sept. 13, 1960, Pub.L. 86–770, § 1, 74 Stat. 912; Oct. 18, 1962, Pub.L. 87–845, § 10, 76A Stat.

699; Apr. 2, 1982, Pub.L. 97–164, Title I, § 132, 96 Stat. 39; Oct. 19, 1996, Pub.L. 104–317, Title VI, § 610(b), 110 Stat. 3860.

§ 1407. Multidistrict litigation

(a) When civil actions involving one or more common questions of fact are pending in different districts, such actions may be transferred to any district for coordinated or consolidated pretrial proceedings. Such transfers shall be made by the judicial panel on multidistrict litigation authorized by this section upon its determination that transfers for such proceedings will be for the convenience of parties and witnesses and will promote the just and efficient conduct of such actions. Each action so transferred shall be remanded by the panel at or before the conclusion of such pretrial proceedings to the district from which it was transferred unless it shall have been previously terminated: *Provided, however,* That the panel may separate any claim, cross-claim, counter-claim, or third-party claim and remand any of such claims before the remainder of the action is remanded.

(b) Such coordinated or consolidated pretrial proceedings shall be conducted by a judge or judges to whom such actions are assigned by the judicial panel on multidistrict litigation. For this purpose, upon request of the panel, a circuit judge or a district judge may be designated and assigned temporarily for service in the transferee district by the Chief Justice of the United States or the chief judge of the circuit, as may be required, in accordance with the provisions of chapter 13 of this title. With the consent of the transferee district court, such actions may be assigned by the panel to a judge or judges of such district. The judge or judges to whom such actions are assigned, the members of the judicial panel on multidistrict litigation, and other circuit and district judges designated when needed by the panel may exercise the powers of a district judge in any district for the purpose of conducting pretrial depositions in such coordinated or consolidated pretrial proceedings.

(c) Proceedings for the transfer of an action under this section may be initiated by—

(i) the judicial panel on multidistrict litigation upon its own initiative, or

(ii) motion filed with the panel by a party in any action in which transfer for coordinated or consolidated pretrial proceedings under this section may be appropriate. A copy of such motion shall be filed in the district court in which the moving party's action is pending.

The panel shall give notice to the parties in all actions in which transfers for coordinated or consolidated pretrial proceedings are contemplated, and such notice shall specify the time and place of any hearing to determine whether such transfer shall be made. Orders of the panel to set a hearing and other orders of the panel issued prior to the order either directing or denying transfer shall be filed in the office of the clerk of the district court in which a transfer hearing is to be or has been held. The panel's order of transfer shall be based upon a record of such hearing at which material evidence may be offered by any party to an action pending in any district that would be affected by the proceedings under this section, and shall be supported by findings of fact and conclusions of law based upon such record. Orders of transfer and such other orders as the panel may make thereafter shall be filed in the office of the clerk of the district court of the transferee district and shall be effective when thus filed. The clerk of the transferee district court shall forthwith transmit a certified copy of the panel's order to transfer to the clerk of the district court from which the action is being transferred. An order denying transfer shall be filed in each district wherein there is a case pending in which the motion for transfer has been made.

(d) The judicial panel on multidistrict litigation shall consist of seven circuit and district judges designated from time to time by the Chief Justice of the United States, no two of whom shall be from the same circuit. The concurrence of four members shall be necessary to any action by the panel.

(e) No proceedings for review of any order of the panel may be permitted except by extraordinary writ pursuant to the provisions of title 28, section 1651, United States Code. Petitions for an extraordinary writ to review an order of the panel to set a transfer hearing and other orders of the panel issued prior to the order either directing or denying transfer shall be filed only in the court of appeals having jurisdiction over the district in which a hearing is to be or has been held. Petitions for an extraordinary writ to review an order to transfer or orders subsequent to transfer shall be filed only in the court of appeals having jurisdiction over the transferee district. There shall be no appeal or review of an order of the panel denying a motion to transfer for consolidated or coordinated proceedings.

(f) The panel may prescribe rules for the conduct of its business not inconsistent with Acts of Congress and the Federal Rules of Civil Procedure.

(g) Nothing in this section shall apply to any action in which the United States is a complainant arising under the antitrust laws. "Antitrust laws" as used herein include those acts referred to in the Act of October 15, 1914, as amended (38 Stat. 730; 15 U.S.C. 12), and also include the Act of June 19, 1936 (49 Stat. 1526; 15 U.S.C. 13, 13a, and 13b) and the Act of September 26, 1914, as added March 21, 1938 (52 Stat. 116, 117; 15 U.S.C. 56); but shall not include section 4A of the Act of October 15, 1914, as added July 7, 1955 (69 Stat. 282; 15 U.S.C. 15a).

(h) Notwithstanding the provisions of section 1404 or subsection (f) of this section, the judicial panel on multidistrict litigation may consolidate and transfer with or without the consent of the parties, for both pretrial purposes and for trial, any action brought under section 4C of the Clayton Act. Added Apr. 29, 1968, Pub.L. 90–296, § 1, 82 Stat. 109; as amended Sept. 30, 1976, Pub.L. 94–435, Title III, § 303, 90 Stat. 1396.

§ 1408. Venue of cases under title 11

Except as provided in section 1410 of this title, a case under title 11 may be commenced in the district court for the district—

(1) in which the domicile, residence, principal place of business in the United States, or principal assets in the United States, of the person or entity that is the subject of such case have been located for the one hundred and eighty days immediately preceding such commencement, or for a longer portion of such one-hundred-and-eighty-

day period than the domicile, residence, or principal place of business, in the United States, or principal assets in the United States, of such person were located in any other district; or

(2) in which there is pending a case under title 11 concerning such person's affiliate, general partner, or partnership. Added July 10, 1984, Pub.L. 98–353, Title I, § 102(a), 98 Stat. 334.

§ 1409. Venue of proceedings arising under title 11 or arising in or related to cases under title 11

(a) Except as otherwise provided in subsections (b) and (d), a proceeding arising under title 11 or arising in or related to a case under title 11 may be commenced in the district court in which such case is pending.

(b) Except as provided in subsection (d) of this section, a trustee in a case under title 11 may commence a proceeding arising in or related to such case to recover a money judgement of or property worth less than $1,000 or a consumer debt of less than $15,000, or a debt (excluding a consumer debt) against a noninsider of less than $10,000, only in the district court for the district in which the defendant resides.

(c) Except as provided in subsection (b) of this section, a trustee in a case under title 11 may commence a proceeding arising in or related to such case as statutory successor to the debtor or creditors under section 541 or 544(b) of title 11 in the district court for the district where the State or Federal court sits in which, under applicable nonbankruptcy venue provisions, the debtor or creditors, as the case may be, may have commenced an action on which such proceeding is based if the case under title 11 had not been commenced.

(d) A trustee may commence a proceeding arising under title 11 or arising in or related to a case under title 11 based on a claim arising after the commencement of such case from the operation of the business of the debtor only in the district court for the district where a State or Federal court sits in which, under applicable nonbankruptcy venue provisions, an action on such claim may have been brought.

(e) A proceeding arising under title 11 or arising in or related to a case under title 11, based on a claim arising after the commencement of such case from the operation of the business of the debtor, may be commenced against the representative of the estate in such case in the district court for the district where the State or Federal courts sits in which the party commencing such proceeding may, under applicable nonbankruptcy venue provisions, have brought an action on such claim, or in the district court in which such case is pending. Added July 10, 1984, Pub.L. 98–353, Title I, § 102(a), 98 Stat. 334; as amended Apr. 20, 2005, Pub.L. 109–8, Title IV, § 410, 119 Stat. 106.

§ 1410. Venue of cases ancillary to foreign proceedings

A case under chapter 15 of title 11 may be commenced in the district court of the United States for the district—

(1) in which the debtor has its principal place of business or principal assets in the United States;

(2) if the debtor does not have a place of business or assets in the United States, in which there is pending against the debtor an action or proceeding in a Federal or State court; or

(3) in a case other than those specified in paragraph (1) or (2), in which venue will be consistent with the interests of justice and the convenience of the parties, having regard to the relief sought by the foreign representative. Added July 10, 1984, Pub.L. 98–353, Title I, § 102(a), 98 Stat. 335; as amended Apr. 20, 2005, Pub.L. 109–8, Title VIII, § 802(c)(4), 119 Stat. 146.

§ 1411. Jury trials

(a) Except as provided in subsection (b) of this section, this chapter and title 11 do not affect any right to trial by jury that an individual has under applicable nonbankruptcy law with regard to a personal injury or wrongful death tort claim.

(b) The district court may order the issues arising under section 303 of title 11 to be tried without a jury. Added July 10, 1984, Pub.L. 98–353, Title I, § 102(a), 98 Stat. 335.

§ 1412. Change of venue

A district court may transfer a case or proceeding under title 11 to a district court for another district, in the interest of justice or for the convenience of the parties. Added July 10, 1984, Pub.L. 98–353, Title I, § 102(a), 98 Stat. 335.

§ 1441. Actions removable generally

(a) Except as otherwise expressly provided by Act of Congress, any civil action brought in a State court of which the district courts of the United States have original jurisdiction, may be removed by the defendant or the defendants, to the district court of the United States for the district and division embracing the place where such action is pending. For purposes of removal under this chapter, the citizenship of defendants sued under fictitious names shall be disregarded.

(b) Any civil action of which the district courts have original jurisdiction founded on a claim or right arising under the Constitution, treaties or laws of the United States shall be removable without regard to the citizenship or residence of the parties. Any other such action shall be removable only if none of the parties in interest properly joined and served as defendants is a citizen of the State in which such action is brought.

(c) Whenever a separate and independent claim or cause of action within the jurisdiction conferred by section 1331 of this title is joined with one or more otherwise non-removable claims or causes of action, the entire case may be removed and the district court may determine all issues therein, or, in its discretion, may remand all matters in which State law predominates.

(d) Any civil action brought in a State court against a foreign state as defined in section 1603(a) of this title may be removed by the foreign state to the district court of the United States for the district and division embracing the place where such action is pending. Upon removal the action shall be tried by the court without jury. Where removal is based upon this subsection, the time limitations of section 1446(b) of this chapter may be enlarged at any time for cause shown.

(e)(1) Notwithstanding the provisions of subsection (b) of this section, a defendant in a civil action in a State court may remove the action to the district court of the United States for the district and division embracing the place where the action is pending if—

(A) the action could have been brought in a United States district court under section 1369 of this title; or

(B) the defendant is a party to an action which is or could have been brought, in whole or in part, under section 1369 in a United States district court and arises from the same accident as the action in State court, even if the action to be removed could not have been brought in a district court as an original matter.

The removal of an action under this subsection shall be made in accordance with section 1446 of this title, except that a notice of removal may also be filed before trial of the action in State court within 30 days after the date on which the defendant first becomes a party to an action under section 1369 in a United States district court that arises from the same accident as the action in State court, or at a later time with leave of the district court.

(2) Whenever an action is removed under this subsection and the district court to which it is removed or transferred under section 1407(j) has made a liability determination requiring further proceedings as to damages, the district court shall remand the action to the State court from which it had been removed for the determination of damages, unless the court finds that, for the convenience of parties and witnesses and in the interest of justice, the action should be retained for the determination of damages.

(3) Any remand under paragraph (2) shall not be effective until 60 days after the district court has issued an order determining liability and has certified its intention to remand the removed action for the determination of damages. An appeal with respect to the liability determination of the district court may be taken during that 60-day period to the court of appeals with appellate jurisdiction over the district court. In the event a party files such an appeal, the remand shall not be effective until the appeal has been finally disposed of. Once the remand has become effective, the liability determination shall not be subject to further review by appeal or otherwise.

(4) Any decision under this subsection concerning remand for the determination of damages shall not be reviewable by appeal or otherwise.

(5) An action removed under this subsection shall be deemed to be an action under section 1369 and an action in which jurisdiction is based on section 1369 of this title for purposes of this section and sections 1407, 1697, and 1785 of this title.

(6) Nothing in this subsection shall restrict the authority of the district court to transfer or dismiss an action on the ground of inconvenient forum.

(f) The court to which a civil action is removed under this section is not precluded from hearing and determining any claim in such civil action because the State court from which such civil action is removed did not have jurisdiction over that claim. As amended Oct. 21, 1976, Pub.L. 94–583, § 6, 90 Stat. 2898; June 19, 1986, Pub.L. 99–336, § 3, 100 Stat. 637; Nov. 19, 1988, Pub.L. 100–702, Title X, § 1016(a), 102 Stat. 4669; Dec. 1, 1990, Pub.L. 101–650, Title III, § 312, 104 Stat. 5114; Dec. 9, 1991, Pub.L. 102–198, § 4, 105 Stat. 1623; Nov. 2, 2002, Pub.L. 107–273, Div. C, Title I, § 11020(b)(3), 116 Stat. 1827.

§ 1442. Federal officers or agencies sued or prosecuted

(a) A civil action or criminal prosecution commenced in a State court against any of the following may be removed by them to the district court of the United States for the district and division embracing the place wherein it is pending:

(1) The United States or any agency thereof or any officer (or any person acting under that officer) of the United States or of any agency thereof, sued in an official or individual capacity for any act under color of such office or on account of any right, title or authority claimed under any Act of Congress for the apprehension or punishment of criminals or the collection of the revenue.

(2) A property holder whose title is derived from any such officer, where such action or prosecution affects the validity of any law of the United States.

(3) Any officer of the courts of the United States, for any Act under color of office or in the performance of his duties;

(4) Any officer of either House of Congress, for any act in the discharge of his official duty under an order of such House.

(b) A personal action commenced in any State court by an alien against any citizen of a State who is, or at the time the alleged action accrued was, a civil officer of the United States and is a nonresident of such State, wherein jurisdiction is obtained by the State court by personal service of process, may be removed by the defendant to the district court of the United States for the district and division in which the defendant was served with process. As amended Oct. 19, 1996, Pub.L. 104–317, Title II, § 206, 110 Stat. 3850.

§ 1442a. Members of armed forces sued or prosecuted

A civil or criminal prosecution in a court of a State of the United States against a member of the armed forces of the United States on account of an act done under color of his office or status, or in respect to which he claims any right, title, or authority under a law of the United States respecting the armed forces thereof, or under the law of war, may at any time before the trial or final hearing thereof be removed for trial into the district court of the United States for the district where it is pending in the manner prescribed by law, and it shall thereupon be entered on the docket of the district court, which shall proceed as if the cause had been originally commenced therein and shall have full power to hear and determine the cause. Added Aug. 10, 1956, c. 1041, § 19(a), 70A Stat. 626.

§ 1443. Civil rights cases

Any of the following civil actions or criminal prosecutions, commenced in a State court may be removed by the defendant to the district court of the United States for the district and division embracing the place wherein it is pending:

(1) Against any person who is denied or cannot enforce in the courts of such State a right under any law providing for the equal civil rights of citizens of the United States, or of all persons within the jurisdiction thereof;

(2) For any act under color of authority derived from any law providing for equal rights, or for refusing to do any act on the ground that it would be inconsistent with such law.

§ 1445. Nonremovable actions

(a) A civil action in any State court against a railroad or its receivers or trustees, arising under sections 1–4 and 5–10 of the Act of April 22, 1908 (45 U.S.C. 51–54, 55–60), may not be removed to any district court of the United States.

(b) A civil action in any State court against a carrier or its receivers or trustees to recover damages for delay, loss, or injury of shipments, arising under section 11706 or 14706 of Title 49, may not be removed to any district court of the United States unless the matter in controversy exceeds $10,000, exclusive of interest and costs.

(c) A civil action in any State court arising under the workmen's compensation laws of such State may not be removed to any district court of the United States.

(d) A civil action in any State court arising under section 40302 of the Violence Against Women Act of 1994 may not be removed to any district court of the United States. As amended July 25, 1958, Pub.L. 85–554, § 5, 72 Stat. 415; Oct. 17, 1978, Pub.L. 95–473, § 2(a)(3)(A), 92 Stat. 1465; Oct. 20, 1978, Pub.L. 95–486, § 9(b), 92 Stat. 1634; Sept. 13, 1994, Pub.L. 103–322, Title IV, § 40302(e)(5), 108 Stat. 1942; Dec. 29, 1995, Pub.L. 104–88, Title III, § 305(b), 109 Stat. 944; Oct. 11, 1996, Pub.L. 104–287, § 3, 110 Stat. 3388.

§ 1446. Procedure for removal

(a) A defendant or defendants desiring to remove any civil action or criminal prosecution from a State court shall file in the district court of the United States for the district and division within which such action is pending a notice of removal signed pursuant to Rule 11 of the Federal Rules of Civil Procedure and containing a short and plain statement of the grounds for removal, together with a copy of all process, pleadings, and orders served upon such defendant or defendants in such action.

(b) The notice of removal of a civil action or proceeding shall be filed within thirty days after the receipt by the defendant, through service or otherwise, of a copy of the initial pleading setting forth the claim for relief upon which such action or proceeding is based, or within thirty days after the service of summons upon the defendant if such initial pleading has·

then been filed in court and is not required to be served on the defendant, whichever period is shorter.

If the case stated by the initial pleading is not removable, a notice of removal may be filed within thirty days after receipt by the defendant, through service or otherwise, of a copy of an amended pleading, motion, order or other paper from which it may first be ascertained that the case is one which is or has become removable, except that a case may not be removed on the basis of jurisdiction conferred by section 1332 of this title more than 1 year after commencement of the action.

(c)(1) A notice of removal of a criminal prosecution shall be filed not later than thirty days after the arraignment in the State court, or at any time before trial, whichever is earlier, except that for good cause shown the United States district court may enter an order granting the defendant or defendants leave to file the notice at a later time.

(2) A notice of removal of a criminal prosecution shall include all grounds for such removal. A failure to state grounds which exist at the time of the filing of the notice shall constitute a waiver of such grounds, and a second notice may be filed only on grounds not existing at the time of the original notice. For good cause shown, the United States district court may grant relief from the limitations of this paragraph.

(3) The filing of a notice of removal of a criminal prosecution shall not prevent the State court in which such prosecution is pending from proceeding further, except that a judgment of conviction shall not be entered unless the prosecution is first remanded.

(4) The United States district court in which such notice is filed shall examine the notice promptly. If it clearly appears on the face of the notice and any exhibits annexed thereto that removal should not be permitted, the court shall make an order for summary remand.

(5) If the United States district court does not order the summary remand of such prosecution, it shall order an evidentiary hearing to be held promptly and after such hearing shall make such disposition of the prosecution as justice shall require. If the United States district court determines that removal shall be permitted, it shall so notify the State court in which prosecution is pending, which shall proceed no further.

(d) Promptly after the filing of such notice of removal of a civil action the defendant or defendants shall give written notice thereof to all adverse parties and shall file a copy of the notice with the clerk of such State court, which shall effect removal and the State court shall proceed no further unless and until the case is remanded.

(e) If the defendant or defendants are in actual custody on process issued by the State court, the district court shall issue its writ of habeas corpus, and the marshal shall thereupon take such defendant or defendants into his custody and deliver a copy of the writ to the clerk of such State court.

(f) With respect to any counterclaim removed to a district court pursuant to section 337(c) of the Tariff Act of 1930, the district court shall resolve such counterclaim in the same manner as an original complaint under the Federal Rules of Civil Procedure, except that the payment of a filing fee shall not be required in such cases and the counterclaim shall relate back to the date of the original complaint in the proceeding before the International Trade Commission under section 337 of that Act. As amended May 24, 1949, c. 139, § 83, 63 Stat. 101; Sept. 29, 1965, Pub.L. 89–215, 79 Stat. 887; July 30, 1977, Pub.L. 95–78, § 3, 91 Stat. 321; Nov. 19, 1988, Pub.L. 100–702, Title X, § 1016(b), 102 Stat. 4669; Dec. 9, 1991, Pub.L. 102–198, § 10(a), 105 Stat. 1626; Dec. 12, 1994, Pub.L. 103–465, Title III, § 321(b)(2), 108 Stat. 4946; Oct. 19, 1996, Pub.L. 104–317, Title VI, § 603, 110 Stat. 3857.

§ 1447. Procedure after removal generally

(a) In any case removed from a State court, the district court may issue all necessary orders and process to bring before it all proper parties whether served by process issued by the State court or otherwise.

(b) It may require the removing party to file with its clerk copies of all records and proceedings in such State court or may cause the same to be brought before it by writ of certiorari issued to such State court.

(c) A motion to remand the case on the basis of any defect other than lack of subject matter jurisdiction must be made within 30 days after the filing of the notice of removal under section 1446(a). If at any time before final judgment it appears that the district court lacks subject matter jurisdiction, the case shall be remanded. An order remanding the case may require payment of just costs and any actual expenses, including attorney fees, incurred as a result of the removal. A certified copy of the order of remand shall be mailed by the clerk to the clerk of the State court. The State court may thereupon proceed with such case.

(d) An order remanding a case to the State court from which it was removed is not reviewable on appeal or otherwise, except that an order remanding a case to the State court from which it was removed pursuant to section 1443 of this title shall be reviewable by appeal or otherwise.

(e) If after removal the plaintiff seeks to join additional defendants whose joinder would destroy subject matter jurisdiction, the court may deny joinder, or permit joinder and remand the action to the State court. As amended May 24, 1949, c. 139, § 84, 63 Stat. 102; July 2, 1964, Pub.L. 88–352, Title IX, § 901, 78 Stat. 266; Nov. 19, 1988, Pub.L. 100–702, Title X, § 1016(c), 102 Stat. 4670; Dec. 9, 1991, Pub.L. 102–198, § 10(b), 105 Stat. 1626; Oct. 1, 1996, Pub.L. 104–219, § 1, 110 Stat. 3022.

§ 1448. Process after removal

In all cases removed from any State court to any district court of the United States in which any one or more of the defendants has not been served with process or in which the service has not been perfected prior to removal, or in which process served proves to be defective, such process or service may be completed or new process issued in the same manner as in cases originally filed in such district court.

This section shall not deprive any defendant upon whom process is served after removal of his right to move to remand the case.

§ 1449. State court record supplied

Where a party is entitled to copies of the records and proceedings in any suit or prosecution in a State court, to be used in any district court of the United States, and the clerk of such State court, upon demand, and the payment or tender of the legal fees, fails to deliver certified copies, the district court may, on affidavit reciting such facts, direct such record to be supplied by affidavit or otherwise. Thereupon such proceedings, trial, and judgment may be had in such district court, and all such process awarded, as if certified copies had been filed in the district court. As amended May 24, 1949, c. 139, § 85, 63 Stat. 102.

§ 1450. Attachment or sequestration; securities

Whenever any action is removed from a State court to a district court of the United States, any attachment or sequestration of the goods or estate of the defendant in such action in the State court shall hold the goods or estate to answer the final judgment or decree in the same manner as they would have been held to answer final judgment or decree had it been rendered by the State court.

All bonds, undertakings, or security given by either party in such action prior to its removal shall remain valid and effectual notwithstanding such removal.

All injunctions, orders, and other proceedings had in such action prior to its removal shall remain in full force and effect until dissolved or modified by the district court.

§ 1451. Definitions

For purposes of this chapter—

(1) The term "State court" includes the Superior Court of the District of Columbia.

(2) The term "State" includes the District of Columbia. Added July 29, 1970, Pub.L. 91–358, Title I, § 172(d)(1), 84 Stat. 591.

§ 1452. Removal of claims related to bankruptcy cases

(a) A party may remove any claim or cause of action in a civil action other than a proceeding before the United States Tax Court or a civil action by a governmental unit to enforce such governmental unit's police or regulatory power, to the district court for the district where such civil action is pending, if such district court has jurisdiction of such claim or cause of action under section 1334 of this title.

(b) The court to which such claim or cause of action is removed may remand such claim or cause of action on any equitable ground. An order entered under this subsection remanding a claim or cause of action, or a decision to not remand, is not reviewable by appeal or otherwise by the court of appeals under section 158(d), 1291, or 1292 of this title or by the Supreme Court of the United States under section 1254 of this title. Added July 10, 1984, Pub.L. 98–353, Title I, § 103(a), 98 Stat. 335; as amended Dec. 1, 1990, Pub.L. 101–650, Title III, § 309(c), 104 Stat. 5113.

§ 1453. Removal of class actions

(a) Definitions.—In this section, the terms "class", "class action", "class certification order", and "class member" shall have the meanings given such terms under section 1332(d)(1).

(b) In general.—A class action may be removed to a district court of the United States in accordance with section 1446 (except that the 1–year limitation under section 1446(b) shall not apply), without regard to whether any defendant is a citizen of the State in which the action is brought, except that such action may be removed by any defendant without the consent of all defendants.

(c) Review of remand orders.—

(1) In general.—Section 1447 shall apply to any removal of a case under this section, except that notwithstanding section 1447(d), a court of appeals may accept an appeal from an order of a district court granting or denying a motion to remand a class action to the State court from which it was removed if application is made to the court of appeals not more than 10 days after entry of the order.

(2) Time period for judgment.—If the court of appeals accepts an appeal under paragraph (1), the court shall complete all action on such appeal, including rendering judgment, not later than 60 days after the date on which such appeal was filed, unless an extension is granted under paragraph (3).

(3) Extension of time period.—The court of appeals may grant an extension of the 60–day period described in paragraph (2) if—

(A) all parties to the proceeding agree to such extension, for any period of time; or

(B) such extension is for good cause shown and in the interests of justice, for a period not to exceed 10 days.

(4) Denial of appeal.—If a final judgment on the appeal under paragraph (1) is not issued before the end of the period described in paragraph (2), including any extension under paragraph (3), the appeal shall be denied.

(d) Exception.—This section shall not apply to any class action that solely involves—

(1) a claim concerning a covered security as defined under section 16(f) (3) of the Securities Act of 1933 (15 U.S.C. 78p(f)(3)) and section 28(f)(5)(E) of the Securities Exchange Act of 1934 (15 U.S.C. 78bb(f)(5)(E));

(2) a claim that relates to the internal affairs or governance of a corporation or other form of business enterprise and arises under or by virtue of the laws of the State in which such corporation or business enterprise is incorporated or organized; or

(3) a claim that relates to the rights, duties (including fiduciary duties), and obligations relating to or created by or pursuant to any security (as defined under section 2(a)(1) of the Securities Act of 1933 (15 U.S.C. 77b(a)(1)) and the regulations issued thereunder). Added

Feb. 18, 2005, Pub.L. 109–2, § 5(a), 119 Stat. 12; as amended May 7, 2009, Pub.L. 111–6, § 6(2), 123 Stat. 1608, 1609.

§ 1602. Findings and declaration of purpose

The Congress finds that the determination by United States courts of the claims of foreign states to immunity from the jurisdiction of such courts would serve the interests of justice and would protect the rights of both foreign states and litigants in United States courts. Under international law, states are not immune from the jurisdiction of foreign courts insofar as their commercial activities are concerned, and their commercial property may be levied upon for the satisfaction of judgments rendered against them in connection with their commercial activities. Claims of foreign states to immunity should henceforth be decided by courts of the United States and of the States in conformity with the principles set forth in this chapter. Added Oct. 21, 1976, Pub.L. 94–583, § 4(a), 90 Stat. 2892.

§ 1603. Definitions

For purposes of this chapter—

(a) A "foreign state", except as used in section 1608 of this title, includes a political subdivision of a foreign state or an agency or instrumentality of a foreign state as defined in subsection (b).

(b) An "agency or instrumentality of a foreign state" means any entity—

(1) which is a separate legal person, corporate or otherwise, and

(2) which is an organ of a foreign state or political subdivision thereof, or a majority of whose shares or other ownership interest is owned by a foreign state or political subdivision thereof, and

(3) which is neither a citizen of a State of the United States as defined in section 1332(c) and (e) of this title, nor created under the laws of any third country.

(c) The "United States" includes all territory and waters, continental or insular, subject to the jurisdiction of the United States.

(d) A "commercial activity" means either a regular course of commercial conduct or a particular commercial transaction or act. The commercial character of an activity shall be determined by reference to the nature of the course of conduct or particular transaction or act, rather than by reference to its purpose.

(e) A "commercial activity carried on in the United States by a foreign state" means commercial activity carried on by such state and having substantial contact with the United States. Added Oct. 21, 1976, Pub.L. 94–583, § 4(a), 90 Stat. 2892; as amended Feb. 18, 2005, Pub.L. 109–2, § 4(b)(2), 119 Stat. 12.

§ 1604. Immunity of a foreign state from jurisdiction

Subject to existing international agreements to which the United States is a party at the time of enactment of this Act a foreign state shall be immune from the jurisdiction of the courts of the United States and of the States except as provided in sections 1605 to 1607 of this chapter. Added Oct. 21, 1976, Pub.L. 94–583, § 4(a), 90 Stat. 2892.

§ 1605. General exceptions to the jurisdictional immunity of a foreign state

(a) A foreign state shall not be immune from the jurisdiction of courts of the United States or of the States in any case—

(1) in which the foreign state has waived its immunity either explicitly or by implication, notwithstanding any withdrawal of the waiver which the foreign state may purport to effect except in accordance with the terms of the waiver;

(2) in which the action is based upon a commercial activity carried on in the United States by the foreign state; or upon an act performed in the United States in connection with a commercial activity of the foreign state elsewhere; or upon an act outside the territory of the United States in connection with a commercial activity of the foreign state elsewhere and that act causes a direct effect in the United States;

(3) in which rights in property taken in violation of international law are in issue and that property or any property exchanged for such property is present in the United States in connection with a commercial activity carried on in the United States by the foreign state; or that property or any property exchanged for such property is owned or operated by an agency or instrumentality of the foreign state and that agency or instrumentality is engaged in a commercial activity in the United States;

(4) in which rights in property in the United States acquired by succession or gift or rights in immovable property situated in the United States are in issue;

(5) not otherwise encompassed in paragraph (2) above, in which money damages are sought against a foreign state for personal injury or death, or damage to or loss of property, occurring in the United States and caused by the tortious act or omission of that foreign state or of any official or employee of that foreign state while acting within the scope of his office or employment; except this paragraph shall not apply to—

(A) any claim based upon the exercise or performance or the failure to exercise or perform a discretionary function regardless of whether the discretion be abused, or

(B) any claim arising out of malicious prosecution, abuse of process, libel, slander, misrepresentation, deceit, or interference with contract rights; or

(6) in which the action is brought, either to enforce an agreement made by the foreign state with or for the benefit of a private party to submit to arbitration all or any differences which have arisen or which may arise between the parties with respect to a defined legal relationship, whether contractual or not, concerning a subject matter capable of settlement by arbitration under the laws of the United States, or to

confirm an award made pursuant to such an agreement to arbitrate, if (A) the arbitration takes place or is intended to take place in the United States, (B) the agreement or award is or may be governed by a treaty or other international agreement in force for the United States calling for the recognition and enforcement of arbitral awards, (C) the underlying claim, save for the agreement to arbitrate, could have been brought in a United States court under this section or section 1607, or (D) paragraph (1) of this subsection is otherwise applicable.

(b) A foreign state shall not be immune from the jurisdiction of the courts of the United States in any case in which a suit in admiralty is brought to enforce a maritime lien against a vessel or cargo of the foreign state, which maritime lien is based upon a commercial activity of the foreign state: *Provided,* That—

(1) notice of the suit is given by delivery of a copy of the summons and of the complaint to the person, or his agent, having possession of the vessel or cargo against which the maritime lien is asserted; and if the vessel or cargo is arrested pursuant to process obtained on behalf of the party bringing the suit, the service of process of arrest shall be deemed to constitute valid delivery of such notice, but the party bringing the suit shall be liable for any damages sustained by the foreign state as a result of the arrest if the party bringing the suit had actual or constructive knowledge that the vessel or cargo of a foreign state was involved; and

(2) notice to the foreign state of the commencement of suit as provided in section 1608 of this title is initiated within ten days either of the delivery of notice as provided in paragraph (1) of this subsection or, in the case of a party who was unaware that the vessel or cargo of a foreign state was involved, of the date such party determined the existence of the foreign state's interest.

(c) Whenever notice is delivered under subsection (b)(1), the suit to enforce a maritime lien shall thereafter proceed and shall be heard and determined according to the principles of law and rules of practice of suits in rem whenever it appears that, had the vessel been privately owned and possessed, a suit in rem might have been maintained. A decree against the foreign state may include costs of the suit and, if the decree is for a money judgment, interest as ordered by the court, except that the court may not award judgment against the foreign state in an amount greater than the value of the vessel or cargo upon which the maritime lien arose. Such value shall be determined as of the time notice is served under subsection (b)(1). Decrees shall be subject to appeal and revision as provided in other cases of admiralty and maritime jurisdiction. Nothing shall preclude the plaintiff in any proper case from seeking relief in personam in the same action brought to enforce a maritime lien as provided in this section.

(d) A foreign state shall not be immune from the jurisdiction of the courts of the United States in any action brought to foreclose a preferred mortgage, as defined in section 31301 of title 46. Such action shall be brought, heard, and determined in accordance with the provisions of chapter 313 of title 46 and in accordance with the principles of law and rules of practice of suits in rem, whenever it appears that had the vessel been privately owned and possessed a suit in rem might have been maintained.

(e) [Repealed.]

(f) [Repealed.]

(g) Limitation on Discovery.—

(1) In General.—(A) Subject to paragraph (2), if an action is filed that would otherwise be barred by section 1604, but for section 1605A, the court, upon request of the Attorney General, shall stay any request, demand, or order for discovery on the United States that the Attorney General certifies would significantly interfere with a criminal investigation or prosecution, or a national security operation, related to the incident that gave rise to the cause of action, until such time as the Attorney General advises the court that such request, demand, or order will no longer so interfere.

(B) A stay under this paragraph shall be in effect during the 12–month period beginning on the date on which the court issues the order to stay discovery. The court shall renew the order to stay discovery for additional 12–month periods upon motion by the United States if the Attorney General certifies that discovery would significantly interfere with a criminal investigation or prosecution, or a national security operation, related to the incident that gave rise to the cause of action.

(2) Sunset.—(A) Subject to subparagraph (B), no stay shall be granted or continued in effect under paragraph (1) after the date that is 10 years after the date on which the incident that gave rise to the cause of action occurred.

(B) After the period referred to in subparagraph (A), the court, upon request of the Attorney General, may stay any request, demand, or order for discovery on the United States that the court finds a substantial likelihood would—

(i) create a serious threat of death or serious bodily injury to any person;

(ii) adversely affect the ability of the United States to work in cooperation with foreign and international law enforcement agencies in investigating violations of United States law; or

(iii) obstruct the criminal case related to the incident that gave rise to the cause of action or undermine the potential for a conviction in such case.

(3) Evaluation of Evidence.—The court's evaluation of any request for a stay under this subsection filed by the Attorney General shall be conducted ex parte and in camera.

(4) Bar on Motions to Dismiss.—A stay of discovery under this subsection shall constitute a bar to the granting of a motion to dismiss under rules 12(b)(6) and 56 of the Federal Rules of Civil Procedure.

(5) Construction.—Nothing in this subsection shall prevent the United States from seeking protective orders or asserting privileges

ordinarily available to the United States. Added Oct. 21, 1976, Pub.L. 94–583, § 4(a), 90 Stat. 2892; as amended Nov. 9, 1988, Pub.L. 100–640, § 1, 102 Stat. 3333; Nov. 16, 1988, Pub.L. 100–669, § 2, 102 Stat. 3969; Dec. 1, 1990, Pub.L. 101–650, Title III, § 325(b)(8), 104 Stat. 5121; Apr. 24, 1996, Pub.L. 104–132, Title II, § 221(a), 110 Stat. 1241; Apr. 25, 1997, Pub.L. 105–11, 111 Stat. 22; Nov. 28, 2001, Pub.L. 107–77, Title VI, § 626(c), 115 Stat. 803; Jan. 10, 2003, Pub.L. 107–117, Div. B, § 208, 115 Stat. 2299; Oct. 6, 2006, Pub.L. 109–304, § 17(f)(2), 120 Stat. 1708; Jan. 28, 2008, Pub.L. 110–181, Div. A, Title X, § 1083(b)(1), 122 Stat. 341.

§ 1605A. Terrorism exception to the jurisdictional immunity of a foreign state

(a) In General.—

(1) No Immunity.—A foreign state shall not be immune from the jurisdiction of courts of the United States or of the States in any case not otherwise covered by this chapter in which money damages are sought against a foreign state for personal injury or death that was caused by an act of torture, extrajudicial killing, aircraft sabotage, hostage taking, or the provision of material support or resources for such an act if such act or provision of material support or resources is engaged in by an official, employee, or agent of such foreign state while acting within the scope of his or her office, employment, or agency.

(2) Claim Heard.—The court shall hear a claim under this section if—

(A)(i)(I) the foreign state was designated as a state sponsor of terrorism at the time the act described in paragraph (1) occurred, or was so designated as a result of such act, and, subject to subclause (II), either remains so designated when the claim is filed under this section or was so designated within the 6–month period before the claim is filed under this section; or

(II) in the case of an action that is refiled under this section by reason of section 1083(c)(2)(A) of the National Defense Authorization Act for Fiscal Year 2008 or is filed under this section by reason of section 1083(c)(3) of that Act, the foreign state was designated as a state sponsor of terrorism when the original action or the related action under section 1605(a)(7) (as in effect before the enactment of this section) or section 589 of the Foreign Operations, Export Financing, and Related Programs Appropriations Act, 1997 (as contained in section 101(c) of division A of Public Law 104–208) was filed;

(ii) the claimant or the victim was, at the time the act described in paragraph (1) occurred—

(I) a national of the United States;

(II) a member of the armed forces; or

(III) otherwise an employee of the Government of the United States, or of an individual performing a contract awarded by the United States Government, acting within the scope of the employee's employment; and

(iii) in a case in which the act occurred in the foreign state against which the claim has been brought, the claimant has afforded the foreign state a reasonable opportunity to arbitrate the claim in accordance with the accepted international rules of arbitration; or

(B) the act described in paragraph (1) is related to Case Number 1:00CV03110 (EGS) in the United States District Court for the District of Columbia.

(b) Limitations.—An action may be brought or maintained under this section if the action is commenced, or a related action was commenced under section 1605(a)(7) (before the date of the enactment of this section) or section 589 of the Foreign Operations, Export Financing, and Related Programs Appropriations Act, 1997 (as contained in section 101(c) of division A of Public Law 104–208) not later than the latter of—

(1) 10 years after April 24, 1996; or

(2) 10 years after the date on which the cause of action arose.

(c) Private Right of Action.—A foreign state that is or was a state sponsor of terrorism as described in subsection (a)(2)(A)(i), and any official, employee, or agent of that foreign state while acting within the scope of his or her office, employment, or agency, shall be liable to—

(1) a national of the United States,

(2) a member of the armed forces,

(3) an employee of the Government of the United States, or of an individual performing a contract awarded by the United States Government, acting within the scope of the employee's employment, or

(4) the legal representative of a person described in paragraph (1), (2), or (3),

for personal injury or death caused by acts described in subsection (a) (1) of that foreign state, or of an official, employee, or agent of that foreign state, for which the courts of the United States may maintain jurisdiction under this section for money damages. In any such action, damages may include economic damages, solatium, pain and suffering, and punitive damages. In any such action, a foreign state shall be vicariously liable for the acts of its officials, employees, or agents.

(d) Additional Damages.—After an action has been brought under subsection (c), actions may also be brought for reasonably foreseeable property loss, whether insured or uninsured, third party liability, and loss claims under life and property insurance policies, by reason of the same acts on which the action under subsection (c) is based.

(e) Special Masters.—

(1) In General.—The courts of the United States may appoint special masters to hear damage claims brought under this section.

(2) Transfer of Funds.—The Attorney General shall transfer, from funds available for the program under section 1404C of the Victims of

Crime Act of 1984 (42 U.S.C. 10603c), to the Administrator of the United States district court in which any case is pending which has been brought or maintained under this section such funds as may be required to cover the costs of special masters appointed under paragraph (1). Any amount paid in compensation to any such special master shall constitute an item of court costs.

(f) Appeal.—In an action brought under this section, appeals from orders not conclusively ending the litigation may only be taken pursuant to section 1292(b) of this title.

(g) Property Disposition.—

(1) In General.—In every action filed in a United States district court in which jurisdiction is alleged under this section, the filing of a notice of pending action pursuant to this section, to which is attached a copy of the complaint filed in the action, shall have the effect of establishing a lien of lis pendens upon any real property or tangible personal property that is—

(A) subject to attachment in aid of execution, or execution, under section 1610;

(B) located within that judicial district; and

(C) titled in the name of any defendant, or titled in the name of any entity controlled by any defendant if such notice contains a statement listing such controlled entity.

(2) Notice.—A notice of pending action pursuant to this section shall be filed by the clerk of the district court in the same manner as any pending action and shall be indexed by listing as defendants all named defendants and all entities listed as controlled by any defendant.

(3) Enforceability.—Liens established by reason of this subsection shall be enforceable as provided in chapter 111 of this title.

(h) Definitions.—For purposes of this section—

(1) the term "aircraft sabotage" has the meaning given that term in Article 1 of the Convention for the Suppression of Unlawful Acts Against the Safety of Civil Aviation;

(2) the term "hostage taking" has the meaning given that term in Article 1 of the International Convention Against the Taking of Hostages;

(3) the term "material support or resources" has the meaning given that term in section 2339A of title 18;

(4) the term "armed forces" has the meaning given that term in section 101 of title 10;

(5) the term "national of the United States" has the meaning given that term in section 101(a)(22) of the Immigration and Nationality Act (8 U.S.C. 1101(a)(22));

(6) the term "state sponsor of terrorism" means a country the government of which the Secretary of State has determined, for purposes of section 6(j) of the Export Administration Act of 1979 (50

587

U.S.C. App. 2405(j)), section 620A of the Foreign Assistance Act of 1961 (22 U.S.C. 2371), section 40 of the Arms Export Control Act (22 U.S.C. 2780), or any other provision of law, is a government that has repeatedly provided support for acts of international terrorism; and

(7) the terms "torture" and "extrajudicial killing" have the meaning given those terms in section 3 of the Torture Victim Protection Act of 1991 (28 U.S.C. 1350 note). Added Jan. 28, 2008, Pub.L. 110–181, Div. A, Title X, § 1083(a)(1), 122 Stat. 338.

§ 1606. Extent of liability

As to any claim for relief with respect to which a foreign state is not entitled to immunity under section 1605 or 1607 of this chapter, the foreign state shall be liable in the same manner and to the same extent as a private individual under like circumstances; but a foreign state except for an agency or instrumentality thereof shall not be liable for punitive damages; if, however, in any case wherein death was caused, the law of the place where the action or omission occurred provides, or has been construed to provide, for damages only punitive in nature, the foreign state shall be liable for actual or compensatory damages measured by the pecuniary injuries resulting from such death which were incurred by the persons for whose benefit the action was brought. Added Oct. 21, 1976, Pub.L. 94–583, § 4(a), 90 Stat. 2894; as amended Oct. 21, 1998, Pub.L. 105–277, Div. A, § 101(h) [Title I, § 117(b)], 112 Stat. 2681–491; Oct. 28, 2000, Pub.L. 106–386, Div. C, § 2002(f)(2), 114 Stat. 1543.

§ 1607. Counterclaims

In any action brought by a foreign state, or in which a foreign state intervenes, in a court of the United States or of a State, the foreign state shall not be accorded immunity with respect to any counterclaim—

(a) for which a foreign state would not be entitled to immunity under section 1605 or 1605A of this chapter had such claim been brought in a separate action against the foreign state; or

(b) arising out of the transaction or occurrence that is the subject matter of the claim of the foreign state; or

(c) to the extent that the counterclaim does not seek relief exceeding in amount or differing in kind from that sought by the foreign state. Added Oct. 21, 1976, Pub.L. 94–583, § 4(a), 90 Stat. 2894; as amended Jan. 28, 2008, Pub.L. 110–181, Div. A, Title X, § 1083(b)(2), 122 Stat. 341.

§ 1608. Service; time to answer; default

(a) Service in the courts of the United States and of the States shall be made upon a foreign state or political subdivision of a foreign state:

(1) by delivery of a copy of the summons and complaint in accordance with any special arrangement for service between the plaintiff and the foreign state or political subdivision; or

(2) if no special arrangement exists, by delivery of a copy of the summons and complaint in accordance with an applicable international convention on service of judicial documents; or

(3) if service cannot be made under paragraphs (1) or (2), by sending a copy of the summons and complaint and a notice of suit, together with a translation of each into the official language of the foreign state, by any form of mail requiring a signed receipt, to be addressed and dispatched by the clerk of the court to the head of the ministry of foreign affairs of the foreign state concerned, or

(4) if service cannot be made within 30 days under paragraph (3), by sending two copies of the summons and complaint and a notice of suit, together with a translation of each into the official language of the foreign state, by any form of mail requiring a signed receipt, to be addressed and dispatched by the clerk of the court to the Secretary of State in Washington, District of Columbia, to the attention of the Director of Special Consular Services—and the Secretary shall transmit one copy of the papers through diplomatic channels to the foreign state and shall send to the clerk of the court a certified copy of the diplomatic note indicating when the papers were transmitted.

As used in this subsection, a "notice of suit" shall mean a notice addressed to a foreign state and in a form prescribed by the Secretary of State by regulation.

(b) Service in the courts of the United States and of the States shall be made upon an agency or instrumentality of a foreign state:

(1) by delivery of a copy of the summons and complaint in accordance with any special arrangement for service between the plaintiff and the agency or instrumentality; or

(2) if no special arrangement exists, by delivery of a copy of the summons and complaint either to an officer, a managing or general agent, or to any other agent authorized by appointment or by law to receive service of process in the United States; or in accordance with an applicable international convention on service of judicial documents; or

(3) if service cannot be made under paragraphs (1) or (2), and if reasonably calculated to give actual notice, by delivery of a copy of the summons and complaint, together with a translation of each into the official language of the foreign state—

(A) as directed by an authority of the foreign state or political subdivision in response to a letter rogatory or request or

(B) by any form of mail requiring a signed receipt, to be addressed and dispatched by the clerk of the court to the agency or instrumentality to be served, or

(C) as directed by order of the court consistent with the law of the place where service is to be made.

(c) Service shall be deemed to have been made—

(1) in the case of service under subsection (a)(4), as of the date of transmittal indicated in the certified copy of the diplomatic note; and

(2) in any other case under this section, as of the date of receipt indicated in the certification, signed and returned postal receipt, or other proof of service applicable to the method of service employed.

(d) In any action brought in a court of the United States or of a State, a foreign state, a political subdivision thereof, or an agency or instrumentality of a foreign state shall serve an answer or other responsive pleading to the complaint within sixty days after service has been made under this section.

(e) No judgment by default shall be entered by a court of the United States or of a State against a foreign state, a political subdivision thereof, or an agency or instrumentality of a foreign state, unless the claimant establishes his claim or right to relief by evidence satisfactory to the court. A copy of any such default judgment shall be sent to the foreign state or political subdivision in the manner prescribed for service in this section. Added Oct. 21, 1976, Pub.L. 94–583, § 4(a), 90 Stat. 2894.

§ 1609. Immunity from attachment and execution of property of a foreign state

Subject to existing international agreements to which the United States is a party at the time of enactment of this Act the property in the United States of a foreign state shall be immune from attachment arrest and execution except as provided in sections 1610 and 1611 of this chapter. Added Oct. 21, 1976, Pub.L. 94–583, § 4(a), 90 Stat. 2895.

§ 1610. Exceptions to the immunity from attachment or execution

(a) The property in the United States of a foreign state, as defined in section 1603(a) of this chapter, used for a commercial activity in the United States, shall not be immune from attachment in aid of execution, or from execution, upon a judgment entered by a court of the United States or of a State after the effective date of this Act, if—

(1) the foreign state has waived its immunity from attachment in aid of execution or from execution either explicitly or by implication, notwithstanding any withdrawal of the waiver the foreign state may purport to effect except in accordance with the terms of the waiver, or

(2) the property is or was used for the commercial activity upon which the claim is based, or

(3) the execution relates to a judgment establishing rights in property which has been taken in violation of international law or which has been exchanged for property taken in violation of international law, or

(4) the execution relates to a judgment establishing rights in property—

(A) which is acquired by succession or gift, or

(B) which is immovable and situated in the United States: *Provided,* That such property is not used for purposes of maintaining a diplomatic or consular mission or the residence of the Chief of such mission, or

(5) the property consists of any contractual obligation or any proceeds from such a contractual obligation to indemnify or hold harmless the foreign state or its employees under a policy of automobile or other liability or casualty insurance covering the claim which merged into the judgment, or

(6) the judgment is based on an order confirming an arbitral award rendered against the foreign state, provided that attachment in aid of execution, or execution, would not be inconsistent with any provision in the arbitral agreement, or

(7) the judgment relates to a claim for which the foreign state is not immune under section 1605A, regardless of whether the property is or was involved with the act upon which the claim is based.

(b) In addition to subsection (a), any property in the United States of an agency or instrumentality of a foreign state engaged in commercial activity in the United States shall not be immune from attachment in aid of execution, or from execution, upon a judgment entered by a court of the United States or of a State after the effective date of this Act, if—

(1) the agency or instrumentality has waived its immunity from attachment in aid of execution or from execution either explicitly or implicitly, notwithstanding any withdrawal of the waiver the agency or instrumentality may purport to effect except in accordance with the terms of the waiver, or

(2) the judgment relates to a claim for which the agency or instrumentality is not immune by virtue of section 1605(a)(2), (3), or (5), 1605(b), or 1605A of this chapter, regardless of whether the property is or was involved in the act upon which the claim is based.

(c) No attachment or execution referred to in subsections (a) and (b) of this section shall be permitted until the court has ordered such attachment and execution after having determined that a reasonable period of time has elapsed following the entry of judgment and the giving of any notice required under section 1608(e) of this chapter.

(d) The property of a foreign state, as defined in section 1603(a) of this chapter, used for a commercial activity in the United States, shall not be immune from attachment prior to the entry of judgment in any action brought in a court of the United States or of a State, or prior to the elapse of the period of time provided in subsection (c) of this section, if—

(1) the foreign state has explicitly waived its immunity from attachment prior to judgment, notwithstanding any withdrawal of the waiver the foreign state may purport to effect except in accordance with the terms of the waiver, and

(2) the purpose of the attachment is to secure satisfaction of a judgment that has been or may ultimately be entered against the foreign state, and not to obtain jurisdiction.

(e) The vessels of a foreign state shall not be immune from arrest in rem, interlocutory sale, and execution in actions brought to foreclose a preferred mortgage as provided in section 1605(d).

(f)(1)(A) Notwithstanding any other provision of law, including but not limited to section 208(f) of the Foreign Missions Act (22 U.S.C. 4308(f)), and except as provided in subparagraph (B), any property with respect to which financial transactions are prohibited or regulated pursuant to section 5(b) of the Trading with the Enemy Act (50 U.S.C. App. 5(b)), section 620(a) of the Foreign Assistance Act of 1961 (22 U.S.C. 2370(a)), sections 202 and 203 of the International Emergency Economic Powers Act (50 U.S.C. 1701–1702), or any other proclamation, order, regulation, or license issued pursuant thereto, shall be subject to execution or attachment in aid of execution of any judgment relating to a claim for which a foreign state (including any agency or instrumentality or such state) claiming such property is not immune under section 1605(a)(7) (as in effect before the enactment of section 1605A) or section 1605A.

(B) Subparagraph (A) shall not apply if, at the time the property is expropriated or seized by the foreign state, the property has been held in title by a natural person or, if held in trust, has been held for the benefit of a natural person or persons.

(2)(A) At the request of any party in whose favor a judgment has been issued with respect to a claim for which the foreign state is not immune under section 1605(a)(7) (as in effect before the enactment of section 1605A) or section 1605A, the Secretary of the Treasury and the Secretary of State should make every effort to fully, promptly, and effectively assist any judgment creditor or any court that has issued any such judgment in identifying, locating, and executing against the property of that foreign state or any agency or instrumentality of such state.

(B) In providing such assistance, the Secretaries—

(i) may provide such information to the court under seal; and

(ii) should make every effort to provide the information in a manner sufficient to allow the court to direct the United States Marshall's office to promptly and effectively execute against that property.

(3) Waiver.—The President may waive any provision of paragraph (1) in the interest of national security.

(g) Property in Certain Actions.—

(1) In General.—Subject to paragraph (3), the property of a foreign state against which a judgment is entered under section 1605A, and the property of an agency or instrumentality of such a state, including property that is a separate juridical entity or is an interest held directly or indirectly in a separate juridical entity, is subject to attachment in aid of execution, and execution, upon that judgment as provided in this section, regardless of—

(A) the level of economic control over the property by the government of the foreign state;

(B) whether the profits of the property go to that government;

(C) the degree to which officials of that government manage the property or otherwise control its daily affairs;

(D) whether that government is the sole beneficiary in interest of the property; or

(E) whether establishing the property as a separate entity would entitle the foreign state to benefits in United States courts while avoiding its obligations.

(2) United States Sovereign Immunity Inapplicable.—Any property of a foreign state, or agency or instrumentality of a foreign state, to which paragraph (1) applies shall not be immune from attachment in aid of execution, or execution, upon a judgment entered under section 1605A because the property is regulated by the United States Government by reason of action taken against that foreign state under the Trading With the Enemy Act or the International Emergency Economic Powers Act.

(3) Third–Party Joint Property Holders.—Nothing in this subsection shall be construed to supersede the authority of a court to prevent appropriately the impairment of an interest held by a person who is not liable in the action giving rise to a judgment in property subject to attachment in aid of execution, or execution, upon such judgment. Added Oct. 21, 1976, Pub.L. 94–583, § 4(a), 90 Stat. 2896; as amended Nov. 9, 1988, Pub.L. 100–640, § 2, 102 Stat. 3333; Nov. 16, 1988, Pub.L. 100–669, § 3, 102 Stat. 3969; Dec. 1, 1990, Pub.L. 101–650, Title III, § 325(b)(9), 104 Stat. 5121; Apr. 24, 1996, Pub.L. 104–132, Title II, § 221(b), 110 Stat. 1242; Oct. 21, 1998, Pub.L. 105–277, Div. A, § 101(h) [Title I, § 117(a)], 112 Stat. 2681–491; Oct. 28, 2000, Pub.L. 106–386, Div. C, § 2002(f)(1), 114 Stat. 1543; Jan. 28, 2008, Pub.L. 110–181, Div. A, Title X, § 1083(b)(3), 122 Stat. 341.

§ 1611. Certain types of property immune from execution

(a) Notwithstanding the provisions of section 1610 of this chapter, the property of those organizations designated by the President as being entitled to enjoy the privileges, exemptions, and immunities provided by the International Organizations Immunities Act shall not be subject to attachment or any other judicial process impeding the disbursement of funds to, or on the order of, a foreign state as the result of an action brought in the courts of the United States or of the States.

(b) Notwithstanding the provisions of section 1610 of this chapter, the property of a foreign state shall be immune from attachment and from execution, if—

(1) the property is that of a foreign central bank or monetary authority held for its own account, unless such bank or authority, or its parent foreign government, has explicitly waived its immunity from attachment in aid of execution, or from execution, notwithstanding any withdrawal of the waiver which the bank, authority or government may purport to effect except in accordance with the terms of the waiver; or

(2) the property is, or is intended to be, used in connection with a military activity and

(A) is of a military character, or

(B) is under the control of a military authority or defense agency.

(c) Notwithstanding the provisions of section 1610 of this chapter, the property of a foreign state shall be immune from attachment and from execution in an action brought under section 302 of the Cuban Liberty and Democratic Solidarity (LIBERTAD) Act of 1996 to the extent that the property is a facility or installation used by an accredited diplomatic mission for official purposes. Added Oct. 21, 1976, Pub.L. 94–583, § 4(a), 90 Stat. 2897; as amended March 12, 1996, Pub.L. 104–114, Title III, § 302(e), 110 Stat. 818.

§ 1631. Transfer to cure want of jurisdiction

Whenever a civil action is filed in a court as defined in section 610 of this title or an appeal, including a petition for review of administrative action, is noticed for or filed with such a court and that court finds that there is a want of jurisdiction, the court shall, if it is in the interest of justice, transfer such action or appeal to any other such court in which the action or appeal could have been brought at the time it was filed or noticed, and the action or appeal shall proceed as if it had been filed in or noticed for the court to which it is transferred on the date upon which it was actually filed in or noticed for the court from which it is transferred. Added Apr. 2, 1982, Pub.L. 97–164, Title III, § 301(a), 96 Stat. 55.

§ 1651. Writs

(a) The Supreme Court and all courts established by Act of Congress may issue all writs necessary or appropriate in aid of their respective jurisdictions and agreeable to the usages and principles of law.

(b) An alternative writ or rule nisi may be issued by a justice or judge of a court which has jurisdiction. As amended May 24, 1949, c. 139, § 90, 63 Stat. 102.

§ 1652. State laws as rules of decision

The laws of the several states, except where the Constitution or treaties of the United States or Acts of Congress otherwise require or provide, shall be regarded as rules of decision in civil actions in the courts of the United States, in cases where they apply.

§ 1653. Amendment of pleadings to show jurisdiction

Defective allegations of jurisdiction may be amended, upon terms, in the trial or appellate courts.

§ 1654. Appearance personally or by counsel

In all courts of the United States the parties may plead and conduct their own cases personally or by counsel as, by the rules of such courts, respectively, are permitted to manage and conduct causes therein. As amended May 24, 1949, c. 139, § 91, 63 Stat. 103.

§ 1655. Lien enforcement; absent defendants

In an action in a district court to enforce any lien upon or claim to, or to remove any incumbrance or lien or cloud upon the title to, real or personal property within the district, where any defendant cannot be served within the State, or does not voluntarily appear, the court may order the absent defendant to appear or plead by a day certain.

Such order shall be served on the absent defendant personally if practicable, wherever found, and also upon the person or persons in possession or charge of such property, if any. Where personal service is not practicable, the order shall be published as the court may direct, not less than once a week for six consecutive weeks.

If an absent defendant does not appear or plead within the time allowed, the court may proceed as if the absent defendant had been served with process within the State, but any adjudication shall, as regards the absent defendant without appearance, affect only the property which is the subject of the action. When a part of the property is within another district, but within the same state, such action may be brought in either district.

Any defendant not so personally notified may, at any time within one year after final judgment, enter his appearance, and thereupon the court shall set aside the judgment and permit such defendant to plead on payment of such costs as the court deems just.

§ 1657. Priority of civil actions

(a) Notwithstanding any other provision of law, each court of the United States shall determine the order in which civil actions are heard and determined, except that the court shall expedite the consideration of any action brought under chapter 153 or section 1826 of this title, any action for temporary or preliminary injunctive relief, or any other action if good cause therefor is shown. For purposes of this subsection, "good cause" is shown if a right under the Constitution of the United States or a Federal Statute (including rights under section 552 of title 5) would be maintained in a factual context that indicates that a request for expedited consideration has merit.

(b) The Judicial Conference of the United States may modify the rules adopted by the courts to determine the order in which civil actions are heard and determined, in order to establish consistency among the judicial circuits. Added Nov. 8, 1984, Pub.L. 98–620, Title IV, § 401(a), 98 Stat. 3356.

§ 1658. Time limitations on the commencement of civil actions arising under Acts of Congress

(a) Except as otherwise provided by law, a civil action arising under an Act of Congress enacted after the date of the enactment of this section may not be commenced later than 4 years after the cause of action accrues.

(b) Notwithstanding subsection (a), a private right of action that involves a claim of fraud, deceit, manipulation, or contrivance in contravention of a regulatory requirement concerning the securities laws, as defined in section 3(a)(47) of the Securities Exchange Act of 1934 (15 U.S.C. 78c(a)(47)), may be brought not later than the earlier of—

(1) 2 years after the discovery of the facts constituting the violation; or

(2) 5 years after such violation. Added Dec. 1, 1990, Pub.L. 101–650, Title III, § 313(a), 104 Stat. 5114; as amended July 30, 2002, Pub.L. 107–204, Title VIII, § 804(a), 116 Stat. 801.

§ 1693.   Place of arrest in civil action

Except as otherwise provided by Act of Congress, no person shall be arrested in one district for trial in another in any civil action in a district court.

§ 1694.   Patent infringement action

In a patent infringement action commenced in a district where the defendant is not a resident but has a regular and established place of business, service of process, summons or subpoena upon such defendant may be made upon his agent or agents conducting such business.

§ 1695.   Stockholder's derivative action

Process in a stockholder's action in behalf of his corporation may be served upon such corporation in any district where it is organized or licensed to do business or is doing business.

§ 1696.   Service in foreign and international litigation

(a) The district court of the district in which a person resides or is found may order service upon him of any document issued in connection with a proceeding in a foreign or international tribunal. The order may be made pursuant to a letter rogatory issued, or request made, by a foreign or international tribunal or upon application of any interested person and shall direct the manner of service. Service pursuant to this subsection does not, of itself, require the recognition or enforcement in the United States of a judgment, decree, or order rendered by a foreign or international tribunal.

(b) This section does not preclude service of such a document without an order of court. Added Oct. 3, 1964, Pub.L. 88–619, § 4(a), 78 Stat. 995.

§ 1697.   Service in multiparty, multiforum actions

When the jurisdiction of the district court is based in whole or in part upon section 1369 of this title, process, other than subpoenas, may be served at any place within the United States, or anywhere outside the United States if otherwise permitted by law. Added Nov. 2, 2002, Pub.L. 107–273, Div. C, Title I, § 11020(b)(4)(A), 116 Stat. 1828.

§ 1711.   Definitions

In this chapter:

(1) Class.—The term "class" means all of the class members in a class action.

(2) Class action.—The term "class action" means any civil action filed in a district court of the United States under rule 23 of the Federal Rules of Civil Procedure or any civil action that is removed to a district court of the United States that was originally filed under a State statute or rule of judicial procedure authorizing an action to be brought by 1 or more representatives as a class action.

(3) Class counsel.—The term "class counsel" means the persons who serve as the attorneys for the class members in a proposed or certified class action.

(4) Class members.—The term "class members" means the persons (named or unnamed) who fall within the definition of the proposed or certified class in a class action.

(5) Plaintiff class action.—The term "plaintiff class action" means a class action in which class members are plaintiffs.

(6) Proposed settlement.—The term "proposed settlement" means an agreement regarding a class action that is subject to court approval and that, if approved, would be binding on some or all class members. Added Feb. 18, 2005, Pub.L. 109–2, § 3(a), 119 Stat. 5.

§ 1712. Coupon settlements

(a) Contingent fees in coupon settlements.—If a proposed settlement in a class action provides for a recovery of coupons to a class member, the portion of any attorney's fee award to class counsel that is attributable to the award of the coupons shall be based on the value to class members of the coupons that are redeemed.

(b) Other attorney's fee awards in coupon settlements.—

(1) In general.—If a proposed settlement in a class action provides for a recovery of coupons to class members, and a portion of the recovery of the coupons is not used to determine the attorney's fee to be paid to class counsel, any attorney's fee award shall be based upon the amount of time class counsel reasonably expended working on the action.

(2) Court approval.—Any attorney's fee under this subsection shall be subject to approval by the court and shall include an appropriate attorney's fee, if any, for obtaining equitable relief, including an injunction, if applicable. Nothing in this subsection shall be construed to prohibit application of a lodestar with a multiplier method of determining attorney's fees.

(c) Attorney's fee awards calculated on a mixed basis in coupon settlements.—If a proposed settlement in a class action provides for an award of coupons to class members and also provides for equitable relief, including injunctive relief—

(1) that portion of the attorney's fee to be paid to class counsel that is based upon a portion of the recovery of the coupons shall be calculated in accordance with subsection (a); and

(2) that portion of the attorney's fee to be paid to class counsel that is not based upon a portion of the recovery of the coupons shall be calculated in accordance with subsection (b).

(d) Settlement valuation expertise.—In a class action involving the awarding of coupons, the court may, in its discretion upon the motion of a party, receive expert testimony from a witness qualified to provide information on the actual value to the class members of the coupons that are redeemed.

(e) Judicial scrutiny of coupon settlements.—In a proposed settlement under which class members would be awarded coupons, the court may approve the proposed settlement only after a hearing to determine whether, and making a written finding that, the settlement is fair, reasonable, and adequate for class members. The court, in its discretion, may also require that a proposed settlement agreement provide for the distribution of a portion of the value of unclaimed coupons to 1 or more charitable or governmental organizations, as agreed to by the parties. The distribution and redemption of any proceeds under this subsection shall not be used to calculate attorneys' fees under this section. Added Feb. 18, 2005, Pub.L. 109–2, § 3(a), 119 Stat. 5.

§ 1713. Protection against loss by class members

The court may approve a proposed settlement under which any class member is obligated to pay sums to class counsel that would result in a net loss to the class member only if the court makes a written finding that nonmonetary benefits to the class member substantially outweigh the monetary loss. Added Feb. 18, 2005, Pub.L. 109–2, § 3(a), 119 Stat. 5.

§ 1714. Protection against discrimination based on geographic location

The court may not approve a proposed settlement that provides for the payment of greater sums to some class members than to others solely on the basis that the class members to whom the greater sums are to be paid are located in closer geographic proximity to the court. Added Feb. 18, 2005, Pub.L. 109–2, § 3(a), 119 Stat. 5.

§ 1715. Notifications to appropriate Federal and State officials

(a) Definitions.—

(1) Appropriate Federal official.—In this section, the term "appropriate Federal official" means—

(A) the Attorney General of the United States; or

(B) in any case in which the defendant is a Federal depository institution, a State depository institution, a depository institution holding company, a foreign bank, or a nondepository institution subsidiary of the foregoing (as such terms are defined in section 3 of the Federal Deposit Insurance Act (12 U.S.C. 1813)), the person who has the primary Federal regulatory or supervisory responsibility with respect to the defendant, if some or all of the matters alleged in the class action are subject to regulation or supervision by that person.

(2) Appropriate State official.—In this section, the term "appropriate State official" means the person in the State who has the primary regulatory or supervisory responsibility with respect to the defendant, or who licenses or otherwise authorizes the defendant to conduct business in the State, if some or all of the matters alleged in the class action are subject to regulation by that person. If there is no primary regulator, supervisor, or licensing authority, or the matters alleged in the class action are not subject to regulation or supervision by that person, then the appropriate State official shall be the State attorney general.

(b) In general.—Not later than 10 days after a proposed settlement of a class action is filed in court, each defendant that is participating in the proposed settlement shall serve upon the appropriate State official of each State in which a class member resides and the appropriate Federal official, a notice of the proposed settlement consisting of—

(1) a copy of the complaint and any materials filed with the complaint and any amended complaints (except such materials shall not be required to be served if such materials are made electronically available through the Internet and such service includes notice of how to electronically access such material);

(2) notice of any scheduled judicial hearing in the class action;

(3) any proposed or final notification to class members of—

(A)(i) the members' rights to request exclusion from the class action; or

(ii) if no right to request exclusion exists, a statement that no such right exists; and

(B) a proposed settlement of a class action;

(4) any proposed or final class action settlement;

(5) any settlement or other agreement contemporaneously made between class counsel and counsel for the defendants;

(6) any final judgment or notice of dismissal;

(7)(A) if feasible, the names of class members who reside in each State and the estimated proportionate share of the claims of such members to the entire settlement to that State's appropriate State official; or

(B) if the provision of information under subparagraph (A) is not feasible, a reasonable estimate of the number of class members residing in each State and the estimated proportionate share of the claims of such members to the entire settlement; and

(8) any written judicial opinion relating to the materials described under subparagraphs (3) through (6).

(c) Depository institutions notification.—

(1) Federal and other depository institutions.—In any case in which the defendant is a Federal depository institution, a depository institution holding company, a foreign bank, or a non-depository institution subsidiary of the foregoing, the notice requirements of this section are satisfied by serving the notice required under subsection (b) upon the person who has the primary Federal regulatory or supervisory responsibility with respect to the defendant, if some or all of the matters alleged in the class action are subject to regulation or supervision by that person.

(2) State depository institutions.—In any case in which the defendant is a State depository institution (as that term is defined in section 3 of the Federal Deposit Insurance Act (12 U.S.C. 1813)), the notice requirements of this section are satisfied by serving the notice required under subsection (b) upon the State bank supervisor (as that term is defined in section 3 of the Federal Deposit Insurance Act (12 U.S.C. 1813)) of the State in which the defendant is incorporated or chartered, if some or all of the matters alleged in the class action are subject to regulation or supervision by that person, and upon the appropriate Federal official.

(d) Final approval.—An order giving final approval of a proposed settlement may not be issued earlier than 90 days after the later of the dates on which the appropriate Federal official and the appropriate State official are served with the notice required under subsection (b).

(e) Noncompliance if notice not provided.—

(1) In general.—A class member may refuse to comply with and may choose not to be bound by a settlement agreement or consent decree in a class action if the class member demonstrates that the notice required under subsection (b) has not been provided.

(2) Limitation.—A class member may not refuse to comply with or to be bound by a settlement agreement or consent decree under paragraph (1) if the notice required under subsection (b) was directed to the appropriate Federal official and to either the State attorney general or the person that has primary regulatory, supervisory, or licensing authority over the defendant.

(3) Application of rights.—The rights created by this subsection shall apply only to class members or any person acting on a class member's behalf, and shall not be construed to limit any other rights affecting a class member's participation in the settlement.

(f) Rule of construction.—Nothing in this section shall be construed to expand the authority of, or impose any obligations, duties, or responsibilities upon, Federal or State officials. Added Feb. 18, 2005, Pub.L. 109–2, § 3(a), 119 Stat. 5.

§ 1738. State and Territorial statutes and judicial proceedings; full faith and credit

The Acts of the legislature of any State, Territory, or Possession of the United States, or copies thereof, shall be authenticated by affixing the seal of such State, Territory or Possession thereto.

The records and judicial proceedings of any court of any such State, Territory or Possession, or copies thereof, shall be proved or admitted in other courts within the United States and its Territories and Possessions by the attestation of the clerk and seal of the court annexed, if a seal exists, together with a certificate of a judge of the court that the said attestation is in proper form.

Such Acts, records and judicial proceedings or copies thereof, so authenticated, shall have the same full faith and credit in every court within the United States and its Territories and Possessions as they have by law or usage in the courts of such State, Territory or Possession from which they are taken.

§ 1738A. Full faith and credit given to child custody determinations

(a) The appropriate authorities of every State shall enforce according to its terms, and shall not modify except as provided in subsections (f), (g), and (h) of this section, any custody determination or visitation determination made consistently with the provisions of this section by a court of another State.

(b) As used in this section, the term—

(1) "child" means a person under the age of eighteen;

(2) "contestant" means a person, including a parent or grandparent, who claims a right to custody or visitation of a child;

(3) "custody determination" means a judgment, decree, or other order of a court providing for the custody of a child, and includes permanent and temporary orders, and initial orders and modifications;

(4) "home State" means the State in which, immediately preceding the time involved, the child lived with his parents, a parent, or a person acting as parent, for at least six consecutive months, and in the case of a child less than six months old, the State in which the child lived from birth with any of such persons. Periods of temporary absence of any of such persons are counted as part of the six-month or other period;

(5) "modification" and "modify" refer to a custody or visitation determination which modifies, replaces, supersedes, or otherwise is made subsequent to, a prior custody or visitation determination concerning the same child, whether made by the same court or not;

(6) "person acting as a parent" means a person, other than a parent, who has physical custody of a child and who has either been awarded custody by a court or claims a right to custody;

(7) "physical custody" means actual possession and control of a child;

(8) "State" means a State of the United States, the District of Columbia, the Commonwealth of Puerto Rico, or a territory or possession of the United States; and

(9) "visitation determination" means a judgment, decree, or other order of a court providing for the visitation of a child and includes permanent and temporary orders and initial orders and modifications.

(c) A child custody or visitation determination made by a court of a State is consistent with the provisions of this section only if—

(1) such court has jurisdiction under the law of such State; and

(2) one of the following conditions is met:

(A) such State (i) is the home State of the child on the date of the commencement of the proceeding, or (ii) had been the child's home State within six months before the date of the commencement of the proceeding and the child is absent from such State because of his removal or retention by a contestant or for other reasons, and a contestant continues to live in such State;

(B)(i) it appears that no other State would have jurisdiction under subparagraph (A), and (ii) it is in the best interest of the child that a court of such State assume jurisdiction because (I) the child and his parents, or the child and at least one contestant, have a significant connection with such State other than mere physical presence in such State, and (II) there is available in such State substantial evidence concerning the child's present or future care, protection, training, and personal relationships;

(C) the child is physically present in such State and (i) the child has been abandoned, or (ii) it is necessary in an emergency to protect the child because the child, a sibling, or parent of the child has been subjected to or threatened with mistreatment or abuse;

(D)(i) it appears that no other State would have jurisdiction under subparagraph (A), (B), (C), or (E), or another State has declined to exercise jurisdiction on the ground that the State whose jurisdiction is in issue is the more appropriate forum to determine the custody or visitation of the child, and (ii) it is in the best interest of the child that such court assume jurisdiction; or

(E) the court has continuing jurisdiction pursuant to subsection (d) of this section.

(d) The jurisdiction of a court of a State which has made a child custody or visitation determination consistently with the provisions of this section continues as long as the requirement of subsection (c)(1) of this section continues to be met and such State remains the residence of the child or of any contestant.

(e) Before a child custody or visitation determination is made, reasonable notice and opportunity to be heard shall be given to the contestants, any parent whose parental rights have not been previously terminated and any person who has physical custody of a child.

(f) A court of a State may modify a determination of the custody of the same child made by a court of another State, if—

(1) it has jurisdiction to make such a child custody determination; and

(2) the court of the other State no longer has jurisdiction, or it has declined to exercise such jurisdiction to modify such determination.

(g) A court of a State shall not exercise jurisdiction in any proceeding for a custody or visitation determination commenced during the pendency of a proceeding in a court of another State where such court of that other State is exercising jurisdiction consistently with the provisions of this section to make a custody or visitation determination.

(h) A court of a State may not modify a visitation determination made by a court of another State unless the court of the other State no longer has jurisdiction to modify such determination or has declined to exercise jurisdiction to modify such determination. Added Dec. 28, 1980, Pub.L. 96–611, § 8(a), 94 Stat. 3569; as amended Nov. 12, 1998, Pub.L. 105–374, § 1, 112 Stat. 3383; Oct. 28, 2000, Pub.L. 106–386, Div. B, Title III, § 1303(d), 114 Stat. 1512.

§ 1738B. Full faith and credit for child support orders

(a) General Rule.—The appropriate authorities of each State—

(1) shall enforce according to its terms a child support order made consistently with this section by a court of another State; and

(2) shall not seek or make a modification of such an order except in accordance with subsections (e), (f), and (i).

(b) Definitions.—In this section:

"child" means—

(A) a person under 18 years of age; and

(B) a person 18 or more years of age with respect to whom a child support order has been issued pursuant to the laws of a State.

"child's State" means the State in which a child resides.

"child's home State" means the State in which a child lived with a parent or a person acting as parent for at least 6 consecutive months immediately preceding the time of filing of a petition or comparable pleading for support and, if a child is less than 6 months old, the State in which the child lived from birth with any of them. A period of temporary absence of any of them is counted as part of the 6–month period.

"child support" means a payment of money, continuing support, or arrearages or the provision of a benefit (including payment of health insurance, child care, and educational expenses) for the support of a child.

"child support order"—

(A) means a judgment, decree, or order of a court requiring the payment of child support in periodic amounts or in a lump sum; and

(B) includes—

(i) a permanent or temporary order; and

603

(ii) an initial order or a modification of an order.

"contestant" means—

(A) a person (including a parent) who—

(i) claims a right to receive child support;

(ii) is a party to a proceeding that may result in the issuance of a child support order; or

(iii) is under a child support order; and

(B) a State or political subdivision of a State to which the right to obtain child support has been assigned.

"court" means a court or administrative agency of a State that is authorized by State law to establish the amount of child support payable by a contestant or make a modification of a child support order.

"modification" means a change in a child support order that affects the amount, scope, or duration of the order and modifies, replaces, supersedes, or otherwise is made subsequent to the child support order.

"State" means a State of the United States, the District of Columbia, the Commonwealth of Puerto Rico, the territories and possessions of the United States, and Indian country (as defined in section 1151 of title 18).

(c) Requirements of Child Support Orders.—A child support order made by a court of a State is made consistently with this section if—

(1) a court that makes the order, pursuant to the laws of the State in which the court is located and subsections (e), (f), and (g)—

(A) has subject matter jurisdiction to hear the matter and enter such an order; and

(B) has personal jurisdiction over the contestants; and

(2) reasonable notice and opportunity to be heard is given to the contestants.

(d) Continuing Jurisdiction.—A court of a State that has made a child support order consistently with this section has continuing, exclusive jurisdiction over the order if the State is the child's State or the residence of any individual contestant unless the court of another State, acting in accordance with subsections (e) and (f), has made a modification of the order.

(e) Authority to Modify Orders.—A court of a State may modify a child support order issued by a court of another State if—

(1) the court has jurisdiction to make such a child support order pursuant to subsection (i); and

(2)(A) the court of the other State no longer has continuing, exclusive jurisdiction of the child support order because that State no longer is the child's State or the residence of any individual contestant; or

604

(B) each individual contestant has filed written consent with the State of continuing, exclusive jurisdiction for a court of another State to modify the order and assume continuing, exclusive jurisdiction over the order.

(f) Recognition of Child Support Orders.—If 1 or more child support orders have been issued with regard to an obligor and a child, a court shall apply the following rules in determining which order to recognize for purposes of continuing, exclusive jurisdiction and enforcement:

(1) If only 1 court has issued a child support order, the order of that court must be recognized.

(2) If 2 or more courts have issued child support orders the same obligor and child, and only 1 of the courts would have continuing, exclusive jurisdiction under this section, the order of that court must be recognized.

(3) If 2 or more courts have issued child support orders for the same obligor and child, and more than 1 of the courts would have continuing, exclusive jurisdiction under this section, an order issued by a court in the current home State of the child must be recognized but if an order has not been issued in the current home State of the child, the order most recently issued must be recognized.

(4) If 2 or more courts have issued child support orders for the same obligor and child, and none of the courts would have continuing, exclusive jurisdiction under this section, a court having jurisdiction over the parties shall issue a child support order, which must be recognized.

(5) The court that has issued an order recognized under this subsection is the court having continuing, exclusive jurisdiction under subsection (d).

(g) Enforcement of Modified Orders.—A court of a State that no longer has continuing, exclusive jurisdiction of a child support order may enforce the order with respect to nonmodifiable obligations and unsatisfied obligations that accrued before the date on which a modification of the order is made under subsections (e) and (f).

(h) Choice of Law.—

(1) In general.—In a proceeding to establish, modify, or enforce a child support order, the forum State's law shall apply except as provided in paragraphs (2) and (3).

(2) Law of state of issuance of order.—In interpreting a child support order including the duration of current payments and other obligations of support, a court shall apply the law of the State of the court that issued the order.

(3) Period of limitation.—In an action to enforce arrears under a child support order, a court shall apply the statute of limitation of the forum State or the State of the court that issued the order, whichever statute provides the longer period of limitation.

(i) Registration for Modification.—If there is no individual contestant or child residing in the issuing State, the party or support enforcement agency seeking to modify, or to modify and enforce, a child support order issued in another State shall register that order in a State with jurisdiction over the nonmovant for the purpose of modification.   Added Oct. 20, 1994, Pub.L. 103–383, § 3(a), 108 Stat. 4064; Aug. 22, 1996, Pub.L. 104–193, Title III, § 322, 110 Stat. 2221; Aug. 5, 1997, Pub.L. 105–33, Title V, § 5554, 111 Stat. 636.

§ 1738C.   Certain acts, records, and proceedings and the effect thereof

No State, territory, or possession of the United States, or Indian tribe, shall be required to give effect to any public act, record, or judicial proceeding of any other State, territory, possession, or tribe respecting a relationship between persons of the same sex that is treated as a marriage under the laws of such other State, territory, possession, or tribe, or a right or claim arising from such relationship.   Added Sept. 21, 1996, Pub.L. 104–199, § 2, 110 Stat. 2419.

§ 1739.   State and Territorial nonjudicial records; full faith and credit

All nonjudicial records or books kept in any public office of any State, Territory, or Possession of the United States, or copies thereof, shall be proved or admitted in any court or office in any other State, Territory, or Possession by the attestation of the custodian of such records or books, and the seal of his office annexed, if there be a seal, together with a certificate of a judge of a court of record of the county, parish, or district in which such office may be kept, or of the Governor, or secretary of state, the chancellor or keeper of the great seal, of the State, Territory, or Possession that the said attestation is in due form and by the proper officers.

If the certificate is given by a judge, it shall be further authenticated by the clerk or prothonotary of the court, who shall certify, under his hand and the seal of his office, that such judge is duly commissioned and qualified; or, if given by such Governor, secretary, chancellor, or keeper of the great seal, it shall be under the great seal of the State, Territory, or Possession in which it is made.

Such records or books, or copies thereof, so authenticated, shall have the same full faith and credit in every court and office within the United States and its Territories and Possessions as they have by law or usage in the courts or offices of the State, Territory, or Possession from which they are taken.

§ 1746.   Unsworn declarations under penalty of perjury

Wherever, under any law of the United States or under any rule, regulation, order, or requirement made pursuant to law, any matter is required or permitted to be supported, evidenced, established, or proved by the sworn declaration, verification, certificate, statement, oath, or affidavit, in writing of the person making the same (other than a deposition, or an oath of office, or an oath required to be taken before a specified official other than a notary public), such matter may, with like force and effect, be supported, evidenced, established, or proved by the unsworn declaration, certificate, verification, or statement, in writing of such person which is subscribed by him, as true under penalty of perjury, and dated, in substantially the following form:

(1) If executed without the United States: "I declare (or certify, verify, or state) under penalty of perjury under the laws of the United States of America that the foregoing is true and correct. Executed on (date).

(Signature)".

(2) If executed within the United States, its territories, possessions, or commonwealths: "I declare (or certify, verify, or state) under penalty of perjury that the foregoing is true and correct. Executed on (date).

(Signature)".

Added Oct. 18, 1976, Pub.L. 94–550, § 1(a), 90 Stat. 2534.

§ 1785. Subpoenas in multiparty, multiforum actions

When the jurisdiction of the district court is based in whole or in part upon section 1369 of this title, a subpoena for attendance at a hearing or trial may, if authorized by the court upon motion for good cause shown, and upon such terms and conditions as the court may impose, be served at any place within the United States, or anywhere outside the United States if otherwise permitted by law. Added Nov. 2, 2002, Pub.L. 107–273, Div. C, Title I, § 11020(b)(4)(B), 116 Stat. 1828.

A case under chapter 15 of title 11 may be commenced in the district court of the United States for the district—

(1) in which the debtor has its principal place of business or principal assets in the United States;

(2) if the debtor does not have a place of business or assets in the United States, in which there is pending against the debtor an action or proceeding in a Federal or State court; or

(3) in a case other than those specified in paragraph (1) or (2), in which venue will be consistent with the interests of justice and the convenience of the parties, having regard to the relief sought by the foreign representative. Added July 10, 1984, Pub.L. 98–353, Title I, § 102(a), 98 Stat. 335; as amended Apr. 20, 2005, Pub.L. 109–8, Title VIII, § 802(c)(4), 119 Stat. 146.

§ 1826. Recalcitrant witnesses

(a) Whenever a witness in any proceeding before or ancillary to any court or grand jury of the United States refuses without just cause to comply with an order of the court to testify or provide other information, including any book, paper, document, record, recording or other material, the court, upon such refusal, or when such refusal is duly brought to its attention, may summarily order his confinement at a suitable place until such time as the witness is willing to give such testimony or provide such information. No period of such confinement shall exceed the life of—

607

(1) the court proceeding, or

(2) the term of the grand jury, including extensions,

before which such refusal to comply with the court order occurred, but in no event shall such confinement exceed eighteen months.

(b) No person confined pursuant to subsection (a) of this section shall be admitted to bail pending the determination of an appeal by him from the order for his confinement if it appears that the appeal is frivolous or taken for delay. Any appeal from an order of confinement under this section shall be disposed of as soon as practicable, but not later than thirty days from the filing of such appeal.

(c) Whoever escapes or attempts to escape from the custody of any facility or from any place in which or to which he is confined pursuant to this section or section 4243 of title 18, or whoever rescues or attempts to rescue or instigates, aids, or assists the escape or attempt to escape of such a person, shall be subject to imprisonment for not more than three years, or a fine of not more than $10,000, or both. Added Oct. 15, 1970, Pub.L. 91–452, Title III, § 301(a), 84 Stat. 932; as amended Oct. 12, 1984, Pub.L. 98–473, Title II, § 1013, 98 Stat. 2142.

§ 1861. Declaration of policy

It is the policy of the United States that all litigants in Federal courts entitled to trial by jury shall have the right to grand and petit juries selected at random from a fair cross section of the community in the district or division wherein the court convenes. It is further the policy of the United States that all citizens shall have the opportunity to be considered for service on grand and petit juries in the district courts of the United States, and shall have an obligation to serve as jurors when summoned for that purpose. As amended Sept. 9, 1957, Pub.L. 85–315, Part V, § 152, 71 Stat. 638; Mar. 27, 1968, Pub.L. 90–274, § 101, 82 Stat. 53.

§ 1870. Challenges

In civil cases, each party shall be entitled to three peremptory challenges. Several defendants or several plaintiffs may be considered as a single party for the purposes of making challenges, or the court may allow additional peremptory challenges and permit them to be exercised separately or jointly.

All challenges for cause or favor, whether to the array or panel or to individual jurors, shall be determined by the court. As amended Sept. 16, 1959, Pub.L. 86–282, 73 Stat. 565.

§ 1873. Admiralty and maritime cases

In any case of admiralty and maritime jurisdiction relating to any matter of contract or tort arising upon or concerning any vessel of twenty tons or upward, enrolled and licensed for the coasting trade, and employed in the business of commerce and navigation between places in different states upon the lakes and navigable waters connecting said lakes, the trial of all issues of fact shall be by jury if either party demands it.

§ 1914. District court; filing and miscellaneous fees; rules of court

(a) The clerk of each district court shall require the parties instituting any civil action, suit or proceeding in such court, whether by original process, removal or otherwise, to pay a filing fee of $350, except that on application for a writ of habeas corpus the filing fee shall be $5.

(b) The clerk shall collect from the parties such additional fees only as are prescribed by the Judicial Conference of the United States.

(c) Each district court by rule or standing order may require advance payment of fees. As amended Nov. 6, 1978, Pub.L. 95–598, Title II, § 244, 92 Stat. 2671; June 19, 1986, Pub.L. 99–336, § 4(a), 100 Stat. 637; Oct. 18, 1986, Pub.L. 99–500, Title I, § 101(b) [Title IV, § 407(a)], 100 Stat. 1783–64; Oct. 30, 1986, Pub.L. 99–591, Title I, § 101(b) [Title IV, § 407(a)], 100 Stat. 3341–64; Oct. 19, 1996, Pub.L. 104–317, Title IV, § 401(a), 110 Stat. 3853; Dec. 8, 2004, Pub.L. 108–447, Div. B, Title III, § 307(a), 118 Stat. 2895; Feb. 8, 2006, Pub.L. 109–171, Title X, § 10001(a), 120 Stat. 183.

§ 1915. Proceedings in forma pauperis

(a)(1) Subject to subsection (b), any court of the United States may authorize the commencement, prosecution or defense of any suit, action or proceeding, civil or criminal, or appeal therein, without prepayment of fees or security therefor, by a person who submits an affidavit that includes a statement of all assets such prisoner possesses that the person is unable to pay such fees or give security therefor. Such affidavit shall state the nature of the action, defense or appeal and affiant's belief that the person is entitled to redress.

(2) A prisoner seeking to bring a civil action or appeal a judgment in a civil action or proceeding without prepayment of fees or security therefor, in addition to filing the affidavit filed under paragraph (1), shall submit a certified copy of the trust fund account statement (or institutional equivalent) for the prisoner for the 6–month period immediately preceding the filing of the complaint or notice of the appeal, obtained from the appropriate official of each prison at which the prisoner is or was confined.

(3) An appeal may not be taken in forma pauperis if the trial court certifies in writing that it is not taken in good faith.

(b)(1) Notwithstanding subsection (a), if a prisoner brings a civil action or files an appeal in forma pauperis, the prisoner shall be required to pay the full amount of a filing fee. The court shall assess and, when funds exist, collect, as a partial payment of any court fees required by law, an initial partial filing fee of 20 percent of the greater of—

(A) the average monthly deposits to the prisoner's account; or

(B) the average monthly balance in the prisoner's account for the 6–month period immediately preceding the filing of the complaint or notice of appeal.

(2) After payment of the initial partial filing fee, the prisoner shall be required to make monthly payments of 20 percent of the preceding month's

income credited to the prisoner's account. The agency having custody of the prisoner shall forward payments from the prisoner's account to the clerk of the court each time the amount in the account exceeds $10 until the filing fees are paid.

(3) In no event shall the filing fee collected exceed the amount of fees permitted by statute for the commencement of a civil action or an appeal of a civil action or criminal judgment.

(4) In no event shall a prisoner be prohibited from bringing a civil action or appealing a civil or criminal judgment for the reason that the prisoner has no assets and no means by which to pay the initial partial filing fee.

(c) Upon the filing of an affidavit in accordance with subsections (a) and (b) and the prepayment of any partial filing fee as may be required under subsection (b), the court may direct payment by the United States of the expenses of (1) printing the record on appeal in any civil or criminal case, if such printing is required by the appellate court; (2) preparing a transcript of proceedings before a United States magistrate in any civil or criminal case, if such transcript is required by the district court, in the case of proceedings conducted under section 636(b) of this title or under section 3401(b) of title 18, United States Code; and (3) printing the record on appeal of such printing is required by the appellate court, in the case of proceedings conducted pursuant to section 636(c) of this title. Such expenses shall be paid when authorized by the Director of the Administrative Office of the United States Courts.

(d) The officers of the court shall issue and serve all process, and perform all duties in such cases. Witnesses shall attend as in other cases, and the same remedies shall be available as are provided for by law in other cases.

(e)(1) The court may request an attorney to represent any person unable to afford counsel.

(2) Notwithstanding any filing fee, or any portion thereof, that may have been paid, the court shall dismiss the case at any time if the court determines that—

(A) the allegation of poverty is untrue; or

(B) the action or appeal—

(i) is frivolous or malicious;

(ii) fails to state a claim on which relief may be granted; or

(iii) seeks monetary relief against a defendant who is immune from such relief.

(f)(1) Judgment may be rendered for costs at the conclusion of the suit or action as in other proceedings, but the United States shall not be liable for any of the costs thus incurred. If the United States has paid the cost of a stenographic transcript or printed record for the prevailing party, the same shall be taxed in favor of the United States.

(2)(A) If the judgment against a prisoner includes the payment of costs under this subsection, the prisoner shall be required to pay the full amount of the costs ordered.

(B) The prisoner shall be required to make payments for costs under this subsection in the same manner as is provided for filing fees under subsection (a)(2).

(C) In no event shall the costs collected exceed the amount of the costs ordered by the court.

(g) In no event shall a prisoner bring a civil action or appeal a judgment in a civil action or proceeding under this section if the prisoner has, on 3 or more prior occasions, while incarcerated or detained in any facility, brought an action or appeal in a court of the United States that was dismissed on the grounds that it is frivolous, malicious, or fails to state a claim upon which relief may be granted, unless the prisoner is under imminent danger of serious physical injury.

(h) As used in this section, the term "prisoner" means any person incarcerated or detained in any facility who is accused of, convicted of, sentenced for, or adjudicated delinquent for, violations of criminal law or the terms and conditions of parole, probation, pretrial release, or diversionary program. As amended May 24, 1949, c. 139, § 98, 63 Stat. 104; Oct. 31, 1951, c. 655, § 51(b, c), 65 Stat. 727; Sept. 21, 1959, Pub.L. 86–320, 73 Stat. 590; Oct. 10, 1979, Pub.L. 96–82, § 6, 93 Stat. 645; Apr. 26, 1996, Pub.L. 104–134, Title I, § 804, 110 Stat. 1321–73.

§ 1915A. Screening

(a) Screening.—The court shall review, before docketing, if feasible or, in any event, as soon as practicable after docketing, a complaint in a civil action in which a prisoner seeks redress from a governmental entity or officer or employee of a governmental entity.

(b) Grounds for Dismissal.—On review, the court shall identify cognizable claims or dismiss the complaint, or any portion of the complaint, if the complaint—

(1) is frivolous, malicious, or fails to state a claim upon which relief may be granted; or

(2) seeks monetary relief from a defendant who is immune from such relief.

(c) Definition.—As used in this section, the term "prisoner" means any person incarcerated or detained in any facility who is accused of, convicted of, sentenced for, or adjudicated delinquent for, violations of criminal law or the terms and conditions of parole, probation, pretrial release, or diversionary program. Added Apr. 26, 1996, Pub.L. 104–134, Title I, § 805, 110 Stat. 1321–75.

§ 1919. Dismissal for lack of jurisdiction

Whenever any action or suit is dismissed in any district court, the Court of International Trade, or the Court of Federal Claims for want of jurisdiction, such court may order the payment of just costs. As amended

Oct. 10, 1980, Pub.L. 96–417, Title V, § 510, 94 Stat. 1743; Oct. 29, 1992, Pub.L. 102–572, Title IX, § 908, 106 Stat. 4519.

§ 1920. Taxation of costs

A judge or clerk of any court of the United States may tax as costs the following:

(1) Fees of the clerk and marshal;

(2) Fees for printed or electronically recorded transcripts necessarily obtained for use in the case;

(3) Fees and disbursements for printing and witnesses;

(4) Fees for exemplification and the costs of making copies of any materials where the copies are necessarily obtained for use in the case;

(5) Docket fees under section 1923 of this title;

(6) Compensation of court appointed experts, compensation of interpreters, and salaries, fees, expenses, and costs of special interpretation services under section 1828 of this title.

A bill of costs shall be filed in the case and, upon allowance, included in the judgment or decree. As amended Oct. 28, 1978, Pub.L. 95–539, § 7, 92 Stat. 2044; Oct. 13, 2008, Pub.L. 110–406, § 6, 122 Stat. 4292.

§ 1924. Verification of bill of costs

Before any bill of costs is taxed, the party claiming any item of cost or disbursement shall attach thereto an affidavit, made by himself or by his duly authorized attorney or agent having knowledge of the facts, that such item is correct and has been necessarily incurred in the case and that the services for which fees have been charged were actually and necessarily performed.

§ 1927. Counsel's liability for excessive costs

Any attorney or other person admitted to conduct cases in any court of the United States or any Territory thereof who so multiplies the proceedings in any case unreasonably and vexatiously may be required by the court to satisfy personally the excess costs, expenses, and attorneys' fees reasonably incurred because of such conduct. As amended Sept. 12, 1980, Pub.L. 96–349, § 3, 94 Stat. 1156.

§ 1961. Interest

(a) Interest shall be allowed on any money judgment in a civil case recovered in a district court. Execution therefor may be levied by the marshal, in any case where, by the law of the State in which such court is held, execution may be levied for interest on judgments recovered in the courts of the State. Such interest shall be calculated from the date of the entry of the judgment, at a rate equal to the weekly average 1–year constant maturity Treasury yield, as published by the Board of Governors of the Federal Reserve System, for the calendar week preceding the date of the judgment. The Director of the Administrative Office of the United

States Courts shall distribute notice of that rate and any changes in it to all Federal judges.

(b) Interest shall be computed daily to the date of payment except as provided in section 2516(b) of this title and section 1304(b) of title 31, and shall be compounded annually.

(c)(1) This section shall not apply in any judgment of any court with respect to any internal revenue tax case. Interest shall be allowed in such cases at the underpayment rate or overpayment rate (whichever is appropriate) established under section 6621 of the Internal Revenue Code of 1954.

(2) Except as otherwise provided in paragraph (1) of this subsection, interest shall be allowed on all final judgments against the United States in the United States Court of Appeals for the Federal circuit, at the rate provided in subsection (a) and as provided in subsection (b).

(3) Interest shall be allowed, computed, and paid on judgments of the United States Court of Federal Claims only as provided in paragraph (1) of this subsection or in any other provision of law.

(4) This section shall not be construed to affect the interest on any judgment of any court not specified in this section. As amended Apr. 2, 1982, Pub.L. 97–164, Title III, § 302(a), 96 Stat. 55; Sept. 13, 1982, Pub.L. 97–258, § 2(m)(1), 96 Stat. 1062; Jan. 12, 1983, Pub.L. 97–452, § 2(d)(1), 96 Stat. 2478; Oct. 22, 1986, Pub.L. 99–514, Title XV, § 1511(c)(17), 100 Stat. 2745; Oct. 29, 1992, Pub.L. 102–572, Title IX, § 902(b)(1), 106 Stat. 4516; Dec. 21, 2000, Pub.L. 106–554, § 1(a)(7)[307(d)(1)], 114 Stat. 2763A–636.

§ 1963. Registration of judgments for enforcement in other districts

A judgment in an action for the recovery of money or property entered in any court of appeals, district court, bankruptcy court, or in the Court of International Trade may be registered by filing a certified copy of the judgment in any other district or, with respect to the Court of International Trade, in any judicial district, when the judgment has become final by appeal or expiration of the time for appeal or when ordered by the court that entered the judgment for good cause shown. Such a judgment entered in favor of the United States may be so registered any time after judgment is entered. A judgment so registered shall have the same effect as a judgment of the district court of the district where registered and may be enforced in like manner.

A certified copy of the satisfaction of any judgment in whole or in part may be registered in like manner in any district in which the judgment is a lien.

The procedure prescribed under this section is in addition to other procedures provided by law for the enforcement of judgments. As amended Aug. 23, 1954, c. 837, 68 Stat. 772; July 7, 1958, Pub.L. 85–508, § 12(o), 72 Stat. 349; Nov. 19, 1988, Pub.L. 100–702, Title X, § 1002, 102 Stat. 4664; Nov. 29, 1990, Pub.L. 101–647, Title XXXVI, § 3628, 104 Stat. 4965; Oct. 19, 1996, Pub.L. 104–317, Title II, § 203, 110 Stat. 3849.

§ 1964. Constructive notice of pending actions

Where the law of a State requires a notice of an action concerning real property pending in a court of the State to be registered, recorded, docketed, or indexed in a particular manner, or in a certain office or county or parish in order to give constructive notice of the action as it relates to the real property, and such law authorizes a notice of an action concerning real property pending in a United States district court to be registered, recorded, docketed, or indexed in the same manner, or in the same place, those requirements of the State law must be complied with in order to give constructive notice of such an action pending in a United States district court as it relates to real property in such State. Added Aug. 20, 1958, Pub.L. 85–689, § 1(a), 72 Stat. 683.

§ 2071. Rule-making power generally

(a) The Supreme Court and all courts established by Act of Congress may from time to time prescribe rules for the conduct of their business. Such rules shall be consistent with Acts of Congress and rules of practice and procedure prescribed under section 2072 of this title.

(b) Any rule prescribed by a court, other than the Supreme Court, under subsection (a) shall be prescribed only after giving appropriate public notice and an opportunity for comment. Such rule shall take effect upon the date specified by the prescribing court and shall have such effect on pending proceedings as the prescribing court may order.

(c)(1) A rule of a district court prescribed under subsection (a) shall remain in effect unless modified or abrogated by the judicial council of the relevant circuit.

(2) Any other rule prescribed by a court other than the Supreme Court under subsection (a) shall remain in effect unless modified or abrogated by the Judicial Conference.

(d) Copies of rules prescribed under subsection (a) by a district court shall be furnished to the judicial council, and copies of all rules prescribed by a court other than the Supreme Court under subsection (a) shall be furnished to the Director of the Administrative Office of the United States Courts and made available to the public.

(e) If the prescribing court determines that there is an immediate need for a rule, such court may proceed under this section without public notice and opportunity for comment, but such court shall promptly thereafter afford such notice and opportunity for comment.

(f) No rule may be prescribed by a district court other than under this section. As amended May 24, 1949, c. 139, § 102, 63 Stat. 104; Nov. 19, 1988, Pub.L. 100–702, Title IV, § 403(a)(1), 102 Stat. 4650.

§ 2072. Rules of procedure and evidence; power to prescribe

(a) The Supreme Court shall have the power to prescribe general rules of practice and procedure and rules of evidence for cases in the United States district courts (including proceedings before magistrates thereof) and courts of appeals.

(b) Such rules shall not abridge, enlarge or modify any substantive right. All laws in conflict with such rules shall be of no further force or effect after such rules have taken effect.

(c) Such rules may define when a ruling of a district court is final for the purposes of appeal under section 1291 of this title. As amended May 24, 1949, c. 139, § 103, 63 Stat. 104; July 18, 1949, c. 343, § 2, 63 Stat. 446; May 10, 1950, c. 174, § 2, 64 Stat. 158; July 7, 1958, Pub.L. 85–508, § 12(m), 72 Stat. 348; Nov. 6, 1966, Pub.L. 89–773, § 1, 80 Stat. 1323; Nov. 19, 1988, Pub.L. 100–702, Title IV, § 401(a), 102 Stat. 4648; Dec. 1, 1990, Pub.L. 101–650, Title III, § 315, 104 Stat. 5115.

§ 2073. Rules of procedure and evidence; method of prescribing

(a)(1) The Judicial Conference shall prescribe and publish the procedures for the consideration of proposed rules under this section.

(2) The Judicial Conference may authorize the appointment of committees to assist the Conference by recommending rules to be prescribed under sections 2072 and 2075 of this title. Each such committee shall consist of members of the bench and the professional bar, and trial and appellate judges.

(b) The Judicial Conference shall authorize the appointment of a standing committee on rules of practice, procedure, and evidence under subsection (a) of this section. Such standing committee shall review each recommendation of any other committees so appointed and recommend to the Judicial Conference rules of practice, procedure, and evidence and such changes in rules proposed by a committee appointed under subsection (a)(2) of this section as may be necessary to maintain consistency and otherwise promote the interest of justice.

(c)(1) Each meeting for the transaction of business under this chapter by any committee appointed under this section shall be open to the public, except when the committee so meeting, in open session and with a majority present, determines that it is in the public interest that all or part of the remainder of the meeting on that day shall be closed to the public, and states the reason for so closing the meeting. Minutes of each meeting for the transaction of business under this chapter shall be maintained by the committee and made available to the public, except that any portion of such minutes, relating to a closed meeting and made available to the public, may contain such deletions as may be necessary to avoid frustrating the purposes of closing the meeting.

(2) Any meeting for the transaction of business under this chapter, by a committee appointed under this section, shall be preceded by sufficient notice to enable all interested persons to attend.

(d) In making a recommendation under this section or under section 2072 or 2075, the body making that recommendation shall provide a proposed rule, an explanatory note on the rule, and a written report explaining the body's action, including any minority or other separate views.

(e) Failure to comply with this section does not invalidate a rule prescribed under section 2072 or 2075 of this title. Added Nov. 19, 1988,

Pub.L. 100–702, Title IV, § 401(a), 102 Stat. 4648; as amended Oct. 22, 1994, Pub.L. 103–394, Title I, § 104(e), 108 Stat. 4110.

§ 2074. Rules of procedure and evidence; submission to Congress; effective date

(a) The Supreme Court shall transmit to the Congress not later than May 1 of the year in which a rule prescribed under section 2072 is to become effective a copy of the proposed rule. Such rule shall take effect no earlier than December 1 of the year in which such rule is so transmitted unless otherwise provided by law. The Supreme Court may fix the extent such rule shall apply to proceedings then pending, except that the Supreme Court shall not require the application of such rule to further proceedings then pending to the extent that, in the opinion of the court in which such proceedings are pending, the application of such rule in such proceedings would not be feasible or would work injustice, in which event the former rule applies.

(b) Any such rule creating, abolishing, or modifying an evidentiary privilege shall have no force or effect unless approved by Act of Congress. Added Nov. 19, 1988, Pub.L. 100–702, Title IV, § 401(a), 102 Stat. 4648.

§ 2075. Bankruptcy rules

The Supreme Court shall have the power to prescribe by general rules, the forms of process, writs, pleadings, and motions, and the practice and procedure in cases under title 11.

Such rules shall not abridge, enlarge, or modify any substantive right.

The Supreme Court shall transmit to Congress not later than May 1 of the year in which a rule prescribed under this section is to become effective a copy of the proposed rule. The rule shall take effect no earlier than December 1 of the year in which it is transmitted to Congress unless otherwise provided by law.

The bankruptcy rules promulgated under this section shall prescribe a form for the statement required under section 707(b)(2)(C) of title 11 and may provide general rules on the content of such statement. Added Oct. 3, 1964, Pub.L. 88–623, § 1, 78 Stat. 1001; as amended Nov. 6, 1978, Pub.L. 95–598, Title II, § 247, 92 Stat. 2672; Oct. 22, 1994, Pub.L. 103–394, Title I, § 104(f), 108 Stat. 4110; Apr. 20, 2005, Pub.L. 109–8, Title XII, § 1232, 119 Stat. 202.

§ 2077. Publication of rules; advisory committees

(a) The rules for the conduct of the business of each court of appeals, including the operating procedures of such court, shall be published. Each court of appeals shall print or cause to be printed necessary copies of the rules. The Judicial Conference shall prescribe the fees for sales of copies under section 1913 of this title, but the Judicial Conference may provide for free distribution of copies to members of the bar of each court and to other interested persons.

(b) Each court, except the Supreme Court, that is authorized to prescribe rules of the conduct of such court's business under section 2071 of this title shall appoint an advisory committee for the study of the rules of practice and internal operating procedures of such court and, in the case of an advisory committee appointed by a court of appeals, of the rules of the judicial council of the circuit. The advisory committee shall make recommendations to the court concerning such rules and procedures. Members of the committee shall serve without compensation, but the Director may pay travel and transportation expenses in accordance with section 5703 of title 5. Added Apr. 2, 1982, Pub.L. 97–164, Title II, § 208(a), 96 Stat. 54; as amended Nov. 19, 1988, Pub.L. 100–702, Title IV, § 401(b), 102 Stat. 4650; Dec. 1, 1990, Pub.L. 101–650, Title IV, § 406, 104 Stat. 5124.

§ 2101. Supreme Court; time for appeal or certiorari; docketing; stay

(a) A direct appeal to the Supreme Court from any decision under section 1253 of this title, holding unconstitutional in whole or in part, any Act of Congress, shall be taken within thirty days after the entry of the interlocutory or final order, judgment or decree. The record shall be made up and the case docketed within sixty days from the time such appeal is taken under rules prescribed by the Supreme Court.

(b) Any other direct appeal to the Supreme Court which is authorized by law, from a decision of a district court in any civil action, suit or proceeding, shall be taken within thirty days from the judgment, order or decree, appealed from, if interlocutory, and within sixty days if final.

(c) Any other appeal or any writ of certiorari intended to bring any judgment or decree in a civil action, suit or proceeding before the Supreme Court for review shall be taken or applied for within ninety days after the entry of such judgment or decree. A justice of the Supreme Court, for good cause shown, may extend the time for applying for a writ of certiorari for a period not exceeding sixty days.

(d) The time for appeal or application for a writ of certiorari to review the judgment of a State court in a criminal case shall be as prescribed by rules of the Supreme Court.

(e) An application to the Supreme Court for a writ of certiorari to review a case before judgment has been rendered in the court of appeals may be made at any time before judgment.

(f) In any case in which the final judgment or decree of any court is subject to review by the Supreme Court on writ of certiorari, the execution and enforcement of such judgment or decree may be stayed for a reasonable time to enable the party aggrieved to obtain a writ of certiorari from the Supreme Court. The stay may be granted by a judge of the court rendering the judgment or decree or by a justice of the Supreme Court, and may be conditioned on the giving of security, approved by such judge or justice, that if the aggrieved party fails to make application for such writ within the period allotted therefor, or fails to obtain an order granting his application, or fails to make his plea good in the Supreme Court, he shall answer for all damages and costs which the other party may sustain by reason of the stay.

(g) The time for application for a writ of certiorari to review a decision of the United States Court of Appeals for the Armed Forces shall be as prescribed by rules of the Supreme Court. As amended May 24, 1949, c. 139, § 106, 63 Stat. 104; Dec. 6, 1983, Pub.L. 98–209, § 10(b), 97 Stat. 1406; June 27, 1988, Pub.L. 100–352, § 5(b), 102 Stat. 663; Oct. 5, 1994, Pub.L. 103–337, Div. A, Title IX, § 924(d)(1)(C), 108 Stat. 2832.

§ 2102.　Priority of criminal case on appeal from State court

Criminal cases on review from State courts shall have priority, on the docket of the Supreme Court, over all cases except cases to which the United States is a party and such other cases as the court may decide to be of public importance.

§ 2104.　Reviews of State court decisions

A review by the Supreme Court of a judgment or decree of a State court shall be conducted in the same manner and under the same regulations, and shall have the same effect, as if the judgment or decree reviewed had been rendered in a court of the United States. As amended June 27, 1988, Pub.L. 100–352, § 5(d)(1), 102 Stat. 663.

§ 2105.　Scope of review; abatement

There shall be no reversal in the Supreme Court or a court of appeals for error in ruling upon matters in abatement which do not involve jurisdiction.

§ 2106.　Determination

The Supreme Court or any other court of appellate jurisdiction may affirm, modify, vacate, set aside or reverse any judgment, decree, or order of a court lawfully brought before it for review, and may remand the cause and direct the entry of such appropriate judgment, decree, or order, or require such further proceedings to be had as may be just under the circumstances.

§ 2107.　Time for appeal to court of appeals

(a) Except as otherwise provided in this section, no appeal shall bring any judgment, order or decree in an action, suit or proceeding of a civil nature before a court of appeals for review unless notice of appeal is filed, within thirty days after the entry of such judgment, order or decree.

(b) In any such action, suit or proceeding in which the United States or an officer or agency thereof is a party, the time as to all parties shall be sixty days from such entry.

(c) The district court may, upon motion filed not later than 30 days after the expiration of the time otherwise set for bringing appeal, extend the time for appeal upon a showing of excusable neglect or good cause. In addition, if the district court finds—

　　(1) that a party entitled to notice of the entry of a judgment or order did not receive such notice from the clerk or any party within 21 days of its entry, and

(2) that no party would be prejudiced,

the district court may, upon motion filed within 180 days after entry of the judgment or order or within 14 days after receipt of such notice, whichever is earlier, reopen the time for appeal for a period of 14 days from the date of entry of the order reopening the time for appeal.

(d) This section shall not apply to bankruptcy matters or other proceedings under Title 11. As amended May 24, 1949, c. 139, §§ 107, 108, 63 Stat. 104; Dec. 9, 1991, Pub.L. 102–198, § 12, 105 Stat. 1627; May 7, 2009, Pub.L. 111–6, § 6(3), 123 Stat. 1608, 1609.

§ 2108. Proof of amount in controversy

Where the power of any court of appeals to review a case depends upon the amount or value in controversy, such amount or value, if not otherwise satisfactorily disclosed upon the record, may be shown and ascertained by the oath of a party to the case or by other competent evidence.

§ 2109. Quorum of Supreme Court justices absent

If a case brought to the Supreme Court by direct appeal from a district court cannot be heard and determined because of the absence of a quorum of qualified justices, the Chief Justice of the United States may order it remitted to the court of appeals for the circuit including the district in which the case arose, to be heard and determined by that court either sitting in banc or specially constituted and composed of the three circuit judges senior in commission who are able to sit, as such order may direct. The decision of such court shall be final and conclusive. In the event of the disqualification or disability of one or more of such circuit judges, such court shall be filled as provided in chapter 15 of this title.

In any other case brought to the Supreme Court for review, which cannot be heard and determined because of the absence of a quorum of qualified justices, if a majority of the qualified justices shall be of opinion that the case cannot be heard and determined at the next ensuing term, the court shall enter its order affirming the judgment of the court from which the case was brought for review with the same effect as upon affirmance by an equally divided court.

§ 2111. Harmless error

On the hearing of any appeal or writ of certiorari in any case, the court shall give judgment after an examination of the record without regard to errors or defects which do not affect the substantial rights of the parties. Added May 24, 1949, c. 139, § 110, 63 Stat. 105.

§ 2113. Definition

For purposes of this chapter, the terms "State court", "State courts", and "highest court of a State" include the District of Columbia Court of Appeals. Added July 29, 1970, Pub.L. 91–358, Title I, § 172(a)(2)(A), 84 Stat. 590.

§ 2201. Creation of remedy

(a) In a case of actual controversy within its jurisdiction, except with respect to Federal taxes other than actions brought under section 7428 of the Internal Revenue Code of 1986, a proceeding under section 505 or 1146 of title 11, or in any civil action involving an antidumping or countervailing duty proceeding regarding a class or kind of merchandise of a free trade area country (as defined in section 516A(f)(10) of the Tariff Act of 1930), as determined by the administering authority, any court of the United States, upon the filing of an appropriate pleading, may declare the rights and other legal relations of any interested party seeking such declaration, whether or not further relief is or could be sought. Any such declaration shall have the force and effect of a final judgment or decree and shall be reviewable as such.

(b) For limitations on actions brought with respect to drug patents see section 505 or 512 of the Federal Food, Drug, and Cosmetic Act. As amended May 24, 1949, c. 139, § 111, 63 Stat. 105; Aug. 28, 1954, c. 1033, 68 Stat. 890; July 7, 1958, Pub.L. 85–508, § 12(p), 72 Stat. 349; Oct. 4, 1976, Pub.L. 94–455, Title XIII, § 1306(b)(8), 90 Stat. 1719; Nov. 6, 1978, Pub.L. 95–598, Title II, § 249, 92 Stat. 2672; Sept. 24, 1984, Pub.L. 98–417, Title I, § 106, 98 Stat. 1597; Sept. 28, 1988, Pub.L. 100–449, Title IV, § 402(c), 102 Stat. 1884; Nov. 16, 1988, Pub.L. 100–670, Title I, § 107(b), 102 Stat. 3984; Dec. 8, 1993, Pub.L. 103–182, Title IV, § 414(b), 107 Stat. 2147.

§ 2202. Further relief

Further necessary or proper relief based on a declaratory judgment or decree may be granted, after reasonable notice and hearing, against any adverse party whose rights have been determined by such judgment.

§ 2241. Power to grant writ

(a) Writs of habeas corpus may be granted by the Supreme Court, any justice thereof, the district courts and any circuit judge within their respective jurisdictions. The order of a circuit judge shall be entered in the records of the district court of the district wherein the restraint complained of is had.

(b) The Supreme Court, any justice thereof, and any circuit judge may decline to entertain an application for a writ of habeas corpus and may transfer the application for hearing and determination to the district court having jurisdiction to entertain it.

(c) The writ of habeas corpus shall not extend to a prisoner unless—

(1) He is in custody under or by color of the authority of the United States or is committed for trial before some court thereof; or

(2) He is in custody for an act done or omitted in pursuance of an Act of Congress, or an order, process, judgment or decree of a court or judge of the United States; or

(3) He is in custody in violation of the Constitution or laws or treaties of the United States; or

(4) He, being a citizen of a foreign state and domiciled therein is in custody for an act done or omitted under any alleged right, title, authority, privilege, protection, or exemption claimed under the commission, order or sanction of any foreign state, or under color thereof, the validity and effect of which depend upon the law of nations; or

(5) It is necessary to bring him into court to testify or for trial.

(d) Where an application for a writ of habeas corpus is made by a person in custody under the judgment and sentence of a State court of a State which contains two or more Federal judicial districts, the application may be filed in the district court for the district wherein such person is in custody or in the district court for the district within which the State court was held which convicted and sentenced him and each of such district courts shall have concurrent jurisdiction to entertain the application. The district court for the district wherein such an application is filed in the exercise of its discretion and in furtherance of justice may transfer the application to the other district court for hearing and determination.

(e)(1) No court, justice, or judge shall have jurisdiction to hear or consider an application for a writ of habeas corpus filed by or on behalf of an alien detained by the United States who has been determined by the United States to have been properly detained as an enemy combatant or is awaiting such determination.

(2) Except as provided in paragraphs (2) and (3) of section 1005(e) of the Detainee Treatment Act of 2005 (10 U.S.C. 801 note), no court, justice, or judge shall have jurisdiction to hear or consider any other action against the United States or its agents relating to any aspect of the detention, transfer, treatment, trial, or conditions of confinement of an alien who is or was detained by the United States and has been determined by the United States to have been properly detained as an enemy combatant or is awaiting such determination. As amended May 24, 1949, c. 139, § 112, 63 Stat. 105; Sept. 19, 1966, Pub.L. 89–590, 80 Stat. 811; Dec. 30, 2005, Pub.L. 109–148, Div. A, Title X, § 1005(e)(1), 119 Stat. 2742; Jan. 6, 2006, Pub.L. 109–163, Div. A, Title XIV, § 1405(e)(1), 119 Stat. 3477; Oct. 17, 2006, Pub.L. 109–366, § 7(a), 120 Stat. 2635.

§ 2242. Application

Application for a writ of habeas corpus shall be in writing signed and verified by the person for whose relief it is intended or by someone acting in his behalf.

It shall allege the facts concerning the applicant's commitment or detention, the name of the person who has custody over him and by virtue of what claim or authority, if known.

It may be amended or supplemented as provided in the rules of procedure applicable to civil actions.

If addressed to the Supreme Court, a justice thereof or a circuit judge it shall state the reasons for not making application to the district court of the district in which the applicant is held.

§ 2243. Issuance of writ; return; hearing; decision

A court, justice or judge entertaining an application for a writ of habeas corpus shall forthwith award the writ or issue an order directing the respondent to show cause why the writ should not be granted, unless it appears from the application that the applicant or person detained is not entitled thereto.

The writ, or order to show cause shall be directed to the person having custody of the person detained. It shall be returned within three days unless for good cause additional time, not exceeding twenty days, is allowed.

The person to whom the writ or order is directed shall make a return certifying the true cause of the detention.

When the writ or order is returned a day shall be set for hearing, not more than five days after the return unless for good cause additional time is allowed.

Unless the application for the writ and the return present only issues of law the person to whom the writ is directed shall be required to produce at the hearing the body of the person detained.

The applicant or the person detained may, under oath, deny any of the facts set forth in the return or allege any other material facts.

The return and all suggestions made against it may be amended, by leave of court, before or after being filed.

The court shall summarily hear and determine the facts, and dispose of the matter as law and justice require.

§ 2244. Finality of determination

(a) No circuit or district judge shall be required to entertain an application for a writ of habeas corpus to inquire into the detention of a person pursuant to a judgment of a court of the United States if it appears that the legality of such detention has been determined by a judge or court of the United States on a prior application for a writ of habeas corpus, except as provided in section 2255.

(b)(1) A claim presented in a second or successive habeas corpus application under section 2254 that was presented in a prior application shall be dismissed.

(2) A claim presented in a second or successive habeas corpus application under section 2254 that was not presented in a prior application shall be dismissed unless—

    (A) the applicant shows that the claim relies on a new rule of constitutional law, made retroactive to cases on collateral review by the Supreme Court, that was previously unavailable; or

    (B)(i) the factual predicate for the claim could not have been discovered previously through the exercise of due diligence; and

      (ii) the facts underlying the claim, if proven and viewed in light of the evidence as a whole, would be sufficient to establish by clear and convincing evidence that, but for constitutional error, no reasonable factfinder would have found the applicant guilty of the underlying offense.

(3)(A) Before a second or successive application permitted by this section is filed in the district court, the applicant shall move in the appropriate court of appeals for an order authorizing the district court to consider the application.

(B) A motion in the court of appeals for an order authorizing the district court to consider a second or successive application shall be determined by a three-judge panel of the court of appeals.

(C) The court of appeals may authorize the filing of a second or successive application only if it determines that the application makes a prima facie showing that the application satisfies the requirements of this subsection.

(D) The court of appeals shall grant or deny the authorization to file a second or successive application not later than 30 days after the filing of the motion.

(E) The grant or denial of an authorization by a court of appeals to file a second or successive application shall not be appealable and shall not be the subject of a petition for rehearing or for a writ of certiorari.

(4) A district court shall dismiss any claim presented in a second or successive application that the court of appeals has authorized to be filed unless the applicant shows that the claim satisfies the requirements of this section.

(c) In a habeas corpus proceeding brought in behalf of a person in custody pursuant to the judgment of a State court, a prior judgment of the Supreme Court of the United States on an appeal or review by a writ of certiorari at the instance of the prisoner of the decision of such State court, shall be conclusive as to all issues of fact or law with respect to an asserted denial of a Federal right which constitutes ground for discharge in a habeas corpus proceeding, actually adjudicated by the Supreme Court therein, unless the applicant for the writ of habeas corpus shall plead and the court shall find the existence of a material and controlling fact which did not appear in the record of the proceeding in the Supreme Court and the court shall further find that the applicant for the writ of habeas corpus could not have caused such fact to appear in such record by the exercise of reasonable diligence.

(d)(1) A 1–year period of limitation shall apply to an application for a writ of habeas corpus by a person in custody pursuant to the judgment of a State court. The limitation period shall run from the latest of—

(A) the date on which the judgment became final by the conclusion of direct review or the expiration of the time for seeking such review;

(B) the date on which the impediment to filing an application created by State action in violation of the Constitution or laws of the United States is removed, if the applicant was prevented from filing by such State action;

(C) the date on which the constitutional right asserted was initially recognized by the Supreme Court, if the right has been newly recognized by the Supreme Court and made retroactively applicable to cases on collateral review; or

(D) the date on which the factual predicate of the claim or claims presented could have been discovered through the exercise of due diligence.

(2) The time during which a properly filed application for State post-conviction or other collateral review with respect to the pertinent judgment or claim is pending shall not be counted toward any period of limitation under this subsection. As amended Nov. 2, 1966, Pub.L. 89–711, § 1, 80 Stat. 1104; Apr. 24, 1996, Pub.L. 104–132, Title I, §§ 101, 106, 110 Stat. 1217, 1220.

§ 2254. State custody; remedies in Federal courts

(a) The Supreme Court, a Justice thereof, a circuit judge, or a district court shall entertain an application for a writ of habeas corpus in behalf of a person in custody pursuant to the judgment of a State court only on the ground that he is in custody in violation of the Constitution or laws or treaties of the United States.

(b)(1) An application for a writ of habeas corpus on behalf of a person in custody pursuant to the judgment of a State court shall not be granted unless it appears that—

(A) the applicant has exhausted the remedies available in the courts of the State; or

(B)(i) there is an absence of available State corrective process; or

(ii) circumstances exist that render such process ineffective to protect the rights of the applicant.

(2) An application for a writ of habeas corpus may be denied on the merits, notwithstanding the failure of the applicant to exhaust the remedies available in the courts of the State.

(3) A State shall not be deemed to have waived the exhaustion requirement or be estopped from reliance upon the requirement unless the State, through counsel, expressly waives the requirement.

(c) An applicant shall not be deemed to have exhausted the remedies available in the courts of the State, within the meaning of this section, if he has the right under the law of the State to raise, by any available procedure, the question presented.

(d) An application for a writ of habeas corpus on behalf of a person in custody pursuant to the judgment of a State court shall not be granted with respect to any claim that was adjudicated on the merits in State court proceedings unless the adjudication of the claim—

(1) resulted in a decision that was contrary to, or involved an unreasonable application of, clearly established Federal law, as determined by the Supreme Court of the United States; or

(2) resulted in a decision that was based on an unreasonable determination of the facts in light of the evidence presented in the State court proceeding.

(e)(1) In a proceeding instituted by an application for a writ of habeas corpus by a person in custody pursuant to the judgment of a State court, a determination of a factual issue made by a State court shall be presumed to be correct. The applicant shall have the burden of rebutting the presumption of correctness by clear and convincing evidence.

(2) If the applicant has failed to develop the factual basis of a claim in State court proceedings, the court shall not hold an evidentiary hearing on the claim unless the applicant shows that—

(A) the claim relies on—

(i) a new rule of constitutional law, made retroactive to cases on collateral review by the Supreme Court, that was previously unavailable; or

(ii) a factual predicate that could not have been previously discovered through the exercise of due diligence; and

(B) the facts underlying the claim would be sufficient to establish by clear and convincing evidence that but for constitutional error, no reasonable factfinder would have found the applicant guilty of the underlying offense.

(f) If the applicant challenges the sufficiency of the evidence adduced in such State court proceeding to support the State court's determination of a factual issue made therein, the applicant, if able, shall produce that part of the record pertinent to a determination of the sufficiency of the evidence to support such determination. If the applicant, because of indigency or other reason is unable to produce such part of the record, then the State shall produce such part of the record and the Federal court shall direct the State to do so by order directed to an appropriate State official. If the State cannot provide such pertinent part of the record, then the court shall determine under the existing facts and circumstances what weight shall be given to the State court's factual determination.

(g) A copy of the official records of the State court, duly certified by the clerk of such court to be a true and correct copy of a finding, judicial opinion, or other reliable written indicia showing such a factual determination by the State court shall be admissible in the Federal court proceeding.

(h) Except as provided in section 408 of the Controlled Substances Act, in all proceedings brought under this section, and any subsequent proceedings on review, the court may appoint counsel for an applicant who is or becomes financially unable financially unable to afford counsel, except as provided by a rule promulgated by the Supreme Court pursuant to statutory authority. Appointment of counsel under this section shall be governed by section 3006A of title 18.

(i) The ineffectiveness or incompetence of counsel during Federal or State collateral post-conviction proceedings shall not be a ground for relief in a proceeding arising under section 2254. As amended Nov. 2, 1966,

Pub.L. 89–711, § 2, 80 Stat. 1105; Apr. 24, 1996, Pub.L. 104–132, Title I, § 104, 110 Stat. 1218.

§ 2255.   Federal custody; remedies on motion attacking sentence

(a) A prisoner in custody under sentence of a court established by Act of Congress claiming the right to be released upon the ground that the sentence was imposed in violation of the Constitution or laws of the United States, or that the court was without jurisdiction to impose such sentence, or that the sentence was in excess of the maximum authorized by law, or is otherwise subject to collateral attack, may move the court which imposed the sentence to vacate, set aside or correct the sentence.

(b) Unless the motion and the files and records of the case conclusively show that the prisoner is entitled to no relief, the court shall cause notice thereof to be served upon the United States attorney, grant a prompt hearing thereon, determine the issues and make findings of fact and conclusions of law with respect thereto. If the court finds that the judgment was rendered without jurisdiction, or that the sentence imposed was not authorized by law or otherwise open to collateral attack, or that there has been such a denial or infringement of the constitutional rights of the prisoner as to render the judgment vulnerable to collateral attack, the court shall vacate and set the judgment aside and shall discharge the prisoner or resentence him or grant a new trial or correct the sentence as may appear appropriate.

(c) A court may entertain and determine such motion without requiring the production of the prisoner at the hearing.

(d) An appeal may be taken to the court of appeals from the order entered on the motion as from a final judgment on application for a writ of habeas corpus.

(e) An application for a writ of habeas corpus in behalf of a prisoner who is authorized to apply for relief by motion pursuant to this section, shall not be entertained if it appears that the applicant has failed to apply for relief, by motion, to the court which sentenced him, or that such court has denied him relief, unless it also appears that the remedy by motion is inadequate or ineffective to test the legality of his detention.

(f) A 1–year period of limitation shall apply to a motion under this section. The limitation period shall run from the latest of—

(1) the date on which the judgment of conviction becomes final;

(2) the date on which the impediment to making a motion created by governmental action in violation of the Constitution or laws of the United States is removed, if the movant was prevented from making a motion by such governmental action;

(3) the date on which the right asserted was initially recognized by the Supreme Court, if that right has been newly recognized by the Supreme Court and made retroactively applicable to cases on collateral review; or

(4) the date on which the facts supporting the claim or claims presented could have been discovered through the exercise of due diligence.

(g) Except as provided in section 408 of the Controlled Substances Act, in all proceedings brought under this section, and any subsequent proceedings on review, the court may appoint counsel, except as provided by a rule promulgated by the Supreme Court pursuant to statutory authority. Appointment of counsel under this section shall be governed by section 3006A of title 18.

(h) A second or successive motion must be certified as provided in section 2244 by a panel of the appropriate court of appeals to contain—

(1) newly discovered evidence that, if proven and viewed in light of the evidence as a whole, would be sufficient to establish by clear and convincing evidence that no reasonable factfinder would have found the movant guilty of the offense; or

(2) a new rule of constitutional law, made retroactive to cases on collateral review by the Supreme Court, that was previously unavailable. As amended May 24, 1949, c. 139, § 114, 63 Stat. 105; Apr. 24, 1996, Pub.L. 104–132, Title I, § 105, 110 Stat. 1220; Jan. 7, 2008, Pub.L. 110–177, Title V, § 511, 121 Stat. 2545.

§ 2283. Stay of State court proceedings

A court of the United States may not grant an injunction to stay proceedings in a State court except as expressly authorized by Act of Congress, or where necessary in aid of its jurisdiction, or to protect or effectuate its judgments.

§ 2284. Three-judge court; when required; composition; procedure

(a) A district court of three judges shall be convened when otherwise required by Act of Congress, or when an action is filed challenging the constitutionality of the apportionment of congressional districts or the apportionment of any statewide legislative body.

(b) In any action required to be heard and determined by a district court of three judges under subsection (a) of this section, the composition and procedure of the court shall be as follows:

(1) Upon the filing of a request for three judges, the judge to whom the request is presented shall, unless he determines that three judges are not required, immediately notify the chief judge of the circuit, who shall designate two other judges, at least one of whom shall be a circuit judge. The judges so designated, and the judge to whom the request was presented, shall serve as members of the court to hear and determine the action or proceeding.

(2) If the action is against a State, or officer or agency thereof, at least five days' notice of hearing of the action shall be given by registered or certified mail to the Governor and attorney general of the State.

(3) A single judge may conduct all proceedings except the trial, and enter all orders permitted by the rules of civil procedure except as provided

in this subsection. He may grant a temporary restraining order on a specific finding, based on evidence submitted, that specified irreparable damage will result if the order is not granted, which order, unless previously revoked by the district judge, shall remain in force only until the hearing and determination by the district court of three judges of an application for a preliminary injunction. A single judge shall not appoint a master, or order a reference, or hear and determine any application for a preliminary or permanent injunction or motion to vacate such an injunction, or enter judgment on the merits. Any action of a single judge may be reviewed by the full court at any time before final judgment. As amended June 11, 1960, Pub.L. 86–507, § 1(19), 74 Stat. 201; Aug. 12, 1976, Pub.L. 94–381, § 3, 90 Stat. 1119; Nov. 8, 1984, Pub.L. 98–620, Title IV, § 402(29)(E), 98 Stat. 3359.

§ 2361. Process and procedure

In any civil action of interpleader or in the nature of interpleader under section 1335 of this title, a district court may issue its process for all claimants and enter its order restraining them from instituting or prosecuting any proceeding in any State or United States court affecting the property, instrument or obligation involved in the interpleader action until further order of the court. Such process and order shall be returnable at such time as the court or judge thereof directs, and shall be addressed to and served by the United States marshals for the respective districts where the claimants reside or may be found.

Such district court shall hear and determine the case, and may discharge the plaintiff from further liability, make the injunction permanent, and make all appropriate orders to enforce its judgment. As amended May 24, 1949, c. 139, § 117, 63 Stat. 105.

§ 2401. Time for commencing action against United States

(a) Except as provided by the Contract Disputes Act of 1978, every civil action commenced against the United States shall be barred unless the complaint is filed within six years after the right of action first accrues. The action of any person under legal disability or beyond the seas at the time the claim accrues may be commenced within three years after the disability ceases.

(b) A tort claim against the United States shall be forever barred unless it is presented in writing to the appropriate Federal agency within two years after such claim accrues or unless action is begun within six months after the date of mailing, by certified or registered mail, of notice of final denial of the claim by the agency to which it was presented. As amended Apr. 25, 1949, c. 92, § 1, 63 Stat. 62; Sept. 8, 1959, Pub.L. 86–238, § 1(3), 73 Stat. 472; July 18, 1966, Pub.L. 89–506, § 7, 80 Stat. 307; Nov. 1, 1978, Pub.L. 95–563, § 14(b), 92 Stat. 2389.

§ 2402. Jury trial in actions against United States

Subject to chapter 179 of this title, any action against the United States under section 1346 shall be tried by the court without a jury, except that any action against the United States under section 1346(a)(1) shall, at

628

the request of either party to such action, be tried by the court with a jury. As amended July 30, 1954, c. 648, § 2(a), 68 Stat. 589; Oct. 26, 1996, Pub.L. 104–331, § 3(b)(3), 110 Stat. 4069.

§ 2403. Intervention by United States or a State; constitutional question

(a) In any action, suit or proceeding in a court of the United States to which the United States or any agency, officer or employee thereof is not a party, wherein the constitutionality of any Act of Congress affecting the public interest is drawn in question, the court shall certify such fact to the Attorney General, and shall permit the United States to intervene for presentation of evidence, if evidence is otherwise admissible in the case, and for argument on the question of constitutionality. The United States shall, subject to the applicable provisions of law, have all the rights of a party and be subject to all liabilities of a party as to court costs to the extent necessary for a proper presentation of the facts and law relating to the question of constitutionality.

(b) In any action, suit, or proceeding in a court of the United States to which a State or any agency, officer, or employee thereof is not a party, wherein the constitutionality of any statute of that State affecting the public interest is drawn in question, the court shall certify such fact to the attorney general of the State, and shall permit the State to intervene for presentation of evidence, if evidence is otherwise admissible in the case, and for argument on the question of constitutionality. The State shall, subject to the applicable provisions of law, have all the rights of a party and be subject to all liabilities of a party as to court costs to the extent necessary for a proper presentation of the facts and law relating to the question of constitutionality. As amended Aug. 12, 1976, Pub.L. 94–381, § 5, 90 Stat. 1120.

§ 2412. Costs and fees

(a)(1) Except as otherwise specifically provided by statute, a judgment for costs, as enumerated in section 1920 of this title, but not including the fees and expenses of attorneys, may be awarded to the prevailing party in any civil action brought by or against the United States or any agency or any official of the United States acting in his or her official capacity in any court having jurisdiction of such action. A judgment for costs when taxed against the United States shall, in an amount established by statute, court rule, or order, be limited to reimbursing in whole or in part the prevailing party for the costs incurred by such party in the litigation.

(2) A judgment for costs, when awarded in favor of the United States in an action brought by the United States, may include an amount equal to the filing fee prescribed under section 1914(a) of this title. The preceding sentence shall not be construed as requiring the United States to pay any filing fee.

(b) Unless expressly prohibited by statute, a court may award reasonable fees and expenses of attorneys, in addition to the costs which may be awarded pursuant to subsection (a), to the prevailing party in any civil action brought by or against the United States or any agency or any official of the United States acting in his or her official capacity in any court having jurisdiction of such action. The United States shall be liable for such fees and expenses to the same extent that any other party would be liable under the common law or under the terms of any statute which specifically provides for such an award.

(c)(1) Any judgment against the United States or any agency and any official of the United States acting in his or her official capacity for costs pursuant to subsection (a) shall be paid as provided in sections 2414 and 2517 of this title and shall be in addition to any relief provided in the judgment.

(2) Any judgment against the United States or any agency and any official of the United States acting in his or her official capacity for fees and expenses of attorneys pursuant to subsection (b) shall be paid as provided in sections 2414 and 2517 of this title, except that if the basis for the award is a finding that the United States acted in bad faith, then the award shall be paid by any agency found to have acted in bad faith and shall be in addition to any relief provided in the judgment.

(d)(1)(A) Except as otherwise specifically provided by statute, a court shall award to a prevailing party other than the United States fees and other expenses, in addition to any costs awarded pursuant to subsection (a), incurred by that party in any civil action (other than cases sounding in tort), including proceedings for judicial review of agency action, brought by or against the United States in any court having jurisdiction of that action, unless the court finds that the position of the United States was substantially justified or that special circumstances make an award unjust.

(B) A party seeking an award of fees and other expenses shall, within thirty days of final judgment in the action, submit to the court an application for fees and other expenses which shows that the party is a prevailing party and is eligible to receive an award under this subsection, and the amount sought, including an itemized statement from any attorney or expert witness representing or appearing in behalf of the party stating the actual time expended and the rate at which fees and other expenses are computed. The party shall also allege that the position of the United States was not substantially justified. Whether or not the position of the United States was substantially justified shall be determined on the basis of the record (including the record with respect to the action or failure to act by the agency upon which the civil action is based) which is made in the civil action for which fees and other expenses are sought.

(C) The court, in its discretion, may reduce the amount to be awarded pursuant to this subsection, or deny an award, to the extent that the prevailing party during the course of the proceedings engaged in conduct which unduly and unreasonably protracted the final resolution of the matter in controversy.

(D) If, in a civil action brought by the United States or a proceeding for judicial review of an adversary adjudication described in section 504(a)(4) of title 5, the demand by the United States is substantially in excess of the judgment finally obtained by the United States and is unreasonable when compared with such judgment, under the facts and circumstances of the case, the court shall award to the party the fees and other expenses related to defending against the excessive demand, unless the party has committed a willful violation of law or otherwise acted in bad faith, or special circumstances make an award unjust. Fees and expenses awarded under this subparagraph shall paid only as a consequence of appropriations provided in advance.

(2) For the purposes of this subsection—

(A) "fees and other expenses" includes the reasonable expenses of expert witnesses, the reasonable cost of any study, analysis, engineering report, test, or project which is found by the court to be necessary for the preparation of the party's case, and reasonable attorney fees (The amount of fees awarded under this subsection shall be based upon prevailing market rates for the kind and quality of the services furnished, except that (i) no expert witness shall be compensated at a rate in excess of the highest rate of compensation for expert witnesses paid by the United States; and (ii) attorney fees shall not be awarded in excess of $125 per hour unless the court determines that an increase in the cost of living or a special factor, such as the limited availability of qualified attorneys for the proceedings involved, justifies a higher fee.);

(B) "party" means (i) an individual whose net worth did not exceed $2,000,000 at the time the civil action was filed, or (ii) any owner of an unincorporated business, or any partnership, corporation, association, unit of local government, or organization, the net worth of which did not exceed $7,000,000 at the time the civil action was filed, and which had not more than 500 employees at the time the civil action was filed; except that an organization described in section 501(c)(3) of the Internal Revenue Code of 1954 (26 U.S.C. 501(c)(3)) exempt from taxation under section 501(a) of such Code, or a cooperative association as defined in section 15(a) of the Agricultural Marketing Act (12 U.S.C. 1141j(a)), may be a party regardless of the net worth of such organization or cooperative association or for purposes of subsection (d)(1)(D), a small entity as defined in section 601 of title 5;

(C) "United States" includes any agency and any official of the United States acting in his or her official capacity;

(D) "position of the United States" means, in addition to the position taken by the United States in the civil action, the action or failure to act by the agency upon which the civil action is based; except that fees and expenses may not be awarded to a party for any portion of the litigation in which the party has unreasonably protracted the proceedings;

(E) "civil action brought by or against the United States" includes an appeal by a party, other than the United States, from a decision of a contracting officer rendered pursuant to a disputes clause in a contract with the Government or pursuant to the Contract Disputes Act of 1978;

(F) "court" includes the United States Court of Federal Claims and the United States Court of Appeals for Veterans Claims;

(G) "final judgment" means a judgment that is final and not appealable, and includes an order of settlement;

(H) "prevailing party", in the case of eminent domain proceedings, means a party who obtains a final judgment (other than by settlement), exclusive of interest, the amount of which is at least as close to the highest valuation of the property involved that is attested to at trial on behalf of the property owner as it is to the highest valuation of the property involved that is attested to at trial on behalf of the Government; and

(I) "demand" means the express demand of the United States which led to the adversary adjudication, but shall not include a recitation of the maximum statutory penalty (i) in the complaint, or (ii) elsewhere when accompanied by an express demand for a lesser amount.

(3) In awarding fees and other expenses under this subsection to a prevailing party in any action for judicial review of an adversary adjudication, as defined in subsection (b)(1)(C) of section 504 of title 5, United States Code, or an adversary adjudication subject to the Contract Disputes Act of 1978, the court shall include in that award fees and other expenses to the same extent authorized in subsection (a) of such section, unless the court finds that during such adversary adjudication the position of the United States was substantially justified, or that special circumstances make an award unjust.

(4) Fees and other expenses awarded under this subsection to a party shall be paid by any agency over which the party prevails from any funds made available to the agency by appropriation or otherwise.

(e) The provisions of this section shall not apply to any costs, fees, and other expenses in connection with any proceeding to which section 7430 of the Internal Revenue Code of 1954 applies (determined without regard to subsections (b) and (f) of such section). Nothing in the preceding sentence shall prevent the awarding under subsection (a) of section 2412 of title 28, United States Code, of costs enumerated in section 1920 of such title (as in effect on October 1, 1981).

(f) If the United States appeals an award of costs or fees and other expenses made against the United States under this section and the award is affirmed in whole or in part, interest shall be paid on the amount of the award as affirmed. Such interest shall be computed at the rate determined under section 1961(a) of this title, and shall run from the date of the award through the day before the date of the mandate of affirmance. As amended July 18, 1966, Pub.L. 89–507, § 1, 80 Stat. 308; Oct. 21, 1980, Pub.L. 96–481, Title II, § 204(a), (c), 94 Stat. 2327, 2329; Sept. 3, 1982, Pub.L. 97–248, Title II, § 292(c), 96 Stat. 574; Aug. 5, 1985, Pub.L. 99–80, §§ 2, 6, 99 Stat. 184, 186; Oct. 29, 1992, Pub.L. 102–572, Title III, § 301(a), Title V, §§ 502(b), 506(a), Title IX, § 902(b)(1), 106 Stat. 4511, 4512, 4513, 4516; Dec. 21, 1995, Pub.L. 104–66, Title I, § 1091(b), 109 Stat. 722; Mar. 29, 1996, Pub.L. 104–121, Title II, § 232, 110 Stat. 863; Nov. 11, 1998, Pub.L. 105–368, Title V, § 512(b)(1)(B), 112 Stat. 3342.

§ 2671. Definitions

As used in this chapter and sections 1346(b) and 2401(b) of this title, the term "Federal agency" includes the executive departments, the judicial and legislative branches, the military departments, independent establishments of the United States, and corporations primarily acting as instrumentalities or agencies of the United States, but does not include any contractor with the United States.

"Employee of the government" includes (1) officers or employees of any federal agency, members of the military or naval forces of the United States, members of the National Guard while engaged in training or duty under section 115, 316, 502, 503, 504, or 505 of title 32, and persons acting on behalf of a federal agency in an official capacity, temporarily or permanently in the service of the United States, whether with or without compensation, and (2) any officer or employee of a Federal public defender organization, except when such officer or employee performs professional services in the course of providing representation under section 3006A of title 18.

"Acting within the scope of his office or employment", in the case of a member of the military or naval forces of the United States or a member of the National Guard as defined in section 101(3) of title 32, means acting in line of duty. As amended May 24, 1949, c. 139, § 124, 63 Stat. 106; July 18, 1966, Pub.L. 89–506, § 8, 80 Stat. 307; Dec. 29, 1981, Pub.L. 97–124, § 1, 95 Stat. 1666; Nov. 18, 1988, Pub.L. 100–694, § 3, 102 Stat. 4564; Oct. 30, 2000, Pub.L. 106–398, § 1[665(b)], 114 Stat. 1654A–169; Nov. 13, 2000, Pub.L. 106–518, Title IV, § 401, 114 Stat. 2421.

§ 2672. Administrative adjustment of claims

The head of each Federal agency or his designee, in accordance with regulations prescribed by the Attorney General, may consider, ascertain, adjust, determine, compromise, and settle any claim for money damages against the United States for injury or loss of property or personal injury or death caused by the negligent or wrongful act or omission of any employee of the agency while acting within the scope of his office or employment, under circumstances where the United States, if a private person, would be liable to the claimant in accordance with the law of the place where the act or omission occurred: *Provided,* That any award, compromise, or settlement in excess of $25,000 shall be effected only with the prior written approval of the Attorney General or his designee.

Subject to the provisions of this title relating to civil actions on tort claims against the United States, any such award, compromise, settlement, or determination shall be final and conclusive on all officers of the Government, except when procured by means of fraud.

Any award, compromise, or settlement in an amount of $2,500 or less made pursuant to this section shall be paid by the head of the Federal agency concerned out of appropriations available to that agency. Payment of any award, compromise, or settlement in an amount in excess of $2,500 made pursuant to this section or made by the Attorney General in any amount pursuant to section 2677 of this title shall be paid in a manner similar to judgments and compromises in like causes and appropriations or funds available for the payment of such judgments and compromises are hereby made available for the payment of awards, compromises, or settlements under this chapter.

The acceptance by the claimant of any such award, compromise, or settlement shall be final and conclusive on the claimant, and shall constitute a complete release of any claim against the United States and against the employee of the government whose act or omission gave rise to the claim, by reason of the same subject matter. As amended Apr. 25, 1949, c. 92, § 2(b), 63 Stat. 62; May 24, 1949, c. 139, § 125, 63 Stat. 106; Sept. 23, 1950, c. 1010, § 9, 64 Stat. 987; Sept. 8, 1959, Pub.L. 86–238, § 1(1), 73 Stat. 471; July 18, 1966, Pub.L. 89–506, §§ 1, 9(a), 80 Stat. 306, 308; Nov. 15, 1990, Pub.L. 101–552, § 8(a), 104 Stat. 2746.

§ 2674. Liability of United States

The United States shall be liable, respecting the provisions of this title relating to tort claims, in the same manner and to the same extent as a private individual under like circumstances, but shall not be liable for interest prior to judgment or for punitive damages.

If, however, in any case wherein death was caused, the law of the place where the act or omission complained of occurred provides, or has been construed to provide, for damages only punitive in nature, the United States shall be liable for actual or compensatory damages, measured by the pecuniary injuries resulting from such death to the persons respectively, for whose benefit the action was brought, in lieu thereof.

With respect to any claim under this chapter, the United States shall be entitled to assert any defense based upon judicial or legislative immunity which otherwise would have been available to the employee of the United States whose act or omission gave rise to the claim, as well as any other defenses to which the United States is entitled.

With respect to any claim to which this section applies, the Tennessee Valley Authority shall be entitled to assert any defense which otherwise would have been available to the employee based upon judicial or legislative immunity, which otherwise would have been available to the employee of the Tennessee Valley Authority whose act or omission gave rise to the claim as well as any other defenses to which the Tennessee Valley Authority is entitled under this chapter. As amended Nov. 18, 1988, Pub.L. 100–694, §§ 4, 9(c), 102 Stat. 4564, 4567.

§ 2675. Disposition by federal agency as prerequisite; evidence

(a) An action shall not be instituted upon a claim against the United States for money damages for injury or loss of property or personal injury or death caused by the negligent or wrongful act or omission of any employee of the Government while acting within the scope of his office or employment, unless the claimant shall have first presented the claim to the appropriate Federal agency and his claim shall have been finally denied by the agency in writing and sent by certified or registered mail. The failure of an agency to make final disposition of a claim within six months after it is filed shall, at the option of the claimant any time thereafter, be deemed a final denial of the claim for purposes of this section. The provisions of this subsection shall not apply to such claims as may be asserted under the Federal Rules of Civil Procedure by third party complaint, cross-claim, or counterclaim.

(b) Action under this section shall not be instituted for any sum in excess of the amount of the claim presented to the federal agency, except where the increased amount is based upon newly discovered evidence not reasonably discoverable at the time of presenting the claim to the federal agency, or upon allegation and proof of intervening facts, relating to the amount of the claim.

(c) Disposition of any claim by the Attorney General or other head of a federal agency shall not be competent evidence of liability or amount of damages. As amended May 24, 1949, c. 139, § 126, 63 Stat. 107; July 18, 1966, Pub.L. 89–506, § 2, 80 Stat. 306.

§ 2676. Judgment as bar

The judgment in an action under section 1346(b) of this title shall constitute a complete bar to any action by the claimant, by reason of the same subject matter, against the employee of the government whose act or omission gave rise to the claim.

§ 2677. Compromise

The Attorney General or his designee may arbitrate, compromise, or settle any claim cognizable under section 1346(b) of this title, after the commencement of an action thereon. As amended July 18, 1966, Pub.L. 89–506, § 3, 80 Stat. 307.

§ 2678. Attorney fees; penalty

No attorney shall charge, demand, receive, or collect for services rendered, fees in excess of 25 per centum of any judgment rendered pursuant to section 1346(b) of this title or any settlement made pursuant to section 2677 of this title, or in excess of 20 per centum of any award, compromise, or settlement made pursuant to section 2672 of this title.

Any attorney who charges, demands, receives, or collects for services rendered in connection with such claim any amount in excess of that allowed under this section, if recovery be had, shall be fined not more than $2,000 or imprisoned not more than one year, or both. As amended July 18, 1966, Pub.L. 89–506, § 4, 80 Stat. 307.

§ 2679. Exclusiveness of remedy

(a) The authority of any federal agency to sue and be sued in its own name shall not be construed to authorize suits against such federal agency on claims which are cognizable under section 1346(b) of this title, and the remedies provided by this title in such cases shall be exclusive.

(b)(1) The remedy against the United States provided by sections 1346(b) and 2672 of this title for injury or loss of property, or personal injury or death arising or resulting from the negligent or wrongful act or omission of any employee of the Government while acting within the scope of his office or employment is exclusive of any other civil action or proceeding for money damages by reason of the same subject matter against the employee whose act or omission gave rise to the claim or against the estate of such employee. Any other civil action or proceeding for money damages arising out of or relating to the same subject matter against the employee or the employee's estate is precluded without regard to when the act or omission occurred.

(2) Paragraph (1) does not extend or apply to a civil action against an employee of the Government—

(A) which is brought for a violation of the Constitution of the United States, or

(B) which is brought for a violation of a statute of the United States under which such action against an individual is otherwise authorized.

(c) The Attorney General shall defend any civil action or proceeding brought in any court against any employee of the Government or his estate for any such damage or injury. The employee against whom such civil action or proceeding is brought shall deliver within such time after date of service or knowledge of service as determined by the Attorney General, all process served upon him or an attested true copy thereof to his immediate superior or to whomever was designated by the head of his department to receive such papers and such person shall promptly furnish copies of the pleadings and process therein to the United States attorney for the district embracing the place wherein the proceeding is brought, to the Attorney General, and to the head of his employing Federal agency.

(d)(1) Upon certification by the Attorney General that the defendant employee was acting within the scope of his office or employment at the time of the incident out of which the claim arose, any civil action or proceeding commenced upon such claim in a United States district court shall be deemed an action against the United States under the provisions of this title and all references thereto, and the United States shall be substituted as the party defendant.

(2) Upon certification by the Attorney General that the defendant employee was acting within the scope of his office or employment at the time of the incident out of which the claim arose, any civil action or proceeding commenced upon such claim in a State court shall be removed without bond at any time before trial by the Attorney General to the district court of the United States for the district and division embracing the place in which the action or proceeding is pending. Such action or proceeding shall be deemed to be an action or proceeding brought against the United States under the provisions of this title and all references thereto, and the United States shall be substituted as the party defendant. This certification of the Attorney General shall conclusively establish scope of office or employment for purposes of removal.

(3) In the event that the Attorney General has refused to certify scope of office or employment under this section, the employee may at any time before trial petition the court to find and certify that the employee was acting within the scope of his office or employment. Upon such certification by the court, such action or proceeding shall be deemed to be an action or proceeding brought against the United States under the provisions of

this title and all references thereto, and the United States shall be substituted as the party defendant. A copy of the petition shall be served upon the United States in accordance with the provisions of Rule 4(d)(4) of the Federal Rules of Civil Procedure. In the event the petition is filed in a civil action or proceeding pending in a State court, the action or proceeding may be removed without bond by the Attorney General to the district court of the United States for the district and division embracing the place in which it is pending. If, in considering the petition, the district court determines that the employee was not acting within the scope of his office or employment, the action or proceeding shall be remanded to the State court.

(4) Upon certification, any action or proceeding subject to paragraph (1), (2), or (3) shall proceed in the same manner as any action against the United States filed pursuant to section 1346(b) of this title and shall be subject to the limitations and exceptions applicable to those actions.

(5) Whenever an action or proceeding in which the United States is substituted as the party defendant under this subsection is dismissed for failure first to present a claim pursuant to section 2675(a) of this title, such a claim shall be deemed to be timely presented under section 2401(b) of this title if—

(A) the claim would have been timely had it been filed on the date the underlying civil action was commenced, and

(B) the claim is presented to the appropriate Federal agency within 60 days after dismissal of the civil action.

(e) The Attorney General may compromise or settle any claim asserted in such civil action or proceeding in the manner provided in section 2677, and with the same effect. As amended Sept. 21, 1961, Pub.L. 87–258, § 1, 75 Stat. 539; July 18, 1966, Pub.L. 89–506, § 5(a), 80 Stat. 307; Nov. 18, 1988, Pub.L. 100–694, §§ 5, 6, 102 Stat. 4564.

§ 2680. Exceptions

The provisions of this chapter and section 1346(b) of this title shall not apply to—

(a) Any claim based upon an act or omission of an employee of the Government, exercising due care, in the execution of a statute or regulation, whether or not such statute or regulation be valid, or based upon the exercise or performance or the failure to exercise or perform a discretionary function or duty on the part of a federal agency or an employee of the Government, whether or not the discretion involved be abused.

(b) Any claim arising out of the loss, miscarriage, or negligent transmission of letters or postal matter.

(c) Any claim arising in respect of the assessment or collection of any tax or customs duty, or the detention of any goods, merchandise, or other property by any officer of customs or excise or any other law enforcement officer, except that the provisions of this chapter and section 1346(b) of this title apply to any claim based on injury or loss of goods, merchandise, or other property, while in the possession of any officer of customs or excise or any other law enforcement officer, if—

(1) the property was seized for the purpose of forfeiture under any provision of Federal law providing for the forfeiture of property other than as a sentence imposed upon conviction of a criminal offense;

(2) the interest of the claimant was not forfeited;

(3) the interest of the claimant was not remitted or mitigated (if the property was subject to forfeiture); and

(4) the claimant was not convicted of a crime for which the interest of the claimant in the property was subject to forfeiture under a Federal criminal forfeiture law.

(d) Any claim for which a remedy is provided by chapter 309 or 311 of title 46 relating to claims or suits in admiralty against the United States.

(e) Any claim arising out of an act or omission of any employee of the Government in administering the provisions of sections 1–31 of Title 50, Appendix.

(f) Any claim for damages caused by the imposition or establishment of a quarantine by the United States.

(g) [Repealed.]

(h) Any claim arising out of assault, battery, false imprisonment, false arrest, malicious prosecution, abuse of process, libel, slander, misrepresentation, deceit, or interference with contract rights: *Provided,* That, with regard to acts or omissions of investigative or law enforcement officers of the United States Government, the provisions of this chapter and section 1346(b) of this title shall apply to any claim arising, on or after the date of the enactment of this proviso, out of assault, battery, false imprisonment, false arrest, abuse of process, or malicious prosecution. For the purpose of this subsection, "investigative or law enforcement officer" means any officer of the United States who is empowered by law to execute searches, to seize evidence, or to make arrests for violations of Federal law.

(i) Any claim for damages caused by the fiscal operations of the Treasury or by the regulation of the monetary system.

(j) Any claim arising out of the combatant activities of the military or naval forces, or the Coast Guard, during time of war.

(k) Any claim arising in a foreign country.

(*l*) Any claim arising from the activities of the Tennessee Valley Authority.

(m) Any claim arising from the activities of the Panama Canal Company.

(n) Any claim arising from the activities of a Federal land bank, a Federal intermediate credit bank, or a bank for cooperatives. As amended July 16, 1949, c. 340, 63 Stat. 444; Sept. 26, 1950, c. 1049, §§ 2(a)(2), 13(5), 64 Stat. 1038, 1043; Aug. 18, 1959, Pub.L. 86–168, Title II, § 202(b), 73 Stat. 389; Mar. 16, 1974, Pub.L. 93–253, § 2, 88 Stat. 50; Apr. 25, 2000, Pub.L. 106–185, § 3(a), 114 Stat. 211; Oct. 6, 2006, Pub.L. 109–304, § 17(f)(4), 120 Stat. 1708.

SELECTED PROVISIONS OF OTHER PROCEDURAL STATUTES

FEDERAL ANTITRUST LAW
Title 15, United States Code

§ 4. Jurisdiction of courts; duty of United States attorneys; procedure

The several district courts of the United States are invested with jurisdiction to prevent and restrain violations of sections 1 to 7 [Sherman Antitrust Act] of this title; and it shall be the duty of the several United States attorneys, in their respective districts, under the direction of the Attorney General, to institute proceedings in equity to prevent and restrain such violations. Such proceedings may be by way of petition setting forth the case and praying that such violation shall be enjoined or otherwise prohibited. When the parties complained of shall have been duly notified of such petition the court shall proceed, as soon as may be, to the hearing and determination of the case; and pending such petition and before final decree, the court may at any time make such temporary restraining order or prohibition as shall be deemed just in the premises.

§ 5. Bringing in additional parties

Whenever it shall appear to the court before which any proceeding under section 4 of this title may be pending, that the ends of justice require that other parties should be brought before the court, the court may cause them to be summoned, whether they reside in the district in which the court is held or not; and subpoenas to that end may be served in any district by the marshal thereof.

§ 15. Suits by persons injured

(a) Amount of recovery; prejudgment interest

Except as provided in subsection (b) of this section, any person who shall be injured in his business or property by reason of anything forbidden in the antitrust laws may sue therefor in any district court of the United States in the district in which the defendant resides or is found or has an agent, without respect to the amount in controversy, and shall recover threefold the damages by him sustained, and the cost of suit, including a reasonable attorney's fee. The court may award under this section, pursuant to a motion by such person promptly made, simple interest on actual damages for the period beginning on the date of service of such person's pleading setting forth a claim under the antitrust laws and ending on the date of judgment, or for any shorter period therein, if the court

639

finds that the award of such interest for such period is just in the circumstances. In determining whether an award of interest under this section for any period is just in the circumstances, the court shall consider only—

(1) whether such person or the opposing party, or either party's representative, made motions or asserted claims or defenses so lacking in merit as to show that such party or representative acted intentionally for delay, or otherwise acted in bad faith;

(2) whether, in the course of the action involved, such person or the opposing party, or either party's representative, violated any applicable rule, statute, or court order providing for sanctions for dilatory behavior or otherwise providing for expeditious proceedings; and

(3) whether such person or the opposing party, or either party's representative, engaged in conduct primarily for the purpose of delaying the litigation or increasing the cost thereof.

(b) Amount of damages payable to foreign states and instrumentalities of foreign states

* * *

§ 15a.   Suits by United States; amount of recovery; prejudgment interest

Whenever the United States is hereafter injured in its business or property by reason of anything forbidden in the antitrust laws it may sue therefor in the United States district court for the district in which the defendant resides or is found or has an agent, without respect to the amount in controversy, and shall recover threefold the damages by it sustained and the cost of suit. The court may award under this section, pursuant to a motion by the United States promptly made, simple interest on threefold the damages for the period beginning on the date of service of the pleading of the United States setting forth a claim under the antitrust laws and ending on the date of judgment, or for any shorter period therein, if the court finds that the award of such interest for such period is just in the circumstances. In determining whether an award of interest under this section for any period is just in the circumstances, the court shall consider only—

(1) whether the United States or the opposing party, or either party's representative, made motions or asserted claims or defenses so lacking in merit as to show that such party or representative acted intentionally for delay or otherwise acted in bad faith;

(2) whether, in the course of the action involved, the United States or the opposing party, or either party's representative, violated any applicable rule, statute, or court order providing for sanctions for dilatory behavior or otherwise providing for expeditious proceedings;

(3) whether the United States or the opposing party, or either party's representative, engaged in conduct primarily for the purpose of delaying the litigation or increasing the cost thereof; and

(4) whether the award of such interest is necessary to compensate the United States adequately for the injury sustained by the United States.

§ 15b. Limitation of actions

Any action to enforce any cause of action under sections 15, 15a, or 15c of this title shall be forever barred unless commenced within four years after the cause of action accrued. No cause of action barred under existing law on the effective date [1956] of this Act shall be revived by this Act.

§ 15c. Actions by State attorneys general

* * *

§ 16. Judgments

(a) Prima facie evidence; collateral estoppel

A final judgment or decree heretofore or hereafter rendered in any civil or criminal proceeding brought by or on behalf of the United States under the antitrust laws to the effect that a defendant has violated said laws shall be prima facie evidence against such defendant in any action or proceeding brought by any other party against such defendant under said laws as to all matters respecting which said judgment or decree would be an estoppel as between the parties thereto: *Provided,* That this section shall not apply to consent judgments or decrees entered before any testimony has been taken. Nothing contained in this section shall be construed to impose any limitation on the application of collateral estoppel, except that, in any action or proceeding brought under the antitrust laws, collateral estoppel effect shall not be given to any finding made by the Federal Trade Commission under the antitrust laws or under section 45 of this title which could give rise to a claim for relief under the antitrust laws.

* * *

(i) Suspension of limitations

Whenever any civil or criminal proceeding is instituted by the United States to prevent, restrain, or punish violations of any of the antitrust laws, but not including an action under section 15a of this title, the running of the statute of limitations in respect of every private or State right of action arising under said laws and based in whole or in part on any matter complained of in said proceeding shall be suspended during the pendency thereof and for one year thereafter: *Provided, however,* That whenever the running of the statute of limitations in respect of a cause of action arising under section 15 or 15c of this title is suspended hereunder, any action to enforce such cause of action shall be forever barred unless commenced either within the period of suspension or within four years after the cause of action accrued.

§ 22. District in which to sue corporation

Any suit, action, or proceeding under the antitrust laws against a corporation may be brought not only in the judicial district whereof it is an inhabitant, but also in any district wherein it may be found or transacts business; and all process in such cases may be served in the district of which it is an inhabitant, or wherever it may be found.

§ 23. Suits by United States; subpoenas for witnesses

In any suit, action, or proceeding brought by or on behalf of the United States subpoenas for witnesses who are required to attend a court of the United States in any judicial district in any case, civil or criminal, arising under the antitrust laws may run into any other district: *Provided,* That in civil cases no writ of subpoena shall issue for witnesses living out of the district in which the court is held at a greater distance than one hundred miles from the place of holding the same without the permission of the trial court being first had upon proper application and cause shown.

§ 25. Restraining violations; procedure

The several district courts of the United States are invested with jurisdiction to prevent and restrain violations of this [Clayton Antitrust] Act, and it shall be the duty of the several United States attorneys, in their respective districts, under the direction of the Attorney General, to institute proceedings in equity to prevent and restrain such violations. Such proceedings may be by way of petition setting forth the case and praying that such violation shall be enjoined or otherwise prohibited. When the parties complained of shall have been duly notified of such petition, the court shall proceed, as soon as may be, to the hearing and determination of the case; and pending such petition, and before final decree, the court may at any time make such temporary restraining order or prohibition as shall be deemed just in the premises. Whenever it shall appear to the court before which any such proceeding may be pending that the ends of justice require that other parties should be brought before the court, the court may cause them to be summoned whether they reside in the district in which the court is held or not, and subpoenas to that end may be served in any district by the marshal thereof.

§ 26. Injunctive relief for private parties; exception; costs

Any person, firm, corporation, or association shall be entitled to sue for and have injunctive relief, in any court of the United States having jurisdiction over the parties, against threatened loss or damage by a violation of the antitrust laws, including sections 13, 14, 18, and 19 of this title, when and under the same conditions and principles as injunctive relief against threatened conduct that will cause loss or damage is granted by courts of equity, under the rules governing such proceedings, and upon the execution of proper bond against damages for an injunction improvidently granted and a showing that the danger of irreparable loss or damage is immediate, a preliminary injunction may issue: *Provided,* That nothing herein contained shall be construed to entitle any person, firm, corporation, or association, except the United States, to bring suit for injunctive relief against any common carrier subject to the jurisdiction of the Surface Transportation Board under subtitle IV of title 49, United States Code. In any action under this section in which the plaintiff substantially prevails, the court shall award the cost of suit, including a reasonable attorney's fee, to such plaintiff.

FEDERAL CIVIL RIGHTS LAW

Title 42, United States Code

§ 1983. Civil action for deprivation of rights

Every person who, under color of any statute, ordinance, regulation, custom, or usage, of any State or Territory or the District of Columbia, subjects, or causes to be subjected, any citizen of the United States or other person within the jurisdiction thereof to the deprivation of any rights, privileges, or immunities secured by the Constitution and laws, shall be liable to the party injured in an action at law, suit in equity, or other proper proceeding for redress, except that in any action brought against a judicial officer for an act or omission taken in such officer's judicial capacity, injunctive relief shall not be granted unless a declaratory decree was violated or declaratory relief was unavailable. For the purposes of this section, any Act of Congress applicable exclusively to the District of Columbia shall be considered to be a statute of the District of Columbia.

§ 1988. Proceedings in vindication of civil rights; attorney's fees; expert fees

(a) Applicability of statutory and common law

The jurisdiction in civil and criminal matters conferred on the district courts by the provisions of this Title, and of Title "CIVIL RIGHTS," and of Title "CRIMES," for the protection of all persons in the United States in their civil rights, and for their vindication, shall be exercised and enforced in conformity with the laws of the United States, so far as such laws are suitable to carry the same into effect; but in all cases where they are not adapted to the object, or are deficient in the provisions necessary to furnish suitable remedies and punish offenses against law, the common law, as modified and changed by the constitution and statutes of the State wherein the court having jurisdiction of such civil or criminal cause is held, so far as the same is not inconsistent with the Constitution and laws of the United States, shall be extended to and govern the said courts in the trial and disposition of the cause, and, if it is of a criminal nature, in the infliction of punishment on the party found guilty.

(b) Attorney's fees

In any action or proceeding to enforce a provision of sections 1981, 1981a, 1982, 1983, 1985, and 1986 of this title, title IX of Public Law 92–318, the Religious Freedom Restoration Act of 1993, the Religious Land Use and Institutionalized Persons Act of 2000, title VI of the Civil Rights Act of 1964, or section 40302 of the Violence Against Women Act of 1994, the court, in its discretion, may allow the prevailing party, other than the United States, a reasonable attorney's fee as part of the costs, except that in any action brought against a judicial officer for an act or omission taken in such officer's judicial capacity such officer shall not be held liable for any costs, including attorney's fees, unless such action was clearly in excess of such officer's jurisdiction.

(c) Expert fees

In awarding an attorney's fee under subsection (b) of this section in any action or proceeding to enforce a provision of section 1981 or 1981a of this title, the court, in its discretion, may include expert fees as part of the attorney's fee.

CALIFORNIA

Code of Civil Procedure

§ 410.10. Basis

A court of this state may exercise jurisdiction on any basis not inconsistent with the Constitution of this state or of the United States.

NEW YORK

Judiciary Law

§ 140–b. General jurisdiction of supreme court

The general jurisdiction in law and equity which the supreme court possesses under the provisions of the constitution [art. VI, § 7] includes all the jurisdiction which was possessed and exercised by the supreme court of the colony of New York at any time, and by the court of chancery in England on the fourth day of July, seventeen hundred seventy-six, with the exceptions, additions and limitations created and imposed by the constitution and laws of the state. Subject to those exceptions and limitations the supreme court of the state has all the powers and authority of each of those courts and may exercise them in like manner.

Civil Practice Law and Rules

Article 2—Limitations of Time

§ 201. Application of article

An action, including one brought in the name or for the benefit of the state, must be commenced within the time specified in this article unless a different time is prescribed by law or a shorter time is prescribed by written agreement. No court shall extend the time limited by law for the commencement of an action.

§ 202. Cause of action accruing without the state

An action based upon a cause of action accruing without the state cannot be commenced after the expiration of the time limited by the laws of either the state or the place without the state where the cause of action accrued, except that where the cause of action accrued in favor of a resident of the state the time limited by the laws of the state shall apply.

§ 203. Method of computing periods of limitation generally

(a) Accrual of cause of action and interposition of claim. The time within which an action must be commenced, except as otherwise expressly prescribed, shall be computed from the time the cause of action accrued to the time the claim is interposed.

(b) Claim in complaint where action commenced by service. In an action which is commenced by service, a claim asserted in the complaint is interposed against the defendant or a co-defendant united in interest with such defendant when:

1. the summons is served upon the defendant; or

2. first publication of the summons against the defendant is made pursuant to an order, and publication is subsequently completed; or

3. an order for a provisional remedy other than attachment is granted, if, within thirty days thereafter, the summons is served upon the defendant or first publication of the summons against the defendant is made pursuant to an order and publication is subsequently completed, or, where the defendant dies within thirty days after the order is granted and before the summons is served upon the defendant or publication is completed, if the summons is served upon the defendant's executor or administrator within sixty days after letters are issued; for this purpose seizure of a chattel in an action to recover a chattel is a provisional remedy; or

4. an order of attachment is granted, if the summons is served in accordance with the provisions of section 6213; or

5. the summons is delivered to the sheriff of that county outside the city of New York or is filed with the clerk of that county within the city of New York in which the defendant resides, is employed or is doing business, or if none of the foregoing is known to the plaintiff after reasonable inquiry, then of the county in which the defendant is known to have last resided, been employed or been engaged in business, or in which the cause of action arose; or if the defendant is a corporation, of a county in which it may be served or in which the cause of action arose; provided that:

(i) the summons is served upon the defendant within sixty days after the period of limitation would have expired but for this provision; or

(ii) first publication of the summons against the defendant is made pursuant to an order within sixty days after the period of limitation would have expired but for this provision and publication is subsequently completed; or

(iii) the summons is served upon the defendant's executor or administrator within sixty days after letters are issued, where the defendant dies within sixty days after the period of limitation would have expired but for this provision and before the summons is served upon the defendant or publication is completed.

6. in an action to be commenced in a court not of record, the summons is delivered for service upon the defendant to any officer author-

ized to serve it in a county, city or town in which the defendant resides, is employed or is doing business, or if none of the foregoing be known to the plaintiff after reasonable inquiry, then in a county, city or town in which defendant is known to have last resided, been employed or been engaged in business, or, where the defendant is a corporation, in a county, city or town in which it may be served, if the summons is served upon the defendant within sixty days after the period of limitation would have expired but for this provision; or, where the defendant dies within sixty days after the period of limitation would have expired but for this provision and before the summons is served upon the defendant, if the summons is served upon his executor or administrator within sixty days after letters are issued.

(c) Claim in complaint where action commenced by filing. In an action which is commenced by filing, a claim asserted in the complaint is interposed against the defendant or a co-defendant united in interest with such defendant when the action is commenced.

(d) Defense or counterclaim. A defense or counterclaim is interposed when a pleading containing it is served. A defense or counterclaim is not barred if it was not barred at the time the claims asserted in the complaint were interposed, except that if the defense or counterclaim arose from the transactions, occurrences, or series of transactions or occurrences, upon which a claim asserted in the complaint depends, it is not barred to the extent of the demand in the complaint notwithstanding that it was barred at the time the claims asserted in the complaint were interposed.

(e) Effect upon defense or counterclaim of termination of action because of death or by dismissal or voluntary discontinuance. Where a defendant has served an answer containing a defense or counterclaim and the action is terminated because of the plaintiff's death or by dismissal or voluntary discontinuance, the time which elapsed between the commencement and termination of the action is not a part of the time within which an action must be commenced to recover upon the claim in the defense or counterclaim or the time within which the defense or counterclaim may be interposed in another action brought by the plaintiff or his successor in interest.

(f) Claim in amended pleading. A claim asserted in an amended pleading is deemed to have been interposed at the time the claims in the original pleading were interposed, unless the original pleading does not give notice of the transactions, occurrences, or series of transactions or occurrences, to be proved pursuant to the amended pleading.

(g) Time computed from actual or imputed discovery of facts. Except as provided in article two of the uniform commercial code or in section two hundred fourteen–a of this chapter, where the time within which an action must be commenced is computed from the time when facts were discovered or from the time when facts could with reasonable diligence have been discovered, or from either of such times, the action must be commenced within two years after such actual or imputed discovery or within the period otherwise provided, computed from the time the cause of action accrued, whichever is longer.

§ 204. Stay of commencement of action; demand for arbitration

* * *

§ 205. Termination of action

(a) New action by plaintiff. If an action is timely commenced and is terminated in any other manner than by a voluntary discontinuance, a failure to obtain personal jurisdiction over the defendant, a dismissal of the complaint for neglect to prosecute the action, or a final judgment upon the merits, the plaintiff, or, if the plaintiff dies, and the cause of action survives, his or her executor or administrator, may commence a new action upon the same transaction or occurrence or series of transactions or occurrences within six months after the termination provided that the new action would have been timely commenced at the time of commencement of the prior action and that service upon defendant is effected within such six-month period. Where a dismissal is one for neglect to prosecute the action made pursuant to rule thirty-two hundred sixteen of this chapter or otherwise, the judge shall set forth on the record the specific conduct constituting the neglect, which conduct shall demonstrate a general pattern of delay in proceeding with the litigation.

(b) Defense or counterclaim. Where the defendant has served an answer and the action is terminated in any manner, and a new action upon the same transaction or occurrence or series of transactions or occurrences is commenced by the plaintiff or his successor in interest, the assertion of any cause of action or defense by the defendant in the new action shall be timely if it was timely asserted in the prior action.

(c) Application. This section also applies to a proceeding brought under the workers' compensation law.

§ 206. Computing periods of limitation in particular actions

[Treatment of actions where a demand is necessary to entitle a person to commence the action and of actions based on misconduct of an agent, on breach of a covenant of seizin or against incumbrances, or on account.]

§ 207. Defendant's absence from state or residence under false name

If, when a cause of action accrues against a person, he is without the state, the time within which the action must be commenced shall be computed from the time he comes into or returns to the state. If, after a cause of action has accrued against a person, that person departs from the state and remains continuously absent therefrom for four months or more, or that person resides within the state under a false name which is unknown to the person entitled to commence the action, the time of his absence or residence within the state under such a false name is not a part of the time within which the action must be commenced. If an action is commenced against a person described above, the time within which service must be made on such person in accordance with subdivisions (a) and (b) of section three hundred six-b of this chapter shall be computed in accordance with this section. This section does not apply:

1. while there is in force a designation, voluntary or involuntary, made pursuant to law, of a person to whom a summons may be delivered within the state with the same effect as if served personally within the state; or

2. while a foreign corporation has one or more officers or other persons in the state on whom a summons against such corporation may be served; or

3. while jurisdiction over the person of the defendant can be obtained without personal delivery of the summons to the defendant within the state.

§ 208. Infancy, insanity

If a person entitled to commence an action is under a disability because of infancy or insanity at the time the cause of action accrues, and the time otherwise limited for commencing the action is three years or more and expires no later than three years after the disability ceases, or the person under the disability dies, the time within which the action must be commenced shall be extended to three years after the disability ceases or the person under the disability dies, whichever event first occurs; if the time otherwise limited is less than three years, the time shall be extended by the period of disability. The time within which the action must be commenced shall not be extended by this provision beyond ten years after the cause of action accrues, except, in any action other than for medical, dental or podiatric malpractice, where the person was under a disability due to infancy. This section shall not apply to an action to recover a penalty or forfeiture, or against a sheriff or other officer for an escape.

§ 209. War

* * *

§ 210. Death of claimant or person liable; cause of action accruing after death and before grant of letters

(a) Death of claimant. Where a person entitled to commence an action dies before the expiration of the time within which the action must be commenced and the cause of action survives, an action may be commenced by his representative within one year after his death.

(b) Death of person liable. The period of eighteen months after the death, within or without the state, of a person against whom a cause of action exists is not a part of the time within which the action must be commenced against his executor or administrator.

(c) Cause of action accruing after death and before grant of letters. In an action by an executor or administrator to recover personal property wrongfully taken after the death and before the issuance of letters, or to recover damages for taking, detaining or injuring personal property within that period, the time within which the action must be commenced shall be computed from the time the letters are issued or from three years after the death, whichever event first occurs. Any distributee, next of kin, legatee or creditor who was under a disability prescribed in section 208 at the time the cause of action accrued, may, within two years after the disability ceases, commence an action to recover such damages or the value of such property as he would have received upon a final distribution of the estate if an action had been timely commenced by the executor or administrator.

§ 211. Actions to be commenced within twenty years

(a) On a bond. An action to recover principal or interest upon a written instrument evidencing an indebtedness of the state of New York or of any person, association or public or private corporation, originally sold by the issuer after publication of an advertisement for bids for the issue in a newspaper of general circulation and secured only by a pledge of the faith and credit of the issuer, regardless of whether a sinking fund is or may be established for its redemption, must be commenced within twenty years after the cause of action accrues. This subdivision does not apply to actions upon written instruments evidencing an indebtedness of any corporation, association or person under the jurisdiction of the public service commission, the commissioner of transportation, the interstate commerce commission, the federal communications commission, the civil aeronautics board, the federal power commission, or any other regulatory commission or board of a state or of the federal government. This subdivision applies to all causes of action, including those barred on April eighteenth, nineteen hundred fifty, by the provisions of the civil practice act then effective.

(b) On a money judgment. A money judgment is presumed to be paid and satisfied after the expiration of twenty years from the time when the party recovering it was first entitled to enforce it. This presumption is conclusive, except as against a person who within the twenty years acknowledges an indebtedness, or makes a payment, of all or part of the amount recovered by the judgment, or his heir or personal representative, or a person whom he otherwise represents. Such an acknowledgment must be in writing and signed by the person to be charged. Property acquired by an enforcement order or by levy upon an execution is a payment, unless the person to be charged shows that it did not include property claimed by him. If such an acknowledgment or payment is made, the judgment is conclusively presumed to be paid and satisfied as against any person after the expiration of twenty years after the last acknowledgment or payment made by him. The presumption created by this subdivision may be availed of under an allegation that the action was not commenced within the time limited.

(c) By state for real property. The state will not sue a person for or with respect to real property, or the rents or profits thereof, by reason of the right or title of the state to the same, unless the cause of action accrued, or the state, or those from whom it claims, have received the rents and profits of the real property or of some part thereof, within twenty years before the commencement of the action.

(d) By grantee of state for real property. An action shall not be commenced for or with respect to real property by a person claiming by virtue of letters patent or a grant from the state, unless it might have been maintained by the state, as prescribed in this section, if the patent or grant had not been issued or made.

(e) For support, alimony or maintenance. An action or proceeding to enforce any temporary order, permanent order or judgment of any court of competent jurisdiction which awards support, alimony or maintenance, regardless of whether or not arrears have been reduced to a money judgment, must be commenced within twenty years from the date of a default in payment. This section shall only apply to orders which have been entered subsequent to the date upon which this section shall become effective.

§ 212. Actions to be commenced within ten years

(a) Possession necessary to recover real property. An action to recover real property or its possession cannot be commenced unless the plaintiff, or his predecessor in interest, was seized or possessed of the premises within ten years before the commencement of the action.

(b) Annulment of letters patent. Where letters patent or a grant of real property, issued or made by the state, are declared void on the ground of fraudulent suggestion or concealment, forfeiture, mistake or ignorance of a material fact, wrongful detaining or defective title, an action to recover the premises may be commenced by the state or by a subsequent patentee or grantee, or his successor in interest, within ten years after the determination is made.

(c) To redeem from a mortgage. An action to redeem real property from a mortgage with or without an account of rents and profits may be commenced by the mortgagor or his successors in interest, against the mortgagee in possession, or against the purchaser of the mortgaged premises at a foreclosure sale in an action in which the mortgagor or his successors in interest were not excluded from their interest in the mortgaged premises, or against a successor in interest of either, unless the mortgagee, purchaser or successor was continuously possessed of the premises for ten years after the breach or non-fulfillment of a condition or covenant of the mortgage, or the date of recording of the deed of the premises to the purchaser.

(d) To recover under an affidavit of support of an alien. An action under section one hundred twenty-two of the social services law to recover amounts paid to or on behalf of an alien for whom an affidavit of support pursuant to section 213A of the immigration and naturalization act has been signed.

§ 213. Actions to be commenced within six years: where not otherwise provided for; on contract; on sealed instrument; on bond or note, and mortgage upon real property; by state based on misappropriation of public property; based on mistake; by corporation against director, officer or stockholder; based on fraud

The following actions must be commenced within six years:

1. an action for which no limitation is specifically prescribed by law;

2. an action upon a contractual obligation or liability, express or implied, except as provided in section two hundred thirteen-a of this article

or article 2 of the uniform commercial code or article 36–B of the general business law;

3. an action upon a sealed instrument;

4. an action upon a bond or note, the payment of which is secured by a mortgage upon real property, or upon a bond or note and mortgage so secured, or upon a mortgage of real property, or any interest therein;

5. an action by the state based upon the spoliation or other misappropriation of public property; the time within which the action must be commenced shall be computed from discovery by the state of the facts relied upon;

6. an action based upon mistake;

7. an action by or on behalf of a corporation against a present or former director, officer or stockholder for an accounting, or to procure a judgment on the ground of fraud, or to enforce a liability, penalty or forfeiture, or to recover damages for waste or for an injury to property or for an accounting in conjunction therewith;

8. an action based upon fraud; the time within which the action must be commenced shall be the greater of six years from the date the cause of action accrued or two years from the time the plaintiff or the person under whom the plaintiff claims discovered the fraud, or could with reasonable diligence have discovered it.

§ 213–a. Actions to be commenced within four years: residential rent overcharge

An action on a residential rent overcharge shall be commenced within four years of the first overcharge alleged and no determination of an overcharge and no award or calculation of an award of the amount of any overcharge may be based upon an overcharge having occurred more than four years before the action is commenced. This section shall preclude examination of the rental history of the housing accommodation prior to the four-year period immediately preceding the commencement of the action.

§ 213–b. Action by a victim of a criminal offense

Notwithstanding any other limitation set forth in this article or in article five of the estates, powers and trusts law, an action by a crime victim, or the representative of a crime victim, as defined in subdivision six of section six hundred twenty-one of the executive law, may be commenced to recover damages from a defendant: (1) convicted of a crime which is the subject of such action, for any injury or loss resulting therefrom within seven years of the date of the crime or (2) convicted of a specified crime as defined in paragraph (e) of subdivision one of section six hundred thirty-two-a of the executive law which is the subject of such action for any injury or loss resulting therefrom within ten years of the date the defendant was convicted of such specified crime.

§ 213–c. Action by victim of conduct constituting certain sexual offenses

Notwithstanding any other limitation set forth in this article, a civil claim or cause of action to recover from a defendant as hereinafter defined, for physical, psychological or other injury or condition suffered by a person as a result of acts by such defendant of rape in the first degree as defined in section 130.35 of the penal law, or criminal sexual act in the first degree as defined in section 130.50 of the penal law, or aggravated sexual abuse in the first degree as defined in section 130.70 of the penal law, or course of sexual conduct against a child in the first degree as defined in section 130.75 of the penal law may be brought within five years. As used in this section, the term "defendant" shall mean only a person who commits the acts described in this section or who, in a criminal proceeding, could be charged with criminal liability for the commission of such acts pursuant to section 20.00 of the penal law and shall not apply to any related civil claim or cause of action arising from such acts. Nothing in this section shall be construed to require that a criminal charge be brought or a criminal conviction be obtained as a condition of bringing a civil cause of action or receiving a civil judgment pursuant to this section or be construed to require that any of the rules governing a criminal proceeding be applicable to any such civil action.

§ 214. Actions to be commenced within three years: for non-payment of money collected on execution; for penalty created by statute; to recover chattel; for injury to property; for personal injury; for malpractice other than medical, dental or podiatric malpractice; to annul a marriage on the ground of fraud

The following actions must be commenced within three years:

1. an action against a sheriff, constable or other officer for the nonpayment of money collected upon an execution;

2. an action to recover upon a liability, penalty or forfeiture created or imposed by statute except as provided in sections 213 and 215;

3. an action to recover a chattel or damages for the taking or detaining of a chattel;

4. an action to recover damages for an injury to property;

5. an action to recover damages for a personal injury except as provided in sections 214–b and 215;

6. an action to recover damages for malpractice, other than medical, dental or podiatric malpractice, regardless of whether the underlying theory is based in contract or tort; and

7. an action to annul a marriage on the ground of fraud; the time within which the action must be commenced shall be computed from the time the plaintiff discovered the facts constituting the fraud, but if the plaintiff is a person other than the spouse whose consent was obtained by fraud, the time within which the action must be commenced shall be computed from the time, if earlier, that that spouse discovered the facts constituting the fraud.

§ 214–a. Action for medical, dental or podiatric malpractice to be commenced within two years and six months; exceptions

An action for medical, dental or podiatric malpractice must be commenced within two years and six months of the act, omission or failure complained of or last treatment where there is continuous treatment for the same illness, injury or condition which gave rise to the said act, omission or failure; provided, however, that where the action is based upon the discovery of a foreign object in the body of the patient, the action may be commenced within one year of the date of such discovery or of the date of discovery of facts which would reasonably lead to such discovery, whichever is earlier. For the purpose of this section the term "continuous treatment" shall not include examinations undertaken at the request of the patient for the sole purpose of ascertaining the state of the patient's condition. For the purpose of this section the term "foreign object" shall not include a chemical compound, fixation device or prosthetic aid or device.

§ 214–b. Action to recover damages for personal injury caused by contact with or exposure to phenoxy herbicides

Notwithstanding any provision of law to the contrary, an action to recover damages for personal injury caused by contact with or exposure to phenoxy herbicides while serving as a member of the armed forces of the United States in Indo-China from January first, nineteen hundred sixty-two through May seventh, nineteen hundred seventy-five, may be commenced within two years from the date of the discovery of such injury, or within two years from the date when through the exercise of reasonable diligence the cause of such injury should have been discovered, whichever is later.

§ 214–c. Certain actions to be commenced within three years of discovery

1. In this section: "exposure" means direct or indirect exposure by absorption, contact, ingestion, inhalation, implantation or injection.

2. Notwithstanding the provisions of section 214, the three year period within which an action to recover damages for personal injury or injury to property caused by the latent effects of exposure to any substance or combination of substances, in any form, upon or within the body or upon or within property must be commenced shall be computed from the date of discovery of the injury by the plaintiff or from the date when through the exercise of reasonable diligence such injury should have been discovered by the plaintiff, whichever is earlier.

3. For the purposes of sections fifty-e and fifty-i of the general municipal law, section thirty-eight hundred thirteen of the education law and the provisions of any general, special or local law or charter requiring as a condition precedent to commencement of an action or special proceeding that a notice of claim be filed or presented within a specified period of time after the claim or action accrued, a claim or action for personal injury or injury to property caused by the latent effects of exposure to any

substance or combination of substances, in any form, upon or within the body or upon or within property shall be deemed to have accrued on the date of discovery of the injury by the plaintiff or on the date when through the exercise of reasonable diligence the injury should have been discovered, whichever is earlier.

4. Notwithstanding the provisions of subdivisions two and three of this section, where the discovery of the cause of the injury is alleged to have occurred less than five years after discovery of the injury or when with reasonable diligence such injury should have been discovered, whichever is earlier, an action may be commenced or a claim filed within one year of such discovery of the cause of the injury; provided, however, if any such action is commenced or claim filed after the period in which it would otherwise have been authorized pursuant to subdivision two or three of this section the plaintiff or claimant shall be required to allege and prove that technical, scientific or medical knowledge and information sufficient to ascertain the cause of his injury had not been discovered, identified or determined prior to the expiration of the period within which the action or claim would have been authorized and that he has otherwise satisfied the requirements of subdivisions two and three of this section.

5. This section shall not be applicable to any action for medical or dental malpractice.

6. This section shall be applicable to acts, omissions or failures occurring prior to, on or after July first, nineteen hundred eighty-six, except that this section shall not be applicable to any act, omission or failure:

(a) which occurred prior to July first, nineteen hundred eighty-six, and

(b) which caused or contributed to an injury that either was discovered or through the exercise of reasonable diligence should have been discovered prior to such date, and

(c) an action for which was or would have been barred because the applicable period of limitation had expired prior to such date.

§ 214–d. Limitations on certain actions against licensed engineers and architects

* * *

§ 214–e. Action to recover damages for personal injury caused by the infusion of such blood products which result in the contraction of the human immunodeficiency virus (HIV) and/or AIDS

Notwithstanding any provision of law to the contrary, any cause of action for an injury or death against a proprietary manufacturer of blood products for damages involving the infusion of such blood products which resulted in the contraction of the human immunodeficiency virus (HIV) and/or AIDS which is barred as of the effective date of this section because the applicable period of limitation has expired is hereby revived, and an action thereon may be commenced and prosecuted provided such action is commenced within two years of the effective date of this section. The provisions of this section shall be inapplicable to any civil action governed by the statute of limitations of another jurisdiction.

§ 215. Actions to be commenced within one year: against sheriff, coroner or constable; for escape of prisoner; for assault, battery, false imprisonment, malicious prosecution, libel or slander; for violation of right of privacy; for penalty given to informer; on arbitration award

The following actions shall be commenced within one year:

1. an action against a sheriff, coroner or constable, upon a liability incurred by him by doing an act in his official capacity or by omission of an official duty, except the non-payment of money collected upon an execution;

2. an action against an officer for the escape of a prisoner arrested or imprisoned by virtue of a civil mandate;

3. an action to recover damages for assault, battery, false imprisonment, malicious prosecution, libel, slander, false words causing special damages, or a violation of the right of privacy under section fifty-one of the civil rights law;

4. an action to enforce a penalty or forfeiture created by statute and given wholly or partly to any person who will prosecute; if the action is not commenced within the year by a private person, it may be commenced on behalf of the state, within three years after the commission of the offense, by the attorney-general or the district attorney of the county where the offense was committed; and

5. an action upon an arbitration award.

6. An action to recover any overcharge of interest or to enforce a penalty for such overcharge.

7. an action by a tenant pursuant to subdivision three of section two hundred twenty-three-b of the real property law.

8.(a) Whenever it is shown that a criminal action against the same defendant has been commenced with respect to the event or occurrence from which a claim governed by this section arises, the plaintiff shall have at least one year from the termination of the criminal action as defined in section 1.20 of the criminal procedure law in which to commence the civil action, notwithstanding that the time in which to commence such action has already expired or has less than a year remaining.

(b) Whenever it is shown that a criminal action against the same defendant has been commenced with respect to the event or occurrence from which a claim governed by this section arises, and such criminal action is for rape in the first degree as defined in section 130.35 of the penal law, or criminal sexual act in the first degree as defined in section 130.50 of the penal law, or aggravated sexual abuse in the first degree as defined in section 130.70 of the penal law, or course of sexual conduct against a child in the first degree as defined in section 130.75 of the penal law, the plaintiff shall have at least five years from the termination of the criminal action as defined in section 1.20 of the criminal procedure law in which to commence the civil action, notwithstanding that the time in which to commence such action has already expired or has less than a year remaining.

§ 217. Proceeding against body or officer; actions complaining about conduct that would constitute a union's breach of its duty of fair representation; four months

1. Unless a shorter time is provided in the law authorizing the proceeding, a proceeding against a body or officer must be commenced within four months after the determination to be reviewed becomes final and binding upon the petitioner or the person whom he represents in law or in fact, or after the respondent's refusal, upon the demand of the petitioner or the person whom he represents, to perform its duty; or with leave of the court where the petitioner or the person whom he represents, at the time such determination became final and binding upon him or at the time of such refusal, was under a disability specified in section 208, within two years after such time.

2.(a) Any action or proceeding against an employee organization subject to article fourteen of the civil service law or article twenty of the labor law which complains that such employee organization has breached its duty of fair representation regarding someone to whom such employee organization has a duty shall be commenced within four months of the date the employee or former employee knew or should have known that the breach has occurred, or within four months of the date the employee or former employee suffers actual harm, whichever is later.

(b) Any action or proceeding by an employee or former employee against an employer subject to article fourteen of the civil service law or article twenty of the labor law, an essential element of which is that an employee organization breached its duty of fair representation to the person making the complaint, shall be commenced within four months of the date the employee or former employee knew or should have known that the breach has occurred, or within four months of the date the employee or former employee suffers actual harm, whichever is later.

Article 3—Jurisdiction and Service, Appearance and Choice of Court

§ 301. Jurisdiction over persons, property or status

A court may exercise such jurisdiction over persons, property, or status as might have been exercised heretofore.

§ 302. Personal jurisdiction by acts of non-domiciliaries

(a) Acts which are the basis of jurisdiction. As to a cause of action arising from any of the acts enumerated in this section, a court may exercise personal jurisdiction over any non-domiciliary, or his executor or administrator, who in person or through an agent:

1. transacts any business within the state or contracts anywhere to supply goods or services in the state; or

2. commits a tortious act within the state, except as to a cause of action for defamation of character arising from the act; or

3. commits a tortious act without the state causing injury to person or property within the state, except as to a cause of action for defamation of character arising from the act, if he

(i) regularly does or solicits business, or engages in any other persistent course of conduct, or derives substantial revenue from goods used or consumed or services rendered, in the state, or

(ii) expects or should reasonably expect the act to have consequences in the state and derives substantial revenue from interstate or international commerce; or

4. owns, uses or possesses any real property situated within the state.

(b) Personal jurisdiction over non-resident defendant in matrimonial actions or family court proceedings. A court in any matrimonial action or family court proceeding involving a demand for support, alimony, maintenance, distributive awards or special relief in matrimonial actions may exercise personal jurisdiction over the respondent or defendant notwithstanding the fact that he or she no longer is a resident or domiciliary of this state, or over his or her executor or administrator, if the party seeking support is a resident of or domiciled in this state at the time such demand is made, provided that this state was the matrimonial domicile of the parties before their separation, or the defendant abandoned the plaintiff in this state, or the claim for support, alimony, maintenance, distributive awards or special relief in matrimonial actions accrued under the laws of this state or under an agreement executed in this state. The family court may exercise personal jurisdiction over a non-resident respondent to the extent provided in sections one hundred fifty-four and one thousand thirty-six and article five–B of the family court act and article five–A of the domestic relations law.

(c) Effect of appearance. Where personal jurisdiction is based solely upon this section, an appearance does not confer such jurisdiction with respect to causes of action not arising from an act enumerated in this section.

(d) Foreign defamation judgment. The courts of this state shall have personal jurisdiction over any person who obtains a judgment in a defamation proceeding outside the United States against any person who is a resident of New York or is a person or entity amenable to jurisdiction in New York who has assets in New York or may have to take actions in New York to comply with the judgment, for the purposes of rendering declaratory relief with respect to that person's liability for the judgment, and/or for the purpose of determining whether said judgment should be deemed non-recognizable pursuant to section fifty-three hundred four of this chapter, to the fullest extent permitted by the United States constitution, provided:

1. the publication at issue was published in New York, and

2. that resident or person amenable to jurisdiction in New York (i) has assets in New York which might be used to satisfy the foreign defamation judgment, or (ii) may have to take actions in New York to comply with the foreign defamation judgment. The provisions of this subdivision shall apply to persons who obtained judgments in defamation

proceedings outside the United States prior to and/or after the effective date of this subdivision.

§ 303.   Designation of attorney as agent for service

The commencement of an action in the state by a person not subject to personal jurisdiction is a designation by him of his attorney appearing in the action or of the clerk of the court if no attorney appears, as agent, during the pendency of the action, for service of a summons pursuant to section 308, in any separate action in which such a person is a defendant and another party to the action is a plaintiff if such separate action would have been permitted as a counterclaim had the action been brought in the supreme court.

§ 307.   Personal service upon the state

* * *

§ 308.   Personal service upon a natural person

Personal service upon a natural person shall be made by any of the following methods:

1.   by delivering the summons within the state to the person to be served; or

2.   by delivering the summons within the state to a person of suitable age and discretion at the actual place of business, dwelling place or usual place of abode of the person to be served and by either mailing the summons to the person to be served at his or her last known residence or by mailing the summons by first class mail to the person to be served at his or her actual place of business in an envelope bearing the legend "personal and confidential" and not indicating on the outside thereof, by return address or otherwise, that the communication is from an attorney or concerns an action against the person to be served, such delivery and mailing to be effected within twenty days of each other; proof of such service shall be filed with the clerk of the court designated in the summons within twenty days of either such delivery or mailing, whichever is effected later; service shall be complete ten days after such filing; proof of service shall identify such person of suitable age and discretion and state the date, time and place of service, except in matrimonial actions where service hereunder may be made pursuant to an order made in accordance with the provisions of subdivision a of section two hundred thirty-two of the domestic relations law; or

3.   by delivering the summons within the state to the agent for service of the person to be served as designated under rule 318, except in matrimonial actions where service hereunder may be made pursuant to an order made in accordance with the provisions of subdivision a of section two hundred thirty-two of the domestic relations law;

4.   where service under paragraphs one and two cannot be made with due diligence, by affixing the summons to the door of either the actual place of business, dwelling place or usual place of abode within the state of the person to be served and by either mailing the summons to such person at his or her last known residence or by mailing the summons by first class

mail to the person to be served at his or her actual place of business in an envelope bearing the legend "personal and confidential" and not indicating on the outside thereof, by return address or otherwise, that the communication is from an attorney or concerns an action against the person to be served, such affixing and mailing to be effected within twenty days of each other; proof of such service shall be filed with the clerk of the court designated in the summons within twenty days of either such affixing or mailing, whichever is effected later; service shall be complete ten days after such filing, except in matrimonial actions where service hereunder may be made pursuant to an order made in accordance with the provisions of subdivision a of section two hundred thirty-two of the domestic relations law;

5. in such manner as the court, upon motion without notice, directs, if service is impracticable under paragraphs one, two and four of this section.

6. For purposes of this section, "actual place of business" shall include any location that the defendant, through regular solicitation or advertisement, has held out as its place of business.

§ 309. Personal service upon an infant, incompetent or conservatee

* * *

§ 310. Personal service upon a partnership

* * *

§ 311. Personal service upon a corporation or governmental subdivision

(a) Personal service upon a corporation or governmental subdivision shall be made by delivering the summons as follows:

1. upon any domestic or foreign corporation, to an officer, director, managing or general agent, or cashier or assistant cashier or to any other agent authorized by appointment or by law to receive service. A business corporation may also be served pursuant to section three hundred six or three hundred seven of the business corporation law. A not-for-profit corporation may also be served pursuant to section three hundred six or three hundred seven of the not-for-profit corporation law;

* * *

§ 312. Personal service upon a court, board or commission

* * *

§ 312–a. Personal service by mail

(a) Service. As an alternative to the methods of personal service authorized by section 307, 308, 310, 311 or 312 of this article, a summons and complaint, or summons and notice, or notice of petition and petition may be served by the plaintiff or any other person by mailing to the person or entity to be served, by first class mail, postage prepaid, a copy of the summons and complaint, or summons and notice or notice of petition and petition, together with two copies of a statement of service by mail and acknowledgement of receipt in the form set forth in subdivision (d) of this section, with a return envelope, postage prepaid, addressed to the sender.

(b) Completion of service and time to answer.

1. The defendant, an authorized employee of the defendant, defendant's attorney or an employee of the attorney must complete the acknowledgement of receipt and mail or deliver one copy of it within thirty (30) days from the date of receipt. Service is complete on the date the signed acknowledgement of receipt is mailed or delivered to the sender. The signed acknowledgement of receipt shall constitute proof of service.

2. Where a complaint or petition is served with the summons or notice of petition, the defendant shall serve an answer within twenty (20) days after the date the signed acknowledgement of receipt is mailed or delivered to the sender.

(c) Affirmation. The acknowledgement of receipt of service shall be subscribed and affirmed as true under penalties of perjury and shall have the same force and effect as an affidavit.

(d) Form. The statement of service by mail and the acknowledgement of receipt of such service shall be in substantially the following form:

Statement of Service by Mail and
Acknowledgement of Receipt by Mail of
Summons and Complaint or Summons and Notice
or Notice of Petition and Petition

A. STATEMENT OF SERVICE BY MAIL

To: (Insert the name and address of the person or entity to be served.) The enclosed summons and complaint, or summons and notice, or notice of petition and petition (strike out inapplicable terms) are served pursuant to section 312–a of the Civil Practice Law and Rules.

To avoid being charged with the expense of service upon you, you must sign, date and complete the acknowledgement part of this form and mail or deliver one copy of the completed form to the sender within thirty (30) days from the date you receive it. You should keep a copy for your records or your attorney. If you wish to consult an attorney, you should do so as soon as possible before the thirty (30) days expire.

If you do not complete and return the form to the sender within thirty (30) days, you (or the party on whose behalf you are being served) will be required to pay expenses incurred in serving the summons and complaint, or summons and notice, or notice of petition and petition in any other manner permitted by law, and the cost of such service as permitted by law will be entered as a judgment against you.

If you have received a complaint or petition with this statement, the return of this statement and acknowledgement does not relieve you of the necessity to answer the complaint or petition. The time to answer expires twenty (20) days after the day you mail or deliver this form to the sender. If you wish to consult with an attorney, you should do so as soon as possible before the twenty (20) days expire.

If you are served on behalf of a corporation, unincorporated association, partnership or other entity, you must indicate under your signature your relationship to the entity. If you are served on behalf of another person and you are authorized to receive process, you must indicate under your signature your authority.

It is a crime to forge a signature or to make a false entry on this statement or on the acknowledgement.

B. ACKNOWLEDGEMENT OF RECEIPT OF SUMMONS AND COMPLAINT OR SUMMONS AND NOTICE OR NOTICE OF PETITION AND PETITION

I received a summons and complaint, or summons and notice, or notice of petition and petition (strike out inapplicable terms) in the above-captioned matter at (insert address). PLEASE CHECK ONE OF THE FOLLOWING;

IF 2 IS CHECKED, COMPLETE AS INDICATED:

1. / /I am not in military service.

2. / /I am in military service, and my rank and branch of service are as follows:

Rank:

_____

Branch of Service:

_____

TO BE COMPLETED REGARDLESS OF MILITARY STATUS:

Date:

_____

(Date this Acknowledgement is executed)

I affirm the above as true under penalty of perjury.

_____

Signature

_____

Print name

_____

Name of Defendant for which acting

_____

Position with Defendant for which acting (i.e., officer, attorney, etc.)

PLEASE COMPLETE ALL BLANKS INCLUDING DATES

(e) Subsequent service. Where a duly executed acknowledgement is not returned, upon the subsequent service of process in another manner permitted by law, the summons or notice of petition or paper served with the summons or notice of petition shall indicate that an attempt previously was made to effect service pursuant to this section.

(f) Disbursements. Where the signed acknowledgement of receipt is not returned within thirty (30) days after receipt of the documents mailed pursuant to subdivision (a) of this section, the reasonable expense of serving process by an alternative method shall be taxed by the court on notice pursuant to section 8402 of this chapter as a disbursement to the party serving process, and the court shall direct immediate judgment in that amount.

§ 313.   Service without the state giving personal jurisdiction

A person domiciled in the state or subject to the jurisdiction of the courts of the state under section 301 or 302, or his executor or administrator, may be served with the summons without the state, in the same manner as service is made within the state, by any person authorized to make service within the state who is a resident of the state or by any person authorized to make service by the laws of the state, territory, possession or country in which service is made or by any duly qualified attorney, solicitor, barrister, or equivalent in such jurisdiction.

§ 314.   Service without the state not giving personal jurisdiction in certain actions

Service may be made without the state by any person authorized by section 313 in the same manner as service is made within the state:

1.   in a matrimonial action; or

2.   where a judgment is demanded that the person to be served be excluded from a vested or contingent interest in or lien upon specific real or personal property within the state; or that such an interest or lien in favor of either party be enforced, regulated, defined or limited; or otherwise affecting the title to such property, including an action of interpleader or defensive interpleader; or

3.   where a levy upon property of the person to be served has been made within the state pursuant to an order of attachment or a chattel of such person has been seized in an action to recover a chattel.

§ 315.   Service by publication authorized

The court, upon motion without notice, shall order service of a summons by publication in an action described in section 314 if service cannot be made by another prescribed method with due diligence.

Rule 316.   Service by publication [method]

* * *

§ 317.   Defense by person to whom summons not personally delivered

A person served with a summons other than by personal delivery to him or to his agent for service designated under rule 318, within or without the state, who does not appear may be allowed to defend the action within one year after he obtains knowledge of entry of the judgment, but in no event more than five years after such entry, upon a finding of the court that he did not personally receive notice of the summons in time to defend and has a meritorious defense. If the defense is successful, the court may direct and enforce restitution in the same manner and subject to the same conditions as where a judgment is reversed or modified on appeal. This section does not apply to an action for divorce, annulment or partition.

Rule 318. Designation of agent for service

A person may be designated by a natural person, corporation or partnership as an agent for service in a writing, executed and acknowledged in the same manner as a deed, with the consent of the agent endorsed thereon. The writing shall be filed in the office of the clerk of the county in which the principal to be served resides or has its principal office. The designation shall remain in effect for three years from such filing unless it has been revoked by the filing of a revocation, or by the death, judicial declaration of incompetency or legal termination of the agent or principal.

Rule 320. Defendant's appearance

(a) Requirement of appearance. The defendant appears by serving an answer or a notice of appearance, or by making a motion which has the effect of extending the time to answer. An appearance shall be made within twenty days after service of the summons, except that if the summons was served on the defendant by delivering it to an official of the state authorized to receive service in his behalf or if it was served pursuant to section 303, subdivision two, three, four or five of section 308, or sections 313, 314 or 315, the appearance shall be made within thirty days after service is complete. If the complaint is not served with the summons, the time to appear may be extended as provided in subdivision (b) of section 3012.

(b) When appearance confers personal jurisdiction, generally. Subject to the provisions of subdivision (c), an appearance of the defendant is equivalent to personal service of the summons upon him, unless an objection to jurisdiction under paragraph eight of subdivision (a) of rule 3211 is asserted by motion or in the answer as provided in rule 3211.

(c) When appearance confers personal jurisdiction, in certain actions; limited appearance. When the court's jurisdiction is not based upon personal service on the defendant, an appearance is not equivalent to personal service upon the defendant:

1. in a case specified in subdivision (3) of section 314, if jurisdiction is based solely upon a levy on defendant's property within the state pursuant to an order of attachment; or

2. in any other case specified in section 314, if an objection to jurisdiction under paragraphs eight [personal jurisdiction] or nine [nonpersonal jurisdiction] of subdivision (a) of rule 3211, or both, is asserted by motion or in the answer as provided in rule 3211, unless the defendant proceeds with the defense after asserting the objection to jurisdiction and the objection is not ultimately sustained.

663

(d) Appearance after first publication. Where the defendant appears during the period of publication of a summons against him, the service by publication shall be deemed completed by the appearance.

Rule 327. Inconvenient forum

(a) When the court finds that in the interest of substantial justice the action should be heard in another forum, the court, on the motion of any party, may stay or dismiss the action in whole or in part on any conditions that may be just. The domicile or residence in this state of any party to the action shall not preclude the court from staying or dismissing the action.

(b) Notwithstanding the provisions of subdivision (a) of this rule, the court shall not stay or dismiss any action on the ground of inconvenient forum, where the action arises out of or relates to a [big commercial] contract, agreement or undertaking to which section 5–1402 of the general obligations law applies, and the parties to the contract have agreed that the law of this state shall govern their rights or duties in whole or in part.

Article 5—Venue

§ 501. Contractual provisions fixing venue

Subject to the provisions of subdivision two of section 510, written agreement fixing place of trial, made before an action is commenced, shall be enforced upon a motion for change of place of trial.

§ 502. Conflicting venue provisions

Where, because of joinder of claims or parties, there is a conflict of provisions under this article, the court, upon motion, shall order as the place of trial one proper under this article as to at least one of the parties or claims.

§ 503. Venue based on residence

(a) Generally. Except where otherwise prescribed by law, the place of trial shall be in the county in which one of the parties resided when it was commenced; or, if none of the parties then resided in the state, in any county designated by the plaintiff. A party resident in more than one county shall be deemed a resident of each such county.

(b) Executor, administrator, trustee, committee, conservator, general or testamentary guardian, or receiver. An executor, administrator, trustee, committee, conservator, general or testamentary guardian, or receiver shall be deemed a resident of the county of his appointment as well as the county in which he actually resides.

(c) Corporation. A domestic corporation, or a foreign corporation authorized to transact business in the state, shall be deemed a resident of the county in which its principal office is located; except that such a corporation, if a railroad or other common carrier, shall also be deemed a resident of the county where the cause of action arose.

(d) Unincorporated association, partnership, or individually-owned business. A president or treasurer of an unincorporated association, suing or being sued on behalf of the association, shall be deemed a resident of any county in which the association has its principal office, as well as the county in which he actually resides. A partnership or an individually-owned business shall be deemed a resident of any county in which it has its principal office, as well as the county in which the partner or individual owner suing or being sued actually resides.

(e) Assignee. In an action for a sum of money only, brought by an assignee other than an assignee for the benefit of creditors or a holder in due course of a negotiable instrument, the assignee's residence shall be deemed the same as that of the original assignor at the time of the original assignment.

(f) Consumer credit transaction. In an action arising out of a consumer credit transaction where a purchaser, borrower or debtor is a defendant, the place of trial shall be the residence of a defendant, if one resides within the state or the county where such transaction took place, if it is within the state, or, in other cases, as set forth in subdivision (a).

§ 504. Actions against counties, cities, towns, villages, school districts and district corporations

* * *

§ 505. Actions involving public authorities

* * *

§ 506. Where special proceeding commenced

* * *

§ 507. Real property actions

The place of trial of an action in which the judgment demanded would affect the title to, or the possession, use or enjoyment of, real property shall be in the county in which any part of the subject of the action is situated.

§ 508. Actions to recover a chattel

The place of trial of an action to recover a chattel may be in the county in which any part of the subject of the action is situated at the time of the commencement of the action.

§ 509. Venue in county designated

Notwithstanding any provision of this article, the place of trial of an action shall be in the county designated by the plaintiff, unless the place of trial is changed to another county by order upon motion, or by consent as provided in subdivision (b) of rule 511.

§ 510. Grounds for change of place of trial

The court, upon motion, may change the place of trial of an action where:

1. the county designated for that purpose is not a proper county; or

2. there is reason to believe that an impartial trial cannot be had in the proper county; or

3. the convenience of material witnesses and the ends of justice will be promoted by the change.

Rule 511. Change of place of trial

(a) **Time for motion or demand.** A demand under subdivision (b) for change of place of trial on the ground that the county designated for that purpose is not a proper county shall be served with the answer or before the answer is served. A motion for change of place of trial on any other ground shall be made within a reasonable time after commencement of the action.

(b) **Demand for change of place of trial upon ground of improper venue, where motion made.** The defendant shall serve a written demand that the action be tried in a county he specifies as proper. Thereafter, the defendant may move to change the place of trial within fifteen days after service of the demand, unless within five days after such service plaintiff serves a written consent to change the place of trial to that specified by the defendant. Defendant may notice such motion to be heard as if the action were pending in the county he specified, unless plaintiff within five days after service of the demand serves an affidavit showing either that the county specified by the defendant is not proper or that the county designated by him is proper.

(c) **Stay of proceedings.** No order to stay proceedings for the purpose of changing the place of trial shall be granted unless it appears from the papers that the change is sought with due diligence.

(d) **Order, subsequent proceedings and appeal.** Upon filing of consent by the plaintiff or entry of an order changing the place of trial by the clerk of the county from which it is changed, the clerk shall forthwith deliver to the clerk of the county to which it is changed all papers filed in the action and certified copies of all minutes and entries, which shall be filed, entered or recorded, as the case requires, in the office of the latter clerk. Subsequent proceedings shall be had in the county to which the change is made as if it had been designated originally as the place of trial, except as otherwise directed by the court. An appeal from an order changing the place of trial shall be taken in the department in which the motion for the order was heard and determined.

FEDERAL RULES OF EVIDENCE

TABLE OF CONTENTS

RULES OF EVIDENCE

*

FEDERAL RULES OF EVIDENCE

Rule 101.

SCOPE

These rules govern proceedings in the courts of the United States and before United States bankruptcy judges and United States magistrate judges, to the extent and with the exceptions stated in rule 1101.

As amended 1987, 1988, 1993.

Rule 102.

PURPOSE AND CONSTRUCTION

These rules shall be construed to secure fairness in administration, elimination of unjustifiable expense and delay, and promotion of growth and development of the law of evidence to the end that the truth may be ascertained and proceedings justly determined.

Rule 103.

RULINGS ON EVIDENCE

(a) Effect of erroneous ruling. Error may not be predicated upon a ruling which admits or excludes evidence unless a substantial right of the party is affected, and

(1) *Objection.* In case the ruling is one admitting evidence a timely objection or motion to strike appears of record, stating the specific ground of objection if the specific ground was not apparent from the context; or

(2) *Offer of proof.* In case the ruling is one excluding evidence, the substance of the evidence was made known to the court by offer or was apparent from the context within which questions were asked.

Once the court makes a definitive ruling on the record admitting or excluding evidence, either at or before trial, a party need not renew an objection or offer of proof to preserve a claim of error for appeal.

(b) Record of offer and ruling. The court may add any other or further statement which shows the character of the evidence, the form in which it was offered, the objection made, and the ruling thereon. It may direct the making of an offer in question and answer form.

(c) Hearing of jury. In jury cases, proceedings shall be conducted, to the extent practicable, so as to prevent inadmissible evidence from being suggested to the jury by any means, such as making statements or offers of proof or asking questions in the hearing of the jury.

(d) Plain error. Nothing in this rule precludes taking notice of plain errors affecting substantial rights although they were not brought to the attention of the court.

As amended 2000.

Rule 104.

PRELIMINARY QUESTIONS

(a) Questions of admissibility generally. Preliminary questions concerning the qualification of a person to be a witness, the existence of a privilege, or the admissibility of evidence shall be determined by the court, subject to the provisions of subdivision (b). In making its determination it is not bound by the rules of evidence except those with respect to privileges.

(b) Relevancy conditioned on fact. When the relevancy of evidence depends upon the fulfillment of a condition of fact, the court shall admit it upon, or subject to, the introduction of evidence sufficient to support a finding of the fulfillment of the condition.

(c) Hearing of jury. Hearings on the admissibility of confessions shall in all cases be conducted out of the hearing of the jury. Hearings on other preliminary matters shall be so conducted when the interests of justice require, or when an accused is a witness and so requests.

(d) Testimony by accused. The accused does not, by testifying upon a preliminary matter, become subject to cross-examination as to other issues in the case.

(e) Weight and credibility. This rule does not limit the right of a party to introduce before the jury evidence relevant to weight or credibility.

As amended 1987.

Rule 105.

LIMITED ADMISSIBILITY

When evidence which is admissible as to one party or for one purpose but not admissible as to another party or for another purpose is admitted, the court, upon request, shall restrict the evidence to its proper scope and instruct the jury accordingly.

Rule 106.

REMAINDER OF OR RELATED WRITINGS OR RECORDED STATEMENTS

When a writing or recorded statement or part thereof is introduced by a party, an adverse party may require the introduction at that time of any other part or any other writing or recorded statement which ought in fairness to be considered contemporaneously with it.

As amended 1987.

ARTICLE II.   JUDICIAL NOTICE

Rule 201.

JUDICIAL NOTICE OF ADJUDICATIVE FACTS

(a) Scope of rule.   This rule governs only judicial notice of adjudicative facts.

(b) Kinds of facts.   A judicially noticed fact must be one not subject to reasonable dispute in that it is either (1) generally known within the territorial jurisdiction of the trial court or (2) capable of accurate and ready determination by resort to sources whose accuracy cannot reasonably be questioned.

(c) When discretionary.   A court may take judicial notice, whether requested or not.

(d) When mandatory.   A court shall take judicial notice if requested by a party and supplied with the necessary information.

(e) Opportunity to be heard.   A party is entitled upon timely request to an opportunity to be heard as to the propriety of taking judicial notice and the tenor of the matter noticed.   In the absence of prior notification, the request may be made after judicial notice has been taken.

(f) Time of taking notice.   Judicial notice may be taken at any stage of the proceeding.

(g) Instructing jury. In a civil action or proceeding, the court shall instruct the jury to accept as conclusive any fact judicially noticed. In a criminal case, the court shall instruct the jury that it may, but is not required to, accept as conclusive any fact judicially noticed.

ARTICLE III. PRESUMPTIONS IN CIVIL ACTIONS AND PROCEEDINGS

Rule 301.

PRESUMPTIONS IN GENERAL IN CIVIL ACTIONS AND PROCEEDINGS

In all civil actions and proceedings not otherwise provided for by Act of Congress or by these rules, a presumption imposes on the party against whom it is directed the burden of going forward with evidence to rebut or meet the presumption, but does not shift to such party the burden of proof in the sense of the risk of nonpersuasion, which remains throughout the trial upon the party on whom it was originally cast.

Rule 302.

APPLICABILITY OF STATE LAW IN CIVIL ACTIONS AND PROCEEDINGS

In civil actions and proceedings, the effect of a presumption respecting a fact which is an element of a claim or defense as to which State law supplies the rule of decision is determined in accordance with State law.

ARTICLE IV. RELEVANCY AND ITS LIMITS

Rule 401.

DEFINITION OF "RELEVANT EVIDENCE"

"Relevant evidence" means evidence having any tendency to make the existence of any fact that is of consequence to the determination of the action more probable or less probable than it would be without the evidence.

Rule 402.

RELEVANT EVIDENCE GENERALLY ADMISSIBLE; IRRELEVANT EVIDENCE INADMISSIBLE

All relevant evidence is admissible, except as otherwise provided by the Constitution of the United States, by Act of Congress, by these rules, or by other rules prescribed by the Supreme Court pursuant to statutory authority. Evidence which is not relevant is not admissible.

Rule 403.

EXCLUSION OF RELEVANT EVIDENCE ON GROUNDS OF PREJUDICE, CONFUSION, OR WASTE OF TIME

Although relevant, evidence may be excluded if its probative value is substantially outweighed by the danger of unfair prejudice, confusion of the issues, or misleading the jury, or by considerations of undue delay, waste of time, or needless presentation of cumulative evidence.

Rule 404.

CHARACTER EVIDENCE NOT ADMISSIBLE TO PROVE CONDUCT; EXCEPTIONS; OTHER CRIMES

(a) Character evidence generally. Evidence of a person's character or a trait of character is not admissible for the purpose of proving action in conformity therewith on a particular occasion, except:

(1) *Character of accused.* In a criminal case, evidence of a pertinent trait of character offered by an accused, or by the prosecution to rebut the same, or if evidence of a trait of character of the alleged victim of the crime is offered by an accused and admitted under Rule 404(a)(2), evidence of the same trait of character of the accused offered by the prosecution;

(2) *Character of alleged victim.* In a criminal case, and subject to the limitations imposed by Rule 412, evidence of a pertinent trait of character of the alleged victim of the crime offered by an accused, or by the prosecution to rebut the same, or evidence of a character trait of peacefulness of the alleged victim offered by the prosecution in a homicide case to rebut evidence that the alleged victim was the first aggressor;

(3) *Character of witness.* Evidence of the character of a witness, as provided in Rules 607, 608, and 609.

(b) Other crimes, wrongs, or acts. Evidence of other crimes, wrongs, or acts is not admissible to prove the character of a person in order to show action in conformity therewith. It may, however, be admissible for other purposes, such as proof of motive, opportunity, intent, preparation, plan, knowledge, identity, or absence of mistake or accident, provided that upon request by the accused, the prosecution in a criminal case shall provide reasonable notice in advance of trial, or during trial if the court excuses pretrial notice on good cause shown, of the general nature of any such evidence it intends to introduce at trial.

As amended 1987, 1991, 2000, 2006.

Rule 405.

METHODS OF PROVING CHARACTER

(a) Reputation or opinion. In all cases in which evidence of character or a trait of character of a person is admissible, proof may be made by testimony as to reputation or by testimony in the form of an opinion. On cross-examination, inquiry is allowable into relevant specific instances of conduct.

(b) Specific instances of conduct. In cases in which character or a trait of character of a person is an essential element of a charge, claim, or defense, proof may also be made of specific instances of that person's conduct.

As amended 1987.

Rule 406.

HABIT; ROUTINE PRACTICE

Evidence of the habit of a person or of the routine practice of an organization, whether corroborated or not and regardless of the presence of eyewitnesses, is relevant to prove that the conduct of the person or organization on a particular occasion was in conformity with the habit or routine practice.

Rule 407.

SUBSEQUENT REMEDIAL MEASURES

When, after an injury or harm allegedly caused by an event, measures are taken that, if taken previously, would have made the injury or harm less likely to occur, evidence of the subsequent measures is not admissible to prove negligence, culpable conduct, a defect in a product, a defect in a product's design, or a need for a warning or instruction. This rule does not require the exclusion of evidence of subsequent measures when offered for another purpose, such as proving ownership, control, or feasibility of precautionary measures, if controverted, or impeachment.

As amended 1997.

Rule 408.

COMPROMISE AND OFFERS TO COMPROMISE

(a) Prohibited uses. Evidence of the following is not admissible on behalf of any party, when offered to prove liability for, invalidity of, or amount of a claim that was disputed as to validity or amount, or to impeach through a prior inconsistent statement or contradiction:

(1) furnishing or offering or promising to furnish—or accepting or offering or promising to accept—a valuable consideration in compromising or attempting to compromise the claim; and

(2) conduct or statements made in compromise negotiations regarding the claim, except when offered in a criminal case and the negotiations related to a claim by a public office or agency in the exercise of regulatory, investigative, or enforcement authority.

(b) Permitted uses. This rule does not require exclusion if the evidence is offered for purposes not prohibited by subdivision (a). Examples of permissible purposes include proving a witness's bias or prejudice; negating a contention of undue delay; and proving an effort to obstruct a criminal investigation or prosecution.

As amended 2006.

Rule 409.

PAYMENT OF MEDICAL AND SIMILAR EXPENSES

Evidence of furnishing or offering or promising to pay medical, hospital, or similar expenses occasioned by an injury is not admissible to prove liability for the injury.

Rule 410.

INADMISSIBILITY OF PLEAS, PLEA DISCUSSIONS, AND RELATED STATEMENTS

Except as otherwise provided in this rule, evidence of the following is not, in any civil or criminal proceeding, admissible against the defendant who made the plea or was a participant in the plea discussions:

(1) a plea of guilty which was later withdrawn;

679

(2) a plea of nolo contendere;

(3) any statement made in the course of any proceedings under Rule 11 of the Federal Rules of Criminal Procedure or comparable state procedure regarding either of the foregoing pleas; or

(4) any statement made in the course of plea discussions with an attorney for the prosecuting authority which do not result in a plea of guilty or which result in a plea of guilty later withdrawn.

However, such a statement is admissible (i) in any proceeding wherein another statement made in the course of the same plea or plea discussions has been introduced and the statement ought in fairness be considered contemporaneously with it, or (ii) in a criminal proceeding for perjury or false statement if the statement was made by the defendant under oath, on the record and in the presence of counsel.

As amended 1975, 1980.

Rule 411.

LIABILITY INSURANCE

Evidence that a person was or was not insured against liability is not admissible upon the issue whether the person acted negligently or otherwise wrongfully. This rule does not require the exclusion of evidence of insurance against liability when offered for another purpose, such as proof of agency, ownership, or control, or bias or prejudice of a witness.

As amended 1987.

Rule 412.

SEX OFFENSE CASES; RELEVANCE OF ALLEGED VICTIM'S PAST SEXUAL BEHAVIOR OR ALLEGED SEXUAL PREDISPOSITION

(a) Evidence generally inadmissible. The following evidence is not admissible in any civil or criminal proceeding involving alleged sexual misconduct except as provided in subdivisions (b) and (c):

(1) Evidence offered to prove that any alleged victim engaged in other sexual behavior.

(2) Evidence offered to prove any alleged victim's sexual predisposition.

(b) Exceptions.

(1) In a criminal case, the following evidence is admissible, if otherwise admissible under these rules:

(A) evidence of specific instances of sexual behavior by the alleged victim offered to prove that a person other than the accused was the source of semen, injury or other physical evidence;

(B) evidence of specific instances of sexual behavior by the alleged victim with respect to the person accused of the sexual misconduct offered by the accused to prove consent or by the prosecution; and

(C) evidence the exclusion of which would violate the constitutional rights of the defendant.

(2) In a civil case, evidence offered to prove the sexual behavior or sexual predisposition of any alleged victim is admissible if it is otherwise admissible under these rules and its probative value substantially outweighs the danger of harm to any victim and of unfair prejudice to any party. Evidence of an alleged victim's reputation is admissible only if it has been placed in controversy by the alleged victim.

(c) Procedure to determine admissibility.

(1) A party intending to offer evidence under subdivision (b) must—

(A) file a written motion at least 14 days before trial specifically describing the evidence and stating the purpose for which it is offered unless the court, for good cause requires a different time for filing or permits filing during trial; and

(B) serve the motion on all parties and notify the alleged victim or, when appropriate, the alleged victim's guardian or representative.

(2) Before admitting evidence under this rule the court must conduct a hearing in camera and afford the victim and parties a right to attend and be heard. The motion, related papers, and the record of the hearing must be sealed and remain under seal unless the court orders otherwise.

Added 1978; as amended 1988, 1994.

Rule 413.

EVIDENCE OF SIMILAR CRIMES
IN SEXUAL ASSAULT CASES

(a) In a criminal case in which the defendant is accused of an offense of sexual assault, evidence of the defendant's commission of another offense or offenses of sexual assault is admissible, and may be considered for its bearing on any matter to which it is relevant.

(b) In a case in which the Government intends to offer evidence under this rule, the attorney for the Government shall disclose the evidence to the defendant, including statements of witnesses or a summary of the substance of any testimony that is expected to be offered, at least fifteen days before the scheduled date of trial or at such later time as the court may allow for good cause.

(c) This rule shall not be construed to limit the admission or consideration of evidence under any other rule.

(d) For purposes of this rule and Rule 415, "offense of sexual assault" means a crime under Federal law or the law of a State (as defined in section 513 of title 18, United States Code) that involved—

(1) any conduct proscribed by chapter 109A of title 18, United States Code;

(2) contact, without consent, between any part of the defendant's body or an object and the genitals or anus of another person;

(3) contact, without consent, between the genitals or anus of the defendant and any part of another person's body;

(4) deriving sexual pleasure or gratification from the infliction of death, bodily injury, or physical pain on another person; or

(5) an attempt or conspiracy to engage in conduct described in paragraphs (1)–(4).

Added 1995.

Rule 414.

EVIDENCE OF SIMILAR CRIMES IN CHILD MOLESTATION CASES

(a) In a criminal case in which the defendant is accused of an offense of child molestation, evidence of the defendant's commission of another offense or offenses of child molestation is admissible, and may be considered for its bearing on any matter to which it is relevant.

(b) In a case in which the Government intends to offer evidence under this rule, the attorney for the Government shall disclose the evidence to the defendant, including statements of witnesses or a summary of the substance of any testimony that is expected to be offered, at least fifteen days before the scheduled date of trial or at such later time as the court may allow for good cause.

(c) This rule shall not be construed to limit the admission or consideration of evidence under any other rule.

(d) For purposes of this rule and Rule 415, "child" means a person below the age of fourteen, and "offense of child molestation" means a crime under Federal law or the law of a State (as defined in section 513 of title 18, United States Code) that involved—

(1) any conduct proscribed by chapter 109A of title 18, United States Code, that was committed in relation to a child;

(2) any conduct proscribed by chapter 110 of title 18, United States Code;

(3) contact between any part of the defendant's body or an object and the genitals or anus of a child;

(4) contact between the genitals or anus of the defendant and any part of the body of a child;

(5) deriving sexual pleasure or gratification from the infliction of death, bodily injury, or physical pain on a child; or

(6) an attempt or conspiracy to engage in conduct described in paragraphs (1)–(5).

Added 1995.

Rule 415.

EVIDENCE OF SIMILAR ACTS IN CIVIL CASES CONCERNING SEXUAL ASSAULT OR CHILD MOLESTATION

(a) In a civil case in which a claim for damages or other relief is predicated on a party's alleged commission of conduct constituting an offense of sexual assault or child molestation, evidence of that party's commission of another offense or offenses of sexual assault or child molestation is admissible and may be considered as provided in Rule 413 and Rule 414 of these rules.

(b) A party who intends to offer evidence under this Rule shall disclose the evidence to the party against whom it will be offered, including statements of witnesses or a summary of the substance of any testimony that is expected to be offered, at least fifteen days before the scheduled date of trial or at such later time as the court may allow for good cause.

(c) This rule shall not be construed to limit the admission or consideration of evidence under any other rule.

Added 1995.

ARTICLE V.   PRIVILEGES

Rule 501.

GENERAL RULE

Except as otherwise required by the Constitution of the United States or provided by Act of Congress or in rules prescribed by the Supreme Court pursuant to statutory authority, the privilege of a witness, person, government, State, or political subdivision thereof shall be governed by the principles of the common law as they may be interpreted by the courts of the United States in the light of reason and experience.   However, in civil actions and proceedings, with respect to an element of a claim or defense as to which State law supplies the rule of decision, the privilege of a witness, person, government, State, or political subdivision thereof shall be determined in accordance with State law.

Rule 502.

ATTORNEY–CLIENT PRIVILEGE AND WORK PRODUCT; LIMITATIONS ON WAIVER

The following provisions apply, in the circumstances set out, to disclosure of a communication or information covered by the attorney-client privilege or work-product protection.

(a) Disclosure made in a Federal proceeding or to a Federal office or agency; scope of a waiver. When the disclosure is made in a Federal proceeding or to a Federal office or agency and waives the attorney-client privilege or work-product protection, the waiver extends to an undisclosed communication or information in a Federal or State proceeding only if:

(1) the waiver is intentional;

(2) the disclosed and undisclosed communications or information concern the same subject matter; and

(3) they ought in fairness to be considered together.

(b) Inadvertent disclosure. When made in a Federal proceeding or to a Federal office or agency, the disclosure does not operate as a waiver in a Federal or State proceeding if:

(1) the disclosure is inadvertent;

(2) the holder of the privilege or protection took reasonable steps to prevent disclosure; and

(3) the holder promptly took reasonable steps to rectify the error, including (if applicable) following Federal Rule Civil Procedure 26(b)(5)(B).

(c) Disclosure made in a State proceeding. When the disclosure is made in a State proceeding and is not the subject of a State-court order concerning waiver, the disclosure does not operate as a waiver in a Federal proceeding if the disclosure:

(1) would not be a waiver under this rule if it had been made in a Federal proceeding; or

(2) is not a waiver under the law of the State where the disclosure occurred.

(d) Controlling effect of a court order. A Federal court may order that the privilege or protection is not waived by disclosure connected with the litigation pending before the court—in which event the disclosure is also not a waiver in any other Federal or State proceeding.

(e) Controlling effect of a party agreement. An agreement on the effect of disclosure in a Federal proceeding is binding only on the parties to the agreement, unless it is incorporated into a court order.

(f) Controlling effect of this rule. Notwithstanding Rules 101 and 1101, this rule applies to State proceedings and to Federal court-annexed and Federal court-mandated arbitration proceedings, in the circumstances set out in the rule. And notwithstanding Rule 501, this rule applies even if State law provides the rule of decision.

(g) Definitions. In this rule:

(1) "attorney-client privilege" means the protection that applicable law provides for confidential attorney-client communications; and

(2) "work-product protection" means the protection that applicable law provides for tangible material (or its intangible equivalent) prepared in anticipation of litigation or for trial.

Added 2008.

ARTICLE VI. WITNESSES

Rule 601.

GENERAL RULE OF COMPETENCY

Every person is competent to be a witness except as otherwise provided in these rules. However, in civil actions and proceedings, with respect to an element of a claim or defense as to which State law supplies the rule of decision, the competency of a witness shall be determined in accordance with State law.

Rule 602.

LACK OF PERSONAL KNOWLEDGE

A witness may not testify to a matter unless evidence is introduced sufficient to support a finding that the witness has personal knowledge of the matter. Evidence to prove personal knowledge may, but need not, consist of the witness' own testimony. This rule is subject to the provisions of rule 703, relating to opinion testimony by expert witnesses.

As amended 1987, 1988.

Rule 603.

OATH OR AFFIRMATION

Before testifying, every witness shall be required to declare that the witness will testify truthfully, by oath or affirmation administered in a form calculated to awaken the witness' conscience and impress the witness' mind with the duty to do so.

As amended 1987.

Rule 604.

INTERPRETERS

An interpreter is subject to the provisions of these rules relating to qualification as an expert and the administration of an oath or affirmation to make a true translation.

As amended 1987.

Rule 605.

COMPETENCY OF JUDGE AS WITNESS

The judge presiding at the trial may not testify in that trial as a witness. No objection need be made in order to preserve the point.

Rule 606.

COMPETENCY OF JUROR AS WITNESS

(a) At the trial. A member of the jury may not testify as a witness before that jury in the trial of the case in which the juror is sitting. If the juror is called so to testify, the opposing party shall be afforded an opportunity to object out of the presence of the jury.

(b) Inquiry into validity of verdict or indictment. Upon an inquiry into the validity of a verdict or indictment, a juror may not testify as to any matter or statement occurring during the course of the jury's deliberations or to the effect of anything upon that or any other juror's mind or emotions as influencing the juror to assent to or dissent from the verdict or indictment or concerning the juror's mental processes in connection therewith. But a juror may testify about (1) whether extraneous prejudicial information was improperly brought to the jury's attention, (2) whether any outside influence was improperly brought to bear upon any juror, or (3) whether there was a mistake in entering the verdict onto the verdict form. A juror's affidavit or evidence of any statement by the juror may not be received on a matter about which the juror would be precluded from testifying.

As amended 1975, 1987, 2006.

Rule 607.

WHO MAY IMPEACH

The credibility of a witness may be attacked by any party, including the party calling the witness.

As amended 1987.

Rule 608.

EVIDENCE OF CHARACTER AND CONDUCT OF WITNESS

(a) Opinion and reputation evidence of character. The credibility of a witness may be attacked or supported by evidence in the form of opinion or reputation, but subject to these limitations: (1) the evidence may refer only to character for truthfulness or untruthfulness, and (2) evidence of truthful character is admissible only after the character of the witness for truthfulness has been attacked by opinion or reputation evidence or otherwise.

(b) Specific instances of conduct. Specific instances of the conduct of a witness, for the purpose of attacking or supporting the witness' character for truthfulness, other than conviction of crime as provided in rule 609, may not be proved by extrinsic evidence. They may, however, in the discretion of the court, if probative of truthfulness or untruthfulness, be inquired into on cross-examination of the witness (1) concerning the witness' character for truthfulness or untruthfulness, or (2) concerning the character for truthfulness or untruthfulness of another witness as to which character the witness being cross-examined has testified.

The giving of testimony, whether by an accused or by any other witness, does not operate as a waiver of the accused's or the witness' privilege against self-incrimination when examined with respect to matters that relate only to character for truthfulness.

As amended 1987, 1988, 2003.

Rule 609.

IMPEACHMENT BY EVIDENCE OF CONVICTION OF CRIME

(a) General rule. For the purpose of attacking the character for truthfulness of a witness,

(1) evidence that a witness other than an accused has been convicted of a crime shall be admitted, subject to Rule 403, if the crime was punishable by death or imprisonment in excess of one year under the law under which the witness was convicted, and evidence that an accused has been convicted of such a crime shall be admitted if the court determines that the probative value of admitting this evidence outweighs its prejudicial effect to the accused; and

(2) evidence that any witness has been convicted of a crime shall be admitted regardless of the punishment, if it readily can be determined that establishing the elements of the crime required proof or admission of an act of dishonesty or false statement by the witness.

(b) Time limit. Evidence of a conviction under this rule is not admissible if a period of more than ten years has elapsed since the date of the conviction or of the release of the witness from the confinement imposed for that conviction, whichever is the later date, unless the court determines, in the interests of justice, that the probative value of the conviction supported by specific facts and circumstances substantially outweighs its prejudicial effect. However, evidence of a conviction more than 10 years old as calculated herein, is not admissible unless the proponent gives to the adverse party sufficient advance written notice of intent to use such evidence to provide the adverse party with a fair opportunity to contest the use of such evidence.

(c) Effect of pardon, annulment, or certificate of rehabilitation. Evidence of a conviction is not admissible under this rule if (1) the conviction has been the subject of a pardon, annulment, certificate of rehabilitation, or other equivalent procedure based on a finding of the rehabilitation of the person convicted, and that person has not been convicted of a subsequent crime that was punishable by death or imprisonment in excess of one year, or (2) the conviction has been the subject of a pardon, annulment, or other equivalent procedure based on a finding of innocence.

(d) Juvenile adjudications. Evidence of juvenile adjudications is generally not admissible under this rule. The court may, however, in a criminal case allow evidence of a juvenile adjudication of a witness other than the accused if conviction of the offense would be admissible to attack the credibility of an adult and the court is satisfied that admission in evidence is necessary for a fair determination of the issue of guilt or innocence.

(e) Pendency of appeal. The pendency of an appeal therefrom does not render evidence of a conviction inadmissible. Evidence of the pendency of an appeal is admissible.

As amended 1987, 1990, 2006.

Rule 610.

RELIGIOUS BELIEFS OR OPINIONS

Evidence of the beliefs or opinions of a witness on matters of religion is not admissible for the purpose of showing that by reason of their nature the witness' credibility is impaired or enhanced.

As amended 1987.

Rule 611.

MODE AND ORDER OF INTERROGATION
AND PRESENTATION

(a) Control by court. The court shall exercise reasonable control over the mode and order of interrogating witnesses and presenting evidence so as to (1) make the interrogation and presentation effective for the ascertainment of the truth, (2) avoid needless consumption of time, and (3) protect witnesses from harassment or undue embarrassment.

(b) Scope of cross-examination. Cross-examination should be limited to the subject matter of the direct examination and matters affecting the credibility of the witness. The court may, in the exercise of discretion, permit inquiry into additional matters as if on direct examination.

(c) Leading questions. Leading questions should not be used on the direct examination of a witness except as may be necessary to develop the witness' testimony. Ordinarily leading questions should be permitted on cross-examination. When a party calls a hostile witness, an adverse party, or a witness identified with an adverse party, interrogation may be by leading questions.

As amended 1987.

Rule 612.

WRITING USED TO REFRESH MEMORY

Except as otherwise provided in criminal proceedings by section 3500 of title 18, United States Code, if a witness uses a writing to refresh memory for the purpose of testifying, either—

(1) while testifying, or

(2) before testifying, if the court in its discretion determines it is necessary in the interests of justice,

an adverse party is entitled to have the writing produced at the hearing, to inspect it, to cross-examine the witness thereon, and to introduce in evidence those portions which relate to the testimony of the witness. If it is claimed that the writing contains matters not related to the subject matter of the testimony the court shall examine the writing in camera, excise any portions not so related, and order delivery of the remainder to the party entitled thereto. Any portion withheld over objections shall be preserved and made available to the appellate court in the event of an appeal. If a writing is not produced or delivered pursuant to order under this rule, the court shall make any order justice requires, except that in criminal cases when the prosecution elects not to comply, the order shall be one striking the testimony or, if the court in its discretion determines that the interests of justice so require, declaring a mistrial.

As amended 1987.

Rule 613.

PRIOR STATEMENTS OF WITNESSES

(a) Examining witness concerning prior statement. In examining a witness concerning a prior statement made by the witness, whether written or not, the statement need not be shown nor its contents disclosed to the witness at that time, but on request the same shall be shown or disclosed to opposing counsel.

(b) Extrinsic evidence of prior inconsistent statement of witness. Extrinsic evidence of a prior inconsistent statement by a witness is not admissible unless the witness is afforded an opportunity to explain or deny the same and the opposite party is afforded an opportunity to interrogate the witness thereon, or the interests of justice otherwise require. This provision does not apply to admissions of a party-opponent as defined in rule 801(d)(2).

As amended 1987, 1988.

Rule 614.

CALLING AND INTERROGATION OF WITNESSES BY COURT

(a) Calling by court. The court may, on its own motion or at the suggestion of a party, call witnesses, and all parties are entitled to cross-examine witnesses thus called.

(b) Interrogation by court. The court may interrogate witnesses, whether called by itself or by a party.

(c) Objections. Objections to the calling of witnesses by the court or to interrogation by it may be made at the time or at the next available opportunity when the jury is not present.

Rule 615.

EXCLUSION OF WITNESSES

At the request of a party the court shall order witnesses excluded so that they cannot hear the testimony of other witnesses, and it may make the order of its own motion. This rule does not authorize exclusion of (1) a party who is a natural person, or (2) an officer or employee of a party which is not a natural person designated as its representative by its attorney, or (3) a person whose presence is shown by a party to be essential to the presentation of the party's cause, or (4) a person authorized by statute to be present.

As amended 1987, 1988, 1998.

ARTICLE VII.   OPINIONS AND EXPERT TESTIMONY

Rule 701.

OPINION TESTIMONY BY LAY WITNESSES

If the witness is not testifying as an expert, the witness' testimony in the form of opinions or inferences is limited to those opinions or inferences which are (a) rationally based on the perception of the witness, (b) helpful to a clear understanding of the witness' testimony or the determination of a fact in issue, and (c) not based on scientific, technical, or other specialized knowledge within the scope of Rule 702.

As amended 1987, 2000.

Rule 702.

TESTIMONY BY EXPERTS

If scientific, technical, or other specialized knowledge will assist the trier of fact to understand the evidence or to determine a fact in issue, a witness qualified as an expert by knowledge, skill, experience, training, or education, may testify thereto in the form of an opinion or otherwise, if (1) the testimony is based upon sufficient facts or data, (2) the testimony is the product of reliable principles and methods, and (3) the witness has applied the principles and methods reliably to the facts of the case.

As amended 2000.

Rule 703.

BASES OF OPINION TESTIMONY BY EXPERTS

The facts or data in the particular case upon which an expert bases an opinion or inference may be those perceived by or made known to the expert at or before the hearing. If of a type reasonably relied upon by experts in the particular field in forming opinions or inferences upon the subject, the facts or data need not be admissible in evidence in order for the opinion or inference to be admitted. Facts or data that are otherwise inadmissible shall not be disclosed to the jury by the proponent of the opinion or inference unless the court determines that their probative value in assisting the jury to evaluate the expert's opinion substantially outweighs their prejudicial effect.

As amended 1987, 2000.

Rule 704.

OPINION ON ULTIMATE ISSUE

(a) Except as provided in subdivision (b), testimony in the form of an opinion or inference otherwise admissible is not objectionable because it embraces an ultimate issue to be decided by the trier of fact.

(b) No expert witness testifying with respect to the mental state or condition of a defendant in a criminal case may state an opinion or inference as to whether the defendant did or did not have the mental state or condition constituting an element of the crime charged or of a defense thereto. Such ultimate issues are matters for the trier of fact alone.

As amended 1984.

Rule 705.

DISCLOSURE OF FACTS OR DATA UNDERLYING EXPERT OPINION

The expert may testify in terms of opinion or inference and give reasons therefor without first testifying to the underlying facts or data, unless the court requires otherwise. The expert may in any event be required to disclose the underlying facts or data on cross-examination.

As amended 1987, 1993.

Rule 706.

COURT APPOINTED EXPERTS

(a) Appointment. The court may on its own motion or on the motion of any party enter an order to show cause why expert witnesses should not be appointed, and may request the parties to submit nominations. The court may appoint any expert witnesses agreed upon by the parties, and may appoint expert witnesses of its own selection. An expert witness shall not be appointed by the court unless the witness consents to act. A witness so appointed shall be informed of the witness' duties by the court in writing, a copy of which shall be filed with the clerk, or at a conference in which the parties shall have opportunity to participate. A witness so appointed shall advise the parties of the witness' findings, if any; the witness' deposition may be taken by any party; and the witness may be called to testify by the court or any party. The witness shall be subject to cross-examination by each party, including a party calling the witness.

(b) Compensation. Expert witnesses so appointed are entitled to reasonable compensation in whatever sum the court may allow. The compensation thus fixed is payable from funds which may be provided by law in criminal cases and civil actions and proceedings involving just compensation under the fifth amendment. In other civil actions and proceedings the compensation shall be paid by the parties in such proportion and at such time as the court directs, and thereafter charged in like manner as other costs.

(c) Disclosure of appointment. In the exercise of its discretion, the court may authorize disclosure to the jury of the fact that the court appointed the expert witness.

(d) Parties' experts of own selection. Nothing in this rule limits the parties in calling expert witnesses of their own selection.

As amended 1987.

ARTICLE VIII. HEARSAY

Rule 801.

DEFINITIONS

The following definitions apply under this article:

(a) Statement. A "statement" is (1) an oral or written assertion or (2) nonverbal conduct of a person, if it is intended by the person as an assertion.

(b) Declarant. A "declarant" is a person who makes a statement.

(c) Hearsay. "Hearsay" is a statement, other than one made by the declarant while testifying at the trial or hearing, offered in evidence to prove the truth of the matter asserted.

(d) Statements which are not hearsay. A statement is not hearsay if—

(1) *Prior statement by witness.* The declarant testifies at the trial or hearing and is subject to cross-examination concerning the statement, and the statement is (A) inconsistent with the declarant's testimony, and was given under oath subject to the penalty of perjury at a trial, hearing, or other proceeding, or in a deposition, or (B) consistent with the declarant's testimony and is offered to rebut an express or implied charge against the declarant of recent fabrication or improper influence or motive, or (C) one of identification of a person made after perceiving the person; or

(2) *Admission by party-opponent.* The statement is offered against a party and is (A) the party's own statement, in either an individual or a representative capacity or (B) a statement of which the party has manifested an adoption or belief in its truth, or (C) a statement by a person authorized by the party to make a statement concerning the subject, or (D) a statement by the party's agent or servant concerning a matter within the scope of the agency or employment, made during the existence of the relationship, or (E) a statement by a coconspirator of a party during the course and in furtherance of the conspiracy. The contents of the statement shall be considered but are not alone sufficient to establish the declarant's authority under subdivision (C), the agency or employment relationship and scope thereof under subdivision (D), or the existence of the conspiracy and the participation therein of the declarant and the party against whom the statement is offered under subdivision (E).

As amended 1975, 1987, 1997.

Rule 802.

HEARSAY RULE

Hearsay is not admissible except as provided by these rules or by other rules prescribed by the Supreme Court pursuant to statutory authority or by Act of Congress.

Rule 803.

HEARSAY EXCEPTIONS; AVAILABILITY OF DECLARANT IMMATERIAL

The following are not excluded by the hearsay rule, even though the declarant is available as a witness:

(1) Present sense impression. A statement describing or explaining an event or condition made while the declarant was perceiving the event or condition, or immediately thereafter.

(2) Excited utterance. A statement relating to a startling event or condition made while the declarant was under the stress of excitement caused by the event or condition.

(3) Then existing mental, emotional, or physical condition. A statement of the declarant's then existing state of mind, emotion, sensation, or physical condition (such as intent, plan, motive, design, mental feeling, pain, and bodily health), but not including a statement of memory or belief to prove the fact remembered or believed unless it relates to the execution, revocation, identification, or terms of declarant's will.

(4) Statements for purposes of medical diagnosis or treatment. Statements made for purposes of medical diagnosis or treatment and describing medical history, or past or present symptoms, pain, or sensations, or the inception or general character of the cause or external source thereof insofar as reasonably pertinent to diagnosis or treatment.

(5) Recorded recollection. A memorandum or record concerning a matter about which a witness once had knowledge but now has insufficient recollection to enable the witness to testify fully and accurately, shown to have been made or adopted by the witness when the matter was fresh in the witness' memory and to reflect that knowledge correctly. If admitted, the memorandum or record may be read into evidence but may not itself be received as an exhibit unless offered by an adverse party.

(6) Records of regularly conducted activity. A memorandum, report, record, or data compilation, in any form, of acts, events, conditions, opinions, or diagnoses, made at or near the time by, or from information transmitted by, a person with knowledge, if kept in the course of a regularly conducted business activity and if it was the regular practice of that business activity to make the memorandum, report, record, or data compilation, all as shown by the testimony of the custodian or other qualified witness, or by certification that complies with Rule 902(11), Rule 902(12), or a statute permitting certification, unless the source of information or the method or circumstances of preparation indicate lack of trustworthiness. The term "business" as used in this paragraph includes business, institution, association, profession, occupation, and calling of every kind, whether or not conducted for profit.

(7) Absence of entry in records kept in accordance with the provisions of paragraph (6). Evidence that a matter is not included in the memoranda reports, records, or data compilations, in any form, kept in accordance with the provisions of paragraph (6), to prove the nonoccurrence or nonexistence of the matter, if the matter was of a kind of which a memorandum, report, record, or data compilation was regularly made and preserved, unless the sources of information or other circumstances indicate lack of trustworthiness.

(8) Public records and reports. Records, reports, statements, or data compilations, in any form, of public offices or agencies, setting forth (A) the activities of the office or agency, or (B) matters observed pursuant to duty imposed by law as to which matters there was a duty to report, excluding, however, in criminal cases matters observed by police officers and other law enforcement personnel, or (C) in civil actions and proceedings and against the Government in criminal cases, factual findings resulting from an investigation made pursuant to authority granted by law, unless the sources of information or other circumstances indicate lack of trustworthiness.

(9) Records of vital statistics. Records or data compilations, in any form, of births, fetal deaths, deaths, or marriages, if the report thereof was made to a public office pursuant to requirements of law.

(10) Absence of public record or entry. To prove the absence of a record, report, statement, or data compilation, in any form, or the nonoccurrence or nonexistence of a matter of which a record, report, statement, or data compilation, in any form, was regularly made and preserved by a public office or agency, evidence in the form of a certification in accordance with rule 902, or testimony, that diligent search failed to disclose the record, report, statement, or data compilation, or entry.

(11) Records of religious organizations. Statements of births, marriages, divorces, deaths, legitimacy, ancestry, relationship by blood or marriage, or other similar facts of personal or family history, contained in a regularly kept record of a religious organization.

(12) Marriage, baptismal, and similar certificates. Statements of fact contained in a certificate that the maker performed a marriage or other ceremony or administered a sacrament, made by a clergyman, public official, or other person authorized by the rules or practices of a religious organization or by law to perform the act certified, and purporting to have been issued at the time of the act or within a reasonable time thereafter.

(13) Family records. Statements of fact concerning personal or family history contained in family Bibles, genealogies, charts, engravings on rings, inscriptions on family portraits, engravings on urns, crypts, or tombstones, or the like.

(14) Records of documents affecting an interest in property. The record of a document purporting to establish or affect an interest in property, as proof of the content of the original recorded document and its execution and delivery by each person by whom it purports to have been executed, if the record is a record of a public office and an applicable statute authorizes the recording of documents of that kind in that office.

(15) Statements in documents affecting an interest in property. A statement contained in a document purporting to establish or affect an interest in property if the matter stated was relevant to the purpose of the document, unless dealings with the property since the document was made have been inconsistent with the truth of the statement or the purport of the document.

(16) Statements in ancient documents. Statements in a document in existence twenty years or more the authenticity of which is established.

(17) Market reports, commercial publications. Market quotations, tabulations, lists, directories, or other published compilations, generally used and relied upon by the public or by persons in particular occupations.

(18) Learned treatises. To the extent called to the attention of an expert witness upon cross-examination or relied upon by the expert witness in direct examination, statements contained in published treatises, periodicals, or pamphlets on a subject of history, medicine, or other science or art, established as a reliable authority by the testimony or admission of the witness or by other expert testimony or by judicial notice. If admitted, the statements may be read into evidence but may not be received as exhibits.

(19) Reputation concerning personal or family history.
Reputation among members of a person's family by blood, adoption,
or marriage, or among a person's associates, or in the community,
concerning a person's birth, adoption, marriage, divorce, death,
legitimacy, relationship by blood, adoption, or marriage, ancestry,
or other similar fact of personal or family history.

(20) Reputation concerning boundaries or general history.
Reputation in a community, arising before the controversy,
as to boundaries of or customs affecting lands in the community,
and reputation as to events of general history important to the
community or State or nation in which located.

(21) Reputation as to character. Reputation of a person's
character among associates or in the community.

(22) Judgment of previous conviction. Evidence of a final
judgment, entered after a trial or upon a plea of guilty (but not
upon a plea of nolo contendere), adjudging a person guilty of a
crime punishable by death or imprisonment in excess of one year,
to prove any fact essential to sustain the judgment, but not including, when offered by the Government in a criminal prosecution for
purposes other than impeachment, judgments against persons other
than the accused. The pendency of an appeal may be shown but
does not affect admissibility.

**(23) Judgment as to personal, family, or general histo-
ry, or boundaries.** Judgments as proof of matters of personal,
family or general history, or boundaries, essential to the judgment,
if the same would be provable by evidence of reputation.

(24) [Transferred to Rule 807]

As amended 1975, 1987, 1997, 2000.

Rule 804.

HEARSAY EXCEPTIONS; DECLARANT UNAVAILABLE

(a) Definition of unavailability. "Unavailability as a witness" includes situations in which the declarant—

(1) is exempted by ruling of the court on the ground of
privilege from testifying concerning the subject matter of the
declarant's statement; or

(2) persists in refusing to testify concerning the subject
matter of the declarant's statement despite an order of the
court to do so; or

(3) testifies to a lack of memory of the subject matter of
the declarant's statement; or

(4) is unable to be present or to testify at the hearing because of death or then existing physical or mental illness or infirmity; or

(5) is absent from the hearing and the proponent of a statement has been unable to procure the declarant's attendance (or in the case of a hearsay exception under subdivision (b)(2), (3), or (4), the declarant's attendance or testimony) by process or other reasonable means.

A declarant is not unavailable as a witness if exemption, refusal, claim of lack of memory, inability, or absence is due to the procurement or wrongdoing of the proponent of a statement for the purpose of preventing the witness from attending or testifying.

(b) Hearsay exceptions. The following are not excluded by the hearsay rule if the declarant is unavailable as a witness:

(1) *Former testimony.* Testimony given as a witness at another hearing of the same or a different proceeding, or in a deposition taken in compliance with law in the course of the same or another proceeding, if the party against whom the testimony is now offered, or, in a civil action or proceeding, a predecessor in interest, had an opportunity and similar motive to develop the testimony by direct, cross, or redirect examination.

(2) *Statement under belief of impending death.* In a prosecution for homicide or in a civil action or proceeding, a statement made by a declarant while believing that the declarant's death was imminent, concerning the cause or circumstances of what the declarant believed to be impending death.

(3) *Statement against interest.* A statement which was at the time of its making so far contrary to the declarant's pecuniary or proprietary interest, or so far tended to subject the declarant to civil or criminal liability, or to render invalid a claim by the declarant against another, that a reasonable person in the declarant's position would not have made the statement unless believing it to be true. A statement tending to expose the declarant to criminal liability and offered to exculpate the accused is not admissible unless corroborating circumstances clearly indicate the trustworthiness of the statement.

(4) *Statement of personal or family history.* (A) A statement concerning the declarant's own birth, adoption, marriage, divorce, legitimacy, relationship by blood, adoption, or marriage, ancestry, or other similar fact of personal or family history, even though declarant had no means of acquiring personal knowledge of the matter stated; or (B) a statement

concerning the foregoing matters, and death also, of another person, if the declarant was related to the other by blood, adoption, or marriage or was so intimately associated with the other's family as to be likely to have accurate information concerning the matter declared.

(5) [Transferred to Rule 807]

(6) *Forfeiture by wrongdoing.* A statement offered against a party that has engaged or acquiesced in wrongdoing that was intended to, and did, procure the unavailability of the declarant as a witness.

As amended 1975, 1987, 1988, 1997.

Rule 805.

HEARSAY WITHIN HEARSAY

Hearsay included within hearsay is not excluded under the hearsay rule if each part of the combined statements conforms with an exception to the hearsay rule provided in these rules.

Rule 806.

ATTACKING AND SUPPORTING CREDIBILITY OF DECLARANT

When a hearsay statement, or a statement defined in Rule 801(d)(2)(C), (D), or (E), has been admitted in evidence, the credibility of the declarant may be attacked, and if attacked may be supported, by any evidence which would be admissible for those purposes if declarant had testified as a witness. Evidence of a statement or conduct by the declarant at any time, inconsistent with the declarant's hearsay statement, is not subject to any requirement that the declarant may have been afforded an opportunity to deny or explain. If the party against whom a hearsay statement has been admitted calls the declarant as a witness, the party is entitled to examine the declarant on the statement as if under cross-examination.

As amended 1987, 1997.

Rule 807.

RESIDUAL EXCEPTION

A statement not specifically covered by Rule 803 or 804 but having equivalent circumstantial guarantees of trustworthiness, is not excluded by the hearsay rule, if the court determines that (A) the statement is offered as evidence of a material fact; (B) the statement is more probative on the point for which it is offered than any other evidence which the proponent can procure through reasonable efforts; and (C) the general purposes of these rules and the interests of justice will best be served by admission of the statement into evidence. However, a statement may not be admitted under this exception unless the proponent of it makes known to the adverse party sufficiently in advance of the trial or hearing to provide the adverse party with a fair opportunity to prepare to meet it, the proponent's intention to offer the statement and the particulars of it, including the name and address of the declarant.

Added 1997.

ARTICLE IX. AUTHENTICATION AND IDENTIFICATION

Rule 901.

REQUIREMENT OF AUTHENTICATION OR IDENTIFICATION

(a) General provision. The requirement of authentication or identification as a condition precedent to admissibility is satisfied by evidence sufficient to support a finding that the matter in question is what its proponent claims.

(b) Illustrations. By way of illustration only, and not by way of limitation, the following are examples of authentication or identification conforming with the requirements of this rule:

(1) Testimony of witness with knowledge. Testimony that a matter is what it is claimed to be.

(2) Nonexpert opinion on handwriting. Nonexpert opinion as to the genuineness of handwriting, based upon familiarity not acquired for purposes of the litigation.

(3) Comparison by trier or expert witness. Comparison by the trier of fact or by expert witnesses with specimens which have been authenticated.

(4) Distinctive characteristics and the like. Appearance, contents, substance, internal patterns, or other distinctive characteristics, taken in conjunction with circumstances.

(5) Voice identification. Identification of a voice, whether heard firsthand or through mechanical or electronic transmission or recording, by opinion based upon hearing the voice at any time under circumstances connecting it with the alleged speaker.

(6) Telephone conversations. Telephone conversations, by evidence that a call was made to the number assigned at the time by the telephone company to a particular person or business, if (A) in

the case of a person, circumstances, including self-identification, show the person answering to be the one called, or (B) in the case of a business, the call was made to a place of business and the conversation related to business reasonably transacted over the telephone.

(7) Public records or reports. Evidence that a writing authorized by law to be recorded or filed and in fact recorded or filed in a public office, or a purported public record, report, statement, or data compilation, in any form, is from the public office where items of this nature are kept.

(8) Ancient documents or data compilation. Evidence that a document or data compilation, in any form, (A) is in such condition as to create no suspicion concerning its authenticity, (B) was in a place where it, if authentic, would likely be, and (C) has been in existence 20 years or more at the time it is offered.

(9) Process or system. Evidence describing a process or system used to produce a result and showing that the process or system produces an accurate result.

(10) Methods provided by statute or rule. Any method of authentication or identification provided by Act of Congress or by other rules prescribed by the Supreme Court pursuant to statutory authority.

Rule 902.

SELF–AUTHENTICATION

Extrinsic evidence of authenticity as a condition precedent to admissibility is not required with respect to the following:

(1) Domestic public documents under seal. A document bearing a seal purporting to be that of the United States, or of any State, district, Commonwealth, territory, or insular possession thereof, or the Panama Canal Zone, or the Trust Territory of the Pacific Islands, or of a political subdivision, department, officer, or agency thereof, and a signature purporting to be an attestation or execution.

(2) Domestic public documents not under seal. A document purporting to bear the signature in the official capacity of an officer or employee of any entity included in paragraph (1) hereof, having no seal, if a public officer having a seal and having official duties in the district or political subdivision of the officer or employee certifies under seal that the signer has the official capacity and that the signature is genuine.

(3) Foreign public documents. A document purporting to be executed or attested in an official capacity by a person authorized by the laws of a foreign country to make the execution or attestation, and accompanied by a final certification as to the genuineness of the signature and official position (A) of the executing or attesting person, or (B) of any foreign official whose certificate of genuineness of signature and official position relates to the execution or attestation or is in a chain of certificates of genuineness of signature and official position relating to the execution or attestation. A final certification may be made by a secretary of an embassy or legation, consul general, consul, vice consul, or consular agent of the United States, or a diplomatic or consular official of the foreign country assigned or accredited to the United States. If reasonable opportunity has been given to all parties to investigate the authenticity and accuracy of official documents, the court may, for good cause shown, order that they be treated as presumptively authentic without final certification or permit them to be evidenced by an attested summary with or without final certification.

(4) Certified copies of public records. A copy of an official record or report or entry therein, or of a document authorized by law to be recorded or filed and actually recorded or filed in a public office, including data compilations in any form, certified as correct by the custodian or other person authorized to make the certification, by certificate complying with paragraph (1), (2), or (3) of this rule or complying with any Act of Congress or rule prescribed by the Supreme Court pursuant to statutory authority.

(5) Official publications. Books, pamphlets, or other publications purporting to be issued by public authority.

(6) Newspapers and periodicals. Printed materials purporting to be newspapers or periodicals.

(7) Trade inscriptions and the like. Inscriptions, signs, tags, or labels purporting to have been affixed in the course of business and indicating ownership, control, or origin.

(8) Acknowledged documents. Documents accompanied by a certificate of acknowledgment executed in the manner provided by law by a notary public or other officer authorized by law to take acknowledgments.

(9) Commercial paper and related documents. Commercial paper, signatures thereon, and documents relating thereto to the extent provided by general commercial law.

(10) Presumptions under Acts of Congress. Any signature, document, or other matter declared by Act of Congress to be presumptively or prima facie genuine or authentic.

(11) Certified domestic records of regularly conducted activity. The original or a duplicate of a domestic record of regularly conducted activity that would be admissible under Rule

803(6) if accompanied by a written declaration of its custodian or other qualified person, in a manner complying with any Act of Congress or rule prescribed by the Supreme Court pursuant to statutory authority, certifying that the record—

    (A) was made at or near the time of the occurrence of the matters set forth by, or from information transmitted by, a person with knowledge of those matters;

    (B) was kept in the course of the regularly conducted activity; and

    (C) was made by the regularly conducted activity as a regular practice.

A party intending to offer a record into evidence under this paragraph must provide written notice of that intention to all adverse parties, and must make the record and declaration available for inspection sufficiently in advance of their offer into evidence to provide an adverse party with a fair opportunity to challenge them.

(12) Certified foreign records of regularly conducted activity. In a civil case, the original or a duplicate of a foreign record of regularly conducted activity that would be admissible under Rule 803(6) if accompanied by a written declaration by its custodian or other qualified person certifying that the record—

    (A) was made at or near the time of the occurrence of the matters set forth by, or from information transmitted by, a person with knowledge of those matters;

    (B) was kept in the course of the regularly conducted activity; and

    (C) was made by the regularly conducted activity as a regular practice.

The declaration must be signed in a manner that, if falsely made, would subject the maker to criminal penalty under the laws of the country where the declaration is signed. A party intending to offer a record into evidence under this paragraph must provide written notice of that intention to all adverse parties, and must make the record and declaration available for inspection sufficiently in advance of their offer into evidence to provide an adverse party with a fair opportunity to challenge them.

As amended 1987, 1988, 2000.

Rule 903.

SUBSCRIBING WITNESS' TESTIMONY UNNECESSARY

The testimony of a subscribing witness is not necessary to authenticate a writing unless required by the laws of the jurisdiction whose laws govern the validity of the writing.

ARTICLE X. CONTENTS OF WRITINGS,
RECORDINGS, AND PHOTOGRAPHS

Rule 1001.

DEFINITIONS

For purposes of this article the following definitions are applicable:

(1) Writings and recordings. "Writings" and "recordings" consist of letters, words, or numbers, or their equivalent, set down by handwriting, typewriting, printing, photostating, photographing, magnetic impulse, mechanical or electronic recording, or other form of data compilation.

(2) Photographs. "Photographs" include still photographs, X-ray films, video tapes, and motion pictures.

(3) Original. An "original" of a writing or recording is the writing or recording itself or any counterpart intended to have the same effect by a person executing or issuing it. An "original" of a photograph includes the negative or any print therefrom. If data are stored in a computer or similar device, any printout or other output readable by sight, shown to reflect the data accurately, is an "original."

(4) Duplicate. A "duplicate" is a counterpart produced by the same impression as the original, or from the same matrix, or by means of photography, including enlargements and miniatures, or by mechanical or electronic re-recording, or by chemical reproduction, or by other equivalent techniques which accurately reproduces the original.

Rule 1002.

REQUIREMENT OF ORIGINAL

To prove the content of a writing, recording, or photograph, the original writing, recording, or photograph is required, except as otherwise provided in these rules or by Act of Congress.

Rule 1003.

ADMISSIBILITY OF DUPLICATES

A duplicate is admissible to the same extent as an original unless (1) a genuine question is raised as to the authenticity of the original or (2) in the circumstances it would be unfair to admit the duplicate in lieu of the original.

Rule 1004.

ADMISSIBILITY OF OTHER EVIDENCE OF CONTENTS

The original is not required, and other evidence of the contents of a writing, recording, or photograph is admissible if—

(1) Originals lost or destroyed. All originals are lost or have been destroyed, unless the proponent lost or destroyed them in bad faith; or

(2) Original not obtainable. No original can be obtained by any available judicial process or procedure; or

(3) Original in possession of opponent. At a time when an original was under the control of the party against whom offered, that party was put on notice, by the pleadings or otherwise, that the contents would be a subject of proof at the hearing, and that party does not produce the original at the hearing; or

(4) Collateral matters. The writing, recording, or photograph is not closely related to a controlling issue.

As amended 1987.

Rule 1005.

PUBLIC RECORDS

The contents of an official record, or of a document authorized to be recorded or filed and actually recorded or filed, including data compilations in any form, if otherwise admissible, may be proved by copy, certified as correct in accordance with rule 902 or testified to be correct by a witness who has compared it with the original. If a copy which complies with the foregoing cannot be obtained by the exercise of reasonable diligence, then other evidence of the contents may be given.

Rule 1006.

SUMMARIES

The contents of voluminous writings, recordings, or photographs which cannot conveniently be examined in court may be presented in the form of a chart, summary, or calculation. The originals, or duplicates, shall be made available for examination or copying, or both, by other parties at reasonable time and place. The court may order that they be produced in court.

Rule 1007.

TESTIMONY OR WRITTEN ADMISSION OF PARTY

Contents of writings, recordings, or photographs may be proved by the testimony or deposition of the party against whom offered or by that party's written admission, without accounting for the nonproduction of the original.

As amended 1987.

Rule 1008.

FUNCTIONS OF COURT AND JURY

When the admissibility of other evidence of contents of writings, recordings, or photographs under these rules depends upon the fulfillment of a condition of fact, the question whether the condition has been fulfilled is ordinarily for the court to determine in accordance with the provisions of rule 104. However, when an issue is raised (a) whether the asserted writing ever existed, or (b) whether another writing, recording, or photograph produced at the trial is the original, or (c) whether other evidence of contents correctly reflects the contents, the issue is for the trier of fact to determine as in the case of other issues of fact.

ARTICLE XI. MISCELLANEOUS RULES

Rule 1101.

APPLICABILITY OF RULES

(a) **Courts and judges.** These rules apply to the United States district courts, the District Court of Guam, the District Court of the Virgin Islands, the District Court for the Northern Mariana Islands, the United States courts of appeals, the United States Claims Court, and to United States bankruptcy judges and United States magistrate judges, in the actions, cases, and proceedings and to the extent hereinafter set forth. The terms "judge" and "court" in these rules include United States bankruptcy judges and United States magistrate judges.

(b) **Proceedings generally.** These rules apply generally to civil actions and proceedings, including admiralty and maritime cases, to criminal cases and proceedings, to contempt proceedings except those in which the court may act summarily, and to proceedings and cases under title 11, United States Code.

(c) **Rule of privilege.** The rule with respect to privileges applies at all stages of all actions, cases, and proceedings.

(d) Rules inapplicable. The rules (other than with respect to privileges) do not apply in the following situations:

(1) *Preliminary questions of fact.* The determination of questions of fact preliminary to admissibility of evidence when the issue is to be determined by the court under rule 104.

(2) *Grand jury.* Proceedings before grand juries.

(3) *Miscellaneous proceedings.* Proceedings for extradition or rendition; preliminary examinations in criminal cases; sentencing, or granting or revoking probation; issuance of warrants for arrest, criminal summonses, and search warrants; and proceedings with respect to release on bail or otherwise.

(e) Rules applicable in part. In the following proceedings these rules apply to the extent that matters of evidence are not provided for in the statutes which govern procedure therein or in other rules prescribed by the Supreme Court pursuant to statutory authority: the trial of misdemeanors and other petty offenses before United States magistrate judges; review of agency actions when the facts are subject to trial de novo under section 706(2)(F) of title 5, United States Code; review of orders of the Secretary of Agriculture under section 2 of the Act entitled "An Act to authorize association of producers of agricultural products" approved February 18, 1922 (7 U.S.C. 292), and under sections 6 and 7(c) of the Perishable Agricultural Commodities Act, 1930 (7 U.S.C. 499f, 499g(c)); naturalization and revocation of naturalization under sections 310–318 of the Immigration and Nationality Act (8 U.S.C. 1421–1429); prize proceedings in admiralty under sections 7651–7681 of title 10, United States Code; review of orders of the Secretary of the Interior under section 2 of the Act entitled "An Act authorizing associations of producers of aquatic products" approved June 25, 1934 (15 U.S.C. 522); review of orders of petroleum control boards under section 5 of the Act entitled "An Act to regulate interstate and foreign commerce in petroleum and its products by prohibiting the shipment in such commerce of petroleum and its products produced in violation of State law, and for other purposes", approved February 22, 1935 (15 U.S.C. 715d); actions for fines, penalties, or forfeitures under part V of title IV of the Tariff Act of 1930 (19 U.S.C. 1581–1624), or under the Anti-Smuggling Act (19 U.S.C. 1701–1711); criminal libel for condemnation, exclusion of imports, or other proceedings under the Federal Food, Drug, and Cosmetic Act (21 U.S.C. 301–392); disputes between seamen under sections 4079, 4080, and 4081 of the Revised Statutes (22 U.S.C. 256–258); habeas corpus under sections 2241–2254 of title 28, United States Code; motions to vacate, set aside or correct sentence under section 2255 of title 28, United States Code; actions for penalties for refusal to transport destitute seamen under section 4578 of the Revised Statutes (46 U.S.C. 679); actions against the United States under the Act entitled "An Act authorizing suits against the United States in admiralty for damage caused by and salvage service rendered to public vessels belonging to the United States, and for other purposes", approved March 3, 1925 (46 U.S.C. 781–790), as implemented by section 7730 of title 10, United States Code.

As amended 1975, 1979, 1982, 1987, 1988, 1993.

Rule 1102.

AMENDMENTS

Amendments to the Federal Rules of Evidence may be made as provided in section 2072 of title 28 of the United States Code. As amended 1991.

Rule 1103.

TITLE

These rules may be known and cited as the Federal Rules of Evidence.

———

[The Act of Congress of January 2, 1975, Pub.L. 93–595, § 1, 88 Stat. 1926, stated that the rules therein set forth, to be known as the Federal Rules of Evidence, "shall take effect on the one hundred and eightieth day beginning after the date of the enactment of this Act. These rules apply to actions, cases, and proceedings brought after the rules take effect. These rules also apply to further procedure in actions, cases, and proceedings then pending, except to the extent that application of the rules would not be feasible, or would work injustice, in which event former evidentiary principles apply." The Rules became effective July 1, 1975. For legislative history, see Michael H. Graham, Handbook of Federal Evidence.]

———

[Rule 801(d) was amended October 16, 1975, Pub.L. 94–113, § 1, 89 Stat. 576, to be effective October 31, 1975.]

———

[Technical corrections to Rules 606(b), 803(23), 804(b), and 1101(e), and an amendment to Rule 410, were made December 12, 1975, Pub.L. 94–149, § 1, 89 Stat. 805.]

———

[Rule 412 was added October 28, 1978, Pub.L. 95–540, § 2, 92 Stat. 2046, to be effective November 28, 1978.]

————

[Rule 1101(a) and (b) was amended November 6, 1978, Pub.L. 95–598, Title II, § 251, 92 Stat. 2673, to be effective October 1, 1979.]

————

[Rule 410 was amended by the order of the Supreme Court of April 30, 1979. 441 U.S. 1005. The effective date of this amendment was delayed by Congress July 31, 1979, Pub.L. 96–42, 93 Stat. 326, until December 1, 1980.]

————

[Rule 1101(a) was amended April 2, 1982, Pub.L. 97–164, Title I, § 142, 96 Stat. 45, to be effective October 1, 1982.]

————

[Rule 704 was amended October 12, 1984, Pub.L. 98–473, Title II, § 406, 98 Stat. 2067.]

————

[Rules 101 and 1101(a) were amended, and gender-specific language was neutralized in numerous Rules, by the order of the Supreme Court of March 2, 1987, to be effective October 1, 1987. 480 U.S. 1023.]

————

[Technical corrections to Rules 101, 602, 608(b), 613(b), 615, 902(3), and 1101(a) and (e) were made by the order of the Supreme Court of April 25, 1988, to be effective November 1, 1988. 485 U.S. 1049.]

————

[Rules 412, 804(a), and 1101(a) were amended November 18, 1988, Pub.L. 100–690, Title VII, §§ 7046, 7075, 102 Stat. 4400, 4405.]

————

[Rule 609(a) was amended by the order of the Supreme Court of January 26, 1990, to be effective December 1, 1990. 493 U.S. 1173.]

————

[Rules 404(b) and 1102 were amended by the order of the Supreme Court of April 30, 1991, to be effective December 1, 1991. 500 U.S. 1001.]

[Rules 101, 705, and 1101(a) and (e) were amended by the order of the Supreme Court of April 22, 1993, to be effective December 1, 1993. 507 U.S. 1187.]

[Rule 412 was amended September 13, 1994, Pub.L. 103–322, Title IV, § 40141(b), 108 Stat. 1919, to be effective December 1, 1994.]

[Rules 413, 414, and 415 were added September 13, 1994, Pub.L. 103–322, Title XXXII, § 320935(a), 108 Stat. 2135, to be effective July 9, 1995.]

[Rules 407, 801(d), 803(24), 804(b), and 806 were amended, and Rule 807 added, by the order of the Supreme Court of April 11, 1997, to be effective December 1, 1997. 520 U.S. 1323.]

[Rule 615 was amended by the order of the Supreme Court of April 24, 1998, to be effective December 1, 1998. 523 U.S. 1235.]

[Rules 103(a), 404(a), 701, 702, 703, 803(6), and 902 were amended by the order of the Supreme Court of April 17, 2000, to be effective December 1, 2000. 529 U.S. 1189.]

[Rule 608(b) was amended by the order of the Supreme Court of March 27, 2003, to be effective December 1, 2003. 538 U.S. 1097.]

[Rules 404(a), 408, 606(b), and 609(a) and (c) were amended by the order of the Supreme Court of April 12, 2006, to be effective December 1, 2006. 547 U.S. 1281.]

[Rule 502 was added September 19, 2008, Pub.L. 110–322, § 1, 122 Stat. 3537.]

LOCAL RULES OF PRACTICE FOR THE UNITED STATES DISTRICT COURT FOR THE NORTHERN DISTRICT OF NEW YORK

SECTION I. SCOPE OF THE RULES— ONE FORM OF ACTION

1.1 Scope of the Rules

(a) Title and Citation. These are the Local Rules of Practice for the United States District Court for the Northern District of New York. They shall be cited as "L.R. . . ."

(b) Effective Date; Transitional Provision. These Rules became effective on **December 1, 2009**. Recent amendments are noted with the phrase (Amended December 1, 2009). [Notations omitted in this version.]

(c) Scope of the Rules; Construction. These Rules supplement the Federal Rules of Civil and Criminal Procedure. They shall be construed to be consistent with those Rules and to promote the just, efficient and economical determination of every action and proceeding.

(d) Sanctions and Penalties for Noncompliance. Failure of an attorney or of a party to comply with any provision of these Rules, General Orders of this District, Orders of the Court, or the Federal Rules of Civil or Criminal Procedure shall be a ground for imposition of sanctions.

(e) Definitions.

1. The word "court," except where the context otherwise requires, refers to the United States District Court for the Northern District of New York.

2. The word "judge" refers either to a United States District Judge or to a United States Magistrate Judge.

3.   The words "assigned judge," except where the context otherwise requires, refer to the United States District Judge or United States Magistrate Judge exercising jurisdiction with respect to a particular action or proceeding.

4.   The words "Chief Judge" refer to the Chief Judge or a judge temporarily performing the duties of Chief Judge under 28 U.S.C. § 136(e).

5.   The word "clerk" refers to the Clerk of the Court or to a deputy clerk whom the Clerk designates to perform services of the general class provided for in Fed. R. Civ. P. 77.

6.   The word "marshal" refers to the United States Marshal of this District and includes deputy marshals.

7.   The word "party" includes a party's representative.

8.   Reference in these Rules to an attorney for a party is in no way intended to preclude a party from appearing pro se, in which case reference to an attorney applies to the pro se litigant.

9.   Where appropriate the "singular" shall include the "plural" and vice versa.

1.2   Availability of the Local Rules

Copies of these Rules are available from the Clerk's office or at the Court's webpage at "www.nynd.uscourts.gov."

2.1   One Form of Action

[Reserved.]

SECTION II.   COMMENCEMENT OF ACTION; SERVICE OF PROCESS, PLEADINGS, MOTIONS AND ORDERS

3.1   Civil Cover Sheet

A completed civil cover sheet on a form available from the Clerk shall be submitted with every complaint, notice of removal, or other document initiating a civil action. This requirement is solely for administrative purposes, and matters appearing on the civil cover sheet have no legal effect in the action.

3.2   Venue

The Court's Civil Case Assignment Plan shall control venue for civil cases filed in the Northern District of New York.

3.3   Complex and Multi-district Litigation

(a) If the assigned judge determines, in his or her discretion, that the case is of such a complex nature that it cannot reasonably be trial ready within eighteen months from the date the complaint is filed, the assigned judge may design and issue a particularized case management order that will move the case to trial as quickly as the complexity of the case allows.

(b) The parties shall promptly notify the Court in writing if any action commenced is appropriate for multi-district litigation.

4.1 Service of Process

(a) Service shall be made in the manner specified in the Federal Rules of Civil Procedure or as required or permitted by statute. The party seeking service of papers shall be responsible for arranging the service. The Clerk is authorized to sign orders appointing persons to serve process.

(b) Upon the filing of a complaint, the Clerk shall issue to the plaintiff General Order 25 which requires, among other things, service of process upon all defendants within sixty (60) days of the filing of the complaint. This expedited service requirement is necessary to ensure adequate time for pretrial discovery and motion practice. In no event shall service of process be completed after the time specified in Fed. R. Civ. P. 4.

(c) At the time the complaint or notice of removal is served, the party seeking to invoke the jurisdiction of this Court shall also serve on all parties the following materials:

    1. Judicial Case Assignment Form;

    2. Joint Civil Case Management Plan Containing Notice of Initial Pretrial Conference;

    3. Notice and Consent Form to Proceed Before a United States Magistrate Judge; and

    4. Notice and Consent Form for the Court Sponsored Alternative Dispute Resolution Procedures.

The Clerk shall furnish these materials to the party seeking to invoke the jurisdiction of the Court at the time the complaint or notice of removal is filed.

5.1 Service and Filing of Papers

(a) All pleadings and other papers shall be served and filed in accordance with the Federal Rules of Civil Procedure and shall be in the form prescribed by L.R. 10.1. The party or its designee shall declare, by affidavit or certification, that it has provided all other parties in the action with all documents it has filed with the Court. See also L.R. 26.2 (discovery material).

(b) In civil actions where the Court has directed a party to submit an order or judgment, that party shall file all such orders or judgments in duplicate, and the Clerk's entry of such duplicate in the proper record book shall be deemed in compliance with Fed. R. Civ. P. 79(b). Such party shall also furnish the Clerk with a sufficient number of additional copies for each party to the action, which the Clerk shall mail with notice of entry in accordance with Fed. R. Civ. P. 77(d).

(c) In a civil action, upon filing a notice of appeal, the appellant shall furnish the Clerk with a sufficient number of copies for mailing in accordance with Fed. R. App. P. 3(d).

(d) Upon filing of a motion pursuant to Fed. R. Civ. P. 65.1, the moving party shall furnish the Clerk with a sufficient number of copies of the motion and notice of the motion in compliance with the mailing provision of that rule.

(e) No paper on file in the Clerk's office shall be removed except pursuant to the Court's order.

(f) All civil complaints submitted to the Clerk for filing shall be accompanied by a summons or, if electing to serve by mail, the approved service by mail forms, together with sufficient copies of the complaint for service on each of the named defendants.

(g) A private process server shall serve every summons, except as otherwise required by statute or rule or as the Court directs for good cause shown. A private process server is any person authorized to serve process in an action brought in the New York State Supreme Court or in the court of general jurisdiction of the State in which service is made.

(h) In the case of a prisoner's civil rights action, or any action where a party has been granted leave to proceed in forma pauperis, the Marshal shall serve the summons and complaint by regular mail pursuant to Fed. R. Civ. P. 4(c)(2). The Marshal shall file the return or other acknowledgment of service with the Court. The return shall constitute prima facie evidence of the service of process. If no acknowledgment of service is filed with the Court, the Marshal shall notify the plaintiff; and, if the plaintiff so requests, the Marshal shall make personal service as provided in Fed. R. Civ. P. 4.

5.1.2 Electronic Case Filing

All cases filed in this Court may be assigned to the Electronic Case Files System ("ECF") in accordance with the Procedural Order on Electronic Case Filing (General Order #22), the provisions of which are incorporated herein by reference, and which the Court may amend from time to time. Copies of General Order #22 are available at the Clerk's office or at the Court's webpage at "www.nynd.uscourts.gov."

5.2 Prepayment of Fees

(a) Filing Fees. A party commencing an action or removing an action from a state court must pay to the Clerk the statutory filing fee before the case will be docketed and process issued. Title 28 U.S.C. § 1915 and L.R. 5.4 govern in forma pauperis proceedings.

(b) Miscellaneous Fees. The Clerk is not required to render any service for which a fee is prescribed by statute or by the Judicial Conference of the United States unless the fee for the service is paid in advance.

5.3 Schedule of Fees

Fee schedules are available at the Clerk's office or at the Court's webpage at "www.nynd.uscourts.gov."

5.4 Civil Actions Filed In Forma Pauperis; Applications for Leave to Proceed In Forma Pauperis

(a) On receipt of a complaint or petition and an application to proceed in forma pauperis, and supporting documentation as required for prisoner litigants, the Clerk shall promptly file the complaint or petition without the payment of fees and assign the action in accordance with L.R. 40.1. The Clerk shall then forward the complaint or petition, application and supporting documentation to the assigned judicial officer for a determination of the in forma pauperis application and the sufficiency of the complaint or petition and, if appropriate, to direct service by the Marshal. Prior to the Marshal serving process pursuant to 28 U.S.C. § 1915(d) and L.R. 5.1(h), the Court shall review all actions filed pursuant to 28 U.S.C. § 1915(g) to determine whether sua sponte dismissal is appropriate. The granting of an in forma pauperis application shall not relieve a party of the obligation to pay all other fees for which that party is responsible regarding the action, including but not limited to copying and/or witness fees.

(b) Whenever a fee is due for a civil action subject to the Prison Litigation Reform Act ("PLRA"), the prisoner must comply with the following procedure:

1.(A) Submit a signed, fully completed and properly certified in forma pauperis application; and

(B) Submit the authorization form issued by the Clerk's office.

2.(A)(i) If the prisoner **has not** fully complied with the requirements set forth in paragraph 1 above, and the action is not subject to sua sponte dismissal, a judicial officer shall, by Court order, inform the prisoner about what he or she must submit in order to proceed with such action in this District ("Order").

(ii) The Order shall afford the prisoner **thirty (30) days** in which to comply with the terms of same. If the prisoner fails to comply fully with the terms of such Order within such period of time, the Court shall dismiss the action.

(B) If the prisoner **has** fully complied with the requirements set forth in paragraph 1 above, and the action is not subject to sua sponte dismissal, the judicial officer shall review the in forma pauperis application. The granting of the application shall in no way relieve the prisoner of the obligation to pay the full amount of the filing fee.

3.   After being notified of the filing of the civil action, the agency having custody of the prisoner shall comply with the provisions of 28 U.S.C. § 1915(b) regarding the filing fee due for the action.

5.5   Filing by Facsimile

Neither the Court nor the Clerk's Office will accept for filing any facsimile transmission without prior authorization from the Court. The party using facsimile transmission to file its papers must accompany any such documents with a cover letter stating that the Court authorized such transmission and the date on which the Court provided that authorization. Violations of this Rule subject the offending party to the Court's full disciplinary powers.

5.6   Service of the Writ in Exclusion and Deportation Cases

(a) After delivery of an alien for deportation to the master of a ship or the commanding officer of an airplane, the writ shall be addressed to, and served on, the master or commanding officer only. Notice to the respondent of the allowance or issuance of the writ shall not be recognized as binding without proper service. Service shall be made by delivery of the original writ to the respondent while the alien is in custody. Service shall not be made on a master after a ship has cast off her moorings.

(b) In case the writ is served on the master of a ship or on the commanding officer of an airplane, such person may deliver the alien at once to the officer from whom such person received the alien for custody until the return day. In such case, the writ shall be deemed returnable promptly; and the custody of the officer receiving the alien shall be deemed that of the respondent, pending disposition of the writ.

5.7 Documents to Be Provided to the Clerk

All pretrial and settlement conference statements shall be provided to the Clerk but not filed. These documents are not for public view. Forms for preparation of pretrial and settlement conference statements are available from the Clerk's office or at the Court's webpage at "www.nynd.uscourts.gov."

6.1 Calculation of Time Periods

[Reserved.]

SECTION III. PLEADINGS AND MOTIONS

7.1 Motion Practice

Introduction—Motion Dates and Times. Unless the Court directs otherwise, the moving party shall make its motion returnable at the **next regularly scheduled motion date at least thirty-one days from the date the moving party files and serves its motion**. The moving party shall select a return date in accordance with the procedures set forth in subdivision (b). If the return date the moving party selects is not the next regularly scheduled motion date, or if the moving party selects no return date, the Clerk will set the proper return date and notify the parties.

Information regarding motion dates and times is specified on the case assignment form that the Court provides to the parties at the commencement of the litigation or the parties may obtain this form from the Clerk's office or at the Court's webpage at "www.nynd.uscourts.gov."

The Court hereby directs the Clerk to set a proper return date in motions that pro se litigants submit for filing that do not specify a return date or fail to allow for sufficient time pursuant to this Rule. Generally, the return date that the Clerk selects should not exceed 30 days from the date of filing. Furthermore, the Clerk shall forward a copy of the revised or corrected notice of motion to the parties.

(a) Papers Required. Except as otherwise provided in this paragraph, all motions and opposition to motions require a memorandum of law, supporting affidavit, and proof of service on all the parties. See L.R. 5.1(a). Additional requirements for specific types of motions, including cross-motions, see L.R. 7.1(c), are set forth in this Rule.

    1. *Memorandum of Law.* No party shall file or serve a memorandum of law that exceeds twenty-five (25) pages in length, unless that party obtains leave of the judge hearing the

motion *prior to filing*. All memoranda of law shall contain a table of contents and, wherever possible, parallel citations. Memoranda of law that contain citations to decisions exclusively reported on computerized databases, e.g., Westlaw, Lexis, Juris, shall include copies of those decisions.

When a moving party makes a motion based upon a rule or statute, the moving party must specify in its moving papers the rule or statute upon which it bases its motion.

A memorandum of law is required for all motions except the following:

(A) a motion pursuant to Fed. R. Civ. P. 12(e) for a more definite statement;

(B) a motion pursuant to Fed. R. Civ. P. 15 to amend or supplement a pleading;

(C) a motion pursuant to Fed. R. Civ. P. 17 to appoint next friend or guardian ad litem;

(D) a motion pursuant to Fed. R. Civ. P. 25 for substitution of parties;

(E) a motion pursuant to Fed. R. Civ. P. 37 to compel discovery; and

(F) a motion pursuant to Fed. R. Civ. P. 55 for default.

2. *Affidavit.* An affidavit must not contain legal arguments but must contain factual and procedural background that is relevant to the motion the affidavit supports.

An affidavit is required for all motions except the following:

(A) a motion pursuant to Fed. R. Civ. P. 12(b)(6) for failure to state a claim upon which relief can be granted;

(B) a motion pursuant to Fed. R. Civ. P. 12(c) for judgment on the pleadings; and

(C) a motion pursuant to Fed. R. Civ. P. 12(f) to strike a portion of a pleading.

3. *Summary Judgment Motions.* Any motion for summary judgment shall contain a Statement of Material Facts. The Statement of Material Facts shall set forth, in numbered paragraphs, each material fact about which the moving party contends there exists no genuine issue. Each fact listed shall set forth a specific citation to the record where the fact is established. The record for purposes of the Statement of Material Facts includes the pleadings, depositions, answers to interrogatories, admissions and affidavits. It does not, however,

include attorney's affidavits. *Failure of the moving party to submit an accurate and complete Statement of Material Facts shall result in a denial of the motion.*

The moving party shall also advise pro se litigants about the consequences of their failure to respond to a motion for summary judgment. See also L.R. 56.2.

The opposing party shall file a response to the Statement of Material Facts. The non-movant's response shall mirror the movant's Statement of Material Facts by admitting and/or denying each of the movant's assertions in matching numbered paragraphs. Each denial shall set forth a specific citation to the record where the factual issue arises. The non-movant's response may also set forth any additional material facts that the non-movant contends are in dispute in separately numbered paragraphs. The Court shall deem admitted *any facts set forth in the Statement of Material Facts that the opposing party does not specifically controvert.*

4. *Motions to Amend or Supplement Pleadings or for Joinder or Interpleader.* A party moving to amend a pleading pursuant to Fed. R. Civ. P. 14, 15, 19–22 must attach an unsigned copy of the proposed amended pleading to its motion papers. Except if the Court otherwise orders, the proposed amended pleading must be a complete pleading, which will supersede the original pleading in all respects. A party shall not incorporate any portion of its prior pleading into the proposed amended pleading by reference.

The motion must set forth specifically the proposed amendments and identify the amendments in the proposed pleading, either through the submission of a red-lined version of the original pleading or other equivalent means.

Where a party seeks leave to supplement a pleading pursuant to Fed. R. Civ. P. 15(d), the party must limit the proposed supplemental pleading to transactions or occurrences or events which have occurred since the date of the pleading that the party seeks to supplement. The party must number the paragraphs in the proposed pleading consecutively to the paragraphs contained in the pleading that it seeks to supplement. In addition to the pleading requirements set forth above, the party requesting leave to supplement must set forth specifically the proposed supplements and identify the supplements in the proposed pleading, either through the submission of a red-lined version of the original pleading or other equivalent means.

Caveat: The granting of the motion does not constitute the filing of the amended pleading. After the Court grants leave, unless the Court otherwise orders, the moving party must file and serve the original signed amended pleading within fourteen (14) days of the Order granting the motion.

(b) Motions.

1. *Dispositive Motions.* The moving party must file all motion papers with the Court and serve them upon the other parties not less than THIRTY–ONE DAYS prior to the return date of the motion. The Notice of Motion must state the return date that the moving party has selected.

The party opposing the motion must file its opposition papers with the Court and serve them upon the other parties not less than SEVENTEEN DAYS prior to the return date of the motion.

The moving party must file its reply papers, which may not exceed ten (10) pages, with the Court and serve them upon the other parties not less than ELEVEN DAYS prior to the return date of the motion.

A surreply is not permitted.

Parties shall file all original motion papers, including memoranda of law and supporting affidavits, if any, in accordance with the Administrative Procedures for Electronic Case Filing (General Order #22) and/or the case assignment form provided to the parties at the commencement of the litigation. The parties need not provide a courtesy copy of their motion papers to the assigned judge unless the assigned judge requests a copy.

2. *Non-Dispositive Motions.* Prior to making any non-dispositive motion before the assigned Magistrate Judge, the parties must make **good faith efforts among themselves to resolve or reduce all differences relating to the non-dispositive issue**. If, after conferring, the parties are unable to arrive at a mutually satisfactory resolution, the party seeking relief must then request a court conference with the assigned Magistrate Judge.

A court conference is a prerequisite to filing a non-dispositive motion before the assigned Magistrate Judge. In the Notice of Motion, the moving party is required to set forth the date that the court conference with the Magistrate Judge was held regarding the issues being presented in the motion. Failure to include this information in the Notice of Motion may result in the Court rejecting the motion papers.

Actions which involve an incarcerated, pro se party are not subject to the requirement that a court conference be held prior to filing a non-dispositive motion.

Unless the Court orders otherwise, the moving party must file all motion papers with the Court and serve them upon the other parties not less than THIRTY–ONE DAYS prior to the return date of the motion.

The party opposing the motion must file its opposition papers with the Court and serve them upon the other parties not less than SEVENTEEN DAYS prior to the return date of the motion.

Reply papers and adjournments are not permitted without the Court's prior permission.

3. *Failure to Timely File or Comply.* The Court shall not consider any papers required under this Rule that are not timely filed or are otherwise not in compliance with this Rule unless good cause is shown. Where a properly filed motion is unopposed and the Court determines that the moving party has met its burden to demonstrate entitlement to the relief requested therein, the non-moving party's failure to file or serve any papers as this Rule requires shall be deemed as consent to the granting or denial of the motion, as the case may be, unless good cause is shown.

Any party who does not intend to oppose a motion, or a movant who does not intend to pursue a motion, shall promptly notify the Court and the other parties of such intention. They should provide such notice at the earliest practicable date, but in any event no less than FOURTEEN DAYS prior to the scheduled return date of the motion, unless for good cause shown. **Failure to comply with this Rule may result in the Court imposing sanctions.**

(c) Cross–Motions. A party may file and serve cross-motions at the time it files and serves its opposition papers to the original motion, i.e., not less than SEVENTEEN DAYS prior to the return date of the motion. If a party makes a cross-motion, it must join its cross-motion brief with its opposition brief, and this combined brief may not exceed twenty-five (25) pages in length, exclusive of exhibits. A separate brief in opposition to the original motion is not permissible.

The original moving party may reply in further support of the original motion and in opposition to the cross-motion with a reply/opposition brief that does not exceed twenty-five (25) pages in length, exclusive of exhibits. The original moving party must file its reply/opposition papers with the Court and serve them on the other parties not less than ELEVEN DAYS prior to the return date of the original motion.

The cross-moving party may not reply in further support of its cross-motion without the Court's prior permission.

(d) Discovery Motions. The following steps are required prior to making any discovery motion pursuant to Rules 26 through 37 of the Federal Rules of Civil Procedure.

1. Parties must make good faith efforts among themselves to resolve or reduce all differences relating to discovery prior to seeking court intervention.

2. The moving party must confer in detail with the opposing party concerning the discovery issues between them in a good faith effort to eliminate or reduce the area of controversy and to arrive at a mutually satisfactory resolution. Failure to do so may result in denial of a motion to compel discovery and/or imposition of sanctions.

3. If the parties' conference does not fully resolve the discovery issues, the party seeking relief must then request a court conference with the assigned Magistrate Judge. Incarcerated, pro se parties are not subject to the court conference requirement prior to filing a motion to compel discovery. The assigned Magistrate Judge may direct the party making the request for a court conference to file an affidavit setting forth the date(s) and mode(s) of the consultation(s) with the opposing party and a letter that concisely sets forth the nature of the dispute and a specific listing of each of the items of discovery sought or opposed. Immediately following each disputed item, the party must set forth the reason why the Court should allow or disallow that item.

4. Following a request for a discovery conference, the Court may schedule a conference and advise all parties of a date and time. The assigned Magistrate Judge may, in his or her discretion, conduct the discovery conference by telephone conference call, initiated by the party making the request for the conference, by video conference, or by personal appearance.

5. Following a discovery conference, the Court may direct the prevailing party to submit a proposed order on notice to the other parties.

6. If a party fails or refuses to confer in good faith with the requesting party, thus requiring the request for a discovery conference, the Court, at its discretion, may subject the resisting party to the sanction of the imposition of costs, including the attorney's fees of the opposing party in accordance with Fed. R. Civ. P. 37.

7. A party claiming privilege with respect to a communication or other item must specifically identify the privilege and the grounds for the claimed privilege. The parties may not make any generalized claims of privilege.

8. The parties shall file any motion to compel discovery that these Rules authorize no later than FOURTEEN DAYS after the discovery cut-off date. See L.R. 16.2. A party shall

accompany any motion that it files pursuant to Fed. R. Civ. P. 37 with the discovery materials to which the motion relates if the parties have not previously filed those materials with the Court.

(e) Order to Show Cause. All motions that a party brings by Order to Show Cause shall conform to the requirements set forth in L.R. 7.1(a)(1) and (2). **Immediately after filing an Order to Show Cause, the moving party must telephone the Chambers of the presiding judicial officer and inform Chambers staff that it has filed an Order to Show Cause.** Parties may obtain the telephone numbers for all Chambers from the Clerk's office or at the Court's webpage at "www.nynd.uscourts.gov." The Court shall determine the briefing schedule and return date applicable to motions brought by Order to Show Cause.

In addition to the requirements set forth in Local Rule 7.1(a)(1) and (2), a motion brought by Order to Show Cause must include an affidavit clearly and specifically showing good and sufficient cause why the standard Notice of Motion procedure cannot be used. The moving party must give reasonable advance notice of the application for an Order to Show Cause to the other parties, except in those circumstances where the movant can demonstrate, in a detailed and specific affidavit, good cause and substantial prejudice that would result from the requirement of reasonable notice.

An Order to Show Cause must contain a space for the assigned judge to set forth (a) the deadline for filing and serving supporting papers, (b) the deadline for filing and serving opposing papers, and (c) the date and time for the hearing.

(f) Temporary Restraining Order. A party may seek a temporary restraining order by Notice of Motion or Order to Show Cause, as appropriate. Filing procedures and requirements for supporting documents are the same as set forth in this Rule for other motions. The moving party must serve any application for a temporary restraining order on all other parties unless Fed. R. Civ. P. 65 otherwise permits. L.R. 7.1(b)(2) governs motions for injunctive relief, other than those brought by Order to Show Cause. L.R. 7.1(e) governs motions brought by Order to Show Cause.

(g) Motion for Reconsideration. Unless Fed. R. Civ. P. 60 otherwise governs, a party may file and serve a motion for reconsideration or reargument no later than FOURTEEN DAYS after the entry of the challenged judgment, order, or decree. All motions for reconsideration shall conform with the requirements set forth in L.R. 7.1(a)(1) and (2). The briefing schedule and return date applicable to motions for reconsideration shall conform to L.R. 7.1(b)(2). A motion for reconsideration of a Magistrate Judge's determination of a non-dispositive matter shall toll the fourteen

(14) day time period to file objections pursuant to L.R. 72.1(b). The Court will decide motions for reconsideration or reargument on submission of the papers without oral argument, unless the Court directs otherwise.

(h) Oral Argument. The parties shall appear for oral argument on all motions that they make returnable before a district court judge, except motions for reconsideration, on the scheduled return date of the motion. In the district court judge's discretion, or on consideration of a request of any party, the district court judge may dispose of a motion without oral argument. Thus, the parties should be prepared to have their motion papers serve as the sole method of argument on the motion.

The parties shall not appear for oral argument on motions that they make returnable before a Magistrate Judge on the scheduled return date of the motion unless the Magistrate Judge sua sponte directs or grants the request of any party for oral argument.

(i) Sanctions for Vexatious or Frivolous Motions or Failure to Comply with this Rule. A party who presents vexatious or frivolous motion papers or fails to comply with this Rule is subject to discipline as the Court deems appropriate, including sanctions and the imposition of costs and attorney's fees to the opposing party.

(j) Adjournments of Dispositive Motions. After the moving party files and serves its motion papers requesting dispositive relief, but before the time that the opposing party must file and serve its opposing papers, the parties may agree to an adjournment of the return date for the motion. However, any such adjournment may not be for more than **THIRTY-ONE DAYS** from the return date that the moving party selected. In addition, the parties may agree to new dates for the filing and service of opposition and reply papers. However, the parties must file all papers with the Court and serve them upon the other parties not less than **ELEVEN DAYS** prior to the newly selected return date of the motion. If the parties agree to such an adjournment, they must file a letter with the Court stating the following: (1) that they have agreed to an adjournment of the return date for the motion, (2) the new return date, (3) the date on which the opposing party must file and serve its opposition papers, and (4) the date on which the moving party must file and serve its reply papers. The parties may not agree to any further adjournment.

If one of the parties seeks an adjournment of not more than **THIRTY-ONE DAYS** from the return date that the moving party selected, but the other parties will not agree to such an adjournment, the party seeking the adjournment must file a letter request with the Court and serve the same upon the other parties, stating the following: (1) that the parties cannot agree to an adjournment, (2) the reason that the party is seeking the adjournment, and (3) the suggested return date for the motion. Within three days of receiving this letter request, the parties who have not agreed to an adjournment may file a letter with the Court and serve the same upon the other parties, setting forth the reasons that they do not agree to the requested adjournment. The Court will then take the request under advisement and, as soon as practicable, will enter an order granting or denying the request and, if granting the request, will set forth new dates for the filing and serving of opposition and reply papers.

If any party seeks an adjournment of the return date that is more than **THIRTY-ONE DAYS** from the return date that the moving party selected, that party must file a letter request with the Court stating the following: (1) why the party needs a longer adjournment and (2) a suggested return date for the motion. The Court will grant such an adjournment only upon a showing of exceptional circumstances. In the alternative or if the Court denies the request for an adjournment, the moving party may **withdraw its motion without prejudice** to refile at a later date. The moving party must refile its motion within the time frame set in the Uniform Pretrial Scheduling Order unless either the assigned District Judge or the assigned Magistrate Judge has granted an extension of the motion-filing deadline.

8.1 Personal Privacy Protection

Parties shall refrain from including, or shall redact where inclusion is necessary, the following personal identifiers from all pleadings that they file with the Court, including exhibits thereto, whether filed electronically or in paper form, unless the Court orders otherwise.

1. *Social security numbers.* If an individual's social security number must be included in a document, use only the last four digits of that number.

2. *Names of minor children.* If the involvement of a minor child must be mentioned, use only the initials of that child.

3. *Dates of birth.* If an individual's date of birth must be included in a document, use only the year.

4. *Financial account numbers.* If financial account numbers are relevant, use only the last four digits of those numbers.

5. *Home Addresses.* If a home address must be used, use only the City and State.

In addition, caution shall be exercised when filing documents that contain the following:

1. personal identifying number, such as a driver's license number;

2. medical records, treatment and diagnosis;

3. employment history;

4. individual financial information; and

5. proprietary or trade secret information.

In compliance with the E–Government Act of 2002, a party wishing to file a document containing the personal data identifiers listed above may

1. file an unredacted version of the document under seal, or

2. file a reference list under seal. The reference list shall contain the complete personal data identifier(s) and the redacted identifier(s) used in its(their) place in the filing. All references in the case to the redacted identifiers included in the reference list will be construed to refer to the corresponding complete personal data identifier. The reference list must be filed under seal and may be amended as of right.

Counsel is strongly urged to discuss this issue with all their clients so that they can make an informed decision about the inclusion of certain information. The responsibility for redacting these personal identifiers **rests solely with counsel and the parties**. The Clerk will not review each pleading for compliance with this Rule. Counsel and the parties are cautioned that failure to redact these personal identifiers may subject them to the Court's full disciplinary power.

Exception: Transcripts of the administrative record in social security proceedings and state-court records relating to a habeas corpus petitions are exempt from this requirement.

9.1   Request for Three–Judge Court

Whenever a party believes that only a three-judge court may grant the relief requested in a lawsuit, the party shall include the words "Three–Judge Court," or the equivalent, immediately following the title of the first pleading in which the party asserts the cause of action requesting a three-judge court. Unless the basis for the request is apparent from the pleading, the party shall set forth the basis for the request in the pleading or in an attached statement. On the convening of a three-judge court, in addition to the original papers on file, the parties shall make the following documents available to the Clerk for distribution: three copies of the pleadings, three copies of the motion papers, and three copies of all memoranda of law.

9.2 Requirement to File a Civil RICO Statement

In any action in which a party asserts a claim under the Racketeer Influenced and Corrupt Organizations Act ("RICO"), 18 U.S.C. § 1961 et seq., the party asserting such a claim shall file a RICO statement within thirty (30) days of the filing of the pleading containing such claim. This statement shall conform to the format that the Court has adopted and shall be entitled "RICO Statement." Parties may obtain copies of General Order #14—CIVIL RICO STATEMENT FILING REQUIREMENTS from the Clerk's office or at the Court's webpage at "www.nynd.uscourts.gov." This statement shall state in detail and with specificity the information requested in the RICO Statement. The Court shall construe the RICO Statement as an amendment to the pleadings.

10.1 Form of Papers

(a) Form Generally. All pleadings, motions, and other documents that a party presents for filing, whether in paper form or in electronic form, shall meet the following requirements:

1. all text, whether in the body of the document or in footnotes, must be a minimum of 12 point type

2. all documents must have one-inch margins on all four sides of the page

3. all text in the body of the document must be double-spaced

4. the text in block quotations and footnotes may be single-spaced

5. extensive footnotes must not be used to circumvent page limitations

6. compacted or other compressed printing features must not be used

7. pages must be consecutively numbered

(b) Additional requirements for all pleadings, motions, and other documents that a party presents for filing in paper form:

1. all documents must be on 8½ x 11 inch white paper of good quality

2. all text must be plainly and legibly written, typewritten, printed or reproduced without erasures or interlineations materially defacing them

3. all documents must be in black or blue ink

    4. pages of all documents must be stapled (or in some other way fastened) together

    5. all documents must be single-sided

    6. the Court, at its discretion, may require the electronic submission of any document in a WordPerfect-compatible format

The Court may reject documents that do not comply with the above-listed requirements.

(c) Information required. The following information must appear on each document that a party files.

    1. A caption, which must include the title of the Court, the title of the action, the civil action number of the case, the initials of the assigned judge(s), and the name or nature of the paper in sufficient detail for identification. **The parties must separately caption affidavits and declarations and *must not* physically attach them to the Notice of Motion or Memorandum of Law.**

    2. Each document must identify the person filing the document. This identification must include an original signature of the attorney or pro se litigant; the typewritten name of that person; the address of a pro se litigant; and the bar roll number, office address, telephone number, e-mail address and fax number of the attorney. **All attorneys of record and pro se litigants must immediately notify the Court of any change of address.** Parties must file the notice of change of address with the Clerk and serve the same on all other parties to the action. The notice must identify each and every action to which the notice applies.

    Attorneys shall update their e-mail address, telephone or fax number through CM/ECF within fourteen (14) days of a change. Detailed instructions are available on the Court's website, http://www.nynd.uscourts.gov/. Attorneys shall notify the Court within fourteen (14) days of any change to their mailing address by completing the automated Update My Information form located on the Court's website: http://www.nynd.uscourts.gov/e-filingregistration/procform13.cfm.

    Failure to keep this information current will result in removal from the roll of the Court.

(d) The record on hearings, unless ordered printed, shall be plainly typewritten and bound in book form, paginated and indexed.

(e) The Court conducts its reviews and deliberations in English. Unless otherwise directed by the Court, any document that a party transmits to the Court (including one in the record on appeal) that is in a language other than English must be accompanied by an English translation that the translator has certified as true and accurate, pursuant to 28 U.S.C. § 1746. Any party who disputes a translation must file notice of its intention to challenge the translation with the Court and all other parties within seven (7) days of receiving the Notice of Electronic Filing for the translation, or, if a non-Filing User, within seven (7) days of receiving the translation. Upon receipt of a notice to challenge a translation, the Court shall establish the procedure and applicable time periods for the challenge to be heard.

11.1 Signing of Pleadings, Motions, and Other Papers; Sanctions

[Reserved.]

12.1 Defenses and Objections—How Presented

[Reserved.]

13.1 Counterclaims and Cross-Claims

[Reserved.]

14.1 Impleader

See L.R. 7.1(a)(4).

15.1 Form of a Motion to Amend and Its Supporting Documentation

See L.R. 7.1(a)(4).

16.1 Civil Case Management

This Court has found that the interests of justice are most effectively served by adopting a systematic, differential case management system that tailors the level of individualized and case-specific management to such criteria as case complexity, time required to prepare a case for trial, and availability of judicial and other resources.

(a) Filing of Complaint/Service of Process. Upon the filing of a complaint, the Clerk shall issue to the plaintiff General Order 25, which requires, among other things, service of process upon all defendants within sixty (60) days of the filing of the complaint. This expedited service requirement is necessary to ensure adequate time for pretrial discovery and motion practice.

(b) Assignment of District Judge/Magistrate Judge. Immediately upon the filing of a civil action, the Clerk shall assign the action or proceeding to a District Judge and may also assign the action or proceeding to a Magistrate Judge pursuant to the Court's assignment plan. When a civil action is assigned to a Magistrate Judge, the Magistrate Judge shall conduct proceedings in accordance with these Rules and 28 U.S.C. § 636 as directed by the District Judge. Once assigned, either judicial officer shall have authority to design and issue a case management order.

(c) Initial Pretrial Conference. Except for cases excluded under section II of General Order 25, an initial pretrial conference pursuant to Fed. R. Civ. P. 16 shall be held within 120 days after the filing of the complaint. The Clerk shall set the date of this conference upon the filing of the complaint. The purpose of this conference is to prepare and adopt a case-specific management plan which will be memorialized in a case management order. See subsection (d) below. In order to facilitate the adoption of such a plan, prior to the scheduled conference, counsel for all parties shall confer among themselves as Fed. R. Civ. P. 26(f) requires and shall use the Civil Case Management Plan form contained in the General Order 25 filing packet. The parties shall file their jointly-proposed plan, or if they cannot reach consensus, each party shall file its own proposed plan with the Clerk at least fourteen (14) business days prior to the scheduled pretrial conference.

(d) Subject Matter of Initial Pretrial Conference. At the initial pretrial conference, the Court shall consider, and the parties shall be prepared to discuss, the following:

1. Deadlines for joinder of parties, amendment of pleadings, completion of discovery, and filing of dispositive motions;

2. Trial date;

3. Requests for jury trial;

4. Subject matter and personal jurisdiction;

5. Factual and legal bases for claims and defenses;

6. Factual and legal issues in dispute;

7. Factual and legal issues upon which the parties can agree or which they can narrow through motion practice and which will expedite resolution of the dispute;

8. Specific relief requested, including method for computing damages;

9. Intended discovery and proposed methods to limit and/or decrease time and expense thereof;

10. Suitability of case for voluntary arbitration;

11. Measures for reducing length of trial;

12. Related cases pending before this or other U.S. District Courts;

13. Procedures for certifying class actions, if appropriate;

14. Settlement prospects; and

15. If the case is in the ADR track, choice of ADR method and estimated time for completion of ADR.

(e) Uniform Pretrial Scheduling Order. Upon completion of the initial pretrial conference, the presiding judge may issue a Uniform Pretrial Scheduling Order setting forth deadlines for joinder of parties, amendment of pleadings, production of expert reports, completion of discovery, and filing of motions; a trial ready date; the requirements for all trial submissions; and if an ADR track case, the ADR method to be used and the deadline for completion of ADR.

(f) Enforcement of Deadlines. The Court shall strictly enforce any deadlines that it establishes in any case management order, and the Court shall not modify these, even upon stipulation of the parties, except upon a showing of good cause.

16.2 Discovery Cut–Off

The "discovery cut-off" is that date by which all responses to written discovery, including requests for admissions, shall be due according to the Federal Rules of Civil Procedure and by which all depositions shall be concluded. Counsel are advised to initiate discovery requests and notice depositions sufficiently in advance of the cut-off date to comply with this Rule. Discovery requests that call for responses or scheduled depositions after the discovery cut-off will not be enforceable except by order of the Court for good cause shown. Parties shall file and serve motions to compel discovery no later than fourteen (14) days after the discovery cut-off. See L.R. 7.1(d)(8).

SECTION IV.   PARTIES

17.1   Actions by or on Behalf of Infants and/or Incompetents

(a) An action by or on behalf of an infant or incompetent shall not be settled or compromised, or voluntarily discontinued, dismissed or terminated, without leave of the Court embodied in an order, judgment or decree. The proceedings on an application to settle or compromise such an action shall conform to the New York State statutes and rules; but the Court, for good cause shown, may dispense with any New York State requirement.

(b) The Court shall authorize payment of a reasonable attorney's fee and proper disbursements from the amount recovered in such an action, whether realized by settlement, execution or otherwise, and shall determine the fee and disbursements after due inquiry as to all charges against the amount recovered.

(c) The Court shall order the balance of the proceeds of the recovery or settlement to be distributed as it deems will best protect the interest of the infant or incompetent.

18.1 Joinder of Claims and Remedies

See L.R. 7.1(a)(4).

19.1 Joinder of Persons Necessary for Just Adjudication

See L.R. 7.1(a)(4).

20.1 Permissive Joinder of Parties

See L.R. 7.1(a)(4).

21.1 Misjoinder and Nonjoinder of Parties

See L.R. 7.1(a)(4).

22.1 Interpleader

[Reserved.]

23.1 Designation of "Class Action" in the Caption

(a) If a party seeks to maintain a case as a class action pursuant to Fed. R. Civ. P. 23, the party shall include the words "Class Action" in the complaint or other pleading asserting a class action.

(b) The plaintiff also shall check the appropriate box on the Civil Cover Sheet at the time of filing the action.

23.2 Certification of a Class Action

As soon as practicable after the commencement of an action designated as a "Class Action," the plaintiff shall file a motion, with the assigned district judge, seeking an order of the Court determining that the plaintiff may maintain the action as a class action.

24.1 Intervention

[Reserved.]

25.1 Substitution of Parties

[Reserved.]

SECTION V. DEPOSITIONS AND DISCOVERY

26.1 Form of Certain Discovery Documents

The parties shall number each interrogatory or request sequentially, regardless of the number of sets of interrogatories or requests. In answering or objecting to interrogatories, requests for admission, or requests to produce or inspect, the responding party shall first state verbatim the propounded interrogatory or request and immediately thereafter the answer or objection.

26.2 Filing Discovery

Parties shall not file notices to take depositions, transcripts of depositions, interrogatories, requests for documents, requests for admissions, disclosures, and answers and responses to these notices and requests unless the Court orders otherwise; provided, however, that a party shall file any discovery material that it expects to use at trial or to support any motion, including a motion to compel or for summary judgment prior to the trial or motion return date. A party shall include with any motion pursuant to Fed. R. Civ. P. 37 the discovery materials to which the motion relates if the parties have not previously filed those materials with the Court.

26.3 Production of Expert Witness Information

There shall be binding disclosure of the identity of expert witnesses. The parties shall make such disclosure, including a curriculum vitae and, unless waived by the other parties, service of the expert's written report pursuant to Fed. R. Civ. P. 26(a)(2)(B), before the completion of discovery in accordance with the deadlines contained in the Uniform Pretrial Scheduling Order or any other Court order. Failure to comply with these deadlines may result in the imposition of sanctions, including the preclusion of testimony, pursuant to Fed. R. Civ. P. 16(f).

If a party expects to call a treating physician as a witness, the party must identify the treating physician in accordance with the timetable provided in the Uniform Pretrial Scheduling Order or other Court order.

26.4 Timing of Discovery

Fed. R. Civ. P. 26(d), which prohibits discovery prior to a meeting and conference between the parties, and Fed. R. Civ. P. 26(f), which directs parties to meet and confer with each other relative to the nature and basis of claims and defenses to a lawsuit, shall not apply to any action in which a party is incarcerated.

27.1 Depositions Before Action or Pending Appeal

[Reserved.]

28.1 Persons Before Whom Depositions Shall Be Taken

[Reserved.]

29.1 Discovery Stipulations

See L.R. 16.1(f); 16.2.

30.1 Depositions

Unless the Court orders otherwise pursuant to Fed. R. Civ. P. 5(d) and 26(c), transcripts of depositions when received and filed by the Clerk, shall then be opened by the Clerk who shall affix the filing stamp to the cover page of the transcripts. See L.R. 26.2.

31.1 Depositions on Written Questions

[Reserved.]

32.1 Use of Depositions in Court Proceedings

[Reserved.]

33.1 Interrogatories

[Reserved.]

34.1 Production of Documents and Things

[Reserved.]

35.1 Physical and Mental Examination of Persons

[Reserved.]

36.1 Requests for Admission

[Reserved.]

37.1 Form of Discovery Motions

See L.R. 7.1(d).

SECTION VI. TRIALS

38.1 Notation of "Jury Demand" in the Pleading

(a) If a party demands a jury trial as Fed. R. Civ. P. 38(b) permits, the party shall place a notation on the front page of the initial pleading which that party signed, stating "Demand for Jury Trial" or an equivalent statement. This notation shall serve as a sufficient demand under Fed. R. Civ. P. 38(b).

(b) In cases removed from state court, a party may file a "Demand for Jury Trial" that is separate from the initial pleading. See Fed. R. Civ. P. 81.3; L.R. 81.3.

39.1 Opening Statements and Closing Arguments

The Court will determine the time to be allotted for opening and closing arguments.

39.2 Submission of Pretrial Papers

The parties shall file all pretrial submissions in accordance with the requirements of the Uniform Pretrial Scheduling Order unless the Court orders otherwise.

40.1 Case Assignment System

Immediately upon the filing of a civil action or proceeding, the Clerk shall assign the action or proceeding to a District Judge and may also assign the action or proceeding to a Magistrate Judge pursuant to the Court's Assignment Plan. When a civil action or proceeding is assigned to a Magistrate Judge, the Magistrate Judge shall conduct proceedings in accordance with these Rules and 28 U.S.C. § 636 as directed by the District Judge. See General Order #12.

40.2 Preferences

Only the following causes shall be entitled to preferences:

1. Issues in bankruptcy framed by an answer to a bankruptcy petition which are triable by a jury;

2. Causes entitled to a preference under any statute of the United States;

3. Causes restored to the calendar for a new trial by the setting aside of a former verdict, by reversal of a former judgment, or after a mistrial;

4. Causes to which a receiver appointed by any court or a trustee or debtor-in-possession in a bankruptcy proceeding is a party;

5. Causes which, in the discretion of the assigned judge, are entitled to a preference for meritorious reasons.

Preferences shall be obtained only by order of the Court on seven-days notice of the application.

40.3 Trial Calendar

The trial calendar number shall be the same as the docket number. No note of issue is required. Each judge shall dispose of cases as the law and the effective administration of justice require.

41.1 Settlements, Apportionments and Allowances in Wrongful Death Actions

In an action for wrongful death,

1. The Court shall apportion the proceeds of the action only where required by statute;

2. The Court shall approve a settlement only in a case covered by subdivision 1; and

3. The Court shall approve an attorney's fee only upon application in accordance with the provisions of the Judiciary Law of the State of New York.

41.2 Dismissal of Actions

(a) Each judge shall from time to time notice for hearing on a dismissal calendar such actions or proceedings assigned to that judge which appear not to have been diligently prosecuted. Whenever it appears that the plaintiff has failed to prosecute an action or proceeding diligently, the assigned judge shall order it dismissed. In the absence of an order by the assigned judge or magistrate judge setting any date for any pretrial proceeding or for trial, the plaintiff's failure to take action for four (4) months shall be presumptive evidence of lack of prosecution. Unless the assigned judge or magistrate judge otherwise orders, each party shall, not less than fourteen (14) days prior to the noticed hearing date, serve and file a certificate setting forth the status of the action or proceeding and whether good cause exists to dismiss it for failure to prosecute. The parties need not appear in person. No explanations communicated in person, over the telephone, or by letter shall be acceptable. If a party fails to respond as this Rule requires, the Court shall issue a written order dismissing the case for failure to prosecute or providing for sanctions or making other directives to the parties as justice requires. Nothing in this Rule shall preclude any party from filing a motion to dismiss an action or proceeding for failure to prosecute under Fed. R. Civ. P. 41(b).

(b) Failure to notify the Court of a change of address in accordance with L.R. 10.1(c)(2) may result in the dismissal of any pending action.

41.3 Actions Dismissed by Stipulation

Stipulations of dismissal shall be signed by each attorney and/or pro se litigant appearing in the action. Any action which is submitted for dismissal by stipulation of the parties shall contain the following language, if applicable: "That no party hereto is an infant or incompetent." For actions involving an infant or incompetent, see L.R. 17.1.

42.1 Separation of Issues in Civil Suits

[Reserved.]

43.1 Examination of Witnesses

[Reserved.]

44.1 Official Records

[Reserved.]

45.1 Subpoenas

See Fed. R. Civ. P. 45.

46.1 Exceptions to Rulings

[Reserved.]

47.1 Grand and Petit Jurors

Grand and petit jurors to serve at stated and special sessions of the Court shall be summoned pursuant to the Jury Selection and Service Act of 1968, as amended, codified in Sections 1861–1867 of Title 28 of the United States Code, and the Plan adopted and approved by the judges of this Court and approved by the Judicial Council for the Court of Appeals for the Second Circuit. The selection of grand and petit jurors is made by random selection from voter registration lists and supplemented by, if available, lists of licensed drivers from the New York State Department of Motor Vehicles. Court sessions, pursuant to 28 U.S.C. § 112, are designated to be held in the Northern District of New York in the cities of Albany, Auburn, Binghamton, Malone, Syracuse, Utica, Watertown and Plattsburgh. For jury selection purposes under § 1869(c) of the Act, this District is divided into divisions from which jurors are selected for the particular place where jury sessions are to be held. The divisions are as follows:

1. ALBANY DIVISION: Albany, Columbia, Greene, Rensselaer, Saratoga, Schenectady, Schoharie, Ulster, Warren and Washington Counties.

2. BINGHAMTON DIVISION: Broome, Chenango, Delaware, Otsego and Tioga Counties.

3. SYRACUSE–AUBURN DIVISION: Cayuga, Cortland, Madison, Onondaga, Oswego, and Tompkins Counties.

4. UTICA DIVISION: Fulton, Hamilton, Herkimer, Montgomery and Oneida Counties.

5. WATERTOWN DIVISION: Jefferson, Lewis and St. Lawrence Counties.

6. MALONE/PLATTSBURGH DIVISION: Clinton, Essex and Franklin Counties.

A copy of the Plan for the NDNY for Random Selection of Grand and Petit Jurors, is available upon request at the Clerk's office or on the Court's webpage at "www.nynd.uscourts.gov."

47.2 Jury Selection

(a) Voir Dire. The Court, the attorneys, or both shall conduct voir dire examination as the Court shall determine. The Court, in its sound discretion, may limit the attorneys' examination in time and subject matter.

(b) Impanelment of the Jury. In its discretion, the Court shall impanel the jury by use of either the "Strike" or "Jury Box" selection method unless the Court determines otherwise.

(c) Peremptory Challenges. Unless the Court orders otherwise, all parties shall alternately exercise their peremptory challenges.

(d) Waiver of Peremptory Challenges. Except when using the strike method, if a party passes or refuses to exercise a peremptory challenge, such action shall constitute a waiver of the right to exercise the challenge.

(e) Names of Potential Jurors During Voir Dire. During the voir dire process, unless otherwise directed by the presiding judicial officer, potential jurors shall be referred to by their assigned juror number. Should an issue develop where the name of the potential juror is germane, the requesting party shall submit a written request to the presiding judicial officer for release of the potential juror's name.

47.3   Assessment of Juror Costs

Whenever any civil action scheduled for jury trial is postponed, settled or otherwise disposed of in advance of the actual trial, then, except for good cause shown, all juror costs, including marshal's fees, mileage and per diem, shall be assessed against the parties and/or their attorneys as the Court directs, unless the parties or their attorneys notify the Court and the Clerk's office at least one full business day prior to the day on which the action is scheduled for trial, so that the Clerk has time to advise the jurors that it shall not be necessary for them to attend. The parties may request an advance estimate of costs from the Clerk.

47.4   Jury Deliberation

Availability of Attorneys During Jury Deliberations. Attorneys shall be available on short notice during jury deliberations in the event of a verdict or a question by the jury. Attorneys shall keep the Clerk informed as to where they will be at all times when the jury is deliberating. Attorneys should not leave the building without the presiding judge's prior approval.

47.5   Jury Contact Prohibition

The following rules apply in connection with contact between attorneys or parties and jurors.

1.   At any time after the Court has called a jury panel from which jurors shall be selected to try cases for a term of Court fixed by the presiding judge or otherwise impaneled, no party or attorney, or anyone associated with the party or the

attorney, shall have any communication or contact by any means or manner with any juror until such time as the panel of jurors has been excused and the term of court ended.

2. This prohibition is designed to prevent all unauthorized contact between attorneys or parties and jurors and does not apply when authorized by the judge while court is in session or when otherwise authorized by the presiding judge.

48.1 Number of Jurors

In civil cases, the Court shall determine the number of jurors, which shall not be less than six nor more than twelve.

49.1 Special Verdicts and Interrogatories

[Reserved.]

50.1 Judgment as a Matter of Law in Actions Tried by Jury; Alternative Motion for New Trial; Conditional Rulings

[Reserved.]

51.1 Instructions to the Jury

When Submitted and Served. See Uniform Pretrial Scheduling Order issued by the court following the initial pretrial conference. See L.R. 16.1(e).

52.1 Proposed Findings in Civil Cases

(a) In civil non-jury trials, each party shall submit proposed findings of fact and conclusions of law sufficiently detailed that, if the Court adopts them, would form an adequate factual basis, supported by anticipated evidence, for the resolution of the case and the entry of judgment.

(b) When Submitted and Served. See Uniform Pretrial Scheduling Order issued by the Court following the initial pretrial conference. See L.R. 16.1(e).

53.1 Masters

[Reserved]

53.2 Master's Fees

The Court, in its discretion, shall fix the compensation of masters. Factors the Court shall consider include expended hours, disbursements, the relative complexity of the matter, and whether the parties have previously consented to a reasonable rate of compensation. The compensation and disbursements shall be paid and taxed as costs in the manner and amounts that the Court directs unless the parties stipulate otherwise.

53.3 Oath of Master, Commissioner, etc.

Every person appointed master, special master, commissioner, special commissioner, referee, assessor or appraiser (collectively referred to as "master") shall take and subscribe an oath, which, except as otherwise prescribed by statute or rule, shall be to the effect that they will faithfully and impartially discharge their duties. The oath shall be taken before any federal or state officer authorized by federal law to administer oaths and shall be filed in the Clerk's office.

SECTION VII. JUDGMENTS

54.1 Taxation of Costs

(a) Procedure for Taxation in Civil Cases. The party entitled to recover costs shall file, within thirty (30) days after entry of judgment, a verified bill of costs on the forms that the Clerk provides. The party seeking costs shall accompany its request with receipts indicating that the party actually incurred the costs that it seeks. The verified bill of costs shall include the date on which the party shall appear before the Clerk for taxation of the costs and proof of service of a copy on the party liable for the costs. Post-trial motions shall not serve to extend the time within which a party may file a verified bill of costs as provided in this Rule, except on an order extending the time. Forms for the preparation of a bill of costs are available from the Clerk's office or at the Court's webpage at "www.nynd.uscourts.gov."

(b) To Whom Payable. Except in criminal cases, suits for civil penalties for violations of criminal statutes, and government cases that the Department of Justice does not handle, all costs taxed are payable directly to the party entitled thereto and not to the Clerk, unless the Court orders otherwise.

(c) Waiver of Costs. Failure to file a bill of costs within the time provided for in this Rule shall constitute a waiver of the taxable costs.

54.2 Jury Cost Assessment

See L.R. 47.3.

54.3 Award of Attorney's Fees

[Reserved]

54.4 Allowances to Attorneys and Receivers

Every attorney and receiver requesting an allowance for services rendered in a civil action in which the Court has appointed a receiver shall, on filing the receiver's report with the Clerk, file a detailed statement of the services rendered and the amount claimed, with a statement of any partial allowance previously made, together with an affidavit of the applicants, stating that no agreement has been made, directly or indirectly, and that no understanding exists for a division of fees between the attorney and the receiver. The petition shall be heard and allowance made on notice as the Court shall direct.

55.1 Certificate of Entry of Default

A party applying to the Clerk for a certificate of entry of default pursuant to Fed. R. Civ. P. 55(a) shall submit an affidavit showing that (1) a party against whom it seeks a judgment for affirmative relief has failed to plead or otherwise defend the action as provided in the Federal Rules of Civil Procedure and (2) it has properly served the pleading to which the opposing party has not responded.

55.2 Default Judgment

(a) By the Clerk. When a party is entitled to have the Clerk enter a default judgment pursuant to Fed. R. Civ. P. 55(b)(1), the party shall submit, with the form of judgment, **the Clerk's certificate of entry of default**, a statement showing the principal amount due, not to exceed the amount demanded in the complaint, giving credit for any payments, and showing the amounts and dates of payment, a computation of the interest to the day of judgment, a per diem rate of interest, and the costs and taxable disbursements claimed. An affidavit of the party or the party's attorney shall be appended to the statement showing that

1. The party against whom it seeks judgment is not an infant or an incompetent person;

2. The party against whom it seeks judgment is not in the military service, or if unable to set forth this fact, the affidavit shall state that the party against whom the moving party seeks judgment by default is in the military service or that the party seeking a default judgment is not able to determine whether or not the party against whom it seeks judgment by default is in the military service;

3. The party has defaulted in appearance in the action;

4. Service was properly effected under Fed. R. Civ. P. 4;

5. The amount shown in the statement is justly due and owing and that no part has been paid except as set forth in the statement this Rule requires; and

6. The disbursements sought to be taxed have been made in the action or will necessarily be made or incurred.

The Clerk shall then enter judgment for principal, interest and costs. If, however, the Clerk determines, for whatever reason, that it is not proper for a default judgment to be entered, the Clerk shall forward the documents submitted in accordance with L.R. 55.2(a) to the assigned district judge for review. The assigned district judge shall then promptly notify the Clerk as to whether the Clerk shall properly enter a default judgment under L.R. 55.2(a).

(b) By the Court. A party shall accompany a motion to the Court for the entry of a default judgment, pursuant to Fed. R. Civ. P. 55(b)(2), with a **clerk's certificate of entry of default** in accordance with Fed. R. Civ. P. 55(a), a **proposed form of default judgment**, and a copy of the pleading to which no response has been made. The moving party shall also include in its application an affidavit of the moving party or the moving party's attorney setting forth facts as required by L.R. 55.2(a).

56.1 Summary Judgment Procedure

See L.R. 7.1 (a)(3).

56.2 Notice to Pro Se Litigants of the Consequences of Failing to Respond to a Summary Judgment Motion

When moving for summary judgment against a pro se litigant, the moving party shall inform the pro se litigant of the consequences of failing to respond to the summary judgment motion. Counsel for the moving party shall send a notice to the pro se litigant that a motion for summary judgment seeks dismissal of some or all of the claims or defenses asserted in their complaint or answer and that the pro se litigant's failure to respond to the motion may result in the Court entering a judgment against the pro se litigant. Parties can obtain a sample notice from the Court's webpage at "www.nynd.uscourts.gov."

57.1 Declaratory Judgment

[Reserved.]

58.1 Entry of Judgment

(a) Upon the verdict of a jury or the decision of the Court, the Clerk shall sign and enter a separate document which shall constitute the judgment. The judgment shall contain no recitals other than a recital of the verdict or any direction of the Court on which the judgment is entered. Unless the Court specifically directs otherwise, the Clerk shall promptly prepare the judgment. The Clerk shall promptly sign and enter the judgment, except that where Fed. R. Civ. P. 58 requires the Court's approval, the Clerk shall first submit the judgment to the Court, which shall manifest approval by signing it or noting approval on the margin. The notation of the judgment in the appropriate docket shall constitute the entry of judgment.

(b) The attorney causing the entry of an order or judgment shall append to, or endorse on, it a list of the names of the parties entitled to be notified of the entry and the names and addresses of their respective attorneys if known.

58.2 Entering Satisfaction of Judgment or Decree

The Clerk shall enter satisfaction of a money judgment recovered or registered in the District as follows:

(a) Upon the payment into Court of the amount, plus applicable interest, and the payment of the Marshal's fees, if any;

(b) Upon the filing of a satisfaction-piece executed and acknowledged by:

1. The judgment-creditor; or

2. The judgment-creditor's legal representative or assigns, with evidence of the representative's authority; or

3. The judgment-creditor's attorney or proctor, if within two years of the entry of the judgment or decree.

(c) If the judgment-creditor is the United States, upon the filing of a satisfaction-piece executed by the United States Attorney.

(d) In admiralty, pursuant to an order of satisfaction; but an order shall not be made on the consent of the proctors only, unless consent is given within two years from the entry of the decree to be satisfied.

(e) Upon the registration of a certified copy of a satisfaction entered in another district.

59.1 New Trial; Amendment of Judgment

See L.R. 7.1(g) (Motions for Reconsideration).

60.1 Relief from Judgment or Order

[Reserved.]

61.1 Harmless Error

[Reserved.]

62.1 Stay of Proceedings

[Reserved.]

62.2 Supersedeas Bond

See L.R. 67.1.

63.1 Disability of a Judge

[Reserved.]

SECTION VIII. PROVISIONAL AND FINAL REMEDIES AND SPECIAL PROCEEDINGS

64.1 Seizure of Person or Property

The Court has adopted a Uniform Procedure for Civil Forfeiture Cases, which is available from the Clerk's office or at the Court's webpage at "www.nynd.uscourts.gov."

Pursuant to Title 19, United States Code, Section 1605, the United States Customs Service, Ogdensburg, New York, shall be appointed the Substitute Custodian and be responsible for the execution of warrants of arrest in rem for assets and/or property seized and forfeited under the laws administered or enforced by the United States Customs Service.

Pursuant to Fed. R. Civ. P. Supp. R. C(3)(b)(ii), personnel of the United States Customs Service, Office of Fines, Penalties and Forfeitures, 127 North Water Street, Ogdensburg, New York, shall be appointed as special process servers in all cases pertaining to assets and/or property seized and forfeited under the laws administered or enforced by the United States Customs Service, to perform the tasks of service by mail, or in person, execution of the warrants of seizure and monition, publication of the notices of the action in newspapers having general circulation in the district in which the res were seized, and filing of all returns of such process with the United States District Court Clerk's Office for the Northern District of New York.

65.1 Injunctions

See L.R. 7.1(f).

65.1.1 Sureties

(a) Whenever a bond, undertaking or stipulation is required, it shall be sufficient, except in bankruptcy or criminal cases, or as otherwise prescribed by law, if the instrument is executed by the surety or sureties only.

(b) Except as otherwise provided by law, every bond, undertaking or stipulation shall be secured by the deposit of cash or government bonds in the amount of the bond, undertaking or stipulation; or be secured by the undertaking or guaranty of a corporate surety holding a certificate of authority from the Secretary of the Treasury; or the undertaking or guaranty of two individual residents of the Northern District of New York, each of whom owns real or personal property within the District worth double the amount of the bond, undertaking or stipulation, over all the debts and liabilities of each of the residents, and over all obligations assumed by each of the residents on other bonds, undertakings or stipulations, and exclusive of all legal exemptions.

(c) In the case of a bond or undertaking, or stipulation executed by individual sureties, each surety shall attach an affidavit of justification, giving full name, occupation, residence and business address and showing that the surety is qualified as an individual surety under subdivision (b) of this Rule.

(d) Members of the bar, administrative officers or employees of this Court, the Marshal, or the Marshal's deputies or assistants shall not act as sureties in any suit, action or proceeding pending in this Court. See L.R. 67.3.

65.2 Temporary Restraining Orders

See L.R. 7.1(f).

66.1 Receiverships

[Reserved.]

67.1 Deposits in Court

(a) A supersedeas bond, where the judgment is for a sum of money only, shall be in the amount of the judgment plus 11% to cover interest and any damage for delay as may be awarded, plus $250 to cover costs.

When a stay shall be effected solely by the giving of the supersedeas bond, but the judgment or order is not solely for a sum of money, the Court, on notice, shall fix the amount of the bond. In all other cases, the Court shall, on notice, grant a stay on the terms it deems proper.

On approval, a party shall file the supersedeas bond with the Clerk, and shall promptly serve a copy thereof, with notice of filing, upon all parties affected thereby. If a party raises objections to the form of the bond or to the sufficiency of the surety, the Court shall provide prompt notice of a hearing to consider such objections.

(b) Order Directing the Investment of Funds. Any order directing the Clerk to invest funds deposited with the registry account of the Court pursuant to 28 U.S.C. § 2041 shall include the following:

1. The amount to be invested; and

2. The type of interest-bearing account in which the funds are to be invested.

(c) Time for Investing Funds. The Clerk shall take all reasonable steps to invest the funds within fourteen (14) days of the filing date of the order.

(d) Fee. Unless the Court orders otherwise, the Clerk shall deduct from income earned on registry funds invested in interest-bearing accounts or instruments a fee of ten percent (10%) on amounts that are invested that are less than $100 million and held for up to 5 years. For amounts that are invested and held for 6–10 years, the fee decreases to seven and one-half percent (7.5%); for amounts that are invested and held for 11–15 years, the fee decreases to five percent (5%); and for amounts that are invested and held for 15 years or more, the fee decreases to two and one-half percent (2.5%).

The Clerk shall deduct the fee before any other distribution of the account and shall deposit the fee in the Treasury of the United States, without further order of this Court. This assessment shall apply to all registry fund investments.

67.2 Withdrawal of a Deposit Pursuant to Fed. R. Civ. P. 67

Any person seeking withdrawal of money deposited in the Court pursuant to Fed. R. Civ. P. 67 and subsequently deposited into an interest-bearing account or instrument as Fed. R. Civ. P. 67 requires shall provide a completed Internal Revenue Service Form W–9 with the motion papers seeking withdrawal of the funds.

67.3 Bonds and Other Sureties

(a) General Requirements. Unless the Court expressly directs otherwise pursuant to the provisions of 18 U.S.C. § 3146 in the supervision of a criminal matter, the principal obligor or one or more sureties qualified under this Rule shall execute every bond, recognizance or other undertaking that the law or court order requires in any proceeding.

(b) Unacceptable Sureties. An attorney or the attorney's employee, a party to an action, or the spouse of a party to an action or of an attorney shall not be accepted as surety on a cost bond, bail bond, appeal bond, or any other bond.

(c) Corporate Surety. A corporate surety on any undertaking in which the United States is the obligee shall be qualified in accordance with the provisions of 6 U.S.C. §§ 6–13, and approved thereunder by the Secretary of the Treasury of the United States. In all other instances, a corporate surety qualified to write bonds in the State of New York shall be an acceptable surety. In all actions, a power of attorney showing authority of the agent signing the bond shall be attached to the bond.

(d) Personal Surety. Persons competent to convey real property who own real property in the State of New York of an unencumbered value of at least the stated penalty of the bond shall obtain consideration for qualification as surety thereon by attaching thereto a duly acknowledged justification showing (1) the legal description of the real property; (2) a complete list of all encumbrances and liens thereon; (3) its market value based upon recent sales of like property; (4) a waiver of inchoate rights of any character and certification that the real property is not exempt from execution; and (5) certification as to the aggregate amount of penalties of all other existing undertakings, if any, assured by the bondsperson as of that date. The Court will review the justifications and certifications for approval or disapproval of the surety.

(e) Cost Bonds. The Court on motion, or upon its own initiative, may order any party to file an original bond for costs or additional security for costs in such an amount and so conditioned as the court by its order shall designate.

(f) Cash Bonds. Cash bonds shall be deposited into the Court's registry only upon execution and filing of a written bond sufficient as to form and setting forth the conditions of the bond. Withdrawal of cash bonds so deposited shall not be made except upon the Court's written order.

(g) Insufficiency—Remedy. An opposing party may raise objections to a bond's form or timeliness or the sufficiency of the surety. If the bond is found to be insufficient, the Court shall order that a party file a sufficient bond within a stated time. If the party does not comply with the order, the Court shall dismiss the case for want of prosecution, or the Court shall take other appropriate action as justice requires.

68.1 Settlement Conferences

See L.R. 16.1.

68.2 Settlement Procedures

(a) On notice to the Court or the Clerk that the parties have settled an action, and upon confirmation of the settlement by all parties, the Court may issue a judgment dismissing the action by reason of settlement. The Court shall issue the order without prejudice to the parties' right to secure reinstatement of the case within thirty (30) days after the date of judgment by making a showing that the settlement was not, in fact, consummated.

(b) If the Court decides not to follow the procedures set forth in L.R. 68.2(a), the parties shall file within thirty (30) days of the notification to the Court, unless otherwise directed by written order, such pleadings as are necessary to terminate the action. If the required documents are not filed within the thirty (30) day period, the Clerk shall place the action on the dismissal calendar.

See also L.R. 17.1 (Actions involving infants and/or incompetents).

69.1 Execution

[Reserved.]

70.1 Judgment for Specific Acts; Vesting Title

[Reserved.]

71.1 Process in Behalf of and Against Persons Not Parties

[Reserved.]

71A.1 Condemnation Cases

[Reserved.]

72.1 Authority of Magistrate Judges

(a) A full-time Magistrate Judge is authorized to exercise all powers and perform all duties permitted by 28 U.S.C. § 636(a), (b), and (c) and any additional duties that are consistent with the Constitution and laws of the United States. Part-time Magistrate Judges are authorized to exercise all of those duties, except that only those Magistrate Judges whom the Court specifically designates are authorized to perform duties allowed under 28 U.S.C. § 636(c) and any additional duties consistent with the Constitution and laws of the United States.

(b) Any party may file objections to a Magistrate Judge's determination of a non-dispositive matter by filing with the Clerk and serving upon all parties their objections. The party must file and serve its objections within fourteen (14) days after being served with the Magistrate Judge's order, must state a return date in accordance with L.R. 7.1(b)(2) and must specifically designate the order or part of the order from which the party seeks relief and the basis for the objection. The parties shall file all supporting and opposition papers in accordance with L.R. 7.1(b)(2). The supporting papers shall include the following documents:

> 1. A designation of the contents of the record on appeal, including the documents, exhibits and other materials the Court is to consider; and

> 2. A memorandum of law.

Opposition papers shall also include a memorandum of law responsive to the appellant's arguments. Unless the Court directs otherwise, it will decide all appeals on submission of the papers without oral argument.

(c) Any party may object to a Magistrate Judge's proposed findings, recommendations, or report issued pursuant to 28 U.S.C. § 636(b)(1)(B) and (C) within fourteen (14) days after being served with a copy of the Magistrate Judge's recommendation. The party must file with the Clerk and serve upon all parties written objections which specifically identify the portions of the proposed findings, recommendations, or report to which it has an objection and the basis for the objection. The party shall file with the Clerk a transcript of the specific portions of any evidentiary proceedings to which it has an objection. Objections may not exceed twenty-five (25) pages without the Court's prior approval. The opposing party may file and serve its response to the objections within fourteen (14) days after being served with a copy of the objections. The objecting party may not file a reply. The Court will proceed in accordance with Fed. R. Civ. P. 72(b) or Rule 8(b) of the Rules Governing Section 2254 Petitions, as applicable.

72.2   Duties of Magistrate Judges

(a) In all civil cases, in accordance with Fed. R. Civ. P. 16, the Magistrate Judge assigned pursuant to L.R. 40.1 is authorized to hold conferences before trial, enter scheduling orders, and modify scheduling orders. The scheduling order may limit the time to join parties, amend pleadings, file and hear motions, and complete discovery. It may also include dates for a final pretrial conference and other conferences, a trial ready date, a trial date, and any other matters appropriate under the circumstances of the case. A schedule cannot be modified except by order of the Court. The Magistrate Judge may explore the possibility of settlement and hold settlement conferences.

(b) The following procedure shall be followed regarding consent of the parties and designation of a Magistrate Judge to exercise civil trial jurisdiction under 28 U.S.C. § 636(c):

1.   Upon the filing of a complaint or petition for removal, the Clerk shall promptly provide to the plaintiff, or the plaintiff's attorney, a notice, as approved by the Court, informing the parties of their right to consent to have the full-time Magistrate Judge conduct all proceedings in the case. Proceedings in the case include hearing and determining all pretrial and post-trial motions, including dispositive motions; conducting a jury or non-jury trial; and ordering the entry of a final judgment. The plaintiff shall attach copies of the notice to the copies of the complaint and summons when served. Additional copies of the notice shall be furnished to the parties at later stages of the proceedings and shall be included with pretrial notices and instructions. The consent form will state that any

appeal lies directly with the Court of Appeals for the Second Circuit.

2. If the parties agree to consent, the attorney for each party or the party, if pro se, must execute the consent form. The parties shall file the executed consent forms directly with the Clerk. No consent form shall be made available, nor shall its contents be made known, to any District Judge or Magistrate Judge, unless all of the parties have executed the consent form. No judge or other court official shall attempt to persuade or induce any party to consent to the reference of any matter to a Magistrate Judge. A District Judge, Magistrate Judge, or other court official may again inform or remind the parties that they have the option of referring the case to a Magistrate Judge. In reminding the parties about the availability of consent to a Magistrate Judge, the judge or other court official must inform the parties that they are free to withhold consent without adverse substantive consequences. The parties may agree to a Magistrate Judge's exercise of civil jurisdiction at any time prior to trial, subject to the approval of the District Judge.

3. When all of the parties have executed and filed the consent forms, the Clerk shall then transmit those forms along with the file to the assigned District Judge for approval and referral of the case to a Magistrate Judge. If the District Judge assigns the case to a Magistrate Judge on consent, authority vests in the Magistrate Judge to conduct all proceedings and to direct the Clerk to enter a final judgment in the same manner as if a District Judge presided over the case.

4. The Clerk shall notify any parties added to an action after consent and reference to a Magistrate Judge of their right to consent to the exercise of jurisdiction by the Magistrate Judge. If an added party does not consent to the Magistrate Judge's jurisdiction, the action shall be returned to the referring District Judge for further proceedings.

(c) Assignment of Magistrate Judges to Serve as Special Masters. A Magistrate Judge shall serve as a special master subject to the procedures and limitations of 28 U.S.C. § 636(b)(2) and Fed. R. Civ. P. 53. Where the parties consent, a Magistrate Judge shall serve as a special master in any civil case without regard to the provisions of Fed. R. Civ. P. 53(b).

(d) Other Duties in Civil Actions. A Magistrate Judge is also authorized to:

1. Conduct proceedings for the collection of civil penalties of not more than $200 assessed under the Federal Boat Safety

Act of 1971, as amended, in accordance with 46 U.S.C. § 4311(d), 12309(c);

2. Conduct examinations of judgment debtors in accordance with Fed. R. Civ. P. 69;

3. Review petitions in civil commitment proceedings under Title III of the Narcotic Rehabilitation Act;

4. Supervise proceedings conducted pursuant to letters rogatory in accordance with 28 U.S.C. § 1782;

5. Exercise general supervision of the Court's civil calendar, conduct calendar and status calls, and determine motions to expedite or postpone the trial of cases for the judges; and

6. Administer oaths and affirmations and take acknowledgments, affidavits, and depositions.

72.3 Assignment of Duties to Magistrate Judges

(a) Immediately upon the filing of a civil action or proceeding, the Clerk shall assign the action or proceeding to a District Judge and may also assign the action or proceeding to a Magistrate Judge pursuant to the Court's Assignment Plan. When a civil action or proceeding is assigned to a Magistrate Judge, the Magistrate Judge shall conduct proceedings in accordance with these Rules and 28 U.S.C. § 636 as directed by the District Judge. See L.R. 40.1.

(b) All civil cases in which the parties have executed and filed consent forms pursuant to 28 U.S.C. § 636(c) and L.R. 72.2(b) shall be transmitted to the assigned District Judge for approval and referral of the case to a Magistrate Judge, who shall then have the authority to conduct all proceedings and to direct the Clerk to enter final judgment. See L.R. 72.2(b)(3).

(c) Prisoner Cases. Any proceedings that an unrepresented prisoner commences shall, unless the Court orders otherwise, be referred to a Magistrate Judge for the purpose of reviewing applications, petitions and motions in accordance with these Rules and 28 U.S.C. § 636.

(d) Social Security Appeal Cases. Upon the filing of the complaint, the Clerk shall assign social security appeal cases in rotation to the District Judges. The assigned District Judge shall immediately refer these cases in rotation to a full-time Magistrate Judge for the purpose of review and submission of a report-recommendation relative to the complaint or, if the Magistrate Judge has been assigned to the case pursuant to 28 U.S.C. § 636(c) and L.R. 72.2(b), for final judgment.

(e) Federal Debt Collection Act Cases.

1. Any action brought pursuant to the Federal Debt Collection Act, 28 U.S.C. § 3001 et seq., shall be handled on an expedited

basis and brought before a Magistrate Judge in Syracuse, New York, or to a District Judge if no Magistrate Judge is available, for an initial determination.

2.   If appropriate, the Court shall issue an order directing the Clerk to issue the writ being sought, except that an application under 28 U.S.C. § 3203 for a writ of execution in a post-judgment proceeding shall not require an order of the Court.

3.   Thereafter, the Clerk shall assign geographically a Magistrate Judge if no Magistrate Judge was previously assigned in accordance with General Order #12.

4.   The assigned Magistrate Judge shall conduct any hearing that may be requested, decide all non-dispositive issues, and issue a report-recommendation on any and all dispositive issues.

5.   The parties shall file any written objections to the report-recommendation within twenty-one (21) days of the filing of same. Without oral argument, the assigned District Judge shall review the report-recommendation along with any objections that the parties have filed.

6.   If a party requests a hearing, the Clerk shall make a good faith effort to schedule the hearing within seven (7) days of the receipt of the request or "as soon after that as possible" pursuant to 28 U.S.C. § 3101(d)(1).

72.4   Habeas Corpus

(a) Petitions under 28 U.S.C. §§ 2241, 2254 and 2255 shall be filed pursuant to the Rules Governing § 2254 Cases in the United States District Courts and the Rules Governing § 2255 Proceedings in the United States District Courts. All memoranda of law filed in Habeas Corpus proceedings shall conform to the requirements set forth in Local Rule 7.1(a)(1).

(b) Subject to the requirement of subsection (c), the petitioner shall file the original verified petition with the Clerk at Syracuse, New York. Applications for a writ of habeas corpus made by persons in custody shall be filed, heard and determined in the district court for the district in which they were convicted and sentenced provided, however, that if the convenience of the parties and witnesses requires a hearing in a different district, such application shall be transferred to any district that the assigned judge finds or determines to be more convenient.

(c) Before a second or successive application is filed in this Court, the applicant shall move in the Second Circuit Court of Appeals for an order authorizing the district court to consider the application.

(d) If the respondent submits the state-court records with its answer to the petition, the respondent must properly identify the records in the answer and arrange them in chronological order. The respondent must also sequentially number the pages of the state-court records so that citations to those records will identify the exact location where the information appears. If documents are separately bound and the citation to the documents is easily identifiable, the respondent does not need to repaginate the documents.

72.5 Habeas Corpus Petitions Involving the Death Penalty; Special Requirements

(a) Applicability. This Rule shall govern the procedures for a first petition for a writ of habeas corpus filed pursuant to 28 U.S.C. § 2254 in which a petitioner seeks relief from a judgment imposing the penalty of death. The Court may deem a subsequent filing relating to a particular petition a first petition under this Rule if a court did not dismiss the original filing on the merits. The District Judge or Magistrate Judge to whom the petition is assigned may modify the application of this Rule. This Rule shall supplement the Rules Governing § 2254 Cases and does not in any regard alter or supplant those rules.

(b) Notices from Office of the Attorney General for the State of New York. The Office of the Attorney General for the State of New York ("Attorney General") shall send to the Clerk (1) prompt notice whenever the New York State Court of Appeals affirms a sentence of death; (2) at least once a month, a list of scheduled executions; and (3) at least once a month, a list of the death penalty appeals pending before the New York State Court of Appeals.

(c) Notice from Petitioner's Counsel. Whenever counsel decides to file a petition in this Court, counsel shall promptly file with the Clerk and serve on the Attorney General a written notice of counsel's intention to file a petition. The notice shall state the name of the petitioner, the district in which the petitioner was convicted, the place of the petitioner's incarceration, the status of the petitioner's state-court proceedings and the scheduled date of execution. The notice is for the Court's information only, and the failure to file the notice shall not preclude the filing of the petition.

(d) Counsel.

1. *Appointment of Counsel.* Each indigent petitioner shall be represented by counsel unless petitioner has clearly elected to proceed pro se and the Court is satisfied, after a hearing, that petitioner's election is intelligent, competent, and voluntary. Where the Court is to appoint counsel, such appointment shall be made at the earliest practicable time. The active judges of this District will

certify a panel of attorneys qualified for appointment in death penalty cases ("qualified panel").

If state appellate counsel is available to continue representation in the federal courts and the assigned District Judge deems counsel qualified to continue representation, there is a presumption in favor of continued representation except when state appellate counsel was also counsel at trial. In light of this presumption, it is expected that any appointed counsel who is willing to continue representation and whom the assigned District Judge has found qualified to do so, would ordinarily file a motion for appointment of counsel on behalf of his or her client together with the client's federal habeas corpus petition. If, however, counsel for any reason wishes to confirm appointment before preparing the petition, counsel may move for appointment as described above before filing the petition.

If state appellate counsel is not available to represent the petitioner in the federal habeas corpus proceeding or if appointment of state appellate counsel would be inappropriate for any reason, the Court may appoint counsel upon application of the petitioner. The Clerk shall have available forms for such application. The Court may appoint counsel from the qualified panel. The assigned District Judge may suggest one or more counsel for appointment. If a petitioner makes an application for appointed counsel before filing the petition, the Clerk shall assign the application to a District Judge and Magistrate Judge in the same manner that the Clerk would assign a non-capital petition. The District Judge and Magistrate Judge so assigned shall be the District Judge and Magistrate Judge assigned when counsel files a petition for writ of habeas corpus.

2. *Second Counsel.* The Guide to Judiciary Policies and Procedures, Appointment of Counsel in Criminal Cases shall govern the appointment and compensation of second counsel.

(e) Filing.

1. *General requirement.* Petitioners shall file petitions as to which venue lies in this District in accordance with the applicable Local Rules. Petitioners shall fill in their petitions by printing or typewriting. In the alternative, the petitioner may typewrite or legibly write a petition which contains all of the information that the form requires. All petitions shall (1) state whether the petitioner has previously sought relief arising out of the same matter from this Court or any other federal court, together with the ruling and reasons given for denial of relief; (2) set forth any scheduled execution date; and (3) contain the wording in full caps and underscored "Death Penalty Case" directly under the case number on each pleading. Counsel for petitioner shall file an original and

three (3) copies of the petition. A pro se petitioner need file only the original.

The Clerk will immediately notify the Attorney General's office when a petition is filed.

When a petitioner who was convicted outside of this District files a petition, the Court will immediately advise the clerk of the district in which the petitioner was convicted.

2. *Emergency motions or applications.* Counsel shall file emergency motions or applications with the Clerk. If time does not permit the filing of a motion or application in person or by mail, counsel may communicate with the Clerk and obtain the Clerk's permission to file the motion by facsimile. Counsel should communicate with the Clerk by telephone as soon as it becomes evident that he or she will seek emergency relief from this Court. The motion or application shall contain a brief account of the prior actions, if any, of this Court and the name of the judge or judges involved in the prior actions.

(f) Assignment to Judges. Notwithstanding the Court's case assignment plan, the Clerk shall assign petitions to judges of the Court as follows: (1) the Clerk shall establish a separate category for these petitions, to be designated with the title "Capital Case"; (2) all active judges of this Court shall participate in the assignments; (3) the Clerk shall assign petitions in the Capital Case category randomly to each of the available active judges of the Court; (4) if a petitioner has previously sought relief in this Court with respect to the same conviction, the petition shall, when practical, be assigned to the judges who were assigned to the prior proceeding; and (5) pursuant to 28 U.S.C. § 636(b)(1)(B), and consistent with law, the Court may designate Magistrate Judges to perform all duties under this Rule, including evidentiary hearings.

(g) Transfer of Venue. Subject to the provisions of 28 U.S.C. § 2241(d), it is the Court's policy that a petition should be heard in the district in which the petitioner was convicted rather than in the district of the petitioner's present confinement. See L.R. 72.4(b). If an order for the transfer of venue is made, the Court will order a stay of execution which shall continue until such time as the transferee court acts upon the petition or the order of stay.

(h) Stays of Execution.

1. *Stay Pending Final Disposition.* Upon the filing of a habeas corpus petition, unless the petition is patently frivolous, the Court shall issue a stay of execution pending final disposition of the matter. Notwithstanding any provision of this paragraph (h), the Court shall not grant or maintain stays of execution, except in accordance with law. Thus, the provisions of this paragraph (h) for

a stay shall be ineffective in any case in which the stay would be inconsistent with the limitations of 28 U.S.C. § 2262 or any other governing statute.

2. *Temporary Stay for Appointment of Counsel.* Where counsel in the state-court proceedings withdraws at the conclusion of the state-court proceedings or is otherwise not available or qualified to proceed, the Court may designate an attorney who will assist an indigent petitioner in filing pro se applications for appointment of counsel and for a temporary stay of execution. Upon the filing of this application, the Court shall issue a temporary stay of execution and appoint counsel. The temporary stay will remain in effect for forty-five (45) days unless the Court extends this time.

3. *Temporary Stay for Preparation of the Petition.* Where the Court appoints new counsel to the case, upon counsel's application for a temporary stay of execution accompanied by a specification of nonfrivolous issues to be raised in the petition, the Court shall issue a temporary stay of execution unless no nonfrivolous issues are presented. The temporary stay will remain in effect for one hundred twenty (120) days to allow newly-appointed counsel to prepare and file the petition. The Court may extend the temporary stay upon a subsequent showing of good cause.

4. *Temporary Stay for Transfer of Venue.* See paragraph (g).

5. *Temporary Stay for Unexhausted Claims.* If the petition indicates that there are unexhausted claims for which a state-court remedy is still available, the Court shall grant the petitioner a sixty (60) day stay of execution in which to seek a further stay from the state court in order to litigate the unexhausted claims in state court. During the proceedings in state court, the Court will stay the proceedings on the petition. After the state-court proceedings have been completed, the petitioner may amend the petition with respect to the newly exhausted claims.

6. *Stay Pending Appeal.* If the Court denies the petition and issues a certificate of appealability, the Court will grant a stay of execution which will continue in effect until the court of appeals acts upon the appeal or the order of stay.

7. *Notice of Stay.* Upon the granting of any stay of execution, the Clerk will immediately notify the appropriate prison superintendent and the Attorney General. The Attorney General shall ensure that the Clerk has a twenty-four (24) hour telephone number for the superintendent.

(i) Procedures for Considering the Petition. Unless the Court summarily dismisses the petition as patently frivolous, the following schedule and procedures shall apply subject to the Court's modification. Requests for enlargement of any time period in this Rule shall comply with these Local Rules.

1. Respondent shall, as soon as practicable, but in any event on or before twenty-one (21) days from the date of service of the petition, file with the Court the following:

(A) Transcripts of the state trial-court proceedings;

(B) Appellant's and respondent's briefs on direct appeal to the Court of Appeals, and the opinion or orders of that Court;

(C) Petitioner's and respondent's briefs in any state-court habeas corpus proceedings and all opinions, orders and transcripts of such proceedings;

(D) Copies of all pleadings, opinions and orders that the petitioner has filed in any previous federal habeas corpus proceeding which arose from the same conviction; and

(E) An index of all materials described in paragraphs (A) through (D) above.

Respondent shall mark and number the materials so that they can be uniformly cited. Respondent shall serve this index upon counsel for petitioner or the petitioner pro se. If time does not permit, the respondent may file the answer without attachments (A) through (D) above, but the respondent shall file these attachments as soon as possible. If any items identified in paragraphs (A) through (D) above are not available, respondent shall state when, if at all, such missing material can be filed.

2. If counsel for petitioner claims that respondent has not complied with the requirements of paragraph (1), or if counsel for petitioner does not have copies of all the documents that respondent filed with the Court, counsel for petitioner shall immediately notify the Court in writing, with a copy to respondent. The Court will provide copies of any missing documents to the petitioner's counsel.

3. Respondent shall file an answer to the petition with accompanying points and authorities within thirty (30) days from the date of service of the petition. Respondent shall attach to the answer any other relevant documents that the parties have not already filed.

4. Within thirty (30) days after respondent has filed the answer, petitioner may file a traverse.

5. There shall be no discovery without leave of the Court.

6. Either party shall make any request for an evidentiary hearing within fifteen (15) days from the filing of the traverse or within fifteen (15) days from the expiration of the time for filing the traverse. The request shall include a specification of which factual issues require a hearing and a summary of what evidence petitioner proposes to offer. Any opposition to the request for an evidentiary hearing shall be made within fifteen (15) days from the filing of the request. The Court will then give due consideration to whether it will hold an evidentiary hearing.

(j) Evidentiary Hearing. If the Court holds an evidentiary hearing, the Court will order the preparation of a transcript of the hearing, which is to be immediately provided to petitioner and respondent for use in briefing and argument. Upon the preparation of the transcript, the Court may establish a reasonable schedule for further briefing and argument about the issues considered at the hearing.

(k) Rulings. The Court's rulings may be in the form of a written opinion, which will be filed, or in the form of an oral opinion on the record in open court, which shall be promptly transcribed and filed. The Clerk will immediately notify the appropriate prison superintendent and the Attorney General whenever relief is granted on a petition. The Clerk will immediately notify the clerk of the United States Court of Appeals for the Second Circuit by telephone of (1) the issuance of a final order denying or dismissing a petition without a certificate of probable cause for appeal or (2) the denial of a stay of execution. If the petitioner files a notice of appeal, the Clerk will transmit the appropriate documents to the United States Court of Appeals for the Second Circuit immediately.

73.1 Magistrate Judges: Trial by Consent

Upon the consent of the parties, a Magistrate Judge shall conduct all proceedings in any civil case, including a jury or non-jury trial and shall order the entry of a final judgment, in accordance with 28 U.S.C. § 636(c). See L.R. 72.2(b)(2).

74.1 Method of Appeal to District Judge in Consent Cases

[Reserved.]

75.1 Proceedings on Appeal from Magistrate Judge to District Judge under Rule 73(d)

[Reserved.]

76.1 Bankruptcy Cases

Reference to Bankruptcy Court. All cases under Title 11 of the United States Code, and all proceedings arising under Title 11, or arising in, or related to, a case under Title 11, are referred to the bankruptcy court of this District pursuant to 28 U.S.C. § 157.

In accordance with the provisions of 28 U.S.C. § 157(e), the Board of Judges has specifically designated the United States Bankruptcy Court Judges of this District to conduct jury trials in all proceedings commenced in cases filed under Title 11 of the United States Code where the right to a jury trial applies and where all the parties have expressly consented thereto.

76.2 Bankruptcy Appeals

(a) When a party files a notice of appeal with the bankruptcy court clerk, and the notice is not timely filed in accordance with Fed. R. Bankr. P. 8002(a), and the party did not file a motion for extension of time in accordance with Fed. R. Bankr. P. 8002(c), the bankruptcy court clerk shall forward the notice of appeal together with a "Certification of Noncompliance" to the Clerk without assembling the record as provided for in Fed. R. Bankr. P. 8007(b). The Clerk shall file the notice and certificate, assign a civil action number, and forward the file to a District Judge to determine whether the party timely filed the notice of appeal or whether to dismiss the appeal as untimely. If the District Judge determines that the party timely filed the appeal or that the appeal should otherwise be perfected, the Clerk shall notify the bankruptcy court clerk to complete the record promptly in accordance with Fed. R. Bankr. P. 8007(b).

(b) The Clerk shall issue a standard bankruptcy appeal scheduling order at the time of the filing of the record on appeal, a copy of which the Clerk shall provide to the parties, the bankruptcy judge from whom the appeal was taken, and the bankruptcy court clerk.

(c) Appeals from a decision of the bankruptcy court shall be in accordance with 28 U.S.C. § 158 and applicable bankruptcy rules. Fed. R. Bankr. P. 8009 respecting the filing of briefs shall not be applicable, and the parties shall file their briefs in accordance with this Court's scheduling order.

76.3 Bankruptcy Record of Transmittal, Certificate of Facts, and Proposed Findings Pursuant to Title 11, Section 110(i)

(a) Upon direction of the bankruptcy judge, the bankruptcy court clerk shall cause to be filed with the Clerk the designated record of transmittal, which shall consist of certified copies of the Memorandum–Decision, Findings of Fact, Conclusions of Law, bankruptcy docket, and transcript of proceedings which relate to the bankruptcy judge's findings. The bankruptcy court clerk shall also provide the Clerk with a list of those individuals to whom the notice of filing shall be given.

(b) Upon receipt of the above, the Clerk shall assign a civil action number, assign a District Judge and issue a scheduling order for the filing of motions pursuant to 11 U.S.C. § 110(i)(1). The Clerk shall serve copies of the scheduling order upon those individuals whom the bankruptcy court clerk designates.

Upon the filing of any motion(s), the Clerk shall schedule and notice all concerned parties of a hearing date. Failure to file motions within the time ordered will be deemed a waiver of the provisions of 11 U.S.C. § 110(i)(1). The Clerk shall prepare and present to the assigned District Judge a proposed order pursuant to the provisions of L.R. 41.2.

SECTION IX.   DISTRICT COURT AND CLERKS

77.1   Hours of Court

[Reserved.]

77.2   Orders

(a) With these exceptions, all orders, whether by consent or otherwise, shall be presented for approval and execution to the assigned judge. The Clerk may sign without submission to the assigned judge the following orders:

1.   Orders specifically appointing persons to serve process in accordance with Fed. R. Civ. P. 4;

2.   Orders on consent for the substitution of attorneys in civil cases where the trial of the action has not been set. See also L.R. 83.2;

3.   Orders restoring an action to the court docket after the filing of a demand for trial de novo pursuant to L.R. 83.7–7 (Consensual Arbitration Program);

4.   Orders on consent satisfying decrees and orders on consent canceling stipulations and bonds.

(b) If the assigned judge instructs the prevailing party to do so, the prevailing party shall submit a proposed order which the opposing party has approved and which contains the endorsement of the opposing party: "Approved as to form."

When the parties are unable to agree as to the form of the proposed order, the prevailing party shall, on seven (7) days notice to all other parties, submit a proposed order and a written explanation for the form of that order. The Court may award costs and attorney's fees against a party whose unreasonable conduct the Court deemed to have required the bringing of the motion. The provisions of L.R. 7.1 shall not apply to such motion, and the Court shall not hear oral argument.

77.3 Sessions of Court

The Court shall be in continuous session in Albany, Binghamton, Syracuse, and Utica. The Court shall from time to time hold sessions in Auburn, Malone and Watertown, or such other place as the Court shall, by order, deem appropriate. Jurors shall serve as the Court directs.

77.4 Court Library

The district court libraries are not open for use by the public.

77.5 Official Newspapers

All process, notices, and orders required to be published shall be published in the proper county in an official newspaper. The Court shall direct the publication of process, notices, and orders in any other newspaper, upon proper showing, as it shall deem advisable. The following are designated as official newspapers:

County	Newspaper	City
Albany	Times Union (D)	Albany, NY
Broome	Binghamton Press/ Sun Bulletin (D)	Binghamton, NY
Cayuga	The Citizen (D)	Auburn, NY
Clinton	Press–Republican (D)	Plattsburgh, NY
Chenango	Evening Sun (D)	Norwich, NY
Columbia	Register Star (D)	Hudson, NY
	The Independent (W)	Hillsdale, NY
Cortland	Cortland Standard (D)	Cortland, NY
Delaware	Walton Reporter (W)	Walton, NY
Essex	Lake Placid News (W)	Lake Placid, NY
Franklin	Adirondack Enterprise (D)	Saranac Lake, NY
Fulton	Leader Herald (D)	Gloversville, NY
Greene	Catskill Daily Mail (D)	Catskill, NY
Hamilton	Post Star (D)	Glens Falls, NY
Herkimer	Telegram (D)	Herkimer, NY
	The Evening Times (D)	Little Falls, NY
Jefferson	Watertown Times (D)	Watertown, NY
	Thousand Island Sun (W)	Alexandria Bay, NY
Lewis	Journal Republican (W)	Lowville, NY
Madison	Oneida Dispatch (D)	Oneida, NY
Montgomery	The Recorder (D)	Amsterdam, NY
Oneida	Utica Observer Dispatch (D)	Utica, NY
	Rome Sentinal (D)	Rome, NY
Onondaga	Post Standard (D)	Syracuse, NY
Oswego	Palladium Times (D)	Oswego, NY
Otsego	The Daily Star	Oneonta, NY
Rensselaer	Times Record (D)	Troy, NY

County	Newspaper	City
St. Lawrence	Ogdensburg Journal (D)	Ogdensburg, NY
	Tribune Press (W)	Gouverneur, NY
	Daily Courier Observer (D)	Massena, NY
Saratoga	Saratogian–Tri City News (D)	Saratoga Springs, NY
Schenectady	Schenectady Gazette (D)	Schenectady, NY
Schoharie	Times Journal (W)	Cobleskill, NY
Tioga	Owego Pennysaver (W)	Owego, NY
Tompkins	Ithaca Journal (D)	Ithaca, NY
Ulster	The Daily Freeman (D)	Kingston, NY
Warren	Post Star (D)	Glen Falls, NY
	Times (D)	Glen Falls, NY
Washington	Whitehall Times (W)	Whitehall, NY

(D) = Daily   (W) = Weekly

77.6 Release of Information

All court personnel, including but not limited to marshals, deputy clerks, court clerks, bailiffs, court reporters, law clerks, secretaries, and probation officers, shall not disclose to any person, without the Court's authorization, information divulged in arguments and hearings held in chambers or otherwise outside the presence of the public or any information relating to a pending case that is not part of the Court's public records.

77.7 Official Station of the Clerk

The Clerk's official station shall be Syracuse. The Clerk shall appoint deputy clerks in such number as are necessary, and they shall be stationed at Albany, Binghamton, Utica, Syracuse and Watertown.

78.1 Motion Days

Listings of the regularly scheduled motion days for all judges shall be available at each Clerk's office and are available on the Court's webpage at "www.nynd.uscourts.gov." The Clerk shall provide notice of the regular motion days for all judges to the parties at the time an action is commenced.

79.1 Custody of Exhibits and Transcripts

(a) Unless the Court orders otherwise, the parties shall not file exhibits and transcripts with the Clerk. Rather, the party that produced them in court shall retain them.

(b) In the case of an appeal or other review by an appellate court, the parties are encouraged to agree with respect to which exhibits and transcripts are necessary for the determination of the appeal. In the absence of agreement and except as provided in this Rule, a party, upon written request of any other party or by Court order, shall make available at the Clerk's office all the original exhibits in the party's possession, or true copies, to enable such other party to prepare the record on appeal. At the same time and place, such other party also shall make available all the original exhibits in that party's possession. All exhibits made available at the Clerk's office, which any party designates as part of the record on appeal, shall be filed with the Clerk, who shall transmit them together with the record on appeal to the clerk of the Second Circuit Court of Appeals. Exhibits and transcripts not so designated shall remain in the custody of the respective attorneys who shall have the responsibility of promptly forwarding them to the clerk of the Second Circuit Court of Appeals on request.

(c) Documents of unusual bulk or weight and physical exhibits, other than documents, shall remain in the custody of the party producing them, who shall permit any party to inspect them for the purpose of preparing the record on appeal and who shall be charged with the responsibility for their safekeeping and transportation to the Second Circuit Court of Appeals.

(d) The party responsible for filing the exhibits and transcripts with the Clerk shall be responsible for removing them (1) if no appeal is taken, within ninety (90) days after a final decision is rendered or (2), if an appeal has been taken, within thirty (30) days after the mandate of the final reviewing court is filed. The Clerk shall notify the parties that fail to comply with this Rule to remove their exhibits. Upon their failure to do so within thirty (30) days, the Clerk shall dispose of these exhibits and transcripts as the Clerk sees fit.

79.2 Books and Records of the Clerk

[Reserved.]

80.1 Stenographic Transcript: Court Reporting Fees

Subject to the provisions of Fed. R. Civ. P. 54(d), the expense of any party in obtaining all or any part of a transcript for the Court's use when the Court so orders and the expense of any party in obtaining all or any part of a transcript for the purposes of a new trial or for amended findings or for appeals shall be a taxable cost against the unsuccessful party. A fee schedule of transcript rates is available on the Court's webpage at "www.nynd.uscourts.gov."

81.1 Removal Bonds

[Reserved.]

81.2 Copies of State Court Proceedings
in Removed Actions

[Reserved.]

81.3 Removed Cases, Demand for Jury Trial

In an action removed from a state court, a party entitled to trial by jury under Fed. R. Civ. P. 38 shall be accorded a jury trial if the party files and serves a demand in accordance with the provisions of Fed. R. Civ. P. 81 and L.R. 38.1. The Court will not consider a motion that a party filed in state court unless that party refiles the motion in this Court in accordance with the Local Rules of Practice for the Northern District of New York.

81.4 Actions Removed Pursuant to 28 U.S.C. § 1452

If removal is based upon 28 U.S.C. § 1452 (Removal of claims related to bankruptcy cases), the removing party shall specifically identify in its Notice of Removal which claims or causes of action it is removing and which of the parties in the state-court action are parties to the removed claims or causes of action.

82.1 Jurisdiction and Venue Unaffected

[Reserved.]

83.1 Admission to the Bar

(a) Permanent Admission. A member in good standing of the bar of the State of New York or of the bar of any United States District Court, or of the highest court in the state in which they reside, whose professional character is good, may be permanently admitted to practice in this Court on motion of a member of the bar of this Court in compliance with the requirements of this Rule. **An admission packet containing all the required forms is available from the Clerk's office and on the Court's webpage at "www.nynd.uscourts.gov."**

Each applicant for permanent admission must file, at least fourteen (14) days prior to the scheduled hearing (unless, for good cause shown, the Court shortens the time), documentation for admission as set forth below. Ordinarily, the Court entertains applications for admission only on regularly scheduled motion days. Documentation required for permanent admission includes the following:

1. *A verified petition for admission* stating the following:

● place of residence and office address;

● the date(s) when and court(s) where previously admitted;

● legal training and trial experience;

● whether the applicant has ever been held in contempt of court, censured, suspended or disbarred by any court and, if so, the facts and circumstances connected therewith; and

● that the applicant is familiar with the provisions of the Judicial Code (Title 28 U.S.C.), which pertain to the jurisdiction of, and practice in, the United States District

Courts; the Federal Rules of Civil Procedure and the Federal Rules of Evidence for the District Courts; the Federal Rules of Criminal Procedure for the District Courts; the Local Rules of the District Court for the Northern District of New York; and the N.Y.S. Lawyer's Code of Professional Responsibility. The applicant shall further affirm faithful adherence to these Rules and responsibilities.

2. *Affidavit of Sponsor.* The sponsor must be a member in good standing of the bar of the Northern District of New York who has personal knowledge of the petitioner's background and character. A form Affidavit of Sponsor is available from the Clerk's office.

3. *Attorney E-Filing Registration Form.* The E-Filing Registration Form must be in the form the Clerk prescribes, which sets forth the attorney's current office address(es); telephone and fax number(s), and e-mail address. A copy of the Attorney E-Filing Registration Form is available on the Court's webpage at "www.nynd.uscourts.gov." See subdivision (e) for requirements when information on the Registration Form changes.

4. *Certificate of Good Standing.* The certificate of good standing must be dated within six (6) months of the date of admission.

5. *The Required Fee.* As prescribed by and pursuant to the Judicial Conference of the United States and the Rules of this Court, the fee for admission to the bar is $150.00.

In addition to the initial admission fee, there shall be a $30.00 biennial registration fee. This fee shall be due and owning on June 1, 2001, and every two years thereafter unless the Board of Judges directs otherwise. Failure to remit this fee will result in the removal of the non-paying attorney from the Court's bar roll. Should the payment of this biennial fee present a significant financial hardship, an attorney may request, by submitting an application to the Chief Judge, that the biennial registration fee be waived.

The Clerk shall deposit the additional $30.00 fee required for admission to the bar and the $30.00 biennial registration fee into the District Court Fund. The Clerk shall be the trustee of the Fund, and the monies deposited in the Fund shall be used only for the benefit of the bench and bar in the administration of justice. All withdrawals from the Fund require the approval of the Chief Judge or a judge designated by the Chief Judge to authorize the withdrawals.

The admission fees and biennial registration fees are waived for all attorneys in the employ of the United States Government.

The biennial registration fees **only** are waived for all attorneys employed by state and local public sector entities.

6. *Oath on Admission.* Applicants must swear or affirm that as attorneys and counselors of this Court, they will conduct themselves uprightly and according to law and that they will support the Constitution of the United States. The applicant signs the Oath on Admission, Form AO 153, in court at the time of the admission.

(b) Applicants who are not admitted to another United States District Court in New York State must appear with their sponsor for formal admission unless the Court, in the exercise of its discretion, waives such appearance. If the applicant is admitted to practice in New York State, the Certificate of Good Standing submitted with the application for admission must be from the appropriate New York State Appellate Division. All requirements of subdivision (a) apply.

If the applicant is from outside New York State, the Certificate of Good Standing may be from the highest court of the state or from a United States District Court. All requirements of subdivision (a) apply.

(c) Applicants who are members in good standing of a United States District Court for the Eastern, Western, or Southern District of New York need not appear for formal admission. They must submit a Certificate of Good Standing from the United States District Court where they are members and a proposed order granting the admission. A sponsor's affidavit is not required. All other requirements of subdivision (a) apply.

(d) Pro Hac Vice Admission. A member in good standing of the bar of any state, or of any United States District Court, may be admitted pro hac vice to argue or try a particular case in whole or in part. In addition to the requirements of L.R. 83.1(a)(1)(3) and (4), an applicant must make a Motion for Pro Hac Vice Admission, which includes the case caption of the particular case for which the applicant seeks admission. See L.R. 10.1(b). In lieu of a written motion for admission, the sponsoring attorney may make an oral motion in open court on the record. In that case, the attorney seeking pro hac vice admission must immediately complete and file the required documents as set forth above.

The pro hac vice admission fee is $30.00. The Clerk deposits all pro hac vice admission fees into the District Court Fund. See L.R. 83.1(a)(5). An attorney admitted pro hac vice must file a written notice of appearance in the case for which the attorney was admitted in accordance with L.R. 83.2.

(e) Registration Form Changes. Every attorney must update their e-mail address, telephone or fax number through CM/ECF within 14 days of a change. Detailed instructions are available on the Court's website, http://www.nynd.uscourts.gov/. Attorneys shall notify the Court within 14 days of any change to their mailing address by completing the automated Update My Information form located on the Court's website: http://www.nynd.uscourts.gov/e-filingregistration/procform13.cfm.

Failure to keep this information current will result in removal from the roll of the Court.

(f) Pro Bono Service. Every member of the bar of this Court shall be available upon the Court's request for appointment to represent or assist in the representation of indigent parties. The Court shall make appointments under this Rule in a manner such that the Court shall not request any attorney to accept more than one appointment during any twelve-month period.

(g) United States Attorney's Office. An attorney appointed by the United States Attorney General as a United States Attorney, an Assistant United States Attorney, or as a Special Assistant United States Attorney under 28 U.S.C. §§ 541–543, who has been admitted to practice before any United States District Court, shall be admitted to practice in this Court upon motion of a member of the bar of this Court. Thereafter, the attorney may appear before this Court on any matter on behalf of the United States. Prior to admission, applicants are required to complete and submit an oath of admission, a verified petition for admission to practice and an attorney E-filing registration form.

83.2 Appearance and Withdrawal of Attorney

(a) Appearance. An attorney appearing for a party in a civil case shall promptly file with the Clerk a written notice of appearance; however, an attorney does not need to file a notice of appearance if the attorney who would be filing the notice of appearance is the same individual who has signed the complaint, notice of removal, pre-answer motion, or answer.

(b) Withdrawal. An attorney who has appeared may withdraw only upon notice to the client and all parties to the case and an order of the Court, upon a finding of good cause, granting leave to withdraw. If the Court grants leave to withdraw, the withdrawing attorney must serve a copy of the order upon the affected party and file an affidavit of service.

Unless the Court orders otherwise, withdrawal of counsel shall not result in the extension of any of the deadlines contained in any case management orders, including the Uniform Pretrial Scheduling Order, see L.R. 16.1(e), or the adjournment of a trial ready or trial date.

83.3   Pro Bono Panel

(a) Description of Panel. In recognition of the need for representation of indigent parties in civil actions, this Court has established the Pro Bono Panel ("Panel") of the Northern District of New York.

1.   The Panel shall include those members of the Criminal Assigned Counsel Panel in this Court. The Court also expects any other attorney admitted to practice in this Court to participate in periodic training that the Court offers and to accept no more than one pro bono assignment per year.

2.   The Court shall maintain a list of Panel members, which shall include the information deemed necessary for the effective administration and assignment of Panel attorneys.

3.   The Court shall select Panel members for assignment upon its determination that the appointment of an attorney is warranted. The Court shall select from the Panel a member who has not received an appointment from the Court during the past year and (1) has attended a training seminar that this Court sponsors, (2) has adequate prior experience closely related to the matter assigned, or (3) has accepted criminal (CJA) assignments from the Court.

4.   Where a pro se party has one or more other cases pending before this Court in which the Court has appointed an attorney, the Court may determine it to be appropriate that the attorney appointed in the other case or cases be appointed to represent the pro se party in the case before the Court.

5.   Where the Court finds that the nature of the case requires specific expertise, and among the Panel members available for appointment there are some with the required expertise, the attorney may be selected from among those included in the group or the Court may designate a specific member of the Panel.

6.   Where the Court finds that the nature of the case requires specific expertise and none of the Panel members available for appointment has indicated that expertise, the Court may appoint an attorney with the required expertise who is not on the Panel.

(b) Application for Appointment of Attorney.

1.   Any application that a party appearing pro se makes for the appointment of an attorney shall include a form of affidavit

stating the party's efforts to obtain an attorney by means other than appointment and indicating any prior pro bono appointments of an attorney to represent the party in cases brought in this Court, including both pending and terminated actions.

2. Failure of a party to make a written application for an appointed attorney shall not preclude appointment.

3. Where a pro se litigant, who was ineligible for an appointed attorney at the time of initial or subsequent requests, later becomes eligible by reason of changed circumstances, the Court may entertain a subsequent application, using the procedures specified above, within a reasonable time after the change in circumstances has occurred.

(c) Factors Used in Determining Whether to Appoint Counsel. Upon receipt of an application for the appointment of an attorney, the Court shall determine whether to appoint an attorney to represent the pro se party. The Court shall make that determination within a reasonable time after the party makes the application. Factors that the Court will take into account in making the determination are as follows:

1. The potential merit of the claims as set forth in the pleading;

2. The nature and complexity of the action, both factual and legal, including the need for factual investigation;

3. The presence of conflicting testimony calling for an attorney's presentation of evidence and cross-examination;

4. The capability of the pro se party to present the case;

5. The inability of the pro se party to retain an attorney by other means;

6. The degree to which the interests of justice shall be served by appointment of an attorney, including the benefit that the Court shall derive from the assistance of an appointed attorney;

7. Any other factors the Court deems appropriate.

(d) Order of Appointment. Whenever the Court concludes that the appointment of an attorney is warranted, the Court shall issue an order directing the appointment of an attorney to represent the pro se party. The Court shall promptly transmit the order to the Clerk. If service of the summons and complaint has not yet been made, the Court shall accompany its appointment order with an order directing service by the United States Marshal or by other appropriate method of service.

(e) Notification of Appointment. After the Court has appointed an attorney, the Clerk shall send the attorney a copy of the order of appointment. Copies of the pleadings filed to date, relevant correspondence, and all other relevant documents shall be forwarded to the Clerk's office nearest to the attorney and made available for immediate review and copying of the necessary papers without charge. In addition to notifying the attorney, the Clerk shall also notify all of the parties to the action of the appointment, together with the name, address and telephone number of the appointed attorney.

(f) Duties and Responsibilities of Appointed Counsel. On receiving notice of the appointment, the attorney shall promptly file an appearance in the action to which the appointment applies unless precluded from acting in the action or appeal, in which event the attorney shall promptly notify the Court and the putative client. Promptly following the filing of an appearance, the attorney shall communicate with the newly-represented party concerning the action. In addition to a full discussion of the merits of the dispute, the attorney shall explore with the party any possibilities of resolving the dispute in other forums, including but not limited to administrative forums. If after consultation with the attorney the party decides to prosecute or defend the action, the attorney shall proceed to represent the party in the action unless or until the attorney-client relationship is terminated as these Rules provide.

In the Court's discretion, the Court may appoint stand-by counsel to act in an advisory capacity. "Stand-by counsel" is not the party's representative; rather, the role of stand-by counsel is to provide assistance to the litigant and the Court where appropriate. The Court may in its discretion appoint counsel for other purposes.

(g) Reimbursement for Expenses. Pro Bono attorneys whom the Court appoints pursuant to this Rule may seek reimbursement for expenses incident to representation of indigent clients by application to the Court. Reimbursement or advances shall be permitted to the extent possible in light of available resources and, absent extraordinary circumstances, shall not exceed $2,000.00. Any expenses in excess of $300.00 should receive the Court's prior approval. If good cause is shown, the Court may approve additional expenses. Appointed counsel should seek reimbursement using the Pro Bono Fund Voucher and Request for Reimbursement Form and should accompany this form with detailed documentation. The Court advises counsel that if they submit a voucher seeking more than $2,000.00 without the Court's prior approval, the Court may reduce or deny the request. The Chief Judge or a judge whom the Chief Judge designates to authorize withdrawals must approve all reimbursements made by withdrawal from the District Fund. **To the extent that appointed counsel seeks reimbursement for expenses that are recoverable as costs to a prevailing party under Fed R. Civ. P. 54,**

the appointed attorney must submit a verified bill of costs on the form the Clerk provides for reimbursement of such expenses.

(h) Attorney's Fees. Except as provided in this subsection, an appointed attorney cannot recover attorney's fees from the Pro Bono Fund. However, in its discretion, the Court may award an appointed attorney for a prevailing party attorney's fees from the judgment or settlement to the extent that the applicable law permits. See, e.g., 28 U.S.C. § 2678 (permitting the attorney for a prevailing party under the Federal Tort Claims Act to recover up to 25% of any judgment or settlement); 42 U.S.C. § 1988(b) (authorizing an additional award of attorney's fees to prevailing parties in civil rights actions).

(i) Grounds for Relief from Appointment. After appointment, an attorney may apply to be relieved from an order of appointment only on one or more of the following grounds, or on such other grounds as the appointing judge finds adequate for good cause shown:

1.   some conflict of interest precludes the attorney from accepting the responsibilities of representing the party in the action;

2.   the attorney does not feel competent to represent the party in the particular type of action assigned;

3.   some personal incompatibility exists between the attorney and the party or a substantial disagreement exists between the attorney and the party concerning litigation strategy; or

4.   in the attorney's opinion the party is proceeding for purposes of harassment or malicious injury or the party's claims or defenses are not warranted under existing law and cannot be supported by a good faith argument for extension, modification or reversal of existing law.

(j) Application for Relief from Appointment. An appointed attorney shall make any application for relief from an order of appointment on any of the grounds set forth in this Rule to the Court promptly after the attorney becomes aware of the existence of such grounds or within such additional period as the Court may permit for good cause shown.

(k) Order Granting Relief from Appointment. If the Court grants an application for relief from an order of appointment, the Court shall issue an order directing the appointment of another attorney to represent the party. Where the application for relief from appointment identifies an attorney affiliated with the moving attorney who is able to represent the party, the order shall direct appointment of the affiliated attorney with the consent of the affiliated attorney. Any other appointment shall be made in accordance with the procedures set forth in these Rules. Alternatively, the Court shall have the discretion not to issue a further order of appointment, in which case the party shall be permitted to prosecute or defend the action pro se.

83.4 Discipline of Attorneys

(a) The Chief Judge shall have charge of all matters relating to discipline of members of the bar of this Court.

(b) Any member of the bar of this Court who is convicted of a felony in any State, Territory, other District, Commonwealth, or Possession shall be suspended from practice before this Court and, upon the judgment of conviction becoming final, shall cease to be a member of the bar of this Court.

On the presentation to the Court of a certified or exemplified copy of a judgment of conviction, the attorney shall be suspended from practicing before this Court and, on presentation of proof that judgment of conviction is final, the name of the attorney convicted shall, by order of the Court, be struck from the roll of members of the bar of this Court.

(c) Any member of the bar of the Northern District of New York who shall resign from the bar of any State, Territory, other District, Commonwealth or Possession while an investigation into allegations of misconduct is pending shall cease to be a member of the bar of this Court.

On the presentation to the Court of a certified or exemplified copy of an order accepting resignation, the name of the attorney resigning shall, by order of the Court, be struck from the roll of members of the bar of this Court.

(d) Any member of the bar of the Northern District of New York who shall be disciplined by a court in any State, Territory, other District, Commonwealth, or Possession shall be disciplined to the same extent by this Court unless an examination of the record resulting in the discipline discloses

   1. that the procedure was so lacking in notice or opportunity to be heard as to constitute a deprivation of due process;

   2. that there was such an infirmity of proof establishing the misconduct as to give rise to the clear conviction that this Court should not accept as final the conclusion on that subject;

   3. that this Court's imposition of the same discipline would result in grave injustice; or

   4. that this Court has held that the misconduct warrants substantially different discipline.

On the filing of a certified or exemplified copy of an order imposing discipline, this Court shall, by order, discipline the attorney to the same extent. It is provided, however, that within thirty (30) days of service on the attorney of the Court's order of discipline, either the attorney or a bar association that the Chief Judge designated in the order imposing discipline shall apply to the Chief Judge for an order to show cause why the discipline imposed in this District should not be modified on the basis of one or more of the grounds set forth in this Rule. The term "bar association" as used in this Rule shall mean the following: The New York State Bar Association or any city or county bar association.

(e) The Court may disbar, suspend or censure any member of the bar of this Court who is convicted of a misdemeanor in any State, Territory, other District, Commonwealth, or Possession, upon such conviction.

Upon the filing of a certified or exemplified copy of a judgment of conviction, the Chief Judge may designate a bar association to prosecute a proceeding against the attorney. The bar association shall obtain an order requiring the attorney to show cause within thirty (30) days after service, personally or by mail, why the attorney should not be disciplined. The Chief Judge may, for good cause, temporarily suspend the attorney pending the determination of the proceeding. Upon receiving the attorney's answer to the order to show cause, the Chief Judge may set the matter for prompt hearing before a court of one or more judges or shall appoint a master to hear and to report findings and a recommendation. After a hearing and report, or if the attorney makes no timely answer or the answer raises no issue requiring a hearing, the Court shall take action as justice requires. In all proceedings, a certificate of conviction shall constitute conclusive proof of the attorney's guilt of the conduct for which the attorney was convicted.

(f) Any attorney who has been disbarred from the bar of a state in which the attorney was admitted to practice shall have his or her name stricken from the roll of attorneys of this Court or, if suspended from practice for a period at such bar, shall be suspended automatically for a like period from practice in this Court.

(g)(1) In addition to any other sanctions imposed in any particular case under these Rules, any person admitted to practice in this Court may be prohibited from practicing in this Court or otherwise disciplined for cause.

(2) Complaints alleging any cause for discipline shall be directed to the Chief Judge and must be in writing. If the Chief Judge deems the conduct alleged in the complaint sanctionable, the Chief Judge shall appoint a panel attorney to investigate and, if necessary, support the complaint. At the same time, the Chief Judge

shall refer the matter to a Magistrate Judge for all pre-disposition proceedings.

(3) The Chief Judge shall appoint a panel of attorneys who are members of the bar of this Court to investigate complaints and, if the complaint is supported by the evidence, to prepare statements of charges and to support such charges at any hearing. In making appointments to the panel, the Chief Judge may solicit recommendations from the Federal Court Bar Association and other bar associations and groups. The Chief Judge shall appoint attorneys to the panel for terms not to exceed four years without limitation as to the number of terms an attorney may serve. The Court may reimburse an attorney from this panel whom the Chief Judge appoints to investigate and support a complaint in accordance with subsection (3) below ("panel attorney") for expenses incurred in performing such duties from the Pro Bono Fund to the extent and in the manner provided in L.R. 83.3(g).

(4) If the panel attorney determines after investigation that the evidence fails to establish probable cause to believe that any violation of the Code of Professional Responsibilities has occurred, the panel attorney shall submit a report of such findings and conclusions to the Chief Judge for the consideration of the active district court judges.

(5) If the panel attorney determines after investigation that the evidence establishes probable cause to believe that one or more violations of the Code of Professional Responsibilities has occurred, the panel attorney shall prepare a statement of charges alleging the grounds for discipline. The Clerk shall cause the Statement of Charges to be served upon the attorney concerned ("responding attorney") by certified mail, return receipt requested, directed to the address of the attorney as shown on the rolls of this Court and, if different, to the last known address of the attorney as shown in any other source together with a direction from the Clerk that the responding attorney shall show cause in writing within thirty days why discipline should not be imposed.

(6) If the responding attorney fails to respond to the statement of charges, the charges shall be deemed admitted. If the responding attorney denies any charge, the assigned Magistrate Judge shall schedule a prompt evidentiary hearing. The Magistrate Judge may grant such pre-hearing discovery as deemed necessary, shall hear witnesses called by the panel attorney supporting the charges and by the responding attorney, and may consider such other evidence included in the record of the hearing that the Magistrate Judge deems relevant and material. A disciplinary charge may not be found proven unless supported by clear and convincing evidence. The Magistrate Judge shall report his or her findings and recom-

mendations in writing to the Chief Judge and shall serve them upon the responding attorney and the panel attorney. The responding attorney and the panel attorney may file objections to the Magistrate Judge's report and recommendations within twenty-one days of the date thereof.

(7) An attorney may not be found guilty of a disciplinary charge except upon a majority vote of the active district judges that such charge has been proven by clear and convincing evidence. Any discipline imposed shall also be determined by a majority vote of the active district judges except that in the event of a tie vote, the Chief Judge shall cast a tie-breaking vote. If the District Judge submitted the complaint under subsection (2) above giving rise to the disciplinary proceeding, that judge shall be recused from participating in the decisions regarding guilt and discipline.

(8) Unless the Court orders otherwise, all documents, records, and proceedings concerning a disciplinary matter shall be filed and conducted confidentially except that, without further order of the Court, the Clerk may notify other licensing jurisdictions of the imposition of any sanctions.

(h) A visiting attorney permitted to argue or try a particular cause in accordance with L.R. 83.1 who is found guilty of misconduct shall be precluded from again appearing in this Court. On entry of an order of preclusion, the Clerk shall transmit to the court of the State, Territory, District, Commonwealth, or Possession where the attorney was admitted to practice a certified copy of the order and of the Court's opinion.

(i) Unless the Court orders otherwise, no action shall be taken pursuant to L.R. 83.4(e) and (f) in any case in which disciplinary proceedings against the attorney have been instituted in the State.

(j) The Court shall enforce the N.Y.S. Lawyer's Code of Professional Responsibilities, as adopted from time to time by the Appellate Division of the State of New York, in construing which the court as a matter of comity will follow decisions of the New York State Court of Appeals and other New York state courts absent an over-arching federal interest and as interpreted and applied by the United States Court of Appeals for the Second Circuit.

(k) Nothing in this Rule shall limit the Court's power to punish contempts or to sanction counsel in accordance with the Federal Rules of Civil or Criminal Procedure or the Court's inherent authority to enforce its rules and orders.

83.5 Contempt

(a) A proceeding to adjudicate a person in civil contempt of court, including a case provided for in Fed. R. Civ. P. 37(b)(2)(D), shall be commenced by the service of a notice of motion or order to show cause.

The affidavit on which the notice of motion or order to show cause is based shall set out with particularity the misconduct complained of, the claim, if any, for resulting damages, and evidence as to the amount of damages that is available to the moving party. A reasonable attorney's fee, necessitated by the contempt proceeding, may be included as an item of damages. Where the alleged contemnor has appeared in the action by an attorney, the notice of motion or order to show cause and the papers on which it is based shall be served on the contemnor's attorney; otherwise service shall be made personally in the manner provided by the Federal Rules of Civil Procedure for the service of summons. If an order to show cause is sought, the order may, on necessity shown, embody a direction to the United States Marshal to arrest and hold the alleged contemnor on bail in an amount fixed by the order, conditioned upon appearance at the hearing and further conditioned upon the alleged contemnor's amenability to all orders of the Court for surrender.

(b) If the alleged contemnor puts in issue the alleged misconduct or the resulting damages, the alleged contemnor shall, on demand, be entitled to have oral evidence taken either before the Court or before a master whom the Court appoints. When by law the alleged contemnor is entitled to a trial by jury, the contemnor shall make a written demand on or before the return day or adjourned day of the application; otherwise the Court will deem that the alleged contemnor has waived a trial by jury.

(c) If the Court finds that the alleged contemnor is in contempt of the Court, the Court shall issue and enter an order

1.   Reciting or referring to the verdict or findings of fact on which the adjudication is based;

2.   Setting forth the amount of the damages to which the complainant is entitled;

3.   Fixing the fine, if any, imposed by the Court, which fine shall include the damages found and naming the person to whom the fine shall be payable;

4.   Stating any other conditions, the performance of which shall operate to purge the contempt;

5.   Directing, in the Court's discretion, the Marshal to arrest and confine the contemnor until the performance of the condition fixed in the order and payment of the fine or until the contemnor is otherwise discharged pursuant to law. The order shall specify the place of confinement. No party shall be required to pay or to advance to the Marshal any expenses for

the upkeep of the prisoner. On an order of contempt, no person shall be detained in prison by reason of the non-payment of the fine for a period exceeding six months. A certified copy of the order committing the contemnor shall be sufficient warrant to the Marshal for the arrest and confinement. The aggrieved party shall also have the same remedies against the property of the contemnor as if the order awarding the fine were a final judgment.

(d) If the alleged contemnor is found not guilty of the charges, the contemnor shall be discharged from the proceeding and, in the discretion of the Court, shall have judgment against the complainant for costs, disbursements and a reasonable attorney's fee.

83.6 Transfer of Cases to Another District

In a case ordered transferred from this District, the Clerk, unless otherwise ordered, shall, upon the expiration of fourteen (14) days, mail to the court to which the case is transferred

    1. Certified copies of the Court's opinion and order compelling the transfer and of the docket entries in the case; and

    2. The originals of all papers on file in the case except for the opinion ordering the transfer of the action.

SECTION X. ALTERNATE DISPUTE RESOLUTION AND GENERAL PROVISIONS

83.7–1 Scope and Effectiveness of Rule

This Rule governs the consensual arbitration program for referral of civil actions to court-annexed arbitration. It may remain in effect until further order of the Court. Its purpose is to establish a less formal procedure for the just, efficient and economical resolution of disputes, while preserving the right to a full trial on demand.

83.7–2 Actions Subject to this Rule

The Clerk shall notify the parties in all civil cases, except as the Rules otherwise direct, that they may consent to non-binding arbitration under this Rule. The notice shall be furnished to the parties at pretrial/scheduling conferences or shall be included with pretrial conference notices and instructions. Consent to arbitration under this Rule shall be discussed at the pretrial/scheduling conference. No party or attorney shall be prejudiced for refusing to participate in arbitration. The Court shall allow the referral of any civil action pending before it to the arbitration process if the parties consent. The plaintiff shall be responsible for securing the execution of a consent form by the parties and for filing the form with the Clerk within fourteen (14) days after the parties receive the form. The parties shall freely and knowingly enter into the consent.

83.7–3 Referral to Arbitration

(a) Time for Referral. The Clerk shall refer every action subject to this Rule to arbitration in accordance with the procedures under this Rule twenty-one (21) days after the filing of the last responsive pleading or within twenty-one (21) days of the filing of a stipulated consent order referring the action to arbitration, whichever event occurs last, except as otherwise provided. If any party notices a motion to dismiss under the provisions of Fed. R. Civ. P. 12(a) and/or (b), or a motion to join necessary parties pursuant to the Federal Rules of Civil Procedure prior to the expiration of the twenty-one (21) day period, the assigned judge shall hear the motion and further proceedings under this Rule shall be deferred pending decision on the motion. If the Court does not dismiss the action on the motion, the Court shall refer the action to arbitration twenty-one (21) days after the filing of the decision.

Motions for summary judgment pursuant to Fed. R. Civ. P. 56 shall be filed and served within twenty-one (21) days following the close of discovery. The filing of a Rule 56 motion shall defer further proceedings under this Rule pending decision on the motion.

(b) Authority of Assigned Judge. Notwithstanding any provision of this Rule, the Clerk shall assign every action subject to this Rule to a judge upon filing in the normal course, in accordance with the Court's Assignment Plan. The assigned judge shall have authority to conduct status and settlement conferences, hear motions and in all other respects supervise the action in accordance with these Rules notwithstanding its referral by consent to arbitration.

(c) Relief from Referral. Any party shall request relief from the operation of this Rule by filing with the Court a motion for the relief within twenty-one (21) days after entry of the initial stipulated consent order which refers the case for arbitration. The assigned judge shall, sua sponte, exempt an action from the application of this Rule where the objectives of arbitration would not be realized because (1) the case involves complex or novel legal issues, (2) legal issues predominate over factual issues, or (3) for other good cause.

83.7–4 Selection and Compensation of Arbitrator

(a) Selection of Arbitrators. The Clerk shall maintain a roster of arbitrators qualified to hear and determine actions under this Rule. The Court shall select arbitrators from time to time from applications submitted by or on behalf of attorneys willing to serve.

To be eligible for selection, an attorney (1) shall have been admitted to practice for not less than five (5) years; (2) shall be a member of the bar of this Court or a member of the New York bar and reside within the Northern District of New York; and (3) shall either (i) for not less than five (5) years have devoted 50% or more of the attorney's professional time to matters involving litigation, or (ii) have substantial experience serving as a "neutral" in dispute resolution proceedings, or (iii) have substantial experience negotiating consensual resolutions to complex problems. Each attorney shall, upon selection, take the oath or affirmation prescribed in 28 U.S.C. § 453 and shall complete any training that the Court requires.

(b) Selection of the Panel. Whenever an action has been referred to arbitration through consent of the parties pursuant to this Rule, the parties shall nominate the arbitrator or arbitrators whom they select to serve as an arbitrator(s) in full compliance with L.R. 83.7–4(a), or the Clerk shall promptly furnish to each party a list of arbitrators whose names shall have been drawn at random from the roster for the division in which the case is pending. If the parties have elected to proceed with a **single** arbitrator, the Clerk shall provide five (5) names for the selection process. If the parties have elected to proceed with a panel of **three** (3) arbitrators, the Clerk shall provide seven (7) names for the selection process.

1. Each side shall be entitled to strike two names from the list. All parties shall sign the list and return it to the Clerk within fourteen (14) days of receipt. Failure of the parties to timely notify the Clerk of strikes shall result in the Clerk's selection of the panel.

2. The Clerk shall promptly notify the person or persons whom the parties did not strike. If the parties have elected to proceed with a single arbitrator, and the arbitrator selected is unable or unwilling to serve, the process of selection under this Rule shall begin anew. If the parties have elected to proceed with a panel of arbitrators and any person whom they select is unable or unwilling to serve, the Clerk shall select an additional individual at random who shall constitute the third member of the panel. If the Clerk is still unable to form a panel of three arbitrators for any reason, the process of selection under this Rule shall begin anew. When a single arbitrator, or when three of the selected arbitrators have agreed to serve, the Clerk shall promptly send written notice of the membership of the panel to each arbitrator and the parties.

(c) Disqualification. No person shall serve as an arbitrator in an action in which any of the circumstances specified in 28

U.S.C. § 455 (conflict of interest) exist or in good faith shall be believed to exist.

(d) Withdrawal by Arbitrator. Any person whose name appears on the roster maintained in the Clerk's office may ask at any time to have his or her name removed or, if selected to serve on a panel, decline to serve but remain on the roster.

(e) Compensation and Reimbursement. Arbitrators shall be paid $250.00 per day or portion of each day of hearing in which they participate serving as a single arbitrator or $100.00 for each day or portion of a day if serving as a member of a panel of three (3). Compensation for an arbitrator's services outside the hearing shall be supported by an affidavit setting forth in detail the time required for pre- and post-hearing matters. When the arbitrators file their decision, each shall submit a voucher, on the form that the Clerk prescribes, for payment by the Administrative Office of the United States Courts of compensation and out-of-pocket expenses necessarily incurred in the performance of their duties under this Rule. No reimbursement shall be made for the cost of office or other space for the hearing.

83.7–5 Arbitration Hearings

(a) Hearing Date. After an answer is filed in a case in which the parties have consented to arbitration and the Court has approved the consent and on completion of the parties' selection of the panel, the arbitration clerk shall send a notice to the attorney setting forth the date, time and location for the arbitration hearing. The date of the arbitration hearing set forth in the notice shall be approximately five (5) months, but in no event later than 180 days, from the date the answer was filed, except that the arbitration proceeding shall not, in the absence of the parties' consent, commence until thirty (30) days after the Court's disposition of any motion to dismiss the complaint, motion for judgment on the pleadings, or motion to join necessary parties if such a motion was filed and served within twenty-one (21) days after the filing of the last responsive pleading. Motions for summary judgment pursuant to Fed. R. Civ. P. 56 shall be filed in accordance with L.R. 83.7–3(a). The Court may modify the 180–day and twenty-one (21) day periods specified in L.R. 83.7 for good cause shown. The notice shall also advise the attorneys that they may agree to an earlier date for the arbitration hearing provided the arbitration clerk is notified within thirty (30) days of the date of the notice.

The notice shall also advise the attorneys that they have 120 days to complete discovery unless the Court orders a shorter or longer period for discovery. If a third party has been brought into the action, this notice shall not be sent until the third party has filed an answer.

(b) Upon entry of the order designating the arbitrator(s), the arbitration clerk shall send to each arbitrator a copy of the order designating the arbitrator, a copy of the court docket sheet and a copy of the guidelines for arbitrators. On receipt of the notice scheduling the case to proceed to arbitration and appointing an arbitrator, the plaintiff's attorney shall promptly forward to the arbitrator copies of all pleadings, including any counterclaim or third-party complaint and respective answer. Thereafter, and at least ten (10) days prior to the arbitration hearing, each attorney shall deliver to the arbitrator(s) and to the adverse attorney pre-marked copies of all exhibits, including expert reports and all portions of depositions and interrogatories to which reference shall be made at the hearing (but not including documents intended solely for impeachment).

(c) Default of a Party. The arbitration hearing shall proceed in the absence of any party who, after notice, fails to be present. If a party fails to participate in the arbitration process in a meaningful manner, the arbitrator(s) shall make that determination and shall support it with specific written findings filed with the Clerk. The Court shall then conduct a hearing, on notice to all attorneys and personal notice to any party adversely affected by the arbitrator's determination, and may impose any appropriate sanctions, including, but not limited to, the striking of any demand for a trial de novo which that party has filed.

(d) Conduct of Hearing. The arbitrator is authorized to administer oaths and affirmations and all testimony shall be given under oath or affirmation. Each party shall have the right to cross-examine witnesses, except as otherwise provided. In receiving evidence, the arbitrator shall be guided by the Federal Rules of Evidence. These rules, however, shall not preclude the arbitrator from receiving evidence that the arbitrator considers to be relevant and trustworthy and that is not privileged. A party desiring to offer a document, otherwise subject to hearsay objections, at the hearing shall serve a copy on the adverse party not less than ten (10) days in advance of the hearing, indicating intent to offer it as an exhibit. Unless the adverse party gives written notice in advance of the hearing of intent to cross-examine the author of the document, the arbitrator shall deem that the adverse party has waived any hearsay objection to the document. Attendance of witnesses and production of documents shall be compelled in accordance with Fed. R. Civ. P. 45.

(e) Transcript or Recording. A party may cause a transcript or recording to be made of the proceedings at its expense but shall, at the request of the opposing party, make a copy available to that party at no charge, unless the parties have otherwise agreed. Except as provided in L.R. 83.7–7(c), no transcript of the proceeding shall be admissible in evidence at any subsequent de novo trial of the action.

(f) Place of Hearing. Hearings shall be held at any location within the Northern District of New York that the arbitrator(s) designates. Hearings may be held in any courtroom or other room in any federal courthouse that the Clerk makes available to the arbitrator(s). When no room is available, the hearing shall be held at any suitable location that the arbitrator(s) selects. In selecting a hearing location, the arbitrator shall consider the convenience of the panel, the parties and the witnesses. The date for the hearing shall not be continued except for extreme and unanticipated emergencies.

(g) Time of Hearing. Unless the parties agree otherwise, hearings shall be held during normal business hours.

(h) Authority of Arbitrator. The arbitrator(s) shall be authorized to make reasonable rules and issue orders necessary for the fair and efficient conduct of the hearing before the arbitrator(s). Any two members of a panel shall constitute a quorum; but, unless the parties stipulate otherwise, the concurrence of a majority of the entire panel shall be required for any action or decision.

(i) Ex Parte Communication. There shall be no ex parte communication between an arbitrator(s) and any attorney or party on any matter related to the action except for purposes of scheduling or continuing the hearing.

83.7–6   Award and Judgment

(a) Filing of Award. The arbitrator(s) shall file the award with the Clerk promptly following the close of the hearing and in any event not more than fourteen (14) days following the close of the hearing. As soon as the arbitrator(s) files the award, the Clerk shall serve copies on the parties.

(b) Form of Award. The award shall state clearly and concisely the name or names of the prevailing party or parties, the party or parties against which the award is rendered, and the precise amount of money and other relief, if any, awarded. The award shall be in writing; and, unless the parties stipulate otherwise, the arbitrator or at least two members of a panel must sign the award. No panel member shall participate in the award without having attended the hearing.

(c) Entry of Judgment on Award. Unless a party has filed a demand for a trial de novo (or a notice of appeal which shall be treated as a demand for trial de novo) within thirty (30) days of the filing of the arbitration award, the Clerk shall enter judgment on the arbitration award in accordance with Fed. R. Civ. P. 58. A judgment so entered shall be subject to the same provisions of law and shall have the same force and effect as a judgment of the Court in a civil action, except that the judgment shall not be subject to review in any other court by appeal or otherwise.

(d) Sealing of Arbitration Awards. The contents of any arbitration award made under this Rule shall not be made known to any judicial officer who might be assigned to preside at the trial of the case or to rule on potentially dispositive motions

1. Until the district court has entered final judgment in the action or the action has been otherwise terminated;

2. Except for purposes of preparing the report required by section 903(b) of the Judicial Improvements and Access to Justice Act; or

3. Except as necessary for the Court to determine whether to assess costs or attorneys' fees under 28 U.S.C. § 655.

83.7–7 Trial De Novo

(a) Time for Demand. If either party files and serves a written demand for a trial de novo within thirty (30) days of entry of judgment on the award, the Clerk shall immediately vacate the judgment and the action shall proceed in the normal manner before the assigned judge.

(b) Restoration to Court Docket. On a demand for a trial de novo, the Clerk shall restore the action to the Court's docket, trial ready, and the action shall be treated for all purposes as if it had not been referred to arbitration. In such a case, any right of trial by jury that a party otherwise would have had, as well as any place on the Court calendar which is no later than that which a party otherwise would have had, is preserved.

(c) Limitation on Admission of Evidence. At the trial de novo, the Court shall not admit any evidence that an arbitration proceeding has occurred, the nature or amount of any award, or any other matter concerning the conduct of the arbitration proceeding unless

1. The evidence would otherwise be admissible in the Court under the Federal Rules of Evidence; or

2. The parties have stipulated otherwise.

(d) Arbitrator's Costs. The party requesting a trial de novo shall deposit the cost of the arbitrator's services as a prerequisite to the trial. If the requesting party fails to obtain judgment in an amount which, exclusive of interest and costs, is more favorable to that party, the Clerk shall retain those funds. However, if that party is successful in obtaining a more favorable result, the Clerk shall return the prepaid costs to the party who deposited them.

(e) Opposing Party's Costs. If a party has rejected an award and the action proceeds to trial, that party shall pay the opposing party's actual costs unless the verdict is more favorable to the rejecting party than the arbitrator's award on that claim. If the opposing party has also rejected that award, however, a party is entitled to costs only if the verdict is more favorable to that party than the arbitrator's award.

1. Actual costs include those costs and fees taxable in any civil action and attorney's fees for each day of trial not to exceed $500.00.

2. For good cause shown, the Court shall order relief from payment of any or all costs.

3. The provisions of L.R. 83.7–7(d) and (e) shall not apply to claims to which the United States or one of its agencies is a party.

83.7–8 Cases Pending Prior to the Implementation of Arbitration

Notwithstanding the provisions of the Rules set forth above, each district judge shall select cases from the docket currently in process and notify the attorneys involved of the availability of the consensual arbitration program. A case shall qualify for referral to arbitration if it complies with the provisions of this Rule.

83.8 [Reserved]

83.9 Commission to Take Testimony

(a) Except as the law otherwise provides, in all actions or proceedings where the taking of depositions of witnesses or of parties is authorized, the procedure for obtaining and using the depositions shall comply with the Federal Rules of Civil Procedure. The party seeking the deposition shall furnish the officer to whom the commission is issued with a copy of the Federal Rules of Civil Procedure pertaining to discovery.

(b) Upon receipt of a deposition, the Clerk, unless otherwise ordered, shall open and file it promptly.

83.10 Student Practice

General Order #13 pertains to the rules regarding student practice in this District. Parties may obtain a copy of General Order #13 from the Clerk's office or on the Court's webpage at "www.nynd.uscourts.gov."

83.11–1 Mediation

(a) Purpose. The purpose of this Rule is to provide a supplementary procedure to the Court's existing alternative dispute resolution procedures. This Rule provides for an earlier resolution of civil disputes resulting in savings of time and cost to litigants and the Court without sacrificing the quality of justice rendered or the right of litigants to a full trial on all issues not resolved through mediation.

(b) Definitions. Mediation is a process by which an impartial person, the mediator, facilitates communication between disputing parties to promote understanding, reconciliation and settlement. The mediator is an advocate for settlement and uses the mediation process to help the parties fully explore any potential area of agreement. The mediator does not serve as a judge or arbitrator and has no authority to render any decision on any disputed issue or to force a settlement. The parties themselves are responsible for negotiating any resolution(s) to their dispute.

83.11–2 Designation and Qualifications of Mediators

(a) Designation of Mediators. The judges of this Court may authorize those persons who are eligible and qualified to serve as mediators under this Rule in such numbers as the Court shall deem appropriate. The Court may withdraw such designation of any mediator at any time. Applications for designation as an ADR panel member are available at the Clerk's office.

(b) List of Mediators. The Alternative Dispute Resolution clerk (ADR clerk) shall maintain a list of court-approved mediators and make that list available to counsel and the public upon request.

(c) Required Qualifications of Mediators.

1. An individual may be designated as a mediator if he or she (1) has practiced law for at least five (5) years; and (2) is a member in good standing of the bar of this Court or of the New York bar and resides within the Northern District of New York; or (3) is a professional mediator who would otherwise qualify as a special master or is a professional whom the Court has determined to be competent to perform the duties of the mediator and has completed appropriate training in the process of mediation as the Court may from time to time determine and direct; and (4) shall attend and complete a mediation training course that the Court sponsors. Upon Court approval as a mediator, every mediator shall take the oath prescribed by 28 U.S.C.§ 453.

2. No person shall serve as a mediator in an action in which any of the circumstances specified in 28 U.S.C. § 455 exists, or may in good faith be believed to exist. Additionally, any mediator may be disqualified for bias or prejudice as provided in 28 U.S.C. § 144. Furthermore, the mediator has a continuing obligation to disclose any information that may cause a party or the court to believe, in good faith, that such mediator should be disqualified.

(d) Removal from the Panel. Membership in the ADR Panel is a privilege, not a right, which the Board of Judges may terminate at any time, as it, in its sole discretion may determine.

(e) Service to the Bar and Court Provided by Mediators. The individuals serving as mediators in the Northern District of New York perform their mediation duties as a pro bono service for the Court, litigants and the bar.

83.11–3 Actions Subject to Mediation

(a) The Court may refer any civil action (or any portion thereof) to mediation under this Rule

    1. By order of referral; or

    2. On the motion of any party; or

    3. By consent of the parties.

(b) The parties may withdraw from mediation any civil action or claim that the Court refers to mediation pursuant to this Rule by application to the assigned judge at least ten (10) days prior to the scheduled mediation session.

(c) Notwithstanding the provisions of the Rules set forth above, each judge shall select cases from the docket currently pending and notify the attorneys involved of the availability of the mediation program.

83.11–4 Procedures for Referral, Selecting the Mediator, and Scheduling the Mediation Session

(a) The parties shall discuss with the Court the possibility and appropriateness of mediation under this Rule at the initial status/scheduling conference of the case that the Court holds in accordance with the provisions of General Order #25.

(b) In every case in which the Court determines that referral to mediation is appropriate pursuant to L.R. 83.11–3, the Court shall enter an order of reference, which shall define the period of time during which the mediation session shall be conducted. The Court intends that mediation under this Rule shall occur at the earliest practical time in an effort to encourage earlier, less costly resolutions of disputes. Referral to mediation under this Rule shall not delay or stay other proceedings, including but not limited to discovery, unless the Court so orders.

(c) Within fourteen (14) days of the order of reference, parties are to select a mediator of their choice from a list of mediators available from the Court and submit the selection to the ADR clerk in the Clerk's office. If the parties do not select a mediator in a timely manner or if the parties cannot agree upon a mediator, the ADR clerk shall select a mediator for them. The ADR clerk shall work with the selected mediator and counsel of record to set a mutually agreeable date for the mediation within the time prescribed in the order of reference.

(d) Mediation sessions under this Rule may be held in any available court space or in any other suitable location agreeable to the mediator and the parties. Consideration shall be given to the convenience of the parties and to the cost and time of travel involved.

(e) There shall be no continuance of a mediation session beyond the time set in the referral order except by order of the Court upon a showing of good cause. If any rescheduling occurs within the prescribed time, the parties or the mediator must notify the ADR clerk and select the location of the rescheduled hearing.

(f) The parties shall promptly report any settlement that occurs prior to the scheduled mediation to the mediator and to the ADR clerk.

83.11–5 The Mediation Session

(a) Memorandum for Mediation. At least two days prior to the mediation session, each party shall provide to the mediator and all other such parties a "memorandum for mediation." This memo shall:

    1.   State the name and role of each person expected to attend;

    2.   Identify each person with full settlement authority;

    3.   Include a concise summary of the parties' claims or defenses;

    4.   Discuss liability and damages; and

    5.   State the relief sought by such party.

The memorandum for mediation shall not exceed five pages, and the parties shall not file these documents in the case or otherwise make them part of the court file.

(b) Attendance Required. The attorneys who are expected to try the case for the parties shall appear and shall be accompanied by an individual with authority to settle the lawsuit. Those latter individuals shall be the parties (if the parties are natural persons) or representatives of parties that are not natural persons. These latter individuals may not be counsel (except in-house counsel). Attorneys for the parties shall notify other interested parties such as insurers or indemnitors who shall attend and are subject to the provisions of this Rule. Only the assigned judge may excuse attendance of any attorney, party, or party's representative. Anyone who wants to be excused from attending the mediation must make such request in writing to the presiding judge at least forty-eight (48) hours in advance of the mediation session.

(c) Good Faith Participation in the Process. Parties and counsel shall participate in good faith, without any time constraints, and put forth their best efforts toward settlement. Typically, the mediator will meet initially with all parties to the dispute and their counsel in a joint session and thereafter separately with each party and their representative. This process permits the mediator and the parties to explore the needs and interests underlying their respective positions, generate and evaluate alternative settlement proposals or potential solutions, and consider interests that may be outside the scope of the stated controversy including matters that the Court may not address. The parties will participate in crafting a resolution of the dispute.

(d) Confidentiality. Mediation is regarded as a settlement procedure and is confidential and private. No participant may disclose, without consent of the other parties, any confidential information acquired during mediation. There shall be no stenographic or electronic record, e.g., audio or video, of the mediation process.

    1. All written and oral communications made in connection with or during the mediation session are confidential.

    2. No communication made in connection with or during any mediation session may be disclosed or used for any purpose in any pending or future proceeding in the U.S. District Court for the Northern District of New York.

    3. Privileged and confidential status is afforded all communications made in connection with the mediation session, including matters emanating from parties and counsel as well as mediators' comments, assessments, and recommendations concerning case development, discovery, and motions. Except for communication between the assigned judge and the mediator regarding noncompliance with program procedures (as set forth in this Rule), *there will be no communications between the Court and the mediator regarding a case that has been designated for mediation.* The parties will be asked to sign an agreement of confidentiality at the beginning of the mediation session.

    4. Parties, counsel and mediators may respond to inquiries from authorized court staff which are made for the purpose of program evaluation. Such responses will be kept in strict confidence.

    5. The mediator may not be required to testify in any proceeding relating to or arising out of the matter in dispute.

Nor may the mediator be subject to process requiring disclosure of information or data relating to or arising out of the matter in dispute.

6. *Immunity.* Mediators, as well as the Mediation Administrator (ADR clerk), shall be immune from claims arising out of acts or omissions incident to service as a court appointee in the mediation program. See, e.g., Wagshal v. Foster, 28 F.3d 1249 (D.C. Cir. 1994).

7. *Default.* Subject to the mediator's approval, the mediation session may proceed in the absence of a party, who, after due notice, fails to be present. The Court may impose sanctions on any party who, absent good cause shown, fails to attend or participate in the mediation session in good faith in accordance with this Rule.

8. *Conclusion of the Mediation Session.* The mediation shall be concluded:

    a. By the parties' resolution and settlement of the dispute;

    b. By adjournment for future mediation by agreement of the parties and the mediator; or

    c. Upon the mediator's declaration of impasse that future efforts to resolve the dispute are no longer worthwhile.

Unless the Court authorizes otherwise, mediation sessions shall be concluded at least fourteen (14) days prior to any final pretrial conference that the Court has scheduled.

If the mediation is adjourned by agreement for further mediation, the additional session shall be concluded within the time the Court orders.

83.11–6 Mediation Report; Notice of Settlement or Trial

(a) Immediately upon conclusion of the mediation, the mediator shall file a mediation report with the ADR clerk, indicating only whether the case settled, settled in part, or did not settle.

(b) In the event the parties reach an agreement to settle the case, the representatives for each party shall promptly notify the ADR clerk and promptly prepare and file the appropriate stipulation of dismissal.

(c) If the parties reach a partial agreement to narrow, withdraw or settle some but not all claims, they shall file a stipulation concisely setting forth the resolved claims with the ADR clerk within five (5) days of the mediation. The stipulation shall bind the parties.

(d) If the mediation session does not conclude in settlement of all the issues in the case, the case will proceed toward trial pursuant to the scheduling orders entered in the case.

83.12–1 Early Neutral Evaluation

The ENE Process. Early neutral evaluation (ENE) is a process in which parties obtain from an experienced neutral (an "evaluator") a nonbinding, reasoned, oral evaluation of the merits of the case. The first step in the ENE process involves the Court appointing an evaluator who has expertise in the area of law in the case. After the parties exchange essential information and position statements early in the pretrial period (usually within 150 to 200 days after a complaint has been filed), the evaluator convenes an ENE session that typically lasts about two hours. At the ENE meeting, each side briefly presents the factual and legal basis of its position. The evaluator may ask questions of the parties and help them identify the main issues in dispute and the areas of agreement. The evaluator may also help the parties explore options for settlement. If settlement does not occur, the evaluator then offers an opinion as to the settlement value of the case, including the likelihood of liability and the likely range of damages. With the benefit of this assessment, the parties are again encouraged to discuss settlement, with or without the evaluator's assistance. The parties may also explore ways to narrow the issues in dispute, exchange information about the case or otherwise prepare efficiently for trial.

The evaluator has no power to impose a settlement or to dictate any agreement regarding the pretrial management of the case. The ENE process, whether or not it results in settlement, is confidential.

83.12–2 Designation and Qualifications of Evaluators

(a) Designation of Evaluators. The judges of this Court may authorize those persons who are eligible and qualified to serve as evaluators under this Rule in such numbers as the Court shall deem appropriate. The Court may withdraw such designation of any evaluator at any time. Applications for designation as an ADR panel member are available at the Clerk's office.

(b) List of Evaluators. The ADR clerk shall maintain a list of court-approved evaluators that shall make the list available to counsel and the public upon request.

(c) Required Qualifications of Evaluators.

1. An individual may be designated as an Early Neutral Evaluator if he or she (1) has practiced law for at least *fifteen* years; and (2) is a member in good standing of the bar of this court or of

the New York bar and resides within the Northern District of New York; or (3) is a professional whom this Court determines to be competent to perform the duties of the evaluator and has completed appropriate training in the process of Early Neutral Evaluation as the Court may from time to time determine and direct. Upon Court approval as an evaluator, every evaluator shall take the oath prescribed by 28 U.S.C. § 453.

2. No person shall serve as an evaluator in an action in which any of the circumstances specified in 28 U.S.C. § 455 exist or may in good faith be believed to exist. Additionally, any evaluator may be disqualified for bias or prejudice as provided in 28 U.S.C. § 144. Furthermore, the evaluator has a continuing obligation to disclose any information which may cause a party or the Court to believe in good faith that such evaluator should be disqualified.

(d) Removal from the Panel. Membership in the ADR Panel is a privilege, not a right, which the Board of Judges may terminate at any time, as it, in its sole discretion, may determine.

(e) Service to the Bar and Court Provided by Evaluators. The individuals serving as evaluators in the Northern District of New York perform their duties as a pro bono service to the Court, litigants, and the bar.

83.12–3 Actions Subject to Early Neutral Evaluation

(a) The Court may refer any civil action (or any portion thereof) to ENE under this Rule

    1. By order of referral;

    2. On the motion of any party; or

    3. By consent of the parties.

(b) The parties may withdraw any civil action or claim that the Court has referred to the ENE Process pursuant to this Rule by application to the assigned judge at least ten (10) days before the scheduled evaluation session.

(c) Notwithstanding the provisions of the rules set forth above, each judge shall select cases from the docket currently pending and notify the attorneys involved of the availability of the ENE Process.

(d) When a case is designated for ENE, the ADR clerk will provide counsel with copies of the judge's designation order, a listing by division of the available early neutral evaluators, and a copy of the ENE procedure guide.

83.12–4 Administrative Procedures and Requirements

(a) In most cases, the Court will issue the ENE order early enough in the pretrial period to allow the ENE session to be held within 150 to 200 days from the filing of the complaint.

(b) When the ADR clerk receives a copy of a judicial order designating a case for ENE, the ADR clerk will give the parties a date by which they must choose an evaluator from the list provided to counsel. If the parties do not select an evaluator by the designated date, the ADR clerk will assign an evaluator with expertise in the subject matter of the lawsuit and notify counsel.

(c) The evaluator will contact all attorneys and set the date and place of the evaluation session. Whenever possible, the evaluator shall hold the ENE session within 150 to 200 days of the filing of the complaint and within forty-five days of the date that the ADR clerk notifies counsel of the identity of the evaluator.

(d) The ADR clerk and evaluators shall schedule ENE proceedings in a manner that does not interfere in any way with the management of case processing or the actions of the referring judge. *No party may avoid or postpone any obligation imposed by the order of reference on any ground related to the ENE process.*

83.12–5 Evaluation Statements

(a) No later than ten (10) days prior to the ENE session, each party shall submit directly to the evaluator, and shall serve on all other parties, a written evaluation statement not to exceed ten (10) pages *excluding exhibits and attachments.*

Such statements must

> 1. Identify person(s), in addition to counsel, who will attend the ENE session and who have decision-making authority;

> 2. Address whether the case involves legal or factual issues the early resolution of which might reduce the scope of the dispute or contribute significantly to settlement negotiations; and

> 3. Identify the discovery that will contribute most to meaningful settlement negotiations.

(b) Parties may also identify persons whose presence at the ENE session might improve significantly the productivity of the session.

(c) Parties shall attach to the evaluation statements, copies of key documents out of which the suit arose (e.g., contracts) or materials that might advance the purposes of the ENE session (e.g., medical reports).

The parties shall NOT file written evaluation statements with the Court. Evaluation statements are considered confidential between the parties and the evaluator.

83.12–6 Attendance at ENE Sessions

(a) The Court requires parties to attend evaluation sessions. The main purposes of an ENE session are to give litigants the opportunity (1) to present their positions; (2) to hear their opponents' view of the issues in dispute; and (3) to hear a neutral assessment of the strengths of each side's case.

(b) When a party to a case is not a natural person (e.g., a corporation), a person *other than the outside counsel* who has authority to enter stipulations and to bind the party in a settlement must attend.

(c) In cases involving insurance carriers, company representatives with settlement authority shall attend.

(d) When a party is a unit of the federal government, an agency representative and counsel from the U.S. Attorney's Office must attend the ENE session.

(e) An attorney for each party who has primary responsibility for handling the trial of the matter must attend the ENE session.

(f) A party or attorney may be excused from attending an ENE session only after petitioning the referring judge in writing no fewer than ten (10) days before the scheduled ENE session. Such a petition must show that attendance at the ENE session would impose an extraordinary or unjustifiable hardship.

(g) Default. Subject to the evaluator's approval, the evaluation session may proceed in the absence of a party, who, after due notice, fails to attend. The Court may impose sanctions on any party who, absent good cause shown, fails to attend or participate in the evaluation session in good faith in accordance with this Rule.

83.12–7 Procedures at ENE Sessions

(a) The evaluator has broad discretion to structure the ENE session. The evaluator will determine the time and place of the session and will structure the session and any follow-up sessions. Rules of Evidence shall not apply and there is no formal examination or cross-examination of witnesses.

(b) The evaluator shall:

    1. Permit each party, or counsel, to make an oral presentation of its position;

    2. Help parties identify areas of agreement and enter stipulations, wherever feasible;

    3. Assess the relative strengths and weaknesses of the parties' positions and explain the reasons for the assessments;

    4. Help parties explore settlement;

5. Estimate, where possible, the likelihood of liability and the range of damages;

6. Help parties develop an information-sharing or discovery plan to expedite settlement discussions or to position the case for disposition by other means; and

7. Determine what, if any, follow-up measures will contribute to case development or settlement (e.g., written reports; telephone reports; additional ENE sessions; or other forms of ADR, such as arbitration, mediation, settlement conference, or consent before a Magistrate Judge).

(c) When an evaluator completes work on a case, the evaluator will, *regardless of case outcome*, submit an evaluator-assessment form to the ADR clerk.

83.12–8 Confidentiality

Early Neutral Evaluation is regarded as a settlement procedure and is confidential and private. No participant may disclose, without consent of the other parties, any confidential information acquired during the ENE session. There shall be no stenographic or electronic record, e.g., audio or video, of the ENE process.

(a) All written and oral communications made in connection with or during any ENE sessions are confidential.

(b) No communication made in connection with or during any ENE sessions may be disclosed or used for any purpose in any pending or future proceeding in this Court.

(c) Privileged and confidential status is afforded all communications made in connection with ENE sessions, including matters emanating from parties and counsel as well as evaluators' comments, assessments, and recommendations concerning case development, discovery and motions. Except for communication between the assigned judge and the evaluator regarding noncompliance with program procedures as set forth in this Rule, *there will be no communications between the Court and the evaluator regarding a case that has been designated for evaluation.* The parties will be asked to sign an agreement of confidentiality at the beginning of the evaluation session.

(d) Parties, counsel, and evaluators may respond to inquiries from authorized court staff which are made for the purposes of program evaluation. Such responses will be kept in strict confidence.

(e) The evaluator may not be required to testify in any proceeding relating to or arising out of the matter in dispute. Nor may the evaluator be subject to process requiring disclosure of information or data relating to or arising out of the matter in dispute.

83.12–9 Role of Evaluators

(a) Evaluators may not compel parties or counsel to conduct or respond to discovery or to file motions.

(b) Evaluators may not determine the issues in a case or impose limits on pretrial activities.

(c) Evaluators, and any parties who encounter a problem during the ENE session and have discussed such problem with the evaluator without obtaining a satisfactory resolution of the matter, shall report to the assigned judge any instances of noncompliance with ENE procedures that, in their view, may disrupt the evaluation process or threaten the integrity of the ENE program.

(d) Immunity. Evaluators, as well as the ADR clerk, shall be immune from claims arising out of acts or omissions incident to service as a court appointee in this Early Neutral Evaluation Program.

83.12–10 Early Neutral Evaluation Report

(a) Immediately upon conclusion of the evaluation session, the evaluator shall file a report with the ADR clerk indicating only whether the case settled, settled in part, or did not settle.

(b) In the event the parties reach an agreement to settle the case, the representatives for each party shall promptly notify the ADR clerk and promptly prepare and file the appropriate stipulation of dismissal.

(c) If the parties reach a partial agreement to narrow, withdraw, or settle some but not all claims, they shall file a stipulation concisely setting forth the resolved claims with the ADR clerk within seven (7) days of the evaluation session. The stipulation shall bind the parties.

(d) If the Early Neutral Evaluation Session does not conclude in settlement of all the issues in the case, the case will proceed toward trial pursuant to the scheduling orders entered in the case.

83.13 Sealed Matters

Cases may be sealed in their entirety, or only as to certain parties or documents, when they are initiated, or at various stages of the proceedings. The Court may on its own motion enter an order directing that a document, party or entire case be sealed. A party seeking to have a document, party or entire case sealed shall submit an application, under seal, setting forth the reason(s) why the document, party or entire case should be sealed, together with a proposed order for the assigned judge's approval. The proposed order shall include language in the "ORDERED" paragraph stating the referenced document(s) to be sealed and should include the phrase "including this sealing order." Upon the assigned judge's approval of the sealing order, the Clerk shall seal the document(s) and the sealing order. A complaint presented for filing with a motion to seal and a proposed order shall be treated as a sealed case, pending approval of the proposed order. Once the Court seals a document or case, it shall remain under seal until a subsequent order, upon the Court's own motion or in response to the motion of a party, is entered directing that the document or case be unsealed.

Pleadings and other papers filed under seal in civil actions shall remain under seal for sixty (60) days following final disposition of the action, i.e., final disposition of the action includes any time allowed by the federal rules to file an appeal in a civil matter, and, if an appeal is filed, sixty (60) days from the date of the filing of the mandate if the action was not remanded for further proceedings. After that time, the Court will unseal all sealed documents and place them in the case record[1] unless the district judge or magistrate judge, upon motion, orders that the pleading or other document remain under seal or be returned to the filing party.

83.14 Production and Disclosure of Documents and Testimony of Judicial Personnel in Legal Proceedings

(a) The purpose of the rule is to implement the policy of the Judicial Conference of the United States with regard

    1. to the production or disclosure of official information or records by the federal judiciary, and

    2. the testimony of present or former judicial personnel relating to any official information acquired by any such individual as part of the individual's performance of official duties, or by virtue of that individual's official status, in federal, state, or other legal proceedings. Implementation of this Rule is subject to the regulations that the Judicial Conference of the United States has established and which are incorporated herein. Parties can obtain a copy of such regulations from the Clerk's office.

(b) Requests that this Rule covers include an order, subpoena, or other demand of a court or administrative or other authority, of competent jurisdiction, under color of law, or any other request by whatever method, for the production, disclosure, or release of information or records by the federal judiciary, or for the appearance and testimony of federal judicial personnel as witnesses as to

---

1. If the case is fully electronic, this will mean that the documents that have been unsealed will be uploaded to CM/ECF and available for public viewing.

matters arising out of the performance of their official duties, in legal proceedings. This includes requests for voluntary production or testimony in the absence of any legal process.

(c) This Rule does not apply to requests that members of the public make, when properly made through the procedures that the Court has established for records or documents, such as court files or dockets, routinely made available to members of the public for inspection or copying.

(d) In any request for testimony or production of records, the party shall set forth a written statement explaining the nature of the testimony or records the party seeks, the relevance of that testimony or those records to the legal proceedings, and the reasons why that testimony or those records, or the information contained therein, are not readily available from other sources or by other means. This explanation shall contain sufficient information for the determining officer to decide whether or not federal judicial personnel should be allowed to testify or the records should be produced. Where the request does not contain an explanation sufficient for this purpose, the determining officer may deny the request or may ask the requester to provide additional information. The request for testimony or production of records shall be provided to the federal judicial personnel from whom testimony or production of records is sought at least twenty-one (21) days in advance of the date on which the testimony or production of records is required. Failure to meet this requirement shall provide a sufficient basis for denial of the request.

(e) In the case of a request directed to a district judge or a magistrate judge, or directed to a current or former member of such a judge's personal staff, the determining officer shall be the district judge or the magistrate judge.

(f) Procedures to be followed:

1. In the case of a request directed to an employee or former employee of the Clerk's office, the determining officer shall be the Clerk. The Clerk shall consult with the Chief Judge for determination of the proper response to a request.

2. In the case of a request directed to an employee or former employee of the Probation Office, the determining officer will be the Chief Probation Officer or his or her designee. The determining officer shall consult with the Chief Judge or his or her designee regarding the proper response to a request. The Chief Probation Officer's designee(s) will be the officer to whom the request is directed and the officer's supervisor or manager. The Chief Judge's designee will be the judge who sentenced the offender who made the request or whose records are the subject of the request. Requests for disclosure, other

than subpoenas, not otherwise covered by memorandum of understanding, statute, rule of procedure, regulation, case law, or court-approved local policy, will be presented to the sentencing judge, or in that judge's absence, the Chief Judge, for approval. All subpoenas will be presented to the Court.

84.1   Forms

[Reserved.]

85.1   Title

[Reserved.]

86.1   Effective Date

See L.R. 1.1(b).

SECTION XI.   CRIMINAL PROCEDURE

[Omitted.]

SECTION XII.   LOCAL RULES OF PROCEDURE FOR ADMIRALTY AND MARITIME CASES

[Omitted.]

INDEX

References are to Federal Rule of Civil Procedure (C),
Federal Rule of Appellate Procedure (A),
Section of 28 U.S.C. (§), or Federal
Rule of Evidence (E)

INDEX

INDEX

810

*

APPENDIX: FORMER FEDERAL RULES OF CIVIL PROCEDURE

Editor's Note
on amendments effective December 1, 2007

On December 1, 2007, massive albeit mainly stylistic amendments to all the Federal Rules of Civil Procedure became effective. Also in the package were minor substantive changes to Rules 4(k), 9(h), 11(a), 14(b), 16(c), 26(g), 30(b), 31(c), 40, 71.1(d), and 78, as well as the addition of Rule 5.2 on privacy protection.

The restyling came about as part of a bigger project, begun in 1992, to clarify and simplify the wording of all the major sets of court rules, supposedly making then easier to use and understand without changing their meaning. See Edward H. Cooper, *Restyling the Civil Rules: Clarity Without Change*, 79 Notre Dame L. Rev. 1761 (2004).

Serious questions exist as to whether the benefits of restyling outweigh the considerable costs of performing this immense task and then in assimilating the product—plus the costs imposed by the inevitable changes of substance inadvertently made by the restylers, and the costs of litigating about those changes. See Edward A. Hartnett, *Against (Mere) Restyling*, 82 Notre Dame L. Rev. 155 (2006).

This appendix provides you with the former Federal Rules of Civil Procedure, as they existed prior to December 1, 2007.

I. SCOPE OF RULES—ONE FORM OF ACTION

Rule 1. SCOPE AND PURPOSE OF RULES

These rules govern the procedure in the United States district courts in all suits of a civil nature whether cognizable as cases at law or in equity or in admiralty, with the exceptions stated in Rule 81. They shall be construed and administered to secure the just, speedy, and inexpensive determination of every action.

Rule 2. ONE FORM OF ACTION

There shall be one form of action to be known as "civil action".

II. COMMENCEMENT OF ACTION; SERVICE OF PROCESS, PLEADINGS, MOTIONS, AND ORDERS

Rule 3. COMMENCEMENT OF ACTION

A civil action is commenced by filing a complaint with the court.

Rule 4. SUMMONS

(a) Form. The summons shall be signed by the clerk, bear the seal of the court, identify the court and the parties, be directed to the defendant, and state the name and address of the plaintiff's attorney or, if unrepresented, of the plaintiff. It shall also state the time within which the defendant must appear and defend, and notify the defendant that failure to do so will result in a judgment by default against the defendant for the relief demanded in the complaint. The court may allow a summons to be amended.

(b) Issuance. Upon or after filing the complaint, the plaintiff may present a summons to the clerk for signature and seal. If the summons is in proper form, the clerk shall sign, seal, and issue it to the plaintiff for service on the defendant. A summons, or a copy of the summons if addressed to multiple defendants, shall be issued for each defendant to be served.

(c) Service With Complaint; by Whom Made.

(1) A summons shall be served together with a copy of the complaint. The plaintiff is responsible for service of a summons and complaint within the time allowed under subdivision (m) and shall furnish the person effecting service with the necessary copies of the summons and complaint.

(2) Service may be effected by any person who is not a party and who is at least 18 years of age. At the request of the plaintiff, however, the court may direct that service be effected by a United States marshal, deputy United States marshal, or other person or officer specially appointed by the court for that purpose. Such an appointment must be made when the plaintiff is authorized to proceed in forma pauperis pursuant to 28 U.S.C. § 1915 or is authorized to proceed as a seaman under 28 U.S.C. § 1916.

(d) Waiver of Service; Duty to Save Costs of Service; Request to Waive.

(1) A defendant who waives service of a summons does not thereby waive any objection to the venue or to the jurisdiction of the court over the person of the defendant.

(2) An individual, corporation, or association that is subject to service under subdivision (e), (f), or (h) and that receives notice of an action in the manner provided in this paragraph has a duty to avoid unnecessary costs of serving the summons. To avoid costs, the plaintiff may notify such a defendant of the commencement of the action and request that the defendant waive service of a summons. The notice and request

(A) shall be in writing and shall be addressed directly to the defendant, if an individual, or else to an officer or managing or general agent (or other agent authorized by appointment or law to receive service of process) of a defendant subject to service under subdivision (h);

(B) shall be dispatched through first-class mail or other reliable means;

(C) shall be accompanied by a copy of the complaint and shall identify the court in which it has been filed;

(D) shall inform the defendant, by means of a text prescribed in an official form promulgated pursuant to Rule 84, of the consequences of compliance and of a failure to comply with the request;

(E) shall set forth the date on which the request is sent;

(F) shall allow the defendant a reasonable time to return the waiver, which shall be at least 30 days from the date on which the request is sent, or 60 days from that date if the defendant is addressed outside any judicial district of the United States; and

(G) shall provide the defendant with an extra copy of the notice and request, as well as a prepaid means of compliance in writing.

If a defendant located within the United States fails to comply with a request for waiver made by a plaintiff located within the United States, the court shall impose the costs subsequently incurred in effecting service on the defendant unless good cause for the failure be shown.

(3) A defendant that, before being served with process, timely returns a waiver so requested is not required to serve an answer to the complaint until 60 days after the date on which the request for waiver of service was sent, or 90 days after that date if the defendant was addressed outside any judicial district of the United States.

(4) When the plaintiff files a waiver of service with the court, the action shall proceed, except as provided in paragraph (3), as if a summons and complaint had been served at the time of filing the waiver, and no proof of service shall be required.

(5) The costs to be imposed on a defendant under paragraph (2) for failure to comply with a request to waive service of a summons shall include the costs subsequently incurred in effecting service under subdivision (e), (f), or (h), together with the costs, including a reasonable attorney's fee, of any motion required to collect the costs of service.

(e) Service Upon Individuals Within a Judicial District of the United States. Unless otherwise provided by federal law, service upon an individual from whom a waiver has not been obtained and filed, other than an infant or an incompetent person, may be effected in any judicial district of the United States:

(1) pursuant to the law of the state in which the district court is located, or in which service is effected, for the service of a summons upon the defendant in an action brought in the courts of general jurisdiction of the State; or

(2) by delivering a copy of the summons and of the complaint to the individual personally or by leaving copies thereof at the individual's dwelling house or usual place of abode with some person of suitable age and discretion then residing therein or by delivering a copy of the summons and of the complaint to an agent authorized by appointment or by law to receive service of process.

(f) Service Upon Individuals in a Foreign Country. Unless otherwise provided by federal law, service upon an individual from whom a waiver has not been obtained and filed, other than an infant or an incompetent person, may be effected in a place not within any judicial district of the United States:

(1) by any internationally agreed means reasonably calculated to give notice, such as those means authorized by the Hague Convention on the Service Abroad of Judicial and Extrajudicial Documents; or

(2) if there is no internationally agreed means of service or the applicable international agreement allows other means of service, provided that service is reasonably calculated to give notice:

(A) in the manner prescribed by the law of the foreign country for service in that country in an action in any of its courts of general jurisdiction; or

(B) as directed by the foreign authority in response to a letter rogatory or letter of request; or

(C) unless prohibited by the law of the foreign country, by

(i) delivery to the individual personally of a copy of the summons and the complaint; or

(ii) any form of mail requiring a signed receipt, to be addressed and dispatched by the clerk of the court to the party to be served; or

(3) by other means not prohibited by international agreement as may be directed by the court.

(g) Service Upon Infants and Incompetent Persons. Service upon an infant or an incompetent person in a judicial district of the United States shall be effected in the manner prescribed by the law of the state in which the service is made for the service of summons or other like process upon any such defendant in an action brought in the courts of general jurisdiction of that state. Service upon an infant or an incompetent person in a place not within any judicial district of the United States shall be effected in the manner prescribed by paragraph (2)(A) or (2)(B) of subdivision (f) or by such means as the court may direct.

(h) Service Upon Corporations and Associations. Unless otherwise provided by federal law, service upon a domestic or foreign corporation or upon a partnership or other unincorporated association that is subject to suit under a common name, and from which a waiver of service has not been obtained and filed, shall be effected:

(1) in a judicial district of the United States in the manner prescribed for individuals by subdivision (e)(1), or by delivering a copy of the summons and of the complaint to an officer, a managing or general agent, or to any other agent authorized by appointment or by law to receive service of process and, if the agent is one authorized by statute to receive service and the statute so requires, by also mailing a copy to the defendant, or

(2) in a place not within any judicial district of the United States in any manner prescribed for individuals by subdivision (f) except personal delivery as provided in paragraph (2)(C)(i) thereof.

(i) Serving the United States, Its Agencies, Corporations, Officers, or Employees.

(1) Service upon the United States shall be effected

(A) by delivering a copy of the summons and of the complaint to the United States attorney for the district in which the action is brought or to an assistant United States attorney or clerical employee designated by the United States attorney in a writing filed with the clerk of the court or by sending a copy of the summons and of the complaint by registered or certified mail addressed to the civil process clerk at the office of the United States attorney and

(B) by also sending a copy of the summons and of the complaint by registered or certified mail to the Attorney General of the United States at Washington, District of Columbia, and

(C) in any action attacking the validity of an order of an officer or agency of the United States not made a party, by also sending a copy of the summons and of the complaint by registered or certified mail to the officer or agency.

(2)(A) Service on an agency or corporation of the United States, or an officer or employee of the United States sued only in an official capacity, is effected by serving the United States in the manner prescribed by Rule 4(i)(1) and by also sending a copy of the summons and complaint by registered or certified mail to the officer, employee, agency, or corporation.

(B) Service on an officer or employee of the United States sued in an individual capacity for acts or omissions occurring in connection with the performance of duties on behalf of the United States—whether or not the officer or employee is sued also in an official capacity—is effected by serving the United States in the manner prescribed by Rule 4(i)(1) and by serving the officer or employee in the manner prescribed by Rule 4 (e), (f), or (g).

(3) The court shall allow a reasonable time to serve process under Rule 4(i) for the purpose of curing the failure to serve:

(A) all persons required to be served in an action governed by Rule 4(i)(2)(A), if the plaintiff has served either the United States attorney or the Attorney General of the United States, or

(B) the United States in an action governed by Rule 4(i)(2)(B), if the plaintiff has served an officer or employee of the United States sued in an individual capacity.

(j) Service Upon Foreign, State, or Local Governments.

(1) Service upon a foreign state or a political subdivision, agency, or instrumentality thereof shall be effected pursuant to 28 U.S.C. § 1608.

(2) Service upon a state, municipal corporation, or other governmental organization subject to suit shall be effected by delivering a copy of the summons and of the complaint to its chief executive officer or by serving the summons and complaint in the manner prescribed by the law of that state for the service of summons or other like process upon any such defendant.

(k) Territorial Limits of Effective Service.

(1) Service of a summons or filing a waiver of service is effective to establish jurisdiction over the person of a defendant

(A) who could be subjected to the jurisdiction of a court of general jurisdiction in the state in which the district court is located, or

(B) who is a party joined under Rule 14 or Rule 19 and is served at a place within a judicial district of the United States and not more than 100 miles from the place from which the summons issues, or

(C) who is subject to the federal interpleader jurisdiction under 28 U.S.C. § 1335, or

(D) when authorized by a statute of the United States.

(2) If the exercise of jurisdiction is consistent with the Constitution and laws of the United States, serving a summons or filing a waiver of service is also effective, with respect to claims arising under federal law, to establish personal jurisdiction over the person of any defendant who is not subject to the jurisdiction of the courts of general jurisdiction of any state.

(*l*) **Proof of Service.** If service is not waived, the person effecting service shall make proof thereof to the court. If service is made by a person other than a United States marshal or deputy United States marshal, the person shall make affidavit thereof. Proof of service in a place not within any judicial district of the United States shall, if effected under paragraph (1) of subdivision (f), be made pursuant to the applicable treaty or convention, and shall, if effected under paragraph (2) or (3) thereof, include a receipt signed by the addressee or other evidence of delivery to the addressee satisfactory to the court. Failure to make proof of service does not affect the validity of the service. The court may allow proof of service to be amended.

(m) **Time Limit for Service.** If service of the summons and complaint is not made upon a defendant within 120 days after the filing of the complaint, the court, upon motion or on its own initiative after notice to the plaintiff, shall dismiss the action without prejudice as to that defendant or direct that service be effected within a specified time; provided that if the plaintiff shows good cause for the failure, the court shall extend the time for service for an appropriate period. This subdivision does not apply to service in a foreign country pursuant to subdivision (f) or (j)(1).

(n) **Seizure of Property; Service of Summons Not Feasible.**

(1) If a statute of the United States so provides, the court may assert jurisdiction over property. Notice to claimants of the property shall then be sent in the manner provided by the statute or by service of a summons under this rule.

(2) Upon a showing that personal jurisdiction over a defendant cannot, in the district where the action is brought, be obtained with reasonable efforts by service of summons in any manner authorized by this rule, the court may assert jurisdiction over any of the defendant's assets found within the district by seizing the assets under the circumstances and in the manner provided by the law of the state in which the district court is located.

Rule 4.1. SERVICE OF OTHER PROCESS

(a) **Generally.** Process other than a summons as provided in Rule 4 or subpoena as provided in Rule 45 shall be served by a United States marshal, a deputy United States marshal, or a person specially appointed for that purpose, who shall make proof of service as provided in Rule 4(*l*).

The process may be served anywhere within the territorial limits of the state in which the district court is located, and, when authorized by a statute of the United States, beyond the territorial limits of that state.

(b) Enforcement of Orders: Commitment for Civil Contempt. An order of civil commitment of a person held to be in contempt of a decree or injunction issued to enforce the laws of the United States may be served and enforced in any district. Other orders in civil contempt proceedings shall be served in the state in which the court issuing the order to be enforced is located or elsewhere within the United States if not more than 100 miles from the place at which the order to be enforced was issued.

Rule 5. SERVING AND FILING PLEADINGS AND OTHER PAPERS

(a) Service: When Required. Except as otherwise provided in these rules, every order required by its terms to be served, every pleading subsequent to the original complaint unless the court otherwise orders because of numerous defendants, every paper relating to discovery required to be served upon a party unless the court otherwise orders, every written motion other than one which may be heard ex parte, and every written notice, appearance, demand, offer of judgment, designation of record on appeal, and similar paper shall be served upon each of the parties. No service need be made on parties in default for failure to appear except that pleadings asserting new or additional claims for relief against them shall be served upon them in the manner provided for service of summons in Rule 4.

In an action begun by seizure of property, in which no person need be or is named as defendant, any service required to be made prior to the filing of an answer, claim, or appearance shall be made upon the person having custody or possession of the property at the time of its seizure.

(b) Making Service.

(1) Service under Rules 5(a) and 77(d) on a party represented by an attorney is made on the attorney unless the court orders service on the party.

(2) Service under Rule 5(a) is made by:

(A) Delivering a copy to the person served by:

(i) handing it to the person;

(ii) leaving it at the person's office with a clerk or other person in charge, or if no one is in charge leaving it in a conspicuous place in the office; or

(iii) if the person has no office or the office is closed, leaving it at the person's dwelling house or usual place of abode with someone of suitable age and discretion residing there.

(B) Mailing a copy to the last known address of the person served. Service by mail is complete on mailing.

(C) If the person served has no known address, leaving a copy with the clerk of the court.

(D) Delivering a copy by any other means, including electronic means, consented to in writing by the person served. Service by electronic means is complete on transmission; service by other consented means is complete when the person making service delivers the copy to the agency designated to make delivery. If authorized by local rule, a party may make service under this subparagraph (D) through the court's transmission facilities.

(3) Service by electronic means under Rule 5(b)(2)(D) is not effective if the party making service learns that the attempted service did not reach the person to be served.

(c) Same: Numerous Defendants. In any action in which there are unusually large numbers of defendants, the court, upon motion or of its own initiative, may order that service of the pleadings of the defendants and replies thereto need not be made as between the defendants and that any cross-claim, counterclaim, or matter constituting an avoidance or affirmative defense contained therein shall be deemed to be denied or avoided by all other parties and that the filing of any such pleading and service thereof upon the plaintiff constitutes due notice of it to the parties. A copy of every such order shall be served upon the parties in such manner and form as the court directs.

(d) Filing; Certificate of Service. All papers after the complaint required to be served upon a party, together with a certificate of service, must be filed with the court within a reasonable time after service, but disclosures under Rule 26(a)(1) or (2) and the following discovery requests and responses must not be filed until they are used in the proceeding or the court orders filing: (i) depositions, (ii) interrogatories, (iii) requests for documents or to permit entry upon land, and (iv) requests for admission.

(e) Filing With the Court Defined. The filing of papers with the court as required by these rules shall be made by filing them with the clerk of court, except that the judge may permit the papers to be filed with the judge, in which event the judge shall note thereon the filing date and forthwith transmit them to the office of the clerk. A court may by local rule permit or require papers to be filed, signed, or verified by electronic means that are consistent with technical standards, if any, that the Judicial Conference of the United States establishes. A local rule may require filing by electronic means only if reasonable exceptions are allowed. A paper filed by electronic means in compliance with a local rule constitutes a written paper for the purpose of applying these rules. The clerk shall not refuse to accept for filing any paper presented for that purpose solely because it is not presented in proper form as required by these rules or any local rules or practices.

Rule 5.1.　CONSTITUTIONAL CHALLENGE TO A STATUTE— NOTICE, CERTIFICATION, AND INTERVENTION

(a) Notice by a Party. A party that files a pleading, written motion, or other paper drawing into question the constitutionality of a federal or state statute must promptly:

(1) file a notice of constitutional question stating the question and identifying the paper that raises it, if:

(A) a federal statute is questioned and neither the United States nor any of its agencies, officers, or employees is a party in an official capacity, or

(B) a state statute is questioned and neither the state nor any of its agencies, officers, or employees is a party in an official capacity; and

(2) serve the notice and paper on the Attorney General of the United States if a federal statute is challenged—or on the state attorney general if a state statute is challenged—either by certified or registered mail or by sending it to an electronic address designated by the attorney general for this purpose.

(b) Certification by the Court. The court must, under 28 U.S.C. § 2403, certify to the Attorney General of the United States that there is a constitutional challenge to a federal statute, or certify to the state attorney general that there is a constitutional challenge to a state statute.

(c) Intervention; Final Decision on the Merits. Unless the court sets a later time, the attorney general may intervene within 60 days after the notice of constitutional question is filed or after the court certifies the challenge, whichever is earlier. Before the time to intervene expires, the court may reject the constitutional challenge, but may not enter a final judgment holding the statute unconstitutional.

(d) No Forfeiture. A party's failure to file and serve the notice, or the court's failure to certify, does not forfeit a constitutional claim or defense that is otherwise timely asserted.

Rule 6. TIME

(a) Computation. In computing any period of time prescribed or allowed by these rules, by the local rules of any district court, by order of court, or by any applicable statute, the day of the act, event, or default from which the designated period of time begins to run shall not be included. The last day of the period so computed shall be included, unless it is a Saturday, a Sunday, or a legal holiday, or, when the act to be done is the filing of a paper in court, a day on which weather or other conditions have made the office of the clerk of the district court inaccessible, in which event the period runs until the end of the next day which is not one of the aforementioned days. When the period of time prescribed or allowed is less than 11 days, intermediate Saturdays, Sundays, and legal holidays shall be excluded in the computation. As used in this rule and in Rule 77(c), "legal holiday" includes New Year's Day, Birthday of Martin Luther King, Jr., Washington's Birthday, Memorial Day, Independence Day, Labor Day, Columbus Day, Veterans Day, Thanksgiving Day, Christmas Day, and any other day appointed as a holiday by the President or the Congress of the United States, or by the state in which the district court is held.

(b) Enlargement. When by these rules or by a notice given thereunder or by order of court an act is required or allowed to be done at or within a specified time, the court for cause shown may at any time in its discretion (1) with or without motion or notice order the period enlarged if request therefor is made before the expiration of the period originally prescribed or as extended by a previous order, or (2) upon motion made after the expiration of the specified period permit the act to be done where the failure to act was the result of excusable neglect; but it may not extend the time for taking any action under Rules 50(b) and (c)(2), 52(b), 59(b), (d) and (e), and 60(b), except to the extent and under the conditions stated in them.

(c) [Abrogated.]

(d) For Motions—Affidavits. A written motion, other than one which may be heard ex parte, and notice of the hearing thereof shall be served not later than 5 days before the time specified for the hearing, unless a different period is fixed by these rules or by order of the court. Such an order may for cause shown be made on ex parte application. When a motion is supported by affidavit, the affidavit shall be served with the motion; and, except as otherwise provided in Rule 59(c), opposing affidavits may be served not later than 1 day before the hearing, unless the court permits them to be served at some other time.

(e) Additional Time After Certain Kinds of Service. Whenever a party must or may act within a prescribed period after service and service is made under Rule 5(b)(2)(B), (C), or (D), 3 days are added after the prescribed period would otherwise expire under subdivision (a).

III. PLEADINGS AND MOTIONS

Rule 7. PLEADINGS ALLOWED; FORM OF MOTIONS

(a) Pleadings. There shall be a complaint and an answer; a reply to a counterclaim denominated as such; an answer to a cross-claim, if the answer contains a cross-claim; a third-party complaint, if a person who was not an original party is summoned under the provisions of Rule 14; and a third-party answer, if a third-party complaint is served. No other pleading shall be allowed, except that the court may order a reply to an answer or a third-party answer.

(b) Motions and Other Papers.

(1) An application to the court for an order shall be by motion which, unless made during a hearing or trial, shall be made in writing, shall state with particularity the grounds therefor, and shall set forth the relief or order sought. The requirement of writing is fulfilled if the motion is stated in a written notice of the hearing of the motion.

(2) The rules applicable to captions and other matters of form of pleadings apply to all motions and other papers provided for by these rules.

(3) All motions shall be signed in accordance with Rule 11.

(c) Demurrers, Pleas, etc., Abolished. Demurrers, pleas, and exceptions for insufficiency of a pleading shall not be used.

Rule 7.1. DISCLOSURE STATEMENT

(a) Who Must File: Nongovernmental Corporate Party. A nongovernmental corporate party to an action or proceeding in a district court must file two copies of a statement that identifies any parent corporation and any publicly held corporation that owns 10% or more of its stock or states that there is no such corporation.

(b) Time for Filing; Supplemental Filing. A party must:

(1) file the Rule 7.1(a) statement with its first appearance, pleading, petition, motion, response, or other request addressed to the court, and

(2) promptly file a supplemental statement upon any change in the information that the statement requires.

Rule 8. GENERAL RULES OF PLEADING

(a) Claims for Relief. A pleading which sets forth a claim for relief, whether an original claim, counterclaim, cross-claim, or third-party claim, shall contain (1) a short and plain statement of the grounds upon which the court's jurisdiction depends, unless the court already has jurisdiction and the claim needs no new grounds of jurisdiction to support it, (2) a short and plain statement of the claim showing that the pleader is entitled to relief, and (3) a demand for judgment for the relief the pleader seeks. Relief in the alternative or of several different types may be demanded.

(b) Defenses; Form of Denials. A party shall state in short and plain terms the party's defenses to each claim asserted and shall admit or deny the averments upon which the adverse party relies. If a party is without knowledge or information sufficient to form a belief as to the truth of an averment, the party shall so state and this has the effect of a denial. Denials shall fairly meet the substance of the averments denied. When a pleader intends in good faith to deny only a part or a qualification of an averment, the pleader shall specify so much of it as is true and material and shall deny only the remainder. Unless the pleader intends in good faith to controvert all the averments of the preceding pleading, the pleader may make denials as specific denials of designated averments or paragraphs or may generally deny all the averments except such designated averments or paragraphs as the pleader expressly admits; but, when the pleader does so intend to controvert all its averments, including averments of the grounds upon which the court's jurisdiction depends, the pleader may do so by general denial subject to the obligations set forth in Rule 11.

(c) Affirmative Defenses. In pleading to a preceding pleading, a party shall set forth affirmatively accord and satisfaction, arbitration and award, assumption of risk, contributory negligence, discharge in bankruptcy, duress, estoppel, failure of consideration, fraud, illegality, injury by fellow servant, laches, license, payment, release, res judicata, statute of frauds, statute of limitations, waiver, and any other matter constituting an avoidance or affirmative defense. When a party has mistakenly designated a defense as a counterclaim or a counterclaim as a defense, the court on terms, if justice so requires, shall treat the pleading as if there had been a proper designation.

(d) Effect of Failure to Deny. Averments in a pleading to which a responsive pleading is required, other than those as to the amount of damage, are admitted when not denied in the responsive pleading. Averments in a pleading to which no responsive pleading is required or permitted shall be taken as denied or avoided.

(e) Pleading to Be Concise and Direct; Consistency.

(1) Each averment of a pleading shall be simple, concise, and direct. No technical forms of pleading or motions are required.

(2) A party may set forth two or more statements of a claim or defense alternately or hypothetically, either in one count or defense or in separate counts or defenses. When two or more statements are made in the alternative and one of them if made independently would be sufficient, the pleading is not made insufficient by the insufficiency of one or more of the alternative statements. A party may also state as many separate claims or defenses as the party has regardless of consistency and whether based on legal, equitable, or maritime grounds. All statements shall be made subject to the obligations set forth in Rule 11.

(f) Construction of Pleadings. All pleadings shall be so construed as to do substantial justice.

Rule 9. PLEADING SPECIAL MATTERS

(a) Capacity. It is not necessary to aver the capacity of a party to sue or be sued or the authority of a party to sue or be sued in a representative capacity or the legal existence of an organized association of persons that is made a party, except to the extent required to show the jurisdiction of the court. When a party desires to raise an issue as to the legal existence of any party or the capacity of any party to sue or be sued or the authority of a party to sue or be sued in a representative capacity, the party desiring to raise the issue shall do so by specific negative averment, which shall include such supporting particulars as are peculiarly within the pleader's knowledge.

(b) Fraud, Mistake, Condition of the Mind. In all averments of fraud or mistake, the circumstances constituting fraud or mistake shall be stated with particularity. Malice, intent, knowledge, and other condition of mind of a person may be averred generally.

(c) Conditions Precedent. In pleading the performance or occurrence of conditions precedent, it is sufficient to aver generally that all conditions precedent have been performed or have occurred. A denial of performance or occurrence shall be made specifically and with particularity.

(d) Official Document or Act. In pleading an official document or official act it is sufficient to aver that the document was issued or the act done in compliance with law.

(e) Judgment. In pleading a judgment or decision of a domestic or foreign court, judicial or quasi-judicial tribunal, or of a board or officer, it is sufficient to aver the judgment or decision without setting forth matter showing jurisdiction to render it.

(f) Time and Place. For the purpose of testing the sufficiency of a pleading, averments of time and place are material and shall be considered like all other averments of material matter.

(g) Special Damage. When items of special damage are claimed, they shall be specifically stated.

(h) Admiralty and Maritime Claims. A pleading or count setting forth a claim for relief within the admiralty and maritime jurisdiction that is also within the jurisdiction of the district court on some other ground may contain a statement identifying the claim as an admiralty or maritime claim for the purposes of Rules 14(c), 38(e), 82, and the Supplemental Rules for Admiralty or Maritime Claims and Asset Forfeiture Actions. If the claim is cognizable only in admiralty, it is an admiralty or maritime claim for those purposes whether so identified or not. The amendment of a pleading to add or withdraw an identifying statement is governed by the principles of Rule 15. A case that includes an admiralty or maritime claim within this subdivision is an admiralty case within 28 U.S.C. § 1292(a)(3).

Rule 10. FORM OF PLEADINGS

(a) Caption; Names of Parties. Every pleading shall contain a caption setting forth the name of the court, the title of the action, the file number, and a designation as in Rule 7(a). In the complaint the title of the action shall include the names of all the parties, but in other pleadings it is sufficient to state the name of the first party on each side with an appropriate indication of other parties.

(b) Paragraphs; Separate Statements. All averments of claim or defense shall be made in numbered paragraphs, the contents of each of which shall be limited as far as practicable to a statement of a single set of circumstances; and a paragraph may be referred to by number in all succeeding pleadings. Each claim founded upon a separate transaction or occurrence and each defense other than denials shall be stated in a separate count or defense whenever a separation facilitates the clear presentation of the matters set forth.

(c) Adoption by Reference; Exhibits. Statements in a pleading may be adopted by reference in a different part of the same pleading or in another pleading or in any motion. A copy of any written instrument which is an exhibit to a pleading is a part thereof for all purposes.

Rule 11. SIGNING OF PLEADINGS, MOTIONS, AND OTHER PAPERS; REPRESENTATIONS TO COURT; SANCTIONS

(a) Signature. Every pleading, written motion, and other paper shall be signed by at least one attorney of record in the attorney's individual name, or, if the party is not represented by an attorney, shall be signed by the party. Each paper shall state the signer's address and telephone number, if any. Except when otherwise specifically provided by rule or statute, pleadings need not be verified or accompanied by affidavit. An unsigned paper shall be stricken unless omission of the signature is corrected promptly after being called to the attention of the attorney or party.

(b) Representations to Court. By presenting to the court (whether by signing, filing, submitting, or later advocating) a pleading, written motion, or other paper, an attorney or unrepresented party is certifying that to the best of the person's knowledge, information, and belief, formed after an inquiry reasonable under the circumstances,—

(1) it is not being presented for any improper purpose, such as to harass or to cause unnecessary delay or needless increase in the cost of litigation;

(2) the claims, defenses, and other legal contentions therein are warranted by existing law or by a nonfrivolous argument for the

extension, modification, or reversal of existing law or the establishment of new law;

(3) the allegations and other factual contentions have evidentiary support or, if specifically so identified, are likely to have evidentiary support after a reasonable opportunity for further investigation or discovery; and

(4) the denials of factual contentions are warranted on the evidence or, if specifically so identified, are reasonably based on a lack of information or belief.

(c) Sanctions. If, after notice and a reasonable opportunity to respond, the court determines that subdivision (b) has been violated, the court may, subject to the conditions stated below, impose an appropriate sanction upon the attorneys, law firms, or parties that have violated subdivision (b) or are responsible for the violation.

(1) *How Initiated.*

(A) *By Motion.* A motion for sanctions under this rule shall be made separately from other motions or requests and shall describe the specific conduct alleged to violate subdivision (b). It shall be served as provided in Rule 5, but shall not be filed with or presented to the court unless, within 21 days after service of the motion (or such other period as the court may prescribe), the challenged paper, claim, defense, contention, allegation, or denial is not withdrawn or appropriately corrected. If warranted, the court may award to the party prevailing on the motion the reasonable expenses and attorney's fees incurred in presenting or opposing the motion. Absent exceptional circumstances, a law firm shall be held jointly responsible for violations committed by its partners, associates, and employees.

(B) *On Court's Initiative.* On its own initiative, the court may enter an order describing the specific conduct that appears to violate subdivision (b) and directing an attorney, law firm, or party to show cause why it has not violated subdivision (b) with respect thereto.

(2) *Nature of Sanction; Limitations.* A sanction imposed for violation of this rule shall be limited to what is sufficient to deter repetition of such conduct or comparable conduct by others similarly situated. Subject to the limitations in subparagraphs (A) and (B), the sanction may consist of, or include, directives of a nonmonetary nature, an order to pay a penalty into court, or, if imposed on motion and warranted for effective deterrence, an order directing payment to the movant of some or all of the reasonable attorneys' fees and other expenses incurred as a direct result of the violation.

(A) Monetary sanctions may not be awarded against a represented party for a violation of subdivision (b)(2).

(B) Monetary sanctions may not be awarded on the court's initiative unless the court issues its order to show cause before a voluntary dismissal or settlement of the claims made by or against the party which is, or whose attorneys are, to be sanctioned.

(3) *Order.* When imposing sanctions, the court shall describe the conduct determined to constitute a violation of this rule and explain the basis for the sanction imposed.

(d) Inapplicability to Discovery. Subdivisions (a) through (c) of this rule do not apply to disclosures and discovery requests, responses, objections, and motions that are subject to the provisions of Rules 26 through 37.

Rule 12. DEFENSES AND OBJECTIONS—WHEN AND HOW PRESENTED—BY PLEADING OR MOTION—MOTION FOR JUDGMENT ON THE PLEADINGS

(a) When Presented.

(1) Unless a different time is prescribed in a statute of the United States, a defendant shall serve an answer

(A) within 20 days after being served with the summons and complaint, or

(B) if service of the summons has been timely waived on request under Rule 4(d), within 60 days after the date when the request for waiver was sent, or within 90 days after that date if the defendant was addressed outside any judicial district of the United States.

(2) A party served with a pleading stating a cross-claim against that party shall serve an answer thereto within 20 days after being served. The plaintiff shall serve a reply to a counterclaim in the answer within 20 days after service of the answer, or, if a reply is ordered by the court, within 20 days after service of the order, unless the order otherwise directs.

(3)(A) The United States, an agency of the United States, or an officer or employee of the United States sued in an official capacity, shall serve an answer to the complaint or cross-claim—or a reply to a counterclaim— within 60 days after the United States attorney is served with the pleading asserting the claim.

(B) An officer or employee of the United States sued in an individual capacity for acts or omissions occurring in connection with the performance of duties on behalf of the United States shall serve an answer to the complaint or cross-claim—or a reply to a counterclaim—within 60 days after service on the officer or employee, or service on the United States attorney, whichever is later.

(4) Unless a different time is fixed by court order, the service of a motion permitted under this rule alters these periods of time as follows:

(A) if the court denies the motion or postpones its disposition until the trial on the merits, the responsive pleading shall be served within 10 days after notice of the court's action; or

(B) if the court grants a motion for a more definite statement, the responsive pleading shall be served within 10 days after the service of the more definite statement.

(b) How Presented. Every defense, in law or fact, to a claim for relief in any pleading, whether a claim, counterclaim, cross-claim, or third-party claim, shall be asserted in the responsive pleading thereto if one is required, except that the following defenses may at the option of the pleader be made by motion: (1) lack of jurisdiction over the subject matter, (2) lack of jurisdiction over the person, (3) improper venue, (4) insufficiency of process, (5) insufficiency of service of process, (6) failure to state a claim upon which relief can be granted, (7) failure to join a party under Rule 19. A motion making any of these defenses shall be made before pleading if a further pleading is permitted. No defense or objection is waived by being joined with one or more other defenses or objections in a responsive pleading or motion. If a pleading sets forth a claim for relief to which the adverse party is not required to serve a responsive pleading, the adverse party may assert at the trial any defense in law or fact to that claim for relief. If, on a motion asserting the defense numbered (6) to dismiss for failure of the pleading to state a claim upon which relief can be granted, matters outside the pleading are presented to and not excluded by the court, the motion shall be treated as one for summary judgment and disposed of as provided in Rule 56, and all parties shall be given reasonable opportunity to present all material made pertinent to such a motion by Rule 56.

(c) Motion for Judgment on the Pleadings. After the pleadings are closed but within such time as not to delay the trial, any party may move for judgment on the pleadings. If, on a motion for judgment on the pleadings, matters outside the pleadings are presented to and not excluded by the court, the motion shall be treated as one for summary judgment and disposed of as provided in Rule 56, and all parties shall be given reasonable opportunity to present all material made pertinent to such a motion by Rule 56.

(d) Preliminary Hearings. The defenses specifically enumerated (1)–(7) in subdivision (b) of this rule, whether made in a pleading or by motion, and the motion for judgment mentioned in subdivision (c) of this rule shall be heard and determined before trial on application of any party, unless the court orders that the hearing and determination thereof be deferred until the trial.

(e) Motion for More Definite Statement. If a pleading to which a responsive pleading is permitted is so vague or ambiguous that a party cannot reasonably be required to frame a responsive pleading, the party may move for a more definite statement before interposing a responsive pleading. The motion shall point out the defects complained of and the details desired. If the motion is granted and the order of the court is not obeyed within 10 days after notice of the order or within such other time as the court may fix, the court may strike the pleading to which the motion was directed or make such order as it deems just.

(f) Motion to Strike. Upon motion made by a party before responding to a pleading or, if no responsive pleading is permitted by these rules, upon motion made by a party within 20 days after the service of the pleading upon the party or upon the court's own initiative at any time, the court may order stricken from any pleading any insufficient defense or any redundant, immaterial, impertinent, or scandalous matter.

(g) Consolidation of Defenses in Motion. A party who makes a motion under this rule may join with it any other motions herein provided for and then available to the party. If a party makes a motion under this rule but omits therefrom any defense or objection then available to the party which this rule permits to be raised by motion, the party shall not thereafter make a motion based on the defense or objection so omitted, except a motion as provided in subdivision (h)(2) hereof on any of the grounds there stated.

(h) Waiver or Preservation of Certain Defenses.

(1) A defense of lack of jurisdiction over the person, improper venue, insufficiency of process, or insufficiency of service of process is waived (A) if omitted from a motion in the circumstances described in subdivision (g), or (B) if it is neither made by motion under this rule nor included in a responsive pleading or an amendment thereof permitted by Rule 15(a) to be made as a matter of course.

(2) A defense of failure to state a claim upon which relief can be granted, a defense of failure to join a party indispensable under Rule 19, and an objection of failure to state a legal defense to a claim may be made in any pleading permitted or ordered under Rule 7(a), or by motion for judgment on the pleadings, or at the trial on the merits.

(3) Whenever it appears by suggestion of the parties or otherwise that the court lacks jurisdiction of the subject matter, the court shall dismiss the action.

Rule 13.   COUNTERCLAIM AND CROSS–CLAIM

(a) Compulsory Counterclaims. A pleading shall state as a counterclaim any claim which at the time of serving the pleading the pleader has against any opposing party, if it arises out of the transaction or occurrence that is the subject matter of the opposing party's claim and does not require for its adjudication the presence of third parties of whom the court cannot acquire jurisdiction. But the pleader need not state the claim if (1) at the time the action was commenced the claim was the subject of another pending action, or (2) the opposing party brought suit upon the claim by attachment or other process by which the court did not acquire jurisdiction to render a personal judgment on that claim, and the pleader is not stating any counterclaim under this Rule 13.

(b) Permissive Counterclaims. A pleading may state as a counterclaim any claim against an opposing party not arising out of the transaction or occurrence that is the subject matter of the opposing party's claim.

(c) Counterclaim Exceeding Opposing Claim. A counterclaim may or may not diminish or defeat the recovery sought by the opposing party. It may claim relief exceeding in amount or different in kind from that sought in the pleading of the opposing party.

(d) Counterclaim Against the United States. These rules shall not be construed to enlarge beyond the limits now fixed by law the right to assert counterclaims or to claim credits against the United States or an officer or agency thereof.

(e) Counterclaim Maturing or Acquired After Pleading. A claim which either matured or was acquired by the pleader after serving a pleading may, with the permission of the court, be presented as a counter-claim by supplemental pleading.

(f) Omitted Counterclaim. When a pleader fails to set up a counter-claim through oversight, inadvertence, or excusable neglect, or when justice requires, the pleader may by leave of court set up the counterclaim by amendment.

(g) Cross–Claim Against Co–Party. A pleading may state as a cross-claim any claim by one party against a co-party arising out of the transaction or occurrence that is the subject matter either of the original action or of a counterclaim therein or relating to any property that is the subject matter of the original action. Such cross-claim may include a claim that the party against whom it is asserted is or may be liable to the cross-claimant for all or part of a claim asserted in the action against the cross-claimant.

(h) Joinder of Additional Parties. Persons other than those made parties to the original action may be made parties to a counterclaim or cross-claim in accordance with the provisions of Rules 19 and 20.

(i) Separate Trials; Separate Judgments. If the court orders separate trials as provided in Rule 42(b), judgment on a counterclaim or cross-claim may be rendered in accordance with the terms of Rule 54(b) when the court has jurisdiction so to do, even if the claims of the opposing party have been dismissed or otherwise disposed of.

Rule 14. THIRD–PARTY PRACTICE

(a) When Defendant May Bring in Third Party. At any time after commencement of the action a defending party, as a third-party plaintiff, may cause a summons and complaint to be served upon a person not a party to the action who is or may be liable to the third-party plaintiff for all or part of the plaintiff's claim against the third-party plaintiff. The third-party plaintiff need not obtain leave to make the service if the third-party plaintiff files the third-party complaint not later than 10 days after serving the original answer. Otherwise the third-party plaintiff must obtain leave on motion upon notice to all parties to the action. The person served with the summons and third-party complaint, hereinafter called the third-party defendant, shall make any defenses to the third-party plaintiff's claim as provided in Rule 12 and any counterclaims against the third-party plaintiff and cross-claims against other third-party defendants as provided in Rule 13. The third-party defendant may assert against the plaintiff any defenses which the third-party plaintiff has to the plaintiff's claim. The third-party defendant may also assert any claim against the plaintiff arising out of the transaction or occurrence that is the subject matter of the plaintiff's claim against the third-party plaintiff. The plaintiff may assert any claim against the third-party defendant arising out of the transaction or occurrence that is the subject matter of the plaintiff's claim against the third-party plain-tiff, and the third-party defendant thereupon shall assert any defenses as provided in Rule 12 and any counterclaims and cross-claims as provided in Rule 13. Any party may move to strike the third-party claim, or for its severance or separate trial. A third-party defendant may proceed under this rule against any person not a party to the action who is or may be liable to the third-party defendant for all or part of the claim made in the action against the third-party defendant. The third-party complaint, if within the admiralty and maritime jurisdiction, may be in rem against a vessel, cargo, or other property subject to admiralty or maritime process in rem, in which case references in this rule to the summons include the warrant of arrest, and references to the third-party plaintiff or defendant include, where appropriate, a person who asserts a right under Supplemental Rule C(6)(a)(i) in the property arrested.

(b) When Plaintiff May Bring in Third Party. When a counterclaim is asserted against a plaintiff, the plaintiff may cause a third party to be brought in under circumstances which under this rule would entitle a defendant to do so.

(c) Admiralty and Maritime Claims. When a plaintiff asserts an admiralty or maritime claim within the meaning of Rule 9(h), the defendant or person who asserts a right under Supplemental Rule C(6)(a)(i), as a third-party plaintiff, may bring in a third-party defendant who may be wholly or partly liable, either to the plaintiff or to the third-party plaintiff, by way of remedy over, contribution, or otherwise on account of the same transaction, occurrence, or series of transactions or occurrences. In such a case the third-party plaintiff may also demand judgment against the third-party defendant in favor of the plaintiff, in which event the third-party defendant shall make any defenses to the claim of the plaintiff as well as to that of the third-party plaintiff in the manner provided in Rule 12 and the action shall proceed as if the plaintiff had commenced it against the third-party defendant as well as the third-party plaintiff.

Rule 15. AMENDED AND SUPPLEMENTAL PLEADINGS

(a) Amendments. A party may amend the party's pleading once as a matter of course at any time before a responsive pleading is served or, if the pleading is one to which no responsive pleading is permitted and the action has not been placed upon the trial calendar, the party may so amend it at any time within 20 days after it is served. Otherwise a party may amend the party's pleading only by leave of court or by written consent of the adverse party; and leave shall be freely given when justice so requires. A party shall plead in response to an amended pleading within the time remaining for response to the original pleading or within 10 days after service of the amended pleading, whichever period may be the longer, unless the court otherwise orders.

(b) Amendments to Conform to the Evidence. When issues not raised by the pleadings are tried by express or implied consent of the parties, they shall be treated in all respects as if they had been raised in the pleadings. Such amendment of the pleadings as may be necessary to cause them to conform to the evidence and to raise these issues may be made upon motion of any party at any time, even after judgment; but failure so to amend does not affect the result of the trial of these issues. If evidence is objected to at the trial on the ground that it is not within the issues made by the pleadings, the court may allow the pleadings to be amended and shall do so freely when the presentation of the merits of the action will be subserved thereby and the objecting party fails to satisfy the court that the admission of such evidence would prejudice the party in maintaining the party's action or defense upon the merits. The court may grant a continuance to enable the objecting party to meet such evidence.

(c) Relation Back of Amendments. An amendment of a pleading relates back to the date of the original pleading when

(1) relation back is permitted by the law that provides the statute of limitations applicable to the action, or

(2) the claim or defense asserted in the amended pleading arose out of the conduct, transaction, or occurrence set forth or attempted to be set forth in the original pleading, or

(3) the amendment changes the party or the naming of the party against whom a claim is asserted if the foregoing provision (2) is satisfied and, within the period provided by Rule 4(m) for service of the summons and complaint, the party to be brought in by amendment (A) has received such notice of the institution of the action that the party will not be prejudiced in maintaining a defense on the merits, and (B) knew or should have known that, but for a mistake concerning the identity of the proper party, the action would have been brought against the party.

The delivery or mailing of process to the United States Attorney, or United States Attorney's designee, or the Attorney General of the United States, or an agency or officer who would have been a proper defendant if named, satisfies the requirement of subparagraphs (A) and (B) of this paragraph (3) with respect to the United States or any agency or officer thereof to be brought into the action as a defendant.

(d) Supplemental Pleadings. Upon motion of a party the court may, upon reasonable notice and upon such terms as are just, permit the party to serve a supplemental pleading setting forth transactions or occurrences or events which have happened since the date of the pleading sought to be supplemented. Permission may be granted even though the original pleading is defective in its statement of a claim for relief or defense. If the court deems it advisable that the adverse party plead to the supplemental pleading, it shall so order, specifying the time therefor.

Rule 16. PRETRIAL CONFERENCES; SCHEDULING; MANAGEMENT

(a) Pretrial Conferences; Objectives. In any action, the court may in its discretion direct the attorneys for the parties and any unrepresented parties to appear before it for a conference or conferences before trial for such purposes as

(1) expediting the disposition of the action;

(2) establishing early and continuing control so that the case will not be protracted because of lack of management;

(3) discouraging wasteful pretrial activities;

(4) improving the quality of the trial through more thorough preparation, and;

(5) facilitating the settlement of the case.

(b) Scheduling and Planning. Except in categories of actions exempted by district court rule as inappropriate, the district judge, or a magistrate judge when authorized by district court rule, shall, after receiving the report from the parties under Rule 26(f) or after consulting with the attorneys for the parties and any unrepresented parties by a scheduling conference, telephone, mail, or other suitable means, enter a scheduling order that limits the time

(1) to join other parties and to amend the pleadings;

(2) to file motions; and

(3) to complete discovery.

The scheduling order may also include

(4) modifications of the times for disclosures under Rules 26(a) and 26(e)(1) and of the extent of discovery to be permitted;

(5) provisions for disclosure or discovery of electronically stored information;

(6) any agreements the parties reach for asserting claims of privilege or of protection as trial-preparation material after production;

(7) the date or dates for conferences before trial, a final pretrial conference, and trial; and

(8) any other matters appropriate in the circumstances of the case.

The order shall issue as soon as practicable but in any event within 90 days after the appearance of a defendant and within 120 days after the complaint has been served on a defendant. A schedule shall not be modified except upon a showing of good cause and by leave of the district judge or, when authorized by local rule, by a magistrate judge.

(c) Subjects for Consideration at Pretrial Conferences. At any conference under this rule consideration may be given, and the court may take appropriate action, with respect to

(1) the formulation and simplification of the issues, including the elimination of frivolous claims or defenses;

(2) the necessity or desirability of amendments to the pleadings;

(3) the possibility of obtaining admissions of fact and of documents which will avoid unnecessary proof, stipulations regarding the authenticity of documents, and advance rulings from the court on the admissibility of evidence;

(4) the avoidance of unnecessary proof and of cumulative evidence, and limitations or restrictions on the use of testimony under Rule 702 of the Federal Rules of Evidence;

(5) the appropriateness and timing of summary adjudication under Rule 56;

(6) the control and scheduling of discovery, including orders affecting disclosures and discovery pursuant to Rule 26 and Rules 29 through 37;

(7) the identification of witnesses and documents, the need and schedule for filing and exchanging pretrial briefs, and the date or dates for further conferences and for trial;

(8) the advisability of referring matters to a magistrate judge or master;

(9) settlement and the use of special procedures to assist in resolving the dispute when authorized by statute or local rule;

(10) the form and substance of the pretrial order;

(11) the disposition of pending motions;

(12) the need for adopting special procedures for managing potentially difficult or protracted actions that may involve complex issues, multiple parties, difficult legal questions, or unusual proof problems;

(13) an order for a separate trial pursuant to Rule 42(b) with respect to a claim, counterclaim, cross-claim, or third-party claim, or with respect to any particular issue in the case;

(14) an order directing a party or parties to present evidence early in the trial with respect to a manageable issue that could, on the evidence, be the basis for a judgment as a matter of law under Rule 50(a) or a judgment on partial findings under Rule 52(c);

(15) an order establishing a reasonable limit on the time allowed for presenting evidence; and

(16) such other matters as may facilitate the just, speedy, and inexpensive disposition of the action.

At least one of the attorneys for each party participating in any conference before trial shall have authority to enter into stipulations and to make admissions regarding all matters that the participants may reasonably anticipate may be discussed. If appropriate, the court may require that a party or its representative be present or reasonably available by telephone in order to consider possible settlement of the dispute.

(d) Final Pretrial Conference. Any final pretrial conference shall be held as close to the time of trial as reasonable under the circumstances. The participants at any such conference shall formulate a plan for trial, including a program for facilitating the admission of evidence. The conference shall be attended by at least one of the attorneys who will conduct the trial for each of the parties and by any unrepresented parties.

(e) Pretrial Orders. After any conference held pursuant to this rule, an order shall be entered reciting the action taken. This order shall control the subsequent course of the action unless modified by a subsequent order. The order following a final pretrial conference shall be modified only to prevent manifest injustice.

(f) Sanctions. If a party or party's attorney fails to obey a scheduling or pretrial order, or if no appearance is made on behalf of a party at a scheduling or pretrial conference, or if a party or party's attorney is substantially unprepared to participate in the conference, or if a party or party's attorney fails to participate in good faith, the judge, upon motion or the judge's own initiative, may make such orders with regard thereto as are just, and among others any of the orders provided in Rule 37(b)(2)(B), (C), (D). In lieu of or in addition to any other sanction, the judge shall require the party or the attorney representing the party or both to pay the reasonable expenses incurred because of any noncompliance with this rule, including attorney's fees, unless the judge finds that the noncompliance was substantially justified or that other circumstances make an award of expenses unjust.

IV. PARTIES

Rule 17. PARTIES PLAINTIFF AND DEFENDANT; CAPACITY

(a) Real Party in Interest. Every action shall be prosecuted in the name of the real party in interest. An executor, administrator, guardian, bailee, trustee of an express trust, a party with whom or in whose name a contract has been made for the benefit of another, or a party authorized by statute may sue in that person's own name without joining the party for whose benefit the action is brought; and when a statute of the United States so provides, an action for the use or benefit of another shall be brought in the name of the United States. No action shall be dismissed on the ground that it is not prosecuted in the name of the real party in interest until a reasonable time has been allowed after objection for ratification of commencement of the action by, or joinder or substitution of, the real party in interest; and such ratification, joinder, or substitution shall have the same effect as if the action had been commenced in the name of the real party in interest.

(b) Capacity to Sue or Be Sued. The capacity of an individual, other than one acting in a representative capacity, to sue or be sued shall be determined by the law of the individual's domicile. The capacity of a corporation to sue or be sued shall be determined by the law under which it was organized. In all other cases capacity to sue or be sued shall be determined by the law of the state in which the district court is held, except (1) that a partnership or other unincorporated association, which has no such capacity by the law of such state, may sue or be sued in its common name for the purpose of enforcing for or against it a substantive right existing under the Constitution or laws of the United States, and (2) that the capacity of a receiver appointed by a court of the United States to sue or be sued in a court of the United States is governed by Title 28, U.S.C. §§ 754 and 959(a).

(c) Infants or Incompetent Persons. Whenever an infant or incompetent person has a representative, such as a general guardian, committee, conservator, or other like fiduciary, the representative may sue or defend on behalf of the infant or incompetent person. An infant or incompetent person who does not have a duly appointed representative may sue by a next friend or by a guardian ad litem. The court shall appoint a guardian ad litem for an infant or incompetent person not otherwise represented in an action or shall make such other order as it deems proper for the protection of the infant or incompetent person.

Rule 18. JOINDER OF CLAIMS AND REMEDIES

(a) Joinder of Claims. A party asserting a claim to relief as an original claim, counterclaim, cross-claim, or third-party claim, may join, either as independent or as alternate claims, as many claims, legal, equitable, or maritime, as the party has against an opposing party.

(b) Joinder of Remedies; Fraudulent Conveyances. Whenever a claim is one heretofore cognizable only after another claim has been prosecuted to a conclusion, the two claims may be joined in a single action; but the court shall grant relief in that action only in accordance with the relative substantive rights of the parties. In particular, a plaintiff may state a claim for money and a claim to have set aside a conveyance fraudulent as to that plaintiff, without first having obtained a judgment establishing the claim for money.

Rule 19. JOINDER OF PERSONS NEEDED FOR JUST ADJUDICATION

(a) Persons to Be Joined if Feasible. A person who is subject to service of process and whose joinder will not deprive the court of jurisdiction over the subject matter of the action shall be joined as a party in the action if (1) in the person's absence complete relief cannot be accorded among those already parties, or (2) the person claims an interest relating to the subject of the action and is so situated that the disposition of the action in the person's absence may (i) as a practical matter impair or impede the person's ability to protect that interest or (ii) leave any of the persons already parties subject to a substantial risk of incurring double, multiple, or otherwise inconsistent obligations by reason of the claimed interest. If the person has not been so joined, the court shall order that the person be made a party. If the person should join as a plaintiff but refuses to do so, the person may be made a defendant, or, in a proper case, an involuntary plaintiff. If the joined party objects to venue and joinder of that party would render the venue of the action improper, that party shall be dismissed from the action.

(b) Determination by Court Whenever Joinder Not Feasible. If a person as described in subdivision (a)(1)–(2) hereof cannot be made a party, the court shall determine whether in equity and good conscience the action should proceed among the parties before it, or should be dismissed, the absent person being thus regarded as indispensable. The factors to be considered by the court include: first, to what extent a judgment rendered in the person's absence might be prejudicial to the person or those already parties; second, the extent to which, by protective provisions in the judgment, by the shaping of relief, or other measures, the prejudice can be lessened or avoided; third, whether a judgment rendered in the person's absence will be adequate; fourth, whether the plaintiff will have an adequate remedy if the action is dismissed for nonjoinder.

(c) Pleading Reasons for Nonjoinder. A pleading asserting a claim for relief shall state the names, if known to the pleader, of any persons as described in subdivision (a)(1)–(2) hereof who are not joined, and the reasons why they are not joined.

(d) Exception of Class Actions. This rule is subject to the provisions of Rule 23.

Rule 20. PERMISSIVE JOINDER OF PARTIES

(a) Permissive Joinder. All persons may join in one action as plaintiffs if they assert any right to relief jointly, severally, or in the alternative in respect of or arising out of the same transaction, occurrence, or series of transactions or occurrences and if any question of law or fact common to all these persons will arise in the action. All persons (and any vessel, cargo or other property subject to admiralty process in rem) may be joined in one action as defendants if there is asserted against them jointly, severally, or in the alternative, any right to relief in respect of or arising out of the same transaction, occurrence, or series of transactions or occurrences and if any question of law or fact common to all defendants will arise in the action. A plaintiff or defendant need not be interested in obtaining or defending against all the relief demanded. Judgment may be given for one or more of the plaintiffs according to their respective rights to relief, and against one or more defendants according to their respective liabilities.

(b) Separate Trials. The court may make such orders as will prevent a party from being embarrassed, delayed, or put to expense by the inclusion of a party against whom the party asserts no claim and who asserts no claim against the party, and may order separate trials or make other orders to prevent delay or prejudice.

Rule 21. MISJOINDER AND NON–JOINDER OF PARTIES

Misjoinder of parties is not ground for dismissal of an action. Parties may be dropped or added by order of the court on motion of any party or of its own initiative at any stage of the action and on such terms as are just. Any claim against a party may be severed and proceeded with separately.

Rule 22. INTERPLEADER

(1) Persons having claims against the plaintiff may be joined as defendants and required to interplead when their claims are such that the plaintiff is or may be exposed to double or multiple liability. It is not ground for objection to the joinder that the claims of the several claimants or the titles on which their claims depend do not have a common origin or are not identical but are adverse to and independent of one another, or that the plaintiff avers that the plaintiff is not liable in whole or in part to any or all of the claimants. A defendant exposed to similar liability may obtain such interpleader by way of cross-claim or counterclaim. The provisions of this rule supplement and do not in any way limit the joinder of parties permitted in Rule 20.

(2) The remedy herein provided is in addition to and in no way supersedes or limits the remedy provided by Title 28, U.S.C. §§ 1335, 1397, and 2361. Actions under those provisions shall be conducted in accordance with these rules.

Rule 23. CLASS ACTIONS

(a) Prerequisites to a Class Action. One or more members of a class may sue or be sued as representative parties on behalf of all only if (1) the class is so numerous that joinder of all members is impracticable, (2) there are questions of law or fact common to the class, (3) the claims or defenses of the representative parties are typical of the claims or defenses of the class, and (4) the representative parties will fairly and adequately protect the interests of the class.

(b) Class Actions Maintainable. An action may be maintained as a class action if the prerequisites of subdivision (a) are satisfied, and in addition:

(1) the prosecution of separate actions by or against individual members of the class would create a risk of

(A) inconsistent or varying adjudications with respect to individual members of the class which would establish incompatible standards of conduct for the party opposing the class, or

(B) adjudications with respect to individual members of the class which would as a practical matter be dispositive of the interests of the other members not parties to the adjudications or substantially impair or impede their ability to protect their interests; or

(2) the party opposing the class has acted or refused to act on grounds generally applicable to the class, thereby making appropriate final injunctive relief or corresponding declaratory relief with respect to the class as a whole; or

(3) the court finds that the questions of law or fact common to the members of the class predominate over any questions affecting only individual members, and that a class action is superior to other available methods for the fair and efficient adjudication of the controversy. The matters pertinent to the findings include: (A) the interest of members of the class in individually controlling the prosecution or defense of separate actions; (B) the extent and nature of any litigation concerning the controversy already commenced by or against members of the class; (C) the desirability or undesirability of concentrating the litigation of the claims in the particular forum; (D) the difficulties likely to be encountered in the management of a class action.

(c) Determining by Order Whether to Certify a Class Action; Appointing Class Counsel; Notice and Membership in Class; Judgment; Multiple Classes and Subclasses.

(1)(A) When a person sues or is sued as a representative of a class, the court must—at an early practicable time—determine by order whether to certify the action as a class action.

(B) An order certifying a class action must define the class and the class claims, issues, or defenses, and must appoint class counsel under Rule 23(g).

(C) An order under Rule 23(c)(1) may be altered or amended before final judgment.

(2)(A) For any class certified under Rule 23(b)(1) or (2), the court may direct appropriate notice to the class.

(B) For any class certified under Rule 23(b)(3), the court must direct to class members the best notice practicable under the circumstances, including individual notice to all members who can be identified through reasonable effort. The notice must concisely and clearly state in plain, easily understood language:

- the nature of the action,

- the definition of the class certified,

- the class claims, issues, or defenses,

- that a class member may enter an appearance through counsel if the member so desires,

- that the court will exclude from the class any member who requests exclusion, stating when and how members may elect to be excluded, and

- the binding effect of a class judgment on class members under Rule 23(c)(3).

(3) The judgment in an action maintained as a class action under subdivision (b)(1) or (b)(2), whether or not favorable to the class, shall include and describe those whom the court finds to be members of the class. The judgment in an action maintained as a class action under subdivision (b)(3), whether or not favorable to the class, shall include and specify or describe those to whom the notice provided in subdivision (c)(2) was directed, and who have not requested exclusion, and whom the court finds to be members of the class.

(4) When appropriate (A) an action may be brought or maintained as a class action with respect to particular issues, or (B) a class may be divided into subclasses and each subclass treated as a class, and the provisions of this rule shall then be construed and applied accordingly.

(d) Orders in Conduct of Actions. In the conduct of actions to which this rule applies, the court may make appropriate orders: (1) determining the course of proceedings or prescribing measures to prevent undue repetition or complication in the presentation of evidence or argument; (2) requiring, for the protection of the members of the class or otherwise for the fair conduct of the action, that notice be given in such manner as the court may direct to some or all of the members of any step in the action, or of the proposed extent of the judgment, or of the opportunity of members to signify whether they consider the representation fair and adequate, to intervene and present claims or defenses, or otherwise to come into the action; (3) imposing conditions on the representative parties or on intervenors; (4) requiring that the pleadings be amended to eliminate therefrom allegations as to representation of absent persons, and that the action proceed accordingly; (5) dealing with similar procedural matters. The orders may be combined with an order under Rule 16, and may be altered or amended as may be desirable from time to time.

(e) Settlement, Voluntary Dismissal, or Compromise.

(1)(A) The court must approve any settlement, voluntary dismissal, or compromise of the claims, issues, or defenses of a certified class.

(B) The court must direct notice in a reasonable manner to all class members who would be bound by a proposed settlement, voluntary dismissal, or compromise.

(C) The court may approve a settlement, voluntary dismissal, or compromise that would bind class members only after a hearing and on finding that the settlement, voluntary dismissal, or compromise is fair, reasonable, and adequate.

(2) The parties seeking approval of a settlement, voluntary dismissal, or compromise under Rule 23(e)(1) must file a statement identifying any agreement made in connection with the proposed settlement, voluntary dismissal, or compromise.

(3) In an action previously certified as a class action under Rule 23(b)(3), the court may refuse to approve a settlement unless it affords a new opportunity to request exclusion to individual class members who had an earlier opportunity to request exclusion but did not do so.

(4)(A) Any class member may object to a proposed settlement, voluntary dismissal, or compromise that requires court approval under Rule 23(e)(1)(A).

(B) An objection made under Rule 23(e)(4)(A) may be withdrawn only with the court's approval.

(f) Appeals. A court of appeals may in its discretion permit an appeal from an order of a district court granting or denying class action certification under this rule if application is made to it within ten days after entry of the order. An appeal does not stay proceedings in the district court unless the district judge or the court of appeals so orders.

(g) Class Counsel.

(1) *Appointing Class Counsel.*

(A) Unless a statute provides otherwise, a court that certifies a class must appoint class counsel.

(B) An attorney appointed to serve as class counsel must fairly and adequately represent the interests of the class.

(C) In appointing class counsel, the court

(i) must consider:

• the work counsel has done in identifying or investigating potential claims in the action,

• counsel's experience in handling class actions, other complex litigation, and claims of the type asserted in the action,

• counsel's knowledge of the applicable law, and

• the resources counsel will commit to representing the class;

(ii) may consider any other matter pertinent to counsel's ability to fairly and adequately represent the interests of the class;

(iii) may direct potential class counsel to provide information on any subject pertinent to the appointment and to propose terms for attorney fees and nontaxable costs; and

(iv) may make further orders in connection with the appointment.

(2) *Appointment Procedure.*

(A) The court may designate interim counsel to act on behalf of the putative class before determining whether to certify the action as a class action.

(B) When there is one applicant for appointment as class counsel, the court may appoint that applicant only if the applicant is adequate under Rule 23(g)(1)(B) and (C). If more than one adequate applicant seeks appointment as class counsel, the court must appoint the applicant best able to represent the interests of the class.

(C) The order appointing class counsel may include provisions about the award of attorney fees or nontaxable costs under Rule 23(h).

(h) Attorney Fees Award. In an action certified as a class action, the court may award reasonable attorney fees and nontaxable costs authorized by law or by agreement of the parties as follows:

(1) *Motion for Award of Attorney Fees.* A claim for an award of attorney fees and nontaxable costs must be made by motion under Rule 54(d)(2), subject to the provisions of this subdivision, at a time set by the court. Notice of the motion must be served on all parties and, for motions by class counsel, directed to class members in a reasonable manner.

(2) *Objections to Motion.* A class member, or a party from whom payment is sought, may object to the motion.

(3) *Hearing and Findings.* The court may hold a hearing and must find the facts and state its conclusions of law on the motion under Rule 52(a).

(4) *Reference to Special Master or Magistrate Judge.* The court may refer issues related to the amount of the award to a special master or to a magistrate judge as provided in Rule 54(d)(2)(D).

Rule 23.1. DERIVATIVE ACTIONS BY SHAREHOLDERS

In a derivative action brought by one or more shareholders or members to enforce a right of a corporation or of an unincorporated association, the corporation or association having failed to enforce a right which may properly be asserted by it, the complaint shall be verified and shall allege (1) that the plaintiff was a shareholder or member at the time of the transaction of which the plaintiff complains or that the plaintiff's share or membership thereafter devolved on the plaintiff by operation of law, and (2) that the action is not a collusive one to confer jurisdiction on a court of the United States which it would not otherwise have. The complaint shall also allege with particularity the efforts, if any, made by the plaintiff to obtain the action the plaintiff desires from the directors or comparable authority and, if necessary, from the shareholders or members, and the reasons for the plaintiff's failure to obtain the action or for not making the effort. The derivative action may not be maintained if it appears that the plaintiff does not fairly and adequately represent the interests of the shareholders or members similarly situated in enforcing the right of the corporation or association. The action shall not be dismissed or compromised without the approval of the court, and notice of the proposed dismissal or compromise shall be given to shareholders or members in such manner as the court directs.

Rule 23.2.   ACTIONS RELATING TO UNINCORPORATED ASSOCIATIONS

An action brought by or against the members of an unincorporated association as a class by naming certain members as representative parties may be maintained only if it appears that the representative parties will fairly and adequately protect the interests of the association and its members. In the conduct of the action the court may make appropriate orders corresponding with those described in Rule 23(d), and the procedure for dismissal or compromise of the action shall correspond with that provided in Rule 23(e).

Rule 24.   INTERVENTION

(a) Intervention of Right. Upon timely application anyone shall be permitted to intervene in an action: (1) when a statute of the United States confers an unconditional right to intervene; or (2) when the applicant claims an interest relating to the property or transaction which is the subject of the action and the applicant is so situated that the disposition of the action may as a practical matter impair or impede the applicant's ability to protect that interest, unless the applicant's interest is adequately represented by existing parties.

(b) Permissive Intervention. Upon timely application anyone may be permitted to intervene in an action: (1) when a statute of the United States confers a conditional right to intervene; or (2) when an applicant's claim or defense and the main action have a question of law or fact in common. When a party to an action relies for ground of claim or defense upon any statute or executive order administered by a federal or state governmental officer or agency or upon any regulation, order, requirement or agreement issued or made pursuant to the statute or executive order, the officer or agency upon timely application may be permitted to intervene in the action. In exercising its discretion the court shall consider whether the intervention will unduly delay or prejudice the adjudication of the rights of the original parties.

(c) Procedure. A person desiring to intervene shall serve a motion to intervene upon the parties as provided in Rule 5. The motion shall state the grounds therefor and shall be accompanied by a pleading setting forth the claim or defense for which intervention is sought. The same procedure shall be followed when a statute of the United States gives a right to intervene.

Rule 25.   SUBSTITUTION OF PARTIES

(a) Death.

(1) If a party dies and the claim is not thereby extinguished, the court may order substitution of the proper parties. The motion for substitution may be made by any party or by the successors or representatives of the deceased party and, together with the notice of hearing, shall be served on the parties as provided in Rule 5 and upon persons not parties in the manner provided in Rule 4 for the service of a summons, and may be served in any judicial district. Unless the motion for substitution is made not later than 90 days after the death is suggested upon the record by service of a statement of the fact of the death as provided herein for the

service of the motion, the action shall be dismissed as to the deceased party.

(2) In the event of the death of one or more of the plaintiffs or of one or more of the defendants in an action in which the right sought to be enforced survives only to the surviving plaintiffs or only against the surviving defendants, the action does not abate. The death shall be suggested upon the record and the action shall proceed in favor of or against the surviving parties.

(b) Incompetency. If a party becomes incompetent, the court upon motion served as provided in subdivision (a) of this rule may allow the action to be continued by or against the party's representative.

(c) Transfer of Interest. In case of any transfer of interest, the action may be continued by or against the original party, unless the court upon motion directs the person to whom the interest is transferred to be substituted in the action or joined with the original party. Service of the motion shall be made as provided in subdivision (a) of this rule.

(d) Public Officers; Death or Separation From Office.

(1) When a public officer is a party to an action in an official capacity and during its pendency dies, resigns, or otherwise ceases to hold office, the action does not abate and the officer's successor is automatically substituted as a party. Proceedings following the substitution shall be in the name of the substituted party, but any misnomer not affecting the substantial rights of the parties shall be disregarded. An order of substitution may be entered at any time, but the omission to enter such an order shall not affect the substitution.

(2) A public officer who sues or is sued in an official capacity may be described as a party by the officer's official title rather than by name; but the court may require the officer's name to be added.

V. DEPOSITIONS AND DISCOVERY

Rule 26. GENERAL PROVISIONS GOVERNING DISCOVERY; DUTY OF DISCLOSURE

(a) Required Disclosures; Methods to Discover Additional Matter.

(1) *Initial Disclosures.* Except in categories of proceedings specified in Rule 26(a)(1)(E), or to the extent otherwise stipulated or directed by order, a party must, without awaiting a discovery request, provide to other parties:

(A) the name and, if known, the address and telephone number of each individual likely to have discoverable information that the disclosing party may use to support its claims or defenses, unless solely for impeachment, identifying the subjects of the information;

(B) a copy of, or a description by category and location of, all documents, electronically stored information, and tangible things that are in the possession, custody, or control of the party and that the disclosing party may use to support its claims or defenses, unless solely for impeachment;

(C) a computation of any category of damages claimed by the disclosing party, making available for inspection and copying as under Rule 34 the documents or other evidentiary material, not privileged or protected from disclosure, on which such computation is based, including materials bearing on the nature and extent of injuries suffered; and

(D) for inspection and copying as under Rule 34 any insurance agreement under which any person carrying on an insurance business may be liable to satisfy part or all of a judgment which may be entered in the action or to indemnify or reimburse for payments made to satisfy the judgment.

(E) The following categories of proceedings are exempt from initial disclosure under Rule 26(a)(1):

(i) an action for review on an administrative record;

(ii) a forfeiture action in rem arising from a federal statute;

(iii) a petition for habeas corpus or other proceeding to challenge a criminal conviction or sentence;

(iv) an action brought without counsel by a person in custody of the United States, a state, or a state subdivision;

(v) an action to enforce or quash an administrative summons or subpoena;

(vi) an action by the United States to recover benefit payments;

(vii) an action by the United States to collect on a student loan guaranteed by the United States;

(viii) a proceeding ancillary to proceedings in other courts; and

(ix) an action to enforce an arbitration award.

These disclosures must be made at or within 14 days after the Rule 26(f) conference unless a different time is set by stipulation or court order, or unless a party objects during the conference that initial disclosures are not appropriate in the circumstances of the action and states the objection in the Rule 26(f) discovery plan. In ruling on the objection, the court must determine what disclosures—if any—are to be made, and set the time for disclosure. Any party first served or otherwise joined after the Rule 26(f) conference must make these disclosures within 30 days after being served or joined unless a different time is set by stipulation or court order. A party must make its initial disclosures based on the information then reasonably available to it and is not excused from making its disclosures because it has not fully completed its investigation of the case or because it challenges the sufficiency of another party's disclosures or because another party has not made its disclosures.

(2) *Disclosure of Expert Testimony.*

(A) In addition to the disclosures required by paragraph (1), a party shall disclose to other parties the identity of any person who may be used at trial to present evidence under Rules 702, 703, or 705 of the Federal Rules of Evidence.

(B) Except as otherwise stipulated or directed by the court, this disclosure shall, with respect to a witness who is retained or specially employed to provide expert testimony in the case or whose duties as an employee of the party regularly involve giving expert testimony, be accompanied by a written report prepared and signed by the witness. The report shall contain a complete statement of all opinions to be expressed and the basis and reasons therefor; the data or other information considered by the witness in forming the opinions; any exhibits to be used as a summary of or support for the opinions; the qualifications of the witness, including a list of all publications authored by the witness within the preceding ten years; the compensation to be paid for the study and testimony; and a listing of any other cases in which the witness has testified as an expert at trial or by deposition within the preceding four years.

(C) These disclosures shall be made at the times and in the sequence directed by the court. In the absence of other directions from the court or stipulation by the parties, the disclosures shall be made at least 90 days before the trial date or the date the case is to be ready for trial or, if the evidence is intended solely to contradict or rebut evidence on the same subject matter identified by another party under paragraph (2)(B), within 30 days after the disclosure made by the other party. The parties shall supplement these disclosures when required under subdivision (e)(1).

(3) *Pretrial Disclosures.* In addition to the disclosures required by Rule 26(a)(1) and (2), a party must provide to other parties and promptly file with the court the following information regarding the evidence that it may present at trial other than solely for impeachment:

(A) the name and, if not previously provided, the address and telephone number of each witness, separately identifying those whom the party expects to present and those whom the party may call if the need arises;

(B) the designation of those witnesses whose testimony is expected to be presented by means of a deposition and, if not taken stenographically, a transcript of the pertinent portions of the deposition testimony; and

(C) an appropriate identification of each document or other exhibit, including summaries of other evidence, separately identifying those which the party expects to offer and those which the party may offer if the need arises.

Unless otherwise directed by the court, these disclosures must be made at least 30 days before trial. Within 14 days thereafter, unless a different time is specified by the court, a party may serve and promptly file a list disclosing (i) any objections to the use under Rule 32(a) of a deposition designated by another party under Rule 26(a)(3)(B), and (ii) any objection, together with the grounds therefor, that may be made to the admissibility of materials identified under Rule 26(a)(3)(C). Objections not so disclosed, other than objections under Rules 402 and 403 of the Federal Rules of Evidence, are waived unless excused by the court for good cause.

(4) *Form of Disclosures.* Unless the court orders otherwise, all disclosures under Rules 26(a)(1) through (3) must be made in writing, signed, and served.

(5) *Methods to Discover Additional Matter.* Parties may obtain discovery by one or more of the following methods: depositions upon oral examination or written questions; written interrogatories; production of documents or things or permission to enter upon land or other property under Rule 34 or 45(a)(1)(C), for inspection and other purposes; physical and mental examinations; and requests for admission.

(b) Discovery Scope and Limits. Unless otherwise limited by order of the court in accordance with these rules, the scope of discovery is as follows:

(1) *In General.* Parties may obtain discovery regarding any matter, not privileged, that is relevant to the claim or defense of any party, including the existence, description, nature, custody, condition, and location of any books, documents, or other tangible things and the identity and location of persons having knowledge of any discoverable matter. For good cause, the court may order discovery of any matter relevant to the subject matter involved in the action. Relevant information need not be admissible at the trial if the discovery appears reasonably calculated to lead to the discovery of admissible evidence. All discovery is subject to the limitations imposed by Rule 26(b)(2)(i), (ii), and (iii).

(2) *Limitations.*

(A) By order, the court may alter the limits in these rules on the number of depositions and interrogatories or the length of depositions under Rule 30. By order or local rule, the court may also limit the number of requests under Rule 36.

(B) A party need not provide discovery of electronically stored information from sources that the party identifies as not reasonably accessible because of undue burden or cost. On motion to compel discovery or for a protective order, the party from whom discovery is sought must show that the information is not reasonably accessible because of undue burden or cost. If that showing is made, the court may nonetheless order discovery from such sources if the requesting party shows good cause, considering the limitations of Rule 26(b)(2)(C). The court may specify conditions for the discovery.

(C) The frequency or extent of use of the discovery methods otherwise permitted under these rules and by any local rule shall be limited by the court if it determines that: (i) the discovery sought is unreasonably cumulative or duplicative, or is obtainable from some other source that is more convenient, less burdensome, or less expensive; (ii) the party seeking discovery has had ample opportunity by discovery in the action to obtain the information sought; or (iii) the burden or expense of the proposed discovery outweighs its likely benefit, taking into account the needs of the case, the amount in controversy, the parties' resources, the importance of the issues at stake in the litigation, and the importance of the proposed discovery in resolving the issues. The court may act upon its own initiative after reasonable notice or pursuant to a motion under Rule 26(c).

(3) *Trial Preparation: Materials.* Subject to the provisions of subdivision (b)(4) of this rule, a party may obtain discovery of documents and tangible things otherwise discoverable under subdivision (b)(1) of this rule and prepared in anticipation of litigation or for trial by or for another party or by or for that other party's representative (including the other party's attorney, consultant, surety, indemnitor, insurer, or agent) only upon a showing that the party seeking discovery has substantial need of the materials in the preparation of the party's case and that the party is unable without undue hardship to obtain the substantial equivalent of the materials by other means. In ordering discovery of such materials when the required showing has been made, the court shall protect against disclosure of the mental impressions, conclusions, opinions, or legal theories of an attorney or other representative of a party concerning the litigation.

A party may obtain without the required showing a statement concerning the action or its subject matter previously made by that party. Upon request, a person not a party may obtain without the required showing a statement concerning the action or its subject matter previously made by that person. If the request is refused, the person may move for a court order. The provisions of Rule 37(a)(4) apply to the award of expenses incurred in relation to the motion. For purposes of this paragraph, a statement previously made is (A) a written statement signed or otherwise adopted or approved by the person making it, or (B) a stenographic, mechanical, electrical, or other recording, or a transcription thereof, which is a substantially verbatim recital of an oral statement by the person making it and contemporaneously recorded.

(4) *Trial Preparation: Experts.*

(A) A party may depose any person who has been identified as an expert whose opinions may be presented at trial. If a report from the expert is required under subdivision (a)(2)(B), the deposition shall not be conducted until after the report is provided.

(B) A party may, through interrogatories or by deposition, discover facts known or opinions held by an expert who has been retained or specially employed by another party in anticipation of litigation or preparation for trial and who is not expected to be called as a witness at trial only as provided in Rule 35(b) or upon a showing of exceptional circumstances under which it is impracticable for the party seeking discovery to obtain facts or opinions on the same subject by other means.

(C) Unless manifest injustice would result, (i) the court shall require that the party seeking discovery pay the expert a reasonable fee for time spent in responding to discovery under this subdivision; and (ii) with respect to discovery obtained under subdivision (b)(4)(B) of this rule the court shall require the party seeking discovery to pay the other party a fair portion of the fees and expenses reasonably incurred by the latter party in obtaining facts and opinions from the expert.

(5) *Claims of Privilege or Protection of Trial–Preparation Materials.*

(A) *Information Withheld.* When a party withholds information otherwise discoverable under these rules by claiming that it is privileged or subject to protection as trial-preparation material, the party shall make the claim expressly and shall describe the nature of the documents, communications, or things not produced or disclosed in a manner that, without revealing information itself privileged or protected, will enable other parties to assess the applicability of the privilege or protection.

(B) *Information Produced.* If information is produced in discovery that is subject to a claim of privilege or of protection as trial-preparation material, the party making the claim may notify any party that received the information of the claim and the basis for it. After being notified, a party must promptly return, sequester, or destroy the specified information and any copies it has and may not use or disclose the information until the claim is resolved. A receiving party may promptly present the information to the court under seal for a determination of the claim. If the receiving party disclosed the information before being notified, it must take reasonable steps to retrieve it. The producing party must preserve the information until the claim is resolved.

(c) Protective Orders. Upon motion by a party or by the person from whom discovery is sought, accompanied by a certification that the movant has in good faith conferred or attempted to confer with other affected parties in an effort to resolve the dispute without court action, and for good cause shown, the court in which the action is pending or alternatively, on matters relating to a deposition, the court in the district where the deposition is to be taken may make any order which justice requires to protect a party or person from annoyance, embarrassment, oppression, or undue burden or expense, including one or more of the following:

(1) that the disclosure or discovery not be had;

(2) that the disclosure or discovery may be had only on specified terms and conditions, including a designation of the time or place;

(3) that the discovery may be had only by a method of discovery other than that selected by the party seeking discovery;

(4) that certain matters not be inquired into, or that the scope of the disclosure or discovery be limited to certain matters;

(5) that discovery be conducted with no one present except persons designated by the court;

(6) that a deposition, after being sealed, be opened only by order of the court;

(7) that a trade secret or other confidential research, development, or commercial information not be revealed or be revealed only in
a designated way; and

(8) that the parties simultaneously file specified documents or
information enclosed in sealed envelopes to be opened as directed by
the court.

If the motion for a protective order is denied in whole or in part, the court
may, on such terms and conditions as are just, order that any party or
other person provide or permit discovery. The provisions of Rule 37(a)(4)
apply to the award of expenses incurred in relation to the motion.

(d) Timing and Sequence of Discovery. Except in categories of
proceedings exempted from initial disclosure under Rule 26(a)(1)(E), or
when authorized under these rules or by order or agreement of the parties,
a party may not seek discovery from any source before the parties have
conferred as required by Rule 26(f). Unless the court upon motion, for the
convenience of parties and witnesses and in the interests of justice, orders
otherwise, methods of discovery may be used in any sequence, and the fact
that a party is conducting discovery, whether by deposition or otherwise,
does not operate to delay any other party's discovery.

(e) Supplementation of Disclosures and Responses. A party who
has made a disclosure under subdivision (a) or responded to a request for
discovery with a disclosure or response is under a duty to supplement or
correct the disclosure or response to include information thereafter acquired if ordered by the court or in the following circumstances:

(1) A party is under a duty to supplement at appropriate intervals
its disclosures under subdivision (a) if the party learns that in some
material respect the information disclosed is incomplete or incorrect
and if the additional or corrective information has not otherwise been
made known to the other parties during the discovery process or in
writing. With respect to testimony of an expert from whom a report is
required under subdivision (a)(2)(B) the duty extends both to information contained in the report and to information provided through a
deposition of the expert, and any additions or other changes to this
information shall be disclosed by the time the party's disclosures under
Rule 26(a)(3) are due.

(2) A party is under a duty seasonably to amend a prior response
to an interrogatory, request for production, or request for admission if
the party learns that the response is in some material respect incomplete or incorrect and if the additional or corrective information has
not otherwise been made known to the other parties during the
discovery process or in writing.

(f) Conference of Parties; Planning for Discovery. Except in
categories of proceedings exempted from initial disclosure under Rule
26(a)(1)(E) or when otherwise ordered, the parties must, as soon as
practicable and in any event at least 21 days before a scheduling conference
is held or a scheduling order is due under Rule 16(b), confer to consider the
nature and basis of their claims and defenses and the possibilities for a
prompt settlement or resolution of the case, to make or arrange for the

disclosures required by Rule 26(a)(1), to discuss any issues relating to preserving discoverable information, and to develop a proposed discovery plan that indicates the parties' views and proposals concerning:

(1) what changes should be made in the timing, form, or requirement for disclosures under Rule 26(a), including a statement as to when disclosures under Rule26(a)(1) were made or will be made;

(2) the subjects on which discovery may be needed, when discovery should be completed, and whether discovery should be conducted in phases or be limited to or focused upon particular issues;

(3) any issues relating to disclosure or discovery of electronically stored information, including the form or forms in which it should be produced;

(4) any issues relating to claims of privilege or of protection as trial-preparation material, including—if the parties agree on a procedure to assert such claims after production—whether to ask the court to include their agreement in an order;

(5) what changes should be made in the limitations on discovery imposed under these rules or by local rule, and what other limitations should be imposed; and

(6) any other orders that should be entered by the court under Rule 26(c) or under Rule 16(b) and (c).

The attorneys of record and all unrepresented parties that have appeared in the case are jointly responsible for arranging the conference, for attempting in good faith to agree on the proposed discovery plan, and for submitting to the court within 14 days after the conference a written report outlining the plan. A court may order that the parties or attorneys attend the conference in person. If necessary to comply with its expedited schedule for Rule 16(b) conferences, a court may by local rule (i) require that the conference between the parties occur fewer than 21 days before the scheduling conference is held or a scheduling order is due under Rule 16(b), and (ii) require that the written report outlining the discovery plan be filed fewer than 14 days after the conference between the parties, or excuse the parties from submitting a written report and permit them to report orally on their discovery plan at the Rule 16(b) conference.

(g) Signing of Disclosures, Discovery Requests, Responses, and Objections.

(1) Every disclosure made pursuant to subdivision (a)(1) or subdivision (a)(3) shall be signed by at least one attorney of record in the attorney's individual name, whose address shall be stated. An unrepresented party shall sign the disclosure and state the party's address. The signature of the attorney or party constitutes a certification that to the best of the signer's knowledge, information, and belief, formed after a reasonable inquiry, the disclosure is complete and correct as of the time it is made.

(2) Every discovery request, response, or objection made by a party represented by an attorney shall be signed by at least one attorney of record in the attorney's individual name, whose address shall be stated. An unrepresented party shall sign the request, response, or objection and state

the party's address. The signature of the attorney or party constitutes a certification that to the best of the signer's knowledge, information, and belief, formed after a reasonable inquiry, the request, response, or objection is:

(A) consistent with these rules and warranted by existing law or a good faith argument for the extension, modification, or reversal of existing law;

(B) not interposed for any improper purpose, such as to harass or to cause unnecessary delay or needless increase in the cost of litigation; and

(C) not unreasonable or unduly burdensome or expensive, given the needs of the case, the discovery already had in the case, the amount in controversy, and the importance of the issues at stake in the litigation.

If a request, response, or objection is not signed, it shall be stricken unless it is signed promptly after the omission is called to the attention of the party making the request, response, or objection, and a party shall not be obligated to take any action with respect to it until it is signed.

(3) If without substantial justification a certification is made in violation of the rule, the court, upon motion or upon its own initiative, shall impose upon the person who made the certification, the party on whose behalf the disclosure, request, response, or objection is made, or both, an appropriate sanction, which may include an order to pay the amount of the reasonable expenses incurred because of the violation, including a reasonable attorney's fee.

Rule 27. DEPOSITIONS BEFORE ACTION OR PENDING APPEAL

(a) Before Action.

(1) *Petition.* A person who desires to perpetuate testimony regarding any matter that may be cognizable in any court of the United States may file a verified petition in the United States district court in the district of the residence of any expected adverse party. The petition shall be entitled in the name of the petitioner and shall show: 1, that the petitioner expects to be a party to an action cognizable in a court of the United States but is presently unable to bring it or cause it to be brought, 2, the subject matter of the expected action and the petitioner's interest therein, 3, the facts which the petitioner desires to establish by the proposed testimony and the reasons for desiring to perpetuate it, 4, the names or a description of the persons the petitioner expects will be adverse parties and their addresses so far as known, and 5, the names and addresses of the persons to be examined and the substance of the testimony which the petitioner expects to elicit from each, and shall ask for an order authorizing the petitioner to take the depositions of the persons to be examined named in the petition, for the purpose of perpetuating their testimony.

(2) *Notice and Service.* At least 20 days before the hearing date, the petitioner must serve each expected adverse party with a copy of the petition and a notice stating the time and place of the hearing. The notice may be served either inside or outside the district or state in the manner

provided in Rule 4. If that service cannot be made with due diligence on an expected adverse party, the court may order service by publication or otherwise. The court must appoint an attorney to represent persons not served in the manner provided by Rule 4 and to cross-examine the deponent if an unserved person is not otherwise represented. Rule 17(c) applies if any expected adverse party is a minor or is incompetent.

(3) *Order and Examination.* If the court is satisfied that the perpetuation of the testimony may prevent a failure or delay of justice, it shall make an order designating or describing the persons whose depositions may be taken and specifying the subject matter of the examination and whether the depositions shall be taken upon oral examination or written interrogatories. The depositions may then be taken in accordance with these rules; and the court may make orders of the character provided for by Rules 34 and 35. For the purpose of applying these rules to depositions for perpetuating testimony, each reference therein to the court in which the action is pending shall be deemed to refer to the court in which the petition for such deposition was filed.

(4) *Use of Deposition.* If a deposition to perpetuate testimony is taken under these rules or if, although not so taken, it would be admissible in evidence in the courts of the state in which it is taken, it may be used in any action involving the same subject matter subsequently brought in a United States district court, in accordance with the provisions of Rule 32(a).

(b) Pending Appeal. If an appeal has been taken from a judgment of a district court or before the taking of an appeal if the time therefor has not expired, the district court in which the judgment was rendered may allow the taking of the depositions of witnesses to perpetuate their testimony for use in the event of further proceedings in the district court. In such case the party who desires to perpetuate the testimony may make a motion in the district court for leave to take the depositions, upon the same notice and service thereof as if the action was pending in the district court. The motion shall show (1) the names and addresses of persons to be examined and the substance of the testimony which the party expects to elicit from each; (2) the reasons for perpetuating their testimony. If the court finds that the perpetuation of the testimony is proper to avoid a failure or delay of justice, it may make an order allowing the depositions to be taken and may make orders of the character provided for by Rules 34 and 35, and thereupon the depositions may be taken and used in the same manner and under the same conditions as are prescribed in these rules for depositions taken in actions pending in the district court.

(c) Perpetuation by Action. This rule does not limit the power of a court to entertain an action to perpetuate testimony.

Rule 28. PERSONS BEFORE WHOM DEPOSITIONS MAY BE TAKEN

(a) Within the United States. Within the United States or within a territory or insular possession subject to the jurisdiction of the United States, depositions shall be taken before an officer authorized to administer oaths by the laws of the United States or of the place where the examination is held, or before a person appointed by the court in which the action is pending. A person so appointed has power to administer oaths and take testimony. The term officer as used in Rules 30, 31 and 32 includes a person appointed by the court or designated by the parties under Rule 29.

(b) In Foreign Countries. Depositions may be taken in a foreign country (1) pursuant to any applicable treaty or convention, or (2) pursuant to a letter of request (whether or not captioned a letter rogatory), or (3) on notice before a person authorized to administer oaths in the place where the examination is held, either by the law thereof or by the law of the United States, or (4) before a person commissioned by the court, and a person so commissioned shall have the power by virtue of the commission to administer any necessary oath and take testimony. A commission or a letter of request shall be issued on application and notice and on terms that are just and appropriate. It is not requisite to the issuance of a commission or a letter of request that the taking of the deposition in any other manner is impracticable or inconvenient; and both a commission and a letter of request may be issued in proper cases. A notice or commission may designate the person before whom the deposition is to be taken either by name or descriptive title. A letter of request may be addressed "To the Appropriate Authority in [here name the country]." When a letter of request or any other device is used pursuant to any applicable treaty or convention, it shall be captioned in the form prescribed by that treaty or convention. Evidence obtained in response to a letter of request need not be excluded merely because it is not a verbatim transcript, because the testimony was not taken under oath, or because of any similar departure from the requirements for depositions taken within the United States under these rules.

(c) Disqualification for Interest. No deposition shall be taken before a person who is a relative or employee or attorney or counsel of any of the parties, or is a relative or employee of such attorney or counsel, or is financially interested in the action.

Rule 29. STIPULATIONS REGARDING DISCOVERY PROCEDURE

Unless otherwise directed by the court, the parties may by written stipulation (1) provide that depositions may be taken before any person, at any time or place, upon any notice, and in any manner and when so taken may be used like other depositions, and (2) modify other procedures governing or limitations placed upon discovery, except that stipulations extending the time provided in Rules 33, 34, and 36 for responses to discovery may, if they would interfere with any time set for completion of discovery, for hearing of a motion, or for trial, be made only with the approval of the court.

Rule 30. DEPOSITIONS UPON ORAL EXAMINATION

(a) When Depositions May Be Taken; When Leave Required.

(1) A party may take the testimony of any person, including a party, by deposition upon oral examination without leave of court except as provided in paragraph (2). The attendance of witnesses may be compelled by subpoena as provided in Rule 45.

(2) A party must obtain leave of court, which shall be granted to the extent consistent with the principles stated in Rule 26(b)(2), if the person to be examined is confined in prison or if, without the written stipulation of the parties,

(A) a proposed deposition would result in more than ten depositions being taken under this rule or Rule 31 by the plaintiffs, or by the defendants, or by third-party defendants;

(B) the person to be examined already has been deposed in the case; or

(C) a party seeks to take a deposition before the time specified in Rule 26(d) unless the notice contains a certification, with supporting facts, that the person to be examined is expected to leave the United States and be unavailable for examination in this country unless deposed before that time.

(b) Notice of Examination: General Requirements; Method of Recording; Production of Documents and Things; Deposition of Organization; Deposition by Telephone.

(1) A party desiring to take the deposition of any person upon oral examination shall give reasonable notice in writing to every other party to the action. The notice shall state the time and place for taking the deposition and the name and address of each person to be examined, if known, and, if the name is not known, a general description sufficient to identify the person or the particular class or group to which the person belongs. If a subpoena duces tecum is to be served on the person to be examined, the designation of the materials to be produced as set forth in the subpoena shall be attached to, or included in, the notice.

(2) The party taking the deposition shall state in the notice the method by which the testimony shall be recorded. Unless the court orders otherwise, it may be recorded by sound, sound-and-visual, or stenographic means, and the party taking the deposition shall bear the cost of the recording. Any party may arrange for a transcription to be made from the recording of a deposition taken by nonstenographic means.

(3) With prior notice to the deponent and other parties, any party may designate another method to record the deponent's testimony in addition to the method specified by the person taking the deposition. The additional record or transcript shall be made at that party's expense unless the court otherwise orders.

(4) Unless otherwise agreed by the parties, a deposition shall be conducted before an officer appointed or designated under Rule 28 and shall begin with a statement on the record by the officer that includes (A) the officer's name and business address; (B) the date, time, and place of the deposition; (C) the name of the deponent; (D) the administration of the oath or affirmation to the deponent; and (E) an identification of all persons present. If the deposition is recorded other than stenographically, the officer shall repeat items (A) through (C) at the beginning of each unit of recorded tape or other recording medium. The appearance or demeanor of deponents or attorneys shall not be distorted through camera or sound-recording techniques. At the end of the deposition, the officer shall state on

the record that the deposition is complete and shall set forth any stipulations made by counsel concerning the custody of the transcript or recording and the exhibits, or concerning other pertinent matters.

(5) The notice to a party deponent may be accompanied by a request made in compliance with Rule 34 for the production of documents and tangible things at the taking of the deposition. The procedure of Rule 34 shall apply to the request.

(6) A party may in the party's notice and in a subpoena name as the deponent a public or private corporation or a partnership or association or governmental agency and describe with reasonable particularity the matters on which examination is requested. In that event, the organization so named shall designate one or more officers, directors, or managing agents, or other persons who consent to testify on its behalf, and may set forth, for each person designated, the matters on which the person will testify. A subpoena shall advise a non-party organization of its duty to make such a designation. The persons so designated shall testify as to matters known or reasonably available to the organization. This subdivision (b)(6) does not preclude taking a deposition by any other procedure authorized in these rules.

(7) The parties may stipulate in writing or the court may upon motion order that a deposition be taken by telephone or other remote electronic means. For the purposes of this rule and Rules 28(a), 37(a)(1), and 37(b)(1), a deposition taken by such means is taken in the district and at the place where the deponent is to answer questions.

(c) Examination and Cross–Examination; Record of Examination; Oath; Objections. Examination and cross-examination of witnesses may proceed as permitted at the trial under the provisions of the Federal Rules of Evidence except Rules 103 and 615. The officer before whom the deposition is to be taken shall put the witness on oath or affirmation and shall personally, or by someone acting under the officer's direction and in the officer's presence, record the testimony of the witness. The testimony shall be taken stenographically or recorded by any other method authorized by subdivision (b)(2) of this rule. All objections made at the time of the examination to the qualifications of the officer taking the deposition, to the manner of taking it, to the evidence presented, to the conduct of any party, or to any other aspect of the proceedings shall be noted by the officer upon the record of the deposition; but the examination shall proceed, with the testimony being taken subject to the objections. In lieu of participating in the oral examination, parties may serve written questions in a sealed envelope on the party taking the deposition and the party taking the deposition shall transmit them to the officer, who shall propound them to the witness and record the answers verbatim.

(d) Schedule and Duration; Motion to Terminate or Limit Examination.

(1) Any objection during a deposition must be stated concisely and in a non-argumentative and non-suggestive manner. A person may instruct a deponent not to answer only when necessary to preserve a privilege, to enforce a limitation directed by the court, or to present a motion under Rule 30(d)(4).

(2) Unless otherwise authorized by the court or stipulated by the parties, a deposition is limited to one day of seven hours. The court must allow additional time consistent with Rule 26(b)(2) if needed for a fair examination of the deponent or if the deponent or another person, or other circumstance, impedes or delays the examination.

(3) If the court finds that any impediment, delay, or other conduct has frustrated the fair examination of the deponent, it may impose upon the persons responsible an appropriate sanction, including the reasonable costs and attorney's fees incurred by any parties as a result thereof.

(4) At any time during a deposition, on motion of a party or of the deponent and upon a showing that the examination is being conducted in bad faith or in such manner as unreasonably to annoy, embarrass, or oppress the deponent or party, the court in which the action is pending or the court in the district where the deposition is being taken may order the officer conducting the examination to cease forthwith from taking the deposition, or may limit the scope and manner of the taking of the deposition as provided in Rule 26(c). If the order made terminates the examination, it may be resumed thereafter only upon the order of the court in which the action is pending. Upon demand of the objecting party or deponent, the taking of the deposition must be suspended for the time necessary to make a motion for an order. The provisions of Rule 37(a)(4) apply to the award of expenses incurred in relation to the motion.

(e) Review by Witness; Changes; Signing. If requested by the deponent or a party before completion of the deposition, the deponent shall have 30 days after being notified by the officer that the transcript or recording is available in which to review the transcript or recording and, if there are changes in form or substance, to sign a statement reciting such changes and the reasons given by the deponent for making them. The officer shall indicate in the certificate prescribed by subdivision (f)(1) whether any review was requested and, if so, shall append any changes made by the deponent during the period allowed.

(f) Certification and Delivery by Officer; Exhibits; Copies.

(1) The officer must certify that the witness was duly sworn by the officer and that the deposition is a true record of the testimony given by the witness. This certificate must be in writing and accompany the record of the deposition. Unless otherwise ordered by the court, the officer must securely seal the deposition in an envelope or package indorsed with the title of the action and marked "Deposition of [here insert name of witness]" and must promptly send it to the attorney who arranged for the transcript or recording, who must store it under conditions that will protect it against loss, destruction, tampering, or deterioration. Documents and things produced for inspection during the examination of the witness must, upon the request of a party, be marked for identification and annexed to the deposition and may be inspected and copied by any party, except that if the person producing the materials desires to retain them the person may (A) offer copies to be marked for identification and annexed to the deposition and to serve thereafter as originals if the person affords to all parties fair opportunity to verify the copies by comparison with the originals, or (B) offer the originals to be marked for identification, after

giving to each party an opportunity to inspect and copy them, in which event the materials may then be used in the same manner as if annexed to the deposition. Any party may move for an order that the original be annexed to and returned with the deposition to the court, pending final disposition of the case.

(2) Unless otherwise ordered by the court or agreed by the parties, the officer shall retain stenographic notes of any deposition taken stenographically or a copy of the recording of any deposition taken by another method. Upon payment of reasonable charges therefor, the officer shall furnish a copy of the transcript or other recording of the deposition to any party or to the deponent.

(3) The party taking the deposition shall give prompt notice of its filing to all other parties.

(g) Failure to Attend or to Serve Subpoena; Expenses.

(1) If the party giving the notice of the taking of a deposition fails to attend and proceed therewith and another party attends in person or by attorney pursuant to the notice, the court may order the party giving the notice to pay to such other party the reasonable expenses incurred by that party and that party's attorney in attending, including reasonable attorney's fees.

(2) If the party giving the notice of the taking of a deposition of a witness fails to serve a subpoena upon the witness and the witness because of such failure does not attend, and if another party attends in person or by attorney because that party expects the deposition of that witness to be taken, the court may order the party giving the notice to pay to such other party the reasonable expenses incurred by that party and that party's attorney in attending, including reasonable attorney's fees.

Rule 31. DEPOSITIONS UPON WRITTEN QUESTIONS

(a) Serving Questions; Notice.

(1) A party may take the testimony of any person, including a party, by deposition upon written questions without leave of court except as provided in paragraph (2). The attendance of witnesses may be compelled by the use of subpoena as provided in Rule 45.

(2) A party must obtain leave of court, which shall be granted to the extent consistent with the principles stated in Rule 26(b)(2), if the person to be examined is confined in prison or if, without the written stipulation of the parties,

(A) a proposed deposition would result in more than ten depositions being taken under this rule or Rule 30 by the plaintiffs, or by the defendants, or by third-party defendants;

(B) the person to be examined has already been deposed in the case; or

(C) a party seeks to take a deposition before the time specified in Rule 26(d).

(3) A party desiring to take a deposition upon written questions shall serve them upon every other party with a notice stating (1) the name and

address of the person who is to answer them, if known, and if the name is not known, a general description sufficient to identify the person or the particular class or group to which the person belongs, and (2) the name or descriptive title and address of the officer before whom the deposition is to be taken. A deposition upon written questions may be taken of a public or private corporation or a partnership or association or governmental agency in accordance with the provisions of Rule 30(b)(6).

(4) Within 14 days after the notice and written questions are served, a party may serve cross questions upon all other parties. Within 7 days after being served with cross questions, a party may serve redirect questions upon all other parties. Within 7 days after being served with redirect questions, a party may serve recross questions upon all other parties. The court may for cause shown enlarge or shorten the time.

(b) Officer to Take Responses and Prepare Record. A copy of the notice and copies of all questions served shall be delivered by the party taking the deposition to the officer designated in the notice, who shall proceed promptly, in the manner provided by Rule 30(c), (e), and (f), to take the testimony of the witness in response to the questions and to prepare, certify, and file or mail the deposition, attaching thereto the copy of the notice and the questions received by the officer.

(c) Notice of Filing. When the deposition is filed the party taking it shall promptly give notice thereof to all other parties.

Rule 32.   USE OF DEPOSITIONS IN COURT PROCEEDINGS

(a) Use of Depositions. At the trial or upon the hearing of a motion or an interlocutory proceeding, any part or all of a deposition, so far as admissible under the rules of evidence applied as though the witness were then present and testifying, may be used against any party who was present or represented at the taking of the deposition or who had reasonable notice thereof, in accordance with any of the following provisions:

(1) Any deposition may be used by any party for the purpose of contradicting or impeaching the testimony of deponent as a witness, or for any other purpose permitted by the Federal Rules of Evidence.

(2) The deposition of a party or of anyone who at the time of taking the deposition was an officer, director, or managing agent, or a person designated under Rule 30(b)(6) or 31(a) to testify on behalf of a public or private corporation, partnership or association or governmental agency which is a party may be used by an adverse party for any purpose.

(3) The deposition of a witness, whether or not a party, may be used by any party for any purpose if the court finds:

(A) that the witness is dead; or

(B) that the witness is at a greater distance than 100 miles from the place of trial or hearing, or is out of the United States, unless it appears that the absence of the witness was procured by the party offering the deposition; or

(C) that the witness is unable to attend or testify because of age, illness, infirmity, or imprisonment; or

(D) that the party offering the deposition has been unable to procure the attendance of the witness by subpoena; or

(E) upon application and notice, that such exceptional circumstances exist as to make it desirable, in the interest of justice and with due regard to the importance of presenting the testimony of witnesses orally in open court, to allow the deposition to be used.

A deposition taken without leave of court pursuant to a notice under Rule 30(a)(2)(C) shall not be used against a party who demonstrates that, when served with the notice, it was unable through the exercise of diligence to obtain counsel to represent it at the taking of the deposition; nor shall a deposition be used against a party who, having received less than 11 days notice of a deposition, has promptly upon receiving such notice filed a motion for a protective order under Rule 26(c)(2) requesting that the deposition not be held or be held at a different time or place and such motion is pending at the time the deposition is held.

(4) If only part of a deposition is offered in evidence by a party, an adverse party may require the offeror to introduce any other part which ought in fairness to be considered with the part introduced, and any party may introduce any other parts.

Substitution of parties pursuant to Rule 25 does not affect the right to use depositions previously taken; and, when an action has been brought in any court of the United States or of any State and another action involving the same subject matter is afterward brought between the same parties or their representatives or successors in interest, all depositions lawfully taken and duly filed in the former action may be used in the latter as if originally taken therefor. A deposition previously taken may also be used as permitted by the Federal Rules of Evidence.

(b) Objections to Admissibility. Subject to the provisions of Rule 28(b) and subdivision (d)(3) of this rule, objection may be made at the trial or hearing to receiving in evidence any deposition or part thereof for any reason which would require the exclusion of the evidence if the witness were then present and testifying.

(c) Form of Presentation. Except as otherwise directed by the court, a party offering deposition testimony pursuant to this rule may offer it in stenographic or nonstenographic form, but, if in nonstenographic form, the party shall also provide the court with a transcript of the portions so offered. On request of any party in a case tried before a jury, deposition testimony offered other than for impeachment purposes shall be presented in nonstenographic form, if available, unless the court for good cause orders otherwise.

(d) Effect of Errors and Irregularities in Depositions.

(1) *As to Notice.* All errors and irregularities in the notice for taking a deposition are waived unless written objection is promptly served upon the party giving the notice.

(2) *As to Disqualification of Officer.* Objection to taking a deposition because of disqualification of the officer before whom it is to be taken is

waived unless made before the taking of the deposition begins or as soon thereafter as the disqualification becomes known or could be discovered with reasonable diligence.

(3) *As to Taking of Deposition*.

(A) Objections to the competency of a witness or to the competency, relevancy, or materiality of testimony are not waived by failure to make them before or during the taking of the deposition, unless the ground of the objection is one which might have been obviated or removed if presented at that time.

(B) Errors and irregularities occurring at the oral examination in the manner of taking the deposition, in the form of the questions or answers, in the oath or affirmation, or in the conduct of parties, and errors of any kind which might be obviated, removed, or cured if promptly presented, are waived unless seasonable objection thereto is made at the taking of the deposition.

(C) Objections to the form of written questions submitted under Rule 31 are waived unless served in writing upon the party propounding them within the time allowed for serving the succeeding cross or other questions and within 5 days after service of the last questions authorized.

(4) *As to Completion and Return of Deposition*. Errors and irregularities in the manner in which the testimony is transcribed or the deposition is prepared, signed, certified, sealed, indorsed, transmitted, filed, or otherwise dealt with by the officer under Rules 30 and 31 are waived unless a motion to suppress the deposition or some part thereof is made with reasonable promptness after such defect is, or with due diligence might have been, ascertained.

Rule 33. INTERROGATORIES TO PARTIES

(a) Availability. Without leave of court or written stipulation, any party may serve upon any other party written interrogatories, not exceeding 25 in number including all discrete subparts, to be answered by the party served or, if the party served is a public or private corporation or a partnership or association or governmental agency, by any officer or agent, who shall furnish such information as is available to the party. Leave to serve additional interrogatories shall be granted to the extent consistent with the principles of Rule 26(b)(2). Without leave of court or written stipulation, interrogatories may not be served before the time specified in Rule 26(d).

(b) Answers and Objections.

(1) Each interrogatory shall be answered separately and fully in writing under oath, unless it is objected to, in which event the objecting party shall state the reasons for objection and shall answer to the extent the interrogatory is not objectionable.

(2) The answers are to be signed by the person making them, and the objections signed by the attorney making them.

(3) The party upon whom the interrogatories have been served shall serve a copy of the answers, and objections if any, within 30 days after the

service of the interrogatories. A shorter or longer time may be directed by the court or, in the absence of such an order, agreed to in writing by the parties subject to Rule 29.

(4) All grounds for an objection to an interrogatory shall be stated with specificity. Any ground not stated in a timely objection is waived unless the party's failure to object is excused by the court for good cause shown.

(5) The party submitting the interrogatories may move for an order under Rule 37(a) with respect to any objection to or other failure to answer an interrogatory.

(c) Scope; Use at Trial. Interrogatories may relate to any matters which can be inquired into under Rule 26(b)(1), and the answers may be used to the extent permitted by the rules of evidence.

An interrogatory otherwise proper is not necessarily objectionable merely because an answer to the interrogatory involves an opinion or contention that relates to fact or the application of law to fact, but the court may order that such an interrogatory need not be answered until after designated discovery has been completed or until a pretrial conference or other later time.

(d) Option to Produce Business Records. Where the answer to an interrogatory may be derived or ascertained from the business records, including electronically stored information, of the party upon whom the interrogatory has been served or from an examination, audit or inspection of such business records, including a compilation, abstract or summary thereof and the burden of deriving or ascertaining the answer is substantially the same for the party serving the interrogatory as for the party served, it is a sufficient answer to such interrogatory to specify the records from which the answer may be derived or ascertained and to afford to the party serving the interrogatory reasonable opportunity to examine, audit or inspect such records and to make copies, compilations, abstracts, or summaries. A specification shall be in sufficient detail to permit the interrogating party to locate and to identify, as readily as can the party served, the records from which the answer may be ascertained.

Rule 34. PRODUCTION OF DOCUMENTS, ELECTRONICALLY STORED INFORMATION, AND THINGS AND ENTRY UPON LAND FOR INSPECTION AND OTHER PURPOSES

(a) Scope. Any party may serve on any other party a request (1) to produce and permit the party making the request, or someone acting on the requestor's behalf, to inspect, copy, test, or sample any designated documents or electronically stored information—including writings, drawings, graphs, charts, photographs, sound recordings, images, and other data or data compilations stored in any medium from which information can be obtained—translated, if necessary, by the respondent into reasonably usable form, or to inspect, copy, test, or sample any designated tangible things which constitute or contain matters within the scope of Rule 26(b) and which are in the possession, custody or control of the party upon whom the request is served; or (2) to permit entry upon designated land or other property in the possession or control of the party upon whom the request is served for the purpose of inspection and measuring, surveying, photographing, testing, or sampling the property or any designated object or operation thereon, within the scope of Rule 26(b).

(b) Procedure. The request shall set forth, either by individual item or by category, the items to be inspected, and describe each with reasonable particularity. The request shall specify a reasonable time, place, and manner of making the inspection and performing the related acts. The request may specify the form or forms in which electronically stored information is to be produced. Without leave of court or written stipulation, a request may not be served before the time specified in Rule 26(d).

The party upon whom the request is served shall serve a written response within 30 days after the service of the request. A shorter or longer time may be directed by the court or, in the absence of such an order, agreed to in writing by the parties, subject to Rule 29. The response shall state, with respect to each item or category, that inspection and related activities will be permitted as requested, unless the request is objected to, including an objection to the requested form or forms for producing electronically stored information, stating the reasons for the objection. If objection is made to part of an item or category, the part shall be specified and inspection permitted of the remaining parts. If objection is made to the requested form or forms for producing electronically stored information— or if no form was specified in the request—the responding party must state the form or forms it intends to use. The party submitting the request may move for an order under Rule 37(a) with respect to any objection to or other failure to respond to the request or any part thereof, or any failure to permit inspection as requested.

Unless the parties otherwise agree, or the court otherwise orders:

(i) a party who produces documents for inspection shall produce them as they are kept in the usual course of business or shall organize and label them to correspond with the categories in the request;

(ii) if a request does not specify the form or forms for producing electronically stored information, a responding party must produce the information in a form or forms in which it is ordinarily maintained or in a form or forms that are reasonably usable; and

(iii) a party need not produce the same electronically stored information in more than one form.

(c) Persons Not Parties. A person not a party to the action may be compelled to produce documents and things or to submit to an inspection as provided in Rule 45.

Rule 35. PHYSICAL AND MENTAL EXAMINATION OF PERSONS

(a) Order for Examination. When the mental or physical condition (including the blood group) of a party, or of a person in the custody or under the legal control of a party, is in controversy, the court in which the action is pending may order the party to submit to a physical or mental examination by a suitably licensed or certified examiner or to produce for examination the person in the party's custody or legal control. The order may be made only on motion for good cause shown and upon notice to the person to be examined and to all parties and shall specify the time, place, manner, conditions, and scope of the examination and the person or persons by whom it is to be made.

(b) Report of Examiner.

(1) If requested by the party against whom an order is made under Rule 35(a) or the person examined, the party causing the examination to be made shall deliver to the requesting party a copy of the detailed written report of the examiner setting out the examiner's findings, including results of all tests made, diagnoses and conclusions, together with like reports of all earlier examinations of the same condition. After delivery the party causing the examination shall be entitled upon request to receive from the party against whom the order is made a like report of any examination, previously or thereafter made, of the same condition, unless, in the case of a report of examination of a person not a party, the party shows that such party is unable to obtain it. The court on motion may make an order against a party requiring delivery of a report on such terms as are just, and if an examiner fails or refuses to make a report the court may exclude the examiner's testimony if offered at trial.

(2) By requesting and obtaining a report of the examination so ordered or by taking the deposition of the examiner, the party examined waives any privilege the party may have in that action or any other involving the same controversy, regarding the testimony of every other person who has examined or may thereafter examine the party in respect of the same mental or physical condition.

(3) This subdivision applies to examinations made by agreement of the parties, unless the agreement expressly provides otherwise. This subdivision does not preclude discovery of a report of an examiner or the taking of a deposition of the examiner in accordance with the provisions of any other rule.

Rule 36. REQUESTS FOR ADMISSION

(a) Request for Admission. A party may serve upon any other party a written request for the admission, for purposes of the pending action only, of the truth of any matters within the scope of Rule 26(b)(1) set forth in the request that relate to statements or opinions of fact or of the application of law to fact, including the genuineness of any documents described in the request. Copies of documents shall be served with the request unless they have been or are otherwise furnished or made available for inspection and copying. Without leave of court or written stipulation, requests for admission may not be served before the time specified in Rule 26(d).

Each matter of which an admission is requested shall be separately set forth. The matter is admitted unless, within 30 days after service of the request, or within such shorter or longer time as the court may allow or as the parties may agree to in writing, subject to Rule 29, the party to whom the request is directed serves upon the party requesting the admission a written answer or objection addressed to the matter, signed by the party or by the party's attorney. If objection is made, the reasons therefor shall be stated. The answer shall specifically deny the matter or set forth in detail the reasons why the answering party cannot truthfully admit or deny the matter. A denial shall fairly meet the substance of the requested admission, and when good faith requires that a party qualify an answer or deny only a part of the matter of which an admission is requested, the party shall specify so much of it as is true and qualify or deny the remainder. An answering party may not give lack of information or knowledge as a reason for failure to admit or deny unless the party states that the party has made reasonable inquiry and that the information known or readily obtainable by the party is insufficient to enable the party to admit or deny. A party who considers that a matter of which an admission has been requested presents a genuine issue for trial may not, on that ground alone, object to the request; the party may, subject to the provisions of Rule 37(c), deny the matter or set forth reasons why the party cannot admit or deny it.

The party who has requested the admissions may move to determine the sufficiency of the answers or objections. Unless the court determines that an objection is justified, it shall order that an answer be served. If the court determines that an answer does not comply with the requirements of this rule, it may order either that the matter is admitted or that an amended answer be served. The court may, in lieu of these orders, determine that final disposition of the request be made at a pre-trial conference or at a designated time prior to trial. The provisions of Rule 37(a)(4) apply to the award of expenses incurred in relation to the motion.

(b) Effect of Admission. Any matter admitted under this rule is conclusively established unless the court on motion permits withdrawal or amendment of the admission. Subject to the provisions of Rule 16 governing amendment of a pre-trial order, the court may permit withdrawal or amendment when the presentation of the merits of the action will be subserved thereby and the party who obtained the admission fails to satisfy the court that withdrawal or amendment will prejudice that party in maintaining the action or defense on the merits. Any admission made by a party under this rule is for the purpose of the pending action only and is not an admission for any other purpose nor may it be used against the party in any other proceeding.

Rule 37. FAILURE TO MAKE DISCLOSURES OR COOPERATE IN DISCOVERY; SANCTIONS

(a) Motion for Order Compelling Disclosure or Discovery. A party, upon reasonable notice to other parties and all persons affected thereby, may apply for an order compelling disclosure or discovery as follows:

(1) *Appropriate Court.* An application for an order to a party shall be made to the court in which the action is pending. An application for an order to a person who is not a party shall be made to the court in the district where the discovery is being, or is to be, taken.

(2) *Motion.*

(A) If a party fails to make a disclosure required by Rule 26(a), any other party may move to compel disclosure and for appropriate sanctions. The motion must include a certification that the movant has in good faith conferred or attempted to confer with the party not making the disclosure in an effort to secure the disclosure without court action.

(B) If a deponent fails to answer a question propounded or submitted under Rules 30 or 31, or a corporation or other entity fails to make a designation under Rule 30(b)(6) or 31(a), or a party fails to answer an interrogatory submitted under Rule 33, or if a party, in response to a request for inspection submitted under Rule 34, fails to respond that inspection will be permitted as requested or fails to permit inspection as requested, the discovering party may move for an order compelling an answer, or a designation, or an order compelling inspection in accordance with the request. The motion must include a certification that the movant has in good faith conferred or attempted to confer with the person or party failing to make the discovery in an effort to secure the information or material without court action. When taking a deposition on oral examination, the proponent of the question may complete or adjourn the examination before applying for an order.

(3) *Evasive or Incomplete Disclosure, Answer, or Response.* For purposes of this subdivision an evasive or incomplete disclosure, answer, or response is to be treated as a failure to disclose, answer, or respond.

(4) *Expenses and Sanctions.*

(A) If the motion is granted or if the disclosure or requested discovery is provided after the motion was filed, the court shall, after affording an opportunity to be heard, require the party or deponent whose conduct necessitated the motion or the party or attorney advising such conduct or both of them to pay to the moving party the reasonable expenses incurred in making the motion, including attorney's fees, unless the court finds that the motion was filed without the movant's first making a good faith effort to obtain the disclosure or discovery without court action, or that the opposing party's nondisclosure, response, or objection was substantially justified, or that other circumstances make an award of expenses unjust.

(B) If the motion is denied, the court may enter any protective order authorized under Rule 26(c) and shall, after affording an opportunity to be heard, require the moving party or the attorney filing the motion or both of them to pay to the party or deponent who opposed the motion the reasonable expenses incurred in opposing the motion, including attorney's fees, unless the court finds that the making of the motion was substantially justified or that other circumstances make an award of expenses unjust.

(C) If the motion is granted in part and denied in part, the court may enter any protective order authorized under Rule 26(c) and may, after affording an opportunity to be heard, apportion the reasonable expenses incurred in relation to the motion among the parties and persons in a just manner.

(b) Failure to Comply with Order.

(1) *Sanctions by Court in District Where Deposition Is Taken.* If a deponent fails to be sworn or to answer a question after being directed to do so by the court in the district in which the deposition is being taken, the failure may be considered a contempt of that court.

(2) *Sanctions by Court in Which Action Is Pending.* If a party or an officer, director, or managing agent of a party or a person designated under Rule 30(b)(6) or 31(a) to testify on behalf of a party fails to obey an order to provide or permit discovery, including an order made under subdivision (a) of this rule or Rule 35, or if a party fails to obey an order entered under Rule 26(f), the court in which the action is pending may make such orders in regard to the failure as are just, and among others the following:

(A) An order that the matters regarding which the order was made or any other designated facts shall be taken to be established for the purposes of the action in accordance with the claim of the party obtaining the order;

(B) An order refusing to allow the disobedient party to support or oppose designated claims or defenses, or prohibiting that party from introducing designated matters in evidence;

(C) An order striking out pleadings or parts thereof, or staying further proceedings until the order is obeyed, or dismissing the action or proceeding or any part thereof, or rendering a judgment by default against the disobedient party;

(D) In lieu of any of the foregoing orders or in addition thereto, an order treating as a contempt of court the failure to obey any orders except an order to submit to a physical or mental examination;

(E) Where a party has failed to comply with an order under Rule 35(a) requiring that party to produce another for examination, such orders as are listed in paragraphs (A), (B), and (C) of this subdivision, unless the party failing to comply shows that that party is unable to produce such person for examination.

In lieu of any of the foregoing orders or in addition thereto, the court shall require the party failing to obey the order or the attorney advising that party or both to pay the reasonable expenses, including attorney's fees, caused by the failure, unless the court finds that the failure was substantially justified or that other circumstances make an award of expenses unjust.

(c) Failure to Disclose; False or Misleading Disclosure; Refusal to Admit.

(1) A party that without substantial justification fails to disclose information required by Rule 26(a) or 26(e)(1), or to amend a prior response to discovery as required by Rule 26(e)(2), is not, unless such failure is harmless, permitted to use as evidence at a trial, at a hearing, or on a motion any witness or information not so disclosed. In addition to or in lieu of this sanction, the court, on motion and after affording an opportunity to be heard, may impose other appropriate sanctions. In addition to requiring payment of reasonable expenses, including attorney's

fees, caused by the failure, these sanctions may include any of the actions authorized under Rule 37(b)(2)(A), (B), and (C) and may include informing the jury of the failure to make the disclosure.

(2) If a party fails to admit the genuineness of any document or the truth of any matter as requested under Rule 36, and if the party requesting the admissions thereafter proves the genuineness of the document or the truth of the matter, the requesting party may apply to the court for an order requiring the other party to pay the reasonable expenses incurred in making that proof, including reasonable attorney's fees. The court shall make the order unless it finds that (A) the request was held objectionable pursuant to Rule 36(a), or (B) the admission sought was of no substantial importance, or (C) the party failing to admit had reasonable ground to believe that the party might prevail on the matter, or (D) there was other good reason for the failure to admit.

(d) Failure of Party to Attend at Own Deposition or Serve Answers to Interrogatories or Respond to Request for Inspection. If a party or an officer, director, or managing agent of a party or a person designated under Rule 30(b)(6) or 31(a) to testify on behalf of a party fails (1) to appear before the officer who is to take the deposition, after being served with a proper notice, or (2) to serve answers or objections to interrogatories submitted under Rule 33, after proper service of the interrogatories, or (3) to serve a written response to a request for inspection submitted under Rule 34, after proper service of the request, the court in which the action is pending on motion may make such orders in regard to the failure as are just, and among others it may take any action authorized under subparagraphs (A), (B), and (C) of subdivision (b)(2) of this rule. Any motion specifying a failure under clause (2) or (3) of this subdivision shall include a certification that the movant has in good faith conferred or attempted to confer with the party failing to answer or respond in an effort to obtain such answer or response without court action. In lieu of any order or in addition thereto, the court shall require the party failing to act or the attorney advising that party or both to pay the reasonable expenses, including attorney's fees, caused by the failure unless the court finds that the failure was substantially justified or that other circumstances make an award of expenses unjust.

The failure to act described in this subdivision may not be excused on the ground that the discovery sought is objectionable unless the party failing to act has a pending motion for a protective order as provided by Rule 26(c).

(e) [Abrogated.]

(f) Electronically Stored Information. Absent exceptional circumstances, a court may not impose sanctions under these rules on a party for failing to provide electronically stored information lost as a result of the routine, good-faith operation of an electronic information system.

(g) Failure to Participate in the Framing of a Discovery Plan. If a party or a party's attorney fails to participate in good faith in the development and submission of a proposed discovery plan as required by Rule 26(f), the court may, after opportunity for hearing, require such party or attorney to pay to any other party the reasonable expenses, including attorney's fees, caused by the failure.

VI. TRIALS

Rule 38. JURY TRIAL OF RIGHT

(a) Right Preserved. The right of trial by jury as declared by the Seventh Amendment to the Constitution or as given by a statute of the United States shall be preserved to the parties inviolate.

(b) Demand. Any party may demand a trial by jury of any issue triable of right by a jury by (1) serving upon the other parties a demand therefor in writing at any time after the commencement of the action and not later than 10 days after the service of the last pleading directed to such issue, and (2) filing the demand as required by Rule 5(d). Such demand may be indorsed upon a pleading of the party.

(c) Same: Specification of Issues. In the demand a party may specify the issues which the party wishes so tried; otherwise the party shall be deemed to have demanded trial by jury for all the issues so triable. If the party has demanded trial by jury for only some of the issues, any other party within 10 days after service of the demand or such lesser time as the court may order, may serve a demand for trial by jury of any other or all of the issues of fact in the action.

(d) Waiver. The failure of a party to serve and file a demand as required by this rule constitutes a waiver by the party of trial by jury. A demand for trial by jury made as herein provided may not be withdrawn without the consent of the parties.

(e) Admiralty and Maritime Claims. These rules shall not be construed to create a right to trial by jury of the issues in an admiralty or maritime claim within the meaning of Rule 9(h).

Rule 39. TRIAL BY JURY OR BY THE COURT

(a) By Jury. When trial by jury has been demanded as provided in Rule 38, the action shall be designated upon the docket as a jury action. The trial of all issues so demanded shall be by jury, unless (1) the parties or their attorneys of record, by written stipulation filed with the court or by an oral stipulation made in open court and entered in the record, consent to trial by the court sitting without a jury or (2) the court upon motion or of its own initiative finds that a right of trial by jury of some or all of those issues does not exist under the Constitution or statutes of the United States.

(b) By the Court. Issues not demanded for trial by jury as provided in Rule 38 shall be tried by the court; but, notwithstanding the failure of a party to demand a jury in an action in which such a demand might have been made of right, the court in its discretion upon motion may order a trial by a jury of any or all issues.

(c) Advisory Jury and Trial by Consent. In all actions not triable of right by a jury the court upon motion or of its own initiative may try any issue with an advisory jury or, except in actions against the United States when a statute of the United States provides for trial without a jury, the court, with the consent of both parties, may order a trial with a jury whose verdict has the same effect as if trial by jury had been a matter of right.

Rule 40. ASSIGNMENT OF CASES FOR TRIAL

The district courts shall provide by rule for the placing of actions upon the trial calendar (1) without request of the parties or (2) upon request of a party and notice to the other parties or (3) in such other manner as the courts deem expedient. Precedence shall be given to actions entitled thereto by any statute of the United States.

Rule 41. DISMISSAL OF ACTIONS

(a) Voluntary Dismissal: Effect Thereof.

(1) *By Plaintiff; by Stipulation.* Subject to the provisions of Rule 23(e), of Rule 66, and of any statute of the United States, an action may be dismissed by the plaintiff without order of court (i) by filing a notice of dismissal at any time before service by the adverse party of an answer or of a motion for summary judgment, whichever first occurs, or (ii) by filing a stipulation of dismissal signed by all parties who have appeared in the action. Unless otherwise stated in the notice of dismissal or stipulation, the dismissal is without prejudice, except that a notice of dismissal operates as an adjudication upon the merits when filed by a plaintiff who has once dismissed in any court of the United States or of any state an action based on or including the same claim.

(2) *By Order of Court.* Except as provided in paragraph (1) of this subdivision of this rule, an action shall not be dismissed at the plaintiff's instance save upon order of the court and upon such terms and conditions as the court deems proper. If a counterclaim has been pleaded by a defendant prior to the service upon the defendant of the plaintiff's motion to dismiss, the action shall not be dismissed against the defendant's objection unless the counterclaim can remain pending for independent adjudication by the court. Unless otherwise specified in the order, a dismissal under this paragraph is without prejudice.

(b) Involuntary Dismissal: Effect Thereof. For failure of the plaintiff to prosecute or to comply with these rules or any order of court, a defendant may move for dismissal of an action or of any claim against the defendant. Unless the court in its order for dismissal otherwise specifies, a dismissal under this subdivision and any dismissal not provided for in this rule, other than a dismissal for lack of jurisdiction, for improper venue, or for failure to join a party under Rule 19, operates as an adjudication upon the merits.

(c) Dismissal of Counterclaim, Cross–Claim, or Third–Party Claim. The provisions of this rule apply to the dismissal of any counter-claim, cross-claim, or third-party claim. A voluntary dismissal by the claimant alone pursuant to paragraph (1) of subdivision (a) of this rule shall be made before a responsive pleading is served or, if there is none, before the introduction of evidence at the trial or hearing.

(d) Costs of Previously Dismissed Action. If a plaintiff who has once dismissed an action in any court commences an action based upon or including the same claim against the same defendant, the court may make such order for the payment of costs of the action previously dismissed as it may deem proper and may stay the proceedings in the action until the plaintiff has complied with the order.

Rule 42.　CONSOLIDATION; SEPARATE TRIALS

(a) Consolidation. When actions involving a common question of law or fact are pending before the court, it may order a joint hearing or trial of any or all the matters in issue in the actions; it may order all the actions consolidated; and it may make such orders concerning proceedings therein as may tend to avoid unnecessary costs or delay.

(b) Separate Trials. The court, in furtherance of convenience or to avoid prejudice, or when separate trials will be conducive to expedition and economy, may order a separate trial of any claim, cross-claim, counterclaim, or third-party claim, or of any separate issue or of any number of claims, cross-claims, counterclaims, third-party claims, or issues, always preserving inviolate the right of trial by jury as declared by the Seventh Amendment to the Constitution or as given by a statute of the United States.

Rule 43.　TAKING OF TESTIMONY

(a) Form. In every trial, the testimony of witnesses shall be taken in open court, unless a federal law, these rules, the Federal Rules of Evidence, or other rules adopted by the Supreme Court provide otherwise. The court may, for good cause shown in compelling circumstances and upon appropriate safeguards, permit presentation of testimony in open court by contemporaneous transmission from a different location.

(b) [Abrogated.]

(c) [Abrogated.]

(d) Affirmation in Lieu of Oath. Whenever under these rules an oath is required to be taken, a solemn affirmation may be accepted in lieu thereof.

(e) Evidence on Motions. When a motion is based on facts not appearing of record the court may hear the matter on affidavits presented by the respective parties, but the court may direct that the matter be heard wholly or partly on oral testimony or deposition.

(f) Interpreters. The court may appoint an interpreter of its own selection and may fix the interpreter's reasonable compensation. The compensation shall be paid out of funds provided by law or by one or more of the parties as the court may direct, and may be taxed ultimately as costs, in the discretion of the court.

Rule 44.　PROOF OF OFFICIAL RECORD

(a) Authentication.

(1) *Domestic.* An official record kept within the United States, or any state, district, or commonwealth, or within a territory subject to the administrative or judicial jurisdiction of the United States, or an entry therein, when admissible for any purpose, may be evidenced by an official publication thereof or by a copy attested by the officer having the legal custody of the record, or by the officer's deputy, and accompanied by a certificate that such officer has the custody. The certificate may be made

by a judge of a court of record of the district or political subdivision in which the record is kept, authenticated by the seal of the court, or may be made by any public officer having a seal of office and having official duties in the district or political subdivision in which the record is kept, authenticated by the seal of the officer's office.

(2) *Foreign.* A foreign official record, or an entry therein, when admissible for any purpose, may be evidenced by an official publication thereof; or a copy thereof, attested by a person authorized to make the attestation, and accompanied by a final certification as to the genuineness of the signature and official position (i) of the attesting person, or (ii) of any foreign official whose certificate of genuineness of signature and official position relates to the attestation or is in a chain of certificates of genuineness of signature and official position relating to the attestation. A final certification may be made by a secretary of embassy or legation, consul general, consul, vice consul, or consular agent of the United States, or a diplomatic or consular official of the foreign country assigned or accredited to the United States. If reasonable opportunity has been given to all parties to investigate the authenticity and accuracy of the documents, the court may, for good cause shown, (i) admit an attested copy without final certification or (ii) permit the foreign official record to be evidenced by an attested summary with or without a final certification. The final certification is unnecessary if the record and the attestation are certified as provided in a treaty or convention to which the United States and the foreign country in which the official record is located are parties.

(b) Lack of Record. A written statement that after diligent search no record or entry of a specified tenor is found to exist in the records designated by the statement, authenticated as provided in subdivision (a)(1) of this rule in the case of a domestic record, or complying with the requirements of subdivision (a)(2) of this rule for a summary in the case of a foreign record, is admissible as evidence that the records contain no such record or entry.

(c) Other Proof. This rule does not prevent the proof of official records or of entry or lack of entry therein by any other method authorized by law.

Rule 44.1. DETERMINATION OF FOREIGN LAW

A party who intends to raise an issue concerning the law of a foreign country shall give notice by pleadings or other reasonable written notice. The court, in determining foreign law, may consider any relevant material or source, including testimony, whether or not submitted by a party or admissible under the Federal Rules of Evidence. The court's determination shall be treated as a ruling on a question of law.

Rule 45. SUBPOENA

(a) Form; Issuance.

(1) Every subpoena shall

(A) state the name of the court from which it is issued; and

(B) state the title of the action, the name of the court in which it is pending, and its civil action number; and

(C) command each person to whom it is directed to attend and give testimony or to produce and permit inspection, copying, testing, or sampling of designated books, documents, electronically stored information, or tangible things in the possession, custody or control of that person, or to permit inspection of premises, at a time and place therein specified; and

(D) set forth the text of subdivisions (c) and (d) of this rule.

A command to produce evidence or to permit inspection, copying, testing, or sampling may be joined with a command to appear at trial or hearing or at deposition, or may be issued separately. A subpoena may specify the form or forms in which electronically stored information is to be produced.

(2) A subpoena must issue as follows:

(A) for attendance at a trial or hearing, from the court for the district where the trial or hearing is to be held;

(B) for attendance at a deposition, from the court for the district where the deposition is to be taken, stating the method for recording the testimony; and

(C) for production, inspection, copying, testing, or sampling, if separate from a subpoena commanding a person's attendance, from the court for the district where the production or inspection is to be made.

(3) The clerk shall issue a subpoena, signed but otherwise in blank, to a party requesting it, who shall complete it before service. An attorney as officer of the court may also issue and sign a subpoena on behalf of

(A) a court in which the attorney is authorized to practice; or

(B) a court for a district in which a deposition or production is compelled by the subpoena, if the deposition or production pertains to an action pending in a court in which the attorney is authorized to practice.

(b) Service.

(1) A subpoena may be served by any person who is not a party and is not less than 18 years of age. Service of a subpoena upon a person named therein shall be made by delivering a copy thereof to such person and, if the person's attendance is commanded, by tendering to that person the fees for one day's attendance and the mileage allowed by law. When the subpoena is issued on behalf of the United States or an officer or agency thereof, fees and mileage need not be tendered. Prior notice of any commanded production of documents and things or inspection of premises before trial shall be served on each party in the manner prescribed by Rule 5(b).

(2) Subject to the provisions of clause (ii) of subparagraph (c)(3)(A) of this rule, a subpoena may be served at any place within the district of the court by which it is issued, or at any place without the district that is within 100 miles of the place of the deposition, hearing, trial, production, inspection, copying, testing, or sampling specified in the subpoena or at any place within the state where a state statute or rule of court permits service

of a subpoena issued by a state court of general jurisdiction sitting in the place of the deposition, hearing, trial, production, inspection, copying, testing, or sampling specified in the subpoena. When a statute of the United States provides therefor, the court upon proper application and cause shown may authorize the service of a subpoena at any other place. A subpoena directed to a witness in a foreign country who is a national or resident of the United States shall issue under the circumstances and in the manner and be served as provided in Title 28, U.S.C. § 1783.

(3) Proof of service when necessary shall be made by filing with the clerk of the court by which the subpoena is issued a statement of the date and manner of service and of the names of the persons served, certified by the person who made the service.

(c) Protection of Persons Subject to Subpoenas.

(1) A party or an attorney responsible for the issuance and service of a subpoena shall take reasonable steps to avoid imposing undue burden or expense on a person subject to that subpoena. The court on behalf of which the subpoena was issued shall enforce this duty and impose upon the party or attorney in breach of this duty an appropriate sanction, which may include, but is not limited to, lost earnings and a reasonable attorney's fee.

(2)(A) A person commanded to produce and permit inspection, copying, testing, or sampling of designated electronically stored information, books, papers, documents or tangible things, or inspection of premises need not appear in person at the place of production or inspection unless commanded to appear for deposition, hearing or trial.

(B) Subject to paragraph (d)(2) of this rule, a person commanded to produce and permit inspection, copying, testing, or sampling may, within 14 days after service of the subpoena or before the time specified for compliance if such time is less than 14 days after service, serve upon the party or attorney designated in the subpoena written objection to producing any or all of the designated materials or inspection of the premises—or to producing electronically stored information in the form or forms requested. If objection is made, the party serving the subpoena shall not be entitled to inspect, copy, test, or sample the materials or inspect the premises except pursuant to an order of the court by which the subpoena was issued. If objection has been made, the party serving the subpoena may, upon notice to the person commanded to produce, move at any time for an order to compel the production, inspection, copying, testing, or sampling. Such an order to compel shall protect any person who is not a party or an officer of a party from significant expense resulting from the inspection, copying, testing, or sampling commanded.

(3)(A) On timely motion, the court by which a subpoena was issued shall quash or modify the subpoena if it

(i) fails to allow reasonable time for compliance;

(ii) requires a person who is not a party or an officer of a party to travel to a place more than 100 miles from the place where that person resides, is employed or regularly transacts business in person, except that, subject to the provisions of clause (c)(3)(B)(iii) of this rule, such a person may in order to attend trial be commanded to travel from any such place within the state in which the trial is held;

(iii) requires disclosure of privileged or other protected matter and no exception or waiver applies; or

(iv) subjects a person to undue burden.

(B) If a subpoena

(i) requires disclosure of a trade secret or other confidential research, development, or commercial information, or

(ii) requires disclosure of an unretained expert's opinion or information not describing specific events or occurrences in dispute and resulting from the expert's study made not at the request of any party, or

(iii) requires a person who is not a party or an officer of a party to incur substantial expense to travel more than 100 miles to attend trial,

the court may, to protect a person subject to or affected by the subpoena, quash or modify the subpoena or, if the party in whose behalf the subpoena is issued shows a substantial need for the testimony or material that cannot be otherwise met without undue hardship and assures that the person to whom the subpoena is addressed will be reasonably compensated, the court may order appearance or production only upon specified conditions.

(d) Duties in Responding to Subpoena.

(1)(A) A person responding to a subpoena to produce documents shall produce them as they are kept in the usual course of business or shall organize and label them to correspond with the categories in the demand.

(B) If a subpoena does not specify the form or forms for producing electronically stored information, a person responding to a subpoena must produce the information in a form or forms in which the person ordinarily maintains it or in a form or forms that are reasonably usable.

(C) A person responding to a subpoena need not produce the same electronically stored information in more than one form.

(D) A person responding to a subpoena need not provide discovery of electronically stored information from sources that the person identifies as not reasonably accessible because of undue burden or cost. On motion to compel discovery or to quash, the person from whom discovery is sought must show that the information sought is not reasonably accessible because of undue burden or cost. If that showing is made, the court may nonetheless order discovery from such sources if the requesting party shows good cause, considering the limitations of Rule 26(b)(2)(C). The court may specify conditions for the discovery.

(2)(A) When information subject to a subpoena is withheld on a claim that it is privileged or subject to protection as trial-preparation materials, the claim shall be made expressly and shall be supported by a description of the nature of the documents, communications, or things not produced that is sufficient to enable the demanding party to contest the claim.

(B) If information is produced in response to a subpoena that is subject to a claim of privilege or of protection as trial-preparation material, the person making the claim may notify any party that received the information of the claim and the basis for it. After being notified, a party must promptly return, sequester, or destroy the specified information and any copies it has and may not use or disclose the information until the claim is resolved. A receiving party may promptly present the information to the court under seal for a determination of the claim. If the receiving party disclosed the information before being notified, it must take reasonable steps to retrieve it. The person who produced the information must preserve the information until the claim is resolved.

(e) Contempt. Failure of any person without adequate excuse to obey a subpoena served upon that person may be deemed a contempt of the court from which the subpoena issued. An adequate cause for failure to obey exists when a subpoena purports to require a nonparty to attend or produce at a place not within the limits provided by clause (ii) of subparagraph (c)(3)(A).

Rule 46. EXCEPTIONS UNNECESSARY

Formal exceptions to rulings or orders of the court are unnecessary; but for all purposes for which an exception has heretofore been necessary it is sufficient that a party, at the time the ruling or order of the court is made or sought, makes known to the court the action which the party desires the court to take or the party's objection to the action of the court and the grounds therefor; and, if a party has no opportunity to object to a ruling or order at the time it is made, the absence of an objection does not thereafter prejudice the party.

Rule 47. SELECTION OF JURORS

(a) Examination of Jurors. The court may permit the parties or their attorneys to conduct the examination of prospective jurors or may itself conduct the examination. In the latter event, the court shall permit the parties or their attorneys to supplement the examination by such further inquiry as it deems proper or shall itself submit to the prospective jurors such additional questions of the parties or their attorneys as it deems proper.

(b) Peremptory Challenges. The court shall allow the number of peremptory challenges provided by 28 U.S.C. § 1870.

(c) Excuse. The court may for good cause excuse a juror from service during trial or deliberation.

Rule 48. NUMBER OF JURORS—PARTICIPATION IN VERDICT

The court shall seat a jury of not fewer than six and not more than twelve members and all jurors shall participate in the verdict unless excused from service by the court pursuant to Rule 47(c). Unless the parties otherwise stipulate, (1) the verdict shall be unanimous and (2) no verdict shall be taken from a jury reduced in size to fewer than six members.

Rule 49. SPECIAL VERDICTS AND INTERROGATORIES

(a) Special Verdicts. The court may require a jury to return only a special verdict in the form of a special written finding upon each issue of fact. In that event the court may submit to the jury written questions susceptible of categorical or other brief answer or may submit written forms of the several special findings which might properly be made under the pleadings and evidence; or it may use such other method of submitting the issues and requiring the written findings thereon as it deems most appropriate. The court shall give to the jury such explanation and instruction concerning the matter thus submitted as may be necessary to enable the jury to make its findings upon each issue. If in so doing the court omits any issue of fact raised by the pleadings or by the evidence, each party waives the right to a trial by jury of the issue so omitted unless before the jury retires the party demands its submission to the jury. As to an issue omitted without such demand the court may make a finding; or, if it fails to do so, it shall be deemed to have made a finding in accord with the judgment on the special verdict.

(b) General Verdict Accompanied by Answer to Interrogatories. The court may submit to the jury, together with appropriate forms for a general verdict, written interrogatories upon one or more issues of fact the decision of which is necessary to a verdict. The court shall give such explanation or instruction as may be necessary to enable the jury both to make answers to the interrogatories and to render a general verdict, and the court shall direct the jury both to make written answers and to render a general verdict. When the general verdict and the answers are harmonious, the appropriate judgment upon the verdict and answers shall be entered pursuant to Rule 58. When the answers are consistent with each other but one or more is inconsistent with the general verdict, judgment may be entered pursuant to Rule 58 in accordance with the answers, notwithstanding the general verdict, or the court may return the jury for further consideration of its answers and verdict or may order a new trial. When the answers are inconsistent with each other and one or more is likewise inconsistent with the general verdict, judgment shall not be entered, but the court shall return the jury for further consideration of its answers and verdict or shall order a new trial.

Rule 50. JUDGMENT AS A MATTER OF LAW IN JURY TRIALS; ALTERNATIVE MOTION FOR NEW TRIAL; CONDITIONAL RULINGS

(a) Judgment as a Matter of Law.

(1) *In General.* If a party has been fully heard on an issue during a jury trial and the court finds that a reasonable jury would not have a legally sufficient evidentiary basis to find for the party on that issue, the court may:

(A) resolve the issue against the party; and

(B) grant a motion for judgment as a matter of law against the party on a claim or defense that, under the controlling law, can be maintained or defeated only with a favorable finding on that issue.

(2) *Motion.* A motion for judgment as a matter of law may be made at any time before the case is submitted to the jury. The motion must specify the judgment sought and the law and facts that entitle the movant to the judgment.

(b) Renewing the Motion After Trial; Alternative Motion for a New Trial. If the court does not grant a motion for judgment as a matter of law made under subdivision (a), the court is considered to have submitted the action to the jury subject to the court's later deciding the legal questions raised by the motion. The movant may renew its request for judgment as a matter of law by filing a motion no later than 10 days after the entry of judgment or—if the motion addresses a jury issue not decided by a verdict—no later than 10 days after the jury was discharged. The movant may alternatively request a new trial or join a motion for a new trial under Rule 59. In ruling on a renewed motion, the court may:

(1) if a verdict was returned:

(A) allow the judgment to stand,

(B) order a new trial, or

(C) direct entry of judgment as a matter of law; or

(2) if no verdict was returned:

(A) order a new trial, or

(B) direct entry of judgment as a matter of law.

(c) Granting Renewed Motion for Judgment as a Matter of Law; Conditional Rulings; New Trial Motion

(1) If the renewed motion for judgment as a matter of law is granted, the court shall also rule on the motion for a new trial, if any, by determining whether it should be granted if the judgment is thereafter vacated or reversed, and shall specify the grounds for granting or denying the motion for the new trial. If the motion for a new trial is thus conditionally granted, the order thereon does not affect the finality of the judgment. In case the motion for a new trial has been conditionally granted and the judgment is reversed on appeal, the new trial shall proceed unless the appellate court has otherwise ordered. In case the motion for a new trial has been conditionally denied, the appellee on appeal may assert error in that denial; and if the judgment is reversed on appeal, subsequent proceedings shall be in accordance with the order of the appellate court.

(2) Any motion for a new trial under Rule 59 by a party against whom judgment as a matter of law is rendered shall be filed no later than 10 days after entry of the judgment.

(d) Same: Denial of Motion for Judgment as a Matter of Law. If the motion for judgment as a matter of law is denied, the party who prevailed on that motion may, as appellee, assert grounds entitling the party to a new trial in the event the appellate court concludes that the trial court erred in denying the motion for judgment. If the appellate court reverses the judgment, nothing in this rule precludes it from determining that the appellee is entitled to a new trial, or from directing the trial court to determine whether a new trial shall be granted.

Rule 51. INSTRUCTIONS TO JURY; OBJECTIONS; PRESERVING A CLAIM OF ERROR

(a) Requests.

(1) A party may, at the close of the evidence or at an earlier reasonable time that the court directs, file and furnish to every other party written requests that the court instruct the jury on the law as set forth in the requests.

(2) After the close of the evidence, a party may:

(A) file requests for instructions on issues that could not reasonably have been anticipated at an earlier time for requests set under Rule 51(a)(1), and

(B) with the court's permission file untimely requests for instructions on any issue.

(b) Instructions. The court:

(1) must inform the parties of its proposed instructions and proposed action on the requests before instructing the jury and before final jury arguments;

(2) must give the parties an opportunity to object on the record and out of the jury's hearing to the proposed instructions and actions on requests before the instructions and arguments are delivered; and

(3) may instruct the jury at any time after trial begins and before the jury is discharged.

(c) Objections.

(1) A party who objects to an instruction or the failure to give an instruction must do so on the record, stating distinctly the matter objected to and the grounds of the objection.

(2) An objection is timely if:

(A) a party that has been informed of an instruction or action on a request before the jury is instructed and before final jury arguments, as provided by Rule 51(b)(1), objects at the opportunity for objection required by Rule 51(b)(2); or

(B) a party that has not been informed of an instruction or action on a request before the time for objection provided under Rule 51(b)(2) objects promptly after learning that the instruction or request will be, or has been, given or refused.

(d) Assigning Error; Plain Error.

(1) A party may assign as error:

(A) an error in an instruction actually given if that party made a proper objection under Rule 51(c), or

(B) a failure to give an instruction if that party made a proper request under Rule 51(a), and—unless the court made a definitive ruling on the record rejecting the request—also made a proper objection under Rule 51(c).

(2) A court may consider a plain error in the instructions affecting substantial rights that has not been preserved as required by Rule 51(d)(1)(A) or (B).

Rule 52. FINDINGS BY THE COURT; JUDGMENT ON PARTIAL FINDINGS

(a) Effect. In all actions tried upon the facts without a jury or with an advisory jury, the court shall find the facts specially and state separately its conclusions of law thereon, and judgment shall be entered pursuant to Rule 58; and in granting or refusing interlocutory injunctions the court shall similarly set forth the findings of fact and conclusions of law which constitute the grounds of its action. Requests for findings are not necessary for purposes of review. Findings of fact, whether based on oral or documentary evidence, shall not be set aside unless clearly erroneous, and due regard shall be given to the opportunity of the trial court to judge of the credibility of the witnesses. The findings of a master, to the extent that the court adopts them, shall be considered as the findings of the court. It will be sufficient if the findings of fact and conclusions of law are stated orally and recorded in open court following the close of the evidence or appear in an opinion or memorandum of decision filed by the court. Findings of fact and conclusions of law are unnecessary on decisions of motions under Rules 12 or 56 or any other motion except as provided in subdivision (c) of this rule.

(b) Amendment. On a party's motion filed no later than 10 days after entry of judgment, the court may amend its findings—or make additional findings—and may amend the judgment accordingly. The motion may accompany a motion for a new trial under Rule 59. When findings of fact are made in actions tried without a jury, the sufficiency of the evidence supporting the findings may be later questioned whether or not in the district court the party raising the question objected to the findings, moved to amend them, or moved for partial findings.

(c) Judgment on Partial Findings. If during a trial without a jury a party has been fully heard on an issue and the court finds against the party on that issue, the court may enter judgment as a matter of law against that party with respect to a claim or defense that cannot under the controlling law be maintained or defeated without a favorable finding on that issue, or the court may decline to render any judgment until the close of all the evidence. Such a judgment shall be supported by findings of fact and conclusions of law as required by subdivision (a) of this rule.

Rule 53. MASTERS

(a) Appointment.

(1) Unless a statute provides otherwise, a court may appoint a master only to:

(A) perform duties consented to by the parties;

(B) hold trial proceedings and make or recommend findings of fact on issues to be decided by the court without a jury if appointment is warranted by

(i) some exceptional condition, or

(ii) the need to perform an accounting or resolve a difficult computation of damages; or

(C) address pretrial and post-trial matters that cannot be addressed effectively and timely by an available district judge or magistrate judge of the district.

(2) A master must not have a relationship to the parties, counsel, action, or court that would require disqualification of a judge under 28 U.S.C. § 455 unless the parties consent with the court's approval to appointment of a particular person after disclosure of any potential grounds for disqualification.

(3) In appointing a master, the court must consider the fairness of imposing the likely expenses on the parties and must protect against unreasonable expense or delay.

(b) Order Appointing Master.

(1) *Notice.* The court must give the parties notice and an opportunity to be heard before appointing a master. A party may suggest candidates for appointment.

(2) *Contents.* The order appointing a master must direct the master to proceed with all reasonable diligence and must state:

(A) the master's duties, including any investigation or enforcement duties, and any limits on the master's authority under Rule 53(c);

(B) the circumstances—if any—in which the master may communicate ex parte with the court or a party;

(C) the nature of the materials to be preserved and filed as the record of the master's activities;

(D) the time limits, method of filing the record, other procedures, and standards for reviewing the master's orders, findings, and recommendations; and

(E) the basis, terms, and procedure for fixing the master's compensation under Rule 53(h).

(3) *Entry of Order.* The court may enter the order appointing a master only after the master has filed an affidavit disclosing whether there is any ground for disqualification under 28 U.S.C. § 455 and, if a ground for disqualification is disclosed, after the parties have consented with the court's approval to waive the disqualification.

(4) *Amendment.* The order appointing a master may be amended at any time after notice to the parties, and an opportunity to be heard.

(c) Master's Authority. Unless the appointing order expressly directs otherwise, a master has authority to regulate all proceedings and take all appropriate measures to perform fairly and efficiently the assigned duties. The master may by order impose upon a party any noncontempt sanction provided by Rule 37 or 45, and may recommend a contempt sanction against a party and sanctions against a nonparty.

(d) Evidentiary Hearings. Unless the appointing order expressly directs otherwise, a master conducting an evidentiary hearing may exercise the power of the appointing court to compel, take, and record evidence.

(e) Master's Orders. A master who makes an order must file the order and promptly serve a copy on each party. The clerk must enter the order on the docket.

(f) Master's Reports. A master must report to the court as required by the order of appointment. The master must file the report and promptly serve a copy of the report on each party unless the court directs otherwise.

(g) Action on Master's Order, Report, or Recommendations.

(1) *Action.* In acting on a master's order, report, or recommendations, the court must afford an opportunity to be heard and may receive evidence, and may: adopt or affirm; modify; wholly or partly reject or reverse; or resubmit to the master with instructions.

(2) *Time to Object or Move.* A party may file objections to—or a motion to adopt or modify—the master's order, report, or recommendations no later than 20 days from the time the master's order, report, or recommendations are served, unless the court sets a different time.

(3) *Fact Findings.* The court must decide de novo all objections to findings of fact made or recommended by a master unless the parties stipulate with the court's consent that:

(A) the master's findings will be reviewed for clear error, or

(B) the findings of a master appointed under Rule 53(a)(1)(A) or (C) will be final.

(4) *Legal Conclusions.* The court must decide de novo all objections to conclusions of law made or recommended by a master.

(5) *Procedural Matters.* Unless the order of appointment establishes a different standard of review, the court may set aside a master's ruling on a procedural matter only for an abuse of discretion.

(h) Compensation.

(1) *Fixing Compensation.* The court must fix the master's compensation before or after judgment on the basis and terms stated in the order of appointment, but the court may set a new basis and terms after notice and an opportunity to be heard.

(2) *Payment.* The compensation fixed under Rule 53(h)(1) must be paid either:

(A) by a party or parties; or

(B) from a fund or subject matter of the action within the court's control.

(3) *Allocation.* The court must allocate payment of the master's compensation among the parties after considering the nature and amount of the controversy, the means of the parties, and the extent to which any party is more responsible than other parties for the reference to a master. An interim allocation may be amended to reflect a decision on the merits.

(i) Appointment of Magistrate Judge. A magistrate judge is subject to this rule only when the order referring a matter to the magistrate judge expressly provides that the reference is made under this rule.

VII. JUDGMENT

Rule 54. JUDGMENTS; COSTS

(a) Definition; Form. "Judgment" as used in these rules includes a decree and any order from which an appeal lies. A judgment shall not contain a recital of pleadings, the report of a master, or the record of prior proceedings.

(b) Judgment upon Multiple Claims or Involving Multiple Parties. When more than one claim for relief is presented in an action, whether as a claim, counterclaim, cross-claim, or third-party claim, or when multiple parties are involved, the court may direct the entry of a final judgment as to one or more but fewer than all of the claims or parties only upon an express determination that there is no just reason for delay and upon an express direction for the entry of judgment. In the absence of such determination and direction, any order or other form of decision, however designated, which adjudicates fewer than all the claims or the rights and liabilities of fewer than all the parties shall not terminate the action as to any of the claims or parties, and the order or other form of decision is subject to revision at any time before the entry of judgment adjudicating all the claims and the rights and liabilities of all the parties.

(c) Demand for Judgment. A judgment by default shall not be different in kind from or exceed in amount that prayed for in the demand for judgment. Except as to a party against whom a judgment is entered by default, every final judgment shall grant the relief to which the party in whose favor it is rendered is entitled, even if the party has not demanded such relief in the party's pleadings.

(d) Costs; Attorneys' Fees.

(1) *Costs Other than Attorneys' Fees.* Except when express provision therefor is made either in a statute of the United States or in these rules, costs other than attorneys' fees shall be allowed as of course to the prevailing party unless the court otherwise directs; but costs against the United States, its officers, and agencies shall be imposed only to the extent permitted by law. Such costs may be taxed by the clerk on one day's notice. On motion served within 5 days thereafter, the action of the clerk may be reviewed by the court.

(2) *Attorneys' Fees.*

(A) Claims for attorneys' fees and related nontaxable expenses shall be made by motion unless the substantive law governing the action provides for the recovery of such fees as an element of damages to be proved at trial.

(B) Unless otherwise provided by statute or order of the court, the motion must be filed no later than 14 days after entry of judgment; must specify the judgment and the statute, rule, or other grounds entitling the moving party to the award; and must state the amount or provide a fair estimate of the amount sought. If directed by the court, the motion shall also disclose the terms of any agreement with respect to fees to be paid for the services for which claim is made.

(C) On request of a party or class member, the court shall afford an opportunity for adversary submissions with respect to the motion in accordance with Rule 43(e) or Rule 78. The court may determine issues of liability for fees before receiving submissions bearing on issues of evaluation of services for which liability is imposed by the court. The court shall find the facts and state its conclusions of law as provided in Rule 52(a).

(D) By local rule the court may establish special procedures by which issues relating to such fees may be resolved without extensive evidentiary hearings. In addition, the court may refer issues relating to the value of services to a special master under Rule 53 without regard to the provisions of Rule 53(a)(1) and may refer a motion for attorneys' fees to a magistrate judge under Rule 72(b) as if it were a dispositive pretrial matter.

(E) The provisions of subparagraphs (A) through (D) do not apply to claims for fees and expenses as sanctions for violations of these rules or under 28 U.S.C. § 1927.

Rule 55. DEFAULT

(a) Entry. When a party against whom a judgment for affirmative relief is sought has failed to plead or otherwise defend as provided by these rules and that fact is made to appear by affidavit or otherwise, the clerk shall enter the party's default.

(b) Judgment. Judgment by default may be entered as follows:

(1) *By the Clerk.* When the plaintiff's claim against a defendant is for a sum certain or for a sum which can by computation be made certain, the clerk upon request of the plaintiff and upon affidavit of the amount due shall enter judgment for that amount and costs against the defendant, if the defendant has been defaulted for failure to appear and is not an infant or incompetent person.

(2) *By the Court.* In all other cases the party entitled to a judgment by default shall apply to the court therefor; but no judgment by default shall be entered against an infant or incompetent person unless represented in the action by a general guardian, committee, conservator, or other such representative who has appeared therein. If the party against whom judgment by default is sought has appeared in the action, the party (or, if appearing by representative, the party's representative) shall be served with written notice of the application for judgment at least 3 days prior to the hearing on such application. If, in order to enable the court to enter judgment or to carry it into effect, it is necessary to take an account or to determine the amount of damages or to establish the truth of any averment by evidence or to make an investigation of any other matter, the court may conduct such hearings or order such references as it deems necessary and proper and shall accord a right of trial by jury to the parties when and as required by any statute of the United States.

(c) Setting Aside Default. For good cause shown the court may set aside an entry of default and, if a judgment by default has been entered, may likewise set it aside in accordance with Rule 60(b).

(d) Plaintiffs, Counterclaimants, Cross–Claimants. The provisions of this rule apply whether the party entitled to the judgment by default is a plaintiff, a third-party plaintiff, or a party who has pleaded a cross-claim or counterclaim. In all cases a judgment by default is subject to the limitations of Rule 54(c).

(e) Judgment Against the United States. No judgment by default shall be entered against the United States or an officer or agency thereof unless the claimant establishes a claim or right to relief by evidence satisfactory to the court.

Rule 56. SUMMARY JUDGMENT

(a) For Claimant. A party seeking to recover upon a claim, counter-claim, or cross-claim or to obtain a declaratory judgment may, at any time after the expiration of 20 days from the commencement of the action or after service of a motion for summary judgment by the adverse party, move with or without supporting affidavits for a summary judgment in the party's favor upon all or any part thereof.

(b) For Defending Party. A party against whom a claim, counter-claim, or cross-claim is asserted or a declaratory judgment is sought may, at any time, move with or without supporting affidavits for a summary judgment in the party's favor as to all or any part thereof.

(c) Motion and Proceedings Thereon. The motion shall be served at least 10 days before the time fixed for the hearing. The adverse party prior to the day of hearing may serve opposing affidavits. The judgment sought shall be rendered forthwith if the pleadings, depositions, answers to interrogatories, and admissions on file, together with the affidavits, if any, show that there is no genuine issue as to any material fact and that the moving party is entitled to a judgment as a matter of law. A summary judgment, interlocutory in character, may be rendered on the issue of liability alone although there is a genuine issue as to the amount of damages.

(d) Case Not Fully Adjudicated on Motion. If on motion under this rule judgment is not rendered upon the whole case or for all the relief asked and a trial is necessary, the court at the hearing of the motion, by examining the pleadings and the evidence before it and by interrogating counsel, shall if practicable ascertain what material facts exist without substantial controversy and what material facts are actually and in good faith controverted. It shall thereupon make an order specifying the facts that appear without substantial controversy, including the extent to which the amount of damages or other relief is not in controversy, and directing such further proceedings in the action as are just. Upon the trial of the action the facts so specified shall be deemed established, and the trial shall be conducted accordingly.

(e) Form of Affidavits; Further Testimony; Defense Required. Supporting and opposing affidavits shall be made on personal knowledge, shall set forth such facts as would be admissible in evidence, and shall show affirmatively that the affiant is competent to testify to the matters stated therein. Sworn or certified copies of all papers or parts thereof referred to in an affidavit shall be attached thereto or served therewith. The court may permit affidavits to be supplemented or opposed by depositions, answers to interrogatories, or further affidavits. When a motion for summary judgment is made and supported as provided in this rule, an adverse party may not rest upon the mere allegations or denials of the adverse party's pleading, but the adverse party's response, by affidavits or as otherwise provided in this rule, must set forth specific facts showing that there is a genuine issue for trial. If the adverse party does not so respond, summary judgment, if appropriate, shall be entered against the adverse party.

(f) When Affidavits Are Unavailable. Should it appear from the affidavits of a party opposing the motion that the party cannot for reasons stated present by affidavit facts essential to justify the party's opposition, the court may refuse the application for judgment or may order a continuance to permit affidavits to be obtained or depositions to be taken or discovery to be had or may make such other order as is just.

(g) Affidavits Made in Bad Faith. Should it appear to the satisfaction of the court at any time that any of the affidavits presented pursuant to this rule are presented in bad faith or solely for the purpose of delay, the court shall forthwith order the party employing them to pay to the other party the amount of the reasonable expenses which the filing of the affidavits caused the other party to incur, including reasonable attorney's fees, and any offending party or attorney may be adjudged guilty of contempt.

Rule 57. DECLARATORY JUDGMENTS

The procedure for obtaining a declaratory judgment pursuant to Title 28 U.S.C. § 2201, shall be in accordance with these rules, and the right to trial by jury may be demanded under the circumstances and in the manner provided in Rules 38 and 39. The existence of another adequate remedy does not preclude a judgment for declaratory relief in cases where it is appropriate. The court may order a speedy hearing of an action for a declaratory judgment and may advance it on the calendar.

Rule 58. ENTRY OF JUDGMENT

(a) Separate Document.

(1) Every judgment and amended judgment must be set forth on a separate document, but a separate document is not required for an order disposing of a motion:

(A) for judgment under Rule 50(b);

(B) to amend or make additional findings of fact under Rule 52(b);

(C) for attorney fees under Rule 54;

(D) for a new trial, or to alter or amend the judgment, under Rule 59; or

(E) for relief under Rule 60.

(2) Subject to Rule 54(b):

(A) unless the court orders otherwise, the clerk must, without awaiting the court's direction, promptly prepare, sign, and enter the judgment when:

(i) the jury returns a general verdict,

(ii) the court awards only costs or a sum certain, or

(iii) the court denies all relief;

(B) the court must promptly approve the form of the judgment, which the clerk must promptly enter, when:

(i) the jury returns a special verdict or a general verdict accompanied by interrogatories, or

(ii) the court grants other relief not described in Rule 58(a)(2).

(b) Time of Entry. Judgment is entered for purposes of these rules:

(1) if Rule 58(a)(1) does not require a separate document, when it is entered in the civil docket under Rule 79(a), and

(2) if Rule 58(a)(1) requires a separate document, when it is entered in the civil docket under Rule 79(a) and when the earlier of these events occurs:

(A) when it is set forth on a separate document, or

(B) when 150 days have run from entry in the civil docket under Rule 79(a).

(c) Cost or Fee Awards.

(1) Entry of judgment may not be delayed, nor the time for appeal extended, in order to tax costs or award fees, except as provided in Rule 58(c)(2).

(2) When a timely motion for attorney fees is made under Rule 54(d)(2), the court may act before a notice of appeal has been filed and has become effective to order that the motion have the same effect under Federal Rule of Appellate Procedure 4(a)(4) as a timely motion under Rule 59.

(d) Request for Entry. A party may request that judgment be set forth on a separate document as required by Rule 58(a)(1).

Rule 59. NEW TRIALS; AMENDMENT OF JUDGMENTS

(a) Grounds. A new trial may be granted to all or any of the parties and on all or part of the issues (1) in an action in which there has been a trial by jury, for any of the reasons for which new trials have heretofore been granted in actions at law in the courts of the United States; and (2) in an action tried without a jury, for any of the reasons for which rehearings have heretofore been granted in suits in equity in the courts of the United States. On a motion for a new trial in an action tried without a jury, the court may open the judgment if one has been entered, take additional testimony, amend findings of fact and conclusions of law or make new findings and conclusions, and direct the entry of a new judgment.

(b) Time for Motion. Any motion for a new trial shall be filed no later than 10 days after entry of the judgment.

(c) Time for Serving Affidavits. When a motion for new trial is based on affidavits they shall be filed with the motion. The opposing party has 10 days after service to file opposing affidavits, but that period may be extended for up to 20 days, either by the court for good cause or by the parties' written stipulation. The court may permit reply affidavits.

(d) On Court's Initiative; Notice; Specifying Grounds. No later than 10 days after entry of judgment the court, on its own, may order a new trial for any reason that would justify granting one on a party's motion. After giving the parties notice and an opportunity to be heard, the court may grant a timely motion for a new trial for a reason not stated in the motion. When granting a new trial on its own initiative or for a reason not stated in a motion, the court shall specify the grounds in its order.

(e) Motion to Alter or Amend Judgment. Any motion to alter or amend a judgment shall be filed no later than 10 days after entry of the judgment.

Rule 60. RELIEF FROM JUDGMENT OR ORDER

(a) Clerical Mistakes. Clerical mistakes in judgments, orders or other parts of the record and errors therein arising from oversight or omission may be corrected by the court at any time of its own initiative or on the motion of any party and after such notice, if any, as the court orders. During the pendency of an appeal, such mistakes may be so corrected before the appeal is docketed in the appellate court, and thereafter while the appeal is pending may be so corrected with leave of the appellate court.

(b) Mistakes; Inadvertence; Excusable Neglect; Newly Discovered Evidence; Fraud, etc. On motion and upon such terms as are just, the court may relieve a party or a party's legal representative from a final judgment, order, or proceeding for the following reasons: (1) mistake, inadvertence, surprise, or excusable neglect; (2) newly discovered evidence which by due diligence could not have been discovered in time to move for a new trial under Rule 59(b); (3) fraud (whether heretofore denominated intrinsic or extrinsic), misrepresentation, or other misconduct of an adverse party; (4) the judgment is void; (5) the judgment has been satisfied, released, or discharged, or a prior judgment upon which it is based has been reversed or otherwise vacated, or it is no longer equitable that the judgment should have prospective application; or (6) any other reason justifying relief from the operation of the judgment. The motion shall be made within a reasonable time, and for reasons (1), (2), and (3) not more than one year after the judgment, order, or proceeding was entered or taken. A motion under this subdivision (b) does not affect the finality of a judgment or suspend its operation. This rule does not limit the power of a court to entertain an independent action to relieve a party from a judgment, order, or proceeding, or to grant relief to a defendant not actually personally notified as provided in Title 28, U.S.C., § 1655, or to set aside a judgment for fraud upon the court. Writs of coram nobis, coram vobis, audita querela, and bills of review and bills in the nature of a bill of review, are abolished, and the procedure for obtaining any relief from a judgment shall be by motion as prescribed in these rules or by an independent action.

Rule 61. HARMLESS ERROR

No error in either the admission or the exclusion of evidence and no error or defect in any ruling or order or in anything done or omitted by the court or by any of the parties is ground for granting a new trial or for setting aside a verdict or for vacating, modifying or otherwise disturbing a judgment or order, unless refusal to take such action appears to the court inconsistent with substantial justice. The court at every stage of the proceeding must disregard any error or defect in the proceeding which does not affect the substantial rights of the parties.

Rule 62. STAY OF PROCEEDINGS TO ENFORCE A JUDGMENT

(a) Automatic Stay; Exceptions—Injunctions, Receiverships, and Patent Accountings. Except as stated herein, no execution shall issue upon a judgment nor shall proceedings be taken for its enforcement until the expiration of 10 days after its entry. Unless otherwise ordered by the court, an interlocutory or final judgment in an action for an injunction or in a receivership action, or a judgment or order directing an accounting in an action for infringement of letters patent, shall not be stayed during the period after its entry and until an appeal is taken or during the pendency of an appeal. The provisions of subdivision (c) of this rule govern the suspending, modifying, restoring, or granting of an injunction during the pendency of an appeal.

(b) Stay on Motion for New Trial or for Judgment. In its discretion and on such conditions for the security of the adverse party as are proper, the court may stay the execution of or any proceedings to enforce a judgment pending the disposition of a motion for a new trial or to alter or amend a judgment made pursuant to Rule 59, or of a motion for relief from a judgment or order made pursuant to Rule 60, or of a motion for judgment in accordance with a motion for a directed verdict made pursuant to Rule 50, or of a motion for amendment to the findings or for additional findings made pursuant to Rule 52(b).

(c) Injunction Pending Appeal. When an appeal is taken from an interlocutory or final judgment granting, dissolving, or denying an injunction, the court in its discretion may suspend, modify, restore, or grant an injunction during the pendency of the appeal upon such terms as to bond or otherwise as it considers proper for the security of the rights of the adverse party. If the judgment appealed from is rendered by a district court of three judges specially constituted pursuant to a statute of the United States, no such order shall be made except (1) by such court sitting in open court or (2) by the assent of all the judges of such court evidenced by their signatures to the order.

(d) Stay upon Appeal. When an appeal is taken the appellant by giving a supersedeas bond may obtain a stay subject to the exceptions contained in subdivision (a) of this rule. The bond may be given at or after the time of filing the notice of appeal or of procuring the order allowing the appeal, as the case may be. The stay is effective when the supersedeas bond is approved by the court.

(e) Stay in Favor of the United States or Agency Thereof. When an appeal is taken by the United States or an officer or agency thereof or by direction of any department of the Government of the United States and the operation or enforcement of the judgment is stayed, no bond, obligation, or other security shall be required from the appellant.

(f) Stay According to State Law. In any state in which a judgment is a lien upon the property of the judgment debtor and in which the judgment debtor is entitled to a stay of execution, a judgment debtor is entitled, in the district court held therein, to such stay as would be accorded the judgment debtor had the action been maintained in the courts of that state.

(g) Power of Appellate Court Not Limited. The provisions in this rule do not limit any power of an appellate court or of a judge or justice thereof to stay proceedings during the pendency of an appeal or to suspend, modify, restore, or grant an injunction during the pendency of an appeal or to make any order appropriate to preserve the status quo or the effectiveness of the judgment subsequently to be entered.

(h) Stay of Judgment as to Multiple Claims or Multiple Parties. When a court has ordered a final judgment under the conditions stated in Rule 54(b), the court may stay enforcement of that judgment until the entering of a subsequent judgment or judgments and may prescribe such conditions as are necessary to secure the benefit thereof to the party in whose favor the judgment is entered.

Rule 63.   INABILITY OF A JUDGE TO PROCEED

If a trial or hearing has been commenced and the judge is unable to proceed, any other judge may proceed with it upon certifying familiarity with the record and determining that the proceedings in the case may be completed without prejudice to the parties. In a hearing or trial without a jury, the successor judge shall at the request of a party recall any witness whose testimony is material and disputed and who is available to testify again without undue burden. The successor judge may also recall any other witness.

VIII.   PROVISIONAL AND FINAL REMEDIES

Rule 64.   SEIZURE OF PERSON OR PROPERTY

At the commencement of and during the course of an action, all remedies providing for seizure of person or property for the purpose of securing satisfaction of the judgment ultimately to be entered in the action are available under the circumstances and in the manner provided by the law of the state in which the district court is held, existing at the time the remedy is sought, subject to the following qualifications: (1) any existing statute of the United States governs to the extent to which it is applicable; (2) the action in which any of the foregoing remedies is used shall be commenced and prosecuted or, if removed from a state court, shall be prosecuted after removal, pursuant to these rules. The remedies thus available include arrest, attachment, garnishment, replevin, sequestration, and other corresponding or equivalent remedies, however designated and regardless of whether by state procedure the remedy is ancillary to an action or must be obtained by an independent action.

Rule 65. INJUNCTIONS

(a) Preliminary Injunction.

(1) *Notice.* No preliminary injunction shall be issued without notice to the adverse party.

(2) *Consolidation of Hearing with Trial on Merits.* Before or after the commencement of the hearing of an application for a preliminary injunction, the court may order the trial of the action on the merits to be advanced and consolidated with the hearing of the application. Even when this consolidation is not ordered, any evidence received upon an application for a preliminary injunction which would be admissible upon the trial on the merits becomes part of the record on the trial and need not be repeated upon the trial. This subdivision (a)(2) shall be so construed and applied as to save to the parties any rights they may have to trial by jury.

(b) Temporary Restraining Order; Notice; Hearing; Duration.
A temporary restraining order may be granted without written or oral notice to the adverse party or that party's attorney only if (1) it clearly appears from specific facts shown by affidavit or by the verified complaint that immediate and irreparable injury, loss, or damage will result to the applicant before the adverse party or that party's attorney can be heard in opposition, and (2) the applicant's attorney certifies to the court in writing the efforts, if any, which have been made to give the notice and the reasons supporting the claim that notice should not be required. Every temporary restraining order granted without notice shall be indorsed with the date and hour of issuance; shall be filed forthwith in the clerk's office and entered of record; shall define the injury and state why it is irreparable and why the order was granted without notice; and shall expire by its terms within such time after entry, not to exceed 10 days, as the court fixes, unless within the time so fixed the order, for good cause shown, is extended for a like period or unless the party against whom the order is directed consents that it may be extended for a longer period. The reasons for the extension shall be entered of record. In case a temporary restraining order is granted without notice, the motion for a preliminary injunction shall be set down for hearing at the earliest possible time and takes precedence of all matters except older matters of the same character; and when the motion comes on for hearing the party who obtained the temporary restraining order shall proceed with the application for a preliminary injunction and, if the party does not do so, the court shall dissolve the temporary restraining order. On 2 days' notice to the party who obtained the temporary restraining order without notice or on such shorter notice to that party as the court may prescribe, the adverse party may appear and move its dissolution or modification and in that event the court shall proceed to hear and determine such motion as expeditiously as the ends of justice require.

(c) Security.
No restraining order or preliminary injunction shall issue except upon the giving of security by the applicant, in such sum as the court deems proper, for the payment of such costs and damages as may be incurred or suffered by any party who is found to have been wrongfully enjoined or restrained. No such security shall be required of the United States or of an officer or agency thereof.

The provisions of Rule 65.1 apply to a surety upon a bond or undertaking under this rule.

(d) Form and Scope of Injunction or Restraining Order. Every order granting an injunction and every restraining order shall set forth the reasons for its issuance; shall be specific in terms; shall describe in reasonable detail, and not by reference to the complaint or other document, the act or acts sought to be restrained; and is binding only upon the parties to the action, their officers, agents, servants, employees, and attorneys, and upon those persons in active concert or participation with them who receive actual notice of the order by personal service or otherwise.

(e) Employer and Employee; Interpleader; Constitutional Cases. These rules do not modify any statute of the United States relating to temporary restraining orders and preliminary injunctions in actions affecting employer and employee; or the provisions of Title 28, U.S.C., § 2361, relating to preliminary injunctions in actions of interpleader or in the nature of interpleader; or Title 28, U.S.C., § 2284, relating to actions required by Act of Congress to be heard and determined by a district court of three judges.

(f) Copyright Impoundment. This rule applies to copyright impoundment proceedings.

Rule 65.1. SECURITY: PROCEEDINGS AGAINST SURETIES

Whenever these rules, including the Supplemental Rules for Admiralty or Maritime Claims and Asset Forfeiture Actions, require or permit the giving of security by a party, and security is given in the form of a bond or stipulation or other undertaking with one or more sureties, each surety submits to the jurisdiction of the court and irrevocably appoints the clerk of the court as the surety's agent upon whom any papers affecting the surety's liability on the bond or undertaking may be served. The surety's liability may be enforced on motion without the necessity of an independent action. The motion and such notice of the motion as the court prescribes may be served on the clerk of the court, who shall forthwith mail copies to the sureties if their addresses are known.

Rule 66. RECEIVERS APPOINTED BY FEDERAL COURTS

An action wherein a receiver has been appointed shall not be dismissed except by order of the court. The practice in the administration of estates by receivers or by other similar officers appointed by the court shall be in accordance with the practice heretofore followed in the courts of the United States or as provided in rules promulgated by the district courts. In all other respects the action in which the appointment of a receiver is sought or which is brought by or against a receiver is governed by these rules.

Rule 67. DEPOSIT IN COURT

In an action in which any part of the relief sought is a judgment for a sum of money or the disposition of a sum of money or the disposition of any other thing capable of delivery, a party, upon notice to every other party, and by leave of court, may deposit with the court all or any part of such sum or thing, whether or not that party claims all or any part of the sum or thing. The party making the deposit shall serve the order permitting deposit on the clerk of the court. Money paid into court under this rule shall be deposited and withdrawn in accordance with the provisions of Title 28, U.S.C., §§ 2041, and 2042; the Act of June 26, 1934, c. 756, § 23, as amended (48 Stat. 1236, 58 Stat. 845), U.S.C., Title 31, § 725v; or any like statute. The fund shall be deposited in an interest-bearing account or invested in an interest-bearing instrument approved by the court.

Rule 68. OFFER OF JUDGMENT

At any time more than 10 days before the trial begins, a party defending against a claim may serve upon the adverse party an offer to allow judgment to be taken against the defending party for the money or property or to the effect specified in the offer, with costs then accrued. If within 10 days after the service of the offer the adverse party serves written notice that the offer is accepted, either party may then file the offer and notice of acceptance together with proof of service thereof and thereupon the clerk shall enter judgment. An offer not accepted shall be deemed withdrawn and evidence thereof is not admissible except in a proceeding to determine costs. If the judgment finally obtained by the offeree is not more favorable than the offer, the offeree must pay the costs incurred after the making of the offer. The fact that an offer is made but not accepted does not preclude a subsequent offer. When the liability of one party to another has been determined by verdict or order or judgment, but the amount or extent of the liability remains to be determined by further proceedings, the party adjudged liable may make an offer of judgment, which shall have the same effect as an offer made before trial if it is served within a reasonable time not less than 10 days prior to the commencement of hearings to determine the amount or extent of liability.

Rule 69. EXECUTION

(a) In General. Process to enforce a judgment for the payment of money shall be a writ of execution, unless the court directs otherwise. The procedure on execution, in proceedings supplementary to and in aid of a judgment, and in proceedings on and in aid of execution shall be in accordance with the practice and procedure of the state in which the district court is held, existing at the time the remedy is sought, except that any statute of the United States governs to the extent that it is applicable. In aid of the judgment or execution, the judgment creditor or a successor in interest when that interest appears of record, may obtain discovery from any person, including the judgment debtor, in the manner provided in these rules or in the manner provided by the practice of the state in which the district court is held.

(b) Against Certain Public Officers. When a judgment has been entered against a collector or other officer of revenue under the circumstances stated in Title 28, U.S.C., § 2006, or against an officer of Congress in an action mentioned in the Act of March 3, 1875, c. 130, § 8 (18 Stat. 401), U.S.C., Title 2, § 118, and when the court has given the certificate of probable cause for the officer's act as provided in those statutes, execution shall not issue against the officer or the officer's property but the final judgment shall be satisfied as provided in such statutes.

Rule 70. JUDGMENT FOR SPECIFIC ACTS; VESTING TITLE

If a judgment directs a party to execute a conveyance of land or to deliver deeds or other documents or to perform any other specific act and the party fails to comply within the time specified, the court may direct the act to be done at the cost of the disobedient party by some other person appointed by the court and the act when so done has like effect as if done by the party. On application of the party entitled to performance, the clerk shall issue a writ of attachment or sequestration against the property of the disobedient party to compel obedience to the judgment. The court may also in proper cases adjudge the party in contempt. If real or personal property is within the district, the court in lieu of directing a conveyance thereof may enter a judgment divesting the title of any party and vesting it in others and such judgment has the effect of a conveyance executed in due form of law. When any order or judgment is for the delivery of possession, the party in whose favor it is entered is entitled to a writ of execution or assistance upon application to the clerk.

Rule 71. PROCESS IN BEHALF OF AND AGAINST PERSONS NOT PARTIES

When an order is made in favor of a person who is not a party to the action, that person may enforce obedience to the order by the same process as if a party; and, when obedience to an order may be lawfully enforced against a person who is not a party, that person is liable to the same process for enforcing obedience to the order as if a party.

IX. SPECIAL PROCEEDINGS

Rule 71A. CONDEMNATION OF PROPERTY

(a) Applicability of Other Rules. The Rules of Civil Procedure for the United States District Courts govern the procedure for the condemnation of real and personal property under the power of eminent domain, except as otherwise provided in this rule.

(b) Joinder of Properties. The plaintiff may join in the same action one or more separate pieces of property, whether in the same or different ownership and whether or not sought for the same use.

(c) Complaint.

(1) *Caption.* The complaint shall contain a caption as provided in Rule 10(a), except that the plaintiff shall name as defendants the property, designated generally by kind, quantity, and location, and at least one of the owners of some part of or interest in the property.

(2) *Contents.* The complaint shall contain a short and plain statement of the authority for the taking, the use for which the property is to be taken, a description of the property sufficient for its identification, the interests to be acquired, and as to each separate piece of property a designation of the defendants who have been joined as owners thereof or of some interest therein. Upon the commencement of the action, the plaintiff need join as defendants only the persons having or claiming an interest in the property whose names are then known, but prior to any hearing involving the compensation to be paid for a piece of property, the plaintiff shall add as defendants all persons having or claiming an interest in that

property whose names can be ascertained by a reasonably diligent search of the records, considering the character and value of the property involved and the interests to be acquired, and also those whose names have otherwise been learned. All others may be made defendants under the designation "Unknown Owners." Process shall be served as provided in subdivision (d) of this rule upon all defendants, whether named as defendants at the time of the commencement of the action or subsequently added, and a defendant may answer as provided in subdivision (e) of this rule. The court meanwhile may order such distribution of a deposit as the facts warrant.

(3) *Filing.* In addition to filing the complaint with the court, the plaintiff shall furnish to the clerk at least one copy thereof for the use of the defendants and additional copies at the request of the clerk or of a defendant.

(d) Process.

(1) *Notice; Delivery.* Upon the filing of the complaint the plaintiff shall forthwith deliver to the clerk joint or several notices directed to the defendants named or designated in the complaint. Additional notices directed to defendants subsequently added shall be so delivered. The delivery of the notice and its service have the same effect as the delivery and service of the summons under Rule 4.

(2) *Same; Form.* Each notice shall state the court, the title of the action, the name of the defendant to whom it is directed, that the action is to condemn property, a description of the defendant's property sufficient for its identification, the interest to be taken, the authority for the taking, the uses for which the property is to be taken, that the defendant may serve upon the plaintiff's attorney an answer within 20 days after service of the notice, and that the failure so to serve an answer constitutes a consent to the taking and to the authority of the court to proceed to hear the action and to fix the compensation. The notice shall conclude with the name of the plaintiff's attorney and an address within the district in which action is brought where the attorney may be served. The notice need contain a description of no other property than that to be taken from the defendants to whom it is directed.

(3) *Service of Notice.*

(A) *Personal Service.* Personal service of the notice (but without copies of the complaint) shall be made in accordance with Rule 4 upon a defendant whose residence is known and who resides within the United States or a territory subject to the administrative or judicial jurisdiction of the United States.

(B) *Service by Publication.* Upon the filing of a certificate of the plaintiff's attorney stating that the attorney believes a defendant cannot be personally served, because after diligent inquiry within the state in which the complaint is filed the defendant's place of residence cannot be ascertained by the plaintiff or, if ascertained, that it is beyond the territorial limits of personal service as provided in this rule, service of the notice shall be made on this defendant by publication in a newspaper published in the county where the property is located, or if there is no such newspaper, then in a newspaper having a general circulation where the property is located, once a week for not less than three successive weeks. Prior to the last publication, a copy of the notice shall also be mailed to a defendant who cannot be personally served as provided in this rule but whose place of residence is then known. Unknown owners may be served by publication in like manner by a notice addressed to "Unknown Owners."

Service by publication is complete upon the date of the last publication. Proof of publication and mailing shall be made by certificate of the plaintiff's attorney, to which shall be attached a printed copy of the published notice with the name and dates of the newspaper marked thereon.

(4) *Return; Amendment.* Proof of service of the notice shall be made and amendment of the notice or proof of its service allowed in the manner provided for the return and amendment of the summons under Rule 4.

(e) Appearance or Answer. If a defendant has no objection or defense to the taking of the defendant's property, the defendant may serve a notice of appearance designating the property in which the defendant claims to be interested. Thereafter, the defendant shall receive notice of all proceedings affecting it. If a defendant has any objection or defense to the taking of the property, the defendant shall serve an answer within 20 days after the service of notice upon the defendant. The answer shall identify the property in which the defendant claims to have an interest, state the nature and extent of the interest claimed, and state all the defendant's objections and defenses to the taking of the property. A defendant waives all defenses and objections not so presented, but at the trial of the issue of just compensation, whether or not the defendant has previously appeared or answered, the defendant may present evidence as to the amount of the compensation to be paid for the property, and the defendant may share in the distribution of the award. No other pleading or motion asserting any additional defense or objection shall be allowed.

(f) Amendment of Pleadings. Without leave of court, the plaintiff may amend the complaint at any time before the trial of the issue of compensation and as many times as desired, but no amendment shall be made which will result in a dismissal forbidden by subdivision (i) of this rule. The plaintiff need not serve a copy of an amendment, but shall serve notice of the filing, as provided in Rule 5(b), upon any party affected thereby who has appeared and, in the manner provided in subdivision (d) of this rule, upon any party affected thereby who has not appeared. The plaintiff shall furnish to the clerk of the court for the use of the defendants at least one copy of each amendment and shall furnish additional copies on the request of the clerk or of a defendant. Within the time allowed by subdivision (e) of this rule a defendant may serve an answer to the amended pleading, in the form and manner and with the same effect as there provided.

(g) Substitution of Parties. If a defendant dies or becomes incompetent or transfers an interest after the defendant's joinder, the court may order substitution of the proper party upon motion and notice of hearing. If the motion and notice of hearing are to be served upon a person not already a party, service shall be made as provided in subdivision (d)(3) of this rule.

(h) Trial. If the action involves the exercise of the power of eminent domain under the law of the United States, any tribunal specially constituted by an Act of Congress governing the case for the trial of the issue of just compensation shall be the tribunal for the determination of that issue; but if there is no such specially constituted tribunal any party may have a trial by jury of the issue of just compensation by filing a demand therefor within the time allowed for answer or within such further time as the court may fix, unless the court in its discretion orders that, because of the character, location, or quantity of the property to be condemned, or for other reasons in the interest of justice, the issue of compensation shall be determined by a commission of three persons appointed by it.

In the event that a commission is appointed the court may direct that not more than two additional persons serve as alternate commissioners to hear the case and replace commissioners who, prior to the time when a decision is filed, are found by the court to be unable or disqualified to perform their duties. An alternate who does not replace a regular commissioner shall be discharged after the commission renders its final decision. Before appointing the members of the commission and alternates the court shall advise the parties of the identity and qualifications of each prospective commissioner and alternate and may permit the parties to examine each such designee. The parties shall not be permitted or required by the court to suggest nominees. Each party shall have the right to object for valid cause to the appointment of any person as a commissioner or alternate. If a commission is appointed it shall have the authority of a master provided in Rule 53(c) and proceedings before it shall be governed by the provisions of Rule 53(d). Its action and report shall be determined by a majority and its findings and report shall have the effect, and be dealt with by the court in accordance with the practice, prescribed in Rule 53(e), (f), and (g). Trial of all issues shall otherwise be by the court.

(i) Dismissal of Action.

(1) *As of Right.* If no hearing has begun to determine the compensation to be paid for a piece of property and the plaintiff has not acquired the title or a lesser interest in or taken possession, the plaintiff may dismiss the action as to that property, without an order of the court, by filing a notice of dismissal setting forth a brief description of the property as to which the action is dismissed.

(2) *By Stipulation.* Before the entry of any judgment vesting the plaintiff with title or a lesser interest in or possession of property, the action may be dismissed in whole or in part, without an order of the court, as to any property by filing a stipulation of dismissal by the plaintiff and the defendant affected thereby; and, if the parties so stipulate, the court may vacate any judgment that has been entered.

(3) *By Order of the Court.* At any time before compensation for a piece of property has been determined and paid and after motion and hearing, the court may dismiss the action as to that property, except that it shall not dismiss the action as to any part of the property of which the plaintiff has taken possession or in which the plaintiff has taken title or a lesser

interest, but shall award just compensation for the possession, title or lesser interest so taken. The court at any time may drop a defendant unnecessarily or improperly joined.

(4) *Effect.* Except as otherwise provided in the notice, or stipulation of dismissal, or order of the court, any dismissal is without prejudice.

(j) Deposit and Its Distribution. The plaintiff shall deposit with the court any money required by law as a condition to the exercise of the power of eminent domain; and, although not so required, may make a deposit when permitted by statute. In such cases the court and attorneys shall expedite the proceedings for the distribution of the money so deposited and for the ascertainment and payment of just compensation. If the compensation finally awarded to any defendant exceeds the amount which has been paid to that defendant on distribution of the deposit, the court shall enter judgment against the plaintiff and in favor of that defendant for the deficiency. If the compensation finally awarded to any defendant is less than the amount which has been paid to that defendant, the court shall enter judgment against that defendant and in favor of the plaintiff for the overpayment.

(k) Condemnation Under a State's Power of Eminent Domain. The practice as herein prescribed governs in actions involving the exercise of the power of eminent domain under the law of a state, provided that if the state law makes provision for trial of any issue by jury, or for trial of the issue of compensation by jury or commission or both, that provision shall be followed.

(*l*) Costs. Costs are not subject to Rule 54(d).

Rule 72. MAGISTRATE JUDGES; PRETRIAL ORDERS

(a) Nondispositive Matters. A magistrate judge to whom a pretrial matter not dispositive of a claim or defense of a party is referred to hear and determine shall promptly conduct such proceedings as are required and when appropriate enter into the record a written order setting forth the disposition of the matter. Within 10 days after being served with a copy of the magistrate judge's order, a party may serve and file objections to the order; a party may not thereafter assign as error a defect in the magistrate judge's order to which objection was not timely made. The district judge to whom the case is assigned shall consider such objections and shall modify or set aside any portion of the magistrate judge's order found to be clearly erroneous or contrary to law.

(b) Dispositive Motions and Prisoner Petitions. A magistrate judge assigned without consent of the parties to hear a pretrial matter dispositive of a claim or defense of a party or a prisoner petition challenging the conditions of confinement shall promptly conduct such proceedings as are required. A record shall be made of all evidentiary proceedings before the magistrate judge and a record may be made of such other proceedings as the magistrate judge deems necessary. The magistrate judge shall enter into the record a recommendation for disposition of the matter, including proposed findings of fact when appropriate. The clerk shall forthwith mail copies to all parties.

A party objecting to the recommended disposition of the matter shall promptly arrange for the transcription of the record, or portions of it as all parties may agree upon or the magistrate judge deems sufficient, unless the district judge otherwise directs. Within 10 days after being served with a copy of the recommended disposition, a party may serve and file specific, written objections to the proposed findings and recommendations. A party may respond to another party's objections within 10 days after being served with a copy thereof. The district judge to whom the case is assigned shall make a de novo determination upon the record, or after additional evidence, of any portion of the magistrate judge's disposition to which specific written objection has been made in accordance with this rule. The district judge may accept, reject, or modify the recommended decision, receive further evidence, or recommit the matter to the magistrate judge with instructions.

Rule 73. MAGISTRATE JUDGES; TRIAL BY CONSENT AND APPEAL

(a) Powers; Procedure. When specially designated to exercise such jurisdiction by local rule or order of the district court and when all parties consent thereto, a magistrate judge may exercise the authority provided by Title 28, U.S.C. § 636(c) and may conduct any or all proceedings, including a jury or nonjury trial, in a civil case. A record of the proceedings shall be made in accordance with the requirements of Title 28, U.S.C. § 636(c)(5).

(b) Consent. When a magistrate judge has been designated to exercise civil trial jurisdiction, the clerk shall give written notice to the parties of their opportunity to consent to the exercise by a magistrate judge of civil jurisdiction over the case, as authorized by Title 28, U.S.C. § 636(c). If, within the period specified by local rule, the parties agree to a magistrate judge's exercise of such authority, they shall execute and file a joint form of consent or separate forms of consent setting forth such election.

A district judge, magistrate judge, or other court official may again advise the parties of the availability of the magistrate judge, but, in so doing, shall also advise the parties that they are free to withhold consent without adverse substantive consequences. A district judge or magistrate judge shall not be informed of a party's response to the clerk's notification, unless all parties have consented to the referral of the matter to a magistrate judge.

The district judge, for good cause shown on the judge's own initiative, or under extraordinary circumstances shown by a party, may vacate a reference of a civil matter to a magistrate judge under this subdivision.

(c) Appeal. In accordance with Title 28, U.S.C. § 636(c)(3), appeal from a judgment entered upon direction of a magistrate judge in proceedings under this rule will lie to the court of appeals as it would from a judgment of the district court.

Rule 74. [Abrogated.]

Rule 75. [Abrogated.]

Rule 76. [Abrogated.]

X. DISTRICT COURTS AND CLERKS

Rule 77. DISTRICT COURTS AND CLERKS

(a) District Courts Always Open. The district courts shall be deemed always open for the purpose of filing any pleading or other proper paper, of issuing and returning mesne and final process, and of making and directing all interlocutory motions, orders, and rules.

(b) Trials and Hearings; Orders in Chambers. All trials upon the merits shall be conducted in open court and so far as convenient in a regular court room. All other acts or proceedings may be done or conducted by a judge in chambers, without the attendance of the clerk or other court officials and at any place either within or without the district; but no hearing, other than one ex parte, shall be conducted outside the district without the consent of all parties affected thereby.

(c) Clerk's Office and Orders by Clerk. The clerk's office with the clerk or a deputy in attendance shall be open during business hours on all days except Saturdays, Sundays, and legal holidays, but a district court may provide by local rule or order that its clerk's office shall be open for specified hours on Saturdays or particular legal holidays other than New Year's Day, Birthday of Martin Luther King, Jr., Washington's Birthday, Memorial Day, Independence Day, Labor Day, Columbus Day, Veterans Day, Thanksgiving Day, and Christmas Day. All motions and applications in the clerk's office for issuing mesne process, for issuing final process to enforce and execute judgments, for entering defaults or judgments by default, and for other proceedings which do not require allowance or order of the court are grantable of course by the clerk; but the clerk's action may be suspended or altered or rescinded by the court upon cause shown.

(d) Notice of Orders or Judgments. Immediately upon the entry of an order or judgment the clerk shall serve a notice of the entry in the manner provided for in Rule 5(b) upon each party who is not in default for failure to appear, and shall make a note in the docket of the service. Any party may in addition serve a notice of such entry in the manner provided in Rule 5(b) for the service of papers. Lack of notice of the entry by the clerk does not affect the time to appeal or relieve or authorize the court to relieve a party for failure to appeal within the time allowed, except as permitted in Rule 4(a) of the Federal Rules of Appellate Procedure.

Rule 78. MOTION DAY

Unless local conditions make it impracticable, each district court shall establish regular times and places, at intervals sufficiently frequent for the prompt dispatch of business, at which motions requiring notice and hearing may be heard and disposed of; but the judge at any time or place and on such notice, if any, as the judge considers reasonable may make orders for the advancement, conduct, and hearing of actions.

To expedite its business, the court may make provision by rule or order for the submission and determination of motions without oral hearing upon brief written statements of reasons in support and opposition.

Rule 79. BOOKS AND RECORDS KEPT BY THE CLERK AND ENTRIES THEREIN

(a) Civil Docket. The clerk shall keep a book known as "civil docket" of such form and style as may be prescribed by the Director of the Administrative Office of the United States Courts with the approval of the Judicial Conference of the United States, and shall enter therein each civil action to which these rules are made applicable. Actions shall be assigned consecutive file numbers. The file number of each action shall be noted on the folio of the docket whereon the first entry of the action is made. All papers filed with the clerk, all process issued and returns made thereon, all appearances, orders, verdicts, and judgments shall be entered chronologically in the civil docket on the folio assigned to the action and shall be marked with its file number. These entries shall be brief but shall show the nature of each paper filed or writ issued and the substance of each order or judgment of the court and of the returns showing execution of process. The entry of an order or judgment shall show the date the entry is made. When in an action trial by jury has been properly demanded or ordered the clerk shall enter the word "jury" on the folio assigned to that action.

(b) Civil Judgments and Orders. The clerk shall keep, in such form and manner as the Director of the Administrative Office of the United States Courts with the approval of the Judicial Conference of the United States may prescribe, a correct copy of every final judgment or appealable order, or order affecting title to or lien upon real or personal property, and any other order which the court may direct to be kept.

(c) Indices; Calendars. Suitable indices of the civil docket and of every civil judgment and order referred to in subdivision (b) of this rule shall be kept by the clerk under the direction of the court. There shall be prepared under the direction of the court calendars of all actions ready for trial, which shall distinguish "jury actions" from "court actions."

(d) Other Books and Records of the Clerk. The clerk shall also keep such other books and records as may be required from time to time by the Director of the Administrative Office of the United States Courts with the approval of the Judicial Conference of the United States.

Rule 80. STENOGRAPHER; STENOGRAPHIC REPORT OR TRANSCRIPT AS EVIDENCE

(a) [Abrogated.]

(b) [Abrogated.]

(c) Stenographic Report or Transcript as Evidence. Whenever the testimony of a witness at a trial or hearing which was stenographically reported is admissible in evidence at a later trial, it may be proved by the transcript thereof duly certified by the person who reported the testimony.

XI. GENERAL PROVISIONS

Rule 81. APPLICABILITY IN GENERAL

(a) To What Proceedings Applicable.

(1) These rules do not apply to prize proceedings in admiralty governed by Title 10, U.S.C. §§ 7651–7681. They do apply to proceedings in bankruptcy to the extent provided by the Federal Rules of Bankruptcy Procedure.

(2) These rules are applicable to proceedings for admission to citizenship, habeas corpus, and quo warranto, to the extent that the practice in such proceedings is not set forth in statutes of the United States, the Rules Governing Section 2254 Cases, or the Rules Governing Section 2255 Proceedings, and has heretofore conformed to the practice in civil actions.

(3) In proceedings under Title 9, U.S.C., relating to arbitration, or under the Act of May 20, 1926, ch. 347, § 9 (44 Stat. 585), U.S.C., Title 45, § 159, relating to boards of arbitration of railway labor disputes, these rules apply only to the extent that matters of procedure are not provided for in those statutes. These rules apply to proceedings to compel the giving of testimony or production of documents in accordance with a subpoena issued by an officer or agency of the United States under any statute of the United States except as otherwise provided by statute or by rules of the district court or by order of the court in the proceedings.

(4) These rules do not alter the method prescribed by the Act of February 18, 1922, c. 57, § 2 (42 Stat. 388), U.S.C., Title 7, § 292; or by the Act of June 10, 1930, c. 436, § 7 (46 Stat. 534), as amended, U.S.C., Title 7, § 499g(c), for instituting proceedings in the United States district courts to review orders of the Secretary of Agriculture; or prescribed by the Act of June 25, 1934, c. 742, § 2 (48 Stat. 1214), U.S.C., Title 15, § 522, for instituting proceedings to review orders of the Secretary of the Interior; or prescribed by the Act of February 22, 1935, c. 18, § 5 (49 Stat. 31), U.S.C., Title 15, § 715d(c), as extended, for instituting proceedings to review orders of petroleum control boards; but the conduct of such proceedings in the district courts shall be made to conform to these rules as far as applicable.

(5) These rules do not alter the practice in the United States district courts prescribed in the Act of July 5, 1935, c. 372, §§ 9 and 10 (49 Stat. 453), as amended, U.S.C., Title 29, §§ 159 and 160, for beginning and conducting proceedings to enforce orders of the National Labor Relations Board; and in respects not covered by those statutes, the practice in the district courts shall conform to these rules so far as applicable.

(6) These rules apply to proceedings for enforcement or review of compensation orders under the Longshoremen's and Harbor Workers' Compensation Act, Act of March 4, 1927, c. 509, §§ 18, 21 (44 Stat. 1434, 1436), as amended, U.S.C., Title 33, §§ 918, 921, except to the extent that matters of procedure are provided for in that Act. The provisions for service by publication and for answer in proceedings to cancel certificates of citizenship under the Act of June 27, 1952, c. 477, Title III, c. 2, § 340 (66 Stat. 260), U.S.C., Title 8, § 1451, remain in effect.

(b) Scire Facias and Mandamus. The writs of scire facias and mandamus are abolished. Relief heretofore available by mandamus or scire facias may be obtained by appropriate action or by appropriate motion under the practice prescribed in these rules.

(c) Removed Actions. These rules apply to civil actions removed to the United States district courts from the state courts and govern procedure after removal. Repleading is not necessary unless the court so orders. In a removed action in which the defendant has not answered, the defendant shall answer or present the other defenses or objections available under these rules within 20 days after the receipt through service or otherwise of a copy of the initial pleading setting forth the claim for relief upon which the action or proceeding is based, or within 20 days after the service of summons upon such initial pleading, then filed, or within 5 days after the filing of the petition for removal, whichever period is longest. If at the time of removal all necessary pleadings have been served, a party entitled to trial by jury under Rule 38 shall be accorded it, if the party's demand therefor is served within 10 days after the petition for removal is filed if the party is the petitioner, or if not the petitioner within 10 days after service on the party of the notice of filing the petition. A party who, prior to removal, has made an express demand for trial by jury in accordance with state law, need not make a demand after removal. If state law applicable in the court from which the case is removed does not require the parties to make express demands in order to claim trial by jury, they need not make demands after removal unless the court directs that they do so within a specified time if they desire to claim trial by jury. The court may make this direction on its own motion and shall do so as a matter of course at the request of any party. The failure of a party to make demand as directed constitutes a waiver by that party of trial by jury.

(d) [Abrogated.]

(e) Law Applicable. Whenever in these rules the law of the state in which the district court is held is made applicable, the law applied in the District of Columbia governs proceedings in the United States District Court for the District of Columbia. When the word "state" is used, it includes, if appropriate, the District of Columbia. When the term "statute of the United States" is used, it includes, so far as concerns proceedings in the United States District Court for the District of Columbia, any Act of Congress locally applicable to and in force in the District of Columbia. When the law of a state is referred to, the word "law" includes the statutes of that state and the state judicial decisions construing them.

(f) References to Officer of the United States. Under any rule in which reference is made to an officer or agency of the United States, the term "officer" includes a district director of internal revenue, a former district director or collector of internal revenue, or the personal representative of a deceased district director or collector of internal revenue.

Rule 82. JURISDICTION AND VENUE UNAFFECTED

These rules shall not be construed to extend or limit the jurisdiction of the United States district courts or the venue of actions therein. An admiralty or maritime claim within the meaning of Rule 9(h) shall not be treated as a civil action for the purposes of Title 28, U.S.C. §§ 1391–1392.

Rule 83. RULES BY DISTRICT COURTS; JUDGE'S DIRECTIVES

(a) Local Rules.

(1) Each district court, acting by a majority of its district judges, may, after giving appropriate public notice and an opportunity for comment, make and amend rules governing its practice. A local rule shall be consistent with—but not duplicative of—Acts of Congress and rules adopted under 28 U.S.C. §§ 2072 and 2075, and shall conform to any uniform numbering system prescribed by the Judicial Conference of the United States. A local rule takes effect on the date specified by the district court and remains in effect unless amended by the court or abrogated by the judicial council of the circuit. Copies of rules and amendments shall, upon

their promulgation, be furnished to the judicial council and the Administrative Office of the United States Courts and be made available to the public.

(2) A local rule imposing a requirement of form shall not be enforced in a manner that causes a party to lose rights because of a nonwillful failure to comply with the requirement.

(b) Procedures When There Is No Controlling Law. A judge may regulate practice in any manner consistent with federal law, rules adopted under 28 U.S.C. §§ 2072 and 2075, and local rules of the district. No sanction or other disadvantage may be imposed for noncompliance with any requirement not in federal law, federal rules, or the local district rules unless the alleged violator has been furnished in the particular case with actual notice of the requirement.

Rule 84.   FORMS

The forms contained in the Appendix of Forms are sufficient under the rules and are intended to indicate the simplicity and brevity of statement which the rules contemplate.

Rule 85.   TITLE

These rules may be known and cited as the Federal Rules of Civil Procedure.

Rule 86.   EFFECTIVE DATE

(a) [Effective Date of Original Rules]. These rules will take effect on the day which is 3 months subsequent to the adjournment of the second regular session of the 75th Congress, but if that day is prior to September 1, 1938, then these rules will take effect on September 1, 1938. They govern all proceedings in actions brought after they take effect and also all further proceedings in actions then pending, except to the extent that in the opinion of the court their application in a particular action pending when the rules take effect would not be feasible or would work injustice, in which event the former procedure applies.

(b) Effective Date of Amendments. The amendments adopted by the Supreme Court on December 27, 1946, and transmitted to the Attorney General on January 2, 1947, shall take effect on the day which is three months subsequent to the adjournment of the first regular session of the 80th Congress, but, if that day is prior to September 1, 1947, then these amendments shall take effect on September 1, 1947. They govern all proceedings in actions brought after they take effect and also all further proceedings in actions then pending, except to the extent that in the opinion of the court their application in a particular action pending when the amendments take effect would not be feasible or would work injustice, in which event the former procedure applies.

(c) Effective Date of Amendments. The amendments adopted by the Supreme Court on December 29, 1948, and transmitted to the Attorney General on December 31, 1948, shall take effect on the day following the adjournment of the first regular session of the 81st Congress.

(d) Effective Date of Amendments. The amendments adopted by the Supreme Court on April 17, 1961, and transmitted to the Congress on April 18, 1961, shall take effect on July 19, 1961. They govern all proceedings in actions brought after they take effect and also all further proceedings in actions then pending, except to the extent that in the opinion of the court their application in a particular action pending when the amendments take effect would not be feasible or would work injustice, in which event the former procedure applies.

(e) Effective Date of Amendments. The amendments adopted by the Supreme Court on January 21, 1963, and transmitted to the Congress on January 21, 1963, shall take effect on July 1, 1963. They govern all proceedings in actions brought after they take effect and also all further proceedings in actions then pending, except to the extent that in the opinion of the court their application in a particular action pending when the amendments take effect would not be feasible or would work injustice, in which event the former procedure applies.

†